Lecture Notes in Artificial Intelligence 3488

Edited by J. G. Carbonell and J. Siekmann

Subseries of Lecture Notes in Computer Science

T0190060

Mohand-Said Hacid   Neil V. Murray
Zbigniew W. Raś   Shusaku Tsumoto (Eds.)

Foundations of Intelligent Systems

15th International Symposium, ISMIS 2005
Saratoga Springs, NY, USA, May 25-28, 2005
Proceedings

 Springer

Volume Editors

Mohand-Said Hacid
Université Claude Bernard Lyon 1
LIRIS - UFR d'Informatique
69622 Villeurbanne Cedex, France
E-mail: mshacid@bat710.univ-lyon.fr

Neil V. Murray
University at Albany, SUNY
Department of Computer Science
Albany, NY 12222, USA
E-mail: nvm@cs.albany.edu

Zbigniew W. Raś
University of North Carolina
Department of Computer Science
Charlotte, NC 28223, USA
E-mail: ras@uncc.edu

Shusaku Tsumoto
Shimane Medical University
School of Medicine, Department of Medical Informatics
89-I Enya-cho, Izumo 693-8501, Japan
E-mail: tsumoto@computer.org

Library of Congress Control Number: 2005925177

CR Subject Classification (1998): I.2, H.3, H.2.8, H.4, H.5.2, K.4.4, F.1

ISSN   0302-9743
ISBN-10   3-540-25878-7 Springer Berlin Heidelberg New York
ISBN-13   978-3-540-25878-0 Springer Berlin Heidelberg New York

This work is subject to copyright. All rights are reserved, whether the whole or part of the material is concerned, specifically the rights of translation, reprinting, re-use of illustrations, recitation, broadcasting, reproduction on microfilms or in any other way, and storage in data banks. Duplication of this publication or parts thereof is permitted only under the provisions of the German Copyright Law of September 9, 1965, in its current version, and permission for use must always be obtained from Springer. Violations are liable to prosecution under the German Copyright Law.

Springer is a part of Springer Science+Business Media

springeronline.com

© Springer-Verlag Berlin Heidelberg 2005
Printed in Germany

Typesetting: Camera-ready by author, data conversion by Scientific Publishing Services, Chennai, India
Printed on acid-free paper   SPIN: 11425274   06/3142   5 4 3 2 1 0

Preface

This volume contains the papers selected for presentation at the 15th International Symposium on Methodologies for Intelligent Systems, ISMIS 2005, held in Saratoga Springs, New York, 25–28 May, 2005. The symposium was organized by SUNY at Albany. It was sponsored by the Army Research Office and by several units of the University at Albany including its Division for Research, College of Arts and Sciences, Department of Computer Science, and Institute for Informatics, Logics, and Security Studies (formerly the Institute for Programming and Logics). ISMIS is a conference series that was started in 1986 in Knoxville, Tennessee. Since then it has been held in Charlotte (North Carolina), Knoxville (Tennessee), Turin (Italy), Trondheim (Norway), Warsaw (Poland), Zakopane (Poland), Lyon (France), and Maebashi City (Japan).

The Program Committee selected the following major areas for ISMIS 2005: intelligent information systems, knowledge discovery and data mining, knowledge information and integration, knowledge representation, logic for artificial intelligence, soft computing, Web intelligence, Web services, and papers dealing with applications of intelligent systems in complex/novel domains.

The contributed papers were selected from almost 200 full draft papers by the Program Committee members: Troels Andreasen, Peter Baumgartner, Boualemn Benatallah, Salima Benbernou, Veronique Benzaken, Petr Berka, Elisa Bertino, Alan Biermann, Jacques Calmet, Sandra Carberry, Juan Carlos Cubero, Luigia Carlucci Aiello, Shu-Ching Chen, Christine Collet, Agnieszka Dardzinska, Ian Davidson, Robert Demolombe, Jitender Deogun, Jon Doyle, Tapio Elomaa, Attilio Giordana, Jerzy Grzymala-Busse, Mirsad Hadzikadic, Reiner Haehnle, Janusz Kacprzyk, Vipul Kashyap, Jan Komorowski, Jacek Koronacki, Tsau Young Lin, Donato Malerba, David Maluf, Davide Martinenghi, Stan Matwin, Natasha Noy, Werner Nutt, James Peters, Jean-Marc Petit, Vijay Raghavan, Jan Rauch, Gilbert Ritschard, Erik Rosenthal, Marie-Christine Rousset, Nahid Shahmehri, Andrzej Skowron, Dominik Slezak, Nicolas Spyratos, V.S. Subrahmanian, Einoshin Suzuki, Domenico Talia, Yuzuru Tanaka, Farouk Toumani, Athena Vakali, Takashi Washio, Alicja Wieczorkowska, Xindong Wu, Xintao Wu, Ronald Yager, Yiyu Yao, and Saygin Yucel.

The list of additional reviewers: Johan Aberg, Marie Agier, Lefteris Angelis, Annalisa Appice, Khalid Belhajjame, Margherita Berardi, Patrick Bosc, Henrik Bulskov, Franck Capello, Costantina Caruso, Michelangelo Ceci, Min Chen, Ioan Chisalita, Laurence Cholvy, Dario Colazzo, Carmela Comito, Antonio Congiusta, Frédéric Cuppens, Anusch Daemi, Fabien De Marchi, Elizabeth Diaz, Devdatt Dubhashi, Peter Gammie, Arnaud Giacometti, Martin Giese, Paul Goutam, Gianluigi Greco, Samira Hammiche, Thomas Herault, Seung Hyun Im, Kimihito Ito, Mikhail Jiline, Kristofer Johannisson, Fabrice Jouanot, Matti Kääriäinen, Svetlana Kiritchenko, Rasmus Knappe, Lotfi Lakhal, Patrick Lambrix, Tine Lassen, Anne Laurent, Dominique Laurent, Alexandre Lefebvre, João Fernando Lima Alcantara, Gabriela Lindemann, Yann Loyer, James Lu, Perry Mar, Carlo Mastroianni, Mirjam Minor, Dagmar Monett,

Dheerendranath Mundluru, Oliver Obst, Raffale Perego, Aarne Ranta, Brigitte Safar, Lorenza Saitta, Eric San Juan, Kay Schröter, Michele Sebag, Biren Shah, Laurent Simon, Giandomenico Spezzano, Diemo Urbig, Thomas Vestskov Terney, Li-Shiang Tsay, Phan-Luong Viet, Richard Waldinger, Christoph Wernhard, Ying Xie, Jianhua Yan, Ke Yin, José Luis Zechinelli Martini, Na Zhao, and Xiaosi Zhou.

We wish to express our thanks to all ISMIS 2005 reviewers and to Alan Biermann, Jaime Carbonell, and Salvatore Stolfo who presented invited talks at the symposium. We express our appreciation to the sponsors of the symposium and to all who submitted papers for presentation and publication in the proceedings. Our sincere thanks go Floriana Esposito, David Hislop, Robert Meersman, Hiroshi Motoda, Raghu Ramakrishnan, Zbigniew Ras (Chair), Lorenza Saitta, Maria Zemankova, Djamel Zighed, and Ning Zhong who served as members of the ISMIS 2005 Steering Committee, and to both Adrian Tanasescu who was responsible for the website and submission site management and Lynne Casper who worked on all aspects of local arrangements. Also, our thanks are due to Alfred Hofmann of Springer for his continuous support.

February, 2005   M.-S. Hacid, N.V. Murray, Z.W. Raś, S. Tsumoto

Table of Contents

Invited Papers

Methodologies for Automated Telephone Answering
Alan W. Biermann, R. Bryce Inouye, Ashley McKenzie 1

Anomaly Detection in Computer Security and an Application to File System Accesses
Salvatore J. Stolfo, Shlomo Hershkop, Linh H. Bui, Ryan Ferster, Ke Wang 14

Regular Papers

1A Knowledge Discovery and Data Mining (1)

A Machine Text-Inspired Machine Learning Approach for Identification of Transmembrane Helix Boundaries
Betty Yee Man Cheng, Jaime G. Carbonell, Judith Klein-Seetharaman 29

Visualization of Similarities and Dissimilarities in Rules Using Multidimensional Scaling
Shusaku Tsumoto, Shoji Hirano 38

Learning Profiles Based on Hierarchical Hidden Markov Model
Ugo Galassi, Attilio Giordana, Lorenza Saitta, Maco Botta 47

Statistical Independence from the Viewpoint of Linear Algebra
Shusaku Tsumoto 56

2A Intelligent Information Systems (1)

Bitmap Index-Based Decision Trees
Cécile Favre, Fadila Bentayeb 65

On Automatic Modeling and Use of Domain-Specific Ontologies
Troels Andreasen, Henrik Bulskov, Rasmus Knappe 74

Using Self-Adaptable Probes for Dynamic Parameter Control of Parallel Evolutionary Algorithms
Xavier Bonnaire, María-Cristina Riff 83

Robust Inference of Bayesian Networks Using Speciated Evolution and
Ensemble
Kyung-Joong Kim, Ji-Oh Yoo, Sung-Bae Cho 92

1B Knowledge Discovery and Data Mining (2)

Mining the Semantic Web: A Logic-Based Methodology
Francesca A. Lisi, Floriana Esposito 102

Analysis of Textual Data with Multiple Classes
Shigeaki Sakurai, Chong Goh, Ryohei Orihara 112

SARM – Succinct Association Rule Mining: An Approach to Enhance
Association Mining
Jitender Deogun, Liying Jiang 121

Learning the Daily Model of Network Traffic
Costantina Caruso, Donato Malerba, Davide Papagni 131

2B Intelligent Information Systems (2)

ARGUS: Rete + DBMS = Efficient Persistent Profile Matching
on Large-Volume Data Streams
Chun Jin, Jaime Carbonell, Phil Hayes 142

Failing Queries in Distributed Autonomous Information System
Zbigniew W. Raś, Agnieszka Dardzińska 152

Evaluation of Two Systems on Multi-class Multi-label Document Classification
Xiao Luo, A. Nur Zincir-Heywood 161

Uncertain Knowledge Gathering: An Evolutionary Approach
Dennis Hooijmaijers, Damien Bright 170

1C Information and Knowledge Integration (1)

Duality in Knowledge Compilation Techniques
Neil V. Murray, Erik Rosenthal 182

Data Protection in Distributed Database Systems
Chun Ruan, Vijay Varadharajan 191

2C Soft Computing (1)

A Softened Formulation of Inductive Learning and Its Use for Coronary
Disease Data
Janusz Kacprzyk, Grażyna Szkatula 200

Subsystem Based Generalizations of Rough Set Approximations
Yiyu Yao, Yaohua Chen 210

1D Clustering (1)

Model-Based Cluster Analysis for Web Users Sessions
George Pallis, Lefteris Angelis, Athena Vakali 219

On Autonomous *k*-Means Clustering
Tapio Elomaa, Heidi Koivistoinen 228

CSI: Clustered Segment Indexing for Efficient Approximate Searching on the
Secondary Structure of Protein Sequences
Minkoo Seo, Sanghyun Park, Jung-Im Won 237

Using Supervised Clustering to Enhance Classifiers
Christoph F. Eick, Nidal Zeidat 248

2D Web Data

Modelling Good Entry Pages on the Web
Theodora Tsikrika, Mounia Lalmas 257

A Query Expression and Processing Technique for an XML Search Engine
Wol Young Lee, Hwan Seung Yong 266

Adapting the Object Role Modelling Method for Ontology Modelling
Peter Spyns 276

Identifying Content Blocks from Web Documents
Sandip Debnath, Prasenjit Mitra, C. Lee Giles 285

1E Information and Knowledge Integration (2)

Building the Data Warehouse of Frequent Itemsets in the DWFIST Approach
*Rodrigo Salvador Monteiro, Geraldo Zimbrão, Holger Schwarz,
Bernhard Mitschang, Jano Moreira de Souza* 294

Normal Forms for Knowledge Compilation
Reiner Hähnle, Neil V. Murray, Erik Rosenthal 304

2E Soft Computing (2)

On the Approximate Division of Fuzzy Relations
Patrick Bosc, Olivier Pivert, Daniel Rocacher 314

Efficient Learning of Pseudo-Boolean Functions from Limited Training Data
Guoli Ding, Jianhua Chen, Robert Lax, Peter Chen 323

1F Knowledge Discovery and Data Mining (3)

Discovering Partial Periodic Sequential Association Rules with Time Lag in
Multiple Sequences for Prediction
Dan Li, Jitender S. Deogun 332

Mining and Filtering Multi-level Spatial Association Rules with ARES
Annalisa Appice, Margherita Berardi, Michelangelo Ceci,
Donato Malerba 342

Association Reducts: A Framework for Mining Multi-attribute Dependencies
Dominik Ślęzak 354

Frequent Pattern Mining with Preferences – Utility Functions Approach
Elena Braynova, Hemant Pendharkar 364

2F Intelligent Information Systems (3)

Semantic-Based Access to Digital Document Databases
F. Esposito, S. Ferilli, T.M.A. Basile, N. Di Mauro 373

Statistical Database Modeling for Privacy Preserving Database Generation
Xintao Wu, Yongge Wang, Yuliang Zheng 382

Scalable Inductive Learning on Partitioned Data
Qijun Chen, Xindong Wu, Xingquan Zhu 391

Agent-Based Home Simulation and Control
B. De Carolis, G. Cozzolongo, S. Pizzutilo, V.L. Plantamura 404

1G Logic for Artificial Intelligence

Aggregates and Preferences in Logic Programming
S. Greco, I. Trubitsyna, E. Zumpano 413

The Chisholm Paradox and the Situation Calculus
Robert Demolombe, Pilar Pozos-Parra 425

A Logic Approach for LTL System Modification
Yulin Ding, Yan Zhang 435

Anticipatory Agents Based on Anticipatory Reasoning
Feng Shang, Jingde Cheng 445

2G Applications (1)

Extracting Emotions from Music Data
Alicja Wieczorkowska, Piotr Synak, Rory Lewis, Zbigniew W. Raś 456

An Intelligent System for Assisting Elderly People
*Alberto Tablado, Arantza Illarramendi, Miren I. Bagüés, Jesús Bermúdez,
Alfredo Goñi* 466

Multi-strategy Instance Selection in Mining Chronic Hepatitis Data
*Masatoshi Jumi, Einoshin Suzuki, Muneaki Ohshima, Ning Zhong,
Hideto Yokoi, Katsuhiko Takabayashi* 475

A Probabilistic Approach to Finding Geometric Objects in Spatial Datasets of
the Milky Way
Jon Purnell, Malik Magdon-Ismail, Heidi Jo Newberg 485

1H Applications (2)

Towards Ad-Hoc Rule Semantics for Gene Expression Data
Marie Agier, Jean-Marc Petit, Einoshin Suzuki 494

Flexible Pattern Discovery with (Extended) Disjunctive Logic Programming
Luigi Palopoli, Simona Rombo, Giorgio Terracina 504

Interactive SOM-Based Gene Grouping: An Approach to Gene Expression
Data Analysis
Alicja Gruźdź, Aleksandra Ihnatowicz, Dominik Ślęzak 514

Some Theoretical Properties of Mutual Information for Student Assessments
in Intelligent Tutoring Systems
Chao-Lin Liu 524

2H Intelligent Information Retrieval (1)

Cooperative Query Answering for RDF
Adrian Tanasescu 535

Intelligent Information Retrieval for Web-Based Design Data Repository
Huijae Lee, Sang Bong Yoo 544

Incremental Collaborative Filtering for Highly-Scalable Recommendation
Algorithms
Manos Papagelis, Ioannis Rousidis, Dimitris Plexousakis,
Elias Theoharopoulos 553

1I Clustering (2)

A Distance-Based Algorithm for Clustering Database User Sessions
Qingsong Yao, Aijun An, Xiangji Huang 562

User-Interest-Based Document Filtering via Semi-supervised Clustering
Na Tang, V. Rao Vemuri 573

A Filter Feature Selection Method for Clustering
Pierre-Emmanuel Jouve, Nicolas Nicoloyannis 583

Automatic Determination of the Number of Fuzzy Clusters Using Simulated
Annealing with Variable Representation
Sanghamitra Bandyopadhyay 594

2I Knowledge Discovery and Data Mining (4)

Experimental Analysis of the Q-Matrix Method in Knowledge Discovery
Tiffany Barnes, Donald Bitzer, Mladen Vouk 603

Clustering Time-Series Medical Databases Based on the Improved Multiscale
Matching
Shoji Hirano, Shusaku Tsumoto 612

Efficient Causal Interaction Learning with Applications in Microarray
Yong Ye, Xintao Wu 622

A Dynamic Adaptive Sampling Algorithm (DASA) for Real World
Applications: Finger Print Recognition and Face Recognition
    Ashwin Satyanarayana, Ian Davidson 631

1J Intelligent Information Retrieval (2)

Catching the Picospams
    Matthew Chang, Chung Keung Poon 641

Personalized Peer Filtering for a Dynamic Information Push
    Melanie Gnasa, Sascha Alda, Nadir Gul, Armin B. Cremers 650

Getting Computers to See Information Graphics So Users Do Not Have to
    Daniel Chester, Stephanie Elzer 660

2J Knowledge Representation

A Data Model Based on Paraconsistent Intuitionistic Fuzzy Relations
    Haibin Wang, Rajshekhar Sunderraman 669

Logical Data Independence Reconsidered
    James J. Lu 678

Estimation of the Density of Datasets with Decision Diagrams
    Ansaf Salleb, Christel Vrain 688

Author Index 699

Methodologies for Automated Telephone Answering

Alan W. Biermann, R. Bryce Inouye, and Ashley McKenzie

Department of Computer Science, Duke University,
Durham NC 27708, USA
{awb, rbi, armckenz}@cs.duke.edu

Abstract. We survey some of the approaches to dialogue representation and processing for modern telephone answering systems. We include discussions of their strong and weak points and some of the performance levels obtained by them.

1 Technologies for the Third Millennium

The advent of ubiquitous computing will bring computers and the Internet into our lives on an almost continuous basis. We will have machines and communication access in our offices, in our vehicles, in our brief cases, on our walls, and elsewhere. We will be able to interact with the world, access the huge Internet resources, do local computations, and much more. But how will we utilize these machines easily enough to really profit from their capabilities? One suggestion is that we should speak to them as we do to humans and receive responses back using natural language ([1],[2],[3]). However, there have been major obstacles to the development of spoken language dialogue machines over the decades and some of these remain a problem today. This paper will address some of the major ideas in the development of dialogue systems and the levels of success that are possible. The focus of much research activity in recent years has been in automatic telephone answering ([4],[5],[6],[7],[3]) but we will also mention projects that study other types of human-machine interaction ([8],[2]).

Our primary concerns in this paper are the overall conception of what a dialogue is and how a computer may represent it and manage it. We present some of the most common and most successful paradigms for dialogue processing. Given these formats, we then discuss related issues including the control of initiative, user modeling, error correction, and dialogue optimization.

2 Paradigms for Dialogue Management

The earliest and probably the most used model for dialogues has been the finite-state machine ([9]). The model enables the designer to systematically specify the sequential steps of a dialogue anticipating what the user may say and designing the responses that are needed. This is a conservative technology that enables

M.-S. Hacid et al. (Eds.): ISMIS 2005, LNAI 3488, pp. 1–13, 2005.
© Springer-Verlag Berlin Heidelberg 2005

precise control of every machine action and prevents surprising behaviors that could result from unanticipated situations.

For the purposes of this paper, we will do examples from the domain of credit card company telephone answering where we have some experience ([10]). We will assume a greatly simplified version of the problem to keep the presentation short but will include enough complexity to make the points. Our model will require the system to obtain the name of the caller and an identifying account code. It also will require the system to obtain the purpose of the call. In our simplified example, we will assume there are only three possible goals: to determine the current balance on the credit card account, to report that the card has been lost and that another needs to be issued, or to request that a new address be registered for this caller.

Figure 1 shows a finite-state solution for this simplified credit card problem. The interaction begins with the machine greeting the user. We omit details of what this might be but a company would have a policy as to what to say. Perhaps it would say something like this: "Hello, this is the XYZ corporation automated credit card information system. What can I do for you today?" The figure shows the kinds of caller comments expected and the machine recognition system and parser have the tasks of recognizing and processing the incoming speech. The figure shows the next steps for the machine's response. Its output system needs an ability to convert a target message into properly enunciated speech. The continuation of the diagram shows the dialogue capabilities of the system. We omit a number of transitions in the diagram that might be included for variations in the interactions, for unusual requests, and for error correction.

An example dialogue that traverses this diagram is as follows:

System: Hello. XYZ credit card management. How can I help you?
Caller: Hello. I need to report a lost credit card.
System: Please give me your name.
Caller: William Smith.
System: Thank you. And your account code?
Caller: X13794.
System: Okay, I will cancel your existing card and issue a new one within 24 hours.

A common problem with the finite state model is that designers become exhausted with the detailed specification of every possible interaction that could occur. The number of states can explode as one accounts for misrecognitions and repeated requests, variations in the strategy of the interactions, different levels of initiative, extra politeness in special cases, and more. This leads to another model for dialogue systems, the form-filling model that assumes there is a set of slots to be filled in the interaction and that processing should evolve around the concept of filling the slots. Here the software can be designed around the slots and the computations needed to fill them. The ordering of the dialogue interactions is not implicitly set ahead of time and the designer need not think about order as much. If any interaction happens to include information to fill a slot, the information is immediately parsed and entered. If an important slot

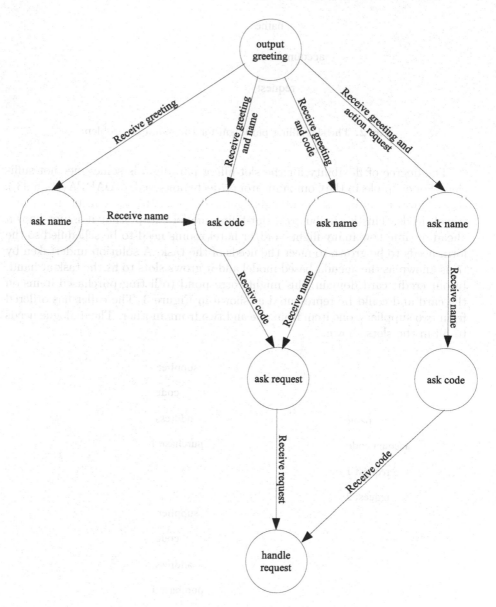

Fig. 1. Finite-state model for the credit card dialogue

exists that is unfilled, the system can initiate dialogue to fill it. Figure 2 shows the simple form that would be associated with our example problem and one can easily imagine dialogues that could evolve from this approach that are not easily accounted for by the finite-state model. A variety of systems have been built around this paradigm with considerable success ([7]).

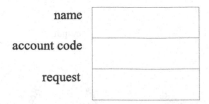

Fig. 2. The slot-filling paradigm for the example problem

The degree of flexibility for the slot-filling paradigm is sometimes not sufficient. For example, in the Communicator project sponsored by DARPA ([4],[6],[3]), the task was to set up a series of flights and hotel reservations to meet the caller's travel needs. This is similar to a slot-filling model except that it is not known ahead of time how many flights and/or hotel rooms need to be scheduled so the form needs to be grown to meet the needs of the task. A solution undertaken by [7] is known as the agenda-based model and it grows slots to fit the task at hand. In our credit card domain, this might correspond to listing purchased items on the card and could be represented as shown in Figure 3. The caller has ordered from two suppliers, one item from one and two from another. The dialogue needs to fill in the slots shown.

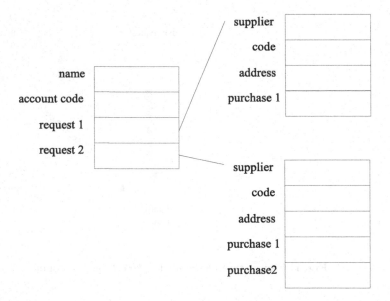

Fig. 3. Model for agenda-based dialogue

A third common paradigm for dialogue is the rule-based system pioneered by Allen, Litman, and Perrault ([11],[12]) and revised by Smith et al. ([8],[13]) Here the emphasis is on achieving goals and the data structures for the information exist within the logical formalisms that control the dialogue. This approach seeks to model problem solving activities of the participants, and dialogue is aimed at achieving a top level goal. STRIPS-style [14] production rules model the legal operators in the problem solving environment and dialogue acts are some of the legal operators useful in solving the problem.

We use the notation of the Prolog programming language adopted by [8],[13] in our example here. The form

```
f :- a, b, c.
```

represents the Prolog assertion that f can be achieved if a, b, and c can be achieved. Processing of the goal f involves attempting to prove goals a, b, and c sequentially. Suppose a and b are known to be true. This is expressed in Prolog as a. and b. The system can then attempt to prove c with a rule of the form

```
c :- d, e, g, h.
```

which leads recursively to a series of partial proofs or a completed proof. However, it may be true that no such rule for c exists in which case the dialogue system resorts to asking the dialogue partner. The missing axiom theory of Smith et al. ([8],[13])assumes that dialogue is carried out to achieve a goal and that the interactions with the dialogue partner address the problem of filling in the facts needed to achieve the goal. In our example, suppose that a participant wishes to achieve the goal f in some situation and the known facts are these:

```
f :- a, b, c.
a.
b.
```

Suppose there is no known rule for achieving c. Then the machine could ask the question c to try to achieve goal f. If the partner can provide the answer that c is true, then f will have been proven. (We will note below that it is good to have a user model which tells us whether it is appropriate to ask c. Perhaps it is not reasonable to ask this particular user this particular question.)

Here is a Prolog-style representation of the rules for solving the credit card problem.

```
handlecall :-
    speak("hello . . ."),
    find(name,acc,req),
    handle(name,acc,req),
    getacknowl(s),
    speak("i am handling this now. goodbye").
find(name,acc,req) :-
    get(s),
    parsename(s,name),
    parseacc(s,acc),
    parsereq(s,req).
parsename(s,name) :- (attempt parse of name).
```

```
parsename(s,name) :-
    speak("please give your name"),
    get(s2),
    parsename(s2,name).
parseacc(s,acc) :- (attempt parse of acc).
parseacc(s,acc) :-
    speak("please give me your account code"),
    get(s3),
    parseacc(s3,acc).
parsereq(s,req) :- (attempt parse of req).
parsereq(s,req) :-
    speak("i can give you your account balance,
        handle a lost card, or record a change of address.
        which of these would you like"),
    get(s4),
    parsereq(s4,req).
handle(name,acc,req) :-
    process(name,acc,req),
    outputyes(name,acc,req).
getacknowl(s) :- (attempt parse acknowledgement).
```

These rules are capable of the following interaction.

System:Hello. XYZ credit card processing.
Caller: Hello, this is William Smith and I have my identifier here,
         X13794.
System:How may I help you?
Caller: Actually, I was shopping at the mall yesterday and when I . . .
System:(no parse possible on incoming sentences) I can give you your
         account balance, handle a lost card, or record a change of address.
         Which of these would you like?
Caller: Ahh, I seem to ahh lost my card.
System:Okay, I will cancel your existing card and issue a new one within
         24 hours.
Caller: Thank you very much.
System:I am handling this now. Goodbye.
Caller: Goodbye.

With some additional rules, one can handle a wide variety of such dialogues.

Processing of this example proceeds as follows. The top level goal, handlecall, is to be achieved and processing calls in the only available rule:

```
handlecall :- speak(), find(), handle(), getacknowl(),speak().
```

It attempts these goals sequentially. The first speak goal is achieved as the system outputs the original message.

"Hello. XYZ credit card processing."

The second top level goal is `find(name,acc,req)` and it invokes the rule

```
find(name,acc,req) :-
    get(s),
    parsename(s,name),
    parseacc(s,acc),
    parsereq(s,req).
```

`get(s)` receives a spoken input `s`. This `s` is used in the second goal `parsename(s,name)` which attempts to find a name in `s`. `s` is this:

`s` = "Hello, this is William Smith and I have my identifier here, X13794."
`parsename(s,name)` finds name = William Smith.

Similarly, `parseacc(s,acc)` is the second goal in `find(name,acc,req)`. It finds

`acc` = X13794.

However, the third goal of `find(name,acc,req)` is `parsereq(s,req)`. It fails and this sends the system looking for another rule:

```
parsereq(s,req) :-
    speak("i can give you your account balance,
        handle a lost card, or record a change of address.
        which of these would you like"),
    get(s4),parsereq(s4,req).
```

This rule outputs a request and obtains this sentence

`s4` = "Ahh, I seem to ahh lost my card."
`parsereq(s4,req)` obtains req = lostcard.

This completes the execution of `find(name,acc,req)` having obtained the name, account code, and caller request. So processing next invokes the top level goal `handle(name,acc,req)` since all arguments are known. The rest of the processing proceeds similarly.

The main advantage of the rule-based methodology is that all processing is goal oriented which models that mechanisms of real human interactions. Typical human-human dialogue will begin with one purpose and then jump to subdialogues to support the main goal. Success or failure of various subdialogues cause movement to other subdialogues, and with good luck, eventual success of the top level dialogue. The rule-based approach enables the designer to identify the significant subgoals of a domain and write rules that address them. Once these rules are created, the dialogue will move effectively to the needed subgoals possibly in a very unpredictable manner. The sequential actions of the participants cannot be known ahead of time and the dialogue machine should proceed as each event requires. Thus the system is capable of dialogues that the designer could never foresee ahead of time.

A second advantage is that initiative is easily adjusted within the context of a rule-based system. It has been shown ([15], [16]) that appropriate initiative decisions can improve dialogue efficiency greatly. The optimum strategy requires the system to take the initiative when it has a direct and predictable path to success. The machine should release initiative to the partner if it has evidence that partner can efficiently lead the interaction to success. A rule-based system can apply variable initiative mechanisms in the context of the rules as described below.

A third reason to use rule-based systems is that they easily enable very complex behaviors that account for variations in user abilities. A natural user model can live within the context of the dialogue rules guiding them to behaviors that are specific to the current user.

Finally, the rule-based approach effectively yields predictive information about the expected user's responses that can be employed for error correction. These ideas are described further below. Systems have been built based on the missing axiom theory in our laboratory addressing the problems of equipment repair ([8], [13]), mystery solving ([16]), and many others.

3   Programming Initiative

Smith, Hipp, and Guinn showed in ([8],[15]) that variable initiative can greatly affect the efficiency of dialogues. We can explore briefly some of the models of dialogue given above and the implementation of variable initiative in each case. In the finite-state model, every input and output is anticipated by the designer and, at significant expense, initiative can be programmed. For aggressive taking of the initiative, states can be coded to demand certain responses from the user and parsing can adjusted to receive only those answers. For more passive behaviors, states can be designed to ask for help and the inputs can be parsed for the large variety of suggestions that may come back.

The most significant observation to make about initiative is that it represents a decision about who will specify the goals to be addressed. Smith and Hipp implemented a variable initiative system with four levels of initiative: *directive, suggestive, declarative,* and *passive.* The strongest level of initiative, directive, has the machine setting all goals and not responding to user answers that may deviate from the computer specified goals. Lower levels of initiative allow more and more variation in the user inputs. The weakest form of initiative for the machine, passive, has the machine wait for user assertions for what to do and it responds to them.

In terms of the rules being used, the rule being processed at each point is selected either on the basis of machine choices or user choices or some compromise between them. The point is that the rule-based architecture provides the proper environment for building in variable initiative because it makes explicit the basis for programming initiative, namely the decision as to who selects the next rule to be invoked. Initiative also involves variations in syntax for requesting and answering. We will not address that issue here.

4   User Modeling

Returning to the credit card example, we need to remember that there are many versions of the assertions a machine might make and the decision as to what to say depends somewhat on the user. If you have an experienced caller who knows about card numbers, it is reasonable to expect an answer from the request "Please give me your account code." However, a naive caller might be surprised by the request and unable to respond. A more sensitive dialogue might be this:

> System: Are you able to find one of your credit card statements?
> Caller: Yes, I have one here.
> System: Can you find that six character code at the upper right corner of
>   the statement?
> Caller: Ahhh. . . Yes, there it is.
> System: Please read me that code?
> Caller: X13794.

This can be implemented by adding a rule to carry out the subdialogue. Here is one of them.

```
parseacc(s,acc) :-
  help(findstatement),
  help(findacconstatement),
  help(readacconstatement).
```

Then a revision to the **speak** routine is added that checks the user model before it speaks anything. If the user model indicates the statement will not be understood, speak fails and some other rule needs to be invoked. In this case, the `parseacc(s,acc)` rule will be invoked which goes through a sequence of help statements. Notice that any of these help statements must also be checked with the user model before those statements are output. Perhaps the caller does not have a credit card statement or does not know what a statement is. Additional rules can be included and they will be automatically invoked if the user model signals for them.

Thus a rule-based system can have a huge variety of behaviors that are styled to the needs of the user. The user model is a simple and natural addition to the basic rule-based system.

This type of user model can be augmented by including probabilities with the assertions about user abilities. Suppose that we want to say to the caller "Please give me your account code." and we are unsure about whether the user will be able to respond helpfully. Over a period of time of usage of the system, we will obtain experience that some percent P of the callers will be able to answer correctly. As such percentages are gathered, it may become possible to optimize the dialogues for minimal length and this has been studied by Inouye ([17]). If there are many questions that may be asked and we know the probability for each one that it will be answered correctly, we can sometimes derive a path through the rules that will minimize the average length of the dialogues.

5   Error Correction

The best way to guarantee correct recognition of incoming speech is to know what the speaker will say before they say it. If a speaker enunciates the Gettysburg Address and your system knows that he or she is doing this, recognition can be perfect. A step in this direction for telephone answering was proposed by Baker et al. [18] who suggested that telephones of the future will have displays and those displays can be used to prompt the speaker before each utterance is made. That is the user can be given suggestions on the form and content of expected responses. In a test within the credit card domain, it was found that the average length of utterances in visually prompted cases was 2.9 words and this was 4.7 if no prompt was available. This led to substantial increases in word recognition rates for prompted inputs.

When a dialogue model is available as described above, one can greatly improve recognition by comparing the incoming utterance with the utterances that the model predicts. Thus in the rule-based example above, one can make reasonable guesses as to what might follow this statement:

>   System: I can give you your account balance, handle a lost card, or record
>   a change of address. Which of these would you like?

Here are some possibilities:

>   Sample utterances for the need account balance case:
>   How much do I owe?
>   What's my acc count balance?
>   Can you please tell me my balance?
>   Account balance, please.

>   For the lost card case:
>   I lost my card.
>   I cannot find my credit card.
>   I need a new card because I seem to have misplaced the old one.
>   I think my card was stolen.

>   For the change of address case:
>   I just moved. I am now at . . .
>   Next week I will be going to California.
>   You have my zip code wrong on my address.
>   My wife has a new job. We will be moving to North Carolina.

Given these possible responses and many more that might resemble them, how do we process the answer coming in from the caller? The methodology presented by Smith and Hipp was to measure the distance by some measure of the incoming utterance to the expected sentences. Thus we might receive the following:

Caller: Ahh, I seem to ahh lost my card.

The methodology is to measure the similarity between this sequence and those that are in the expected set. We will not pursue the details of this case except to reference two examples. Hipp ([8]) used a Hamming distance measure with the more important words weighted more heavily. Chu-Carroll ([19]) computed a representative word count vector for each classification (need balance, lost card, or change of address) and then computed that vector for the incoming utterance. The classification with the closest vector was selected as the most likely intended meaning. We used this system in our AMITIES system ([10]).

We developed a very attractive additional technique for handling the problem of identifying the caller ([10]). Suppose there are a million card holders for our XYZ company and we need to identify the caller with high probability. Huge problems arise because the pronunciation of names can vary, many new names may be entered into the database regularly, several people may have the same name, people may use nicknames, and so forth. We decided to place a probability on every record in the database before the call came in giving the likelihood that this individual was calling. Then as the information came in giving the name, account code, address, and so forth, we updated the probability for each record that this person was the one calling. Despite high error rates by the recognizer on the individual items spoken, the system could select the correct record with great accuracy. On a database of one million names with the caller spelling out six fields of information (name, account code, etc.), the machine identified the caller with 96.7 percent accuracy.

6   Success Finally

After several decades of optimism and many false starts, spoken language interfaces are beginning to work. Telephone systems for checking flight arrival and departure are installed and working well. Many other applications such as providing stock market quotes and call directory services are running routinely and successfully. Where more complicated negotiations are needed, experimental systems are showing promising results. In the early 1990's, Smith and Hipp reported success rates for equipment repair in the range of about 80 percent ([8], [13]). More recently, the recent DARPA Communicator project reported success rates for airline, hotel and auto rental reservations at the rate of mid 60's to about 70 percent for the best systems that were created ([3]). With these successes, some installed and some on the way, one can expect many more successful applications in the coming years.

Acknowledgement

The authors gratefully acknowledge the ongoing financial support by SAIC of our work on spoken language systems. This project has also been supported by National Science Foundation Grant 0121211 and Defense Advanced research Projects Agency Grant N66001-01-1-8941.

References

1. Rudnicky, A., Hauptmann, A., Lee, K.F.: Survey of current speech technology. Communications of the ACM **37** (1994) 52–57
2. van Kuppevelt, J., Smith, R.W., eds.: Current and New Directions in Discourse and Dialogue. Kluwer Academic Publishers, Dordrecht (2003)
3. Walker, M.A., Hirschman, L., Aberdeen, J.: Evaluation for darpa communicator spoken dialogue systems. In: Proceedings of the Second International Conference on Language Resources and Evaluation, Athens, Greece (2000)
4. Levin, E., Narayanan, S., Pieraccini, R., Biatov, K., Bocchieri, E., Fabbrizio, G.D., Eckert, W., Lee, S., Pokrovsky, A., Rahim, M., Ruscitti, P., Walker, M.: The at&t-darpa communicator mixed initiative spoken dialog system. In: Proceedings of the International Conference on Spoken Language Processing, ICSLP00. (2000)
5. Levin, E., Pieraccini, R., Eckert, W.: A stochastic model of human-machine interaction for learning dialog strategies. IEEE Transactions on Speech and Audio Processing (2000) 11–23
6. Rudnicky, A., Bennett, C., Black, A., Chotomongcol, A., Lenzo, K., Oh, A., Singh, R.: Task and domain specific modelling in the carnegie mellon communicator system. In: Proceedings of the International Conference on Spoken Language Processing, ICSLP00. (2000)
7. Rudnicky, A., Xu, W.: An agenda-based dialog management architecture for spoken language systems. In: IEEE Automatic Speech Recognition and Understanding Workshop. (1999)
8. Smith, R.W., Hipp, D.R.: Spoken Natural Language Dialog Systems. Oxford University Press, New York (1994)
9. Cohen, P.: Models of dialogue. In: Proceedings of the Fourth NEC Research Symposium. (1994)
10. Hardy, H., Biermann, A., Inouye, R., McKenzie, A., Strzalkowski, T., Ursu, C., Webb, N., Wu, M.: Data-driven strategies for an automated dialogue system. In: Proceedings of the 42nd Annual Meeting of the Association for Computational Linguistics. (2004)
11. Allen, J., Perrault, C.: Analyzing intention in utterances. Artificial Intelligence **15** (1980) 143–178
12. Litman, D., Allen, J.: A plan recognition model for subdialogs in conversations. Cognitive Science **11** (1987) 163–200
13. Smith, R.W., Hipp, D.R., Biermann, A.W.: An architecture for voice dialog systems based on prolog-style theorem proving. Computational Linguistics **21** (1995) 281–320
14. Fikes, R., Nilsson, N.: Strips: A new approach to the application of theorem proving to problem solving. Artificial Intelligence **2** (1971) 189–208
15. Guinn, C.: Mechanisms for mixed-initiative human-computer collaborative discourse. In: Proceedings of the 34th Annual Meeting of the Association for Computational Linguistics. (1996)

16. Guinn, C.I.: Meta-Dialogue Behaviors: Improving the Efficiency of Human-Machine Dialogue. PhD thesis, Duke University (1994)
17. Inouye, R.B.: Minimizing the length of non-mixed initiative dialogs. In: Companion Volume to the Proceedings of the Association for Computational Linguistics. (2004) 13–18
18. Baker, K., McKenzie, A., Biermann, A., Webelhuth, G.: Constraining user response via multimodal interface. International Journal of Speech Technology **7** (2004) 251–258
19. Chu-Carroll, J., Carpenter, B.: Vector-based natural language call routing. Computational Linguistics **25** (1999) 361–388

Anomaly Detection in Computer Security and an Application to File System Accesses*

Salvatore J. Stolfo, Shlomo Hershkop, Linh H. Bui, Ryan Ferster, and Ke Wang

Columbia University, New York, NY 10027, USA
{sal, shlomo, lhb2001, rlf92, kewang}@cs.columbia.edu

Abstract. We present an overview of anomaly detection used in computer security, and provide a detailed example of a host-based Intrusion Detection System that monitors file systems to detect abnormal accesses. The File Wrapper Anomaly Detector (FWRAP) has two parts, a sensor that audits file systems, and an unsupervised machine learning system that computes normal models of those accesses. FWRAP employs the Probabilistic Anomaly Detection (PAD) algorithm previously reported in our work on Windows Registry Anomaly Detection. FWRAP represents a general approach to anomaly detection. The detector is first trained by operating the host computer for some amount of time and a model specific to the target machine is automatically computed by PAD. The model is then deployed to a real-time detector. In this paper we describe the feature set used to model file system accesses, and the performance results of a set of experiments using the sensor while attacking a Linux host with a variety of malware exploits. The PAD detector achieved impressive detection rates in some cases over 95% and about a 2% false positive rate when alarming on anomalous processes.

Keywords: Host-Based Intrusion Detection, Anomaly Detection, File System, Wrapping

1 Introduction

Widely used commercial Intrusion Detection Systems (IDS) are based on signature matching algorithms. These algorithms match audit data of network or host activity to a database of signatures which correspond to known attacks. This approach, like virus detection algorithms, requires previous knowledge of an attack and is not effective on new attacks.

Anomaly Detection is an important alternative detection methodology that has the advantage of defending against new threats not detectable by signature-based systems. In general, anomaly detectors build a description of **normal** activity, by training a model of a system under typical operation, and compare

---

* This work has been supported in part by a contract from DARPA, Application-layer IDS, Contract No. F30602-00-1-0603.

M.-S. Hacid et al. (Eds.): ISMIS 2005, LNAI 3488, pp. 14–28, 2005.
© Springer-Verlag Berlin Heidelberg 2005

the normal model at run time to detect deviations of interest. Anomaly Detectors may be used over any audit source to both train and test for deviations from the norm. Anomaly detection algorithms may be specification-based or data mining or machine learning-based [11, 12], and have been applied to network intrusion detection [9, 11] and also to the analysis of system calls for host based intrusion detection [4, 6, 10, 23].

Specification or behavior based anomaly detectors such as the STAT approach [19], represent normal execution of a system using programmer supplied state transition or finite state machine representations [14]. Anomalies are detected at run-time when the execution of a process or system violates the predefined normal execution model. Data mining or machine learning-based anomaly detectors automatically learn a normal model without human intervention.

Anomaly detection systems are more art than science. A number of design choices are necessary to build an effective detector. First, one must design a monitor or auditing sensor that is able to extract data from some system or component, and do so without wasting resources and minimizing the impact on the system being monitored.

One must also design a set of informative "features" that are extracted from the audit data that provides the means of computing an effective model able to distinguish attacks from normal execution. Subsequently, one must understand what "attacks" may be buried in that audit data, i.e. whether sufficient information is manifest in the data to identify an attack from normal data. In approaches based upon machine learning, the design process is further complicated by "noise". Too frequently in research on anomaly detection, authors state the requirement that the training data must be purely normal and attack-free. This is unrealistic in most cases of computer security auditing where systems are under constant attack and monitoring generates vast quantities of data including attacks. Hand-cleaning data to exclude noise, or attack information, or to label data accurately, is simply not possible. Hence, anomaly detection algorithms must be sensitive to noise and produce models that are robust.

Some approaches to host-based anomaly detection have focused on monitoring the operating system's (OS) processes during program execution and alerting on anomalous sequences of system calls. For example, OS wrappers monitor each system call or DLL application and test a set of rules for "consistent" program execution [2]. This presumes that a program's legitimate system call execution can be specified correctly by a set of predefined rules. Alternatively, some have implemented machine learning techniques that model sequences of normal execution traces and thus detect run time anomalies that exhibit abnormal execution traces [6].

There are several important advantages to auditing at the OS level. This approach may provide *broad coverage* and *generality*; for a given target platform it may have wide applicability to detect a variety of malicious applications that may run on that platform.

However, there are several disadvantages to anomaly detection at the OS monitoring level. *Performance* (tracing and analyzing system calls) is not cheap;

there is a substantial overhead for running these systems, even if architected to be as lightweight as possible. Second, the adaptability and extensibility of these systems complicates their use as updates or patches to a platform may necessitate a complete retraining of the OS trace models.

Furthermore, OS system call tracing and anomaly detection may have another serious deficiency; they may suffer from *mimicry attack* [20], since the target platform is widely available for study by attackers to generate exploits that appear normal when executed.

We have taken an alternative view of host-based anomaly detection. Anomalous process executions (possibly those that are malicious) may be detected by monitoring the trace of events as they appear on attempts to alter or damage the machine's permanent store. Thus, a malicious attack that alters only runtime memory would not necessarily be detected by this monitor, while the vast majority of malicious attacks which do result in changes to the permanent store of the host might leave a trace of anomalous file system events. In this case, the two very important host based systems to defend and protect are the Registry (in Window's case) and the file system (in both Window's and Unix cases). The file system is the core permanent store of the host and any malicious execution intended to damage a host will ultimately set its sights upon the file system. A typical user or application will not behave in the same manner as a malicious exploit, and hence the behavior of a malicious exploit is likely able to be detected as an unusual or unlikely set of file system accesses.

The File Wrapper Anomaly Detection System (FWRAP) is presented in this paper as an exemplary application of anomaly detection to computer security applications. FWRAP is a host-based detector that utilizes file wrapper technology to monitor file system accesses. The file wrappers implemented in FWRAP are based upon work described in [25] and operate in much the same fashion as the wrapper technology described in [2]. The wrappers are implemented to extract a set of information about each file access including, for example, date and time of access, host, UID, PID, and filename, etc. Each such file access thus generates a record describing that access.

Our initial focus here is to regard the set of file system access records as a database, and to model the *likely records* in this database. Hence, any record analyzed during detection time is tested to determine whether it is consistent with the database of training records. This modeling is performed by the **P**robabilistic **A**nomaly **D**etection algorithm (PAD) introduced in our prior work on the Windows registry [1]. We report on experiments using alternative threshold logic that governs whether the detector generates an alarm or not depending upon the scores computed by PAD. The PAD detector achieved impressive detection rates in some cases over 95% and about a 2% false positive rate when alarming on anomalous processes.

The rest of the paper is organized as follows. Section 2 briefly describes alternative anomaly detection algorithms and a brief description of the PAD algorithm. Section 3 discusses the architecture of the FWRAP sensor. Section 4 describes the audit data and features computed that are input to PAD to generate models of normal file accesses. We then detail results of various experiments running real malware against a Linux host. Section 5 describes the experimental setup and the results and findings. Section 5 describes the open problems in anomaly detection research and how this work can be extended.

2   Alternative Anomaly Detection Algorithms

Anomaly detection systems for computer security, and host-based intrusion detection specifically, were first proposed by Denning [3]. The concept was later implemented in NIDES [9] to model normal network behavior in order to detect deviant network traffic that may correspond to an attack against a network computer system.

A variety of other work has appeared in the literature detailing alternative algorithms to establish normal profiles, applied to a variety of different audit sources, some specific to user commands for masquerade detection [16, 13, 21], others specific to network protocols and LAN traffic for detecting denial of service attacks [12, 18] or Trojan execution, or application or system call-level data for malware detection [6], to name a few.

A variety of different modeling approaches have been described in the literature to compute baseline profiles. These include probabilistic models or statistical outlier detection over (temporal) data [4, 24]; comparison of statistical distributions (or histogram distance metrics) [22], one-class supervised machine learning [13, 21] and unsupervised cluster-based algorithms [5, 15]. Some approaches consider the correlation of multiple models [7, 23]. One-class Support Vector Machines have also been applied to anomaly detection in computer security [8]. W. Lee et al. [11] describe a framework and system for auditing and data mining and feature selection for intrusion detection. This framework consists of classification, link analysis and sequence analysis for constructing intrusion detection models.

In general, in the case that an audit source is a stream or temporally ordered data, a variety of models may be defined for an audit source and a detector may be computed to generate an alarm if a violation is observed based upon volume and velocity statistics. Volume statistics represent the amount of data observed per unit of time, while velocity statistics model the changes in frequency of the data over time. In practice, a number of simple algorithms work surprisingly well. For example, computing "moving averages" over time to estimate the average state of a system, and detecting "bursts" by, for example, noting when the volume or velocity of events exceeds one or two standard deviations from the mean works effectively in detecting distributed denial of service attacks, or scanning/probing activities.

One of the most cruical design choices in designing an anomaly detector is the choice of algorithm, the feature sets and the training methodology. Fundamentally, the issue is whether the resultant models can effectively detect truly abnormal events that correspond to an attack. A fuller treatment evaluating anomaly detection algorithms and their coverage is given by Maxion [17].

The performance of the various anomaly detectors also varies with a number of tunable parameters including the amount and quality of training data (amount of noise present), the threshold settings and the particular decision logic used, and whether the detectors output is validated by correlating with other information. For example, probabilistic based algorithms typically score data by estimating the likelihood of that data. Cluster-based or SVM-based algorithms employ a distance metric or a density measure to estimate whether a datum is normal, or a member of a minority cluster. In either case, a threshold needs to be set to determine whether a data under test is or is not normal. The calibration of this tunable threshold greatly affects the performance of any anomaly detection system, either generating too few true positives, or too many false positives.

Furthermore, computer systems are highly dynamic and rarely reach a stable state. Any normal model computed for one period of time will undoubtedly go stale at some future time. Thus, anomaly detectors require updating and adaption to shifting environments. Detecting when retraining is necessary, or the time "epoch" when a detector ought to be retrained is very much a matter of the specific environment being modeled. In many cases, these issues, calibration, environment shift, and adaptive re-training, are core design requirements necessitating a lot of study, design and engineering for successful systems to be deployed. Bad choices will lead to faulty systems that are either blind to real attacks, or generate so many false alarms as to provide no useful information.

In our prior work, we proposed and developed a number of anomaly detection algorithms. Several cluster-based algorithms were explored [15, 5] as well as probabilistic modeling for sequence data [4], and for database records [1]. The PAD algorithm inspects feature values in its training data set, and estimates the probability of occurrence of each value using a Bayesian estimation technique. PAD estimates a full conditional probability mass function and thus estimates the relative probability of a feature value conditioned on other feature values and the expected frequency of occurrence of each feature. One of the strengths of the PAD algorithm is that it also models the likelihood of seeing new feature values at run-time that it may not have encountered during training. We assume that normal events will occur quite frequently, and abnormal events will occur with some very low probability. Our experiments and application of PAD have been shown to be robust and effective models are trainable in any environment where "noise" is a minority of the training data.

In the following sections we provide an exemplar anomaly detector. We present the FWRAP anomaly detector that audits host-based file systems during a training period, and detects abnormal file accesses at detection time using the PAD algorithm. Anomalous processes are noted by FWRAP when a sufficient number of anomalous file accesses are detected by PAD. We test the effectiveness of the detector by running real exploits against a Windows machine and meausure the detector accuracy over varying threshold settings. We begin with a description of the FWRAP architecture.

3   FWRAP System Architecture

Several requirements drove the design of the FWRAP system. The file system sensor had to be lightweight, easily portable to different systems, and complete, in the sense that it is able to monitor all file system accesses without loss of information. Perhaps the most important requirement is that the system must be transparent to the user.

Previous work by Zadok [25] proposed a mountable file system for Unix and Windows which would allow additional extensions to the underlying operating system without having to modify kernel level functionality. The FiST technology developed in that work has been extended to provide a security mechanism via file system auditing modules via a Vnode interface. We implemented a FiST audit module that forms the basis of the FWRAP audit sensor. Figure 1 illustrates the architecture that we developed as a standalone real time application on a single Linux host.

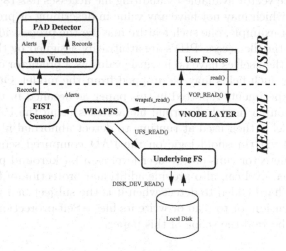

Fig. 1. The Architecture of FWRAP IDS

Once all subsystem file accesses are logged its a straightforward matter to provide the means of reading from the log, formatting the data and sending it to the PAD module for analysis. A typical snippet of a line of text sent to the PAD module is as follows.

```
Mar  9 19:03:14 zeno kernel:
snoopfs detected access by uid 0, pid 1010, to file cat
```

This record was generated when the root user accesses a file named 'cat' on a machine named 'zeno'. We modified a C program to format this data for PAD exemplified by the following (partial) record.

```
<rec><Month str>Mar</Month> <Day i>9</Day> <Time str>19:03:14</Time>
<IP str>zeno</IP> <UID i>0</UID> <PID i>1010</PID> <File str>cat</File></rec>
```

3.1   PAD Detector

The data gathered by monitoring each file access is a rich set of information that describes in great detail a single file access. Each record is treated as a feature vector used by PAD for training a normal model that describes normal file accesses.

PAD models each feature and pairs of features as a conditional probability. A single feature produces a "first order consistency check" that scores the likelihood of observing a feature value at run time. PAD also models the likelihood of observing a new feature value at run-time that was not observed during training. Second order consistency checks score the likelihood of a particular feature value conditioned on a second feature. Thus, given n features in a training record, PAD generates n first order consistency checks, and $n * (n - 1)$ second order consistency checks. Although it is possible to use higher order consistency checks, the computational overhead and space constraints make it infeasible for the current implementation of PAD.

The feature vector available by auditing file accesses has 18 fields of information, some of which may not have any value in describing or predicting a normal file access. For example, one such feature may be the process identifier, PID, associated with the file access. PID's are arbitrarily assigned by the underlying OS and in and of themselves have no intrinsic value as a predictor of a file access. As an expediency such fields may be dropped from the model. Only 7 features are used in the experiments reported in this paper as detailed in the next section.

After training a model of normal file accesses using the PAD algorithm the resultant model is then used at runtime to detect abnormal file accesses. Alerts are generated via threshold logic on the PAD computed scores. As shown in Figure 1 the detector runs on the user level as a background process. Having it run on the user level can also provide additional protection of the system as the sensor can be hard-coded to detect when it is the subject of a process that aims to kill its execution, or to read or write its files. (Self-protection mechanisms for FWRAP are beyond the scope of this paper.)

3.2   FWRAP Features

The FWRAP data model consists of 7 features extracted or derived from the audit data provided by the FWRAP sensor.

Several of the features describe intrinsic values of the file access, for example, the name of the file, and the user id. We also encode information about the characteristics of the file involved in the access, specifically the frequency of touching the file. This information is discretized into a few categories rather than represented as a continuous valued feature. We generally follow a strategy suggested by the Windows OS. Within the add/change applications function of control panel in Windows, the frequency of use of an application is characterized as "frequently", "sometimes" and "rarely". Since it is our aim to port FWRAP to Windows (exploiting whatever native information Windows may provide and to correlate FWRAP with RAD), we decided in this experimental implementation of FWRAP on Linux to follow the same principle for the Unix file system but with a slightly finer level of granularity than suggested by Windows. Hence, we measured file accesses over a trace for several days, and discretized the frequency of use of a file into the four categories as described below.

The entire set of features used by in this study to model file system accesses are as follows:

UID. This is the user ID running the process

WD. The working directory of a user running the process

CMD. This is the command line invoking the running process

DIR. This is the parent directory of the touched file.

FILE. This is the name of the file being accessed. This allows our algorithm to locate files that are often or not often accessed in the training data. Many files are accessed only once for special situations like system or application installation. Some of these files can be changed during an exploit.

PRE-FILE. This is the concatenation of the three previous accessed files. This feature codes information about the sequence of accessed files of normal activities such as log in, Netscape, statx, etc. For example, a login process typically follows a sequence of accessed files such as .inputrc, .tcshrc, .history, .login, .cshdirs, etc.

FREQUENCY. This feature encodes the access frequency of files in the training records. This value is estimated from the training data and discretized into four categories:

1. NEVER (for processes that don't touch any file)
2. FEW (where a file had been accessed only once or twice)
3. SOME (where a file had been accessed about 3 to 10 times)
4. OFTEN (more than SOME).

Alternative discretization of course are possible. We computed the standard deviations from the average frequency of access files from all user processes in the training records to define the category ranges. An access frequency falls into the range of FEW or OFTEN categories often occurs for a file touched by the kernel or a background process.

Examples of typical records gathered from the sensors with these 7 features are:

```
500 /home/linhbui login /bin dc2xx10
725-705-cmdline Some    1205,Normal

500 /home/linhbui kmod /Linux_Attack kmod
1025-0.3544951178-0.8895221054 Never    1253,Malicious
```

The last items (eg., "1253,Malicious) are tab separated from the feature values and represent an optional comment, here used to encode ground truth used in evaluating performance of the detector. The first record with pid=1205 was generated from a normal user activity. The second was captured from an attack running the kmod program to gain root access. The distinction is represented by the labels "normal" and "malicious". These labels are not used by the PAD algorithm. They exist solely for testing and evaluating the performance of the computed models.

Another malicious record is

```
0 /home/linhbui sh /bin su meminfo-debug-insmod Some
1254,Malicious
```

This record illustrates the results of an intruder who gained root access. The working directory (WD) is still at /home/linhbui but the UID now has changed to 0. A record of this nature ought to be a low probability event.

4   Experiments

We deployed the FWRAP audit sensor on a "target host" machine in our lab environment, an Intel Celeron 800MHz PC with 256 RAM, running Linux 2.4 with an ext2 file-system. The data gathered by the sensor was logged and used for experimental evaluation on a separate machine. The latter test machine is far faster and provided the means of running multiple experiments to measure accuracy and performance of the PAD implementation. The target host was part of a Test Network Environment which allowed us to run controlled executions of malicious programs without worrying about noise from outside the network corrupting our tests, nor inadvertently allowing leakage of an attack to other systems. Data was not gathered from a simulator, but rather from runtime behavior of a set of users on the target machine.

We collected data from the target host for training over 5 days of normal usage from a group of 5 users. Each user used the machine for their work, logging in, editing some files on terminal, checking email, browsing some website, etc. The root user performed some system maintenance as well as routine sysadmin tasks.

The logged data resulted in a data set of 275,666 records of 23 megabytes which we used to build a PAD model on the other "test machine". This model will be referred to as the "clean model", although we note that PAD can tolerate noise. The size of the model was 486 megabytes prior to any pruning and compression.

Once the model was computed, one of the users on the target machine volunteered to be the "Attacker", who then used the target machine for 3 experiments each lasting from 1 to 3 hours. The malicious user ran three different exploits and three Trojan exploits from their home account. These exploits are publicly available on the Internet. The user was asked to act maliciously and to gain root privileges using the attack exploits on hand. Once root control was acquired, the user further misused the host by executing programs which placed back-doors in the system. The system was monitored while the attacks were run. The resultant monitoring produced records from the FWRAP sensors. These records were then tested and scored by the PAD model.

The PAD analysis was run on the test machine, a dual processor 1500 MHz with 2GB of ram. The total time to build the model of the 23 MB of training data was three minutes, with memory usage at 14%. Once, the model was created, we ran the model against the test data from the 3 experiments, while varying the thresholds to generate a ROC curve. Each detection process took 15 seconds with 40% of CPU usage and 14% of memory.

These performance statistics were measured on the test machine, not on the target host where the data was gathered. This experimental version was implemented to test the efficacy of the approach and has not been optimized for high efficiency and minimal resource consumption for deployment on the target machine. Even so, the analysis of the computational performance of the sensor measured during the experiments indicates that although training the model is resource intensive, run-time detection is far less expensive. A far more efficient professionally engineered version of FWRAP would reduce resource consumption considerably. That effort would make sense only if the sensor achieves the goal of detecting anomalous events indicative of a security breach.

It should be noted that the RAD sensor/detector using PAD running on Windows has been upgraded to run exceptionally fast, with a very small amount of memory and CPU footprint. (The current Windows implementation of PAD requires less than 1 MB of space and the run-time detector consumes at most 5% of CPU, barely discernible.) This newer implementation of PAD is being ported to Linux so that FWRAP will also be far more efficient than the present prototype reported in this paper. The version reported here is the first proof of concept implementation without the performance enhancements implemented on the Windows platform.

5   Results

This section describes the results of a subset of experiments we ran. Space does not permit a full treatment and comparative evaluation of alternative alert decision logic.

The PAD algorithm evaluates each file access record output by the sensor by comparing the PAD scores to a threshold value. Each record produces 49 scores for each consistency check (7 first order + 7x6 second order). The minimum score over all consistency checks is then tested against the threshold. If the minimum score is below the threshold, an alert is generated for that record.

An example of the PAD output with threshold = 0.1 is as follows: 8.873115 8.39732 7.69225 4.057663 0.485905 0.323076 6.527675 8.34453 7.464175 3.727299 0.0 0.0 5.971592 8.344 7.464175 3.727299 0.0 0.0 5.79384 7.45713 7.454335 4.060443 0.0 0.0 4.97851 3.732753 3.723643 4.039242 0.0 0.0 3.982627 0.458721 0.371057 0.439515 0.14842 0.0 0.221132 0.302689 0.20546 0.258604 0.090151 0.0 0.067373 5.978326 5.81323 5.015466 4.060443 0.0 0.0 :
1254,Malicious (Min score 0.0)

A process is identified as malicious if more than some minimum number of records it generates is scored as an anomaly. This number is a second threshold. We tested varying threshold levels applied to the PAD scores under different thresholds governing the number of anomalous records used to generate a final alert.

The decision process is evaluated by varying the percentage of anomalous records that are generated by a process in order to raise an alert. For example, a process might be considered malicious if it generates one anomalous record, or all of its records are anomalous, or some percentage of its records are deemed anomalous. We vary this percentage in the following experiments from 10% to 80%.

We define "Detection Rate" as the percentage of all process labeled "malicious" that produced PAD scores below the threshold. The "False Positive Rate" is the percentage labeled "normal" that likewise produced records with PAD scores that were below the threshold. We illustrate the different detection rates and false positive rates over different threshold settings in tabular form. The results indicate that the per-process detection logic provides excellent detection rate and lower false positive rates. This leads to the observation that a malicious process typically generates a considerable number of anomalous events, while many normal processes occasionally generate a few anomalous events. This is not surprising as the same results were discovered in the RAD experiments [1].

Table 1, **Table 2**, and **Table 3** detail the results on a Per Process basis. The best results are 95% detection with about 2% false positive rates in experiment 1, 97% accuracy with 7% false positives in experiment 2 and 100% with 8% false positive in experiment 3. Note that the results from experiment 1 are relatively better with respect to false positive rates than those from experiments 2 and 3. The primary reason concerns that amount of training performed during the different experiments. Experiment 1 had far more training data establishing the perhaps obvious point that as the sensor models more events its detection accuracy increases.

In the first experiment implemented on the target machine, there were 5,550 processes generated during the 3 hour period. 121 processes were generated during the attack period (i.e. the time between the initial launching of the attacking exploits and the Trojan software execution after he gained root access). However, only 22 processes generated during this time were spawned by the attack.

Many of the false positives were from processes that were simply not run as a part of the training session but were otherwise normal file system programs.

Table 1. Experiment 1, per-process detection. Number of processes: 5550, number of malicious processes: 22

Threshold	Detection Rate	False Positive
1.1	1.0	0.027090
1.0	0.954545	0.02727
0.9	0.909091	0.026690
0.8	0.909091	0.026345
0.7	0.863636	0.025927
0.6	0.863636	0.025381
0.5	0.772727	0.023363
0.4	0.772727	0.021145
0.3	0.727273	0.020981
0.2	0.727273	0.020909
0.1	0.727273	0.020163

Table 2. Experiment 2, per-process detection. Number of processes: 1344, number of malicious processes: 37

Threshold	Detection Rate	False Positive
1.3	1.0	0.072485
1.2	0.972973	0.071741
1.1	0.972973	0.071145
1.0	0.972973	0.070104
0.9	0.972973	0.068616
0.8	0.972973	0.0675
0.7	0.972973	0.066532
0.6	0.945946	0.062961
0.5	0.945946	0.057553
0.4	0.945946	0.057328
0.3	0.918919	0.057276
0.2	0.918919	0.057180
0.1	0.918919	0.046897

Table 3. Experiment 3, per-process detection. Number of processes: 1279, number of malicious processes: 72

Threshold	Detection Rate	False Positive
0.8	1.0	0.08889
1.7	0.98611	0.08850
0.6	0.97222	0.08647
0.5	0.86111	0.07732
0.4	0.80555	0.07544
0.3	0.79166	0.07498
0.2	0.79166	0.07357
0.1	0.77777	0.07107

False positives also occurred when processes were run under varying conditions. Command shell execution and file execution of a new application caused false positives to appear. Applications generate processes in different ways depending upon their underlying system call initiation. Furthermore, programs which require a network connection to run correctly caused a false alarm when executed without a network connection. These false alarms arise because the model has not seen behavior from all the different execution behaviors of a given program.

6   Conclusions

By using file system access on a Linux system, we are able to label all processes as either attacks or normal, with high accuracy and low false positive rates. We observe that file system accesses are apparently quite regular and well modeled by PAD. Anomalous accesses are rather easy to detect. Furthermore, malicious process behavior generates a relatively significant number of anomalous events, while normal processes can indeed generate anomalous accesses as well.

The work reported in this paper is an extension of our research on anomaly detection. The PAD algorithm has been previously applied to network traffic, as well as the Windows Registry, as described earlier in this paper. There are a number of open research issues that we are actively pursuing. These issues involve calibration, pruning, feature selection, concept (or environment) drift, correlation and resiliency to attack.

Briefly, we seek automatic means of building anomaly detectors for arbitrary audit sources that are well behaved, and are easy to use. With respect to calibration, one would ideally like a system such as FWRAP to self-adjust its thresholding to minimize false positives while revealing sufficient evidence of a true anomaly indicative of an abuse or an attack. It is important to understand, however, that anomaly detection models should be considered part of the evidence, and not be depended upon for the whole detection task. This means anomaly detector outputs should be correlated with other indicators or other anomaly detection models computed over different audit sources, different features or different modeling algorithms, in order to confirm or deny that an attack is truly occurring. Thus, it would be a mistake to entirely focus on a well calibrated threshold for a single anomaly detector simply to reduce false positives. It may in fact be a better strategy to generate more alerts, and possibly higher numbers of false positives, so that the correlation of these alerts with other confirmatory evidence reveals the true attacks that otherwise would go undetected (had the anomaly detector threshold been set too low).

In the experiments run to date PAD produces fine grained models that are expensive in memory. There are several enhancements that have been implemented in the Windows implementation of PAD for the RAD detector to alleviate its memory consumption requirements. These include pruning of features after an analytical evaluation that would indicate no possible consistency check violation would be possible for a feature at run-time.

Finally, two questions come to most minds when they first study anomaly detectors of various kinds; how long should they be trained, and when should they be retrained. These issues are consistently revealed due to a common phenomenon, concept (or environment) drift. What is modeled at one point in time represents the "normal data" drawn from the environment for a particular training epoch, but the environment may change (either slowly or rapidly) which necessitates a change in model.

The particular features being drawn from the environment have an intrinsic range of values; PAD is learning this range, and modeling the inherent "variability" of the particular feature values one may see for some period of time. Some features would not be expected to vary widely over time, others may be expected to vary widely. PAD learns this information (or an approximation) for the period of time it observes the data. But it is not known if it has observed enough. RAD's implementation on Windows provides the means of automatically retraining a model under a variety of user controlled schedules or performance measures. RAD includes a decision procedure, and a feedback control loop that provides the means to determine whether PAD has trained enough, and deems when it may be necessary to retrain a model if its performance should degrade. The same techniques are easily implemented for FWRAP as well.

References

1. F. Apap, A. Honig, S. Hershkop, E. Eskin and S. Stolfo. Detecting Malicious Software by Monitoring Anomalous Windows Registry Accesses. Fifth International Symposium on Recent Advances in Intrusion Detection, RAID-2002. Zurich, Switzerland, 2002.
2. R. Balzer. Mediating Connectors. 19th IEEE International Conference on Distributed Computing Systems Workshop, 1994.
3. D. E. Denning, An intrusion detection model. IEEE Transactions on Software Engineering, 222, SE-13, 1987
4. E. Eskin. Anomaly Detection Over Noisy Data Using Learned Probability Distributions. In Proceedings of the 17th Intl Conf. on Machine Learning (ICML-2000), 2000.
5. E. Eskin, A. Arnold, M. Prerau, L. Portnoy and S. J. Stolfo. A Geometric Framework for Unsupervised Anomaly Detection: Detecting Intrusions in Unlabeled Data. Data Mining for Security Applications. Kluwer 2002.
6. S. Forrest and S. A. Hofmeyr and A. Somayaji and T. A. Longstaff. A Sense of Self for UNIX Processes IEEE Symposium on Security and Privacy, 120-128, 1996
7. A. K. Ghosh, A. Schwartzbard, M. Schatz. Learning Program Behavior Profiles for Intrusion Detection. Workshop Intrusion Detection and Network Monitoring 1999.
8. K. A Heller, K. M Svore, A. D. Keromytis, and S. J. Stolfo. One Class Support Vector Machines for Detecting Anomalous Window Registry Accesses. 3rd IEEE Conference Data Mining Workshop on Data Mining for Computer Security. November 19, 2003.
9. H. S. Javitz and A. Valdes. The NIDES Statistical Component: Description and Justification. Technical report. SRI International, 1993.
10. W. Lee and S. J. Stolfo and P. K. Chan. Learning patterns from UNIX processes execution traces for intrusion detection AAAI Workshop on AI Approaches to Fraud Detection and Risk Management, 50-56, 1997
11. W. Lee and S. Stolfo. 1999. A Framework for Constructing Features and Models for Intrusion Detection Systems. In Proceedings of 1999 IEEE Symposium on Computer Security and Privacy and the Proceedings of the 8th ACM SIGKDD Int. Conf. on Knowledge Discovery and Data Mining. 1999.
12. M. V. Mahoney AND P. K. Chan. Detecting Novel Attacks by Identifying anomalous Network Packet Headers. Florida Institute of Technology Technical Report CS-2001-2, 1999.
13. R. Maxion, and T. Townsend. Masquerade Detection Using Truncated Command Lines. International Conference on Dependable Systems and Networks (DSN-02), Washington, D.C., 2002.
14. C. C. Michael and A. Ghosh. Simple, State-based approaches to Program-based Anomaly Detection. ACM Trans. on Information and System Security, TISSEC. Vol. 5., 2002.

15. L. Portnoy, E. Eskin and S. J. Stolfo. Intrusion detection with unlabeled data using clustering'. Proceedings of ACM CSS Workshop on Data Mining Applied to Security (DMSA-2001). Philadelphia, PA, 2001.
16. M. Schonlau, W. DuMouchel, W. Ju, A. F. Karr, M. Theus, and Y. Vardi. Computer intrusion: Detecting masquerades. Statistical Science, 16(1):58-74, February 2001.
17. K M.C. Tan and Roy A. Maxion. Why 6? Defining the Operational Limits of stide, an Anomaly-Based Intrusion Detector. IEEE Symp. On Security and Privacy. 2002.
18. C. Taylor and J. Alves-Foss. NATE: Network Analysis of Anomalous Traffic Events, a low-cost approach. In Proceedings New Security Paradigms Workshop, 2001.
19. G. Vigna, F. Valeur and R. Kemmerer. Designing and Implementing a Family of Intrusion Detection Systems. Proc. 9th European software engineering conference, 2003.
20. D. Wagner and P. Soto. Mimicry attacks on host based intrusion detection systems. Ninth ACM Conference on Computer and Communications Security, 2002.
21. K. Wang and S. Stolfo. One-Class Training for Masquerade Detection. 3rd IEEE International Conference on Data Mining, Workshop on Data Mining for Security Applications, Florida, Nov., 2003.
22. K. Wang, S. J. Stolfo. Anomalous Payload-based Network Intrusion Detection. RAID2004, France, September 2004.
23. C. Warrender, S. Forrest, and B. Pearluter. Detecting Intrusions Using System Calls: Alternative Data Models. IEEE Computer Society, 1999.
24. N. Ye. A Markov Chain Model of Temporal Behavior for Anomaly Detection. In Proceedings of the 2000 IEEE Workshop on Information Assurance and Security, United States Military Academy, West Point, NY. 2000.
25. E. Zadok and Jason Nieh. FiST: A Language for Stackable File Systems. Usenix Technical Conference. June 2000

A Machine Text-Inspired Machine Learning Approach for Identification of Transmembrane Helix Boundaries

Betty Yee Man Cheng[1], Jaime G. Carbonell[1],
and Judith Klein-Seetharaman[1, 2]

[1] Language Technologies Institute, Carnegie Mellon University,
5000 Forbes Avenue, Pittsburgh, PA, 15213, USA
{ymcheng, jgc}@cs.cmu.edu
[2] Department of Pharmacology, University of Pittsburgh,
200 Lothrop Street, Pittsburgh, PA, 15261, USA
judithks@cs.cmu.edu

Abstract. In this paper, we adapt a statistical learning approach, inspired by automated topic segmentation techniques in speech-recognized documents to the challenging protein segmentation problem in the context of G-protein coupled receptors (GPCR). Each GPCR consists of 7 transmembrane helices separated by alternating extracellular and intracellular loops. Viewing the helices and extracellular and intracellular loops as 3 different topics, the problem of segmenting the protein amino acid sequence according to its secondary structure is analogous to the problem of topic segmentation. The method presented involves building an n-gram language model for each 'topic' and comparing their performance in predicting the current amino acid, to determine whether a boundary occurs at the current position. This presents a distinctly different approach to protein segmentation from the Markov models that have been used previously and its commendable results is evidence of the benefit of applying machine learning and language technologies to bioinformatics.

1 Introduction

Predicting the function of a protein from its amino acid sequence information alone is one of the major bottlenecks in understanding genome sequences and an important topic in bioinformatics. Mapping of protein sequence to function can be viewed as a multi-step cascaded process: the primary sequence of amino acids encodes secondary structure, tertiary or 3-dimensional structure, and finally quaternary structure, a functional unit of multiple interacting protein subunits. Proteins are divided broadly into two classes, soluble proteins and transmembrane proteins. The problem of predicting secondary structure from the primary sequence in soluble proteins has been viewed predominantly as a 3-state classification problem with the state-of-the-art performance at 76% when multiple homologous sequences are available [1]. The problem of predicting secondary structure in transmembrane proteins has been limited to predicting the transmembrane portions of helices in helical membrane proteins [2, 3]. Here, accuracy is more difficult to assess because there is a very limited number of transmembrane proteins with known 3-dimensional structure, and membrane lipids are

M.-S. Hacid et al. (Eds.): ISMIS 2005, LNAI 3488, pp. 29–37, 2005.
© Springer-Verlag Berlin Heidelberg 2005

usually not included in these structures. For both soluble and transmembrane proteins, a large portion of inaccuracy comes from the boundary cases. However, in many biological applications, knowing the precise boundaries is critical. This paper addresses a subproblem of the general protein segmentation problem by limiting the context to G-protein coupled receptors, an important superfamily of helical transmembrane proteins where the order and type of secondary structures within each protein are known. However, the approach can be extended to any helical transmembrane protein. In order to address structural segmentation in proteins with high accuracy, we combine domain insights from structural biology with machine learning techniques proven for the analogous task of topic segmentation in text mining.

1.1 G Protein Coupled Receptors

G Protein Coupled Receptors (GPCRs) are transmembrane proteins that serve as sensors to the external environment. There are now more than 8000 GPCR sequences known [4], but only a single known 3-dimensional structure, namely that of rhodopsin [5, 6]. This is due to the fact that the structures of transmembrane proteins are difficult to determine by the two main techniques that give high-resolution structural information, NMR spectroscopy and x-ray crystallography. However, detailed information about the structure of individual GPCRs is urgently needed in drug design as approximately 60% of currently approved drugs target GPCR proteins [7]. The distribution of hydrophobic amino acids suggests a common secondary structure organization of alternating alpha helices and loops (Fig. 1): there are seven transmembrane helices, an (extracellular) N-terminus, three extracellular loops, a (cytoplasmic) C-terminus, and three cytoplasmic loops.

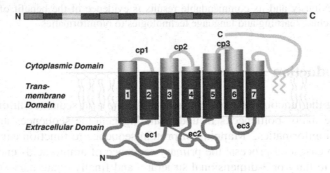

Fig. 1. Schematic of the amino acid sequence and secondary structure of a GPCR. Extracellular and cytoplasmic loops are colored dark grey and light grey respectively

Due to insufficient real training data for predicting the boundaries of transmembrane helices in GPCR, the training and testing data used in this study (except for rhodopsin) are synthetic. They are predictions based on hydrophobicity, which have been accepted by the majority of biologists as the closest estimates to the true boundaries. Because our approach does not use hydrophobicity information directly, a consensus between our predictions and the hydrophobicity predictions can be interpreted as additional evidence that the particular predicted boundary point is correct.

1.2 Related Work

A number of algorithms have been proposed to predict transmembrane domains in proteins using only amino acid sequence information, from the first Kyte-Doolittle approach based on hydrophobicity plots [8] to the more recent algorithms TMHMM [9] and PRED-TMR [10]. Most of these methods are either window-based or make use of Markov models. Window-based algorithms predict the secondary structure of the central amino acid in the window by examining the residues in the local window, using information such as frequencies of individual amino acids in each type of secondary structure, correlations among positions within the window, and evolutionary information via multiple sequence alignment of homologous sequences. Recently, improvements have also been found in considering interactions in the sequence outside the fixed window [11].

Like in most areas of computational biology, Markov models have been found to be useful in predicting the locations of transmembrane helices and are among the most successful prediction methods, including MEMSAT [12], HMMTOP [13] and TMHMM [9]. The models differ in the number of states, where each state is a Markov model on its own, representing different regions of the helices, extracellular or cytoplasmic loops.

Due to the lack of a standard dataset, the performance of the various approaches to predicting transmembrane alpha helices is controversial. Recently, a server was established that compares the performance of different methods using a single testing dataset with both soluble and transmembrane proteins. However, the training dataset is not uniform across the methods, making the results of the comparison unreliable [3, 14]. Moreover, since these methods are available only as programs pre-trained on different datasets, a fair comparison between these methods and our own is not possible.

2 Approach

In human languages, topic segmentation has many applications, particularly in speech and video where there are no document boundaries. Beeferman et al. [15] introduced a new statistical approach to segmentation in human languages based on exponential models to extract topicality and cue-word features. In essence, Beeferman and his colleagues calculated the predictive ratio of a topic model vs. a background model, and where significant changes (discontinuities) were noted, a boundary hypothesis is generated. Other features of the text string cuing boundaries were also used to enhance performance. Here, we adapted their notion of topicality features for GPCR segmentation.

2.1 Segmentation in Human Languages

Beeferman et al. [15] used the relative performance of two language models, a long-range model and a short-range model, to help predict the topic boundaries. The long-range model was trained on the entire corpus, while the short-range model was trained on only data seen since the last (predicted) boundary. This causes the short-range model to be more specifically targeted to the current topic and as a result, it performs better than the long-range model while inside the current topic. However, at a topic boundary, the short-range model's performance would suddenly drop below the long-range model's performance because it is too specific to the last topic instead of the general corpus, and it would need to see a certain amount of data from the new topic before it can again outperform the long-range model. This was tracked using topical-ity measure — the log ratio of the short-range model's performance to the long-range model's performance in predicting the current word. Beeferman et al. [15] used this to detect the general position of the topic boundary, and cue-words (words that often occur near a topic boundary) to fine-tune the prediction.

2.2 GPCR Segmentation

Since the type and order of segments in the GPCR secondary structure is known (Fig. 1), we built a language model for each of the segments and compared the probability each of them assigns to the current amino acid to determine the location of the seg-ment boundary. The reason for not building a short-range model and a long-range model as in Beeferman et al. [15] is that the average length of a protein segment is 25 amino acids — too short to train a language model. Previous segmentation experi-ments using mutual information [16] and Yule's association measure [17] have shown the helices to be much more similar to each other than to the extracellular and cyto-plasmic loops. Similarly, the N-terminus and C-terminus have been shown to be very similar to the extracellular and cytoplasmic loops respectively. Moreover, since no two helices, extracellular or cytoplasmic segments occur consecutively, 3 segment models for helices, extracellular domains and intracellular domains are sufficient.

Each of the segment models is an interpolation of 6 basic probability models — a unigram model, a bigram model and 4 trigram models, where a 'gram' is a single amino acid. One of the trigram models, as well as the unigram and bigram models, uses the complete 20 amino acid alphabet. The other 3 trigram models make use of three reduced alphabets where a group of amino acids sharing a common physio-chemical property, such as hydrophobicity, is reduced to a single alphabet letter:

1. LVIM, FY, KR, ED, AG, ST, NQ, W, C, H, P
2. LVIMFYAGCW, KREDH, STNQP, and
3. LVIMFYAGCW, KREDHSTNQP.

The reason for using reduced amino acid alphabets is because sometimes a position in a primary sequence may call for any amino acid with a certain biochemical prop-erty rather than a specific amino acid, for example, hydrophobicity in transmembrane proteins.

2.2.1 Boundary Determination

As expected from the limited context of the trigram models, the relative performance of the 3 segment models fluctuates significantly, making it difficult to pinpoint loca-tions where one model begins to outperform another overall. To smooth out the fluc-tuations, we compute running averages of the log probabilities. Figure 2 shows the running averages of the log probabilities over a window size of ±2.

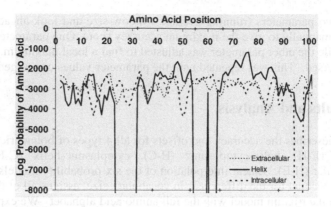

Fig. 2. Running averages of log probabilities at each position in D3DR_RAT sequence. Vertical dashed and dotted lines show the "true" and predicted boundaries respectively

While running averages minimize the fluctuations, we still do not want the system to label a position as a boundary point if the model for the next segment outperforms the current segment model only for a few positions. An example is the region in figure 2 between position 10 and 20 where the helix model performs better than the extracellular loop model temporarily before losing to the extracellular model again. Thus, we set a look-ahead interval: the model for the next segment must outperform the current segment model at the current position and at every position in the look-ahead interval for the current position to be labeled a segment boundary.

3   Evaluation

3.1 Dataset

The data set used in this study is the set of full GPCR sequences uploaded to GPCRDB [18] in September 2002. The headers of the sequence files contain the predicted segment boundaries taken as the synthetic "truth" in our training and testing data. This header information was retrievable only for a subset of these sequences, 1298 GPCRs. Ten-fold cross validation was used to evaluate our method.

3.2 Evaluation and Parameter Optimization

Two evaluation metrics were used: average offset and accuracy. Offset is the absolute value of the difference between the predicted and "true" boundary positions. An average offset was computed across all boundaries and for each of the 4 boundary types: extracellular-helix,   helix-cytoplasmic,   cytoplasmic-helix,   and   helix-extracellular. In computing accuracy, we assigned a score of 1 to a perfect match between the predicted and true boundary, a score of 0.5 for an offset of ±1, and a score of 0.25 for an offset of ±2. The scores for all the boundaries in all the proteins were averaged to produce an accuracy score.

The two parameters (running average window size and look-ahead interval) were adjusted manually to give the maximum accuracy score. One parameter was held constant, while the other parameter was adjusted to find a local maximum. Then the roles were reversed. This was repeated until the parameter values converged.

4 Results and Analysis

Table 1 describes the accuracy and offsets for all 4 types of boundaries — extracellular-helix (E-H), helix-cytoplasmic (H-C), cytoplasmic-helix (C-H), and helix-extracellular (H-E). Linear interpolation of the six probability models, after normalization to account for the differences in vocabulary size, assigns all of the interpolation weight to the trigram model with the full amino acid alphabet. We experimented with "Trained" interpolation weights (i.e. only trigram model with full amino acid alphabet), and pre-set weights to use "All" the models or only the 4 "Trigram" models. The window-size for running averages and the look-ahead interval in each case were optimized. Note there is little variance in the offset over the 4 types of boundaries.

Table 1. Evaluation results of boundary prediction. "Trained": trained interpolation weights, window-size ±2, look-ahead 5. "All": 0.1 for unigram and bigram model, 0.2 for trigram model, window-size ±5, look-ahead 4. "Trigram": 0.25 for each trigram model, window-size ±4, look-ahead 4

Weights	Accuracy	Offset				
		E-H	H-C	C-H	H-E	Avg
Trained	0.2410	35.7	35.4	34.5	36.5	35.5
All	0.2228	47.9	47.5	44.9	48.2	47.2
Trigram	0.2293	50.4	50.2	47.6	50.6	49.8

Using only the trigram model with the full amino acid alphabet shows a 5.1% improvement over using all 4 trigram models, which in turn shows a 2.9% improvement over including the unigram and bigram models. This suggests that the unigram and bigram models and reduced alphabets are not very useful in this task. However, the unigram and bi-gram models help in lessening the offset gap between predicted and true boundaries when they are more than 2 positions apart.

4.1 Discrepancy Between Accuracy and Offset

The accuracy in all of our results ranges from 0.22 to 0.24, suggesting an offset of ±2 positions from the synthetic boundaries. However, our measured offsets lie between 35 and 50. This is because the offset measure (in the trained interpolation weights case) has a large standard deviation of 160 and a maximum of 2813 positions. A histogram of the offsets (Fig. 3) shows a distribution with a very long tail, suggesting that large offsets between our predictions and the synthetic true boundaries are rare. After removing the 10% of proteins in our dataset with the largest offset averaged across their 14 boundaries, the average offset decreases from 36 to 11 positions. This result suggests that the large offsets are localized in a small number of proteins instead of being general for the dataset.

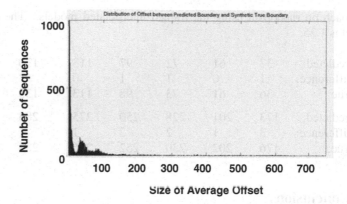

Fig. 3. Histogram of the number of sequences with the given average offset from the trained interpolated models. Note that the bars for the small offsets have been cut off at 1000 in the graph below for visibility

The distribution of offsets shows a local maximum at 36 amino acids, approximately the length of a helix plus a loop. This suggests that we may be missing the beginning of a helix and not predicting any boundaries as a result until the next helix approximately 35 positions later. To test this hypothesis, we re-evaluate our boundary predictions ignoring their order. That is, we measure the offset as the minimal absolute difference between a predicted boundary point and any synthetic true boundary point for the same sequence. The distribution of the new offsets is plotted in figure 4. The lack of a peak at position 36 confirms our hypothesis that the large offsets when evaluated in an order-specific fashion are due to missing the beginning of a helix and becoming asynchronized.

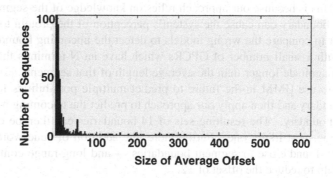

Fig. 4. Histogram of the order-independent offsets from the trained interpolated models. Bars for the small offsets have been cut off at 100 in the graph below for visibility

4.2 The Only Truth: Rhodopsin OPSD_HUMAN

As described in Section 1.1, rhodopsin is the only GPCR for which there is experimental evidence of the segment boundary positions. Below are the predictions of our approach on rhodopsin using the trained interpolated models. The average position offset is 1.35.

Predicted:	37	61	72	97	113	130	153
Difference:	1	0	1	1	0	3	1
True:	36	61	73	98	113	133	152
Predicted:	173	201	228	250	275	283	307
Difference:	3	1	2	2	1	1	2
True:	176	202	230	252	276	284	309

5 Conclusions

In this paper, we addressed the problem of protein segmentation in the limited domain of GPCR where the order and type of secondary structure segments are known. We developed a new statistical approach to protein segmentation that is distinctly different from the fixed window and Markov model based methods currently used. Taking the different types of segments as "topics" in the protein sequence, we adapted a topic segmentation approach for human languages to this biological problem. We built a language model for each of the different segment types present in GPCRs, and by comparing their performance in predicting the current amino acid, we determine whether a segment boundary occurs at the current position. Each of the segment models is an interpolated model of a unigram, a bigram and 4 trigram language models.

The results from our approach is promising, with an accuracy of 0.241 on a scale where 0.25 is an offset of ±2 positions from the synthetic boundaries predicted by hydrophobicity profiles. When the gap between the predicted boundary and the synthetic "true" boundary is 3 or more amino acids wide, the gap tends to be much larger than 3. This is because our approach relies on knowledge of the segment order and a 'missed' boundary can cause the system's perception of the protein to be misaligned, leading it to compare the wrong models to detect the upcoming boundaries. This occurred with a small number of GPCRs which have an N-terminus that is several orders of magnitude longer than the average length of that segment. For such proteins, we plan to use HMM in the future to predict multiple possibilities for the first segment boundary and then apply our approach to predict the upcoming boundaries given the first boundary. The resulting sets of 14 boundaries can then be evaluated to determine the most likely one. Furthermore, the addition of "cue-words" — n-grams frequently found close to segment boundaries — and long-range contact information should help to reduce the offset of ±2.

Acknowledgements

This research was supported by National Science Foundation Large Information Technology Research grant NSF 0225656.

References

1. Rost, B., *Review: protein secondary structure prediction continues to rise.* J Struct Biol, 2001. **134**(2-3): p. 204-218.
2. Chen, C.P., A. Kernytsky, and B. Rost, *Transmembrane helix predictions revisited.* Protein Science, 2002. **11**(12): p. 2774-2791.
3. Chen, C.P. and B. Rost, *State-of-the-art in membrane protein prediction.* Applied Bioinformatics, 2002. **1**(1): p. 21-35.
4. Bateman, A., et al., *The Pfam protein families database.* Nucleic Acids Res, 2002. **30**(1): p. 276-80.
5. Okada, T., et al., *Functional role of internal water molecules in rhodopsin revealed by X-ray crystallography.* Proc Natl Acad Sci U S A, 2002. **99**(9): p. 5982-5987.
6. Palczewski, K., *Crystal structure of rhodopsin: implication for vision and beyond. Mechanisms of activation.* Scientific World Journal, 2002. **2**(1 Suppl 2): p. 106-107.
7. Muller, G., *Towards 3D structures of G protein-coupled receptors: a multidisciplinary approach.* Current Medical Chemistry, 2000. **7**(9): p. 861-888.
8. Kyte, J. and R.F. Doolittle, *A simple method for displaying the hydropathic character of a protein.* J Mol Biol, 1982. **157**(1): p. 105-32.
9. Sonnhammer, E.L., G. von Heijne, and A. Krogh, *A hidden Markov model for predicting transmembrane helices in protein sequences.* Proc Int Conf Intell Syst Mol Biol, 1998. **6**: p. 175-182.
10. Pasquier, C., et al., *A novel method for predicting transmembrane segments in proteins based on a statistical analysis of the SwissProt database: the PRED-TMR algorithm.* Protein Engineering, 1999. **12**(5): p. 381-385.
11. Schmidler, S.C., J.S. Liu, and D.L. Brutlag, *Bayesian segmentation of protein secondary structure.* Journal of Computational Biology, 2000. **7**(1-2): p. 233-248.
12. Jones, D.T., W.R. Taylor, and J.M. Thornton, *A model recognition approach to the prediction of all-helical membrane protein structure and topology.* Biochemistry, 1994. **33**(10): p. 3038-3049.
13. Tusnady, G.E. and I. Simon, *Principles governing amino acid composition of integral membrane proteins: application to topology prediction.* J Mol Biol, 1998. **283**(2): p. 489-506.
14. Kernytsky, A. and B. Rost, *Static benchmarking of membrane helix predictions.* Nucleic Acids Research, 2003. **31**(13): p. 3642-3644.
15. Beeferman, D., A. Berger, and J. Lafferty, *Statistical Models for Text Segmentation.* Machine Learning, Special Issue on Natural Language Learning, 1999. **34**(1-3): p. 177-210.
16. Weisser, D. and J. Klein-Seetharaman, *Identification of Fundamental Building Blocks in Protein Sequences Using Statistical Association Measures.* 2004: ACM SIG Proceedings. p. in press.
17. Ganapathiraju, M., et al. *Yule values tables from protein datasets of different categories: emphasis on membrane proteins.* in *Biological Language Conference.* 2003. Pittsburgh, PA, USA.
18. Horn, F., et al., *GPCRDB: an information system for G-protein coupled receptors.* Nucleic Acids Research, 1998. **26**(1): p. 275-279.

Visualization of Similarities and Dissimilarities in Rules Using Multidimensional Scaling

Shusaku Tsumoto and Shoji Hirano

Department of Medical Informatics,
Shimane University, School of Medicine,
Enya-cho Izumo City, Shimane 693-8501 Japan
hirano@ieee.org, tsumoto@computer.org

Abstract. One of the most important problems with rule induction methods is that it is very difficult for domain experts to check millions of rules generated from large datasets. The discovery from these rules requires deep interpretation from domain knowledge. Although several solutions have been proposed in the studies on data mining and knowledge discovery, these studies are not focused on similarities between rules obtained. When one rule r_1 has reasonable features and the other rule r_2 with high similarity to r_1 includes unexpected factors, the relations between these rules will become a trigger to the discovery of knowledge. In this paper, we propose a visualization approach to show the similar and dissimilar relations between rules based on multidimensional scaling, which assign a two-dimensional cartesian coordinate to each data point from the information about similiaries between this data and others data. We evaluated this method on two medical data sets, whose experimental results show that knowledge useful for domain experts could be found.

1 Introduction

One of the most important problems with rule induction methods is that it is very difficult for domain experts to check millions of rules generated from large datasets. Moreover, since the data collection is deeply dependent on domain knowledge, rules derived by datasets need deep interpretation made by domain experts. For example, Tsumoto and Ziarko reported the following case in analysis of a dataset on meningitis [1].

Even though the dataset is small, the number of records is 198, they obtained 136 rules with high confidence (more than 0.75) and support (more than 20). Here are the examples which are unexpected to domain experts.

1. [WBC 12000] & [Gender=Female] & [CSFcell 1000] => Virus meningitis
   (Accuracy: 0.97, Coverage: 0.55)
2. [Age > 40] & [WBC > 8000] => Bacterial meningitis
   (Accuracy: 0.80, Coverage: 0.58)

M.-S. Hacid et al. (Eds.): ISMIS 2005, LNAI 3488, pp. 38–46, 2005.
© Springer-Verlag Berlin Heidelberg 2005

```
3. [WBC > 8000] & [Gender=Male] => Bacterial menigits
   (Accuracy: 0.78, Coverage: 0.58)
4. [Gender=Male] & [CSFcell>1000] => Bacterial meningitis
   (Accuracy: 0.77, Coverage: 0.73)
```

The factors in these rules unexpected to domain experts are gender and age, which have not been pointed out in the literature on meningitis [2].

Since these detected patterns may strongly depend on the characteristics of data, Tsumoto and Ziarko searched for the hidden factors. For this analysis, several groupings of attributes are processed into the dataset.

The results obtained from the secondary analysis of processed data show that both $[Gender = male]$ and $[Age > 40]$ are closely related with chronic diseases, which is a risk factor of bacterial meningitis. The first attribute-value pair, $[Gender = male]$ is supported by 70 cases in total 198 records: 48 cases are bacterial meningitis, all of which suffered from chronic diseases (25 cases: diabetes mellitus, 17 cases: liver cirrhosis and 6 cases: chronic sinusitis.) On the other hand, $[Age > 40]$ is supported by 121 cases: 59 cases are bacterial meningitis, 45 cases of which suffered from chronic diseases (25 cases: diabetes mellitus, 17 cases: liver cirrhosis and 3 cases: chronic sinusitis.) Domain explanation was given as follows: chronic diseases, especially diabetes mellitus and liver cirrhosis degrade the host-defence to microorganisms as immunological deficiency and chronic sinusitis influences the membrane of brain through the cranial bone. Epidemiological studies show that women before 50 having mensturation suffer from such chronic diseases less than men.

This example illustrates that deep interpretation based on data and domain knowledge is very important for discovery of new knowledge. Especially, the above example shows the importance of similarities between rules. When one rule r_i has reasonable features and the other rule r_j with high similarity to r_i includes unexpected factors, the relations between these rules will become a trigger to the discovery of knowledge.

In this paper, we propose a visualization approach to show the similarity relations between rules based on multidimensional scaling, which assign a two-dimensional cartesian coordinate to each data point from the information about similiaries between this data and others data. We evaluated this method on three medical data sets. Experimental results show that several knowledge useful for domain experts could be found.

2   Similarity of Rules

Let $sim(a, b)$ denote a similarity between objects a and b. Formally, similarity relation should hold the following relations:

1. An object a is similar to oneself: $sim(a, a)$.
2. If $sim(a, b)$, then $sim(b, a)$. (Symmetry)

It is notable that the second property is the principal axiom for the similarity measure. In this section, we define three types of similarity measures for rules which hold the above relations. As shown in the subsection 1, rules are composed of (1) relation between attribute-value pairs (proposition) and (2) values of probabilistic indices (and its supporting sets). Let us call the former component a **syntactic** part and the latter one a **semantic** part. Two similarities are based on the characteristics of these parts.

2.1 Syntactic Similarity

Syntatic similarity is defined as the similarity between conditional parts of the same target concept. In the example shown in Section 1, the following two rules have similar conditional parts:

```
R2. [Age > 40] & [WBC > 8000] => Bacterial meningitis
    (Accuracy: 0.80, Coverage: 0.58)


R3. [WBC > 8000] & [Gender=Male] => Bacterial menigits
    (Accuracy: 0.78, Coverage: 0.58)
```

The difference between these two rules are $[Age > 40]$ and $[Gender = Male]$. To measure the similarity between these two rules, we can apply several indices of two-way contigency tables. Table 1 gives a contingency table for two rules,

Table 1. Contingency Table for Similarity

		$Rule_j$		
		$Observed$	$Not\ Observed$	Total
$Rule_i$	$Observed$	a	b	$a + b$
	Not $Observed$	c	d	$c + d$
	Total	$a + c$	$b + d$	$a + b$ $+ c + d$

$Rule_i$ and $Rule_j$. The first cell a (the intersection of the first row and column) shows the number of matched attribute-value pairs.

2.2 Similarities

From this table, several kinds of similarity measures can be defined [3, 4]. The best similarity measures in the statistical literature are seven measures shown in Table 2. It is notable that these indices satisfies the property on symmetry shown in the beginning of this section.

2.3 Semantic Similarity: Covering

The other similarity which can be defined from the definition of the rule is based on the *meaning* of the relations between formulas f_i and f_j from the viewpoint of set-theoretical point of view. Let us assume that we have two rules:

Table 2. Definition of Similarity Measures

(1) Matching Number	a
(2) Jaccard's coefficient	$a/(a+b+c)$
(3) χ^2-statistic	$N(ad-bc)^2/M$
(4) point correlation coefficient	$(ad-bc)/\sqrt{M}$
(5) Kulczynski	$\frac{1}{2}(\frac{a}{a+b}+\frac{a}{a+c})$
(6) Ochiai	$\frac{a}{\sqrt{(a+b)(a+c)}}$
	$=\sqrt{\alpha_R(D)\kappa_R(D)}$
(7) Simpson	$\frac{a}{min\{(a+b),(a+c)\}}$
	$=min(\alpha_R(D),\kappa_R(D))$

$$N - a + b + c + d,\ M = (a+b)(b+c)(c+d)(d+a)$$

$$f_i \to D\left(\alpha_{f_i}(D), \kappa_{f_i}(D)\right)$$
$$f_j \to D\left(\alpha_{f_j}(D), \kappa_{f_j}(D)\right)$$

As shown in the last subsection, syntactic similarity is defined as $sim(f_i, f_j)$ from the viewpoint of syntactic representations. Since f_i and f_j have meanings (supporting sets), f_{iA} and f_{jA}, respectively, where A denotes the given attribute space. Then, we can define $sim(f_{iA}, f_{jA})$ by using a contingency table: Table 1 in the same way.

2.4   From Assymmetric Indices to Symmetric Ones

Since a similarity measure between two rules is symmetric, it may not capture assymetrical information between two rules. To extract simmilarities and dissimilarities information, we defined the following two measures:

$$average(R, D) = \frac{1}{2}(\frac{a}{a+b} + \frac{a}{a+c}),\quad and$$
$$difference(R, D) = \frac{1}{2}|\frac{a}{a+b} - \frac{a}{a+c}|$$

where the difference is equivalent to the dissimilarity. It is notable that the difference has a meaning if $a \neq 0$. If $a = 0$, the difference will be maximum. We assume that $difference(R, D)$ is equal to 1.0 if the intersection a is equal to 0.

3   Multidimensional Scaling

3.1   Problems with Clustering

After calculating the similarity relations among rules and deriving similarity matrix, patterns with respect to similarities will be investigated. Usually, data miners apply clustering methods to the similarity matrix obtained from given datasets [3]. However, clustering have several problems: most of clustering methods, hierarchical or nearnest neighbor based methods, forces grouping given examples, attributes or classes into one or several classses, with one dimension. This limitation is already given as a formal form of similarity function, $sim(a, b)$. As a mapping, similarity function is given as $O \times O \rightarrow R$, where O and R denote a set of objects and real number, respectively.

Since each object may have many properties, one dimensional analysis may not be sufficient for detecting the similarity between two objects. In these cases, the increase of the dimensionality gives a wider scope for reasoning about similarities. Multidimensional scaling (MDS) is one solution for dimensionality, which uses two-dimensional plane to visualize the similarity relations between objects.

3.2   How MDS Works

Metric MDS. The most important function of MDS is to recover cartesian coordinates (usually, two-dimensional) from a given similarity matrix. For recovery, we assume that a similarity is given as an inner product of two vectors for objects. Although we need three points to recover coordinates, but one point is fixed as the origin of the plane.

Let us assume that the coordinates of two objects x_i and x_j are given as: $(x_{i1}, x_{i2}, \cdots, x_{ip})$ and $(x_{j1}, x_{j2}, \cdots, x_{jp})$, where p is the number of dimension of the space. Let k denote the origin of the space $(0, 0, \cdots, 0)$. Then, here, we assume that the distance betweeen x_i and x_j d_{ij} is given as the formula of distance, such as Eucledian, Minkowski, and so on. MDS based on this assumption is called *metric MDS*. Then, the similarity between i and j s_{ij} is given as:

$$s_{ij} = d_{ik}d_{jk}\cos\theta = \sum_{m=1}^{p} x_{im}x_{jm}$$

From the triangle ijk, the following formula holds:

$$d_{ij}^2 = d_{ik}^2 + d_{jk}^2 - 2d_{ik}d_{jk}\cos\theta.$$

Therefore, similarity should hold the following formula.

$$s_{ij} = \frac{d_{ik}^2 + d_{jk}^2 - d_{ij}^2}{2}$$

Since s_{ij} is given as $\sum_{m=1}^{p} x_{im}x_{jm}$, the similarity matrix for s_{ij} is given as:

$$\mathbf{Z} = \mathbf{X}\mathbf{X}^\mathbf{T},$$

where $\mathbf{X}^\mathbf{T}$ denotes the transposition matrix of $\mathbf{X}$. To obtain $\mathbf{X}$, we consider the minimization of an objective function Q defined as:

$$Q = \sum_i \sum_j \left(z_{ij} - \sum_{m=1}^{p} x_{im}x_{jm}\right)^2.$$

For this purpose, we apply *EckartandYoung* decomposition [5] in the following way. first, we calculate eigenvalues, denoted by $\lambda_1, \cdots, \lambda_p$, and eigenvectors of $\mathbf{Z}$, denoted by $\mathbf{v^1}, \cdots, \mathbf{v^p}$. Then by using a diagnoal matrix of eigenvalues, denoted by $\mathbf{\Lambda}$ and a matrix with eigenvectors, denoted by $\mathbf{Y}$, we obtain the following formula:

$$\mathbf{X} = \mathbf{Y}\mathbf{\Lambda}\mathbf{Y^T},$$

where

$$\mathbf{\Lambda} = \begin{pmatrix} \lambda_1 & 0 & \cdots\cdots\cdots & 0 \\ 0 & \lambda_2 & 0\cdots \quad \cdots & 0 \\ \cdots\cdots & & \lambda_i & \cdots\cdots \\ 0 & 0 & \cdots & \lambda_{p-1} \quad 0 \\ 0 & 0 & \cdots & 0 \quad \lambda_p \end{pmatrix} \quad and \quad \mathbf{Y} = \left(\mathbf{v^1}, \mathbf{v^2}, \cdots, \mathbf{v^p}\right).$$

From this decomposition, we obtain $\mathbf{X}$ as $\mathbf{X} = \mathbf{Y}\mathbf{\Lambda}^{1/2}$.

Nonmetric MDS. The above metric MDS can be applied to the case only when the difference between similarities has the meaning. In other words, the similarity index holds the property of interval calculus (interval scale). If the similarity index holds the property of order, we should not apply the above calculus to the similarity matrix, but we should apply nonmetric MDS method. Here, we will introduce Kruskal method, which is one of the most well-known nonmetric MDS method [6].

First, we calculate given similarities s_{ij} into distance data d_{ij}^* (dissimilarity). Next, we estimate the coordinates of x_i and x_j from the minimization of *Stress* function, defined as:

$$S = \sqrt{\frac{\sum\sum_{i<j}(d_{ij} - d_{ji}^*)^2}{\sum\sum d_{ij}^2}},$$

where the distance d_{ij} is defined as a Minkowski distance:

$$d_{ij} = \left(\sum_{m=1}^{P} |x_{im} - x_{jm}|^t\right)^{1/t},$$

where t denotes the Minkowski constant. For the minimization of S, optimization methods, such as gradient method are applied and the dimensionality and t will be estimated. Since the similarity measures given above do not hold the property of distance (triangular inequality), we adopt nonmetric MDS method to visualize similarity relations.

3.3   Process for Visualization

Process for Visualization is given as follows:

1. Induce rules with accuracy and coverage from a given dataset.
2. Construct a Synctactic similarity matrix for rules for a target concept.

3. Construct a Dependency Matrix for rules for a target concept.
4. Construct Average and Difference matrices from a Dependence matrix.
5. Apply nonmetric MDS methods to Synctactic matrix.
6. Apply nonmetric MDS methods to Average and Difference matrices.

Average and Difference matrix is calculated as follows. Let $M_{dep}(D)$, $M_{avg}(D)$ and $M_{diff}(D)$ denote a dependency, average, difference matrix for a target concept D, respectively. From the definition of average and difference measure shown in 2.4, $M_{avg}(D)$ and $M_{diff}(D)$ are obtained as:

$$M_{avg}(D) = \frac{1}{2}(M_{dep}(D) + M_{dep}^T(D)), \tag{1}$$

$$M_{diff}(D) = \frac{1}{2}|M_{dep}(D) - M_{dep}^T(D)|, \tag{2}$$

where $M_{dep}^T(D)$ denotes the transposition of $M_{dep}(D)$.

4 Experimental Results

We applied the combination of rule induction and nonmetric MDS to a medical dataset on differential diagnosis of headache, which has 52119 esamples, 45 classes and 73 attributes. In these experiments, rule induction based on rough sets [7] is applied, where δ_α and δ_κ were set to 0.75 and 0.5 for rule induction, respectively. For similarity measures, we adopt Kulczynski's similarity and calculate similarity measures from accuracy and coverage of rules obtained from data.

Due to the limitation of space, we focus on the most interesting visualized patterns for each datasets. First, Figure 1, 2 and 3 show the pattern of synctatic, average and difference similarity of rules for headache $m.c.h.$, respectively. The figures suggest two groups of the features of descriptors from average and three groups from different. While the descriptors in the right upper region in Figure 2 are those which are regularly used for the differential diagnosis of headache, the left lower group shows the descriptors used for special types of $m.c.h.$, which we call emotional-evoked $m.c.h.$ and occupational $m.c.h.$. Thus, these patterns match with expert's knowledge.

However, Figure 3 gives a different pattern: two groups are scattered in different ways, which suggests that the left lower group in Figure 2 does not give overlapped intersections between rules, while the lower upper group has high overlapped region.

5 Conclusion

In this paper, we propose a visualization approach to show the similar relations between rules based on multidimensional scaling, which assign a two-dimensional cartesian coordinate to each data point from the information about similiaries between this data and others data. As similarity for rules, we define three types of similarities: syntactic, semantic (covering based) and semantic (indice based).

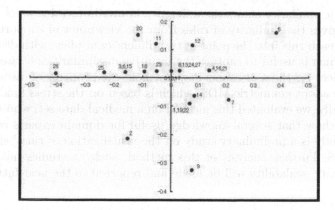

Fig. 1. Patterns of Similar Rules for *m.c.h.* (Synctactic Similarity: Headache)

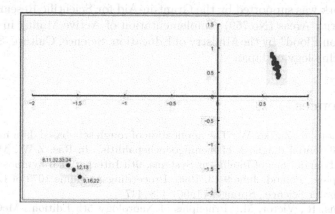

Fig. 2. Patterns of Similar Rules for *m.c.h.* (Semantic Similarity(Average): Headache)

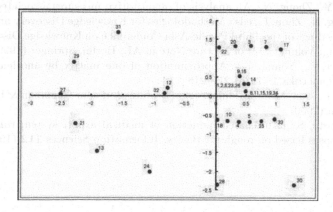

Fig. 3. Patterns of Similar Rules for *m.c.h.* (Semantic Similarity(Difference): Headache)

Syntactic similarity shows the difference in attribute-value pairs, semantic similarity gives the similarity of rules from the viewpoint of supporting sets. MDS assigns each rule into the point of two-dimensional plane with distance information, which is useful to capture the intuitive dissimilarities between rules. Since the indices for these measures may not hold the property of distance (transitivity), we adopt nonmetric MDS, which is based on the stress function.

Finally, we evaluated this method on a medical data set, whose experimental results show that several knowledge useful for domain experts could be found. This study is a preliminary study on the visualization of rules' similarity based on MDS. Further analysis of this method, such as studies on computational complexity, scalability will be made and reported in the near future.

Acknowledgement

This work was supported by the Grant-in-Aid for Scientific Research (13131208) on Priority Areas (No.759) "Implementation of Active Mining in the Era of Information Flood" by the Ministry of Education, Science, Culture, Sports, Science and Technology of Japan.

References

1. Tsumoto, S., Ziarko, W.: The application of rough sets-based data mining technique to differential diagnosis of meningoenchepahlitis. In Ras, Z.W., Michalewicz, M., eds.: Foundations of Intelligent Systems, 9th International Symposium, ISMIS '96, Zakopane, Poland, June 9-13, 1996, Proceedings. Volume 1079 of Lecture Notes in Computer Science., Springer (1996) 438–447
2. Adams, R., Victor, M.: Principles of Neurology 5th Edition. McGraw-Hill, New York (1993)
3. Everitt, B.: Cluster Analysis. 3rd edn. John Wiley & Son, London (1996)
4. Yao, Y., Zhong, N.: An analysis of quantitative measures associated with rules. In Zhong, N., Zhou, L., eds.: Methodologies for Knowledge Discovery and Data Mining, Proceedings of the Third Pacific-Asia Conference on Knowledge Discovery and Data Mining. Volume 1574 of Lecture Note in AI., Berlin, Springer (1999) 479–488
5. Eckart, C., Young, G.: Approximation of one matrix by another of lower rank. Psychometrika 1 (1936) 211–218
6. Cox, T., Cox, M.: Multidimensional Scaling. 2nd edn. Chapman & Hall/CRC, Boca Raton (2000)
7. Tsumoto, S.: Automated induction of medical expert system rules from clinical databases based on rough set theory. Information Sciences 112 (1998) 67–84

Learning Profiles Based on Hierarchical Hidden Markov Model

Ugo Galassi[1], Attilio Giordana[1], Lorenza Saitta[1], and Maco Botta[2]

[1] Dipartimento di Informatica, Università Amedeo Avogadro
Spalto Marengo 33, Alessandria, Italy
[2] Dipartimento di Informatica, Universitá di Torino,
C.so Svizzera 185, 10149 Torino, Italy

Abstract. This paper presents a method for automatically constructing a sophisticated user/process profile from traces of user/process behavior. User profile is encoded by means of a Hierarchical Hidden Markov Model (HHMM). The HHMM is a well formalized tool suitable to model complex patterns in long temporal or spatial sequences. The method described here is based on a recent algorithm, which is able to synthesize the HHMM structure from a set of logs of the user activity. The algorithm follows a bottom-up strategy, in which elementary facts in the sequences (motives) are progressively grouped, thus building the abstraction hierarchy of a HHMM, layer after layer. The method is firstly evaluated on artificial data. Then a user identification task, from real traces, is considered. A preliminary experimentation with several different users produced encouraging results.

1 Introduction

Building profiles for processes and for interactive users, is an important task in intrusion detection. This paper presents the results obtained with a recent induction algorithm algorithm [2], which is based on Hierarchical Hidden Markov Model [5]. The algorithm discovers typical "motives" [1] of a process behavior, and correlates them into a hierarchical model. Motives can be interleaved with possibly long gaps where no regular behavior is detectable. We assume that motives could be affected by noise due to non-deterministic causes. Noise is modeled as insertion, deletion and substitution errors according to a common practice followed in Pattern Recognition. An approach to deal with such kind of noisy patterns, which reported impressive records of successes in speech recognition [10] and DNA analysis [4], is the one based on Hidden Markov Model (HMM) [11]). However, applying HMM does not reduce to simply running a learning algorithm but it requires a considerable effort in order to individuate a suitable structure for the HMM. A formal framework to design and train complex HMMs

---

[1] A motif is a subsequence of consecutive elementary events typical of a process.

M.-S. Hacid et al. (Eds.): ISMIS 2005, LNAI 3488, pp. 47–55, 2005.
© Springer-Verlag Berlin Heidelberg 2005

is represented by the Hierarchical Hidden Markov Model (HHMM) [5]. The problem of estimating HMM and HHMM parameters has been widely investigated while little has been done in order to learn their structure. A few proposals can be found in the literature in order to learn the structure of HMM. A novelty, in this sense, is represented by a recent paper by Botta et Al. [2], which proposes a method for automatically inferring from sequences, and possibly domain knowledge, both the structure and the parameters of complex HHMMs.

In this paper, the learning algorithm proposed in [2] is briefly overviewed and then is experimentally evaluated on three *profiling* case studies. The first two cases are built on a suite of artificial traces automatically generated by a set of given HHMMs. The challenge for the algorithm is to reconstruct the original model from the traces. It will be shown that the algorithm is able to learn HHMMs very similar to the original ones, in presence of noise and distractors.

The third case study refers to the problem of constructing a discriminative model for a user typing on a keyboard [1, 3, 8]. The results reported with a set of 20 different users are encouraging.

2   The Hierarchical Hidden Markov Model

A Hierarchical Hidden Markov Model is a generalization of the Hidden Markov Model, which is a stochastic finite state automaton [11] defined by a tuple $\langle S, O, A, B, \pi \rangle$, where:

- S is a set of states, and O is a set of atomic events (observations),
- A is a probability distribution governing the transitions from one state to another. Specifically, any member $a_{i,j}$ of A defines the probability of the transition from state s_i to state s_j, given s_i.
- B is a probability distribution governing the emission of observable events depending on the state. Specifically, an item $b_{i,j}$ belonging to B defines the probability of producing event O_j when the automaton is in state s_i.
- π is a distribution on S defining, for every $s_i \in S$, the probability that s_i is the initial state of the automaton.

A difficulty, related to a HMM defined in this way, is that, when the set of states S grows large, the number of parameters to estimate (A and B) rapidly becomes intractable.

A second difficulty is that the probability of a sequence being generated by a given HMM decreases exponentially with its length. Then, complex and sparse events become difficult to discover.

The HHMM proposed by Fine, Singer and Tishby [5] is an answer to both problems. On one hand, the number of parameters to estimate is strongly reduced by assigning a null probability to many transitions in distribution A, and to many observations in distribution B. On the other hand, it allows a possibly long chain of elementary events to be abstracted into a single event, which can be handled as a single item. This is obtained by exploiting the regular languages property of being closed under substitution, which allows a large finite state automaton to be transformed into a hierarchy of simpler ones.

More specifically, numbering the hierarchy levels with ordinals increasing from the highest towards the lowest level, observations generated in a state s_i^k by a stochastic automaton al level k are sequences generated by an automaton at level $k + 1$. Moreover, no direct transition may occur between the states of different automata in the hierarchy. An example of HHMM is given in Figure 1.

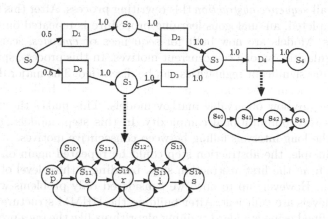

Fig. 1. Example of Hierarchical Hidden Markov Model. Circles denotes states with observable emission, whereas rectangles denote *gaps*

The advantage of the hierarchical structure, as defined by [5], may help very much the inference of the entire structure of the automaton by part of an induction algorithm.

The research efforts about HHMM mostly concentrate on the algorithms for estimating the probabilities governing the emissions and the transition from state to state. In the seminal paper by Fine et al. [5], the classical Baum-Welch algorithm is extended to the HHMM. In a more recent work, Murphy and Paskin [9] derive a linear (approximated) algorithm by mapping a HHMM into a Dynamic Bayesian Network.

3   Learning Algorithm Overview

The basic algorithm [2] is bottom-up and constructs the HHMM hierarchy starting from the lowest level. The first step consists in searching for possible motives, i.e., short chains of consecutive symbols that appear frequently in the learning traces, and building a HMM for each one of them. This step is accomplished by means of classical methods used in DNA analysis [4,7]. As, motif models are constructed independently one from another, it may happen that models for spurious motives be constructed. At the same time, it may happen that relevant motives be disregarded just because their frequency is not high enough. Both kinds of errors will be fixed at a second time. The HMMs learned so far, are then used as feature constructors. Each HMM is labeled with a different *name* and the original sequences are rewritten into the new alphabet defined by the set of names given to the models. In other words, every sub-sequence in the input sequences, which can be attributed to a specific HMM, is replaced by the corresponding name.

The subsequences between two motives, not attributed to any model, are considered gaps and will be handled by means of special construct called *gap*. We will call *sequence abstraction* this rewriting process. After this basic cycle has been completed, an analogous learning procedure is repeated on the abstracted sequences. Models are now built for sequences of *episodes*, searching for long range regularities among co-occurrent motives. In this process, spurious motives not showing significant regularities can be discarded. The major difference, with respect to the first learning step, is that the models built from the abstract sequences, are now observable markov models. This makes the task easier and decreases the computational complexity. In this step, models (*gaps*) are built also for the long intervals falling between consecutive motives.

In principle, the abstraction step could be repeated again on the sequences obtained from the first abstraction step, building a third level of the hierarchy, and so on. However, up to now, we considered only problems where two hierarchical levels are sufficient. After building the HHMM structure in this way, it can be refined using standard training algorithms like the ones proposed in [5, 9]. However, two other refinement techniques are possible.

The first technique concerns the recovery of motives lost in the primary learning phase because not having a sufficient statistical evidence. As said above, this missed information has actually been modeled by *gaps*. A nice property of the HHMM is that sub-models in the hierarchy have a loose interaction with one another, and so their structure can be reshaped without changing the global structure. Then, the model of a gap can be transformed into the model of a motif later on, when further data will be available.

The second method consists in repeating the entire learning cycle using as learning set only the portion of the sequences where the instance of the previously learned HHMM have been found with sufficient evidence. Repeating the procedure allows more precise models to be learned for motives, because false motives will no longer participate to the learning procedure. The details about the implementation can be found in [2].

4   Evaluation on Artificial Traces

A specific testing procedure has been designed in order to monitor the capability of the algorithm of discovering "known patterns" hidden in trace artificially generated by a handcrafted HHMMs. Random noise and spurious motives have been added to all sequences filling the gaps between consecutive motives, in order to make the task more difficult.

Three target HHMMs, each one constructed according to a two level hierarchy have been used to generate a set of 72 learning tasks (24 for every model). Every learning task consists of a set of 330 traces. The 90% of the sequences contain an instance of a target HHMM that should be discovered by the learning program, whereas the 10% contain sequences of spurious motives non generated by the target HHMM. The sequence length ranges from 80 to 120 elementary events.

The structure for the high level of the three models is shown in Figure 2. Every state at the high level emits a string (motif) generated by an HMM at the low level, indicated with a capital letter (A,B,C,D,E). A different HMM (F) has been used to generate spurious motives. The gaps between motives have been filled with subsequences containing random noise.

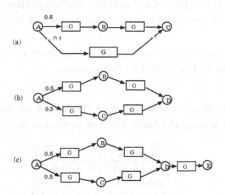

Fig. 2. HHMM used for evaluation on artificial data

The evaluation of the obtained results has been done on the base of the *bayes classification error* between two (or more) HHMMs). Formally, given two HHMMs, λ_1 and λ_2, and the set L of all possible traces, which can be generated by λ_1 or λ_2, the Bayes classification error $C(\lambda_1, \lambda_2)$ is defined as:

$$C(\lambda_1, \lambda_2) = \sum_{x \in L} [min(p(\lambda_1|x), p(\lambda_2|x)]p(x) \tag{1}$$

being $p(\lambda_1|x)$ and $p(\lambda_2|x)$ the probability that, given a trace x, it has been generated by λ_1 or λ_2, respectively, and $p(x)$ the a priori probability of x. We notice that the upper-bound for $C(\lambda_1, \lambda_2)$is 0.5, when λ_1 and λ_2 are identical. In general, for N models, the upper-bound is given by the expression $1 - 1/N$.

In general, expression (1) cannot be computed because L is too large. Therefore, we adopted an approximate evaluation made using a subset of L stochastically sampled.

The bayes classification error 1 intervenes in the evaluation procedure in two different ways. A first way is to measure the quality of the learned models. A perfect learner should learn a model identical to the one used to generate the traces. Therefore, a learned model has to be considered as much accurate as much close to 0.5 the classification error, between it and the original model, is.

The second way is to estimate the difficulty of the learning task. It is reasonable to assume that the difficulty of identifying a model hidden in a set of traces grows along with the similarity among the motives belonging to the model and the spurious motives. Moreover, the difficulty grows also when the motives belonging to a same model become similar each other, because it becomes more difficult to discover the correspondence between a motif and the hidden state it has been emitted from. Therefore, the experimentation has been run using different versions of models A, B, C, D, E, F with different bayes classification error among them.

The results obtained under three different conditions of difficulty are summarized in Table 1. The similarity between the six kinds of motives has been varied from 0.2 to 0.55. For every setting, the experiment has been repeated 8 times for each one of the three models. The reported results are the average over the 8 runs. In all cases, the bayes classification error has been estimated using a set of traces obtained by collecting 500 sequences generated from each one of the models involved in the specific comparison.

Table 1. Bayes classification error between the target model and the learned model, versus the confusion among the basic motives (reported in the first line)

Motives	0.2	0.4	0.55
Model (a)	0.48	0.46	0.45
Model (b)	0.47	0.42	0.42
Model (c)	0.43	0.42	0.41

It appears that the performances suffer very little from the similarity among the motif models, and in all cases, the similarity between the original model and the learned model is very high ($C(\lambda_1, \lambda_2)$, is close to 0.5).

5   Evaluation of the Generalization Capabilities

The second case study has the goal of evaluating the ability of the algorithm at correctly generalizing the nominal form of motives in presence of noise. The generalization of the learned HHMM is assessed by considering the maximum likelihood sequence, it generates. In the best case this should be identical to the one generated by the original model, used to construct the dataset. For this group of experiments, HHMMs, which generate sequences of names of towns in a predefined order, have been used. Such HHMMs also model the presence of noise in the data, in form of insertion, deletion and substitution errors. The gaps between the names are filled by symbols randomly chosen in the alphabet defined by the union of the letters contained in the names. Moreover, random subsequences, up to 15 characters long, have been added at the beginning and the end of each sequence. The global length of the sequences ranges from 60 to 120 characters. The difficulty of the task has been controlled by varying the degree of noise.

One set of experiments has been designed in this framework. More specifically, a sequence of problems has been generated varying the number of words ($5 \leq w \leq 8$), the word length ($5 \leq L \leq 8$) and the noise level ($N \in \{0\%, 5\%, 10\%, 15\%\}$. For every triple $< w, L, N >$, 10 different datasets has been generated for a total of 640 learning problems.

Table 2. Performances obtained with *town names* dataset. The sequence length ranges from 60 to 140 characters. The CPU time, for solving a problem, ranges from 42 to 83 seconds on a Pentium IV 2.4Ghz

		After the first cycle				After refinement			
		Noise Level				Noise Level			
w	L	0%	5%	10 %	15%	0%	5%	10 %	15%
5	5	0.03	0.06	0.06	0.08	0.04	0.04	0.04	0.04
5	6	0.06	0.12	0.12	0.09	0.03	0.03	0.03	0.03
5	7	0.00	0.02	0.03	0.05	0.00	0.00	0.02	0.00
5	8	0.02	0.04	0.02	0.04	0.00	0.00	0.00	0.00
6	5	0.06	0.11	0.04	0.04	0.10	0.06	0.00	0.03
6	6	0.06	0.10	0.06	0.19	0.05	0.00	0.00	0.00
6	7	0.03	0.03	0.02	0.05	0.02	0.00	0.00	0.00
6	8	0.01	0.04	0.05	0.05	0.00	0.00	0.04	0.00
7	5	0.02	0.05	0.11	0.17	0.02	0.05	0.01	0.10
7	6	0.01	0.10	0.05	0.14	0.04	0.02	0.05	0.04
7	7	0.00	0.06	0.02	0.05	0.00	0.00	0.02	0.05
7	8	0.01	0.06	0.09	0.11	0.01	0.00	0.09	0.09
8	5	0.00	0.00	0.01	0.00	0.00	0.00	0.01	0.00
8	6	0.03	0.08	0.10	0.14	0.03	0.06	0.06	0.14
8	7	0.00	0.01	0.01	0.08	0.00	0.00	0.00	0.00
8	8	0.01	0.03	0.08	0.09	0.01	0.00	0.00	0.0

The most important results are summarized in Table 2. The error rate is evaluated as the edit distance (i.e. the minimum number of corrections) between the maximum likelihood sequence (maximum consensus) generated by the Viterbi algorithm [6] from the original HHMM and the one generated from the learned HHMM. When, an entire word is missed, the corresponding error is set equal to the its length. Experiments in table 2, reporting an error rate much higher than the others, have missed words. In all cases, the learning cycle has been iterated twice, as explained in Section 3. It appears that the average error rate after one refinement cycle decreases of about 50% with respect to the first learning step.

From Table 2, it appears that the model extracted from the data without noise is almost error free. Moreover, the method seems to be little sensitive with respect to the sequence length while the error rate roughly increases proportionally to the noise in the original model (the 15% of noise corresponds to an average error rate of about 19%).

6   User Identification

The task consists in learning to identify a user from the its typing style on a keyboard. The basic assumption is that every user has a different way of typing that becomes particularly evident when he types words which are specifically important for him, such its name or words referring to his job. Assimilating such words to motives characteristic of a user, it is possible to learn a discriminating HHMM on the basis of them.

Two experiments have been done. In the first, a group of 20 users have been asked to type a sentence of 22 syllables on the same keyboard. A transparent program recorded, for every typed key, the duration and the delay two consecutive strikes creating a trace for every typing session. Each user provided ten repetitions of the sentence. Then, a dataset of 200 traces has been obtained, which has been partitioned into a learning set of 140 traces and a testing set of 60 traces. According to a standard procedure in machine learning, 20 HHMMs have been learned from the learning set. Then, the 20 HHMMs have been used to classify the traces in the testing set, according to the following standard procedure. For each HHMM M and for each trace t the forward-backward algorithm [11] is applied in order to estimate the probability for t of being generated by M. Then, t is attributed to the HHMM that has shows the highest probability. If such a HHMM is the model of the the user that has generated t, the classification is considered correct. Otherwise it is counted as a misclassification error. However, it may happen that all HHMMs show a null probability when t does not belong the language of anyone of them. This is considered a rejection error. In, the specific case, 76% of the traces have been correctly classified with a very good margin (a strong difference between the probability assigned by the correct model and the other ones). An analysis of the misclassified data has shown that they are by to the presence of serious typing errors (it is quite rare that a sequence in the dataset does not show any typing correction). As the number of repetitions for a single user is small, the algorithm was not able to learn also the error modalities for each one of them.

In the second experiment, a volunteer (not belonging to the group of 20 users in the first experiment) provided 140 repetitions of the same sentence used in the first experiment. A set of 100 of them has been used to build a model of the user. The HHMM learned by the algorithm contained 11 motif models at the low level corresponding to 11 states at the high level. It has been evaluated using the remaining 40 traces of the volunteer and the 200 traces used in the first experiment. The results have been excellent: on the 40 traces belonging to the volunteer, the log-odds of the probability of the trace assigned by the model was always very high (from +140 to +190), whereas on the 200 traces of the other users it was always very low (from -10 to +10).

The experiment shows that, increasing the size of the dataset, the algorithm has been able to learn a very accurate model.

7   Conclusions

We have proposed a method for automatically synthesizing complex profiles based on HHMMs from traces. In preliminary tests on artificial datasets, the method succeeded in reconstructing non trivial two level HHMMs, whereas the results obtained on a task of user identification are very encouraging. It is worth noticing that, in this case, the goal was not to compete with the results obtained by task specific algorithms[1, 3, 8], but to test how a general purpose algorithm performed on a non trivial task for which it was not customized. In fact, the learning algorithm has been simply run on the datasets dedicating few hours to prepare the experiment. Even if the experimentation is not extensive enough for a definitive conclusion, the results look interesting. In particular, we consider very promising the fact that the distance between the models of the different users is very large.

Acknowledgments

The present work has been supported by the FIRB Project: WebMinds.

References

1. S. Bleha, C. Slivinsky, and B. Hussein. Computer-access security systems using keystroke dynamics. *IEEE Transactions on Pattern Analysis and Machine Intelligence*, PAMI-12(12):1217–1222, 1990.
2. M. Botta, U. Galassi, and A.Giordana. Learning complex and sparse events in long sequences. In *Proceedings of the European Conference on Artificial Intelligence, ECAI-04*, Valencia, Spain, August 2004.
3. M. Brown and S.J. Rogers. User identification via keystroke characteristics of typed names using neural networks. *International Journal of Man-Machine Studies*, 39:999–1014, 1993.
4. R. Durbin, S. Eddy, A. Krogh, and G. Mitchison. *Biological sequence analysis*. Cambridge University Press, 1998.
5. S. Fine, Y Singer, and N. Tishby. The hierarchical hidden markov model: Analysis and applications. *Machine Learning*, 32:41–62, 1998.
6. G. D. Forney. The viterbi algorithm. *Proceedings of IEEE*, 61:268–278, 1973.
7. D. Gussfield. *Algorithms on Strings, Trees, and Sequences*. Cambridge University Press, 1997.
8. R. Joyce and G. Gupta. User authorization based on keystroke latencies. *Communications of the ACM*, 33(2):168–176, 1990.
9. K. Murphy and M. Paskin. Linear time inference in hierarchical hmms. In *Advances in Neural Information Processing Systems (NIPS-01)*, volume 14, 2001.
10. L. Rabiner and B. Juang. *Fundamentals of Speech Recognition*. Prentice Hall, Englewood Cliffs, NY, 1993.
11. L.R. Rabiner. A tutorial on hidden markov models and selected applications in speech recognition. *Proceedings of IEEE*, 77(2):257–286, 1989.

Statistical Independence from the Viewpoint of Linear Algebra

Shusaku Tsumoto

Department of Medical Informatics,
Shimane University, School of Medicine,
89-1 Enya-cho Izumo 693-8501 Japan
tsumoto@computer.org

Abstract. A contingency table summarizes the conditional frequencies of two attributes and shows how these two attributes are dependent on each other with the information on a partition of universe generated by these attributes. Thus, this table can be viewed as a relation between two attributes with respect to information granularity. This paper focuses on statistical independence in a contingency table from the viewpoint of granular computing, which shows that statistical independence in a contingency table is a special form of linear dependence. The discussions also show that when a contingency table is viewed as a matrix, its rank is equal to 1.0. Thus, the degree of independence, rank plays a very important role in extracting a probabilistic model from a given contingency table.

1 Introduction

Statistical independence between two attributes is a very important concept in data mining and statistics. The definition $P(A, B) = P(A)P(B)$ show that the joint probability of A and B is the product of both probabilities. This gives several useful formula, such as $P(A|B) = P(A)$, $P(B|A) = P(B)$. In a data mining context, these formulae show that these two attributes may not be correlated with each other. Thus, when A or B is a classification target, the other attribute may not play an important role in its classification.

Although independence is a very important concept, it has not been fully and formally investigated as a relation between two attributes.

In this paper, a statistical independence in a contingency table is focused on from the viewpoint of granular computing.

The first important observation is that a contingency table compares two attributes with respect to information granularity. It is shown from the definition that statistifcal independence in a contingency table is a special form of linear depedence of two attributes. Especially, when the table is viewed as a matrix, the above discussion shows that the rank of the matrix is equal to 1.0. Also, the results also show that partial statistical independence can be observed.

The second important observation is that matrix algebra is a key point of analysis of this table. A contingency table can be viewed as a matrix and several

M.-S. Hacid et al. (Eds.): ISMIS 2005, LNAI 3488, pp. 56–64, 2005.
© Springer-Verlag Berlin Heidelberg 2005

operations and ideas of matrix theory are introduced into the analysis of the contingency table.

The paper is organized as follows: Section 2 discusses the characteristics of contingency tables. Section 3 shows the conditions on statistical independence for a 2×2 table. Section 4 gives those for a $2 \times n$ table. Section 5 extends these results into a multi-way contingency table. Section 6 discusses statistical independence from matrix theory. Finally, Section 7 concludes this paper.

2   Contingency Table from Rough Sets

2.1   Rough Sets Notations

In the subsequent sections, the following notations is adopted, which is introduced in [7]. Let U denote a nonempty, finite set called the universe and A denote a nonempty, finite set of attributes, i.e., $a : U \to V_a$ for $a \in A$, where V_a is called the domain of a, respectively. Then, a decision table is defined as an information system, $A = (U, A \cup \{\mathcal{D}\})$, where $\{\mathcal{D}\}$ is a set of given decision attributes. The atomic formulas over $B \subseteq A \cup \{\mathcal{D}\}$ and V are expressions of the form $[a = v]$, called descriptors over B, where $a \in B$ and $v \in V_a$. The set $F(B, V)$ of formulas over B is the least set containing all atomic formulas over B and closed with respect to disjunction, conjunction and negation. For each $f \in F(B, V)$, f_A denote the meaning of f in A, i.e., the set of all objects in U with property f, defined inductively as follows.

1. If f is of the form $[a = v]$ then, $f_A = \{s \in U | a(s) = v\}$
2. $(f \wedge g)_A = f_A \cap g_A;\ (f \vee g)_A = f_A \vee g_A;\ (\neg f)_A = U - f_a$

By using this framework, classification accuracy and coverage, or true positive rate is defined as follows.

Definition 1.
Let R and D denote a formula in $F(B, V)$ and a set of objects whose decision attribute is given as $\lceil$, respectively. Classification accuracy and coverage(true positive rate) for $R \to \mathcal{D}$ is defined as:

$$\alpha_R(D) = \frac{|R_A \cap D|}{|R_A|}(= P(D|R)),\ and\ \kappa_R(D) = \frac{|R_A \cap D|}{|D|}(= P(R|D)),$$

where $|A|$ denotes the cardinality of a set A, $\alpha_R(D)$ denotes a classification accuracy of R as to classification of $\mathcal{D}$, and $\kappa_R(D)$ denotes a coverage, or a true positive rate of R to $\mathcal{D}$, respectively.

2.2   Two-Way Contingency Table

From the viewpoint of information systems, a contingency table summarizes the relation between two attributes with respect to frequencies. This viewpoint has already been discussed in [10, 11]. However, this study focuses on more statistical interpretation of this table.

Definition 2. *Let R_1 and R_2 denote binary attributes in an attribute space A. A contingency table is a table of a set of the meaning of the following formulas:* $|[R_1 = 0]_A|, |[R_1 = 1]_A|, |[R_2 = 0]_A|, |[R_1 = 1]_A|, |[R_1 = 0 \wedge R_2 = 0]_A|, |[R_1 = 0 \wedge R_2 = 1]_A|, |[R_1 = 1 \wedge R_2 = 0]_A|, |[R_1 = 1 \wedge R_2 = 1]_A|, |[R_1 = 0 \vee R_1 = 1]_A|(= |U|)$. *This table is arranged into the form shown in Table 1, where:* $|[R_1 = 0]_A| = x_{11} + x_{21} = x_{.1}, |[R_1 = 1]_A| = x_{12} + x_{22} = x_{.2}, |[R_2 = 0]_A| = x_{11} + x_{12} = x_{1.}, |[R_2 = 1]_A| = x_{21} + x_{22} = x_{2.}, |[R_1 = 0 \wedge R_2 = 0]_A| = x_{11}, |[R_1 = 0 \wedge R_2 = 1]_A| = x_{21}, |[R_1 = 1 \wedge R_2 = 0]_A| = x_{12}, |[R_1 = 1 \wedge R_2 = 1]_A| = x_{22}, |[R_1 = 0 \vee R_1 = 1]_A| = x_{.1} + x_{.2} = x_{..}(= |U|)$.

Table 1. Two way Contingency Table

	$R_1 = 0$	$R_1 = 1$	
$R_2 = 0$	x_{11}	x_{12}	$x_{1.}$
$R_2 = 1$	x_{21}	x_{22}	$x_{2.}$
	$x_{.1}$	$x_{.2}$	$x_{..}$

$$(= |U| = N)$$

From this table, accuracy and coverage for $[R_1 = 0] \rightarrow [R_2 = 0]$ are defined as:

$$\alpha_{[R_1=0]}([R_2 = 0]) = \frac{|[R_1 = 0 \wedge R_2 = 0]_A|}{|[R_1 = 0]_A|} = \frac{x_{11}}{x_{.1}},$$

and

$$\kappa_{[R_1=0]}([R_2 = 0]) = \frac{|[R_1 = 0 \wedge R_2 = 0]_A|}{|[R_2 = 0]_A|} = \frac{x_{11}}{x_{1.}}.$$

2.3   Multi-way Contingency Table

Two-way contingency table can be extended into a contingency table for multi-nominal attributes.

Definition 3. *Let R_1 and R_2 denote multinominal attributes in an attribute space A which have m and n values. A contingency tables is a table of a set of the meaning of the following formulas:* $|[R_1 = A_j]_A|, |[R_2 = B_i]_A|, |[R_1 = A_j \wedge R_2 = B_i]_A|, |[R_1 = A_1 \wedge R_1 = A_2 \wedge \cdots \wedge R_1 = A_m]_A|, |[R_2 = B_1 \wedge R_2 = A_2 \wedge \cdots \wedge R_2 = A_n]_A|$ *and* $|U|$ *($i = 1, 2, 3, \cdots, n$ and $j = 1, 2, 3, \cdots, m$). This table is arranged into the form shown in Table 1, where:* $|[R_1 = A_j]_A| = \sum_{i=1}^{m} x_{1i} = x_{.j}, |[R_2 = B_i]_A| = \sum_{j=1}^{n} x_{ji} = x_{i.}, |[R_1 = A_j \wedge R_2 = B_i]_A| = x_{ij}, |U| = N = x_{..}$ *($i = 1, 2, 3, \cdots, n$ and $j = 1, 2, 3, \cdots, m$).*

Table 2. Contingency Table ($m \times n$)

	A_1	A_2	$\cdots$	A_n	Sum
B_1	x_{11}	x_{12}	$\cdots$	x_{1n}	$x_{1\cdot}$
B_2	x_{21}	x_{22}	$\cdots$	x_{2n}	$x_{2\cdot}$
$\vdots$	$\vdots$	$\vdots$	$\ddots$	$\vdots$	$\vdots$
B_m	x_{m1}	x_{m2}	$\cdots$	x_{mn}	$x_{m\cdot}$
Sum	$x_{\cdot 1}$	$x_{\cdot 2}$	$\cdots$	$x_{\cdot n}$	$x_{\cdot\cdot} = |U| = N$

3   Statistical Independence in 2 × 2 Contingency Table

Let us consider a contingency table shown in Table 1. Statistical independence between R_1 and R_2 gives:

$$P([R_1 = 0], [R_2 = 0]) = P([R_1 = 0]) \times P([R_2 = 0])$$
$$P([R_1 = 0], [R_2 = 1]) = P([R_1 = 0]) \times P([R_2 = 1])$$
$$P([R_1 = 1], [R_2 = 0]) = P([R_1 = 1]) \times P([R_2 = 0])$$
$$P([R_1 = 1], [R_2 = 1]) = P([R_1 = 1]) \times P([R_2 = 1])$$

Since each probability is given as a ratio of each cell to N, the above equations are calculated as:

$$\frac{x_{11}}{N} = \frac{x_{11} + x_{12}}{N} \times \frac{x_{11} + x_{21}}{N}$$
$$\frac{x_{12}}{N} = \frac{x_{11} + x_{12}}{N} \times \frac{x_{12} + x_{22}}{N}$$
$$\frac{x_{21}}{N} = \frac{x_{21} + x_{22}}{N} \times \frac{x_{11} + x_{21}}{N}$$
$$\frac{x_{22}}{N} = \frac{x_{21} + x_{22}}{N} \times \frac{x_{12} + x_{22}}{N}$$

Since $N = \sum_{i,j} x_{ij}$, the following formula will be obtained from these four formulae.

$$x_{11}x_{22} = x_{12}x_{21} \ \text{or} \ x_{11}x_{22} - x_{12}x_{21} = 0$$

Thus,

Theorem 1. *If two attributes in a contingency table shown in Table 1 are statistical indepedent, the following equation holds:*

$$x_{11}x_{22} - x_{12}x_{21} = 0 \tag{1}$$

$\square$

It is notable that the above equation corresponds to the fact that the determinant of a matrix corresponding to this table is equal to 0. Also, when these four values are not equal to 0, the equation 1 can be transformed into:

$$\frac{x_{11}}{x_{21}} = \frac{x_{12}}{x_{22}}.$$

Let us assume that the above ratio is equal to $C(constant)$. Then, since $x_{11} = Cx_{21}$ and $x_{12} = Cx_{22}$, the following equation is obtained.

$$\frac{x_{11} + x_{12}}{x_{21} + x_{22}} = \frac{C(x_{21} + x_{22})}{x_{21} + x_{22}} = C = \frac{x_{11}}{x_{21}} = \frac{x_{12}}{x_{22}}. \tag{2}$$

It is notable that this discussion can be easily extended into a $2xn$ contingency table where $n > 3$. The important equationwill be extended into

$$\frac{x_{11}}{x_{21}} = \frac{x_{12}}{x_{22}} = \cdots = \frac{x_{1n}}{x_{2n}} = \frac{x_{11} + x_{12} + \cdots + x_{1n}}{x_{21} + x_{22} + \cdots + x_{2n}} = \frac{\sum_{k=1}^{n} x_{1k}}{\sum_{k=1}^{n} x_{2k}} \tag{3}$$

Thus,

Theorem 2. *If two attributes in a contingency table $(2 \times k(k = 2, \cdots, n))$ are statistical indepedent, the following equations hold:*

$$x_{11}x_{22} - x_{12}x_{21} = x_{12}x_{23} - x_{13}x_{22} = \cdots = x_{1n}x_{21} - x_{11}x_{n3} = 0 \tag{4}$$

$\square$

It is also notable that this equation is the same as the equation on collinearity of projective geometry [2].

4 Statistical Independence in $m \times n$ Contingency Table

Let us consider a $m \times n$ contingency table shown in Table 2. Statistical independence of R_1 and R_2 gives the following formulae:

$$P([R_1 = A_i, R_2 = B_j]) = P([R_1 = A_i])P([R_2 = B_j])$$
$$(i = 1, \cdots, m, j = 1, \cdots, n).$$

According to the definition of the table,

$$\frac{x_{ij}}{N} = \frac{\sum_{k=1}^{n} x_{ik}}{N} \times \frac{\sum_{l=1}^{m} x_{lj}}{N}. \tag{5}$$

Thus, we have obtained:

$$x_{ij} = \frac{\sum_{k=1}^{n} x_{ik} \times \sum_{l=1}^{m} x_{lj}}{N}. \tag{6}$$

Thus, for a fixed j,

$$\frac{x_{i_a j}}{x_{i_b j}} = \frac{\sum_{k=1}^{n} x_{i_a k}}{\sum_{k=1}^{n} x_{i_b k}}$$

In the same way, for a fixed i,

$$\frac{x_{ij_a}}{x_{ij_b}} = \frac{\sum_{l=1}^{m} x_{lj_a}}{\sum_{l=1}^{m} x_{lj_b}}$$

Since this relation will hold for any j, the following equation is obtained:

$$\frac{x_{i_a 1}}{x_{i_b 1}} = \frac{x_{i_a 2}}{x_{i_b 2}} \cdots = \frac{x_{i_a n}}{x_{i_b n}} = \frac{\sum_{k=1}^{n} x_{i_a k}}{\sum_{k=1}^{n} x_{i_b k}}. \tag{7}$$

Since the right hand side of the above equation will be constant, thus all the ratios are constant. Thus,

Theorem 3. *If two attributes in a contingency table shown in Table 2 are statistical indepedent, the following equations hold:*

$$\frac{x_{i_a 1}}{x_{i_b 1}} = \frac{x_{i_a 2}}{x_{i_b 2}} \cdots = \frac{x_{i_a n}}{x_{i_b n}} = const. \tag{8}$$

for all rows: i_a and i_b ($i_a, i_b = 1, 2, \cdots, m$).

$\square$

5   Contingency Matrix

The meaning of the above discussions will become much clearer when we view a contingency table as a matrix.

Definition 4. *A corresponding matrix $C_{T_{a,b}}$ is defined as a matrix the element of which are equal to the value of the corresponding contingency table $T_{a,b}$ of two attributes a and b, except for marginal values.*

Definition 5. *The rank of a table is defined as the rank of its corresponding matrix. The maximum value of the rank is equal to the size of (square) matrix, denoted by r.*

The contingency matrix of Table $2(T(R_1, R_2))$ is defined as $C_{T_{R_1, R_2}}$ as below:

$$\begin{pmatrix} x_{11} & x_{12} & \cdots & x_{1n} \\ x_{21} & x_{22} & \cdots & x_{2n} \\ \vdots & \vdots & \ddots & \vdots \\ x_{m1} & x_{m2} & \cdots & x_{mn} \end{pmatrix}$$

5.1   Independence of 2×2 Contingency Table

The results in Section 3 corresponds to the degree of independence in matrix theory. Let us assume that a contingency table is given as Table 1. Then the corresponding matrix $(C_{T_{R_1, R_2}})$ is given as:

$$\begin{pmatrix} x_{11} & x_{12} \\ x_{21} & x_{22} \end{pmatrix},$$

Then,

Proposition 1. *The determinant of $det(C_{T_{R_1, R_2}})$ is equal to $x_{11}x_{22} - x_{12}x_{21}$,*

Proposition 2. *The rank will be:*

$$rank = \begin{cases} 2, & if \ det(C_{T_{R_1,R_2}}) \neq 0 \\ 1, & if \ det(C_{T_{R_1,R_2}}) = 0 \end{cases}$$

From Theorem 1,

Theorem 4. *If the rank of the corresponding matrix of a 2times2 contingency table is 1, then two attributes in a given contingency table are statistically independent. Thus,*

$$rank = \begin{cases} 2, & dependent \\ 1, & statistical \ independent \end{cases}$$

This discussion can be extended into $2 \times n$ tables.

Theorem 5. *If the rank of the corresponding matrix of a $2 \times n$ contigency table is 1, then two attributes in a given contingency table are statistically independent. Thus,*

$$rank = \begin{cases} 2, & dependent \\ 1, & statistical \ independent \end{cases}$$

5.2   Independence of 3×3 Contingency Table

When the number of rows and columns are larger than 3, then the situation is a little changed. It is easy to see that the rank for statistical independence of a $m \times n$ contingency table is equal 1.0 as shown in Theorem 3. Also, when the rank is equal to $\min(m,n)$, two attributes are dependent.

Then, what kind of structure will a contingency matrix have when the rank is larger than 1,0 and smaller than $\min(m,n) - 1$? For illustration, let us consider the following $3times3$ contingecy table.

Example. Let us consider the following corresponding matrix:

$$A = \begin{pmatrix} 1 & 2 & 3 \\ 4 & 5 & 6 \\ 7 & 8 & 9 \end{pmatrix}.$$

The determinant of A is:

$$det(A) = 1 \times (-1)^{1+1} det \begin{pmatrix} 5 & 6 \\ 8 & 9 \end{pmatrix}$$
$$+2 \times (-1)^{1+2} det \begin{pmatrix} 4 & 6 \\ 7 & 9 \end{pmatrix}$$
$$+3 \times (-1)^{1+3} det \begin{pmatrix} 4 & 5 \\ 7 & 8 \end{pmatrix}$$
$$= 1 \times (-3) + 2 \times 6 + 3 \times (-3) = 0$$

Thus, the rank of A is smaller than 2. On the other hand, since $(123) \neq k(456)$ and $(123) \neq k(789)$, the rank of A is not equal to 1.0 Thus, the rank of A is equal to 2.0. Actually, one of three rows can be represented by the other two rows. For example,

$$(4\,5\,6) = \frac{1}{2}\{(1\,2\,3) + (7\,8\,9)\}.$$

Therefore, in this case, we can say that two of three pairs of one attribute are dependent to the other attribute, but one pair is statistically independent of the other attribute with respect to the linear combination of two pairs. It is easy to see that this case includes the cases when two pairs are statistically independent of the other attribute, but the table becomes statistically dependent with the other attribute.

In other words, the corresponding matrix is a mixture of statistical dependence and independence. We call this case *contextual independent*. From this illustration, the following theorem is obtained:

Theorem 6. *If the rank of the corresponding matrix of a 3×3 contigency table is 1, then two attributes in a given contingency table are statistically independent. Thus,*

$$rank = \begin{cases} 3, & dependent \\ 2, & contextual\ independent \\ 1, & statistical\ independent \end{cases}$$

It is easy to see that this discussion can be extended into $3 \times n$ contingency tables.

5.3   Independence of $m \times n$ Contingency Table

Finally, the relation between rank and independence in a multi-way contingency table is obtained from Theorem 3.

Theorem 7. *Let the corresponding matrix of a given contingency table be a $m \times n$ matrix. If the rank of the corresponding matrix is 1, then two attributes in a given contingency table are statistically independent. If the rank of the corresponding matrix is $\min(m, n)$, then two attributes in a given contingency table are dependent. Otherwise, two attributes are contextual dependent, which means that several conditional probabilities can be represented by a linear combination of conditional probabilities. Thus,*

$$rank = \begin{cases} \min(m, n) & dependent \\ 2, \cdots, \min(m, n) - 1 & contextual\ independent \\ 1 & statistical\ independent \end{cases}$$

6   Conclusion

In this paper, a contingency table is interpreted from the viewpoint of granular computing and statistical independence. From the definition of statistical independence, statistical independence in a contingency table will holds when the equations of collinearity(Equation 6) are satisfied. In other words, statistical independence can be viewed as linear dependence. Then, the correspondence between contingency table and matrix, gives the theorem where the rank of the contingency matrix of a given contingency table is equal to 1 if two attributes are statistical independent. That is, all the rows of contingency table can be described by one row with the coefficient given by a marginal distribution. If the rank is maximum, then two attributes are dependent. Otherwise, some probabilistic structure can be found within attribute -value pairs in a given attribute, which we call contextual independence. Thus, matrix algebra is a key point of the analysis of a contingency table and the degree of independence, rank plays a very important role in extracting a probabilistic model.

References

1. Butz, C.J. Exploiting contextual independencies in web search and user profiling, *Proceedings of World Congress on Computational Intelligence (WCCI'2002)*, CD-ROM, 2002.
2. Coxeter, H.S.M. *Projective Geometry, 2nd Edition*, Springer, New York, 1987.
3. Polkowski, L. and Skowron, A.(Eds.) *Rough Sets and Knowledge Discovery 1*, Physica Verlag, Heidelberg, 1998.
4. Polkowski, L. and Skowron, A.(Eds.) *Rough Sets and Knowledge Discovery 2*, Physica Verlag, Heidelberg, 1998.
5. Pawlak, Z., *Rough Sets*. Kluwer Academic Publishers, Dordrecht, 1991.
6. Rao, C.R. *Linear Statistical Inference and Its Applications, 2nd Edition*, John Wiley & Sons, New York, 1973.
7. Skowron, A. and Grzymala-Busse, J. From rough set theory to evidence theory. In: Yager, R., Fedrizzi, M. and Kacprzyk, J.(eds.) *Advances in the Dempster-Shafer Theory of Evidence*, pp.193-236, John Wiley & Sons, New York, 1994.
8. Tsumoto S and Tanaka H: Automated Discovery of Medical Expert System Rules from Clinical Databases based on Rough Sets. In: *Proceedings of the Second International Conference on Knowledge Discovery and Data Mining 96*, AAAI Press, Palo Alto CA, pp.63-69, 1996.
9. Tsumoto, S. Knowledge discovery in clinical databases and evaluation of discovered knowledge in outpatient clinic. *Information Sciences*, **124**, 125-137, 2000.
10. Yao, Y.Y. and Wong, S.K.M., A decision theoretic framework for approximating concepts, *International Journal of Man-machine Studies*, **37**, 793-809, 1992.
11. Yao, Y.Y. and Zhong, N., An analysis of quantitative measures associated with rules, N. Zhong and L. Zhou (Eds.), *Methodologies for Knowledge Discovery and Data Mining, Proceedings of the Third Pacific-Asia Conference on Knowledge Discovery and Data Mining*, LNAI **1574**, Springer, Berlin, pp. 479-488, 1999.
12. Ziarko, W., Variable Precision Rough Set Model. *Journal of Computer and System Sciences*, 46, 39-59, 1993.

Bitmap Index-Based Decision Trees

Cécile Favre and Fadila Bentayeb

ERIC - Université Lumière Lyon 2,
Bâtiment L, 5 avenue Pierre Mendès-France
69676 BRON Cedex – FRANCE
{cfavre, bentayeb}@eric.univ-lyon2.fr

Abstract. In this paper we propose an original approach to apply data
mining algorithms, namely decision tree-based methods, taking into account not only the size of processed databases but also the processing
time. The key idea consists in constructing a decision tree, within the
DBMS, using bitmap indices. Indeed bitmap indices have many useful
properties such as the count and bit-wise operations. We will show that
these operations are efficient to build decision trees. In addition, by using bitmap indices, we don't need to access raw data. This implies clear
improvements in terms of processing time.

Keywords: Bitmap indices, databases, data mining, decision trees,
performance.

1 Introduction

Mining large databases efficiently has been the subject of many research studies
during the last years. However, in practice, the long processing time required by
data mining algorithms remains a critical issue. Indeed, traditional data mining algorithms operate on main memory, which limits the size of the processed
databases. There are three approaches to overcome this limit. The first way
consists in preprocessing data by using feature selection [11] or sampling [4, 18]
techniques. The second way is to increase the scalability, by optimising data
accesses [6, 15] or algorithms [1, 7]. The third way consists in integrating data
mining methods within DataBases Management Systems (DBMSs) [5]. Many
integrated approaches have been proposed. They usually use SQL extensions for
developing new operators [8, 12, 16] or new languages [9, 10, 19]. This trend has
been confirmed with the integration of data mining tools in commercial solutions
[13, 17], but these are real "black boxes" requiring also the use of Application
Programming Interfaces (APIs).

In opposition to these different solutions, recent works have proposed to integrate decision tree-based methods within DBMSs, using only the tools offered
by these latter. The analogy is made between building successive partitions,
representing different populations, and successive relational views modeling the
decision tree [2]. Building views tend to increase processing time due to multiple
accesses. This can be improved by using a contingency table as proposed in [3].

M.-S. Hacid et al. (Eds.): ISMIS 2005, LNAI 3488, pp. 65–73, 2005.
© Springer-Verlag Berlin Heidelberg 2005

Instead of applying data mining algorithms to the training set, we apply them to the contingency table which is much smaller. In this paper, we propose to improve processing time by reducing not only the size of the training set, but also the data accesses. Indeed, our approach is to use bitmap indices to represent the training set and apply data mining algorithms on these indices to build our decision tree. The population frequencies of a given node in the decision tree are obtained by applying counting and low-cost boolean operations on selected bitmap indices. To run these operations, the DBMS does not need to access raw data. Thus, in opposition to the integrated approaches proposed in the literature, our approach presents three advantages: (1) no extension of the SQL language is needed; (2) no programming through an API is required and (3) no access data sources is necessary. To validate our approach, we implemented the ID3 (Induction Decision Tree) method [14] as a PL/SQL stored procedure, named *ID3_Bitmap*. To prove that our implementation of ID3 works properly, we successfully compared the output of our procedure with the output of an existing and validated data mining in-memory software, Sipina [20]. Moreover, we showed that with bitmap indices we did not have a size limit when dealing with large databases as compared to in-memory software, while obtaining linear processing times.

The remainder of this paper is organized as follows. First, we present the principle of bitmap indices in Section 2. In Section 3, we present our bitmap-based approach for decision tree-based methods. Section 4 details our implementation of ID3 method, presents the experimental results and the complexity study. We finally conclude this paper and provide future research directions in Section 5.

2   Bitmap Indices

A bitmap index is a data structure used to efficiently access large databases. Generally, the purpose of an index is to provide pointers to rows in a table containing given key values. In a common index, this is achieved by storing a list of rowids for each key corresponding to the rows with that key value. In a bitmap index, records in a table are assumed to be numbered sequentially from 1. For each key value, a bitmap (array of bits) is used instead of a list of rowids. Each bit in the bitmap corresponds to an existing rowid. If the bit is set to "*1*", it means that the row with the corresponding rowid contains the key value ; otherwise the bit is set to "*0*". A mapping function converts the bit position to an actual rowid, so the bitmap index provides the same functionality as a regular index even though it uses a different representation internally.

2.1   Example

To illustrate how bitmap indices work, we use the Titanic database as an example. Titanic is a table containing 2201 tuples described by four attributes *Class*, *Age*, *Gender* and *Survivor* (Table 1). A bitmap index built on the *Survivor* attribute is presented in Table 2.

Table 1. Titanic Database

Class	Age	Gender	Survivor
1st	Adult	Female	Yes
3rd	Adult	Male	Yes
2nd	Child	Male	Yes
3rd	Adult	Male	Yes
1st	Adult	Female	Yes
2nd	Adult	Male	No
1st	Adult	Male	Yes
Crew	Adult	Female	No
Crew	Adult	Female	Yes
2nd	Adult	Male	No
3rd	Adult	Male	No
Crew	Adult	Male	No
...	...	...	...

Table 2. *Survivor* Bitmap Index

	Rowid	..	12	11	10	9	8	7	6	5	4	3	2	1
Survivor	No	..	1	1	1	0	1	0	1	0	0	0	0	0
	Yes	..	0	0	0	1	0	1	0	1	1	1	1	1

2.2 Properties

Bitmap indices are designed for efficient queries on multiple keys. Hence, queries are answered using bit-wise operations such as intersection (AND), and union (OR). Each operation takes two bitmaps of the same size and the operator is applied on corresponding bits. In the resulting bitmap, every "1" bit marks the desired tuple. Thus counting the number of tuples is even faster. For some select queries "SELECT COUNT()...WHERE ... AND ...", those logical operations could provide answers without returning to data sources. In addition to standard operations, the SQL engine can use bitmap indices to efficiently perform special set-based operations using combinations of multiple indices. For example, to find the total number of *"male survivors"*, we can simply perform the logical AND operation between bitmaps representing *Survivor="Yes"* and *Gender="Male"*, then count the number of *"1"* (Table 3).

Table 3. Bitmap(**Survivor**=*"Yes"*) **AND** Bitmap(**Gender**=*"Male"*)

Rowid	..	12	11	10	9	8	7	6	5	4	3	2	1
Survivor="Yes"	..	0	0	0	1	0	1	0	1	1	1	1	1
Gender="Male"	..	1	1	1	0	0	1	1	0	1	1	1	0
AND	..	0	0	0	0	0	1	0	0	1	1	1	0

3   Bitmap-Based Decision Trees Methods

Induction trees are among the most popular supervised data mining methods proposed in the literature. They may be viewed as a succession of smaller and smaller partitions of an initial training set. They take as input a set of objects (tuples, in the relational databases vocabulary) described by a collection of predictive attributes. Each object belongs to one of a set of mutually exclusive classes (attribute to be predicted). Induction tree construction methods apply successive criteria on the training population to obtain these partitions, wherein the size of one class is maximized. In the ID3 algorithm, the discriminating power of an attribute for segmenting a node of the decision tree is expressed by a variation of entropy and more precisely, its entropy of Shannon.

3.1   Principle

In this paper, we propose to integrate decision tree-based methods within DBMSs. To achieve this goal, we only use existing structures, namely, bitmap indices, that we exploit through SQL queries. Bitmap indices improve select queries performance by applying count and bit-wise logical operations such as AND. This type of queries coincides exactly to those we need to build a decision tree and more precisely to define the nodes' frequencies. Indeed, as we have shown in Table 3, to find the total number of the *"male survivors"*, SQL engine performs logical AND and COUNT operations onto bitmap indices and gets the result. In the case of a decision tree-based method, this query may correspond to a segmentation step for obtaining the population frequency of the class *Survivor="Yes"* in the node *Gender="Male"*.

To show that our approach is efficient and relevant, we introduced the use of bitmap indices into the ID3 method. This induces changes in the computation of the information gain for each predictive attribute. Thus, in our approach, for an initial training set, we create its associated set of bitmap indices for predictive attributes and the attribute to be predicted. Then, the ID3 algorithm is applied onto the set of bitmap indices rather than the whole training set. For the root node of the decision tree, the population frequencies are obtained by simply counting the total number of *"1"* in the bitmaps built on the attribute to be predicted. For each other node in the decision tree, we generate a new set of bitmaps, each one corresponding to the class in the node. The bitmap characterizing each class in the current node is obtained by applying the AND operation between the bitmap associated to the current node and the bitmaps corresponding to the successive nodes from the root to the current node. To get the population frequency of each class in this node, we count the total number of *"1"* in the resulting bitmap. Since the information gain is based on population frequencies, it is also computed with bitmap indices.

3.2   Running Example

To illustrate our approach, let us take the Titanic database as an example (Table 1). The aim is to predict which classes of the Titanic passengers are more likely to survive the wreck. Those passengers are described by different attributes which are: *Class*={*1st*; *2nd*; *3rd*; *Crew*}; *Age*={*Adult*; *Child*}; *Gender*={*Female*; *Male*} and *Survivor*={*No*; *Yes*}.

For each predictive attribute (*Gender*, *Class* and *Age*) and the attribute to be predicted (*Survivor*), we create its corresponding bitmap index (Table 4). Thus, our learning population is precisely composed of these four different bitmap indices. Hence, we apply the decision tree building method directly on this set of bitmap indices.

Table 4. Bitmap Indices for Titanic's Database

		Rowid ‖ ..	12	11	10	9	8	7	6	5	4	3	2	1
Class	Crew	‖ ..	1	0	0	1	1	0	0	0	0	0	0	0
	1st	..	0	0	0	0	0	1	0	1	0	0	0	1
	2nd	..	0	0	1	0	0	0	1	0	0	1	0	0
	3rd	..	0	1	0	0	0	0	0	0	1	0	1	0
Age	Child	..	0	0	0	0	0	0	0	0	0	1	0	0
	Adult	..	1	1	1	1	1	1	1	1	1	0	1	1
Gender	Female	‖ ..	0	0	0	1	1	0	0	1	0	0	0	1
	Male	..	1	1	1	0	0	1	1	0	1	1	1	0
Survivor	No	..	1	1	1	0	1	0	1	0	0	0	0	0
	Yes	..	0	0	0	1	0	1	0	1	1	1	1	1

To obtain the root node of the decision tree, we have to determine the population frequency of each class. In our running example, these frequencies are obtained by counting the number of "*1*" in the bitmaps associated to *Survivor*= "*Yes*" and *Survivor*= "*No*" respectively (Fig. 1).

$$COUNT_1(Bitmap(Survivor = "Yes")) \longrightarrow \boxed{Yes\ 711}$$
$$COUNT_1(Bitmap(Survivor = "No")) \longrightarrow \boxed{No\ 1490}$$ ***Survivor***

Fig. 1. Root node

Then, the variation of entropy indicates that the segmentation attribute is *Gender*. The population of the root node is then divided into two sub-nodes corresponding to the rules *Gender*= "*Male*" and *Gender*= "*Female*" respectively. Each sub-node is composed of two sub-populations, those that survived and those that did not. To obtain the population frequencies of the node *Gender*= "*Male*" , we apply the logical operation AND firstly between the *Gender*= "*Male*" bitmap and the *Survivor*= "*Yes*" bitmap and secondly between the *Gender*= "*Male*" bitmap and the *Survivor*= "*No*" bitmap. Then we count the total number of "*1*" in the corresponding *And_bitmap* (Table 5). The same process is performed for the node *Gender*="*Female*" (Fig. 2). This process is repeated for all the other predictive attributes to obtain the final decision tree.

Table 5. AND-bitmaps for the node *Gender= "Male"*

Rowid	..	12	11	10	9	8	7	6	5	4	3	2	1
Survivor="Yes"	..	0	0	0	1	0	1	0	1	1	1	1	1
Gender="Male"	..	1	1	1	0	0	1	1	0	1	1	1	0
AND	..	**0**	**0**	**0**	**0**	**0**	**1**	**0**	**0**	**1**	**1**	**1**	**0**
Survivor="No"	..	1	1	1	0	1	0	1	0	0	0	0	0
Gender="Male"	..	1	1	1	0	0	1	1	0	1	1	1	0
AND	..	**1**	**1**	**1**	**0**	**0**	**0**	**1**	**0**	**0**	**0**	**0**	**0**

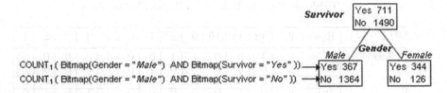

Fig. 2. Nodes of the first level of the decision tree

4 Validation

4.1 Implementation

We have implemented the ID3 method using bitmap indices as a PL/SQL stored procedure, namely *ID3_Bitmap*, under Oracle 9i, which is part of a broader package named *decision_tree* that is available on-line[1]. This stored procedure allows us to create the necessary bitmap indices for a given training set and then build the decision tree. Since Oracle uses by default B-Tree indices, we forced it to use bitmap indices. The nodes of the decision tree are built by using an SQL query that is based on the AND operation applied on its own bitmaps and its parent bitmaps. Then, the obtained *And_bitmaps* are used to count the population frequency of each class in the node with simple COUNT queries. These counts are used to determine the criterion that helps either partitioning the current node into a set of disjoint sub-partitions based on the values of a specific attribute or concluding that the node is a leaf, i.e., a terminal node. In the same way, to compute the information gain for a predictive attribute, our implementation uses bitmap indices rather than the whole training set.

4.2 Experimental Results

In order to validate our bitmap-based approach and compare its performances to classical in-memory data mining approaches, we tested it on the Titanic training set (Table 1). To have a significant database size, we duplicated the records of Titanic database. Moreover, these tests have been carried out in the same environment: a PC with 128 MB of RAM and the Personal Oracle DBMS version

---

[1] http://bdd.univ-lyon2.fr/download/decision_tree.zip

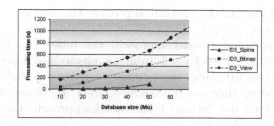

Fig. 3. Processing time with respect to database size

9i (Fig. 3). First, we compared the processing times of $ID3\_Bitmap$ to those of a classical in-memory implementation of ID3 available in the Sipina data mining software [20]. We clearly observe that $ID3\_Bitmap$ allowed us mining large databases without size limit comparing with $ID3\_Sipina$, while obtaining linear processing times with respect to the database size. For databases over 50 Mo, with the hardware configuration used for the tests, Sipina is unable to build a decision tree as compared to our method. Secondly, we compared the processing times of our $ID3\_Bitmap$ with the view-based approach $ID3\_View$ [2]. The results we obtain clearly underline the gain (40%) induced by $ID3\_Bitmap$, that has a much lower processing time than $ID3\_View$ on an average.

4.3   Complexity Study

Our objective is to confirm, from a theoretical point of view, the results obtained by our approach. For this study we place ourselves in the worst case, i.e. the indices are too large to be loaded in memory.

Let N be the total number of tuples in the training set, K the number of attributes, L the average length, in bits, of each attribute and A the average number of values of each attribute.

First we evaluate the size of training sets. The size of the initial training set is $N * L * K$ bits. For our bitmap-based approach, this initial training set is replaced by the set of bitmap indices. Thus K bitmap indices are created with an average number of A bitmaps for each index. Each bitmap has a size of N bits. In this case, the size of the training set is $N * A * K$ bits. As regards to the size of the training set and thus the loading time, our approach is preferable if $A < L$, which corresponds to a majority of cases.

In terms of time spent to data reading, we consider that a bit is read in one time unit.

The total number of nodes on the ith depth level can be approximated by A^{i-1}. Indeed we suppose that the obtained decision tree is complete and balanced. To reach level $i + 1$ from an unspecified level i of the tree, each training set must be read as many times as there are predictive attributes remaining at this level, i.e. $(K - i)$.

In the classical approach, as the size of the training set is $N * L * K$, reading time for level i (in time units) is $(K - i) * N * L * K * A^{i-1}$. Hence, to build the whole decision tree, in the classical approach, the reading time is : $\sum_{i=1}^{K}(K - i) * N * L * K * A^{i-1}$.

In our bitmap index-based approach, the index size is approximated by $N * A$ bits. To reach level $i + 1$ from an unspecified level i of the tree, for a given predictive attribute, the number of index to read is $i + 1$. Thus, at level i, the reading time is : $(i + 1)(K - i)N * A^i$. Hence, to build the whole decision tree with our bitmap index-based approach, the reading time is : $\sum_{i=1}^{K}(i + 1)(K - i)N * A^i$.

To evaluate the gain in time, we build the following ratio:

$$R = \frac{time\ with\ classical\ approach}{time\ with\ bitmap\ index-based\ approach} = \frac{\frac{KL}{A}\sum_{i=1}^{K}(K\ i)*A^i}{\sum_{i=1}^{K}(K-i)(i+1)*A^i}.$$

After computing we obtain : $R = \dfrac{\frac{KL}{A}\sum_{i=1}^{K}(K-i)*A^i}{\sum_{i=1}^{K}(K-i)*A^i+\sum_{i=1}^{K}i(K-i)*A^i}$

$$R^{-1} = \frac{A}{KL}\left(1 + \frac{\sum_{i=1}^{K}i(K-i)*A^i}{\sum_{i=1}^{K}(K-i)*A^i}\right) = \frac{A}{KL}(1 + G)$$

As we consider the polynomials of higher degree, G is of complexity K. Thus R^{-1} is of complexity $\frac{A}{L}$. Indeed $R^{-1} = \frac{A}{KL}(1 + K) = \frac{A}{L}(1 + \frac{1}{K})$ and $\frac{1}{K}$ is insignificant. Our approach is interesting if the ratio R^{-1} is lower than one, that means if $A < L$, which corresponds to a majority of the cases.

5   Conclusion and Perspectives

These last years, an important research effort has been made to apply efficiently data mining methods on large databases. Traditional data mining algorithms operate on main memory, which limits the size of the processed databases. Recently, a new approach has emerged. It consists in integrating data mining methods within DBMSs using only the tools offered by these latter. Following the integrated approach, we proposed in this paper an original method for applying decision trees-based algorithms on large databases. This method uses bitmap indices which have many useful properties such as the count and the bit-wise operations that can be used through SQL queries. Our method has two major advantages: it is not limited by the size of the main memory and it improves processing times because there is no need to access data sources since our method uses bitmap indices rather than the whole training set. To validate our approach, we implemented the ID3 method, under the form of a PL/SQL stored procedure into the Oracle DBMS. We showed that our bitmap-based implementation allowed us mining bigger databases as compared to the in-memory implementations while obtaining linear processing times with respect to the database size.

There are different perspectives opened by this study. We plan to implement other data mining methods using bitmap indices. More precisely, extending our approach to deal with the OR operator in the case for example of the CART method allowing grouping attribute values into classes. Moreover, we intend to compare the performances of these implementations to their equivalent in-memory software on real-life databases.

References

1. R. Agrawal, H. Mannila, R. Srikant, and et al. Fast discovery of association rules. In *Advances in Kowledge Discovery and Data Mining*, pages 307–328, 1996.
2. F. Bentayeb and J. Darmont. Decision tree modeling with relational views. In *XIIIth International Symposium on Methodologies for Intelligent Systems (ISMIS 02), France*, 2002.
3. F. Bentayeb, J. Darmont, and C. Udréa. Efficient integration of data mining techniques in dbmss. In *8th International Database Engineering and Applications Symposium (IDEAS 04), Portugal*, 2004.
4. J. H. Chauchat and R. Rakotomalala. A new sampling strategy for building decision trees from large databases. In *7th Conference of the International Federation of Classification Societies (IFCS 00), Belgium*, 2000.
5. S. Chaudhuri. Data mining and database systems: Where is the intersection? *Data Engineering Bulletin*, 21(1):4–8, 1998.
6. B. Dunkel and N. Soparkar. Data organization and access for efficient data mining. In *ICDE*, pages 522–529, 1999.
7. J. Gehrke, R. Ramakrishnan, and V. Ganti. Rainforest - a framework for fast decision tree construction of large datasets. In *24th International Conference on Very Large Data Bases (VLDB 98), USA*, 1998.
8. I. Geist and K. U. Sattler. Towards data mining operators in database systems: Algebra and implementation. 2nd International Workshop on Databases, Documents, and Information Fusion (DBFusion 2002).
9. J. Han, Y. Fu, W. Wang, K. Koperski, and O. Zaiane. DMQL: A data mining query language for relational databases. In *SIGMOD'96 Workshop on Research Issues in Data Mining and Knowledge Discovery (DMKD'96), Canada*, 1996.
10. T. Imielinski and A. Virmani. Msql: A query language for database mining. *DataMining and Knowledge Discovery : An International Journal*, 3:373–408, 1999.
11. H. Liu and H. Motoda. *Feature Selection for knowledge discovery and data mining*. Kluwer Academic Publishers, 1998.
12. R. Meo, G. Psaila, and S. Ceri. A new SQL-like operator for mining association rules. In *The VLDB Journal*, pages 122–133, 1996.
13. Oracle. Oracle 9i data mining. White paper, June 2001.
14. J. R. Quinlan. Induction of decision trees. *Machine Learning*, 1:81–106, 1986.
15. G. Ramesh, W. Maniatty, and M. Zaki. Indexing and data access methods for database mining, 2001.
16. S. Sarawagi, S. Thomas, and R. Agrawal. Integrating mining with relational database systems: Alternatives and implications. In *ACM SIGMOD International Conference on Management of Data (SIGMOD 98), USA*, 1998.
17. S. Soni, Z. Tang, and J. Yang. Performance study microsoft data mining algorithms. Technical report, Microsoft Corp., 2001.
18. H. Toivonen. Sampling large databases for association rules. In *In Proc. 1996 Int. Conf. Very Large Data Bases*, 1996.
19. H. Wang, C. Zaniolo, and C. R. Luo. Atlas : a small but complete sql extension for data mining and data streams. In *29th VLDB Conference. Germany*, 2003.
20. D. A. Zighed and R. Rakotomalala. Sipina-w(c) for windows: User's guide. Technical report, ERIC laboratory, University of Lyon 2, France, 1996.

On Automatic Modeling and Use of Domain-Specific Ontologies

Troels Andreasen, Henrik Bulskov, and Rasmus Knappe

Department of Computer Science,
Roskilde University,
P.O. Box 260, DK-4000 Roskilde, Denmark
{troels, bulskov, knappe}@ruc.dk

Abstract. In this paper, we firstly introduce an approach to the modeling of a domain-specific ontology for use in connection with a given document collection. Secondly, we present a methodology for deriving conceptual similarity from the domain-specific ontology. Adopted for ontology representation is a specific lattice-based concept algebraic language by which ontologies are inherently generative. The modeling of a domain specific ontology is based on a general ontology built upon common knowledge resources as dictionaries and thesauri. Based on analysis of concept occurrences in the object document collection the general ontology is restricted to a domain specific ontology encompassing concepts instantiated in the collection. The resulting domain specific ontology and similarity can be applied for surveying the collection through key concepts and conceptual relations and provides a means for topic-based navigation. Finally, a measure of concept similarity is derived from the domain specific ontology based on occurrences, commonalities, and distances in the ontology.

1 Introduction

The use of ontologies can contribute significantly to the structure and organization of concepts and relations within a knowledge domain.

The introduction of ontologies into tools for information access provides foundation for enhanced, knowledge-based approaches to surveying, indexing and querying of document collections.

We introduce in this paper the notion of an *instantiated ontology*, as a subontology derived from a general ontology and restricted by the set of instantiated concepts in a target document collection. As such, this instantiated ontology represents a conceptual organization reflecting the document collection, and reveals domain knowledge, for instance about the thematic areas of the domain which in turn facilitates means for a topic-based navigation and visualization of the structure within the given domain.

The primary focus of this paper concerns the modeling and use of ontologies. We introduce, in section 2, to a formalism for representation of ontologies. Section 3 describes the modeling of general and instantiated ontologies, respectively

M.-S. Hacid et al. (Eds.): ISMIS 2005, LNAI 3488, pp. 74–82, 2005.
© Springer-Verlag Berlin Heidelberg 2005

and illustrates the use of instantiated ontologies for surveying, visualization of both a given domain, but also queries or sets of domain concepts. Finally, in section 4, we derive a measure of conceptual similarity, based on the structure and relations of the ontology.

Both modeling and use of ontologies relies on the possibility to identify concept occurrences in – or generate conceptual descriptions of – text. To this end we assume a processing of text by a simplified natural language parser providing concept occurrences in the text. This parser may be applied for indexing of documents as well as for interpreting queries. The most simplified principle used here is basically a nominal phrase bracketing and an extract of nouns and adjectives that are combined by a *"noun* CHR *adjective"*-pattern concept (CHR representing a "characterized by" relation).

Thus, for instance, for the sentence *Borges has been widely hailed as the foremost contemporary Spanish-American writer*, the parser may produce the following:

$$borges, writer[\text{CHR}:contemporary, \text{CHR}:foremost, \text{CHR}:spanish\_american]$$

Concept expressions, that are the key to modelling and use of ontologies, are explained in more detail below, we refer, however, to [2] for a discussion of general principles behind parsing for concepts.

2 Representation of Ontologies

The purpose of the ontology is to define and relate concepts that may appear in the document collection or in queries to this.

We define a generative ontology framework where a basis ontology situates a set of atomic term concepts **A** in a concept inclusion lattice. A concept language (description language) defines a set of well-formed concepts, including both atomic and compound term concepts.

The concept language used here, ONTOLOG[8], defines a set of semantic relations **R** that can be used for "attribution" (feature-attachment) of concepts to form compound concepts. The set of available relations may vary with different domains and applications. We may choose $\mathbf{R} = \{\text{WRT}, \text{CHR}, \text{CBY}, \text{TMP}, \text{LOC}, \ldots\}$, for *with respect to, characterized by, caused by, temporal, location,* respectively.

Expressions in ONTOLOG are concepts situated in the ontology formed by an algebraic lattice with concept inclusion (ISA) as the ordering relation.

Attribution of concepts – combining atomic concepts into compound concepts by attaching attributes – can be written as feature structures. Simple attribution of a concept c_1 with relation r and a concept c_2 is denoted $c_1[r: c_2]$.

Given atomic concepts **A** and relations **R**, the set of well-formed terms **L** of the ONTOLOG language is defined as follows.

- if $x \in \mathbf{A}$ then $x \in \mathbf{L}$
- if $x \in \mathbf{L}$, $r_i \in \mathbf{R}$ and $y_i \in \mathbf{L}, i = 1, \ldots, n$
  then $x[r_1: y_1, \ldots, r_n: y_n] \in \mathbf{L}$

It appears that compound terms can be built from nesting, for instance, $c_1[r_1\colon c_2[r_2\colon c_3]]$ and from multiple attribution as in $c_1[r_1\colon c_2, r_2\colon c_3]$.

The attributes of a term with multiple attributes $T = x[r_1\colon y_1, \ldots, r_n\colon y_n]$ are considered as a set, thus we can rewrite T with any permutation of $\{r_1\colon y_1, \ldots, r_n\colon y_n\}$.

3   Modeling Ontologies

One objective in the modelling of domain knowledge is for the domain expert or knowledge engineer to identify significant concepts in the domain.

Ontology modelling in the present context is, compared to other works within the ontology area, a limited approach. The modelling consists of two parts. Firstly an inclusion of knowledge from available knowledge sources into a general ontology and secondly a restriction to a domain-specific part of the general ontology. The first part involves modeling of concepts in a generative ontology using different knowledge sources. In the second part a domain-specific ontology is retrieved as a subontology of the general ontology. The restriction to this subontology is build based on the set of concepts that appears (is instantiated) in the document collection and the result is called an instantiated ontology.

3.1   The General Ontology

Sources for knowledge base ontologies may have various forms. Typically a taxonomy can be supplemented with for instance word and term lists as well as dictionaries for definition of vocabularies and for handling of morphology.

We will not go into details on the modeling here but just assume the presence of a taxonomy in the form of a simple taxonomic concept inclusion relation $\mathrm{ISA_{KB}}$ over the set of atomic concepts $\mathbf{A}$. $\mathrm{ISA_{KB}}$ and $\mathbf{A}$ expresses the domain and world knowledge provided. $\mathrm{ISA_{KB}}$ is assumed to be explicitly specified – e.g. by domain experts – and would most typically not be transitively closed.

Based on $\widehat{\mathrm{ISA}}_{\mathrm{KB}}$, the transitive closure of $\mathrm{ISA_{KB}}$, we can generalize into a relation over all well-formed terms of the language $\mathbf{L}$ by the following:

- if $x\ \widehat{\mathrm{ISA}}_{\mathrm{KB}}\ y$ then $x \leq y$
- if $x[\ldots] \leq y[\ldots]$ then also
    $x[\ldots, r\colon z] \leq y[\ldots]$, and
    $x[\ldots, r\colon z] \leq y[\ldots, r\colon z]$,
- if $x \leq y$ then also
    $z[\ldots, r\colon x] \leq z[\ldots, r\colon y]$

where repeated $\ldots$ in each case denote zero or more attributes of the form $r_i\colon w_i$.

The general ontology $O = (\mathbf{L}, \leq, \mathbf{R})$ thus encompasses a set of well-formed expressions $\mathbf{L}$ derived from the concept language with a set of atomic concepts $\mathbf{A}$, an inclusion relation generalized from an expert provided relation $\mathrm{ISA_{KB}}$ and a supplementary set of semantic relations $\mathbf{R}$, where for $r \in \mathbf{R}$ we obviously have that $x[r\colon y] \leq x$ and that $x[r\colon y]$ is in relation r to y. Observe that $\mathbf{L}$ is infinite and that O thus is generative.

3.2   The Domain-Specific Ontology

Apart from the general ontology O, the target document collection contributes to the construction of the domain ontology. We assume a processing of the target document collection, where an indexing of text in documents, formed by sets of concepts from $\mathbf{L}$, is attached. In broad terms the domain ontology is a restriction of the general ontology to the concepts appearing in the target document collection.

More specifically the generative ontology is, by means of concept occurrence analysis over the document collection, transformed into a domain specific ontology restricted to include only the concepts instantiated in the documents covering that particular domain. We thus introduce the domain specific ontology as an "instantiated ontology" of the general ontology with respect to the target document collection.

The instantiated ontology $O_{\widehat{I}}$ appears from the set of all instantiated concepts I, firstly by expanding I to $\widehat{I}$ – the transitive closure of the set of terms and subterms of term in I – and secondly by producing the subontology consisting of $\widehat{I}$ connected by relations from O between elements of $\widehat{I}$.

The subterms of a term c is obtained by the decomposition $\tau(c)$. $\tau(c)$ is defined as the set of all subterms of c, which thus includes c and all attributes of subsuming concepts for c.

$$t(c) = \{x | c \le x[\dots, r\colon y] \vee c \le y[\dots, r\colon x], x, y \in \mathbf{L}, r \in \mathbf{R}\}$$

$$\tau(c) = \textit{closure of } \{c\} \textit{ with respect to } t$$

For a set of terms we define $\tau(C) = \bigcup_{c \in C} \tau(c)$. As an example, we have that

$$\tau(c_1[r_1\colon c_2[r_2\colon c_3]]) = \{c_1[r_1\colon c_2[r_2\colon c_3]], c_1[r_1\colon c_2], c_1,$$
$$c_2[r_2\colon c_3], c_2, c_3\}.$$

Let $\omega(C)$ for a set of terms C be the transitive closure of C with respect to $\le$. Then the expansion of the set of instantiated concepts I becomes:

$$\widehat{I} = \omega(\tau(I))$$

Now, the C-restiction subontology $O_C = (C, \le, \mathbf{R})$ with respect to a given set of concepts C, is the subontology of O over concepts in C connected by $\le$ and $\mathbf{R}$. Thus the instantiated ontology $O_{\widehat{I}} = (\widehat{I}, \le, \mathbf{R}) = (\omega(\tau(I)), \le, \mathbf{R})$ is the $\widehat{I}$-restiction subontology of O.

Finally we define ISA as the transitive reduction of $\le$ and consider $(\widehat{I}, \text{ISA}, \mathbf{R})$ for visualization and as basis for similarity computation below.

3.3   Modeling Domain-Specific Ontologies – An Example

Consider the knowledge base ontology ISA_{KB} shown in Figure 1a. In this case we have $\mathbf{A} = \{cat, dog, bird, black, brown, red, animal, color, noise, anything\}$ and $\mathbf{L}$ includes $\mathbf{A}$ and any combination of compound terms combining elements of

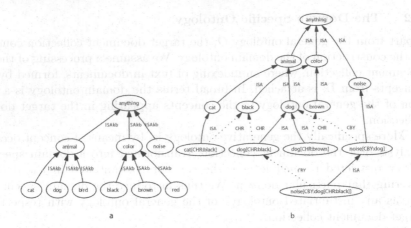

a   b

Fig. 1. a) An example knowledge base ontology ISA_KB **b)** A simple instantiated ontology based on figure a and the set of instantiated concepts *cat*[CHR:*black*], *dog*[CHR:*black*], *dog*[CHR:*brown*], *noise*[CBY:*dog*[CHR:*black*]]

A with attributes from **A** by relations from **R**, due to the generative quality of the ontology. Now assume a miniature target document collection with the following instantiated concepts:

$$I = cat[\text{CHR}:black], dog[\text{CHR}:black], dog[\text{CHR}:brown],$$
$$noise[\text{CBY}:dog[\text{CHR}:black]]$$

The decomposition $\tau(I)$ includes any subterm of elements from I, while $\widehat{I} = \omega(\tau(I))$ adds the subsuming $\{animal, color, anything\}$:

$$\widehat{I} = \{cat, dog, black, brown, animal, color, noise, anything,$$
$$cat[\text{CHR}:black], dog[\text{CHR}:black], dog[\text{CHR}:brown],$$
$$noise[\text{CBY}:dog], noise[\text{CBY}:dog[\text{CHR}:black]]\}$$

where the concepts *red* and *bird* from **A** are omitted because they are not instantiated.

The resulting instantiated ontology $(\widehat{I}, \leq, \mathbf{R})$ is transitively reduced into the domain-specific ontology $(\widehat{I}, \text{ISA}, \mathbf{R})$ as shown in figure 1b.

3.4   Visualization of Instantiated Ontologies

As the instantiated ontology is a restriction of a general ontology with respect to a set of concepts, it can be used for providing structured descriptions. The restriction could be with respect to the sets of concepts in a particular target document collection. But it could also comprise the set of concept of a query, the set of concept in a complete search result, or any set of concept selected by the user or the querying system.

The notion of instantiated ontologies has as such applications with respect to navigation and surveying of the topics covered by the domain in question, where the domain could be the instantiated ontology of any of the suggested restrictions above.

As the concepts instantiated in the document collection expresses a structuring of the information available, we can it to address one of the difficulties users have to overcome when querying information systems, which concerns the transformation of their information need into the descriptions used by the system.

Consider the following example, where we have a document collection with the following four instantiated concepts

$$I = \{stockade[\text{CHR}:old], rampart[\text{CHR}:old], church[\text{CHR}:old], palisade\}$$

and a global ontology constructed from version 1.6 of the WordNet lexicon [6], the Suggested Upper Merged Ontology (SUMO) [7], and the mid-level ontology (MILO) [7] designed to bridge the high-level ontology SUMO and WordNet.

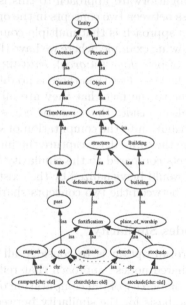

Fig. 2. A simple instantiated ontology, based on WordNet, SUMO and MILO and the four concepts $stockade[\text{CHR}:old], rampart[\text{CHR}:old], church[\text{CHR}:old], palisade$

The instantiated ontology reveals two different aspects covered by the document collection, 1) different kinds of fortifications and 2) a place of worship. On a more general level the instantiated ontology describes buildings and the abstract notion of something dated back in time.

Another use of instantiated ontologies is for visualizing user queries. When users pose queries to the system using polysemous concepts, the instantiated ontology constructed from the query can be used to visualize the different senses known to the system. If for example a user poses a query $Q = \{bank, huge\}$, then the system cannot use the concept *huge* to resolve the context/diambuiguate *bank*, since *huge* can be used in connection with different senses of *bank*.

One possible way to incorporate the knowledge visualized is to the user to identify which sense meant, and use the disambiguated concept in the query evaluation.

4   Deriving Similarity

As touched upon elsewhere in this paper a domain ontology, that reflects a document collection, may provide an excellent means to survey and give perspective to the collection. However as far as access to documents is concerned ontology reasoning is not the most obvious evaluation strategy and it may well entail scaling problems. Applying measures of similarity derived from the ontology is a way to replace reasoning with simple computation still influenced by the ontology. A well-known and straightforward approach to this is the shortest path approach [5, 9], where closeness between two concepts in the ontology imply high similarity. A problem with this approach is that multiple connections are ignored.

Consider the following example, where we have three concepts, all of which are assumed subclasses of pet: *dog*[CHR:*grey*], *cat*[CHR:*grey*] and *bird*[CHR:*yellow*]. If we consider only the ISA-edges then there is no difference in similarity between any pair of them due to the fact that they are all specializations of pet. If we on the other hand also consider the semantic edges (CHR), then we can add the aspect of shared attribution to the computation of similarity. In our example, we can, by including the the the CHR-edges, capture the intuitive difference in similarity between two grey pets compared to the similarity between a grey and a yellow pet. This difference would be visualized by the existence of a path, that includes the shared concept, between the two concepts sharing attribution.

4.1   Shared Nodes Similarity

To differentiate here an option is to consider all paths rather than only the shortest path. A "shared nodes" approach that reflects multiple paths, but still avoids the obvious complexity of full computation of all paths is presented in [1]. In this approach the basis for the similarity between two concepts c_1 and c_2 is the set of "upwards reachable" concepts (nodes) shared between c_1 and c_2. This is, with $\alpha(x) = \omega(\tau(x))$, the intersection $\alpha(x) \cap \alpha(y)$.

Similarity can be defined in various ways, one option being, as described in [3], a weighted average, where $\rho \in [0, 1]$ determines the degree of influence of the nodes reachable from x respectively y.

$$sim(x, y) = \rho \frac{|\alpha(x) \cap \alpha(y)|}{|\alpha(x)|} + (1 - \rho) \frac{|\alpha(x) \cap \alpha(y)|}{|\alpha(y)|} \tag{1}$$

As it appears the upwards expansion $\alpha(c)$ includes not only all subsuming concepts $\{c_i \mid c \leq c_i\}$ but also concepts that appears as direct or nested attributes to c or to any subsuming concept of these attributes. The latter must be included if we want to cope with multiple connections and want to consider for instance two concepts more similar if they bear the same color.

4.2 Weighted Shared Nodes Similarity

However, a further refinement seems appropriate here. If we want two concepts to be more similar if they have an immediate subsuming concept (e.g. $cat[$CHR:$black]$ and $cat[$CHR:$brown]$ due to the subsuming cat) than if they only share an attribute (e.g. $black$ shared by $cat[$CHR:$black]$ and $dog[$CHR:$black]$ we must differentiate and cannot just define $\alpha(c)$ as a crisp set. The following is a generalization to fuzzy set based similarity.

First of all notice that $\alpha(c)$ can be derived as follows. Let the triple (x, y, r) be the edge of type r from concept x to concept y, E be the set of all edges in the ontology, and T be the top concept. Then we have:

$$\alpha(T) = \{T\}$$
$$\alpha(c) = \{c\} \cup (\cup_{(c,c_i,r)\in E}\alpha(c_i))$$

A simple modification that generalizes $\alpha(c)$ to a fuzzy set is obtained through a function $weight(r)$ that attach a weight to each relation type r. With this function we can generalize to:

$$\alpha(T) = \{1/T\}$$
$$\alpha(c) = \{c\} \cup (\cup_{(c,c_i,r)\in E} weight(r) * \alpha(c_i))$$
$$= \{c\} \cup (\cup_{(c,c_i,r)\in E} \Sigma_{\mu(c_{ij})/c_{ij}\in\alpha(c_i)} weight(r) * \mu(c_{ij})/c_{ij})$$

$\alpha(c)$ is thus the fuzzy set of nodes reachable from the concept c and modified by weights of relations $weight(r)$. For instance from the instantiated ontology in figure 1b, assuming relation weights $weight($ISA$) = 1$, $weight($CHR$) = 0.5$ and $weight($CBY$) = 0.5$, we have:

$\alpha(noise[$CBY:dog
$[$CHR:$black]) = 1/noise[$CBY:$dog[$CHR:$black] + 1/noise + 0.5/dog[$CHR:$black] +$
$0.5/dog + 0.5/animal + 0.25/black + 0.25/color + 1/anything$

For concept similarity we can still use the parameterized expression (1) above, applying minimum for fuzzy intersection and sum for fuzzy cardinality:

$\alpha(cat[$CHR:$black]) \cap \alpha(dog[$CHR:$black]) = 0.5/black + 0.5/color + 1/animal +$
$1/anything$

$|\alpha(cat[$CHR:$black]) \cap \alpha(dog[$CHR:$black])| = 3.0$

The similarities between $dog[$CHR:$black]$ and other concepts in the ontology are, when collected in a fuzzy subset of similar concepts (with $similar(x) = \Sigma sim(x,y)/y$) and $\rho = \frac{4}{5}$ the following:

$similar(dog[$CHR:$black]) = 1.00/dog[$CHR:$black]+0.68/dog+0,6/cat[$CHR:$black]+$
$0.6/noise[$CBY:$dog[$CHR:$black]+0,52/animal+0,45/black+0,45/cat+0,39/color+$
$0,36/anything + 0,34/brown + 0.26/noise$

5   Conclusion

Firstly, we have introduced the notion of a domain-specific ontology as a restriction of a general ontology to the concepts instantiated in a document collection, and we have demonstrated its applications with respect to navigation and surveying of a target document collection.

Secondly, we have presented a methodology for deriving similarity using the domain-specific ontology by means of weighted shared nodes. The proposed measure incorporates multiple aspects when calculating overall similarity between concepts, but also respects the structure and relations of the ontology.

It should be noted that modelling of similarity functions is far from objective. It is not possible to define optimal functions, neither in the general nor in the domain specific case. The best we can do is to specify flexible, parameterized functions on the basis of obvious 'intrinsic' properties of intuitive interpretation, and then to adjust and evaluate these functions on an empirical basis.

References

1. Andreasen, T., Bulskov, H. and Knappe, R.: On Querying Ontologies and Databases, Flexible Query Answering Systems, 6th International Conference, FQAS 2004, Lyon, France, June 24-26, 2004, Proceedings
2. Andreasen, T.; Jensen, P. Anker; Nilsson, J. Fischer; Paggio, P.; Pedersen, B.S.; Thomsen, H. Erdman: Content-based Text Querying with Ontological Descriptors, in Data & Knowledge Engineering 48 (2004) pp 199-219, Elsevier, 2004.
3. Andreasen, T., Bulskov, H., and Knappe, R.: Similarity from Conceptual Relations, pp. 179–184 in Ellen Walker (Eds.): 22nd International Conference of the North American Fuzzy Information Processing Society, NAFIPS 2003, Chicago, Illinois USA, July 24–26, 2003, Proceedings
4. Beckwith, R.; Miller, G. A. & Tengi, R. (Eds.): Design and implementation of the WordNet lexical database and searching software, http://www.cogsci.princeton.edu/ wn/5papers.ps.
5. Bulskov, H.; Knappe, R. & Andreasen, T.: On Measuring Similarity for Conceptual Querying, LNAI 2522, pp. 100–111 in Andreasen T.; Motro A.; Christiansen H.; Larsen H.L.(Eds.): Flexible Query Answering Systems 5th International Conference, FQAS 2002, Copenhagen, Denmark, October 27–29, 2002, Proceedings
6. Miller, George: WordNet: An On-line Lexical Database, International Journal of Lexiography, Volume 3, Number 4, 1990
7. Niles, I.; Pease, A.: Towards a Standard Upper Ontology, in Chris Welty and Barry Smith (eds.): Proceedings of the 2nd International Conference on Formal Ontology in Information Systems (FOIS-2001), Ogunquit, Maine, October 17-19, 2001.
8. Nilsson, J. Fischer: A Logico-algebraic Framework for Ontologies – ONTOLOG, in Jensen, P. Anker & Skadhauge, P. (eds.): Proceedings of the First International OntoQuery Workshop – Ontology-based interpretation of NP's, Department of Business Communication and Information Science, University of Southern Denmark, Kolding, 2001
9. Rada, Roy; Mili, Hafedh; Bicknell, Ellen & Blettner, Maria: Development and Application of a Metric on Semantic Nets, IEEE Transactions on Systems, Man, and Cybernetics, Volume 19, Number 1, pp. 17–30, 1989

Using Self-Adaptable Probes for Dynamic Parameter Control of Parallel Evolutionary Algorithms*

Xavier Bonnaire and María-Cristina Riff

Department of Computer Science,
Universidad Técnica Federico Santa María, Valparaíso, Chile
{Xavier.Bonnaire, María-Cristina.Riff}@inf.utfsm.cl

Abstract. Controlling parameters during execution of parallel evolutionary algorithms is an open research area. Some recent research have already shown good results applying self-calibrating strategies. The motivation of this work is to improve the search of parallel genetic algorithms using monitoring techniques. Monitoring results guides the algorithm to take some actions based on both the search state and the values of its parameters. In this paper, we propose a parameter control architecture for parallel evolutionary algorithms, ba sed on self-adaptable monitoring techniques. Our approach provides an efficient and low cost monitoring technique to design parameters control strategies. Moreover, it is completely independant of the implementation of the evolutionary algorithm.

1 Introduction

When we design an evolutionary algorithm to address a specific problem we need to define a representation, and a set of operators to solve the problem. We also need to choose parameters values which we expect to give the algorithm the best performance. This process of finding adequate parameter values is a time-consuming task and considerable effort has already gone into automating this process [8]. Researchers have used various methods to find good values for the parameters, as these can affect the performance of the algorithm in a significant way. The best known mechanism to do that is *tuning parameters* on the basis of experimentation, something like a generate and test procedure. Taking into account that a run of an evolutionary algorithm is an intrinsically dynamic adaptive process, we could expect that a dynamic adaptation of the parameters during the search could help to improve the performance of the algorithm, [4], [15], [17], [7]. The idea of adapting and self-adapting parameters during the run is not new, but we need to manage a compromise between both the improvement of the search and the adaptation cost. A number of recent publications have shown that parallel implementation is a promising choice to make evolutionary algorithms faster

---

* Supported by Fondecyt Project 1040364.

M.-S. Hacid et al. (Eds.): ISMIS 2005, LNAI 3488, pp. 83–91, 2005.
© Springer-Verlag Berlin Heidelberg 2005

[3], [12]. However, parallel evolutionary algorithms with multiple populations are difficult to configure because they are controlled by many parameters, more than a sequential approach, and that's obviously affects their efficiency and accuracy. A parallel approach includes other kind of parameters like the size of the populations, the number of the populations, the rate of migration. Researchers have recently proposed new approaches for self-calibrating parallel evolutionary algorithm [9], [10], [11], [16]. These strategies are frequently included into the algorithm and they allow to change its parameters values during the execution. The key idea here is to monitor the search to be able to trigger actions from parameters control strategies, in order to improve the performance of the parallel evolutionary algorithms. In this paper, we propose a parameter control architecture for parallel evolutionary algorithms, based on self-adaptable monitoring technique. This paper is organized as follows: In the next section we briefly describe the mechanisms for dynamic parameter control. In section 3 we introduce the architecture for monitoring. In section 4 we present the performance evaluation of the architecture. Finally, section 5 presents the conclusions and future work.

2   Dynamic Parameter Control

We can classify the parameter selection process in two different methods: *tuning* and *parameter control*, [6]. Tuning as mentioned above implies a generate and test procedure, in order to define which are the "best" parameters values for an evolutionary algorithm. Usually, these parameters values are fixed for all the runs of the algorithm. We can expect that the "best" parameters values depend on the step of the algorithm we are. For that reason, the idea to design strategies to allow the algorithm to change its parameters values during its execution appears as a promising way to improve the performance of an evolutionary algorithm. In this context many ideas have been proposed in the research community, between them we find self-adaptability process where the individuals include information that can influence the parameters values and their evolution could use some criteria to produce changes, [13], [14], [4]. A recent research [7] defines an algorithm which is able to adapt its parameters during the execution as a self-calibrating algorithm. They propose a strategy to change the population size of the genetic algorithm taking into account the state of the search. The advantage of changing the parameters values during the execution becames more relevant when we are tackling NP-complete problems. The frame of this research is parallel evolutionary algorithms which could potentially include more parameters than sequential ones. For instance, Lis in [9] considers control of one parameter only: mutation probability. She adapts mutation rates in a parallel GA with a farming model. At the beginning the master processor creates an initial population and sends portions of the population to the slave processors. The sub-populations evolve independently on the slave processors. After a predetermined interval of number of generations the slave processors send their best individual to the master processor. Then the master processor gathers these individuals and sends the best individual to the slave processors. The mechanism of adaptation is related to the mutation probability in the slave processors. If the best individual was obtained from a slave processor with a low mutation rate then it implies to reduce in all slave processors their mutation probabilities, in the same way if it came from a slave processor with a high mutation rate the slaves mutation probabilities will be increased. Combining forms of control is much more difficult as the interactions of even static parameter settings for different components of single evolutionary algorithms are not well understood, as they often depend on the objective function and representation that are used. Several empirical studies have been performed to investigate the interactions between various parameters of an EA, [5]. In [10] Lis & Lis introduced a strategy for self-adapting parallel genetic algorithm for the dynamic mutation probability, crossover rate and population size. Their work is a good idea to control various parameters at the same time for a parallel genetic algorithm. More recently, Tongchim et al, [16] proposed an adaptive algorithm that can adjust parameters of genetic algorithms according to the computed performance. This performance is directly related to the fitness of each population. Their parallel genetic algorithm uses a ring architecture to send and to receive the messages. Each node has two set of parameters, it chooses the best of them according to the fitness evaluation. The messages from a node to its neighboor include the best set of its parameter values. Another research work which proposes an architecture for massive parallelization of compact genetic algorithm is presented in [11]. In their approach the architecture is controlled by a master process who is charged to receive and to send information to the nodes or "workers". The communication is only between master and worker, and it only occurs when both have accomplished m iterations, and when a change of parameter values has been produced in the node.

All of the approaches mentioned above do not include an observation task. The idea of observation allows to take actions according to the state detected by the monitoring technique. For instance, in a traditional genetic algorithm context, when we detect that after a number of generations the algorithm is not able to converge and it is doing too much exploration, a natural action could be either to increase the crossover probability or to reduce the mutation probability. We can think about more sophisticated actions, such reducing the number of individuals of the population, migrating a set of individuals from a node which has the best fitness value to another one, or also mixed actions triggered by the observation of a set of conditions. We introduce in this paper an architecture which is able to implement efficient parameter control strategies using the idea of monitoring the evolution, and take some actions during the execution in order to accelerate the convergence process.

3   The Architecture Proposed

We suppose in this paper that a Parallel Genetic Algorithm (PGA) is a set of workers processes running on one or more nodes of a cluster or a grid, and a set of one or more controllers that implement control parameters strategies. Figure 1 shows our Dynamic Parameters Control Architecture (DPCA). Several

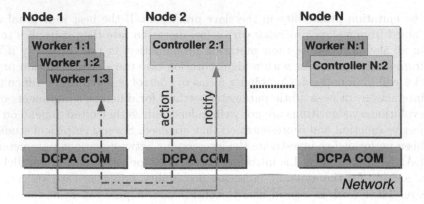

Fig. 1. Architecture DPCA

workers can be on the same node as well as several controllers. The key idea in our proposition is that the controllers are able to detect some special conditions about the workers, and then can trigger actions to modify one or more parameters of the worker (operator probability, population size, migration frequency, etc...). A Worker condition can be a variable condition like the fitness value (the fitness has not changed since the last n generations), or the population state (the population became uniform or to sparced), etc... The action triggered by a controller depends on the control strategy that has been implemented by the GA designer. Next section will show that controllers strategies can be dynamically modified during the GA execution. To detect a special condition on a worker, DPCA uses self adaptable probes to monitor the workers state [1], [2]. Monitoring can brings significant overhead when the observation is systematic, for example if a notification is sent each time a given state changes. Our self adaptable probes provide a way for the workers to hardly reduce this overhead by sending a notifications only when it is strictly necessary. To do this, a self adaptable probe is composed of one or more monitoring conditions. For example, we can implement a monitoring condition on the fitness value. The probe notification is an event based mechanism. When a least one monitoring condition is satisfied in a probe, the probe sends a notification about the associated resource. A controller that receives the notification can then trigger a corresponding action, according to a control parameter strategy. A typical GA worker structure (written in pseudo C language) in DPCA is shown in figure 2. The Monitoring() function in DPCA has the code shown in figure 3.

The Notify() primitive sends a message on the network to inform the controllers that a particular condition has been satisfied on a worker. A controller can then take an action according to its parameter control strategy. The ReceiveActions() is a non blocking primitive that checks if some actions have been received from a controller. If the ActionSet is not empty, the ExecuteActions() primitive executes all the requested actions atomically (that is during the actual generation). All possible actions on the worker parameters must be initially

```
Begin /* Main Loop */
while (gen < maxgen )
   ActionSet = ReceiveActions()
   ExecuteActions(ActionSet)
   SelectIndividuals( population )
   Transform( ind )
   fitness = EvaluatePopulation( population )
   Monitoring()
   gen = gen + 1
endwhile
End  /* Main Loop */
```

Fig. 2. GA worker structure

```
Monitoring()
Begin
for condition in ConditionSet
   if ( condition() == true )
   then
      Notify( condition )
      return;
   endif
endfor
End
```

Fig. 3. Monitoring Function in DPCA

present into the worker. That is all the primitives required to change the parameters must be implemented. From the controllers and the workers point of view, all actions have an identification number (an integer). The correspondence between the identifier and the action itself is a convention between the controllers and the workers. The workers then binds this identifier with their corresponding internal primitive. For example, *action25* is known by both workers and controllers to be "Modify the population size". On the worker side, identifier 25 will be binded to the ModifyPopulationSize() primitive. On the controller side, the parameter control strategy, must decide which actions should be taken when monitoring conditions occur, in which order, etc...It is illustrated in figure 4.

A condition that checks every 100 generations if the fitness value has at least decreased 0.5 since the last notification can be the code shown in figure 5.

The controller can pass arguments to the worker when it triggers the action. The number of arguments depends on the action. A worker can have as many actions as necessary. An action can also modify more than one parameter at the same time, it is just a matter of convention between the controller and the worker.A typical action to change the population size parameter on the worker side can be the code shown in figure 6.

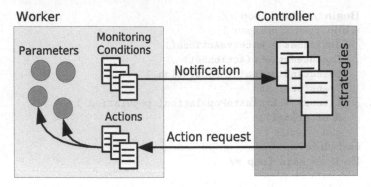

Fig. 4. Worker Controler Interactions

```
Boolean Condition1()
Begin
if ( gen modulo 100 ≠ 0 ) return false
if Δ(lastfitness, fitness) >= 0.5 return true
else return false
End
```

Fig. 5. Example of a Boolean Condition

```
ModifyPopulationSize( newsize )
Begin
ResizePopulation( population, newsize );
popsize = newsize;
End
```

Fig. 6. Example of a tipycal action

3.1   DPCA Communication System

DPCA uses a multicast model where messages are signed with a message *protocol*, a message *type*, a message *sub-type*, and a message *context*. Each message also contains a data part. The *protocol, type*, and *sub-type* are integer fields. The *context* field is a string. The communication system is based on the Publish/Subscribe paradigm. The controllers subscribe to messages send by the workers, and the workers subscribe to message send by the controllers. The subscription uses the message signature. If we suppose that the protocol for DPCA is 1. Workers and Controllers can agree than a worker monitoring notification for the fitness value (condition 1) will be as follow:

Protocol	1	*DPCA protocol (convention)*
Type	NOTIFICATION	*Monitoring notification*
Sub-Type	1	*fitness condition 1*
Context	"nodeid:workerid"	*Worker identifier*
Data	"fitnessvalue"	*The actual fitness value*

To be able to receive this message, the controller must subscribe to the following message signature: <1, NOTIFICATION, 1, "nodeid:workerid">. Note that all fields of a subscription can accept wildcard values (-1 for integer, "*" for strings) to simplify the subscription, and also to be unaware of the number of workers for example.

On the other side, if the controller wants to react to this monitoring notification, and according to its current parameter control strategy it requires to change the population size (action 25), it will send to the worker the following message:

Protocol	1	*DCPA protocol*
Type	REQUEST	*Action request*
Sub-Type	25	*Action 25 requested*
Context	"nodeid:workerid"	*Worker identifier*
Data	"newpopsize"	*Argument*

This will required from the worker to be subscribed to the following signature: <1, REQUEST, 25, "nodeid:workerid">.

Note that, as the ReceiveActions() primitive is a non blocking one, a controller reaction to a notification can be taken into account by the worker after executing a few more generations. It depends on the network load, the controller reaction speed, etc... This is a normal behavior if we want to build a reactive architecture where the workers won't block waiting for some controller requests.

Because the DPCA communication model is based on a publish/subscribe technique, the message exchange between workers and controllers is location independent. Workers and Controllers can be on any nodes of the cluster or the grid. The subscription mechanism also supports to dynamically add new workers or new controllers during the execution. It also provides an easy way to build different logical organization of the workers and controllers:

- All workers are managed by only one controller. That is, this controller could implement a unique control parameter strategy.
- Each worker has its own controller, with a dedicated strategy.
- Several controllers can control the parameters of a given worker. For example, a controller can only react to a given monitoring condition.
- A set of workers is managed by a set of controllers.

It is also possible for a controller to unsubscribe to all monitoring notification and terminate independently of the workers execution. It is thus easy to stop a controller, and to start a new one with another parameter control strategy. It is then possible to test the efficiency of a strategy for a given algorithm or problem that is been solved, without having to restart the whole computation. Additionally, all workers have the following three special actions:

- Action 1: Allows a controller to delete a monitoring condition into a given worker: < 1, REQUEST, 1, "nodeid:workerid", "condition_id" >.
- Action 2: Allows a controller to add a new monitoring condition into a given worker: <1, REQUEST, 2, "nodeid:workerid", "condition_id:path_to_new _code" >, the last argument gives the path in the filesystem where to find the object code file corresponding to the new condition. The new condition code is dynamically loaded and linked into the worker.
- Action 3: Allows, in the same way as Action 2, a controller to modify an existing monitoring condition into a given worker: <1, REQUEST, 3, "nodeid:workerid", "condition_id:path_to_new_code" > Note that the use of wildcards in the context field allows a controller to address the whole set of workers.

Therefore, a controller can also include in its parameter control strategy, a way to refine the monitoring conditions of a given worker or of all workers. Refining monitoring conditions can be very useful in the case of self adapting GAs that change themselves their parameters. It could become necessary for a controller to start to receive monitoring information about the use of a given operator that was not of interest before.

4   Evaluation of the Performance

DPCA has shown good performance in term of overhead introduced to the monitored processes. The minimum additional time required for the process execution is about 2.5% of the initial execution time. This includes the monitoring code, and the network accesses. The maximum overhead that has been observed, with systematic monitoring of a ressource, is about 20% of additional time to execution the process. A reasonable overhead, that is when using reasonable monitoring conditions should not exceed 5% of additional execution time.

5   Conclusions

The monitoring architecture that we proposed in this paper can significantly contribute to design efficient parallel evolutionary algorithms. It allows to take advantage of the power of cluster computing, providing a low cost observation system needed to build a dynamic parameter control system. The self-adaptables probes used to handle the parameter variations significantly reduce the overhead of the monitoring while offering a good observation technique. Our architecture allows to easily design different parameter control strategies through the controllers and can dynamically handle news strategies. DPCA allows to manages multiple parameter control strategies with different controllers. Each controller can adapt the monitoring associated to the workers it manages by dynamically adding, changing or deleting monitoring conditions. Moreover, testing new control parameters strategies can be done without restarting the whole computing process. One of the best promising research area is to use similar techniques than those that are used for the dynamic change of monitoring condition to be able to modify the GA itself during its execution. This kind of modification of the execution code could allows to insert new operators in the GA or also to modify the way it handles the population.

References

[1] Boutros C. and Bonnaire X. *Cluster Monitoring Platform Based on Self-Adaptable Probes.* In *Proceedings of the 12th Symposium on Computer Architecture and High Performance Computing,* 2000.

[2] Boutros C., Bonnaire X. and Folliot B. *Flexible Monitoring Platform to Build Cluster Management Services.* In *Proceedings of the IEEE International Conference on Cluster Computing- CLUSTER 2000,* 2000.

[3] Cantu-Paz E. *Dessigning efficient and accurate parallel genetic algorithms* PhD Thesis, University of Illinois at Urbana Champaign, 1999.

[4] Davis L. *Adapting Operator Probabilities in Genetic Algorithms* In *Proceedings of 3rd. International Conf. on Genetic Algorithms and their Applications,* 1989

[5] Deb K. and Agrawal S. *Understanding Interactions among Genetic Algorithms Parameters* In *Foundations of Genetic Algorithms, 5, pp 265-286,* 1998

[6] Eiben A., Hinterding R. and Michalewicz Z. *Parameter Control in Evolutionary Algorithms* IEEE Transactions on evolutionary computation, 3(2):124–141, 1999.

[7] Eiben A. E., Marchiori E. and Valko V.A. *Evolutionary Algorithms with on-the-fly Population Size Adjustment* PPSN VIII, LNCS 3242, pp. 41-50, 2004.

[8] Hinterding R., Michalewicz Z. and Eiben A. *Adaptation in Evolutionary Computation: A Survey* In *Proceedings of 4th. IEEE International Conf. on Evolutionary Computation,* 1997.

[9] Lis J. *Parallel Genetic Algorithm with the Dynamic Control Parameter* In *Proceedings of 3rd. IEEE International Conf. on Evolutionary Computation,* 1996.

[10] Lis J., and Lis M. *Self-adapting Parallel Genetic Algorithm with the Dynamic Mutation Probability, Crossover Rate and Population Size* In *Proceedings of 1st. Polish Nat. Conf. Evolutionary Computation,* 1996.

[11] Lobo F., Lima C. and Mártires H. *An architecture for massive parallelization of the compact genetic algorithm* Proceedings GECCO 2004, pp. 412-413, 2004.

[12] Nuñez A. and Riff M-C. *Evaluating Migration Strategies for a graph-based evolutionary algorithm for CSP* Foundations of Intelligent Systems, ISMIS'2000, LNCS/LNAI 1932, 2000.

[13] Pettinger J. and Everson R. *Controlling Genetic Algorithms with Reinforcement Learning* Proceedings of the GECCO 2002.

[14] Riff M-C and Bonnaire Xavier *Inheriting Parents Operators: A New Dynamic Strategy to improve Evolutionary Algorithms* Foundations of Intelligent Systems, ISMIS'2002, LNCS/LNAI 2366, pp. 333-341, 2002.

[15] Smith J. and Fogarty T.C. *Operator and parameter adaptation in genetic algorithms* In *Soft Computing, 1(2):81-87* , 1997.

[16] Tongchim, S. and Chongstitvatana, P. *Parallel genetic algorithm with parameter adaptation* Information Processing Letters, Volume 82, Issue 1, pp. 47-54, 2002.

[17] Tuson A. and Ross P. *Adapting Operator Settings in Genetic Algorithms* In *Evolutionary Computation, (6):2, pp. 161-184,* 1998.

Robust Inference of Bayesian Networks Using Speciated Evolution and Ensemble

Kyung-Joong Kim, Ji-Oh Yoo, and Sung-Bae Cho

Dept. of Computer Science, Yonsei University,
134 Shinchon-dong, Sudaemoon-ku, Seoul 120-749, Korea
{uribyul, taiji391}@sclab.yonsei.ac.kr
sbcho@cs.yonsei.ac.kr

Abstract. Recently, there are many researchers to design Bayesian network structures using evolutionary algorithms but most of them use the only one fittest solution in the last generation. Because it is difficult to integrate the important factors into a single evaluation function, the best solution is often biased and less adaptive. In this paper, we present a method of generating diverse Bayesian network structures through fitness sharing and combining them by Bayesian method for adaptive inference. In the experiments with Asia network, the proposed method provides with better robustness for handling uncertainty owing to the complicated redundancy with speciated evolution.

1 Introduction

One commonly used approach to deal with uncertainty is a Bayesian network (BN) which represents joint probability distributions of domain. It has already been recognized that the BN is quite easy to incorporate expert knowledge. BN and associated schemes constitute a probabilistic framework for reasoning under uncertainty that in recent years has gained popularity in the community of artificial intelligence. From an informal perspective, BN is directed acyclic graph (DAG), where the nodes are random variables and the arcs specify the dependency between these variables. It is difficult to search for the BN that best reflects the dependency in a database of cases because of the large number of possible DAG structures, given even a small number of nodes to connect. Recently, there are many researchers to design BN structures using evolutionary algorithms but most of them use the only one fittest solution in the last generation [1].

The main problem with standard evolutionary algorithms appears that they eventually converge to an optimum and thereby loose their diversity necessary for efficiently exploring the search space and its ability to adapt to a change in the environment when a change occurs. In this paper, we present a method of generating diverse evolutionary Bayesian networks through fitness sharing and combining them by Bayes rule. It is promising to use multiple solutions which have different characteristics because they can deal with uncertainty by complementing each other for better robustness. Several works are concerned with machine learning based on evolutionary computation (EC) and combining the solutions found in the last population [2, 3, 4]. Fig. 1 shows the basic idea of the proposed method. To show the usefulness of the method, we conduct experiments with a benchmark problem of ASIA network.

M.-S. Hacid et al. (Eds.): ISMIS 2005, LNAI 3488, pp. 92–101, 2005.
© Springer-Verlag Berlin Heidelberg 2005

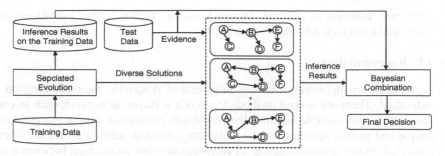

Fig. 1. The proposed ensemble model of speciated Bayesian networks

2 Evolutionary Bayesian Networks

As indicated by [5], evolutionary algorithm is suitable for dynamic and stochastic optimization problems but there are a few works to deal with the issue using evolutionary Bayesian network. One important approach to learning Bayesian networks from data uses a scoring metric to evaluate the fitness of any given candidate network for the database, and applies a search procedure to explore the set of candidate networks [6]. Because learning Bayesian networks is, in general, an NP-hard problem and exact methods become infeasible, recently some researchers present a method for solving this problem of the structure learning of Bayesian network from a database of cases based on evolutionary algorithms [7].

Larranaga *et al.* carry out performance analysis on the control parameters of the genetic algorithms (population size, local optimizer, reproduction mechanism, probability of crossover, and mutation rate) using simulations of the ASIA and ALARM networks [1]. Also, they propose searching for the best ordering of the domain variables using genetic algorithms [8]. Wong *et al.* have developed a new approach (MDLEP) to learn Bayesian network structures based on the Minimum Description Length (MDL) principle and evolutionary programming (EP) [9]. Wong *et al.* propose a novel data mining algorithm that employs cooperative co-evolution and a hybrid approach to discover Bayesian networks from data [10]. They divide the network learning problem of *n* variables into *n* sub-problems and use genetic algorithms for solving the sub-problems.

3 Speciated Evolutionary Bayesian Network Ensemble

The system sets each BN with random initial structures. The fitness of Bayesian network for training data is calculated using general Dirichlet prior score metric (DPSM). Yang reports that DPSM performs better than other scoring metrics [11]. Fitness sharing using MDL difference measure which needs only small computational cost rescales the original fitness for diversity. Once the fitness is calculated, genetic algorithm selects the best 80% individuals to apply genetic operators. The genetic operators, crossover and mutation, are applied to those selected individuals. After applying genetic operations, the new set of individuals forms a new population. It finishes when stop criterion is satisfied. Using clustering, representative individuals are selected and combined with Bayesian scheme.

3.1 Representation

In evolutionary algorithm, it is very important to determine the representation of an individual. There are several methods to encode a Bayesian network such as connection matrix and variable ordering list. Although connection matrix representation is simple and genetic operators can be easily implemented, additional "repair" operation is needed. In the structure learning of Bayesian network an ordering between nodes of the structure is often assumed, in order to reduce the search space. In variable ordering list, a Bayesian network structure can be represented by a list L with length n, where its elements l_j verify

$$\text{if } l_j \in Pa(l_i) \text{ then } j < i, \ (l_j, l_i \in V)$$

Although variable ordering list can reduce search space, it has a shortcoming that only one Bayesian network structure can be constructed from one ordering.

In this paper, we devise a new chromosome representation which combines both of them. It does not need a "repair operator" but also provides enough representation power for searching diverse Bayesian network structures. In this representation, a Bayesian network structure can be represented by a variable ordering list L with length n, and $n \times n$ connectivity matrix C. The definition of L is the same as the above formula but an element of matrix C is used for representing an existence of arcs between variables.

$$c_{ij} = \begin{cases} 1 & \text{if there is an arc between } x_i \text{ and } x_j \ (i > j), \\ 0 & \text{otherwise.} \end{cases}$$

Lower left triangle describes the connection link information.

3.2 Genetic Operators

The crossover operator exchanges the structures of two Bayesian networks in the population. Since finding an optimal ordering of variables resembles the traveling salesman problem (TSP), Larranaga et al. use genetic operators that were developed for the TSP problem [8]. In their work, cycle crossover (CX) operator gives the best results and needs a small population size to give good results while other crossover operators require larger population sizes. CX operator attempts to create an offspring from the parents where every position is occupied by a corresponding element from one of the parents. The $n \times n$ connection matrix can be represented as a string with length $_nC_2$, because only lower left triangle area in the matrix describes useful information. Two connection matrix represented as a string can be exchanged by using 1-point crossover.

The displacement mutation operator (DM) is used for mutation of variable order. The combination of cycle crossover and the mutation operator shows better results in extensive tests [8]. The operator selects a substring at random. This substring is removed from the string and inserted in a random place. Mutation operator for the connection matrix performs one of the two operations: addition of a new connection and deletion of an existing connection. If the connection link does not exist and the connection entry of the BN matrix is '0', a new connection link is created. If the connection link already exists, it removes the connection link.

3.3 Fitness Evaluation

In order to induce a Bayesian network from data, researchers proposed a variety of score metrics based on different assumptions. Yang *et al.* compared the performance of five score metrics: uniform prior score metric (UPSM), conditional uniform prior score metric (CUPSM), Dirichlet prior score metric (DPSM), likelihood-equivalence Bayesian Dirichlet score metric (BDe), and minimum description length (MDL) [11]. They concluded that the tenth-order DPSM is the best score metric. If the Dirichlet distribution is assumed, then the score metric can be written as

$$P(B,D) = P(B) \prod_{i=1}^{n} \prod_{j=1}^{q_i} \frac{\Gamma(N'_{ij})}{\Gamma(N'_{ij} + N_{ij})} \times \prod_{k=1}^{r_i} \frac{\Gamma(N'_{ijk} + N_{ijk})}{\Gamma(N'_{ijk})}.$$

Here, N_{ijk} denotes the number of cases in the given database D in which the variable x_i takes the kth value ($k = 1, 2, ..., r_i$), and its parent $Pa(x_i)$ is instantiated as the jth value ($k = 1, 2, ..., q_i$), and $N_{ij} = \sum_{k=1}^{r_i} N_{ijk}$. N'_{ijk} is the corresponding Dirichlet distribution orders and $N'_{ij} = \sum_{k=1}^{r_i} N'_{ijk}$. As [11], we investigate a special case where the Dirichlet orders are set to a constant, say $N'_{ijk} = 10$.

3.4 Fitness Sharing with MDL Measure

There are several ways to simulate speciation. In this paper, fitness sharing technique is used. Fitness sharing decreases the fitness of individuals in densely populated area and shares the fitness with other BN's. Therefore, it helps genetic algorithm search broader solution space and generate more diverse BN's. With fitness sharing, the genetic algorithm finds diverse solution. The population of BN's is defined as $\{B_1, B_2, ..., B_{pop\_size}\}$.

Given that f_i is the fitness of an individual B_i and $sh(d_{ij})$ is a sharing function, the shared fitness fs_i is computed as follows :

$$fs_i = \frac{f_i}{\displaystyle\sum_{j=1}^{pop\_size} sh(d_{ij})}$$

The sharing function $sh(d_{ij})$ is computed using the distance value d_{ij} which means the difference of individuals B_i and B_j as follows:

$$sh(d_{ij}) = \begin{cases} 1 - \dfrac{d_{ij}}{\sigma_s}, & 0 \le d_{ij} < \sigma_s \\ 0, & d_{ij} \ge \sigma_s \end{cases}$$

Here, σ_s means the sharing radius. σ_s is set with a half of the mean of distances between each BN in initial population. If the difference of the individuals is larger than σ_s, they do not share the fitness. Only the individuals that have smaller distance value than σ_s can share the fitness. Fitness of individuals on the highest peak decreases when the individuals in the area are dense.

Although there is no consensus on the distance measure for the difference of individuals B_i and B_j, an easily acceptable measure is structural difference between them. Lam defines the structural difference measure in the minimum description length principle which is well established in machine learning [12]. To compute the description length of the differences we need develop an encoding scheme for representing these differences. It is clear that the structure of B_i can be recovered from the structure of B_j and the following information.

- A list of the reverse arcs
- The missing arcs of B_i
- The additional arcs of B_i

Let r, m, and a be, respectively, the number of reverse, missing, and additional arcs in B_i, with respect to a network B_j. Since there are $n(n-1)$ possible directed arcs, we need $\log_2[n(n-1)]$ bits. The description length B_i given B_j is as follows.

$$DL(B_i \mid B_j) = DL(B_j \mid B_i) = (r + m + a)\log_2[n(n-1)]$$

Because it is formally defined and has low computational cost, we have adopted the measure to calculate the difference between Bayesian networks.

3.5 Combination of Multiple Bayesian Networks

Single linkage clustering is used to select representative Bayesian networks from a population of the last generation. The number of individuals for the combination is automatically determined by the predefined threshold value. Bayesian method takes each BN's significance into accounts by allowing the error possibility of each BN to affect the ensemble's results [13].

The number of selected BN's is K. $B = \{B_1, B_2, \ldots, B_K\}$. B denotes the set of the BN's. Q is the target node. M is the number of states of Q that has $g_1, g_2, \ldots, g_M$ states. The kth BN produces the probability that Q is in state i using Bayesian inference, and it is defined as $P_i(k)$. Using training data, $P(P_i(k) > 0.5 \mid Q = q_i)$ is calculated. Finally, $P(Q = q_i \mid B_1, B_2, \ldots, B_k)$ is represented as follows.

$$P(Q = q_i \mid B_1, B_2, \ldots, B_k) = \prod_{k=1}^{K} \frac{P(P_i(k) > 0.5 \mid Q = q_i)}{P_i(k)}$$

4 Experimental Results

The ASIA network, introduced by Lauritzen and Spiegelhalter [14] to illustrate their method of propagation of evidence considers a small piece of fictitious qualitative medical knowledge. Fig. 2 presents the structure of the ASIA network. The ASIA network is a small Bayesian network that calculates the probability of a patient having tuberculosis, lung cancer or bronchitis respectively based on different factors, for exa mple whether or not the patient has been to Asia recently.

There are several techniques for simulating BN's, and we have used probabilistic logic sampling, with which we develop a database of 1000 cases. Population size is 50 and the maximum generation number is 1000. Crossover rate is 0.5, selection rate is 0.8 and mutation rate is 0.01.

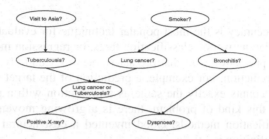

Fig. 2. The network structure for a benchmark problem

Randomly selected 100 cases from the 1000 cases are used as test data while the remaining data are used for training. Because the size of the network is relatively small, both of genetic algorithm without speciation and that with speciation can find near-optimal solutions. Unlike other classifiers such as neural networks and support vector machine, Bayesian network can infer the probability of unobserved target states given the observed evidences. It is assumed that "Tuberculousis," "Lung cancer," "Bronchitis," and "Lung cancer or Tuberculosis" nodes are unobserved target variables and the remaining nodes are observed variables. The four nodes are regarded as target nodes and represent whether a person gets a disease. Although the data are generated from the original ASIA network, inference results for the data using the original network may be incorrect because there are only four observed variables.

Using single linkage clustering method, the last generation of speciated evolution is clustered and there are five clusters when threshold value is 90. If the number of individuals in the cluster is more than two, the one with the highest fitness is chosen. An individual labeled as 49 in the largest cluster shows the best fitness (-2123.92) while the others' fitness are ranged from -2445.52 to -2259.57. Although the fitness values of four individuals in other clusters are relatively smaller than the best one, the combination can be stronger one by complementing each other. Inference accuracies of original network, the best individual from simple genetic algorithm without speci-ation (Fig. 3), and the combination of the speciated Bayesian networks (Fig. 4) for the "Lung cancer or Tuberculosis" node are 98%, 98%, and 99%, respectively. For "Tu-berculousis," "Lung cancer," and "Bronchitis" nodes, they show the same accuracy. Both of the best individual in simple genetic algorithm and the individual labeled as 49 in the speciation have a similar structure with the original network. However, the other four networks in the speciation have more complex structures than the original network. Table 1 summarizes the inference results of the case where only the combi-nation of BN's produces correct result.

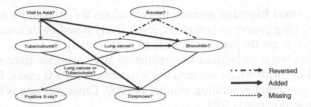

Fig. 3. The best individual evolved using simple genetic algorithm without speciation

Predictive accuracy is the most popular technique for evaluating models, whether they are Bayesian networks, classification trees, or regression models [15]. However, a fundamental problem lies in that predictive accuracy entirely disregards the confidence of the prediction. For example, a prediction of the target variable with a probability of 0.51 counts exactly the same as a prediction with a probability of 1.0. In recognition of this kind of problem, there is a growing movement to employ cost-sensitive classification methods. Good invented a cost neutral assessment measure [16]. Good's definition is

$$IR = \sum_i [1 + \log_2 P(x_i = v)]$$

where i indexes the test cases, v is the actual class of the ith test case and $P(x_i)$ is the probability of that event asserted by the learner.

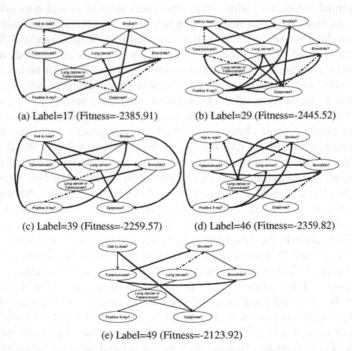

(a) Label=17 (Fitness=-2385.91)   (b) Label=29 (Fitness=-2445.52)

(c) Label=39 (Fitness=-2259.57)   (d) Label=46 (Fitness=-2359.82)

(e) Label=49 (Fitness=-2123.92)

Fig. 4. The five individuals evolved using genetic algorithm with speciation

Table 1. Inference results of "Lung cancer or Tuberculosis" when "Visit to Asia" is "No visit," "Smoker" is "Non-Smoker," "Positive X-ray" is "Abnormal" and "Dyspnoea" is "Present." The original value of "Lung cancer or Tuberculosis" is "True." (T=True, F=False)

	The original network	The best individual in simple GA	Label 17	Label 29	Label 39	Label 46	Label 49	The combination of five BN's
	False	False	False	True	True	True	False	True
P(T)	0.494	0.471	0.118	0.709	0.676	0.576	0.464	0.503
P(F)	0.506	0.529	0.882	0.291	0.324	0.424	0.536	0.497

Table 2. Information rewards for inferring "Bronchitis" when "Dyspnoea" is unobservable. Experimental results are the average of ten runs

The original network	The best individual in simple GA	The best individual in speciation	The combination of BN's
-2.08	-3.14 ± 0.18	-3.02 ± 0.22	0.86 ± 0.24

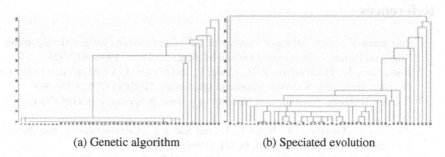

(a) Genetic algorithm   (b) Speciated evolution

Fig. 5. The comparison of dendrograms

The combination of the speciated BN's can improve the predictability even when some variables are unobserved. Table 2 summarizes information reward values for the situation and the combination of BN's shows the best performance. If the reward value is high, it means that the classifier performs well. Although the best individual in the speciated evolution returns similar reward value with that from the best individual in genetic algorithm, the combination returns improved information reward value that is larger than that of original network. Fig. 5 shows the comparison of dendrogram. In Fig. 5(a), 40 individuals in the left side form one cluster and they are almost the same. Meanwhile, 40 individuals in the left side in Fig. 5(b) form a number of clusters.

5 Conclusion

In this paper, we have proposed an ensemble of multiple speciated Bayesian networks using Bayesian combination method. Although some Bayesian networks in ensemble provides incorrect inference, the ensemble network can perform correctly by reflecting each Bayesian network's behavior in training data and reducing the effect of incorrect results. Experimental results on ASIA network show that the proposed method can improve simple genetic algorithm which converges to only one solutions (sometimes the best solution performs poorly in changed environments) and the fusion of results from speciated networks can improve the inference performance by compensating each other. Future work of this research is to develop real-world applications based on the proposed method. Highly dynamic problems such as robot navigation, user context recognition, and user modeling can be considered as candidates.

Acknowledgements

This research is supported by the 21st century frontier R&D program of ministry of science and technology in Korea.

References

1 Larranaga, P., *et al.*: Structure learning of Bayesian networks by genetic algorithm. IEEE Trans. on Pattern Analysis and Machine Intelligence, 18(9) (1996) 912-926
2 Immamura, K., Heckendorn, R. B., Soule, T., and Foster, J. A.: Abstention reduces errors-Decision abstaining N-version genetic programming. GECCO (2002) 796-803
3 Iba, H.: Bagging, boosting, and bloating in genetic programming. GECCO (1999) 1053-1060
4 Anglano, C., Giordana, A., Bello, G. L., and Saitta, L.: Coevolutionary, distributed search for inducing concept description. ECML (1998) 322-333
5 Branke, J.: Evolutionary Optimization in Dynamic Environments. Kluwer (2001)
6 Neapolitan, R. E.: Learning Bayesian Networks. Prentice Hall (2003)
7 Neil, J. R., and K. B. Korb.: The evolution of causal models: A comparison of Bayesian metrics and structure priors. Pacific-Asia Conference on Knowledge Discovery and Data Mining (1999)
8 Larranaga, P., *et al.*: Learning Bayesian network structures by searching for the best ordering with genetic algorithm. IEEE Trans. on Systems, Man and Cybernetics – Part (A), 26(4) (1996) 487-493
9 Wong, M. L., Lam, W., and Leung, K.S.: Using evolutionary programming and minimum description length principle for data mining of Bayesian networks. IEEE Trans. on Pattern Analysis and Machine Intelligence, 21(2) (1999) 174-178
10 Wong, M. L., Lee, S.Y., and Leung, K.S.: Data mining of Bayesian networks using cooperative coevolution. Decision Support Systems (2004) (in press)
11 Yang, S. and Chang, K.-C.: Comparison of score metrics for Bayesian network learning. IEEE Trans. on Systems, Man and Cybernetics-Part A, 32(3) (2002) 419-428
12 Lam, W.: Bayesian network refinement via machine learning approach. IEEE Trans. on Pattern Analysis and Machine Intelligence, 20(3) (1998) 240-251
13 Xu, L., Krzyzak, A. and Suen, C.Y.: Methods of combining multiple classifiers and their applications to handwriting recognition. IEEE Trans. on Systems, Man and Cybernetics, SMC-22(3) (1992) 418-435

14 Lauritzen, S. L. and Spiegelhalter, D. J.: Local computations with probabilities on graphical structures and their applications on expert systems. Journal Royal Statistical Society B, 50(2) (1988) 157-224

15 Korb, K. B. and Nicholson, A. E.: Bayesian Artificial Intelligence. CHAPMAN & HALL, (2003)

16 Good, I.: Relational decisions. Journal of the Royal Statistical Society B, 14 (1952) 107-114

Mining the Semantic Web:
A Logic-Based Methodology

Francesca A. Lisi and Floriana Esposito

Dipartimento di Informatica, University of Bari, Italy
{lisi, esposito}@di.uniba.it

Abstract. This paper deals with mining the logical layer of the Semantic Web. Our approach adopts the hybrid system $\mathcal{AL}$-log as a knowledge representation and reasoning framework and Inductive Logic Programming as a methodological apparatus. We illustrate the approach by means of examples taken from a case study of frequent pattern discovery in data of the on-line CIA World Fact Book.

1 Background and Motivation

The Semantic Web is the vision of the WWW enriched by machine-processable information which supports the user in his tasks [3]. Its architecture consists of several layers, each of which is equipped with an ad-hoc mark-up language. Therefore it poses several challenges in the field of Knowledge Representation and Reasoning (KR&R), mainly attracting people doing research on Description Logics (DLs) [1]. E.g., the design of OWL (http://www.w3.org/2004/OWL/) for the *ontological layer* has been based on DLs derived from $\mathcal{ALC}$ [17]. Also ORL [6], recently proposed for the *logical layer*, extends OWL 'to build rules on top of ontologies'. It bridges the expressive gap between DLs and Horn clausal logic (or its fragments) in a way that is similar in the spirit to *hybridization* in KR&R systems such as $\mathcal{AL}$-log [5]. The Semantic Web is also gaining the attention of the Machine Learning and Data Mining communities, thus giving rise to the new application area of Semantic Web Mining [2]. Most work in this area simply extends previous work to the new application context, e.g. [12], or concentrates on the RDF/RDFSchema layer, e.g. [13]. Yet OWL and ORL raise research issues that are of greater interest to these communities. A crucial issue is the definition of *generality orders* for inductive hypotheses. Indeed many approaches in machine learning, e.g. Inductive Logic Programming (ILP) [15], and data mining, e.g. Mannila's framework for frequent pattern discovery [14], are centered around the mechanism of generalization and propose algorithms based on a search process through a partially ordered space of inductive hypotheses.

In this paper we show how our ILP framework for learning in $\mathcal{AL}$-log [9, 10, 8] can be considered as a logic-based methodology for mining the logical layer of the Semantic Web. Our goal is to show that $\mathcal{AL}$-log, though less expressive than ORL, is powerful enough to satisfy the actual needs of expressiveness in many

M.-S. Hacid et al. (Eds.): ISMIS 2005, LNAI 3488, pp. 102–111, 2005.
© Springer-Verlag Berlin Heidelberg 2005

Table 1. Syntax and semantics of $\mathcal{ALC}$

bottom (resp. top) concept	$\bot$ (resp. $\top$)	$\emptyset$ (resp. $\Delta^{\mathcal{I}}$)
atomic concept	A	$A^{\mathcal{I}} \subseteq \Delta^{\mathcal{I}}$
role	R	$R^{\mathcal{I}} \subseteq \Delta^{\mathcal{I}} \times \Delta^{\mathcal{I}}$
individual	a	$a^{\mathcal{I}} \in \Delta^{\mathcal{I}}$
concept negation	$\neg C$	$\Delta^{\mathcal{I}} \setminus C^{\mathcal{I}}$
concept conjunction	$C \sqcap D$	$C^{\mathcal{I}} \cap D^{\mathcal{I}}$
concept disjunction	$C \sqcup D$	$C^{\mathcal{I}} \cup D^{\mathcal{I}}$
value restriction	$\forall R.C$	$\{x \in \Delta^{\mathcal{I}} \mid \forall y \ (x,y) \in R^{\mathcal{I}} \to y \in C^{\mathcal{I}}\}$
existential restriction	$\exists R.C$	$\{x \in \Delta^{\mathcal{I}} \mid \exists y \ (x,y) \in R^{\mathcal{I}} \land y \in C^{\mathcal{I}}\}$
equivalence axiom	$C \equiv D$	$C^{\mathcal{I}} = D^{\mathcal{I}}$
subsumption axiom	$C \sqsubseteq D$	$C^{\mathcal{I}} \subseteq D^{\mathcal{I}}$
concept assertion	$a : C$	$a^{\mathcal{I}} \in C^{\mathcal{I}}$
role assertion	$\langle a, b \rangle : R$	$(a^{\mathcal{I}}, b^{\mathcal{I}}) \in R^{\mathcal{I}}$

Semantic Web applications. In the rest of this section we briefly introduce $\mathcal{AL}$-log and the aforementioned learning framework.

1.1 Knowledge Representation and Reasoning with $\mathcal{AL}$-Log

The system $\mathcal{AL}$-log [5] integrates two KR&R systems. The **structural sub-system** Σ is based on $\mathcal{ALC}$ [17] and allows for the specification of knowledge in terms of classes (*concepts*), binary relations between classes (*roles*), and instances (*individuals*). Complex concepts can be defined from atomic concepts and roles by means of constructors (see Table 1). Also Σ can state both is-a relations between concepts (*axioms*) and instance-of relations between individuals (resp. couples of individuals) and concepts (resp. roles) (*assertions*). An *interpretation* $\mathcal{I} = (\Delta^{\mathcal{I}}, \cdot^{\mathcal{I}})$ for Σ consists of a domain $\Delta^{\mathcal{I}}$ and a mapping function $\cdot^{\mathcal{I}}$. In particular, individuals are mapped to elements of $\Delta^{\mathcal{I}}$ such that $a^{\mathcal{I}} \neq b^{\mathcal{I}}$ if $a \neq b$ (*unique names* assumption). If $\mathcal{O} \subseteq \Delta^{\mathcal{I}}$ and $\forall a \in \mathcal{O} : a^{\mathcal{I}} = a$, $\mathcal{I}$ is called $\mathcal{O}$-*interpretation*. The main reasoning task for Σ is the *consistency check*. This test is performed with a *tableau calculus* that starts with the tableau branch $S = \mathcal{T} \cup \mathcal{M}$ and adds assertions to S by means of *propagation rules* like

- $S \to_{\sqcup} S \cup \{s : D\}$ if
  1. $s : C_1 \sqcup C_2$ is in S,
  2. $D = C_1$ and $D = C_2$,
  3. neither $s : C_1$ nor $s : C_2$ is in S
- $S \to_{\sqsubseteq} S \cup \{s : C' \sqcup D\}$ if
  1. $C \sqsubseteq D$ is in S,
  2. s appears in S,
  3. C' is the NNF concept equivalent to $\neg C$
  4. $s : \neg C \sqcup D$ is not in S

- $S \rightarrow_\perp \{s : \perp\}$ if
  1. $s : A$ and $s : \neg A$ are in S, or
  2. $s : \neg\top$ is in S,
  3. $s : \perp$ is not in S

until either a contradiction is generated or an interpretation satisfying S can be easily obtained from it [5]. The **relational subsystem** Π extends DATALOG [4] by using the so-called *constrained* DATALOG *clause*, i.e. clauses of the form

$$\alpha_0 \leftarrow \alpha_1, \ldots, \alpha_m \& \gamma_1, \ldots, \gamma_n$$

where $m \geq 0$, $n \geq 0$, α_i are DATALOG atoms and γ_j are *constraints* of the form $s : C$ where s is either a constant or a variable already appearing in the clause, and C is an $\mathcal{ALC}$ concept. A constrained DATALOG clause of the form $\leftarrow \beta_1, \ldots, \beta_m \& \gamma_1, \ldots, \gamma_n$ is called *constrained* DATALOG *query*. For an $\mathcal{AL}$-log *knowledge base* $\mathcal{B} = \langle \Sigma, \Pi \rangle$ to be acceptable, it must satisfy the following conditions: (i) The set of predicate symbols appearing in Π is disjoint from the set of concept and role symbols appearing in Σ; (ii) The alphabet of constants used in Π coincides with $\mathcal{O}$; (iii) For each clause in Π, each variable occurring in the constraint part occurs also in the DATALOG part. The interaction between Σ and Π allows the notion of *substitution* to be straightforwardly extended from DATALOG to $\mathcal{AL}$-log. It is also at the basis of a model-theoretic semantics for $\mathcal{AL}$-log. An *interpretation* $\mathcal{J}$ for $\mathcal{B}$ is the union of an $\mathcal{O}$-interpretation $\mathcal{I}_\mathcal{O}$ for Σ and an Herbrand interpretation $\mathcal{I}_\mathcal{H}$ for Π_D (i.e. the set of DATALOG clauses obtained from the clauses of Π by deleting their constraints). The notion of *logical consequence* paves the way to the definition of *correct answer* and *answer set* similarly to DATALOG. Reasoning for an $\mathcal{AL}$-log knowledge base $\mathcal{B}$ is based on *constrained SLD-resolution*, i.e. an extension of SLD-resolution with the tableau calculus to deal with constraints. *Constrained SLD-refutation* is a complete and sound method for answering queries, being the definition of *computed answer* and *success set* analogous to DATALOG. A big difference from DATALOG is that the derivation of a constrained empty clause does not represent a refutation but actually infers that the query is true in those models of $\mathcal{B}$ that satisfy its constraints. Therefore in order to answer a query it is necessary to collect enough derivations ending with a constrained empty clause such that every model of $\mathcal{B}$ satisfies the constraints associated with the final query of at least one derivation.

1.2   Learning in $\mathcal{AL}$-Log

In our framework for learning in $\mathcal{AL}$-log the **language** $\mathcal{L}$ **of hypotheses** admits only constrained DATALOG clauses that are compliant with the properties of *linkedness* and *connectedness* [15] and the bias of *Object Identity* (OI) [18]. In this context the OI bias can be considered as an extension of the unique names assumption from the semantics of $\mathcal{ALC}$ to the syntax of $\mathcal{AL}$-log. It boils down to the use of substitutions whose bindings avoid the identification of terms. The **space of hypotheses** is ordered according to the generality relation $\succeq_\mathcal{B}$ (called $\mathcal{B}$-*subsumption* [9]) that can be tested by resorting to constrained SLD-resolution. Therefore the $\mathcal{ALC}$ machinery plays a role during learning.

```
<owl:Class rdf:ID="MiddleEastCountry">
  <owl:sameAs>
    <owl:intersectionOf rdf:parseType="Collection">
      <owl:Class rdf:ID="AsianCountry" />
      <owl:Restriction>
        <owl:onProperty rdf:resource="#Hosts" />
        <owl:someValuesFrom rdf:resource="#MiddleEasternEthnicGroup" />
      </owl:Restriction>
    </owl:intersectionOf>
  </owl:sameAs>
</owl:Class>
```

Fig. 1. Definition of the concept `MiddleEastCountry` in OWL

Theorem 1. *Let H_1, H_2 be two constrained* DATALOG *clauses, $\mathcal{B}$ an $\mathcal{AL}$-log knowledge base, and σ a Skolem substitution for H_2 w.r.t. $\{H_1\} \cup \mathcal{B}$. We say that $H_1 \succeq_\mathcal{B} H_2$ iff there exists a substitution θ for H_1 such that (i) $head(H_1)\theta = head(H_2)$ and (ii) $\mathcal{B} \cup body(H_2)\sigma \vdash body(H_1)\theta\sigma$ where $body(H_1)\theta\sigma$ is ground.*

Since $\succeq_\mathcal{B}$ is a quasi-order [9], a refinement operator has been proposed to search $(\mathcal{L}, \succeq_\mathcal{B})$ [10]. Also $\succeq_\mathcal{B}$ can be exploited to make the evaluation of hypotheses more efficient [8]. Though this learning framework is valid whatever the scope of induction (prediction/description) is, it is implemented in the system $\mathcal{AL}$-QuIn[1] [10, 8] as regards the case of characteristic induction (description).

2   Semantic Web Mining with $\mathcal{AL}$-QuIn

The system $\mathcal{AL}$-QuIn solves a variant of the frequent pattern discovery problem which takes concept hierarchies into account, thus yielding descriptions of a data set at multiple granularity levels. More formally, given

- a data set **r** including a taxonomy $\mathcal{T}$ where a reference concept C_{ref} and task-relevant concepts are designated,
- a multi-grained language $\mathcal{L} = \{\mathcal{L}^l\}_{1 \leq l \leq maxG}$
- a set $\{minsup^l\}_{1 \leq l \leq maxG}$ of support thresholds

the problem of *frequent pattern discovery at l levels of description granularity*, $1 \leq l \leq maxG$, is to find the set $\mathcal{F}$ of all the patterns $P \in \mathcal{L}^l$ frequent in **r**, namely P's with support s such that (i) $s \geq minsup^l$ and (ii) all ancestors of P w.r.t. $\mathcal{T}$ are frequent in **r**.

In $\mathcal{AL}$-QuIn, the data set **r** is actually an $\mathcal{AL}$-log knowledge base.

Example 1. As a running example, we consider an $\mathcal{AL}$-log knowledge base $\mathcal{B}_{CIA}$ that enriches DATALOG facts[2] extracted from the on-line 1996 CIA World Fact

---

[1] A previous version of $\mathcal{AL}$-QuIn is described in [11].

[2] http://www.dbis.informatik.uni-goettingen.de/Mondial/mondial-rel-facts.flp

Book[3] with $\mathcal{ALC}$ ontologies[4]. The structural subsystem Σ of $\mathcal{B}_{CIA}$ focus on the concepts Country, EthnicGroup, Language, and Religion. Axioms like

```
AsianCountry ⊑ Country.
MiddleEasternEthnicGroup ⊑ EthnicGroup.
MiddleEastCountry ≡ AsianCountry ⊓ ∃Hosts.MiddleEasternEthnicGroup.
IndoEuropeanLanguage ⊑ Language.
IndoIranianLanguage ⊑ IndoEuropeanLanguage.
MonotheisticReligion ⊑ Religion.
ChristianReligion ⊑ MonotheisticReligion.
MuslimReligion ⊑ MonotheisticReligion.
```

define four taxonomies, one for each concept above. Note that Middle East countries (concept MiddleEastCountry, whose definition in OWL is reported in Figure 1) have been defined as Asian countries that host at least one Middle Eastern ethnic group. Assertions like

```
'ARM':AsianCountry.
'IR':AsianCountry.
'Arab':MiddleEasternEthnicGroup.
'Armenian':MiddleEasternEthnicGroup.
<'ARM','Armenian'>:Hosts.
<'IR','Arab'>:Hosts.
'Armenian':IndoEuropeanLanguage.
'Persian':IndoIranianLanguage.
'Armenian Orthodox':ChristianReligion.
'Shia':MuslimReligion.
'Sunni':MuslimReligion.
```

belong to the extensional part of Σ. In particular, Armenia ('ARM') and Iran ('IR') are two of the 14 countries that are classified as Middle Eastern.

The relational subsystem Π of $\mathcal{B}_{CIA}$ expresses the CIA facts as a constrained DATALOG program. The extensional part of Π consists of DATALOG facts like

```
language('ARM','Armenian',96).
language('IR','Persian',58).
religion('ARM','Armenian Orthodox',94).
religion('IR','Shia',89).
religion('IR','Sunni',10).
```

whereas the intensional part defines two views on language and religion:

```
speaks(CountryID, LanguageN)←language(CountryID,LanguageN,Perc)
                & CountryID:Country, LanguageN:Language
```

---

[3] http://www.odci.gov/cia/publications/factbook/
[4] The ontology available at http://www.daml.org/2003/09/factbook/factbook-ont for the same domain is not good for our illustrative purposes because it contains only atomic concepts and shallow concept hierarchies.

```
<owlx:Rule>
  <owlx:antecedent>
    <owlx:classAtom>
      <owlx:class="&MiddleEastCountry" /><owlx:Variable owlx:name="_X">
    </owlx:classAtom>
    <owlx:classAtom>
      <owlx:class="&Religion" /><owlx:Variable owlx:name="_Y">
    </owlx:classAtom>
    <owlx:individualPropertyAtom owlx:property="&believes">
      <owlx:Variable owlx:name="_X"><owlx:Variable owlx:name="_Y">
    </owlx:individualPropertyAtom>
  </owl:antecedent>
  <owlx:consequent>
    <owlx:individualPropertyAtom owlx:property="&q">
      <owlx:Variable owlx:name="_X">
    </owlx:individualPropertyAtom>
  </owlx:consequent>
</owlx:Rule>
```

Fig. 2. Representation of the $\mathcal{O}$-query Q_1 in ORL

$$\text{believes(CountryID, ReligionN)} \leftarrow \text{religion(CountryID,ReligionN,Perc)}$$
$$\& \text{ CountryID:Country, ReligionN:Religion}$$

that can deduce new DATALOG facts when triggered on $\mathcal{B}_{\text{CIA}}$.

The language $\mathcal{L}$ for a given problem instance is implicitly defined by a declarative bias specification that allows for the generation of expressions, called $\mathcal{O}$-queries, relating individuals of C_{ref} to individuals of the task-relevant concepts. More formally, an $\mathcal{O}$-*query* Q to an $\mathcal{AL}$-log knowledge base $\mathcal{B}$ is a (linked, connected, and OI-compliant) constrained DATALOG clause of the form

$$Q = q(X) \leftarrow \alpha_1, \ldots, \alpha_m \& X : C_{ref}, \gamma_2, \ldots, \gamma_n$$

where X is the *distinguished variable*. The $\mathcal{O}$-query $Q_t = q(X) \leftarrow \&X : C_{ref}$ is called *trivial* for $\mathcal{L}$.

Example 2. We want to describe Middle East countries (individuals of the reference concept) with respect to the religions believed and the languages spoken (individuals of the task-relevant concepts) at three levels of granularity ($maxG = 3$). To this aim we define $\mathcal{L}_{\text{CIA}}$ as the set of $\mathcal{O}$-queries with $C_{ref} =$ MiddleEastCountry that can be generated from the alphabet $\mathcal{A} = \{$believes/2, speaks/2$\}$ of DATALOG binary predicate names, and the alphabets

$\Gamma^1 = \{$Language, Religion$\}$
$\Gamma^2 = \{$IndoEuropeanLanguage, ..., MonotheisticReligion, ...$\}$
$\Gamma^3 = \{$IndoIranianLanguage, ..., MuslimReligion, ...$\}$

of $\mathcal{ALC}$ concept names for $1 \leq l \leq 3$. Examples of $\mathcal{O}$-queries in $\mathcal{L}_{\text{CIA}}$ are:

$Q_0 = $ q(X) $\leftarrow$ & X:MiddleEastCountry
$Q_1 = $ q(X) $\leftarrow$ believes(X,Y) & X:MiddleEastCountry, Y:Religion
$Q_2 = $ q(X) $\leftarrow$ believes(X,Y), speaks(X,Z) & X:MiddleEastCountry,
     Y:MonotheisticReligion, Z:IndoEuropeanLanguage
$Q_3 = $ q(X) $\leftarrow$ believes(X,Y), speaks(X,Z) & X:MiddleEastCountry,
     Y:MuslimReligion, Z:IndoIranianLanguage

where Q_0 is the trivial $\mathcal{O}$-query for $\mathcal{L}_{\text{CIA}}$, $Q_1 \in \mathcal{L}^1_{\text{CIA}}$, $Q_2 \in \mathcal{L}^2_{\text{CIA}}$, and $Q_3 \in \mathcal{L}^3_{\text{CIA}}$. A representation of Q_1 in ORL is reported in Figure 2.

The *support* of an $\mathcal{O}$-query $Q \in \mathcal{L}$ w.r.t. $\mathcal{B}$ supplies the percentage of individuals of C_{ref} that satisfy Q and is defined as

$$supp(Q, \mathcal{B}) = \mid answerset(Q, \mathcal{B}) \mid / \mid answerset(Q_t, \mathcal{B}) \mid$$

where $answerset(Q, \mathcal{B})$ is the set of correct answers to Q w.r.t. $\mathcal{B}$, i.e. the set of substitutions θ_i for the distinguished variable of Q such that there exists a correct answer to $body(Q)\theta$ w.r.t. $\mathcal{B}$.

Example 3. The substitution $\theta = \{$X/'ARM'$\}$ is a correct answer to Q_1 w.r.t. $\mathcal{B}_{\text{CIA}}$ because there exists a correct answer $\sigma = \{$Y/ 'Armenian Orthodox'$\}$ to $body(Q_1)\theta$ w.r.t.$\mathcal{B}_{\text{CIA}}$. Furthermore, since $\mid answerset(Q_1, \mathcal{B}_{\text{CIA}}) \mid = 14$ and $\mid answerset(Q_t, \mathcal{B}_{\text{CIA}}) \mid = \mid$ MiddleEastCountry $\mid = 14$, then $supp(Q_1, \mathcal{B}_{\text{CIA}}) = 100\%$.

The system $\mathcal{AL}$-QuIn implements the *levelwise search* [14] for frequent pattern discovery. This method is based on the following assumption: If a generality order $\succeq$ for the language $\mathcal{L}$ of patterns can be found such that $\succeq$ is monotonic w.r.t. the evaluation function *supp*, then the resulting space $(\mathcal{L}, \succeq)$ can be searched breadth-first starting from the most general pattern in $\mathcal{L}$ by alternating candidate generation and candidate evaluation phases. In particular, candidate patterns of a certain level k are obtained by refinement of the frequent patterns discovered at level $k-1$. In $\mathcal{AL}$-QuIn patterns are ordered according to $\mathcal{B}$-subsumption (which has been proved to fulfill the abovementioned condition of monotonicity [11]). The search starts from the trivial $\mathcal{O}$-query in $\mathcal{L}$ and iterates through the generation-evaluation cycle for a number of times that is bounded with respect to both the granularity level l ($maxG$) and the depth level k ($maxD$). In the following we illustrate the features of $\succeq_\mathcal{B}$ in this context.

Example 4. We want to check whether Q_1 $\mathcal{B}$-subsumes the $\mathcal{O}$-query

$Q_4 = $ q(A) $\leftarrow$ believes(A,B) & A:MiddleEastCountry, B:MonotheisticReligion

belonging to $\mathcal{L}^2_{\text{CIA}}$. Let $\sigma = \{$A/a, B/b$\}$ a Skolem substitution for Q_4 w.r.t. $\mathcal{B}_{\text{CIA}} \cup \{Q_1\}$ and $\theta = \{$X/A, Y/B$\}$ a substitution for Q_1. The condition (i) of Theorem 1 is immediately verified. It remains to verify that (ii) $\mathcal{B}' = $

$\mathcal{B}_{\text{CIA}} \cup \{$believes(a,b), a:MiddleEastCountry, b:MonotheisticReligion$\}$
$\models$believes(a,b) & a:MiddleEastCountry, b:Religion.

We try to build a constrained SLD-refutation for

$$Q^{(0)} = \leftarrow \text{believes(a,b)} \ \& \ \text{a:MiddleEastCountry, b:Religion}$$

in $\mathcal{B}'$. Let $E^{(1)}$ be believes(a,b). A resolvent for $Q^{(0)}$ and $E^{(1)}$ with the empty substitution $\sigma^{(1)}$ is the constrained empty clause

$$Q^{(1)} = \leftarrow \ \& \ \text{a:MiddleEastCountry, b:Religion}$$

The consistency of $\Sigma'' = \Sigma' \cup \{\text{a:MiddleEastCountry, b:Religion}\}$ needs now to be checked. The first unsatisfiability check operates on the initial tableau $S_1^{(0)} = \Sigma' \cup \{\text{a:}\neg\text{MiddleEastCountry}\}$. The application of the propagation rule $\rightarrow_\perp$ to $S_1^{(0)}$ produces the final tableau $S_1^{(1)} = \{\text{a:}\perp\}$. Therefore $S_1^{(0)}$ is unsatisfiable. The second check starts with $S_2^{(0)} = \Sigma' \cup \{\text{b:}\neg\text{Religion}\}$. The rule $\rightarrow_\sqsubseteq$ w.r.t. $\text{MonotheisticReligion}\sqsubseteq\text{Religion}$, the only one applicable to $S_2^{(0)}$, produces $S_2^{(1)} = \Sigma \cup \{\text{b:}\neg\text{Religion, b:}\neg\text{MonotheisticReligion}\sqcup\text{Religion}\}$. By applying $\rightarrow_\sqcup$ to $S_2^{(1)}$ w.r.t. Religion we obtain $S_2^{(2)} = \Sigma \cup \{\text{b:}\neg\text{Religion, b:Religion}\}$ which brings to the final tableau $S_2^{(3)} = \{\text{b:}\perp\}$ via $\rightarrow_\perp$.

Having proved the consistency of Σ'', we have proved the existence of a constrained SLD-refutation for $Q^{(0)}$ in $\mathcal{B}'$. Therefore we can say that $Q_1 \succeq_\mathcal{B} Q_4$. Conversely, $Q_4 \not\succeq_\mathcal{B} Q_1$. Similarly it can be proved that $Q_2 \succeq_\mathcal{B} Q_3$ and $Q_3 \not\succeq_\mathcal{B} Q_2$.

Example 5. It can be easily verified that Q_1 $\mathcal{B}$-subsumes the following query

$$Q_5 = \text{q(A)} \leftarrow \text{believes(A,B), believes(A,C)} \ \& \ \text{A:MiddleEastCountry, B:Religion}$$

by choosing $\sigma = \{\text{A/a, B/b, C/c}\}$ as a Skolem substitution for Q_5 w.r.t. $\mathcal{B}_{\text{CIA}} \cup \{Q_1\}$ and $\theta = \{\text{X/A, Y/B}\}$ as a substitution for Q_1. Note that $Q_5 \not\succeq_\mathcal{B} Q_1$ under the OI bias. Indeed this bias does not admit the substitution $\{\text{A/X, B/Y, C/Y}\}$ for Q_5 which would make possible to verify conditions (i) and (ii) of Theorem 1.

Example 6. Note that $\succeq_\mathcal{B}$ relations can be verified by comparing the answer sets of the two $\mathcal{O}$-queries at hand. E.g., Armenia satisfies Q_2 but not to Q_3, thus confirming that $Q_3 \not\succeq_\mathcal{B} Q_2$. This is quite interesting for the following reasons. Armenia, as opposite to Iran (which satisfies all the patterns from Q_1 to Q_5), is a well-known borderline case for the geo-political concept of Middle East, though the Armenian is usually listed among Middle Eastern ethnic groups. In 1996 the on-line CIA World Fact Book considered Armenia as part of Asia. But modern experts tend nowadays to consider it as part of Europe, therefore out of Middle East. This trend emerges from the fact that, among the characterizations of the Middle East reported in this section, Armenia satisfies only the weakest one.

3   Conclusions

Methodologies for Semantic Web Mining can not ignore the features of standard mark-up languages for the Semantic Web. In particular mining the logical layer requires approaches able to deal with representations combining Horn clauses and DLs. The system $\mathcal{AL}$-QuIN implements a framework for learning in $\mathcal{AL}$-log which goes beyond the potential of traditional ILP as discussed in [9, 10, 8]. Furthermore the existence of an implementation makes a difference from related approaches, notably the framework for learning in CARIN-$\mathcal{ALN}$ [16, 7]. In this paper we have presented the intended application of $\mathcal{AL}$-QuIN in Semantic Web Mining. For the future, we wish to extend the underlying learning framework to more expressive hybrid languages so that $\mathcal{AL}$-QuIN can cope with larger fragments of ORL. This will allow us - as soon as huge ORL data sources will be made available - to evaluate extensively the application.

Acknowledgement. This work is supported by the COFIN-PRIN 2003 project "Tecniche di Intelligenza Artificiale per il Reperimento di Informazione di Qualità sul Web" funded by the *Ministero dell'Istruzione, dell'Università, e della Ricerca Scientifica.*

References

1. F. Baader, D. Calvanese, D. McGuinness, D. Nardi, and P.F. Patel-Schneider, editors. *The Description Logic Handbook: Theory, Implementation and Applications.* Cambridge University Press, 2003.
2. B. Berendt, A. Hotho, and G. Stumme. Towards semantic web mining. In I. Horrocks and J.A. Hendler, editors, *International Semantic Web Conference*, volume 2342 of *Lecture Notes in Computer Science*, pages 264–278. Springer, 2002.
3. T. Berners-Lee, J. Hendler, and O. Lassila. The Semantic Web. *Scientific American*, May, 2001.
4. S. Ceri, G. Gottlob, and L. Tanca. *Logic Programming and Databases.* Springer, 1990.
5. F.M. Donini, M. Lenzerini, D. Nardi, and A. Schaerf. $\mathcal{AL}$-log: Integrating Datalog and Description Logics. *J. of Intelligent Information Systems*, 10(3):227–252, 1998.
6. I. Horrocks and P.F. Patel-Schneider. A Proposal for an OWL Rules Language. In *Proc. of the 13th Int. World Wide Web Conference*, pages 723–731. ACM, 2004.
7. J.-U. Kietz. Learnability of description logic programs. In S. Matwin and C. Sammut, editors, *Inductive Logic Programming*, volume 2583 of *Lecture Notes in Artificial Intelligence*, pages 117–132. Springer, 2003.
8. F.A. Lisi and F. Esposito. Efficient Evaluation of Candidate Hypotheses in $\mathcal{AL}$-log. In R. Camacho, R. King, and A. Srinivasan, editors, *Inductive Logic Programming*, volume 3194 of *LNAI*, pages 216–233. Springer, 2004.
9. F.A. Lisi and D. Malerba. Bridging the Gap between Horn Clausal Logic and Description Logics in Inductive Learning. In A. Cappelli and F. Turini, editors, *AI*IA 2003: Advances in Artificial Intelligence*, volume 2829 of *Lecture Notes in Artificial Intelligence*, pages 49–60. Springer, 2003.
10. F.A. Lisi and D. Malerba. Ideal Refinement of Descriptions in $\mathcal{AL}$-log. In T. Horvath and A. Yamamoto, editors, *Inductive Logic Programming*, volume 2835 of *Lecture Notes in Artificial Intelligence*, pages 215–232. Springer, 2003.
11. F.A. Lisi and D. Malerba. Inducing Multi-Level Association Rules from Multiple Relations. *Machine Learning*, 55:175–210, 2004.
12. A. Maedche and S. Staab. Discovering Conceptual Relations from Text. In W. Horn, editor, *Proc. of the 14th European Conference on Artificial Intelligence*, pages 321–325. IOS Press, 2000.

13. A. Maedche and V. Zacharias. Clustering Ontology-Based Metadata in the Semantic Web. In T. Elomaa, H. Mannila, and H. Toivonen, editors, *Principles of Data Mining and Knowledge Discovery*, volume 2431 of *Lecture Notes in Computer Science*, pages 348–360. Springer, 2002.
14. H. Mannila and H. Toivonen. Levelwise search and borders of theories in knowledge discovery. *Data Mining and Knowledge Discovery*, 1(3):241–258, 1997.
15. S.-H. Nienhuys-Cheng and R. de Wolf. *Foundations of Inductive Logic Programming*, volume 1228 of *Lecture Notes in Artificial Intelligence*. Springer, 1997.
16. C. Rouveirol and V. Ventos. Towards Learning in CARIN-$\mathcal{ALN}$. In J. Cussens and A. Frisch, editors, *Inductive Logic Programming*, volume 1866 of *Lecture Notes in Artificial Intelligence*, pages 191–208. Springer, 2000.
17. M. Schmidt-Schauss and G. Smolka. Attributive concept descriptions with complements. *Artificial Intelligence*, 48(1):1–26, 1991.
18. G. Semeraro, F. Esposito, D. Malerba, N. Fanizzi, and S. Ferilli. A logic framework for the incremental inductive synthesis of Datalog theories. In N.E. Fuchs, editor, *Proc. of the 7th Int. Workshop on Logic Program Synthesis and Transformation*, volume 1463 of *Lecture Notes in Computer Science*, pages 300–321. Springer, 1998.

Analysis of Textual Data with Multiple Classes

Shigeaki Sakurai[1], Chong Goh[1,2], and Ryohei Orihara[1]

[1] Corporate Research & Development Center, Toshiba Corporation
[2] Carnegie Mellon University

Abstract. This paper proposes a new method for analyzing textual data. The method deals with items of textual data, where each item includes various viewpoints and each viewpoint is regarded as a class. The method inductively acquires classification models for 2-class classification tasks from items labeled by multiple classes. The method infers classes of new items by using these models. Lastly, the method extracts important expressions from new items in each class and extracts characteristic expressions by comparing the frequency of expressions. This paper applies the method to questionnaire data described by guests at a hotel and verifies its effect through numerical experiments.

1 Introduction

As computers and network environments have become ubiquitous, many kinds of questionnaires are now conducted on the Web. A simple means of analyzing responses to questionnaires is required. The responses are usually composed of selective responses and textual responses. In the case of the selective responses, the responses can be analyzed relatively easily using statistical techniques and data mining techniques. However, the responses may not correspond to the opinions of respondents because the respondents have to select appropriate responses from among those given by the designers of the questionnaires. Also, the designers are unable to receive unexpected responses because only those expected by the designers are available. On the other hand, in the case of the textual responses, the respondents can freely describe their opinions. The designers are able to receive more appropriate responses that reflect the opinions of the respondents and may be able to receive unexpected responses. Therefore, textual responses are expected to be analyzed using text mining techniques. Even though many text mining techniques [2] [3] [8] [9] have previously been studied, textual data has not always been analyzed sufficiently. Since analysis may be undertaken for various purposes and there are various types of textual data, it is difficult to construct a definitive text mining technique. The text mining technique must reflect the features of the textual data. In this paper, we propose a new analysis method that deals with textual data that includes multiple viewpoints. The method is designed to deal with free-form textual responses, to classify textual responses to questionnaires according to various viewpoints, and to discover characteristic expressions corresponding to

M.-S. Hacid et al. (Eds.): ISMIS 2005, LNAI 3488, pp. 112–120, 2005.
© Springer-Verlag Berlin Heidelberg 2005

each viewpoint. We apply the proposed method to the analysis of textual responses given by guests at a hotel and verify its effect through numerical experiments.

2   Analysis of Textual Responses

2.1   Analysis Targets

Many kinds of comments may be expressed in textual responses to questionnaires. It is important to investigate all textual responses in detail and to include measures that resolve problems in the responses. However, the amount of textual responses that analysts can investigate is limited. Even if they could investigate all textual responses, it would be impracticable to include all required measures due to constraints regarding cost, time, etc. Therefore, it is necessary to show rough trends for the textual responses and to extract the important topics from them. Thus, we propose a method that classifies textual data into various viewpoints and extracts important expressions corresponding to each viewpoint.

2.2   Analysis Policy

Respondents to a questionnaire can freely describe their opinions in textual responses, and the respondents can provide responses that include multiple viewpoints. For example, in the case of a questionnaire for guests at a hotel, a guest may provide a textual response that includes three viewpoints, e.g. bad aspects of the hotel, good aspects of the hotel, and requests to the hotel. If the respondents classified their responses according to the viewpoints and put them into columns, the analyst's task would be easy. However, since the respondents would be likely to find such a questionnaire troublesome, a low response rate would be likely. It is necessary to allow textual responses that include multiple viewpoints in order to ease the burden on respondents.

We first consider a method that uses passage extraction techniques [6] [10] for that purpose. The techniques can extract specific parts of textual data and are used effectively in a question answering task. However, it is necessary for many passage extraction techniques to measure the distance between a standard sentence and parts of the textual data. In the case of analysis of textual responses to questionnaires, it is difficult to decide what corresponds to a standard sentence. Therefore, we can not extract the specific parts using the techniques.

Next, we consider classifying each textual response by using a classification model. The classification model has to identify textual responses that include a single viewpoint and textual responses that include multiple viewpoints. It is difficult for the model to identify the former responses with the latter responses, because the former responses may be a part of the latter responses. A large number of training examples are required to inductively learn the model, because the latter responses are composed of combinations of the former responses. Therefore, a method based on a classification model is not always appropriate.

Thus, we try to acquire classification models corresponding to viewpoints. Here, the classification models can identify whether or not a textual response corresponds to a viewpoint. The models are acquired from training example sets that correspond to viewpoints. We can identify viewpoints that correspond to each textual response by using the models and can also extract expressions from textual responses included in a specific viewpoint. Here, it should be noted that the expressions are not always related to the specific viewpoints. This is the reason they can be related to other viewpoints that simultaneously occur with the specific viewpoint. However, the number is much smaller than the number of expressions related to the specific viewpoint. Therefore, we can extract expressions that correspond to each viewpoint by comparing the number of expressions extracted in each viewpoint. We consider that the classification and the extraction can analyze textual responses to questionnaires.

2.3   Analysis Flow

We constructed a new analysis method based on the policy described in subsection 2.2. The method is composed of five processes as shown in Figure 1. Here, the method deals with a language without word segmentation, such as Japanese. In the following, the processes are explained.

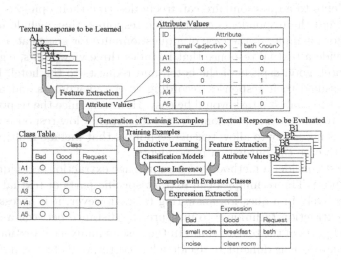

Fig. 1. Analysis flow

Feature Extraction Process: The process decomposes each textual response into words with corresponding parts of speech by using morphological analysis [5]. The process extracts words, if their tf-idf values are bigger than or equal to a threshold and their parts of speech are included in a designated set of parts of speech. The process regards the extracted words as attributes. The process also evaluates whether or not the words are included in a textual response. If the words are included, the process gives 1s to the corresponding attributes.

Table 1. Training examples corresponding to the viewpoint "Bad"

ID	Attribute			Class
	small <adjective>	$\cdots$	bath <noun>	
A1	1	$\cdots$	0	c_1
A2	0	$\cdots$	0	c_0
A3	0	$\cdots$	1	c_0
A4	1	$\cdots$	1	c_1
A5	0	$\cdots$	0	c_1

Otherwise, the process gives 0s to them. Therefore, a column vector as shown at the upper-right side in Figure 1 is assigned to each textual response.

Generation Process of Training Examples: The process selects a viewpoint in the class table. The process evaluates whether the viewpoint is assigned in a textual response or not. If the viewpoint is assigned, the process assigns the class c_1 to the textual response. Otherwise, the process assigns the class c_0 to it. The process generates the training example set corresponding to the viewpoint by integrating attribute values with the classes. Table 1 shows an example of training examples corresponding to the viewpoint "Bad".

Inductive Learning Process: The process acquires classification models from each training example set by solving 2-class classification tasks. Each model corresponds to a viewpoint. In this paper, the process uses a support vector machine (SVM) [4] to acquire the models, because many papers [1] [7] have reported that an SVM gives high precision ratios for text classification. The process acquires classification models described with hyperplanes by using an SVM.

Class Inference Process: The process applies textual responses to be evaluated to each classification model. Here, each textual response is characterized by words extracted from the textual responses to be learned. The process infers classes, c_0s or c_1s, corresponding to the textual responses to be evaluated for each viewpoint. In Figure 1, three kinds of classes corresponding to the viewpoints "Bad", "Good", and "Request" are assigned to the responses B1 $\sim$ B5.

Expression Extraction Process: The process extracts expressions from the textual responses with class c_1. Here, the expressions are words that are specific parts of speech or phrases that are specific sequences of parts of speech such as <adjective> and <noun>. The words and the sequences are designated by analysts. The process calculates the frequency of the expressions in each viewpoint and assigns the viewpoint with the maximum frequency to the expressions. Lastly, the process extracts expressions that are bigger than or equal to a threshold. The expressions are regarded as characteristic expressions in the viewpoints.

For example, assume that five textual responses are given. Here, two textual responses include the expression "small room", two textual responses include the expression "clean room", and one textual response includes the expressions "small room" and "clean room". Also, assume that textual responses with "small room" are classified into "Bad" and textual responses with "clean room" are classified into "Good". In the case of "Good", "clean room" occurs 3 times and "small room" occurs once. Similarly, in the case of "Bad", "clean room" occurs once and "small room" occurs 3 times. Therefore, we can extract "clean room" as an expression relating to "Good" and "small room" as an expression relating to "Bad".

3   Numerical Experiments

3.1   Experimental Method

We used textual responses to a questionnaire collected from guests at a hotel. Each textual response contains comments on the hotel. The comments have three viewpoints: bad aspects of the hotel, good aspects of the hotel, and requests to the hotel. Analysts read each textual response and assigned three viewpoints to each textual response. Thus, some textual responses have multiple viewpoints and other textual responses have a single viewpoint. We collected a total of 1,643 textual responses with viewpoints assigned by analysts not as a single set but as the result of 4 separate attempts. The data sets D1, D2, D3, and D4 corresponding to 4 attempts are related such that D2 $\subseteq$ D3 and D4 = D1 + D3. The frequency of the textual responses in the data set is shown in Table 2. In Table 2, "Yes" indicates the number that includes a viewpoint and "No" indicates the number that does not include a viewpoint.

Table 2. Distribution of comments

	D1		D2		D3		D4	
	Yes	No	Yes	No	Yes	No	Yes	No
Bad	48	59	603	714	693	843	741	902
Good	62	45	707	610	823	713	885	758
Request	51	56	457	860	506	1,030	557	1,086
Total	107		1,317		1,536		1,643	

In order to evaluate the difference in the feature extraction process, we used 9 lexical filters and 5 thresholds of tf-idf values. Each filter extracts the part of speech designated by Table 3. That is, a filter L1 extracts adjectives and a filter L9 extracts all words. Also, the thresholds are changed in the range 0.000 ~ 0.020.

At first, we performed numerical experiments by using D1. We extracted attributes from textual responses included in D1 by using a lexical filter and a threshold. 10-Cross validation experiments were applied to textual responses with attribute values and a single viewpoint. Also, the 10-Cross validation experiments were performed for three viewpoints. Moreover, these numerical experiments were performed for each lexical filter and each threshold. We calculated

Table 3. Lexical filter

Filter	Part of speech	Filter	Part of speech	Filter	Part of speech
L1	adjective	L4	adjective, verb	L7	adjective, verb, noun
L2	verb	L5	adjective, noun	L8	L7, numeral, symbol, alphabet, desinence, interjection, unknown
L3	noun	L6	verb, noun	L9	All parts of speech

the precision ratio defined by Formula (1) for each viewpoint, each filter, and each threshold.

$$\text{precision ratio} = \frac{\text{Number of correctly classified textual responses}}{\text{Number of textual responses}} \qquad (1)$$

Next, we performed numerical experiments by using D2, D3, and D4. We extracted attributes from textual data included in each data set, where we used a lexical filter and a threshold selected by the former experiments. The number of attributes was about 1,400. We also performed 10-Cross validation experiments for each viewpoint and each data set, and calculated precision ratios.

Lastly, we extracted expressions from textual responses in D1. We selected lexical filters and thresholds that corresponded to maximum precision ratios and acquired classification models for each viewpoint. We set 2 as the threshold of the expression extraction process and extracted nouns. We investigated which textual responses included extracted words and classified extracted words into four categories: correct category, wrong category, mixed category, and neutral category. Here, correct category indicates that an extracted word corresponds to its viewpoint, wrong category indicates it does not correspond to its viewpoint, mixed category indicates it corresponds to its viewpoint and also corresponds to other viewpoints, and neutral category indicates it is not related to all viewpoints. We calculated frequency ratios defined by Formula (2) for the correct category, the wrong category, and the mixed category.

$$\text{frequency ratio} = \frac{\text{Number of expressions of each category}}{\text{Number of expressions except the neutral category}} \qquad (2)$$

3.2   Experimental Results

Table 4 shows results for changing lexical filters and thresholds. Each cell shows average precision ratios in three viewpoints. The last row shows average values when using the same threshold and the last column shows average values when using the same lexical filter.

Figure 2 shows results for changing data sets. Solid lines in the figures indicate results for "Bad", "Good", and "Request". A solid heavy line indicates average values for three viewpoints. Here, we used a lexical filter L9 and a threshold 0.005, because the filters and the threshold give a model with a stable precision ratio, as shown in Table 4.

Lastly, Table 5 shows frequency ratios for D1.

Table 4. Precision ratio for thresholds and filters in D1

Filter	Threshold					Average
	0.000	0.005	0.010	0.015	0.020	
L1	0.667	0.667	0.664	0.673	0.660	0.666
L2	0.508	0.508	0.514	0.520	0.539	0.518
L3	0.586	0.586	0.592	0.579	0.583	0.585
L4	0.660	0.660	0.629	0.617	0.648	0.643
L5	0.676	0.676	0.695	0.664	0.695	0.681
L6	0.651	0.651	0.626	0.617	0.611	0.631
L7	0.682	0.682	0.707	0.657	0.664	0.679
L8	0.688	0.688	0.688	0.654	0.667	0.677
L9	0.698	0.698	0.682	0.685	0.667	0.686
Average	0.646	0.646	0.644	0.630	0.637	0.641

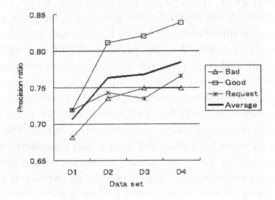

Fig. 2. Precision ratio for data sets

3.3   Discussion

Setting of Viewpoints: In this analysis task, we used three viewpoints. The viewpoints can not always apply to all analysis tasks. However, the viewpoints can apply to analysis of the customer voice in the service field. We have large amounts of data in the field. Therefore, we consider that the viewpoints have a wide range of application tasks.

Influence of Lexical Filters: The textual responses describe the impressions of the guests. Expressions that include adjectives and nouns are important. They lead to the correct viewpoint classification. We believe this is the reason the lexical filters that included adjectives and nouns provided comparatively high precision ratios. On the other hand, the morphological analysis engine sometimes leads to incorrect word segmentation. In particular, the engine tends to fail in the case of word segmentation for text that includes new words and proper nouns. This causes the engine to identify the words as unknown words, or to segment

Table 5. Frequency ratio of expressions

	Bad	Good	Request
Correct	0.887	0.512	0.800
Wrong	0.065	0.198	0.086
Mixed	0.048	0.291	0.114

the words at wrong positions and assign wrong parts of speech to the words. The L9 lexical filter is able to deal with new words and proper nouns because the filter extracts all parts of speech. Therefore, the L9 filter gives the highest precision ratio. However, the filter causes an increase in attributes. The L5 or L7 filters should be used, if calculation speed and memory size are important considerations. This is the reason the numbers of their attributes are comparatively small and their average precision ratios are almost equal to the L9 filter.

Influence of the Thresholds: The number of attributes increases as the threshold of the feature extraction process becomes low. When an inductive learning method uses large amounts of attributes, the method tends to acquire a classification model which excessively depends on training examples. It is necessary to select an appropriate threshold. However, in these textual responses, the difference in the thresholds does not lead to a big difference in precision ratios. The thresholds are not relatively sensitive. We believe the reason behind this result is the low number of irrelevant words, because each textual response deals with limited topics and is described in a comparatively short sentence.

Influence of Increase in Textual Responses: The precision ratio becomes higher as the number of textual responses increases. The case of D4 is about 8% higher than the case of D1. We believe this is why a more appropriate classification model is acquired by using many textual responses. On the other hand, the precision curves do not always converge. If more training examples are used, the proposed method may give a higher precision ratio.

Validation of Extracted Expressions: In the case of "Bad" and "Request", frequency ratios of "Correct" are comparatively high and the proposed method extracts valid expressions. On the other hand, in the case of "Good", the frequency ratio of "Correct" is low. We believe this is the reason many "Good" textual responses are accompanied by topics of other classes. That is, the classification model for "Good" tends to classify a textual response as "Good". If some guests assign topics to "Good" and other guests assign the topics to "Bad" or "Request", the expressions corresponding to the topics tend to acquire the maximum frequency in the case of "Good". Therefore, the frequency ratio of "Mixed" becomes high and the frequency ratio of "Correct" becomes low in the case of "Good". In the future, it will be necessary to devise a method that identifies topics with multiple viewpoints.

According to the above discussion, we believe that the proposed method is able to classify textual responses to questionnaires and extract valid expressions to some extent. The method therefore makes it possible for analysts to easily acquire new knowledge from textual responses.

4   Summary and Future Work

This paper proposes a new analysis method in order to analyze textual responses to questionnaires. The method was applied to questionnaire data collected from guests at a hotel. We show that precision ratios based on classification models were improved by an increase in training examples. We also show that the method extracted valid expressions of textual responses. We believe the method is efficient for analyzing textual responses to questionnaires.

In the future, we hope to develop a method that extracts more characteristic expressions. In this paper, we adopted a simple method based on frequency, but the method extracts many words included in the neutral category. The frequency of words included in the neutral category must be reduced. We also hope to develop a system in which the method is applied via a graphical user interface, and will also attempt to apply the method to other types of questionnaire data.

References

1. A. Cardoso-Cachopo and A. L. Oliveira, "An Empirical Comparison of Text Categorization Methods," Proceedings of the 10th International Symposium on String Processing and Information Retrieval, 183-196, 2003.
2. R. Feldman and H. Hirsh, "Mining Text using Keyword Distributions," Journal of Intelligent Information Systems, 10:281-300, 1998.
3. Marti A. Hearst, M. A. Hearst, "Untangling Text Data Mining," Proceedings of the 37th Annual Meeting of the Association for Computational Linguistics, 1999.
4. C. -W. Hsu, C. -C. Chang, and C. -J. Lin, "A Practical Guide to Support Vector Classification," http://www.csie.ntu.edu.tw/~ cjlin/libsvm/.
5. Y. Ichimura, Y. Nakayama, M. Miyoshi, T. Akahane, T. Sekiguchi, and Y. Fujiwara, "Text Mining System for Analysis of a Salesperson's Daily Reports," Proceedings of Pacific Association for Computational Linguistics 2001, 127-135, 2001.
6. A. Ittycheriah, M. Franz, W. -J. Zhu, and A. Ratnaparkhi, "IBM's Statistical Question Answering System," Proceedings of the 8th Text Retrieval Conference, 2000.
7. L. M. Manevitz and M. Yousef, "One-Class SVMs for Document Classification," Journal of Machine Learning Research, 2:139-154, 2001.
8. S. Sakurai, Y. Ichimura, A. Suyama, and R. Orihara, "Acquisition of a Knowledge Dictionary for a Text Mining System using an Inductive Learning Method," IJCAI 2001 Workshop on Text Learning: Beyond Supervision, 45-52, 2001.
9. P. -N. Tan, H. Blau, S. Harp, and R. Goldman, "Textual Data Mining of Service Center Call Records," Proceedings of the 6th International Conference on Knowledge Discovery and Data Mining, 417-423, 2000.
10. S. Tellex, B. Katz, J. Lin, and A. Fernandes, "Quantitative Evaluation of Passage Retrieval Algorithms for Question Answering," Proceedings of the 26th Annual Conference ACM SIGIR Conference on Research and Development in Information Retrieval, 2003.

SARM — Succinct Association Rule Mining: An Approach to Enhance Association Mining*

Jitender Deogun and Liying Jiang

Department of Computer Science and Engineering,
University of Nebraska - Lincoln, Lincoln, NE, 68588-0115, USA
{deogun, ljiang}@cse.unl.edu

Abstract. The performance of association rule mining in terms of computation time and number of redundant rules generated deteriorates as the size of database increases and/or support threshold used is smaller. In this paper, we present a new approach called *SARM — succinct association rule mining*, to enhance the association mining. Our approach is based on our understanding of the mining process that items become less useful as mining proceeds, and that such items can be eliminated to accelerate the mining and to reduce the number of redundant rules generated. We propose a new paradigm that an item becomes less useful when the most interesting rules involving the item have been discovered and deleting it from the mining process will not result in any significant loss of information. SARM generates a compact set of rules called *succinct association rule* (SAR) set that is largely free of redundant rules. SARM is efficient in association mining, especially when support threshold used is small. Experiments are conducted on both synthetic and real-life databases. SARM approach is especially suitable for applications where rules with small support may be of significant interest. We show that for such applications SAR set can be mined efficiently.

1 Introduction

Association rule mining is one of the most important data mining techniques. Association rules are of the form $X \Rightarrow Y$, where X is the *antecedent*, and Y the *consequent* of the rule. *Support* of $X \Rightarrow Y$ indicates the percentage of transactions in dataset that contain both X and Y. *Confidence* of $X \Rightarrow Y$ denotes the probability of a transaction containing Y given that it contains X. Association rule mining is to find rules that have support and confidence greater than user-specified *minimum support* (s_{min}) and *confidence* (c_{min}) threshold values.

Apriori algorithm [4] is the well known standard method for association mining, and most of the later algorithms follow the framework of Apriori. Real world studies, however, show that association rule mining is still faced with the

---

* This research was supported in part by NSF Grant No. EIA-0091530, USDA RMA Grant NO. 02IE08310228, and NSF EPSCOR, Grant No. EPS-0346476.

M.-S. Hacid et al. (Eds.): ISMIS 2005, LNAI 3488, pp. 121–130, 2005.
© Springer-Verlag Berlin Heidelberg 2005

problems of time-inefficiency, especially for applications on large databases when minimum support threshold used is small [8]. While in many cases, small s_{min} is desirable, and it is important to improve the mining efficiency when s_{min} used is small. Another problem in association mining is that often too many rules are generated, many of which are redundant [6]. In this paper, to solve the problem of time inefficiency and rule redundancy in association mining, we propose approach called *SARM— succinct association rule mining*. The SARM approach generates a set of *succinct association rules* (SAR) that contains most of the interesting and useful rules and can be mined efficiently.

A key factor that causes the inefficiency and redundancy in association rule mining is the large amount of items in a database. It maybe noted that the mining complexity is exponentially proportional to the dimension of the database [7]. We claim that some items might lose their usefulness from the point of view of information as the mining proceeds. That is, at a certain point in the mining process, if there are interesting rules involving the item that have not been discovered yet, then the item is useful and important to the mining process at this point. Therefore, an item loses its usefulness or importance as the mining progresses and the interesting rules involving it are discovered. We define the SARM paradigm as follows: *if the most interesting rules involving an item have been discovered, then such item becomes less useful, and deleting it from the mining accelerates the mining and reduces the number of redundant rules generated as well.* Finding the point at which most of the interesting rules involving the item have been discovered during the mining process is based the model of *maximal potentially useful* (MaxPUF) association rules [2], which are a set of rules that are most informational and interesting. If the MaxPUF rules of an item have been mined, we show that such an item becomes less useful and deleting it from the mining process will not result in any significant loss of information.

2   Related Work

The SARM approach is based on the *maximal potentially useful* (MaxPUF) pattern model. We give a brief review for background knowledge of our work in [2, 3]. To facilitate interesting pattern discovery, we develop a logic model of data mining that integrates *formal concept analysis* (FCA) [5] and *probability logic* [1] in [3]. Probability logic extends first-order logic with probability expression capability. It defines a language that includes predicate symbols, object variables, statistical probability operation "[ ]". Predicate symbols represent conjunctions of attributes, and Object variables define the domain of a set of objects of interest. Operation "[ ]" computes the probability of a proposition represented by predicate symbols over a set of objects.

Definition 1. *Concept. If P is a predicate symbol and x an object variable, P_x is a concept, or simply denoted as P if the domain is clear from the context. If $P_1,...,P_j$ are concepts of the same domain, $P = P_1... \wedge P_j$ is a concept.*

If $P = \bigwedge_{i=1}^{n} P_i$, we say P is a *superconcept* of P_i and P_i is a *subconcept* of P, $1 \leq i \leq n$. The set of all concepts for given context form a lattice under superconcept/subconcept relation [2,5]. Moreover, we define all superconcepts and subconcepts of a concept Q as the *relative concepts* of Q.

Definition 2. Elementary and Conditional Pattern. *If P is a concept, then $[P] = r$ $(0 \leq r \leq 1)$ is an elementary pattern. If P, Q are concepts and $P \neq \emptyset$, then $[Q|P] = r$ is a conditional pattern. Q is called conSequent Concept (SC), and P conDition Concept (DC) of the pattern. Probability r is called confidence of the pattern, and $r = \frac{[QP]}{[P]}$. A pattern is an elementary or a conditional pattern.*

We can logically formulate an association rule as a conditional pattern. *DC* of the conditional pattern represents the *antecedent* of the rule and *SC* represents the *consequent* of the rule. *Probability* of the pattern denotes the *confidence* of the rule. *Support* of the antecedent, the consequent and the rule is equal to the *probability* of the corresponding elementary patterns. For example, if we have an rule $A \Rightarrow B$ with confidence c and support s, then the corresponding conditional pattern is $[B|A] = c$, and $sup(A) = [A]$, $sup(B) = [B]$, $s = sup(AB) = [AB]$.

Definition 3. MaxPUF patterns and Valid DC. *Let c_{min} be the user-defined minimum confidence threshold, a pattern $[B|A] = r$, if $r \geq c_{min}$, and there is no patterns in the form of $[B|A'] = r'$ where $r' \geq c_{min}$ and $A' \subset A$, then $[B|A] = r$ is a MaxPUF pattern of consequent concept B, and A is called a valid DC of B.*

The interestingness of a pattern is tightly related to the confidence of the pattern. No doubt, high confidence patterns are interesting. However, MaxPUF patterns are the most informational and potentially useful patterns among all the high confidence patterns. Among all high-confidence patterns of a certain *SC*, MaxPUF patterns are the patterns *DC* of which has smallest number of items. The *DC*s of a MaxPUF pattern is the point of articulation in the concept lattice [2]. Below this point, no high-confidence pattern can be constructed with the *relative concepts* of the *Valid DC*. A *Valid DC* is the most informational condition concept, because it is the minimal condition concept such that the *SC* occurs at high enough frequency. A further narrower condition concept (*DC*), is not as interesting as *Valid DC*, because the additional items are very likely minor condition factors or trivial factors. In this sense, *Valid DC* can be seen as the set of main conditional factors to assure the occurrence of the consequent concept. As a *Valid DC* is the most informational concept among all of its relative concepts, we state that a MaxPUF pattern is most informational pattern among all the patterns of a consequent concept (*SC*).

3   SARM — Succinct Association Rule Mining

In association mining, an attempt to obtain more complete information results in much higher cost in terms of computation time and in addition a larger number of redundant rules generated. To strike a balance between these two extremes, we do not mine the entire set of useful rules, rather, we want to efficiently discover a subset of rules that contains most of the informational rules while only as small number of redundant rules as possible are generated.

As the mining process is to first generate candidate frequent itemsets and then validate the candidates, to accelerate the procedure, our thought process is to reduce the number of candidates that are not useful. The number of candidates is largely determined by the number of total items in the dataset. For example, if one more items is added to the dataset, at each pass, the number of candidates is at least doubled. In this sense, if we can efficiently reduce the number of items, we can greatly reduce the number of candidates generated and the related computation of support. Therefore, to accelerate the rule mining, we consider how to effectively reduce the number of unimportant items in the mining process. The importance of an item is related to the notion of redundant rules.

Assertion. Rules of the following types are redundant: *1) rules with low confidence; 2) rules that is not MaxPUF rule and has consequent identical to a MaxPUF rule; 3) the rules information of which can be deducted or implied from the rules already generated.*

At the beginning of association mining, all the items are important. However, as mining progresses, some items become less important or less informational, because useful rules involving these items have already been discovered. Thus we could delete such items from the mining process and not consider them in further computations. Now the problem is which are these items?

Assume after generating frequent k-itemsets in the mining, instead of continuing to generate $(k+1)$-itemsets, we first generate high-confidence patterns using k-itemsets. Suppose that we discover a pattern $[B|A] = r$, where $r \geq c_e > c_{min}$. Here c_e is a user-defined parameter that we call *elimination confidence threshold*. c_e is a relatively high value, we usually define c_e higher than 0.7. What will happen if we delete itemset B from the dataset? There are six types of patterns that will be affected by the deletion of itemset B, which are 1)$[B|AX] = r$, 2)$[BY|AX] = r$, 3) $[Y|BA] = r$, 4) $[B|Y] = r$, 5) $[Y|B] = r$, 6) $[BY|A] = r$, where A, X and Y represent arbitrary itemsets.

Discussion on Missing Patterns. First of all, if these patterns have confidence lower than c_{min}, then they are redundant and thus these patterns should not be mined. So in the following discussions, we assume that these patterns, if mined, will have confidence higher than c_{min}.

Case 1. For patterns of the form $[B|AX]$, we argue they are not as useful as pattern $[B|A]$ because $[B|A]$ is the MaxPUF pattern of consequent concept B. Based on the Assertion in Section 3.1, pattern $[B|AX]$ is redundant compared to the MaxPUF pattern $[B|A]$. It is desirable that such patterns are not mined.

Case 2. After B is deleted, no patterns of the form $[Y|BA]$ will be discovered. We argue that if we could discover the pattern $[Y|A]$, then $[Y|A]$ is the MaxPUF pattern of $[Y|BA]$ and thus $[Y|BA]$ is redundant in presence of $[Y|A]$.

Lemma 1. Assume a pattern $[B|A] \geq c_e$ and $[Y|BA] \geq c_{min}$, then $[Y|A] \geq c_{min} * c_e$, and $[[Y|A] \geq c_{min}] \geq \frac{1-c_{min}}{1-c_{min} \cdot c_e}$, that is, the probability that $[Y|A] \geq c_{min}$ is greater than $\frac{1-c_{min}}{1-c_{min} \cdot c_e}$.

Proof: *Since* $[B|A] = \frac{supp(AB)}{supp(A)} = c \Rightarrow supp(AB) = supp(A) \cdot r$, *and* $[Y|AB] = \frac{supp(YAB)}{supp(AB)} = \frac{supp(YAB)}{supp(A) \cdot r} \geq c_{min} \Rightarrow \frac{supp(YAB)}{supp(A)} \geq r \cdot c_{min}$, *then* $[Y|A] = \frac{supp(YA)}{supp(A)} \geq \frac{supp(YAB)}{supp(A)} \geq r \cdot c_{min} \geq c_e \cdot c_{min}$. *As* $[c_{min} \cdot c_e \geq c_{min}] \geq \frac{1-c_{min}}{1-c_{min} \cdot c_e}$, therefore, $[[Y|A] \geq c_{min}] \geq \frac{1-c_{min}}{1-c_{min} \cdot c_e}$. ∎

Case 3. $[BY|AX]$ implies two pieces of information: $[B|AX]$ and $[Y|AX]$. The mining of $[Y|AX]$ is not affected by deletion of B. $[B|AX]$ is less useful compared to its MaxPUF pattern $[B|A]$. Because we use high c_e value, $[B|A]$ suggest that A may always imply B, then AX also imply B. Therefore, $[B|AX]$ and $[Y|AX]$ together imply the information of $[BY|AX]$ and make $[BY|AX]$ redundant.

Case 4. The discovery of $[B|Y]$ can be formulated as discovering the MaxPUF patterns, SC of which is B. If B is an interesting consequent concept (SC), we can start a special process to find all of its MaxPUF patterns.

Case 5. For patterns $[Y|B]$, there are two cases. First if Y is a 1-itemset, the mining $[Y|B]$ is not affected by deletion of B. On the other hand, if $Y = \{y_1, y_2, ..., y_k\}$ $(k > 1)$ and $[Y|B] \geq c_{min}$, it is easy to see that $[y_i|B] \geq c_{min}$ $(1 \leq i \leq k)$. As y_i is 1-itemset, mining of $[y_i|B]$ is not affected by the deletion of B. Then we only need a complementary process to discover patterns with k-itemset SC $(k > 1)$ from the patterns that have 1-itemset SC and an identical DC, which is B in this case. We introduce this process in Section 4.

Case 6. Similar strategy in Case 5 is used for patterns of the form $[BY|A]$. That is, can we discover this pattern based on $[B|A]$ and $[Y|A]$, which are patterns with 1-itemset SC and an identical DC, which is A in this case.

Succinct Association Rule Set. From the above discussions, we can see if we delete the SCs of high-confidence patterns during the mining process, we are still able to discover most of the useful patterns/rules. As it is not necessary to discover all the rules, which results in many redundant ones, we propose SARM, a novel approach for improving the efficiency of association mining and at the same time discovering most of the useful rules. In general, SARM approach is a mining process involves dynamic elimination of items during the mining process. That is, after discovering the frequent k-itemsets, if we can construct a pattern $[B|A] \geq c_e$ from a k-itemsets, we prohibit the SC of the pattern, which is B in this case, from generating candidate $(k+1)$-itemsets. SARM generates a set of association rules we call *succinct association rule* (SAR) set. As association rules can be represented as patterns, the formal definition of SAR set is given as follows using the format of patterns.

Definition 4. Succinct Pattern Set. *Let* $I = \{i_1, i_2, ..., i_m\}$ *represent the set of items in a database,* c_{min} *and* c_e *respectively be minimum and elimination confi-*

dence thresholds. Succinct pattern set is a set of patterns of the form $[X|Y] = r$ where $0 \leq< c_{min} \leq r \leq 1$, and meet the condition that in the set, if there is a rule of the form $[B|A] \geq c_e$, then there is no rule of the form $[B_1|A_1] = r_1$ such that $B \subseteq B_1 \cup A_1$ and $|A| + |B| > |A_1| + |B_1|$.

Lemma 2. *1-itemset deletion property.* In SARM, if pattern $[B|A] = r$ is generated from a k-itemset and $r \geq c_e$, then B is a 1-itemset and A is a $(k-1)$-itemset.

This Lemma can be proven by contradiction. Assume k-itemsets are generate in the kth pass. If there is a pattern $[B|A] \geq c_e$, where $B = \{b_1, ..., b_m\}$ ($k > m > 1$), then in the $(k - m + 1)^{th}$ pass, we must have discovered the pattern $[b_1|A] \geq c_e$, which results in the deletion of item b_1. And similar case is for other b_i. As b_i has been deleted before $k^t h$ pass, the pattern $[B|A]$ will not exist. It is a contradiction.

Some patterns of the form $[BY|A]$ and $[Y|B]$ are not included in the SAR set, to prevent information loss, SARM includes a special complementary process to discover such patterns whenever deemed necessary. SARM approach explores only the most informational patterns. In SARM, after an item has been explored with adequate information, it is eliminated and does not take part in any future mining process. The deletion of some items will greatly reduce the number of candidate patterns, and at the same time, it is safe from loss of information. SARM is a good model for the objective to accelerate association rule mining and have an overview of the most useful patterns. The SAR set may not contain some special patterns, but it retains most of the informational association rules and is largely free of redundant rules.

4   The SARM Algorithm

The SARM approach has two parts, the main part, mining the SAR set, and the other is a complementary process to mine patterns not included in SAR set.

Mining the SAR Set. SARM algorithm combines itemset discovery and rule mining, and use rule mining results to help eliminate less important item, which is shown in Figure 1. SARM algorithm commits several passes to discover frequent itemsets from 1-itemsets to l-itemsets. Each pass includes three main steps. The first step is to generate candidate k-itemsets (CS_k) and check the support of them to find the set of frequent k-itemsets (FS_k). This is similar to Apriori. But different from Apriori, before continue to generate candidate $(k+1)$-itemsets, in the second step, we use the discovered frequent k-itemsets to build up association rules. If a rule has confidence higher than c_e, we delete the consequent item, i.e., we prune the FS_k to generate FSC_k, so that none of itemsets in FSC_k includes the eliminated items. In general, FSC_k is the set of FS_k except those itemsets that include the items in EC. In the third step, use FSC_k to generate candidate frequent $(k + 1)$-itemsets (CS_{k+1}). The process is repeated until no candidate itemsets can be generated.

Algorithm: $SARM$ $(\mathcal{D}, I, s_{min}, c_{min}, c_e)$
Input: 1)Database $\mathcal{D}$, 2)s_{min}, 3)c_{min} and 4)elimination confidence (c_e).
Output: SAR set satisfying s_{min}, c_{min}, and c_e.
1)Discover all frequent 1-itemsets, store into FS_1;
2)$FSC_1 = FS_1$; $k = 2$;
3)$CS_2 = \{c \mid c = f1 \cap f2, |c| = 2, \forall f1, f2 \in FSC_1\}$;
4)FS_2=Gen-FS(CS_2);
5)EC=Gen-rule(FS_2);
6)$FSC_2 = FS_2 - \{f \mid f \in FS_2, f \cap EC \neq \emptyset\}$;
7)while $(FSC_k \neq \emptyset)$
8) $k++$;
9) $CS_k = \{c \mid c = f1 \cap f2, |c| = k, \forall f1, f2 \in FSC_{k-1}\}$;
10) FS_k=Gen-FS(CS_k);
11) EC=Gen-rule(FS_k);
12) $FSC_k = FS_k - \{f \mid f \in FS_k, f \cap EC \neq \emptyset\}$;
13)end while

Fig. 1. SARM: Succinct Association Rules Mining Algorithm

The Complementary Process. The complementary process is to generate patterns with k-itemset SC $(k > 1)$ from the patterns with 1-itemset SC and an identical DC.

Lemma 3. It is possible that pattern $[X_1 X_2 ... X_i | A] \geq c_{min}$ only if for $\forall X_j$, $[X_j | A] \geq c_{min}, 1 \leq j \leq i$.

Based on Lemma 4, to the discover the patterns SC of which is a k-itemset $(k \geq 2)$, it depends on the patterns SC of which is 1-itemset. The idea is, check the discovered patterns, only if two or more 1-itemset SCs have a common DC, we can construct a candidate pattern, DC of which is the common DC and SC is a combination of the 1-itemset SCs. For example, assume there are two discovered patterns $[1|3]$ and $[2|3]$, where the common $DC=(3)$, then $[1,2|3]$ should be a candidate pattern because it is possible $[1,2|3] \geq c_{min}$.

5   Experiments and Analysis

The experiments are designed to test the efficiency of the proposed algorithm for mining SAR set, compare the SAR set with the set of rules discovered by Apriori-like algorithms and evaluate the set of SAR. Comprehensive performance studies are conducted on both synthetic and real-life datasets. The programs are coded in C++, and experiments are conducted on a 950 MHz Intel Pentium-3 PC with 512 MB main memory.

Figure 2 and 3 show the experimental results on the synthetic database. For T40 databases, SARM is 5 to 20 times faster. The improvement increases almost exponentially as s_{min} decreases. This demonstrates that SARM model is efficient and suitable for applications requiring small s_{min}. The decrease of running time is due to reduction in the number of candidates generated in SARM

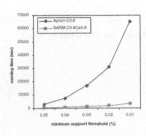
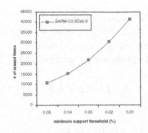
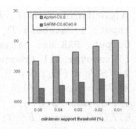

Fig. 2. Varying Support for Database T40I10D200K

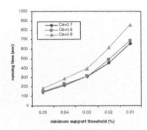
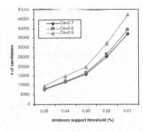
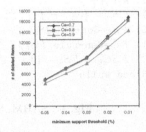

Fig. 3. Performance Study for Different c_e Value on Database T25I6D100K

and correspondingly less supporting computations are needed as some items are deleted during the mining process. Following Lemma 1, it is noted that a huge enough value for c_e must be chosen so that patterns of the form $[Y|A] \geq c_{min}$ can be effectively discovered. In the experiments, we choose $c_e = 0.9, 0.8, 0.7$, and $c_{min} = 0.6$, then based on Lemma 1, it is estimated that $[[Y|A] \geq c_{min}]$ is respectively greater than $82\%, 77\%, 69\%$. From Figure 3, we see that as c_e decreases, the execution time decreases, so do the number of candidates and rules generated (see Figure 3). These are natural results since smaller c_e will result in more items satisfying the elimination threshold earlier and thus being deleted earlier, and then smaller number of candidates and rules are generated. The SAR set is much smaller than general association rule set, for T25 data, the number of rules in SAR set is 25 times smaller than that of Apriori rules on average, and 70 to 190 times smaller for T40 data.

Experiments on Real-life Databases. We further evaluate the SAR set that is generated from the real-life databases. The data is collected from the weather station at Clay Center, Nebraska. We intend to discover rules that demonstrate the relations between weather events and environmental indices. We use quality metrics *Precision* and *Recall* to evaluate the rule set. Precision is defined as the percentage of interesting rules discovered among all the rules discovered by an algorithm, and recall is defined as the percentage of rules discovered by an algorithm to the number of rules that exist in the given datasets. Based on the definitions, the *recall* of the conventional rule set discovered by Apriori algorithm can be deemed as 100% because we can assume that all the rules that exist in the database are the rules discovered by Apriori. Table 1 shows the comparison

Table 1. SAR Set Evaluation

$c_{min} = 0.8$	# Rules	Recall(%)	Precision(%)
Apriori	2423	100	4.95
SAR($c_e = 0.95$)	595	91.67	20.79
SAR($c_e = 0.9$)	303	76.67	30.36
SAR($c_e = 0.8$)	157	66.67	50.96

of general rule set and SAR set with respect to the recall and precision. The precision of the SAR set is five to eleven times higher than general rule set generated by Apriori with different c_e value used. This demonstrates that SAR set is largely free of redundant rules. The recall of the SAR set is reasonably high, which shows that SAR set can discover most of the useful association rules. We also notice that the length of the longest rules in SAR set is generally half of that in general rule set. That is, SARM tends to discover short useful patterns. This fact complies with the principle of MaxPUF association rules that we believe if shorter condition can predict a consequent, then the rules with longer condition to predict the same consequent are redundant.

6   Conclusions

In this paper, we investigate the issues affecting the efficiency of association mining in terms of computation time and the number of redundant rules generated, especially when a smaller s_{min} is used in context of large databases. We show that items become less informational and thus less important as the mining proceeds. Thus, dynamically deleting such items during the mining process not only improves the mining efficiency but also effectively prevents the generation of a large number of trivial or redundant rules. Based on our hypothesis, we propose a new model called SARM, which generates a compact rule set called SAR set. We develop an algorithm to discover the SAR set, which combines the discovery of frequent itemsets and generation of rules, in a way to accelerate the mining process. The experimental results on synthetic databases show that SARM is 5 to 20 times faster than Apriori algorithm as s_{min} decreases. We evaluate the SAR set generated from real-life databases, and show that SAR set retains most of the useful rules and is largely free of redundant rules, the precision increases five to eleven times as compared to rules generated by Apriori, and at the same time, the recall value remains high. We believe that SARM is an efficient and useful model for generating most informational patterns in large databases.

References

1. F. Bacchus. *Representing and Reasoning With Probabilistic Knowledge*. MIT, 1990.
2. J. Deogun, L. Jiang, and V. Raghavan. Discovering maximal potentially useful association rules based on probability logics. In *Proc. of Rough Sets and Current Trends in Computing, 4th International Conf.*, 2004.

3. J. Deogun, L. Jiang, Y. Xie, and V. Raghavan. Probability logic modeling of knowledge discovery in databases. In *Proc. of Foundations of Intelligent Systems, 14th International Symposium (ISMIS)*, 2003.
4. R. Agrawal etc. Mining association rules between sets of items in large databases. In *Proc. of ACM SIGMOD Intern. Conf. on Management of Data*, 1993.
5. B. Ganter and R. Wille. *Formal Concept Analsis: Mathematical Foundations*. Springer-Verlag, Berlin, 1999.
6. M. Kryszkiewicz. Closed set based discovery of representative association rules. In *Advances in Intelligent Data Analysis, 4th International Conf.*, 2001.
7. S. Orlando and etc. A scalable multi-strategy algorithm for counting frequent sets. In *Proc. of the 5th Intern. Workshop on High Performance Data Mining*, 2002.
8. Zijian Zheng, Ron Kohavi, and Llew Mason. Real world performance of association rule algorithms. In *Proc. of the 7th ACM SIGKDD International Conf. on Knowledge Discovery and Data Mining*, 2001.

Learning the Daily Model of Network Traffic

Costantina Caruso, Donato Malerba, and Davide Papagni

Dipartimento di Informatica, Università degli Studi di Bari,
Via E. Orabona 4 - 70126 Bari - Italy
{caruso, malerba}@di.uniba.it, davidepapagni@libero.it

Abstract. Anomaly detection is based on profiles that represent normal behaviour of users, hosts or networks and detects attacks as significant deviations from these profiles. In the paper we propose a methodology based on the application of several data mining methods for the construction of the "normal" model of the ingoing traffic of a department-level network. The methodology returns a daily model of the network traffic as a result of four main steps: first, daily network connections are reconstructed from TCP/IP packet headers passing through the firewall and represented by means of feature vectors; second, network connections are grouped by applying a clustering method; third, clusters are described as sets of rules generated by a supervised inductive learning algorithm; fourth, rules are transformed into symbolic objects and similarities between symbolic objects are computed for each couple of days. The result is a longitudinal model of the similarity of network connections that can be used by a network administrator to identify deviations in network traffic patterns that may demand for his/her attention. The proposed methodology has been tested on log files of the firewall of our University Department.

Keywords: Anomaly detection, daily model, data mining, machine learning, symbolic data analysis, network traffic analysis.

1 Introduction and Related Work

Intrusion detection is the process [1] of monitoring the events occurring in a computer system or network and analysing them for signs of intrusions, defined as the attempts to bypass the security mechanisms of a computer or a network.

The two analysis strategies are *misuse detection* and *anomaly detection*. While the former is based on extensive knowledge, provided by human experts, of patterns associated with known attacks, the latter is based on profiles that represent normal behaviour of users, hosts or networks and detects attacks as significant deviations from these profiles. The misuse detection strategy is based on matching the input streams to a signatures database, so as it can detect only known attacks and its effectiveness strongly depends on how frequently the database is updated. On the contrary, anomaly detection is potentially able to recognize new types of attacks, but it requires to define first what can be considered a *normal* behaviour for the observed entity (which can be a computer system, a particular user, etc.), and thereafter to decide how to label a specific activity as abnormal [2].

M.-S. Hacid et al. (Eds.): ISMIS 2005, LNAI 3488, pp. 131–141, 2005.
© Springer-Verlag Berlin Heidelberg 2005

To overcome difficulties met in manually defining a model of normality for anomaly detection, it has been proposed to apply data mining and machine learning methods to clean data [3] [4], that is, data certainly containing no anomalies. However, this approach presents at least two issues. Firstly, clean data are difficult to obtain because, if we use real data, it is very hard to guarantee that there are no attacks in them, while simulated data represent only a limited view of the behaviour of a real system (computer or network) and the model trained over them will be difficult to update. Secondly, it is difficult to make anomaly detection systems adaptive because they cannot be trained in real-time given that they require clean data.

In the literature, various methods have been proposed for constructing normal models from *simulated* data, either clean (i.e. normal) or anomalous. In [5] a normal sequences model is built by means of look ahead pairs and contiguous sequences. Lee & Stolfo [6] build a prediction model for anomalies by training decision trees over normal data, while Ghosh & Schwartzbard [7] use a neural network to obtain the model. In [8] unlabeled data for anomaly detection are analyzed by looking at user profiles and by comparing an intrusive activity vs. a normal activity. A survey of techniques used for anomaly detection is given in [9].

When dealing with large volumes of network or system data collected in real-time, it is impracticable to apply supervised learning methods, which require a pre-classification of activities as normal or anomalous. This justifies the interest for some unsupervised learning techniques and, more in general, for descriptive data mining methods, whose aim is that of finding the intrinsic structures, relations, or affinities in data but no classes or labels are assigned a priori.

In this paper we propose a methodology for the construction of a daily model of the network traffic, that starts with the application of a clustering (unsupervised) method to feature vectors representing daily network connections reconstructed from TCP/IP packet headers passing through a firewall. Clusters are then described as sets of rules generated by a supervised inductive learning algorithm. The last steps of the proposed methodology consist of the transformation of rules into symbolic objects and in the subsequent computation of similarities between symbolic objects for each couple of days. The result is a longitudinal model of the similarity of network connections that can be used by a network administrator to identify deviations in network traffic patterns that may demand for his/her attention.

The paper is organized as follows. In the next section the collection and preprocessing of real log files of a firewall is illustrated, while in Section 3 the generation of descriptions, expressed as sets of rules, for daily network connections is explained. The transformation of rules into symbolic objects and the formulation of the dissimilarity measure used in our analysis are both described in Section 4. A discussion on discovered longitudinal models for the traffic of our departmental network concludes the paper.

2   Data Collection and Preprocessing

The source data set is formed by four successive weeks of firewall logs of our Department, from May 31st to June 27th, 2004. A transaction is a single logged packet, each of which is described by the following attributes: counter (integer), date, time, protocol (tcp/udp/icmp), direction (inbound/outbound), action (accept, drop, rejected, refused), source IP, destination IP, service port, source port, length, rule, diagnostic message, sys_message and others. Files have been cleaned from our service traffic generated by internal servers or internal broadcast. No missing or incorrect values have been observed in extracted data.

The target dataset is built by reconstructing the entire connections from single packets. In our analysis we have used only accepted ingoing connections and we have a file for every day that contains all the connections opened and closed in that day. There are very few connections between two days that have been discarded. Since the goal is to create the daily description of our connections, we have chosen to work with few but fundamental attributes, namely:

a. *StartHalfHour* (integer): The original time field of a packet has the format hh:mm:ss. We have chosen to map this value to the range [0, 47] by dividing a day into 48 intervals, each of half an hour: a connection belongs to the time interval it starts in.
b. *Protocol* (nominal): udp, tcp; few icmp values have been dropped when generating training data.
c. *DestinationIP* (integer): this field, which is composed of four bytes, can only have the value of our network addresses, so we have considered only the last byte (values 0..255).
d. *SourceIP* (nominal): this field has a very high cardinality because it represents the entire IPv4 space.
e. *ServicePort* (nominal): the requested service (http, ftp, smtp and many other ports).
f. *NumPackets* (integer): the number of connection packets.
g. *Length* (integer): the time length of the connection.
h. *NationCode* (nominal): the two digit code of the nation the source IP belongs to.
i. *NationTimeZone* (integer): the time zone of the nation the source IP belongs to, expressed as difference from GMT value; in some cases this is a mean value (e.g. for Russia or USA).

The features set above describes quite precisely a connection, however the high cardinality of *SourceIP*, if treated as nominal feature, may cause some problems in subsequent data mining steps. In a set of preliminary experiments performed on the first week of available data, we tested the importance of *SourceIP* when the source of a connection is also described by two redundant, but less precise, features such as *NationCode* or *NationTimeZone*. We observed that *SourceIP* behaves as a *masking variable* [10] and adds a bit of noise to clustering, therefore we decided to drop it in subsequent experiments. At the end of the pre-processing step, two different feature sets have been considered, one including only *NationCode* and the other including only *NationTimeZone*.

3   Describing Daily Network Connections

Clustering. Clustering is a global model of discovery and summarization used as a basis for more precise models [11] and it widely employed in different sciences. In this work two different clustering algorithms, namely K-means and EM, have been considered, so that a comparison of possibly different results is possible [10].

K-means is very simple and reasonably efficient. It distributes instances between clusters deterministically by trying to minimize the distance (in our case the Euclidean one) between an instance and its cluster's centroid. The EM (expectation-maximization) algorithm distributes instances probabilistically. It tries to maximize likelihood looking for the most feasible parameters' values, in particular, the number of clusters. Both K-means and EM are implemented in the data mining package Weka [12] which we used in our experiments.

One of the most important problems in a clustering task is to determine the optimal number k of clusters. The parameter k has been determined by applying a cross-validation procedure on clustering results generated by the EM algorithm. More precisely, data are randomly divided in 10 subsets containing almost the same number of instances, and EM is run on every subset; k is initially set to 1 and incremented by 1 if the log-likelihood averaged over the ten runs increases.

For a fair comparison of the two clustering methods, EM is executed first, keeping the results for the best k obtained by cross-validation, and then K-means is tested for the same k value of EM.

Classification Rules. Both clustering techniques presented above have the disadvantage that they do not provide intensional descriptions of the clusters obtained. Intensional descriptions are essential in our context, since they provide the network administrator with human-interpretable patterns of network traffic. To overcome this limitation, several conceptual clustering techniques have been proposed in the literature [13], [14]. However, conceptual clustering methods are known to be rather slow. Therefore, we adopt a two-stepped approach. First, we apply a non-conceptual clustering algorithm, either EM or k-means, in order to decrease the size of the problem. Then we generate a set of rules whose consequents represent the cluster membership, that is, rules discriminate the resulting clusters.

The rules, which provide an intensional description of clusters, are generated by means of the algorithm PART [15]. PART combines two rule learning paradigms, namely divide-and-conquer and separate-and-conquer, and is characterized by high efficiency. It adopts the separate-and-conquer strategy in that it builds a rule, removes the instances it covers, and continues creating rules recursively for the remaining instances until none are left. However, the generation of each rule differs from the standard separate-and-conquer strategy, since it is based on the rule conversion of the path to the leaf with the largest coverage in a pre-pruned decision tree built for the current set of instances (hence the combination with the divide-and-conquer strategy). The time taken to generate a rule set of size r is $O(r{\cdot}a{\cdot}N{\cdot}\log N)$, where a is the number of attributes or features and N is the number of training examples. It is noteworthy that no pruning of the resulting rule set is performed, since our goal is that of precisely describing the phenomena rather than increasing predictive accuracy.

By testing two distinct clustering algorithms on two different data sets corresponding to the two feature sets (one with *NationCode* and one with *NationTimeZone*), we collect four sets of rules for each day. Some statistics are reported shown on Table 1 for three days of June 2004. The average value of the number of generated rules is generally greater than one hundred for the first features set while it is more manageable for the second set. It is worthwhile to notice that in this way we can drastically reduce data to treat and to store: daily model of network traffic is given by few hundreds of rules vs. thousands of network connections. The proposed daily model is light and at the same time adaptive because it is easily able to follow network variability; a network traffic change implies that one of its components can disappear or appear and, in our approach, this means that a rule disappears or appears.

By examining the distribution of instances per cluster, we notice that while EM tends to create one big cluster and many other significantly smaller, K-means tends to evenly distribute instances among clusters.

Table 1. Values of instances, clusters and rules obtained on June 4th, 5th, and 6th, 2004

Day	Instances	Clusters EM/K-means		Rules generated by PART			
		1st feature set	2nd feature set	1st feature set		2nd feature set	
				EM	K-means	EM	K-means
June 4th, 2004	20,130	4	4	156	143	138	38
June 5th, 2004	40,270	5	3	98	188	10	22
June 6th, 2004	16,302	2	6	179	90	45	33

4 Building a Longitudinal Model of Similarities

The rule set generated by PART for every day is a *static* representation of daily network traffic. However, the network administrator needs to compare patterns of network traffic over time in order to:

- understand which events have to be considered recurrent or random
- observe how characteristics of network connections vary upon time.

To build a longitudinal model of network traffic from daily sets of rules, we propose to compute similarities between rules derived for a user-defined time window. Rules correspond to homogeneous classes or groups of connections, that is, to *second-order objects* according to the terminology commonly used in symbolic data analysis (*first-order objects* correspond to the description of individual connections) [16].

Second order objects are described by *set-valued* or *modal* variables. A variable Y defined for all elements k of a set E is termed *set-valued* with the domain $\mathcal{Y}$ if it takes its values in $P(\mathcal{Y})=\{U \mid U \subseteq \mathcal{Y} \}$, that is the power set of $\mathcal{Y}$. When $Y(k)$ is finite for each k, then Y is called *multi-valued*. A single-valued variable is a special case of set-valued variable for which $|Y(k)|=1$ for each k. When an order relation $\prec$ is defined on $\mathcal{Y}$ then the value returned by a set-valued variable can be expressed by an interval

[α,β], and Y is termed an *interval* variable. More generally, a *modal* variable is a set-valued variable with a measure or a (frequency, probability or weight) distribution associated to $Y(k)$. The description of a class or a group of individuals by means of either set-valued variables or modal variables is termed *symbolic object* (SO). Specifically, a *Boolean symbolic object* (BSO) is described by set-valued variables only, while a *probabilistic symbolic object* (PSO), is described by modal variables with a relative frequency distribution associated to each of them.

A set of symbolic data, which involves the same variables to describe different (possibly overlapping) classes of individuals, can be described by a single table, called *symbolic data table*, where rows correspond to distinct symbolic data while columns correspond descriptive variables. Symbolic data tables are more complex to be analysed than standard data tables, since each item at the intersection of a row and a column can be either a finite set of values, or an interval or a probability distribution. The main goal of the research area known as *symbolic data analysis* is that of investigating new theoretically sound techniques to analyse such tables [16].

Many proposals of dissimilarity measures for BSOs have been reported in literature [17]. They have been implemented in a software package developed for the three-years IST project ASSO (Analysis System of Symbolic Official Data) (http://www.assoproject.be/).

Therefore, to provide the network administrator with a dynamic representation of network traffic, we propose to transform rules into symbolic objects and then to compute the dissimilarities between different SOs of different days by means of the ASSO software. The most similar and recurrent SOs in a fixed time window represent the dominant behaviour of network, similar and less frequent events are its secondary aspects while symbolic objects very different from other ones are anomalies.

Transformation of rules into symbolic objects is straightforward. For instance, the following rule, obtained by K-means on the first features subset on June 4th, 2004:

```
ServicePort=10131 AND StartHalfHour>41 AND Nation-
Code=DE : c3
```

is transformed in this SO:

```
[StartHalfHour=[42,47]] ∧ [Protocol=*] ∧ [Destina-
tionIP=*] ∧ [service=10131] ∧ [NumPackets=*] ∧
[Length=*] ∧ [NationCode=DE].
```

The symbol "*", which represents the whole domain, is assigned to variables not present in the rule antecedent.

To execute this step, the DISS module of the ASSO software has been used; the dissimilarity measure selected for our analysis is that proposed by Gowda and Diday [18].

The rules found for a given day are compared with rules of all previous days within a time window. To simplify computation at this stage, the ten rules with highest support have been chosen for each day. The result is a daily dissimilarity matrix, that is, a table of dissimilarities values between a day and its previous ones. Every element is a dissimilarity measure D and it is represented by "DxRy" where x is the day and y is the number of the rule with respect to the same day. The matrix has as many columns

Table 2. Structure of daily dissimilarity matrix

	so1g$_i$	so2g$_i$	...	soN$_i$g$_i$
so1g$_1$	D(so1g$_1$,so1g$_i$)	D(so1g$_1$,so2g$_i$)	...	D(so1g$_1$,soN$_i$g$_i$)
so2g$_1$	D(so2g$_1$,so1g$_i$)	D(so2g$_1$,so2g$_i$)	...	D(so2g$_1$,soN$_i$g$_i$)
...	...	...	...	...
soN$_1$g$_1$	D(soN$_1$g$_1$,so1g$_i$)	D(soN$_1$g$_1$,so2g$_i$)	...	D(soN$_1$g$_1$,soN$_i$g$_i$)
so1g$_2$	D(so1g$_2$,so1g$_i$)	D(so1g$_2$,so2g$_i$)	...	D(so1g$_2$,soN$_i$g$_i$)
...	...	...	...	...
soN$_2$g$_2$	D(soN$_2$g$_2$,so1g$_i$)	D(soN$_2$g$_2$,so2g$_i$)	...	D(soN$_2$g$_2$,soN$_i$g$_i$)
...	...	...	...	...
so1g$_{i-1}$	D(so1g$_{i-1}$,so1g$_i$)	D(so1g$_{i-1}$,so2g$_i$)	...	D(so1g$_{i-1}$,soN$_i$g$_i$)
...	...	...	...	...
soN$_{i-1}$g$_{i-1}$	D(soN$_{i-1}$g$_{i-1}$,so1g$_i$)	D(soN$_{i-1}$g$_{i-1}$,so2g$_i$)	...	D(soN$_{i-1}$g$_{i-1}$,soN$_i$g$_i$)

as the SOs of the referenced day while the number of its rows is equal to the sum of the SOs of all previous days. The structure of this matrix for the ith day (i>2) is shown in Table 2, where N$_i$ represents the number of SOs of the ith day.

To identify similar rules between the present day and the previous ones a numerical threshold (dissMax) has been fixed; given a rule *r*, all the rules whose dissimilarity from *r* is less then dissMax are considered similar to *r*. An example of the possible output is given in the following, where rules similar to Rule 1 of the 4th day (June 3rd, 2004) are shown:

```
Day 4 similar rules found (dissMax = 2.0)
>> Rule 1: /* of the 4ᵗʰ day */
DestinationIP <= 87 AND NationTimeZone >-4 AND Star-
tHalfHour > 26 : c1 /* cluster identifier */
- Similar rules (1):
> Rule 3 of day 3 (diss=1.7528): NationTimeZone > -6
AND StartHalfHour > 25: c0.
```

By consulting the lists of similar rules the network administrator is able to recognize sets of connections that are recurrent and other less frequent or random sets. In this way, the network administrator can learn more and more detailed information about network traffic.

Further information about a rule or its corresponding symbolic object so$_n$g$_m$ (*n*-th rule of *m*-th day) can be obtained by computing its dissimilarity mean value:

$$avgDiss(so_n g_m) = \frac{\sum_{i=m-w}^{m-1} \sum_{j=1}^{n_i} D(so_n g_m, so_j g_i)}{\sum_{i=m-w}^{m-1} n_i} \tag{1}$$

where *w* is the chosen time window (the number of previous days considered) and n_i is the number of rules of the jth day. The dissimilarity mean value measures "how much" a rule is similar to all the rules previously seen. By using a graphical representation (see Fig. 1), the high values of the calculated means can identify rules very dissimilar from other ones while the low values put in evidence rules similar to the previous ones in the fixed time window w.

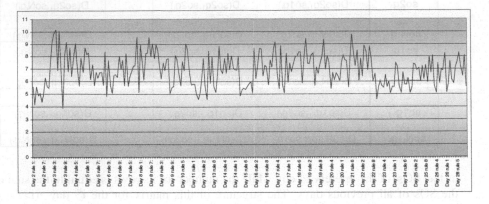

Fig. 1. The dissimilarity mean value of the rules generated by PART for clusters results obtained by EM algorithm and 1st feature set

Another interesting parameter is the minimum value of dissimilarity of a rule; indeed, a rule with high mean dissimilarity could be similar to few others but very dissimilar from the remaining ones and the mean value is not able to capture this situation. Therefore we compute, with the formula (2), the minimum value of dissimilarity amongst a fixed rule and all the rules of the previous days:

$$minDiss(so_ng_m) = \min_{i=m-w}^{m-1} \min_{j=1}^{n_i} D(so_ng_m, so_jg_i) \tag{2}$$

Dominant aspects of the network (i.e. frequent rules) can be reasonably represented by a set of recurrent similar rules whose mean and minimal dissimilarity values are low; secondary (but legal) aspects can have high mean dissimilarity values, while anomalies where domain expert attention must concentrate on, should have high values for both parameters.

5   Analysis of Results and Discussion

The main aim of this work is to investigate the potentialities of a new methodology in order to identify and learn patterns in the network traffic. The experiments have been made on the network traffic of our department but the features used are general and so this methodology can be applied to the traffic of every network active device.

One of the problem in learning network traffic is the huge quantity of data which pass daily through the network. It is important to reduce treated data by representing them with relatively few patterns. In our experiments we managed to compress the original firewall logs of 950 MB total size in 27 small dissimilarity matrices. For our experiments, we used a Pentium IV with 512 MB Ram, 80 GB HD, CPU 2,4 GHz. The cleaning and preprocessing phases, the clustering phase, the rules generation phase and the DISS phase needed respectively 60 seconds, 15 minutes (EM) or 8 minutes (K-means), 15 minutes and 1 minute for each daily files.

We cannot report here all the graphs obtained by graphical representation of the mean and minimal dissimilarities but we try to summarize the main quantitative peculiarities observed in using K-means or EM as clustering algorithm and SP3.1 or SP3.2 as a feature subset. In our graphs, the mean dissimilarity fluctuates in a limited range of values since the fourth day (we chose w = 3). The mean values of extracted rules vary in a wider range when data are clusterized by EM rather than by K-means. In fact, the mean dissimilarity values obtained by K-means are generally lower of 1 unit than those obtained by EM, so that rules obtained by EM seems "more different" each other. The other aspect to underline is that the graphs obtained by EM and K-means have similar behaviour along the time: they generally show high and low peaks nearly at the same points. The first three days represent a transient period, for both the clustering algorithms, when the SP3.1 features subset is used, while this phenomenon does not show up for SP3.2. Although the graphs obtained with the two feature subsets have similar behaviour, mimimum and maximum points are respectively higher and lower with SP3.2 subset than with SP3.1. This suggests that the feature *NationTimeZone* puts more in evidence very similar or dissimilar rules.

The behaviour of mean dissimilarity and minimal one is the same: they respectively grown or decrease at the same time but the graphical representations obtained by the difference of mean and minimal dissimilarity show that this value is higher in the experiments with EM algorithm.

These results confirm that the proposed methodology is promising as to the most interesting aspect, that is, learning of network behaviour patterns along time by building a longitudinal model. A limit of this work is that we considered only syntactic dissimilarity measures according to which the more syntactically different two rules are the more dissimilar they are. However it may happen that two rules with several different attribute-value pairs represent the same network event. Therefore, it is important to investigate dissimilarity measures based on their actual coverage, that is, the observations that they daily share.

6 Conclusions and Future Work

For a network administrator it is important to have a complete description of the connections behaviour so to understand the development of his/her own network. This aspect is becoming more and more relevant and in fact commercial firewalls include modules which, though the computation of simple descriptive statistics, try to inform the security officer on the qualitative nature of network traffic. Firewalls have no means to give information about the mass of connections. The built-in modules permit to analyse every aspect of packet streams; some firewalls also possess an SQL dialect to query its own logs but SQL queries give answers about something the user already know or "suspect".

Personal experience as netadmins teaches us that some types of attack strategies against the network are discovered by chance. Often, netadmins have to read the firewall logs to notice anomalous connections neither intrusion detection systems nor firewall itself would be able to notice. Although a firewall offers a privileged viewpoint with respect to other points in the network because of its concentration of all the pass-through traffic, the network security can only be guaranteed by agents distributed in different points that collaborate each other; a firewall is just one of this point.

These considerations justify some interest towards the application of data mining techniques to firewall logs in order to develop better tools for network security. In the paper we have proposed a methodology based on the application of several data mining methods for the construction of the "normal" model of the ingoing traffic of a department-level network. The methodology returns a daily model of the network traffic as a result of four main steps: 1) description of daily network connections; 2) clustering; 3) generation of sets of rules for each cluster; 4) conversion of rules into symbolic objects and computation of dissimilarities between symbolic objects.

As future work, we intend to achieve better computational performance and a better degree of automation. Moreover, to reach a better degree of automation we intend to investigate the problem of automatically selecting the threshold *dissMax* with respect to which rule similarity is compared. All results obtained as mean and minimum values will be further analysed by means of mathematical techniques to gain more insights on the dynamics of curves. Another research direction concerns the consideration of other essential information sources, like network servers logs or systems logs, for the tasks of intrusion detection and intrusion prevention. We also intend to investigate the use of coverage-based dissimilarity measures as alternative to syntax-based measures. Finally, we intend to develop further research on how to transform daily experience in effectual and stable knowledge which is able to distinguish among different types of anomalies.

Acknowledgments

The work presented in this paper is partial fulfillment of the research objective set by the ATENEO-2003 project on "Metodi di apprendimento automatico e di data mining per sistemi di conoscenza basati sulla semantica ".

References

1. Lazarević, A., Srivastava, J., Kumar, V.: Tutorial on the Pacific-Asia Conference on Knowledge Discovery in Databases (2003)
2. Axelsson, S.: IDS: A Survey and a Taxonomy (2000)
3. Bridges, S., Vaughn, R.: Intrusion Detection via Fuzzy Data Mining (2000)
4. Barbara, D. et al.: ADAM: A Testbed for Exploring the Use of Data Mining in Intrusion Detection, SIGMOD 2001
5. Hofmeyr, S.A., Forrest, S., Somayaji, A.: Intrusion Detection Using Sequences of System Calls. Journal of Computer Security, (1998) 6:151-180
6. Lee, W., Stolfo, S.J.: Data Mining approach for Intrusion Detection. Proceedings of the 1998 USENIX Security Symposium (1998)
7. Ghosh, A., Schwartzbard, A.: A Study in Using Neural Networks for Anomaly and Misuse Detection. Proceedings of the 8th USENIX Security Symposium (1999)

8. Lane, T., Brodley, C.E.: Sequence Matching and Learning in Anomaly Detection for Computer Security. AAAI Workshop: AI Approaches to Fraud Detection and Risk Management, pages 43-49. AAAI Press (1997)

9. Warrender, C., Forrest, S., Pearlmutter, B.: Detecting Intrusions Using Systems Calls: Alternative Data Models. IEEE Symposium on Security and Privacy. IEEE Computer Society (1999) 133-145

10. Milligan G.W., Clustering Validation: Results and Implications for Applied Analyses. World Scientific Publications, River Edge, NJ, USA (1996)

11. Fayyad, U., Piatetsky-Shapiro, G., Smyth, P., Uthurusamy, R. Advances in knowledge discovery and data mining. AAAI Press/ The MIT Press (1996)

12. http://www.cs.waikato.ac.nz/ml/weka

13. Michalski, R. S., Stepp, R. E.: Learning from Observation: Conceptual Clustering. In R. S. Michalski, J. G. Carbonell and T. M. Michell (Eds.), Machine Learning: An Artificial Intelligence Approach. Morgan Kauffmann, San Mateo, CA (1983) 331-363

14. Fisher, D. H. Knowledge Acquisition via Incremental Conceptual Clustering. Machine Learning (1987) 2:139-172

15. Witten I., Frank E., Generate Accurate Rule Sets Without Global Optimisation. Machine Learning: Proceedings of the 15th International Conference, Morgan Kaufmann Publishers, San Francisco, USA (1998)

16. Bock, H.H., Diday, E.: Symbolic Objects. In Bock, H.H, Diday, E. (eds.): Analysis of Symbolic Data. Exploratory Methods for extracting Statistical Information from Complex Data, Series: Studies in Classification, Data Analysis, and Knowledge Organisation, Vol. 15, Springer-Verlag, Berlin (2000) 54-77

17. Esposito, F. , Malerba, D., Tamma, V.: Dissimilarity Measures for Symbolic Objects. Chapter 8.3 in in H.-H. Bock and E. Diday (Eds.), Analysis of Symbolic Data. Exploratory methods for extracting statistical information from complex data, Series: Studies in Classification, Data Analysis, and Knowledge Organization, vol. 15, Springer-Verlag:Berlin, (2000), 165-185.

18. Gowda, K. C., Diday, E.: Symbolic Clustering Using a New Dissimilarity Measure. In Pattern Recognition, Vol. 24, No. 6 (1991) 567-578

ARGUS: Rete + DBMS = Efficient Persistent Profile Matching on Large-Volume Data Streams

Chun Jin[1], Jaime Carbonell[1], and Phil Hayes[2]

[1] Language Technologies Institute, School of Computer Science,
Carnegie Mellon University, Pittsburgh, PA 15213 USA
{cjin, jgc}@cs.cmu.edu
[2] Dynamix Technologies, 12330 Perry Highway, Wexford, PA 15090 USA
phayes@dynamixtechnologies.com

Abstract. Efficient processing of complex streaming data presents multiple challenges, especially when combined with intelligent detection of hidden anomalies in real time. We label such systems Stream Anomaly Monitoring Systems (SAMS), and describe the CMU/Dynamix ARGUS system as a new kind of SAMS to detect rare but high value patterns combining streaming and historical data. Such patterns may correspond to hidden precursors of terrorist activity, or early indicators of the onset of a dangerous disease, such as a SARS outbreak. Our method starts from an extension of the RETE algorithm for matching streaming data against multiple complex persistent queries, and proceeds beyond to transitivity inferences, conditional intermediate result materialization, and other such techniques to obtain both accuracy and efficiency, as demonstrated by the evaluation results outperforming classical techniques such as a modern DMBS.

1 Introduction

Efficient processing of complex streaming data presents multiple challenges. Among data intensive stream applications, we identify an important sub-class which we call Stream Anomaly Monitoring Systems (SAMS). A SAMS monitors transaction data streams or other structured data streams and alerts when anomalies or potential hazards are detected. The system is expected to deal with very-high data-rate streams, many millions of records per day, yet the matches of the anomaly conditions should be very infrequent. However, the matches may generate very high-urgency alerts, may be fed to decision-making systems, and may invoke significant actions. The conditions for anomalies or potential hazards are formulated as persistent queries over data streams by experienced analysts. The data streams are composed of homogeneous records such as money transfer transaction records or hospital inpatient admission records.

Examples motivating a SAMS can be found in many domains including banking, medicine, and stock trading. For instance, given a data stream of FedWire money transfers, an analyst may want to find linkages between big money transfer transactions connected to suspected people or organizations. Given data streams from all the hospitals in a region, a SAMS may help with early alerting of potential diseases or bio-terrorist events. In a stock trading domain, connections between trading transactions with certain

M.-S. Hacid et al. (Eds.): ISMIS 2005, LNAI 3488, pp. 142–151, 2005.
© Springer-Verlag Berlin Heidelberg 2005

features may draw an analyst's attention to check whether insider information is being illegally used.

In this paper, we are concerned with optimal incremental evaluation plans of rarely matching persistent queries over high data rate streams and large-volume historical data archives. We focus on exploring the very-high-selectivity query property to produce good/optimal incremental evaluation plans to solve the performance problem posed by the very-large-volume historical data and very-high stream data rates.

The basic algorithm for the incremental evaluation is a variant of the Rete algorithm which is widely used in rule-based production systems. The Rete match algorithm [7] is an efficient method for matching a large collection of patterns to a large collection of objects. By storing partially instantiated (matched) patterns, Rete saves a significant computation that would otherwise have to be re-computed repetitively in recursive matching of the newly produced working elements. The adapted Rete for stream processing adopts the same idea of storing intermediate results (partial results) of the persistent queries matched against the historical data. New data items arriving at the system may match with the intermediate results to significantly speed up producing the new query results. This is particularly useful when intermediate result size is much smaller than the size of the original data to be processed. This is exactly the case for many SAMS queries. The historical data volume is very large, yet intermediate results may be minimized by exploiting the very-high-selectivity query property.

ARGUS is a prototype SAMS that exploits the adapted Rete algorithm, and is built upon the platform of Oracle DBMS. It also explores transitivity inferences, and conditional intermediate result materialization, and will further incorporate complex computation sharing functionality and the Dynamix Matcher [6] into the system. The Dynamix Matcher is an integrated part of the ARGUS project that can perform fast simple-query filtering before joins and aggregations are processed by Rete; it has also been used for commercial applications. In ARGUS, a persistent query is translated into a procedural network of operators on streams and relations. Derived (intermediate) streams or relations are conditionally materialized as DBMS tables. A node of the network, or the operator, is represented as one or more simple SQL queries that perform the incremental evaluation. The whole network is wrapped as a DBMS stored procedure.

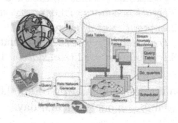

Fig. 1. ARGUS System Architecture

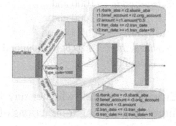

Fig. 2. A Rete network for Example 4

In this paper, we present some SAMS query examples, describe the Rete-based ARGUS design and extensions, and conclude with preliminary performance results, and related work.

2   SAMS Query Examples

We choose the FedWire money transfer domain for illustration and experiments in this paper. It has a single data stream that contains money transfer transaction records. We present seven persistent query examples (one is also presented with the formulated SQL query) which cover the SAMS query scope: selection, join, aggregation, and using views. For more details, and more thorough analysis of the results please see [11].

Example 1. The analyst is interested in knowing if there exists a bank, which received an incoming transaction over 1,000,000 dollars and performed an outgoing transaction over 500,000 dollars on the same day.

Example 2. For every big transaction, the analyst wants to check if the money stayed in the bank or left it within ten days.

Example 3. For every big transaction, the analyst wants to check if the money stayed in the bank or left it within ten days by transferring out in several smaller transactions. The query generates an alert whenever the receiver of a large transaction (over $1,000,000) transfers at least half of the money further within ten days of this transaction.

Example 4. For every big transaction of type code 1000, the analyst wants to check if the money stayed in the bank or left within ten days. An additional sign of possible fraud is that transactions involve at least one intermediate bank. The query generates an alert whenever the receiver of a large transaction (over $1,000,000) transfers at least half of the money further within ten days using an intermediate bank.

SELECT *
FROM $transaction\ r1,\ transaction\ r2,$
        $transaction\ r3$
WHERE $r2.type\_code = 1000$ and
$r3.type\_code = 1000$ and
$r1.type\_code = 1000$ and
$r1.amount > 1000000$ and
$r1.rbank\_aba = r2.sbank\_aba$ and
        (continue)

$r1.benef\_account = r2.orig\_account$ and
$r2.amount > 0.5 * r1.amount$ and
$r1.tran\_date <= r2.tran\_date$ and
$r2.tran\_date <= r1.tran\_date + 10$ and
$r2.rbank\_aba = r3.sbank\_aba$ and
$r2.benef\_account = r3.orig\_account$ and
$r2.amount = r3.amount$ and
$r2.tran\_date <= r3.tran\_date$ and
$r3.tran\_date <= r2.tran\_date + 10;$

Example 5. Check whether any bank has incoming transactions of $100,000,000 or more and outgoing transactions of $50,000,000 or more on one particular day.

Example 6. Get the transactions of Citibank and Fleet on a particular day.

Example 7. The analyst is interested in knowing whether Citibank has conducted a transaction on a particular day with the amount exceeding 1,000,000 dollars.

3   ARGUS Profile System Design

Figure 1 shows the SAMS dataflow and the ARGUS system architecture. Analysts selectively formulate the conditions of anomalies or potential hazards as persistent queries, and register them with the system. Data records in streams arrive continuously. Registered queries are scheduled periodic executions over the new data records, and return any new results as alerts. The ARGUS system contains two components, the database created on the Oracle DBMS, and the Rete construction module, ReteGenerator, which translates persistent queries into Rete networks. Wrapped in a stored procedure, a Rete network encodes an instance of the adapted Rete algorithm. Registering a persistent query in the database includes creating and initializing the intermediate tables based on the historical data, and storing and compiling the Rete network procedure.

QueryTable is a system table that records query information, one entry per query. Each entry contains the query ID, the procedure name to call, the query priority, and a boolean flag indicating whether the query is active or not. $Do\_queries()$ is a system level procedure that finds all the active Rete networks from QueryTable in the order of their priorities, and executes them one by one. New data arrive continuously and are appended to data tables. The active Rete networks are scheduled periodical runs on new data arrivals, and generate alerts when any persistent query matches the new data.

3.1   Adapted Rete Algorithm

Let n and m denote the old data sets, and Δn and Δm the new much smaller incremental data sets, respectively. By Relational Algebra, a selection operation σ on data $n + \Delta n$ is equivalent to $\sigma(n + \Delta n) = \sigma(n) + \sigma(\Delta n)$. $\sigma(n)$ is the set of old results that is materialized. To evaluate incrementally, only the computation on Δn is needed ($\sigma(\Delta n)$). Similarly, for a join operation $\bowtie$ on $(n + \Delta n)$ and $(m + \Delta m)$, we have $(n + \Delta n) \bowtie (m + \Delta m) = n \bowtie m + \Delta n \bowtie m + n \bowtie \Delta m + \Delta n \bowtie \Delta m$. $n \bowtie m$ is the set of old results that is materialized. Only the computations on $\Delta n \bowtie m + n \bowtie \Delta m + \Delta n \bowtie \Delta m$ portion are needed, which can be decomposed to three joins. When Δn and Δm are small compared to n and m, the time complexity of the incremental join is linear with $O(n + m)$.

Figure 2 shows a Rete network for Example 4. A satisfied result set contains joins of three tuples each of which satisfies a set of selection predicates, identified as Pattern 1, Pattern 2, and Pattern 3, respectively. To allow incremental evaluation, each intermediate result storage comprises two parts, the main part that stores intermediate results for historical data, and the delta part that stores the intermediate results for new data.

In summary, a Rete network performs incremental query evaluation over the delta part (new stream data) and materializes intermediate results. The incremental evaluation makes the execution much faster. However, a potential problem is that when any materialized intermediate table grows very large, thus requiring many I/O operations, the performance degrades severely. Fortunately, since queries are expected to be satisfied infrequently, there are usually highly selective conditions that make the intermediate tables fairly small. We investigated several optimization techniques to minimizing the sizes of intermediate result tables.

3.2   Translating SQL Queries into Rete Networks

A query may contain multiple SQL statements and a single SQL statement may contain unions of multiple SQL terms. Multiple SQL statements allow an analyst to define views. Each SQL term is mapped to a sub-Rete network. These sub-Rete networks are then connected to form the statement-level sub-networks. And the statement-level sub-networks are further connected based on the view references to form the final query-level Rete network. For more details, please see [11].

ReteGenerator. ReteGenerator contains three components: the SQL Parser, the Rete Topology Constructor, and the Rete Coder. The SQL Parser parses a query (a set of SQLs) to a set of parse trees. The Rete Topology Constructor rearranges the connections of nodes in the sub-parse tree of each SQL term to obtain the desired sub-Rete network topologies. And the Rete Coder generates the Rete network code and corresponding DDL statements in Oracle PL/SQL language by traversing the reconstructed parse trees and instantiating the code templates.

The Rete Topology Constructor takes three steps to construct the sub-Rete network topology for each SQL term based on its *where_clause* sub-parse tree. First, predicates are classified based on the tables they use. Second, the classified predicate sets are sorted based on the number of tables that the sets contain. Finally, the new subtree is reconstructed bottom-up. Single-table predicate sets correspond to leaf nodes. A new node joining two existing nodes is selectively created if a join predicate set exists. The process continues until all nodes are merged into a single node. Figure 3 shows the reconstructed *where_clause* subtree of the query Example 4.

Aggregation and Union. An SQL term may contain groupby/having clauses. If it also contains a *where_clause*, the Rete network is generated for the *where_clause* and the output of the Rete network is stored in a table, which will be the input to the groupby/having clauses. Then the system does the operations of grouping/having on the whole input table, and finds the difference between the current results and the previous results. These grouping operations on whole input sets will be replaced by incremental aggregation in future.

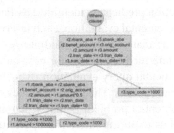

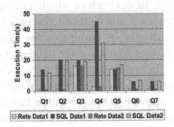

Fig. 3. The Reconstructed Where_clause Sub-tree for Example 4

Fig. 4. Execution Times of Q1-Q7

3.3   Improvements on Rete Network

Transitivity Inference. Transitivity Inference explores the transitivity property of comparison operators, such as $>$, $<$, and $=$, to infer hidden selective single-table conditions from a set of existing conditions. For example, in Example 4, the query has the following conditions (the first is very selective): $r1.amount > 1000000$, $r2.amount > r1.amount * 0.5$, and $r3.amount = r2.amount$. The first two conditions imply a selective condition on $r2$: $r2.amount > 500000$. Further, the third condition and the newly derived condition imply another selective condition on $r3$: $r3.amount > 500000$. These inferred conditions have significant impact on performance. The first level intermediate tables, filtered by the highly selective selection predicates, are made very small, which saves significant computation on subsequent joins.

Conditional Materialization. If intermediate results grow large, for instance in join queries where single-table selection predicates are not selective and transitivity inference is not applicable, pipelined operation is preferable to materialization. Assume Transitivity Inference is not applicable by turning the module off, Example 4 is such a query. The two single-table selection predicates ($r2.type\_code = 1000$, $r3.type\_code = 1000$) are highly non-selective, the sizes of the intermediate results are close to that of the original data table. Aware of the table statistics, or indicated by users, such a materialization can be conditionally skipped, which we call Conditional Materialization. In our experiments, Rete network Q11 is a Conditional Rete network for Example 4 while Q10 is another one for the same example. They are similar except that Q11 does not materialize the results of the two non-selective selection predicates.

User-Defined Join Priority. Join priority specifies the join order that the Rete network should take. It is similar to the reordering of join operators in traditional query optimization. The ReteGenerator currently accepts user-defined join priority. We are working on applying query optimization techniques based on table statistics and cost models to automatically decide the optimal join order.

3.4   Current Research

We are designing complex extensions to incorporate computation sharing, cost-based optimization, incremental aggregation, and the Dynamix Matcher. Computation sharing among multiple queries adds much more complexity to the system. We are developing the schemes to index query predicates and predicate sets, and algorithms to identify and rearrange predicate sets to minimize intermediate result sizes in the shared networks. Cost-based optimization automatically decides the join order and the choice of conditional materialization based on table statistics. Incremental aggregation aggregates data items by maintaining sufficient statistics instead of the whole group items. For example, by preserving the SUM and COUNT, up-to-date AVERAGE can be calculated without accessing the historical data. The Dynamix Matcher is a fast query matching system for large-scale simple queries that exploits special data structures. We are working on the scheme of rerouting the partial query evaluations to Dynamix Matcher when they can be efficiently carried out by the Dynamix Matcher.

4   Experimental Results

4.1   Experiment Setting

The experiments compared performance of the prototype ARGUS to the Oracle DBMS that ARGUS was built upon, and were conducted on an HP computer with 1.7G CPU and 512M RAM, running Windows XP.

Data Conditions. The data conditions are derived from a database of synthesized Fed-Wire money transfer transactions. The database D contains 320,006 records. The timestamps of the data span 3 days. We split the data in two ways, and most of the experiments were conducted on both data conditions:

- Data1. Old data: the first $300,000$ records of D. New data: the remaining $20,006$ records of D. This data set provides alerts for most of the queries being tested.
- Data2. Old data: the first $300,000$ records of D. New data: the next $20,000$ records of D. This data set does not generate alerts for most of the queries being tested.

Queries. We tested eleven Rete networks created for the seven queries described in Section 2. Q1-Q7 are the Rete networks for the seven examples created in a common setting, respectively: no hidden condition is added to the original queries, and Transitivity Inference module is turned on. Q8 and Q10 are variants of Example 2 and 4 that are generated without Transitivity Inference. Q9 is the variant of Example 4 whose original SQL query is enhanced with hidden conditions. Q11 is a Conditional Rete network of Example 4.

When running the original SQL queries, we combined the historical (old) data and the new data (stream). It takes some time for Rete networks to initialize intermediate results, yet it is a one-time operation. Rete networks provide incremental new results, while original SQL queries only provide whole sets of results.

4.2   Results Interpretation

Figure 4 summarizes the results of running the queries Q1-Q7 on the two data conditions. For most of the queries, Rete networks with Transitivity Inference gain significant improvements over directly running the SQL queries. For more details, please see [11].

Aggregation. Q3 and Q5 are the two queries involving aggregations. Q3's Rete network has to join with the large original table. And Rete's incremental evaluation scheme is not applicable to Q5. This leads to limited or zero improvement of the Rete procedures. We expect incremental aggregation will provide noticeable improvements to these queries.

Transitivity Inference. Example 2 and 4 are queries that benefit from Transitivity Inference. Figure 5 shows the execution times for these two examples. The inferred condition $amount > 500000$ is very selective with selectivity factor of 0.1%. Clearly, when Transitivity Inference is applicable and the inferred conditions are selective, a Rete network runs much faster than its non-TI counterpart and the original SQL.

Note that in Figure 5 $SQL\ TI\ (Q9)$, Example 4 with manually added conditions, runs significantly faster than the original one. This suggests that this type of complex transitivity inference is not applied in the DBMS query optimization, and may be a potential new query optimization method for a traditional DBMS.

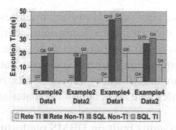
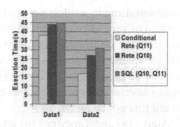

Fig. 5. "Rete TI": Rete generated with Transitivity Inference. "Rete Non-TI": Rete without Transitivity Inference. "SQL Non-TI": Original SQL query. "SQL TI". Original SQL query with hidden conditions manually added

Fig. 6. Effect of Conditional Materialization. Comparing the execution times of Conditional Rete, Non-Conditional Rete, and SQL for Example 4 on Data1 and Data2

Conditional Materialization. Assume Transitivity Inference is not applicable by turning the module off for Example 4, we obtain a Rete network Q10, and a Conditional Rete network Q11. Figure 6 compares the execution times of the Conditional Rete network, the Rete network, and original SQL. It is clear that if non-selective conditions are present, Conditional Rete is superior to the original Rete network.

5   Related Work

TREAT [13] is a variant form of Rete that skips the materialization of intermediate join nodes but joins all nodes in one step. Match Box algorithm [16] pre-computes a rule's binding space, and then has each binding independently monitor working memory for the incremental formation of tuple instantiations. LEAPS [14] is a lazy matching scheme that collapses the space complexity required by Rete to linear.

A generalization of Rete and TREAT, Gator [9] is a non-binary bushy tree instead of a binary bushy tree like Rete, applied to a scalable trigger processing system [10], in which predicate indexing provides computation sharing among common predicates. The work on Gator networks is more general than ours with respect to employing non-binary discrimination networks with cost model optimizations. However, [9] explores only single tuple updates at a time, does not consider aggregation operators, and is used for trigger condition detection instead of stream processing.

Our work is closely related to several Database research directions, including Active Databases [8][20][18], materialized view maintenance [3], and Stream Database systems. Some recent and undergoing stream projects, STREAM [2], TelegraphCQ [4], and Aurora [1], etc., develop general-purpose Data Stream Management Systems, and focus on general stream processing problems, such as high data rates, bursting data arrivals, and various query output requirements, etc. Compared to these systems, ARGUS tries to solve the performance problem caused by very-large-volume historical data and high data rates by exploiting the very-high-selectivity property of SAMS queries, particularly optimizing incremental query evaluations.

OpenCQ, WebCQ [12], and NiagaraCQ [5] are continuous query systems for Internet databases with incremental query evaluation schemes over data changes. NiagaraCQ's incremental query evaluation is similar to Rete networks. However, it addresses the problem of very large number of queries instead of very-large volume data and high data rates, and the optimization strategy is sharing as much computation as possible among multiple queries. Distinguishably, ARGUS attempts to minimize the intermediate result sizes in both single-query Rete networks and shared multi-query Rete networks. ARGUS applies several techniques such as transitivity inference and conditional materialization toward this goal.

Alert [18] and Tapestry [19] are two early systems built on DBMS platforms. Alert uses triggers to check the query conditions, and modified cursors to fetch satisfied tuples. This method may not be efficient in handling high data rates and the large number of queries in a stream processing scenario. Similar to ARGUS, Tapestry's incremental evaluation scheme is also wrapped in a stored procedure. However, its incremental evaluation is realized by rewriting the query with sliding window specifications on the append-only relations (streams). This approach becomes inefficient when the append-only table is very large. Particularly, it has to do repetitive computations over large historical data whenever new data is to be matched in joins.

There is some relevant work on inferring hidden predicates [15][17]. However, they deal with only the simplest case of equi-join predicates without any arithmetic operators. ARGUS deals with general 2-way join predicates with comparison operators and arithmetic operators for Transitivity Inference.

6   Conclusion

Dealing with very-large volume historical data and high data rates presents special challenges for a Stream Anomaly Monitoring System. In ARGUS, Rete networks provide the basic framework for incremental query evaluation, and the very-high-selectivity property of SAMS queries is exploited to minimize intermediate result sizes and speed up performance significantly. The techniques include transitivity inference, user-defined join priority, and conditional materialization. The later two will be replaced by a more general cost-based optimization method that will subsume them. We are also extensively expanding the system to incorporate multi-query computation sharing, incremental aggregation, and the Dynamix Matcher.

Acknowledgements. This work was supported in part by ARDA, NIMD program under contract NMA401-02-C-0033. The views and conclusions are those of the authors, not of the U.S. government or its agencies. We thank Chris Olston for his helpful suggestions and comments, and Bob Frederking, Eugene Fink, Cenk Gazen, Dwight Dietrich, Ganesh Mani, Aaron Goldstein, and Johny Mathew for helpful discussions.

References

1. D. J. Abadi and etc. Aurora: a new model and architecture for data stream management. *The VLDB Journal*, 12(2):120–139, 2003.
2. B. Babcock, S. Babu, M. Datar, R. Motwani, and J. Widom. Models and Issues in Data Stream Systems. In *Proc. of the 21st ACM SIGMOD-SIGACT-SIGART Symp. PODS*, 2002.

3. J. A. Blakeley and etc. Updating Derived Relations: Detecting Irrelevant and Autonomously Computable Updates. *ACM Trans. on Database Systems (TODS)*, 14(3):369–400, 1989.
4. S. Chandrasekaran and etc. TelegraphCQ: Continuous Dataflow Processing for an Uncertain World. In *Proc. of the 2003 Conf. on Innovative Data Systems Research*.
5. J. Chen and etc. Design and Evaluation of Alternative Selection Placement Strategies in Optimizing Continuous Queries. In *Proc. of the 18th Intl. Conf. on Data Engineering*, 2002.
6. E. Fink, A. Goldstein, P. Hayes, and J. Carbonell. Search for Approximate Matches in Large Databases. In *Proc. of the 2004 IEEE Intl. Conf. on Systems, Man, and Cybernetics*.
7. C. L. Forgy. Rete: A Fast Algorithm for the Many Pattern/Many Object Pattern Match Problem. *Artificial Intelligence*, 19(1):17–37, 1982.
8. L. Haas and etc. Startburst Mid-Flight: As the Dust Clears. *IEEE Trans. on Knowledge and Data Engineering*, 2(1):143–160, 1990.
9. E. N. Hanson, S. Bodagala, and U. Chadaga. Optimized Trigger Condition Testing in Ariel Using Gator Networks. Technical Report TR-97-021, CISE Dept., Univ. of Florida, 1997.
10. E. N. Hanson and etc. Scalable Trigger Processing. In *Proc. of the 15th Intl. Conf. on Data Engineering*, 1999.
11. C. Jin and J. Carbonell. ARGUS: Rete + DBMS = Efficient Continuous Profile Matching on Large-Volume Data Streams. Tech. Report CMU-LTI-04-181, Carnegie Mellon Univ. 2004 URL: www.cs.cmu.den/čjin/publications/Rete.pdf.
12. L. Liu, W. Tang, D. Buttler, and C. Pu. Information Monitoring on the Web: A Scalable Solution. *World Wide Web Journal*, 5(4), 2002.
13. D. P. Miranker. *TREAT: A New and Efficient Match Algorithm for IA Production Systems*. Morgan Kaufmann, 1990.
14. D. P. Miranker and D. A. Brant. An algorithmic basis for integrating production systems and large databases. In *Proc. of the Sixth Intl. Conf. on Data Engineering*, 1990.
15. K. Ono and G. Lohman. Measuring the Complexity of Join Enumeration in Query Optimization. In *Proc. of 16th Intl. Conf. on VLDB*, pages 314–325, 1990.
16. M. W. Perlin. The match box algorithm for parallel production system match. Technical Report CMU-CS-89-163, Carnegie Mellon Univ., 1989.
17. H. Pirahesh and etc. A Rule Engine for Query Transformation in Starburst and IBM DB2 C/S DBMS. In *Proc. of 13th Intl. Conf. on Data Engineering*, pages 391–400, 1997.
18. U. Schreier, H. Pirahesh, R. Agrawal, and C. Mohan. Alert: An Architecture for Transforming a Passive DBMS into an Active DBMS. In *Proc. of 17th Intl. Conf. on VLDB*, 1991.
19. D. Terry, D. Goldberg, D. Nichols, and B. Oki. Continuous Queries over Append-Only Databases. In *Proc. of the 1992 ACM SIGMOD Intl. Conf.*
20. J. Widom and S. Ceri, editors. *Active Database Systems*. Morgan Kaufmann, 1996.

Failing Queries in Distributed Autonomous Information System

Zbigniew W. Raś[1,2] and Agnieszka Dardzińska[3]

[1] UNC-Charlotte, Department of Computer Science, Charlotte, N.C. 28223, USA
[2] Polish Academy of Sciences, Institute of Computer Science,
Ordona 21, 01-237 Warsaw, Poland
[3] Bialystok Technical Univ., Dept. of Mathematics,
ul. Wiejska 45A, 15-351 Bialystok, Poland

Abstract. There are two basic cases when Query Answering System (QAS) for a Distributed Autonomous Information System ($DAIS$) may give no answer to a submitted query. Let us assume that q is that query which is submitted to an information system S representing one of the sites in $DAIS$. Systems in $DAIS$ can be incomplete, have hierarchical attributes, and we also assume that there are no objects in S which descriptions are matching q. In such a case, QAS will fail and return the empty set of objects. Alternatively, it may relax query q as it was proposed in [7], [8], [2]. It means that q is replaced either automatically or with a help from user by a new more general query. Clearly, the ultimate goal is to find a generalization of q which is possibly the smallest. Smaller generalizations of queries always guarantee higher confidence in objects returned by QAS. Such QAS is called cooperative. We may also encounter failing query problem when some of the attributes listed in q are outside the domain of S. We call them foreign for S. In such a case, we extract definitions of foreign attributes for S at other sites in $DAIS$ and next used them in QAS to solve q. However, to do that successfully, we have to assume that both systems agree on the ontology of their common attributes [14], [15], [16]. Such definitions are used to identify which objects in S may satisfy that query. The corresponding QAS is called collaborative. This paper shows that cooperation can be used as a refinement tool for the collaboration strategy dealing with failing query problem as presented in [14], [15].

1 Introduction

Distributed Autonomous Information System ($DAIS$) is a system that connects a number of autonomous information systems using network communication technology. In this paper, we assume that some of these systems may have hierarchical attributes and some of them are incomplete. Incompleteness is understood by allowing to have a set of weighted attribute values as a value of an attribute. Additionally, we assume that the sum of these weights has to be equal 1. The definition of an information system of type λ and distributed autonomous

M.-S. Hacid et al. (Eds.): ISMIS 2005, LNAI 3488, pp. 152–160, 2005.
© Springer-Verlag Berlin Heidelberg 2005

information system used in this paper was given by Raś and Dardzińska in [15]. The type λ is used to monitor the weights assigned to values of attributes by *Chase* algorithm [5], if they are greater than or equal to λ. If the weight assigned by *Chase* to one of the attribute values is less than the threshold value λ, then this attribute value is ruled out. Semantic inconsistencies among sites are due to different interpretations of attributes and their values among sites (for instance one site can interpret the concept *young* differently than another site). Ontologies ([9], [10], [17], [18], [19], [1], [20], [6]) are usually used to handle differences in semantics among information systems. If two systems agree on the ontology associated with attribute *young* and its values, then attribute *young* can be used as a semantical bridge between these systems. Different interpretations are also due to the way each site is handling null values. Null value replacement by a value predicted either by statistical or some rule-based methods is quite common before queries are answered by *QAS*. In [14], the notion of *rough semantics* and a method of its construction was proposed. The rough semantics can be used to model and nicely handle semantic inconsistencies among sites due to different interpretations of incomplete values.

There are some cases when Query Answering System (*QAS*) for a Distributed Autonomous Information System (*DAIS*) may fail to return a satisfactory answer to a submitted query. For instance, let us assume that an information system S has hierarchical attributes and there is no single object in S which description is matching a query submitted by a user. By generalizing that query, we may identify objects in S which descriptions are nearest to the description submitted by the user. We may also faced failing query problem when some of the attributes listed in a query q are outside the domain of a queried information system S. The way to solve this problem is to extract definitions of such attributes at one of the remote sites for S in *DAIS* and next used them by *QAS* to identify objects in S satisfying q. This problem is similar to the problem when the granularity of the attribute value used in a query q is less general than the granularity of the corresponding attribute used in S. By replacing this attribute value in q by the one used in S, we retrieve objects from S which possibly satisfy q. Alternatively, we may compute definitions of this attribute value at one of the remote sites for S in *DAIS* and next used them by *QAS* to enhance the process of identifying which objects in S satisfy that query. However, before doing that, we need to know that both systems involved in this process agree on the ontology of their common attributes [14], [15], [16]. In this paper, we present a new strategy for failing query problem in *DAIS*.

2   Query Processing with Incomplete Data

In real life, information about objects is collected and stored in information systems residing at many different locations, built independently. These systems are usually incomplete and their attributes may have different granularity levels. For instance, at one system, concepts *child, young,middle-aged, old, senile* may represent the domain of attribute *age*. At the other information system, we may use just integers to define that domain. If these two systems agree on the ontology related to attribute *age* and its values, then they can use this attribute when they communicate with each other. It is very possible that an attribute is missing in one information system while it occurs at many others. Assume now that user submits a query to a Query Answering System (QAS) of S (called a client), which can not answer it due to the fact that some of the attributes used in a query are either missing in S or their granularity is more specific than the granularity of the same attributes at S. In all such cases, system S can collaborate with other information systems (called servers) to get definitions of these attributes from them. These new definitions form a knowledge base which is used to chase (see [4]) that missing values or discover more precise values that can replace the current values of attributes at S. Algorithm Chase for $DAIS$, based on rules, was given by Raś and Dardzińska in [4]. This algorithm can be easily modified so it can be used for refinement of object descriptions in S. But before that, semantic inconsistencies due to different interpretations of incomplete values among sites have to be somehow resolved. For instance, it can be done by taking rough semantics [14], mentioned earlier. In any case, collaborating sites have to agree on the ontology associated with their common attributes. For simplicity reason, in this paper, we are not considering ontology associated with users.

Definition 1:
We say that $S = (X, A, V)$ is a partially incomplete information system of type λ, if S is an incomplete information system and the following three conditions hold:

- $a_S(x)$ is defined for any $x \in X$, $a \in A$,

- $(\forall x \in X)(\forall a \in A)[(a_S(x) = \{(a_i, p_i) : 1 \leq i \leq m\}) \rightarrow \sum_{i=1}^{m} p_i = 1]$,

- $(\forall x \in X)(\forall a \in A)[(a_S(x) = \{(a_i, p_i) : 1 \leq i \leq m\}) \rightarrow (\forall i)(p_i \geq \lambda)]$.

Now, let us assume that S_1, S_2 are partially incomplete information systems, both of type λ. The same objects (from X) are stored in both systems and the same attributes (from A) are used to describe them. The meaning and granularity of values of attributes from A in both systems S_1, S_2 is also the same. Additionally, we assume that $a_{S_1}(x) = \{(a_{1i}, p_{1i}) : 1 \leq m_1\}$ and $a_{S_2}(x) = \{(a_{2i}, p_{2i}) : 1 \leq m_2\}$.

We say that containment relation Ψ holds between S_1 and S_2, if the following two conditions hold:

- $(\forall x \in X)(\forall a \in A)[card(a_{S_1(x)}) \geq card(a_{S_2(x)})]$,

- $(\forall x \in X)(\forall a \in A)[[card(a_{S_1}(x)) = card(a_{S_2}(x))] \rightarrow$
$$[\sum_{i \neq j} |p_{2i} - p_{2j}| > \sum_{i \neq j} |p_{1i} - p_{1j}|]].$$

Instead of saying that containment relation holds between S_1 and S_2, we can equivalently say that S_1 was transformed into S_2 by containment mapping

Ψ. This fact can be presented as a statement $\Psi(S_1) = S_2$ or $(\forall x \in X)(\forall a \in A)[\Psi(a_{S_1}(x)) = \Psi(a_{S_2}(x))]$. Similarly, we can either say that $a_{S_1}(x)$ was transformed into $a_{S_2}(x)$ by Ψ or that containment relation Ψ holds between $a_{S_1}(x)$ and $a_{S_2}(x)$.

So, if containment mapping Ψ converts an information system S to S', then S' is more complete than S. Saying another words, for a minimum one pair $(a, x) \in A \times X$, either Ψ has to decrease the number of attribute values in $a_S(x)$ or the average difference between confidences assigned to attribute values in $a_S(x)$ has to be increased by Ψ. To clarify this definition, let us assume that $a_{S_1}(x) = \{(a_1, \frac{1}{3}), (a_2, \frac{2}{3})\}$ and $a_{S_2}(x) = \{(a_1, \frac{1}{5}), (a_2, \frac{4}{5})\}$. Clearly S_2 is closer to a complete system than S_1 with respect to $a(x)$, since our uncertainty in the value of attribute a for x is lower in S_2 than in S_1.

To give an example of a containment mapping Ψ, let us take two information systems S_1, S_2 both of the type λ, represented as Table 1 and Table 2.

Table 1. Information System S_1

X	a	b	c	d	e
x_1	$\{(a_1, \frac{1}{3}), (a_2, \frac{2}{3})\}$	$\{(b_1, \frac{2}{3}), (b_2, \frac{1}{3})\}$	c_1	d_1	$\{(e_1, \frac{1}{2}), (e_2, \frac{1}{2})\}$
x_2	$\{(a_2, \frac{1}{4}), (a_3, \frac{3}{4})\}$	$\{(b_1, \frac{1}{3}), (b_2, \frac{2}{3})\}$		d_2	e_1
x_3		b_2	$\{(c_1, \frac{1}{2}), (c_3, \frac{1}{2})\}$	d_2	e_3
x_4	a_3		c_2	d_1	$\{(e_1, \frac{2}{3}), (e_2, \frac{1}{3})\}$
x_5	$\{(a_1, \frac{2}{3}), (a_2, \frac{1}{3})\}$	b_1	c_2		e_1
x_6	a_2	b_2	c_3	d_2	$\{(e_2, \frac{1}{3}), (e_3, \frac{2}{3})\}$
x_7	a_2	$\{(b_1, \frac{1}{4}), (b_2, \frac{3}{4})\}$	$\{(c_1, \frac{1}{3}), (c_2, \frac{2}{3})\}$	d_2	e_2
x_8		b_2	c_1	d_1	e_3

It can be easily checked that the values assigned to $e(x_1)$, $b(x_2)$, $c(x_2)$, $a(x_3)$, $e(x_4)$, $a(x_5)$, $c(x_7)$, and $a(x_8)$ in S_1 are different than the corresponding values in S_2. In each of these eight cases, an attribute value assigned to an object in S_2 is less general than the value assigned to the same object in S_1. It means that $\Psi(S_1) = S_2$.

Again, let us assume that $S_1 = (X, A, V_1)$, $S_2 = (X, A, V_2)$ are partially incomplete information systems, both of type λ. Although attributes in both systems are the same, they differ in granularity of their values. We assume that $a_{S_1}(x) = \{(a_{1i}, p_{1i}) : 1 \le i \le m_1\}$ and $a_{S_2}(x) = \{a_1\}$.

We say that containment relation Φ holds between S_2 and S_1, if the following two conditions hold:

Table 2. Information System S_2

X	a	b	c	d	e
x_1	$\{(a_1,\frac{1}{3}),(a_2,\frac{2}{3})\}$	$\{(b_1,\frac{2}{3}),(b_2,\frac{1}{3})\}$	c_1	d_1	$\{(e_1,\frac{1}{3}),(e_2,\frac{2}{3})\}$
x_2	$\{(a_2,\frac{1}{4}),(a_3,\frac{3}{4})\}$	b_1	$\{(c_1,\frac{1}{3}),(c_2,\frac{2}{3})\}$	d_2	e_1
x_3	a_1	b_2	$\{(c_1,\frac{1}{2}),(c_3,\frac{1}{2})\}$	d_2	e_3
x_4	a_3		c_2	d_1	e_2
x_5	$\{(a_1,\frac{3}{4}),(a_2,\frac{1}{4})\}$	b_1	c_2		c_1
x_6	a_2	b_2	c_3	d_2	$\{(e_2,\frac{1}{3}),(e_3,\frac{2}{3})\}$
x_7	a_2	$\{(b_1,\frac{1}{4}),(b_2,\frac{3}{4})\}$	c_1	d_2	e_2
x_8	$\{(a_1,\frac{2}{3}),(a_2,\frac{1}{3})\}$	b_2	c_1	d_1	e_3

- $(\forall i \leq m_1)[a_{1i}$ is a child of a_1 in the ontology part representing hierarchical attribute $a]$,

- either $\{a_{1i} : 1 \leq i \leq m_1\}$ does not contain all children of a_1 or weights in $\{p_{1i} : 1 \leq i \leq m_1\}$ are not all the same.

Instead of saying that containment relation holds between S_2 and S_1, we can equivalently say that S_2 was transformed into S_1 by containment mapping Φ. This fact can be written as $\Phi(S_2) = S_1$ or $(\forall x \in X)(\forall a \in A)[\Phi(a_{S_2}(x)) = \Phi(a_{S_1}(x))]$. Similarly, we can either say that $a_{S_2}(x)$ was transformed into $a_{S_1}(x)$ by Φ or that containment relation Φ holds between $a_{S_2}(x)$ and $a_{S_1}(x)$.

So, if containment mapping Φ converts an information system S to S', then information about any object in S' is more precise than about the same object in S. Clearly, if $\{a_{1i} : 1 \leq i \leq m\}$ contains all children of a_1, then semantically a_1 has the same meaning as $\{(a_{1i}, 1/m) : 1 \leq i \leq m\}$.

3   How to Handle Failing Queries in DAIS

Assume now that a query $q(B)$ is submitted to system $S = (X, A, V)$, where B is the set of all attributes used in q and that $A \cap B \neq \emptyset$. All attributes in $B - [A \cap B]$ are called foreign for S. If S is a part of $DAIS$, then for definitions of foreign attributes for S we may look at its remote sites (see [14]). We assume here that two information systems can collaborate only if they agree on the ontology of attributes which are present in both of them. Clearly, the same ontology does not mean that a common attribute is of the same granularity at both sites. Similarly, the granularity of values of attributes used in a query may differ from the granularity of values of the same attributes in S. In [14], it was shown that query $q(B)$ can be processed at site S by discovering definitions of values of attributes from $B - [A \cap B]$ at any of the remote sites for S and use them to answer $q(B)$. With each rule discovered at a remote site, a number of additional rules (implied by that rule) is also discovered. For instance, let us assume that two attributes *age* and *salary* are used to describe objects at a remote site which ascribes to the ontology given below:

- age(child($\leq$17),
      young(18,19,...,29),
      middle-aged(30,31,...,60),
      old(61,62,...,80),
      senile(81,82,...,$\geq$100))

- salary(low($\leq$10K,20K,30K,40K),
        medium(50K,60K,70K),
        high(80K,90K,100K),
        very-high(110K,120K,$\geq$130K))

Now, assume that the rule $(age, young) \longrightarrow (salary, 40K)$ is extracted at the remote site. Jointly with that rule, the following rules are also discovered:

- $(age, young) \longrightarrow (salary, low)$,
- $(age, N) \longrightarrow (salary, 40K)$, where $N = 18, 19, ..., 29$,
- $(age, N) \longrightarrow (salary, low)$, where $N = 18, 19, ..., 29$.

If both attributes are used in S and the granularity of values of the attribute *salary* in S is more general than the granularity of values of the same attribute used in some rules listed above, then these rules can be used by containment mapping Φ to convert S into a system S'. Information about objects, with respect to attribute *salary*, is more precise in S' than in S. This conversion is necessary, if only the granularity of values of the attribute *salary* used in query $q(B)$ is the same as its granularity used in rules in Φ. Otherwise, we would be forced to replace the user query by more general one in order to match the granularity of values of attributes used in S. Clearly, the user will be more pleased if his query is kept untouched.

Assume now that $L(D) = \{(t \rightarrow v_c) \in D : c \in G(A)\}$ (called a knowledge-base) is a set of all rules extracted at a remote site for $S = (X, A, V)$ by $ERID(S, \lambda_1, \lambda_2)$, where $G(A)$ is the set of attributes in S which values are more general than the corresponding values of attributes used in $q(B)$. Parameters λ_1, λ_2 represent thresholds for minimum support and minimum confidence, correspondingly. *ERID* is the algorithm for discovering rules from incomplete information systems, presented by Dardzińska and Raś in [4]. The type of incompleteness in [15] is the same as in this paper if we only assume that any attribute value a_1 in S can be replaced by $\{(a_{1i}, 1/m) : 1 \leq i \leq m\}$, where $\{a_{1i} : 1 \leq i \leq m\}$ is the set of all children of a_1 in the ontology associated with a_1.

By replacing values of attributes in $G(A)$, describing objects in S, by values which are finer, we can easily arrive to a new system $\Phi(S)$ in which $q(B)$ will fail (we get either the empty set of objects or set of weighted objects with weights below some threshold value provided by user). In this paper we propose an objective strategy to find an optimal subset of $G(A)$ for the refinement process of attribute values. But before it is presented, another issue has to be discussed first.

Foreign attributes for S can be seen as attributes which are 100% incomplete in S, that means values (either exact or partially incomplete) of such attributes have to be ascribed to all objects in S. Stronger the consensus among sites on a value to be ascribed to x, *finer* the result of the ascription process for x can be expected. Assuming that systems S_1, S_2 store the same sets of objects and use the same attributes to describe them, system S_1 is *finer* than system S_2, if $\Psi(S_2) = S_1$.

But, before we continue this discussion any further, we have to decide first on the interpretation of functors *or* and *and*, denoted in this paper by $+$ and $*$, correspondingly. We adopt the semantics of terms proposed by Raś & Joshi in [16] as their semantics has all the properties required for the query transformation process to be sound [see [16]]. It was proved that, under their semantics, the following distributive property holds: $t_1 * (t_2 + t_3) = (t_1 * t_2) + (t_1 * t_3)$.

So, let us assume that $S = (X, A, V)$ is an information system of type λ and t is a term constructed in a standard way (for predicate calculus expression) from values of attributes in V seen as *constants* and from two functors $+$ and $*$. By $N_S(t)$, we mean the standard interpretation of a term t in S defined as (see [16]):

- $N_S(v) = \{(x, p) : (v, p) \in a(x)\}$, for any $v \in V_a$,
- $N_S(t_1 + t_2) = N_S(t_1) \oplus N_S(t_2)$,
- $N_S(t_1 * t_2) = N_S(t_1) \otimes N_S(t_2)$,

where, for any $N_S(t_1) = \{(x_i, p_i)\}_{i \in I}$, $N_S(t_2) = \{(x_j, q_j)\}_{j \in J}$, we have:

- $N_S(t_1) \oplus N_S(t_2) =$
$$\{(x_i, p_i)\}_{i \in (I-J)} \cup \{(x_j, p_j)\}_{j \in (J-I)} \cup \{(x_i, max(p_i, q_i))\}_{i \in I \cap J},$$
- $N_S(t_1) \otimes N_S(t_2) = \{(x_i, p_i \cdot q_i)\}_{i \in (I \cap J)}.$

Now, we are ready to discuss the failing query problem in $DAIS$. Let $S = (X, A, V)$ represents the client site in $DAIS$. For simplicity reason, we assume that $A = A_1 \cup A_2 \cup \{a, b, d\}$, $V_a = \{a_1, a_2, a_3\}$, $V_b = \{b_{1,1}, b_{1,2}, b_{1,3}, b_{2,1}, b_{2,2}, b_{2,3}, b_{3,1}, b_{3,2}, b_{3,3}\}$, $V_d = \{d_1, d_2, d_3\}$, and that the semantics of hierarchical attributes $\{a, b, c, d\}$, used in $DAIS$, is a part of $DAIS$ ontology defined as:

- $a(a_1[a_{1,1}, a_{1,2}, a_{1,3}], a_2[a_{2,1}, a_{2,2}, a_{2,3}], a_3[a_{3,1}, a_{3,2}, a_{3,3}])$
- $b(b_1[b_{1,1}, b_{1,2}, b_{1,3}], b_2[b_{2,1}, b_{2,2}, b_{2,3}], b_3[b_{3,1}, b_{3,2}, b_{3,3}])$
- $c(c_1[c_{1,1}, c_{1,2}, c_{1,3}], c_2[c_{2,1}, c_{2,2}, c_{2,3}], c_3[c_{3,1}, c_{3,2}, c_{3,3}])$
- $d(d_1[d_{1,1}, d_{1,2}, d_{1,3}], d_2[d_{2,1}, d_{2,2}, d_{2,3}], d_3[d_{3,1}, d_{3,2}, d_{3,3}])$

So, the set $\{a_1, a_2, a_3\}$ represents the values of attribute a at its first granularity level. The set $\{a_{1,1}, a_{1,2}, a_{1,3}, a_{2,1}, a_{2,2}, a_{2,3}, a_{3,1}, a_{3,2}, a_{3,3}\}$ represents the values of attribute a at its second granularity level. Attributes in $\{b, c, d\}$ have a similar representation. Clearly, $a_{i,j}$ is finer than a_i, for any i, j.

Now, we assume that query $q = a_{i,1} * b_i * c_{i,3} * d_i$ is submitted to S. There is number of options for solving q.

The first step to solve the query is to generalize $a_{i,1}$ to a_i and $c_{i,3}$ to c. This way query q is replaced by a new query $q_1 = a_i * b_i * d_i$. Now, either there are objects in S satisfying q_1 or further generalization of q_1 is needed. In the first case, we can only say that objects matching q_1, may satisfy q. Further generalization of q will decrease the chance that the retrieved objects will match q. Since the granularity of attributes used in q_1 is the same as the granularity of attributes in S, we can use cooperative query answering approach (see [7], [8], [2]) to find the nearest objects in S matching q_1. If there is a number of objects in S satisfying q_1, then we can use knowledge discovery methods to check which of these objects should satisfy the property $a_{i,1} * c_{i,3}$ and the same should satisfy query q. To be more precise, we search $DAIS$ for a site which has overlapping attributes with S, including attributes a, c. The granularity level of attributes a, c has to be the same as their granularity level in q. For instance, if S_1 is identified as such a site, we extract from S_1 definitions of $a_{i,1}$ and $c_{i,3}$ in terms of the overlapping attributes between S and S_1. These definitions are used to identify which objects retrieved by q_1 should also match query q.

Distributive property $t_1 * (t_2 + t_3) = (t_1 * t_2) + (t_1 * t_3)$, mentioned earlier, is important because of the replacement of values of attributes either in q or in q_1 by terms which are in disjunctive form. For instance, if $d_i \longrightarrow a_{i,1}$ and $c_i \longrightarrow a_{i,1}$ are extracted at remote sites for S, then $d_i + c_i$ may replace $a_{i,1}$ in q.

Finally, we can check what values of the attribute a and of the attribute c are implied by $d_i * b_{i,2}$ at remote sites for S and if any of these implications (rules) have high confidence and high support. This information is used to identify which objects in S can be seen as the closest match for objects described by q.

References

1. Benjamins, V. R., Fensel, D., Prez, A. G. (1998) Knowledge management through ontologies, in *Proceedings of the 2nd International Conference on Practical Aspects of Knowledge Management (PAKM-98)*, Basel, Switzerland.
2. Chu, W., Yang, H., Chiang, K., Minock, M., Chow, G., Larson, C. (1996) Cobase: A scalable and extensible cooperative information system, in *Journal of Intelligent Information Systems*, Vol. 6, No. 2/3, 223-259
3. Dardzińska, A., Raś, Z.W. (2003) Rule-Based Chase Algorithm for Partially Incomplete Information Systems, in **Proceedings of the Second International Workshop on Active Mining (AM'2003)**, Maebashi City, Japan, October, 2003, 42-51
4. Dardzińska, A., Raś, Z.W. (2003) On Rules Discovery from Incomplete Information Systems, in **Proceedings of ICDM'03 Workshop on Foundations and New Directions of Data Mining**, (Eds: T.Y. Lin, X. Hu, S. Ohsuga, C. Liau), Melbourne, Florida, IEEE Computer Society, 2003, 31-35
5. Dardzińska, A., Raś, Z.W. (2003) Chasing Unknown Values in Incomplete Information Systems, in **Proceedings of ICDM'03 Workshop on Foundations and New Directions of Data Mining**, (Eds: T.Y. Lin, X. Hu, S. Ohsuga, C. Liau), Melbourne, Florida, IEEE Computer Society, 2003, 24-30

6. Fensel, D., (1998), *Ontologies: a silver bullet for knowledge management and electronic commerce*, Springer-Verlag, 1998
7. Gaasterland, T. (1997) Cooperative answering through controlled query relaxation, in *IEEE Expert*, Vol. 12, No. 5, 48-59
8. Godfrey, P. (1997) Minimization in cooperative response to failing database queries, in *International Journal of Cooperative Information Systems*, Vol. 6, No. 2, 95-149
9. Guarino, N., ed. (1998) Formal Ontology in Information Systems, IOS Press, Amsterdam
10. Guarino, N., Giaretta, P. (1995) Ontologies and knowledge bases, towards a terminological clarification, in *Towards Very Large Knowledge Bases: Knowledge Building and Knowledge Sharing*, IOS Press
11. Pawlak, Z. (1991) Rough sets-theoretical aspects of reasoning about data, Kluwer, Dordrecht
12. Pawlak, Z. (1991) Information systems - theoretical foundations, in **Information Systems Journal**, Vol. 6, 1981, 205-218
13. Raś, Z.W. (1994) Dictionaries in a distributed knowledge-based system, in **Concurrent Engineering: Research and Applications**, Conference Proceedings, Pittsburgh, Penn., Concurrent Technologies Corporation, pp. 383-390
14. Raś, Z.W., Dardzińska, A. (2004) Ontology Based Distributed Autonomous Knowledge Systems, in **Information Systems International Journal**, Elsevier, Vol. 29, No. 1, 2004, 47-58
15. Raś, Z.W., Dardzińska, A. (2004) Query answering based on collaboration and chase, in **Proceedings of FQAS 2004 Conference**, Lyon, France, LNCS/LNAI, No. 3055, Springer-Verlag, 125-136
16. Raś, Z.W., Joshi, S. Query approximate answering system for an incomplete DKBS, in **Fundamenta Informaticae Journal**, IOS Press, Vol. 30, No. 3/4, 1997, 313-324
17. Sowa, J.F. (2000a) Ontology, metadata, and semiotics, in B. Ganter & G. W. Mineau, eds., *Conceptual Structures: Logical, Linguistic, and Computational Issues*, LNAI, No. 1867, Springer-Verlag, Berlin, 2000, pp. 55-81
18. Sowa, J.F. (2000b) Knowledge Representation: Logical, Philosophical, and Computational Foundations, Brooks/Cole Publishing Co., Pacific Grove, CA.
19. Sowa, J.F. (1999a) Ontological categories, in L. Albertazzi, ed., *Shapes of Forms: From Gestalt Psychology and Phenomenology to Ontology and Mathematics*, Kluwer Academic Publishers, Dordrecht, 1999, pp. 307-340.
20. Van Heijst, G., Schreiber, A., Wielinga, B. (1997) Using explicit ontologies in KBS development, in *International Journal of Human and Computer Studies*, Vol. 46, No. 2/3, 183-292.

Evaluation of Two Systems on Multi-class Multi-label Document Classification

Xiao Luo and A. Nur Zincir-Heywood

Faculty of Computer Science, Dalhousie University,
6050 University Avenue, Halifax, NS, Canada B3H 1W5
{luo, zincir}@cs.dal.ca

Abstract. In the world of text document classification, the most general case is that in which a document can be classified into more than one category, the multi-label problem. This paper investigates the performance of two document classification systems applied to the task of multi-class multi-label document classification. Both systems consider the pattern of co-occurrences in documents of multiple categories. One system is based on a novel sequential data representation combined with a kNN classifier designed to make use of sequence information. The other is based on the "Latent Semantic Indexing" analysis combined with the traditional kNN classifier. The experimental results show that the first system performs better than the second on multi-labeled documents, while the second performs better on uni-labeled documents. Performance therefore depends on the dataset applied and the objective of the application.

1 Introduction

Text documents classification is one of the tasks of content-based document management. It is a problem of assigning a document into one or more classes. In multi-class document classification, there are more than two classes, however documents can be uni-labeled. On the other hand, in multi-label classification, a document may fall into more than one class, thus a multi-label classifier should be employed. For example, given classes "North America", "Asia", "Europe", a news article about the trade relationship between U.S.A and France may be labeled both to the "North America" and the "Europe" classes.

In this paper, we investigate the performance of two document classification systems regarding the task of multi-class multi-label document classification. Both of the systems consider the patterns of co-occurrences in documents or categories, and solve the high dimensionality problem of the traditional vector space model. The first system is based on a novel document representation technique developed by the authors – a hierarchical Self Organizing Feature Map (SOM) architecture – to encode the documents by first considering the relationships between characters, then words, and then word co-occurrences. After which, word and word co-occurrence sequences were constructed to represent each document. This system automates the identification of typical document characteristics, while considering the significance of the order of

M.-S. Hacid et al. (Eds.): ISMIS 2005, LNAI 3488, pp. 161–169, 2005.
© Springer-Verlag Berlin Heidelberg 2005

words in a document. In the second system, documents are first represented using the traditional vector space model (VSM), and then Latent Semantic Indexing is used to encode the original vectors into a lower dimensional space. It constructs the association within documents and terms from a "Semantic" view. The k-Nearest Neighbour (kNN) classification algorithm is employed at the stage categorization of both systems. However, to make use of the sequence information that the first system captures, new similarity function designed by the authors is employed, whereas kNN is applied using cosine similarity function to the second system. To evaluate both of the systems, experiments are performed on a subset of Reuters-21578 data set. The results show that the first system performs better than the second one on the multi-labeled documents; while the second performs better on the uni-labeled documents. The overall performances of both systems are very competitive, however the first system emphasizes the significant order of the words within a document, whereas the second system emphasizes the semantic association within the words and documents.

The rest of the paper is organized as follows: Section 2 presents the system framework and the data preprocessing applied to both systems. Section 3 describes the encoded data representation model designed by the authors, whereas section 4 presents the alternative Latent Semantic Indexing algorithm. The classification algorithm employed is described in section 5. Experiments performed and results obtained are presented in section 6. Finally, conclusions are drawn and future work is discussed in section 7.

2   System Framework and Document Pre-processing

The principle interest in this work is the scheme used to express co-occurrences consequently; the pre-processing and classification stages remain the same for both systems. Pre-processing removes all tags and non-textual data from the original document. Then a simple part-of-speech (POS) tagging algorithm [3] is used to select nouns from the document after which special nouns are removed. What is left is used as the input for both of the representation systems.

3   The Encoded Sequential Document Representation

In this document representation, we make use of the ability of an unsupervised learning system – Self Organizing Feature Map (SOM) – to provide approximations of a high dimensional input in a lower dimensional space [5, 6]. The SOM acts as an encoder to represent a large input space by finding a smaller set of prototypes.

Thus, in this work, a hierarchical SOM architecture is developed to understand the documents by first encoding the relationships between characters, words, and then words co-occurrences. The hierarchical nature of the model and the corresponding U-matrix of trained SOMs are shown in Figure 1. In this model, the system is defined by the following three steps:

1) Input for the First-Level SOMs: The assumption at this level is that the SOM forms a codebook for the patterns in characters that occur in a specific document category. In order to train an SOM to recognize patterns in characters, the document data must be formatted in such a way as to distinguish characters and highlight the

relationships between them. Characters can easily be represented by their ASCII representation. However, for simplicity, we enumerated them by the numbers 1 to 26, i.e. no differentiation between upper and lower case. The relationships between characters are represented by a character's position, or time index, in a word. It should be noted that it is important to repeat these words as many times as they occur in the documents, so that the neurons on the SOM will be more excited by the characters of the more frequent words and their information will be more efficiently encoded.

2) Input for the Second-Level SOMs: The assumption at this level is that the 2nd level SOM forms a codebook for the patterns in words that occur in a specific document category. When a character and its index are run through a trained first-level SOM, the closest neurons (in the Euclidian sense), or *Best Matching Units* (*BMUs*), are used to represent the input space. A two-step process is used to create a vector for each word, k, which is input to the first-level SOM of each document:

- Form a vector of dimension equal to the number of neurons (r) in the first-level SOM, where each entry of the vector corresponds to a neuron on the first-level SOM, and initialize each entry of the vector to 0.
- For each character of word k,

  o   Observe which neurons n_1, n_2, ..., n_r are closest.
  o   Increase entries in the vector corresponding to the 3 most affected *BMUs* by $1/j$, $1 \leq j \leq 3$.

Hence, each vector represents a word through the sum of its characters. The results given by the second-level SOM are clusters of words on the second-level SOM.

3) Input for the Third-Level SOMs: The assumption at this level is that the SOM forms a codebook for the patterns in word co-occurrence that occur in a specific document category. In the context of this architecture, word co-occurrence is simply a group of consecutive words in a document. The consecutive words are from a single document with a sliding window of size 3. The input space of the third-level SOM is formed in a similar manner to that in the second-level, except that each word in the word co-occurrences is encoded in terms of the indexes of the 3 closest *BMUs* resulting from word vectors passed through the second-level SOMs. Thus, the length of the input vector to the third-level SOM is 9. The results given by third-level SOM are clusters of word co-occurrence on the third-level SOM.

After training the SOMs, we analyzed the results of the trained second and third level SOMs. We observed that documents from the same category always excited the same or similar parts of the second and third level SOMs respectively, as well as sharing *BMU* sequences with each other, Figures 2-3. Moreover, we observed that the different categories have their own characteristic most frequent *BMU* sequences. Based on these observations, we propose a document representation system where each document has two sequence representations: The first one is based on the second-level SOM, i.e. the word based sequence representation. The other is based on the third-level SOM, i.e. the word co-occurrence based sequence representation. These two sequence representations are combined together during the classification stage. The sequence representation (word/word co-occurrence) is defined as a two dimensional vector. The first dimension of the vector is the index of the *BMUs* on the second (third) level SOM; the second dimension is the Euclidean distance to the corresponding *BMUs*.

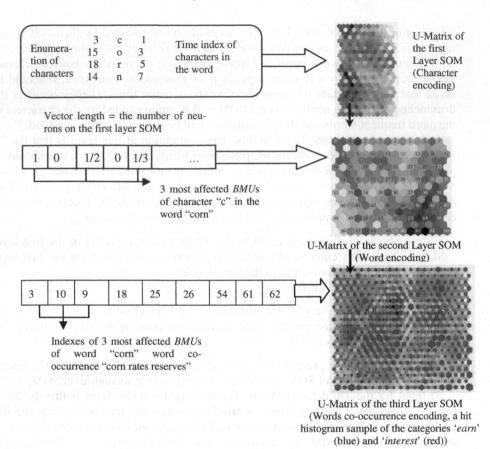

Vector length = the number of neurons on the first layer SOM

3 most affected *BMU*s of character "c" in the word "corn"

Indexes of 3 most affected *BMU*s of word "corn" word co-occurrence "corn rates reserves"

Fig. 1. An overview of the hierarchical SOMs encoding architecture

4 Latent Semantic Indexing (LSI)

A lot of research has been performed using Latent Semantic Indexing (LSI) for information retrieval with many good results for text retrieval, in particular [2, 4]. However, very little consideration has been given to the performance of LSI on multi-class multi-label document classification problems. LSI emphasizes capturing words or term co-occurrences based on the semantics or "latent" associations. The mapping of the original vectors into new vectors is based on Singular Value Decomposition (SVD) applied to the original data vectors [1, 7]. Usually, the original document vectors are constructed using the so-called vector space model and the TF/IDF weighting schema. There are many TF/IDF weighting schemas. The one we used here is:

$$P_{ij} = tf_{ij} \cdot log \ (N/df_i) \tag{1}$$

P_{ij}: Weight of term t_j in document d_i
tf_{ij}: Frequency of term t_j in document d_i

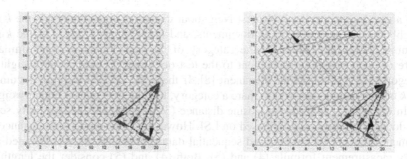

Fig. 2. BMU sequences of two documents from category "Earn" on the second-level SOM

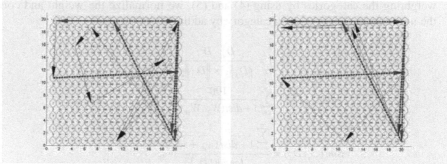

Fig. 3. BMU sequences of two documents from category "Earn" on the third-level SOM

N: Total number of documents in corpus
df_i: Number of documents containing term t_j

Moreover, LSI omits all but the k largest singular values. Here, k is an appropriate value to represent the dimension of the low-dimensional space for the corpus. Hence, the approximation of $A_{n \times m}$ becomes [7]:

$$\hat{A}_{n \times m} = U_{n \times k} S_{k \times k} V_{m \times k}^{T}$$ (2)

A_{nxm}- is a $n \times m$ matrix representing documents
$U_{n \times r} - (u_1, u_2, ...u_r)$ is the term-concept matrix
$S_{r \times r} - diag(\partial_1, \partial_2, ...\partial_r)$, S_{ii} is the strength of concept i
$V_{m \times r} - (v_1, v_2..., v_r)$ is the document-concept matrix

In the experiments performed here, a large range of k values (from 25 to 1125) was explored to fully investigate its efficiency on the multi-class multi-label documents classification.

5 The Document Classification Algorithm Employed

The k-Nearest Neighbour (kNN) classifier algorithm has been studied extensively for text categorization by Yang and Liu [8]. The kNN algorithm is quite simple: To classify a test document, the k-Nearest Neighbour classifier algorithm finds the k nearest neighbours among the training documents, and uses category labels of the k nearest training documents to predict the category of the test document. The similarity in score of each neighbour document to the test document is used as the weight of the categories of the neighbour document [8]. If there are several training documents in the k nearest neighbour, which share a category, the category gets a higher weight.

In this work, we used the Cosine distance (3) to calculate the similarity score for the document representation based on LSI. However, since the Cosine distance measurement does not fit the encoded sequential data representation, we designed a similarity measurement formula (4) and (5). Both (4) and (5) consider the length of the shared *BMU* sequences, in which (4) emphasizes the similarity degree of the *BMU*s in a sequence, while (5) emphasizes the length of the document to be measured. After weighting the categories by using (4) and (5), we normalize the weight and combine the normalized weight of each category by adding them together.

$$Sim\,(D_i,D_j) = \frac{D_i \cdot D_j}{\|D_i\|_2 \times \|D_j\|_2} \tag{3}$$

$$Sim(D_i,D_j) = \sum_{k=1}^{n} \frac{100}{1 + dist(W_{ik},W_{jk})} \times n \tag{4}$$

$$Sim(D_i,D_j) = \frac{\sum_{k=1}^{n} \frac{1}{1 + dist(w_{ik} + w_{jk})}}{length(D_j)} \tag{5}$$

D_i: Test document to be categorized.
D_j: Document in the training set.
n : Total number of *BMU*s in common *BMU* sequences of D_i and D_j.
W: Euclidean distance of a word to the corresponding *BMU*
$dist(W_{ik}, W_{jk})$: The distance between W and the corresponding *BMU* in the common *BMU* sequences of D_i and D_j. This shows the similarity between words (word co-occurrences)
$length(D_j)$: Length of the document in the training set in terms of *BMU* sequences.

6   Experimental Setup and Results

In this work, we employed a well-known multi-class multi-label document data set - Reuters-21578[1]. There are a total of 12612 news stories in this collection. These stories are in English, where 9603 are pre-defined as the training set, and 3299 are pre-defined as the test set. In our experiments, all 9603 training files are used, which belong to 118 categories. In order to fully analyze the performance of the systems for the multi-class multi-label document classification problem, we chose 6 of the top 10 categories of the Reuters-21578 data set to test the categorization performance. These categories are "Earn", "Money-fx", "Interest", "Grain", "Wheat" and "Corn". The

---

[1] Reuters data set, http://www.daviddlewis.com/resources/testcollections/reuters21578/

relationships between these categories in the training set are shown in Figure 4, and are the same as their relationships in the test set. Moreover, there are 8231 nouns left after pre-processing; where it is these nouns that are used to build the SOM and LSI representations.

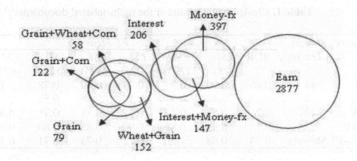

Fig. 4. Size and relationship of the six categories in the training set

Facing a multi-labeled (N labels) test document, we classify the test document to the top N weighted categories. The F1-measure is used to measure performance. We experiment with four kNN limits for the SOM representation — k = 3, 5, 10 and 15, whereas seven kNN limits (k = 25, 115, 225, 425, 525, 625, and 1125) for the LSI representation. In this case, our experiments show that "k = 5" gives the best performance in terms of the Macro F1-measure score.

$$R = \frac{TP}{TP+FN} \quad (6) \qquad P = \frac{TP}{TP+FP} \quad (7) \qquad F1-measure = \frac{2RP}{R+P} \quad (8)$$

TP : Positive examples, classified to be positive.
FN : Positive examples, classified to be negative.
FP: Negative examples, classified to be positive.

Tables 1 and 2 show most of the results on multi-labeled documents and uni-labeled documents, respectively. Table 3 shows the Macro F1-measure of the multi-labeled and uni-labeled documents. It is apparent that both systems have very competitive performance on the task of multi-class multi-label document classification. From the returned Macro-F1 value, the system based on the sequential document representation performs better than the system based on LSI. On the other hand, LSI works better, where each document is based on a single topic. The experiments show that LSI does work better on the uni-labeled documents on some k values (25 or 125). However, it works worse on the multi-labeled documents whatever the k value is.

The encoded sequential document representation can capture the characteristic sequences for documents and categories. Good performance is achieved by utilizing the sequence information for classification. The results show that it works better for the relatively larger categories, such as "Money+Interest", "Grain+Wheat" and "Earn". We conclude the reasons behind this is: This data representation is based on the machine-learning algorithm to capture the characteristic word or word co-occurrences for categories, so the more frequent the word or word co-occurrences are, the more easily it can be caught and represented by the neurons of the hierarchical SOM based architecture developed here. In the experimental corpus, the larger categories present more frequent word or word co-occurrences to the architecture.

Table 1. Classification results of the multi-labeled documents[2,3]

Category	Size in Test set	F1-Measure							
		SDR	LSI (25)	LSI (125)	LSI (225)	LSI (425)	LSI (525)	LSI (625)	LSI (1125)
M+I	43	0.86	0.79	0.73	0.74	0.80	0.78	0.78	0.67
G+C	34	0.55	0.44	0.54	0.59	0.59	0.58	0.52	0.56
G+W	49	0.76	0.62	0.43	0.71	0.73	0.71	0.69	0.65
G+C+W	22	0.75	0.98	0.88	0.90	0.85	0.80	0.86	0.76
Micro-F1 Measure		0.74	0.68	0.61	0.72	0.73	0.71	0.70	0.65

Table 2. Classification results of the uni-labeled documents[3]

Category	Size in Test set	F1-Measure							
		SDR	LSI (25)	LSI (125)	LSI (225)	LSI (425)	LSI (525)	LSI (625)	LSI (1125)
Earn	1087	0.97	0.97	0.97	0.96	0.96	0.96	0.95	0.94
Money	136	0.61	0.68	0.67	0.64	0.58	0.58	0.56	0.56
Interest	88	0.44	0.54	0.61	0.56	0.57	0.58	0.58	0.51
Grain	44	0.35	0.40	0.35	0.34	0.30	0.29	0.23	0.29
Micro-F1 Measure		0.88	0.89	0.89	0.88	0.87	0.87	0.86	0.85

Table 3. The overall classification results of multi-labeled and uni-labeled documents[2]

	SDR	LSI (25)	LSI (125)	LSI (225)	LSI (425)	LSI (525)	LSI (625)	LSI (1125)
Macro-F1	0.81	0.78	0.75	0.80	0.80	0.75	0.75	0.75

7 Conclusion and Future Work

Through this work, we explored the performance of two document classification systems regarding the task of multi-class multi-label document classification. Both of the systems consider the patterns of co-occurrences in documents or categories, and solve the high dimensionality problem associated with the traditional vector space model. However, the first system considers the term co-occurrences from the aspect of the order of the terms within documents, while the Latent Semantic Indexing considers

---

[2] M+I: "Money-fx+Interest"; G+C: "Grain+Corn"; G+W: "Grain+Wheat"; G+C+W: "Grain+Corn+Wheat".

[3] SDR: Sequential Document Representation; LSI (n): Latent Semantic Indexing with k value=n.

the term co-occurrences from the aspect of semantic association within them and documents.

The experimental results show that the SOM representation performs better than the LSI on the multi-labeled documents; while LSI performs better on the uni-labeled documents. The over all performances of both systems are very competitive. The encoding mechanism of the SOM system can efficiently work on both textual and non-textual data. Since the order and the frequency of patterns are maintained as they appear before input to the encoding architecture, it is expected to perform better for other data classification applications such as medical or business information systems where sequence information is more significant and important. Moreover, it can be used for online data classification without seeing all the terms or patterns in the whole corpus. The methodology of the LSI system is easy to use and discovered the semantic associations between the terms within the documents. It is very accurate when each document is on a single topic and the terms are partitioned among the topics such that each topic distribution has high probability on its own terms.

The idea of sequential data representation for document classification is new, more improvements such as looking into the integration of different sizes of the SOMs for the encoding architecture, investigating other styles of representations on top of the encoding architecture, will be done in the future. In addition, other classifiers, which explicitly support sequence classification, will also be analyzed and utilized in the later research.

References

1. Ando, R. K., Lee L.: Iterative Residual Rescaling: An Analysis and Generalization of LSI. Proceedings of the ACM SIGIR'01 (2001) 154-162
2. Berry, M. W., Dumais, S. T., O'Brien G. W.: Using Linear Algebra for Intelligent Information Retrieval. SIAM Review, 37(4) (1995) 573-595
3. Brill, E.: A Simple Rule Based Part of Speech Tagger. Proceedings of the 3rd Conference on Applied Natural Language Processing (1992) 152-155
4. Deerwester, S., Dumais, S. T., Landauer, T. K., Furnas, G. W. and Harshman, R. A.: Indexing by Latent Semantic Analysis. Journal of the Society for Information Science 41(6) (1990) 391-407
5. Haykin, S.: Neural Networks - A Comprehensive Foundation, Chapter-9: Self-Organizing Maps. Second Edition, Prentice Hall (1999) ISBN 0-13-273350-1
6. Luo, X., Zincir-Heywood, A. N.: A Comparison of SOM Based Document Categorization Systems. Proceedings of the IEEE International Joint Conference on Neural Networks (2003) 1786-1791
7. Papadimitriou, C. H., Raghavan, P., Tamaki, H., Vempala, S.: Latent Semantic Indexing: A probabilistic Analysis. Proceedings of the 17th ACM Symposium on the Principles of Database Systems (1998) 159-168
8. Yang Y., Liu X.: A Re-examination of Text Categorization Methods. Proceedings of the ACM SIGIR'99 (1999) 42-49

Uncertain Knowledge Gathering: An Evolutionary Approach

Dennis Hooijmaijers and Damien Bright

School of Computer and Information Science,
University of South Australia,
Mawson Lakes SA 5095, Australia
{dennis.hooijmaijers, damien.bright}@unisa.edu.au

Abstract. Information and the knowledge pertaining to it are important to making informed decisions. In domains where knowledge changes quickly, such as business and open source intelligence gathering there is a need to represent and manage the collection of dynamic information from multiple sources. Some of this information may be transitory due to its situated context and time-limited value (eg driven by a changing business market). Ontologies offer a way to model concepts and relationships from information sources and for dynamic domains it is important to look at how to support evolution of knowledge represented in an ontology, the change management of an ontology and how to maintain consistency when mapping and merging knowledge from multiple sources to an ontology base. One of the difficulties is that often contradictions can occur and sources may be unreliable. In this paper we introduce a technique for merging knowledge while ensuring that the reliability of that knowledge is captured and present a model which supports ontology evolution through the inclusion of trust and belief measures.

1 Introduction

This paper introduces an evolutionary approach for the management of information models which need to reflect evolving knowledge related to uncertain and/or dynamically changing domains. This is often driven by the need to keep track of changing relationships in a dynamic operating environment such as a rapidly changing market in a business domain or intelligence gathering operations. There is increasing interest in open source intelligence gathering (OSINT) [18] where there are multiple sources of information in the public domain with contradictions and unreliability associated with the sources. For business there is interest in OSINT for time critical decision making in dynamic domains (eg rapidly changing markets, portfolio management) and also its use in business competitive intelligence (CI) [20]. As support for standardized methods of knowledge exchange gains momentum, ontologies [1] are increasingly being used to store information models and the need to keep track of an ontology's development has resulted in increasing research work in the area of ontology evolution [2-4]. Our notion of an ontology follows that of [1] where an ontology is defined as metadata that explicitly defines the semantics of terminology in a ma-

M.-S. Hacid et al. (Eds.): ISMIS 2005, LNAI 3488, pp. 170–181, 2005.
© Springer-Verlag Berlin Heidelberg 2005

chine readable format. In this paper we use the ontology web language (OWL) [5] as a standardized way of representing an information model as part of the proposed system. There has been research work looking at how to analyze dynamic information sources such as the internet and then through techniques such as text mining, natural language processing and other processes create models of how concepts relate to each other [18]. For the system presented here we assume that a process has already been applied (associated with what we term an information gathering (IG) agent which is defined as an entity responsible for gathering and processing information into an information source) to convert information sources into a common ontological form (OWL) but that there may still exist issues such as semantic heterogeneity (ie same name used for different concepts or different names used for the same concept) across sources.

Ontology evolution can be described as the adaptation of an ontology to reflect the changing state of a domain [3] which may include the change management process by which the ontology is kept consistent [6]. Building up a correct ontology for a specific domain can be a time intensive activity and generally requires a knowledge or domain expert. Domain experts perform a variety of tasks involved with managing information for a specific domain, while knowledge experts usually create the semantics and terminology of a specific domain. A domain expert is often required to resolve conflicts, handle uncertainty, and to make decisions, such as how data items may relate to each other across multiple sources. This necessity to compare, contrast and resolve differences between multiple sources is part of the process of information fusion [7]. This process can often be broken down to a mapping and merging problem [8]. Knowledge of the semantics involved in the context of information can be used to discover and make decisions about appropriate merges and relationships; this is known as a mapping. Our approach to this problem assumes that decisions will be made by one or more decision makers (DMs) who utilize a knowledge management system. The role of the system in this context is to facilitate the storage and revision of an information model resulting from the fusion of sources supplied by multiple IG agents, as discussed by [8], with the DM making decisions about uncertain or inaccurate knowledge representation derived from the source. Not all sources are equal in terms of reliability and because of the time critical nature of the system it is up to the DM to decide on their confidence in sources at the time the information needs to be merged. Because there may be different DMs who have different levels of domain knowledge we propose that this operation should be modified both by the DM's confidence in the source (can be considered in terms of a belief measure) and also the reputation of the DM or system trust in the DM (ie how much should the system trust the assignment of belief values?).

There is extensive research [7-9] into automated approaches for knowledge fusion problems but for domains where knowledge is transient, uncertain or incomplete there is a need to continually capture domain knowledge and this generally requires some mechanism for rapid assimilation to enhance decisions based on the information and the knowledge describing it. Merging of ontologies, based on interaction with a user through the use of automatically generated suggestions is a feature of tools such as PROMPT [7] and Chimaera [9]. Tools like Protégé-2000 [13] also provide editing functionality that can help support some of the requirements of ontology evolution. However there is still a need to effectively capture knowledge through user interaction (especially for the mapping problem) where this knowledge is not always static or certain and these tools currently provide no mechanism for representing this uncertainty. The main contribution of this paper is the proposal of a knowledge management system based on evolving ontologies to support evolutionary change resulting from uncertainty in domain knowledge and the discussion of results obtained using preliminary experiments with an initial prototype. Part of this includes the aim of minimizing the level of human interaction when performing an information fusion using evolving ontologies, in particular to postpone the need for a domain expert to validate the ontology. The use of uncertainty in stored relationships reflects the need to represent uncertainty present in domain knowledge. This could be due to incomplete or inaccurate information (eg as a result of the lack of domain knowledge by a user who needs to store information) or the need to keep track of a dynamic set of relationships which change due to nature of the domain.

This paper is structured as follows: In section 2 a brief overview of related work is presented. Section 3 introduces our model of an evolutionary ontology. Section 4 provides an overview of our proposed system model and the initial prototype implementation. Section 5 discusses a relevant case study from an intelligence gathering domain and finally section 6 is our conclusion and discussion of future work.

2 Related Work

Ontologies are becoming widely used as a representation language and are used to assist in the fusion of information [7, 10]. Many tools supply assistance to domain experts when the fusion of ontologies is necessary. One limitation of all current implementations is that it is assumed that the ontologies being merged are static structures and the knowledge contained is certain. This limits the use of these tools in real world situations where knowledge is subjective and the creators of the knowledge are not always completely certain on the correct semantics of the concepts contained within. An ontology consists of a hierarchy that relates classes via properties [11]. The property and hierarchy relationships are where we propose the uncertainty may occur. Although not yet supported by tools there has been recent work by [17] to apply a Bayesian approach to uncertainty modeling using OWL ontologies and a draft by W3C [23] on how to represent n-ary relations in OWL which presents patterns which could be used to handle belief values.

McGuinness et al [9] propose Chimaera as an ontology fusion tool. Chimaera's has a suggestion algorithm based on pattern matching. Chimaera searches through the first model and then using a set of reasons searches through the second model for a match. Another tool OntoMerge [8] was originally designed to convert ER models from database schema to an ontology, in a process called "Ontolization"[8]. Dou states that the process of Ontolization can't be fully automatic because only domain experts know the meanings and relationships of the terms. Thus it is only possible, for software, to provide assistance with this process. This manual mapping is utilised by OntoMerge to provide a mechanism for merging ontologies, which was proven to be a requirement for the translation process [7]. OntoMerge uses first-order logic to provide predicate axioms to map the source ontologies onto target ontology. Another ontology fusion tool is PROMPT, proposed by Noy et al [11]. PROMPT is a plug-in component for Protégé-2000 [4]. PROMPT was developed to provide a semi-automatic approach to merging ontologies by providing automation where attainable, and guidance where it is unable to decide upon the correct results. These tools supply suggestions in regards to the fusion of models. This implies that the user performs the fusion not the tool. This causes problems as the user's knowledge, in the domain, must be sufficient to ensure they know which suggestions to accept and additionally which extra mappings are required to ensure a successful fusion. The tools ability to quickly locate likely fusions would minimize the task of a domain expert to search through the models.

Ontology evolution is part of providing richer knowledge models [2]. When discussing ontology evolution versioning is a key concept [2,3] which allows the user to highlight the differences between two ontologies. The reason behind this is that as ontologies change the applications using them do not. This causes problems in that the static applications are expecting the ontology to be static and then manipulate the dynamic data described. Versioning allows the application to access the version of the ontology that it expects to use. In regards to our work the application using the ontology expects there to be changes and actively searches for possible solutions (based on belief values) of the ontology. This means that it is assumed applications are mostly concerned with the most relevant current state (or view) of the domain for a problem or decision at hand (eg the right information at the right time). Previous states supply a framework and a basis for the evolution but once the evolution is performed the previous state is fully incorporated with the new knowledge.

When evolving ontologies it is necessary to perform consistency checking to ensure the ontology is valid [3]. This need complicates the process of evolution as the ontology must remain consistent. Stanjanovic [3] further propose that the evolution process should be supervised and offer advice. Since the evolution process we are implementing revolves around the merging of new knowledge to the existing ontology we can leverage suggestion algorithms in current ontology merging tools to supply this advice. While supervision should be performed by a domain expert by including beliefs in the ontology structures we hope to assist the user in making informed decisions on an evolving knowledgebase.

3 Evolutionary Ontology Model

Often in time critical scenarios it is not possible to have a knowledge expert on hand to assist with knowledge management. In domains where new information is constantly being provided for decision making purposes there is a need for rapid merging of both the information and the relating semantic knowledge. This need for quick assimilation and the unavailability of a knowledge expert often leaves the task of merging in the hands of less qualified staff. Thus it is necessary to firstly ensure the knowledge is converted to a standardized representation language, like OWL [5]. This conversion can be easily achieved if a direct one to one mapping exists. If no one to one mapping exists the conversion can still be performed but it may contain errors. The challenge then is the resolution of semantic problems that may exist, such as the terminology used, the ambiguity of concepts or the semantic structure. A knowledge expert would be able to solve these discrepancies, but in time critical scenarios the knowledge expert often forms a "bottle neck" [13] that may be detrimental to achieving a deadline. To overcome the error of the semantics uncertain relationships can be made transient until they are confirmed or rejected and belief factors can be assigned to these transitory relationships in order to provide the end user with insight into the ontology and those relationships that may be incorrect. At some point the ontology will need to be "cleaned up" by a knowledge expert to remove erroneous relationships, ensure correct terminology and to reinforce correct semantics. In a time critical scenario it is useful to keep superfluous knowledge, with uncertainty, to allow for quick decisions to be made and this motivates our notion of an evolutionary ontology.

3.1 Ontology Evolution Process

The Evolutionary Ontology Model proposed in this paper aims at providing a mechanism for input, from multiple sources, into an evolving base ontology, σ_{base}. For such ontology to near completeness we need to add additional concepts (classes) and semantic relationships (properties or inheritance hierarchy) over time usually in the form of a new ontology, σ_{new}. Changes are driven by merging of new information and knowledge (converted to a standardized ontological form) with the base ontology. Therefore we can define a merge, M, of the two ontologies, such that the new knowledge is reflected in the resultant base ontology, σ^*_{base}, for each σ_{new}, as follows:

$$M(\sigma_{base}, \sigma_{new}) \rightarrow \sigma^*_{base} \tag{1}$$

To achieve this it is not enough to simply insert the set of relationships, R_{new}, into the set of original relationships R_{base}. There is often extra information and context that needs to be considered when inserting new relationships or concepts. An IG agent, in this work, is considered to be a provider of new information and the knowledge that pertains to it, that may be stored in a personal ontology. This is provided to a decision maker (DM) who makes decisions based on the information that the ontology describes. A major concern when accepting input from an IG agent is the correctness of the supplied information and knowledge. This is broken down into how strong is the DM's *belief* in the relationships in the agent's personal ontology and how strong is the system's *trust* in the DM. The aim is to capture these beliefs so that the structure of the ontology allows different *views* on the changing state of a domain model.

3.2 Ontology Change Operations

Critical to evolutionary ontologies is examining the operations used to manipulate and evolve the ontology. These operations are mainly derived from graph theory as shown in [13] and include the addition, modification and removal of concepts (nodes) and relationships (arcs). These operations provide a solid basis for the evolution of ontologies. In addition to standard operations [4] we propose additional operations, strengthen belief and weaken belief as well as specializing the add relationship and remove relationship to include belief and trust factors and to weaken belief. These additional operations allow for the system to capture beliefs about the relationships between knowledge concepts. The add relationship operation will need to ensure that the relationship doesn't exist and if it does will need to strengthen the belief of that relationship while the remove relationship operation needs to weaken the belief of the relationship. Once the belief is sufficiently small it may be more efficient for an ontology management process to remove this relationship.

The ontology model we use, OWL [5], consists of a set of nodes which in this solution can be considered to be concrete concepts. These nodes are connected by a mutable set of relationships that represent possible solution spaces of how these concepts relate. When multiple relationships occur between two concepts it is necessary to place limitations to ensure that only the most correct solutions are shown using views. A view is a selection (subset) of relationships designed to reduce the number of relationships, between two concepts, that are displayed to the DM. Views allow the DM to filter the solution space to select the best possible solution (relationship between two concepts) for their scenario. All views will contain a base set of relationships confirmed by a knowledge expert (i.e. the belief is 100%). Currently this can is achieved in two ways: a "max belief" view that shows the most probable relationships between concepts or a "max belief and max trust" view which shows the maximum belief of the input sources with the highest trust. The beliefs are evolutionary in nature, as other sources may concur or conflict with the current knowledge.

3.3 Assigning Belief and Trust Values

There are a number of formal models which have been applied to decision making and reasoning with uncertain, vague or incomplete information. These include Bayesian reasoning, belief networks, the Dempster-Shafer theory of evidence, fuzzy logic and general probability theory (see [16] for a review of uncertainty formalisms).

In non-standard probability models belief functions are used to allow a decision maker to assign bounds on probabilities linked to events without having to come up with exact probabilities which are often unavailable. We have chosen to use belief functions to represent the system belief in a relationship contained in the base ontology combined with belief revision based on the Certainty Factor (CF) Model developed by Buchanan and Shortliffe [19] in their work with the rule-based medical expert system MYCIN. Because of its simplicity and more natural appeal to users over the use of strict probability theory the CF model has been widely used to handle uncertainty in a range of rule-based expert systems. Certainty factors can be viewed as relative measures that do not translate to a measure of absolute belief. [16] indicates that CFs can be viewed as representing "changes of belief". Therefore they are useful in the heuristic approach (based on combining CFs) which we have adopted for belief revision under uncertainty. Certainty factors can be used to manage incrementally acquired evidence (eg from expert assessment) with different pieces of evidence having different certainty values. The CF model does not have a rigourous mathematical foundation like the Dempster-Shafer model but can be shown to approximate standard probability theory (see [16]) in many situations. CFs are numerical values in range [-1.0,1.0]. To support the required reinforcement and weakening operations we used a CF- combining function (eg see Stanford CF calculus [19]) which provides the necessary framework.

In this model system belief in a relationship is quantified (via a belief function) as a value in the range [0,1] which can be interpreted as a percentage value and stored as association information for a relationship. The ontology model stores the highest level of trust of a DM who has provided knowledge that causes a reinforcement of belief in or creation operation on a relationship. The advantage of keeping the highest trust value ensures that the current DM or user of the system can differentiate between multiple novice DMs of the past and one expert DM's view on a relationship.

In this initial proposal a CF is used to reflect the DM confidence in an information source being processed. This CF is then scaled based on the system trust in the DM. The idea of trust used in this proposal is based on work in reputation systems [14]. The machine belief B (R_m) is restricted to the range [0,1] and can be viewed as the degree of system belief that a relationship should exist based on the accumulated decision making evidence to date. This is because the machine belief B (R_m) determines whether a relationship R_m remains in the ontology or not with negative values having no meaning and a value reaching zero signifying that a relationship has expired and should be removed. Values of machine belief B are not able to be decremented below zero. The DM's overall certainty u_t is a standard CF in the range [-1,1] which needs to be applied to a selected relationship in an information source model being processed. Positive values represent an incremental belief and negative values represent an incremental disbelief in a relationship. Each selection utilizes a trust modifier, φ, (a scalar in the range [0,1]) which when applied to the DM's initial certainty u_1 in the IG agent from which the information originated (ie the DM confidence in the information source) acts as a weight to provide the overall certainty u_t. This is calculated using:

$$u_t = \varphi * u_1 \qquad (2)$$

The trust modifier, φ, represents the reputation of the DM (ie the amount of trust the system has in the DM based on their reputation or rating). This simple approach to representing trust has been adopted in the initial prototype of the system. The scale used for the trust modifier has a set of possible categories or levels ("Novice", "Intermediate", "Advanced", "Domain Expert", "Knowledge Expert") mapped to a set of numerical values in the range [0,1] which can be interpreted as percentages in the range [0%,100%]. This initial set of categories can easily be extended to provide a finer grained set of trust levels. The overall certainty u_t will be negative when weakening the belief in a relationship and positive to strengthen. To strengthen the system's current belief, B_i (R_m), on a relationship, R_m, the new knowledge concerning the existence of the relationship represented through the calculated value of u_t, with ($u_t >$ 0) the resultant machine belief B_f (R_m) can be revised using:

$$B_f (R_m) = B_i (R_m) + u_t - (B_i (R_m)* u_t) \qquad (3)$$

To weaken the belief, B_i (R_m), the new knowledge about the relationship represented by u_t, with ($u_t < 0$) and the machine belief is revised using:

$$B_f (R_m) = (u_t + B_i (R_m)) / (1- MIN (|B_i (R_m) |, | u_t |)) \qquad (4)$$

When a relationship is added between two concepts that already have existing relationships it is necessary to weaken the belief of all existing relationships. When a source has a different relationship between two concepts the implication is of contradicting the existing relationships. The "clean-up" process is performed by a knowledge expert ($\varphi = 1$). The process involves removing incorrect relationships and strengthening the belief in correct relationships to have no uncertainty. This can be performed at any time but should be conducted at regular intervals.

4 System Prototype

The system (see Fig 1) created aims to capture the beliefs and trust factors of relationships in an ontology. It is necessary to provide mechanisms for the DM to supply the necessary information to determine beliefs. This has been achieved by providing a mechanism for entering belief factors when a relationship between two concepts is created in the base ontology. The DM simply annotates their belief to the relationship. The system uses a trust factor in the DM to scale the new knowledge in regards to the impact on the current knowledge base. This is a procedure utilized to ensure that a source is verified before supplying its knowledge to the knowledge base. Once the verification is obtained the new knowledge can be merged into the existing knowledge base. For this system the fusion is currently performed by Protégé-2000 with the PROMPT plug-in [7]. This follows a series of suggestions to assist the DM in merging the concepts in the new knowledge to the current base ontology.

Once the merging and updating of beliefs is completed the DM is able to examine the ontology by use of views. Once a view is selected the DM is then able to provide a view of the instance data (information) and how it semantically interacts. An additional part of the system implemented involves editing of the ontology. This is achieved using Protégé-2000 and allows for the maintenance of the ontology in situations where incorrect concepts have been introduced. This allows the knowledge expert to adjust the ontology to ensure there is consistency.

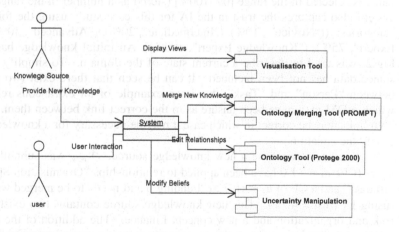

Fig. 1. System Overview showing the main system components

5 Case Study

Intelligence gathering is an important part of defense operations and often relies on channels of new information and knowledge originating from varied and different sources [22]. An Intelligence Analyst (IA), the decision maker, often needs to make informed decisions based on the knowledge and provide a solution of how the knowledge concepts work together to be able to provide their intelligence documentation. There is increased use of open source intelligence gathering from public domains like the internet to aid intelligence operations. Often the knowledge in these situations is uncertain while in other situations the IG agent providing the knowledge may be circumspect and require verification. In time critical situations the sheer volume of knowledge coming to the IA can make this a labour intensive task with decisions being made quickly and often ignoring some components of knowledge. Thus the IA needs to make multiple decisions to ensure the best possible presentation of the information and knowledge for their superiors. The following steps would be complementary with the needs of an IA in this type of scenario:

1. Decide on the standardization if necessary
2. Decide on how to complete the Merge of new knowledge
3. Decide on an appropriate view that provides the best solution space
4. Send up the chain of command to aid command level decisions

Using our proposed system and this procedure the IA would convert, if necessary, the information and knowledge to OWL, while including their confidence in the information source model. The IA then utilizes the fusion mechanism to fuse the new knowledge allowing for multiple solution spaces to be created. The process is repeated if new knowledge is obtained or if the Intelligence Documentation is rejected. The IA is required to categorize the sources providing the information and knowledge. This categorization is based on confidence or belief levels where a good proven source of information may have a higher belief value then an untried source. A belief value is selected in the range [0%,100%] (stored as a number in the range [0,1]). The system also captures the trust in the IA for this case study using the following trust categories: (("Novice" , 10%), ("Intermediate", 20%), ("Advanced", 40%), ("Domain Expert", 75%), ("Knowledge Expert", 100%)). An initial knowledge base, shown in Fig 2, was used to describe a current state of the domain. To simplify the view instance data has not been included. It can be seen that there exist two relationships between "Person" and "Task", this is an example of an extraneous relationship in which a DM may have been unsure as to the correct link between them. Alternately both links may be correct in which case it may be necessary for a knowledge expert to clarify the situation.

To this knowledgebase a new knowledge source, σ_{new}, was submitted by an IG agent (CFs u_1 = +1.0 have been applied to relationships "Organisation Sponsors" and "Budget" and a CF of u_1 = +0.7 to "Funding") and needs to be merged with the σ_{base} (using IA trust = 40%). This new knowledge source contains two existing concepts task and organization and a new concept Finance. The addition of the new concept and the relationships between the existing concepts is a merge operation by PROMPT and requires the belief to be adjusted by trust and CF values as shown in Fig 2 using eqns. (2) and (3). The relationship in σ_{new} between "Organisation" and "Task", "Organisation Sponsors", is different to the relationship between the same concepts in σ_{base}, "Organisation Tasks". This will create an extraneous relationship between these concepts and in turn weaken the beliefs of all other relationships between them, using eqn. (4), as shown in Fig 3.

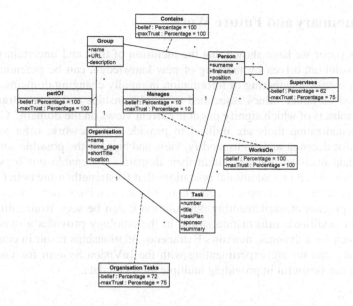

Fig. 2. Knowledgebase σ_{base} representing a current state of the domain

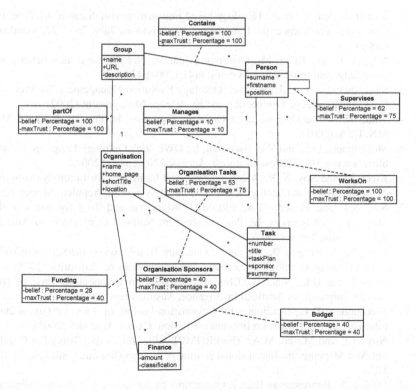

Fig. 3. Updated Knowledgebase $\sigma_{base}*$ after a new knowledge source σ_{new} is added

6 Summary and Future Work

In this paper we have shown that the inclusion of trust and uncertainty during ontology evolution, driven by merging of new knowledge, can be potentially valuable to the time critical gathering of information in rapidly changing domains. The approach is based on belief values associated with relationships and uses extraneous relationships subsets of which signify possible current views on the domain. Current merging and visualization tools are utilized to provide a framework, offer suggestions and allow for decision makers to modify, view and employ the possible solutions to problems and decision making within their domain. To enable ontology evolution we have introduced two additional operations that (i) strengthen the belief that a relationship between two concepts is correct and (ii) weaken the belief. Although we are still in the process of implementing our solution it can be seen from initial experiments that the additional information stored in the ontology provides a dynamic modeling approach for a dynamic domain. Extraneous relationships result in complex ontology structure and we are experimenting with the InVision System for visualization [21] which can be useful in providing multiple views on data.

References

1. Van Harmelen, F., et al.: Ontology-based information visualisation. In: Proc. of Fifth International Conference on Information Visualisation, July 25 - 27, London, England (2001).
2. Noy, N. F. and Klein, M.: Ontology evolution: Not the same as schema evolution. In: Knowledge and Information Systems, 6(4), (2004) 428-440.
3. Stojanovic, L., et al.: User-driven Ontology Evolution Management. In: Proc. of 13th Intl' Conf. on Knowledge Engineering and Knowledge Management (2002).
4. Sindt, T.: Formal Operations for Ontology Evolution. In: Proc. of ICET'03, Minneapolis, MN, USA, (2003).
5. McGuinness, D.L. and Van Harmelen, F.: OWL Web Ontology Language Overview 2003, http://www.w3.org/TR/owl-features/, Accessed November (2004).
6. Klein, M. and Noy, N. F.: A component-based framework for ontology evolution. In Proc. of the Workshop on Ontologies and Distributed Systemsm, Acpulco, Mexico (2003).
7. Noy, N.F. and Musen, M.A.: PROMPT: Algorithm and Tool for Automated Ontology Merging and Alignment. In: Proc. of the 17th National Conference on Artificial Intelligence, Austin, Texas (2000).
8. Dou, D., McDermott, D., and Qi, P.: Ontology Translation on the Semantic Web. In: Proc. of Int'l Conf. on Ontologies, Databases and Applications of Semantics (2003).
9. McGuinness, D.L., et al.: The Chimaera Ontology Environment. In: Proc. of The 17th National Conference on Artificial Intelligence, Austin, Texas (2000).
10. McGuinness, D.L.: Ontologies for Information Fusion. In: Proc. of Fusion 2003 The 6th International Conference on Information Fusion, Cairns, Australia (2003).
11. Noy, N.F. and Musen, M.A.: The PROMPT Suite: Interactive Tools For Ontology Merging And Mapping. In: International Journal of Human-Computer Studies, 59, (2003) 983–1024.
12. Dahl, F.A.: Representing Human Uncertainty by Subjective Likelihood Estimates. Preprint 2004 series, ISSN 0806-3842, Department of Mathematics, University of Oslo (2004).

13. Gennari, J.H., et al.: The Evolution of Protege: An Environment for Knowledge-Based Systems Development. Tech. Report SMI-2002-0943, Stanford Medical Informatics (2002).
14. Resnick, P., Zeckhauser, R., Friedman, E., and Kuwabara, K.: Reputation Systems. In: Communications of the ACM, 43(12), (2000) 45-48.
15. Noy, N. F., Kunnatur, S., Klein, M., and Musen, M. A.: Tracking changes during ontology evolution. In: 3rd Int. Semantic Web Conference (ISWC2004), Hiroshima, Japan (2004).
16. Parsons, S. and Hunter, A.: A Review of uncertainty formalisms. In: Applications of Uncertainty Formalisms, Lecture Notes in Computer Science, volume 1455, Springer (1998).
17. Ding, Z., Peng, Y., Pan, R.: A Bayesian Approach to Uncertainty Modeling in OWL Ontology. In: Proc. of the Int. Conf. on Advances in Intelligent Systems , November (2004).
18. Noble, D.F.: Assessing the Reliability of open Source Information. In: Proc. of 7th International Conference on Information Fusion, Stockholm, Sweden (2004).
19. Buchanan, B.G and Shortliffe, E.H.: Rule-Based Expert Systems. Reading, MA: AddisonWesley, (1984).
20. Johnson, C.H. (Editor): Competitive Intelligence: Where are the ethical limits. In: Special issue, Ethics in Economics, Nos. 3 & 4 (1998)
21. Pattison, T.R. and Phillips, M.P: View Coordination Architecture for Information Visualization. In: Australian Symposium on Information Visualisation, Sydney, Australia (2001).
22. Gauvin, M., Boury-Brisset, A.C., Auger, A.: Context, Ontology and Portfolio: Key Concepts for a Situational Awareness Knowledge Portal. In: Proc. of the 37th Hawaii International Conference on System Sciences (2004).
23. Noh, N., Rector, A.: Defining N-ary Relations on the Semantic Web: Use with Individuals W3C Working Draft, http://www.w3.org/TR/2004/WD-swbp-n-aryRelations-20040721/, Accessed December (2004).

Duality in Knowledge Compilation Techniques*

Neil V. Murray[1] and Erik Rosenthal[2]

[1] Department of Computer Science, State University of New York, Albany, NY 12222, USA
nvm@cs.albany.edu
[2] Department of Mathematics, University of New Haven, West Haven, CT 06516, USA
erosenthal@newhaven.edu

Abstract. Several classes of propositional formulas have been used as target languages for knowledge compilation. Some are based primarily on c-paths (essentially, the clauses in disjunctive normal form); others are based primarily on d-paths. Such duality is not surprising in light of the duality fundamental to classical logic. There is also duality among target languages in terms of how they treat links (complementary pairs of literals): Some are link-free; others are pairwise-linked (essentially, each pair of clauses is linked). In this paper, both types of duality are explored, first, by investigating the structure of existing forms, and secondly, by developing new forms for target languages.

1 Introduction

Several classes of propositional formulas have been used as target languages for knowledge compilation, including *Horn clauses, ordered binary decision diagrams, tries*[1], and sets of *prime implicates/implicants*—see, for example, [2, 3, 8, 12, 20, 21]. The discovery of formula classes that have properties that are useful for target languages is ongoing. Within the past several years, *decomposable negation normal form* [6] (DNNF), linkless formulas called *full dissolvents* [15], *factored negation normal form* [9] (FNNF), and *pairwise-linked* clause sets, in which every pair of clauses contain complementary literals (called EPCCL in [10]), have been investigated as target languages. It is not surprising that dualities arise when comparing target languages, but the extent of their prevalence may be surprising.

Most research has restricted attention to *conjunctive normal form* (CNF). This may be because the structure of *negation normal form* (NNF) can be quite complex. However, there is growing interest in target languages that are subclasses of NNF. Decomposable negation normal form, studied by Darwiche [5, 6], is one such class. They are linkless and have the property that atoms are not shared across conjunctions. Every DNNF formula is automatically a *full dissolvent*—the end result of applying path dissolution to a formula until it is linkless. Although linkless, full dissolvents may share atoms across conjunctions. It turns out that many of the applications of DNNF depend primarily on

---

* This research was supported in part by the National Science Foundation under grant CCR-0229339.
[1] A variation of a tree, often used to store dictionaries.

M.-S. Hacid et al. (Eds.): ISMIS 2005, LNAI 3488, pp. 182–190, 2005.
© Springer-Verlag Berlin Heidelberg 2005

the linkless property and are available and equally efficient with full dissolvents [15]. Moreover, full dissolvents can be advantageous both in time and in the size of the resulting formula.

The class FNNF of factored negation normal form formulas is introduced in [9]. They provide a canonical representation of arbitrary boolean functions. They are closely related to BDDs, but there is a DPLL-like tableau procedure for computing them that operates in PSPACE.

The pairwise-linked formulas introduced by Hai and Jigui [10] appear to be structurally quite different from—and rather unrelated to—DNNF, full dissolvents, or to FNNF formulas. For one thing, pairwise-linked formulas are in CNF and the others are not; for another, pairwise-linked formulas have many links while the others are link-free. It turns out, however, that these classes are closely related, not only through traditional **AND/OR**-based duality, but also through a kind of link-based duality. These formula classes are examined in light of both types of duality; the resulting insight leads to new compilation techniques and to new target languages.

A brief summary of the basics of NNF formulas is presented in Section 2.1. There is also a short discussion of *negated form* (NF), which is useful as the assumed input language since any logical formula whatsoever can be converted to equivalent negated form in linear time. Path dissolution is described in Section 2.2; greater detail can be found in [13]. Decomposable negation normal form is also described in that section.

The class of pairwise-linked clause sets is examined in Section 3.1. Several new observations are made, and an alternative to the compilation technique of [10] is proposed that does not require subsumption checks. This is generalized to *d-path linked formulas* in Section 3.2. Section 4 focuses on duality relationships: Both traditional and/or based duality and link-based.

Proofs are omitted due to lack of space; they can be found in [16].

2   Linkless Normal Forms

There is growing interest [3, 11, 5, 6, 13, 19, 22] in non-clausal representations of logical formulas. The NNF representation of a formula often has a considerable space advantage, and many CNF formulas can be *factored* into an NNF equivalent that is exponentially smaller. Similar space saving can be realized using structure sharing, for example with tries. On the other hand, there is experimental evidence [13] that factoring a CNF formula can provide dramatic improvements in performance for NNF based systems.

Linkless formulas have several properties desirable for knowledge compilation. In [9], *factored negation normal form* (FNNF) and *ordered factored negation normal form* (OFNNF), both linkless, are introduced. The latter is a canonical representation of *any* logical formula (modulo a given variable ordering of any superset of the set of variables that appear in the formula). The FNNF of a formula can be obtained with Shannon expansion. The dual Shannon expansion and the dual of FNNF are described in Section 3.2.

2.1   Negated Form and Negation Normal Form

A logical formula is said to be in *negated form* (NF) if it uses only three binary connectives, $\wedge, \vee, \Leftrightarrow$, and if all negations are at the atomic level. Negated from is introduced in [9] and is useful as an input form because any logical formula can be converted to negated form in linear time (and space). An NF formula that contains no $\Leftrightarrow$'s is in negation normal form (NNF).

Two literal occurrences are said to be *c-connected* if they are conjoined within the formula (and *d-connected* if they are disjoined within the formula). A *c-path* (*d-path*) is a maximal set of c-connected (d-connected) literal occurrences. A *link* is a complementary pair of c-connected literals.

Related to factoring is the *Shannon expansion* of a formula $\mathcal{G}$ on the atom p, also known as *semantic factoring*; it is defined by the identity, $\mathcal{G} \equiv (p \wedge \mathcal{G}[\text{true}/p]) \vee (\neg p \wedge \mathcal{G}[\text{false}/p])$, where $\mathcal{G}[\beta/p]$ denotes the replacement of all occurrences of atom p by β in $\mathcal{G}$. Observe that any formula $\mathcal{G}$ may be replaced by the formula on the right. In fact, this rule can be applied to any subformula, and, in particular, to the smallest part of the formula containing all occurrences of the variable being factored. The term semantic factoring reflects the fact that all occurrences of the atom p within the subformula under consideration have in effect been 'factored' into one positive and one negative occurrence. Darwiche's *conditioning* operation, the original Prawitz Rule [18], BDDs, and Step 4 in Rule III of the Davis-Putnam procedure [7] are closely related to Shannon expansion.

2.2   Path Dissolution and Decomposable Negation Normal Form

Path dissolution [13] is an inference mechanism that works naturally with formulas in negation normal form. It operates on a link by restructuring the formula so that all paths through the link are deleted. The restructured formula is called the *dissolvent*; the c-paths of the dissolvent are precisely the c-paths of the original formula except those through the activated link. Path dissolution is strongly complete in the sense that any sequence of link activations will eventually terminate, producing a linkless formula called the *full dissolvent*. The paths that remain are models of the original formula. Full dissolvents have been used effectively for computing the prime implicants and implicates of a formula [19, 20]. Path dissolution has advantages over clause-based inference mechanisms, even when the input is in CNF, since CNF can be factored. The time savings is often significant, and the space savings can be dramatic.

Let $\mathbf{atoms}(\mathcal{F})$ denote the atom set of a formula $\mathcal{F}$. An NNF formula $\mathcal{F}$ is said to be in *decomposable negation normal form* (DNNF) if $\mathcal{F}$ satisfies the *decomposability property*: If $\alpha = \alpha_1 \wedge \alpha_2 \wedge ... \wedge \alpha_n$ is a conjunction in $\mathcal{F}$, then $i \neq j$ implies that $\mathbf{atoms}(\alpha_i) \cap \mathbf{atoms}(\alpha_j) = \emptyset$; i.e., no two conjuncts of α share an atom. Observe that a DNNF formula is necessarily linkless since a literal and its complement cannot be conjoined—after all, they share the same atom. The structure of formulas in DNNF is much simpler than the more general NNF. As a result, many operations on DNNF formulas can be performed efficiently. Of course, obtaining DNNF can be expensive, but if this is done once as a preprocessing step, the "expense" can be spread over many queries.

2.3   Testing for Entailment

One common query of a knowledge base $\mathcal{K}$ is the question,"Does $\mathcal{K}$ logically entail a clause C?" A yes answer is equivalent to $(\mathcal{K} \wedge \neg C)$ being unsatisfiable. Both DNNF formulas and full dissolvents, which are linkless, can answer such a query in time linear in the size of the knowledge base[2] For DNNF formulas, this is accomplished by converting $(\mathcal{K} \wedge \neg C)$ to DNNF with a technique called *conditioning* [6]. If the resulting DNNF reduces to empty, then the answer to the query is yes.

Full dissolvents can also determine entailment in linear time. If a knowledge base $\mathcal{K}$ is a full dissolvent, $\mathcal{K}$ contains no links, and all links in $\mathcal{K} \wedge \neg C$ go between $\mathcal{K}$ and $\neg C$; i.e., between $\mathcal{K}$ and a unit. Dissolving on such links strictly decreases the size of the formula. Each operation is no worse than linear in the amount by which the formula shrinks, so the total time required to dissolve away all links is linear in the size of $\mathcal{K}$. The formula that is produced is again linkless, and if this formula is empty, the answer to the query is yes.

There is another approach for answering this query; it is based on Nelson's Theorem, a proof of which can be found in [19]:

Theorem 1. In any non-empty formula $\mathcal{K}$ in which no c-path contains a link, i.e., if $\mathcal{K}$ is a full dissolvent, then every implicate of $\mathcal{K}$ is subsumed by some d-path of $\mathcal{K}$.   □

A clause C can then be tested for entailment as follows: First, consider the subformula of $\mathcal{K}$ consisting of all complements of literals of C. Then C is entailed if this subgraph contains a full d-path through $\mathcal{K}$. This computation can be done in time linear in the size of $\mathcal{K}$—for a proof see [15].

3   Pairwise-Linked Formulas

In Section 2, classes of linkless formulas used as target languages for knowledge compilation were described. The opposite approach is considered in this section: Classes of formulas with many links are explored. As we shall see in Section 4, there is a duality to these two approaches.

3.1   Pairwise-Linked Clause Sets

Hai and Jigui introduced pairwise-linked clause sets in [10]. They call them *EPCCL Theories*: *E*ach *P*air (of clauses) *C*ontains *C*omplementary *L*iterals. This class of formulas has a number of nice properties, including the fact that satisfiability can be determined in linear time. The authors provide an elegant proof of this result, included here, with a clever combination of the inclusion/exclusion principle and the observation that every proper subset of the complete matrix, defined below, on m variables is satisfiable.

A *maximal term* on m variables is a clause that contains all m variables (positively or negatively). The *complete matrix* (see [1]) on m variables is the clause set $\mathcal{C}_m$ consisting of all 2^m maximal terms. It is easy to see that $\mathcal{C}_m$ is minimally unsatisfiable; that is,

---

[2] Linear time is not very impressive: The knowledge base is typically exponential in the size of the original formula.

C_m is unsatisfiable, but every subset is satisfiable. The authors use their *extension rule*, defined below, to extend any (non-tautological) clause[3] to a logically equivalent set of maximal terms. They observe that a clause set is thus unsatisfiable if and only if extending every clause to maximal terms produces all of C_m, i.e., exactly 2^m clauses. As a result, satisfiability can be reduced to a counting problem. The authors use the inclusion/exclusion principle, stated below, to do this count in linear time on pairwise-linked clause sets.

The extension rule can be defined as follows: Let C be a clause, and let p be an atom not appearing in C. Then the clause set $C' = \{C \vee p, C \vee \bar{p}\}$ is the extension of C with respect to p. Observe that C' is logically equivalent to C. With repeated applications of extension, a set of maximal terms equivalent to any clause can be obtained. If m is the size of maximal terms, then $2^{m-|C|}$ is the size of the equivalent set of maximal terms.

The inclusion/exclusion principle can be stated as follows: Let $P_1, P_2, ..., P_n$ be any collection of finite sets. Then $(*)$ $|\cup_{i=1}^n P_i| = \sum_{i=1}^n |P_i| - \sum_{1 \le i < j \le n} |P_i \cap P_j| + ... + (-1)^{n+1}|P_1 \cap P_2 \cap ... \cap P_n|$.

Given a set $\mathcal{F} = \{C_1, ..., C_n\}$ of clauses (with m variables), let P_i denote the set of maximal terms obtained by extending C_i. Then $\mathcal{F}$ is equivalent to $\cup_{i=1}^n P_i$ and thus is satisfiable iff $\left| \cup_{i=1}^n P_i \right| < 2^m$. Observe that, for pairwise-linked clause sets, since the C_i's are pairwise linked, the sets P_i are pairwise disjoint. Thus, while for arbitrary clause sets the inclusion/exclusion principle may be impractical to use, for pairwise-linked clause sets, the formula $(*)$ reduces to $|\cup_{i=1}^n P_i| = \sum_{i=1}^n |P_i|$.

The satisfiability of a pairwise-linked clause set can thus be determined in linear time by determining whether $\sum_{i=1}^n |P_i| = \sum_{i=1}^n 2^{m-|C_i|}$ is 2^m. Determining whether a clause is entailed by a pairwise-linked clause set can also be done in polynomial time. If $\mathcal{F}$ is the clause set, and $C = \{p_1, p_2, ..., p_k\}$ is the clause, then $\mathcal{F} \models C$ iff $\mathcal{F} \wedge \neg C$ is unsatisfiable. Since $\neg C$ can be thought of as a set of unit clauses, whether $\mathcal{F} \models C$ can be determined by finding a pairwise-linked clause set that is equivalent to $\mathcal{F} \cup \bigcup_{i=1}^k \{p_i\}$. The computation time will be polynomial if the equivalent pairwise-linked clause set can be constructed in polynomial time.

The method used by Hai and Jigui to accomplish this is simple and elegant. If $\{p\}$ is a unit clause to be added to $\mathcal{F}$, partition $\mathcal{F}$ into three sets of clauses: Let $\mathcal{F}_1$ be the set of clauses containing $\bar{p}$, let $\mathcal{F}_2$ be the set of clauses containing p, and let $\mathcal{F}_3$ be the remaining clauses. The clauses of $\mathcal{F}$ are of course already pairwise linked, so we need only be concerned about links between one clause in $\mathcal{F}$ and the unit clause $\{p\}$. The clauses in $\mathcal{F}_1$ are already linked to $\{p\}$, and $\{p\}$ subsumes each clause in $\mathcal{F}_2$, so they may be deleted. If C is a clause in $\mathcal{F}_3$, then extend C with respect to p, producing $C \cup \{\bar{p}\}$ and $C \cup \{p\}$. The latter is subsumed by p and thus may be deleted. We thus have a pairwise linked clause set that is logically equivalent to $\mathcal{F} \cup \{\{p\}\}$. Observe that the method used to produce this clause set amounts to the following: Add the unit $\{p\}$ to the given pairwise-linked clause set, delete all clauses subsumed by the unit, and add $\bar{p}$ to all clauses not containing $\bar{p}$. This process is clearly linear in the size of the original clause set $\mathcal{F}$ and thus is at most quadratic for adding several unit clauses. The results of this discussion are summarized in the next theorem.

---

[3] Tautologies cannot be extended to maximal terms because they contain an atom and its negation.

Theorem 2. (Hai and Jigui [10]) If $\mathcal{F}$ is a set of pairwise-linked clauses, then determining whether $\mathcal{F}$ is satisfiable can be done in time linear in the size of $\mathcal{F}$, and whether $\mathcal{F}$ entails a given clause can be determined in polynomial time. □

A note of caution: The extension rule can be used to create an equivalent pairwise-linked set of clauses $\mathcal{F}'$ from any clause set $\mathcal{F}$, and these operations are polynomial in $\mathcal{F}'$. However, $\mathcal{F}'$ may be exponentially larger than $\mathcal{F}$.

Quite a bit more can be said about pairwise-linked clause sets. Recall that a literal occurring in a clause set is said to be *pure* if its complement does not occur in the clause set. It is well known (and very easy to verify) that a clause set is unsatisfiable if and only if the clause set produced by removing all clauses containing pure literals is unsatisfiable. The next theorem may therefore be surprising — see [16] for a proof.

Theorem 3. Let $\mathcal{F}$ be an unsatisfiable set of tautology-free pairwise-linked clauses. Then $\mathcal{F}$ contains no pure literals. □

It is often desirable to work with minimally unsatisfiable clause sets, but, typically, it is not easy to find such a set, even knowing that the clause set is unsatisfiable. The next theorem may therefore also be surprising. (The proof — see [16] — is immediate from observations in [10], but there is also an elegant proof that relies only on first principles.)

Theorem 4. Let $\mathcal{F}$ be an unsatisfiable set of tautology-free pairwise-linked clauses. Then $\mathcal{F}$ is minimally unsatisfiable. □

3.2 DPL Formulas

The class of pairwise-linked formulas discussed in Section 3.1 is restricted to CNF. Not surprisingly, there is a corresponding class of NNF formulas that contains the CNF class as a special case; they are called *d-path linked* (DPL) formulas. Satisfiability of certain DPL formulas can also be determined in polynomial time, and so there is the potential advantage that such an NNF formula may be exponentially smaller than the equivalent pairwise-linked clause set.

An NNF formula $\mathcal{G}$ is said to be d-path linked if every pair of distinct d-paths is linked, and if no d-path contains more than one occurrence of an atom. Note that the latter condition forces each d-path, which is an occurrence set, to correspond exactly to a non-tautological clause in a CNF equivalent of $\mathcal{G}$; i.e., the set of d-paths is an equivalent pairwise-linked clause set.

It may seem that working with DPL formulas is impractical. Determining whether an NNF formula is d-path linked would appear to be as hard as determining whether a clause set is pairwise-linked, and it would appear that few arbitrary NNF formulas are in this class. A DPL formula can be obtained by factoring a pairwise-linked clause set, but then the full cost of producing the clause set must be paid. Nevertheless, the situation is more promising than this.

A compilation algorithm is presented in [10] that requires CNF input and produces a pairwise-linked clause set as output. At the heart of the algorithm is a triply-nested loop; at the innermost level resides a subsumption check. Here, a compilation algorithm is introduced that does not use subsumption and that compiles arbitrary formulas directly into DPL formulas. The key to the algorithm is the *dual Shannon expansion* of a formula $\mathcal{G}$, which is defined to be $\neg SE(\neg \mathcal{G}, p) = (p \lor \mathcal{G}[\text{false}/p]) \land (\neg p \lor \mathcal{G}[\text{true}/p])$.

The dual of the FNNF operator is a DPL formula called *disjunctive factored negation normal form*; it is defined using duality by D-FNNF$(L, \mathcal{F}) = \neg \text{FNNF}(L, \neg \mathcal{F})$.

If p_i is chosen so that i is maximal, the result is called ordered D-FNNF and denoted D-OFNNF. The remarks about FNNF apply in a straightforward but dual manner to these formulas. Thus a knowledge base will compile to a formula that can be regarded as a binary tree with root 1, and whose leaves do not have leaf siblings. Branches of D-FNNF (FNNF) trees correspond to d-paths (c-paths). Just as FNNF formulas have no c-links, in D-FNNF there are no d-links. But it is evident from the definition that the d-paths are pairwise linked: The left and right subtrees are rooted at p and $\neg p$, respectively, and so all branches within the left subtree contain p, and all branches within the right subtree contain $\neg p$.[4]

If a knowledge base $\mathcal{K}$ is compiled by the D-OFNNF operator, the question, Given clause $C = \{p_1, \ldots, p_n\}$, does $\mathcal{K}$ entail C, i.e., is $\mathcal{K} \wedge \neg C$ unsatisfiable? can be answered as follows: Substitute 0 for p_i and 1 for $\neg p_i$, $1 \le i \le n$, throughout D-OFNNF$(L, \mathcal{K})$ and apply the $SIMP$ rules. If the query is entailed by $\mathcal{K}$, the tree simplifies to 0. This process is linear in D-OFNNF$(L, \mathcal{K})$. It is interesting to note that for an arbitrary entailment $\mathcal{F} \models C$, determining whether $\mathcal{F} \wedge \neg C$ is unsatisfiable cannot done by substituting constants; indeed, this is an $\mathcal{NP}$-complete problem. But for a D-OFNNF tree, simplification alone is sufficient because the D-OFNNF of an unsatisfiable formula is a root labeled 0.[5]

It is not always necessary to perform all the substitutions and simplifications to determine whether the query is entailed. Suppose C is an implicate of $\mathcal{K}$—i.e., suppose $\mathcal{K} \models C$. Then $\neg C \models \neg \mathcal{K}$, so an assignment making all literals of C false must falsify $\mathcal{K}$. This viewpoint is useful because, just as branches of an OFNNF formula represent satisfying interpretations, D-OFNNF branches represent falsifying ones; i.e., setting all literals on a branch to false falsifies the formula. Thus, the set of literals labeling a branch is an implicate of the formula. Recall that an implicate is *prime* if it is minimal in the sense that no proper subset is also an implicate.

Lemma 1. Let $\mathcal{F}$ be an arbitrary logical formula, and let $\mathcal{I}_P$ be a clause containing q such that $\mathcal{F} \wedge \neg(\mathcal{I}_P - \{q\})$ is not unsatisfiable. Then $\mathcal{I}_P$ is a prime implicate of $\mathcal{F}$ iff $\mathcal{I}_P - \{q\}$ is a prime implicate of $\mathcal{F} \wedge \neg q$. $\square$

Theorem 5. Let the nodes on branch B in D-OFNNF$(L, \mathcal{K})$ be labeled $q_1, \ldots, q_m$, in that order, so that q_m is the leaf. Then there is a unique subset $\mathcal{I}_P$ of $\{q_1, \ldots, q_m\}$ that is a prime implicate of $\mathcal{K}$. Moreover, $\mathcal{I}_P$ contains q_m. $\square$

Theorem 5 provides another way to test a clause $C = \{p_1, \ldots, p_n\}$ for entailment. Suppose the tree is stored so that each node has a bit vector indicating the branch leading to it from the root. The occurrences of p_n in the tree may be scanned, and each node's vector can be examined to determine whether $p_1, \ldots, p_{n-1}$ are on that branch. Such branches are *consistent with* C. If a consistent branch is found in which p_n is not a leaf, then C is not entailed by $\mathcal{K}$ (since the assignment falsifying every literal on this branch falsifies C but not $\mathcal{K}$). If no such branch is found, substitute 0 for p_n and 1 for $\neg p_n$, apply $SIMP$, and repeat for p_{n-1}. Queries for which the answer is yes require as

---

[4] In a dual manner, an FNNF formula represents a pairwise d-linked DNF clause set.

[5] But let us not forget that building D-OFNNF may be expensive.

much computation time with either approach, but if the answer is no, this method may terminate more quickly.

4   Dualities

That duality should arise in a variety of ways in the study of propositional languages is hardly surprising. But in this setting it is so pervasive that a brief synopsis may be illuminating.

Perhaps the most familiar duality is that of CNF and DNF. The latter is (conjunctive) link-free, but typically has many d-links; the former is free of d-links but may have many c-links. From Nelson's Theorem [17], we know that the prime implicants of a tautology-free CNF formula are present as non-contradictory c-paths, and the prime implicates of a contradiction-free DNF formula are present as non-tautological d-paths. It turns out that producing implicants and implicates syntactically is the result not of CNF/DNF per se, but of the absence of links, which is a side effect of converting to CNF or to DNF.

Computing the full dissolvent of a formula removes links without producing DNF; similarly, the disjunctive dual of dissolution produces a formula without d-links. This leads to a version of Nelson's Theorem based only on the absence of links [19].

The work of Hai and Jigui [10] pointed towards an additional layer of duality— namely that implicates can be extracted not only from c-linkless formulas, but also from pairwise-linked clause sets. Thus entailment testing is facilitated either by removing links or by adding enough of them. An immediate consequence is that a DNF clause can be polynomially[6] checked for being a prime implicant of a pairwise d-linked DNF formula.

In [15, 9], Shannon expansion is used to compile to DNNF and to FNNF; these target languages are regarded essentially as c-linkless. But of course FNNF is an NNF generalization of a pairwise d-linked DNF formula, and this realization led the authors to develop D-FNNF, an NNF generalization of a pairwise c-linked CNF formula, using the dual of Shannon expansion. It is by now obvious that the prime implicant status of literal conjunctions can be conveniently tested using OFNNF.

Nelson's Theorem provides a duality between the type of link that is absent and the type of query that is easily answered. The additional duality between many links and the absence of links induces a symmetry: Both prime implicants and prime implicates can be tested with both pairwise-linked formulas and with link-free formulas. This link-based duality — link-free versus d-path linked — appears to be heretofore unnoticed.

References

1. Bibel, W., Tautology testing with a generalized matrix method, *Theoretical Computer Science* **8** (1979), 31–44.
2. Bryant, R. E., Symbolic Boolean manipulation with ordered binary decision diagrams, *ACM Computing Surveys* **24, 3** (1992), 293–318.

---

[6] We repeat the caveat that the pairwise-linked formula may be large.

3. Cadoli, M., and Donini, F. M., A survey on knowledge compilation, *AI Communications* **10** (1997), 137–150.
4. Chatalic, P. and Simon, L., Zres: The old Davis-Putnam procedure meets ZBDDs. *Proc. CADE'17*, David McAllester, ed., LNAI 1831 (June 2000), Springer-Verlag, 449-454.
5. Darwiche, A., Compiling devices: A structure-based approach, Proc. *International Conference on Principles of Knowledge Representation and Reasoning (KR98)*, Morgan-Kaufmann, San Francisco (1998), 156–166.
6. Darwiche, A., Decomposable negation normal form, *J.ACM* **48,4** (2001), 608–647.
7. Davis, M. and Putnam, H. A computing procedure for quantification theory. *J.ACM* **7**, 1960, 201–215.
8. Forbus, K.D. and de Kleer, J., *Building Problem Solvers*, MIT Press, Mass. (1993).
9. Hähnle, R., Murray, N.V., and Rosenthal, E. Normal forms for knowledge compilation, *Proc ISMIS 2005*, Saratoga Springs, NY, *LNAI*, Springer-Verlag, to appear.
10. Hai, L. and Jigui, S., Knowledge compilation using the extension rule, *J. Automated Reasoning*, 32(2), 93-102, 2004.
11. Henocque, L., The prime normal form of boolean formulas. Submitted. Preliminary version available as a technical report at http://www.lsis.org/fiche.php?id=74&page=.
12. Marquis, P., Knowledge compilation using theory prime implicates, Proc. *International Joint Conference on AI (IJCAI)* (1995), Morgan-Kaufmann, San Mateo, California, 837-843.
13. Murray, N.V., and Rosenthal, E. Dissolution: Making paths vanish. *J.ACM* **40,3** (July 1993), 504–535.
14. Murray, N.V., and Rosenthal, E. On the relative merits of path dissolution and the method of analytic tableaux, *Theoretical Computer Science* **131** (1994), 1–28.
15. Murray, N.V. and Rosenthal E., Tableaux, path dissolution, and decomposable negation normal form for knowledge compilation, *Proc TABLEAUX 2003*, Rome, Italy, *LNAI* 2796 (M. Mayer and F. Pirri, Eds.), Springer-Verlag, 165-180.
16. Murray, N.V., and Rosenthal, E. Knowledge compilation and duality, Technical Report SUNYA-CS-04-07, Dept of Computer Science, SUNY Albany, October, 2004.
17. Nelson, R.J., Simplest normal truth functions, *J. of Symbolic Logic* **20**, 105-108 (1955).
18. Prawitz, D. A proof procedure with matrix reduction. *Lecture Notes in Mathematics* **125**, Springer-Verlag, 1970, 207–213.
19. Ramesh, A., Becker, G. and Murray, N.V. CNF and DNF considered harmful for computing prime implicants/implicates. *J. of Automated Reasoning* **18**,3 (1997), Kluwer, 337–356.
20. Ramesh, A. and Murray, N.V. An application of non-clausal deduction in diagnosis. *Expert Systems with Applications* **12**,1 (1997), 119-126.
21. Selman, B., and Kautz, H., Knowledge compilation and theory approximation, *J.ACM* **43,2** (1996), 193-224.
22. Walsh, T., Non-clausal reasoning, *Workshop on Disproving Non-Theorems, Non-Validity, and Non-Provability*, IJCAR 2004, Cork, Ireland.

Data Protection in Distributed Database Systems

Chun Ruan[1] and Vijay Varadharajan[1,2]

[1] School of Computing and Information Technology,
University of Western Sydney, Penrith South DC, NSW 1797 Australia
{chun, vijay}@cit.uws.edu.au
[2] Department of Computing, Macquarie University, North Ryde,
NSW 2109 Australia
vijay@ics.mq.edu.au

Abstract. In this paper, we propose an authorization model for distributed databases. Multiple object granularity of authorizations, such as global relations, fragments and attributes, are supported. Administrative privilege can be delegated from one subject to another to provide decentralized authorization administration. Authorization propagations along both the relation fragmentation tree and the subject group-subgroup hierarchical tree are also considered. Further more, conflict resolution policy is provided that supports well controlled delegations and exceptions. Overall the system provides a very flexible framework for specifying and evaluating the authorizations in distributed database systems.

Keywords: distributed database, authorization.

1 Introduction

Distributed database (DDB) is a database which logically belongs to the same entity but physically distributed in different sites connected by networks [1]. DDB technology combines both distribution and integration. The distribution aspect is provided by distributing the data across the sites in the network, while the integration aspect is provided by logically integrating the distributed data so that it appears to the users as a single, homogenous DB. Centralized DB, by contrast, requires both logical and physical integration.

Authorization models for distributed database should deal with both distribution and integration of DDB. On the distribution side, decentralized authorization administration is needed since the data itself is distributed and no one would know exactly what access right is suitable for every user. This means administrative privileges should be able to be delegated from one user to another and therefore multiple administrators may exist for a database or a specific relation. On the integration side, one should be able to grant authorizations on relations regardless of the real locations of those relations. That is, users can grant authorizations on relations of DDB as if they were put in the same site.

M.-S. Hacid et al. (Eds.): ISMIS 2005, LNAI 3488, pp. 191–199, 2005.
© Springer-Verlag Berlin Heidelberg 2005

We will use authorization propagation technique to realize this. The authorizations will propagate to all the proper physical copies of relations automatically.

Granularity is another important issue for an authorization model of DDB; namely, what is the basic unit or granule to which the access control can be applied. The granularity of the object can range from an individual attribute of a relation to a whole relation or even the entire DB. In a distributed database, a global relation can be divided into several segments by using vertical segmentation, horizontal segmentation or hybrid segmentation. These segments can be further divided into smaller segments, and so on. Therefore even more granules naturally exist in a DDB. In general, the finer the granularity of data objects supported, the more precise can be the access control. However, on the other hand, a fine granularity system will incur a much higher administration overhead than a coarse granularity system. Perhaps a more attractive method is to adopt multiple granularity so that the best suitable granule can be selected for by users based on their needs. In our model, we will support multiple granules for both the object and subject.

An additional key issue about the authorization of DDB is the type of authorizations supported. Early authorization models in distributed database systems only allowed the specification of positive authorizations. They use the *closed world* policy, which means that the lack of an authorization is assumed to be a negative authorization. More flexible authorization models allow the specification of negative authorizations to explicitly express an access to be denied. In this case, since it allows both positive and negative authorizations, conflicts may arise. Basically, if a user is granted both positive and negative authorizations on the same object, we say that these two authorizations *conflict* with each other. Solving conflict problem is an important but difficult issue. Currently, major conflict resolution policies proposed are *Negative (Positive) take precedence*, *More specific take precedence*, *Strong and Weak*, and *Time take precedence*. However, when administrative privileges can be delegated between subjects, the policies mentioned above suffer from the following problem [6]: when some user u_1 delegates some privilege to another user u_2, u_1 will lose control of the privilege for the further delegate and grant. As a result this may lead to some undesired situations such as, through giving u_1 a negative authorization, u_2 may be able to deny u_1 to exercise the same privilege which is delegated from u_1 to u_2. In [6], we proposed a new predecessor-take-precedence based policy to handle the conflicts in authorization delegations which can overcome the above problem. The policy is based on the authorization delegation relation. It traces the delegation path explicitly and gives higher priority to the predecessors than the successors. We will extend this policy to apply to DDB in this paper.

Different authorization models have been proposed. The authorization model for DBMS System R presented in [4] is considered as the milestone in the history of authorization of DBS. Objects to be protected are tables and views, decentralised administration method is used as the owner can grant authorizations with the grant option, which allows the grantee to further grant privileges, with or without grant option, to other users. The model has been extended in several directions. [7] extends the model to allow subjects to be groups. Authorization granted to the groups apply to all its members. [2, 3] introduces the negative authorization into the model, and *Negative take precedence* and *Strong and Weak* policies are used to solve the conflicts, respectively. [5] proposed a flexible model to support multiple security policies.

However, so far, there has not been much work that addresses authorization delegation and conflict resolution in a distributed database environment. Although authorization inheritance and multiple granularity are not new in DDB, they are becoming more difficult to handle when authorization delegations and both positive and negative authorizations are supported. This is because conflicts may happen at all levels of granularity, which may involve explicit authorizations, delegated authorizations and propagated authorizations. In this paper, we will propose a model which supports both positive and negative authorizations. Multiple object granularity of authorizations, such as global relations, fragments and attributes, are supported. Administrative privilege can be delegated from one subject to another to provide decentralized authorization administration. Authorization propagations on object, such as propagations along the relation fragmentation tree, and subject, such as propagations along the group hierarchical tree, are also considered. Further more, Conflict resolution policy is provided that supports controlled delegations and exceptions by taking into account of both subject delegation relation and database relation fragmentation. Overall the system provides a very flexible framework for specifying and evaluating the authorizations in distributed database systems.

2   Distributed Database Systems

A distributed database can be defined as a logically integrated collections of shared data which is physically distributed across the nodes of a computer network. A distributed database management system therefore is the software to manage a distributed database in such a way that the distribution aspects are transparent to the user.

Distributed database systems (DDB) are divided into two separate types: homogeneous distributed database management systems and heterogeneous distributed database management systems. In this paper, we only consider homogeneous distributed database systems. A homogeneous DDB resembles a centralized DB, but instead of storing all the data at one site, the data is distributed across a number of sites in a network. Note that there are no local users; all users access the underlying DBs through the global interface. The global schema is the union of all underlying local data descriptions and user views are defined against this global schema.

To handle the distribution aspects, two additional levels are added to the standard three-level ANSI-SPARC schemas. The fragmentation schema describes how the global relation are divided amongst the local DBs. The allocation schema then specifies at which site each fragment is stored. A fragment can be allocated to more than one site. That is, replication of fragments is easily supported. The optimizer can then select the most efficient materialization of the relation.

There are two primary methods of fragmentation: horizontal relation fragmentation and vertical relation fragmentation. Horizontal fragmentation involves the splitting of the relation along tuples (rows). Vertical fragmentation involves the partitioning of relations along attributes, or columns. A third partition technique, hybrid relation fragmentation, involves the combination of vertical and horizontal fragmentation methods.

Example 1. Figure 1 gives an example of hybrid fragmentation. The global relation E is composed of five attributes: EMP_ID: employee identification number; EMP_NAME: employee name EMP_DEPT: employee department; EMP_SALARY: employee yearly salary; EMP_SKILL: employee position.

E is vertically fragmented to $E1$ and $E2$. $E1$ contains only position data while $E2$ contains only payroll data. $E1$ is further horizontally fragmented to $E11, E12$ and $E13$ based on the employee department number as follows: $E1$: department number $= D1$; $E2$: department number $= D2$; $E3$: department number $= D3$; For physical allocation, $E11, E12$ and $E13$ are located at site 1, site 2 and site 3 respectively, denoted by $E11^1, E12^2$ and $E13^3$. $E2$ has three physical copies $E2^1, E2^2$ and $E2^3$ which are located at site 1, site 2 and site 3 respectively.

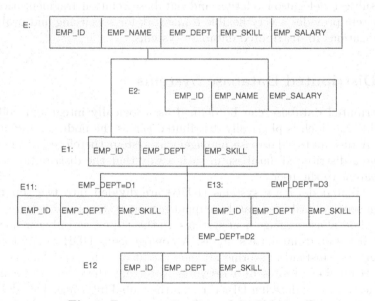

Fig. 1. Fragmentation Tree of the Relation E

3   The Authorization Model

Let S be a finite set of subjects (users, groups, subgroups), O be a finite set of objects (global relations, fragments, attributes), R be a finite set of access rights (read, insert, delete, select, update, etc.), and T be a finite set of grant types. Then we have the following definition for authorization.

Definition 1. (Authorization) *An* authorization *is a 5-ary tuple* (s, o, t, r, g), *where* $s \in S, o \in O$, $t \in T$, $r \in R$, $g \in S$.

Intuitively, an authorization (s, o, t, r, g) states that grantor g has granted subject s the access right r on object o with grant type t. Three grant types are considered: $T = \{*, +, -\}$, where

$*$: delegable, which means that the subject has been granted the administrative privilege of access right r.
$+$: positive, which means that the subject has been granted the access right r.
$-$: negative, which means that the subject has been denied the access right r.

Here we assume that an administrative privilege subsumes a positive authorization. We believe this applies to most situations and can simplify our model specification. For example, a project Manager creates a file and delegates its administration privilege to all the project Team Leaders. This means that the Team Leaders can not only access the file but also grant authorizations to the team members.

Definition 2. (Authorization State) *An* authorization state *is the set of all authorizations at a given time.*

In this paper, we will usually use $\mathcal{A}$ and a (possibly with subscripts) to denote an authorization state and a single authorization respectively, and use $a.s$, $a.o$, $a.t$, $a.r$, $a.g$ to denote the corresponding components of subject, object, type, access right and grantor in a respectively.

Example 2. Consider Figure 1 again. Suppose Manager (Mgr) is the owner of the global relation E, *select* is an access right on E. There is a Technical Director (TD) who manages three technical departments. There are also Head of Department 1 (HoD1), Head of Department 2 (HoD2) and Head of Department 3 (HoD3) responsible for each of the three departments. In addition, we have five Financial Officers (FO1,...,FO5) who form a group called Financial Officer Group(FOG). The manager delegates the *select* right on E to the Technical Director, but excludes the right on $E2$(financial information). The manager also delegates the *select* right on $E2$ to the Financial Officer Group. The Technical Director then delegates the *select* right on each department employees' information to each Head of Department. However, the manager denies Head of Department 1 to *select* his/her department's employee's information for some reason (such as temporary suspension of his/her position). This authorization state $\mathcal{A}$ consists of the following authorizations:

$a_1 = (TD, E, *, select, Mgr)$;
$a_2 = (TD, E2, -, select, Mgr)$;
$a_3 = (FOG, E2, *, select, Mgr)$;
$a_4 = (HoD1, E11, *, select, TD)$;

$a_5 = (HoD2,\text{E}12, *, select, TD)$;
$a_6 = (HoD3,\text{E}13, *, select, TD)$;
$a_7 = (HoD1,\text{E}11, -, select, Mgr)$.

Definition 3. (Delegation Relation $<_{o,r}$ on Subjects) *For any subjects* $s_1, s_2 \in S$, *object* $o \in O$, *and right* $r \in R$, *we say* $s_1 <_{o,r} s_2$, *if there exists an authorization* $(s_2, o, r, *, s_1)$ *in* $\mathcal{A}$.

From the above definition, it is clear that if s_1 grants s_2 a delegable type authorization on o and r, then $s_1 <_{o,r} s_2$. A *path* of length n in relation $<_{o,r}$ from s_1 to s_2 is a finite sequence: $s_1, x_1, ..., x_{n-1}, s_2$, beginning with s_1 and ending with s_2, such that $s_1 <_{o,r} x_1$, $x_1 <_{o,r} x_2$, ..., $x_{n-1} <_{o,r} s_2$. The connectivity relation for $<_{o,r}$, denoted by $<_{o,r}^+$, is defined as $s_1 <_{o,r}^+ s_2$ if there is some path in $<_{o,r}$ from s_1 to s_2. The relation $<_{o,r}^+$ is called *delegation-connectivity* relation. Intuitively, $s_1 <_{o,r}^+ s_2$ means that s_1 grants or transitively grant s_2 a delegable type authorization on o and r.

Example 3. Let the authorization state be the one shown in Example 2, then we have: $Mgr <_{E,select} TD$, $Mgr <_{E2,select} FOG$, $TD <_{E11,select} HoD1$, $TD <_{E12,select} HoD2$ and $TD <_{E13,select} HoD3$.

3.1   Authorization Propagation

As mentioned in last section, the authorization propagation can help to simplify the authorization specification by allowing implicit authorizations to be derived automatically from the explicit authorizations according to some existing rules. In our model, we support authorization propagations from groups to their subgroups on the subject side, and from global relations to their fragments, physical copies and attributes on the object side.

To implement the authorization propagations along subjects, we define a relation $<_S$ which is a partial order denoting group-subgroup relation between subjects. That is, if s is in s', then $s' <_S s$. Each subject is a member of one or several user groups. For the sake of simplicity, we assume that groups are disjoint but they can be nested.

Also, to implement the authorization propagations along objects, we define another relation $<_O$ which is a partial order on objects. $<_O$ can denote the fragmentation relation(the parent-child relation in the fragmentation tree), fragment allocation relation and relation-attribute relation. That is, $o' <_O o$ iff o is a fragment of o', or o is an physical copy of o', or o is an attribute of o'. For example, if a relation R has two fragments R_1 and R_2, then $R <_O R_1$ and $R <_O R_2$. If fragment R_1 has two physical copies R_1^1 and R_1^2, then $R_1 <_O R_1^1, R_1 <_O R_1^2$. If a relation R has an attribute $R.a$, then $R <_O R.a$.

In addition, for the purpose of solving conflicts using the more specific-take-precedence principle, we will give every authorization a label recording the levels at which the subject and object locate with respect to the partial orders $<_S$ and $<_O$, respectively. We define a function *label* as follows. Let a be any authorization in $\mathcal{A}$, then $label(a) = (l_s, l_o)$, where l_s is the level of the subject in the hierarchial tree defined by $<_S$, and l_o is the level of the object in the fragmentation tree defined by $<_O$. Note that, if o is an attribute, then l_o is the level of the relation to which the attribute belongs. For example, in Figure 1, $E1.EMP\_DEPT$ has level 1 whereas $E11.EMP\_DEPT$ has level 2. The global relation always has the level 0. In fact, a label of an explicit authorization reflects the specific degree of this authorization in terms of subject and object. The larger the value of l_s or l_o, the smaller the subject or object. For the authorizations inferred through propagations, their labels will be the same as the original authorizations' from which they are generated. Now we can define the following propagation rule based on the partial orders $<_S$ and $<_O$.

Definition 4. (Authorization Propagation) *For any given authorization (s, o, t, r, g) in an authorization state, if $s <_S s'$ then (s', o, t, r, g) is also in the state and $label((s', o, t, r, g)) = label((s, o, t, r, g))$. Also, if $o <_O o'$, then (s, o', t, r, g) is also in the state and $label((s, o', t, r, g)) = label((s, o, t, r, g))$.*

Example 4. Let the authorization state be the one shown in Example 2. In Figure 1, we have $E <_O E1$, $E <_O E2$, $E1 <_O E11 <_O E11^1$, $E1 <_O E12 <_O E12^2$, $E1 <_O E13 <_O E13^3$, $E2 <_O E2^1, E2 <_O E2^2$, $E2 <_O E2^3, ...$

On the subject side, a financial officer group has been defined. Therefore we have $FOG <_S FO1$, $FOG <_S FO2$, $FOG <_S FO3$, $FOG <_S FO4$, $FOG <_S FO5$. The following are labels for the authorizations:

$label(a_1) = (0, 0)$, $label(a_2) = (0, 1)$, $label(a_3) = (0, 1)$, $label(a_4) = (0, 2)$, $label(a_5) = (0, 2)$, $label(a_6) = (0, 2)$, $label(a_7) = (0, 2)$

The authorizations will propagate along both the subject and object hierarchies. On the object side, from a_1, we can get

$a_8 = (TD, E1, *, select, Mgr)$
$a_9 = (TD, E2, *, select, Mgr)$
$a_{10} = (TD, E11, *, select, Mgr)$
$a_{11} = (TD, E12, *, select, Mgr)$
$a_{12} = (TD, E13, *, select, Mgr)$
...

And $label(a_8) = label(a_9) = label(a_{10}) = label(a_{11}) = label(a_{12}) = label(a_1)$ $= (0, 0)$. On the subject side, from a_3, we can get

$a_{13} = (FO1, E2, *, select, Mgr)$
$a_{14} = (FO2, E2, *, select, Mgr)$
...

$a_{17} = (FO5, E2, *, select, Mgr)$
...

And $label(a_{13}) = ...label(a_{17}) = label(a_3) = (0, 1)$

3.2   Conflict Resolution

Definition 5. (Conflict of Authorizations) *For any two authorizations a_1 and a_2 in $\mathcal{A}$, a_1 conflicts with a_2 if $a_1.s = a_2.s$, $a_1.o = a_2.o$, $a_1.r = a_2.r$, but $a_1.t \neq a_2.t$.*

Since there are three grant types in our model, we can have three kinds of conflicts, i.e. $*$ with $+$, $*$ with $-$ and $+$ with $-$. $*$ and $+$ are conflicting in that $*$ has administrative privilege while $+$ does not.

Conflicts are further divided into comparable conflicts and incomparable conflicts according to the delegation-connectivity relation among the subjects.

Definition 6. (Comparable Conflicts) *Suppose a_1 and a_2 are any two conflicting authorizations on object o and right r. Then a_1 and a_2 are comparable if $a_1.g <^+_{o,r} a_2.g$ or $a_2.g <^+_{o,r} a_1.g$. Otherwise they are incomparable.*

In the path of the delegation relation, we will give higher priorities to the predecessors than the successors. Considering all the rights of an object should be first delegated from the owner of the object, the owner has the highest priority and can therefore still control the object despite of the delegation of the administrative privilege.

Definition 7. (Overriding Authorization Rule 1) *For any two comparable conflicting authorizations $a_1 = (s, o, t, r, g)$ and $a_2 = (s, o, t', r, g')$ in $\mathcal{A}$, a_1 overrides a_2 if $g <^+_{o,r} g'$.*

For incomparable conflicts, their grantors' priorities are not comparable in terms of the delegation relation. We first solve them based on the smaller granularity taking precedence principle. This policy is important to support exception when authorization delegation and propagation are supported. Recall that larger values of l_o or l_s represents smaller granularity. To solve the conflicts, the granularity of object is considered first. If they are the same, the granularity of subject is then considered. Therefore, we define $(l_s, l_o) < (l'_s, l'_o)$ if $(l_o < l'_o)$ or $(l_o = l'_o)$ and $(l_s < l'_s)$.

Definition 8. (Overriding Authorization Rule 2) *For any two incomparable conflicting authorizations $a_1 = (s, o, t, r, g)$ and $a_2 = (s, o, t', r, g')$ in $\mathcal{A}$, a_1 overrides a_2 if $label(a_2) < label(a_1)$.*

For the incomparable conflicts that can not be resolved through the above overriding rule, they are resolved according to the grant types of authorizations. We will use the *positive-take-precedence* based policy, or *optimistic* policy in order to achieve the maximum degree of data sharing, a key objective of distributed databases. The corresponding priority sequence is: $- < + < *$.

Definition 9. (Overriding Authorization Rule 3) *For any two conflicting incomparable authorizations $a_1 = (s, o, t, r, g)$ and $a_2 = (s, o, t', r, g')$ in $\mathcal{A}$, a_1 overrides a_2 if $label(a_1) \not< label(a_2), label(a_2) \not< label(a_1)$, and $t' < t$.*

Example 5. We continue to consider the given authorization state in Example 2. a_2 conflicts with a_9 (inferred through propagation in Example 4). Since the grantors of the two authorizations are the same, we consider their labels next. $label(a_9) = (0,0) < label(a_2) = (0,1)$, so a_2 overrides a_9. Also a_7 conflicts with a_4. Since a_4's grantor is TD, and a_7's grantor is Mgr, and Mgr$<_{E11,select}$ TD, a_7 overrides a_4.

Definition 10. (Consistent Authorization State) *An authorization state* $\mathcal{A}$ *is consistent if it satisfies the following two conditions:*

1. *For any subject s, object o, access type t and right r, if (s, o, t, r, g) is in $\mathcal{A}$, then there exists g' such that $(g, o, *, r, g')$ is also in $\mathcal{A}$.*
2. *For any subject s, object o, and right r, if both (s, o, t, r, g) and (s, o, t', r, g') are in $\mathcal{A}$, then $t = t'$.*

We assume that for every object o, only the owner of o has been initially granted all the rights on o with delegatable type by the system when the object is created. We require the authorization state should always keep consistent. That is, the authorizations whose grantors have no relevant administrative privilege and the authorizations which are overridden must be deleted from the state.

4 Conclusions

In this paper, we have proposed an authorization model for distributed databases. The model supports authorization delegations, authorization propagations along both the database relation fragmentation tree and subject hierarchical tree, and multiple object granularity. A conflict resolution method is also presented which has taken into consideration of both subject delegation relation and database relation fragmentation. We intend to implement the model and integrate it in actual distributed relational databases for the future work.

References

1. D. Bell and J. Grimson, *Distributed Database Systems*, Addison-Wesley Publishing Company, 1992.
2. E. Bertino, P. Samarati, and S. Jajodia, An extended authorization model for relational databases. *IEEE Transaction on Knowledge and Data Engineering*, Vol. 9, No. 1, 1997.
3. E. Bertino, S. Jajodia, P. Samarati, Supporting multiple access control policies in database systems. *Proc. of the IEEE Symposium on Research in Security and Privacy*, Oakland(CA), 1996.
4. P.P. Griffiths and B.W. Wade, An authorization mechanism for a relational database system. ACM Trans. on Database Systems, 1(3):242-255, 1976.
5. S. Jajodia, P. Samarati, and V.S. Subrahmanian, and B. Bertino, A unified framework for enforcing multiple access control policies. *Proceedings of ACM SIGMOD Conference on Management of Data*, 1997.
6. C. Ruan and V. Varadharajan, Resolving conflicts in authorization delegations, 2002. *Proceedings of the 7th Australasian Conference on Information Security and Privacy*, pp 271-285, 2002.
7. P.F. Wilms and B.G. Linsday, A database authorization mechanism supporting individual and group authorization. *Distributed Data Sharing Systems*, pp 273-292, 1982.

A Softened Formulation of Inductive Learning and Its Use for Coronary Disease Data

Janusz Kacprzyk and Grażyna Szkatuła

Systems Research Institute, Polish Academy of Sciences,
ul. Newelska 6, 01-447 Warsaw, Poland
{szkatulg, kacprzyk}@ibspan.waw.pl

Abstract. We present an improved inductive learning method to derive classification rules that correctly describe most of the examples belonging to a class and do not describe most of the examples not belonging to this class. The problem is represented as a modification of the set covering problems solved by a genetic algorithm. Its is employed to medical data on coronary disease, and the results seem to be encouraging.

1 Introduction

In learning from examples, traditionally, we seek a classification rule satisfying *all* positive examples and *no* negative examples. These requirements are often too strict, and some softening may help. Here, we follow Zadeh's computing with words and perceptions paradigm (cf. Zadeh and Kacprzyk [20]), using fuzzy logic at the level of soft problem formulation, and non-fuzzy techniques at the solution level of its solution. We postulate: (1) *a partial completeness*, i.e. that the classification rule must correctly describe (have the same attribute values), say, *most* of the positive examples, (2) *a partial consistency*, i.e. that the classification rule must describe, say, *almost none* of the negative examples, (3) *convergence*, i.e. the classification rule must be derived in a *finite* number of steps, (4) the classification rule of a *minimal "length"* is to be found, e.g. with the minimum number of attributes (or, more generally being "simple").

Examples are described (cf. Michalski [19]) by a set of K "attribute - value" pairs $e = \bigwedge_{j=1}^{K} [a_j \# v_j]$ where a_j denotes attribute j with value v_j and # is a relation as, e.g., =, <, >, ≈,≥, etc. For instance, for the attributes: *height, color_of_hair, color_of_eyes*, we can describe the look of a person as [*height* = "high"] ∧ [*color_of_hair* = "blond"] ∧ [*color_of_eyes* = "blue"].

We propose a modified inductive learning procedure based on Michalski's [19] star-type methodology, related to our previous work (cf. Kacprzyk and Szkatuła [10 – 18]). A pre-processing of data is first performed based on an analysis of how frequent the values of the particular attributes occur. These frequencies are used to define

M.-S. Hacid et al. (Eds.): ISMIS 2005, LNAI 3488, pp. 200–209, 2005.
© Springer-Verlag Berlin Heidelberg 2005

typical values by deriving weights associated with those values. The problem is a modification of set covering, and solved by a genetic algorithm (IP2_GA).

2   A Softened Problem Formulation of Inductive Learning

Sets of examples U and attributes $A = \{a_1,...,a_K\}$ are finite. $V_{a_j} = \{v_{i_1}^{a_j},...,v_{i_j}^{a_j}\}$ is a domain of a_j, $j=1,...,K$, $V = \bigcup_{j=1,...,K} V_{a_j}$. $f : U \times A \to V$ is function, called an *informational function*, $f(e,a_j) \in V_{a_j}$, $\forall a_j \in A$, $\forall e \in U$. Each $e \in U$, with K attributes, $A = \{a_1,...,a_K\}$, is written $e = \bigwedge\limits_{j=1}^{K} [a_j = v_i^{a_j}]$, where $v_i^{a_j} = f(e,a_j) \in V_{a_j}$ denotes attribute a_j taking on value $v_i^{a_j}$ for example e. An e in (1) is composed of K "attribute-value" pairs, denoted $s_j = [a_j = v_i^{a_j}]$ (selectors). The conjunction of $l \leq K$ "attribute-value" pairs, i.e.

$$C^I = \bigwedge_{j \in I} s_j = \bigwedge_{j \in I} [a_j = v_i^{a_j}] = [a_{j_1} = v_i^{a_{j_1}}] \wedge ... \wedge [a_{j_l} = v_i^{a_{j_l}}] \tag{1}$$

where $I = \{j_1, j_2,..., j_l\} \subseteq \{1,..., K\}$ is called a *complex*.

Let us have example e and a complex $C^I = [a_{j_1} = v_i^{a_{j_1}}] \wedge ... \wedge [a_{j_l} = v_i^{a_{j_l}}]$ that corresponds to the set of indices $I = \{j_1,..., j_l\} \subseteq \{1,..., K\}$. The set of indices $\{j_1,..., j_l\}$ is equivalent to a vector $x = [x_j]^T$, $j = 1,..., K$, such that $x_j = 1$ if a selector $s_j = [a_j = v_i^{a_j}]$ occurs in C^I, and 0 otherwise. Complex C^I *covers* example e if all conditions on attributes given as selectors are covered by (equal to) the values of the respective attributes in e, i.e. $f(C^I, a_j) = f(e, a_j), \forall j \in I$.

Now, a_d is a decision attribute and $V_{a_d} = \{v_{i_1}^{a_d},..., v_{i_d}^{a_d}\}$ is a domain of a_d. Each example $e \in U$ is described by a set of attributes $\{a_1, a_2,..., a_K\} \cup \{a_d\}$. So, attribute a_d determines a partition $\{Y_{v_{i_1}^{a_d}}, Y_{v_{i_2}^{a_d}},..., Y_{v_{i_d}^{a_d}}\}$ of set U, where

$Y_{v_{i_t}^{a_d}} = \{e \in U : f(e, a_d) = v_{i_t}^{a_d}\}$, $v_{i_t}^{a_d} \in V_{a_d}$ for $t = 1,...d$. Set $Y_{v_{i_t}^{a_d}}$ is called the

t-th *decision class* (for $v_{i_t}^{a_d} \in V_{a_d}$), $Y_{v_{i_1}^{a_d}} \cup ... \cup Y_{v_{i_d}^{a_d}} = U$, $Y_{v_i^{a_d}} \cap Y_{v_j^{a_d}} = \varnothing$ *for*

$i \neq j$.

Suppose that we have a set of *positive* and *negative examples*:

$$S_P(Y_{v_{i_t}^{a_d}}) = \{e \in U : f(e, a_d) = v_{i_t}^{a_d}\} \tag{2}$$

$$S_N(Y_{v_{i_t}^{a_d}}) = \{e \in U : f(e, a_d) \neq v_{i_t}^{a_d} \text{ and } \forall e' \in S_P(Y_{v_{i_t}^{a_d}})$$

$$\exists a_j \in P, f(e, a_j) \neq f(e', a_j)\} \tag{3}$$

and $S_P(Y_{v_{i_t}^{a_d}}) \cap S_N(Y_{v_{i_t}^{a_d}}) = \varnothing$ and $S_P(Y_{v_{i_t}^{a_d}}) \neq \varnothing$, $S_N(Y_{v_{i_t}^{a_d}}) \neq \varnothing$.

The rule "IF C^I THEN $[a_d = v_{i_t}^{a_d}]$" is called an *"elementary" rule* for class $Y_{v_{i_t}^{a_d}}$, where C^I is a description of example in terms of attributes $a_j, j \in I$, and this example belongs to class $Y_{v_{i_t}^{a_d}}$. We consider the classification rules:

$$\text{IF } C^{I_1} \cup ... \cup C^{I_L} \text{ THEN } [a_d = v_{i_t}^{a_d}] \tag{4}$$

with: $I_1, ..., I_L \subseteq \{1, ..., K\}$, $C^{I_l} = \bigwedge_{j \in I_l} [a_j = v_i^{a_j}]$, $l = 1, ..., L$.

Suppose we have P positive examples, $e^m \in S_P(Y_{v_{i_t}^{a_d}})$, $m = 1, ..., P$, and N negative examples, $e^n \in S_N(Y_{v_{i_t}^{a_d}})$, $n = 1, ..., N$. For each a_j, each possible value occurs at some intensity (frequency). If it occurs more frequently in the positive examples and less frequently in the negative ones, then it is somehow typical and should rather appear in the rule sought. So, we introduce the function, for each a_j, $j = 1, ..., K$ and $v \in V_{a_j}$

$$g_j(v) = \frac{1}{P} \sum_{m=1}^{P} \delta(e^m, v) - \frac{1}{N} \sum_{n=1}^{N} \delta(e^n, v) \tag{5}$$

for each $v \in V_{a_j}$, where: $\delta(e^m, v) = \begin{cases} 1 & \text{for } v_i^{a_j} = v \\ 0 & \text{otherwise} \end{cases}$, and: $e^m \in S_P$,

$v_i^{a_j} = f(e^m, a_j) \in V_{a_j}$; and analogously for $\delta(e^n, v)$. So, we may expresses to what degree the particular values $v \in V_{a_j}$ of attribute a_j occurs more often in the positive than negative examples.

We assume that $g_j(v)$ is used as a weight of value $v \in V_{a_j}$ of each a_j (cf. Kacprzyk and Szkatula [15, 16]).

Example e_W with weights is $e_W = \bigwedge\limits_{j=1}^{K} [a_j = v_i^{a_j}; g_j(v_i^{a_j})]$, i.e. is a conjunction of

weighted selectors, $s_j^W = [a_j = v_i^{a_j}; g_j(v_i^{a_j})]$, that is

$$C_W^I = \bigwedge_{j \in I \subseteq \{1,...,K\}} s_j^W \tag{6}$$

and is called a *weighted complex*. Notice that for C_W^I x has the elements $x_j = 1$ for

$j \in I$, while, for $j \in \{1,2,...,K\} \setminus I$, $x_j = 0$. For C_W^I its *weighted length* is:

$$d_W(C_W^I) =$$

$$= \sum_{j \in I} (1 - g_j(v_i^{a_j})) \cdot x_j + \sum_{j \in \{1,2,...,K\} \setminus I} (1 - g_j(v_i^{a_j})) \cdot x_j = \sum_{j=1}^{K} (1 - g_j(v_i^{a_j})) \cdot x_j \tag{7}$$

which reflects a higher relevance of those values of attributes which occur more often
in the positive than in negative examples.

The *length of the weighted classification rule* $R_W = C_W^{I_l} \cup ... \cup C_W^{I_L}$ is

$$d_{R_W}(C_W^{I_1} \cup ... \cup C_W^{I_L}) = \max_{l=1,...,L} d_W(C_W^{I_l}) \tag{8}$$

We look for an optimal classification rule $R_W^* = C_W^{I_1*} \cup ... \cup C_W^{I_L*}$ such that

$$\min_{I_1,...,I_L} d_{R_W}(C_W^{I_1} \cup ... \cup C_W^{I_L}) \tag{9}$$

As the (exact) solution of (11) is very difficult, an auxiliary problem is solved (cf.
Kacprzyk and Szkatula [11]) whose solution is in general very close but much easier,
i.e. an $R_W^* = C_W^{I_1*} \cup ... \cup C_W^{I_L*}$ is sough such that

$$\min_{I_1} d_W(C_W^{I_1}), ..., \min_{I_L} d_W(C_W^{I_L}) \tag{10}$$

3   Solution by Using the IP2_GA Method

For $e^P \in S_P$, and all the negative examples $e^{P+n} \in S_N$, $n = 1,...,N$, we construct a
0-1 matrix $Z_{N*K} = [z_{nj}]$, $n = 1,...,N$, $j = 1,...,K$, defined as

$$z_{nj} = \begin{cases} 1 & \text{for } f(e^P, a_j) = f(e^{P+n}, a_j) \\ 0 & \text{for } f(e^P, a_j) \neq f(e^{P+n}, a_j) \end{cases} \tag{11}$$

whose rows correspond to the consecutive negative examples $e^{P+n} \in S_N$, $n = 1,...,N$ and columns to the attributes $a_1,...,a_K$; $z_{nj} = 1$ occurs if a_j takes on different values in the positive and negative example, i.e. $f(e^P, a_j) \neq f(e^{P+n}, a_j)$, and $z_{nj} = 0$ otherwise. There are no rows with all elements equal 0 since the sets of positive and negative examples are disjoint (and non-empty). Thus, for any positive and negative example there is always at least one attribute with a different value in these examples.

Consider now the following inequality

$$\sum_{j=1}^{K} z_{nj} x_j \geq \gamma_n , \qquad n = 1,...,N \qquad (12)$$

where $\gamma = [\gamma_1,...,\gamma_N]^T$ is a 0-1 vector, and $x_j \in \{0,1\}$, for $j = 1,...,K$.

Any vector x satisfying $Zx \geq \gamma$ (12) determines therefore uniquely some complex such that the partial completeness and consistence are satisfied. It describes at least one example from the set of positive examples, and it does not describe most of the examples from the set of negative examples. If vector x does not describe the n-th negative example, then $\gamma_n = 1$; and $\gamma_n = 0$ otherwise.

The minimization in (10), using inequality (12), is

$$\min_{x:Zx \geq \gamma} \sum_{j=1}^{K} (1 - g_j(v_i^{a_j})) \cdot x_j \qquad (13)$$

The minimization over the set of indices I_l may be replaced by the minimization with respect to x which yields [cf. (7)] an $R_W^* = C_W^{I_1^*} \cup ... \cup C_W^{I_L^*}$ such that

$$\min_{x:Z^1 x \geq \gamma} d_W(C_W^{I_1}),..., \min_{x:Z^L x \geq \gamma} d_W(C_W^{I_L}) \qquad (14)$$

Each minimization with respect to x in (14) is therefore equivalent to the determination of a 0-1 vector x^* which uniquely determines the complex of the shortest weighted length. On the other hand, the satisfaction of $Zx \geq \Lambda$ (Λ is a unit vector) guarantees that such a complex would not describe all negative examples. If rules defining class $Y_{v_{i_t}^{a_d}}$ must describe *almost none* of the negative examples, problem (13) can be written as a modification of the set covering problem

$$\min_{x,\gamma} \sum_{j=1}^{K} c_j x_j , \text{ subject to } \sum_{j=1}^{K} z_{nj} x_j \geq \gamma_n , \quad n = 1,...,N \qquad (15)$$

with an additional constraint: $\sum_{n=1}^{N} \gamma_n \geq N - rel$, where $c_j = (1 - g_j(v_i^{a_j}))$, $z_{nj} \in \{0,1\}$,

$x_j \in \{0,1\}$, $j = 1,...,K$, $\gamma = [\gamma_1,...,\gamma_N]^T$, $\gamma_n \in \{0,1\}$, $rel \geq 0$.

This is the same as the original set covering problem with the exception that no more then *rel* rows are uncovered. Then, clearly no more then *rel* rows can be deleted. We may, in deleting rows, loose some information about the problem. This reduction cannot always be applied. In the set covering problem (cf. Beasley and Chu [4]) there is only constraint, and $\gamma = [\gamma_1,...,\gamma_N]^T$ is a unit vector. Problem (15) is the problem of covering at least N-*rel* rows of an N-row, K-column, zero-one matrix (z_{nj}) by a subset of the columns at minimal cost c_j. We define $x_j = 1$ if column j with cost $c_j > 0$ is in the solution, and $x_j = 0$ otherwise. Then, most rows (at least N-*rel* rows) are covered by at least one column. It always has a feasible solution (a unit vector x of K element), due to the required disjointness of the sets of positive and negative examples and the way the matrix Z was constructed.

So, we seek a 0-1 vector x at minimum cost and a a 0-1 vector $\gamma = [\gamma_1,...,\gamma_N]^T$ which determines the covered rows, $\gamma_n = 1$ if row n is covered by solution x, and $\gamma_n = 0$, otherwise. By assumption, at least N-*rel* rows must be covered by x.

The set covering problem is a well-known NP-complete combinatorial optimization problem. A number of optimal and faster heuristic algorithms have been proposed, cf. Grossman and Wool [9]. Beasley and Chu [4] presented a genetic algorithm, with modified operations.

For solving (14) we propose a new procedure, IP2_GA, based on a genetic algorithm. We assume that the classification rules must correctly describe *most of the examples*, at least $A_{learning}$; the measure of classification accuracy $A_{learning}$ is the percentage of examples correctly classified. We assume a K-bit binary string which represents a potential solution, K is the number of variables. One for bit j implies that column j is in solution x^l, i.e. that x^l_j is in the solution. In IP2_GA in each iteration all solutions are evaluated with respect to their completeness and consistency.

The fitness of an individual solution x is

$$eval(x) = f(x) - g_{max} \frac{K}{N} \sum_{n=1}^{N} f_n(x) \tag{16}$$

$$f(x) = \sum_{j=1}^{K} c_j x_j; \quad f_n(x) = \begin{cases} 0 & for \ \sum_{j=1}^{K} z_{nj} \cdot x_j > 0 \\ 1 & for \ \sum_{j=1}^{K} z_{nj} \cdot x_j = 0 \end{cases}; \ g_{max} = \max\{g_j : j = 1,...,K\},$$

$n=1,...,N$; x_j is the value of column j in the string and c_j is the cost of column j.

The structure of a new population is chosen by a stochastic universal sampling (cf. Baker [1]). The consecutive steps of IP2_GA are:

Step 1. Initialize: $S = S_P$, i.e. the whole set of examples is initially assumed to contain the positive ones, S_N is a set of negative examples, and $R^*_W = \emptyset$, i.e. the initial set of complexes is assumed empty, iteration $j = 0$, given parameter $rel \geq 0$.

Step 2. Iteration $j = j + 1$. Determine the weights G by analyzing (pre-processing) of the examples due to (4).

Step 3. Determine an appropriate starting point; a good one may be a centroid (cf. Kacprzyk and Szkatula [13, 15]) that is a (possibly non existing) example in which the attributes take on values that occur most often in the positive examples and seldom in the negative examples. In the set of positive examples we find the closest positive example e^P to centroid, as the starting point for the next iterations.

Step 4. For the e^P we form the matrix $Z_{N*K} = [z_{nj}]$, $n = 1,...,N$, $j = 1,...,K$, due to (13) and form a modification of the set covering problem, due to (15).

Step 5. We apply a genetic algorithm.
   Step 1'. Set $t = 1$. Generate an initial population of random solutions $P(t) = \{x^1, x^2,..., x^P\}$, and evaluate the fitness $eval(x^l)$ of individuals in the population.
   Step 2'. For the first solutions a crossover operator is applied. Two solutions are chosen and form two new solutions.
   Step 3'. A mutation operator is applied to each solution in the population.
   Step 4'. The new solution generated by the crossover and mutation procedures may not be feasible. We evaluate the fitness $eval(x^l)$ of new individuals in the population.
   Step 5'. If a termination condition is satisfied, then STOP, and the best solution is the one with the smallest fitness; otherwise, go to Step 6'.
   Step 6'. Select a new population $P(t+1)$ from $P(t)$ and return to Step 2'.

The 0-1 vector $x^* = [x_1^*,...,x_K^*]^T$ found determines uniquely the complex $C_W^{I_j^*}$, and the 0-1 vector $\gamma = [\gamma_1,...,\gamma_N]^T$ determines the fulfilled constraints. The complex can not describe more than rel examples (given $rel \geq 0$). Now, we can go to Step 6.

Step 6. Include the complex $C_W^{I_j^*}$ found in Step 5 into the classification rule sought R_W^* (i.e. that with the minimal weighted length), $R_W^* := R_W^* \cup C_W^{I_j^*}$, and discard from the set of examples S all examples covered by that complex.

Step 7. If the set of examples S remaining is *small enough*, STOP and the rule sought is R_W^*, is the one sought; otherwise, return to Step 2.

4 Using IP2_GA to Solve a Coronary Heart Disease Problem

Several factors of blood, both morphological as well as of plasma, can indicate some illness. Only very basic blood examination is unfortunately so far widely considered though, e.g., blood viscosity may change due to some physical and psychical conditions of people, both ill and well.

We have 90 examples, either ill or healthy persons, 60 of them are a training set and 30 are for testing. The 12 blood factors (attributes) are measured: *lk1* - blood viscosity for coagulation quickness 230/s, *lk2* - blood viscosity for coagulation quickness 23/s, *lk3* - blood viscosity for coagulation quickness 15/s, *lp1* - plasma viscosity for coagulation quickness 230/s, *lp2* - plasma viscosity for coagulation quickness 23/s, *agr* - aggregation level of red blood cells, *fil* - blood cells capacity to change shape, *fib* - fibrin level in plasma, *ht* - hematocrite value, *sas* - sial acid rate in blood serum, *sak* - sial acid rate in blood cells, *ph* - acidity of blood.

The learning problem is formulated as to find classification rules into the classes:

class 1: no coronary disease,
class 2: coronary disease.

We use IP2_GA (with elements of a genetic algorithm) and IP2_GRE (with elements of a greedy algorithm), and assume that the classification rules must correctly describe *most of the learning examples* belonging to class 1 and 2, at least $A_{learning}$, by assumption. The results are shown in Tables 1 and 2, and we denote: IP2_GRE1 - $A_{learning} = 100\ \%$, IP2_GRE2 - $A_{learning} \geq 97\ \%$, IP2_GA1 - $A_{learning} = 100\ \%$ and IP2_GA2 - $A_{learning} \geq 90\ \%$. The percentage of correct classifications is the measure of classification accuracy, in percentage. The computational results are given below. A better classification accuracy for testing examples was obtained by using the classification rules correctly describes *most* of the training examples.

Table 1. Parameters describing the process of finding a classification rule for class 1/2

Algorithm	Number of iterations for class 1/class 2	Number of selectors in rule for class 1/class 2
IP2_GRE1	16/19	43/55
IP2_GRE2	13/17	2633
IP2_GA1	18/19	46/49
IP2_GA2	13/19	26/37

Table 2. Some paameters describing the process of classification the patients

Algorithm	$A_{learning}$ %, by assumption	Classification accuracy, $A_{testing}$ achieved
IP2_GRE1	100 %	90.0 %
IP2_GRE2	at least 97 %	96.7 %
IP2_GA1	100 %	73.4 %
IP2_GA2	at least 90 %	96.7 %

5 Concluding Remarks

We proposed an improved inductive learning procedure IP2_GA, based on a genetic algorithm. Results seem to be very encouraging.

Bibliography

1. Baker J.E. (1987) Reducing bias and inefficiency in the selection algorithm. In: Genetic Algorithms and Their Applications: Proceedings of the 2nd International Conference on Genetic Algorithms. (ed.) J.J. Grefenstette, 14-21, LEA, Cambridge, MA.
2. Balas E. (1980) Cutting planes from conditional bounds: a new approach to set covering. *Mathematical Programming Study* 12, 19-36.
3. Balas E. and Padberg M.W. (1979) Set partitioning - A survey. In: N. Christofides (ed.) *Combinatorial Optimisation*, Wiley, New York.
4. Beasley J.E., Chu P.C. (1994) *A genetic algorithm for the set covering problem.* Technical Report, The Management School, Imperial College.
5. Beasley J.E. (1996) A genetic algorithm for the set covering problem. *European Journal of Operational Research* 94, 392-404.
6. Christofides N. and Korman S. (1975) A computational survey of methods for the set covering problem. *Management Science* 21, 591-599.
7. Chvatal V. (1979) A greedy heuristic for the set-covering problem. *Math. of Oper. Res.* 4 (3) 233-235.
8. Garfinkel R. S. and Nemhauser G.L. (1978) *Integer programming.* John Wiley & Sons, New York-London-Sydney-Toronto.
9. Grossman T. and Wool A. (1995) Computational experience with approximation algorithms for the set covering problem. Working paper, Theoretical Division and CNLS, Los Alamos National Laboratory.
10. Kacprzyk J., Szkatuła G. (1994) Machine learning from examples under errors in data, Proceedings of Fifth International Conference in Information Processing and Management of Uncertainty in Knowledge-Based Systems IPMU'94 Paris France, Vol.2, 1047-1051
11. Kacprzyk J. and Szkatuła G. (1995) Machine learning from examples under errors in data. In B. Bouchon-Meunier, R.R. Yager and L.A. Zadeh (eds.): Fuzzy Logic and Soft Computing, World Scientific, Singapore, 1995, pp. 31 - 36.
12. Kacprzyk J. and Szkatuła G. (1996) An algorithm for learning from erroneous and incorrigible examples, *Int. J. of Intelligent Syst.* 11, 565 - 582.
13. Kacprzyk J. and Szkatuła G (1997a) An improved inductive learning algorithm with a preanalysis od data", In Z.W. Raś and A. Skowron (eds.): Foundations of Intelligent Systems (Proceedings of 10th ISMIS'97 Symposium, Charlotte, NC, USA), Springer-Verlag, Berlin, 157 - 166.
14. Kacprzyk J. and Szkatuła G. (1997b) Deriving IF-THEN rules for intelligent decision support via inductive learning", in N.Kasabov et al. (eds.): Progress in Connectionist-Based Information Systems (Proceedings of ICONIP'97, ANZIIS'97 and ANNES'97 Conference, Dunedin, New Zealand), Springer, Singapore, vol. 2, 818 - 821.
15. Kacprzyk J. and Szkatuła G. (1998) IP1 - An Improved Inductive Learning Procedure with a Preprocessing of Data. In L. Xu, L.W. Chan, I. King and A. Fu (eds.): Intelligent Data Engineering and Learning. Perspectives on Financial Engineering and Data Mining (Proceedings of IDEAL'98, Hong Kong), Springer, Hong Kong, pp. 385-392, 1998.

16. Kacprzyk J. and Szkatuła G. (1999) An inductive learning algorithm with a preanalysis od data. *Int. J. of Knowledge - Based Intelligent Engineering Systems*, vol. 3, 135-146.
17. Kacprzyk J. and Szkatuła G. (2002) An integer programming approach to inductive learning using genetic algorithm. In: Proceedings of the 2002 Congress on Evolutionary Computation, CEC'02, Honolulu, Hawaii, pp. 181-186.
18. Kacprzyk J. and Szkatuła G. (2002) An integer programming approach to inductive learning using genetic and greedy algorithms, In L.C. Jain and J. Kacprzyk (eds.): New Learning Paradigms in Soft Computing, Physica-Verlag, Heidelberg and New York, 2002, pp. 322-366.
19. Michalski R.S. (1983) A theory and methodology of inductive learning. In: R. Michalski, J. Carbonell and T.M. Mitchell (Eds.), Machine Learning. Tioga Press.
20. Zadeh L.A. and J. Kacprzyk (1999) Computing with Words in Information/Intelligent Systems. Vol. Foundations, Vol. 2 Applications, Physica-Verlag, Heidelberg and New York.

Subsystem Based Generalizations of Rough Set Approximations

Yiyu Yao and Yaohua Chen

Department of Computer Science, University of Regina
Regina, Saskatchewan, Canada S4S 0A2
{yyao, chen115y}@cs.uregina.ca

Abstract. Subsystem based generalizations of rough set approximations are investigated. Instead of using an equivalence relation, an arbitrary binary relation is used to construct a subsystem. By exploring the relationships between subsystems and different types of binary relations, we examine various classes of generalized approximation operators. The structures of subsystems and the properties of approximation operators are analyzed.

1 Introduction

Successful applications of the rough set theory depend on the understanding of its basic notions, various views, interpretations and formulations of the theory, and potentially useful generalizations of the basic theory [13, 14, 16, 19, 21]. This paper makes a further contribution by investigating another type of less studied, subsystem based generalizations of rough set approximations.

A basic notion of rough set theory is the lower and upper approximations, or approximation operators [5, 7, 13]. There exist several definitions of this concept, commonly known as the element based, granule based, and subsystem based definitions [19]. Each of them offers a unique interpretation of the theory. They can be used to investigate the connections to other theories, and to generalize the basic theory in different directions [16, 19].

The element based definition establishes a connection between approximation operators and the necessity and the possibility operators of modal logic. Based on the results from modal logics, one can generalize approximation operators by using any binary relations [20]. Under the granule based definition, one may view rough set theory as a concrete example of granular computing [18]. Approximation operators can be generalized by using coverings of the universe [8, 22], or neighborhood systems [15]. The subsystem based definition relates approximation operators to the interior and closure operators of topological spaces [11, 12], the closure operators of closure systems [17], and operators in other algebraic systems [1, 3, 17].

The subsystem based formulation of the rough set theory was first developed by Pawlak [5]. An equivalence relation is used to define a special type of topological space, in which the family of all open sets is the same as the family of all

M.-S. Hacid et al. (Eds.): ISMIS 2005, LNAI 3488, pp. 210–218, 2005.
© Springer-Verlag Berlin Heidelberg 2005

closed sets. With this subsystem, the lower and upper approximation operators
are in fact the interior and closure operators, respectively [5]. Skowron [11] studied such topological spaces in the context of information tables. Wiweger [12]
used generalized approximation operators, as interior and closure operators, by
considering the family of open sets and the family of closed sets, respectively,
in a topological space. Cattaneo [1] further generalized the subsystem based
definition in terms of an abstract approximation space, consisting of a poset,
a family of inner definable elements, and a family of outer definable elements.
The approximation operators are defined based on the two subsystems of definable elements [1]. Järvinen [3] and Yao [17] studied generalized subsystem based
definitions in other algebraic systems.

Except the Pawlak's formulation, studies on subsystem based formulation
assume that one or two subsystems are given. This imposes a limitation on the
applications of the formulation, as the construction of the subsystems may be
a challenging task. Recently, Shi [10] presented some results linking subsystems
and binary relations, based on a relational interpretation of approximation operators suggested by Yao [15]. In this paper, we present a more complete study
on this topic. More specifically, we study different subsystems constructed from
different types of binary relations. Properties of subsystems and the induced
generalized approximation operators are analyzed with respect to properties of
binary relations.

2   Rough Set Approximations

Suppose U is a finite nonempty set called the universe and $E \subseteq U \times U$ is an
equivalence relation on U, that is, E is reflexive, symmetric, and transitive.
The pair $apr = (U, E)$ is called a Pawlak's approximation space [5, 7]. In the
subsystem based development, the rough set approximation operators are defined
in two steps. With respect to an approximation space, one first constructs a
subsystem of the power set 2^U, and then approximates a subset of the universe
from below and above by two subsets in the subsystem.

An equivalence relation E induces a partition U/E of the universe. The partition U/E consists of a family of pairwise disjoint subsets of the universe U,
whose union is the universe, namely, $U = \bigcup[x]_E$, where $[x]_E = \{y \in U \mid xEy\}$
is the equivalence class containing x. All elements of $[x]_E$ cannot be differentiated from x under the equivalence relation E. The equivalence class $[x]_E$ is
therefore a smallest subset of U that can be identified with respect to E, that
is, elements of $[x]_E$ can be separated from other elements of U using E. Any
nonempty subset of $[x]_E$ cannot be properly identified. The equivalence classes
are called elementary sets. A union of elementary sets can also be identified and
thus is a composed set that is definable [5, 13].

By adding the empty set $\emptyset$ and making U/E closed under set union, we
obtain a family of subsets $\sigma(U/E)$, which is a subsystem of the power set 2^U,
i.e., $\sigma(U/E) \subseteq 2^U$. It can be seen that $\sigma(U/E)$ is closed under set complement,
intersection, and union. It is an σ-algebra of subsets of U generated by the

family of equivalence classes U/E, that is, U/E is the basis of the σ-algebra $\sigma(U/E)$. It is also a sub-Boolean algebra of the Boolean algebra given by the power set 2^U.

An approximation space $apr = (U, E)$ defines uniquely a topological space $(U, \sigma(U/E))$, in which $\sigma(U/E)$ is the family of all open and closed sets [5]. Moreover, the family of open sets is the same as the family of closed sets. With respect to the subsystem $\sigma(U/E)$, rough set approximations can be defined [5]. Specifically, the lower approximation of an arbitrary set A is defined as the greatest set in $\sigma(U/E)$ that is contained in A, and the upper approximation of A is defined as the smallest set in $\sigma(U/E)$ that contains A. As pointed out by Pawlak [5], they correspond to the interior and closure of A in the topological space $(U, \sigma(U/E))$.

Formally, rough set approximations can be expressed by the following sub-system based definition [5, 13]: for $A \subseteq U$,

$$\underline{apr}(A) = \bigcup \{X \mid X \in \sigma(U/E), X \subseteq A\}$$
$$\overline{apr}(A) = \bigcap \{X \mid X \in \sigma(U/E), A \subseteq X\}. \tag{1}$$

They satisfy all properties of interior and closure operators and additional properties [5, 13]. The subsystem $\sigma(U/E)$ can be recovered from the approximation operators as follows:

$$\sigma(U/E) = \{X \mid \underline{apr}(X) = X\}$$
$$= \{X \mid \overline{apr}(X) = X\}. \tag{2}$$

It in fact consists of the fixed points of approximation operators. The condition $\underline{apr}(A) = A = \overline{apr}(A)$ is often used to study the definability of a subset A of the universe [6, 9].

3   Generalized Rough Set Approximations

We use subsystems constructed from a non-equivalence relation to generalize the subsystem based definition.

3.1   Remarks on Subsystem Based Formulation

For the generalization of the subsystem based definition, we want to keep some of the basic properties of the approximation operators. The generalized approximation operators must be well defined. For those purposes, we point out several important features of subsystem based definition.

The approximation operators defined by Equation (1) are dual operators with respect to set complement ^{c}, that is, they satisfy the conditions:

$$(\text{L0}) \qquad \underline{apr}(A) = (\overline{apr}(A^c))^c,$$
$$(\text{U0}) \qquad \overline{apr}(A) = (\underline{apr}(A^c))^c,$$

The duality of the approximation operators can be easily verified from the definition and the fact that the subsystem $\sigma(U/E)$ is closed under set complement, intersection and union.

In Equation (1), the lower approximation operator is well defined as long as the subsystem is closed under union. Similarly, the upper approximation operator is well defined as long as the subsystem is closed under intersection. The need for a single subsystem is in fact sufficient, but not necessary. In general, one may use two subsystems [1, 17]. The subsystem for the lower approximation operator must be closed under union and the subsystem for the upper approximation operator must be closed under intersection. In order to keep the duality of approximation operators, elements of two subsystems must be related to each other through set complement [17].

Approximation operators satisfy the following additional properties:

$$
\begin{array}{ll}
\text{(L1)} & \underline{apr}(\emptyset) = \emptyset, \\
\text{(U1)} & \overline{apr}(U) = U, \\
\text{(L2)} & \underline{apr}(A) \subseteq A, \\
\text{(U2)} & A \subseteq \overline{apr}(A), \\
\text{(L3)} & \underline{apr}(A) = \underline{apr}(\underline{apr}(A)), \\
\text{(U3)} & \overline{apr}(A) = \overline{apr}(\overline{apr}(A)), \\
\text{(L4)} & A \subseteq B \Rightarrow \underline{apr}(A) \subseteq \underline{apr}(B), \\
\text{(U4)} & A \subseteq B \Rightarrow \overline{apr}(A) \subseteq \overline{apr}(B).
\end{array}
$$

These properties can be easily derived from the subsystem based definition. Properties (L1) and (U1) are special cases of (L2) and (U2), respectively. Properties (L3) and (U3) are related to the fact that the subsystem $\sigma(U/E)$ consists of the fixed points of the approximation operators. Properties (L4) and (U4) show the monotonicity of approximation operators with respect to set inclusion. Those properties are direct consequences of the subsystem based definition. It is reasonable to expect that generalized definitions keep those properties.

3.2   Construction of Subsystems

Let R denote a binary relation on the universe U. For two elements $x, y \in U$, if xRy, we say that y is R-related to x. For any element $x \in U$, its successor neighborhood $R_s(x)$ is defined as [15]:

$$
R_s(x) = \{y \mid xRy\}. \tag{3}
$$

When the relation R is an equivalence relation, $R_s(x)$ is the equivalence class containing x. For a subset of universe $A \subseteq U$, its successor neighborhood can be defined by extending the successor neighborhood:

$$
R_s(A) = \bigcup_{x \in A} R_s(x). \tag{4}
$$

By the definition, we have $R_s(\emptyset) = \emptyset$.

Independent of the properties of the binary relation, the successor neighborhood operator R_s have the properties: for $A, B \subseteq U$,

(s1) $R_s(A \cap B) \subseteq R_s(A) \cap R_s(B)$,

(s2) $R_s(A \cup B) = R_s(A) \cup R_s(B)$,

(s3) $A \subseteq B \Longrightarrow R_s(A) \subseteq R_s(B)$.

Property (s2) trivially follows from the definition. Properties (s1) and (s3) follow from property (s2).

Let $\mathcal{O}(U)$ denote the family of neighborhoods $R_s(X)$ for all $X \subseteq U$. That is,

$$\mathcal{O}(U) = \{R_s(X) \mid X \subseteq U\}. \tag{5}$$

The family of their complements is given by:

$$\mathcal{C}(U) = \{X^c \mid X \in \mathcal{O}(U)\}. \tag{6}$$

Independent of the properties of the binary relation, the two families have the properties:

(o1) $\emptyset \in \mathcal{O}(U)$,

(c1) $U \in \mathcal{C}(U)$,

(o2) $\mathcal{O}(U)$ is closed under set union,

(c2) $\mathcal{C}(U)$ is closed under set intersection.

By properties (c1) and (c2), $\mathcal{C}(U)$ is a closure system [2]. In general, $\mathcal{O}(U)$ is not closed under set intersection and $\mathcal{C}(U)$ is not closed under union. Furthermore, the two families are not necessarily the same.

By the properties of the two subsystems and discussion in the last subsection, we can conclude that they have all the desired properties for the generalization of approximation operators.

With respect to a binary relation, one can define other types of neighborhoods, such as the predecessor neighborhoods, predecessor or successor neighborhoods, and predecessor and successor neighborhood [15]. The corresponding subsystems can be similarly constructed.

3.3   Rough Set Approximations

Based on the two families $\mathcal{O}(U)$ and $\mathcal{C}(U)$, we define a pair of lower and upper approximation operators by generalizing Equation (1):

$$\underline{apr}(A) = \bigcup \{X \mid X \in \mathcal{O}(U), X \subseteq A\},$$

$$\overline{apr}(A) = \bigcap \{X \mid X \in \mathcal{C}(U), A \subseteq X\}. \tag{7}$$

By properties (o2) and (c2), this definition is well defined [17]. Furthermore, the operator $\overline{apr}$ is the closure operator of the closure system $\mathcal{C}(U)$.

The generalized approximation operators are dual operators satisfying properties (L0)-(L4) and (U0)-(U4). The two subsystems can be recovered from the the fixed points of lower and upper approximations:

$$\mathcal{O}(U) = \{X \mid \underline{apr}(X) = X\},$$
$$\mathcal{C}(U) = \{X \mid \overline{apr}(X) = X\}.$$

The generalized formulation therefore preserves the basic important features of the original formulation.

Example 1. This simple example illustrates the main ideas of the generalized approximation operators. Consider a universe $U = \{a, b, c\}$. A binary relation R is given by:

$$aRa, \ aRb, \ bRa, \ bRb, \ cRb.$$

From Equation (3), R-related elements for each member of U are given by:

$$R_s(a) = \{a, b\}, \ R_s(b) = \{a, b\}, \ R_s(c) = \{b\}.$$

The subsystems $\mathcal{O}(U)$ and $\mathcal{C}(U)$ are:

$$\mathcal{O}(U) = \{\emptyset, \{b\}, \{a, b\}\},$$
$$\mathcal{C}(U) = \{U, \{a, c\}, \{c\}\}.$$

According to the definition of approximation operators, we have:

$$
\begin{aligned}
\underline{apr}(\emptyset) &= \emptyset, & \overline{apr}(\emptyset) &= \{c\}, \\
\underline{apr}(\{a\}) &= \emptyset, & \overline{apr}(\{a\}) &= \{a, c\}, \\
\underline{apr}(\{b\}) &= \{b\}, & \overline{apr}(\{b\}) &= U, \\
\underline{apr}(\{c\}) &= \emptyset, & \overline{apr}(\{c\}) &= \{c\}, \\
\underline{apr}(\{a, b\}) &= \{a, b\}, & \overline{apr}(\{a, b\}) &= U, \\
\underline{apr}(\{a, c\}) &= \emptyset, & \overline{apr}(\{a, c\}) &= \{a, c\}, \\
\underline{apr}(\{b, c\}) &= \{b\}, & \overline{apr}(\{b, c\}) &= U, \\
\underline{apr}(U) &= \{a, b\}, & \overline{apr}(U) &= U.
\end{aligned}
$$

One can establish a close relationship between subsystem based formulation and granule based formulation. Specifically, we can express the lower approximation of A as the union of some successor neighborhoods, which leads to the granule based definition [15]:

$$\underline{apr}(A) = \bigcup \{R_s(x) \mid x \in U, R_s(x) \subseteq A\}. \tag{8}$$

In a special case, we have $\underline{apr}(R_s(x)) = R_s(x)$ and $\underline{apr}(R_s(A)) = R_s(A)$. It should be pointed out that the family of neighborhoods $\{R_s(x) \neq \emptyset \mid x \in U\}$ is not necessarily a covering of the universe.

3.4   Classes of Generalized Rough Set Approximations

Binary relations can be classified based on their properties. Additional properties of a binary relation may induce further structures on the subsystems. Consequently, we can also study classes of approximation operators according to the properties of binary relations.

The following list summarizes the properties of binary relations:

inverse serial :   for all $x \in U$, there exists a $y \in U$ such that yRx,
$$\bigcup_{x \in U} R_s(x) = U,$$

serial :   for all $x \in U$, there exists a $y \in U$ such that xRy,

for all $x \in U, R_s(x) \neq \emptyset$,

reflexive :   for all $x \in U, xRx$,

for all $x \in U, x \in R_s(x)$,

symmetric :   for all $x, y \in U, xRy \Longrightarrow yRx$,

for all $x, y \in U, x \in R_s(y) \Longrightarrow y \in R_s(x)$,

transitive :   for all $x, y, z \in U, [xRy, yRz] \Longrightarrow xRz$,

for all $x, y, z \in U, [y \in R_s(x), z \in R_s(y)] \Longrightarrow z \in R_s(x)$,

for all $x, y \in U, y \in R_s(x) \Longrightarrow R_s(y) \subseteq R_s(x)$.

If a relation R is inverse serial, the subsystems have the properties:

(o3) $U \in \mathcal{O}(U)$,
(c3) $\emptyset \in \mathcal{C}(U)$.

Consequently, the approximation operators have the properties:

(L5) $\underline{apr}(U) = U$,
(U5) $\overline{apr}(\emptyset) = \emptyset$.

If the relation is serial, for every $x \in U$, there exists a $y \in U$ such that xRy, namely, $R_s(x) \neq \emptyset$. This implies the properties:

(o4)   The system $\mathcal{O}(U)$ contains at least a nonempty subset of U,
(c4)   The system $\mathcal{C}(U)$ contains at least a proper subset of U.

For the approximation operators, the corresponding properties are:

(L6)   There exists a subset A of U such that $\underline{apr}(A) \neq \emptyset$,
(U6)   There exists a subset A of U such that $\overline{apr}(A) \neq U$.

A reflexive relation is both inverse serial and serial. The induced approximation operators satisfy properties (L5), (L6), (U5), and (U6).

If the binary relation R is reflexive and transitive, $(U, \mathcal{O}(U))$ is a topological space with $\mathcal{O}(U)$ as the family of open sets [4, 8]. In this case, we have:

(o5) $\mathcal{O}(U)$ is closed under set intersection,

(c6) $\mathcal{C}(U)$ is closed under set union.

Then, we have additional properties of approximation operators:

$$(\text{L7}) \qquad \underline{apr}(A \cap B) = \underline{apr}(A) \cap \underline{apr}(B),$$
$$(\text{U7}) \qquad \overline{apr}(A \cup B) = \overline{apr}(A) \cup \overline{apr}(B).$$

The approximation operators are indeed the topological interior and closure operators.

If the binary relation is an equivalence relation, $R_s(x)$ is the equivalence class containing x. The two systems become the same, that is, $\mathcal{O}(U) = \mathcal{C}(U)$. This leads to the following properties of approximation operators:

$$(\text{L8}) \qquad \underline{apr}(A) = \overline{apr}(\underline{apr}(A)),$$
$$(\text{L8}) \qquad \overline{apr}(B) = \underline{apr}(\overline{apr}(A)).$$

It is clear that the standard rough set approximation operators have all the properties we have discussed so far.

4   Conclusion

The subsystem based formulation provides an important interpretation of the rough set theory. It allows us to study the rough set theory in the contexts of many algebraic systems. This leads naturally to the generalization of rough set approximations.

By extending the subsystem based definition, we examine the generalized approximation operators by using non-equivalence relations. Two subsystems are constructed from a binary relation, and approximation operators are defined in term of the two subsystems. The generalized approximation operators preserve many of the basic features of the standard rough set approximation operators. The properties of binary relations, subsystems, and approximation operators are linked together. Several classes of approximation operators are discussed with respect to different types of binary relations.

A connection is also established between subsystem based formulation and granule based formulation. In general, it is useful to study further their relationships to the element based formulation.

References

1. Cattaneo, G. Abstract approximation spaces for rough theories, in: *Rough Sets in Knowledge Discovery*, Polkowski, L. and Skowron, A. (Eds), Physica-Verlag, Heidelberg, 59-98, 1998.

2. Cohn, P.M. *Universal Algebra*, Harper and Row Publishers, New York, 1965.
3. Järvinen, J. On the structure of rough approximations, *Proceedings of the Third International Conference on Rough Sets and Current Trends in Computing*, LNAI 2475, 123-130, 2002.
4. Kortelainen, J. On relationship between modified sets, topological spaces and rough sets, *Fuzzy Sets System*, **61**, 91-95, 1994.
5. Pawlak, Z. Rough sets, *International Journal of Computer and Information Sciences*, **11**, 341-356, 1982.
6. Pawlak, Z. Rough classification, *International Journal of Man-Machine Studies*, **20**, 469-483, 1984.
7. Pawlak, Z. *Rough Sets: Theoretical Aspects of Reasoning about Data*, Kluwer Academic Publishers, Boston, 1991.
8. Pomykala, J.A. Approximation operations in approximation space, *Bulletin of the Polish Academy of Sciences, Mathematics*, **35**, 653-662, 1987.
9. Pomykala, J.A. On definability of nondeterministic information system, *Bulletin of the Polish Academy of Sciences, Mathematics*, **36**, 193-210, 1988.
10. Shi, H.Y. *A Study of Constructive Methods of Rough Sets*, M.Sc. Thesis, Lakehead University, Canada, 2004.
11. Skowron, A. On topology in information systems, *Bulletin of the Polish Academy of Sciences, Mathematics*, **36**, 477-479, 1989.
12. Wiweger, A. On topological rough sets, *Bulletin of the Polish Academy of Sciences, Mathematics*, **37**, 89-93, 1989.
13. Yao, Y.Y. Two views of the theory of rough sets in finite universe, *International Journal of Approximate Reasoning*, **15**, 291-317, 1996.
14. Yao, Y.Y. Constructive and algebraic methods of the theory of rough sets, *Information Sciences*, **109**, 21-47, 1998.
15. Yao, Y.Y. Relational interpretations of neighborhood operators and rough set approximation operators, *Information Sciences*, **111**, 239-259, 1998.
16. Yao, Y.Y. Generalized rough set models, in: *Rough Sets in Knowledge Discovery*, Polkowski, L. and Skowron, A. (Eds.), Physica-Verlag, Heidelberg, 286-318, 1998.
17. Yao, Y.Y. On generalizing Pawlak approximation operators, *Rough Sets and Current Trends in Computing, Proceedings of the 1st International Conference, (RSCTC 1998)*, LNAI 1424, 298-307, 1998.
18. Yao, Y.Y. Information granulation and rough set approximation, *International Journal of Intelligent Systems*, **16**, 87-104, 2001.
19. Yao, Y.Y. On generalizing rough set theory, *Rough Sets, Fuzzy Sets, Data Mining, and Granular Computing, Proceedings of the 9th International Conference (RSFD-GrC 2003)*, LNAI 2639, 44-51, 2003.
20. Yao, Y.Y. and Lin, T.Y. Generalization of rough sets using modal logic, *Intelligent Automation and Soft Computing, An International Journal*, **2**, 103-120, 1996.
21. Yao, Y.Y., Wong, S.K.M., and Lin, T.Y. A review of rough set models, in: *Rough Sets and Data Mining: Analysis for Imprecise Data*, Lin, T.Y. and Cercone, N. (Eds.), Kluwer Academic Publishers, Boston, 47-75, 1997.
22. Zakowski, W. Approximations in the space (U, Π), *Demonstratio Mathematica*, XVI, 761-769, 1983.

Model-Based Cluster Analysis for Web Users Sessions

George Pallis, Lefteris Angelis, and Athena Vakali

Department of Informatics,
Aristotle University of Thessaloniki,
54124, Thessaloniki, Greece
gpallis@ccf.auth.gr
{lef, avakali}@csd.auth.gr

Abstract. One of the main issues in Web usage mining is the discovery of patterns in the navigational behavior of Web users. Standard approaches, such as clustering of users' sessions and discovering association rules or frequent navigational paths, do not generally allow to characterize or quantify the unobservable factors that lead to common navigational patterns. Therefore, it is necessary to develop techniques that can discover hidden and useful relationships among users as well as between users and Web objects. *Correspondence Analysis* (CO-AN) is particularly useful in this context, since it can uncover meaningful associations among users and pages. We present a model-based cluster analysis for Web users sessions including a novel visualization and interpretation approach which is based on CO-AN.

1 Introduction

The explosive growth of the Web and the increased number of users have led more and more organizations to put their information on the Web and provide sophisticated Web-based services such as distance education, on-line shopping etc. However, the continuous growth in the size and use of the Internet is increasing the difficulties in managing the information. Thus, an urgent need exists for developing new techniques in order to improve the Web performance.

In this context, cluster analysis can be considered as one of the most important aspects in the Web mining process for discovering meaningful groups (interesting distributions or patterns over the considered data sets) as well as interpreting and visualizing the key behaviors exhibited by the users in each cluster. The clustering problem is about partitioning a given data set into clusters (groups) such that the data points in the same cluster are more similar to each other than points in different clusters.

Here, we focus on clustering Web users based on their navigation behavior. Specifically, a Web user may visit a Web site from time to time and spend arbitrary amount of time between consecutive visits. To deal with the unpredictable nature of Web browsing, a new concept, *session*, was introduced as the unit of interaction between a user and a Web server. By clustering the users navigation sessions, the Web developer may understand the browsing behavior of users better and may provide more suitable and customized services to the users. In particular, the knowledge discovered from these sessions will certainly contribute in the construction and maintenance of real-time intelligent Web servers that are able to dynamically adapt their designs to satisfy the future users' needs.

M.-S. Hacid et al. (Eds.): ISMIS 2005, LNAI 3488, pp. 219–227, 2005.
© Springer-Verlag Berlin Heidelberg 2005

Therefore, understanding how users navigate a Web site is an essential step for Web sites developers to customize content (generating pages on a user's previous activities) and to consider creative caching and prefetching schemes to deliver content as quickly as possible.

The main problem with clustering algorithms is that it is difficult to assess the quality of the clusters returned and interpret these results by extracting useful inferences for the users' navigation behavior. Therefore, in most applications the resulting clustering scheme needs some evaluation regarding its validity [10]. Evaluating and assessing the results of a clustering algorithm is the main challenge of cluster validity. Up to now, several clustering validation approaches have been proposed in the literature [4, 8, 9, 10, 11].

The purpose of this paper is to present a comprehensive methodology including clustering at users' sessions, evaluation of clustering results and interpretation of the results. All these steps use advanced statistical methods which help not only to evaluate the clustering scheme but also to discover useful associations among clusters.

In [11], we introduced a probabilistic validation algorithm for model-based clustering, which is based on the χ^2 statistic. Here, we further proceed into presenting a detailed analysis for model-based clustering scheme[1] on a busy Web server and propose an efficient interpretation and visualization technique in order to extract useful conclusions for the underlying clusters. The main novelty in our work is that we find the equilibrium distribution of Web users clusters, each considered as a Markov chain (which represents the probability of a user to access a particular Web page in infinite number of clicks, independently of its previous pages that he has visited) and then we apply on them a correspondence analysis in order to further interpret the clustering results, uncovering meaningful associations among users and Web pages. More specifically, the main technical contributions of this work can be summarized as follows:

- We present a detailed framework for model-based cluster analysis for Web users sessions, studying the equilibrium distribution of each cluster;
- We introduce a visualization method for interpreting the equilibrium distribution of clusters based on correspondence analysis;
- The methods described were tested on a real data set collected from a busy Web server (msn.com).

To the best of our knowledge, there are not previous research works dealing with the interpretation and visualization of model-based clustering schemes using the concept of correspondence analysis [7]. Existing works on model-based clustering largely concentrate on a specific model or application, without providing a visualization method. The main reason is the high complexity which have these implementations [1]. A notable exception is the work in [2] where an interesting visualization tool was presented.

The rest of the paper is organized as follows. In Section 2, we present in detail the framework for model-based cluster analysis for grouping the Web users' sessions. The experimental results are given in Section 3. Finally, we conclude the paper and give some remarks for future research.

---

[1] Each cluster is represented by a probability model and the sessions are grouped according to the order in which users request Web pages.

2   The Clustering Procedure

The procedure for clustering Web users sessions is not a straightforward task but it consists of 4 steps. The first step is the preprocessing of Web log files[2] in order to mine the Web users' sessions. Then, we assign the sessions into the appropriate clusters. The third step is to validate the clusters which have been created in the previous step. Finally, the last step of the clustering procedure is to visualize and interpret the clusters. In the next paragraphs, we present in detail the above procedure.

2.1   Web Data Preprocessing

Web log data are undergone a certain pre-processing, such as invalid data cleaning and session identification. Data cleaning removes the records which do not include useful information for the users' navigation behavior, such as graphics, javascripts etc. The remaining page requests are categorized into different categories. The process of grouping the Web pages into categories is a usual practice, since it improves the data management and in addition eliminates the complexity of the underlying problem (since the number of page categories is smaller than the number of Web pages in a Web site) [2, 11]. In particular, the individual pages are grouped into semantically similar groups (as determined by the Web site administrator).

Moreover, we use heuristic methods to identify the Web access sessions, based on IP and time-outs [3]. We consider that we have an ordered set of traces with respect to the IPs. Therefore, a new session is created when a new IP address is encountered or if the visiting page time does not exceed 30 minutes for the same IP address.

2.2   The Clustering Algorithm

The way that users navigate in a Web site depends on several factors such as user's interest, site structure etc. In this framework, we assume that a user arrives at the Web site in a particular time and is assigned to one of the underlying clusters with some probability. In the next paragraphs, we present the model-based approach which we follow in order to cluster the Web users' sessions:

- **Representation of clusters:** Each cluster consists of Web users' sessions. To model heterogeneity of them we use a mixture of first-order Markov chains, where each cluster in a mixture represents a behavior described by a single Markov chain. Specifically, Markov models can be viewed as stochastic generalizations of finite-state automata, when both transitions between states and generation of output symbols are governed by probability distributions. In our framework, a useful representation of such a model is the transition matrix of size $V \times V$ (where V is the number of categories which are denoted by A_1, A_2, ..., A_V) describing the probability that a user will go to a certain page category given (s)he is viewing the current page category and a vector of V initial probabilities describing how likely is that a user will begin his/her navigation session in a given page category.

---

[2] Web log files provide information about activities performed by a user from the moment the user enters a Web site to the moment the same user leaves it.

- **Clustering users' sessions:** Each cluster has a data-generating model with different estimate parameters for each one. Therefore, this model can be well defined, if only we estimate the parameters of each model component, the probability distribution used to assign users to the various clusters and the number of components. We cluster users' sessions by learning a mixture of first-order Markov models using the EM algorithm. The EM algorithm originates from [5] and in [2] a method for employing on EM on users' sessions is proposed. It alternates two steps:

  - **The expectation E-step**: Given a set of parameter estimates the E-step calculates the conditional expectation of the complete-data log likelihood given the observed data and the parameter estimates.
  - **The maximization M-step**: Given a complete-data log likelihood, the M-step finds the parameter estimates to maximize the complete-data log likelihood from the E-step.

  The two steps are iterated until convergence (i.e. a local optimal solution is reached). Concerning the complexity of the EM algorithm, it depends on the complexity of the E and M steps at each iteration. For example, in our case (Markov mixtures) the complexity is linear in the sum of the lengths of all sessions. Note, that for more complex mixture models the complexity can be higher.

- **Number of clusters:** The number of clusters may be determined by using several probabilistic criteria, such as BIC (Bayesian Information Criterion), bayesian approximations, or bootstrap methods [1, 6]. Formally, we assume that there are K clusters C_1, C_2, ..., C_K and each of them is generated from its own probability distribution. Once the model is specified, we use the EM algorithm and probabilistic out-of-sample evaluation to determine the best number of clusters. A model is fitted on a subsample of sessions (the so-called training data set) and then scored on the remaining data (the so-called testing data set). Thus, we get an objective measure of how well each model fits the data. The model with the minimum out-of-sample predictive log score is selected.

2.3   Cluster Validation

An important issue in cluster analysis is the evaluation of clustering results to find the partitioning that best fits the underlying data. Towards this direction, we propose an efficient validation technique for model-based clustering approaches, where each cluster is represented by an ergodic Markov chain. By the term "ergodic", we mean a Markov chain that has the following two properties: 1) each node can reach any other node (all states intercommunicate), and 2) the chain is not periodic (all states have period one).

In order to validate the clustering scheme, we consider the equilibrium distribution of each cluster produced by the algorithm. These distributions represent the probabilities of a user to access each state in infinite number of states independently of its initial state. Then, the validation is performed by testing the homogeneity of the equilibrium distribution by the χ^2 test. More specifically, χ^2 testing is used to test the homogeneity among multiple clusters with probabilistic distributions by constructing a contingency table. This statistic is used to assess evidence that two or more distributions are dissimilar. Considering that in model-based approach the clusters represent a probabilistic distribution, we can directly apply the test of homogeneity by fitting the state frequen-

Table 1. A Contingency Table for Chi-square Testing

Clusters	States				
	A_1	A_2	...	A_V	sum
C_1	O_{11}	O_{12}	...	O_{1V}	Y_1
C_2	O_{21}	O_{22}	...		Y_2
...	...	...	...	...	...
C_K	O_{K1}	O_{K2}	...	O_{KV}	Y_K
sum	X_1	X_2	...	X_V	S

cies in the cluster into the contingency table, which rejects the fact that our modeling simplifies the testing.

In our framework, the states represent the page categories. Table 1 is the contingency table for testing. A contingency table test (or test of independence) is one that tests the hypothesis that the data are cross-classified in independent ways. In particular, O_{ij} stands for the frequency of A_j state in cluster C_i. O_{ij} is computed by multiplying the relative frequency of A_j state with the number of sessions that belong to cluster C_i. X_i is the sum of all the O_{ij} in i-th column and Y_j is the sum of all the O_{ij} in j-th raw. In this framework, we want to test the following hypothesis (for all the states and clusters of the underlying model):

Null Hypothesis (Ho): The distributions of the states in each cluster are all the same.
Testing: The following equation computes the χ^2 statistic:

$$\chi^2(C_1, C_2, ..., C_K) = \sum_{i=1}^{K} \sum_{j=1}^{V} \frac{(O_{ij} - Y_i \times \frac{X_j}{S})^2}{Y_i \times \frac{X_j}{S}}$$

A large value of the χ^2 criterion shows that the equilibrium distributions for each cluster are significantly different, which in turn is an indication of the heterogeneity among clusters. Therefore, we should know a critical χ^2 value that is the boundary of the area of hypothesis' rejection in a contingency table test. In order to find this critical value, we should define the level of significance (α) and the degrees of freedom (df). In statistics, it is known that a χ^2 has asymptotically a χ^2 distribution with (K-1)×(V-1) df. Therefore, if the value of χ^2 distribution is greater than a critical value, such as $\chi^2_{(K-1)\times(V-1);\alpha}$, we can reject the Ho at the α level of significance. Otherwise, there is no much evidence to reject Ho.

2.4 Cluster Interpretation and Visualization

Interpreting the navigation behaviors exhibited by the Web users in each cluster is important for a number of tasks, such as managing the Web site, identifying malicious visitors, and targeted advertising. It also helps to understand the navigation patterns of different user groups and therefore helps in organizing the Web site to better suit the users' needs. Furthermore, interpreting the results of clusters contributes to identify and provide customized services and recommendations to Web users.

Here, we introduce a model-based clustering interpretation approach by analyzing the contingency tables, that have been occurred in validation process, as described in the previous Section. In particular, an analysis of these tables includes examining row and column discrete variables and testing for independence via the χ^2 statistic. However, the number of variables can be quite large, and the χ^2 test does not reveal the dependence structure. Thus, in order to analyze the clusters in a more efficient way, we propose to use the correspondence analysis method.

Correspondence analysis (CO-AN) is a standard multi-variate statistical analysis method aiming to analyze and visualize simple two-way and multi-way contingency tables containing some measure of correspondence between the rows and columns. Thus, one of the goals of CO-AN is to describe the relationships between the categories for each variable, as well as the relationship between the variables. In this context, CO-AN can be used in order to interpret and visualize the Web users' navigation behaviors.

The rows and the columns of the contingency table as described in Table 1 represent distributions of the categorical variables. In order to measure their similarity and depict them geometrically, CO-AN uses a distance based on the χ^2 statistic. The object of CO-AN is to explain the total variation in the underlying correspondence table. In essence, the correspondence map, that is occurred by this analysis, is a graphical tool which helps the researcher easily to notice relationships within this table. When interpreting a correspondence map it is often helpful to refer back to the original correspondence table. Therefore, CO-AN can be proved a very useful tool for Web site developers since it could be used to graphically provide a meaningful interpretation of clusters as well as, the relationship among users' navigation behaviors. For instance, they might find which Web page categories are associated with each others, with respect to users' sessions. Then, the Web developer may arrange the structure of the Web site so that these pages are interlinked together.

CO-AN may also have several applications in commercial Web sites [1]. CO-AN of Web users sessions through e-commerce Web sites can provide valuable insights into customer behavior and provide clues about whether improvements in site design might be useful. Moreover, CO-AN method may be used to recommend new products to Web site visitors, based on their browsing behavior. It may also be used to understand what factors influence the way customers make purchases on a Web site.

3   Experimental Evaluation

3.1   Data Set

The methods described were tested on a real data set. In particular, the data set comes from Internet Information Server (IIS) logs for msnbc.com and news-related portions of msn.com[3].

In our experiments, there are 17 categories, which are presented in detail in Figure 2. Each category includes a number of URLs and the data set consists of approximately 6,000 users' sessions, with an average of 5,7 page views per session. The number of URLs per category ranges from 10 to 5000. Then, we select some of the sessions as (80% of

---

[3] Msnbc.com anonymous web data: http://kdd.ics.uci.edu/databases/msnbc/msnbc.html.

the total data) training data set and the rest as testing data set in order to determine the number of clusters.

3.2   Cluster Analysis: Validation and Interpretation

The first task is to define an optimal value for the number of clusters. As we mentioned in the previous Section, we choose the number of clusters minimizing the out-of-sample predictive score. We tested several out-of-sample log-likelihoods for varying number of clusters and found that the minimum value is achieved for the choice of 9 clusters. Then, we cluster the users' navigation sessions as described in Section 3. Based on our data set, the result is χ^2= 7040,3 with 128 df. Considering that the $\chi^2_{128;0,005}$=127.81, we conclude that the resulted clusters are an effective choice.

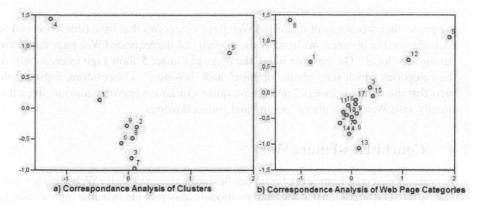

a) Correspondance Analysis of Clusters   b) Correspondence Analysis of Web Page Categories

Fig. 1. Correspondence Analysis of Web Page Categories

Once the clustering algorithm has been described, it is now time to obtain some graphs and interpret their behavior. In this context, Figure 1a illustrates which clusters have common characteristics with each other. As can be seen by this Figure, each cluster is represented by a point. Thus, we observe that the users identified as belonging to clusters 2 and 8 have some common characteristics (i.e. their distances are sufficiently small) while the users belonging to clusters 4 and 5 seem to be different (i.e. the points representing these clusters are isolated).

CO-AN can also be used to graphically display the relationship among Web page categories. As we described above, Web requests are not recorded at the finest level of detail (at the level of URL) but they are rather recorded at the level of page category (as determined by the Web site administrator). Figure 1b illustrates the associations between Web page categories that have occurred using CO-AN. From this Figure, we observe that Web users who visit Web pages about "weather" they do not visit Web pages about "opinion" (the points representing these categories are isolated). In this framework, we also find that the Web pages about "bulletin board service (bbs)" are usually directly associated with Web pages about "travel".

Therefore, a deep knowledge for the inside of each cluster can draw useful and mean-ingful inferences for the users' navigation behavior. More specifically, Figure 2 depicts

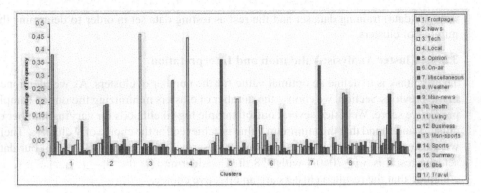

Fig. 2. The Percentage Frequency of Web Page Categories for each Cluster

the percentage frequency of requested Web page categories that have been observed for each cluster. For instance, in cluster 3, the majority of the requested Web page categories belongs to "local". On the other hand, the users in cluster 5 show high interest only for the categories which refer about "opinion" and "business". Furthermore, Figure 2 depicts that the users in clusters 2 and 8 have quite similar navigation behavior, since they usually visit Web pages about "on-air" and "miscellaneous".

4   Conclusions-Future Work

This paper presents a framework for model-based cluster analysis for Web users sessions. Taking into consideration that the Markov models may provide valuable information for users' navigation behavior which is often hidden, it is necessary to develop techniques that can discover hidden meaningful relationships among users as well as between users and Web objects. Towards this direction, statistical analysis helps to explore this hidden information in order to enhance the Web performance. Therefore, CO-AN is particularly useful in this context, since it can uncover semantic associations among users and pages.

For the future, we plan to apply the whole methodology described here in a Web log file in order to further analyze and interpret the results. Another goal is to develop an automatic mechanism in order to deliver the appropriate content to the interested users in a timely, scalable, and cost-effective manner.

References

1. Baldi P., Frasconi P., Smyth P. Modeling the Internet and the Web. Wiley Press,USA, 2003.
2. Cadez I. V., Heckerman D., Meek C., Smyth P., White S. Model-based Clustering and Visualization of Navigation Patterns on a Web Site. Journal of Data Mining and Knowledge Discovery, 7 (4), pp. 399-424, 2003.
3. Chen Z., Fu A., Tong F. Optimal Algorithms for Finding User Access Sessions from very Large Web Logs. World Wide Web: Internet and Information Systems, 6, pp. 259-279, 2003.
4. Chen K., Liu L. Validating and Refining Clusters via Visual Rendering. *In Proc. of the International Conference on Data Mining (ICDM 2003)*, Melbourne, Florida pp. 501-504, Dec. 2003.

5. Dempster A. P., Lsird N. M., Rubin D. B. Maximum Likelihood from Incomplete Data via the EM Algorithm. Statistics Society B, 39, pp. 1-22, 1977.
6. Fraley C., Raftery A. How Many Clusters? Which Clustering Method? Answers via Model-based Cluster Analysis. Computer Journal, 41, pp. 578-588, 1998.
7. Greenacre M.J. Correspondence Analysis in Practice. Academic Press, 1993.
8. Gunter S., Bunke H. Validation Indices for Graph Clustering. Pattern Recognition Letters 24 (8), pp. 1107-1113, 2003.
9. Halkidi M., Batistakis Y., Vazirgiannis M. On Clustering Validation Techniques. J. Intell. Inf. Syst. 17 (2-3), pp. 107-145, 2001.
10. Kohavi R. Study of Cross-Validation and Bootstrap for Accuracy Estimation and Model Selection. *In Proc. of the 14th International Joint Conference on A.I., Vol. 2,* Canada, 1995.
11. Pallis G., Angelis L., Vakali A., Pokorny J. A Probabilistic Validation Algorithm for Web Users' Clusters. *In Proc. of the IEEE International Conference on Systems, Man and Cybernetics (SMC 2004),* Hague, Holland, 2004.

On Autonomous k-Means Clustering

Tapio Elomaa and Heidi Koivistoinen

Institute of Software Systems, Tampere University of Technology,
P.O. Box 553, FI-33101 Tampere, Finland
{tapio.elomaa, heidi.koivistoinen}@tut.fi

Abstract. Clustering is a basic tool in unsupervised machine learning and data mining. One of the simplest clustering approaches is the iterative k-means algorithm. The quality of k-means clustering suffers from being confined to run with fixed k rather than being able to dynamically alter the value of k. Moreover, it would be much more elegant if the user did not have to supply the number of clusters for the algorithm.

In this paper we consider recently proposed autonomous versions of the k-means algorithm. We demonstrate some of their shortcomings and put forward solutions for their deficiencies. In particular, we examine the problem of automatically determining a good initial candidate as the number of clusters.

1 Introduction

In unsupervised learning instances without predefined classification are obtained and the task is to learn relevant information from them. The most common approach is clustering [1, 2], where one aims at finding a natural categorization of the given instances in mutually exclusive or partially overlapping classes. A simple and widely used clustering algorithm is k-means clustering [3, 4, 5]: Given k initial (e.g., random) cluster centers $C = \{c_1, \ldots, c_k\}$ for the metric observations $X = \{x_1, \ldots, x_n\}$, iterate the following until the cluster centers do not change.

1. For each observation point $x_i \in X$ determine the center $c_j \in C$ that is closest to it and associate x_i with the corresponding cluster.
2. Recompute the center locations (as the center of the mass of points associated with them).

The basic assumption underlying k-means is that there is a metric on the set of data points. It is required, e.g., in order to be able to compute the mean values. The metric is a distance function d that obeys the following three properties:

- positiveness: $d(x, y) = 0$ if and only if $x = y$,
- symmetry: $d(x, y) = d(y, x)$, and
- triangle inequality: $d(x, z) \leq d(x, y) + d(y, z)$.

The iterative approach minimizes the squared error — the squared Euclidean distance between the cluster centers and the observations associated with them.

M.-S. Hacid et al. (Eds.): ISMIS 2005, LNAI 3488, pp. 228–236, 2005.
© Springer-Verlag Berlin Heidelberg 2005

One can view k-means clustering to be an instantiation of the generic Expectation Maximization (EM) algorithm [6] with assumptions on spherical Gaussian clusters, instance space partitioning by clusters, and equal weights on the underlying mixture model [7].

The obvious shortcomings of the basic k-means clustering are that the number of clusters needs to determined in advance and the computational cost with respect to the number of observations, clusters, and iterations. Though, k-means is efficient in the sense that only the distance between a point and the k cluster centers — not all other points — needs to be (re)computed in each iteration. Typically the number of observations n is much larger than k.

Recently there have been many approaches trying to alleviate both of these problems. Variations of k-means clustering that are supposed to cope without prior knowledge of the number of cluster centers have been presented [8, 9]. Several proposals for scaling up clustering and, in particular, k-means for massive data sets have been proposed [10, 11, 12, 13]. Quite often these studies assume that a particular distance measure is applied. Moore [13] and Elkan [14] have shown how the triangle inequality can be used for any distance function to reduce the number of distance calculations required during the execution of k-means by carrying information over from iteration to iteration.

In this paper we review autonomously working variations of k-means clustering. I.e., k-means algorithms which, equipped with a statistical or other criterion, try to determine whether the current k-clustering of the given data is a good one, or could a better one be obtained by altering the number of clusters k. Obviously, the need to consider different values of k puts autonomous algorithms in danger of being far too inefficient. Our experiments demonstrate that they, in fact, do not scale up well in time consumption. The G-means algorithm [9] does not determine how to choose the initial value of k. In the X-means algorithm [8] the user is required to provide an upper and lower bound for the value of k. We try to avoid losing autonomous behavior by using efficient geometric schedule [15] to determine a lower bound for k.

The remainder of this paper is organized as follows. In Section 2 we review recent improvements on some aspects of k-means clustering. In particular, we concentrate on automatic detection of the suitable number of clusters and accelerating the execution of the k-means algorithm. In Section 3 we briefly study Hamerly and Elkan's [9] G-means algorithm. Approximating the number of clusters prior to running the autonomous algorithm is the topic of Section 4. In Section 5 we present and empirical evaluation of the proposed approach. Finally, Section 6 presents the concluding remarks of this study.

2   Improving k-Means Clustering

The k-means algorithm is known to converge to a local minimum of the average squared distance from the points to their cluster centers. Unfortunately, the basic iterative algorithm is also known to be notoriously slow for databases of practical interest. Obviously, initializing the cluster centers in an informative way — rather than randomly — may lead to faster convergence and better clustering quality [7, 16]. An approach that is often used to improve the quality of k-means clustering is to run the algorithm with many different initializations [5].

2.1   Determining the (Right) Value of k

Not only the center locations but also their number has a significant impact on the final result of k-means clustering. Obviously, zero-error clustering can be obtained by making each different data point its own cluster, but such grouping of the data is of no value. In practice, the parameter k is most often chosen by the user based on her assumptions, experience, and prior knowledge. Choosing a too large value for k further slows down the algorithm and unnecessarily splits the natural clusters that exist in the data. A too small value for k, on the other hand, requires that some of the existing natural clusters be represented by a single cluster center.

Ideally the value of k should automatically adapt to the input data. There are two possible directions to proceed: One can either increase the number of clusters as required or start with a sufficiently large number of cluster centers and reduce their number whenever possible. For example the minimum description length (MDL) method of Bischof, Leonardis, and Selb [17] follows the latter approach.

The X-means algorithm of Pelleg and Moore [8], on the other hand, works by creating new clusters by splitting an existing one in two whenever a better fit to the data is obtained. The splitting decision in X-means is based on the *Bayesian information criterion* (BIC). Moreover, X-means also caches information that remains unchanged over iterations. The empirical experiments of Pelleg and Moore [8] demonstrate X-means to be more efficient than the original k-means and to produce better clusterings. However, the statistical power of BIC has been questioned [9]. It is claimed that BIC tends to overfit by choosing too many cluster centers when the data is not strictly spherical.

The G-means algorithm of Hamerly and Elkan [9] neither requires the user to supply the number of cluster centers in advance and also works by splitting clusters in two. The decision whether to split a cluster or not is based on a statistical test (Anderson-Darling) measuring if the data currently assigned to a cluster center appear to be Gaussian. If the data do not appear to be Gaussian, it is divided in two in an attempt to improve the overall Gaussian fit. According to experiments [9] G-means often outperforms X-means, the reason being that BIC is ineffective in penalizing for the model's complexity. G-means is not free from all parameter values, since the user is required to supply a value for the significance level of the statistical test. However, the significance level of a statistical test is somewhat more intuitive than the number of clusters.

2.2   Accelerating k-Means Clustering

Pelleg and Moore [18] combined an additional data structure, kd-tree, to k-means clustering. The kd-tree represents a hyper-rectangular partitioning of the instance space. By this additional data structure one can update centers in bulk rather than point by point. By geometric reasoning Pelleg and Moore are able to show how points contained in hyper-rectangles of the kd-tree can be updated all at once. The same technique underlies the acceleration method of X-means algorithm, *blacklisting* [8].

Moore [13] continued this line of research further by defining another data structure, *anchors hierarchy*. Similarly as in using kd-trees, the intent is to take advantage of a data structure that, by using cached sufficient statistics, summarizes statistical information from a large data set. The anchors hierarchy only respects triangle inequality, which is the only (non-trivial) requirement that can be posed to a distance metric.

Also Elkan [14] proposed to accelerate k-means through the use of triangle inequality. His algorithm keeps track of the distances between cluster centers. By combining these distances with known distances between a data point and its cluster center, the point's distance from some other cluster centers can be ignored because they are known to be further away from the point in question. Thus, the number of distance calculations in k-means can be reduced radically.

His observation is that cluster centers that are further away from the current cluster center c of an instance x than twice the distance between x and c cannot become the center "owning" x. Therefore, there is no need to explicitly calculate the distance between x and such a center. This observation also holds for those centers for which an upper bound of the distance from c rather than the exact distance is known.

As a decision problem minimum error clustering is a computationally hard problem. Therefore, it is natural to try to approximate the solution. Many different approaches, often based on subsampling, which achieve excellent efficiency with guaranteed performance for this problem have been developed [19, 20].

3   *G*-Means Algorithm

Let us review closer Hamerly and Elkan's [9] G-means algorithm. It starts by using k-means clustering to associate the given observations to the given initial clusters. The number of initial clusters may of course be one or the algorithm can be initialized otherwise. The clusters are then checked using a statistical test to detect whether all their associated data follows Gaussian distribution. If not, the cluster is partitioned further in an attempt to find Gaussian sub-clusters. G-means$(X, \alpha, \{ c_1, \ldots, c_k \})$

1. $C \leftarrow k\text{-means}(X, \{ c_1, \ldots, c_k \})$;
   % Let $X_c \subseteq X$ denote the data assigned to $c \in C$
2. **while** $\exists c \in C$ such that X_c does not follow Gaussian distribution according to a statistical test (at confidence level α) **do**
   (a) Determine two new cluster centers c_a and c_b;
   (b) $C \leftarrow C \setminus \{ c \} \cup \{ c_a, c_b \}$;
   (c) $G\text{-means}(X_c, \alpha, \{ c_a, c_b \})$;
3. $k\text{-means}(X, C)$;

The potential new cluster centers that may replace center c are $c \pm m$, where m is as follows. Determine the main principal component s of the data. Let its

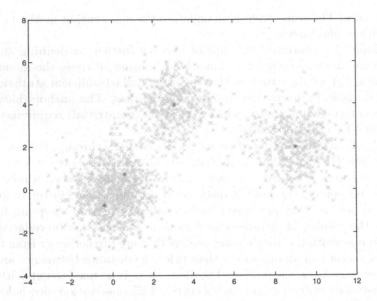

Fig. 1. Clusters of 1000, 500, and 500 instances. G-means divides the densest cluster needlessly in two

eigenvalue be λ. Then $m = s\sqrt{2\lambda/\pi}$. The idea is to place the new cluster centers to their expected locations under the assumption that the associated data does not come from a single Gaussian distribution.

Observe that once k-means has stabilized the cluster centers (Step 1), any instance $x \in X_c$ that is associated with a cluster c, that subsequently is subject to a division, is improbable to be associated with any other cluster than one of the newly created clusters, c_a and c_b. Thus, there is no need to (re)calculate the distances between instances and cluster centers other than the new ones. Therefore, one can implement the rest of the algorithm by recursive partitioning of the identified clusters. This makes G-means a relatively efficient algorithm. Moreover, the implementation of the algorithm orders the data so as to avoid needless recalculations. However, at the end one must rerun k-means to ensure that all data points are associated with correct cluster centers.

By Hamerly and Elkan's [9] experiments X-means and G-means are equally good at finding the correct k and maximizing the BIC statistic on spherically distributed data. For non-spherical data, on the other hand, G-means is substantially better at finding the correct ks. Fig. 1, demonstrates a situation where G-means, nevertheless, overestimates the number of clusters in a very clear-cut three-cluster spherical data. The cluster on the left contains twice as many instances as those on the right.

Another problem still affecting G-means is its inefficiency for data that actually contains many clusters. The growth rate appears to be exponential. For example, we ran G-means with data that had 500 true clusters. The algorithm was able to come up with a clustering having 502 clusters, which is a very good result considering the large number of clusters. The time required to produce this result was on average somewhat above 8 minutes on a PC, while data with 600 clusters already requires over 1 hour and 20 minutes to come up with a result of 607 clusters.

4 Prior Approximation of the Number of Clusters

A straightforward way to improve G-means is to start the algorithm from a more realistic lower bound of the number of required clusters than 1. However, we do not want to destroy the autonomous behavior of the algorithm by requiring the user to supply the lower bound. Instead, we aim at developing an efficient automatic analysis of the input data to provide such a bound for G-means.

There are several ways to choose the locations of the k initial cluster centers. Methods proposed in the literature include [7]: choose random locations, run k clustering problems, take the mean of the whole data and randomly perturb it k times, take the k densest bins along any of the coordinates. Moreover, one can iterate the algorithm with different initial selections [5] — at least for relatively small data sets.

Determining a suitable value for k is a model selection problem, which is being tackled by X-means and G-means during model construction. However, as our preceding example demonstrates, even these algorithms would benefit from a better initial value for the number of eventual clusters. The squared error of k-means clustering monotonically decreases with increasing number of clusters. Therefore, it cannot be used as the basis of model selection.

None of the simple cluster localization methods mentioned above lend themselves as a useful method of initializing k. The approach of Bradley and Fayyad [7,16] works by repetitively subsampling the data, clustering each subsample to k means and, finally, clustering over the cluster centers obtained in different repetitions. Thus, this initialization smooths the approximations obtained from different repetitions.

What X-means does exactly is the following. Assuming a user supplied lower and upper bound for the number of clusters, it finds all locally optimal k-means clusterings within this range, evaluates them using the BIC criterion, and at the end returns the clustering that evaluates the best.

We combine the clustering of subsamples idea of Bradley and Fayyad [7] with the BIC scoring of k-means clusterings idea of Pelleg and Moore [8]. However, as we need to have a conservative sampling strategy that never over-estimates and BIC is known to be weak to penalize against the growth of the number of clusters, we rather employ the Anderson-Darling test used in G-means anyway. In summary, our initialization approach is the following.

1. Draw a subsample S of m instances of the data.
2. Using progressive sampling with a geometric schedule [15] for values $k = 2^1, 2^2, 2^3, \ldots$ execute k-means(S, k); evaluate the resulting clustering using the statistical criterion.

Table 1. Average results over 15 repetitions of the empirical evaluation

		G-MEANS			G-MEANS2	
INSTANCES	CLUSTERS	TIME	CLUSTERS	INIT. k	TIME	CLUSTERS
50	100	4.9 ±0.8	96.0 ±2.0	17.1 ±1.1	4.6 ±0.4	98.4 ±0.4
	200	21.4 ±18.9	191.7 ±4.7	34.1 ±2.1	17.2 ±3.3	197.7 ±0.3
	300	37.3 ±4.6	288.7 ±2.3	59.7 ±4.3	40.3 ±6.2	295.3 ±3.7
	400	73.1 ±8.5	381.9 ±0.9	68.3 ±4.3	72.7 ±7.5	393.5 ±6.5
	500	118.9 ±7.3	488.1 ±5.9	102.4 ±25.6	120.0 ±10.6	491.7 ±0.3
	600	181.6 ±56.0	591.1 ±8.1	128.0 ±0.0	173.7 ±49.4	591.5 ±0.5
	700	251.0 ±18.9	683.7 ±4.3	128.0 ±0.0	227.2 ±38.0	687.9 ±2.1
100	100	8.3 ±1.1	97.1 ±0.9	34.1 ±2.1	7.4 ±0.1	99.1 ±0.1
	200	34.8 ±5.0	197.5 ±2.5	68.3 ±1.5	35.1 ±24.5	198.5 ±0.5
	300	84.8 ±12.3	302.2 ±0.8	128.0 ±0.0	87.3 ±14.8	297.1 ±0.1
	400	155.9 ±1.2	398.2 ±2.8	128.0 ±0.0	157.0 ±21.0	396.9 ±1.1
	500	247.0 ±30.0	518.1 ±0.9	256.0 ±0.0	241.1 ±12.6	495.1 ±1.1
	600	417.3 ±17.4	607.1 ±7.1	256.0 ±0.0	420.9 ±8.8	593.7 ±3.7
	700	570.6 ±208.9	703.2 ±4.8	256.0 ±0.0	557.9 ±140.78	695.2 ±5.8

3. Stop geometric sampling when the criterion does not improve anymore or $k = \lfloor \log m \rfloor$.

4. Choose the k and the associated clustering that obtained the best score.

Altogether there are at most $\log m$ calls for k-means, but all with a small sample of the data. As long as $m \ll n$, one can expect that the time spent in searching for the lower bound of k is easily regained in time savings during the execution of G-means.

5   Empirical Evaluation

We now compare G-means algorithm without prior approximation of the number of clusters with the approach outlined above (G-means2). Of course, our approach cannot be competitive when there are only few true clusters in the data. Therefore, our evaluation will be carried out using generated data that contains quite many clusters. The data was generated randomly: the desired number of random (but clearly separable) cluster centers of 50 or 100 instances each were first drawn. The required number of instances were drawn equiprobably around the centers. The range of the number of clusters ranges from 100 to 700. In our experiments the number of repetitions is 15.

Table 1 summarizes the results of our experiments with the significance parameter α value 0.5 in choosing the initial cluster center candidates. The table gives for each experiment the number of instances per cluster, the number of true clusters, the average time (in seconds) and the average number of found clusters for G-means, the average initial k value chosen by the geometric sampling schedule, and the average time and number of clusters for G-means2.

As a general trend of these experiments we can observe that G-means2 is on the average slightly more efficient (counting in the random sampling phase) than the original algorithm. The advantage with these numbers of clusters, though, is not as large as we would have expected in advance. Moreover, it also approximates the true number of clusters on the average more faithfully than G-means.

G-means2 does not obtain a larger edge on time consumption probably due to the fact that the cluster centers chosen by subsampling can be way off of true cluster center locations. Therefore, the algorithm may have to loop through a large number of clusters that need to be divided, while in the original k-means one can always determine some of the eventually formed clusters not to need further attention. Also, the geometric sampling strategy may sometimes lead to grave under-estimates of the number of required clusters. In these cases the modified algorithm usually ends up spending more time than the original one.

The fact that G-means2 on the average comes up with a more correct number of clusters than the original algorithm is an added bonus that we did not expect in advance. On the other hand, it is not surprising that if the recursive algorithm is allowed to start from a better lower bound for the required number of clusters than 1, it will end up with better end result. Both algorithms, though, are on the average off by only one or two per cents.

6   Conclusion and Further Work

We have proposed to use subsampling for determining a starting value for the search of the number of clusters, not only the locations of the initial cluster centers. In this process we employ the geometric sampling schedule and a statistical test to decide when to stop growing the initial value. Our empirical experiments demonstrate this to be a promising approach: it leads on the average to better results than executing G-means starting from one initial cluster.

We intend to study more refined, but still efficient, methods of choosing the number and locations of the cluster centers. If the chosen initial value of k now is 2^i, then there is still room to look for a higher value within the range $2^i \ldots 2^{i+1}$. Moreover, at the moment we do not know comprehensively the significance of the α parameter in determining the initial cluster centers. It is also possible to consider other ways of determining the initial value of k than using the Anderson-Darling test. Model selection is a widely studied topic in machine learning, and one of the approaches arising in there could be employed to this task as well.

Of course, it is also our plan to carry out a wider experimental study of the algorithm. So far only similarly generated random data was included in the tests. We intend to test the algorithm also with real-world data sets.

Acknowledgements

We thank Greg Hamerly for giving his Matlab-code of G-means at our disposal.

References

1. Fisher, D.: Knowledge acquisition via incremental conceptual clustering. Machine Learning **2** (1987) 139–172
2. Jain, A.K., Murty, M.N., Flynn, P.J.: Data clustering: a review. ACM Computing Surveys **31** (1999) 264–323
3. MacQueen, J.B.: On convergence of k-means and partitions with minimum average variance (abstract). Annals of Mathematical Statistics **36** (1965) 1084
4. Forgy, E.: Cluster analysis of multivariate data: Efficiency vs. interpretability of classifications. Biometrics **21** (1965) 768
5. Duda, R.O., Hart, P.E.: Pattern Classification and Scene Analysis. John Wiley & Sons (1973)
6. Dempster, A.P., Laird, N.M., Rubin, D.B.: Maximum likelihood from incomplete data via the EM algorithm. J. Royal Statistical Society, Series B **39** (1977) 1–38
7. Bradley, P.S., Fayyad, U.M.: Refining initial points for k-means clustering. In: Proc. 15th Intl. Conf. on Machine Learning, Morgan Kaufmann (1998) 91–99
8. Pelleg, D., Moore, A.: X-means: Extending k-means with efficient estimation of the number of clusters. In: Proc. 17th Intl. Conf. on Machine Learning, Morgan Kaufmann (2000) 727–734
9. Hamerly, G., Elkan, C.: Learning the k in k-means. In: Advances in Neural Information Processing Systems 16. MIT Press (2004)
10. Ng, R.T., Han, J.: Efficient and effective clustering methods for spatial data mining. In: Proc. 20th Intl. Conf. on Very Large Data Bases, Morgan Kaufmann (1994) 144–155
11. Zhang, T., Ramakrishnan, R., Livny, M.: Birch: An efficient data clustering method for very large databases. In: Proc. ACM SIGMOD Intl. Conf. on Management of Data, ACM Press (1995) 103–114
12. Guha, S., Rastogi, R., Shim, K.: Cure: An efficient clustering algorithm for large datasets. In: Proc. ACM SIGMOD Intl. Conf. on Management of Data, ACM Press (1998) 73–84
13. Moore, A.W.: The anchors hierarchy: Using the triangle inequality to survive high dimensional data. In: Proc. 16th Conf. on Uncertainty in Artificial Intelligence, Morgan Kaufmann (2000) 397–405
14. Elkan, C.: Using the triangle inequality to accelerate k-means. In: Proc. 20th Intl. Conf. on Machine Learning, AAAI Press (2003) 147–153
15. Provost, F., Jensen, D., Oates, T.: Efficient progressive sampling. In: Proc. 5th ACM SIGKDD Intl. Conf. on Knowledge Discovery and Data Mining, ACM Press (1999) 23–32
16. Fayyad, U.M., Reina, C., Bradley, P.S.: Initialization of iterative refinement clustering. In: Proc. 4th Intl. Conf. on Knowledge Discovery and Data Mining, AAAI Press (1998) 194–198
17. Bischof, H., Leonardis, A., Selb, A.: MDL-principle for robust vector quantisation. Pattern Analysis and Applications **2** (1999) 59–72
18. Pelleg, D., Moore, A.W.: Accelerating exact k-means algorithms with geometric reasoning. In: Proc. 5th Intl. Conf. on Knowledge Discovery and Data Mining, AAAI Press (1999) 277–281
19. Har-Peled, S., Mazumdar, S.: On coresets for k-means and k-median clustering. In: Proc. 36th Annual Symp. on Theory of Computing, ACM Press (2004) 291–300
20. Kumar, A., Sabharwal, Y., Sen, S.: A simple linear time $(1 + \varepsilon)$-approximation algorithm for k-means clustering in any dimensions. In: Proc. 45th Annual IEEE Symp. on Foundations on Computer Science, IEEE Press (2004) 454–462

CSI: Clustered Segment Indexing for Efficient Approximate Searching on the Secondary Structure of Protein Sequences*

Minkoo Seo, Sanghyun Park, and Jung-Im Won

Department of Computer Science, Yonsei University, Korea
{mkseo, sanghyun, jiwon}@cs.yonsei.ac.kr

Abstract. Approximate searching on the primary structure (i.e., amino acid arrangement) of protein sequences is an essential part in predicting the functions and evolutionary histories of proteins. However, because proteins distant in an evolutionary history do not conserve amino acid residue arrangements, approximate searching on proteins' secondary structure is quite important in finding out distant homology. In this paper, we propose an indexing scheme for efficient approximate searching on the secondary structure of protein sequences which can be easily implemented in RDBMS. Exploiting the concept of *clustering* and *lookahead*, the proposed indexing scheme processes three types of secondary structure queries (i.e., exact match, range match, and wildcard match) very quickly. To evaluate the performance of the proposed method, we conducted extensive experiments using a set of actual protein sequences. According to the experimental results, the proposed method was proved to be faster than the existing indexing methods up to 6.3 times in exact match, 3.3 times in range match, and 1.5 times in wildcard match, respectively.

Keywords: Indexing method, Secondary structure of proteins, Approximate searching.

1 Introduction

It is well known to biologists that the amino acid arrangements of proteins determine their structures and functions. Therefore, it is possible to predict the functions, roles, structures, and categories of newly discovered proteins by searching for the proteins whose amino acid arrangements are similar to those of newly discovered proteins [1, 18].

However, the amino acid arrangement of one protein is rarely preserved in another protein if the two proteins are distant in an evolutionary history [5, 15]. Therefore, approximate searching on protein structures, rather than on amino

* This work was supported by the Korea Research Foundation Grant. (KRF-2004-003-D00302)

M.-S. Hacid et al. (Eds.): ISMIS 2005, LNAI 3488, pp. 237–247, 2005.
© Springer-Verlag Berlin Heidelberg 2005

acid arrangements, is more important in finding out distant homology. Among structure searching algorithms, comparing structural arrangements based on the secondary structure elements is gaining more popularity in conjunction with database approaches [5, 14].

The secondary structures are expressed using the three characters: E (beta sheets), H (alpha helices), and L (turns or loops). These characters tend to occur contiguously rather than interspersedly [3, 11]. For example, '$HHLLLLLEEE$' is more likely to occur than '$HLLELLEELH$'.

Exploiting this property, Hammel et al. [11] proposed a segment-based indexing method. The method combines consecutive characters of a same type into a single segment and then builds a B$^+$-tree on two attributes of segments: (1) Type which denotes the type of consecutive characters, and (2) Len which denotes the number of consecutive characters. For example, '$HHLLLLLEEE$' is segmented into '$HH/LLLLL/EEE$' and expressed as $(H, 2)(L, 5)(E, 3)$.

Although the segmentation enables an efficient searching on the secondary structures, it has innate limitations. First, the pair of (Type, Len) does not have uniform distribution. According to our preliminary experimentation with 80,000 proteins, 87% of E segments have a length between 3 and 6, 62% of H segments have a length between 5 and 14, and 41% of L segments are of length between 3 and 6. Therefore, if every segment in a query is close to one of these *hot spots*, each index search will produce lots of intermediate results and thus the overall search performance may be worse than the full table scan. Secondly but more importantly, the number of distinct (Type, Len) pairs is not large enough to provide good selectivity. Our investigation on 80,000 proteins indicates that the total number of distinct (Type, Len) pairs is about 300 but the total number of segments to be indexed is more than 3 millions. Therefore, the average number of segments with the same (Type, Len) pair is more than 10,000.

In this paper, we propose CSI (Clustered Segment Indexing), an efficient indexing scheme for approximate searching on the secondary structure of protein sequences. The proposed indexing scheme exploits the concept of *clustering* and *lookahead* to overcome the aforementioned limitations. A pre-determined number of neighboring segments are grouped into a cluster which is then represented by three attributes: (1) CluStr which denotes the type string of the cluster obtained by concatenating the Type attributes of the underlying segments, (2) CluLen which denotes the length of the cluster obtained by summing up the Len attributes of the underlying segments, and (3) CluLA which denotes the lookahead of the cluster obtained by concatenating the Type attributes of the segments *following* the cluster. It is obvious that the triple (CluStr, CluLen, CluLA) for clusters is more discriminative than the pair (Type, Len) for segments. Therefore, by using a cluster as an indexing and query processing unit, it becomes possible to reduce both the number of intermediate results and the overall query processing time.

2   Related Work

BLAST [2] is the most widely used tool for approximate searching on DNA and protein sequences. BLAST is based on the sequential scan method basically, but it makes use of heuristic algorithms to reduce the number of sequences to be aligned against a query. However, BLAST still has two main drawbacks [18]: (1) entire data set should be loaded into a main memory for fast searching, and (2) since it is based on sequential access, its execution time is directly proportional to the number of sequences in the database. Due to these drawbacks, index-based approaches for approximate searching are demanding.

Suffix trees [16] have been recognized as the best index structure for string or sequence searching, but they have been notorious for large space requirement. Recently, algorithms for building a suffix tree from a data set larger than a main memory were proposed [13]. However, the internal structure of suffix trees is not suitable for pagination and therefore it is not easy to incorporate suffix trees into database systems [16, 17].

RAMdb [7] is an indexing system for the primary structures of protein sequences and was proved, by experiments, to be faster than heuristic approaches up to 800 times. However its search performance deteriorates when the length of a query is not close to that of the interval used for indexing. In addition, RAMdb is an indexing system mainly for the primary structures of protein sequences and therefore it is not easy to apply the proposed idea directly to the secondary structures of protein sequences.

Hammel et al. [11] proposed the segment-based indexing method. The method combines the consecutive characters of the same type into a single segment, and then builds a B^+-tree index on the number and type of consecutive characters. As mentioned in the previous section, however, this segment-based approach does not support good selectivity, thus resulting in an innate limitation of search performance.

VAST [10] and DALI [12] support three dimensional structure-based similarity search algorithms. VAST is motivated by the fact that the number of secondary structure elements (SSEs) is much smaller than the number of C_α and C_β atoms [15]. Hence, VAST performs substructure alignments in three steps: (1) rapid identification of SSE pair alignments, (2) clustering identified SSEs into groups, and (3) scoring the best substructure alignment. DALI, on the other hand, compares C_α atoms using distance matrices. For each protein, a distance matrix which resembles a dot matrix is populated. Each dot in the matrix represents the distance between C_α atoms along the polypeptide chain and between C_α atoms within the protein structure [15]. Therefore, by comparing matrices, DALI can find the proteins whose three dimensional structures are similar to that of a given query. CSI is different from VAST and DALI in that it searches for similar proteins by comparing types and lengths, rather than three dimensional coordinates, of their secondary structure elements.

3   Clustered Segment Table

A segment in a protein is defined as consecutive characters of the same secondary structure type, and can be expressed by its Type and Len attributes. A segment itself has a limitation in selectivity. Therefore, we group a pre-determined number of neighboring segments into a cluster and express it using more discriminative attributes. The procedure to construct clustered segment tables is as follows:

1. Convert each protein sequence S into a series of segments. Let N_S be the number of segments obtained from S.
2. For each k from 0 to $min(\lfloor log_2(N_s) \rfloor, MaxK)$, do the following:
   (a) Using the sliding window of size 2^k, generate a set of clusters, each of which is composed of 2^k neighboring segments.
   (b) Store each cluster into the clustered segment table named CST_k.

In the above procedure, $MaxK$ is a system parameter used to control the total number of clustered segment tables being constructed. Let $(T_1, L_1)(T_2, L_2)...$ (T_{2^k}, L_{2^k}) be 2^k neighboring segments where T_i is Type and L_i is Len of the ith segment. Then the cluster is represented concisely as (CluStr $= T_1 \cdot T_2 \cdot ... \cdot T_{2^k}$, CluLen $= L_1 + L_2 + ... + L_{2^k}$).

There may be a series of segments following a cluster. The Type attributes of such segments can be concatenated, producing the lookahead, CluLA, of the cluster. The maximum length of CluLA is controlled by a system parameter $MaxCluLA$ for space efficiency. The overall schema for each clustered segment table is shown in Table 1. For example, as shown in Table 2, two clustered

Table 1. Schema of each clustered segment table

Field Name	Description
ID	The identifier of the protein from which a cluster is made.
Loc	The beginning position of the cluster.
CluStr	The type string of the cluster obtained by concatenating the Type attributes of the underlying segments.
CluLen	The length of the cluster obtained by summing up the Len attributes of the underlying segments.
CluLA	The type string obtained by concatenating the Type attributes of the segments following the cluster.

Table 2. Clustered segment tables, CST_0 and CST_1, from $S_1 =$ '$EEEHHLLEEE$'

\(CST_0\)					\(CST_1\)				
ID	Loc	CluStr	CluLen	CluLA	ID	Loc	CluStr	CluLen	CluLA
S_1	0	E	3	HL	S_1	0	EH	5	LE
S_1	3	H	2	LE	S_1	3	HL	4	E
S_1	5	L	2	E	S_1	5	LE	5	
S_1	7	E	3						

segment tables, CST_0 and CST_1, are constructed from $S_1 = \text{'}EEEHHLLEEE\text{'}$ when $MaxK = 1$ and $MaxCluLA = 2$.

After populating all the tuples of CST_k, the tuples are sorted according to CluStr, CluLen, and CluLA for the sake of locality. As the final step, we build a B^+-tree on CluStr and CluLen attributes for each CST_k. It is also worth mentioning that the duplication of information in CST_k will bring about more storage consumption than the segment table. Hence, we store each character using 2 bits like: $L = 00_2$, $H = 10_2$, and $E = 11_2$.

4 Query Processing

4.1 Overall Query Processing Algorithm

Suppose that $MaxK + 1$ tables, CST_0, CST_1, ..., and CST_{MaxK}, were created along with their associated B^+-tree indices. The overall query processing algorithm which uses these tables and associated indices to process a query is as follows:

1. Convert a query Q into a series of segments. Let N_Q denote the number of segments obtained from Q.
2. Determine the target table CST_k by computing the expression $k = min(\lfloor log_2 (N_Q) \rfloor, MaxK)$.
3. Decompose the segmented query into n $(=\lceil N_Q/2^k \rceil)$ non-overlapping subqueries, each of which has 2^k segments in it. The last two subqueries may overlap each other when N_Q is not a multiple of 2^k.
4. For each subquery q_i $(i=1,2,\ldots,n)$, do the following:
   (a) Compute its CluStr, CluLen, and CluLA values. Let qCluStr, qCluLen, and qCluLA denote these three values, respectively.
   (b) Search the table CST_k for the tuples whose CluStr, CluLen, and CluLA match with qCluStr, qCluLen, and qCluLA, respectively. The B^+-tree index for CST_k is used at this step.
5. Perform the sort-merge on n sets of intermediate results using their ID and Loc as joining attributes.
6. Perform the post-processing to detect and discard false matches.

4.2 Exact Match Query

Exact match queries are expressed as $Q = < T_1(L_1)\ T_2(L_2)\ \ldots\ T_{N_Q}(L_{N_Q}) >$ where T_i $(\in \{E, H, L\})$ and L_i represent the type and length of the ith segment of Q, respectively. Suppose that we already chose the target table CST_k and decomposed the query into n subqueries, each of which consists of 2^k segments. The algorithm for processing exact match queries is shown in Algorithm 1.

The result of subquery q_i is stored in N_i. If the number of tuples in N_i is less than a predefined threshold ϵ, then we believe that irrelevant answers have been filtered out sufficiently. Therefore, if this happens, we directly go to the merging step (Line 5) without considering the remaining subqueries.

Algorithm 1: ProcessExactMatchQuery

    Input   : Query Q, Clustered segment table CST_k, Threshold ϵ
    Output: Set of answers

1 **for** *(each subquery q_i from Q)* **do**

2 | Let $qCluStr$, $qCluLen$, and $qCluLA$ be $CluStr$, $CluLen$ and $CluLA$ of q_i, respectively;

3 | N_i := ExecuteQuery("select * from CST_k where CluStr = qCluStr
                             and CluLen = qCluLen and CluLA = qCluLA");

4 | **if** *(count(N_i) < ϵ)* **then**
        | ⌊ break;

5 Merge all N_i into N using ID and Loc as joining attributes;
6 answers := PostProcessing(N);
7 return answers;

4.3   Range Match Query

Range match queries are expressed as $Q =< T_1(Lb_1\ Ub_1)\ T_2(Lb_2\ Ub_2)\ \ldots\ T_{N_Q}(Lb_{N_Q}\ Ub_{N_Q}) >$ where Lb_i and Ub_i represent the minimum and maximum length of the ith segment of Q, respectively. In a range match query, the search condition of CluLen for each subquery q_i has the form of 'CluLen between qLb and qUb' where qLb is the sum of the minimum lengths and qUb is the sum of the maximum lengths of the underlying segments of q_i. Therefore, when the difference of qLb and qUb is large, the cost for processing q_i becomes high due to an enlarged search space for CluLen.

To overcome the problem of an enlarged search space of a subquery q_i, we propose the *selective clustering method* (SCM) where q_i is decomposed into a set of *secondary* subqueries and then a secondary subquery with the smallest *estimated* search space is chosen and executed in replacement of q_i. In detail, when a subquery q_i has 2^k segments, its secondary subqueries are generated from $2^{k'}$ underlying segments of q_i for each k' in $[0, k]$.

For example, let us consider the subquery $q_1 = (qCluStr = EH, qCluLen = [3 + 3, 5 + 6], qCluLA = L)$ from the query $Q = < E(3\ 5)H(3\ 6)L(3\ 7) >$. Let $q_{i,j}$ denote the jth secondary subquery of the subquery q_i. Then, in SCM, three secondary subqueries are generated from q_1. When $k' = 0$, we obtain two secondary subqueries, $q_{1,1} = (qCluStr = E, qCluLen = [3, 5], qCluLA = HL)$ and $q_{1,2} = (qCluStr = H, qCluLen = [3, 6], qCluLA = L)$, each of which has 2^0 segment in it. Similarly, when $k' = 1$, we obtain one secondary subquery, $q_{1,3} = (qCluStr = EH, qCluLen = [6, 11], qCluLA = L)$, which has 2^1 segments in it. Among these secondary subqueries, we choose the most selective one by estimating the number of tuples to be retrieved by each secondary subquery, and execute it in replacement of q_1.

Algorithm 2: Estimate_SizeOf_ResultSet

Input : Secondary subquery $q_{i,j}$

Output: Predicted number of tuples in the result set

1 Let $qCluStr$ be $CluStr$ of $q_{i,j}$;

2 Let [qLb, qUb] of $q_{i,j}$ be the range of $qCluLen$;

3 Suppose that $q_{i,j}$ is composed of 2^{qK} segments;

4 N_1 := ExecuteQuery("select sum(#Clusters) from CluStrHistogram where hK=qK");

5 N_2 := ExecuteQuery("select #Clusters from CluStrHistogram where hK=qK and hCluStr=qCluStr");

6 N_3 := ExecuteQuery("select #Clusters from CluLenHistogram where hK=qK and hCluLen between qLb and qUb");

7 return $N_3 \times N_2/N_1$;

In the estimation of selectivities, we use two histograms, one for CluLen and the other for CluStr. The algorithm for estimating the number of tuples to be retrieved by each secondary subquery is presented in Algorithm 2.

4.4 Wildcard Match Query

Wildcard match queries are specified as $Q = < T_1(Lb_1 \ Ub_1) \ T_2(Lb_2 \ Ub_2) \ldots$
$T_{N_Q}(Lb_{N_Q} \ Ub_{N_Q}) >$ where T_i takes a value from $\{E, H, L, ?\}$. The meanings of Lb_i and Ub_i are same as before. Note that T_i may take '?' to express that the ith segment can be of any secondary structure type. To accommodate this wildcard type, we just use 'CluStr like qCluStr' predicate in Algorithm 1 (Line 3) instead of 'CluStr=qCluStr' predicate.

We also apply SCM to this type of query because it has the problem of an enlarged search space for both CluStr and CluLen. Since qCluStr may contain '?', we use 'hCluStr like qCluStr' predicate in Algorithm 2 (Line 5) instead of 'hCluStr=qCluStr'.

Table 3. Schemas of CluLen and CluStr histograms

CluLen Histogram		CluStr Histogram	
Field Name	Description	Field Name	Description
hK	k value of a cluster	hK	k value of a cluster
hCluLen	CluLen value of the cluster	hCluStr	CluStr value of the cluster
#Clusters	Number of clusters whose k value is the same as hK and CluLen value is the same as hCluLen	#Clusters	Number of clusters whose k value is the same as hK and CluStr value is the same as hCluStr

5   Performance Evaluation

In obtaining the secondary structures of proteins, we applied PREDATOR [8, 9] to the amino acid arrangements of proteins downloaded from PIR [19]. To verify the effectiveness of the proposed method CSI, we compared its performance with those of the three segmentation-based methods, MISS(1), MISS(2), and SSS. MISS(n) chooses the most selective n segments from a query and treats each of them as a subquery. It then executes each subquery using a B^+-tree on the segment table. SSS chooses the most selective segment from a query and executes it by performing a full table scan on the segment table.

5.1   Parameter Setting

To determine the values of two system parameters, $MaxK$ and $MaxCluLA$, we first performed the preliminary experiments with a data set of 80,000 protein sequences.

MaxK. The *selectivity*, a ratio of the number of tuples retrieved by a search to the total number of tuples stored in a table, was used as a measure for determining the optimal value of $MaxK$. Figure 1 shows the selectivity of a pair (CluStr, CluLen) for each clustered segment table CST_k. It is clear from the figure that the selectivity becomes better as k increases but it is saturated after k exceeds 3. Therefore, we set 3 as the optimal value of $MaxK$.

MaxCluLA. The selectivity becomes better as the value of $MaxCluLA$ increases. To measure the degree of improvement in selectivity (DIS), we use the following formula:

$$DIS = \frac{selectivity\ of\ (CluStr, CluLen)\ -\ selectivity\ of\ (CluStr, CluLen, CluLA)}{selectivity\ of\ (CluStr, CluLen)}$$

Figure 2 shows the degree of improvement in selectivity for each value of $MaxCluLA$. According to the result, the degree of improvement grows as the value of $MaxCluLA$ increases but the growth is almost saturated after the value of $MaxCluLA$ exceeds 8. Therefore, we set 8 as the optimal value of $MaxCluLA$.

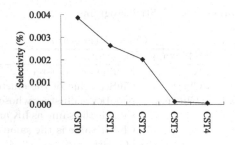

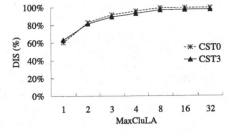

Fig. 1. Selectivity of (CluStr, CluLen) for each clustered segment table CST_k

Fig. 2. Degree of improvement in selectivity (DIS) for each value of $MaxCluLA$

5.2   Query Processing Time

Query Processing Time with Various Numbers of Segments in a Query.
While changing the number of segments, N_Q, in a query, we measured the query
processing times of four methods, CSI, MISS(1), MISS(2), and SSS. For this
experiment, we used a data set of 80,000 protein sequences from which queries
were randomly extracted.

For the simplicity of experimentations, we let only the segment in the middle
of range match and wildcard match queries have a range in its length specification. Considering the distribution of segment lengths, we set the size of the

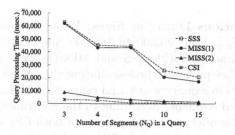

Fig. 3. Exact match query processing
times with increasing N_Q

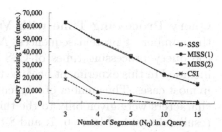

Fig. 4. Range match query processing times with increasing N_Q

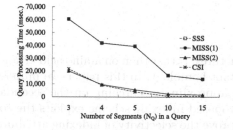

Fig. 5. Wildcard match query processing
times with increasing N_Q

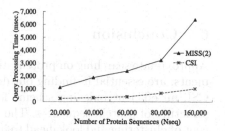

Fig. 6. Exact match query processing
times with increasing N_{seq}

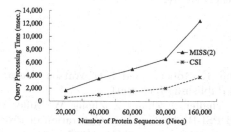

Fig. 7. Range match query processing
times with increasing N_{seq}

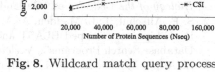

Fig. 8. Wildcard match query processing
times with increasing N_{seq}

range as 30. In case of wildcard match queries, only the segment in the middle had the wildcard character '?'. Figure 3, 4, and 5 shows the query processing times of four methods for exact match, range match, and wildcard match queries, respectively.

According to the experimental results, query processing times of all methods decrease as N_Q increase. This is because more segments with high selectivity are contained in queries as N_Q increases. If N_Q is large, CSI gets extra benefit by choosing a larger k value when deciding a clustered segment table to be searched. As a result, CSI was 1.7~13.0 times, 1.3~6.0 times, and 1.0~3.4 times faster than the best one of the other methods in exact match, range match, and wildcard match, respectively.

Query Processing Time with Various Data Set Sizes. While increasing the number of protein sequences, N_{seq}, from 20,000 to 160,000, we measured the query processing times of CSS and MISS(2). SSS and MISS(1) were not included in this experiment because they proved to be less efficient than MISS(2) in most cases. The number of segments in a query was 5, and ranges and wildcard characters were given only to the third segment. According to the experimental results shown in Figure 6, 7, and 8 the query processing times of both CSI and MISS(2) were proportional to the data set size, and CSI was 4.3~6.3 times, 3.0~3.3 times, and 1.4~1.5 times faster than MISS(2) in exact match, range match, and wildcard match, respectively.

6   Conclusion

Approximate searching on protein structures, rather than on amino acid arrangements, are essential in finding out distant homology. In this paper, we proposed CSI, an efficient indexing scheme for approximate searching on the secondary structure of protein sequences. The proposed indexing scheme exploits the concept of clustering and lookahead to improve the selectivity of indexing attributes. Algorithms for exact match, range match, and wildcard match queries were also proposed and evaluated. The experimental results revealed that CSI is faster than MISS(2) up to 6.3 times, 3.3 times, and 1.5 times in exact match, range match, and wildcard match queries, respectively.

References

1. B. Alberts, D. Bray, J. Lweis, M. Raff, K. Roberts, and J. D. Watson, *Molecular Biology of the Cell, 3rd ed.*, Garland Publishing Inc., 1994.
2. S. F. Altschul, T. L. Madden, A. A. Schaffer, J. Zhang, Z. Zhang, W. Miller, and D. J. Lipman, "Gapped BLAST and PSI-BLAST: A New Generation of Protein Database Search Programs", *Nucleic Acids Research*, 25(17), 1997.
3. Z. Aung, W. Fu, and K.-L. Tan, "An Efficient Index-based Protein Structure Database Searching Method", *Proc. IEEE DASFAA Conf.*, 2003.

4. A. D. Baxevanis and B. F. F. Ouellette. *BIOINFORMATICS: A Practical Guide to the Analysis of Genes and Proteins, 2nd ed.* WILEY INTERSCIENCE, 2001.
5. O. Camoglu, T. Kahveci, and A. K. Singh, "Towards Index-based Similarity Search for Protein Structure Databases", *Proc. IEEE Computer Society Bioinformatics Conf.*, pp. 148-158, 2003.
6. I. Eidhammer and I. Jonassen, "Protein Structure Comparison and Structure Patterns - An Algorithmic Approach", *ISMB tutorial*, 2001.
7. C. Fondrat and P. Dessen, "A Rapid Access Motif Database(RAMdb) with a Searching Algorithm for the Retrieval Patterns in Nucleic Acids or Protein Databanks", *Computer Applications in the Bioscience*, 11(3), pp. 273-279, 1995.
8. D. Frishman and P. Argos, "Seventy-five Accuracy in Protein Secondary Structure Prediction", *Proteins*, 27(3), pp. 329-335, 1997.
9. D. Frishman and P. Argos, "Incorporation of Long-Distance Interactions into a Secondary Structure Prediction Algorithm", *Protein Engineering*, 9(2), pp. 133-142, 1996.
10. J. F. Gibrat, T. Madel, and S. H. Bryant, "Surprising Similarities in Structure Comparison", *Current Opinion in Structural Biology*, 6(3), pp. 377-385, 1996.
11. L. Hammel and J. M. Patel, "Searching on the Secondary Structure of Protein Sequence", In *Proc. VLDB Conf.*, 2002.
12. L. Holm and C. Sander, "Protein Structure Comparison by Alignment of Distance Matrices", *J. Molecular Biology*, 233(1), pp. 123-138, 1993.
13. E. Hunt, M. P. Atkinson, and R. W. Irving, "Database Indexing for Large DNA and Protein Sequence Collections", *VLDB Journal*, 11(3), pp. 256-271, 2002.
14. P. Koehl, "Protein Structure Similarities", *Current Opinion in Structural Biology*, 11(3), pp. 348-353, 2001.
15. D. W. Mount, *Bioinformatics.* Cold Spring Harbor Laboratory Press, 2000.
16. G. A. Stephen, *String Searching Algorithms*, World Scientific Publishing, 1994.
17. H. Wang, C.-S. Perng, W. Fan, S. Park, and P. S. Yu, "Indexing Weighted Sequences in Large Databases", *Proc. IEEE ICDE Conf.*, pp 63-74, 2003.
18. H. E. Williams, "Genomic Information Retrieval", *Proc. Australasian Database Conf.*, pp. 27-35, 2003.
19. C. H. Wu, L.-S. L. Yeh, H. Huang, L. Arminski, J. Castro-Alvear, Y. Chen, Z. Hu, P. Kourtesis, R. S. Ledley, B. E. Suzek, C. R. Vinayaka, J. Zhang, and W. C. Barker, "The Protein Information Resource", *Nucleic Acids Research*, 31(1), pp. 345–347, 2003.

Using Supervised Clustering to Enhance Classifiers

Christoph F. Eick and Nidal Zeidat

Department of Computer Science, University of Houston,
Houston, TX 77204-3010, USA
{ceick, nzeidat}@cs.uh.edu

Abstract. This paper centers on a novel data mining technique we term *supervised clustering*. Unlike traditional clustering, supervised clustering is applied to classified examples and has the goal of identifying class-uniform clusters that have a high probability density. This paper focuses on how data mining techniques in general, and classification techniques in particular, can benefit from knowledge obtained through supervised clustering. We discuss how better nearest neighbor classifiers can be constructed with the knowledge generated by supervised clustering, and provide experimental evidence that they are more efficient and more accurate than a traditional 1-nearest-neighbor classifier. Finally, we demonstrate how supervised clustering can be used to enhance simple classifiers.

1 Introduction

This paper centers on a novel data mining technique we term *supervised clustering*. Clustering is, typically, applied to a set of unclassified examples using particular error functions, e.g. an error function that minimizes the distances inside a cluster keeping clusters tight. *Supervised clustering*, on the other hand, deviates from traditional clustering in that it is applied on classified examples with the objective of identifying clusters that have high probability density with respect to a single class. Moreover, in supervised clustering, we also like to keep the number of clusters small, and objects are assigned to clusters using a notion of closeness with respect to a given distance function.

Fig. 1, that depicts examples belonging to two classes, illustrates the differences between traditional and supervised clustering. A traditional clustering algorithm would, very likely, identify the four clusters depicted in Figure 1.a. A supervised clustering algorithm that maximizes class purity, on the other hand (see Fig. 1.b), would split cluster **A** into two clusters **E** and **F**. Another characteristic of supervised clustering is that it tries to keep the number of clusters low. Consequently, clusters **B** and **C** would be merged into a single cluster **G** without compromising class purity while reducing the number of clusters.

Our previous work [4, 13] centered on the design and implementation of algorithms for supervised clustering and on comparative studies that evaluate different supervised clustering algorithms with respect to quality of solutions found and runtime. In this paper, we will discuss how local and regional learning techniques can benefit from background knowledge that has been generated through supervised clustering.

M.-S. Hacid et al. (Eds.): ISMIS 2005, LNAI 3488, pp. 248–256, 2005.
© Springer-Verlag Berlin Heidelberg 2005

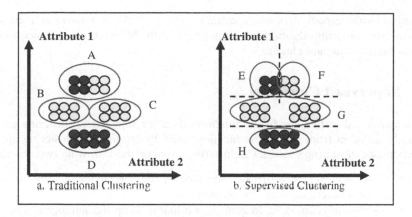

Fig. 1. Differences between traditional clustering and supervised clustering

Section 2 discusses related work. Section 3 introduces supervised clustering in more details. Section 4 presents experimental results that show the benefits of supervised clustering. Section 5 concludes the paper.

2   Related Work

There are two approaches can be viewed as supervised clustering approaches. Sinkkonen et al. propose a very general approach called *discriminative clustering* [7] that minimizes distortion within clusters. Distortion, in their context, represents the loss of mutual information between the auxiliary data (e.g., classes) and the clusters caused by representing each cluster by a prototype. The technique seeks to produce clusters that are internally as homogeneous as possible in conditional distributions $p(c|x)$ of the auxiliary variable, c (i.e., belong to a single class), with respect to a clustering x. Similarly, Tishby et. al. introduce the *information bottleneck method* [9]. Based on that method, they propose an agglomerative clustering algorithm [8] that minimizes information loss with respect to $p(c|a)$ with c being a class and a being an attribute.

However, there has been some work that has some similarity to our research under the heading of semi-supervised clustering. The idea of semi-supervised clustering is to enhance a clustering algorithm by using side information in the clustering process that usually consists of a "small set" of classified examples; the objective of the clustering process then is to optimize class purity (examples with different class labels should belong to different clusters) in addition to the traditional objectives of a clustering algorithm. Demiriz [3] proposes an evolutionary clustering algorithm in which solutions consist of k centroids and the objective of the search process is to obtain clusters that minimize (the sum of) cluster dispersion and cluster impurity. Basu et al. [1] centers on modifying the K-means clustering algorithm to cope with prior knowledge. Xing [12] (and similarly [2]) takes the classified training examples and transforms those into constraints (points that are known to belong to different classes need to have a distance larger than a given threshold) and derives a modified distance function that minimizes the distance between points in the dataset that are known to be similar with respect to these constraints using classical numerical methods. The K-means clustering algorithm in conjunction with the modified distance function is then used to compute clusters.

3 Supervised Clustering

As mentioned earlier, the fitness functions used for *supervised* clustering are significantly different from the fitness functions used by *traditional* clustering algorithms. Supervised clustering evaluates a clustering based on the following two criteria:

- *Class impurity, Impurity(X)*. Measured by the percentage of minority examples in the different clusters of a clustering X.
- *Number of clusters, k*. In general, we like to keep the number of clusters low; trivially, having clusters that only contain a single example is not desirable, although it maximizes class purity.

3.1 A Fitness Function for Supervised Clustering

In particular, we used the following fitness function in our experimental work (lower values for q(X) indicate 'better' clustering solution X).

$$q(X) = \text{Impurity}(X) + \beta * \text{Penalty}(k) \tag{1}$$

where $\text{Impurity}(X) = \dfrac{\text{\# of Minority Examples}}{n}$, and $\text{Penalty}(k) = \begin{cases} \sqrt{\dfrac{k-c}{n}} & k \geq c \\ 0 & k < c \end{cases}$

with n being the total number of examples and c being the number of classes in a dataset. The parameter β ($0 < \beta \leq 2.0$) determines the penalty that is associated with the number of clusters, k, in a clustering: higher values for β imply larger penalties for a higher number of clusters. The objective of Penalty(k) is to dampen the algorithm's natural tendency to increase the number of clusters. However, this dampening ought not to be linear because the effect of increasing the number of clusters from k to $k+1$ has much stronger effect on the clustering outcome when k is low than when k is high. Consequently, we selected a non-linear function for Penalty(k) that has higher slope when k is low. Finding the best, or even a good, clustering X with respect to the fitness function q is a challenging task for a supervised clustering algorithm [13].

3.2 Representative-Based Supervised Clustering Algorithms

There are many possible algorithms for supervised clustering. Our work centers on the development of *representative-based* supervised clustering algorithms. Representative-based clustering aims at finding a set of representative objects in a dataset O, and creates clusters by assigning objects to the cluster of their closest representative. Representative-based supervised clustering algorithms seek to accomplish the following goal: *Find a subset O_R of O such that the clustering X obtained by using the objects in O_R as representatives minimizes q(X).*

As part of our research, several representative-based clustering algorithms have been proposed [4,13], 3 of which are briefly described below:

1. SPAM is a variation of the popular traditional clustering algorithm PAM [5] that uses q(X) as its fitness function.
2. SRIDHCR starts with a randomly chosen initial set of representatives. The algorithm, then, greedily tries to improve this solution by inserting or deleting single representatives. Moreover, the algorithm is restarted r times.
3. SCEC uses evolutionary computing and evolves a population of solutions over a fixed number of generations based on the principle of the survival of the fittest. The genetic composition of solutions is changed by applying mutation and crossover operators.

3.3 Relationship to Local and Regional Learning

One way to characterize inductive learning techniques is to analyze if and to which extent they support the notion of locality. A k-nearest neighbor classifier is an example of a local learning technique (assuming it uses a low k-value); only objects that are very close to the object to be classified are used to predict the class label of that object. Other techniques subdivide the search space into different regions and use regional knowledge to fit the best model to each region. A good example for such a regional technique is a regression tree. In contrast to local techniques, a much larger number of examples are used to predict the class of an unseen example. Finally, global techniques try to fit a single model to the complete dataset. A good example for a global technique is classical regression analysis that tries to find a single curve that minimizes a prediction error with respect to all the examples that belong to the dataset.

As we will discuss in Section 4 of this paper, the parameter β plays key role in determining whether the patterns identified by supervised clustering are local (i.e., high value for β) or are regional (i.e., lower values for β).

4 Benefits of Supervised Clustering

4.1 Supervised Clustering for Creating Summaries and Background Knowledge

Figure 2 shows how cluster purity and the number of clusters k for the best solution found, changes as the value of parameter β increases for the Vehicle and the Diabetes datasets (the results were obtained by running algorithm SRIDHCR). As can be seen in Figure 2, as β increases, more penalty is associated with using the same number of clusters and the algorithm tries to use a lower number of clusters resulting in decreasing cluster purity. It is interesting to note that the Vehicle dataset seems to contain smaller regions with above average purities. Consequently, even if β increases beyond 0.5 the value of k remains quite high for that dataset. The Diabetes dataset, on the other hand, does not seem to contain such localized patterns; as soon as β increases beyond 0.5, k immediately reaches its minimum value of 2 (there are only two classes in the Diabetes dataset).

In general, we claim that supervised clustering is useful for creating background knowledge with respect to a given dataset. Examples include:

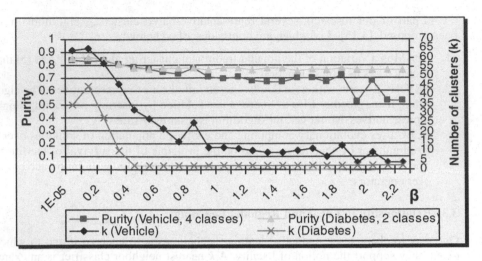

Fig. 2. How Purity(k) and k change as the value of   increases

1. It shows how instances of a particular class distribute in the attribute space; this information is of value for "discovering" subclasses of particular classes.
2. Maps for domain experts can be created that depict class densities in clusters and that identify which clusters share decision boundaries with each other.
3. Statistical summaries can be created for each cluster.
4. Meta attributes, such as various radiuses, distances between representatives, etc. can be generated, and their usefulness for enhancing classifiers can be explored.

4.2 Using Cluster Prototypes for Dataset Editing to Enhance NN-Classifiers

The objective of *dataset editing* [11] is to remove examples from a training set in order to enhance the accuracy of a classifier. In this paper, we propose using supervised clustering for *editing* a dataset O to produce a reduced subset O_r consisting of cluster representatives that have been selected by a supervised clustering algorithm. A 1-Nearest-Neighbor (1-NN) classifier, that we call nearest-representative (NR) classifier, is then used for classifying new examples using subset O_r instead of the original dataset O. We call this approach *supervised clustering editing* (SCE for short).

Figure 3 gives an example that illustrates how supervised clustering is used for dataset editing. Figure 3.a shows a dataset that has not been clustered yet. Figure 3.b shows the same dataset partitioned into 6 clusters using a supervised clustering algorithm. Cluster representatives are marked with circles around them. Figure 3.c shows the resulting subset O_r after the application of supervised clustering editing.

In general, an editing technique reduces the size of a dataset, n, to a smaller size k; we define the dataset compression rate of an editing technique as follows:

$$Compression\ Rate = 1 - \frac{k}{n} \qquad (3)$$

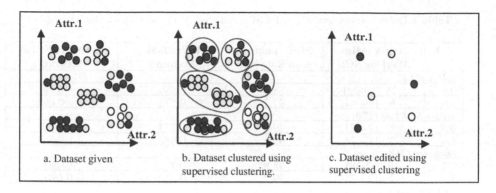

Fig. 3. Editing a dataset using supervised clustering

We applied our editing technique on a benchmark of 8 datasets obtained from [6]. Since β directly affects the size of reduced set O_r (larger β values produce smaller O_r sets while smaller β values tend to produce larger O_r sets) and in order to explore different compression rates, two different values for parameter β were used: 1.0 and 0.4. Prediction accuracies were measured using 10-fold cross-validation. Representatives for the nearest representative (NR) classifier were computed using the SRIDHCR algorithm. In our experiments, SRIDHCR was restarted 50 times, and the best solution (i.e., set of representatives) found in the 50 runs was used as the edited subset for the NR classifier. We also computed prediction accuracy for a traditional 1-NN classifier that uses all training examples when classifying a new example. Table 4 reports the accuracies obtained using the edited subset and the original dataset as well as the average dataset compression rates for supervised clustering editing. Due to the fact that the supervised clustering algorithm has to be run 10 times, once for each fold, Table 4 also reports the average, minimum, and maximum number of representatives found in the 10 runs.

Inspecting the results in Table 4, we can see that the SCE approach accomplished significant improvement in accuracy for the Heart-Stat Log, Diabetes, Waveform, and Iris-Plants datasets, outperforming the traditional 1-NN-classifier. Further inspecting the second and third columns of Table 4, we notice that with the exception of the Glass and the Segmentation datasets, SCE accomplishes compression rates of more than 94% without a significant loss in prediction accuracy for the other 6 datasets.

The reader might ask why it is necessary to develop supervised clustering algorithms for the purpose of editing. Couldn't the same objective be accomplished by clustering examples of each class separately using a traditional clustering algorithm, such as PAM [5]? Figure 4, that shows examples of a dataset consisting of 2 classes 'X' and 'O', illustrates why this is not a good idea. If this dataset is edited using supervised clustering, the red (underlined) O example and the purple (underlined) X example would be picked as representatives. On the other hand, if examples of each class are clustered separately, the blue (italic) *O* example and the purple (underlined) X example would be picked as the representatives. Note that the blue (italic) *O* representative is **not** a good choice for dataset editing, because it "attracts" examples belonging to the class 'X' which leads to misclassifications.

Table 4. Dataset compression rates for SCE and prediction accuracy for the NR and 1-NN

B	Avg. k [Min-Max] for SCE	SCE Compression Rate (%)	NR Prediction Accuracy	1-NN Prediction Accuracy
Glass (214)				
0.4	25 [19-29]	88.4	0.589	0.692
1.0	6 [6 – 6]	97.2	0.575	0.692
Heart-Stat Log (270)				
0.4	2 [2 – 2]	99.3	0.833	0.767
1.0	2 [2 – 2]	99.3	0.838	0.767
Diabetes (768)				
0.4	9 [2-18]	98.8	0.736	0.690
1.0	2 [2 – 2]	99.7	0.745	0.690
Vehicle (846)				
0.4	38 [26-61]	95.5	0.667	0.700
1.0	14 [9-22]	98.3	0.665	0.700
Heart-H (294)				
0.4	2	99.3	0.793	0.783
1.0	2	99.3	0.809	0.783
Waveform (5000)				
0.4	28 [20-39]	99.4	0.841	0.768
1.0	4 [3-6]	99.9	0.837	0.768
Iris-Plants (150)				
0.4	3 [3 – 3]	98.0	0.973	0.947
1.0	3 [3 – 3]	98.0	0.953	0.947
Segmentation (2100)				
0.4	30 [24-37]	98.6	0.919	0.956
1.0	14	99.3	0.889	0.956

```
O    OOx      X      X
O    OOx      X      X
O    OOx      X      X
```

Fig. 4. Supervised clustering editing vs. clustering each class separately

4.3 Using Supervised Clustering to Enhance Simple Classifiers

Another capability of supervised clustering is that it can be used to enhance classifiers by using regional knowledge. Referring to Figure 1 again, we could transform the problem of classifying examples belonging to the two classes "black circles" and "white circles" into the "simpler" problem of classifying the examples that belong to clusters E, F, G, and H. The reduced complexity can be attributed to the fact that those 4 "clusters" are linearly separable (note the dotted lines in Fig. 1.b) whereas the original 2 classes are not. Vilalta et. al. [10] proposed a methodology that first clusters the examples of each class separately using a traditional clustering algorithm, and then learns a classifier by treating the so obtained clusters as separate classes.

We propose to use supervised clustering for class decomposition instead of clustering each class separately using traditional clustering algorithm because supervised clustering has the tendency to merge clusters of the same class if found close to each others, such as cluster G in Figure 1.b. To test this idea, we conducted an experiment where we compared the prediction accuracy of a traditional Naïve Bayes classifier with a Naïve Bayes classifier that treats each cluster as a separate class. We used 4 UCI datasets as a benchmark. We used SRIDHCR supervised clustering algorithm (with β set to 0.25) to obtain the clusters. The results reported in Table 5 indicate that using class decomposition improved the prediction accuracy for 3 of the 4 datasets tested. Furthermore, analyzing the results further, we see that the accuracy improvement for the Vehicle dataset (23.23%) is far higher than that for the Diabetes dataset (0.52%). This result is consistent with the analysis presented in section 4.1.

Table 5. Prediction accuracy of "Naive Bayes" and "Naive Bayes with class decomposition"

Dataset	Naïve Bayes (NB)	NB with Class Decomposition	Improvement
Diabetes	76.56	77.08	0.52%
Heart-H	79.73	70.27	−9.46%
Segment	68.00	75.045	7.05%
Vehicle	45.02	68.25	23.23%

5 Conclusion

In this paper a novel data mining technique we named *supervised clustering* was introduced that, unlike traditional clustering, assumes that the clustering algorithm is applied to classified examples and has the objective of identifying clusters that have a high probability density with respect to a single class. We discussed how local and regional knowledge that has been generated by supervised clustering can be used to enhance classifiers. We also demonstrated how regional knowledge generated by supervised clustering can be used for enhancing simple classifiers. We also believe that running a supervised clustering algorithm gives valuable information about how the examples of the dataset distribute over the attribute space.

In addition to developing efficient and scalable supervised clustering algorithms, our future work centers on using supervised clustering for dataset compression, for learning subclasses, and for distance function learning.

References

1. Basu, S., Bilenko,M., Mooney, R.: Semi-supervised Clustering by Seeding. In Proceedings of the Nineteenth International Conference on Machine Learning (ICML'02). Sydney, Australia, July 2002. 19-26,
2. Bar-Hillel, A., Hertz, T., Shental, N., Weinshall, D.: Learning Distance Functions Using Equivalence Relations. In Proc. ICML'03, Washington DC, August 2003.
3. Demiriz, A., Benett, K.-P., Embrechts, M.J.: Semi-supervised Clustering using Genetic Algorithms. In Proc. ANNIE'99.
4. Eick, C., Zeidat, N., Zhao, Z..: Supervised Clustering – Algorithms and Benefits. Proc. ICTAI'04, Boca Raton, FL, November 2004.

5. Kaufman, L., Rousseeuw P. J.: Finding Groups in Data: an Introduction to Cluster Analysis. John Wiley & Sons, 1990.
6. University of California at Irving, Machine Learning Repository. http://www.ics.uci.edu/~mlearn/MLRepository.html
7. Sinkkonen, J., Kaski, S., and Nikkila, J.: Discriminative Clustering: Optimal Contingency Tables by Learning Metrics. In Proc. ECML'02. Helsinki, Finland, August 2002.
8. Slonim, N. and Tishby, N.: Agglomerative Information Bottleneck. Neural Information Processing Systems (NIPS'99).
9. Tishby, N., Periera, F.C., and Bialek, W.: The Information Bottleneck Method. In proceedings of the 37th Allerton Conference on Communication and Computation, 1999.
10. Vilalta, R., Achari, M., and Eick C.: Class Decomposition Via Clustering: A New Framework For Low-Variance Classifiers. In Proceedings of the Third IEEE International Conference on Data Mining (ICDM'03), Melbourne, FL, November 2003.
11. Wilson, D.L.: Asymptotic Properties of Nearest Neighbor Rules Using Edited Data. IEEE Transactions on Systems, Man, and Cybernetics, 2:408-420, 1972.
12. Xing, E.P., Ng, A., Jordan, M., Russell, S.: Distance Metric Learning with Applications to Clustering with Side Information. Advances in Neural Information Processing 15, MIT Press, 2003.
13. Zeidat, N., Eick, C.: Using k-medoid Style Algorithms for Supervised Summary Generation. Proc. MLMTA'04, Las Vegas, June 2004.

Modelling Good Entry Pages on the Web

Theodora Tsikrika and Mounia Lalmas

Department of Computer Science, Queen Mary University of London,
London E1 4NS, UK
{theodora, mounia}@dcs.qmul.ac.uk
http://qmir.dcs.qmul.ac.uk

Abstract. Being a *good entry page* to a Web site reflects how well the
page enables a user to obtain optimal access, by browsing, to relevant
and quality pages within the site. Our aim is to model a measure of
how good an entry page is, as a combination of evidence of the properties exhibited by the Web pages, which belong to the same site and
are structurally related to it. The proposed model is formally expressed
within *Dempster-Shafer's Theory of Evidence* and can be applied in the
context of Web Information Retrieval tasks.

Keywords: Web Information Retrieval, best entry pages, formal model,
Dempster-Shafer theory of evidence

1 Introduction

The aim of Information Retrieval (IR) systems is to assist users in satisfying their
information needs by providing them with a ranked list of documents relevant to
their queries. In the context of the Web, where hypermedia document authoring
is encouraged, a document on a single topic may be distributed over a number of
pages, which belong to a single site and are linked to each other. Users, however,
consider it redundant for a Web IR system to return many relevant pages from
the same site [3], since, in practice, they are able to easily reach all these pages
by browsing, when given an appropriate entry page to the site [1].

Therefore, Web IR systems should quantify not only how relevant Web pages
are, but also how good they are as entry pages to the site they belong. A *Good
Entry Page* (GEP) measure should reflect how well a page enables a user to
obtain optimal access, by browsing, to the relevant pages within the site. Web
IR systems could then employ this measure in order to *focus* retrieval [5], by
presenting to the user, not all the relevant pages from a site, but only the one
considered to be its *Best Entry Page* (BEP).

We could also consider a more generalised view of a GEP measure, where
being a GEP is determined not only in reference to the relevance of the pages
it provides access to, but also with respect to other properties of these pages.
In the Web, for instance, where there can exist thousands or even millions of
pages relevant to a topic, other properties of Web pages, such as their *quality*, are
taken into account when retrieving them. However, quality is a subjective notion

M.-S. Hacid et al. (Eds.): ISMIS 2005, LNAI 3488, pp. 257–265, 2005.
© Springer-Verlag Berlin Heidelberg 2005

and can be interpreted in different ways. Here, we consider that the quality of a Web page can be captured by its *authority* [6] or its *utility* [10] on the topic. An authoritative page can be defined as a page that is not only topically relevant, but it is also a "trusted source of correct information" [13]. A *topical utility* (or hub [6]) page, on the other hand, provides a comprehensive list of links to authoritative pages on the topic.

In this paper, we adopt this generalised view and our aim is to quantify how good a page is as an entry page to a site, in reference to a particular property. This reflects how well a page enables the user to obtain access to other pages, belonging to the same site and exhibiting this property with respect to the topic. In Web IR, various approaches, such as spreading activation mechanisms[11] and site compression techniques [1] have been used in quantifying GEPs, by exploiting the structural relations among pages belonging to the same site. The underlying assumption is that a GEP measure should reflect not only the relevance or quality of a page, but also that of the pages within the site, that are accessible from it, by browsing.

To achieve our aim, we model Web pages and the properties they exhibit in ways that enable us to model a GEP measure of a page as a combination of evidence of the properties of the pages, which are structurally related to it and belong to the same site. This model is formally expressed within *Dempster-Shafer's (D-S) Theory of Evidence* [12]. D-S is a theory of uncertainty, that allows the explicit representation of combination of evidence, which allows us to model the aggregation of the properties of pages.

The paper is organised as follows. Section 2 contains a brief introduction to D-S theory. The model is described in Section 3 and some concluding remarks are provided in Section 4.

2 Dempster-Shafer's Theory of Evidence

In this section, we describe the main concepts of Dempster-Shafer's (D-S) Theory of Evidence [4, 12]. The combination of evidence, expressed by Dempster's combination rule, makes the use of D-S theory particularly attractive in this work, since it allows the expression of the aggregation of the properties of structurally related pages, which belong to the same site.

Frame of Discernment. Suppose that we are concerned with the value of some quantity u and that the (non-empty) set of its possible values is Θ. In the D-S framework, this set Θ of mutually exhaustive and exclusive events is called a *frame of discernment*. Propositions are represented as subsets of this set. An example of a proposition is "the value of u is in A" for some $A \subseteq \Theta$. For $A = \{a\}$, $a \in \Theta$, "the value of u is a" constitutes a *basic proposition*. *Non-basic propositions* are defined as the union of basic propositions. Therefore, propositions are in a one-to-one correspondence with the subsets of Θ.

Basic Probability Assignment. Beliefs can be assigned to propositions to express their certainty. The beliefs are usually computed based on a density function $m : \wp(\Theta) \rightarrow [0,1]$ called a basic probability assignment (bpa): $m(\emptyset) = 0$ and $\sum_{A \subseteq \Theta} m(A) = 1$. $m(A)$ represents the belief exactly committed to A, that is the exact evidence that the value of u is in A. If there is positive evidence for the value of u being in A, then $m(A) > 0$ and A is called a *focal element*. The proposition A is said to be discerned. No belief can ever be assigned to the false proposition (represented as $\emptyset$). The sum of all non-null bpas must equate 1. The focal elements and the associated bpas define a *body of evidence*.

A δ-*discounted bpa* $m^{\delta}(.)$ can be obtained from the original bpa m as follows: $m^{\delta}(A) = \delta m(A), \forall A \subseteq \Theta, A \neq \Theta$ and $m^{\delta}(\Theta) = \delta m(\Theta) + 1 - \delta$, with $0 \leq \delta \leq 1$. The discounting factor δ represents some form of meta-knowledge regarding the reliability of the body of evidence, which could not be encoded in m.

Belief Function. Given a body of evidence with bpa m, one can compute the total belief provided by the body of evidence for a proposition. This is done with a belief function $Bel : \wp(\Theta) \mapsto [0,1]$ defined upon m as follows: $Bel(A) = \sum_{B \subseteq A} m(B)$. $Bel(A)$ is the total belief committed to A, that is the total positive effect the body of evidence has on the value of u being in A.

Dempster's Combination Rule. This rule aggregates two independent bodies of evidence with bpas m_1 and m_2 defined with the same frame of discernment Θ, into one body of evidence defined by a bpa m on the same frame Θ:

$$m(A) = m_1 \oplus m_2(A) = \frac{\sum_{B \cap C = A} m_1(B) m_2(C)}{\sum_{B \cap C \neq \emptyset} m_1(B) m_2(C)}$$

Dempster's combination rule, then, computes a measure of agreement between two bodies of evidence concerning various propositions discerned from a common frame of discernment. The rule focuses only on those propositions that both bodies of evidence support. The denominator of the above equation is a normalisation factor that ensures that m is a bpa.

3   Description of the Model

Being a good entry page to a site with respect to a specific topic and in reference to a particular property, reflects how well the page enables the user to obtain access to pages within this site, which are exhibiting this property with respect to the topic. Our aim is to model a measure of *topical GEP* of a page, as a combination of evidence of the properties of the pages which are structurally related to it and belong to the same site.

First, we describe the properties exhibited by Web pages (Section 3.1) and define a frame of discernment based on these properties (Section 3.2). Web pages are represented as bodies of evidence within the defined frame of discernment (Section 3.3). The aggregation of the bodies of evidence, corresponding to pages which are structurally related to a particular page, allows us to model a measure of the topical GEP of a page (Section 3.4). Finally we extend the model, by presenting a refinement of the frame of discernment (Section 3.5).

3.1   Properties of Objects

We consider that each Web page exhibits a number of properties. These are either determined with respect to a particular topic (*topic-dependent properties*) or are considered to be intrinsic attributes of the pages (*topic-independent properties*). In this work, we concentrate on the topic-dependent properties of topical relevance, topical authority and topical utility, on the one hand, and the topic-independent properties of authority and utility, on the other, which reflect the quality of a Web page irrespective of any specific topic.

The authority of a Web page is usually determined by *link analysis ranking algorithms*, which view the Web's link structure as a network of recommendations[1] between pages [13]. When a page is pointed by other quality pages, it is considered to be recommended by them and therefore regarded as an authority. When a link analysis ranking algorithm takes into account the whole of the Web's link structure [9], a topic-independent measure of a page's authority is determined. This can then be combined with a topical relevance measure, in order to estimate the page's topical authority. In this case, the topical authority property of a page is directly related both to its topical relevance property, and to its topic-independent authority property.

Link analysis ranking algorithms can also be applied to a sub-network of the Web's link structure, generated by the links between the top ranked topical relevant pages, already retrieved by a Web IR system, and their immediate neighbours (forming the *base set* of pages). In this case, the measure of the page's authority, as this is determined by the algorithm, becomes topic-dependent and the relation among the properties indirect. HITS algorithm [6] and its extensions [2] adopt this approach in quantifying the topical authority of a page.

The same applies to the topical utility of a Web page, which can be quantified, either as a direct combination of its topical relevance with a topic-independent measure of its utility [10], or by employing an appropriate link analysis ranking algorithm [6] on the network of links connecting the pages in the base set.

To capture these relations and dependencies among the properties of a Web page, we introduce the notion of *composite* properties to refer to the ones that are related to the more *elementary* properties of a page. In our case, the topical authority and the topical utility of a page constitute its composite properties. These are related to the elementary properties of topical relevance and topic-independent authority of the page and to topical relevance and topic-independent utility of the page, respectively.

3.2   Frame of Discernment

To define a frame of discernment based on the above properties, we consider $\mathbb{E} = \{e_1, \cdots, e_E\}$ to be the set of elementary properties and $\mathbb{C} = \{c_1, \cdots, c_C\}$ the set of composite properties, with $c_i \subseteq \mathbb{E}$. The frame of discernment Θ is constructed based on the set $\mathbb{E}$. The elements of the frame are defined as the mutually

---

[1] This network takes into account only inter-domain links, since the underlying assumption is that they are the ones conveying endorsement [6].

exclusive propositions, which are derived by considering all the possible boolean conjunctions of all the elements $e_i \in \mathbb{E}$, containing either e_i or its negation $\neg e_i$. There are 2^E elements in Θ and each is denoted as $\theta_{b_1 b_2 \cdots b_n}$, where $b_1 b_2 \cdots b_n$ is an n-bit binary number, such that $\theta_{b_1 b_2 \cdots b_n}$ corresponds to the proposition "$x_1 \wedge x_2 \wedge \cdots \wedge x_n$", where $x_i = e_i$ if $b_i = 1$ and $x_i = \neg e_i$ if $b_i = 0$.

Since we consider that the set of elementary properties of a Web page consists of the topical relevance R exhibited by the page, its topic-independent authority A and topic-independent utility U, we define $\mathbb{E} = \{R, A, U\}$. Each element $\theta_{b_1 b_2 \cdots b_n} \in \Theta$ corresponds to the property $\theta_{b_1 b_2 \cdots b_n}$ exhibited by a Web page. For instance, θ_{100} corresponds to $\{R \wedge \neg A \wedge \neg U\}$, reflecting that the page is exhibiting topical relevance, but not authority or utility. Therefore, θ_{100} provides a more refined representation of the notion of relevance compared to that provided by the proposition $\{R\}$. The latter corresponds to $\theta_{100} \vee \theta_{101} \vee \theta_{110} \vee \theta_{111}$, and reflects the topical relevance as this is exhibited by a page, without specifying whether the authority or utility of the page have been considered. Consequently, θ_{100} corresponds to the topical relevance as this is defined in classical IR, where authority or utility are not considered. In essence, we consider that a page can exhibit any of the properties defined in Θ or any of the elementary or composite properties, which were described in the previous section, and can be expressed in terms of the propositions in Θ.

3.3   Representation of Objects

In our framework, each Web page is referred to as an *object* and is represented by a body of evidence defined in Θ, through a set a focal elements for which there is positive evidence. Therefore, the focal elements can be used as propositions modelling the properties exhibited by the objects. Every elementary property $e_i \in \mathbb{E}$ exhibited by an object, meaning that there is positive evidence supporting it, defines a focal element, the proposition p_i. Every composite property c_k also defines a focal element, the proposition $p_k = \bigwedge_l p_l$, where each p_l is the proposition associated to the elementary property e_l for $e_l \in c_k$.

If we consider an object o to exhibit the following properties: $p_1 = \{R\}$, $p_2 = \{A\}$, $p_3 = \{U\}$ and $p_4 = \{R \wedge A\}$, then these properties are defined in terms of the propositions in Θ as: $p_1 = \theta_{100} \vee \theta_{101} \vee \theta_{110} \vee \theta_{111}$, $p_2 = \theta_{010} \vee \theta_{011} \vee \theta_{110} \vee \theta_{111}$, $p_3 = \theta_{001} \vee \theta_{011} \vee \theta_{101} \vee \theta_{111}$ and $p_4 = \theta_{110} \vee \theta_{111}$. If we further assume that object o exhibits property $p_5 = \{R \wedge \neg A \wedge \neg U\}$, then $p_5 = \theta_{100}$ (Figure 1).

A bpa m represents the uncertainty associated to a property and $m(p)$ corresponds to the degree to which an object exhibits property p. The value of $m(p)$ is estimated by employing an appropriate Web IR approach. For instance, if p corresponds to the topical authority of an object, $m(p)$ could be estimated using HITS algorithm [6] or one of its modifications [2]. However, we are not interested in which approach has been actually employed, just in that $m(p)$ has been estimated. The higher the $m(p)$, the more the object exhibits this property, whereas $m(p) = 0$ means that there is no evidence that the object exhibits property p.

From the definition of the bpa, each body of evidence must assign the same total amount of belief to the entire set of properties exhibited by the objects

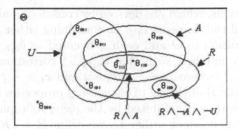

Fig. 1. Example of an object in the frame of discernment

and which define the frame of discernment. One approach in ensuring that this condition holds is to treat it as an *uncommitted belief*, which can be used to represent the uncertainty (overall ignorance) associated with the available evidence regarding the properties exhibited by an object. It is defined as $1 - \sum_{p_k \in \Theta} m(p_k)$ and it is assigned as the bpa value of the proposition corresponding to the frame of discernment. If not null, this proposition constitutes a focal element.

For the object o defined above, if we suppose that $m(p_1) = 0.2$, $m(p_2) = 0.1$, $m(p_3) = 0.05$, $m(p_4) = 0.15$ and $m(p_5) = 0.1$, then the uncommitted belief $m(\Theta) = 1 - (0.2 + 0.1 + 0.05 + 0.15 + 0.1) = 0.4$. The belief $Bel(R) = m(p_1) + m(p_4) + m(p_5) = 0.2 + 0.15 + 0.1 = 0.45$ can be considered to reflect the overall relevance exhibited by the object.

3.4   Object Aggregation

To model a measure of the topical GEP of a page, we consider the combination of evidence of the properties of the pages which belong to the same site and are accessible from it. However, there is a tendency of users and it is more intuitive for them to browse down from starting points [7]. Therefore, they consider a GEP as one that enables them to access pages that are deeper in the hierarchy of the site. In this work, we concentrate on users following hierarchical down links[2] and consider only this kind of structural relation between Web pages.

In our framework, a page containing hierarchical down links is represented as an *aggregate object*. This object is derived from the aggregation of the bodies of evidence of its *component objects*, which are the objects linked by it with hierarchical down links and the object corresponding to the page itself. For instance, consider a site consisting of five pages connected by hierarchical down links (Figure 2a). Page 3 is then represented as aggregate object a_3 derived from the aggregation of o_1, o_2 and o_3 (Figure 2b). The aggregate object a_3 corresponds to the same Web page as object o_3. We use Dempster's combination rule to compute the body of evidence of the aggregate object a_3: $m_{a_3} = m_1 \oplus m_2 \oplus m_3$. Uncommitted belief is also assigned to the aggregate object.

---

[2] Hierarchical down links are intra-domain Web links whose source is higher in the directory path than their target.

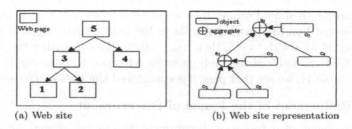

(a) Web site   (b) Web site representation

Fig. 2. Web Site

Table 1. Aggregation process

Step 1 of the aggregation							
object o_1	m_{o_1}	object o_2	m_{o_2}	object o_3	m_{o_3}	aggregate a_3	m_{a_3}
R	0.8	R	0.6	Θ	1	R	0.92
Θ	0.2	Θ	0.4			Θ	0.08

Fading factor - Step 2 of the aggregation							
aggregate a_3	$m_{a_3}^{\beta_3}$	object o_4	m_{o_4}	object o_5	m_{o_5}	aggregate a_5	m_{a_5}
R	0.46	Θ	1	Θ	1	R	0.46
Θ	0.54					Θ	0.54

The aggregation process is applied to the whole site starting with the pages deepest in the hierarchy, where no aggregation is performed. At the first step, we move up one level in the hierarchy to the page which has links to these pages and compute the body of evidence of the aggregate object (a_3 in our example).

In our example, consider that pages 1 and 2 are retrieved, whereas pages 3, 4 and 5 are not. We consider the objects o_1 and o_2, corresponding to the retrieved pages, to exhibit the property $\{R\}$, with belief 0.8 and 0.6 respectively, whereas there is no evidence regarding any other properties for these or for the rest of the objects. The uncommitted belief is then equal to: $m_1(\Theta) = 0.2$, $m_2(\Theta) = 0.4$, and $m_3(\Theta) = m_4(\Theta) = m_5(\Theta) = 1$.

In the first step of the aggregation process (Table 1), Dempster's combination rule yields the aggregate object a_3, exhibiting property R with belief 0.92. Despite page 3 not being initially retrieved, it still can be considered to exhibit topical relevance, by reflecting that of its descendants. We consider the overall belief $Bel_a(R)$ (which is equal to $m_a(R)$ in this case) to reflect a measure of the topical GEP of a page in reference to property R. One can see that the belief in a property increases, when there is positive evidence for that property in more than one of the bodies of evidence being aggregated. Within this step of the aggregation, we could to model the contribution of each of the component objects forming an aggregate object, by using discounted bpas. The extent of each contribution could capture the uncertainty related to the structure of the site. For instance, if an object o has n hierarchical down links to objects o_i, their contribution could be set to $\frac{1}{n}$, whereas that of object o itself could be set to 1.

Before moving one level up in the hierarchy to the next step of the aggregation, a *fading factor* [8] is applied to the aggregate objects already formed. As aggregate objects reflect information deeper in the hierarchy, the contribution of this information should diminish as we move further up. This is modelled by a β_i-*discounted* bpa m^{β_i}, where β_i reflects the fading factor applied to aggregate object a_i. If we set $\beta_3 = 0.5$, then $m_{a_5} = 0.46$. By comparing the values of the topical GEP measure of the Web pages in reference to property R (depicted in bold in Table 1), we see that page 3 is considered the best entry page to the site.

3.5   Refinement of the Frame of Discernment

The refinement of a frame of discernment Θ (*coarse frame*) into a frame of discernment V (*refined frame*) is defined by splitting each element of Θ into a set of elements, that can be viewed as the latter representing more precise items of information than the former.

For instance, element $\theta_{100} \in \Theta$, reflects the proposition "the Web page exhibits topical relevance, but not authority or utility". This could be split into k elements $\theta_{100\_r_i}$, each corresponding to "the Web page exhibits topical relevance, as this is determined by retrieval algorithm r_i, but not authority or utility", where r_i with $i = 1, ..., k$ corresponds to a ranking approach that can be applied in order to determine the topical relevance of an object. For instance, consider that θ_{100} is split into 2 elements of V, each more precise than θ_{100}: θ_{100_p} denoting "the Web page exhibits topical relevance as this is determined by the probabilistic model, but not authority or utility" and θ_{100_v} denoting "the Web page exhibits topical relevance as this is determined by the vector space model, but not authority or utility".

The refinement is formally defined by $\omega : 2^\Theta \rightarrow 2^V$: (i) $\omega(p) \neq 0$ for all $p \in \Theta$, meaning that every element in Θ is split into elements in V; (ii) $\omega(p) \cap \omega(p') = 0$ if $p \neq p'$ for all $p, p' \in \Theta$, meaning that two elements cannot be split into the same element, and (iii) $\bigcup_{p \in \Theta} \omega(p) = V$, meaning that the result of a refinement is a frame of discernment. For instance, refinement for element θ_{100} is expressed as: $\omega(\theta_{100}) = \{\theta_{100\_p}, \theta_{100\_v}\}$. The refinement function is also extended to a set $A \subseteq \Theta$: $\omega(A) = \bigcup_{p \in A} \omega(p)$, where $\omega(A)$ consists of all the elements in V that are obtained by splitting all the elements in A. Therefore, this refinement function links two frames of discernment, such that one is defined in terms of the other. If the properties exhibited by a Web page are modelled by the coarse frame, then the refinement function can give us a more detailed representation in terms of how these properties are actually determined.

Let Bel_Θ and Bel_V be the belief functions defined on Θ and V, respectively. These belief functions must satisfy the criteria that these two frames are *compatible*, which means that the two frames must agree on the information defined in them. Therefore, although refining a set means that more precise items of information are obtained, the union of these items carries the same information as the original set. The belief functions are compatible, if for given set A on the frame Θ, the following holds: $Bel_\Theta(A) = Bel_V(\omega(A))$.

4   Conclusions

We presented a model expressed within the theoretical framework of Dempster-Shafer's theory of evidence, which quantifies a measure of how good a Web page is as an entry page to a Web site. Web pages are represented in terms of topic-dependent and topic-independent properties. Structurally related pages belonging to the same site are combined using Dempster's combination rule, to produce an aggregate, which exhibits properties reflecting those of its structurally related components. We consider that the belief assigned to a particular property of an aggregate object corresponds to a measure of its topical GEP, in reference to that property.

In this work, we considered only intra-domain hierarchical down links to reflect the structural relations between Web pages. The next step is to consider other kinds of intra- and inter-domain structural relations. Currently, we are performing large-scale experiments to evaluate our approach using test collections of Web documents.

References

1. E. Amitay, D. Carmel, A. Darlow, R. Lempel, and A. Soffer. Topic distillation with knowledge agents. In *Proceedings of 11th Text Retrieval Conference (TREC-2002)*, *NIST Special Publication 500-251. Gaitensburg, MD*, 2002.
2. K. Bharat and M. Henzinger. Improved algorithms for topic distillation in a hyperlinked environment. In *Proceedings of ACM SIGIR*, pages 104–111, 1998.
3. N. Craswell and D. Hawking. Overview of the trec-2002 web track. In *Proceedings of 11th Text Retrieval Conference (TREC-2002), NIST Special Publication 500-251. Gaitensburg, MD*, 2002.
4. A. P. Dempster. A generalization of bayesian inference. *Journal of Royal Statistical Society*, 30:205–447, 1968.
5. G. Kazai, M. Lalmas, and T. Roelleke. Focussed structured document retrieval. In *Proceedings of String Processing and Information Retrieval*, 2002.
6. J. Kleinberg. Authoritative sources in a hyperlinked environment. *Journal of the ACM*, 46(5):604–632, 1999.
7. M. Lalmas and E. Moutogianni. A dempster-shafer indexing for the focussed retrieval of hierarchically structured documents: Implementation and experiments on a web museum collection. In *Proceedings of RIAO*, pages 442–456, 2000.
8. M. Marchiori. The quest for correct information on the web: hyper search engines. In *Proceedings of the sixth international conference on World Wide Web*, pages 1225–1235. Elsevier Science Publishers Ltd., 1997.
9. L. Page, S. Brin, R. Motwani, and T. Winograd. The pagerank citation ranking: Bringing order to the web. Technical report, Stanford Digital Library Technologies Project, 1998.
10. V. Plachouras, I. Ounis, and G. Amati. A utility-oriented hyperlink analysis model for the web. In *Proceedings of the First Latin American Web Congress (LA-WEB 2003)*, 2003.
11. V. Plachouras, I. Ounis, G. Amati, and C. J. van Rijsbergen. University of glasgow at the web track of trec 2002. In *Proceedings of 11th Text Retrieval Conference (TREC-2002), NIST Special Publication 500-251. Gaitensburg, MD*, 2002.
12. G. Shafer. *A mathematical theory of evidence*. Princeton University Press, Princeton, NJ, 1976.
13. P. Tsaparas. *Link Analysis Ranking*. PhD thesis, Department of Computer Science, University of Toronto, 2004.

A Query Expression and Processing Technique for an XML Search Engine[*]

Wol Young Lee and Hwan Seung Yong

Department of Computer Science and Engineering,
Ewha Institute of Science and Technology, Seoul, Korea
{wylee, hsyong}@ewha.ac.kr

Abstract. One of the virtues of XML is that it allows complex structures to be easily expressed. This allows XML to be used as an intermediate, neutral, and standard form for representing many types of structured or semistructured documents that arise in a great variety of applications. To support for efficient queries against XML data, many query languages have been designed. The query languages require the users to know the structure of the XML documents and specify path-based search conditions on the structure. This path-based query against XML documents is a natural consequence of the hierarchical structure of XML. However, it is also desirable to allow the users to formulate no path queries against XML documents, to complement the current path-based queries. In this paper, we have developed a query expression and processing technique supporting non-navigational content-based queries for an XML search engine.

1 Introduction

The past few years have been a dramatic increase in the popularity and adoption of XML, as it includes semantic information within documents describing semi-structured data. This makes it possible to overcome the shortcomings of existing markup languages such as HTML and support data exchange in e-business environments. The increasing adoption of XML has also raised new challenges. One of the key issues is the information retrieval against large collections of XML documents. To allow for numerous data search, many query languages have been developed [1-4]. These query languages require users to know the structure of XML documents, including all the element and attribute names, data types of the data values, and the hierarchical structure of the elements. Since a search condition needs to involve an element/attribute name, which appears somewhere in the hierarchical structure of an XML document, these query languages force the users to specify the navigational access paths to the elements/attributes that are involved in search conditions. This makes it difficult for the users to query XML documents.

To complement navigational path-based queries, there have been researches for a keyword-based search engine [6-9]. However, it is difficult for users to search exact

[*] This work was supported by Korea Science and Engineering Foundation (KOSEF) (R01-2003-000-10395-0).

M.-S. Hacid et al. (Eds.): ISMIS 2005, LNAI 3488, pp. 266–275, 2005.
© Springer-Verlag Berlin Heidelberg 2005

results because the keyword-based search engine makes use of only limited information. On the other hand, if users would like to search in navigational query expressions as considering XML properties, users have to use very complex expressions according to document structure. For example, suppose users want the following query against Fig. 1.

Q1: Search book title information of which publisher is 'Morgan Kaufmann', release year is '1999', and whose authors include 'Serge Abiteboul'.

```
<book>
    <isbn>1</isbn>
    <year>1999</year>
    <publisher>Morgan Kaufmann
    </publisher>
    <title>Data on the web</title>
    <author>Serge Abiteboul</author>
    <author>Peter Buneman</author>
    <author>Dan Suciu</author>
</book>
```

(a) elements

```
<book>
    <general_info isbn= "1" year="1999"
        publisher="Morgan Kaufmann">
    </general_info>
    <detail_info  title=" Data on the web"
        author=" 'Serge Abiteboul'
        'Peter Buneman' 'Dan Suciu'">
    </detail_info>
</book>
```

(b) attributes

```
<book>
    <isbn no= "1"></isbn>
    <year yyyy="1999"></year>
    <title name="Data on the web"></title>
    <publisher name="Morgan Kaufmann">
    </publisher>
    <author name1="Serge Abiteboul"
        name2="Peter Buneman"
        name3= "Dan Suciu"></author>
</book>
```

(c) intervening of attributes

```
<book>
    <isbn><no>1</no></isbn>
    <year><yyyy>1999</yyyy></year>
    <title><name>Data on the web</name>
    </title>
    <publisher><name>Morgan Kaufmann
    </name></publisher>
    <author><name>Serge Abiteboul</name>
        <name>Peter Buneman</name>
        <name>Dan Suciu </name></author>
</book>
```

(d) intervening of elements

```
<year>1999
    <publisher>Morgan Kaufmann
    <book>
        <isbn>1</isbn>
        <title>Data on the web</title>
        <author>Serge Abiteboul </author>
        <author>Peter Buneman </author>
        <author>Dan Suciu</author>
    </book> ...
    </publisher>...
</year>
```

(e) *publisher* is nested in *year*

```
<publisher>Morgan Kaufmann
    <year yyyy="1999">
    <book>
        <isbn>1</isbn>
        <title>Data on the web</title>
        <author>Serge Abiteboul </author>
        <author>Peter Buneman</author>
        <author>Dan Suciu</author>
    </book> ...
    </year>...
</publisher>
```

(f) *year* is nested in *publisher*

Fig. 1. Various document representations

If the names are represented as element names and their values are directly assigned as element values like Fig. 1(a), then the users can get desired results by expressing as //year="1999" and //publisher="Morgan Kaufmann" and //author="Serge Abiteboul". However, the users have to differently express a path expression if the names are represented not as elements but attributes on documents like Fig. 1(b). In this case, if the users use XQuery-like expressions, the users have to represent as //@year="1999" and //@publisher="Morgan Kaufmann" and //@author="Serge Abiteboul". If arbitrary data are inserted between the data names and their values like Fig. 1(c) and (d) the users have to know the fact and query expressions are differently represented by a way describing data. The users have to express as //year/@yyyy="1999" and //publisher/@name ="Morgan Kaufmann" and //author/@name="Serge Abiteboul" or //year/@*   ="1999"   and   //publisher/@*   ="Morgan   Kaufmann"   and //author/@*="Serge Abiteboul" against Fig. 1(c). Against Fig. 1(d), the users have to express as //year/yyyy="1999" and //publisher/name="Morgan Kaufmann" and //author/name=" Serge Abiteboul" or //year/*="1999" and //publisher/*="Morgan Kaufmann" and //author/*="Serge Abiteboul". Furthermore, the document may be created as a nested relationship between data names like Fig. 1(e) and (f). In this case, the users have to express the nested relationship among the data as //year="1999"//publisher="Morgan Kaufmann"//author="Serge Abiteboul" against Fig. 1(e). Against Fig. 1(f), the users have to express an inverse nested relationship because the two documents are opposite in the upper and lower relationship of *year* and *publisher* even though both Fig. 1(e) and (f) have a nested relationship.

Insofar as XML gives rise to hierarchical structure, and navigational access to selected parts of an XML document is a natural access pattern, the navigational query expressions clearly make sense. However, for query Q1, we would like to be able to state the search conditions simply as

publisher = "Morgan Kaufmann" and year = "1999" and author = "Serge Abiteboul"

regardless of the structure of the XML documents[5]. We believe non-navigational content-based query expression for XML, and general semi-structured data, are also desirable. In other words, we believe that both navigational and non-navigational query expressions are necessary to support all query needs against XML databases. Specially, the non-navigational content-based queries provide the following contributions.

- The non-navigational content-based queries allow users to query about all document types regardless of document structures. That is, the users need not worry about path representations because the users query by using only data names and their values as SQL-like queries.
- On distributed environments or web data, users do not generally know the exact navigational paths of documents. Also every site may have different structures. But our approach allows users to query on these many sites without knowledge about XML schema like search engines if users know data names and their values. Furthermore, even on local systems, our work can be applied to the case that imports documents created by many people without a common schema.
- Existing HTML web search engines support keyword-based searches because the past web data were expressed using HTML. However, data is increasingly represented as XML because of its various good points. Our research result can be applied to XML web search engines because XML uses tags to represent data. That is, our research can improve the accuracy of XML web search engine by using tag names, element names, besides values in query expressions.

2 Related Work

Up to now, many XML query languages [1-4] were developed. As a commercial product, Oracle XML DB query in an extended SQL because it deals with XML data and relational databases in a tightly coupled method. DB2 XML Extender uses 'contains' operator for information retrieval systems. Also, SQL 2000 server supports XPath-based query expressions and accesses SQL servers through URL. Navigational query languages mainly support XPath [4] and use regular path expressions to relax somewhat query expressions.

Query expressions of current XML query languages are very complex or difficult because of irregular properties of XML. Therefore, there were researches on keyword-based searches to overcome this difficulty [6-9]. These researches used a structure concept to search text data by connecting keyword searches with a structure. But it is difficult that keyword-based searches get exact results because keyword-based query expressions express only data values even though the techniques consider document structures.

3 A Query Expression for an XML Search Engine

Example 3.1. For example, suppose that users want to try the query Q1. If the users would like to query regardless of document structures, the users express the search conditions in a condition clause and a return condition in a result clause of as follows.

Condition:	publisher = "Morgan Kaufmann" and year = "1999" and author = "Serge Abiteboul"
Result:	title

---- CQ1

The non-navigational content-based query expression for an XML search engine can be formally defined as follows.

> *Expression*   ::= *Predicate ("and" | "or")Predicate*
> *Predicate*   ::= *DataName "=" DataValue*
> *DataValue*   ::= *string*

where DataName is either an element name or an attribute name. The DataName-DataValue pairs of the search condition can have various paths on documents. Therefore, to process the search condition, first of all, we have to know all possible paths of the condition clause. For simplicity, we do not distinguish attributes from elements.

First, all possible paths among the DataName-DataValue pairs can have a non-nested or nested relationship on documents. That is, in CQ1, *publisher, year,* and *author* have a non-nested relationship like Fig. 1(a)-(d) or a nested relationship like Fig 1(e) and (f). Second, there may be intervening elements and/or an attribute between an element name and its corresponding value. An XML document of the same content as that represented in Fig. 1(a) may easily be represented as in Fig. 1(c) and (d). Here, *yyyy* intervenes between *year* and "1999", *name* intervenes between *publisher* and "Morgan Kauffmann", and *name* intervenes between *author* and "Serge Abiteboul". In general, there may be an arbitrary number of element or attribute names between the element name and its corresponding value that match the search predicate in a query. Furthermore, there may be the other intervening elements between elements like *book* between *publisher* and *author* of Fig. 1(e) and (f). If we analyze all possible paths against the search condition of non-navigational content-based queries, they can be classified like Table 1. Here, the location of intervening data means whether the intervening element/attribute is located in ancestor or descendant of data of the condition clause. A query processor has to search all the analyzed paths to process the non-navigational content-based queries. We will show the processing steps in section 4.

Table 1. All possible paths among the data of a condition clause

(a) all paths using only data of the condition clause

Relationship among data	Paths
Non-nested	Path X
Nested	Path N

(b) all paths intervening arbitrary data

Relationship among data	Location of intervening data	Paths
Non-nested	ancestor	Path *a*-X
	descendant	Path *d*-X
Nested	ancestor	Path *a*-N
	descendant	Path *d*-N

4 A Query Processing Technique for an XML Search Engine

The processing of a content-based query expression consists of three steps.

Step (a): Evaluate each predicate (i.e., search condition) to find a matching (DataName, DataValue) pair in an XML document.

Step (b): Do the Boolean processing of all search conditions to find only those XML documents that satisfy all search conditions.

Step (c): For each matching document, process the result clause processing to return appropriate parts of the document.

Since the users not use the document structure while querying, the results may not be always be correct. But, in this paper, we will not report some solutions for the problem.

We propose region-numbering scheme [11] to process non-navigational content-based queries. The node identifiers of the numbering scheme represent a hierarchical relationship between nodes. We can search all possible paths for non-navigational content-based queries if we make use of this relationship. Also, if two nodes have a non-nested relationship, then the query processor has to compute nearest common ancestor (NCA) [10]. The reason is to prevent the tree traversal of a single subtree from "over-flowing" into another subtree by designating a special level during computing NCA. For example, suppose the root of an XML tree is named *books*, and its child node is named *book* like Fig. 2. Then the query evaluation involving *books* should be confined to within each *book* document instance, and, for example, the search predicate on *author* in one *book* document should not be combined with the search predicate on *year* in another *book* document. For this, we ignore the outside data of special regions by designating a base level.

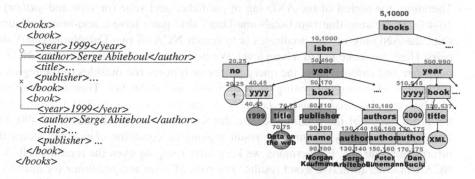

Fig. 2. Base level for NCA   **Fig. 3.** Tree representation for a document

4.1 Query Processing Algorithm

To search the results that satisfy all possible paths, our query processor processes three steps like Algorithm 1. Suppose we want to query CQ1 against Fig. 3.

First, like Fig. 4, our query processor searches the regions of "Morgan Kaufmann", "1999", and "Serge Abiteboul". It also searches the regions of *publisher, year*, and *author*. And then, select the regions of *publisher* (80-110), *year* (30-490), and *author* (130-140) including the regions of the values. Here, *publisher* and its value (or *year* and its value) become Path *d-X* and Path *d-N*.

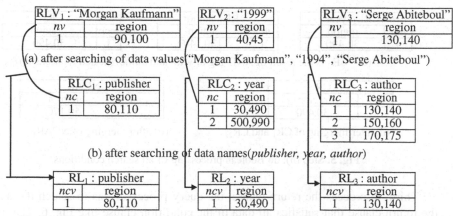

Fig. 4. Step (a): process each search condition separately

Second, the query processor has to do the AND-ing of *publisher* and *year, year* and *author,* and *publisher* and *author* like Fig. 5.

In the case that two DataName-DataValue pairs have a nested relationship, the AND-ing of two predicates is to select the one DataName including the region of another DataName by comparing the region of two DataName-DataValue pairs. Therefore, the region of the AND-ing of *publisher* and *year* (or *year* and *author*) is 30-490. In the case that two DataName-DataValue pairs have a non-nested relationship, the AND-ing of two predicates is to search NCA of two DataName-DataValue pairs. Here, we make use of a base level. We designate the base level as 4 for NCA of *publisher* and *author.* Then, the query processor ignores the outsides of the region of the base level during computing NCA of *author* and *publisher.* Therefore, the result of AND-ing of *publisher* and *author* is NCA and its region is 50-170. Consequently, the result region of the condition clause that satisfies three predicates is 30-490. The query processor does merging the result regions of condition clause and stores the information into CR. Furthermore, we keep after merging even the region of NCA in NCAR in order to derive exact results. The path of *year* and *publisher* (or *author*) is Path *a*-N and the path of *publisher* and *author* are Path X. In the case of Path N or Path *a*-N, the query processor considers a bidirectional relationship between two node name-value pairs.

RL$_1$: publisher		RL$_2$: year		CR$_1$	
ncv	region	ncv	region	ncr	region
1	80,110	1	30,490	1	30,490

(a)   CR$_1$ is the result of AND-ing of *publisher* and *year*(nested relationship)

RL$_1$: publisher		RL$_3$: author		NCAR$_1$	
ncv	region	ncv	region	ncr	region
1	80,110	1	130,140	1	50,170

(b) NCAR$_1$ is the result of AND-ing of *publisher* and *author* (non-nested relationship)

RL$_2$: year		RL$_3$: author		CR$_2$	
ncv	region	ncv	region	ncr	region
1	30,490	1	130,140	1	30,490

(c)   CR$_2$ is the result of AND-ing of *year* and *author*(nested relationship)

CR		NCAR	
ncr	region	nn	region
1	30,490	1	50,170

(d) after merging of CR$_1$ and CR$_2$ (e) after merging of NCAR$_1$

Fig. 5. Step (b): do Boolean processing of all search conditions

Third, to process the return clause, the query processor has to search the data of the return clause that satisfies all data of the condition clause like Fig. 6. The region of *title* that satisfies both the result region of condition clause (30-490) and the region of NCA (50-170) is 70-75. In the case that the region of *title* is 530-537, the query processor ignores this result because it does not satisfy both NCAR and CR. There-fore, the result of CQ1 is <title>Data on the web</title>.

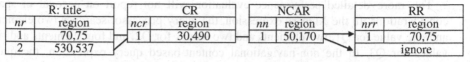

R: title-		CR		NCAR		RR	
nr	region	*ncr*	region	*nn*	region	*nrr*	region
1	70,75	1	30,490	1	50,170	1	70,75
2	530,537						ignore

(a) RR is the result comparing R with CR and NCA

Fig. 6. Step (c): do the result clause processing

Algorithm 1. Query Processing Algorithm

Input: *n* element/attribute names (C_1, C_2,..., C_n) and their values (V_1, V_2,..., V_n)

// step (a): process each search condition separately

While (V_i) {
  Search regions of V_i, store the regions into RLV_i, and count the number of the regions (*nv*)
}

While (C_i) {
  Search regions of C_i, store the regions RLC_i, and count the number of the regions (*nc*)
}

For (*i*=1; *i* < *nv*; *i*++)
  For (*j*=1; *j* < *nc*; *j*++)
    If (RLC_i includes RLV_i) {
    Store the regions into RL_i
    Count the number of the regions (*ncv*)
    }

// step (b): do Boolean processing of all search conditions

For (*i*=1; *i* < *ncv*-1; *i*++)
  For (*j*=*i*+1; *j* < *ncv*; *j*++)
    If (RL_i and RL_j have a nested relationship)
    Store the upper region of RL_i and RL_j into CR_i.
    Else
      Compute NCA of RL_i and RL_j and store the regions of NCA into $NCAR_i$

// step (c): do the result clause processing

Search regions of R and count the number of the regions (*nr*)

If (R satisfies CR and NCAR)
  Store the R into RR
Else
  Ignore the R
Return the information of RR

---

5   Experimental Results

To compare non-navigational content-based queries with path-based navigational queries, we test on Xhive-6.0 known as a native XML-server [12] with 'book' data providing in X-Hive Corporation. We select XQuery as a path-based query language. The system is providing 19 files of small size with slightly different document struc-tures. We have extended the total data size by 10.9 MB. Query statements for testing are as Table 2. Q1 has one predicate and Q2 and Q3 has two predicate. We test both XQuery and content-based queries on our processor. And we perform XQuery statements on X-Hive server to compare with our processor.

The more detailed performance evaluation will not report on account of space considerations. In the XQuery expression, the query processor searches two elements and one value for Q1, two elements and two values for Q2, and four elements and two values for Q3. In the non-navigational content-based query expression, the query processor searches one element and one value for Q1 and two elements and two values for Q2 and Q3. Our query processor generally has an effect on the time searching data and the size of results. The query processor does not traverse the path because users do not express a path in the condition clause. However, the query processor traverses the entire path because XQuery represent a complex path in the condition clause. Therefore content-based query time is the faster than it of XQuery expression. They take ordering of Q1, Q2, and Q3. We can also recognize that our query processing time for both content-based queries and XQuery is faster than it on X-Hive server.

Table 2. Example queries for comparing with X-Hive server

Queries	XQuery	Content-based queries
Q1	for $c in doc ("UN Charter")//chapter where $c/@number = "5" return $c/title/text()	Condition: chapter="5" Result: title
Q2	for $c in doc ("UN Charter")//chapter where $c/@number = "5" or $c/@number = "10" return $c/title/text()	Condition: chapter="5" or chapter="10" Result: title
Q3	for $c in doc ("UN Charter")//chapter where $c//article/@number = "9" and $c//section/title = "COMPOSITION" return $c/title/text()	Condition: article="9" and section="composition" Result: title

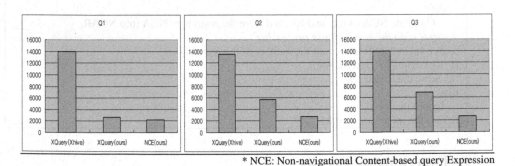

* NCE: Non-navigational Content-based query Expression

Fig. 7. Performance evaluation on X-Hive and our query processor

The performance of the both non-navigational content-based queries and path-based navigational expressions are open to discussion. We believe that we can improve query speed by optimization such as an indexing technique, reduction in the number of searches and comparisons, and so on.

6 Conclusions and Future Work

XML data model can create many various document types because it allows users to create an irregular structure of documents. It is a reason requiring more knowledge about document structures to query. In this paper, for more easy queries, we developed a technique for schema independent queries. For this work, we designed a query expression called content-based queries for an XML search engine. Also, in order to process the query expression, we classified all possible paths among data and developed an algorithm capable of searching these paths. In the future, we will measure time updating documents and optimize non-navigational content-based query processing time.

Acknowledgement. We would like to thank Dr. Won Kim for his comments on this paper.

References

[1] S. Adler, A. Berglund, J. Caruso, S. Deach, T. Graham, P. Grosso, E. Gutentag, A. Milowski, S. Parnell, J. Richman, and S. Zilles, Extensible Stylesheet Language (XSL) Version 1.0, W3C Proposed Recommendation Aug. 2001

[2] S. Abiteboul, D. Quass, J. McHugh, J. Widom, and J. L. Wiener, The Lorel query language for semistructured data, International Journal on Digital Libraries, Apr. 1997

[3] S. Boag, D. Chamberlin, M. F. Fernandez, D. Florescu, J. Robie, J. Siméon, XQuery 1.0: An XML Query Language, W3C Working Draft 16 Aug. 2002

[4] W3C Consortium, XML Path Language (XPath) Version 1.0, W3C Recommendation 16 Nov. 1999

[5] W. Kim, W. Lee, and H. Yong, On Supporting Structure-Agnostic queries for XML, in *Journal of Object Technology*, vol. 3, no. 7, July-August 2004, pp. 27-35.

[6] L. Guo, F. Shao, C. Botev, J. Shanmugasundaram, XRANK: Ranked keyword search over XML documents, Proc. of the ACM SIGMOD Int. Conf. on Management of Data, 2003

[7] S. Cohen, J. Mamou, Y. Kanza, and Y. Sagiv, XSEarch: A semantic search engine for XML, Proc. of the VLDB Conf., 2003

[8] D. Carmel, Y. S. Maarek, M. Mandelbrod, Y. Mass, and A. Soffer, Searching XML documents via XML fragments, Proc. of the 26th Int. ACM SIGIR Conf., 2003

[9] V. Hristidis, Y Papakonstantinou, and A. Balmin, Keyword proximity search on XML graph, Proc. of Int. Conf. on Data Engineering, 2003

[10] Dov Harel and Robert Endre Tarjan, Fast algorithms for finding nearest common ancestors, SIAM Journal on Computing, v.13 n.2, p.338-355, May 1984

[11] M. P. Consens and T. Milo, Algebra for querying text regions: expressive power and optimization, Journal of computer and system sciences, 1998.

[12] X-Hive Corporation, X-Hive/DB 6.0, X-Hive Corporation, 2001, available at http://www.x-hive.com/

Adapting the Object Role Modelling Method for Ontology Modelling

Peter Spyns

Vrije Universiteit Brussel – STAR Lab,
Pleinlaan 2, Gebouw G-10, B-1050 Brussel, Belgium
{Peter.Spyns}@vub.ac.be
http://www.starlab.vub.ac.be

Abstract. A recent evolution in the areas of artificial intelligence, database semantics and information systems is the advent of the Semantic Web that requires that software agents and web services exchange meaningful and unambiguous messages. A prerequisite for this kind of interoperability is the usage of
an ontology. Currently, not many step-wise ontology engineering methodologies exist. This paper describes an outline of such a methodology based on
ORM, a DB conceptual modelling method. The new methodology is to be situated in the ontology engineering framework of DOGMA, developed at VUB
STAR Lab. One of the distinctive characteristics is that language related issues
are taken into account from the on-set.

1 Introduction

A recent evolution in the areas of artificial intelligence, database semantics and information systems is the advent of the Semantic Web. Exchange of meaningful messages is only possible when the intelligent devices or agents share a common conceptual system representing their "world", as is the case for human communication.
Nowadays, a formal representation of such (partial) intensional definition of a conceptualisation of an application domain is called an ontology [4]. The latter is understood as a vocabulary with semantically precise and formally defined terms that stand
for concepts and their inter-relationships in an application domain. There are only a
few ontology-modelling methodologies available that describe in detail the different
steps. Few of these takes into account the fundamental difference between a term on
the language level and a concept label on the meaning level. Therefore, VUB STAR
Lab has defined a novel stepwise ontology-modelling methodology that is based on
an existing conceptual schema modelling methodology [13] called Object Role Modelling (ORM [5, 6]).

The paper is organised as follows. The following Section (2) shortly explains what
the VUB STAR Lab DOGMA framework is about, and introduces the Object Role
Modelling methodology. Subsequently, Section 3 details the novel DOGMA ontology-modelling methodology by listing the various steps. Section 4 contains the discussion, Section 5 the related work while Section 6 ends the paper by outlining the future work and by giving some concluding remarks. Unfortunately, due to the space

M.-S. Hacid et al. (Eds.): ISMIS 2005, LNAI 3488, pp. 276–284, 2005.
© Springer-Verlag Berlin Heidelberg 2005

restrictions, many aspects cannot be discussed in depth. We have strived to provide a bird's eye view on the methodology.

2 Background

DOGMA: Developing Ontology Guided Mediation for Agents

VUB STAR Lab has its own ontology engineering framework called "Developing Ontology Guided Mediation for Agents" aka DOGMA. A DOGMA-inspired ontology is defined in a logic sense, i.e. as a "representationless" mathematical object that forms the range of a classical interpretation mapping from a first order language (assumed to lexically represent an application), to a set of possible ("plausible") conceptualisations of the real world domain. A double articulation of a DOGMA ontology [17] has been introduced by decomposing it formally into an *ontology base* and into instances of their explicit ontological commitments (see Figure 1). The latter become reified in our architecture as a separate mediating layer called the *commitment layer* [9].

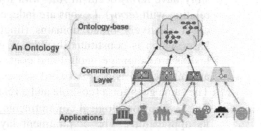

Fig. 1. The double articulation of a DOGMA ontology (reproduced from [9])

This very much resembles classical database modelling theory and practice. From his experience with database design methodology, Meersman identifies a number of issues that have serious methodological implications for ontology development [11]:

1. There is no such thing as *absolute meaning* or *semantics*. Meaning can only result from agreements reached between ontology engineers, domain experts and users.
2. Meaning facilitates communication about a universe of discourse and is represented independent of natural language, but necessarily must be rooted and described in natural language.
3. In a particular natural language, it is hard to reach agreement on terms with which to refer to concepts correctly and unambiguously.
4. Domain constraints, rules and procedures are necessary to achieve an understanding about a domain of interest's semantics, but reaching agreement on them is notoriously difficult.

The DOGMA framework has been refined to explicitly add the distinction between the language and conceptual levels[1] by formalising the context and introducing language identifiers.

---

[1] The UMLS Metathesaurus additionally distinguishes a third level called "strings" as it includes specific terminological combinations abounding in medical classifications (e.g., 'heart disease, not elsewhere classified') and expressions typical of the telegraphic style in (dictated) medical reporting (e.g., 'blood pressure, abnormal') [10]. We haven't yet studied our corpora thoroughly for these kinds of constructs, but at first sight they seem to be rare.

- An <u>ontology base</u> consists of intuitively plausible conceptualisations of a real world domain, i.e. specific binary[2] fact types, called *meta-lexons*, formally noted as a triple <concept$_1$ – relationship – concept$_2$>. They are abstracted (see below) from *lexons*, written as sextuples <(γ,λ): term$_1$, role, co-role, term$_2$> [3]. Informally we say that a *lexon* is a fact that may hold for some domain, expressing that within the context γ and for the natural language λ the *term$_1$* may plausibly have *term$_2$* occur in *role* with it (and inversely *term$_2$* maintains a *co-role* relation with *term$_1$*). Lexons are independent of specific applications and should cover relatively broad domains (linguistic level). Lexons constitute a lexon base, which is constituted by lexons grouped by context and language. Meta-lexons are language-neutral and context-independent (conceptual level). Terms are mapped to concepts (word senses) via the context-language combination. The same goes for a (co-)role and a relationship.
- The <u>layer of ontological commitments</u> mediates between the ontology base and its applications. The commitment layer is organised as a set of ontological commitments, each being an explicit instance of an (intensional) first-order interpretation of a task in terms of the ontology base [9]. Each commitment is a consistent set of rules (or axioms) in a given syntax that adds specific semantics to a selection of meta-lexons of the ontology base.

The ontology base is meant to reach a common and agreed understanding about the ontology terminology and hence is aimed at human understanding. Natural language terms are associated, via the language and context combination, to a unique word sense represented by a concept label (e.g. the WordNet [1] identifier *person#2*). With each word sense, a gloss or explanatory information is associated that describes that notion. Notice that there is a m:n relationship between natural language terms and word senses (to account for synonymy, homonymy and translation equivalents). Going from the language level to the concept level corresponds with converting the lexons into meta-lexons (see below).

The commitment layer, with its formal constraints, is meant for interoperability issues between information systems, software agents and web services, as is currently promoted in the Semantic Web area. These kinds of constraints are mathematically founded and concern rather typical DB schema constraints (cardinality, optionality etc. – see below). The choice for certain constructs/constraints rather than others has been mainly inspired by the tradition of ORM DB modelling, its application inside the DOGMA theoretical framework, and some practical experiences. As the ORM formalisme can be almost completely (except for the external uniqueness constraint – see below) transformed into *SHIQ* Description Logic [8], it is, in principle, possible to convert the commitments into OWL DL and vice versa.

---

[2] On the ontology level (opposed to conceptual database models), we believe that the elementariness of the pieces of a conceptualisation facilitates agreement and reusability [13: p.63]. Note that also RDF statements represent binary facts.

[3] The notions of 'role' and 'co-role' are ORM constructs that indicate the logical predicate (or relationship type that holds between two object types) and its inverse. A role (and co-role) is "a sentence with one or more "object holes" in it – each hole is filled by a term or noun phrase that identifies an object" [5:p.3].

The Object Role Modelling Methodology

The ORM conceptual modelling methodology has been selected because of its strong foundation in natural language, which it inherited from its predecessor called "a Natural Information Analysis Method" (NIAM) [19]. The latter distinguishes between a lexical (label) and non-lexical (thing) objects, and supported subclassing and an extensive set of declarable integrity constraint types [12]. The natural language aspects of NIAM mainly concerned methodological support for the negotiation and agreement process to specify information requirements as conceptual semantic networks, or verbalisations of them, that were readable by non-computer experts and yet could be readily transformed into database designs [11]. Especially this latter feature presents an important advantage as many domain experts have no knowledge engineering or modelling skills. We maintain the ORM graphical notation for the constraints (not shown here) [4].

3   The DOGMA Ontology-Modelling Methodology (DOM^2)

Based on the reasoning made above, we propose to have the ontology engineering process done in two major steps: (i) a linguistic stage (steps 1 & 2) and (ii) a conceptual stage (steps 4 & 9). It must be pointed out that DOM^2 still lacks aspects of distributed collaborative modelling. We hope that we can draw upon existing practices from the terminology community to refine the method. For the sake of easiness, the EON2002 travel domain text [16] will be taken as example.

DOM^2 Step 1: Verbalise Information Examples as Elementary Facts

In many cases, we shall start from scratch with a specific application at hand. As, by definition, ontologies should be shared, care should be taken not to limit the domain world to the one of the application. On the other hand, one must beware of modelling the "entire world". By preference, the data sources collected for the domain ontology should already have an agreed and common character (e.g., standard text, reference classification, ...). If these sources do not exist, domain specialists and other stakeholders have to agree whether or not to include specific entity types.

The first step is to begin with familiar examples of relevant information, and express these as elementary facts. Suppose that there exists a textual description of the domain. The complexity of the text must be reduced to simple sentences expressing elementary facts. An elementary fact is a simple assertion, or atomic proposition, about the universe of discourse. They state that particular objects play particular roles. As mentioned by Halpin [6:p.61], an elementary fact cannot be split into smaller units of information. As long as a sentence contains words like 'and', 'or', 'if', 'not', 'all' or 'some', it does not express an elementary fact. E.g.: "a travel agency works for customers" or "an airport is close to a city".

---

[4] We refer the interested reader to [6] and [19] for more details.

DOM² Step 2: Create Lexons (per Context and Language)

It is the hope and expectation that NLP techniques will be able to deliver lexons after text processing, just as reverse database engineering techniques could do for existing databases and conceptual models. A critical reader will remark that the knowledge acquisition bottleneck is now moved to the next step (see the following Section). However, an important reduction of the cognitive load for a human (entire text → set of lexons) has taken place. E.g., a text of 43K words (on VAT regulation) has been reduced to a set of 817 lexons [14]. In the absence of automated techniques, it is better to choose existing natural language words (or combinations) for terms and roles of a lexon. Many modelling approaches express roles or relationships by verbs. At this stage, domain experts are organising their world in an intuitive and informal way. Nevertheless, the less ambiguity exists about the intuitive meaning of words used for the terms and roles, the better. E.g., by choosing carefully a role name, a modeller can indicate that the role might have a transitive nature. Also, for each modeling task, a context γ and language identifier λ must be provided.

E.g., <(travel_domain,English.UK): lodging, is_included_in, includes, trip >

DOM² Step 3: Create Meta-lexons

Meta-lexons are created by "replacing" the language terms or words (i.e. the terms and roles for a specific language and context) of the lexons by labels identifying concepts and conceptual relationships. Their definitions might already be available (e.g. word sense descriptions in WordNet [1], technical term and definition collections) and thus commonly agreed upon and/or generally accepted. Others have to be construed on the spot as WordNet mostly covers non-technical vocabulary. We recommend doing it in the same format and style as WordNet, thereby also creating (multilingual) synsets. Terminologists, ontology engineers and domain experts have to work together to achieve this. As concepts and relationships stand for a unique notion or sense, the context and language identifiers become superfluous.

E.g., in English as used in the U.K. and for the travel domain context, the noun 'trip' is associated with the meaning as defined in WordNet and labeled by "trip#1(n)" [5].

– *trip*: **trip#1(n)**: (a journey for some purpose (usually including the return); "he took a trip to the shopping center") [sense 1 of 7 for the noun].

DOM² Step 4: Specify Uniqueness Constraints

There are two types of uniqueness constraints that need to be specified:

1. *Internal uniqueness constraints:* this indicates that in a particular instance of a binary fact type, there can be only one instance of the concept involved in the relationship. For instance, if we consider the meta-lexon <x, has, y>, then an internal

---

[5] In the following examples, we use simple words instead of the WordNet labels or numerical identifiers for simplicity – even if meaning ambiguity or semantic fuzziness can occur.

uniqueness constraint on the role *has*, is verbalised as "<u>each</u> *x has* <u>at most one</u> *y*". E.g., <u>each</u> *airport is_located_in* <u>at most one</u> *city*.

2. *External uniqueness constraints:* this specifies that in each instantiation of a combination (or "join") of two or more meta-lexons, there can only be one instance of the concept with the constrained roles involved. Consider the meta-lexons <*x, has, y*> and <*x, has, z*>. If there is an external uniqueness constraint imposed on the role *has* in both meta-lexons, this may be verbalised as "each *y* and *z* combination *has* at most one *x*". E.g., <u>each</u> *type* <u>and</u> *name* <u>combination</u> *identify* <u>at most one</u> plane [6].

DOM² Step 5: Specify Mandatory Constraints

The specification of mandatory constraints involves the specification of the following:

1. *Simple mandatory constraints:* a simple mandatory constraint indicates that every instance of a concept must necessarily participate in the relationship on which the constraint is defined. Returning to the meta-lexon <*x, has, y*> a simple mandatory constraint defined on the role *has* is verbalised as "<u>every</u> *x has* <u>at least one</u> *y*". E.g., <u>each</u> *trip is_done_with* <u>at least one</u> *means_of_transport*.

2. *Disjunctive mandatory constraints:* a disjunctive mandatory constraint defined on a concept occuring in one or more meta-lexons implies that the concept must necessarily be involved in at least one (but possibly more) of the relationships specified. Consider the meta-lexons <*x, has, y*> and <*x, has, z*> and suppose that a disjunctive mandatory constraint has been defined on *x*. Verbalising this yields "*x has* <u>either</u> *y* <u>or</u> *z* <u>(or both)</u>". E.g., a *means_of_transport subsumes city_transport* <u>and/or</u> *travel_transport*.

DOM² Step 6: Specify Subset, Equality, Exclusion and Subtype Constraints

As the title of this Section suggests, this activity involves specifying the following:

1. *Value constraints:* value constraints indicate which values an instance of a concept may assume. In this sense, it could also be called an object type constraint. An enumeration of the days of the week is one example of a value constraint. It is debatable whether value constraints should belong to an ontology as instances, in principle, are not part of an ontology, at least in our understanding (intensional vs. extensional).

2. *Subsets:* this constraint specifies that the existence of one meta-lexon implies the existence of another. That is, if an instance of the "implying" meta-lexon exists, then an instance of the "implied" meta-lexon also necessarily exists. For instance, if the meta-lexon <*x, has, y*> has a subset constraint on the meta-lexon <*x, has, z*>, this may be verbalised as "<u>if</u> *x has y*, <u>then</u> *x has z*". E.g., "<u>if</u> a *name identifies* a *company*, <u>then</u> that *name identifies* an *plane*.

3. *Equality:* the equality constraint indicates that two instance populations are equal. E.g., "<u>if</u> a *country locates* a *city*, <u>then</u> that *country is_located_in* a *continent* <u>as well</u>."

---

[6] The (meta-)lexons are no longer natural language sentences, so they don't have to follow the grammar rules of English or any other natural language.

4. *Exclusion:* this specifies that if a concept occurs in more than one meta-lexon, it cannot be involved in more than one of the roles. Suppose that the meta-lexons <*x, has, y*> and <*x, has, z*> have an exclusion constraint defined on the role *has*. This is verbalised as "no *x has* both *y* and *z*". E.g., "A *flight* stops_in or starts_in an *airport*."

5. *Subtypes:* subtyping specifies that one concept type is a subtype of another (similar to object-oriented design). E.g., each *travel_transportation* must be a *ship*, or a *car*, or a *plane*, or a *train*, or a *ferry*, or a *motorbike*." In many case, subtyping is combined with disjunctive mandatoriness.

DOM² Step 7: Specify Occurrence Frequency

Before conducting final checks, another specification needs to be made:

Occurrence frequency: an occurrence frequency constraint is a generalised version of an internal uniqueness constraint, namely when $n > 1$. That is, an occurrence frequency constraint specifies that n instances of a particular concept must be involved in a particular relationship. It is possible to specify the cardinality as *exactly n, greater than or equal to n, or greater than n. E.g., "a chain consist_of at least two hotel."*

DOM² Step 8: Final Checks

Final checks imply checking for consistency in the commitments that have been specified. This includes ensuring that different constraints do not contradict one another. Currently, no tools have been implemented to support automatic checking.

4 Discussion

Of course, there remain a large number of open questions or areas for further refinement and research. Due to space restrictions, we only mention one pending issue. It concerns the transformation of a lexon role and co-role into a meta-lexon relationship. Do the role and co-role have to be merged into one conceptual relationship? Or do we keep two relationships and formally consider them as separate ones? Currently, we choose to combine the two relationships (represented by a combination of the two labels) in a single meta-lexon. The meta-lexon will be transformed to two separate RDF triples, if needed. In a later stage, the conversion of the DOGMA commitments into Description Logic formulas is foreseen so that automated consistency checking [8] becomes possible. Implementing business logics (reasoning or inferencing) would also benefit from this.

5 Related Work

Currently there hardly exist, at least to our knowledge, comprehensive cookbooks or methodologies (based on a formal and scientific framework) that covers how to actually create from scratch and deploy a *multilingual* ontology-based application. One example are the ONIONS and ONIONS-II [3] methodologies that have been successfully applied to several domains (bio-medical, legal, fishery). Other existing ontology engineering methods build on the CommonKADS [15] knowledge engineering methodology and/or are based on questionnaires for typical expert knowledge elicitation [7]. Others, e.g., Methontology [2], try to encompass the entire knowledge life cycle, but do not provide detailed but generic guidelines (cook book style) on how to construct a domain ontology. Another difference is that the methodologies mentioned origin from a knowledge engineering and AI background, while the methodology proposed in this paper clearly goes back to a widely adapted database modelling methodology ORM, itself being a descendant from NIAM having a strong emphasis on natural language. As DB conceptual modelling methods are quite widespread, we estimate that using a related ontology-modelling methodology will smoothen the process for DB modellers to get acquainted with ontologies.

6 Future Work and Conclusion

This paper provides an overview of the DOM^2 that focuses specifically on how to model an application domain ontology. Another, more encompassing ontology engineering life cycle, methodology called AKEM is also under development at VUB STAR Lab. It is currently being applied to model financial fraud [20]. As both are complementary, the next aim is to integrate both methodologies into one overall ontology engineering lifecycle methodology with the consideration of the context of actual applications. As such, it would offer an DB-inspired alternative to existing methods like Methontology. In addition, the new ontology engineering methodology would also reserve the correct place for linguistic related issues from the on-set. In order to consolidate and refine the new methodology, many real life modelling exercises should be undertaken in the future. A first one was to apply the methodology to innovation management [18]. In particular, the methodology still needs to be adapted for a collaborative modelling scenario to guarantee the consensuality of an ontology.

Acknowledgment

This research has been financed by the Flemish IWT GBOU 2001 #010069 "Onto-Basis" project. In addition, we particularly like to thank Hannes Pretorius (currently at the T.U Eindhoven, dept. of Mathematics and Computer Science – Visualisation Group) for his summary of the commitment modelling steps.

References

[1] Fellbaum C. (ed.), (1998), Wordnet, An Electronic Lexical Database, Cambridge, MIT Press
[2] Fernández M., Gómez-Pérez A., & Juristo N., (1996), Methontology: From Ontological Art Towards Ontological Engineering, In ECAI Workshop on Ontological Engineering, p. 41-51
[3] Gangemi A., Guarino N., Masolo C., Oltramari A., & Schneider L., (2003), Sweetening Ontologies with DOLCE. Proceedings of EKAW 2002. Siguenza, Spain.

[4] Guarino N., (1998), Formal Ontologies and Information Systems, in Guarino N. (ed), Proc. of FOIS98, IOS Press, pp.3-15

[5] Halpin T., (1998), Object-Role Modeling: an overview, [white paper], htpp://www.orm.org

[6] Halpin T., (2001), Information Modeling and Relational Databases: from conceptual analysis to logical design, Morgan-Kaufmann, San Francisco.

[7] Hameed A., Sleeman D. & Preece A., (2002), OntoManager: A workbench Environment to facilitate Ontology Management and Interoperability, In, Sure Y. & Angele J. (eds.), (2002), Proceedings of the OntoWeb-SIG3 Workshop at the 13th International Conference on Knowledge Engineering and Knowledge Management EKAW 2002.

[8] Hoorne K., (2003), Checking consistency of Ontological Commitments by Employing an Inference Engine, unpublished MSc thesis, Vrije Universiteit Brussel, Belgium

[9] Jarrar M. & Meersman R., (2002), Formal Ontology Engineering in the DOGMA Approach, in Meersman R., Tari Z. et al., (eds.), On the Move to Meaningful Internet Systems 2002: CoopIS, DOA, and ODBASE; Confederated International Conferences CoopIS, DOA, and ODBASE 2002 Proceedings, LNCS 2519, Springer Verlag, pp. 1238 – 1254

[10] McCray A., Bodenreider O., & Burgun A., (2001), Evaluting UMLS Strings for Natural Language Processing, in Proceedings of the AMIA Annual Symposium, pp. 448 – 452

[11] Meersman R., (2001), Ontologies and Databases: More than a Fleeting Resemblance, In, d'Atri A. and Missikoff M. (eds), OES/SEO 2001 Rome Workshop, Luiss Publications.

[12] Meersman R., (2001), Reusing certain database design principles, methods and techniques for ontology theory, construction and methodology, Technical Report 01, Brussel

[13] Meersman R., (2002), Semantic Web and Ontologies: Playtime or Business at the Last Frontier in Computing ?, In, NSF-EU Workshop on Database and Information Systems Research for Semantic Web and Enterprises, pp .61 – 67.

[14] Reinberger M.-L., Spyns P., A.J. Pretorius & Daelemans W., Automatic initiation of an ontology, in Meersman R. Tari Z. et al. (eds.), Proceedings of the OTM 2004 Conferences (part I), LNCS 3290, Springer Verlag, pp. 600 – 617

[15] Schreiber A., Akkermans J., Anjewierden A., De Hoog R., Shadbolt N., Van De Velde W., & Wielinga B., (2000), Knowledge Engineering and Management: The CommonKADS Methodology, MIT Press.

[16] Sure Y., & Angele J., (eds.), (2002), Proc. of the First International Workshop on Evaluation of Ontology based Tools (EON 20002), vol. 62 of CEUR Workshop Proceedings (http://CEUR-WS.org/Vol-62/)

[17] Spyns P., Meersman R. & Jarrar M., (2002), Data modelling versus Ontology engineering, In, Sheth A. & Meersman R. (eds.), SIGMOD Record Special Issue 31 (4): 12 – 17.

[18] Spyns P., Van Acker S., Wynants M., Jarrar M. & Lisovoy A., (2004), Using a novel ORM-based ontology modelling method to build an experimental Innovation Router, in Motta E., Shadboldt N., Stutt A. & Gibbins N. (eds.), Proc. of EKAW2004, LNAI Springer, pp. 82-98

[19] Verheyen G. & van Bekkum P., (1982), NIAM, aN Information Analysis Method". In, Olle T., Sol H. & Verrijn-Stuart A., (eds), IFIP Conference on Comparative Review of Information Systems Methodologies, Noord-Holland.

[20] Zhao G, Kingston J., Kerremans K., Coppens F., Verlinden R., Temmerman R. & Meersman R., (2004). Engineering an Ontology of Financial Securities Fraud, in Meersman R., Tari Z., Corrado A. et al. (eds.), Proceedings of the OTM 2004 Workshops, LNCS 3292, Springer Verlag, pp. 605 – 620

Identifying Content Blocks
from Web Documents

Sandip Debnath[1], Prasenjit Mitra[1,2], and C. Lee Giles[1,2]

[1] Department of Computer Science and Engineering,
[2] School of Information Sciences and Technology,
Penn State University, University Park, PA 16802, USA
debnath@cse.psu.edu, {pmitra, giles}@ist.psu.edu

Abstract. Intelligent information processing systems, such as digital libraries or search engines index web-pages according to their informative content. However, web-pages contain several non-informative contents, e.g., navigation sidebars, advertisements, copyright notices, etc. It is very important to separate the informative "primary content blocks" from these non-informative blocks. In this paper, two algorithms, *FeatureExtractor* and *K-FeatureExtractor* are proposed to identify the "primary content blocks" based on their features. None of these algorithms require any supervised learning, but still can identify the "primary content blocks" with high precision and recall. While operating on several thousand web-pages obtained from 15 different websites, our algorithms significantly outperform the Entropy-based algorithm proposed by Lin and Ho [14] in both precision and run-time.

Keywords: Electronic Publishing, Data Mining, Information Systems Applications.

1 Introduction

An end-user is mainly interested in the *primary informative content* of these web-pages. However, a substantial part of web-pages is not very informative in nature. So these parts or blocks (defined later) are seldom sought by the users. We refer to such blocks as *non-content blocks* which includes advertisement blocks, image-maps, plug-ins, logos, counters, search boxes, category information, navigational links, related links, footers and headers, and copyright information among others. In this paper, we address the problem of identifying the primary informative content of a web-page. An added advantage of this is that after identifying all the blocks, we can delete the non-content blocks. This contraction is useful in situations where large parts of the web are crawled, indexed and stored. Since the non-content blocks are often a significant part [1] of dynamically generated web-pages, eliminating them results in significant savings with respect to storage and

---

[1] sometimes the non-content blocks' total size is as much as 65-70% of the whole page-size.

M.-S. Hacid et al. (Eds.): ISMIS 2005, LNAI 3488, pp. 285–293, 2005.
© Springer-Verlag Berlin Heidelberg 2005

index file-size. We have designed and implemented two algorithms, *FeatureExtractor*, and *K-FeatureExtractor*, which can identify the primary content blocks in a web-page. First, the algorithms partition the web-page into blocks based on heuristics. Lin and Ho [14] have proposed an entropy-based algorithm that partitions a web-page into blocks on the basis of HTML tables. In contrast, not only do we consider HTML tables, but also other tags and heuristics to partition a web-page. Secondly, our algorithms classifies each block as either a content block or a non-content block. Both **FeatureExtractor** and **K-FeatureExtractor**) produce excellent precision and recall values and above all, do not use any manual input and require no complex machine learning process. While operating on several thousand web-pages obtained from 15 news websites, our algorithms significantly outperform their nearest competitor - the Entropy-based blocking algorithm proposed by Lin and Ho [14].

The rest of the paper is organized as follows. In section 2 we have discussed the related work. We define the concept of "blocks" and a few related terms in section 3, describe our algorithms in sections 4 and 5, and outline our performance evaluation plan and the dataset in section 6. We then compare our algorithms with the **LH** algorithm in section 7 and conclude thereafter.

2   Related Work

Yi and Liu [17, 15] have proposed an algorithm for identifying non-content blocks of web-pages using "Style Tree". Since our algorithms use simple heuristics to determine non-content blocks, it does not incur the overhead of constructing "Style Tree"s. Another work that is closely related is the work by Lin and Ho [14]. Their algorithm tries to partition a web-page into blocks and identify content blocks. They used the entropy of the keywords used in a block to determine whether the block is redundant. We believe that we have a more comprehensive definition of blocks and demonstrate that we have designed and implemented an algorithm that gives better precision and recall values than their algorithm. Bar-Yossef and Rajagopalan [3] have proposed a method to identify frequent templates of web-pages and pagelets (identical to our blocks). Yi and Liu argue that their entropy-based method supersedes the template identification method. We show that our method produces better result than the entropy-based method. Kushmerick [12, 11] has proposed a feature-based method that identifies Internet advertisements in a web-page. Their algorithm generates rules from training examples using a manually-specified procedure that states how the features to be used can be identified. This manual specification is dependent upon applications. Our algorithms do not require any manual specification or training data set.

Information extraction systems try to extract useful information from either structured, or semi-structured documents. Systems like Tsimmis [4] and Araneus [2] depend on manually provided grammar rules. In Information Manifold [10, 13], Whirl [6], or Ariadne [1], the systems tried to extract information using a query system that is similar to database systems. In Wrapper systems [12], the wrappers are automatically created without the use of hand-coding. Kushmerick et. al. [12, 11] have found an inductive learning technique. Their algorithm learns a resource's wrapper by reasoning about a sample of the resource's pages. In Roadrunner [7], a subclass of regular expression grammar (UFRE or Union Free Regular Expression) is used. In Softmealy [9], a novel web wrapper representation formalism has been presented based on a finite-state transducer (FST) and contextual rules. For other semi-structured wrapper generators like Stalker [16], a hierarchical information-extraction technique converts the complexity of mining into a series of simpler extraction tasks. Most of these approaches are geared toward learning the regular expressions or grammar induction [5] of the inherent structure or the semi-structure and so computational complexities are quite high.

These efforts are to extract information that originally comes from databases, which is very structured in nature. Our work concentrates on web-pages where the underlying information is unstructured text. Our preliminary work [8] shows great improvements in extracting informative blocks from web-pages. We described our **ContentExtractor** algorithm in [8] which uses multiple web-pages from same source and find repetitive similar blocks. By eliminating these repetitive blocks it improved the precision and recall of finding content blocks. In [8] we mentioned **FeatureExtractor** algorithm very briefly. Here we introduce **K-FeatureExtractor** algorithm and to describe it properly, we believe that an introduction of **FeatureExtractor** was necessary. **K-FeatureExtractor** even outperform **ContentExtractor** in runtime.

3   Blocks in Web Pages

A block (or web-page block) $\mathcal{B}$ is a portion of a web-page enclosed within an open-tag and its matching close-tag, where the open and close tags belong to an ordered tag-set $\mathcal{T}$ that includes tags like <TR>, <P>, <HR>, and <UL>.

Heuristics
Out of all these tags, web authors extensively use <TABLE> for layout design. We devised a list of tags to partition a web-page into blocks. <TABLE> comes as the first or tag in that list. <TR>, <P>, <HR>, and <UL> etc. are the next few partitioning tags in that list, in order. We selected the order of the tags based on our observations of web-page design. For example, <TABLE> comes as the first partitioning tag since we see more instances of <UL> in <TR> / <TD> (sub-element of <TABLE>) than <TABLE>s coming inside <LI> (sub-element of <UL>). Our algorithms partition a web-page into blocks, based on the first tag in our list. It continues sub-partitioning the already-identified blocks based on the next listed tags. The partitioning algorithm is illustrated in next section.

Block Features
Blocks may include other smaller blocks, and have features like text, images, applets, javascript, etc. Most, but not all, features are associated with their respective standard tags. For example, an image is always associated with the

tag <IMG>, however, the text feature has no standard tag. For tag-associated features we used the W3C [2] guidelines to make the list of features. We can update this list as time and version of HTML pages change, without doing any fundamental change in our algorithms.

4   Algorithm: FeatureExtractor

We describe our algorithms **FeatureExtractor** and **K-FeatureExtarctor** here. As some parts of these two algorithms are similar, we show them both in Algorithm 1 to save space.

FeatureExtractor takes an HTML page, a desired feature and a sorted tag set (for block-partitioning purpose). It first partitions the page into blocks with the help of *GetBlockSet* routine. It then calculates the probability of individual blocks for the desired feature. It takes those blocks in the winner set for which the probability of the desired feature is more than the combined probability of the rest of the feature. In the next step, within the winner set, it finds the block with the highest probability value and extracts the information (in case of text feature it extracts the text part) from the block.

GetBlockSet
GetBlockSet takes a tag from the tag-set one by one and calls the *GetBlocks* routine for each of the already-generated blocks. New sub-blocks created by *GetBlocks* are added to the block set and the generating main block is removed from the set. *First* gives the first element of an ordered set, and *Next* gives the consecutive elements.

GetBlocks
GetBlocks takes a full or part of an HTML document, and a tag as its input. It partitions the document into blocks according to the input tag. For example, for <TABLE> input tag it will produce a tree with all the table blocks.

5   Algorithm: K-FeatureExtractor

FeatureExtractor shows high precision and recall for most of the websites in our dataset. However, for web-pages with multiple important text blocks, a typical reader may be interested in all of them, instead of just the winner block (from **FeatureExtractor**). General shopping sites, review sites, chat forums etc. comes under this category. Undoubtedly **FeatureExtractor**, shows poor performance. To overcome this we improved **FeatureExtractor**. This improved algorithm, **K-FeatureExtractor**, is also shown in algorithm 1. Here, instead of taking just the winner from the winner-basket, we apply a K-means clus-

---

[2] World Wide Web Consortium or http://www.w3c.org/TR/html4/

Algorithm 1: (K)-FeatureExtractor

Input : Set of HTML pages H, Sorted Tag Set $\mathcal{T}$, Desired Feature $\mathcal{F}_I$

Output : Content Block(s) of H and its content. It returns the contents as well as identifications of the blocks to assist the block-level calculation of b-Precision and b-Recall

Feature : Feature set $\mathcal{F}_S$ used for block separation sorted according to importance taken from $\mathcal{T}$

begin

$\quad B \longleftarrow GetBlockSet(H, \mathcal{F})$

$\quad$ **for** *each* $b \in B$ **do**

$\quad\quad P_1 \longleftarrow Pr(\mathcal{F}_I | \mathcal{F})$

$\quad\quad$ **if** $P_1 > 0.5$ **then**

$\quad\quad\quad \mathcal{W} \longleftarrow \mathcal{W} \cup b$

$\quad$ **for** *each* $b \in \mathcal{W}$ **do**

$\quad\quad P_b \longleftarrow Pr(\mathcal{F}_I | \mathcal{F}, \mathcal{W})$

$\quad$ //In case of FeatureExtractor we used the following method

$\quad W_s \longleftarrow Sort(\mathcal{W})$

$\quad$ //Winner block

$\quad B_w \longleftarrow First(W_s)$

$\quad C \longleftarrow ContentOfBlock(B_w)$

$\quad$ Return (B_w, C)

$\quad$ //In case of K-FeatureExtractor we used the following method

$\quad W_s \longleftarrow KMeansClustering(\mathcal{W})$

$\quad$ //Winner blockset

$\quad W_s{}^w \longleftarrow FirstCluster(W_s)$

$\quad C \leftarrow \phi$

$\quad$ **for** *each* $B_w \in W_s{}^w$ **do**

$\quad\quad C \longleftarrow C \cup ContentOfBlock(B_w)$

$\quad$ Return (W_s, C)

$\quad$ **Function: GetBlockSet**

$\quad$ **Input** : HTML page H, Sorted tag-set $\mathcal{T}$

$\quad$ **Output** : Set of Blocks in H

$\quad$ **begin**

$\quad\quad B \longleftarrow H$; // set of blocks, initially set to H.

$\quad\quad f \longleftarrow Next(\mathcal{T})$

$\quad\quad$ **while** $f \neq \emptyset$ **do**

$\quad\quad\quad b \longleftarrow First(B)$

$\quad\quad\quad$ **while** $b \neq \emptyset$ **do**

$\quad\quad\quad\quad$ **if** b *contains* f **then**

$\quad\quad\quad\quad\quad B^N \longleftarrow GetBlocks(B, f)$

$\quad\quad\quad\quad\quad B \longleftarrow (B - b) \cup B^N$

$\quad\quad\quad\quad b \longleftarrow Next(B)$

$\quad\quad\quad f \longleftarrow Next(\mathcal{T})$

$\quad$ **end**

end

---

tering to select the best probability block-cluster from the preliminary winning basket. After the clustering is done, the high probability cluster is taken and the corresponding *text* contents of all those blocks are combined as the output (the desired feature is *text* here). Both results from **K-FeatureExtractor** and **FeatureExtractor** are shown in table 2.

6   Evaluation Plan

Lin and Ho [14] used *precision* and *recall* to evaluate their algorithm. Although it is confusing and somewhat different from their usual application in "Information Retrieval", we use the same terms (added with a "b-" for blocks) (in order to avoid confusion).

Metric Used
Precision is defined as the ratio of the number of relevant items (actual primary content blocks) r found and the total number of items (primary content blocks suggested by an algorithm) t found. For block level precision, we call it as $b - Precision$. $b - Precision = \frac{r}{t}$. Recall is defined as the ratio of the number of relevant items found and the desired number of relevant items. The number of missed relevant items is m. In case of blocks we call it as $b - Recall$. $b - Recall = \frac{r}{r+m}$. We define the F-measure here as b-F-measure and define it as $b - F - measure = \frac{2*(b-Precision)*(b-Recall)}{(b-Precision)+(b-Recall)}$

Table 1. Details of the dataset. Categories are not shown due to the enormous size of the latex table. But interested reader can find the categories in [8]

Site	Web-address	Number of Web-pages
ABC	http://www.abcnews.com	415
BB	http://www.bloomsberg.com	510
BBC	http://www.bbc.co.uk	890
CBS	http://www.cbsnews.com	370
CNN	http://www.cnn.com	717
FOX	http://www.foxnews.com	476
FOX23	http://www.fox23news.com	658
IE	http://www.indianexpress.com	269
IT	http://www.indiatimes.com	454
MSNBC	http://www.msnbc.com	647
YAHOO	http://news.yahoo.com	505
Shopping	http://www.shopping.com	100
Amazon	http://www.amazon.com	100
Barnes And Noble	http://www.bn.com	100
Epinion	http://www.epinions.com	100

Data Set
Similar to Lin and Ho, we chose several news websites. We also chose shopping and book websites. We crawled these sites to collect documents. The details of the dataset are shown in Table 1 and in [8].

We took 15 different websites whose design and page-layouts are completely different. Unlike Lin and Ho's dataset [14] that is obtained from one fixed category of news sections (only one of them is "Miscellaneous" news from CDN), we took random news pages from a particular website (details in [8]). This makes the dataset a good mix of a wide variety of HTML layouts which is necessary to compare the robustness of **LH** algorithm and ours

7   Performance Comparison

b-Precision and b-Recall
The b-precision and b-recall values for each website are shown in table 2. Our algorithms outperform **LH** in all cases. The results from **LH** algorithm are less precise than those obtained by **K-FeatureExtractor**.

Execution Time
Figure 1 shows execution time taken by algorithms (*LH,* and *(K)-FeatureExtractor*) averaged over all test web-pages. From the figure it is clear that our algorithms outperform the *LH* algorithm by huge margin.

Table 2. Block level Precision and Recall values from *LH* algorithm, *FeatureExtractor*, and *K-FeatureExtractor*. For cases where these results are same for *FeatureExtractor* and *K-FeatureExtractor* we mentioned it once

Site	b-Prec of LH	b-Recall of LH	b-F-measure of LH	b-Prec of FE/K-FE	b-Recall of FE/K-FE	b-F-measure of FE/K-FE
ABC	0.811	0.99	**0.89**	1.00	1.00	**1.00**
BB	0.882	0.99	**0.93**	1.00	1.00	**1.00**
BBC	0.834	0.99	**0.905**	1.00	1.00	**1.00**
CBS	0.823	1.00	**0.902**	0.98	0.977	**0.978**
CNN	0.856	1.00	**0.922**	0.98	0.98	**0.98**
FOX	0.82	1.00	**0.901**	1.00	0.99/1.00	**0.994/1.00**
FOX23	0.822	1.00	**0.902**	1.00	1.00	**1.00**
IE	0.77	0.95	**0.85**	0.93	0.99	**0.959**
IT	0.793	0.99	**0.878**	0.96	0.98	**0.969**
MSNBC	0.802	1.00	**0.89**	0.92	1.00	**0.95**
YAHOO	0.730	1.00	**0.84**	1.00	0.95	**0.974**
Shopping	0.79	1.00	**0.88**	1.00	0.25/0.99	**0.4/0.994**
Amazon	0.771	0.99	**0.86**	1.00	0.35/0.967	**0.51/0.983**
Barnes And Noble	0.81	1.00	**0.895**	1.00	0.34/0.968	**0.50/0.983**
Epinion	0.79	1.00	**0.88**	1.00	0.289/0.956	**0.45/0.977**

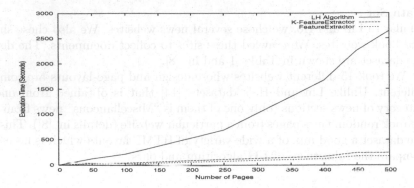

Fig. 1. Run-times for the **LH**, **FeatureExtractor**, and **K-FeatureExtractor** algorithms. The vertical axis represents the time of execution (in seconds) for a number of pages (plotted in the horizontal axis). It is clear that our algorithms outperform the **LH** algorithm in large margin. **K-FeatureExtractor** even outperforms **ContentExtractor** [8]

8   Conclusions and Future Work

We devised simple, yet powerful, and modular algorithms, to identify primary content blocks from web-pages. Our algorithms outperformed the LH algorithm significantly, in b-precision and run-time. In the next step, we will try to identify the semantics of the content to generate markup. The storage requirement for indices, the efficiency of the markup algorithms, and the relevancy measures of documents should also improve since now only the relevant parts of the documents are considered.

Acknowledgements

We acknowledge the help from several graduate students at Penn State University, specially from Pradeep B. Teregowda, and Isaac Councill.

References

1. José Luis Ambite, Naveen Ashish, Greg Barish, Craig A. Knoblock, Steven Minton, Pragnesh J. Modi, Ion Muslea, Andrew Philpot, and Sheila Tejada. Ariadne: a system for constructing mediators for Internet sources. In *SIGMOD*, pages 561–563, 1998.
2. Paolo Atzeni, Giansalvadore Mecca, and Paolo Merialdo. Semistructured and structured data in the web: Going back and forth. In *Workshop on Management of Semistructured Data*, 1997.
3. Ziv Bar-Yossef and Sridhar Rajagopalan. Template detection via data mining and its applications. In *Proceedings of WWW 2002*, pages 580–591, 2002.

4. Sudarshan Chawathe, Hector Garcia-Molina, Joachim Hammer, Kelly Ireland, Yanis Papakonstantinon, Jeffrey Ullman, and Jennifer Widom. The tsimmis project: integration of heterogeneous information sources. In *Proceedings of the 10th meeting og Information Processing Society of Japan*, pages 7–18, 1994.
5. Boris Chidlovskii, Jon Ragetli, and Maarten de Rijke. Wrapper generation via grammar induction. In *Machine Learning: ECML 2000, 11th European Conference on Machine Learning, Barcelona, Catalonia, Spain, May 31 - June 2, 2000, Proceedings*, volume 1810, pages 96–108. Springer, Berlin, 2000.
6. William W. Cohen. A web-based information system that reasons with structured collections of text. In Katia P. Sycara and Michael Wooldridge, editors, *Proceedings of the 2nd International Conference on Autonomous Agents (Agents'98)*, pages 400–407, New York, 9–13, 1998. ACM Press.
7. Valter Crescenzi, Giansalvatore Mecca, and Paolo Merialdo. Roadrunner: Towards automatic data extraction from large web sites. In *Proceedings of the 27th International Conference on Very Large Data Bases*, pages 109–118, 2001.
8. Sandip Debnath, Prasenjit Mitra, and C. Lee Giles. Automatic extraction of informative blocks from webpages. In *the upcoming proceedings of the Special Track on Web Technologies and Applications in the ACM Symposium of Applied Computing*, 2005.
9. C. Hsu. Initial results on wrapping semistructured web pages with finite-state transducers and contextual rules. In *AAAI-98 Workshop on AI and Information Integration*, pages 66–73. AAAI Press, 1998.
10. Thomas Kirk, Alon Y. Levy, Y Sagiv, and Divesh Srivastava. The information manifold. In *Proceedings of the AAAI Spring Symposium: Information Gathering from Heterogeneous Distributed Environments*, pages 85–91, 1995.
11. Nicholas Kushmerick. Wrapper induction: Efficiency and expressiveness. *Artificial Intelligence*, 118(1-2):15–68, 2000.
12. Nickolas Kushmerick, Daniel S. Weld, and Robert B. Doorenbos. Wrapper induction for information extraction. In *International Joint Conference on Artificial Intelligence (IJCAI)*, pages 729–737, 1997.
13. Alon Y. Levy, Divesh Srivastava, and Thomas Kirk. Data model and query evaluation in global information systems. *Journal of Intelligent Information Systems - Special Issue on Networked Information Discovery and Retrieval*, 5(2):121–143, 1995.
14. Shian-Hua Lin and Jan-Ming Ho. Discovering informative content blocks from web documents. *Proceedings of the eighth ACM SIGKDD international conference on Knowledge discovery and data mining*, pages 588–593, 2002.
15. Bing Liu, Kaidi Zhao, and Lan Yi. Eliminating noisy information in web pages for data mining. In *Proceedings of the ninth ACM SIGKDD international conference on Knowledge discovery and data mining*, pages 296–305, 2003.
16. Ion Muslea, Steven Minton, and Craig A. Knoblock. Hierarchical wrapper induction for semistructured information sources. *Autonomous Agents and Multi-Agent Systems*, 4(1/2):93–114, 2001.
17. Lan Yi, Bing Liu, and Xiaoli Li. Visualizing web site comparisons. In *Proceedings of the eleventh international conference on World Wide Web*, pages 693–703, 2002.

Building the Data Warehouse of Frequent Itemsets in the DWFIST Approach

Rodrigo Salvador Monteiro[1,2], Geraldo Zimbrão[1,3], Holger Schwarz[2],
Bernhard Mitschang[2], and Jano Moreira de Souza[1,3]

[1] Computer Science Department, Graduate School of Engineering, Federal University
of Rio de Janeiro, PO Box 68511, ZIP code: 21945-970, Rio de Janeiro, Brazil
{salvador, zimbrao, jano}@cos.ufrj.br
[2] Institute f. Parallel & Distributed Systems, University of Stuttgart,
Universitaetsstr. 38, 70569 Stuttgart
{salvadro, hrschwar, mitsch}@informatik.uni-stuttgart.de
[3] Computer Science Department, Institute of Mathematics, UFRJ, Brazil

Abstract. Some data mining tasks can produce such great amounts of data that
we have to cope with a new knowledge management problem. Frequent itemset
mining fits in this category. Different approaches were proposed to handle or
avoid somehow this problem. All of them have problems and limitations. In
particular, most of them need the original data during the analysis phase, which
is not feasible for data streams. The DWFIST (Data Warehouse of Frequent
ItemSets Tactics) approach aims at providing a powerful environment for the
analysis of itemsets and derived patterns, such as association rules, without
accessing the original data during the analysis phase. This approach is based on
a Data Warehouse of Frequent Itemsets. It provides frequent itemsets in a
flexible and efficient way as well as a standardized logical view upon which
analytical tools can be developed. This paper presents how such a data
warehouse can be built.

1 Introduction

Advances in data gathering mechanisms, the use of bar codes in most commercial
products, and information on many business and governmental transactions have been
flooding us with data, creating an urgent need for new techniques and tools to intelli-
gently and automatically support the transformation of this data into useful knowledge
[2]. Also, recent applications, such as network traffic analysis, web click stream mining, power consumption measurement, sensor network data analysis, and dynamic
tracing of stock fluctuation are some examples where a new kind of data arises, the so
called stream data. A data stream is continuous and potentially infinite. This new kind
of data is also a valuable source of potentially useful knowledge.

The research field of data mining has provided many different techniques to explore the data and reveal different kinds of pattern or non-pattern behavior. More recently, some of these techniques have been adapted to cope with tight requirements
imposed by stream data.

Mining frequent patterns in transactional data, in particular the pattern domain of
itemsets, is a technique that deserves special attention due to its large applicability

M.-S. Hacid et al. (Eds.): ISMIS 2005, LNAI 3488, pp. 294–303, 2005.
© Springer-Verlag Berlin Heidelberg 2005

[12]. The most recognized one is to support association rule mining [1]. Iceberg cube computation [6], associative classification [5], frequent pattern-based clustering [7] and generalized rule mining [8] are examples where frequent itemsets are useful.

The DWFIST approach mainly addresses two issues on frequent itemset mining not solved so far: (1) provide flexible frequent itemset mining capabilities without accessing the original data during the analysis phase; and (2) provide a conceptual view (dimensional model) for pattern analysis that is familiar to business professionals and suitable for the analysis of huge volumes of data.

The main component of the DWFIST approach is the Data Warehouse of Frequent Itemsets. It organizes the whole set of transactions by disjoint partitions and stores information about the frequent itemsets holding on each partition. Different partitions can be combined to obtain the frequent itemsets with approximate support guarantees holding on any set of partitions. For instance, one can request the frequent itemsets holding on Mondays, holidays, every first working day of the month, and so on. These are examples of calendar-based [14] frequent itemset mining that, so far, was not possible to be performed on stream data. The Data Warehouse of Frequent Itemsets also provides a standardized logical view upon which analytical tools can be developed independently.

The set of frequent itemsets holding on a set of transactions retains important information about the pattern behavior. The storage requirements for frequent itemsets are orders of magnitude lower than the ones for the original transactions. The set of frequent patterns usually does not change dramatically over time [9], also reducing storage requirements. At last, measurements in [9] affirm that current frequent itemset mining algorithms are able to cope with tight time constraints imposed by a stream data scenario. These features make it feasible to store frequent itemsets for further detailed analysis for a huge set of transactions or a data stream.

The remainder of the paper is organized as follows. Section 2 discusses the existing approaches. The DWFIST approach is presented in Section 3. Section 4 details how a Data Warehouse of Frequent Itemsets can be built. Section 5 concludes the work.

2   Related Work

This section briefly presents the related works. More information on major related work and the basic ideas of our approach is provided in [11].

The OLAP Mining approach [3] integrates on-line analytical processing (OLAP) with data mining. It provides an interesting solution for analyzing the results of data mining tasks. This approach has two major shortcomings in our context: First, it is restricted to data mining tasks for which the result can be represented as a data cube. For frequent itemset mining there is no such representation [3]. Secondly, it needs to access the original data during the analysis.

In [10] an approach for market basket analysis storing the support counts in a fact table is presented. It stores the support counting for every pair of items that appear together in any transaction. The number of possible combinations grows exponentially with the number of items. Also, the information about all combinations is likely to require more storage than the original transactions, which is infeasible for data streams. Furthermore, it only handles itemsets with two items.

Inductive Databases [4,12] are databases that contain inductive generalizations about the data, which is called the database theory. In such a database the user can simply query the database theory using a conventional query language. However, the database theory relates to the data stored in the database and so, once again, we need the original data available during the analysis phase. Sophisticated analysis operations, such as OLAP operations (drill-down, roll-up, pivot, slice, dice, etc), to explore the database theory are not in the scope of the Inductive Databases approach.

The PANDA project [15] studies current state-of-the-art in pattern management and explores novel theoretical and practical aspects of a Pattern Base Management System. It deals with patterns in a broad sense, considering no predefined pattern types. The main focus lies in devising a general and extensible model for patterns. As it gains in generality it does not provide a standardized logical view for frequent itemsets representation. Also, as in the Inductive Databases approach, no sophisticated analysis operations are considered.

The work presented in [9] proposes a new model for mining frequent patterns from data streams, the FP-Stream. This model is capable of answering user queries considering multiple time granularities. A fine granularity is important for recent changes whereas a coarse granularity is adequate for long-term changes. FP-Stream supports this kind of analysis by a tilted-time window, which keeps storage requirements very low. One of its drawbacks is that it prevents some kinds of analysis, e.g., calendar-based pattern analysis.

At last, many condensed representations [8] for frequent itemsets were proposed which aim at representing a set of frequent itemsets in a more compact way. Some representations can be applied in our approach to represent the set of itemsets holding on a partition.

3   The DWFIST Approach

The acronym DWFIST stands for Data Warehouse of Frequent ItemSets Tactics. The Oxford Dictionary and Thesaurus defines Tactics as: skilful device; scheme, strategy. In this sense, the DWFIST approach aims at providing a skilful environment to explore and analyze patterns based on frequent itemset on transactional data. Figure 1 presents the components of the DWFIST approach. The focus of this work is on the Data Warehouse of Frequent Itemsets. Its main task is to organize and provide all information on frequent itemsets required by the other components. Due to space constraints we do not describe the other components here.

The research field of Data Warehouse has been extremely successful in providing efficient and effective ways to analyze huge amounts of data. Although data warehouse techniques cannot be directly applied to store and analyze frequent itemset patterns, they can be adapted while keeping their principles and lessons learned. Storing frequent itemsets may sound strange at first as one could argue that it is better to store the original data and obtain the frequent patterns upon ad-hoc request. We would like to draw the readers' attention to some important remarks. First, it is not always possible to store the original data. It is usually infeasible to store the whole stream data and at the same time it is still extremely interesting to analyze different kinds of patterns holding on the stream. Second, by pre-processing the frequent itemsets we are able to reduce the computational effort required during the analysis tasks performed by a user. Finally, it is also possible to store the frequent itemsets in addition to the original data. The redundant information can be justified as far as it publishes the data in such a way that can be more effectively analyzed [10].

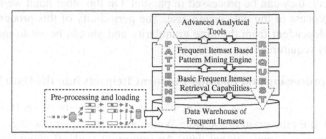

Fig. 1. Components of the DWFIST approach

4   The Data Warehouse of Frequent Itemsets

The Data Warehouse of Frequent Itemsets, although presenting some peculiarities, can be seen for many purposes as a regular Data Warehouse (DW). Therefore, many considerations presented in [10] are applicable. We will keep our focus on the particular features.

4.1   Requirements

It must be possible to answer queries specifying constraints on the original transactions using the information stored in the Data Warehouse of Frequent Itemsets. A sample data source and some queries are presented in Figure 2. Later in Section 4.5 we return to this example explaining how the queries are answered.

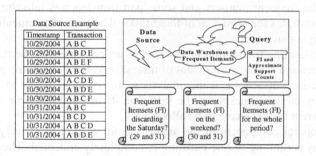

Fig. 2. Data source and query examples

Another important requirement refers to the feasibility of coping with the tight time constraints imposed by data streams. In a data warehouse we want to store the frequent itemsets holding on different partitions of transactions. As far as we are able to compute the frequent itemsets holding on each partition before the next partition is ready to be processed, we cope with this requirement. Measurements presented in [9] affirm that current algorithms for frequent itemset mining are able to cope with time constraints imposed by a stream data scenario. As different partitions are completely independent, they can be processed in parallel. On the other hand we have to consider the load process of the data warehouse. The periodicity of this process must be completely independent from the time granularity and should be set to meet analysis and availability requirements.

4.2 Pre-processing and Loading Frequent Itemsets into the Data Warehouse

In order to pre-process the frequent itemsets a granularity of analysis should be defined. It defines the grain of the Data Warehouse of Frequent Itemsets, thus defining a partition over the transactional data. An important tradeoff should be considered. A more specific analysis grain provides more flexibility for analysis. However, the more specific the analysis grain, the more support counts need to be stored, which increases the storage requirements. The conventional data warehouse rule for storing data at the most granular level must be broken in our approach because it is infeasible to store the most granular level. Nevertheless, we still want to analyze the pattern behavior. Hence, some storage requirements tests have to be carried out to identify the appropriate granularity of analysis.

As in any data warehouse, the temporal information plays an important role. Hence, the analysis grain should have a temporal component. Other components can also be used to define the grain. As an example, an analysis grain could be defined as the frequent itemsets per store per hour. By defining such a grain it must be clear that it will be not possible to analyze the pattern behavior for periods shorter than an hour or more detailed space units than a store. At the other hand, all possible combinations of each per store per hour partition can be analyzed.

Once the analysis grain is defined, three main tasks specific to our approach should be implemented and performed in the data staging area: separate and accumulate transactions for each partition; mine the frequent itemsets holding on each partition; and load the frequent itemsets and some partition features into the data warehouse. Figure 3 illustrates the sequence of these tasks. They are supplemented by other regular data staging area tasks.

A new incoming transaction is analyzed in order to identify the partition it belongs to. Each partition for the current slot of time should have one corresponding bucket to accumulate its transactions. If the analysis grain is defined only by a temporal component then only one bucket will be sufficient. If the analysis grain has other components, different buckets have to be allocated.

The temporal component of the analysis grain is used to identify when the set of transactions pertaining to one partition is completely collected. The complete sets of transactions are passed to the next step where the mining is performed. However, it is always possible to receive delayed transactions. These exceptions should be handled separately from the regular procedures to avoid delaying them. In such cases, we have to identify which partition the delayed transaction belongs to. Afterwards, we may apply two different treatment procedures. One possibility is to adjust the partition features, correcting the number of transactions and the minimum support, which will be

introduced in the mining phase. The other possibility is to perform the mining operation again, but this applies only when the source transactions of the partitions are still
available. The first treatment procedure is particularly interesting because it does not
need to access the original transactions and is extremely simple to be processed.

The frequent itemset mining is performed on each completely collected set of
transactions comprising one partition. A minimum support threshold should be

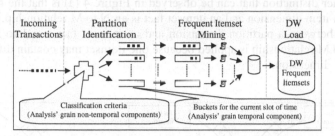

Fig. 3. Overview of the Data Staging Area

specified. The initial threshold value is not a definitive commitment. The minimum
support threshold can be changed freely over time as well as customized thresholds
for different partitions can be specified. The only constraint is that each partition is
associated with only one minimum support threshold. The frequent itemset mining results in a list of frequent itemsets holding on the partition's transactions.

The frequent itemsets, their support counts, the number of partition's transactions
and the applied minimum support threshold should be stored in some intermediate
storage area before the final load into the data warehouse takes place. This intermediate storage area provides isolation between the mining process and the data warehouse load process. By this isolation, it is possible, for example, to define a daily data
warehouse load procedure having an hourly mining granularity. As soon as one partition is mined and its information stored in the intermediate storage area, the partition's transactions can be discarded.

Finally, the information stored in the intermediate storage area will be periodically
loaded into the data warehouse. At this step, many conventional data warehouse issues arise and should be treated the same way as in regular data warehouses. Some
examples of such issues are: assigning surrogate keys, creating new dimension instances, dealing with slowly changing dimension, etc. The isolation provided by the
intermediate storage area makes it feasible to take care of such issues while coping
with tight time constraints imposed by incoming transactions arrival rate.

4.3 Conceptual View

We present a conceptual schema for the Data Warehouse of Frequent Itemsets. Figure
4 presents this schema using the StarER notation [13]. Beside the concepts of dimensional modeling, we need to make a distinction between two different types of dimensions, namely the item dimension and the partition dimension.

An item dimension describes similar items that can appear as part of a frequent
itemset. If there are different groups of items with different features, different item

dimensions should be provided in order to better describe and classify them. As an example, in the context of medical procedures, the hospital materials can be represented in one item dimension and the medical staff in another one.

A partition dimension partitions the original set of transactions into disjoint sets. Each partition dimension describes one component of the granularity of analysis. Temporal and spatial dimensions are typical candidate partition dimensions.

Another distinction that can be observed in Figure 4 (a) is that the relationship between an item dimension and an itemset fact is an N to M relationship, while the relationship between a partition dimension and an itemset fact is a 1 to N relationship. The N to M relationship is applied because one itemset may contain different items of the same dimension.

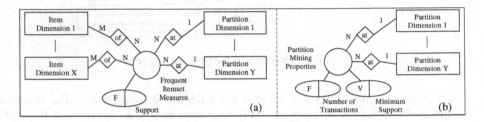

Fig. 4. StarER conceptual schema

It is interesting to relate the information stored in the intermediate storage area with our conceptual schema. The frequent itemsets and their support counts are represented in the schema of Figure 4 (a). A support count is a fact attribute and a frequent itemset is represented by the relationships with item dimensions. The number of transactions per partition and the applied minimum support threshold are represented in the schema of Figure 4 (b) as fact attributes. Note that the schema presented in Figure 4 (b) has only partition dimensions because the partition mining properties are the same for every frequent itemset of the same partition.

4.4 Logical View

A standardized logical schema is presented in Figures 5. In the logical design we introduce one itemset dimension for each item dimension as can be seen in Figure 5 (a). The itemset dimension works as a bridge table. Multivalued dimensions (N:M relationship with the fact table) are commonly solved with the help of a bridge table [10]. Analytical tools usually try to hide the existence of bridge table. The same should be done with the itemset dimension. That is why we do not represent them at the conceptual level.

The itemset dimension should contain one identifier for each distinct itemset, which will be used as a foreign key in the fact table and also to group the items into itemsets. The logical schema presented in Figure 5 (b) is straightforward derived from the conceptual schema presented in Figure 4 (b).

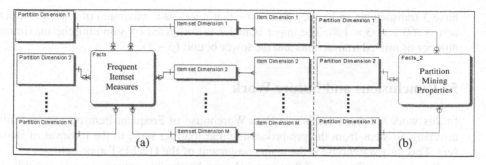

Fig. 5. Logical schema

4.5 Retrieving Frequent Itemsets from the Data Warehouse

After presenting the concepts of the DW we can return to the example in Figure 2 and depict how the query examples can be answered. Figure 6 presents the frequentitem-sets that would be stored in the DW using a daily granularity of analysis and a mini-mum support of 60% for all three partitions. For the sake of simplicity, we use the same minimum support for the queries. Any higher minimum support could be re-quested and a subset of the presented answer would be provided. Obviously, lower supports are not supported.

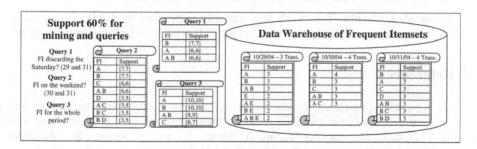

Fig. 6. Examples of Frequent Itemset Retrieval from the DW

The result of a query is the union of the frequent itemsets of the partitions that sat-isfy the constraints excluding the frequent itemsets with support count below the re-quested minimum support. For example, Query 2 is the complete union once that no frequent itemset is guaranteed to be below the request minimum support (60% of 8 = 4.8). The stored support counts are summed providing a lower bound. The upper bound is computed considering the partitions where the itemset is missing. For in-stance, considering the item "C" reported in Query 3 we have the lower bound 6 as the sum of support counts in partitions "10/30/2004" and "10/31/2004". The item "C" is missing in partition "10/29/2004" and this partition satisfy Query 3 constraints. Us-ing the number of transactions and the minimum support stored for this partition we can easily calculate the maximum number of missed transactions. In this case, we have 3 transactions and a support of 60% that gives us a maximum of 1 missed transaction (60% of 3 = 1.8). The upper bound 7 is computed by summing the maximum number of missed transactions and the lower bound (6 + 1).

5   Conclusions and Future Work

In this work we presented how a Data Warehouse of Frequent Itemsets can be built, covering all steps from the pre-processing and loading stage to the retrieval of itemsets. This data warehouse is the main component of the DWFIST approach.

The main contributions of this approach are: the flexible pattern analysis capabilities provided by the combination of partitions, even when the original data is not available anymore; a standardized logical view upon which analytical tools can be developed; and a conceptual view (dimensional model) for pattern analysis that is familiar to business professionals. Our approach can be used with stream data sources, providing analytical capabilities not supported so far, as for example, calendar-based patterns analysis.

As future work we will investigate existing analytical techniques and develop new ones to explore the Data Warehouse of Frequent Itemsets. Also, existing automatic exploration methods can be adapted to explore the patterns and new ones can be developed. These issues will be considered in other components of the DWFIST approach. Besides, we intend to evaluate the use of different condensed representations of frequent itemsets. Furthermore, supporting frequent itemsets at different levels of the item hierarchy (hierarchical mining) is another future task.

Acknowledgements. This work was partially supported by CNPq as a Sandwich Program, during which Monteiro is a visitor PhD student at University of Stuttgart.

References

1. Agrawal, R., Imielinski, T., and Swami, A.: "Mining Association Rules between Sets of Items in Large Databases". Proc. ACM SIGMOD Conf., pp. 207-216, Washington, 1993.
2. Fayyad, U. M., Piatetsky-Shapiro, G., Smyth, P., and Uthurusamy, R.: "Advances in Knowledge Discovery and Data Mining". AAAI Press, 1998.
3. Han, J.: "OLAP Mining: An Integration of OLAP with Data Mining". Proceedings of the 1997 IFIP Conference on Data Semantics (DS-7), pp. 1-11, Leysin, Switzerland, Oct 1997.
4. Imielinski, T., and Mannila, H.: "A database perspective on knowledge discovery". Communications of ACM, vol. 39, pp. 58-64, 1996.
5. Liu, B., Hsu, W., and Ma, Y.: "Integrating classification and association rule mining." In Proceedings KDD'98, pp. 80–86, AAAI Press, New York, USA, 1998.
6. Beyer, K., and Ramakrishnan, R.:. "Bottom-up computation of sparse and iceberg cubes". In Proc. ACM-SIGMOD Int. Conf. Management of Data (SIGMOD'99), pp. 359-370, 1999.
7. Wang, H.; Yang, J.; Wang, W.; and Yu, P. S.: "Clustering by pattern similarity in large data sets". In Proc. ACM-SIGMOD Int. Conf. on Management of Data, pp. 418-427, 2002.
8. Mannila, H., and Toivonen, H.: "Multiple Uses of Frequent Sets and Condensed Representations". In Proceedings KDD'96, pp. 189-194, AAAI Press, Portland, 1996.
9. Giannella, C., Han, J., Pei, J., Yan, X., and Yu, P.S.: "Mining Frequent Patterns in Data Streams at Multiple Time Granularities". H. Kargupta et al. Eds. Data Mining: Next Generation Challenges and Future Directions, AAAI/MIT Press, 2003.

10. Kimball, R., and Ross, M.: "The Data Warehouse Toolkit: The Complete Guide to Dimensional Modelling", Wiley Publishers, second edition, ISBN 0471200247, April 2002.
11. Monteiro, R. S., Zimbrão, G., and Souza, J. M.: "An Analytical Approach for Handling Association Rule Mining Results". Proc. AusDM Workshop, Canberra, Australia, 2003.
12. Boulicaut, J.: "Inductive databases and multiple uses of frequent itemsets: the cInQ approach". In Database support for Data Mining Applications, R. Meo et al. Eds., LNCS 2682. pp. 3-26, 2004.
13. Tryfona, N., Busborg, F., and Christiansen, J. G. B.: "starER: A Conceptual Model for Data Warehouse Design". Proc. Int. Workshop on Data Warehousing and OLAP, pp. 3-8, 1999.
14. Li, Y., Ning, P., Wang, X. S., and Jajodia, S.: "Discovering calendar-based temporal association rules". Proc. Int. Symp. Temp. Representation and Reasoning,pp.111-118, 2001.
15. The PANDA Project, http://dke.cti.gr/panda/, 2004.

Normal Forms for Knowledge Compilation*

Reiner Hähnle[1], Neil V. Murray[2], and Erik Rosenthal[3]

[1] Department of Computing Science, Chalmers University of Technology,
S-41296 Gothenburg, Sweden
reiner@cs.chalmers.se
[2] Department of Computer Science, State University of New York,
Albany, NY 12222, USA
nvm@cs.albany.edu
[3] Department of Mathematics, University of New Haven,
West Haven, CT 06516, USA
erosenthal@newhaven.edu

Abstract. A class of formulas called *factored negation normal form* is introduced. They are closely related to BDDs, but there is a DPLL-like tableau procedure for computing them that operates in PSPACE. *Ordered factored negation normal form* provides a canonical representation for any boolean function. Reduction strategies are developed that provide a unique *reduced factored negation normal form*. These compilation techniques work well with *negated form* as input, and it is shown that any logical formula can be translated into negated form in linear time.

1 Introduction

The last decade has seen a virtual explosion of applications of propositional logic. One emerging technique is *knowledge compilation*: preprocessing the underlying propositional theory. While knowledge compilation is intractable, it is done once, in an off-line phase, with the goal of making frequent on-line queries efficient. This paper is primarily concerned with off-line compilation.

Horn clauses, *binary decision diagrams* (BDDs), *ordered binary decision diagrams* (OBDDs), *tries*, and sets of *prime implicates/implicants* have all been proposed as targets of such compilation—see, for example, [2, 3, 6, 8, 9, 16, 17]. *Decomposable negation normal form* (DNNF) is a class of formulas studied by Darwiche [4, 5]. They are linkless, in negation normal form (NNF), and have the property that atoms are not shared across conjunctions. There are other target languages that employ NNF, although most research has restricted attention to conjunctive normal form (CNF). This may be because the structure of NNF formulas can be surprisingly complex. A comprehensive analysis of that structure can be found in [12] and in [13]. That analysis includes operations on NNF formulas that facilitate the use of NNF in systems.

* This research was supported in part by the National Science Foundation under grant CCR-0229339.

M.-S. Hacid et al. (Eds.): ISMIS 2005, LNAI 3488, pp. 304–313, 2005.
© Springer-Verlag Berlin Heidelberg 2005

Each of these potential target languages has both advantages and disadvantages. For example, DNNF is well suited for consequence testing and for finding minimal cardinality models. On the other hand, often a graph structure is employed that is not amenable to construction in PSPACE. The graph structure used by reduced BDDs has this same shortcoming. Even when the final result is small, there may be intermediate stages in the construction of such a BDD that are exponentially large. One nice feature of BDDs is that imposing an ordering on the variables (OBDDs) provides a canonical representation of every boolean function. Even with a fixed atom ordering, this is not the case for DNNF.

In this paper, several normal forms are developed, all based on tree representations of formulas rather than graphs. The first is *negated form* (NF), which uses only three binary connectives, $\land, \lor, \Leftrightarrow$, and all negations are at the atomic level. Moreover, it can be obtained from *any* logical formula in linear time and space. Also developed is *factored negation normal form* (FNNF), which is closely related to BDDs. Restricting the order of the variables produces *ordered factored negation normal form* (OFNNF), closely related to OBDDs. Redundancies can be removed to produce *reduced ordered factored negation normal form* (ROFNNF), closely related to ROBDDs. The main difference between BDDs and FNNF is that the former are graph-based representations, while the latter are tree-based.

The size of a tree is typically exponential in the size of its branches. In theorem proving, the space of all deductions is often conveniently represented as a tree. Linear procedures such as Davis-Putnam-Logeman-Loveland (DPLL) are relatively efficient with memory by keeping only one branch in memory at a time. A DPLL-like procedure that stores a tree with polynomial branches offline thus requires only PSPACE for construction of the tree. This applies to FNNF formulas, and they can indeed be computed in PSPACE. Since ROBDDs typically employ structure sharing, they cannot be computed in PSPACE. The OFNNF formulas can also be computed in PSPACE and, in addition, there is a canonical OFNNF representation (modulo the ordering) of any boolean function.

A DPLL-like procedure for computing FNNF is described that can be seen as a strengthening of the KE tableau system [11, 1] with the requirement that "enough" cuts be performed. Imposing an order on the cuts yields OFNNF. Even though the procedure can be viewed as a tableau procedure, it can be augmented by many standard inference techniques taken from other paradigms.

The techniques introduced for computing these normal forms can be regarded as knowledge compilation techniques. They work well with NF as input; because of the generality and space efficiency of NF, it is henceforth assumed that input formulas are always in NF. The NF class of formulas is developed in Section 2.1. In that same section it is shown that any logical formula can be translated into negated form in linear time. In Section 2.2, DNNF is described. FNNF is a subclass of DNNF that is developed and proved to be unique in Section 2.3. A tableau-based compilation procedure that produces FNNF and operates in

PSPACE is presented in Section 3. Section 4 presents reduction techniques and a proof of the uniqueness of RFFNF. Proofs are omitted and can be found in [15].

2   Negated Form and Factored Negation Normal Form

Given arbitrary propositional formulas $\mathcal{F}$, $\mathcal{G}$, and $\mathcal{S}$, let $\mathbf{atoms}(\mathcal{F})$ denote the atom set of $\mathcal{F}$, and let the expression $\mathcal{S}[\mathcal{G}/\mathcal{F}]$ represent the result of replacing each occurrence of $\mathcal{F}$ as a subformula of $\mathcal{S}$ with $\mathcal{G}$. The following simplification rules will be used throughout this paper; they are stated up to commutativity. Assume that $\mathcal{F}$ and $\mathcal{G}$ are arbitrary subformulas of $\mathcal{S}$; p is an atom. We use $\Leftrightarrow$ to denote the biconditional and $\equiv$ to denote (meta-level) logical equivalence. The rules are familiar; for example, **SR1** is DeMorgan's laws.

SR1 $\mathcal{S}[\neg\mathcal{F} \vee \neg\mathcal{G}/\neg(\mathcal{F} \wedge \mathcal{G})]$; $\mathcal{S}[\neg\mathcal{F} \wedge \neg\mathcal{G}/\neg(\mathcal{F} \vee \mathcal{G})]$;
SR2 $\mathcal{S}[\neg\mathcal{F} \Leftrightarrow \mathcal{G}/\neg(\mathcal{F} \Leftrightarrow \mathcal{G})]$; $\mathcal{S}[\mathcal{F} \Leftrightarrow \neg\mathcal{G}/\neg(\mathcal{F} \Leftrightarrow \mathcal{G})]$;
SR3 $\mathcal{S}[\mathcal{F}/\neg\neg\mathcal{F}]$;   **SR4** $\mathcal{S}[\mathcal{F}/\mathcal{F} \vee \mathcal{F}]$; $\mathcal{S}[\mathcal{F}/\mathcal{F} \wedge \mathcal{F}]$;
SR5 $\mathcal{S}[\mathcal{F}/\mathcal{F} \vee 0]$; $\mathcal{S}[\mathcal{F}/\mathcal{F} \wedge 1]$;   **SR6** $\mathcal{S}[0/\mathcal{F} \wedge 0]$; $\mathcal{S}[1/\mathcal{F} \vee 1]$;
SR7 $\mathcal{S}[\neg\mathcal{F}/\mathcal{F} \Leftrightarrow 0]$; $\mathcal{S}[\mathcal{F}/\mathcal{F} \Leftrightarrow 1]$;   **SR8** $\mathcal{S}[0/p \wedge \neg p]$; $\mathcal{S}[1/p \vee \neg p]$;
SR9 $\mathcal{S}[0/\mathcal{F} \Leftrightarrow \neg\mathcal{F}]$; $\mathcal{S}[1/\mathcal{F} \Leftrightarrow \mathcal{F}]$.

2.1   Negated Form

A logical formula is said to be in *negated form* (NF) if it contains variables plus the logical constants 0 and 1, if the only binary connectives are $\wedge$, $\vee$, and $\Leftrightarrow$, and if all negations are at the atomic level. Negated form differs from NNF (negation normal form) in that $\Leftrightarrow$ is allowed. In particular, an NF formula without occurrences of $\Leftrightarrow$ is in NNF.

The next lemma is obvious.

Lemma 1. Applications of the simplification rules produce equivalent formulas and preserve both negated form and negation normal form.   □

Theorem 1. Any propositional logical formula (with arbitrary binary connectives) can be transformed into negated form in linear time.   □

Henceforward, assume that, unless otherwise stated, NF formulas have been simplified with rules SR5–SR7 (the ones that remove truth constants). Thus, unless otherwise stated, the only NF formulas containing truth constants are 0 and 1 themselves. The notation $NF(\mathcal{S})$ will be used to denote an NF equivalent of a formula $\mathcal{S}$ that has been so simplified.

2.2   Decomposable Negation Normal Form

An NNF formula $\mathcal{F}$ (possibly containing boolean constants) is said to be in *decomposable negation normal form* (DNNF) if $\mathcal{F}$ satisfies the *decomposability property*: If $\alpha = \alpha_1 \wedge \alpha_2 \wedge \cdots \wedge \alpha_n$ is a conjunction in $\mathcal{F}$, then $i \neq j$ implies that

$\mathbf{atoms}(\alpha_i) \cap \mathbf{atoms}(\alpha_j) = \emptyset$; i.e., no two conjuncts of α share an atom. Observe that a DNNF formula is necessarily linkless since a literal and its complement cannot be conjoined—after all, they share the same atom. The structure of formulas in DNNF is much simpler than the more general NNF. Moreover, since DNNF formulas are link-free, many operations can be performed efficiently with respect to the size of the DNNF formula. A good reference for DNNF is [5]. The relationship between DNNF and full dissolvents is explored in [14]; that paper also provides simplifications for some results in [5].

2.3   Factored Negation Normal Form

This section introduces *factored negation normal form* (FNNF) and *ordered factored negation normal form* (OFNNF), the latter of which is a canonical representation of *any* logical formula (modulo a given variable ordering). In particular, while negated form is very convenient, it is not required for the definition or for the structure theorems of FNNF. However, simplification rules that eliminate constants are necessary. The rules SR1–SR9 are for negated form, but the extensions if other logical connectives are present are easily obtainable.

Given any logical formula $\mathcal{G}$ and atom p, the *Shannon expansion* of $\mathcal{G}$ with respect to p, $SE(\mathcal{G}, p)$, is the formula $(p \wedge \mathcal{G}[1/p]) \vee (\neg p \wedge \mathcal{G}[0/p])$.

This rule is often used for computing normal forms, and it is central to the computation of BDDs [2]. In [14] the rule appears as *semantic factoring*. It is easy to see that $\mathcal{G}$ is logically equivalent to $SE(\mathcal{G}, p)$ (even if p does not occur in $\mathcal{G}$!). Note that the Shannon expansion of a formula in negated form is also in negated form.

Example 1. Consider the NF formula $((\neg r \wedge p) \vee s) \wedge (\neg p \vee (q \wedge r))$. Shannon expansion of this formula with respect to p (with simplification) yields $(p \wedge ((\neg r \vee s) \wedge q \wedge r)) \vee (\neg p \wedge q)$.

Let $SIMP(\mathcal{G})$ denote the result of iteratively simplifying $\mathcal{G}$ with **SR5–SR8**; the Shannon expansion together with $SIMP$ is then sufficient to define factored negation normal form: Let $L = \{p_1, \ldots, p_n\}$ be a set of atoms. Given a formula $\mathcal{F}$ with $\mathbf{atoms}(\mathcal{F}) \subseteq L$, define $FNNF(\mathcal{F}, L)$ recursively as follows:

$$FNNF(\mathcal{F}, L) = \begin{cases} SIMP(\mathcal{F}) & L = \emptyset \\ SIMP \left(\begin{array}{c} (p_i \wedge FNNF(\mathcal{F}[1/p_i], \ L - \{p_i\})) \\ \vee \\ (\neg p_i \wedge FNNF(\mathcal{F}[0/p_i], \ L - \{p_i\})) \end{array} \right) & p_i \in L \end{cases}$$

If p_i is chosen to be the atom in L with maximal subscript, then the resulting FNNF is *ordered factored negation normal form*, denoted $OFNNF(\mathcal{F}, L)$.

Example 2. Let $\mathcal{F}$ be the formula $\neg((p_1 \rightarrow p_3) \Leftrightarrow \neg(p_2 \vee (p_3 \wedge \neg p_1)))$ with $L = \{p_1, p_2, p_3\}$. The negated form $\mathcal{F}'$ of $\mathcal{F}$ is $(p_1 \wedge \neg p_3) \Leftrightarrow (\neg p_2 \wedge (\neg p_3 \vee p_1))$. It is easy to verify that $OFNNF\mathcal{F}'), \{p_1, p_2, p_3\}$ is

$$(p_3 \wedge (p_2 \vee (\neg p_2 \wedge \neg p_1))) \vee (\neg p_3 \wedge ((p_2 \wedge \neg p_1) \vee (\neg p_2 \wedge p_1)))$$

Remark 1.

- The FNNF of any tautology (contradiction) is the constant 1 (0).
- $FNNF(\mathcal{F}, L) = (p \wedge \mathcal{H}_1) \vee (\neg p \wedge \mathcal{H}_2)$ may be regarded as a binary tree with root 1, whose subtrees are rooted at p and $\neg p$, whose other nodes are literals, and whose parent relation is conjunction. Due to SR8, no leaf has a leaf sibling. An atom occurs only once on a branch; thus $FNNF(\mathcal{F}, L)$ is linkless and in DNNF.
- All irrelevant variables — i.e., variables whose truth values are irrelevant to the truth value of the formula — that are processed after the last relevant variable is processed will not appear in $OFNNF(\mathcal{F}, L)$. The same thing happens with FNNF in subtrees in which irrelevant variables are processed at the end.

Example 3. Consider the NF formula from Example 1 with atom ordering $p > q > r > s$. The result of applying the OFNNF operator on its atom set is (in tree notation) is shown on the right. The redundancy exhibited in the right part of the tree is discussed in Section 4.

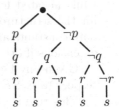

Theorem 2 below states that OFNNF yields a unique representation of any logical formula *when it is computed for a given atom set in a given order*. That is, if $\mathcal{F} \equiv \mathcal{G}$, then $OFNNF(\mathcal{F}, L)$ is syntactically identical to $OFNNF(\mathcal{G}, L)$. In general, we write $\mathcal{F} \doteq \mathcal{G}$ when $\mathcal{F}$ is syntactically identical to $\mathcal{G}$.

The next lemma is trivial, but the observation is useful.

Lemma 2. *If $\mathcal{F}$ is a logical formula with p not occurring in $\mathcal{F}$, then $SE(\mathcal{F}, p) = (p \wedge \mathcal{F}) \vee (\neg p \wedge \mathcal{F})$. Moreover, if $\mathcal{F}$ is logically equivalent to $\mathcal{G}$ and if γ is 1 or 0, then $\mathcal{F}[\gamma/p] \equiv \mathcal{G}[\gamma/p]$, whether or not p occurs in either $\mathcal{F}$ or in $\mathcal{G}$.*   □

Theorem 2. *Let $\mathcal{F}_1$ and $\mathcal{F}_2$ be logically equivalent formulas with atom sets L_1 and L_2, and let $L = L_1 \cup L_2$. Then $OFNNF(\mathcal{F}_1, L) \doteq OFNNF(\mathcal{F}_2, L)$.*   □

3   A Tableau Procedure for Computing FNNF

In this section, a PSPACE tableau procedure for computing the FNNF of a given formula with respect to a given atom set is developed.

Shannon expansion is closely related to D'Agostino and Mondadori's KE tableaux [1, 11]. Recall that the rules of KE tableaux, in the NNF case, consist of atomic cut and α- and β-rules, as depicted in Fig. 1 (top). The notation follows Smullyan's well-known uniform notation for propositional formulas.

These rules are too restrictive for our purpose, because negative premises must be literals. Instead Massacci's simplification rules [10] are used (Fig. 1,

$$
KE \quad \frac{}{p \mid \neg p} \qquad \frac{\alpha_1 \wedge \alpha_2}{\begin{array}{c}\alpha_1 \\ \alpha_2\end{array}} \quad \frac{\neg\beta_1}{\begin{array}{c}\beta_1 \vee \beta_2 \\ \beta_2\end{array}} \quad \frac{\neg\beta_2}{\begin{array}{c}\beta_1 \vee \beta_2 \\ \beta_1\end{array}} \quad \frac{\neg p}{\begin{array}{c}p \\ \times\end{array}}
$$

$$
Simplification \quad \frac{}{p \mid \neg p} \qquad \frac{(\alpha_1 \wedge \alpha_2)}{\begin{array}{c}\alpha_1 \\ \alpha_2\end{array}} \quad \frac{\phi}{\begin{array}{c}(\psi[\phi]) \\ \psi[1/\phi]\end{array}} \quad \frac{\neg p}{\begin{array}{c}(\psi[p]) \\ \psi[0/p]\end{array}}
$$

$$
FNNF \qquad \begin{array}{c}\mathcal{B} \\ / \backslash \\ 0 \quad \mathcal{B}'\end{array} \mapsto \begin{array}{c}\mathcal{B} \\ | \\ \mathcal{B}'\end{array} \qquad \begin{array}{c}\mathcal{B} \\ | \\ 0\end{array} \mapsto 0 \qquad \begin{array}{c}\mathcal{B} \\ / \backslash \\ 1 \quad \mathcal{B}'\end{array} \mapsto \begin{array}{c}\mathcal{B} \\ | \\ 1\end{array} \quad \begin{array}{c}\mathcal{B} \\ | \\ \mathcal{B}'\end{array} \mapsto \mathcal{B} \qquad \begin{array}{c}\mathcal{B} \\ | \\ 1 \\ | \\ \mathcal{B}'\end{array} \mapsto \begin{array}{c}\mathcal{B} \\ | \\ \mathcal{B}'\end{array} \qquad \begin{array}{c}\mathcal{B} \\ / \backslash \\ p \quad \neg p\end{array} \mapsto \begin{array}{c}\mathcal{B} \\ | \\ 1\end{array}
$$

Fig. 1. KE tableaux, Simplification (Massacci), and FNNF tableaux rules

middle). We call them *formula simplification rules*. The formula simplification rules are applicable to arbitrary formulas including ⇔, not only to β-formulas. In contrast to standard tableaux, some of these rules are *destructive*; this is indicated by enclosing in parentheses those premises that are deleted after rule application. This is justified: In each case the deleted premise is implied by the remaining premise and the conclusion.

The formula simplification rules subsume the KE β-rules since the truth functional simplification rules (**SR1–SR9**) are always applied to new formulas (for details see [15]). Nevertheless, these rules alone do not produce FNNF. The problem is that the *SIMP* rules must be applied to the tableaux itself, not just within formulas. To this end define the additional *FNNF Tableaux Rules* depicted schematically in Fig. 1 (bottom), where $\mathcal{B}$ stands for a partial (possibly empty) tableau branch.

Observe that all of these rules are destructive. Under these rules, a saturated FNNF tableau is regarded as an FNNF formula. In other words, the tableau structure corresponds exactly to the formula structure: branches correspond to conjunctions and branch points to disjunctions.

The five FNNF rules lift, respectively, **SR5** (∨), **SR6** (∧), **SR6** (∨), **SR5** (∧), and **SR8** (∨) to the tableau level. (**SR8** for conjunction is not required, see below).

Formally, the FNNF tableau procedure works on a formula in NF and applies the simplification and FNNF rules exhaustively in the following precedence order: first truth functional simplification and tautology elimination, then the α-rule, then the formula simplification rules, and finally the cut rule. Call the result a *saturated FNNF tableau*. Clearly, in a saturated FNNF tableau, all nodes are literals or else the entire tree reduces to 1 or to 0.

An OFNNF tableaux is defined analogously to OFNNF formulas: The cut rule must be applied to an atom with maximal index.

Theorem 3. If T is a saturated OFNNF tableau for $\mathcal{F}$ and L with $\mathbf{atoms}(\mathcal{F}) \subseteq L$, then T^* is the OFNNF of $\mathcal{F}$ with respect to L. In particular, the OFNNF tableau procedure is sound and complete for NF formulas.   □

With a standard depth-first backtracking strategy, this tableau procedure gives a PSPACE algorithm for computing OFNNF for a given NF formula and atom set.

4   Techniques for Space Reduction

4.1   Sibling Reduction

The FNNF of a formula is typically exponential in size, and so eliminating redundancies can be beneficial. One way to do this is by *sibling reduction*, which is based on the following observation: If the Shannon expansion of $\mathcal{F}$ with respect to p is $SE(\mathcal{F}, p) = (p \wedge \mathcal{F}[1/p]) \vee (\neg p \wedge \mathcal{F}[0/p])$, then $\mathcal{F}[1/p] \equiv \mathcal{F}[0/p]$ if and only if p is redundant (or not present!) in $\mathcal{F}$. The point is, $\mathcal{F}[1/p] \equiv \mathcal{F}[0/p]$ means that the truth value of $\mathcal{F}$ is unaffected by the truth value of p. Observe that this is unlikely to be easily detectable unless the variables are ordered; i.e., unless we are dealing with OFNNF.

Consider now what this condition means in the OFNNF tree of $\mathcal{F}$. First, in light of Theorem 2, the two subtrees descending from p and $\neg p$ are identical. More importantly, one of these subtrees may be removed, as may both p and $\neg p$. This process of removing identical sibling subtrees is called *sibling reduction*.

The tree that results from repeated applications of sibling reduction until there are no identical sibling subtrees is called the *reduced factored negation normal form* (ROFNNF), and we write $ROFNNF(\mathcal{F}, L)$, where L is an ordered list of atoms that contains all the atoms of $\mathcal{F}$. A few observations are in order.

Remark 2.

- If the sibling subtrees descending from every occurrence of p and $\neg p$ are identical, then p is redundant in the entire formula.
- If L is the atom set of $\mathcal{F}$, ordered so that all redundant atoms appear after the non-redundant atoms, then the redundant atoms will be removed by $SIMP$ (**SR5** and **SR6**).
- Sibling reduction can be applied to logically equivalent descendents of p and $\neg p$, but this is co-NP complete.
- Hashing is often employed with BDDs. Construction of the hash function is merely overhead and comparing hash values is essentially constant time. But checking collisions is linear in the subtree sizes, which may in turn be exponential in the size of the input formula.

There may be many identical sibling subtrees in an OFNNF tree. Applying sibling reduction to subtrees of a larger subtree that is identical to its sibling could render the larger siblings no longer identical. It may therefore be surprising that reduced factored negation normal form is unique.

Theorem 4. Let $\mathcal{F}_1$ and $\mathcal{F}_2$ be logically equivalent formulas with atom sets L_1 and L_2; let $L = L_1 \cup L_2$. Then $ROFNNF(\mathcal{F}_1, L) \doteq ROFNNF(\mathcal{F}_2, L)$. $\square$

Recall Remark 1: Irrelevant variables processed at the end do not appear in the OFNNF of a formula. Note that, if p is an irrelevant variable, after the Shannon expansion on p, the two subtrees will necessarily be logically equivalent. As a result, when the OFNNF is constructed, the two subtrees will be identical. Thus p will be eliminated from the ROFNNF. In particular, all irrelevant variables will be eliminated from the ROFNNF, *regardless of the order in which they are processed.*

4.2   Linear Reductions

Recall that the FNNF operation can be regarded as tableaux with atomic cut and simplification, as described by Massacci [10]. In that and in other investigations, Massacci observed that simplification *should always be applied whenever possible in a tableau proof.* That is, it cannot hurt and will sometimes provide an exponential speedup at polynomial cost.

The view here is that simplification is itself only one of several techniques that may be applied within a tableau setting. *Any* inference, deduction, rewrite, or simplification technique may be employed prior to a new tableau branching step. (In the extreme, the root of the initial tableaux can always be closed by invoking a theorem-prover on its formulas.)

There is no way to know in advance whether logical inference or decomposition via tableau branching will be more efficient. However, an inference is called a *linear reduction* operation ($\rightsquigarrow$) if it introduces no new branches, does not grow the formula set, and can be done in polynomial time. Examples include Massacci's simplification, unit resolution and subsumption, and unit dissolution.

The use of linear reductions will introduce overhead but is guaranteed to produce some offsetting savings, even when the desired output is simply FNNF or OFNNF and not ROFNNF. In the worst case, a Shannon expansion step is proportional in cost to the size of the formula to which it is applied. So a reduction in size will always yield some benefit. But for ROFNNF, linear reductions also have the potential to make the recognition of identical sibling subtrees immediate.

One simple case is when the variable chosen for expansion, p, does not occur in the formula being expanded, $\mathcal{G}$; the left and right subtrees are clearly identical. Detecting this when p does occur in $\mathcal{G}$ is in general intractable, but linear reductions sometimes do this.

In Fig. 2 (left), if p occurs only in $\mathcal{G}$, p is redundant. This becomes evident only after unit dissolution on q and $\neg q$ removes $\mathcal{G}$ and thus every occurrence of p from the branch.

Somewhat more subtle opportunities are possible. Suppose a branch has the formulas shown in Fig. 2 on the right. Suppose further that $\neg q$ occurs in $\mathcal{G}$.

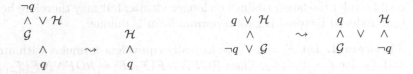

Fig. 2. Unit Dissolution and the Prawitz Rule as Linear Reductions

None of the various NC-resolution options involving q and $\neg q$ are linear reductions. However, we may dissolve on these formulas using the Prawitz Rule [13], producing an equivalent formula of equal size, shown on the right.

Now unit dissolution applies to any occurrence of $\neg q$ in $\mathcal{G}$ (or to any occurrence of q in $\mathcal{H}$). This may eliminate some variables on the branch, but in any case the formulas subject to further expansion have been simplified and reduced in size. Therefore, we assume that linear reductions are given highest priority and applied exhaustively first; only then is the next atomic cut and subsequent simplification activated.

References

1. D'Agostino, M., and Mondadori, M. The taming of the cut, *Journal of Logic and Computation* 4(3) (1994), 285–319.
2. Bryant, R. E., Symbolic Boolean manipulation with ordered binary decision diagrams, *ACM Computing Surveys* **24, 3** (1992), 293–318.
3. Cadoli, M., and Donini, F. M., A survey on knowledge compilation, *AI Communications* **10** (1997), 137–150.
4. Darwiche, A., Compiling devices: A structure-based approach, Proc. *International Conference on Principles of Knowledge Representation and Reasoning (KR98)*, Morgan-Kaufmann, San Francisco (1998), 156–166.
5. Darwiche, A., Decomposable negation normal form, *J.ACM* **48,4** (2001), 608–647.
6. Forbus, K.D. and de Kleer, J., *Building Problem Solvers*, MIT Press, Cambridge, Mass. (1993).
7. Goubault, J. and Posegga, J. BDDs and automated deduction. *Proceedings of the 8th International Symposium on Methodologies for Intelligent Systems*, Charlotte, NC, Oct. 1994. In *LNAI*, Springer-Verlag, Vol. 869, 541–550.
8. Hsiang, J. and Huang, G.S., Some Fundamental Properties of Boolean Ring Normal Forms, DIMACS series on Discrete Mathematics and Computer Science Vol. 35: The Satisfiability Problem, AMS, 587–602, 1997.
9. Marquis, P., Knowledge compilation using theory prime implicates, Proc. *IJCAI'95*, Morgan-Kaufmann, San Mateo, California, 837-843.
10. Massacci, Fabio. Simplification: A General Constraint Propagation Technique for Propositional and Modal Tableau. *Proc. TABLEAUX'98*, Oosterwijk, The Netherlands, 1998. In *LNAI* (H. de Swart, Ed.), Springer-Verlag, Vol. 1397, 217–232.
11. Mondadori M. Classical Analytical Deduction, part I & II. Annali dell' Università di Ferrara, Nuova Serie, sezione III, Filosofia, Discussion Paper, n. 1 & 5, Università degli Studi di Ferrara, Italy, 1988.
12. Murray, N.V. and Rosenthal, E. Inference with path resolution and semantic graphs. *J. ACM* **34**,2 (1987), 225–254.

13. Murray, N.V., and Rosenthal, E. Dissolution: Making paths vanish. *J.ACM* **40,3** (July 1993), 504–535.
14. Murray, N.V. and Rosenthal E., Tableaux, Path Dissolution, and Decomposable Negation Normal Form for Knowledge Compilation, In *Proceedings* of the *TABLEAUX 2003*, Rome, Italy, September 2003. In *LNAI* (M. C. Mayer & F. Pirri, Eds.), Springer-Verlag, Vol. 2796.
15. Hähnle, R., Murray, N.V., and Rosenthal, E. Normal forms for knowledge compilation, Technical Report SUNYA-CS-04-06, Department of Computer Science, University at Albany - SUNY, October, 2004.
16. Ramesh, A. and Murray, N.V. An application of non-clausal deduction in diagnosis. *Expert Systems with Applications* **12,**1 (1997), 119-126.
17. Selman, B., and Kautz, H., Knowledge compilation and theory approximation, *J.ACM* **43,2** (1996), 193-224.

On the Approximate Division of Fuzzy Relations

Patrick Bosc, Olivier Pivert, and Daniel Rocacher

IRISA/ENSSAT, Technopole Anticipa BP 80518,
22305 Lannion Cedex – France

Abstract. Boolean queries may turn out to be too limited to answer certain users needs and it is desirable to envisage extended queries by introducing preferences in the conditions. In this paper, an extension of the division operator, called the approximate division, is studied where the operand relations are fuzzy ones (i.e., are made of weighted tuples) and the universal quantifier underlying the division is softened. The objective is twofold: i) to point out that fuzzy sets provide a convenient framework for the desired extension and ii) to show that the result of the approximate division is a quotient (in reference to the characterization of the quotient of two integers), which provides a well founded semantics.

1 Introduction

Many research works in the database area aim at enriching the capabilities offered by the systems. In particular, some efforts have been devoted to the expression and the interpretation of fuzzy queries in the relational framework (see [2] for instance). The most common operations of the relational algebra (e.g., selection and join) have been studied in order to take into account levels of preference. On the contrary, the division operation has not been so much investigated [1, 3, 4, 5, 6, 7] and different extensions have been proposed with various motivations and contexts. A typical division query is: "find the stores which have orders in quantity greater than 35 on all the products priced under $127" where the dividend is the relation made of the relevant orders, and the divisor is the designated subset of products. In the following, two aspects are taken into account in the extension of the division:

- dividend and divisor relations are fuzzy ones and the term division of fuzzy relations is then used. A fuzzy relation represents a fuzzy (or gradual) concept and is made of weighted tuples, each of which being more or less compatible with this concept. For instance, from a relation p giving the price of a set of products, one can build a fuzzy relation "high-priced products" (hpp) where the grade of each tuple expresses the extent to which this tuple describes a high-priced product;
- the division operation is made more tolerant by a relaxation of the constraint tied to the universal quantifier underlying a division. Such a division is called an approximate division and it applies to both regular and fuzzy relations.

The objective of this paper is to show that the two directions envisaged may lead to a division whose result is a quotient (in relation with the properties of the quotient of

M.-S. Hacid et al. (Eds.): ISMIS 2005, LNAI 3488, pp. 314–322, 2005.
© Springer-Verlag Berlin Heidelberg 2005

integers), provided that appropriate choices are made. This question is mainly a matter of semantics insofar as sound (well founded) extensions of the division are then obtained and the term division is appropriate.

The rest of the paper is organized as follows. In section 2, the definition of the regular division operation is recalled along with the two properties which characterize a quotient. The principle used to adapt the division to fuzzy relations is also briefly given. Section 3 is devoted to the notion of approximate division founded on the weakening of the universal quantifier sustaining the regular division. The approximate division of fuzzy relations is then defined. The property of its result in terms of a quotient is examined in section 4. The last section concludes the paper by summarizing the principal contributions and pointing out some lines for future research.

2 Some Reminders About the Division

2.1 The Usual Division

The division of relation r of schema $R(A, X)$ by relation s of schema $S(B)$ where A and B are compatible sets of attributes is defined as:

$$div(r, s, \{A\}, \{B\}) = t = \{x \mid (x \in dom(X)) \wedge (\forall a, (a \in s) \Rightarrow (<a, x> \in r))\} \quad (1)$$

where $dom(X)$ denotes the domain of attribute X. In other words, an element x belongs to the result t if and only if it is associated in r with *at least all* the values a appearing in s. The justification of the term "division" assigned to this operation relies on the fact that a property similar to that of the quotient of integers holds. The resulting relation t obtained with this definition has the double characteristic of a quotient, namely:

$$\forall u, (u \in t) \Rightarrow (prod(\{u\}, s) \subseteq r) \quad (2a)$$
$$\forall t_1, (t_1 \supset t) \Rightarrow (\exists u, (u \in t_1) \wedge (prod(\{u\}, s) \nsubseteq r)) \quad (2b)$$

where $prod(r_1, r_2)$ denotes the Cartesian product of the relations r_1 and r_2.

It turns out that if the divisor is empty, the result cannot be calculated in practice, since it is the entire domain of X, which is not represented in a database system. Consequently, it is assumed that the divisor relation is not empty.

2.2 The Division of Fuzzy Relations

The context considered now is that of flexible queries where conditions call on preferences instead of Boolean criteria. The answer to such a query is made of a set of elements rank-ordered according to their fitting with respect to preferences. From now on, it will be assumed that predicates of flexible queries are modeled by fuzzy sets [2]. Formally, a fuzzy relation is defined as a fuzzy subset of the Cartesian product of domains of values. Hence, a fuzzy relation r of schema $R(A, B, C)$ is a set of weighted triples $t = <a, b, c>$, denoted by $\mu_r(t)/t$, where $\mu_r(t)$ stands for the membership degree of t in r, i.e., its compatibility with the fuzzy concept associated with this relation. A regular relation is a special case where all the degrees equal 1. A flexible query involves operators applying to fuzzy relations and returning a fuzzy relation, which are obtained through a natural extension of the usual algebraic operators. For instance, the selection of a fuzzy relation r by means of the fuzzy condition f-cond is defined as:

$$\mu_{sel(r, \text{ f-cond})}(t) = \top(\mu_r(t), \mu_{\text{f-cond}}(t)) \tag{3}$$

where H stands for a triangular norm generalizing the conjunction, e.g., the minimum or the product.

Let us consider the relations o and p describing orders and products, whose respective schemas are O(np, store, qty) and P(np, name, price). By analogy with a query calling on a division such as "find the stores which have orders in quantity greater than 35 on *all* the products priced under $127", one may envisage the query aiming at the determination of *the extent* to which any store has orders on *all* the *fairly cheap* products in a *high* quantity, which is expressed thanks to a division of fuzzy relations, namely div(hq-o, fcp-p, {np}, {np}), where the fuzzy relations hq-o and fcp-p are defined as follows:

hq-o = project(select(o, qty = "high"), {np, store}) ;
fcp-p = project(select(p, price = "fairly cheap"), {np}).

Such an extension entails to replace the regular implication by a fuzzy one (i.e., an application from $[0, 1]^2$ to $[0, 1]$), denoted by $\Rightarrow_f$) in formula 1. This leads to:

$$\forall x \in dom(X), \mu_{div(r, \text{ s, } \{A\}, \{B\})}(x) = \inf_s \mu_s(a) \Rightarrow_f \mu_r(a, x) \tag{4}$$

The corresponding double characterization of the result t as a quotient, initially provided by formulas (2a) and (2b), becomes:

$$\forall x, (x \in supp(t) \wedge \mu_t(x) = d) \Rightarrow (prod(\{d/<x>\}, s)) \subseteq r \tag{5a}$$
$$\forall x, (x \in dom(X) \wedge \mu_t(x) = d) \Rightarrow (\forall d1 > d, prod(\{d1/<x>\}, s) \not\subseteq r) \tag{5b}$$

where supp(r), the support of a fuzzy relation r, is defined as: $\{u \mid \mu_r(u) > 0\}$.

The question that arises is about the influence of the choice of the fuzzy implication on the properties of the result of the division. It turns out that only R-implications ensure that the result delivered by expression 4 is a quotient, if we limit ourselves to the case where the Cartesian product is computed by means of a triangular norm. An R-implication is a function from $[0, 1]^2$ to $[0, 1]$, denoted by $\Rightarrow_{R-i}$, which satisfies a number of axioms such as the decreasing (resp. increasing) monotony with respect to the first (resp. second) argument, $(0 \Rightarrow_f a) = 1$, $(a \Rightarrow_f 1) = 1$ and $(1 \Rightarrow_f a) = a)$. It is defined as:

$$p \Rightarrow_{R-i} q = \sup_{[0, 1]} \{u \mid \top(p, u) \leq q\} \tag{6}$$

The minimal element of R-implications, which is obtained by choosing $\top(a, b) = \min(a, b)$ in formula 6, is Gödel implication:

$$p \Rightarrow_{G\ddot{o}} q = 1 \text{ if } p \leq q, \text{ q otherwise.}$$

The family of R-implications has other representatives, for instance Goguen (resp. Lukasiewicz) implication:

$$p \Rightarrow_{Gg} q \text{ (resp. } p \Rightarrow_{Lu} q) = 1 \text{ if } p \leq q, q/p \text{ (resp. } 1 - p + q) \text{ otherwise,}$$

obtained with $\tau(a, b) = a \times b$ (resp. $\max(a + b - 1, 0)$).

It can be easily shown that if t denotes the result of the division obtained using expression 4 with the norm τ, properties 5a and 5b hold, provided that the Cartesian product is based on the same norm (τ) and the inclusion is straightforwardly extended to fuzzy relations as follows:

$$r \subseteq s \Leftrightarrow \forall x \in X, \mu_r(x) \leq \mu_s(x)).$$

Example 1. Let us consider the following fuzzy relations r and s whose respective schemas are R(A, X) and S(B):

$r = \{0.7/<a_1, x>, 0.4/<a_2, x>, 1/<a_3, x>, 1/<a_1, y>, 0.6/<a_2, y>, 0.2/<a_3, y>, 1/<a_1, z>\}$
$s = \{1/<a_1>, 0.5/<a_2>, 0.3/<a_3>\}.$

If the norm "minimum" is chosen in expression 6, Gödel implication is obtained and the result t of the division of r by s (formula 4) is:

$$\mu_t(x) = \inf(1 \Rightarrow_{G\ddot{o}} 0.7, 0.5 \Rightarrow_{G\ddot{o}} 0.4, 0.3 \Rightarrow_{G\ddot{o}} 1) = \inf(0.7, 0.4, 1) = 0.4,$$
$$\mu_t(y) = \inf(1 \Rightarrow_{G\ddot{o}} 1, 0.5 \Rightarrow_{G\ddot{o}} 0.6, 0.3 \Rightarrow_{G\ddot{o}} 0.2) = \inf(1, 1, 0.2) = 0.2,$$
$$\mu_t(z) = \inf(1 \Rightarrow_{G\ddot{o}} 1, 0.5 \Rightarrow_{G\ddot{o}} 0, 0.3 \Rightarrow_{G\ddot{o}} 0) = \inf(1, 0, 0) = 0.$$

The Cartesian product of each element and s, using the norm "minimum", leads to:

$\{0.4/<a_1, x>, 0.4/<a_2, x>, 0.3/<a_3, x>\}, \{0.2/<a_1, y>, 0.2/<a_2, y>, 0.2/<a_3, y>\}, \{\}.$

Each of these relations is (strictly) included in r and expression 5a holds. The presence of the tuples $0.4/<a_2, x>$ and $0.2/<a_3, y>$ in the first two Cartesian products is a token of the fact that t is maximal (according to expression 5b). Moreover, if a positive degree is used instead 0 for the third Cartesian product, one gets a non empty relation with the elements $<a_2, z>$ and $<a_3, z>\}$ which are not at all present in r. ◆

It must be noticed that here again, the result cannot be computed in practice when the divisor is the empty relation, but also when it is not a normalized relation (i.e., a fuzzy relation where at least one element has the degree 1), which extends the notion of an empty relation. Indeed, in such a case, any element of the domain may receive a positive degree even if it is completely absent from the dividend.

Example 2. Let us consider the following fuzzy relations r and s whose respective schemas are R(A, X) and S(B):

$r = \{0.7/<a_1, x>, 0.4/<a_2, x>, 1/<a_3, x>, 1/<a_1, y>, 0.6/<a_2, y>, 0.2/<a_3, y>, 1/<a_1, z>\}$
$s = \{0.8/<a_1>, 0.5/<a_2>, 0.3/<a_3>\}.$

If the norm $H(a, b) = \max(a + b - 1, 0)$ is chosen in expression 6, Lukasiewicz implication is obtained and the result t of the division of r by s (formula 4) is:

$\mu_t(x) = \inf(0.8 \Rightarrow_{Lu} 0.7, 0.5 \Rightarrow_{Lu} 0.4, 0.3 \Rightarrow_{Lu} 1) = \inf(0.9, 0.9, 1) = 0.9,$

$\mu_t(y) = \inf(0.8 \Rightarrow_{Lu} 1, 0.5 \Rightarrow_{Lu} 0.6, 0.3 \Rightarrow_{Lu} 0.2) = \inf(1, 1, 0.9) = 0.9,$

$\mu_t(z) = \inf(0.8 \Rightarrow_{Lu} 1, 0.5 \Rightarrow_{Lu} 0, 0.3 \Rightarrow_{Lu} 0) = \inf(1, 0.5, 0.7) = 0.5,$

and for any other element w of the domain, the degree is:

$\mu_t(w) = \inf(0.8 \Rightarrow_{Lu} 0, 0.5 \Rightarrow_{Lu} 0, 0.3 \Rightarrow_{Lu} 0) = \inf(0.2, 0.5, 0.7) = 0.2.$ ◆

In the following, it will be assumed that the divisor fuzzy relation is normalized.

3   The Approximate Division

The principle retained for defining the approximate division is to replace the universal quantifier underlying the division (see formula 1) by the relative fuzzy quantifier "almost all" [8]. The approximate division obtained, denoted by app-div, constitutes a weakening of the constraint imposed by the non-approximate division. This line of extension makes it possible to consider queries of the form:

"find the extent to which any store has been ordered *almost all* the products whose price is less than $127 in a quantity greater than 35"

which calls on an *approximate division* of *regular* relations, or:

"find the extent to which any store has been ordered *almost all fairly cheap products in a high quantity*"

which is a matter of *approximate division* of *fuzzy* relations. It is worth mentioning that this type of division can be of interest beyond the strict relational framework, e.g., in information retrieval in order to get the documents related to *almost all* the keywords of a specified set.

The quantifier "almost all" is modeled by a function from the unit interval to itself. The idea is to ignore *up to a certain point* some of the values of the divisor which are weakly (or even not at all) associated with a given x appearing in the dividend. Then, in the same spirit as formula 4, the approximate division of the fuzzy relation r whose schema is (A, X) by the fuzzy relation s whose schema is (B) is defined as:

$$\forall x \in \text{dom}(X), \mu_{\text{div-app}(r, s, \{A\}, \{B\})}(x) = \inf_s \max(\alpha_i, w_i) \tag{7}$$

where α_i is the ith smallest implication value $(\mu_s(a_j) \Rightarrow_f \mu_r(a_j, x))$ and $w_i = \mu_{\text{almost all}}(1 - i/n)$, i.e., the degree of ignorance obtained from the quantifier "almost all" for relation s whose support contains n elements (n implication values come into play in formula 7).

It can be noticed that in formula 7, w_i plays the role of a guaranteed level of satisfaction when i elements are ignored.

As R-implications are required to deliver a quotient for the division of fuzzy relations, they are still used for the approximate division. Such a choice guarantees that the approximate division is a true generalization of the division: it is easy to see that if the universal quantifier is used (which is a limit case of "almost-all"), formula 7 boils down to formula 4, since all the grades of ignorance (w_i) equal 0. Similarly, it is easy to check that the result of the approximate division is a superset of that returned by the non-approximate one. Last, let us mention that the divisor relation must be normalized so that the computation can be performed whatever the fuzzy implication used.

Example 3. Let us consider the following extensions of the fuzzy relations r and s whose respective schemas are R(A, X) and S(B):

$$r = \{0.1/<a_1, u>, 0.1/<a_2, u>, 0.2/<a_3, u>, 0.5/<a_4, u>, 0.7/<a_5, u>,$$
$$0.9/<a_6, u>, 1/<a_7, u>, 1/<a_8, u>, 0.2/<a_9, u>, 0.5/<a_{10}, u>,$$
$$0.3/<a_1, v>, 0.3/<a_2, v>, 1/<a_3, v>, ..., 1/<a_{10}, v>\}$$
$$s = \{1/<a_1>, 0.9/<a_2>, 0.9/<a_3>, 0.9/<a_4>, 0.9/<a_5>, 0.8/<a_6>, 0.4/<a_7>,$$
$$0.7/<a_8>, 0.2/<a_9>, 0.1/<a_{10}>\}$$

Let "almost all" be the quantifier defined as:

$\mu_{almost-all}(k) = 0$ for $k \in [0, 0.75]$, $\mu_{almost-all}(k) = 1$ for $k \in [0.95, 1]$,
$\mu_{almost-all}(k)$ is linearly increasing for $k \in [0.75, 0.95]$.

In the perspective of the approximate division of r by s (when s has 10 elements), this quantifier generates the grades (of ignorance):

$$w_1 = 0.75, w_2 = 0.25, w_3 = ... = w_{10} = 0.$$

Applying formula 7 with Lukasiewicz implication, the obtained result is:

$$\mu_{div-app(r, s, \{A\}, \{B\})}(u) = \inf(\max(0.1, 0.75), \max(0.2, 0.25), \max(0.3, 0),$$
$$\max(0.6, 0), \max(0.8, 0), \max(1, 0), \max(1, 0),$$
$$\max(1, 0), \max(1, 0), \max(1, 0)) = 0.25$$
$$\mu_{div-app(r, s, \{A\}, \{B\})}(v) = \inf(\max(0.3, 0.75), \max(0.4, 0.25), \max(1, 0),$$
$$\max(1, 0), \max(1, 0), \max(1, 0), \max(1, 0),$$
$$\max(1, 0), \max(1, 0), \max(1, 0)) = 0.4$$

For u, the values 0.1 and 0.2 are disregarded thanks to w_1 and w_2, while for v, only 0.3 is ignored thanks to w_1. The result of the non-approximate division of r and s, t1 = $\{0.1/<u>, 0.3/<v>\}$, is (strictly) included in t = $\{0.25/<u>, 0.4/<v>\}$.♦

4 Characterizing the Result of the Approximate Division

The characterization of the result delivered by the approximate division (expression 7) cannot be based directly on expressions 5a and 5b. Some modifications must be performed so as to reflect that the universal quantifier has been softened into "almost all". Moreover, the Cartesian product and the inclusion operators to be used must be appropriately specified. All these aspects are dealt with in subsection 4.1, while the fact that the approximate division delivers a quotient is studied in subsection 4.2.

4.1 Adaptation of the Characterization Formulas

The regular inclusion used in expressions 5a and 5b must be changed into an approximate one (denoted by $\subseteq_a$), in order to account for the relaxation of the universal quantifier involved in the approximate division. Consequently, the expressions characterizing the result t of an approximate division of fuzzy relations are the following:

$$\forall x, (x \in \text{supp}(t) \wedge \mu_t(x) = d) \Rightarrow (\text{prod}(\{d/\!<\!x\!>\}), s)) \subseteq_a r \qquad (8a)$$
$$\forall x, (x \in \text{dom}(X) \wedge \mu_t(x) = d) \Rightarrow (\forall d_1 > d, \text{prod}(\{d_1/\!<\!x\!>\}), s) \not\subseteq_a r) \qquad (8b)$$

It is now necessary to specify the Cartesian product and inclusion operations appearing in expressions 8a and 8b. Here again, the Cartesian product is founded on the generative norm of the considered R-implication. The approximate inclusion must be somehow the counterpart of the approximate division and it must be designed so that: i) its result is a Boolean one in order to assess whether or not a relation is approximately included in another relation, and ii) it is able to ignore some elements which do not comply with the regular inclusion. From these two points, the following approximate inclusion ($\subseteq_a$) is defined in relation with the approximate division:

prod($\{d/\!<\!x\!>\}$, s) $\subseteq_a$ r $\Leftrightarrow$ the maximal degree appearing in prod($\{d/\!<\!x\!>\}$, s)
is not greater than $w_q = \mu_{\text{almost all}}(1 - q/n)$ where
n denotes the cardinality of the support of s and
q is the number of elements of prod($\{d/\!<\!x\!>\}$, s)
not included in r (in the regular sense), $\qquad (9)$

Example 4. Let us consider the data of example 3, where the approximate division of relation r by s produced the result t = $\{0.25/\!<\!u\!>, 0.4/\!<\!v\!>\}$. The Cartesian product (using the norm $\tau(x, y) = \max(x + y - 1, 0)$) of $\{0.25/\!<\!u\!>\}$ with s gives:

$\{0.25/\!<\!a_1, u\!>, 0.15/\!<\!a_2, u\!>, 0.15/\!<\!a_3, u\!>, 0.15/\!<\!a_4, u\!>, 0.15/\!<\!a_5, u\!>, 0.05/\!<\!a_6, u\!>\}$.

According to formula 9, this relation is approximately included in r, since the maximal degree appearing in this relation is 0.25, two elements ($<\!a_1, u\!>$ and $<\!a_2, u\!>$) are not included in r and 0.25 = w_2. Similarly, the Cartesian product of $\{0.4/\!<\!v\!>\}$ with s, using the same norm as before delivers the relation:

$\{0.4/\!<\!a_1, v\!>, 0.3/\!<\!a_2, v\!>, 0.3/\!<\!a_3, v\!>, 0.3/\!<\!a_4, v\!>, 0.3/\!<\!a_5, v\!>,$
$0.2/\!<\!a_6, v\!>, 0.1/\!<\!a_8, v\!>\}$,

which is also approximately included in r since it is possible to ignore the element $<\!a_1, v\!>$ ($0.4 < w_1$). Upgrading the degree 0.25 associated with u to $d_1 = 0.25^+$ ($0.25 < 0.25^+ \le 1$) leads to a Cartesian product pr_1 involving in particular the two following elements that must be ignored: $\{0.25^+/\!<\!a_1, u\!>, d_2/\!<\!a_2, u\!>\}$ where $0.15 < d_2 \le 0.9$. Such a relation pr_1 is therefore not approximately included in r ($0.25^+ > w_2$). It can easily be checked that it is the same if the degree (d = 0.4) assigned to v is increased to 0.4^+, since at least two values of the Cartesian product are not included in r. It turns out that the expressions (8a) and (8b) hold. ◆

4.2 Approximate Division and Quotient

As mentioned earlier, this subsection is intended for giving the proof that the situation observed in the previous example is general, i.e., that the result returned by the approximate division defined by expression 7 is a quotient (formulas 8a and 8b hold).

Let $s = \{\mu_1/<a_1>, \ldots, \mu_n/<a_n>\}$ and let r be a fuzzy relation containing the tuples: $\{v_1/<u, a_1>, \ldots, v_n/<u, a_n>\}$ (some of the v_i's may be equal to 0), such that:

$$0 \leq \alpha_1 = (\mu_{i_1} \Rightarrow_{R\text{-}i} v_{i_1}) \leq \ldots \leq \alpha_n = (\mu_{i_n} \Rightarrow_{R\text{-}i} v_{i_n}) \leq 1,$$

where the fuzzy implication $\Rightarrow_{R\,i}$ is generated by the norm $\top$. Let "almost all" be the quantifier such that:

$$w_i = \mu_{\text{almost all}}(1 - i/n) \text{ with } k = \sup \{j \mid w_j > 0\} \text{ and } w_1 \geq \ldots \geq w_n = 0.$$

The approximate division of r by s is performed according to formula 7 and it is assumed that q ($1 \leq q \leq k$) implication values are ignored to a certain extent, i.e., $\forall i \in [1, q]$, $w_i > \alpha_i$. Then: $\mu_{\text{div-app}(r, s, \{A\}, \{B\})}(u) = d = \min(w_q, \alpha_{q+1})$.

Case 1. $d = w_q \leq \alpha_{q+1}$. When the Cartesian product pr of $\{d/<x>\}$ and s is performed, the degrees obtained are such that:

$$\forall k \in [1, q], \tau(d, \mu_{i_k}) > v_{i_k}, \text{ since } d > \alpha_k \text{ and } \alpha_k = \sup \{u \mid \tau(u, \mu_{i_k}) \leq v_{i_k}\}$$
$$\forall k \in [q+1, n], \tau(d, \mu_{i_k}) \leq v_{i_k}, \text{ since } d \leq \alpha_k.$$

Thus, exactly q elements of pr are not included in r. The divisor s being normalized (as assumed at the end of section 2.2), the maximal degree of pr is d itself (H (d, 1) = d for any norm). Hence, since $d = w_q$, and according to formula 9, prod($\{d/<x>\}$, s)) is approximately included in r and formula 8a holds.

To check the validity of expression 8b, let x be an element of the domain of X with $\mu_t(x) = d$ and let d_1 be a degree such that $1 \geq d_1 > d$. The Cartesian product of $\{d_1/<x>\}$ and s is such that at least q of its elements have a degree greater than the one in r (that was already the case with d as written above). Due to the normalization of the divisor s, the maximal degree of pr is d1 itself and d1 > w_q. Thus:

$$\text{prod}(\{d/<x>\}, s)) \not\subseteq_a r,$$

where $\circ_a$ is defined by expression 9, which establishes the validity of expression 8b.

Case b. $d = \alpha_{q+1} < w_q$. When the Cartesian product pr of $\{d/<x>\}$ and s is performed, the degrees obtained are such that:

$$\forall k \in [1, q], \tau(d, \mu_{i_k}) \geq v_{i_k}, \text{ since } d \geq \alpha_k \text{ and } \alpha_k = \sup \{u \mid \tau(u, \mu_{i_k}) \leq v_{i_k}\}$$
$$\forall k \in [q+1, n], \tau(d, \mu_{i_k}) \leq v_{i_k}, \text{ since } d \leq \alpha_k.$$

Therefore, at most q elements of pr are not included in r. At this point, a reasoning similar to that made for case 1 allows to prove that both expression 8a and 8b hold.

5 Conclusion

An extended version of the division of (fuzzy) relations has been dealt with in this paper. The key question raised by such an extension concerns the semantics and properties of the obtained operator. In particular, it is of prime importance to assess if this is a quotient, i.e., the largest relation, which, once composed with the divisor, delivers a result included in the dividend.

The principle of the considered extension is based on the weakening of the universal quantifier underlying the regular division, which becomes "almost all". It has been shown that the result of such an extended division is a quotient provided that: i) the grades issued from the weakened quantifier allow to ignore up to a certain point unsatisfactory elements, ii) the inclusion used in the double characterization of a quotient is defined in association with the approximate division, i.e., is able to ignore elements which are not included in the regular sense, and iii) the divisor relation is normalized. One of the interests of this work is to show that fuzzy sets provide an appropriate framework for modeling queries calling on divisions of fuzzy relations, while ensuring some semantic property as to the result obtained.

This work can be pursued according to several directions. A first one concerns the investigation of non-normalized (or empty) divisor relations. A second topic is about the expression of the (approximate) division operation in a user-oriented query language, such as SQL. In this respect, the algebraic rewriting of the division is worthy of investigation, since it is the basis of one of the expressions of the division in SQL.

References

1. Bosc P., Dubois D., Pivert O., Prade H.: Flexible queries in relational databases - the example of the division operator. Theoretical Computer Science **171** (1997) 281-301.
2. Bosc P., Buckles B., Petry F., Pivert O.: Fuzzy databases. In : Fuzzy Sets in Approximate Reasoning and Information Systems, Bezdek J., Dubois D., Prade H. eds (1999) 403-468.
3. Cubero J.C., Medina J.M., Pons O., Vila M.A.: The generalized selection: an alternative way for the quotient operations in fuzzy relational databases. Proc. of the 5th IPMU Conference, Paris, France (1994) 23-30.
4. Dubois D., Prade H.: Semantics of quotient operators in fuzzy relational databases. Fuzzy Sets and Systems **78** (1996) 89-94.
5. Mouaddib N.: The nuanced relational division. Proc. of the 2nd IEEE International Conference on Fuzzy Systems (FUZZ-IEEE'93), San Francisco, USA (1993) 419-424.
6. Umano M., Fukami S.: Fuzzy relational algebra for possibility-distribution-fuzzy-relational model of fuzzy data. Journal of Intelligent Information Systems **3** (1994) 7-28.
7. Yager R.R.: Fuzzy quotient operators for fuzzy relational databases. Proc. of the International Fuzzy Engineering Symposium (IFES'91), Yokohama, Japan (1991) 289-296.
8. Zadeh L.A.: A computational approach to fuzzy quantifiers in natural languages. Computer Mathematics with Applications **9** (1983) 149-183.

Efficient Learning of Pseudo-Boolean Functions from Limited Training Data

Guoli Ding[1], Jianhua Chen[2], Robert Lax[1], and Peter Chen[2]

[1] Mathematics Department, Louisiana State University,
Baton Rouge, LA 70803, USA
{ding, lax}@math.lsu.edu
[2] Computer Science Department, Louisiana State University,
Baton Rouge, LA 70803, USA
{jianhua, chen}@csc.lsu.edu

Abstract. Pseudo-Boolean functions are generalizations of Boolean functions. We present a new method for learning pseudo-Boolean functions from limited training data. The objective of learning is to obtain a function f which is a good approximation of the target function f^*. We define suitable criteria for the "goodness" of an approximating function. One criterion is to choose a function f that minimizes the "expected distance" with respect to a distance function d (over pairs of pseudo-Boolean functions) and the uniform distribution over all feasible pseudo-Boolean functions. We define two alternative "distance measures" over pairs of pseudo-Boolean functions, and show that they are are actually equivalent with respect to the criterion of minimal expected distance. We outline efficient algorithms for learning pseudo-Boolean functions according to these criteria. Other reasonable distance measures and "goodness" criteria are also discussed.

1 Introduction

In real-world applications of machine learning, it is quite possible to encounter situations where available data is small in quantity, expensive to obtain, and so on. In fact, we face such a scenario in our study on security and terrorist profiling and recognition: there is a very small amount of terrorist data available for learning the patterns of terrorists. Other possible scenarios include machine learning in medical and legal fields where data may be quite difficult to acquire due to economic/legal reasons. It is highly desirable to develop a methodology for learning from limited training data.

To motivate the learning problems, imagine the following situation: You are given a small set of data points of the form $D = \{\langle s_i, p_i \rangle : 1 \leq i \leq m\}$ where each s_i is a 0-1 vector of dimension n and each p_i is a real number in the interval $[-1, +1]$. The vectors s_i represent attributes of some instances (such as being a young person, tall, etc.) and the values p_i represent such instance's rating as a possible terrorist. Your task is to develop a method that learns from this data set D some patterns that can be used for predicting the ratings of unseen

M.-S. Hacid et al. (Eds.): ISMIS 2005, LNAI 3488, pp. 323–331, 2005.
© Springer-Verlag Berlin Heidelberg 2005

instances as possible terrorists. Since the data D may be rather limited in size, your method has to take this factor into consideration. Here the "patterns" will be modeled as *pseudo-Boolean* functions which are generalizations of Boolean functions.

Our proposed framework handles this learning task by finding a pseudo-Boolean function f that is a good approximation to the target function f^*. The training data D are seen as constraints $f^*(s_i) = p_i$ $(1 \le i \le m)$ on the eligible hypotheses, and each consistent hypothesis is deemed equally probable. This is essentially the Bayesian approach to learning. (Note that the *hard* constraints imposed by the data can be easily relaxed by allowing a margin $\gamma > 0$.) Since each eligible pseudo-Boolean function can be represented as a linear function, i.e., a vector in multi-dimensional space, the target function f^* can be seen as a vector of random variables. So selecting a function f as an approximation of f^* can be cast as selecting a prototype vector as values for the random variables minimizing some suitable measure of "approximation error". This leads to the "explicit learning" problem addressed in this paper. Compared with existing works [7] [8] for learning linear functions, our method considers the factor of small training sample size and is thus more realistic. Moreover, we make use of efficient, randomized computational geometry algorithms [3][4][6] for the learning task. Our method recognizes the important role of the *centroid* of the polyhedron for the *version space*, and thus it bears a strong resemblance to the *Bayes Point Machine*[5] model of learning. However, we arrived at the conclusion from a different perspective - namely the pseudo-Boolean functions rather than linear classifiers.

This paper is organized as follows. In Section 2, we give the preliminary definitions and concepts about pseudo-Boolean functions and their representations. Section 3 further discusses the special class of pseudo-Boolean functions which are the focus of this paper. We then formulate the explicit pseudo-Boolean function learning problem in Section 4. The solution to the learning problem is described in Sections 5 and 6. We omit the proofs of the propositions/lemmas in the paper due to space limits.

2   Representing Pseudo-Boolean Functions

Let n be a positive integer and B^n be the set of all n-dimensional 0-1 vectors. A *pseudo-Boolean* function f is a mapping from B^n to R, the set of real numbers. The set of all these functions is denoted by $\mathcal{F}_n$. Notice that f is just an ordinary *boolean* function if its range is $\{0, 1\}$. We use R^t to denote the t-dimensional Euclidean space in our discussions.

Let $\mathcal{H}$ be a class of pseudo-Boolean functions. Suppose there exists a function f^* which is the "target" of learning. We are given no other information about f^* except a small set of training data points in the form $\{< x_i, f^*(x_i) > | 1 \le i \le m\}$. We want to learn from this training data set a function f which is a "good" approximation of the target f^*. More detailed formulation specifying the "goodness" of a hypothesis $h \in \mathcal{H}$ will be described in Section 4.

One way to represent a pseudo-Boolean function f is to list values of $f(x)$, for all $x \in B^n$. Therefore, we may consider f as a 2^n-dimensional vector, which we denote by $v(f)$. Let us denote by R^{B^n} the set of all vectors whose coordinates are indexed by members of B^n. Then it is clear that the mapping $v \colon \mathcal{F}_n \to R^{B^n}$, is a one-to-one correspondence. Representing a pseudo-Boolean function by a vector in R^{B^n} is very inefficient, but we need it to study the behavior of these functions.

A *multi-linear polynomial* on $V = \{x_1, x_2, ..., x_n\}$ is an expression:

$$\sum_{Z \subseteq V} \alpha_Z \prod_{z \in Z} z, \tag{1}$$

where $\prod_{z \in \emptyset} z$ is defined to be 1.

For example, for the case $V = \{x_1, x_2, x_3, x_4, x_5\}$, we can have a pseudo-Boolean function f represented by multi-linear polynomial expression $f = 2x_1 x_3 + 4.8x_2 x_5 - 7.2x_4$. Clearly, pseudo-Boolean functions can be seen as weighted sum of Boolean terms.

Let 2^V be the set of all subsets of V and let R^{2^V} be the set of all vectors whose coordinates are indexed by members of 2^V. Then each multi-linear polynomial given in form (1) can be considered as the vector $\alpha = (\alpha_Z : Z \in 2^V) \in R^{2^V}$. Clearly, expression (1), and thus α, defines a pseudo-Boolean function $f_\alpha \in \mathcal{F}_n$. It is well known [1] that every pseudo-Boolean function can be uniquely expressed by a multi-linear polynomial, we conclude that the mapping $c : \alpha \mapsto f_\alpha$, is a one-to-one correspondence from R^{2^V} to $\mathcal{F}_n$. Clearly, $|2^V| = 2^n$ and R^{2^V} is actually R^{2^n}, the 2^n-dimensional Euclidean space.

We have seen that each pseudo-Boolean function can be expressed by its value vector in R^{B^n}, as well as its coefficient vector in R^{2^V}. Our question is: what is the connection between these two expressions. The following result says that they differ only by a full rank linear transformation. Let $u = v \circ c$, the composition of mappings v and c. Namely, u maps a coefficient vector α in R^{2^V} (for the function f_α) to the function's value vector β in R^{B^n}. The following shows that the mapping u is a one-to-one mapping.

Proposition 1. *There exists a full rank square matrix M such that, for all $\beta \in R^{B^n}$ and $\alpha \in R^{2^V}$, $\beta = u(\alpha)$ if and only if $\beta = M\alpha$.*

3   Special Class of Pseudo-Boolean Functions

3.1   Compact Expressions

In applications, we often consider functions that have a compact (polynomial size) multi-linear polynomial expression. Examples of these include linear functions and quadratic functions. This is the motivation for our following definition.

Let $\mathcal{T}$ be a set of subsets of $V = \{x_1, x_2, ..., x_n\}$ such that $|\mathcal{T}|$ is bounded above by a polynomial function of n, i.e., $\mathcal{T}$ contains only polynomially many subsets of V. Put $|T| = \tau$. We define $\mathcal{B}_T$ to be the set of all pseudo-Boolean functions that can be expressed as

$$\sum_{Z \in T} \alpha_Z \prod_{z \in Z} z, \qquad (2)$$

In the rest of this paper, we focus on $\mathcal{B}_T$, the class of pseudo-Boolean functions that have a compact multi-linear polynomial expression. Like before, we can consider each $f \in \mathcal{B}_T$ as a vector $(\alpha_Z : Z \in T)$. Let R^T be the set of vectors whose coordinates are indexed by members of T. Then, R^T is a subspace of R^{2^V} - in fact, $R^T = R^\tau$.

We may also consider the value vector of functions in $\mathcal{B}_T$. It follows from Proposition 1 that these vectors also form a subspace.

Proposition 2. $\{\beta \in R^{B^n} : \beta = v(f), f \in \mathcal{B}_T\}$ *is a subspace.*

3.2   A Special Class of Pseudo-Boolean Functions

Let t be a positive integer. A bounded subset P of R^t is called a *polyhedron* if, for some positive integer m, there exist an $m \times t$ matrix A and a vector $b \in R^m$ such that $P = \{x \in R^t : Ax \le b\}$.

In most applications, we are only interested in certain special functions in $\mathcal{B}_T$. The following are two examples.

Example 1. $\mathcal{H}_1 = \{f \in \mathcal{B}_T : 0 \le f(x) \le 1, \ \forall x \in B^n\}$.

Example 2. $\mathcal{H}_2 = \{f \in \mathcal{B}_T : -1 \le \alpha_Z \le 1, \ \forall Z \in T\}$.

In general, let $\mathcal{H} \subseteq \mathcal{B}_T$ be a class of functions that we are interested in. Let

$$R^{B^n}(\mathcal{H}) = \{\beta \in R^{B^n} : \beta = v(f), f \in \mathcal{H}\}, \text{ and}$$
$$R^T(\mathcal{H}) = \{\alpha \in R^T : f_\alpha \in \mathcal{H}\}.$$

Clearly, $R^T(\mathcal{H}_2)$ is a polyhedron in R^T (in fact, it is a hypercube). It is also clear, by Proposition 2, that $R^{B^n}(\mathcal{H}_1)$ is a polyhedron in R^{B^n}. At this point, an interesting question is: are $R^T(\mathcal{H}_1)$ and $R^{B^n}(\mathcal{H}_2)$ polyhedra? That is, if the vectors form a polyhedron in one space, what happens in the other space?

Let M be the matrix defined in Proposition 1. Let M_T be the submatrix of M that consists of columns indexed by all $Z \in T$. Since M has full rank, it follows that M_T also has full rank. M_T defines the one-to-one mapping from $R^T(\mathcal{H})$ to $R^{B^n}(\mathcal{H})$. Therefore, we deduce the following from Proposition 1 immediately (the *dimension* of a polyhedron is explained in more detail later).

Proposition 3. $R^{B^n}(\mathcal{H}) = \{\beta \in R^{B^n} : \beta = M_T \alpha, \alpha \in R^T(\mathcal{H})\}$. *Moreover,* $R^{B^n}(\mathcal{H})$ *is a polyhedron of dimension d if and only if $R^T(\mathcal{H})$ is a polyhedron of dimension d.*

We will consider classes $\mathcal{H}$ so that $R^{B^n}(\mathcal{H})$ or $R^T(\mathcal{H})$ is a polyhedron. The last proposition says that one is a polyhedron if and only if the other is as well. In particular, we consider $\mathcal{H}$ of the following form:

$$\mathcal{H} = \{f \in \mathcal{B}_T : -1 \le \alpha_Z \le 1, \forall Z \in T; f^*(x^i) = p_i, i = 1, 2, ..., m\},$$

where $(x^1, p_1), ..., (x^m, p_m)$ are the training data. It is easy to see that $R^T(\mathcal{H})$ is a polyhedron.

4   Formulation of the Learning Problem

The general formulation of the learning problem is the following: Given the training data D, we want to learn a function f (and thus a vector in $R^{B^n}(\mathcal{H})$, and equivalently a vector in $R^T(\mathcal{H})$) that f minimizes the expected distance $E[d(f, f^*)]$, where $d(f_1, f_2)$ is a "distance" measure, or metric, on the space of pseudo-Boolean functions. We show that the centroid of $R^{B^n}(\mathcal{H})$ is a solution to the above learning problem when the metric $d(f_1, f_2)$ is given by the square of the Euclidean distance between the vectors $v(f_1)$, $v(f_2)$ in the polyhedron $R^{B^n}(\mathcal{H})$.

4.1   Measuring the Distance

Let us first define two metrics $d(f_1, f_2)$ on the space $\mathcal{H}$. We show that the two metrics lead to the same choice of the "best" approximation of f^* when we want to choose the function f that minimizes $E[d(f, f^*)]$, the expected distance between the function f and the target function f^* drawn with uniform distribution. The first metric is defined as the square of the Euclidean distance between the vectors $v(f_1)$ and $v(f_2)$ in $R^{B^n}(\mathcal{H})$:

$$d_0(f_1, f_2) = [Euclid(v(f_1), v(f_2))]^2 = \sum_{x \in B^n} (f_1(x) - f_2(x))^2.$$

Here "$Euclid(v_1, v_2)$" denotes the Euclidean distance between the vectors v_1, v_2 in multidimensional space. Notice that this metric generalizes the traditional Hamming distance on Boolean functions. The other metric is defined by the square of the Euclidean distance between the coefficient vectors: we define

$$d_1(f_1, f_2) = [Euclid(\boldsymbol{\alpha}^{(1)}, \boldsymbol{\alpha}^{(2)})]^2 = \sum_{Z \in T} (\alpha_Z^{(1)} - \alpha_Z^{(2)})^2,$$

where $\boldsymbol{\alpha}^{(i)}$ is the vector of length τ associated to f_i (for $i = 1, 2$).

Other possible distance metrics that may be of interest for further studies (but we will not discuss them further in this paper): $d_2(f_1, f_2) = \sum_{Z \in T} |\alpha_Z^{(1)} - \alpha_Z^{(2)}|$, $d_3(f_1, f_2) = \sqrt{d_1(f_1, f_2)}$, and $d_4(f_1, f_2) = \max_{Z \in T} |\alpha_Z^{(1)} - \alpha_Z^{(2)}|$.

4.2   The Learning Problems

Formulation 1: Optimize the Expected Value.

Now suppose we are given training data D and we want to learn an unknown function f^*. Recall that the function f^* is equally likely to be any function in $\mathcal{H}$ (or equally likely to correspond to any point in the polyhedron $R^{B^n}(\mathcal{H})$). For a fixed $f \in \mathcal{H}$ and a metric $d(f_1, f_2)$, we may view the function $f^* \mapsto d(f, f^*)$ as a random variable on $\mathcal{H}$, induced from the uniformly distributed random vector in $R^{B^n}(\mathcal{H})$ (or $R^T(\mathcal{H})$ in case the distance measure is based on $R^T(\mathcal{H})$). Then, for each $f \in \mathcal{H}$, put $\rho(f) = E(d(f, f^*))$, the expected value of this random variable. Then $\rho(f)$ can be seen as a measure of the "approximation error" of f. We are ready now to state our formulation of the learning problem:

Problem 1. Select f that minimizes $\rho(f)$, over all $f \in \mathcal{H}$.

Formulation 2: Optimize the Worst-Case Scenario.
    For a fixed distance mesaure d, and for each $f \in \mathcal{H}$, let

$$\rho_1(f) = \max_{g \in \mathcal{H}} d(f, g).$$

Suppose f is used to approximate f^*. Then, in the worst case, the difference between f and f^* is $\rho_1(f)$.

Problem 2. Select f that minimizes $\rho_1(f)$, over all $f \in \mathcal{H}$. Equivalently, we want to find $f \in \mathcal{H}$ and the smallest real number r such that $d(f, f^*) \leq r$ is guaranteed for any f^* in $\mathcal{H}$.

    For each $f \in \mathcal{H}$, and each positive real number r, the *ball* with center f and radius r is $B(f, r) = \{g \in \mathcal{H} : d(f, g) \leq r\}$.

Proposition 4. $\rho_1(f) = \min_{\mathcal{H} \subseteq B(f,r)} r.$

    It is easy to see that Problem 2 is to find $f \in \mathcal{H}$ and the smallest ball centered at f that contains $\mathcal{H}$.

    In subsequent discussions, we focus on solutions to Problem 1.

5   Solution to the Learning Problem

5.1   Centroid

Let t be a positive integer. A subset F of R^t is called an *affine subspace* if there is a subspace S of R^t and a vector b in R^t such that $F = \{b + s : s \in S\}$. The *dimension* of F is the dimension of S. For any subset X of R^t, let $A(X)$ be the set of affine combinations of vectors in X (An affine combination of vectors is a linear combination of these vectors so that the sum of the coefficients equals 1). It is well known that $A(X)$ is an affine subspace and $A(X) \subseteq F$ for all affine subspaces F with $X \subseteq F$.

    Let P be a polyhedron in R^t and let $F = A(P)$, with dimension d. The *dimension* of P is defined to be the dimension of $A(P)$. Let μ_F be the d-dimensional Lebesgue measure on F. Then the *centroid* of P is defined to be $\bar{x} = (\bar{x}_1, \bar{x}_2, ..., \bar{x}_t)$, where for each $i = 1, 2, ..., t$, $\bar{x}_i = \frac{\int_P x_i d\mu_F}{\int_P d\mu_F}$.

5.2   Centroid Is the Solution for Distance Measure d_0

For any $y = (y_1, y_2, ..., y_t) \in R^t$, let $\lambda_y(x): R^t \to R$ be given by:

$$\lambda_y(x) = (x_1 - y_1)^2 + (x_2 - y_2)^2 + ... + (x_t - y_t)^2$$

where $x = (x_1, x_2, ..., x_t)$.

Let $P \subseteq R^t$ be a d-dimensional polyhedron. Let $F = A(P)$ and let μ_F be the d-dimensional Lebesgue measure on F. Let

$$\Lambda(y) = \frac{\int_P \lambda_y(x) d\mu_F}{\int_P d\mu_F}.$$

The interpretation of $\Lambda(y)$ is the following. For any point x in R^t, $\lambda_y(x)$ is the "distance" between x and y. If x is chosen at random from P, then the expected "distance" between x and y is $\Lambda(y)$.

Proposition 5. $\Lambda(y)$ *is minimized at* $\bar{x}$, *the centroid of* P.

Note that when the polyhedron P is $R^{B^n}(\mathcal{H})$, the measure $\lambda_y(x)$ for any two points $x, y \in P$ is precisely $d_0(f_x, f_y)$ as defined previously. Thus the above proposition indicates that the centroid of $R^{B^n}(\mathcal{H})$ is the solution to the learning problem 1. Let $\bar{x}$ be the centroid of $R^{B^n}(\mathcal{H})$ and let $\bar{f}$ be the corresponding function in $\mathcal{H}$. We know that $\bar{f}$ is the best approximation to the target function under the distance measure d_0, and $\bar{f}$ can be obtained by computing the centroid of $R^{B^n}(\mathcal{H})$.

However, computing the centroid of a polyhedron in the 2^n-dimensional space is not very efficient. We show next that $R^T(\mathcal{H})$ is a polyhedron in τ-dimensional space and its centroid also corresponds to $\bar{f}$ under the distance measure d_1.

5.3   Relationship Between Distance Measures d_0 and d_1

Let $d \le m$ be positive integers and let $\Phi = (\varphi_1, \varphi_2, ..., \varphi_m)$, where each φ_i is a differentiable function with variables $\xi_1, \xi_2, ..., \xi_d$. Let K be the $m \times d$ matrix with $K_{ij} = \partial \varphi_i / \partial \xi_j$. Let $|L|$ denote the determinant of square matrix L. Then we define $J(\Phi) = \sqrt{\sum |K'|^2}$, where the sum is taken over all $d \times d$ submatrices K' of K. For any $\Omega \subseteq R^d$, let $\Phi(\Omega) = \{\Phi(\omega) : \omega \in \Omega\}$.

Suppose Φ is a one-to-one function and $J(\Phi)$ is nowhere zero on R^d. Then $\Gamma = \Phi(R^d)$ is a d-dimensional manifold. Let μ_Γ be the d-dimensional Lebesgue measure on Γ. The following is a classical result in calculus, for example, see [9].

Lemma 1. *Let* $\Omega \subset R^d$ *be Lebesgue measurable and let* f *be a continuous function defined on* $\Phi(\Omega)$. *Suppose* Φ *is a one-to-one function from* R^d *to* Γ, *and* $J(\Phi) \ne 0$ *on* R^d. *Then* $\int_{\Phi(\Omega)} f \, d\mu_\Gamma = \int_\Omega (f \circ \Phi) J(\Phi) \, d\xi$.

In our application, we consider the following situation. Let $d \le t \le m$. Let $\Phi_1 : R^d \to R^t$ and $\Phi_2 : R^t \to R^m$ such that $\Phi_1(\xi) = \zeta_0 + E_1 \xi$ and $\Phi_2(\zeta) = \varsigma_0 + E_2 \zeta$, where $\zeta_0 \in R^t$, $\varsigma_0 \in R^m$, E_1 is a $t \times d$ matrix of rank d, and E_2 is an $m \times t$ matrix of rank t. Let $\Phi = \Phi_2 \circ \Phi_1$. Clearly, $J(\Phi_1)$, $J(\Phi_2)$, and $J(\Phi)$ are non-zero constants. Let μ_1 and μ_2 be the d-dimensional Lebesgue measures on $\Phi_1(R^d)$ and $\Phi(R^d) = \Phi_2(\Phi_1(R^d))$, respectively.

Lemma 2. *Let $\Omega \subset R^d$ be Lebesgue measurable and let f be a continuous function defined on $\Phi(\Omega)$. Then $\int_{\Phi(\Omega)} f \, d\mu_2 = \int_{\Phi_1(\Omega)} (f \circ \Phi_2) \frac{J(\Phi)}{J(\Phi_1)} d\mu_1$.*

The following proposition shows that the centroid of $R^{B^n}(\mathcal{H})$ is mapped to the centroid of $R^{\mathcal{T}}(\mathcal{H})$ and thus $\rho(f)$ is minimal under $d_0(h, g)$ if and only if $\rho(f)$ is minimal under the distance measure $d_1(h, g)$ for any $h, g \in \mathcal{H}$. Thus these two measures are equivalent with respect to the goodness criteria of minimizing ρ.

Let P be a polyhedron in R^t and m be a positive integer and let D be an $m \times t$ matrix with rank t. Let $Q = \{Dx : x \in P\}$.

Proposition 6. *The centroid of Q is $D\bar{x}$.*

6   Efficient Algorithm for Computing the Centroid of $R^{\mathcal{T}}$

We already assumed that $\tau = |\mathcal{T}|$ is bounded above by a polynomial function of n. In other words, we only consider functions that have a "short" expression. In addition, we assume that $R^{\mathcal{T}}(H)$ is given by a separation oracle. That is, for any given point $x \in R^{\mathcal{T}}$, the oracle can tell in unit time if x belongs to $R^{\mathcal{T}}(H)$. In case $x \notin R^{\mathcal{T}}(H)$, the oracle also provides a hyperplane that separates x from $R^{\mathcal{T}}(H)$. For example, when $R^{\mathcal{T}}(H)$ is polyhedron with polynomially many faces, then it has such an oracle.

The centroid can be approximated with the following randomized algorithm: generate a sequence $\alpha^{(1)}, \alpha^{(2)}, \ldots$ of points at random from P and compute $c^{(i)} = (\alpha^{(1)} + \alpha^{(2)} + \ldots + \alpha^{(i)})/i$, for all i. Then the limit of $c^{(i)}$ is the centroid. Kannan, Lovász, and Simonovits [6–Section 5.1] give details on how to draw a good sample of points and they give a bound, with high probability, on the error in the approximation of the centroid using such a randomized algorithm. Also see [5].

Proposition 7. *The centroid of $R^{\mathcal{T}}(H)$ can be approximated by a randomized algorithm in polynomial time.*

Suppose $b \in B^n$ and we only want to approximate/predict the value of $f^*(b)$.

Proposition 8. *The expected value of $f^*(b)$ is $\bar{f}(b)$.*

Polynomial time randomized algorithms for approximating the volume of a polyhedron have been studied in [3][4][6].

7   Conclusions

A new framework for learning pseudo-Boolean functions is presented. We focus on a special class of pseudo-Boolean functions with polynomial-size expression, with the coefficient vectors of the functions forming a bounded polyhedron. We define several distance metrics for measuring the difference between pseudo-Boolean functions and then formulate the learning problems as selecting an approximation that minimizes expected/maximal distance to any feasible candidate function. We show that two distance measures based on the value vectors and on the coefficient vectors of pseudo-Boolean functions leads to the same best choice of the approximation function under the criterion of minimizing expected distance. Efficient, randomized computational-geometry algorithm for centroid calculation is utilized for the learning task. Our method is suitable for applications in which training data is rather limited and yet one would like to make useful and reliable predictions on the future data points. Applications to terrorist detection and classification clearly present such a situation since training data for terrorists are rather scarce.

Acknowledgments

The authors would like to thank Nigel Gwee of the Computer Science Department of LSU for helpful discussions on topics related to this work. This research was partially supported by National Science Foundation grant: ITR-0326387 and AFOSR grants: F49620-03-1-0238, F49620-03-1-0239, and F49620-03-1-0241.

References

1. E. Boros and P. L. Hammer. Pseudo-Boolean Optimization. *Discrete Appl. Math.*, 123 (1-3), 155–225, 2002.
2. J. Chen, P. Chen, G. Ding, R. Lax. A New Method for Learning Pseudo-Boolean Functions with Applications in Terrorist Profiling. *Proceedings of IEEE Int. Conf. on Cybernetics and Intelligent Systems*, Singapore, December 2004.
3. M. Dyer, A. Frieze, R. Kannan. A random polynomial time algorithm for approximating the volume of convex bodies. *J. Assoc. Comput. Mach.* 38(1), 1–17, 1991.
4. M. Grötschel, L. Lovász, A. Schrijver. *Geometric algorithms and combinatorial optimization.* Second corrected edition. Algorithms and Combinatorics, 2. Springer-Verlag, Berlin, 1993.
5. R. Herbrich, T. Graepel, C. Campbell. Bayes Point Machines. *Journal of Machine Learning Research* 1(2001), pp.245-279.
6. R. Kannan, L. Lovasz, M. Simonovits. Random walks and an $O^*(n^5)$ volume algorithm for convex bodies. *Random structures and Algorithms*, 11(1997), 1-50.
7. N. Littlestone. Learning quickly when irrelevant attributes abound: A new linear threshold algorithm. *Machine Learning*, 2(4): 285-318, 1988.
8. N. Littlestone, P.M. Long, M.K. Warmuth. On-line learning of linear functions. Technical Report, UCSC-CRL-91-29, University of California at Santa Cruz, Oct. 1991.
9. R. Sikorski. *Advanced Calculus, Functions of Several Variables.* Warszawa: Polish Scientific Publishers, 1969.
10. V.N. Vapnik. *The Nature of Statistical Learning Theory.* New York: Springer-Verlag, 1995.

Discovering Partial Periodic Sequential Association Rules with Time Lag in Multiple Sequences for Prediction*

Dan Li and Jitender S. Deogun

Department of Computer Science and Engineering,
University of Nebraska-Lincoln, Lincoln NE 68588-0115

Abstract. A periodic pattern indicates something persistent and predictable, so it is important to identify and characterize the periodicity. This paper presents an approach for mining partial periodic association rules in temporal databases. This approach allows the discovery of periodic episodes such that the events in an episode are not limited to a fixed order. Moreover, this approach treats the antecedent and consequent of a rule separately and allows time lag between them. Thus, rules discovered are useful in many applications for prediction. The approach is implemented using two algorithms based on two data structures, *event-based linked list* and *window-based linked list*.

1 Introduction

Periodicity detection in time-related databases is a challenging data mining problem in many applications. Since a periodic pattern indicates something persistent and predictable, it is important to identify and characterize the periodicity. Several algorithms have been developed for detecting periodicity in large datasets [2, 3, 4, 7, 9]. Most previous methods for periodicity detection are based on mining periodic symbolic patterns, where the occurrences of each item in a pattern have fixed order. Focusing on symbol sequences rather than time-related sequences limits the flexibility of algorithms. Many pruning strategies applied to symbol sequences for periodicity search cannot be applied to time-based sequences. This paper addresses the problem of periodicity search while focusing on temporal properties of datasets.

Sequential pattern discovery has been investigated extensively in recent years [1, 6, 8, 10]. All these work focus on the discovery of frequent episodes such that each episode is a set of events occurring together within user-specified time interval. The mining of cyclic association rules has been addressed in [9], where each cyclic association rule is present in each cycle with 100% support. The perfectness

---

* This research was supported in part by NSF Digital Government Grant No. EIA-0091530, USDA RMA Grant NO. 02IE08310228, and NSF EPSCOR, Grant No. EPS-0346476.

M.-S. Hacid et al. (Eds.): ISMIS 2005, LNAI 3488, pp. 332–341, 2005.
© Springer-Verlag Berlin Heidelberg 2005

in periodicity leads to a key idea used in designing efficient cyclicassociation rule mining algorithms, although this perfectness is not easy to satisfy in real world applications. The algorithm for discovering calendar-based temporal association rules has been presented in [7]. The use of calendar schema makes the discovered temporal association rules easy to understand. At the same time, however, this pre-specified calendar schema transforms the original time-related sequential databases into non-temporal transactional databases because the algorithm only takes care of the records occurring at user-specified time stamps.

This paper presents algorithms for discovering partial periodic sequential association rules which allow mismatch considering all possible cycles. In addition, most previous work on periodic association rule mining focuses on the discovery of periodic patterns and the antecedent and the consequent in a rule are merely determined by rule confidence once a periodic pattern is discovered. In this paper, antecedent and consequent episodes are treated separately for the purpose of prediction. The concept of time lag has been addressed in the previous work [6]. Here, this concept is extended to periodic pattern discovery.

2   Preliminaries

Event sequences are time-related input datasets. Formally, an *event sequence* is a triple (t_B, t_D, S) where t_B is the beginning time, t_D is the ending time, and S is a finite, time-ordered sequence of events [8]. For example, $S = (e_{t_B}, e_{t_{B+1p}}, e_{t_{B+2p}}, \ldots e_{t_{B+dp}} = e_{t_D})$ is a sequence of events, where p is the step size between events, d is the total number of steps in the time interval from time t_B to time t_D, and $D = B + dp$. Each e_{t_i} is a member of a class of events ξ, and $t_i \leq t_{i+1}$ for all $i = B, \ldots, D - 1p$. A sequence of events S includes events from a single class of events ξ. Each event sequence has its own class of events.

A *window* on an event sequence S is an event subsequence $W = \{e_{t_j}, \ldots, e_{t_k}\}$, where $t_B \leq t_j$, and $t_k \leq t_D + p$ [5, 8]. The width of the window W, defined as $width(W) = t_k - t_j$, is the time interval of interest. In our system, the value of the window width is user-specified, so that users can control the closeness of the event occurrences. To process the data, we use a *sliding window*, which is defined as the process of sequentially moving the window of width win one step at a time through the data.

An episode in an event sequence is a combination of events with a partially specified order [5, 8]. It occurs in a sequence if there are occurrences of the events in an order consistent with the given order, within a given time bound (window width). Formally, an *episode* Q is a pair $(V, type)$, where V is a collection of events and *type* specifies the type of episode. The episode type is *parallel* if no order is specified and *serial* if the events of the episode have a fixed order. An episode is *injective* if no event type occurs more than once in the episode. The *episode length* is defined as the number of events in the episode.

Given a period p, the set of all windows W on S, with $width(W) = win$ and window offset j (starting from 0), is denoted as $\mathcal{W}(S, p, win, w_j)$. The *support* of a partial periodic episode is defined as the fraction of windows in which the episode occurs. Given an event sequence S and a period p, the support of an episode Q of a given type in S is:

$$sup(Q, S, p, win, w_j) = \frac{|w \in W(S, p, win, w_j) : Q \text{ occurs in } w|}{|W(S, p, win, w_j)|}$$

where win is the window width and w_j indicates the window offset of episode Q regarding period p. Given a support threshold min_sup, Q is a *frequent partial periodic episode* if $sup(Q, S, p, win, w_j) \geq min\_sup$. The support threshold allows the user to control the set of episode of interest. We use $W(S, p, win, p_i)$ to denote the set of all windows W on S, with $width(W) = win$ occurring in the ith (starting from 0) period.

Sometimes events that occur at one time stamp are associated with events that occur at future time stamps. For example, it may be several months after an El Niño episode before the impact is felt in the Northeastern United States. Therefore, it is meaningful to take the time lag into consideration when we explore periodic association rules between ocean parameters and climatic indices. To implement time lag, we use two sliding windows. One is for the events in the antecedent set, and the other is for the events in the consequent set [6]. The offset between these two windows is user specified time lag value.

The sequence S can be a combination of multiple sequences $S_1, S_2, ..., S_n$. An episode can contain events from each of the n sequences. After the frequent partial periodic episodes are found for the antecedent and the consequent independently, we combine the frequent episodes to form partial periodic association rules. Given a period p, a partial periodic association rule r is of the form $\alpha[p, win_a] \Rightarrow_{lag} \beta[p, win_c]$, where α and β are frequent partial periodic episodes, win_a and win_c specify the window width for the antecedent and the consequent episodes respectively, and lag indicates the time lag between the antecedent and the consequent episodes. The *confidence* of a periodic association rule is the conditional probability that periodic episode β occurs, given that periodic episode α occurs, under the time constraints specified by the rule [6].

3   Generating Frequent Partial Periodic Association Rules

3.1   Main Idea

Most algorithms for frequent pattern discovery are variants of Apriori [1]. The Apriori algorithm starts by scanning all the transactions in the dataset and computing the frequent single items. Next, a pass over the dataset is made at level $(k+1)$ to find all the frequent $(k+1)$-itemsets. This process is repeated until all frequent itemsets are enumerated. Apriori uses the downward closed property of itemset support to prune the search space — the property that all subsets of a frequent itemset must also be frequent. Thus only the frequent k-itemsets are used to construct candidate $(k + 1)$-itemsets.

Apriori-like algorithms have been proposed recently to discover periodic patterns in sequential databases [2, 3, 4, 7, 9]. We develop another version of Apriori algorithm by integrating two properties discussed below:

1. Rather than only discovering symbolic periodic patterns in fixed order [2, 3], our algorithm provides more flexibility by finding all periodic patterns with either fixed order or non-fixed order based on the concepts of parallel and serial episodes with user-specified window width. Since the problem of mining serial episodes is similar to the problem of mining symbolic patterns, we only address the problem of discovering periodic parallel episodes.

2. Unlike previous algorithms that divide time-related datasets into discrete time segments [4, 7, 9], our approach uses a sliding window to find all periodic patterns at any offset given a period p.

If an episode Q occurs periodically, its occurrences in the sequence will form an arithmetic series, which can be captured by four parameters: period, window width, window offset, and support. Thus, given a period p, window width win, and support threshold min_sup, the problem of mining frequent partial periodic episodes is to find all the triples $\langle Q, w, sup \rangle$, where Q is an episode with window width win, w is the offset position of windows at which episode Q occurs repeatedly, and $sup \geq min\_sup$ is the support of the episode.

3.2   Data Structures

We define two data structures to accommodate sparse or dense input datasets. One is called *event-based linked list*; the other is called *window-based linked list*. For an event-based linked list, each event type in event sequences is associated with a two-dimensional linked list. The first dimension records the window offset given a period p, and the second dimension records the period number in which the event occurs. For a window-based linked list, each window offset is associated with a two-dimensional linked list. The first dimension represents the period segments, and the second dimension records the events that occur in a particular period. For these two linked lists, the number of windows is $(p - win + 1)$, given a period p and window width win.

Example 1. Consider the event sequence presented in Figure 1. Let period $p = 5$ and window width $win = 2$. The event-based linked list and window-based linked list for this sequence are shown in Figure 1 and Figure 2 , respectively.

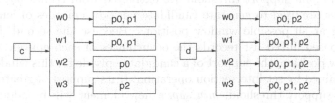

Fig. 1. Example Event-Based Linked List

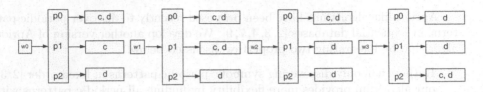

Fig. 2. Example Window-Based Linked List

3.3   Algorithm Development

Figure 3 shows the algorithm for building event-based linked list and window-based linked list with a single scan of event sequences. Once the linked lists are built, all the triples $\langle Q_1, w, sup \rangle$ can be discovered. Here, Q_1 is a frequent periodic episode of length 1, w indicates the window offset where Q_1 occurs repeatedly, and sup is the support of episode Q_1. Based on the principle of the Apriori algorithm, the next step is to find the set of frequent periodic episodes of length $(k+1)$ based on the set of frequent periodic episodes of length k where $(k \geq 1)$. This process is different for two different data structures.

```
Algorithm: Build_Linklists(EventList, WindowList, p, win, S)
1) while (S still has event){
2)    Read event e from S // suppose pos is the position of e in S
3)    Get the index i of e in the domain of event types;
4)    win_offset = pos mod p;
5)    period_num = pos/p;
6)    if (win_offset > (p − win)){
7)       Add period_num to EventList[i][p − win];
8)       Add i to WindowList[p − win][period_num];}
9)    else{
10)      for (j = win_offset − win + 1; j ≤ win_offset; j + +){
11)         Add period_num to EventList[i][j];
12)         Add i to WindowList[j][period_num];}}}
```

Fig. 3. Building Event-Based and Window-Based Linked Lists

For an event-based linked list, at each iteration k, the episodes that meet the minimum support threshold are extracted from triples $\langle Q_k, w, sup \rangle$. These episodes are used to generate candidate periodic episodes of length $(k + 1)$ occurring at all possible window positions. Because the second dimension in an event-based linked list records the occurrences of each episode for a particular window position, the support of a candidate episode for this window position can be obtained by set intersection operation. If its support is greater than or equal to the support threshold, min_sup, a new element will be added to the linked list with corresponding window position and list of occurrences. This process is repeated until no more candidates can be generated.

For a window-based linked list, the algorithm deals with each window position separately. This means the algorithm repeatedly generates candidate episodes of length $(k + 1)$ for different window positions. Each window position needs a database pass to compute the support of each candidate. The algorithm terminates if no more candidates can be generated. There are three major differences between event-based and window-based algorithms. First, the event-based algorithm needs only a single database pass to find frequent periodic episodes of length 1, while the window-based algorithm needs l passes, where l is the maximal length of frequent periodic episodes. Second, the linked list for the event-base algorithm will be modified if a new frequent episode is discovered during each iteration. However, the window-based linked list stays the same once being built. Third, the event-based algorithm generates the candidate set of episodes for all window positions at once, but the window-based algorithm generates the candidate set separately for different window positions. These differences indicate that each algorithm has its own advantages and disadvantages. Experiments and analysis demonstrate these differences.

The event-based algorithm needs to store the actual occurrences of each frequent periodic episode, i.e., the linked list records all the periods where an episode occurs regarding a particular window offset. This could be a problem if events occur frequently. To overcome this, we apply the idea presented in [10] to the event-based algorithm, i.e., we only track the differences of occurrences between two episodes. This reduces the storage size dramatically for dense databases. The set that stores the differences of occurrences between two episodes α and β is denoted as $diffset(\alpha, \beta)$. An interested reader can refer to [10] for the details of implementation.

After the frequent partial periodic episodes are found for the antecedent and the consequent independently, periodic association rules are generated. Each periodic antecedent episode α at window position w_α joins its occurrences with each occurrence of each periodic consequent episode β at window position w_β, as long as condition $0 \leq (w_\beta - w_\alpha) \leq lag$ is satisfied. Here, lag is the user-specified time lag between the antecedent and the consequent.

4   Experiments and Analysis

All experiments were performed on a 2.0Ghz Pentium 4 PC with 768MB of memory, running Windows XP. Algorithms were coded with C#. The description of datasets used for testing the performance of algorithms is shown in Table 1. The first dataset is a synthetic dataset which is constructed randomly. This dataset includes events from 25 sequences occurring at 5000 time stamps. The weather data is collected at the automated weather station in Clay Center, NE, from 1950-1999, for drought assessment and drought risk management [6]. The data for the climatic indices are grouped into seven categories, extremely dry, severely dry, moderately dry, near normal, moderately wet, severely wet, and extremely wet. The weather data used in the experiments are monthly 1-month, 3-month, 6-month, 9-month, and 12-month SPI from this seven categories. Thus,

Table 1. Description of Datasets

Dataset	File Size (KB)	Timestamps	Num. Events	Num. Seq.	Avg. Occ. per Event
Synthetic	1089	5000	125	25	1000
Weather	46	600	35	5	85

the weather dataset includes 35 events from five sequences. Figure 4 shows the algorithm computation time as the support threshold, min_sup, changes from 0.45 to 0.7 on the synthetic data. The system is implemented with three methods, event-based without diffset, event-based with diffset, and window-based methods. We test these methods using different combinations of period p and window width win. First, we set the window width to a constant value, 4, and set the period length to three values, 20, 30, and 40. Then, the experiments were done by setting the period length to a constant value, 20, and changing the value of window width from 4 to 5. Generally, from this group of charts, we observe that:

1. The smaller the support threshold is, the more gap in system running time between the two event-based methods. This is because the smaller threshold results in more candidates, and in turn, more set intersection operations are needed to compute the support of a candidate episode. When event-based linked list is used to record the occurrences of each episode, the time used for set intersection increases sharply as the support threshold decreases. However, when we apply diffset to linked list, the space needed to save the linked list decreases on the synthetic data compared to original linked list. This reduction in storage size results in less running time for set intersection.

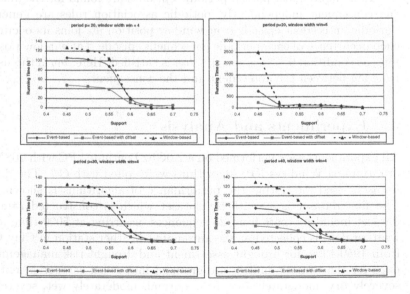

Fig. 4. Running Time vs. Support on Synthetic Data

Table 2. Comparison of Storage Size (Byte) on Synthetic Dataset

Support	Event-based	Apply of Diffset	Reduction
0.7	5561	2285	3276
0.65	242189	122708	119481
0.6	2850298	1687389	1162909
0.55	9482931	6348244	3134687
0.5	11904827	8304380	3600447
0.45	12860022	8947218	3912804

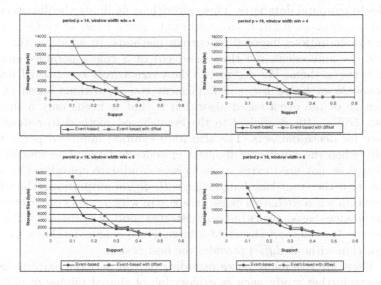

Fig. 5. Storage Size vs. Support on Weather Data

Table 2 shows that as the support threshold becomes smaller, the reduction of storage size between event-based linked list and the linked list with diffset increases.

2. Figure 4 also shows that the window-based algorithm runs faster than the event-based algorithm as the support threshold increases. Although the window-based algorithm needs more database scans compared to the event-based algorithm, the time used for the database scan is less than the time used for linked list storage and set intersection when the support becomes greater.

3. As the window width increases, so does the periodic episode generation time. This is reasonable because a wide window includes more events from multiple sequences, and in turn, generates more candidates.

Next, the experiments were done on the weather data. According to Table 1, the weather dataset used in these experiments contains events occurring at 600 time stamps. All three methods run fast on this dataset. Generally, the average running time for event-based, event-based with diffset and window-based algorithms is 0.015s, 0.046s and 0.021s, respectively. Figure 5 shows the storage size on the weather data when two event-based methods are considered. Different from the results on the synthetic data, the experiments show that diffset requires more space to store the occurrences of episodes. This is because the events in weather data occur less frequently than the events in the synthetic data.

5   Conclusion

This paper presents efficient algorithms for mining partial periodic association rules in temporal databases. These algorithms facilitate the discovery of frequent periodic episodes without any constraint on the order of events, thus overcoming the limitations imposed by current methods. In addition, these algorithms treat the antecedent and the consequent of a rule separately and allow time lag between them. We design two data structures, *event-based linked list* and *window-based linked list*, and implement two algorithms based on them. The strength of the event-based algorithm is that it needs only a single database pass. *Diffset* [10] is applied to the event-based method to reduce the storage space for dense datasets. The algorithm exhibits improved performance, especially when the number of frequent episodes is large. The window-based algorithm does not need extra space to save candidate episodes. Our experiments show that the event-based algorithm with *diffset* outperforms the window-based algorithm when we have a dense database in which events occur more frequently. The window-based algorithm demonstrates good performance when the value of user-specified support threshold is large. For a sparse database, the event-based algorithm without *diffset* provides the best results.

There are still many issues regarding partial periodic pattern discovery that deserve further study, such as exploration of shared mining of periodicity with multiple periods. These problems will be studies and reported in the future.

References

1. R. Agrawal and R. Srikant. Mining sequential patterns. In *Eleventh International Conference on Data Engineering*, pages 3–14, Taipei, Taiwan, 1995.
2. H. Cao, David W. Cheung, and N. Mamoulis. Discovering partial periodic patterns in discrete data sequences. In *Proceedings of The 8th Pacific-Asia Conference on Knowledge Discovery and Data Mining (PAKDD 2004)*, Sydney, Australia, 2004.
3. J. Han, G. Dong, and Y. Yin. Efficient mining of partial periodic patterns in time series database. In *Fifteenth International Conference on Data Engineering*, pages 106–115, Sydney, Australia, 1999. IEEE Computer Society.
4. J. Han, W. Gong, and Y. Yin. Mining segment-wise periodic patterns in time-related databases. In *Fourth International Conference on Knowledge Discovery and Data Mining*, pages 214–218, 1998.
5. S. Harms, J. Deogun, J. Saquer, and T. Tadesse. Discovering representative episodal association rules from event sequences using frequent closed episode sets and event constraints. In *Proceedings of the 2001 IEEE International Conference on Data Mining*, pages 603–606, San Jose, CA, November 29 - December 2 2001.

6. S. Harms, J. Deogun, and T. Tadesse. Discovering sequential association rules with constraints and time lags in multiple sequences. In *Proceedings of the 2002 International Symposium on Methodologies for Intelligent Systems (ISMIS '02)*, pages 432–442, Lyon, France, June 2002.

7. Yingjiu Li, Peng Ning, Xiaoyang Sean Wang, and Sushil Jajodia. Discovering calendar-based temporal association rules. In *TIME*, pages 111–118, 2001.

8. H. Mannila, H. Toivonen, and A. I. Verkamo. Discovering frequent episodes in sequences. In *Proceedings of the First International Conference on Knowledge Discovery and Data Mining*, pages 210–215, Montreal, Canada, August 1995.

9. B. Ozden, S. Ramaswamy, and A. Silberschatz. Cyclic association rules. In *ICDE*, pages 412–421, 1998.

10. Mohammed J. Zaki and Karam Gouda. Fast vertical mining using diffsets. In *Proceedings of the ninth ACM SIGKDD international conference on Knowledge discovery and data mining*, pages 326–335, 2003.

Mining and Filtering Multi-level Spatial Association Rules with ARES

Annalisa Appice, Margherita Berardi, Michelangelo Ceci, and Donato Malerba

Dipartimento di Informatica, Università degli Studi,
via Orabona, 4 - 70126 Bari - Italy
{appice, berardi, ceci, malerba}@di.uniba.it

Abstract. In spatial data mining, a common task is the discovery of spatial association rules from spatial databases. We propose a distributed system, named ARES that takes advantage of the use of a multi-relational approach to mine spatial association rules. It supports spatial database coupling and discovery of multi-level spatial association rules as a means for spatial data exploration. We also present some criteria to bias the search and to filter the discovered rules according to user's expectations. Finally, we show the applicability of our proposal to two different real world domains, namely, document image processing and geo-referenced analysis of census data.

1 Introduction

Spatial data mining investigates the problem of extracting pieces of knowledge from data describing spatial objects, which are characterized by a geometrical representation (e.g. point, line, and region in a 2D context) and a position with respect to some reference system. The relative positioning of spatial objects defines implicitly spatial relations of different nature, such as directional and topological. The goal of spatial data mining methods is to extract spatial patterns, that is, patterns involving spatial relations between mined objects such that they are certain, previously unknown, and potentially useful for the specific application [10].

In [13] the authors have proposed a spatial data mining method, named SPADA (Spatial Pattern Discovery Algorithm), that discovers spatial association rules, that is, association rules involving spatial objects and relations. It is based on an Inductive Logic Programming (ILP) approach to (multi-) relational data mining [5] and permits the extraction of multi-level spatial association rules, that is, association rules involving spatial objects at different granularity levels. For each granularity level, SPADA operates in three different phases: i) pattern generation; ii) pattern evaluation; iii) rule generation and evaluation.

In this paper, we describe the integration of SPADA in a full-fledged spatial data mining system, named ARES (Association Rules Extractor from Spatial data), that assists data miners in the complex process of extracting the units of analysis from the spatial database, specifying the background knowledge on the application domain and defining some form of search bias. The last aspect is particularly relevant, since the

M.-S. Hacid et al. (Eds.): ISMIS 2005, LNAI 3488, pp. 342–353, 2005.
© Springer-Verlag Berlin Heidelberg 2005

number of discovered patterns or association rules is usually high and the interest of most of them does not fulfill user expectations. The new spatial data mining tool has been applied to two different domains, namely, document image processing and geo-referenced analysis of census data, thus proving the generality of the proposed solution.

The paper is organized as follows. The problem of mining spatial association rules is reported in Section 2. In Section 3, some related works are presented. Section 4 describes the ARES distributed architecture that supports the interface of SPADA with a spatial database by generating high-level logic descriptions of spatial data. Some filtering mechanisms implemented in SPADA are described in Section 5. Finally, the application of ARES to two case studies is described in Sections 6.

2 Mining Spatial Association Rules

The discovery of spatial association rules is a descriptive mining task aiming to detect associations between *reference objects* (*ro*) and some *task-relevant objects* (*tro*). The former are the main subject of the description, while the latter are spatial objects that are relevant for the task in hand and are spatially related to the former.

In general, association rules are a class of regularities that can be expressed by the implication: $P \Rightarrow Q$ (s, c), where P and Q are a set of literals, called *items*, such that $P \cap Q = \emptyset$, the support s estimates the probability $p(P \cup Q)$, and the confidence c, estimates the probability $p(Q \mid P)$. The conjunction $P \wedge Q$ is called *pattern*. A *spatial pattern* expresses a spatial relationship among spatial objects and can be expressed by means of predicate calculus. A *spatial association rule* is an association rule whose corresponding pattern is spatial. An example of spatial association rule is:

$$is\_a(X, large\_town), intersects(X,Y), is\_a(Y, road) \Rightarrow$$
$$intersects(X, Z), is\_a(Z, road), Z \neq Y (91\%, 100\%)$$

to be read as "If a large town X intersects a road Y then X intersects a road Z distinct from Y with 91% support and 100% confidence." By taking into account some kind of taxonomic knowledge on task-relevant objects it is possible to obtain descriptions at different granularity levels (*multiple-level association rules*). For instance, a finer-grained association rules can be the following:

$$is\_a(X, large\_town), intersects(X, Y), is\_a(Y, regional\_road) \Rightarrow$$
$$intersects(X, Z), is\_a(Z, main\_trunk\_road), Z \neq Y (65\%, 71\%)$$

The problem of mining association rules solved by SPADA can be formally stated as follows:

Given a spatial database (SDB), a set of reference objects S, some sets R_k, $1 \leq k \leq m$, of task-relevant objects, a background knowledge BK including some hierarchies H_k on objects in R_k , M granularity levels in the descriptions (1 is the highest while M is the lowest), a language bias LB that constrains the search space and a couple of thresholds *minsup[l]* and *minconf[l]* for each granularity level;

Find strong multi-level spatial association rules. Each R_k is typically a layer of the spatial database while hierarchies define *is-a* (i.e., taxonomical) relations of spatial objects in the same layer.

To deal with several hierarchies at once in a uniform manner, objects in them are mapped to one or more of the M user-defined description granularity levels so that frequency of patterns as well as strength of rules depend on the level l of granularity with which patterns/rules describe data. To be more precise, a pattern P ($s\%$) at level l is *frequent* if $s{\geq}minsup[l]$ and all ancestors of P with respect to H_k are frequent at their corresponding levels. An association rule $Q \rightarrow R$ ($s\%$, $c\%$) at level l is *strong* if the pattern $Q{\cup}R$ ($s\%$) is frequent and $c{\geq}minconf[l]$.

3 Related Works

The problem of mining multi-level association rules has its roots in the seminal work by Han and Fu [6], where the authors proposed an improved version of the Apriori algorithm [1] to handle multiple level association rules by remapping the original database and performing the mining by a progressive deepening of the levels. A slight variant of this approach has been adopted by Koperski and Han [11] and implemented in the system GeoMiner [7] in the context of spatial data mining.

A different solution is adopted in the work by Morimoto [17], where different types of patterns, called "Frequent neighboring class sets" are extracted. In particular, first the spatial dataset is partitioned by considering closeness relations and then the patterns are discovered on single partitions.

Another solution is proposed by Ding [4], where rules are extracted from RSI (Remote Sensed Imagery) data by means of the Peano Count Tree (P-tree) structure, which is a lossless representation of the image data. By using P-trees, association rule mining algorithm with fast support calculation and significant pruning techniques is possible. Although RSI data can be considered a kind of spatial data, rules discovered are not "spatial" in a strict sense.

All solutions reported above suffer from severe limitations due to the restrictive data representation formalism, known as *single-table assumption* [5]. More specifically, it is assumed that data to be mined are represented in a single table (or relation) of a relational database, such that each tuple represents an independent unit of the sample population and columns correspond to properties of units. In spatial data mining applications this assumption turns out to be a great limitation. Indeed, different geographical objects may have different properties, which can be properly modeled by as many data tables as the number of object types. The ILP system WARMR [3] overcomes this limitation by resorting to multi-relational data mining. It supports the discovery of frequent DATALOG patterns by adapting Mannila and Toivonen's levelwise method [16] to the case of conjunctive formulas which are organized according to θ-subsumption. Although it has been presented as a system able to use *is-a* hierarchies, WARMR is not a system for mining multi-level association rules because it lacks of mechanisms for taxonomic reasoning [13]. Moreover, the transformation of frequent patterns into association rules requires the specification of a list of possible patterns that can occur in the antecedent or consequent of a rule. Therefore, the specification of a bias for the output rules is a must and not an additional opportunity given to the user to filter some rules. Finally, WARMR is not integrated in a system for spatial data analysis that supports users to extract both spatial and apatial properties of either reference objects or task-relevant object.

Therefore, to the best of our knowledge, SPADA can be considered the only multi-relational data mining method especially conceived for spatial data mining tasks and implemented in a system, named ARES, that supports the user in all preprocessing steps.

4 The Architecture of ARES

ARES has a distributed architecture based on a client-server model (see Figure 1). SPADA is on the server side, so that several data mining tasks can be run concurrently by multiple users. SPADA is implemented in Prolog and allows to specify both the background knowledge *BK* (hierarchies are expressed by a collection of ground atoms that define the binary predicate *is_a*, while domain specific knowledge is expressed as sets of definite clauses) and a language bias *LB* that constrains the search for patterns.

On the client side, the system includes a Graphical User Interface (GUI) implemented as Java application, which provides the user with facilities for controlling all parameters of the data mining process as well as the module RUDE (relative unsupervised discretization algorithm), which discretizes a numerical attribute of a relational database in the context defined by other attributes [14].

The SDB (Oracle Spatial) can run on a third computation unit. Many spatial features (relations and attributes) can be extracted from spatial objects stored in the SDB. The feature extraction requires complex data transformation processes to make spatial relations explicit and representable as ground Prolog atoms. Therefore, a middle layer module is required to make possible a loose coupling between SPADA and the SDB by generating features of spatial objects. The module, named FEATEX (Feature Extractor), is implemented as an Oracle package of procedures and functions, each of which computes a different feature [2]. According to their nature, features extracted by FEATEX can be distinguished as geometrical, directional and topological features. Geometrical features (e.g. area, length) are based on principles of Euclidean geometry, directional features (e.g. north, south,) regard relative spatial orientation in 2D, while topological features (e.g. crosses, on top) are relations preserving themselves under topological transformations such as translation, rotation, and scaling. In addition, hybrid features (e.g. roughly parallel), which merge properties of two or more feature categories, can be also extracted by FEATEX.

On the client side, the system WISDOM++ [15] can be used to extract spatial data from document image and store them in the SDB. The process performed by WISDOM++ consists of the preprocessing of the raster image of a scanned paper document, the segmentation of the preprocessed raster image into basic layout components, the classification of basic layout components according to the type of content (e.g., text, graphics, etc.), the identification of a more abstract representation of the document layout (layout analysis), the classification of the document in one of predefined categories (e.g. business letter, scientific paper) on the basis of its layout and content, and the identification of semantically relevant layout components (e.g. title, abstract of a scientific paper) called logical components (*document image understanding* [15]). The final representation includes both layout structure (extracted in the layout analysis) and logical structure (semantic information extracted by means of document classification and understanding) computed on the original image. A further processing step stores the output structures in the SDB. WISDOM++ makes use of an Oracle Database to store intermediate data.

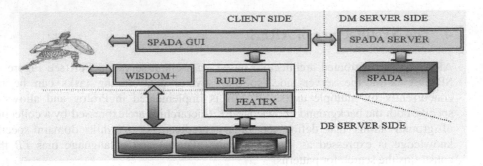

Fig. 1. ARES architecture

In order to handle spatial data provided by WISDOM++, FEATEX has been extended to allow features of layout components to be extracted (see section 5.1).

5   Filtering Patterns and Association Rules

The efficiency of the data mining process is very important to tackle real-world problems. In order to improve the efficiency of the search process, SPADA associates each candidate pattern with backward pointers to parent patterns both at the same granularity level (intra-space parenthood) and at higher granularity levels (inter-space parenthood). Backward pointers are profitably exploited in the pattern generation phase to prevent the generation of some infrequent patterns [12]. In a more recent release of SPADA (3.0), backward pointers are also exploited in the pattern evaluation phase. Indeed, by associating each pattern with the list of support objects, it is possible to perform the evaluation of each pattern solely on the support objects of its intra-space parenthood instead of the whole set S of reference objects. An additional caching technique compensates the overhead in looking for the parenthood of each pattern, since it has a cost, which increases with the number of stored patterns.

The above mentioned efficiency improvements are based on the monotonicity property of the generality order that is defined for spatial patterns with respect to the support of the patterns themselves. This is a nice example of an "intelligent" exploitation of general properties to prune the search space and reduce the number of expensive tests. However, this approach does not take into account user preferences and expectations. In real-world applications, such as urban site accessibility [2], a large number of spatial patterns can be generated even for a few hundred spatial objects. Nevertheless, most of discovered patters are useless for the application at hand. Therefore, it is important to allow the user to specify his/her bias for interesting solutions, and then to exploit this bias to improve both the efficiency of the system and the quality of the discovered rules. In SPADA 3.0, the language bias LB is expressed as a set of constraint specifications for either patterns or association rules. Users may specify the following pattern constraint:

pattern_constraint(AtomList, Min_occur, Max_occur)

where *AtomList* is a list of atoms (for atomic constraints) or a list of atom lists (for conjunctive constraints), while *Min_occur (Max_occur)* is positive number which specifies the minimum (maximum) number of constraints in the *AtomList* that must be satisfied. When Max_occur = '_' no limitation is imposed on the maximum number of constraints. For instance, the following:

pattern_constraint(crossed_by_green_area(_,_), crossed_by_urban_area(_,_)],1,_)

specifies that at least one of the binary spatial predicates *crossed_by_green_area* and *crossed_by_urban_area* must occur in the patterns filtered by SPADA, while the following:

pattern_constraint([[crossed_by_green_area(_,_), crossed_by_urban_area (_,_)], [crossed_only_by_road(_)]], 1, _).

specifies that at least one of either the spatial predicates *crossed_by_green_area* and *crossed_by_urban_area* or the spatial predicate *crossed_only_by_road* must occur in the patterns filtered by SPADA. It is noteworthy that this specification allows users to define both conjunctive and disjunctive constraints.

During the rule generation phase, patterns that do not satisfy a pattern constraint are filtered out. This means that they are generated and evaluated anyway. This late exploitation of pattern constraints is due to the fact that if a pattern *P* does not satisfy a constraint (e.g. the lack of the predicate *crossed_by_green_area*), it is still possible that *P* descendants (i.e., more specific patterns) satisfy it. Therefore, pattern constraints do not prune the pattern space, but improve the efficiency of the mining process, since they prevent the generation of useless rules, and hence their evaluation.

A further pattern constraint takes into account the typing mechanism of the variables to be included in the rules. A variable *X* is untyped when it does not appear as first argument of a binary is-a atom in the rule. In some applications, the occurrence of untyped variables in a rule is undesirable. Therefore, users can specify the constraint *max_rules_untyped_vars(n)*, where *n* denotes the maximum number of untyped variables in the rules being generated. As in the previous case, the specification of this constraint affects the rule generation phase.

Users may specify constraints either on the antecedent or on the consequent of spatial association rules through one of the following facts:

body_constraint(AtomList, Min_occur, Max_occur).
head_constraint(AtomList, Min_occur, Max_occur).

where *AtomList, Min_occur* and *Max_Occur* have the same meaning as in the pattern constraint described above. For instance, the constraint *head_constraint([mortality_ rate(_)], 1, 1)* specifies that a single occurrence of the unary predicate *high_mortality* must be in the head of the rules. As for pattern constraints, head and body constraints affect the rule generation phase. The main property of all described constraints is that they do not prevent the generation of candidate rules but only the evaluation of their confidence.

In addition to constraints above, SPADA 3.0 users can specify the fact: *rule_head_length (Min_occur, Max_occur)* in order to fix the minimum (*Min_occur*) and the maximum number (*Max_occur*) of predicates to be included in the head of generated rules. For instance, by combining the rule filters *head_constraint([mortality_rate(_)], 1, 1)* and *rule_head_length(1, 1)* the user can ask for the generation of rules containing only the predicate *mortality_rate* in the head. Rules in this form may be employed for spatial subgroup mining that is the discovery of interesting group of spatial objects with respect to a certain property of interest, as well as for classification purposes.

6 The Application: Two Case Studies

In this section, we describe the application of SPADA to two distinct real-world problems, namely mining document images and mining geo-referenced census data. In the former problem, spatial objects are layout components extracted by means of WISDOM++. Layout components are in the same page of a document and have a common geometrical representation: they are all rectangles with edges parallel to the axes associated to the left and top border of a page. As result of the document understanding process, layout components may be associated with some components of the document logical structure, whose hierarchical organization defines the hierarchy of task-relevant objects. Discovered spatial association rules can be used in a generative way. For instance, if a part of the document is hidden or missing, strong spatial association rules can be used to predict the location of missing layout/logical components [9]. This problem is also related to document reformatting [8].

In the second problem, the goal is to perform a joint analysis of both socio-economic factors represented in census data and geographical factors represented in topographic maps. The discovery of interesting association rules on geographically distributed socio-economic phenomena can be a valuable support to good public policy. In this case, spatial objects are territorial units for which census data are collected as well as entities of the transport network (roads and rails), while the hierarchies are either based on layers of the topographic map or defined on the basis of a conceptual categorization or urban areas.

6.1 Document Image Processing

In this application SPADA takes as input a collection of ground facts describing both the layout and the logical structures of the documents processed by WISDOM++. Spatial features (relations and attributes) are used to describe the logical structure of a document image. In particular, we use FEATEX to extract locational features such as the coordinates of the centroid of a logical component, geometrical features such as the dimensions of a logical component, and topological features such as relations between two components. We use the *aspatial* feature *type_of* that specifies the content type of a logical component (e.g. *image, text, horizontal line*). In addition there are other aspatial features, called *logical* features which define the label associated to the logical components. They are: *affiliation, page_number, figure, caption, index_term, running_head, author, title, abstract, formulae, subsection_title, section_title, biografy, references, paragraph, table, undefined.*

The specification of the domain specific knowledge allows SPADA to associate information on page order to layout components, since the presence of some logical components may depend on the order page (e.g. *author* is in the first page). An example related to the first page is

at_page(X,first) :- part_of(Y,X), page(Y,first).

The specification of the hierarchy (Figure 2) allows the system to extract spatial association rules at different granularity levels.

In this task, the *ro* are the logical components associated with logical features different from *undefined*. The *tro* are all the logical components. This is specified by means of the language bias *LB*. In particular, we ask for rules containing at least one binary spatial predicate:

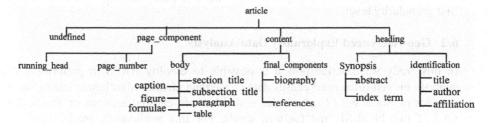

Fig. 2. Hierarchy of logical components

pattern_constraint([only_middle_coumnl(_,_),only_left_row(_,_), ... , on_top(_,_)],1).

Furthermore, we are interested in rules containing the *ro* in the antecedent. For instance, if we use *abstract* as *ro* the constraint is:

body_constraint([abstract(_)], 1).

We investigate the applicability of the proposed solution on 19 real-world documents, which are scientific papers published as either regular or short in the IEEE Transactions on Pattern Analysis and Machine Intelligence in the January and February 1996 issues. Each paper is a multi-page document and has a variable number of pages and layout components per page, for a total of 179 document images and 2,998 layout components. Eight hundred and eleven layout components with no clear logical meaning are labelled as *undefined*. All logical labels belong to the lowest level of the hierarchy reported in the previous section. The number of logical components is 2,177. The number of features to describe the documents presented to SPADA is 78,789, about 440 features for each page document. Average running time per document image is 1.32 secs (237.52/179), therefore this application of SPADA to document images seems scalable to larger collections of documents. The number of mined association rules is 398 at the first level, 468 at the second level, 638 at the third level and 674 at the fourth level. Many spatial patterns involving logical components (e.g., affiliation, title, author, abstract and index term) in the first page of an article are found. SPADA has found several spatial associations involving all logical components, references and biography excluded. This can be explained by the observation that the first page generally has a more regular layout structure and contains several distinct logical components. An example of association rule discovered by SPADA is:

$is\_a(author,A) \Rightarrow on\_top(A,B),\ is\_a(B,heading),\ height(B,[1..174]),\ type\_text(A)$
$$(82.6\%,\ 82.6\%)$$

This means that 19 logical components which represent the *author* of some paper are textual components on top of a logical component B that is the *heading* of the paper, with height between 1 and 174. At a lower granularity level, a similar rule is found where the logical component *B* is specialized as *abstract*:

$is\_a(author,A) \Rightarrow on\_top(A,B),\ is\_a(B,abstract),\ height(B,[1..174]),\ type\_text(A)$
$$(82.6\%,\ 82.6\%)$$

The rule has the same confidence and support reported for the rule inferred at the first granularity level.

6.2 Geo-referenced Exploratory Data Analysis

In this study we describe how it is possible to employ ARES in performing data analysis on geo-referenced census data concerning Greater Manchester, one of the five counties of North West England, that is divided into censual sections or wards, for a total of two hundreds and fourteen wards. For this application, spatial analysis is enabled by the availability of vectorized boundary of wards as well as vector geographical data about transport network, waters, green and urban areas that allow us to investigate the mortality rate (i.e. percentage of deaths with respect to the number of inhabitants) from a spatial viewpoint according to deprivation indices. Geographical layers are taken from the Meridian product of the Ordnance Survey. In particular, we decide to mine spatial association rules relating wards, which play the role of *ro*, with topological related road network (i.e. motorways, primary roads, A- and B- roads), rail network, water network (i.e. rivers, canals and waters), green area (i.e. parks and woods) and urban area (i.e. small and large areas) as *tro*.

Therefore, by using FEATEX we extract facts concerning topological relationships between wards and roads, rails, waters, green areas and urban areas reported in the spatial database for that area. An example of fact extracted by FEATEX is *crosses(ward_135, urbareaL_151)*. The number of facts is 784,107. Despite the complexity of the spatial computation performed by FEATEX to extract these facts, the results are still not appropriate for the goals of our data analysis tasks. Therefore, a domain specific knowledge should be expressed in form of a set of rules. Some of the rules used in this data mining task are:

crossed_by_urbanarea(X,Y) :- crosses(X,Y), is_a(Y,urban_area).
crossed_by_urbanarea(X,Y) :- inside(X,Y), is_a(Y,urban_area).
not_crossed_by_urbanarea(X) :- is_a(X,ward), \+ crossed_by_urbanarea(X,_).

Here the use of the predicate *is_a* hides the fact that a hierarchy has been defined for spatial objects belonging to urban area layer (see Figure 3). Similarly, four different hierarchies have been defined to describe road network, rail network, water network and green area. The hierarchies have depth three and are straightforwardly mapped into three granularity levels. Hence, these hierarchies are used to complete the domain specific knowledge by adding rules describing topological relationships and/or not-relationschips between wards and green area, transport and water net.

Until now, all extracted data and user-defined background knowledge are purely spatial. However, we can observe that the mortality rate of an area cannot be defined on the basis of the geographical environment alone. We select four deprivation indecies, namely Townsend index, Carstairs index, Jarman index and DoE index, we discretize them with RUDE and generate the following four binary predicates for SPADA: *townsend_idx, carstairs_idx, jarman_idx* and *doe_idx*. The first argument of the predicate refers to a ward, while the second argument is an interval returned by RUDE. The Townsend index is a measure of multiple deprivation that is computed at ward level according to the percentage of households that are not owner occupied, percentage of households with no car, percentage of households with more than one person per room and percentage of persons who are unemployed. Similarly, Carstairs index, Jarman index and DoE index are calculated using census data to measure socio-economical deprivation of a ward.

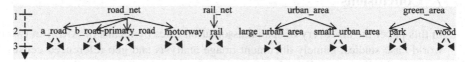

Fig. 3. Spatial hierarchies defined for four Greater Manchester layers: road net, rail net, urban area and green area

To complete the problem statement we specify a declarative bias both to constrain the search space and to filter out some uninteresting spatial association rules. In particular, we rule out all spatial relations directly extracted by means of FEATEX. Moreover, by specifying the rule filters *head_constraint([mortality_rate(_)], 1, 1)* and *rule_head_length(1, 1)* we ask for rules containing only the predicate *mortality_rate* in the head. After some tuning of the parameters *min_sup* and *min_conf* for each granularity level, we decide to run the system with the following parameter values: *min_sup*[1]=0.1, *min_sup*[2]=0.1, *min_sup*[3]=0.05, *min_conf*[1]=0.3, *min_conf*[2]=0.2, *min_conf*[3]=0.1.

Despite the above constraints, SPADA generates 413 rules from a set of 100791 candidates. A rule returned by SPADA at the first level is the following:

*is_a(A, ward), crossed_by_urbanarea(A, B), is_a(B, **urban_area**), townsendidx_rate(A, high) ⇒ mortality_rate(A, high)   (40.72%, 72.47%)*

which states that a high mortality rate is observed in a ward *A* that includes an urban area *B* and has a high value of Townsend index. The support (40.72%) and the high confidence (72.47%) confirm a meaningful association between a geographical factor such as living in deprived urban areas and a social factor such as the mortality rate. It is noteworthy that SPADA generates the following rule:

is_a(A,ward), crossed_by_urbanarea(A,B), is_a(B, urban_area) ⇒
mortality_rate(A, high)   *(56.7%, 60.77%)*

which has a greater support and a ower confidence. These two association rules show together an unexpected association between Townsend index and urban areas. Apparently, this means that this deprivation index is unsuitable for rural areas.

At a granularity level 2, SPADA specializes the task relevant object B by generating the following rule which preserve both support and confidence:

*is_a(A,   ward),   crossed_by_urbanarea(A,   B),   is_a(B,   **urban_areaL**),*
townsendidx_rate(A,high) ⇒ *mortality_rate(A, high)*   *(40.72%, 72.47%)*

This rule clarifies that the urban area B is large.
Similarly, SPADA discovers association rules involving low mortality wards:

is_a(A,   ward),   crossed_by_urbanarea(A,   B),   is_a(B,   urban_area),
townsendidx_rate(A, low) ⇒ *mortality_rate(A, low)*   *(21.13%, 56. 94%)*

This rule, extracted at the first granularity level, states that a low valued Townsend index ward *A* that (partly) includes an urban area *B* presents a low mortality rate.

7 Conclusions

In this paper the discovery of spatial association rules by means of ARES in two real-world case studies, namely document image analysis and geo-referenced census data analysis, is illustrated. We also present some criteria to reduce the pattern search space and to filter extracted rules in order to discover interesting association rules according to user preferences. This is achieved by exploiting the high expressive power of rule miner SPADA 3.0, integrated in ARES, as well as by endowing SPADA 3.0 of a powerful language for bias specification. Results show that ARES mines interesting rules at different granularity levels. For future work we plan to investigate the improvement of ARES in order to implement a tight-coupling between SPADA and the spatial database.

Acknowledgments

We thank Jim Petch, Keith Cole and Mohammed Islam (University of Manchester) for collecting data made available through Manchester Computing in the context of the IST European project SPIN (Spatial Mining for Data of Public Interest).

The work presented in this paper is partial fulfillment of the research objective set by the ATENEO-2004 project on "Metodi di Data Mining Multi-relazionale per la scoperta di conoscenza in basi di dati".

References

1. R. Agrawal, R. Srikant: Fast algorithms for mining association rules. *In Proc. of the International Conference on Very Large Data Bases*, 1994, pp. 487-499.
2. A. Appice , M. Ceci, A. Lanza, F.A. Lisi. and D. Malerba , Discovery of Spatial Association Rules in Georeferenced Census Data: A Relational Mining Approach, *Intelligent Data Analysis*, 7, 6 2003, pp. 541-566.
3. L. Dehaspe, H. Toivonen: Discovery of frequent Datalog patterns. *Data Mining and Knowledge Discovery*, 3(1), 1999, pp. 7-36.
4. Q. Ding: Association Rule Mining on Remotely Sensed Imagery Using P-Trees. *Phd Thesis*. North Dakota State University of Agriculture and Applied Science. 2002
5. S. Džeroski and N. Lavrac, Relational Data Mining, Springer-Verlag, Berlin, 2001.
6. J. Han, Y. Fu: Discovery of multiple-level association rules from large databases., *Proc. of the 21st International Conference on Very Large Data Bases, VLDB'95*, 1995, pp. 420-431
7. J. Han, K. Koperski, N. Stefanovic: GeoMiner: A System Prototype for Spatial Data Mining. *Proceedings of the ACM-SIGMOD International Conference on Management of Data*. SIGMOD'97 Record 26, 2, 1997, pp. 553-556.
8. L. Hardman, L. Rutledge and D. Bulterman, Automated generation of hypermedia presentation from pre-existing tagged media objects, *Proc. Of the 2nd. Workshop on Adaptive Hypertext and Hypermedia*, 1998.
9. K. Hiraki., J.H. Gennari, Y. Yamamoto and Y. Anzai, Learning Spatial Relations from Images, *Machine Learning Workshop*, Chicago, 1991, pp. 407 - 411.
10. K. Koperski, J. Adhikary and J. Han, Spatial Data Mining: Progress and Challenges. Proc. ACM SIGMOD Workshop on Research Issues on Data Mining and Knowledge Discovery, Montreal, Canada, 1996
11. K. Koperski, J. Han: Discovery of Spatial Association Rules in Geographic Information Databases. *Advances in Spatial Databases*. LNCS 951, Springer-Verlag, 1995, pp. 47-66.
12. F.A. Lisi and D. Malerba: Efficient Discovery of Multiple-level Patterns. *Decimo Convegno Nazionale su Sistemi Evoluti per Basi di Dati SEBD'2002*, 2002, 237-250.
13. F.A.Lisi and D. Malerba, Inducing Multi-Level Association Rules from Multiple Relations. *Machine Learning*, vol 55, pp. 175-210, 2004.
14. M.C. Ludl and G. Widmer, Relative Unsupervised Discretization for Association Rule Mining: *PKDD2000*, LNCS 1910, Springer-Verlag, 2000, pp. 148-158
15. D. Malerba, M. Ceci and M. Berardi, XML and Knowledge Technologies for Semantic-Based Indexing of Paper Documents, *DEXA 2003*, LNCS 2736, Springer, Berlin, 2003, pp. 256-265.
16. H. Mannila, H. Toivonen: Levelwise Search and Borders of Theories in Knowledge Discovery. *Data Mining and Knowledge Discovery* 1(3), 1997. pp. 241-258.
17. Y. Morimoto: Mining frequent neighboring class sets in spatial databases. *KDD '01*, 2001, pp. 353- 358.

Association Reducts: A Framework for Mining Multi-attribute Dependencies

Dominik Ślęzak

Department of Computer Science, University of Regina,
Regina, SK, S4S 0A2, Canada
Polish-Japanese Institute of Information Technology,
Koszykowa 86, 02-008 Warsaw, Poland

Abstract. We introduce the notion of an association reduct. It is an analogy to association rules at the level of global dependencies between the sets of attributes. Association reducts represent important complex relations, beyond usually considered "single attribute – single attribute" similarities. They can also express approximate dependencies in terms of, for instance, the information-theoretic measures. Finally, association reducts can be extracted from data using algorithms adapted from the domain of association rules and the theory of rough sets.

Keywords: Association Rules, Feature Reduction, Entropy Measure.

1 Introduction

Association rules [1] proved to be helpful for deriving and understanding the data based knowledge. They provide a clear representation of data dependencies. The rules' premises and consequences are conjunctions of atomic formulas (descriptors), often called templates or patterns. They involve the database attributes (columns) and their values. Many algorithms have been developed to extract both exact and approximate association rules from various types of data.

Valuable knowledge derivable from data can be represented at various levels. Rules expressed by means of the attribute-value descriptors can be replaced by global attribute dependencies. There is a growing interest in handling such dependencies. Among many applicable models, one could base on *reducts* developed within the theory of rough sets – irreducible subsets of attributes preserving information about the other, possibly preset attributes [7].

We propose a novel approach to capturing global relationships involving (the sets of) attributes. We introduce the notion of an *association reduct*, corresponding both to association rules and the rough set reducts. An association reduct is a pair (B_l, B_r) of disjoint subsets of attributes such that all data-supported patterns involving B_l (approximately) determine those involving B_r.

An association reduct (B_l, B_r) is *most informative* when B_l contains a few attributes while B_r – possibly many of them. Imagine that we found a *promising* set of attributes B (the analogy of a large *itemset* in the *Apriori* algorithm [1]).

M.-S. Hacid et al. (Eds.): ISMIS 2005, LNAI 3488, pp. 354–363, 2005.
© Springer-Verlag Berlin Heidelberg 2005

We want to decompose it as $B = B_l \cup B_r$, where possibly small B_l would (approximately) determine the rest of B. This is the minimal *information reduct problem* studied in the theory of rough sets (cf. [2,9]). In this way, we justify a usage of both words – "association" and "reduct" – in the proposed approach.

Association reducts are capable of representing more compound knowledge than "single attribute – single attribute" dependencies. A difference is as if we compared the arbitrary association rules with those involving only single-attribute descriptors at both rule sides. Generally, one could refer to the feature selection problem in *knowledge discovery in databases* [4], where attributes may be of no interest separately while together they provide a huge information gain. Therefore, we are convinced that association reducts provide a promising new means for the data based knowledge representation.

The paper is organized as follows: Section 2 contains basic notions concerning association rules; Section 3 – basic notions concerning the rough set information and decision reducts; Section 4 presents the main idea of association reducts; Section 5 – their informative properties; Section 6 – their approximate extension based on entropy; Section 7 provides basic algorithmic framework for extraction of approximate association reducts from data. Section 8 summarizes the paper.

2   Basic Notions – Association Rules

Association rules were originally introduced for *basket data* (cf. [1]). Then, many other applications were developed. People started to mine rules within databases of more general type, given qualitative and quantitative columns as the generators of *literals* occurring in the conditions and consequences.

We present the definition of an association rule within the framework of *information systems* – the data tables $\mathbb{A} = (U, A)$ consisting of the *attributes* (features, columns) $a \in A$ and *objects* (cases, records) $u \in U$ [7]. Every attribute corresponds to the function $a : U \to V_a$ labeling objects with the a's values from the set V_a. The attribute-value pairs (a, v_a), $a \in A$, $v_a \in V_a$, called *descriptors* correspond to literals or items in the association rule terminology.

Example 1. The information system on the previous page has attributes $A = \{Outlook, Temp., Humid., Wind, Sport\}$ and objects $U = \{u_1, \ldots, u_{14}\}$. The attribute functions take a form, e.g., $Outlook : U \to \{Sunny, Overcast, Rain\}$. There are 12 descriptors. For instance, $(Outlook, Sunny)$ is supported by $u_1, u_2, u_8, u_9, u_{11}$. We will refer to this information system in all further examples.

The problem of mining association rules is to generate all rules that have *support* and *confidence* greater than the user-specified thresholds. Consider the rule *cond* $\Rightarrow$ *cons*, where *cond* and *cons* are conjunctions of disjoint sets of descriptors. By $\|cond\|_{\mathbb{A}}$, $\|cons\|_{\mathbb{A}} \subseteq U$ we denote the subsets of objects satisfying *cond* and *cons* in the system $\mathbb{A}$. The rule's support and confidence are derived as

$$supp(cond \wedge cons) = \frac{card(\|cond\|_{\mathbb{A}} \cap \|cons\|_{\mathbb{A}})}{card(U)} \tag{1}$$

U	Outlook	Temp.	Humid.	Wind	Sport
u_1	Sunny	Hot	High	Weak	No
u_2	Sunny	Hot	High	Strong	No
u_3	Overcast	Hot	High	Weak	Yes
u_4	Rain	Mild	High	Weak	Yes
u_5	Rain	Cold	Normal	Weak	Yes
u_6	Rain	Cold	Normal	Strong	No
u_7	Overcast	Cold	Normal	Strong	Yes
u_8	Sunny	Mild	High	Weak	No
u_9	Sunny	Cold	Normal	Weak	Yes
u_{10}	Rain	Mild	Normal	Weak	Yes
u_{11}	Sunny	Mild	Normal	Strong	Yes
u_{12}	Overcast	Mild	High	Strong	Yes
u_{13}	Overcast	Hot	Normal	Weak	Yes
u_{14}	Rain	Mild	High	Strong	No

$$conf(cond \Rightarrow cons) = \frac{card(\|cond\|_A \cap \|cons\|_A)}{card(\|cond\|_A)} \qquad (2)$$

Example 2. Consider patterns $cond = (Outlook, Sunny) \wedge (Temp., Hot)$ and $cons = (Humid., High) \wedge (Sport, No)$. We obtain $supp(cond \wedge cons) = 0.14$ and $conf(cond \Rightarrow cons) = 1.0$. If we choose $cond = (Outlook, Sunny)$, then we get the support equal to 0.36 and the confidence equal to 0.6.

Usually, the association rule mining is divided onto two steps. First we find all enough supported *itemsets*. The original, still popular method is the *Apriori* algorithm [1]. Fig. 1 presents its possibly simplest version.

1) $L_1 = \{$large 1-itemsets$\}$
2) **for** $(k = 2; L_{k-1} \neq \emptyset; k + +)$ **do begin**
3) $C_k = apriorigen(L_{k-1});$ //generation of new candidates of length k
4)   **forall** candidates $c \in C_k$ **do**
5)   calculate $supp(c);$
6)   **end**
7) $L_k = \{c \in C_k : supp(c) \geq minsup\};$
8) **end**
9) $Answer = \bigcup_k L_k;$

Fig. 1. *Apriori* algorithm [1]. $apriorigen(L_{k-1})$ generates k-long candidates by matching previously found $(k-1)$-long itemsets with the support not less than $minsup$

Example 3. For $minsup = 0.4$ we obtain $L_1 = \{(Temp., Mild), (Humid., High),$ $(Humid., Normal), (Wind, Weak), (Wind, Strong), (Sport, Yes)\}$ and then we get $L_2 = \{(Humid., Normal) \wedge (Sport, Yes), (Wind, Weak) \wedge (Sport, Yes)\}$.

The second step of the association rule generation tries to split every itemset resulting from *Apriori* (or one of its modifications) onto disjoint conditional and consequence parts. The rule's support does not change in this step. The user-specified confidence threshold $minconf$ decides how many descriptors can be moved to the consequence side. We refer the reader to [1] for classical design of algorithms deriving rules from itemsets. A number of more up-to-date approaches can be obviously found in the literature (cf. [4, 8]).

3   Basic Notions – Information and Decision Reducts

The attribute reduction is one of the main steps of the *knowledge discovery in databases* [4]. Once we selected the data dimensions, we should examine whether their number can be *reduced*, before using data mining algorithms. Such a space simplification helps unless we loose some important attributes, non-replaceable by the others. In general, we should consider dependencies among the *sets* of attributes. This is because attributes which seem to be less informative separately may provide crucial information together. Methodology which seems to pay the most attention to this phenomenon originates from the theory of rough sets [7]. We recall its basic notions corresponding to the reduction problems.

Definition 1. *(cf. [7]) Let* $\mathbb{A} = (U, A)$ *and subset* $B \subseteq A$ *be given. We say that* B *is an* information reduct *in* $\mathbb{A}$*, if and only if* B *determines* $A \setminus B$*, that is*

$$\text{for every conjunction } \wedge_{b \in B} (b, v_b) \text{ such that } supp(\wedge_{b \in B}(b, v_b)) > 0 \text{ there}$$
$$\text{exists some } \wedge_{a \notin B} (a, v_a) \text{ such that } conf(\wedge_{b \in B}(b, v_b) \Rightarrow \wedge_{a \notin B}(a, v_a)) = 1 \quad (3)$$
$$\text{and there is no proper subset} B' \subsetneq B such that B' determines A \setminus B' in \mathbb{A}.$$

Information reducts seem to correspond to the association rules, now considered at the global level. Indeed, a reduct $B \subseteq A$ generates *exact* rules $\wedge_{b \in B}(b, v_b)$ $\Rightarrow \wedge_{a \notin B}(a, v_a)$. One can also consider *approximate* reducts as corresponding to the rules with confidence less than 1. We will go back to this topic in Section 6.

Example 4. The only information reduct in the considered information system is $B = \{Outlook, Temp., Humid., Wind\}$. It determines $A \setminus B = \{Sport\}$. We cannot further reduce B. For instance, if we take $B' = \{Outlook, Temp., Humid.\}$, then criterion (3) fails for $(Outlook, Sunny) \wedge (Temp., Hot) \wedge (Humid., High)$.

In the supervised learning problems one often distinguishes features called *decisions*. The notion of an information system can then take the form of a *decision system* $\mathbb{A} = (U, C, D)$ with disjoint sets of *conditions* C and *decisions* D.

Definition 2. *(cf. [7]) Let decision system* $\mathbb{A} = (U, C, D)$ *and subset* $B \subseteq C$ *be given. We say that* B *is a* decision reduct *in* $\mathbb{A}$*, if and only if* B *determines* D *and there is no proper subset* $B' \subsetneq B$ *such that* B' *determines* D *in* $\mathbb{A}$*.*

Intuitively, decision reducts correspond to *decision rules* (cf. [2]) in the same way as information reducts correspond to association rules. Some connections, however, can be drawn also between association rules and decision reducts [5].

4   Foundations of Association Reducts

Our main objective is to extend intuition and formalism behind methodology of association rules onto the level of global dependencies among attributes. A general idea is to operate with subsets of attributes just like we used to operate with conjunctions of descriptors in case of association rules. Determination of the rule consequences by conditions will be now understood in terms of global requirement (3). Approximate determination will be studied in Sections 6, 7.

Definition 3. *Let* $\mathbb{A} = (U, A)$ *and subsets* $B_l, B_r \subseteq A$, $B_l \cap B_r = \emptyset$, *be given. We say that* association reduct $B_l \Rightarrow B_r$ *occurs in* $\mathbb{A}$, *if and only if* B_l *determines* B_r *and there is no proper subset* $B_l' \subsetneq B_l$ *such that* B_l' *determines* $(B_l \setminus B_l') \cup B_r$.

As we can see, the association reduct is a pair of subsets defining its left, conditional part B_l, and its right, consequence part B_r. Association reduct is *non-improvable* in sense that it is impossible to move any element from its left part to the right part without loosing constraints for the global determination (3).

Example 5. For the previously considered information system, reducts {*Outlook*, *Temp.*, *Wind*} $\Rightarrow$ {*Sport*} and {*Outlook*, *Humid.*, *Wind*} $\Rightarrow$ {*Sport*} occur. Consider the first one. {*Outlook*, *Temp.*}, {*Outlook*, *Wind*}, {*Temp.*, *Wind*} do not determine {*Wind*, *Sport*}, {*Temp.*, *Sport*}, and {*Outlook*, *Sport*}, respectively. Hence, conditions of Definition 3 are satisfied.

Association reducts can be easily compared with information reducts:

Proposition 1. *Let* $\mathbb{A} = (U, A)$ *and subsets* $B_l, B_r \subseteq A$, $B_l \cap B_r = \emptyset$, *be given. Association reduct* $B_l \Rightarrow B_r$ *occurs in* $\mathbb{A}$, *if and only if* B_l *is an information reduct in the subsystem* $\mathbb{B} = (U, B)$, *where* $B = B_l \cup B_r$.

Example 6. If we restrict the considered system to *Outlook*, *Temp.*, *Wind*, *Sport*, then {*Outlook*, *Temp.*, *Wind*} becomes the information reduct. Similarly, we get the reduct {*Outlook*, *Humid.*, *Wind*} for *Outlook*, *Humid.*, *Wind*, *Sport*.

As a conclusion, once we find good, *promising* subsets of attributes, we can search for information reducts to get the association reducts. Although the problem of finding optimal information reducts is NP-hard (cf. [9]), there exist numerous heuristic approaches developed within the theory of rough sets (cf. [2]).

5   Most Informative Association Reducts

In Section 1 we claimed that an association reduct (B_l, B_r) is *most informative* when $card(B_l)$ is possibly small comparing to $card(B_r)$. Indeed, it seems to provide maximum information in case a small subset of attributes enables to (approximately) determine a large subset of other attributes.

Definition 4. *Let* $\mathbb{A} = (U, A)$ *and subsets* $B_l, B_r \subseteq A$, $B_l \cap B_r = \emptyset$, *be given. We say that association reduct* $B_l \Rightarrow B_r$ *is* non-extendible *in* $\mathbb{A}$, *if and only if there is no proper superset* $B_r' \supsetneq B_r$, $B_l \cap B_r' = \emptyset$, *such that* B_l *determines* B_r'.

Example 7. The association reducts $\{Outlook, Temp., Wind\} \Rightarrow \{Sport\}$ and $\{Outlook, Humid., Wind\} \Rightarrow \{Sport\}$ are both non-extendible. This is because the represented dependencies cannot be extended to $\{Outlook, Temp., Wind\} \Rightarrow \{Humid., Sport\}$ and $\{Outlook, Humid., Wind\} \Rightarrow \{Temp., Sport\}$, respectively.

Example 8. There is also the third association reduct in the considered system: $\{Outlook, Temp., Humid., Wind\} \Rightarrow \{Sport\}$. It satisfies both Definitions 3 and 4. However, its importance is discussible. We could *reduce* its conditional part by $Temp.$ or $Humid.$ and still obtain a non-extendible association reduct. The problem is that this kind of *reduction* is not analyzed in Definitions 3 and 4 yet.

Definition 5. *Let* $\mathbb{A} = (U, A)$ *and subsets* $B_l, B_r \subseteq A$, $B_l \cap B_r = \emptyset$, *be given. We say that association reduct* $B_l \Rightarrow B_r$ *is irreducible in* $\mathbb{A}$, *if and only if there is no proper subset* $B'_l \subsetneq B_l$ *such that* B'_l *determines* B_r.

Proposition 2. *Let* $\mathbb{A} = (U, A)$ *and subsets* $B_l, B_r \subseteq A$, $B_l \cap B_r = \emptyset$, *be given. Association reduct* $B_l \Rightarrow B_r$ *is irreducible in* $\mathbb{A}$, *if and only if* B_l *is a decision reduct for the decision system* $\mathbb{B} = (U, B_l, B_r)$ *and an information reduct for the information system* $\mathbb{B} = (U, B)$, $B = B_l \cup B_r$.

The *most informative* association reducts should be both non-extendible and irreducible. Only then their informative power cannot be strengthened by neither reducing the set of conditions nor extending the set of consequences. Such reducts provide a kind of optimal knowledge base about the attribute dependencies.

Non-extendibility and irreducibility could be also required for the association rules. It may be compared with other ideas of decreasing the number of rules generated by standard approaches (see e.g. [8]).

Example 9. Consider the *Apriori* algorithm with $minsup = 0.1$. We obtain both $(Temp., Cold) \wedge (Humid., Normal) \in L_2$ and $(Outlook, Rain) \wedge (Temp., Cold) \wedge (Humid., Normal) \in L_3$. Then, for the confidence threshold $minconf = 1.0$, we obtain rules $(Temp., Cold) \Rightarrow (Humid., Normal)$ and $(Outlook, Rain) \wedge (Temp., Cold) \Rightarrow (Humid., Normal)$. In some domains, like medical data mining, the experts would prefer a longer rule as more reliable. On the other hand, the *Ockham's Razor* principle suggests removal of any unnecessary conditions.

6 Approximate Reducts Based on Entropy

In real-life data we cannot count too frequently on the exact dependencies among attributes. Moreover, even if we observe them, we would prefer *approximate* dependencies involving less conditions and, possibly, more consequences. In case of association rules this is regulated by the confidence threshold. In case of reducts, one could think about a threshold reflecting *average* confidence of the corresponding rules. Actually, we need also a kind of *average* support threshold if we want to adapt the *Apriori* algorithm for finding association reducts.

One of the functions studied in the context of the average support and confidence of *approximate* rough set reducts takes the form of *information entropy*

[3]. For simplicity, let us represent any $B \subseteq A$ as $B = \{b_1, \ldots, b_m\}$ and denote by V_i the value set of $b_i \in B$. Entropy of B can be then expressed as $H(B) =$

$$= \sum_{v_1, \ldots, v_m : supp((b_1, v_1) \wedge \ldots \wedge (b_m, v_m)) > 0} \left[\frac{- supp((b_1, v_1) \wedge \ldots \wedge (b_m, v_m)) *}{\log(supp((b_1, v_1) \wedge \ldots \wedge (b_m, v_m)))} \right] \quad (4)$$

It is shown (cf. [9]) that $H(B)$ equals to minus logarithm of geometric average of the support of patterns (conjunctions of descriptors) generated by the objects $u \in U$ within $\mathbb{B} = (U, B)$. In the same way, the *conditional entropy*

$$H(B_r | B_l) = H(B_l \cup B_r) - H(B_l) \quad (5)$$

corresponds to the average *confidence* of rules generated within decision system $\mathbb{B} = (U, B_l, B_r)$. We have always $H(B_r | B_l) \geq 0$, where equality holds if and only if B_l determines B_r. It leads to the following extension of rough set reducts:

Definition 6. *(cf. [9]) Let the threshold $\beta \geq 0$ and $\mathbb{A} = (U, A)$ be given. We say that $B \subseteq A$ is an β-approximate information reduct, if and only if*

$$H(A \setminus B | B) \leq \beta \quad (6)$$

and there is no proper subset $B' \subsetneq B$ which satisfies inequality $H(A \setminus B' | B') \leq \beta$.

Definition 7. *(cf. [9]) Let the threshold $\beta \geq 0$ and $\mathbb{A} = (U, C, D)$ be given. We say that $B \subseteq C$ is an β-approximate decision reduct, if and only if*

$$H(D | B) \leq \beta \quad (7)$$

and there is no proper subset $B' \subsetneq B$ which satisfies inequality $H(D | B') \leq \beta$.

The above notions are equivalent to the information and decision reducts, respectively, for the *average confidence threshold* $\beta = 0$. For $\beta > 0$ we can obtain, however, much shorter reducts which still provide *almost* exact information about the other attributes or distinguished decisions. Let us follow this entropy based interpretation also in case of *most informative* association reducts: [1]

Definition 8. *Let $\beta \geq 0$, $\mathbb{A} = (U, A)$, and $B_l, B_r \subseteq A$, $B_l \cap B_r = \emptyset$, be given. β-approximate association reduct $B_l \Rightarrow_\beta B_r$ occurs in $\mathbb{A}$, if and only if*

$$H(B_r | B_l) \leq \beta \quad (8)$$

and there is neither proper subset $B'_l \subsetneq B_l$ nor proper superset $B'_r \supsetneq B_r$ for which $H(B_r | B'_l) \leq \beta$ and/or $H(B'_r | B_l) \leq \beta$ would still hold.

Proposition 3. *Let $\beta \geq 0$, $\mathbb{A} = (U, A)$, and $B_l, B_r \subseteq A$, $B_l \cap B_r = \emptyset$, be given. $B_l \Rightarrow B_r$ satisfies the requirements of Definitions 3, 4, 5, if and only if $B_l \Rightarrow_\beta B_r$ satisfies the requirements of Definition 8 for $\beta = 0$.*

---

[1] Because of the lack of space, we decide to consider at once the most informative approximate association reducts, with the requirements for non-extendability and irreducibility directly involved in Definition 8. It is well illustrated by Proposition 3.

7 Mining Approximate Association Reducts

Let us specify a framework for mining approximate association reducts. We follow the original approach to extraction of association rules and focus on reducts satisfying the user-defined thresholds. In Fig. 2 we modify the *Apriori* algorithm to search for the largest attribute sets with the preset requirement for averagely high support of generated patterns. Namely, we are interested in α-*promising* sets B such that $H(B) \leq \alpha$, for the user-defined $\alpha > 0$ (please refer to the interpretation of H mentioned in the previous section, based on [9]).

1) $P_1 = \{$promising 1-attributesets$\}$
2) **for** $(k = 2; P_{k-1} \neq \emptyset; k + +)$ **do begin**
3) $C_k = apriorisetgen(P_{k-1});$ //generation of new candidates of cardinality k
4)   **forall** candidates $B \in C_k$ **do**
5)   calculate entropy $H(B);$
6)   **end**
7) $P_k = \{B \in C_k : H(B) \leq \alpha\};$
8) **end**
9) $Answer = reduce(\bigcup_k P_k);$

Fig. 2. *AprioriSet* algorithm. Function $apriorisetgen(P_{k-1})$ matches previously found subsets with entropy not greater than the user-defined threshold $\alpha > 0$. Function $reduce(\bigcup_k P_k)$ deletes redundant subsets. It means that in case of $B, B' \in Answer$ such that $B' \subsetneq B$, the subset B' will be removed from the *Answer* set

Restriction to $Answer = reduce(\bigcup_k P_k)$ assures that the results will further provide only non-extendible (approximate) association reducts. Obviously, the analogous approach can be followed in case of large itemsets (cf. [1, 8]).

Example 10. We want to obtain the attribute subsets generating conjunctions of descriptors supported by at least two objects on average. We should search for the sets with entropy not exceeding $\alpha = -\log(2/14) \approx 2.8$. We obtain $P_1 = \{\{Outlook\}, \{Temp.\}, \{Humid.\}, \{Wind\}, \{Sport\}\}; P_2 = \{\{Outlook, Humid.\}$ $\{Outlook, Wind\}, \{Outlook, Sport\}, \{Temp., Humid.\}, \{Temp., Wind\}, \{Temp.,$ $Sport\}, \{Humid., Wind\}, \{Humid., Sport\}, \{Wind, Sport\}\}; P_3 = \{\{Humid.,$ $Wind, Sport\}\}; P_4 = P_5 = \emptyset$. *AprioriSet* gives $Answer = \{\{Outlook, Humid.\},$ $\{Outlook, Wind\}, \{Outlook, Sport\}, \{Temp., Humid.\}, \{Temp., Wind\}, \{Temp.,$ $Sport\}, \{Humid., Wind, Sport\}\}$. These are the sets which can be further analyzed to get approximate reducts $B_l \Rightarrow_\beta B_r$ satisfying $H(B_l \cup B_r) \leq 2.8$.

The time complexity of *AprioriSet* is potentially exponential, as it is in case of *Apriori*. The following result emphasizes the expected difficulties. Fortunately, a number of speeding-up [1] and heuristic [6] techniques can be adapted.

Theorem 1. *For any constant $\alpha > 0$, the problem of finding maximal sets B satisfying inequality $H(B) \leq \alpha$ is NP-hard.* [2]

---

[2] The proof is skipped because the lack of space. Generally, it involves the problem of finding maximal *almost* independent sets in undirected graphs.

Proposition 4. *Let $\alpha > 0$, $\beta \geq 0$, and $\mathbb{A} = (U, A)$ be given. $B_l \Rightarrow_\beta B_r$ is a β-approximate association reduct satisfying $H(B_l \cup B_r) \leq \alpha$, if and only if $B_l \cup B_r$ belongs to Answer resulting from AprioriSet for α, B_l is a β-approximate decision reduct in decision system $\mathbb{B} = (U, B_l, B_r)$ and a β-approximate information reduct in information system $\mathbb{B} = (U, B_l \cup B_r)$.*

Example 11. We would like to find the β-approximate association reducts for $\beta = -\log(0.65) \approx 0.74$. It means that we want the generated rules to have average confidence not below 0.65. Given the results of Example 10, dependencies $\{Sport\} \Rightarrow_\beta \{Humid.\}$, $\{Humid., Wind\} \Rightarrow_\beta \{Sport\}$ are the only solutions.

The problems of the search of approximate decision and information reducts are NP-hard as well [9]. We would probably not be able to apply the exhaustive reduct search to large real-life data sets, as we actually did in the above example. Still, we can use well established heuristics, like e.g. the order-based hybrid genetic algorithm developed in [10] for approximate entropy reducts, as well as modifications of other rough set based attribute reduction techniques (cf. [2]).

8   Conclusions and Directions for Further Research

We introduced the association reducts representing approximate relationships among the sets of attributes. We discussed their relations to association rules, as well as to other types of reducts developed so far within the theory of rough sets. We discussed requirements for the most informative association reducts, capable of representing the most valuable data based knowledge.

We presented the main intuitions behind association reducts without an extensive algorithmic and experimental study. We adapted the most basic association rule mining methods. More up-to-date techniques should be considered with regards to association reducts, to take the full advantage of this novel framework for knowledge representation in real-life applications. The experiments with real-life data sets should follow the initial algorithmic studies in the nearest future.

Acknowledgements. Research reported in this paper was supported by the research grant from Natural Sciences and Engineering Research Council of Canada.

References

1. Agrawal, R., Mannila, H., Srikant, R., Toivonen, H., Verkamo, A.I.: Fast discovery of assocation rules. In: Advances in Knowledge Discovery and Data Mining. AAAI/MIT Press (1996) pp. 307–328.
2. Bazan, J., Nguyen, H.S., Nguyen, S.H, Synak, P., Wróblewski, J.: Rough Set Algorithms in Classification Problem. In: Rough Set Methods and Applications. Physica Verlag (2000) pp. 49–88.
3. Kapur, J.N., Kesavan, H.K.: Entropy Optimization Principles with Applications. Academic Press (1992).

4. Kloesgen, W., Żytkow, J.M. (eds): Handbook of Data Mining and Knowledge Discovery. Oxford University Press (2002).
5. Nguyen, H.S., Nguyen S.H.: Rough Sets and Association Rule Generation. Fundamenta Informaticae 40/4, IOS Press (1999) pp. 310–318.
6. Nguyen, S.H., Nguyen H.S.: Pattern extraction from data. Fundamenta Informaticae 34/1-2, IOS Press (1998) pp. 129–144.
7. Pawlak, Z.: Rough sets – Theoretical aspects of reasoning about data. Kluwer Academic Publishers (1991).
8. Phan-Luong, V.: The Representative Basis for Association Rules. In: Proc. of ICDM'2001. San Jose, California (2001) pp. 639–640.
9. Ślęzak, D.: Approximate Entropy Reducts. Fundamenta Informaticae 53/3-4, IOS Press (2002) pp. 365–390.
10. Ślęzak, D., Wróblewski, J.: Order-based genetic algorithms for the search of approximate entropy reducts. In: Proc. of RSFDGrC'2003. Chongqing, China (2003).

Frequent Pattern Mining with Preferences–Utility Functions Approach

Elena Braynova and Hemant Pendharkar

Department of Computer Science, Worcester State College,
Worcester, MA 01602
{ebraynova, hpendharkar}@worcester.edu

Abstract. The notion of preference naturally occurs in every context where one talks about human decisions or choice. Users, faced with a huge amount of data but often not equipped with a complete knowledge of the nature of the data, seek ways to obtain not necessarily all but the best or most preferred solutions. In this paper, we study preferences in the context of frequent pattern mining using the utility function approach. We also seek to provide a framework for investigating data mining problems involving preferences. We consider the problem of preference frequent pattern mining and N-best frequent pattern mining. We define preferences analytically, investigate their properties and classify them. We also provide some preference frequent pattern mining algorithms and show how they can be used for efficient N-best data mining.

1 Introduction

It is known that frequent pattern mining plays an essential role in many important data mining problems. For most problems, a minimum support threshold, defined by a user, is assumed to be available. However, setting such a threshold is usually difficult. A user does not know what value for the threshold can be considered good enough. If the threshold set is too low a large number of frequent patterns are generated forcing the user to sift through all of them to find useful ones. That reduces the efficiency and effectiveness of mining. If the threshold set is too high, there is the distinct possibility of losing many interesting patterns. If we could find many more frequent patterns rather than less frequent ones then the user could stop mining right away. The problem becomes more complicated when a user has to find frequent patterns that satisfy specific properties.

The research literature on preferences is extensive. It encompasses preference logics [1, 2, 3], preference reasoning [4, 5, 6], decision theory [7, 8], and preference database querying [9, 10, 11, 12, 13]. The first attempt to address the issue of user preferences in the context of frequent patter mining was done by S. Jagannath [14]. The author presents the use of utility functions to express user preferences and formulates several pattern mining problems. Another approach for preference-based pattern mining is proposed by J. Pei and al. [15]. They model the problem using a directed graph.

M.-S. Hacid et al. (Eds.): ISMIS 2005, LNAI 3488, pp. 364–372, 2005.
© Springer-Verlag Berlin Heidelberg 2005

In this paper we consider preference-based frequent pattern mining using the utility function approach. We believe that this approach is very natural and useful in many mining problems. In this paper we define the concept of preference frequent pattern mining and N-best frequent pattern mining, define preferences analytically, investigate some of their properties and classify them, design algorithms of preference frequent pattern mining for some classes of preferences, and show how these preferences can be pushed into the frequent pattern growth mining. We also demonstrate how preference based frequent pattern mining algorithms can be used for N-best frequent pattern mining and discuss the efficiency of the proposed algorithms.

2 Problem Definition

Let $I=\{i_1, i_2, ..., i_n\}$ be a set of items, where an item is an object with some predefined attributes (for example, profit, weight, price, etc.). An itemset is a subset of the set of items I. In this paper we write an itemset as a string of items, omitting the parentheses. For example, itemset $\{a, b, c\}$ is written as abc. A transaction $t=<tid, I_t>$ is a tuple where tid is the identifier of the transaction and I_t is an itemset. A transaction database T is a set of transactions. We say that an itemset X is contained in a transaction $t=<tid, I_t>$, if and only if $X \subseteq I_t$. The *support* of itemset X, denoted as $sup(X)$, is the number of transactions in T containing X. Given a support threshold ξ, $1 \le \xi \le |T|$, we say that X is frequent if $sup(X) \ge \xi$. The problem of frequent pattern mining is to find the complete set of frequent patterns from a given database, given a support threshold.

Problem Definition 2.1 Preference Frequent Pattern Mining: Given a transaction database T, a support threshold ξ, and a preference P_f. The problem of mining frequent patterns with respect to preference P_f is to find the complete set of frequent itemsets and output them to a user in the preference order, in other words, more preferable itemsets are output prior than less preferable ones.

Example 2.1. Let Table1 be our transaction database T, with a set of items $I=\{a, b, c, d, e, f, g, h\}$. Let support threshold be ξ, $\xi=2$ and preference be P_f, $P_f=Larger$ *support*. The corresponding preference based frequent pattern mining problem is, Find the complete set of frequent patterns for the given database and output larger supported itemsets before the less supported ones.

Table 1

Transaction ID	Items in transaction
1	a, b, c, d, f
2	b, c, d, f, g, h
3	a, c, d, e, f
4	a, e, f, g

The result of the above preference frequent pattern mining is the following partially ordered list of itemsets: $\{c, f, cf\}$, $\{d, cd, df, cdf\}$, $\{a, b, e, g, ac, ad, af, bc, bd, bf, ce, cg, ef, fg, acd, acf, adf, bcd, bcf, bdf, cef, cfg, acdf, bcdf\}$.

The itemsets in the parentheses $\{ \}$ can be output in any order. They have the same preference value for the user. In general, for any frequent pattern mining problem, with the above preference, any itemset of support k, $k \in N$, $k \geq \xi$, must be output rather than any itemset of support i, $i < k$, $i \geq \xi$.

Different preferences on the same transaction database and same threshold, in general, will produce differently ordered lists of itemsets.

Problem Definition 2.2 N-best Frequent Pattern Mining: Given a transaction database T, a support threshold ξ, a nonnegative number N, and a preference P_f. The problem of *N-best frequent pattern mining with respect to preference P_f* is to find N most preferable frequent itemsets and output them to a user in the preference order.

Example 2.2. Let Table1 be our transaction database T, with a set of items $I=\{a, b, c, d, e, f, g, h\}$. Let the support threshold be ξ, $\xi=2$, $N=9$, and the preference $P_f=Larger$ *support*. Then the problem of N-best frequent pattern mining with respect to preference P_f is: *Find 9 frequent itemsets with the largest support presented in the database.*

The result of the above N-best frequent pattern mining is the following partially ordered list of itemsets: $\{c, f, cf\}$, $\{d, cd, df, cdf\}$, $\{x, y\}$, where x and y are any two itemsets from $\{a, b, e, g, ac, ad, af, bc, bd, bf, ce, cg, ef, fg, acd, acf, adf, bcd, bcf, bdf, cef, cfg, acdf, bcdf\}$. The above two problems are very similar. If we know how to organize the search process according to given preferences, we will be able to find N-best frequent patterns quickly. One possible solution is to find the complete set of frequent itemsets using any frequent pattern mining algorithm; compute preference value for each frequent pattern and order the itemsets based on their preference values and output the partially ordered list of the itemsets or N first itemsets of the list to a user.

In the above approach steps 1 and 2 are distinct and hence performed independently. The natural questions that arise are: *Can we combine them? Can we push the ordering with respect to P_f into the mining process? Can we organize the search process such that more preferable itemsets are found earlier than less preferable ones?*

In this paper we propose several *find-order* algorithms thus pushing preferences deep into the mining process. We use ideas similar to constraint frequent pattern mining [16, 18] and preference frequent pattern mining [14, 15].

3 Preferences–Definitions, Properties, Classification

In this section, we model preference frequent pattern mining problem using the utility function approach, define preferences analytically, observe some of their properties and classify them. In this paper we use a simplified concept of utility function to measure a user's preference over frequent itemsets.

Definition 3.1. Given $I=\{i_1, i_2,..., i_n\}$ set of items, where an item is an object with some predefined attributes and a utility function $f:2^I \rightarrow R$, where R is a set of real numbers. A *preference relation* P_f is an order relation corresponding to the utility function f.

Any utility function f defines a preference relation P_f over $2^I \times 2^I$. Any preference relation P_f satisfies the following properties:

- $P_f(X, Y)$ *if and only if* $f(X) > f(Y)$
- $P_f(X,Y)$ and $P_f(Y,X)$ *if and only if* $f(X) = f(Y)$
- $P_f(X,Y)$ and $P_f(Y,X)$ *implies* $P_f(X,Y)$.

Definition 3.2. For any itemsets X and Y ($X, Y \subset I$) we say that X *is preferred over Y* if and only if $P_f(X, Y)$ and write that as $X >_P Y$, omitting subscript f for P_f. We say that X *and Y are equally desirable* if and only if $P_f(X, Y)$ and $P_f(Y, X)$, and write that as $X \sim_P Y$, omitting the subscript f for P_f.

Example 3.1. Here are examples of some widely used utility functions and the preference relations defined by them. In the examples below, X and Y are itemsets, and we assume that each item has a numerical attribute, for example a price attribute.

1. *Find the complete set of frequent itemsets for a given database and output itemsets containing more expensive items before the itemsets containing less expensive ones*, can be defined using utility function f, where $f(X) = max_X(item\_price)$, largest item price over the items contained in the itemset.
2. *Find the complete set of frequent itemsets for a given database and output more expensive (in total) itemsets before the less expensive ones*, can be defined using utility function f, where $f(X) = sum_X(item\_price)$, the sum is taken over all items in the itemset X.
3. Preferences: *Larger average price, Smaller average price, Larger median price, Smaller median price*, can be easily defined using corresponding utility functions (mean and median - functions).

Now let us introduce a few more definitions that will be used for preferences classification. For the sake of brevity, we refer to a preference relation P_f as preference P, omitting subscript f, and describe them informally in the following way: $P = Larger/Smaller\ f(.)$, where $f(.)$ is an appropriate utility function depending on the items in an itemset.

Definition 3.3. Given a preference P. Let $L(P)$ be a result of frequent pattern mining with respect to (w.r.t) P. $L(P)$ is a partially ordered list of frequent itemsets and the order of $L(P)$ is defined by the preference P. We say that P^{-1} is the inverse of P if and only if for any given transaction database T and any threshold ξ: $(\Re(L(P-1)))^{-1} = \Re(L(P))$, where $\Re(X)$ is an order of a set X.

By this definition, two preferences are inverses of each other if and only if the orders of the mining results determined by the preferences are mutually inverse.

Definition 3.4. A preference P is called strictly increasing (strictly decreasing) if and only if $\forall X$, $X \subseteq I$ and $\forall X'$, $X' \subset X$ ($X' \neq X$): $X >_P X'$ ($X' >_P X$)

Example 3.2. $P = Larger\ length$ is a strictly increasing preference. $P' = Smaller\ length$ is a strictly decreasing preference.

Definition 3.5. A preference P is called *increasing* (*decreasing*) if and only if for $\forall X$, $X \subseteq I$ and $\forall X'$, $X' \subset X$. $X >_P X'$ or $X \sim_P X'$ ($X' >_P X$ or $X \sim_P X'$).

Example 3.3. $P=Larger\ support$ is an increasing preference. $P'=Smaller\ support$ is a decreasing preference. It is easy to show that the preference $P_A=containment\ of\ A$, is increasing, too.

Definition 3.6. Given an order $\mathfrak{R}$ of I. We say that P is *increasing* (*decreasing*) w. r. t. $\mathfrak{R}$ if and only if for any $X=\{x_{i1}, x_{i2},...,x_{ik}\}$ and $Y=\{x_{j1}, x_{j2},...,x_{jl}\}$ $ik > jl$ holds $X>_P Y$ or $X\sim_P Y$ ($Y>_P X$ or $X\sim_P Y$).

Example 3.4. $P=Larger\ max(item\_attribute)$ is increasing w.r.t. value-ascending order of the items over the corresponding item's attribute. $P=Larger\ support(.)$ is neither increasing w.r.t $\mathfrak{R}$ nor decreasing w.r.t. $\mathfrak{R}$, for any items order $\mathfrak{R}$. There are also preferences that are neither decreasing, nor increasing.

Definition 3.7. A preference P is called *convertible increasing* (*decreasing*) w.r.t. $\mathfrak{R}$ if and if there is an order $\mathfrak{R}$ on items such that for $\forall X, X \subseteq I$ and $\forall X', X'$ – a prefix of X: $X>_P X'$ or $X\sim_P X'$ ($X'>_P X$ or $X\sim_P X'$).

Example 3.5. The preference $P=Larger\ average(t)$, where t is a real-value attribute of the items, is convertible increasing w.r.t. the value-ascending order of items over the attribute t.

Theorem 1. The following statements are true:

1. P is *strictly increasing* (*strictly decreasing*) if and only if P^{-1} is *strictly decreasing* (*strictly increasing*).
2. P is *increasing* (*decreasing*) if and only if P^{-1} is *decreasing* (*increasing*).
3. P is *increasing* (*decreasing*) w.r.t. $\mathfrak{R}$ if and only if when P^{-1} is *decreasing* (*increasing*)) w.r.t. $\mathfrak{R}^1$.
4. P is *convertible increasing* (*convertible decreasing*) w.r.t. $\mathfrak{R}$ if and only if P^{-1} is *convertible decreasing* (*convertible increasing*) w.r.t. $\mathfrak{R}^1$.

Proof. The proof of the Theorem follows directly from the definitions 3.3–3.7.   □

Theorem 2. The following statements are true:

1. Any *increasing* (*decreasing*) w.r.t. $\mathfrak{R}$ preference is *convertible increasing* (*decreasing*) w.r.t. $\mathfrak{R}$.
2. Any *strictly increasing* (*strictly decreasing*) preference is *increasing* (*decreasing*).
3. Any *increasing* (*decreasing*) preference is *convertible increasing* (*convertible decreasing*) w.r.t. some order $\mathfrak{R}$.

Proof. The proof of the Theorem follows directly from the definitions 3.3–3.7.   □

Example 3.6. The preference $P=Larger\ support$ is increasing, but not strictly increasing. It can be easily verified that the preference $P=Larger\ median(.)$ is neither increasing, nor decreasing.

Definition 3.8. A preference P is called *convertible* if and only if there is an order $\mathcal{R}$ of the itemset I such that P is convertible increasing or convertible decreasing w.r.t $\mathcal{R}$.

Example 3.7. It can be shown that the preference $P=Larger\ sum(.)$ is neither convertible increasing, nor convertible decreasing if items have different sign attribute values.

Lemma 1. The following statements hold:

1. A preference P is *convertible increasing w.r.t.* $\mathcal{R}$ if and only if there exists such order $\mathcal{R}$ over I that for any itemset X and item $a \in I$ such that for $\forall x \in X$, $x\mathcal{R}a$, holds the following: $X \cup \{a\} >_P X$ or $X \cup \{a\} \sim_P X$.
2. A preference P is *convertible decreasing w.r.t.* $\mathcal{R}$ if and only if there exists such order $\mathcal{R}$ over I that for any itemset X and item $a \in I$ such that for $\forall x \in X$, $x\mathcal{R}a$, holds the following: $X >_P X \cup \{a\}$ or $X \sim_P X \cup \{a\}$.

The notion of prefix monotone functions [16] will be used to examine other preferences properties.

Theorem 3. A preference P_f (a preference relation defined by the utility function f) is *convertible increasing w.r.t.* $\mathcal{R}$ if and only if the function f is a prefix increasing function. A preference P_f is a *convertible decreasing w.r.t.* $\mathcal{R}$ if and only if the function f is a prefix decreasing function.

Proof. The proof follows from statements in [16] and Lemma1.   □

Definition 3.9. A preference P is called *strongly convertible* if and only if there exists an order $\mathcal{R}$ over the set of items I such that P is convertible increasing w.r.t. $\mathcal{R}$ and P is convertible decreasing w.r.t. $\mathcal{R}^1$.

Theorem 4. A preference P_f is *strongly convertible* if and only if there exists an order $\mathcal{R}$ over a set of items I such that the utility function f defining P_f is a prefix decreasing w.r.t. $\mathcal{R}$ and a prefix increasing w.r.t. $\mathcal{R}^1$.

Proof. The proof follows from Definition2.9 and Theorem3.   □

Example 3.8 The preferences: *Larger average(.), Smaller average(.), Larger median(.), Smaller median(.)* are strongly convertible preferences.

4 Mining Algorithms

In this section we propose preference-based frequent pattern mining algorithms for some of the preference classes. The general idea is to push preferences into search process as deeply as possible and organize the search such that more preferable items are found prior to finding less preferable ones. We use the ideas similar to pushing constraints into mining process [16, 18] and approach proposed in [14]. All considered algorithms are based on the frequent pattern growth method [17]. The Algorithm for frequent pattern mining with increasing (decreasing) w.r.t. order $\mathcal{R}$ preference P_f can be formulated as follows.

Algorithm1 Increasing w.r.t. $\mathcal{R}(T, \xi, P_f)$:

1. Scan T once, compute the items frequency.
2. Scan T second time: Eliminate non-frequent items. Order the frequent items such that if $X=\{x_{i1}, x_{i2},..., x_{ik}\}, Y=\{x_{j1}, x_{j2},...,x_{jl}\}$, and $ik>jl$ then $f(X) \geq f(Y)$. This can be done since it follows from the existence of such order $\mathcal{R}$, def.3.6.
3. Let $I=\{x_1, x_2,...,x_n\}$ be the frequent items list written in the order $\mathcal{R}$. Search for frequent items in the following projected databases: $T/x_1, T/x_2,...,T/x_n$. For any $k=1,...,n$ search T/x_k only completed the search of T/x_{k-1}. Output the projection bases in the order of projections.

Algorithm 2-Increasing (T, ξ, P_f):

1. Scan T once, compute the items frequency.
2. Scan T second time: Eliminate non-frequent items. Order the frequent items in value-descending order of $f(.)$: $I=\{x_1, x_2, ..., x_n\}$.
3. Find $X_{max} \subseteq 2^I$: $f(X_{max})=max_X\{f(X)\}$, where $X \subseteq 2^I$; take $F=\{f(x_1), f(x_2), ..., f(x_n)\}$, $F'=\emptyset$, $\psi=max(F)$; construct T/X_{max}, $F'=\{f(X_{max}\ y)/y\ is\ a\ frequent\ item\ in\ T/X_{max}\}$, $F=F \cup F'-\{\psi\}$.
4. Until there are non-empty projected databases of T, do the following: $\psi=max(F)$, $X_{max}=\{X_{max} \subseteq 2^I: f(X_{max})=max(F)\}$; construct T/X_{max} and for each considered projected database T/X_{max}: $F'=\{f(X_{max}\ y)/y\ is\ a\ frequent\ item\ in\ T/X_{max}\}$, $F=F \cup F'-\{\psi\}$.
5. Output the projection bases in the order of projections

The algorithm for frequent pattern mining with convertible increasing (convertible decreasing) w.r.t. $\mathcal{R}$ preference P_f is the same as Algorithm 2. Each of the above algorithms can be used for N-best frequent pattern mining, where *best* is defined by a user specified preference.

5 Algorithms Efficiency

We analyze the efficiency of the algorithms in terms of item set size, the output size, and given N for N-best frequent pattern mining. Let $|I|=n$, output size be equal to m, and N be a given nonnegative integer.

Theorem 5. Execution of each of the Algorithms 1-2 requires m database projections and m preference-function recomputations and items sortings, one for each of the projected databases

Proof. Follows directly from the algorithms. □

Theorem 6. Given a nonnegative integer N, N-best frequent pattern search based on any of the Algorithms 1-2 requires N database projections, N preference function recomputations and item sortings, one for each of the projected databases

Proof. Follows directly from the algorithms. □

Based on the above results we can conclude that preference-based algorithms are interesting not only by themselves but also in N-best mining context. The N-best frequent mining algorhihms get more efficient as the ratio m/N increases.

6 Related Work

The current work is a generalization of constraint mining ideas to preference mining [16, 18, 19, 20, 21]. This far, we know only a few papers that discuss preference-based frequent pattern mining problem [14, 15, 19]. In [14] the author formulates several pattern mining problems using utility function approach and provides algorithms for their solutions. The authors of [15] discuss preference-based mining using graph approach. The authors of [19] investigate the problem of frequent patterns mining with larger profit. The problem is a special case of our problem, where the preference is given in the form *Larger sum(profit(t))*, t is an item of a frequent itemset X. Data mining with filters a concept, that is close to preference/constraint mining, is considered in [21]. Different approaches to the evaluation of interestingness and usefulness of association rules are investigated in [22, 23, 24, 25, 26, 27].

7 Conclusions

In this paper we defined the concept of preference frequent pattern mining and N-best frequent pattern mining based on utility function approach, describe preferences ana-lytically, investigated some their properties, and classified some of them. We provided algorithms for the following preference classes: increasing (decreasing) w.r.t. $\Re$, increasing (decreasing), convertible increasing (convertible decreasing) w.r.t. $\Re$, N-best frequent patterns and studied their efficiency.

Acknowledgements. The authors would like to express many thanks to Jian Pei for introducing them to the problem and fruitful discussions.

References

1. S.O.Hansson. Prefernce Logic. In D.Gabbay, editor, Handbook of Philosophical Logic, Vol. 8, 2001.
2. S.M.Mantha. First-Order Preference Theories and their Applications. Ph.D. thesis, University of Utah, 1991.
3. G.H.von Wright. The Logic of Preference. Edinburgh University Press, 1963.
4. C.Boutilier, R.I.Braman, H.H.Hoos, and D.Poole. Reasoning with Conditional Ceteris Paribus Preference Statements. In Symposium on Uncertainty in Artificial Intelligence, 1999.
5. S-W.Tan and J.Pearl. Specification and Evaluation of Preferences under Uncertainty. In International Conference on Principles of Knowledge Representation and Reasoning, 1994.
6. M.P.Wellman and J.Doyle. Preferential Semantics for Goals. In National Conference on Artificial Intelligence, 1991.

7. P.Fishburn. Preference Structures and their Numerical Representations. Theoretical Computer Science, 217: 359-383, 1999.
8. P.Fishburn. Utility Theory for Decision Making. Wiley & Sons, 1970.
9. R.Agrawal and E.L.Wimmers. A Framework for Expressing and Combining Preferences. In ACM SIGMOD International Conference on Management of Data, 297-306, 2000.
10. S. Borzsonyi, D.Kossman, and K.Stocker. The Skyline Operator. In IEEE International Conference on Data Engineering, 421-430, 2001.
11. K.Govindarajan, B.Jayaraman, and S.Mantha. Preference Queries in Deductive Databases. New Generation Computing, 57-86, 2001.
12. M.Lacroix and P.Lavency. Preferences: Putting More Knowledge into Queries. In International Conference on Very Large Databases, 217-225, 1987.
13. J.Chomicki. Querying with Intrinsic Preferences. In EDBT, 2002.
14. S. Jagannath. Utility Guided Pattern Mining,. NCSU MS Thesis, 2003
15. J.Pei, private communication
16. J.Pei, J.Han, and L.V.S. Lakshmanan. Mining frequent itemsets with convertible constraints. In Proc 2001 Int. Conf. Data Engineering (ICDE'01).
17. J.Han, J. Pei, and Y.Yin. Mining frequent patterns without candidate generation. In Proc. 2000 ACM-SIGMOD Int. Conf. Management of Data (SIGMOD'00).
18. J.Han and J. Pei. Can we push more constraints into frequent pattern mining? In Proc. 2000 ACM-SIGKDD Int. Conf.Knowlegde Discovery in Databases (KDD'00).
19. J.Han, S.Zhou. Profit Mining: From Patterns to Auctions. EDRT'02.
20. Y-L.Cheung, A.W-C.Fu. Mining Frequent Itemsets without Support Threshold: with and without Item Constraints.
21. R.Sawai, M.Tsukamoto, Y-H.Loh, T.Terada, and S.Nishio. Functional Properties of Information Filtering. In Proc. of the 27th VLDB Conference. 2001.
22. W.Wang, J.Yang, P.Yu. WAR: Weighted Association Rules for Item Intensities. In Knowledge and Information Systems Journal (KAIS), 6, 203-229, 2004.
23. Y.Yao, Y.Chen, X.Yang. A Measurement-Theoretic Foundation of Rule Interestingness Evaluation. ICDM 2003 Workshop on Foundations of Data Mining.
24. A.A.Fretas. On Rule Interestingness measures. In Knowledge-Based Systems, 12, 309-315, 1999.
25. T.Y.Lin, Y.Y.Yao, E.Louie. Value Added Association Rules. In Proc. of PAKDD. 2002.
26. A. Silberschatz, A.Tuzhilin. On Subjective Measures of Interestingness in Knowl- edge Discovery. In Proc. of KDD. 1995.
27. Y.Yao, N.Zhong. An Analysis of Quantitative Measures associated with Rules. In Proc. of PAKDD, 1999.

Semantic-Based Access
to Digital Document Databases

F. Esposito, S. Ferilli, T.M.A. Basile, and N. Di Mauro

Dipartimento di Informatica, University of Bari, Italy
{esposito, ferilli, basile, ndm}@di.uniba.it

Abstract. Discovering significant meta-information from document collections is a critical factor for knowledge distribution and preservation. This paper presents a system that implements intelligent document processing techniques, by combining strategies for the layout analysis of electronic documents with incremental first-order learning in order to automatically classify the documents and their layout components according to their semantics. Indeed, an in-deep analysis of specific layout components can allow the extraction of useful information to improve the semantic-based document storage and retrieval tasks. The viability of the proposed approach is confirmed by experiments run in the real-world application domain of scientific papers.

1 Introduction

Since having documents in electronic form makes their management significantly easier, much research in the last years looked for approaches to handle the huge amount of legacy documents in paper format according to the semantics of their components [8]. Conversely, almost all documents nowadays are generated directly in digital format, and stored in distributed repositories whose main concerns and problems consist in the acquisition and organization of the information contained therein. Manually creating and maintaining an updated index is clearly infeasible, due to the potentially huge amount of data to be handled, tagged and indexed. Hence a strong motivation for the research concerned with methods that can provide solutions for automatically acquiring new knowledge.

This paper deals with the application of intelligent techniques to the management of a collection of scientific papers on the Internet, aimed at automatically extracting from the documents significant information, useful to properly store and retrieve them. In this application domain, to identify the subject and context of a paper, an important role is played by components such as title, authors, abstract and bibliographic references. Three processing stages are typically needed to identify a document significant components: Layout Analysis, Document Classification and Document Understanding. We propose to exploit Machine Learning techniques to carry out the last two steps. In particular, the need for expressing relations among layout components requires the use of symbolic first-order techniques, while the continuous flow of new document calls for *incremental* abilities that can revise a faulty knowledge previously acquired.

M.-S. Hacid et al. (Eds.): ISMIS 2005, LNAI 3488, pp. 373–381, 2005.
© Springer-Verlag Berlin Heidelberg 2005

In the following we present DOMINUS, a system that can extract the layout structure from electronic documents and applies incremental symbolic learning techniques to tag them.

2   DOMINUS: Document Analysis

The availability of large, heterogeneous repositories of electronic documents is increasing rapidly, and the need for flexible, sophisticated document manipulation tools is growing correspondingly. These tools can benefit by exploiting the *logical structure*, a hierarchy of visually observable organizational components of a document, such as paragraphs, lists, sections, etc. While Document analysis is traditionally concerned with scanned images, in this paper we take into account electronic documents, whose advantages over paper ones include compact and lossless storage, easy maintenance, efficient retrieval and fast transmission.

Some of the major advantages of digital documents are their explicit structure, possibly described by a hierarchy of physical (columns, paragraphs, textlines, words, tables, figures, etc.) or logical (titles, authors, affiliations, abstracts, etc.) components, or both. This structural information can be very useful in indexing and retrieving the information contained in the document. Physical layout and logical structure analysis of document images is a crucial stage in a document processing system. In particular, we focus on documents in PostScript (PS) or Portable Document Format (PDF), and propose a new approach, based primarily on layout information, for discovering a full logical hierarchy.

2.1   Basic PostScript Analysis

POSTSCRIPT [1] is a simple interpretative programming language with powerful graphical capabilities. Its primary application is to describe the appearance of text, graphical shapes, and sampled images on printed or displayed pages. PDF is an evolution of POSTSCRIPT rapidly gaining acceptance as a promising file format for electronic documents. Like POSTSCRIPT, it is an open standard, enabling integrated solutions from a broad range of vendors.

Our layout analysis process uses a preprocessing algorithm, named pstopl, that takes as input a PDF or PS document (such as the PDF version of this paper) and transforms it into its corresponding *XML basic representation*, that describes the initial digital document as a set of pages, each of which is composed of *basic blocks*. It uses Ghostscript, a software package that provides a POSTSCRIPT and PDF interpreter, able to convert POSTSCRIPT files to many raster formats, display them on screen, and print them. Specifically, pstopl performs a syntactic transformation from POSTSCRIPT to XML. A similar algorithm is pstoedit [6], that translates POSTSCRIPT and PDF graphics into other vector formats. More technically, pstopl rewrites basic POSTSCRIPT operators by turning each instruction into an object id, described by means of the following predicates:

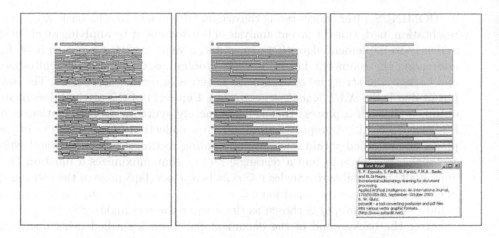

Fig. 1. Word, line and final layout analysis representations automatically extracted from the last page of *this paper*, plus an excerpt from the references

```
box(id, XY0, XY1, font, dimension, RGB, row, text) for the text;
stroke(id, XY0, XY1, RGB, thickness) for the lines;
fill(id, XY0, XY1, RGB) for the Monochromat Areas;
image(id, XY0, XY1) for the Raster Image;
page(n, w, h) for the Pages.
```

where XY0 and XY1 are the top-left and bottom-right coordinates of the bounding box respectively; font and dimension are the font-type and size of the text; RGB is the color of the bounding box content in #rrggbb format; row is the number of the row in the document where the bounding box is placed; text is the text contained; thickness is referred to the lines; n, w and h are, respectively, the number, width and height of the page. For example, the POSTSCRIPT instruction to display a text becomes an object describing a text with attributes for the geometry (location on the page) and appearance (font, colour, etc.) as reported in the following excerpt of a pstopl output.

```
box(1,108.3,753.2,176.5,738.3,Times-Bold,28,#000000,738,"Notions").
stroke(14, 63.7178, 189.721, 230.279, 189.721, #010101, 6).
fill(1173, 305.124, 172.98, 550.201, 172.184, #000000).
image(13, 92.76, 280.561, 204.84, 195.841).
page(1, 595, 841).
```

2.2 Geometric Layout Analysis

Objects in the layout of a document are spatially organized in *frames*, defined as collections of objects completely surrounded by white space. There is no exact correspondence between the layout notion of a frame and a logical notion such as a *paragraph*: two columns on a page correspond to two separate frames, while a paragraph might begin in one column and continue into the next one.

DOMINUS, after transforming the original document into its basic XML representation, performs the layout analysis of the document by applying an efficient and easy-to-implement algorithm named doc, a variant of that reported in [3] for addressing the geometric layout analysis problem. doc analyzes the whitespace and background structure of documents in terms of rectangular covers. The output of doc is the *XML layout structure* (see Figure 1) of the original document, obtained through a process that is not a merely syntactic transformation from PS/PDF to XML. As reported in [3], given a collection of rectangles C in the plane, all contained within some given bounding rectangle r_b, the *maximal white rectangle problem* is to find a rectangle $\bar{r} \subset r_b$ that maximizes a function $Q(\cdot)$ among all the possible rectangles $r \subseteq r_b$, where r overlaps none of the rectangles in C, and Q satisfies the condition $r \subseteq r' \Rightarrow Q(r) \leq Q(r')$ for any two rectangles r and r' (in our case, Q is chosen as the area of the rectangle).

After the background of the document has been identified using doc, it is possible to compute its complement, thus obtaining the desired output consisting of two levels of description. The former refers to single blocks filled with the same kind of content, the latter consists in rectangular frames each of which may be made up of many blocks of the former type. Thus, the overall description of the document includes both kinds of objects, plus information on which frames include which blocks and on the actual spatial relations between frames and between blocks in the same frame (e.g., above, touches, etc.). This allows to maintain both levels of abstraction independently.

The following improvements of the basic algorithm reported in [3] were introduced in doc as reported in Algorithm 2.2:

Lines: line segments in a document are considered first, and divide the document layout into two parts.

Reducing Basic Blocks: to improve the efficiency of doc, two preliminary phases are applied to the XML basic representation. The basic blocks identified by pstopl often correspond to fragments of words, so that a first aggregation based on their overlapping or adjacency is needed in order to obtain blocks surrounding whole words. A further aggregation could be performed, based on proximity, to have blocks that group words in lines (see Figure 1). This yields the *XML line-level description* of the document, that contains fewer blocks than the XML basic description and represents the actual input to the document layout analysis algorithm based on whitespace and background structure analysis.

Rejecting Small White Rectangles: doc uses a threshold, α, on the dimensions and/or area of the rectangles to be found in order to avoid the extraction of non-significant backgrounds such as inter-word or inter-line spaces.

Stop Criterion: since doc finds iteratively the maximal white rectangles, a stop criterion was needed. It was empirically defined as the moment in which the area of the new white rectangle represents a percentage of the total white area in the document (computed by subtracting the sum of all the areas of the basic blocks from the whole area of the document) less than a given threshold, β.

In the resulting XML description of the original document obtained by DOMI-NUS, each logical component has been identified and described (by means of its geometric attributes and relationships with respect to other components) and can be tagged according to the sematic role it plays into the document (e.g., title, abstract, author, etc.).

Algorithm 1 Pseudo-code of the optimization of the Breuel Algorithm

---

function findLayout(M: bound (page's margin); O: obstacles; α, β: float) :
WhiteRectangles: Set of Rectangles

group_blocks_in_words(O,O'); /* *Identify blocks surrounding whole words* */
group_words_in_lines(O',O"); /* *Identify blocks grouping words in lines* */
enqueue(C,(M,O")); /* *C is a priority queue based on obstacles' area* */
WhiteArea := area(M) - area(O"); percIncr := 1;
while not isempty(C) and (percIncr > β) **do**
  (B,Obstacles) = dequeue(C);
  percIncr := area(b) / WhiteArea;
  if (obstacles == $\emptyset$ and area(B) > α) **then**
    WhiteRectangles := WhiteRectangles $\cup$ {B};
    filter(C,B); /* *Split each element of C that overlaps B by using B as a pivot* */
  else
    p = pickpivot(obstacles); /* *The lines are a preferential pivot* */
    b_0 = (p.x1,b.y0,b.x1,b.y1), b_1 = (b.x0,b.y0,p.x0,b.y1)
    b_2 = (b.x0,p.y1,b.x1,b.y1), b_3 = (b.x0,b.y0,b.x1,p.y0)
    for i := 0 .. 3 **do**
      if (area(b_i) > 0 and b_i is not included in any bound of C) **then**
        sub_obstacles = {u $\in$ obstacles | u overlaps b_i}
        enqueue(C,(b_i,sub_obstacles))
Return WhiteRectangles

---

3   DOMINUS: Document Classification/Understanding

The need of automatically labelling the huge amount of documents in a Digital Library environment, along which their significant components, in order to help the automatic organization of the document collection for a more efficient storage and retrieval process, suggested the use of a concept learning system to infer rules for such task. One dimension along with concept learning algorithms can be characterized is whether they operate in an incremental or non-incremental way. The former revise the current concept definition in response to each newly observed training instance, if necessary. The latter infer concepts requiring the whole set of the training instances to be available at the beginning of the learning process. The appropriateness of these two approaches has to be evaluated according to the learning task at hand: in the case of evolutionary environments in which the instances/information come sequentially, as in digital documents collections, an incremental algorithm is preferable since revising an existing hypothesis is more efficient and less expensive than generating a hypothesis from scratch each time a new instance is observed. Furthermore, the purpose of discovering significant knowledge to be used as meta-information for the content-based retrieval and management of document collections cannot leave aside the complexity of the domain, due to the great number of interesting layout components, and their relations, to be discovered in the documents. This suggests the exploitation of symbolic first-order logic as a powerful representation language to handle such a situation. Based on these considerations, we decided to adopt INTHELEX [5] as a system to learn rules for the automatic identification of logical components.

INTHELEX is an incremental Inductive Logic Programming [7] system able to induce conceptual descriptions from positive and negative examples. Specifically, the hypotheses are represented as sets of first-order constant-free clauses whose body describes the definition of the concept in the head. The system incorporates two refinement operators to restore the correctness of the theory, one for generalizing hypotheses that reject positive examples, and the other for specializing hypotheses that explain negative examples. Furthermore, whenever a new example is taken into account the system checks if any sub-concept can be recognized by deduction in its description according to the definitions learned thus far and the background knowledge, in which case the information concerning those concepts is added (properly instantiated) to the example description. Another peculiarity of the system is that it is able to exploit multistrategy operators for shifting the representation language (abstraction) and/or to hypothesize unseen information (abduction).

In order to exploit INTHELEX, a suitable first-order logic representation of the document must be provided. Thus, once the layout components of a document are automatically discovered as explained in the previous section, the next step concerns the description of the pages, blocks and frames according to their size, spatial [9] and membership relations. Dealing with multi-page documents, the document description must be enriched with *page information* such as: the page number; whether the page is at the beginning, in the middle or at the end of the document; whether the page is the last one; the total number of pages in a document. As pointed out, the layout analysis process ends with a set of rectangles in which each single page is divided. Such rectangles are described by means of their type (text, graphic, line) and their horizontal and vertical position in the document. Furthermore, the algebraic relations $\subset$ and $\supset$ are exploited to express the inclusion between pages and frames and between blocks and frames. The other relation that can be described between rectangles is the spatial one. It is applied to all the blocks belonging to the same frame and to all the adjacent frames (given a rectangle r, the set of rectangles A that are adjacent to r is made up of all the $r_i \in A$ such that r_i is the nearest rectangle of r in the same plane). Fixed a rectangle r, one can ideally divide the plane containing it in 25 parts, as reported in Figure 2. Then, the relation between r and the other rectangles is described in terms of the occupied planes with respect to r. Moreover, such kind of representation of the planes allows the introduction in the example description of the topological relations [4, 9], including closeness, intersection and overlapping between rectangles. However, the topological information can be deduced

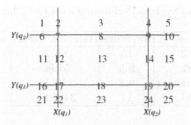

Fig. 2. Representation Planes for a rectangle according to [9]

by the spatial relationships, and thus it can be included by the learning system during the learning process exploiting deduction and abstraction.

In order to evaluate the proposed document processing technique, some experiments were designed based on a dataset made up of 108 documents (scientific papers) coming from online repositories. Specifically, 31 papers were formatted according to the Springer-Verlag LNCS style, 32 according to the Elsevier journals one, 20 according to the ICML proceedings style and other 25 according to the ECAI proceedings style. Each document was pre-processed and automatically described in a first-order logic language, along the features above mentioned. Each document instance obtained in such a way was considered a positive example for the class it belongs to, and as a negative example for all the other classes to be learned. The system performance was evaluated according to a 10-fold cross-validation methodology, ensuring that all the learning and test sets contained the same proportion of positive and negative examples. Furthermore, the system was provided with background knowledge expressing topological relations, and abstraction was exploited to discretize numeric values of size and position. In the following, some examples of both are given.

Fragment of background knowledge for topological relations:

```
over_alignment(B1,B2):-
    occupy_plane_9(B1,B2),not(occupy_plane_4(B1,B2)).
over_alignment(B1,B2) :-
    occupy_plane_10(B1,B2), not(occupy_plane_5(B1,B2)).
left_alignment(B1,B2) :-
    occupy_plane_17(B1,B2), not(occupy_plane_16(B1,B2)).
left_alignment(B1,B2) :-
    occupy_plane_22(B1,B2), not(occupy_plane_21(B1,B2)).
touch(B1,B2) :-
    occupy_plane_17(B1,B2),not(occupy_plane_13(B1,B2)).
touch(B1, B2) :-
    occupy_plane_18(B1,B2),not(occupy_plane_13(B1,B2)).
```

Extract of abstraction theory for rectangles width discretization:

```
width_very_small(X):-              width_small(X):-
    rectangle_width(X,Y),              rectangle_width(X,Y),
    Y >= 0,Y =< 0.023.                 Y > 0.023,Y =< 0.047.
```

Table 1. System Performance on the Classification Phase

Class	Revisions	RunTime (sec.)	Accuracy %
LNCS	15	165.70	93.1
ICML	8.5	51.86	98
Elsevier	9.8	118.34	98
ECAI	11	3108.98	97

Table 2. System Performance on the Understanding Phase

LNCS	Revisions	RunTime (sec.)	Accuracy %
title	11.29	33.467	95.93
author	12.27	47.88	95.39
abstract	16.48	133.706	93.06
references	13.29	50.94	95.24
ICML	**Revisions**	**RunTime (sec.)**	**Accuracy %**
title	12.13	51.668	97.87
author	11.7	29.07	97.12
abstract	10.73	111.130	97.51
references	11.17	76.224	97.54

```
width_medium_small(X):-          width_medium(X):-
  rectangle_width(X,Y),             rectangle_width(X,Y),
  Y > 0.047,Y =< 0.125.             Y > 0.125,Y =< 0.203.
```

In general, due to the different layout components that could be interesting for a specific class of documents but not for others, the image understanding phase must be preceded by a classification process in order to recognize the correct class the document belongs to. Hence, a first experiment on the inference of rules for the classification step was run, showing good system performance in terms of execution time, predictive accuracy and number of theory revisions, as reported in Table 1. The lowest accuracy refers to LNCS, which could be expected due to the less strict check for conformance to the layout standard by the editor. The worst runtime for the ECAI class can be explained by the fact that this is actually a generalization of ICML (from which it differs because of the absence of two horizontal lines above and below the title), which makes hard the revision task for the learning system, as confirmed by the greater number of revisions needed to learn the former with respect to the latter. Anyway, the high predictive accuracy for this class should ensure that few revisions will be needed. Moreover, taking into account that each learning set was made up of 97 examples, an average of 11 revisions can be in any case considered a positive results, since only one revision every 6.5 examples is needed, on average, in the worst case (LNCS). A second experiment concerning the image understanding phase, aimed at learning rules able to identify the layout components, was performed on the *title, authors, abstract* and *references* layout components of the documents belonging to the LNCS and ICML documents. These two classes were chosen since they represent two distinct kinds of layout (a single-column the former, a double-column the latter). In Table 2 the averaged results of the 10 folds along with the execution time, predictive accuracy and number of theory revisions are reported. As it is possible to note, also in this experiment the system showed good performance, specifically as regards the references on which we intend to base additional processing steps.

4 Conclusion and Future Work

This paper presented a proposal for embedding intelligent techniques in the electronic documents processing task. Specifically, incremental first-order learning strategies are exploited for automatically classifying the documents and their layout components according to their semantics. In particular, we focused on the domain of scientific papers, for which we believe that an in-deep analysis of specific layout components, such as the bibliographic references, can improve the identification of the subject and context of the paper. In this respect, we are currently working on the improvement of some initial research already present in the literature [2] and on the development of new, knowledge-based ones. More future work will concern the improvement of layout analysis algorithm, by developing more effective methods for basic-block aggregation and by defining flexible parameters based on the structure of the specific document under processing.

References

1. Adobe Systems Incorporated. *PostScript language reference manual – 2nd ed.* Addison Wesley, 1990.
2. D. Besagni and A. Belaid. Citation recognition for scientific publications in digital libraries. In *Proceedings of the 1st International Workshop on Document Image Analysis for Libraries (DIAL 2004), 23-24 January 2004, Palo Alto, CA, USA*, pages 244–252. IEEE Computer Society, 2004.
3. T.M. Breuel. Two geometric algorithms for layout analysis. In *Workshop on Document Analysis Systems*, 2002.
4. M. Egenhofer. Reasoning about binary topological relations. In Gunther O. and Schek H.-J., editors, *Second Symposium on Large Spatial Databases*, volume 525 of *LNCS*, pages 143–160. Springer, 1991.
5. F. Esposito, S. Ferilli, N. Fanizzi, T.M.A. Basile, and N. Di Mauro. Incremental multistrategy learning for document processing. *Applied Artificial Intelligence: An Internationa Journal*, 17(8/9):859–883, September-October 2003.
6. W. Glunz. pstoedit - a tool converting postscript and pdf files into various vector graphic formats. (http://www.pstoedit.net).
7. S. Muggleton and L. De Raedt. Inductive logic programming: Theory and methods. *Journal of Logic Programming*, 19/20:629–679, 1994.
8. G. Nagy. Twenty years of document image analysis in PAMI. *IEEE Transactions on Pattern Analysis and Machine Intelligence*, 22(1):38–62, 2000.
9. D. Papadias and Y. Theodoridis. Spatial relations, minimum bounding rectangles, and spatial data structures. *International Journal of Geographical Information Science*, 11(2):111–138, 1997.

Statistical Database Modeling for Privacy Preserving Database Generation*

Xintao Wu, Yongge Wang, and Yuliang Zheng

UNC Charlotte
{xwu, yonwang, yzheng}@uncc.edu

Abstract. Testing of database applications is of great importance. Although various studies have been conducted to investigate testing techniques for database design, relatively few efforts have been made to explicitly address the testing of database applications which requires a large amount of representative data available. As testing over live production databases is often infeasible in many situations due to the high risks of disclosure of confidential information or incorrect updating of real data, in this paper we investigate the problem of generating synthetic database based on a-priori knowledge about production database. Our approach is to fit general location model using various characteristics (e.g., constraints, statistics, rules) extracted from production database and then generate synthetic data using model learnt. As characteristics extracted may contain information which may be used by attacker to derive some confidential information, we present a disclosure analysis method which is based on cell suppression technique. Our method is effective and efficient to remove aggregate private information during data generation.

1 Introduction

Database application software testing is by far the most popular activity currently used by developers or vendors to ensure high software quality. A significant issue in database testing consists in the availability of representative data. Although application developers usually have some local development data for local functional testing, however, this small amount of data can not fulfill the requirements of some testing phases such as performance testing where a large amount of data is needed. On the other hand, testing over live production databases is often infeasible in many situations due to the high risks of disclosure of confidential information or incorrect updating of real data. Hence, synthetic data generation becomes an appealing alternative.

There have been some prior investigations into data generation , however, the available data generation tools [3, 4] are built either for testing data mining algorithms or for assessing the performance of database management systems, rather than for testing complex real world database applications. Hence, they lack the required flexibility to produce more realistic data needed for software testing, i.e., the generated data also need to satisfy all the constraints and business rules underlying the live data. The authors

---

* This research was supported by USA National Science Foundation Grant CCR-0310974.

M.-S. Hacid et al. (Eds.): ISMIS 2005, LNAI 3488, pp. 382–390, 2005.
© Springer-Verlag Berlin Heidelberg 2005

in [1] investigate how to populate the database with meaningful data that satisfy various database constraints (e.g., not-NULL, uniqueness, referential integrity constraints, domain constraints, and semantic constraints). Although the data generated look more realistic then pure synthetic data, it still cannot fulfill the testing requirement as they do not take into consideration statistical distributions of underlying data. The authors in [6] point out the importance of providing meaningful, representative data with realistic skew, sparcity and data distributions for benchmarking database system performance. In terms of performance testing, the performance may be totally different when testing database applications using two databases with different distributions. Hence, it will be imperative that the data is both valid and resembling real data in terms of statistical distribution since the statistical nature of the data determines query performance.

Recently, the authors in [7] have proposed a general framework for privacy preserving database application testing and investigated the method of generating synthetic database based on a-priori knowledge (e.g., constraints, statistics, rules etc.) about the current production database. In addition to valid (in terms of constraints and rules) and resembling real data (in terms of statistical distribution), the data generated needs to preserve privacy, i.e., the generated data should not disclose any confidential information that the database owner would not want to reveal. Since the synthetic database is generated from a-priori knowledge about the live database, it is important to preclude confidential information from a-priori knowledge.

In this paper, we propose to use the general location model to model database and use model learnt to generate synthetic database. We will examine in detail how to extract statistics and rules to estimate parameters of the general location model and how to resolve the potential disclosure of confidential information in data generation using model learnt.

2   The General Location Model Revisited

Let $A_1, A_2, \cdots, A_p$ denote a set of categorical attributes and $Z_1, Z_2, \cdots, Z_q$ a set of numerical ones in a table with n entries. Suppose A_j takes possible domain values $1, 2, \cdots, d_j$, the categorical data $\mathbf{W}$ can be summarized by a contingency table with total number of cells equal to $D = \prod_{j=1}^{p} d_j$. Let $\mathbf{x} = \{x_d : d = 1, 2, \cdots, D\}$ denote the number of entries in each cell. Clearly $\sum_{d=1}^{D} x_d = n$.

The general location model [5] is defined in terms of the marginal distribution of $\mathbf{A}$ and the conditional distribution of $\mathbf{Z}$ given $\mathbf{A}$. The former is described by a multinomial distribution on the cell counts $\mathbf{x}$,

$$\mathbf{x} \mid \pi \sim M(n, \pi) = \frac{n!}{x_1! \cdots x_D!} \pi_1{}^{x_1} \cdots \pi_D{}^{x_D}$$

where $\pi = \{\pi_d : d = 1, 2, \cdots, D\}$ is an array of cell probabilities corresponding to $\mathbf{x}$. Given $\mathbf{A}$, the rows $z_1^T, z_2^T, \cdots, z_n^T$ of $\mathbf{Z}$ are then modeled as conditionally multivariate normal. We assume that

$$z_i \mid u_i = E_d, \mu_d, \Sigma \sim N(\mu_d, \Sigma)$$

Table 1. An Example of Mortgage Dataset

| | | Categorical | | | | Numerical | | |
SSN	Name	Zip	Race	Age	Gender	Balance	Income	InterestPaid
1		28223	Asian	20	Male	10k	85k	2k
2		28223	Asian	30	Female	15k	70k	18k
3		28262	Black	20	Male	50k	120k	35k
.		.	.	.	.	.	.	.
n		28223	Black	25	Male	80k	110k	15k

is independent for $i = 1, 2, \cdots, n$, where μ_d is a q-vector means corresponding to cell d, and Σ is a $q \times q$ covariance matrix. The parameters of the general location model can be written as $\theta = (\pi, \mu, \Sigma)$, where $\mu = (\mu_1, \mu_2, \cdots, \mu_D)^T$ is a $D \times q$ matrix of means. The maximum likelihood estimates of θ is as follows:

$$\hat{\pi}_d = \frac{x_d}{n}$$

$$\hat{\mu}_d^T = x_d^{-1} \sum_{i \in B_d} z_i^T$$

$$\hat{\Sigma} = \frac{1}{n} \sum_{d=1}^{D} \sum_{i \in B_d} (z_i - \hat{\mu}_d)(z_i - \hat{\mu}_d)^T \tag{1}$$

where $B_d = \{i : \mu_i = E_d\}$ is the set of all tuples belonging to cell d.

An Illustrating Example. Table 1 shows a data example of Mortgage dataset of customers with n tuples. Let us assume SSN and Name are confidential information and should be marked out. The remaining attributes are grouped into two parts: categorical attributes and numerical attributes. Each categorical attribute has its own domains, e.g., Gender with two domain values {Male, Female}. The categorical part can be summarized by a 4-dimensional contingency table with total number of cells equal to $D =| Zip | \times | Race | \times | Age | \times | Gender |$, where $||$ denote the size of domain values. We use x_d, $d = 1, 2, \cdots, D$ to denote the number of tuples in each cell. In general, tuples contained in one given table is a subset of the cartesian product of some domains. In other words, some cells may not contain any tuple due to either integrity constraints or the limited sample size. In this paper, we assume the domains for each categorical attribute are fixed while the volume of data is changing.

The general location model assumes the numerical attributes (i.e., Balance, Income, InterestPaid) of tuples in each cell follow a multivariate normal distribution. For example, the Balance, Income and InterestPaid of customers in the cell $\{28223, Asian, 20, Male\}$ follow a 3-variate normal distribution with parameter μ_1, Σ_1, where μ_1 is a 3-vector means and Σ_1 is a 3×3 covariance matrix while those in the cell $\{28223, Asian, 20, Female\}$ may follow a 3-variate normal distribution with different means and covariance matrix.

It is straightforward to see we can easily generate a dataset when the parameters of general location model are given. Generally, it invloves two steps. First, we estimate the number of tuples in each cell d and generate x_d tuples. All x_d tuples from this cell have the same categorical attribute values inherited from the cell location of contingency table. Second, we estimate the mean and covariance matrix for those tuples in this cell and generate numerical attribute values based on the multi-variate normal model. In general, some columns' distribution may be functionally dependent on those of other columns, hence we would like to derive an approximate joint distribution of those independent columns which is used to generate synthetic data for performance testing.

3   Database Modeling via the General Location Model

Our approach is to derive an approximate statistical model from the characteristics (e.g., constraints, statistics, rules, and data summary) of the real databases and generate a synthetic data set using model learned. A major advantage of our system over [1] is that, in addition to constraints, we extract more complex characteristics (e.g., statistics and rules) from data catalog and data and use them to build statistical model. As we discussed in introduction, even if one synthetic database satisfies all constraints, it does not mean it can fulfill users' testing requirement as it may have different data distribution than production database. Our intuition is that, for database applications, if two databases are approximately the same from a statistical viewpoint, then the performance of the application on the two databases should also be approximately the same [1]. Furthermore, our system includes one disclosure analysis component which helps users remove those characteristics which may be used by attackers to derive confidential information in production database. As all information used to generate synthetic data in our system are contained in characteristics extracted, our disclosure analysis component can analyze and preclude the potential disclosure of confidential information at the characteristics (i.e., statistics and rules) level instead of data level. In section 3.1, we first present how to extract various characteristics from production databases and how to fit general location model using characteristics extracted. We then present how to analyze the model and check whether it contains confidential information in section 3.2.

3.1   Model Learning

The characteristics of production databases can be extracted from three parts: DDL, Data Dictionary, and Data. In order to ensure that the data is close looking or statistically similar to real data, or at least from the point of view of application testing, we need to have the statistical descriptions, S, and non-deterministic rules, $\mathcal{NR}$, of real data in production databases. These two sets describe the statistical distributions or patterns of underlying data and may affect the size of relations derived as a result of the evaluations of queries the application will need to execute. Hence, they are imperative for the statistical nature of the data that determines the query performance of database application.

Extracting Characteristics from Data Dictionary. Data dictionary consists of read-only base tables that store information about the database. When users execute an SQL

---

[1] Here we assume that file organizations, sorted fields, and index structures of the production database x are not private information and the synthetic data generator use these information to build the synthetic database in the same way that production database has been built.

command (e.g., CREATE TABLE, CREATE INDEX, or CREATE SEQUENCE) to create an object, all of the information about column names, column size, default values, constraints, index names, sequence starting values, and other information are stored in the form of metadata to the data dictionary. Most commercial DBMSs also collect statistical information regarding the distribution of values in a column to be created. This statistical information can be used by the query processor to determine the optimal strategy for evaluating a query. As the data in a column changes, index and column statistics can become out-of-dated and cause the query optimizer to make less-than-optimal decisions on how to process a query. SQL server automatically updates this statistical information periodically as the data in the tables changes. In our system, we have one component which simply accesses tables in data dictionary and fetch characteristics related.

Extracting Characteristics from Data. The statistics information about columns extracted directly from data dictionary is usually with high granularity which may be insufficient to derive relatively accurate model. In practice it is usually true that users can collect more statistics at low granularity from original data or a sample of real data themselves.

```
SELECT     Zip, Race, Age, Gender, COUNT(*),
           AVG(Balance), AVG(Income), AVG(InterestPaid),
           VAR_POP(Balance), VAR_POP(Income), VAR_POP(InterestPaid),
           COVAR_POP(Balance,Income), COVAR_POP(Balance,InterestPaid),
           COVAR_POP(Income,InterestPaid)
FROM       Mortgage
GROUP BY Zip, Race, Age, Gender
HAVING     COUNT(*) > 5
```

Fig. 1. Example of extracting statistics using SQL

Figure 1 presents one SQL command to extract statistics at the finest granularity level. It returns all information needed to derive parameters of general location model. For example, the value from aggregate function COUNT(*) is the estimate, x_d, of the number of tuples in each cell while the values from aggregate functions (i.e., AVG, VAR_POP, COVAR_POP) are the estimates of mean vectors and covariance matrices respectively of the multi-variate normal distribution of each cell. It is worth pointing out all aggregate functions can be used with GROUP BY clause with CUBE or ROLLUP option if we want to extract statistics at all possible granularities.

Q1: SELECT AVG(Income), AVG(InterestP aid) FROM Mortgage WHERE Zip = z AND Race = r
Q2: SELECT AVG(Income) FROM Mortgage WHERE Age = a AND Zip = z

Fig. 2. Workload example of Mortgage database

Statistics 1: SELECT   Zip, Race, COUNT(*), AVG(Balance), AVG(InterestPaid)
              FROM   Mortgage
              GROUP BY Zip, Race
              HAVING   COUNT(*) > 5

Statistics 2: SELECT   Zip, Age, COUNT(*), AVG(Income)
              FROM   Mortgage
              GROUP BY Zip, Age
              HAVING   COUNT(*) > 5

Fig. 3. SQLs of extracting statistics for workload

In practice, it may be infeasible to extract statistics at the finest level because statistics at the finest level may contain too much information and may be exploited by attackers to derive some confidential information about production databases. As our goal is to generate synthetic data for database application testing, we may extract statistics which are only related to queries in workload of database software. For the workload which contains two queries shown in Figure 2, it is clear that the distribution of underlying data at some high level (instead of at the finest level) is sufficient to capture the relation with the execution time of queries in workload. For example, the approximate distribution on $Zip, Race$ would satisfy the performance requirements of Q1 in workload. In this case, we may only extract statistics necessary for query performance of queries. Figure 3 presents two SQL commands to extract statistics for two queries shown in Figure 2.

Extracting Characteristics from Rule Sets. To derive the deterministic rule set $\mathcal{R}$, we take advantage of the database schema, which describes the domains, the relations, and the constraints the database designer has explicitly specified. Some information (function dependencies, correlations, hierarchies etc.) can be derived from database integrity constraints such as foreign keys, check conditions, assertions, and triggers. Furthermore, users may apply some data mining tools to extract non-deterministic rules $\mathcal{NR}$ from production database. The non-deterministic rule set $\mathcal{NR}$ helps describe the statistical distributions or patterns of underlying data and may affect the size of relations derived as a result of the evaluations of queries the application will need to execute. Formally, each rule in $\mathcal{R}$ and $\mathcal{NR}$ can be represented as a declarative rule and is generally of the form:

IF $<premise>$ THEN $<conclusion>$ [with support s and confidence c].

The rules may include exact, strong, and probabilistic rules based on the support and confidence. We note here that complex predicates and external function references may be contained in both the condition and action parts of the rule. Anyone with subject matter expertise will be able to understand the business logic of the data and can develop the appropriate conditions and actions, which will then form the rule set.

Figure 4 shows two examples of non-deterministic rules for Mortgage database. We can interpret Rule 1 as there are 1000 customers with Zip = 28223, Race = Asian,

Rule 1:   IF Zip = 28223, Race = Asian, and Age in (25, 40) THEN Balance is in (20k,30k)
          with support s = 900 and confidence c= 90 %.

Rule 2:   IF Zip = 28262 THEN Race = White with support s = 5000 and confidence c = 80 %

Fig. 4. Example of non-deterministic rules for Mortgage dataset

and Age in (25, 40) and 90 % of them with Balance in the range of (20k, 30k). It is
straightforward to see these rules can be mapped to statistics of general location model
at some granularity. For example, the number of data entries in cell (28223, Asian, 25-40,
All) is 1000 and we can derive average balance of data entries in this cell from the clause
Balance in (20k,30k) with confidence c= 90 %.

Table 2. Parameter constraints of general location model

	Zip	Race	Age	Gender	COUNT(*)	Balance	Income	InterestPaid
Balance > 1000	All	All	All	All		>1000		
Statistics 1	28223	Asian	All	All	2800	23000		75000
	28223	Black	All	All	3100	35000		89000
	.	.	.	.	.	.	.	.
	28262	White	All	All	2500	123000		112000
Statistics 2	28223	All	20	All	300		56000	
	28223	All	21	All	570		38000	
	.	.	.	.	.	.	.	.
	28262	All	40	All	210		73000	
Rule 1	28223	Asian	25-40	All	900	(20k,30k)		
Rule 2	28262	All	All	All	5000			
	28262	White	All	All	4000			

Fitting Model Using Characteristics. It is easy to see all characteristics (i.e., $\mathcal{S}$, $\mathcal{R}$,
$\mathcal{NR}$) extracted from production database can be mapped to constraints of parameters of
general location model at the finest level. Table 2 shows parameter constraints derived
from examples (e.g., constraint Balance > 1000, two statistics from Figure 3, and two
rules from Figure 4.) we discussed previously.

Given those constraints, we can apply linear programming techniques to derive parameters of general location model at the finest level. However, it is infeasible to apply
linear programming techniques directly in practice due to high complexity (the number
of variables is linear of the number of cells D while the number of constraints is large).
As we know, the problem of estimating the cell entries at the finest granularity subject
to some linear constraints is known to be NP-hard. In our system, we combine some
heuristics to derive parameters from high level constraints. For example, from Rule 1,
we can initialize the number of tuples in those 30 cells (28223, Asian, Age, Gender)
where Age is in (25,40) and Gender in {Male, Female} as 30 ($\frac{900}{15\times2}$) when we assume
the tuples are uniformly distributed among Age and Gender in cell (28223, Asian, Age,
Gender).

3.2 Disclosure Analysis

Disclosures which can occur as a result of inferences by attackers include two classes: identity disclosure and value disclosure. Identity disclosure relates to the disclosure of the identity of an individual in the database while value disclosure relates to the disclosure of the value of a certain confidential attribute of that individual.

Given characteristics $\mathcal{DB} = \{\mathcal{S} \cup \mathcal{R} \cup \mathcal{NR}\}$ and a set of confidential information $\bar{\mathcal{DB}} = \{\bar{S} \cup \bar{R} \cup \bar{NR}\}$, our initial problem is to find a $\hat{\mathcal{DB}}$ such that 1) $\hat{\mathcal{DB}} \subseteq \mathcal{DB}$ and 2) no confidential information in $\bar{\mathcal{DB}}$ can be entailed from $\hat{\mathcal{DB}}$ within a given bound. All the information are contained in the parameters of the general location model, i.e., $\theta = (\pi, \mu, \Sigma)$. From section 2, we know 1) π is only used for multinomial distribution and can be estimated using $\hat{\pi}_d = \frac{x_d}{n}$, where x_d is the number of entries in cell d; and 2) μ, Σ is only used for multi-variate normal distribution of numerical attributes for those entries in a given cell d. As π_d is only related to categorical attributes and μ, Σ are only related to numerical attributes, we can analyze them separately.

Identity Disclosure. This problem is referred as determining upper and lower bounds on the cells of the cross-classification given a set of margins [2]. Upper and lower bounds induced by some fixed set of marginal on the cell entries of a contingency table are of great importance in measuring the disclosure risk associated with the release of these marginal totals. If the induced upper and lower bounds are too tight or too close to the actual sensitive value in a confidential cell entry, the information associated with that cell may be disclosed.

In our system, from characteristics $\mathcal{DB} = \{\mathcal{S} \cup \mathcal{R} \cup \mathcal{NR}\}$, we extract a set of cells, $\mathcal{C}^0$, and the number of entries in each cell $c \in \mathcal{C}^0$. From a list of private rules and statistics, $\bar{\mathcal{DB}} = \{\bar{S} \cup \bar{R} \cup \bar{NR}\}$, we similarly extract a list of confidential cells, $\mathcal{C}^1$. For each confidential cell $c \in \mathcal{C}^1$, a confidential range $[x_c^l, x_c^u]$ which contains the true value of the number of entries, x_c, is derived. $[x_c^l, x_c^u]$ here denotes the confidential range which database owner does not want attackers to predict. It is clear that predicting confidential value within a smaller confidential range constitutes compromise. Now our identity disclosure problem is to find a set of cells, $\mathcal{C}^2$, which can be released for data generation, such that 1) $\mathcal{C}^2 \subseteq \mathcal{C}^1$ and 2) no confidential information x_c ($c \in \mathcal{C}^1$) can be predicted in range $[x_c^l, x_c^u]$ from the information contained in $\mathcal{C}^2$.

Value Disclosure. Value disclosure represents the situation where attackers are able to estimate or infer the value of a certain confidential numerical attribute of an entity or a group of entities with a level of accuracy than a pre-specified level. Here an entity or a group of entities can be characterized by cell they locate in. Attackers may use various techniques to estimate and predict the confidential values of individual customers. The accuracy with which attackers are able to predict the confidential attribute determines whether disclosure occurs.

In our scenario, all numerical attribute values are generated from multi-variate normal distributions. We expect database owner specifies a confidential range $[z^l, z^u]$ (z is a confidential numerical attribute) for an entity or a group of entities. Our problem is to make sure that a given set of μ, Σ, which are used for data generation, can not be used by attackers to derive confidential values for an entity or a group of entities in a small confidential bound. We are currently investigating this problem especially when non-confidential attributes and linear combination attributes exist in data set.

4   Conclusions and Future Work

In this paper we investigated how to generate synthetic database using the general location model which is built using various characteristics extracted from production database. Our synthetic database generated has similar distributions or patterns as production database while preserving privacy, hence it can be used for database application testing. There are some aspects of this work that merit further research. Among them, we are trying to figure out how to better screen out confidential information from released characteristics. Another area for future work is centered on refining the architecture of the data generator itself. This could include changes to allow further use of real world data sources (e.g., historical data) for increased realism and more rapid adjustment to emerging data trends or perturbation.

References

1. D. Chays, S. Dan, P. Frankl, F. Vokolos, and E. Weyuker. A framework for testing database applications. In *Proceedings of the ISSTA*. Portland, Oregon, 2000.
2. A. Dobra and S. E. Fienberg. Bounds for cell entries in contingency tables induced by fixed marginal totals with applications to disclosure limitation. *Statistical Journal of the United Nations ECE*, 18:363–371, 2001.
3. Niagara. http://www.cs.wisc.edu/niagara/datagendownload.html.
4. Quest. http://www.quest.com/datafactory.
5. J.L. Schafer. *Analysis of Incomplete Multivariate Data*. Chapman Hall, 1997.
6. J. Stephens and M. Poess. Mudd: A multi-dimensional data generator. In *Proceedings of the 4th International Workshop on Software and Performance*, pages 104–109, 2004.
7. X. Wu, Y. Wang, and Y. Zheng. Privacy preserving database application testing. In *Proceedings of the ACM Workshop on Privacy in Electronic Society*, pages 118–128, 2003.

Scalable Inductive Learning on Partitioned Data

Qijun Chen, Xindong Wu, and Xingquan Zhu

Department of Computer Science, University of Vermont,
33 Colchester Avenue,
Burlington, Vermont 05405, USA
{qchen, xwu, xqzhu}@cs.uvm.edu

Abstract. With the rapid advancement of information technology, scalability has become a necessity for learning algorithms to deal with large, real-world data repositories. In this paper, scalability is accomplished through a data reduction technique, which partitions a large data set into subsets, applies a learning algorithm on each subset sequentially or concurrently, and then integrates the learned results. Five strategies to achieve scalability (Rule-Example Conversion, Rule Weighting, Iteration, Good Rule Selection, and Data Dependent Rule Selection) are identified and seven corresponding scalable schemes are designed and developed. A substantial number of experiments have been performed to evaluate these schemes. Experimental results demonstrate that through data reduction some of our schemes can effectively generate accurate classifiers from weak classifiers generated from data subsets. Furthermore, our schemes require significantly less training time than that of generating a global classifier.

1 Introduction

Research in inductive learning has made substantial progress over the years and a number of algorithms have been developed. AQ [1], C4.5 [2], CART [3], CN2 [4], Bagging [5], and HCV [6] are some of the most popular ones. Two criteria are commonly used to evaluate the performance of a specific algorithm: accuracy and efficiency. Accuracy indicates how well the learned concepts match previously unseen data, and efficiency means how fast these concepts can be learned. Improving the accuracy and efficiency of learning algorithms has been a central research issue with much of the existing effort concentrating on problems with a relatively small amount of data. However, in reality, many databases of customers, operations, scientific data, and other sorts of data are growing rapidly [7]. As a result, modern learning systems are confronted with vast amounts of information and face the challenges of discovering knowledge from the ever-growing data [8]. The question is can we apply our learning algorithms directly to these real-world data? Furthermore, many of the existing approaches require all the training data to be resident in main memory before being processed. Even with the fast development of the hardware technology, such a requirement is still untenable in most real-world cases. It is found that both manual data mining and the direct application of today's mining techniques can be problematic when data sets exceed 100 megabytes [9-11]. In certain cases, data is inherently

M.-S. Hacid et al. (Eds.): ISMIS 2005, LNAI 3488, pp. 391–403, 2005.
© Springer-Verlag Berlin Heidelberg 2005

distributed and can only be localized, it would be infeasible to bring all the data together and compute one primary "global" classifier.

The above observations motivated our research in scalable learning algorithms.
Here scalability is defined as the ability to process a large data set or physically distributed datasets.

As existing learning algorithms have a solid foundation, it would be inadvisable to
design scalable learning schemes from the scratch. So rather than changing the underlying principles of those algorithms, our approach seeks to solve the scalability problem through data reduction, which partitions the data set into subsets, applies a learning algorithm on each subset, and then integrates the learning results. When partitioning the data, some common approaches like random sampling, stratified sampling
[10], and duplicate compaction can be adopted with each subset being sized to fit into
the memory for efficient processing (we use stratified sampling in our system). It is
anticipated that the speed improvement would be more substantial when the computation complexity is more than linear to the data set size. As in distributed environments, each subset is disjointed with each other. Accuracy generally suffers as a result
of data partitioning [12]. Our objective is to seek to minimize the impact of information loss from partitioning.

Due to the size of large databases and the amount of intensive computation involved in data analysis, parallel and distributed data mining has been a crucial
mechanism for large-scale data mining applications. Existing research in this area has
focused on the study of the degree of parallelism, synchronization, data locality issues, and optimization techniques for global rule mining [13-14]. Parallel and distributed data mining can be combined with our data partition strategy. If each of the
partitions is still large, we can apply a parallel or distributed algorithm to discover
rules from each partition, and then apply the strategies designed in this paper.

2   Inductive Learning on Partitioned Data

2.1   Rule-Example Conversion (REC)

The Rule-Example Conversion scheme borrows some techniques from Multiple-
Layer Incremental Induction Learning [6]. Rule generation and rule conversion are
the two major steps in this scheme. Rule generation induces a set of rules from one
subset of the training examples through some inductive learning algorithm. Rule conversion converts rules into examples. An example set P_c which is converted from a
rule set R would be much smaller than the base set P (if R is induced from P) as the
number of rules in R is usually much smaller than the number of examples in P. Such
a converted example set represents some essence information from one subset and can
be easily utilized by other subsets to improve their learning. The detailed algorithm is
given in Fig.1.

Converting a rule into an example can be done as follows. Given rule R_k: $A_{k1} = a_{k1}, A_{k2} = a_{k2}, .. A_{km} = a_{km}$ => Class = C_{jk}. the corresponding converted example I_k will
be defined in attribute A_{kl} (where $l \in [1, m]$) with the value a_{kl}. For those undefined
attributes, we use # (a Don't Care value) to fill them. Correspondingly the class label
for this instance would be C_{jk}.

```
Procedure RuleExampleConversion (NumOfPar)
DataPartition(NumOfPar);
TempRuleSet = ϕ; TempDataSet = ϕ;
For (j=1; j < NumOfPar; j++)
    RuleSet_j = Induce(Partition_j ∪ TempDataSet);
    TempDataSet = Convert(RuleSet_j);
FinalRuleSet = Induce(Partition_{NumOfPar} ∪
        TempDataSet);
Return FinalRuleSet
```

Fig. 1. Rule Example Conversion

```
Procedure RuleWeighting (NumOfPar)
DataPartition(NumOfPar);
For (j=1; j <= NumOfPar; j++)
    RuleSet_j = Induce(Partition_j);
FinalRuleSet = RuleWeighting(NumOfPar,
        RuleSet_1,...,RuleSet_{NumOfPar});
Return FinalRuleSet
```

Fig. 2. Rule Weighting

2.2 Rule Weighting (RW)

Compared with the Rule-Example Conversion scheme, which learns and refines the classifier (a rule set) sequentially, Rule Weighting can process each subset concurrently. This scheme is based on the assumption that the more the subsets agree with a particular rule, the more reliable this rule will be. Therefore we give each rule a weight proportional to its number of occurrences in all rule sets RS_j ($j \in [1, n]$). Such weights can be utilized during deduction. Rules with higher weights will have a stronger influence on the final prediction. Rule Weighting consists of two steps: 1) inducing a rule set RS_j from each subset P_j ($j \in [1, n]$); and 2) integrating rule sets RS_j ($j \in [1, n]$). The algorithm is given in Fig.2.

2.3 Iteration

The Iteration strategy is inspired by the windowing technique [15]. Suppose a classifier C is induced using a subset of the training examples. This classifier can be used to classify examples in another subset or the same subset. Those misclassified examples represent the information unknown or vague to C. Incorporating such examples in the next iteration of learning might be helpful in generating a more powerful classifier. It is expected that: 1) the size of the misclassified set will be much smaller than the size of a single subset and 2) inducing on the expanded set, which includes the misclassified examples, will not add computational cost significantly.

Theoretically, Iteration is not appropriate for noisy data. For example, in very noisy environments, most of the noisy data will be forwarded to the training data in the final iteration, as noisy data will always deny rules that are generally consistent with the training set. As a result the final data set will have a higher percentage of noise than that in the whole training set.

2.3.1 Simple Iteration (IT)

Simple Iteration works through repeatedly replenishing the initial training subset with the misclassified examples from other subsets. First, a classifier C_1 is induced from P_1. C_1 is then used to classify examples in P_2. Misclassified examples from P_2 are forwarded to P_1. Such steps are repeated until all subsets are consumed. The detailed algorithm is provided in Fig. 3.

Procedure *Iteration (NumOfPar)*
DataPartition(NumOfPar);
Partition₁' = Partition₁;
TempDataSet = ∅;
For (j=1; j < NumOfPar; j++)
Cⱼ = Induce(Partition₁');
TempDataSet = Misclassified(Cⱼ, Partitionⱼ₊₁);
Partition₁' = Partition₁' ∪ TempDataSet;
FinalClassifier = Induce(Partition₁');
Return FinalClassifier

Fig. 3. Simple Iteration

Procedure *IterationVoting (NumOfPar)*
DataPartition(NumOfPar);
Partition₁' = Partition₁;
For (j=1; j <= NumOfPar; j++)
Cⱼ = Induce(Partitionⱼ ');
TempDataSet = Misclassified(Cⱼ, Partitionⱼ);
Partitionⱼ₊₁' = Partitionⱼ ∪ TempDataSet
FinalClassifier = CombineByVoting(C₁ , .. ,
C_{NumOfPar});
Return FinalClassifier

Fig. 4. Iteration and Voting

2.3.2 Iteration and Voting (IV)

In IT, the first partition is used to generate the initial classifier. Only misclassified examples from other subsets are incorporated to generate the final classifier, which is thus biased towards the first subset. The quality of the final classifier relies mostly on the data quality of the first subset. Furthermore, IT uses the classifier generated in the final iteration to represent the final learning results while knowledge learned in the intermediate stages is wasted. To compensate for the two shortfalls of IT, VT performs induction and deduction on the same subset in each iteration. Misclassified examples are forwarded to the subsequent subset. The final classifier is the combination of the classifiers generated through Voting. The detailed algorithm is provided in Fig. 4.

2.4 Good Rule Selection

2.4.1 Good Rule Selection (GRS)

"Good rules" are not only useful in providing an accurate prediction, but also in help-ing "shrink" the learning space as in integrative windowing [16]. Suppose we have a rule set RS_{syn}, which is synthesized from a set of rule sets induced from the subsets of the training data. Some of the rules will be labeled as "good" if their prediction accu-racies over an evaluation set meet or exceed the predefined accuracy threshold. Based on our assumption that these rules are "good", most of the examples in the training set would be correctly classified by "good" rules. Thus, we remove all the examples covered by these "good" rules from the original training set and form a new data set with the remaining examples. We call this set an "uncovered" set P_u. P_u represents some knowledge, which is lost through partitioning and can only be recovered by coalescing the "minority" examples in each subset. A strong classifier can be gener-ated through synthesizing rules induced from P_u and good rules in RS_{syn}. Based on this idea, GRS works through combining three operations: induction, evaluation, and synthesis, as shown in Fig. 5.

Procedure *GoodRuleSelection (NumOfPar)*

DataPartition(NumOfPar);

For (j=1; j <= NumOfPar; j++)

    RuleSet$_j$ = Induce(Partition$_j$);

    Rules$_{whole}$ = Append(Rules$_{whole,}$, RuleSet$_j$);

RuleSet$_{syn}$ =Synthesize(Rules$_{whole}$, Partition$_{sample}$);

RuleSet$_{syn}$' = LabelGoodRules(RuleSet$_{syn}$,

        Partition$_{eval}$);

Partion$_u$=FindUncoverd(TrainingSet,RuleSet$_{syn}$);

RuleSet$_u$ = Induce(Partition$_u$);

Rules$_{whole}$ = Append(Rules$_{whole,}$, RuleSet$_u$);

RuleSet$_{syn}$ = Synthesize(Rules$_{whole}$, Partition$_{sample}$);

Return FinalRuleSet

Fig. 5. Good Rule Selection

Procedure *DataDepRuleSelection(NumOfPar)*

DataPartition(NumOfPar);

Rules$_{whole}$ = Φ;

For (j=1; j <= NumOfPar; j++)

    RuleSet$_j$ = Induce(Partition$_j$);

    Rules$_{whole}$ = Append(Rules$_{whole,}$, RuleSet$_j$)

For (j=1; j <= NumOfPar; j++)

    RuleSet$_j$' = Synthesize(Rules$_{whole}$, Partition$_j$);

FinalRuleSet = CombineByVoting(RuleSet$_1$',...,

        RuleSet$_{NumOfPar}$');

Return FinalRuleSet

Fig. 6. Data Dependent Rule Selection

The "rule synthesis operation" is a mechanism used by C4.5Rules to select and order rules (as C4.5Rules uses a first-hit strategy during deduction). Given a data set P and a set of rules, the synthesizer will first partition the rules into k categories (k is the number of classes in the training set) according to the class label each rule deduces. For each category of rules, a synthesizer will choose a "best" rule subset R_p so that R_p causes the minimum ratio of false firing on data set P. All these rule subsets are then ordered by the false firing ratio on data set P. In each subset, the rules are ordered by their error rate.

2.4.2 Good Rule Selection and Voting (GRSV)

GRSV integrates both Voting and GRS. We refine the granularity of weighted elements by weighting rules rather than the classifiers. Furthermore, a special voting member RS_{syn}, which is synthesized from rules collected from rule sets RS_j ($j \in [1,n]$), is incorporated. Similar to GRS, some of the rules in RS_{syn} and RS_j ($j \in [1,n]$) will be labeled as "good" after evaluation. "Good" rules are given higher weights when they

---

Procedure *GoodRuleVoting (NumOfPar)*

DataPartition(NumOfPar); Rules$_{whole}$ = Φ;

For (j=1; j <= NumOfPar; j++)

    RuleSet$_j$ = Induce(Partition$_j$);

    Rules$_{whole}$ = Append(Rules$_{whole,}$, RuleSet$_j$);

RuleSet$_{syn}$ = Synthesize(Rules$_{whole}$, Partition$_{sample}$);

RuleSet$_{syn}$' = LabelGoodRules(RuleSet$_{syn}$, Partition$_{eval}$);

For (j=1; j <= NumOfPar; j++)

    RuleSet$_j$' = LabelGoodRules(RuleSet$_j$, Partition$_{eval}$);

FinalRuleSet = CombineByWeightedVoting(RuleSet$_{syn}$', RuleSet$_1$', .., RuleSet$_{NumOfPar}$');

Return FinalRuleSet

Fig. 7. Good Rule Selection & Voting

are used to deduce a class label for testing examples. "Good" rules in RS_{syn} have higher weights than those in RS_j ($j \in [1,n]$) as RS_{syn} is constructed from a global view. The detailed algorithm is given in Fig. 7.

2.5 Data Dependent Rule Selection (DDRS)

In the Good Rule Selection scheme, a synthesizer can generate a sifted and ordered rule set RS_{syn} from RS_{whole}. This sifted rule set RS_{syn} has the highest prediction power over the data set P. However, in a distributed environment, each local site can access the rules generated from other sites. Can such rules help generate a stronger local classifier? Similar to Good Rule Selection, first a rule set RS_j ($j \in [1,n]$) is induced from each subset of the training examples. Following that all the rules in RS_j ($j \in [1,n]$) are gathered together to form a set of rules RS_{whole}. We use RS_{whole} and each data subset P_j to generate a new local rule set RS_j' ($j \in [1,n]$) through the synthesizer. Finally, rue sets RS_j' ($j \in [1,n]$) are combined through Voting. One advantage of the Data Dependent Rule Selection scheme is that it avoids revealing confidential information caused by exchanging raw data directly. The detailed algorithm is given in Fig. 6.

3 Experimental Evaluations

This section presents the experimental results for the seven schemes discussed the above section. Major findings for each scheme are provided. Not all the data sets were used in different schemes due to the adjustments made during the experiments and the limitations of some schemes. Also different underlying inductive learning algorithms were chosen for different schemes.

3.1 Test Methodologies

The data sets used in the experiments are mainly from UCI data repository [17], and one artificial data set named "Ibm" [18]. In presenting our results in this section, we use the following terminologies to indicate the different experiment conditions:

- We use HCV, C4.5, and C4.5Rules as the underlying inductive learning algorithms.
- We call the classifier generated from a subset of the training data a base classifier. We use *Avg-base* and *Max-base* to represent the average accuracy and the highest accuracy of the base classifiers respectively.
- P_n is the nth subset (or partition) for a given dataset.
- T_n is the threshold for good rule selection, where n indicates that a good rule should have a prediction accuracy higher than n percent over the evaluation set.
- VT is the results of simple voting mechanism.

3.2 Rule-Example Conversion (REC)

Table 1 shows the experimental results of REC and the major findings are listed below:

- Generally REC does not maintain the accuracy of the global classifier. Such an accuracy degradation can be caused by two things: 1) losing information as a result of partitioning, and 2) overgeneralization in REC as one rule that covers many examples in one subset is treated only as one example in another subset.

- It is expected that REC dilutes the effects of noise as examples converted from the rules are not supposed to be noisy. Further investigation is needed to verify the accuracy improvement in the data set Monk2 where the results of P_7 and P_9 beat the global classifier.
- Limitations of REC are found through implementation: inability to process continuous attributes and exclusive conditions of a rule in the rule-example conversion. For example, suppose we have a rule: A1 < 1 and A2 != b => Class 1. How should such a rule be processed? How many examples should be generated from this rule?
- As we can see from the above analysis, REC is not very effective to generate knowledge, which can further be used by different iterations of learning.

Table 1. Rule-example conversion results

Dataset	C4.5	P_3	P_5	P_7	P_9	P_{11}
Car	**89.6**	85.8	85.1	77.8	79.2	77.8
H-r	**92.9**	78.6	46.4	75	71.4	67.9
Monk1	**75.7**	70.8	70.8	75	75	75
Monk2	65	63.9	55.1	**67.1**	**67.1**	62.5
Monk3	**97.2**	**97.2**	80.6	80.6	80.6	80.6
Vote	**97**	**97**	**97**	95.6	**97**	**97**

Table 2. Rule weighting results (HCV)

Dataset	HCV	P_3	P_5	P_7	P_9
Car	**91.319**	90.278	88.542	88.194	84.722
H-r	**78.571**	67.857	**82.143**	57.143	78.571
Monk1	**100**	73.38	72.685	76.157	65.278
Monk2	**65.509**	60.185	63.194	59.259	60.185
Monk3	97.222	**98.148**	96.991	97.222	97.222
Vote	**97.037**	96.296	**97.037**	**97.037**	96.296

3.3 Rule Weighting (RW)

Table 2 lists the results for RW and the major findings are given below:

- RW does not maintain the accuracy of the global classifier consistently. A better result is achieved sometimes; nevertheless, accuracy boosting does not occur regularly.
- It is quite rare for one particular rule to appear repeatedly in different rule sets. This can be caused by the complexity of the rule space or rule pruning in different stages. Therefore effective rule weighting cannot be achieved.

3.4 Simple Iteration (IT)

Tables 3 to 4 show the results for Simple Iteration and the major findings are given below:

- Similar to the RW scheme, accuracy boosting does occur sometimes, but it is unknown when such improvements will happen.
- Table 4 shows the performance of IT on the Connect dataset, which contains 10% of manually injected noise [19]. Severe accuracy droppings can be seen at some spots, which demonstrate the poor performance of IT in a noisy environment. Furthermore, IT cannot maintain the performance of Voting with noisy data.

Table 3. Simple iteration results (HCV)

Dataset	HCV	$P_3(\%)$	$P_5(\%)$	$P_7(\%)$	$P_9(\%)$	$P_{11}(\%)$
Car	**91.319**	90.972	88.889	85.764	87.847	87.153
H-r	78.571	75.00	75.00	**85.714**	64.286	82.143
Monk1	**100**	76.157	91.204	80.324	78.009	77.546
Monk2	65.509	64.583	59.722	64.815	62.731	**67.361**
Monk3	**97.222**	**97.222**	88.889	**97.222**	87.963	94.676
Vote	**97.037**	95.556	94.815	97.037	**97.037**	94.074

Table 4. Simple iteration results from a noisy dataset (10% class noise)

Dataset	C4.5Rules	Approach	$P_4(\%)$	$P_8(\%)$	$P_{12}(\%)$	$P_{16}(\%)$	$P_{20}(\%)$
Con-nect	75.2%	IT	62.40	49.60	62.70	72.30	51.20
		VT	78.40	76.00	74.20	74.10	72.90

3.5 Iteration and Voting (IV)

Tables 5 and 6 present the results for Iteration & Voting and the major findings are given below:

- As shown in Table 8, IV does not maintain the accuracy of the global classifier consistently.
- Iteration&Voting can outperform Voting consistently. Such an accuracy boosting becomes more significant when the number of subsets increases. Therefore Iteration strategy can recover some of the lost knowledge caused by partitioning. This conclusion is further confirmed from experimental results on a large set, as shown in Table 6.
- Iteration & Voting outperforms both Iteration and Voting. Therefore the integration of the two techniques, Voting and Iteration, can boost the accuracy of the final classifier.
- To find out whether IV is more capable than Iteration in noisy environments, we tried IV on Connect. The results in Table 6 demonstrate that IV outperforms both IT and Voting in noisy data. Unexpectedly, IV can even outdo the global classifier sometimes in noisy environments.

Table 5. Iteration and voting results

Dataset	C4.5Rules	Approach	$P_3(\%)$	$P_5(\%)$	$P_7(\%)$	$P_9(\%)$	$P_{11}(\%)$	$P_{13}(\%)$	$P_{15}(\%)$
Car	93.80	IV	91.70	91.70	89.90	89.60	87.80	88.50	86.50
		VT	92.40	86.50	88.50	87.80	87.80	87.50	84.70
Ibm	80.80	IV	**81.00**	77.00	79.00	76.00	75.50	71.80	75.00
		VT	77.80	76.00	72.80	70.20	73.50	70.50	69.00

Table 6. Iteration and voting results from large/noisy dataset

Dataset	C4.5Rules	Approach	$P_4(\%)$	$P_8(\%)$	$P_{12}(\%)$	$P_{16}(\%)$	$P_{20}(\%)$
Connect (noise free)	85.9%	IV	85.50	83.50	82.90	82.80	81.50
		VT	82.30	81.70	79.90	81.00	79.60
Connect (10% class noise)	75.2%	IV	75.20	77.90	77.60	78.00	78.80
		IT	62.40	49.60	62.70	72.30	51.20
		VT	78.40	76.00	74.20	74.10	72.90

3.6 Good Rule Selection (GRS)

Table 7 shows the experimental results of GRS and the major findings are listed below:

- GRS can achieve a higher accuracy than the global classifier sometimes. However, regularities of accuracy improvement cannot be found.
- Generally, the higher the specified 'good' rule accuracy threshold, the higher the accuracy of the final rule set will be. Since less rules will be labeled as 'good' rules, the uncovered data set will have more examples, and consequently, the higher the quality of the rules generated from the uncovered set.
- One drawback of this scheme is found through implementation: the size of the uncovered set is uncontrollable, as it relies on the accuracy threshold for 'good' rules and the initial data quality. So this scheme cannot deal with a situation where the uncovered data set is too large to be processed with one iteration of learning.

Table 7. Good rule selection results

Dataset	C4.5Rules	T_n	$P_3(\%)$	$P_5(\%)$	$P_7(\%)$	$P_9(\%)$	$P_{11}(\%)$
Car	93.80%	T_{95}	91.70	93.40	93.40	91.00	94.10
		T_{90}	91.70	93.40	93.40	89.90	94.10
		T_{85}	89.20	91.00	89.90	89.90	88.50
		T_{80}	89.20	91.70	88.50	89.90	86.10
		T_{70}	89.90	92.70	88.50	87.50	86.10
Ibm	80.80%	T_{95}	78.50	79.20	80.20	81.80	78.00
		T_{90}	78.50	78.00	80.20	78.50	77.20
		T_{85}	78.00	78.50	77.00	78.80	77.50
		T_{80}	76.00	83.50	77.00	78.80	77.50
		T_{70}	74.00	77.80	76.20	76.50	76.00

3.7 Good Rule Selection and Voting (GRSV)

Table 8 shows the results of GRSV. The major findings are listed below:

- GRSV does not maintain the accuracy of the global classifier as the number of subset increases.
- Overall, GRSV outperforms Voting. The increased granularity of the weighted element and good rule labeling are useful in generating a more accurate classifier. But a consistent accuracy improvement can be achieved only when the accuracy threshold >= 90%, which means the rules to be considered as "good" should be indeed good.

Table 8. Good rule selection and voting results

Dataset	C4.5Rules	Approach	$P_3(\%)$	$P_5(\%)$	$P_7(\%)$	$P_9(\%)$	$P_{11}(\%)$
Car	93.80%	T_{95}	94.10	91.00	89.90	87.80	88.20
		T_{90}	93.40	91.00	89.60	87.80	88.20
		T_{85}	92.70	90.60	89.60	87.80	87.50
		T_{80}	92.00	90.60	89.60	87.80	87.50
		T_{70}	92.40	91.00	89.60	88.20	87.80
		Voting	92.40	86.50	88.50	87.80	87.80
Ibm	80.80%	T_{95}	78.80	77.50	74.50	71.50	74.20
		T_{90}	77.80	75.50	74.50	71.20	74.50
		T_{85}	77.50	75.50	74.20	72.80	73.80
		T_{80}	77.50	75.50	75.80	73.80	74.00
		T_{70}	76.80	76.00	75.50	74.80	73.80
		Voting	77.80	76.00	72.80	70.20	73.50

3.8 Data Dependent Rule Selection (DDRS)

Table 9 shows the results of DDRS as compared with Voting.

- Significant accuracy improvement can be found from DDRS as the number of subsets increases. Therefore incorporating rules generated from other learning processes can help local learning and compensate information loss caused by partitioning.
- Contrary to DDRS, GRSV performs well when the number of subsets is small. Therefore it is expected that combining these two strategies can help generate a more accurate classifier.

Table 9. Data dependent rule selection results

Dataset	C4.5Rules	Approach	$P_3(\%)$	$P_5(\%)$	$P_7(\%)$	$P_9(\%)$	$P_{11}(\%)$	$P_{13}(\%)$	$P_{15}(\%)$
Car	0.938	DDRS	92.70	89.60	88.20	87.80	89.60	91.30	86.80
		SV	92.40	86.50	88.50	87.80	87.80	87.50	84.70
		GRSV-DDRS	93.40	89.90	88.90	88.20	89.60	91.30	87.20
Ibm	0.808	DDRS	77.00	75.20	73.50	75.20	76.20	76.50	76.00
		SV	77.80	76.00	72.80	70.20	73.50	70.50	69.00
		GRSV-DDRS	77.80	76.00	73.80	75.20	76.50	76.20	75.80

3.9 Time Complexity Analysis

Table 10 lists the time expense of different schemes as compared with that of C4.5Rules (on Connect). Due to the limitations of REC and RW (incapability in dealing with continuous attributes and exclusive conditions in rules), no experimental results of these two schemes are provided. The following conclusions can be drawn from these results:

- All the schemes evaluated in this paper have significantly less time expense (training plus classification) than that of running C4.5Rules over the whole data set. This conforms that if a learning algorithm's time complexity is more than linear in the number of examples, processing small, fixed size samples sequentially can reduce the complexity.

Table 10. Time expense comparison (Connect, in seconds)

C4.5Rules	Approach	$P_8(s)$	$P_{16}(s)$	$P_{24}(s)$	$P_{32}(s)$	$P_{40}(s)$
4661(s)	GRSV	38	22	19	18	13
	DDRS	401	476	561	667	585
	IV	240	121	84	58	49

3.10 Experiment Summary

Tables 11 to 12 summarize the experimental results (Car and Splice) of all the schemes we investigated. We can see that most of our integration schemes can outperform Avg-base and Max-base. Therefore sampling of the training data is definitely not sufficient to generate accurate classifiers and integration is necessary and helpful.

Table 11. Comparisons from 7 schemes on Car dataset

Classifier	Global Classifier	Approach	$P_3(\%)$	$P_5(\%)$	$P_7(\%)$	$P_9(\%)$	$P_{11}(\%)$
C4.5	89.60%	REC	85.80	85.10	77.80	79.20	77.80
		Max-Base	87.50	84.40	83.70	81.90	79.50
		Avg-Base	84.70	81.32	79.88	79.08	76.92
C4.5Rules	93.80%	IT	91.00	92.40	92.70	96.50	94.40
		IV	91.70	91.70	89.90	89.60	87.80
		GRS	91.70	93.40	93.40	91.00	94.10
		DDRS	92.70	89.60	88.20	87.80	89.60
		GRSV	94.10	91.00	89.90	87.80	88.20
		GRSV-DDRS	93.40	89.90	88.90	88.20	89.60
		VT	92.40	86.50	88.50	87.80	87.80
		Max-base	89.60	89.60	86.80	86.50	84.70
		Avg-base	87.60	85.90	84.30	81.00	79.00
HCV	91.32%	RW	90.28	88.54	88.19	84.72	83.55
		IT	90.97	88.89	85.76	87.85	87.15
		Max-base	88.19	82.63	86.80	84.37	79.86
		Avg-base	84.72	79.23	79.61	75.46	75.03

However, none of our schemes can maintain the accuracy of the global classifier as the number of subsets increases. Iteration and Data Dependent Rule Selection are the two most promising strategies. Combined with Voting, they can generate schemes, which outperform Voting consistently. Furthermore Data Dependent Rule Selection is the best scheme to compensate the information loss caused by partitioning as the number of subsets increases.

Table 12. Comparisons from 5 schemes on Splice dataset

C4.5Rules	Approach	$P_6(\%)$	$P_9(\%)$	$P_{12}(\%)$	$P_{15}(\%)$	$P_{18}(\%)$	$P_{21}(\%)$
	IT	89.90	92.00	90.30	86.70	91.70	88.90
	IV	93.60	94.20	93.80	93.00	92.40	90.10
	GRS	93.60	94.20	93.80	93.00	92.40	90.10
	GRSV	94.00	93.80	94.20	93.20	93.00	90.50
93.60%	DDRS	94.40	94.00	93.80	94.00	94.00	94.00
	GRS-DDRS	93.80	94.00	93.80	94.00	94.00	94.20
	VT	93.40	93.60	93.80	93.00	90.30	87.70
	Avg-base	86.77	86.07	84.89	82.06	79.37	76.71
	Max-base	90.50	91.80	92.40	90.50	87.70	84.30

4 Conclusions

In this paper, we have addressed the problem of inductive learning on large or distributed data repositories. Five strategies (Rule-Example Conversion, Rule Weighting, Iteration, Good Rule Selection, and Data Dependent Rule Selection) and seven schemes have been investigated.

Among all the schemes we designed and evaluated, Iteration &Voting, and Data Dependent Rule Selection are the two most promising integration schemes, which can outperform Voting consistently. In addition, our study shows that classifiers trained individually from the subsets of a large data set are not as accurate as integrating a collection of separately learned classifiers. Therefore integration is necessary. The integration technique yields significantly higher accuracy than a classifier trained from a random subset (an average of 10% improvement). Furthermore, our integration schemes require significantly less training time than that of generating a global classifier over the global data set (an average of 90% improvement).

Many possibilities exist to extend the existing empirical evaluations and work on some related challenging issues, e.g., how many partitions are needed to generate optimal results, whether there exists an error bound for the proposed methods, and what is the accuracy loss due to partitioning. The research achievements on these issues can essentially benefit many real-world applications which have suffered significantly from their large data volumes.

References

1. Michalski R., Mozetic I., Hong J., & Lavrac N., The multipurpose incremental leaning system AQ51 and its testing application to three medical do mains. *Proc. of AAAI*, 1986.
2. Quinlan J., *C4.5: programs for machine learning*. CA: Morgan Kaufmann, 1993.
3. Breiman L., Friedman J. H., Olshen R.A., & Stone C. J., Classification and regression trees, *Belmont, CA, 1984*.
4. Clark P. & Niblett T., The CN2 induction algorithm. *Machine Learning*, 3:261-285, 1989.
5. Breiman L., Bagging predictors, *TR 421*, Dept. of Statistics, UC Berkeley, CA, 1994.
6. Wu X., *Knowledge Acquisition from Databases*, Ablex Publishing Corp, 1995.
7. Fayyad U., Piatetsky-Shapiro G., & Smyth P., From data mining to knowledge discovery: An overview. *In Advances in Knowledge Discovery and Data Mining*, Menlo Park, 1996.
8. Wu X. & Lo W., Multi-layer incremental induction. *Proc. of PRICAI*, pp. 24-32, 1998.
9. Provost F. & Kolluri V., Scaling up inductive algorithms: An overview. *Proc. of KDD*, CA, pp. 239–242, 1997.
10. Provost F. & Kolluri V., A survey of methods for scaling up inductive algorithms. *Data Mining and Knowledge Discovery*, 1999.
11. Huber H., From large to huge: A statistician's reaction to KDD and DM. *Proc. of KDD*, CA, pp. 304–308, 1997.
12. Chan P., An extensible meta-Learning approach for scalable and accurate inductive learning, *Ph.D. thesis*, Columbia Univ., 1996.
13. Cheung D., Ng V., Fu A., & Fu Y., Efficient Mining of Association Rules in Distributed Databases, *IEEE Transactions on Knowledge and Data Engineering*, 8(1996), 6: 911-922.
14. Wu X. & Zhang S., Synthesizing High-Frequency Rules from Different Data Sources, *IEEE Transactions on Knowledge and Data Engineering*, 15(2003), 2: 353-367.
15. Quinlan J., Learning efficient classification procedures and their application to chess endgames. *Machine Learning: An AI approach*, CA: Morgan Kaufmann, 1983.
16. Fürnkranz J., Integrative windowing. *J. of Artificial Intelligence Research* 8:129–164, 1998.
17. Blake C. & Merz C., *UCI Repository of machine learning databases*, 1998.
18. IBM Almaden Research, Synthetic data generator, http://www.almaden.ibm.com /software/quest/Resources /datasets/syndata.html#classSynData
19. Zhu X., Wu X., & Chen Q., Eliminating Class Noise in Large Datasets. *Proc. of ICML*, pp. 920-927, 2003.

Agent-Based Home Simulation and Control

B. De Carolis, G. Cozzolongo, S. Pizzutilo, and V.L. Plantamura

Dipartimento di Informatica -Università di Bari
http://www.di.uniba.it/intint

Abstract. In this paper, we propose an approach to the simulation of control of an intelligent home aiming at understanding which is the impact of embedded and pervasive technology on people daily life. In this vision, the house is seen as an intelligent environment made up of independent and distributed devices interacting to support user's goals and tasks. Achieving this aim requires giving, to these intelligent artifacts, an appropriate level of autonomy, distribution, adaptation, proactiveness, etc. Therefore, in some way, they share the same characteristics as agents. C@sa is a multiagent system aiming at modeling, controlling and simulating house behavior according to user and context features.

1 Introduction

Home Automation aims at handling the house control and management from several viewpoints (appliances, security, communications, comfort, ...) with the main objective of making the life of inhabitants easier. Most of the time, solutions to this problem result in using new complex remote controls or new computer-based interfaces.

Currently, houses are being networked, bringing the internet to the home and allowing new services. In the future home environment, the user will be overwhelmed by a multitude of devices with complex capabilities, different access network interfaces and different multimedia and control services. Introducing new visible technology does not always produce an improvement of the quality of interaction. Then, to change this trend, making home automation systems more accepted and spread through different user categories, the challenge is to create environments in which technology is present but invisible to users, as in Weiser's vision [1].

Ambient Intelligence (AmI) solutions, in which the interaction become pervasive and more natural, may help in making the house services fruition easy, natural and adapted to the user needs [2]. In the AmI information technology paradigm, people interact with a "real-digital" environment that is aware of their presence and of the context in which they are interacting. The environment perceives people presence, adapts and answers in a proactive manner to their needs, habits, emotional states, etc.. In this vision, people will be surrounded by intelligent and intuitive interfaces embedded into objects of daily use that will be able to recognize them and to react to their presence in a transparent way. Then, an AmI environment is composed of independent and distributed devices (artifacts) interacting to support user-centered goals and tasks. The key characteristics of these intelligent artifacts are autonomy, distribution, adaptation, proactiveness, etc: therefore, in a way, they share the characteristics of

M.-S. Hacid et al. (Eds.): ISMIS 2005, LNAI 3488, pp. 404–412, 2005.
© Springer-Verlag Berlin Heidelberg 2005

agents. As envisaged in [3], agent technologies impact ambient intelligence since they can be used as an abstraction metaphor for the design of complex, distributed computational systems as a way of implementing these systems and implementing intelligent interaction with the user [4].

Following this distinction, we propose a MultiAgent System (MAS) which is aimed, on one side, at simulating control of an intelligent home from the functional viewpoint and, on the other side, at providing an interface layer for interacting with the house. In this paper, we discuss how an agent-based organization of the house control may help in achieving the goal of a National project[1] to support architectural designers in testing the requirements of an intelligent house, in order to define guidelines for the integration of these technologies in tomorrow houses. In particular, the paper is structured as follows: in Section 2 we outline the architectural requirements of an agent-based system simulating the behavior of an intelligent house. In this Section we describe which is the role of each agent constituting the MAS and its organization and emphasize how the house behavior is decided. Section 3 illustrates the simulation and control 3D interface that allows to monitor the house behavior. Section 4 reports some information about the system implementation. Conclusions and future work directions are illustrated in the last Section.

2 Architectural Requirements of an Intelligent Home

There are several projects concerning the development of a Smart Home; for instance. Adaptive House [5] focuses on the development of a home that programs itself by observing the lifestyle and desires of the inhabitants, and learns to anticipate and accommodate their needs. In this system the control is handled by neural network reinforcement learning and prediction techniques. In the MavHome project [6] the smart home is seen as an intelligent agent that perceives its environment through the use of sensors, and can act upon the environment through the use of actuators. The home has certain overall goals, such as minimizing the cost of maintaining the home and maximizing the comfort of its inhabitants. The IHome Environment is another example of intelligent home that uses the MAS technology as a way to control the behavior of house appliances from the resource consumption and coordination viewpoint [7] . The UMASS simulated IHome environment is controlled by intelligent agents that are associated with particular appliances (i.e. WaterHeater, CoffeeMaker, Heater, A/C, DishWasher, etc.).

In developing our infrastructure, we were concerned about control, simulation and interaction with the home environment not only at a low abstraction level (single appliances behavior) but also at a higher level of abstraction, closer to the user needs and goals. In our opinion, ambient intelligence artifacts are likely to be function-specific (though possibly configurable to tasks) and will need to interact with numerous other AmI artifacts present in the environment in order to achieve their goals and meet users' expectations. Our research focuses mainly on the software that provides the infrastructure for intelligent control of devices within a home, to design and

---

[1] PRIN 03 – "L'ambiente domestico informatizzato: progetto e verifica dell'integrazione di utente, tecnologia e prodotto"- Università di Bari and Siena, Politecnico di Milano.

406

406B. De Carolis et al.

evaluate a system architecture which: i) allows to manage the house from the services viewpoint rather than from the room or device one; ii) adapts the house behavior to the inhabitant's needs, adjusting the control of devices according to their "influence sphere"; iii) allows to test the relationship between users and their home. We have developed a first prototype of a MAS, called C@sa, in which we propose a hierarchical organization of different types of agents: operators, supervisor and interactors. Let's see in more detail the role of each of them.

2.1 The Operator Agent

An operator agent (Oi) controls and model the behavior of a simple artifact (device, appliance, etc.). As shown in Figure 1, it is defined by a set of attributes describing the state of the artifact and a set of behaviors describing the task that the user or another agent can perform on it. Each task is associated with a formal description that can be used with two aims: controlling the artifact and generating natural language explanation of its use [8]. So for instance, if the user does not know how to use an appliance,

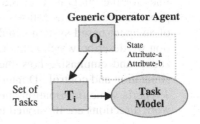

Fig. 1. Operator Agent

he/she may ask explanations to the house that can use the formal model as a knowledge base for generating help [9].

Then, taking inspiration from the functional view of an agent presented in [10], the entire house can be seen as a macro-entity whose reasoning process is driven by sensing user actions and context parameters and whose output is shown through some changes in the house appearance (controlled by some effectors). In this view, the operator agent can be defined as belonging to one or more of the following families: i) **context_sensor (CS)**: this agent measures the value of one or more device attributes (e.g. temperature, humidity, motion, etc.); ii) **effector (E)**: this agent directly affects the state and/or other attributes of the device (e.g., heating on at 26°, air conditioning off, stereo playing *a song*, ...).

2.2 The Supervisor Agent

Operator agents represent the entire home and are, in some way, related to each other (dependent, interacting, etc.). In particular, the state of a device may influence another device and therefore the house behavior.

Since, in order to meet the user's desires, artifacts and therefore operator agents need to interact with other ones, they need to be coordinated according to the recognized user needs.

This is the role of the **Supervisor** agent (Sk) which, according to the current context situation and to the presumed preferences and needs of the user in that context, reasons on how to coordinate the agents belonging to its *influence sphere* (Figure 2). In our system, an influence sphere, is defined in function of the type of service to be provided to the house inhabitants and not in function of house zones (rooms) like in other systems [11]. Examples of influence sphere are the following: comfort, security, wellness and entertainment. Therefore, we specialize the decisional behavior of each Supervisor agent according to the influence sphere it controls.

The Agent's decisional behavior is determined by an influence diagram that models the relationship between decisions (e.g. device actions), random uncertain quantities (e.g. user goals) and values (e.g. utility of the action).

Figure 3 shows the model that a generic supervisor agent uses for deciding the utility of an action on the user. In particular, in this influence diagram:

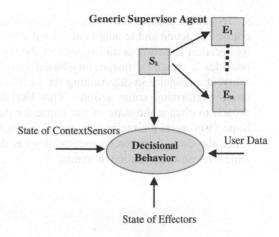

Fig. 2. Schema of a Generic Supervisor Agent

- the *square box* denotes the decision about performing an action at time t_i;
- the *round nodes* are chance variables and, in this abstract model they represent the house and user situation before $(t_i;)$ and after (t_{i+1}) action execution; they describe *sensors* situation and how they influence the *context*; obviously, since the house adapts its decision to the user in order to meet his/her requirements, the *user situation* at a given time is inferred accordingly;

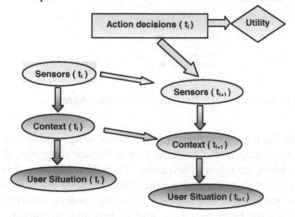

Fig. 3. A General Decision Schema of a Supervisor

- the *rhombus nodes* represent the utility value for the user when an *action i* is executed on the *device i*.

Then, the global semantics of this schema is: given a certain context configuration defined by the values coming from the sensors, there is a probability function that indicates the possible user goals and preferences in that situation, these two values are used to calculate the utility for the user if the Supervisor agent performs an action.

An example of Supervisor is the Comfort agent, which decides the appropriate atmosphere setting and controls the behavior of the involved operator agents, according to some contextual parameters (i.e.weather conditions, internal temperature, etc.). According to some definitions of comfort, it concerns mainly *light settings* (intensity and colour), *internal temperature*, *intrusiveness* of *communication* systems, etc. [11, 12]. However, what comes out from attempting to define comfort is that it is highly subjective.

To enable a Supervisor Agent to reason about the trade-off of different possible courses of action and to adapt behaviorally to changing environment, we implemented its decision behavior as an instance of the abstract diagram illustrated in Figure 3. It provides a dynamic, uncertainty-based knowledge representation for modeling the inherent ambiguity in determining the likelihood of the agent to meet the user expectation performing some actions. This likelihood provides a decision-theoretic approach to change the state of the house for pursuing the goal of the Supervisor. The Supervisor agent maintains a model of the user's needs within a target influence zone. Since the decision-theoretic methodology is domain-independent, it is readily extensible over new application domains.

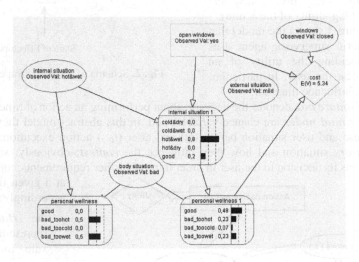

Fig. 4. A portion of the decisional behavior of the Comfort Agent

Figure 4 shows a portion of the network representing the reasoning behavior of the Comfort Supervisor Agent. According to the semantics of influence diagrams, decisions concerning the same problem are taken in sequence. Then, the decision of *turning on the air conditioning at a certain temperature* rather than *opening the window* is influenced by some contextual parameters that can be derived by context_sensors (i.e. internal_temperature, humidity, user heart beat rate, and so on) and, eventually, by some other more static parameters concerning data about the user (i.e. age, environmental attitude, and so on). These data can be retrieved in the user profile.

For instance, in the case that at time t_i "the internal situation is *hot&wet*, the body parameters denote a non comfortable situation and consequently the personal wellness is *bad_toohot/toowet*" then, the decision of *opening the windows* (if closed) is not convenient if the *external situation* would make worst the personal wellness at time t_{i+1}. In the considered example, the Comfort Supervisor will find an improvement of the personal wellness after opening the windows.

This diagram aims at giving an idea of the general model of the Comfort Influence Sphere. Therefore, employing a structured view of an environment provides two major advantages when attempting to control the home. Firstly, the control can be achieved on any node of the network with a guarantee that all causally dependent nodes will change accordingly. For instance, the node representing the wellness level can be forced into a specific state and all dependent nodes' states will subsequently be changed, if a state change is necessary. Secondly, it can be used also for detecting problems with sensors data (for instance, if the user feels bad because is hot and the internal temperature is 10° C, then, probably there is a problem with that sensor).

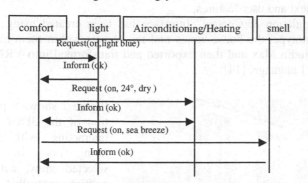

Fig. 5. Exchange of ACL messages between SA and OAs

Once the Supervisor Agent decides what to do, it has to ask the Operator Agents, involved in the decision, to performed the required action. This is done using a protocol in which the agents use ACL (Agent Communication Language) [13], whose content is expressed in XML, for communicating. Figure 5 illustrates the exchange of ACL messages between the Comfort Supervisor and the Operator Agents in its influence sphere.

3 The Interactor Agent

In our project we envisage two different interaction levels (Figure 6) directed to different categories of users: i) the *environment simulation and control interface* to be used especially by architectural designer for testing their hypothesis and ii) the *user interface* level to be used by *house inhabitants*.

In the first case, the interface has to help the end user in simulating context situations and in testing consequent house reactions. In the second case, the house inhabitants should be able to interact naturally with the house appliances or directly (i.e.

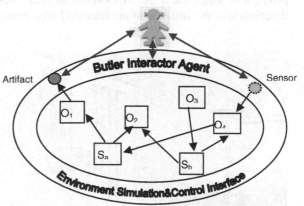

Fig. 6. Interaction paradigms with the smart home

voice commands, tangible interfaces, touch screens, and so on) or indirectly delegating tasks to a "house assistant" (i.e. the virtual butler agent, a robot, etc.) or implicitly (i.e. through sensors perception of relevant data).

In this first phase of the project, we are mainly concerned with the implementation of the level of interaction aiming at simulating and controlling what is happening in the house given some context and user features.

The "Environment Simulation & Control" Interface has been created using 3D Graphics. In this first prototype, the house zones and the objects within them have been realized using 3D Studio Max and then exported and transformed into VRML (Virtual Reality Modeling Language, [14]).

Figure 7 shows a portion of the 3DUI for interacting with the living room. In this selected view, active entities controlled by operator agents are the *internal temperature sensor,* the *air-conditioner* and the *windows.*

Fig. 7. 3DUI showing a portion of the living room

In order to use the 3DUI for simulation and control purposes, it has been necessary to establish a connection with C@sa. This, at the moment, has been made through a protocol in which the house MAS sends an ACL message whose content is the XML description of the situation in the selected house zone.

This message will be received by a Java class able to parse it and to render, at the interface level, what is specified in the message. Figure 8 shows a situation change in which the operator agent controlling the air-conditioner changed its state to "on" after a decision.

Fig. 8. 3DUI showing the air-conditioner cooling the room

Then, the 3DUI interface sends an ACL message specifying a state change or the need to read some state attributes to the operator agent responsible for that device.

A change, obviously has an effect of the decisional behavior of the supervisor agent controlling a certain influence sphere. In this case, actions in the virtual world are collected by the usage model [15] that according to the type of action has update the tables of the Influence Diagram after a number of actions of that kind belonging to the same influence sphere and performed in the same context (calculated as a significant percentage on the total number of interaction). We are still investigating on the weight to be associated to every type of action given a certain influence sphere and some context features.

4 Implementation Issues

There are several agent development frameworks that facilitate the building of multi-agent systems. Among these, the JADE project [16], which is a FIPA compliant framework, showed to be appropriate for developing the described infrastructure. In particular, we had to include the Agent Decisional Behaviour, modelled with Belief and Decision Network Java Applet [17], in the Supervisor Agent Class. The communication among the agents representing the house infrastructure is formalized using ACL messages which allows the information and knowledge exchange through a set of communicative acts. In particular, in order to use a more database and device neutral, readable and easy to parse format, we encoded the content of ACL messages in XML.

5 Conclusions and Future Work Directions

The idea of a house equipped with technical and life-enhancing devices is already old. What is new in this field is the added value of the transparency and interactiveness of ambient intelligence where, following Weiser's vision, the technological devices fade into the background and are embedded into daily objects.

According to this point of view, we have designed and developed a MAS called C@sa aiming at modeling and simulating the behaviour of an intelligent home. The idea at the bases of its organization is that the house is not divided into rooms, but is seen as a set of *Influence Spheres* denoting the type of service that are provided to the house's inhabitants (i.e. the comfort, the security, wellness, etc.). Then, the control of each influence sphere is delegated to a Supervisor Agent that drives the behaviour of Operator Agents representing the devices belonging to that sphere. This aim is achieved using a decisional behaviour modelled as an Influence Diagram. In this phase of the project we are testing the system behaviour using a 3D simulation nterface. The collected data will be used not only for system evaluation by architects involved in the system but also as a set of examples to recognize behaviour patterns and add prediction capabilities to our system.

In our future work, we plan also to evaluate the centralized decision behaviour, presented in this paper, with a distributed one in which global decisions about a service are taken by the Supervisor Agent and decision local to a single device are taken by the correspondent Operator Agent.

Acknowledgements

Research described in this paper has been performed in the scope of the National Project PRIN03 "L'ambiente domestico informatizzato: progetto e verifica dell'integrazione di utente, tecnologia e prodotto". We wish to thank those who cooperated in implementing the system described in this paper: Rosa Sarcina, Grazia Ricco, Anna Rowe and Vincenzo Silvestri. In particular, we thanks Fiorella de Rosis for her useful comments on the MAS organization. and Fabio Abbattista for his suggestions on the 3DUI.

References

1. Weiser M. The Computer for the 21st Century. Scientific American, September 1991.
2. Shadbolt N.Ambient Intelligence. IEEE Intelligent Systems.July/August(Vol.18, No.4).
3. Grill, T. Ibrahim I.K., Kotsis G. Agents for Ambient Intelligence - Support or Nuisance.ÖGAI Journal 23/1.http://www.tk.uni-linz.ac.at/download/oegai_article_final. pdf
4. Maes, P., Agents that Reduce Work and Information Overload. Communications of the ACM 37 (7), pp. 30-40, 1994.
5. Mozer, M. C. (2004). Lessons from an adaptive house. In D. Cook & R. Das (Eds.), Smart environments: Technologies, protocols, and applications. J. Wiley & Sons.
6. Rao S. and D. J. Cook, Predicting Inhabitant Actions Using Action and Task Models with Application to Smart Homes, *International Journal of Artificial Intelligence Tools*, 13(1), pages 81-100, 2004.
7. Lesser, V., Atighetchi, M., Benyo, B. et al.. *The UMASS intelligent home project*. In Proceedings of the Third Annual Conference on Autonomous Agents, pages 291--298, Seattle, USA, 1999.
8. de Rosis, F. Pizzutilo, S., De Carolis B.: Formal description and evaluation of user-adapted interfaces. Int. J. Hum.-Comput. Stud. 49(2): 95-120, 1998.
9. de Rosis, F., De Carolis B., Pizzutilo, S. Automated Generation of Agent Behaviour from Formal Models of Interaction. Advanced Visual Interfaces : 193-200, 2000.
10. Russell, S. and Norvig, P. Artificial Intelligence: a Modern Approach. Prentice Hall.
11. Spronk, B. A House Is Not A Home: Witold Rybczynski Explores The History Of Domestic Comfort. *Aurora Online*, 2001
12. Allen, B., van Berlo, A.,Ekberg, J., Fellbaum, K., Hampicke, M.,Willems, C. Design Guidelines on Smart Homes. (www.stakes.fi/cost219/smarthousing.htm): Printed by AFONSO Lonay (CH), Oct. 1999
13. FIPA: www.fipa.org
14. VRML: http://www.vrmlsite.com/
15. Fink J. and Kobsa A. User Modeling in Personalized City Tours. Artificial Intelligence Review 18(1), 33-74, 2002
16. JADE: http://jade.tilab.com/
17. Belief and Decision Networks Applet: http://www.cs.ubc.ca/labs/lci/CIspace/Version4/ bayes/index.html.

Aggregates and Preferences in Logic Programming

S. Greco, I. Trubitsyna, and E. Zumpano

DEIS, Univ. della Calabria, 87030 Rende, Italy
{greco, irina, zumpano}@deis.unical.it

Abstract. The present work proposes a new semantics for logic program with preference rules and studies logic programs enriched with
both aggregates and preference rules. The interest of research literature
in handling user preferences to express a partial order on rules and literals is reflected by an extensive number of proposals. The association of
aggregates and preferences is, here, used to also express a partial order
on global models, other than on literals and rules, so that optimization
problems can be expressed in a simple and elegant way. The use of aggregates makes logic languages more flexible and intuitive, without any
additional computational complexity.

1 Introduction

The effort of ranking and returning the preferred information is an increasingly
key goal in AI applications ranging from information filtering and extraction
to user profiling. The increased interest of research literature on preferences
is reflected by an extensive number of proposals allowing the specification of
flexible and powerful preferences. Logic programming plays a significant role in
this line of research and different proposals have been developed for representing
and reasoning about users' preferences.

Most of the approaches propose an extension of Gelfond and Lifschitz's extended logic programming by adding preference information [6, 7, 11, 17, 22, 23].
Some other approaches attempt to extend the well founded semantics to logic
programs with preferences [19] and in [22] it is proposed an extension of van-
Gelder's alternating fixpoint theory and it is shown it can be used as a general
semantics for logic programs with priority. A preference is expressed using a binary relation on objects of some given type. The most common form of preference
consists in specifying a strict partial order on rules [6, 7, 11, 17, 22, 23], whereas
more sophisticated forms of preferences also allow specifying priorities between
conjunctive (disjunctive) knowledge with preconditions [3, 6, 17]. The literature
distinguish between *static* and *dynamic* preferences. Static preferences are fixed
at the time a theory is specified, i.e. they are "external" to the logic program
[17, 18], whereas dynamic preferences appear within the logic program and are
determined "on the fly" [6, 7, 3, 20]. A first category of approaches [7, 11, 17, 23]
uses a two level technique, i.e. preferences are used at a meta-level in order
to define an alternative semantics. The basic idea underlying these approaches,

M.-S. Hacid et al. (Eds.): ISMIS 2005, LNAI 3488, pp. 413–424, 2005.
© Springer-Verlag Berlin Heidelberg 2005

though very different, consists in selecting just those answer sets that can be generated in an "order-preserving way". A second category of approaches [1, 3] utilizes extra conditions on the standard answer-sets of the preference free program to further check if an ordinary answer set S is a "preferred answer set".

A framework of prioritized logic programming, having a mechanism of explicit representation of priorities, was introduced by Sakama and Inoue in [18]. A *prioritized logic program* (*PLP*) is a pair $(\mathcal{P}, \Phi)$, where $\mathcal{P}$ is a standard program and Φ is a set of priorities. The approach studies how to represent and reason with static preferences among literals under strict partial order. The semantics of a *PLP* is given as preferred answer sets which are defined as answer sets of $\mathcal{P}$ and satisfy the set of priorities in Φ. Different frameworks for reasoning with priorities in logic programming have been proposed such as ordered logic programs [7], preferred answer sets of extended logic programs [1], logic programs with ordered disjunction [2].

The present work is a contribution in the direction of realizing prioritized reasoning in logic programming. Specifically, the novelty of this paper consists in considering Datalog-like languages with preferences, as proposed by Sakama and Inoue [17], enriched with the use of aggregates, as proposed in [13]. The use of aggregate predicates makes logic languages more flexible and intuitive, and their combination with preferences, as will be shown in the following, allows preferences to be defined on global models and optimization problems to be expressed in a simple and elegant way. The paper proposes a new semantics of preferred stable models with both aggregates and preference rules, which seems to better capture the intuitive meaning of programs. Moreover, the complexity of computing preferred answer sets in the presence of prioritized program with dynamic preferences and aggregates is analyzed. It will be shown that the problem of checking if there exists a preferred stable model is Σ_2^P-*complete*, whereas deciding if a literal is true is Σ_3^P-*complete* and Π_3^P-*complete* under, respectively, brave and cautious reasoning. Thus, the introduction of aggregates predicates and dynamic preferences does not increase the complexity of computing preferred stable models w.r.t. *PLP* in [17].

2 Preliminaries

A *disjunctive Datalog rule* r is a clause of the form:

$$A_1 \vee \cdots \vee A_k \leftarrow B_1, \cdots, B_m, not\, C_1, \cdots, not\, C_n, \qquad k + m + n > 0,$$

where $A_1, \cdots, A_k, B_1, \cdots, B_m, C_1, \cdots, C_n$ are atoms. The disjunction $A_1 \vee \cdots \vee A_k$ is the *head* of r, while the conjunction $B_1, \cdots, B_m, not\, C_1, \cdots, not\, C_n$ is the *body* of r. A *(disjunctive) logic program* is a finite set of rules. A *not*-free (resp. $\vee$-free) program is called *positive* (resp. *normal*). The *Herbrand Universe* $U_{\mathcal{P}}$ of a program $\mathcal{P}$ is the set of all constants appearing in $\mathcal{P}$, and its *Herbrand Base* $B_{\mathcal{P}}$ is the set of all ground atoms constructed from the predicates appearing in $\mathcal{P}$ and the constants from $U\mathcal{P}$. A term, (resp. an atom, a literal, a rule or a program) is *ground* if no variables occur in it. In the following we assume the existence of rules with empty head, called *denials*, which define constraints[1], i.e. rules which are satisfied only if the body is false. An interpretation of $\mathcal{P}$ is any subset of $\mathcal{B}_{\mathcal{P}}$. An interpretation M for $\mathcal{P}$ is a model of $\mathcal{P}$ if M satisfies all rules in $ground(\mathcal{P})$. The minimal model semantics, defined for positive $\mathcal{P}$, assigns to $\mathcal{P}$ the set of its *minimal models* $\mathcal{MM}(\mathcal{P})$, where a model M for $\mathcal{P}$ is minimal, if no proper subset of M is a model for $\mathcal{P}$. The more general *disjunctive stable model semantics* also applies to programs with (unstratified) negation [10]. Disjunctive stable model semantics generalizes stable model semantics, previously defined for normal programs [9]. For any interpretation M, denote with $\mathcal{P}^M$ the ground positive program derived from $ground(\mathcal{P})$ by 1) removing all rules that contain a negative literal $not\ a$ in the body and $a \in M$, and 2) removing all negative literals from the remaining rules. An interpretation M is a (disjunctive) stable model of $\mathcal{P}$ if and only if $M \in \mathcal{MM}(\mathcal{P}^M)$. For general $\mathcal{P}$, the stable model semantics assigns to $\mathcal{P}$ the set $\mathcal{SM}(\mathcal{P})$ of its *stable models*. It is well known that stable models are minimal models (i.e. $\mathcal{SM}(\mathcal{P}) \subseteq \mathcal{MM}(\mathcal{P})$) and that for negation free programs, minimal and stable model semantics coincide (i.e. $\mathcal{SM}(\mathcal{P}) = \mathcal{MM}(\mathcal{P})$). We denote with $DAT^{\vee,not}$ the full language here considered (Datalog rules with disjunctive heads and, possibly unstratified, negation) and with DAT^{not} the restriction of $DAT^{\vee,not}$ where rules are normal (i.e. disjunction free). For a given language $\mathcal{L}$, with a little abuse of notation, we also denote with $\mathcal{L}$ the set of all possible programs which can be written in $\mathcal{L}$. An *exclusive disjunctive datalog rule* r is a clause of the form $A_1 \oplus \cdots \oplus A_k \leftarrow B_1, \cdots, B_m, not\ C_1, \cdots, not\ C_n$. The rule r can be rewritten into k rules of the form: $A_i \leftarrow B_1, \cdots, B_m,\ not\ C_1, \cdots, not\ C_n,\ not\ A_1, \cdots, not\ A_{i-1}, not\ A_{i+1}, \cdots, not\ A_k$ with $i \in [1..k]$.

2.1   Sets, Bugs, Lists and Aggregate Functions

In this section we introduce an extension of Datalog to manage complex terms and aggregates. In particular, we introduce standard SQL functions which are applied to complex terms and a nondeterministic function which selects (nondeterministically) one element from a complex term.

Bugs and Sets. A (ground) *bug term* S is of the form $\{s_1, ..., s_n\}$, where s_j $(1 \leq j \leq n)$ is a constant and the sequence in which the elements are listed is immaterial. Moreover, a bug term $\{s_1, ..., s_n\}$ is called *set term* if the number of occurrences of every s_j, for $1 \leq j \leq n$, is immaterial. Thus, the three sets $\{a, b\}$, $\{b, a\}$ and $\{b, a, b\}$ coincide, while the two bugs $\{a, b\}$ and $\{b, a, b\}$ are different. Note that the enumeration of the elements of a set term can be given either directly or by specifying the conditions for collecting their elements (*grouping variables*). Grouping variables may occur in the head of clauses with the following format: $p(x_1, ..., x_h, \langle y_1 \rangle, ..., \langle y_k \rangle, \langle\langle y_{k+1} \rangle\rangle, ..., \langle\langle y_m \rangle\rangle) \leftarrow B_1, ..., B_n$ where $B_1, ..., B_n$ are the goals of the rules, p is the head predicate symbol with

---

[1] Under total semantics a denial rule of the form $\leftarrow B$ can be rewritten into standard rules of the form $p \leftarrow B, not\ p$.

arity $h + m$, y_i for $1 \leq i \leq m$, is a grouping variable, and $x_1, ..., x_h$ are the other arguments (terms or other grouping variables). To the grouping variable $\langle\langle Y \rangle\rangle$ (resp. $\langle Y \rangle$) will be assigned the bug (resp. set) $\{Y\theta \mid \theta$ is a substitution for r such that $B_1\theta, ..., B_n\theta$ are true$\}$.

Aggregate Functions. We consider logic rules with built-in aggregate functions, such as $min, max, count, sum$ and avg which are applied to sets and bugs. An aggregate term is of the form $f(S)$ where S is a grouping variable and $f \in \{min, max, count, sum, avg\}$ is an aggregate function. Note that since grouping variables may only occur in the head of rules, aggregate terms only occur in the head of rules too. Observe that $min\langle\langle S \rangle\rangle = min\langle S \rangle$ and $max\langle\langle S \rangle\rangle = max\langle S \rangle$.

Example 1. Consider the database D consisting of the following facts: q(a,2,x), q(a,3,y), q(b,4,x), q(b,7,y), q(b,4,z) and the following program P:

$$
\begin{array}{llll}
p_1(X, \langle Y \rangle) & \leftarrow q(X, Y, Z) & p_2(X, \langle\langle Y \rangle\rangle) & \leftarrow q(X, Y, Z) \\
p_3(X, min\langle Y \rangle) & \leftarrow q(X, Y, Z) & p_4(X, max\langle Y \rangle) & \leftarrow q(X, Y, Z) \\
p_5(X, count\langle Y \rangle) & \leftarrow q(X, Y, Z) & p_6(X, count\langle\langle Y \rangle\rangle) & \leftarrow q(X, Y, Z) \\
p_7(X, sum\langle Y \rangle) & \leftarrow q(X, Y, Z) & p_8(X, sum\langle\langle Y \rangle\rangle) & \leftarrow q(X, Y, Z) \\
p_9(X, avg\langle Y \rangle) & \leftarrow q(X, Y, Z) & p_{10}(X, avg\langle\langle Y \rangle\rangle) & \leftarrow q(X, Y, Z)
\end{array}
$$

The evaluation of the above rules gives the following facts:

$$
\begin{array}{llll}
p_1(a, \{2, 3\}), & p_1(b, \{4, 7\}), & p_2(a, \{2, 3\}), & p_2(b, \{4, 7, 4\}), \\
p_3(a, 2), & p_3(b, 4), & p_4(a, 3), & p_4(b, 7), \\
p_5(a, 2), & p_5(b, 2), & p_6(a, 2), & p_6(b, 3), \\
p_7(a, 5), & p_7(b, 11), & p_8(a, 5), & p_8(b, 15), \\
p_9(a, 2.5), & p_9(b, 5.5), & p_{10}(a, 2.5), & p_{10}(b, 5).
\end{array}
$$

□

Nondeterministic Predicates: Choice. Other than classical aggregate operators, we also consider a nondeterministic function, called *choice*, which selects nondeterministically one element from a set, bug or list. A choice term is of the form $choice\langle S \rangle$ where S is a list of variables. Clearly, the candidate results for $choice\langle S \rangle$, and $choice\langle\langle S \rangle\rangle$ coincide. In the following we only consider programs whith aggregates and choice, but we disallow the use of set and bug constructors without aggregates and choice, i.e. the derived facts are standard Datalog atoms.

Example 2. Consider the following program:

$$
\begin{array}{ll}
p(1, \text{fish}, 20) \oplus p(1, \text{beef}, 18) & \leftarrow \\
p(2, \text{red}, 10) \oplus p(2, \text{white}, 8) \oplus p(2, \text{beer}, 5) & \leftarrow \\
p(3, \text{pie}, 3) \oplus p(3, \text{ice-cream}, 2) & \leftarrow
\end{array}
$$

defining different dinner dishes. Each model computes a set of dishes and each dish has associated a cost. The same result can be obtained though the single rule: q(X, choice$\langle Z \rangle$) ← p(X, Y, Z)   where p is a relation containing all atoms reported in the above disjunctive rules. Assuming to consider only the set of dishes whose global cost is lesser than 30:

$$
\begin{array}{l}
qs(sum\langle C \rangle) \leftarrow q(X, C) \\
\leftarrow qs(S), S \geq 30
\end{array}
$$

then the above program has 12 stable models, but only 6 satisfy this bound. □

2.2   Prioritized Logic Programs

In this section we briefly review prioritized logic program proposed in [18]. A *(partial) preference relation* $\preceq$ among atoms is defined as follows. Given two atoms e_1 and e_2, the statement $e_1 \preceq e_2$ (called *priority*) means that e_2 has higher priority than e_1. Moreover, if $e_1 \preceq e_2$ and $e_2 \preceq e_3$, then $e_1 \preceq e_3$. A priority statement $e_1 \preceq e_2$ means that for each a_1 instance of e_1 and for each a_2 instance of e_2 it is $a_1 \preceq a_2$. The statement $e_1 \prec e_2$ stands for $e_1 \preceq e_2$ and $e_2 \not\preceq e_1$ Clearly, if $e_1 \prec e_2$, the sets of ground instantiations of e_1 and e_2 has empty intersection. A *prioritized logic program* (PLP) is a pair $(\mathcal{P}, \Phi)$ where $\mathcal{P}$ is a disjunctive program and Φ is a set of priorities. Φ^* denotes the set of priorities which can be reflexively or transitively derived from Φ,

Definition 1. *Given a PLP $(\mathcal{P}, \Phi)$, the relation $\sqsubseteq$ is defined over the stable models of $\mathcal{P}$ as follows. For any stable models M_1, M_2 and M_3 of $\mathcal{P}$*

1. $M_1 \sqsubseteq M_1$,
2. $M_1 \sqsubseteq M_2$ *if a)* $\exists e_2 \in M_2 - M_1$, $\exists e_1 \in M_1 - M_2$ *such that* $(e_1 \preceq e_2) \in \Phi^*$ *and b)* $\not\exists e_3 \in M_1 - M_2$ *such that* $(e_2 \prec e_3) \in \Phi^*$,
3. *if* $M_1 \sqsubseteq M_2$ *and* $M_2 \sqsubseteq M_3$, *then* $M_1 \sqsubseteq M_3$.   □

If $M_1 \sqsubseteq M_2$ we say that M_2 is *preferable* to M_1. Moreover, we write $M_1 \sqsubset M_2$ if $M_1 \sqsubseteq M_2$ and $M_1 \neq M_2$. An interpretation M is a *preferred* stable model of (P, Φ) if M is a stable model of P and $M \sqsubseteq N$ implies $N \sqsubseteq M$ for any stable model N. The set of preferred stable models of (P, Φ) will be denoted by $\mathcal{PSM}(P, \Phi)$. Note that the relation $\Phi_1 \subseteq \Phi_2$ between two PLPs $(\mathcal{P}, \Phi_1)$ and $(\mathcal{P}, \Phi_2)$ does not imply $\mathcal{PSM}(\mathcal{P}, \Phi_1) \subseteq \mathcal{PSM}(\mathcal{P}, \Phi_2)$. As showed in [18] it is possible to express priorities among conjunctions and disjunctions of atoms, priorities among rules and priorities with preconditions $(e_1 \preceq e_2) \leftarrow B$). More details on PLP can be found in [18] (see also [4, 23] for related material).

We recall that deciding the existence of a preferred stable model is $\Sigma_P^2 - complete$ and deciding whether a literal is true in some (resp. all) preferable stable model of (P, Φ) is Σ_P^3-complete (resp. Σ_P^3-complete).

2.3   Answer Set Optimization

We here provide a brief overview of the technique proposed in [3]. An answer set optimization program ASO is a pair (P_{Gen}, P_{Pref}). P_{Gen} (Generation Program) is used to generate answer set, that is define the space of acceptable solutions. P_{Pref} (Preference Program) defines context-dependent preferences and is used to compare answer sets of P_{Gen}, that is to form a preference ordering of acceptable solutions. Intuitively, the rules in P_{Gen} can be thought of as hard constraints on the answer set; whereas rules of P_{Pref} can be thought of as soft constraints describing conditions under which one answer set is to be considered better than another.

Definition 2. *Let A be a set of atoms. A preference program over A is a finite set of rules of the form: $C_1 > ... > C_k \leftarrow a_1, ..., a_n, not\ b_1, ..., not\ b_m$ where $a_i s$ and $b_j s$ are literals and $C_i s$ are boolean combinations over A.*   □

A boolean combination is a formula built of atoms in A by means of disjunctions, conjunctions, strong ($\neg$) and default (*not*) negation with the restriction that strong negation is allowed to appear only in front of atoms and default negation only in front of literals. P_{Pref} determines a preference ordering on the answer sets described by the generating program P_{PGen}.

Definition 3. *Let $P_{Pref} = r_1, ..., r_n$ be a preference program and let S be an answer set, then S induces a satisfaction vector $V_s = (v_s(r_1), ..., v_s(r_n))$ where:*

- *$v_s(r_j) = I$ if r_j is Irrelevant to S, i.e.*
  - *the body of r_j is not satisfied in S or*
  - *the body of r_j is satisfied, but none of the C_is is satisfied in S.*
- *$v_s(r_j) = min\{i : S \models C_i\}$.* □

In the comparison of models it is assumed that I is equal to 1 (i.e., $v_{S_j}(r_i) = I$ is equivalent to $v_{S_j}(r_i) = 1$).

Definition 4. *Let S_1 and S_2 be an answer sets. We write $V_{S_1} \geq V_{S_2}$ if $v_{S_1}(r_i) \geq v_{S_2}(r_i)$ for every $i \in 1, ..., n$. We write $V_{S_1} > V_{S_2}$ if $V_{S_1} \geq V_{S_2}$ and for some $i \in 1, ..., n$ $v_{S_1}(r_i) > v_{S_2}(r_i)$.* □

The complexity of *ASO* programs depends on the class of generating programs. For disjunctive programs we have the same complexity of prioritized programs, while for disjunction-free programs the complexity is one level lower.

3   Extended Prioritized Logic Programs

In this section we propose a technique which captures some intuitions of the techniques proposed by [3, 18], but differs from both of them.

Syntax

We use a syntax similar to that proposed in [3]. Given two atoms A_1 and A_2, the statement $A_2 > A_1$ means that A_2 has higher priority than A_1. A *(partial) preference relation* > among atoms is defined as follows.

Definition 5. *An (extended) preference rule is of the form*

$$A_1 > A_2 > \cdots > A_k \leftarrow B_1, ..., B_m, not\, C_1, ..., not\, C_n$$

where $A_1, ..., A_k, B_1, ..., B_m, C_1, ..., C_n$ are (ground) atoms.

An (extended) prioritized program is a pair $(\mathcal{P}, \Phi)$ where $\mathcal{P}$ is a disjunctive program and Φ is a set of (extended) preference rules. □

The intuitive meaning of a preference rule $A_1 > A_2 > \cdots > A_k \leftarrow B_1, ..., B_m,$ $not\, C_1, ..., not\, C_n$ is that if the body of the rule is true, then A_i is preferred to A_{i+1}, for $1 \leq i < k$. Preference rules with variables stand for ground rules obtainable by replacing variables with constants.

A preference rule with only two atoms in the head of the form: $A_1 > A_2 \leftarrow B_1, ..., B_m, not\, C_1, ..., not\, C_n$ will be called *binary* preference rule, whereas preference rules with empty bodies will be called *preference facts*. Binary preference rules with empty bodies will be also called *standard preferences*. A prioritized program is said to be in standard form if all preference rules are standard.

Extended preferences rules can be rewritten into standard preferences. A preference rule of the form $A_1 > A_2 > \cdots > A_k \leftarrow B_1, ..., B_m, not\, C_1, ..., not\, C_n$ is equivalent to $k - 1$ (binary) rules of the form $A_i > A_{i+1} \leftarrow B_1, ..., B_m, not\, C_1, ..., not\, C_n$ $1 \le i \le k - 1$ and each binary preference rule of the above form can be rewritten into a standard preference $A_i' > A_{i+1}'$ where A_i' and A_{i+1}' are two new atoms defined as $A_j' \leftarrow A_j, B_1, ..., B_m, not\, C_1, ..., not\, C_n$ *for* $j \in \{i, i + 1\}$.

Definition 6. *Given a set of preference rules Φ, $st(\Phi)$ denotes the pair (P_Φ, Φ_2) where Φ_2 is the set of standard preferences derived from Φ; and P_Φ is the set of new rules introduced during the derivation of Φ_2.* □

Note that, in the above definition, Φ_2 is defined only on atoms defined in P_Φ and for a given preference $a > b \leftarrow body$ in Φ, where body can be a possibly empty conjunction of literals, we introduce two rules $a' \leftarrow a, body$ and $b' \leftarrow b, body$ in P_Φ and the preference $a' > b'$ in Φ_2.

Example 3. Consider the program $\langle \mathcal{P}, \Phi \rangle$:

$$a \oplus b \leftarrow \qquad\qquad\qquad a > b \leftarrow$$
$$c \oplus d \leftarrow \qquad\qquad\qquad c > d \leftarrow a$$
$$\qquad\qquad\qquad\qquad d > c \leftarrow b$$

The (standard) prioritized program $\langle \mathcal{P}_\Phi, \Phi_2 \rangle$ is:

$$a_1 \leftarrow a \qquad\qquad\qquad a_1 > b_1 \leftarrow$$
$$b_1 \leftarrow b \qquad\qquad\qquad c_2 > d_2 \leftarrow$$
$$c_2 \leftarrow a, c \qquad\qquad\qquad d_3 > c_3 \leftarrow$$
$$d_2 \leftarrow a, d$$
$$c_3 \leftarrow b, c$$
$$d_3 \leftarrow b, d$$

□

Semantics

The preference among (ground) atoms is defined by the binary relation $\succeq$ defined as follows. Given an extended prioritized program $\langle \mathcal{P}, \Phi \rangle$, and a stable model M for $\langle \mathcal{P} \cup P_\Phi, \Phi_2 \rangle$, $M^{\mathcal{P}}$ and $M^{\mathcal{P}_\Phi}$ denote, respectively, the set of atoms defined (or inferred by rules) in $\mathcal{P}$ and $\mathcal{P}_\Phi$. As previously observed, the priorities in Φ_2 are defined only on atoms belonging to $M^{\mathcal{P}_\Phi}$. Therefore, given a prioritized program $\langle \mathcal{P}, \Phi \rangle$ and two stable models M and N for $\mathcal{P} \cup P_\Phi$, the comparison of M and N is defined by only considering the atoms defined in $\mathcal{P}_\Phi$.

Definition 7. *Let $\langle \mathcal{P}, \Phi \rangle$ be a prioritized program, $\langle \mathcal{P}_\Phi, \Phi_2 \rangle$ be the standard prioritized program derived from Φ and M a stable model for $\mathcal{P} \cup P_\Phi$. Then,*

- $A \succeq A$, for each $A \in M^{P_\Phi}$,
- $A_2 \succeq A_1$ if there is a ground fact $A_2 > A_1$ in Φ_2 and $A_2, A_1 \in M^{P_\Phi}$,
- $A_2 \succeq A_0$, if $A_2 \succeq A_1$ and $A_1 \succeq A_0$,
- $A_2 \succeq A_1$, if there are two rules $A_2 \leftarrow Body_2$ and $A_1 \leftarrow Body_1$ in P_Φ and two atoms $A_4 \succeq A_3$ in M^{P_Φ} such that
  - $A_4 \in Body_2$ or there is a rule $A_4 \leftarrow Body_4$ in P_Φ s.t. $Body_4 \subseteq Body_2$, and
  - $A_3 \in Body_1$ or there is a rule $A_3 \leftarrow Body_3$ in P_Φ s.t. $Body_3 \subseteq Body_1$. $\square$

Example 4. Consider the program (P, Φ):

$$a \oplus b \leftarrow; \quad c \leftarrow a; \quad d \leftarrow b;$$
$$a > b$$

The preference $a > b$ implies, other than $a \succeq b$, also the preference $c \succeq d$. $\square$

The above semantics extends the derivation of preferences among atoms as it considers, other than transitive closure, also the definition of prioritized atoms. In this way, a preference $A_i \succeq A_j$ is also "propagated" on atoms which depend on A_i and A_j. The semantics of an extended prioritized program $\langle P, \Phi \rangle$, will be given in terms of the standard prioritized program $\langle P \cup P_\Phi, \Phi_2 \rangle$.

Definition 8. *Given a (standard) prioritized program (P, Φ), the relation $\sqsupseteq$ is defined over the stable models of P as follows. For any stable models M_1 and M_2 and M_3 of P*

1. $M_1 \sqsupseteq M_1$,
2. $M_2 \sqsupseteq M_1$ if
   - $\forall$ pair $(e_2 \in M_2, e_1 \in M_1)$ either $\exists e_1' \in M_1$ s.t. $e_2 \succeq e_1'$ or $\exists e_2' \in M_2$ s.t. $e_2' \succeq e_1$,
   - there is no pair of atoms $(e_1'' \in M_1, e_2'' \in M_2)$ s.t. $e_1'' \succeq e_2''$;
3. if $M_2 \sqsupseteq M_1$ and $M_1 \sqsupseteq M_0$, then $M_2 \sqsupseteq M_0$. $\square$

If $M_2 \sqsupseteq M_1$ we say that M_2 is *preferable* to M_1. Moreover, we write $M_2 \sqsupset M_1$ if $M_2 \sqsupseteq M_1$ and $M_2 \neq M_1$. An interpretation M is a *preferred* stable model for a standard prioritized program (P, Φ) if M is a stable model of P and $N \sqsupseteq M$ implies $M \sqsupseteq N$ for any stable model N.

Definition 9. *Given an extended prioritized program $\langle P, \Phi \rangle$, an interpretation M for P is a preferred stable model if there is a preferred stable model N for $\langle P \cup P_\Phi, \Phi_2 \rangle$ such that $M = N^P$. The set of preferred stable models of $\langle P, \Phi \rangle$ will be denoted by $\mathcal{EPSM}(P, \Phi)$.* $\square$

Example 5. Consider the program $\langle P \cup P_\Phi, \Phi_2 \rangle$ of Example 4. From the preference rules we derive, other than $a_1 \succeq b_1$, $c_2 \succeq d_2$ and $d_3 \succeq c_3$, the further preferences $c_2 \succeq c_3$, $c_2 \succeq d_3$, $d_2 \succeq c_3$ and $d_2 \succeq d_3$, The stable models of $P \cup P_\Phi$ are $M_1 = \{a, c, a_1, c_2\}, M_2 = \{a, d, a_1, d_2\}, M_3 = \{b, c, b_1, c_3\}$ and $M_4 = \{b, d, b_1, d_3\}$.

The preferences among models are $M_1 \sqsupset M_2$ (as $a_1 \succeq a_1$ and $c_2 \succeq d_2$), $M_2 \sqsupset M_4$ (as $a_1 \succeq b_1$ and $d_2 \succeq d_3$) and $M_4 \sqsupset M_3$ (as $b_1 \succeq b_1$ and $d_3 \succeq c_3$). Therefore, the preferred model of $\langle P \cup P_\Phi, \Phi_2 \rangle$ is M_1 and, consequently, the preferred model of $\langle P, \Phi \rangle$ is $M_1^P = \{a, c\}$. $\square$

Example 6. Consider the following prioritized program:

fish $\oplus$ beef $\leftarrow$ white $>$ red $>$ beer $\leftarrow$ fish
red $\oplus$ white $\oplus$ beer $\leftarrow$ red $\vee$ beer $>$ white $\leftarrow$ beef
pie $\oplus$ ice-cream $\leftarrow$ pie $>$ ice-cream $\leftarrow$ beer
$\leftarrow$ beef, pie
$\leftarrow$ fish, ice-cream

The rewriting in standard form of the preference rules is as follows:

white$_1$ $\leftarrow$ white, fish   white$_1$ $>$ red$_1$ $>$ beer$_1$
red$_1$ $\leftarrow$ red, fish   red$_2$ $\vee$ beer$_2$ $>$ white$_2$
beer$_1$ $\leftarrow$ beerfish   pie$_3$ $>$ ice-cream$_3$
white$_2$ $\leftarrow$ white, beef
red$_2$ $\leftarrow$ red, beef
beer$_2$ $\leftarrow$ beer, beef
pie$_3$ $\leftarrow$ pie, beer
ice-cream$_3$ $\leftarrow$ ice-cream, beer

The above program has six stable models:

$M_1 = \{$fish, white, pie, white$_1\}$ $M_4 = \{$beef, white, ice-cream, white$_2\}$
$M_2 = \{$fish, red, pie, red$_1\}$ $M_5 = \{$beef, red, ice-cream, red$_2\}$
$M_3 = \{$fish, beer, pie, beer$_1$, pie$_3\}$ $M_6 = \{$beef, beer, ice-cream, beer$_2$, ice-cream$_3\}$

As $M_1 \sqsupset M_2$ (as white$_1 \succeq$ red$_1$), $M_2 \sqsupset M_3$ (as red$_1 \succeq$ beer$_1$), $M_5 \sqsupset M_4$ (as red$_2 \succeq$ white$_2$) and $M_6 \sqsupset M_4$ (as beer$_2 \succeq$ white$_2$), the preferred models are M_1, M_5 and M_6. Consequently, the preferred models of $\langle \mathcal{P}, \Phi \rangle$ are: $N_1 = M_1 - \{$red$_1\}$, $N_5 = M_5 - \{$white$_2\}$ and $N_6 = M_6 - \{$beer$_2$, ice-cream$_3\}$. $\square$

Observe that in the above example $M_3 \not\sqsupset M_6$ as neither beer$_1$ is comparable with any elements in M_6, nor beer$_2$ is comparable with any elements in M_3. We observe that the technique proposed by Sakama and Inoue gives also the preference $M_3 \sqsupset M_6$ which, from our point of view, is not intuitive. This is confirmed by the approach proposed by Brewka which states that $M_3 \not\sqsupset M_6$. Comparing more deeply the two models M_3 and M_6 we have that for the computation of M_3 after selected fish, we first select beer (which is the worst choice w.r.t. the first preference rule) and, then, we select pie (which is the best choice w.r.t. the third preference rule). In the computation of M_6, after selected beef, we first select beer (which is the best choice w.r.t. the second preference rule) and, then, we select ice-cream, which is the worst choice w.r.t. the third preference rule, but the only possible choice in the presence of beef. Therefore, it seems to us that the preference of M_3 with respect to M_6 is not intuitive. Moreover, the technique proposed by Brewka seems, in some case, not capturing the intuitive meaning of preferences.

Example 7. Consider, for instance, the program of Examples 4 and 5 with the constraint $\leftarrow$ a, c. The modified program has only three models: M_2, M_3 and M_4. Moreover, while our technique and the technique proposed by Sakama and Inoue state that only M_2 is a preferred model as $M_2 \sqsupset M_3$ and $M_2 \sqsupset M_4$, Brewka's technique states that also M_4 is a preferred model as $M_2 \not\sqsupset M_4$. $\square$

In our approach the fact that two priorities p_i and p_j depend, respectively, on two atoms a_i, a_j such that $a_i \succeq a_j$ means that $p_i \succeq p_j$. On the other side, the approach proposed by Brewka does not take into account dependencies among priorities.

4   Combining Preferences and Aggregates

In this section we study the combination of aggregates and preferences. A prioritized logic program with aggregates is a pair $(\tilde{\mathcal{P}}, \tilde{\Phi})$ where $\tilde{\mathcal{P}}$ is an extended disjunctive program with aggregates and $\tilde{\Phi}$ is a stratified prioritized program with aggregates. As said before, we assume that rules are aggregate stratified, that is, that there is no recursion through aggregates. The language obtained by adding aggregates to $P\text{-}DAT^{\vee,not}$ (resp. $P\text{-}DAT^{not}$) will be denoted by $P\text{-}DAT^{\vee,not,\mathcal{A}}$ (resp. $P\text{-}DAT^{not,\mathcal{A}}$). We start by considering two examples.

Example 8. **Min Coloring.** The following program $\mathcal{P}_8$ expresses the classical optimization problem computing a coloring for a graph G:

$$
\begin{aligned}
&\texttt{col(X, C)} \oplus \texttt{no\_col(X, C)} \leftarrow \texttt{node(X), color(C)} \\
&\texttt{col\_node(X)} \qquad\qquad \leftarrow \texttt{col(X, C)} \\
&\texttt{gn\_col(countd}\langle\texttt{X}\rangle) \qquad \leftarrow \texttt{col(X, C)}.
\end{aligned}
$$

The second and third rules above compute the colored nodes and the number of used colors. The constraints:

$$
\begin{aligned}
&\leftarrow \texttt{node(X), not col\_node(X)} \\
&\leftarrow \texttt{col(X, C}_1\texttt{), col(X, C}_2\texttt{), C}_1 \neq \texttt{C}_2 \\
&\leftarrow \texttt{edge(X, Y), col(X, C), col(Y, C)}
\end{aligned}
$$

state that i) every node must be colored, ii) a node cannot be colored with two different colors, and iii) two connected nodes cannot be colored with the same color. Every stable model of the program $\mathcal{P}_8$ defines a coloring of the graph. The prioritized rule: Φ_8: $\texttt{gn\_col(X)} > \texttt{gn\_col(Y)} \leftarrow \texttt{X} \leq \texttt{Y}$ gives preference to coloring using a minimum number of colors. Thus, $\langle \mathcal{P}_8, \Phi_8 \rangle$ computes stable models defining colorings using a minimal number of colors.   □

For disjunctive extended prioritized logic programs with aggregates the following results holds.

Theorem 1. *Let $(\mathcal{P}, \Phi)$ be a $P\text{-}DAT^{\vee,not,\mathcal{A}}$ program. Then*

1. *Deciding the existence of a preferred stable model is Σ_P^2-complete.*
2. *Deciding whether a literal is true in some preferable stable model of $(\mathcal{P}, \Phi)$ is Σ_P^3-complete.*
3. *Deciding whether a literal is true in every preferable stable model of $(\mathcal{P}, \Phi)$ is Π_P^3-complete.*   □

Thus, the above theorem shows that the computational complexity does not increase with the introduction of aggregates. This is also true when considering normal programs instead of disjunctive programs.

Corollary 1. *Let* $(\mathcal{P}, \Phi)$ *be a* $P\text{-}DAT^{not,\mathcal{A}}$ *program. Then i) Deciding whether a literal is true in some preferable stable model of* $(\mathcal{P}, \Phi)$ *is* Σ_P^2*-complete. ii) Deciding whether a literal is true in every preferable stable model of* $(\mathcal{P}, \Phi)$ *is* Π_P^2*-complete.* □

5   Conclusions

This paper extends prioritized logic programs in order to cope with preferences and aggregates and proposes a different semantics for logic programs with preference rules which seems to capture the intuitive meaning of programs where other semantics seem to fail. Complexity analysis is also performed showing that the use of a different semantics and the introduction of aggregates do not increase the complexity of computing preferred stable models.

References

1. Brewka, G., Eiter, T., Preferred Answer Sets for Extended Logic Programs. *Artificial Intelligence*, 109(1-2): 297–356, 1999.
2. Brewka, G., Logic programming with ordered disjunction. *AAAI/IAAI*,100-105, 2002.
3. Brewka, G., Niemela, I., Truszczynski, M., Answer Set Optimization. *IJCAI*, 2003.
4. Buccafurri, F., Faber, W., Leone, N., Disjunctive deductive databases with inheritance. *Int. Conf. on Logc Programming*, 79-93, 1999.
5. Brewka, G., Complex Preferences for Answer Set Optimization, *KR*, 213-223, 2004.
6. Delgrande, J., P., Schaub, T., Tompits, H., Logic Programs with Compiled Preferences. *ECAI* 464-468, 2000.
7. Delgrande, J., P., Schaub, T., Tompits, H., A Framework for Compiling Preferences in Logic Programs. *TPLP*   3(2): 129-187, 2003.
8. Eiter, T., Gottlob, G., Mannila, H., Disjunctive Datalog. *TODS*, 22(3):364–418, 1997.
9. Gelfond, M., Lifschitz, V. The Stable Model Semantics for Logic Programming, *Proc. of Fifth Conf. on Logic Programming*, 1070–1080, 1988.
10. Gelfond, M. Lifschitz, V., Classical Negation in Logic Programs and Disjunctive Databases, *New Generation Computing*, 9:365–385, 1991.
11. Gelfond, M. Son, T.C., Reasoning with prioritized defaults. *LPKR*, 164-223, 1997.
12. Govindarajan, K., Jayaraman, B., and Mantha, S., Preference Logic Programming. *ICLP*, 731-746, 1995.
13. Greco, S., Dynamic Programming in Datalog with Aggregates. *IEEE Trans. Knowl. Data Eng.*, 11(2): 265-283, 1999.
14. Greco, S., Saccà, D., Search and Optimization Problems in Datalog. *Computational Logic: Logic Programming and Beyond*, 61-82, 2002.
15. Papadimitriou, C. H., *Computational Complexity*. Addison-Wesley, 1994.
16. Przymusinski, T., Stable semantics for disjunctive programs, *NGC*9(3/4), 401-424, 1991.
17. Sakama, C., Inoue, K., Representing priorities in logic programs. *JICSLP*, 82-96, 1996.

18. Sakama, C., Inoue, K., Priorized logic programming and its application to commonsense reasoning. *Artificial Intelligence*, No. 123, 185-222, 2000.
19. Schaub, T., Wang , K., A Comparative Study of Logic Programs with Preference. *IJCAI*, 597-602, 2001.
20. Wakaki, T., Inoue, K., Sakama, C., Nitta, K., Computing Preferred Answer Sets in Answer Set Programming. *LPAR Conf.*, 259-273, 2003.
21. Wang, X, You, J. H., Yuan, L. Y., Nonmonotonic reasoning by monotonic inferences with priority conditions. *NMELP*, 91-109, 1996.
22. Wang, K., Zhou, L., Lin, F., Alternating Fixpoint Theory for Logic Programs with Priority. *Computational Logic*, 164-178, 2000.
23. Zhang, Y., Foo, N., Answer sets for prioritized logic programs. *ILPS*, 69-83, 1997.

The Chisholm Paradox and the Situation Calculus

Robert Demolombe[1] and Pilar Pozos-Parra[2]

[1] ONERA-Toulouse, 2 Avenue E. Belin BP 4025, 31055 Toulouse, France
Robert.Demolombe@cert.fr
[2] Department of Computing, Macquarie University, NSW 2109, Australia
pilar@ics.mq.edu.au

Abstract. Deontic logic is appropriate to model a wide variety of legal arguments, however this logic suffers from certain paradoxes of which the so-called Chisholm paradox is one of the most notorious. We propose a formalisation of the Chisholm set in the framework of the situation calculus. We utilise this alternative to modal logic for formalising the obligations of the agent and avoiding the Chisholm paradox. This new approach makes use of the notion of obligation fluents together with their associated successor state axioms. Furthermore, some results about automated reasoning in the situation calculus can be applied in order to consider a tractable implementation.

1 Introduction

Deontic logic, the logic of obligations and permissions, is appropriate to model a wide variety of legal arguments, however this logic suffers from certain paradoxes of which the so-called Chisholm paradox is one of the most notorious. The Chisholm paradox [1] comes from the formalisation of secondary obligations (they are also called "contrary-to-duties") which are obligations that come into force when primary obligations have been violated. Let us consider, for instance, the following practical example. A driver who drives on a motorway has the obligation to stay below the speed limit of 60 miles per hour. Then, if he goes above this limit he has the obligation to pay a penalty. Chisholm has proposed a set of sentences defining secondary obligations in natural language that are used to check whether a proposed formal logic can be applied to represent these sentences without leading to unexpected properties such as: inconsistency, redundancy, pragmatic oddity or others. The translation of these sentences from natural language to formal logics raises some difficult problems. Many logics have been proposed in the literature to solve the Chisholm paradox. A weakness of the approaches is their practical drawbacks. The purpose of this paper is to propose a simple representation of the Chisholm set in the framework of situation calculus which avoids unexpected properties and can be used for practical applications.

The situation calculus offers formalisms for reasoning about actions and their effects on the world [2], on agent's mental states [3], and on obligations [4].

M.-S. Hacid et al. (Eds.): ISMIS 2005, LNAI 3488, pp. 425–434, 2005.
© Springer-Verlag Berlin Heidelberg 2005

These approaches propose a solution to the corresponding "frame problem", namely the problem of specifying which properties of the world, beliefs, goals, intentions or obligations remain unchanged after the execution of an action. The technical advantage of situation calculus with respect to modal logic is that it allows quantifiers that range over actions. In [2] the properties of the world that undergo change are represented by *fluents*. To solve the frame problem the *successor state axioms* were introduced. The formalisms proposed in [3, 4] consider the introduction of suitable new fluents such as *belief, goal* and *intention fluents* (or *obligation fluents*) that represent the mental states (or ideal worlds). Their successor state axioms are introduced in order to solve the corresponding frame problem in the mental states (or in ideal worlds). Although the scope of beliefs, goals, intentions and obligations in the proposals is limited to accept only literals, the method utilized for automated reasoning about ordinary fluent change [5] can easily be extended to consider cognitive and social change. We employ this proposal to represent the Chisholm set. Due to the ability of situation calculus to have an explicit representation of each situation it has been possible to solve the Chisholm paradox.

The remainder of the paper is organised as follows. Section 2 briefly describes the situation calculus and its use in the representation of issues involving the evolution of the world and mental states. Section 3 presents the formalisation of obligations. In Section 4, we propose a representation of the Chisholm set that avoids inconsistency and redundancy. In Section 5, we consider an alternative representation in order to avoid the pragmatic oddity problem. We conclude with a discussion of some issues and future work.

2   Situation Calculus

2.1   Dynamic Worlds

The situation calculus involves three basic components: actions, situations and fluents. It is assumed that every change is caused by an action. Situations are sequences of actions which represent possible histories of the world. Fluents are world's properties (in general, relations) that may change. If s represents an arbitrary situation, and a an action, the result of performing a in s is a situation which is denoted by the term $do(a, s)$. The fluents are represented by predicates whose last argument is of type *situation*. For any fluent p and situation s, the expression $p(s)$ denotes the truth value of p in s. The evolution of a fluent p is represented by the successor state axiom of the form:[1]

$$(\mathbf{S_p})\quad p(do(a, s)) \leftrightarrow \Upsilon_p^+(a, s) \vee (p(s) \wedge \neg \Upsilon_p^-(a, s))$$

where $\Upsilon_p^+(a, s)$ represents the exact conditions under which p turns from false to true when a is performed in s, and similarly $\Upsilon_p^-(a, s)$ represents the precise

---

[1] In what follows, it is assumed that all the free variables are universally quantified.

conditions under which p turns from true to false when a is performed in s. It is assumed that no action can turn p to be both true and false in a situation, i.e.

$(\mathbf{C_{S_p}})$ $\neg \exists s \exists a (\Upsilon_p^+(a,s) \wedge \Upsilon_p^-(a,s))$

2.2   Dynamic Mental States

Mental states are represented by cognitive (belief, goal or intention) fluents which are syntactic combinations of modal operators and standard fluents or their negations. We say that the cognitive fluent $\mathcal{M}_i p$ holds in situation s iff the attitude of i about p is positive in situation s, and represent it as $\mathcal{M}_i p(s)$. Similarly $\mathcal{M}_i \neg p(s)$ represents the fact that the fluent $\mathcal{M}_i \neg p$ holds in situation s: the attitude of i about $\neg p$ is positive in the situation s.[2]

   In this case, the evolution of the mental state needs to be represented by two axioms. Each axiom allows the representation of two out of four attitudes of i concerning the fluent p, namely $\mathcal{M}_i p(s)$ and $\neg \mathcal{M}_i p(s)$, or $\mathcal{M}_i \neg p(s)$ and $\neg \mathcal{M}_i \neg p(s)$. The corresponding successor state axioms for an agent i and a fluent p are of the form:

- $\mathcal{M}_i p(do(a,s)) \leftrightarrow \Upsilon_{\mathcal{M}_i p}^+(a,s) \vee (\mathcal{M}_i p(s) \wedge \neg \Upsilon_{\mathcal{M}_i p}^-(a,s))$
- $\mathcal{M}_i \neg p(do(a,s)) \leftrightarrow \Upsilon_{\mathcal{M}_i \neg p}^+(a,s) \vee (\mathcal{M}_i \neg p(s) \wedge \neg \Upsilon_{\mathcal{M}_i \neg p}^-(a,s))$

where $\Upsilon_{\mathcal{M}_i p}^+(a,s)$ are the precise conditions under which the attitude of i (with regard to the fact that p holds) changes from one of negative to positive (for example in the case of beliefs, it turns from one of disbelief to belief) when a is performed in s, and similarly $\Upsilon_{\mathcal{M}_i p}^-(a,s)$ are the precise conditions under which the state of i changes from one of positive to negative. The conditions $\Upsilon_{\mathcal{M}_i \neg p}^+(a,s)$ and $\Upsilon_{\mathcal{M}_i \neg p}^-(a,s)$ have a similar interpretation (with regard to the fact that p does not hold). As in the successor state axioms, some constraints must be imposed to prevent the derivation of inconsistent mental states [3].

3   Deontic Modalities

In the last section we outlined the approach that allows designing of cognitive agents (an example of a planning application can be found in [3]). However, in the development of multiagent systems not only is the cognitive aspect crucial, but social issues such as norms also play an important role. For example, in a planning application, the agent must include in her plan only the "permitted" actions. Since deontic modalities (which deal with obligations, permissions and prohibitions) consider ideal behaviour, the integration of such modalities into a cognitive model makes it possible to draw the distinction between both real and mental entities as well as real and ideal behaviours.

---

[2] We abuse of notation $\mathcal{M}_i p$ and $\mathcal{M}_i \neg p$ in order to have an easy identification of the agent and proposition. An "adequate" notation should be $\mathcal{M}ip$ and $\mathcal{M}inotp$.

3.1   Dynamic Norms

As in the case of mental states, a deontic (obligation or prohibition) fluent is a syntactic combination of a modal operator and a standard fluent. We say that the *obligation fluent Op* holds in situation s iff the "law"[3] says that p must hold in the situation s and we represent it as $Op(s)$. Similarly $Fp(s)$ represents the fact that the *prohibition fluent Fp* holds in the situation s: the law says that p must not hold in the situation s. $O\neg p(s)$ (be obliged not) may be used to represent prohibition notion $Fp(s)$ (be forbidden). Furthermore, the relationship among obligation, permission and prohibition is considered in the *successor deontic state axioms*, specifically in the constraints that the Υ's must satisfy.

In this case, the four interpretations are: $Op(s)$, the law says that p must hold in situation s (p is obligatory); $\neg Op(s)$, the law says that it is not the case that p must hold in s (p is not obligatory); $Fp(s)$, the law says that p must not hold in s (p is forbidden); and $\neg Fp(s)$, the law says that p can hold in s (p is permitted). Deontic fluents, unlike cognitive fluents, do not require the agent's identification since they are considered universals, i.e. every agent must obey the law. However, the parameterisation of agents allows the introduction of rules applied only to a subset of the community. For example: the people who are older that 18 years have right to vote, $\forall s, x, y(agent\_age(x, y, s) \wedge y >= 18 \rightarrow \neg Fvote(x, s))$.

The successor deontic state axioms for a fluent p are of the form:

$(\mathbf{S_{Op}})\ Op(do(a, s)) \leftrightarrow \Upsilon^+_{Op}(a, s) \vee (Op(s) \wedge \neg \Upsilon^-_{Op}(a, s))$

$(\mathbf{S_{Fp}})\ Fp(do(a, s)) \leftrightarrow \Upsilon^+_{O\neg p}(a, s) \vee (Fp(s) \wedge \neg \Upsilon^-_{O\neg p}(a, s))$

where $\Upsilon^+_{Op}(a, s)$ are the precise conditions under which p turns from not obligatory to obligatory (to oblige) when a is performed in s. Similarly $\Upsilon^-_{Op}(a, s)$ are the precise conditions under which p turns from obligatory to not obligatory (to waive). $\Upsilon^+_{O\neg p}(a, s)$ are the precise conditions under which p turns from permitted to forbidden (to forbid) when a is performed in s. Finally $\Upsilon^-_{O\neg p}(a, s)$ are the precise conditions under which p turns from forbidden to permitted (to permit) when a is performed in s. Change in deontic fluents is usually defined in terms of actions of the type "to create" or "to abrogate" a law. A violation of the law causes the corresponding obligation comes into force. So the change in fluents defining the secondary obligations is defined in terms of violations of the law. Note the resemblance between the successor deontic state axioms and $(\mathbf{S_p})$. Hence for practical applications the method used for automated reasoning about the real world can be easily adapted to the deontic context.

A violated obligation is represented by $\neg p(s_1) \wedge Op(s_1)$: in s_1, p does not hold but in the same situation s_1, the law says that p must be. A violated prohibition is represented by $p(s_1) \wedge Fp(s_1)$: in s_1, p holds but in the same situation, the law says that p must not be.

---

[3] "Law" is the term utilised for denoting the normative entity.

3.2   Consistency Properties

As in successor state axioms, some constraints must be imposed to prevent the derivation of inconsistent norms.

To enforce consistent obligations, we need the following axiom:

- $\forall a \forall s \neg (\Upsilon_{Op}^{+}(a,s) \wedge \Upsilon_{Op}^{-}(a,s))$

To enforce consistent permissions (p cannot be permitted and forbidden at the same time), the following axiom is necessary:

- $\forall a \forall s \neg (\Upsilon_{O\neg p}^{+}(a,s) \wedge \Upsilon_{O\neg p}^{-}(a,s))$

To assure that p is not forbidden and obliged simultaneously, we need an axiom of the form:

- $\forall a \forall s \neg (\Upsilon_{Op}^{+}(a,s) \wedge \Upsilon_{O\neg p}^{+}(a,s))$

Note that we can, for instance, have $\neg Op(S_1) \wedge \neg Fp(S_1)$ that means: p is not obligatory nor forbidden in S_1. A similar formula in the epistemic context represents the ignorance (lack of knowledge) of the agent about p: $\neg Bp(S_1) \wedge \neg B\neg p(S_1)$. So such a formula represents the "passivity" (lack of interest) of the law about p.

4   Chisholm Paradox

Let's consider the Chisholm set that consists of four sentences of the following form:

1. p ought to be,
2. if p is, then q ought not to be,
3. if p is not, then q ought to be,
4. p is not.

The first sentence denotes a primary obligation: p should ideally be. The third one denotes a secondary (contrary-to-duty or CTD) obligation, i.e. an obligation about q comes into force when the obligation about p (the primary obligation) is violated. If the obligation about p is obeyed, the secondary obligation (or sanction) must not be effective (second sentence). The last sentence denotes the violation of the primary obligation. Let's consider the following example: let p be "to be a law-abiding citizen (non-delinquent)" and q "to be in prison". Intuitively we have: (1) the agent ought to be law-abiding, (2) if the agent is law-abiding, the agent ought not to be in prison, (3) if the agent is not law-abiding, the agent ought to be in prison, and (4) the agent is not law-abiding. The set of statements is intuitively consistent and none of four sentences seems to be redundant. The problem of finding a representation of the set which is consistent and non-redundant is called the problem of the Chisholm paradox.

If we try to formalise the Chisholm set in the framework of the Standard Deontic Logic (SDL), the reconciliation between consistence and redundancy does not take place. A usual way to represent the sentences in SDL is the following:

1'. $O(p)$,
2'. $O(p \rightarrow \neg q)$,
3'. $\neg p \rightarrow O(q)$,
4'. $\neg p$.

Using the properties of the system KD, which are satisfied by SDL, we can infer the following inconsistency: there is simultaneously an obligation to be in prison and a prohibition to be (obligation not to be) in prison. Furthermore, it is questionable that 2' and 3' are represented in a different form. However, if we replace, for instance, 3' by 3''. $O(\neg p \rightarrow q)$, we can deduce 3'' from 1' and the axiom $O(A) \rightarrow O(A \vee B)$. Similarly, if we replace 2' by 2''. $p \rightarrow O(\neg q)$, the sentence 2'' can be deduced from 4'. Both substitutions lead to redundancy in the set of sentences. In the SDL representation, contrary to intuition, everything is formalized in a static perspective. So the difference between the rules (first three sentences) that must be obeyed "all the time" and the facts (last sentence) that hold "sometimes" cannot be represented. Using deontic fluents, the sentences are represented as follows:[4]

C_1. $\forall s\ Op(s)$,
C_2. $\forall s\ (p(s) \rightarrow Fq(s))$,
C_3. $\forall s\ (\neg p(s) \rightarrow Oq(s))$,
C_4. $\neg p(S_1)$,

where S_1 denotes a situation in which p does not hold. In this context it denotes a situation in which the agent is not law-abiding. The definition of the evolution of deontic fluents and their initial settings must satisfy the constraints $C_1 - C_3$. Without loss of generality, we consider only one agent. To create the successor deontic state axioms, let's simplify the problem and consider solely static ideal worlds, i.e. the primary and CTD obligations are considered fixes in the sense that there is not an abrogation of the rules. However, we consider that the real world may change, and certainly the CTD obligation about q changes whenever p changes. The representation of deontic fluents evolution is of the form:

A_1. $Op(do(a, s)) \leftrightarrow \top$
A_2. $Fq(do(a, s)) \leftrightarrow \Upsilon_p^+(a, s) \vee (Fq(s) \wedge \neg \Upsilon_p^-(a, s))$
A_3. $Oq(do(a, s)) \leftrightarrow \Upsilon_p^-(a, s) \vee (Oq(s) \wedge \neg \Upsilon_p^+(a, s))$

where the successor state axiom of p is of the form ($\mathbf{S_p}$) (see Section 1). To define the initial situation we consider two cases:

(i) when $S_1 = S_0$, i.e. initially the primary obligation has been violated, so the initial settings must be of the form: $\neg p(S_0)$, $Op(S_0)$, $\neg Fq(S_0)$ and $Oq(S_0)$.
(ii) when initially the primary obligation is obeyed, the initial settings must be of the form: $p(S_0)$, $Op(S_0)$, $Fq(S_0)$ and $\neg Oq(S_0)$.

---

[4] Note the similarity of the first sentences with the *state constraints*. They also describe global properties that must hold in all situations. The difference is that the obligations take effect over the idealised world while the state constraints take effect over the real world.

Using the consistency property ($\mathbf{Cs_p}$) about p (see Section 2.1), we can prove deontic consistency, in particular we can prove $\neg \exists s\ (Oq(s) \wedge Fq(s))$, meaning the obligation and prohibition about q do not come into force simultaneously.

Following the example, suppose that the agent becomes a delinquent if she executes some of the following actions: *steal*, *kidnap*, *kill* or *rape*; and she becomes a non-delinquent after the end of her conviction (action *free*). So the successor state axiom of p is of the form:

$$p(do(a,s)) \leftrightarrow a = free \vee p(s) \wedge \neg(a = steal \vee a = kidnap \vee a = kill \vee a = rape)$$

Suppose that the agent is in prison if the police imprison her (action *imprison*) and she is not in prison after she is released (action *free*). So the successor state axiom of q is of the form:

$$q(do(a,s)) \leftrightarrow a = imprison \vee q(s) \wedge \neg(a = free)$$

We obtain the following successor deontic state axioms:

$$Op(do(a,s)) \leftrightarrow \top$$
$$Fq(do(a,s)) \leftrightarrow a = free \vee Fq(s) \wedge \neg(a = steal \vee a = kidnap \vee a = kill \vee a = rape)$$
$$Oq(do(a,s)) \leftrightarrow a = steal \vee a = kidnap \vee a = kill \vee a = rape \vee Oq(s) \wedge \neg(a = free)$$

In the following, the compact notation $do([a_1, a_2, \ldots, a_n], s)$ represents $do(a_n, \ldots, do(a_2, do(a_1, s)) \ldots)$ when $n > 0$ and s when $n = 0$. Now, suppose the following facts: initially the agent was law-abiding, $p(S_0)$. She bought a house, but it was so expensive that she had a loan from the bank. The rates were so high that she began to despair and stole from the bank. So the agent finally becomes a delinquent, $\neg p(do([buy, borrow, despair, steal], S_0))$. In S_0, the obligation has not been violated, so the initial settings are: the agent ought to be law-abiding and not be in prison $Op(S_0), \neg Oq(S_0)$; and it is forbidden to be in prison $Fq(S_0)$. From the successor deontic state axioms we can, for example, deduce $Op(do(buy, S_0)), \neg Oq(do[buy, borrow], S_0)), Fq(do([buy, borrow, despair], S_0))$, which mean: the agent ought to be law-abiding after buying her house, it is not obligatory that she be in prison after she has a loan from the bank, and it is not permitted to be in prison after feeling despair, respectively. What happens after she steals from the bank? In $S_1 = do([buy, borrow, despair, steal], S_0)$, we have: $\neg p(S_1), Op(S_1), Oq(S_1)$ and $\neg Fq(S_1)$, i.e. the agent becomes a delinquent, she ought to be law-abiding, she ought to be in prison and it is not forbidden to be in prison, respectively.

5   Pragmatic Oddity

Note that under the proposed representation $A_1 - A_3, C_4$, we can deduce $Op(S_1)$ and $Oq(S_1)$. In S_1, the agent must be law-abiding and must be in prison, i.e. in the ideal world, in S_1, the agent is law-abiding and is in prison! This kind of problem has been called "pragmatic oddity". To solve the problem, we will distinguish the primary and CTD obligations, just as Carmo and Jones proposed in [6]. Thus, the timeless obligations, such as the primary obligations, are called *ideal obligations* (the set of all ideal obligations defines the ideal world) and the circumstance dependent obligations, such as CTD obligations, are called *situation dependent obligations* (the set of all situation dependent obligations about s defines the obligations in s).[5] So if $p(s)$ is a fluent, the ideal obligation about p is represented by the deontic predicate symbols Op which means that, in the ideal world, p must hold forever. The situation dependent obligation about p is represented by the deontic fluent $Op(s)$, meaning p must hold in the situation s. Clearly, the simultaneous introduction of an ideal and situation dependent obligation about p, is not allowed. Note that only the situation dependent obligations need to be revised. Therefore, the proposed representation of the Chisholm set suffers a small modification in order to avoid the pragmatic oddity problem. The successor deontic state axiom A_1, as well as the initial setting about p, are replaced by the situation independent predicate Op. The representation of first sentence is of the form:

A_1'. Op

So the set A_1', A_2, A_3 and C_4 can be utilised for representing the Chisholm set, which reconcile consistency and non-redundancy. Moreover, it avoids the pragmatic oddity problem. For instance, $Op \wedge Oq(S_1)$ is interpreted as: the agent must ideally be law-abiding but in S_1 she is obliged to be in prison.

The representation satisfies all requirements, proposed by Carmo and Jones in [7], that an adequate formalisation of the Chisholm set should meet, i.e.

a. consistency,
b. logical independence of the members,
c. applicability to timeless and actionless CTD-examples,
d. analogous logical structures for the two conditional sentences (2) and (3),
e. capacity to derive actual obligations (in our case situation dependent obligations),
f. capacity to derive ideal obligations,
g. capacity to represent the fact that a violation of an obligation has occurred,
f. capacity to avoid pragmatic oddity.

The approach proposed in [6] also seems to consider these requirements. However, the pragmatic oddity problem reappears if we add a second level of CTD obligations, such as:

5. if p is not and q is not, then r ought to be,
6. q is not,

which is represented by the following constraints:

C_5. $\forall s\ (\neg p(s) \wedge \neg q(s) \rightarrow Or(s))$,
C_6. $\neg q(S_1)$.

---

[5] In order to avoid the belief that the obligations are only concerned with the actual situation, the term *actual obligations* is not used to indicate the second type of obligations, as Carmo and Jones proposed.

We propose the following representation of the evolution of Or:

$A_5.$ $Or(do(a,s)) \leftrightarrow (\Upsilon_p^-(a,s) \wedge \Upsilon_q^-(a,s)) \vee (\Upsilon_p^-(a,s) \wedge \neg q(s) \wedge \neg \Upsilon_q^+(a,s)) \vee$
$(\Upsilon_q^-(a,s) \wedge \neg p(s) \wedge \neg \Upsilon_p^+(a,s)) \vee (Or(s) \wedge \neg(\Upsilon_p^+(a,s) \vee \Upsilon_q^+(a,s)))$

Following the example, we have (5) if the agent is a delinquent and she is not in prison, then there must be a warning sign: "delinquent on the loose", and (6) the agent is not in prison. The successor deontic state axiom of Or, after reducing some terms using the set of unique name axioms for actions [5], is of the form:

$Or(do(a,s)) \leftrightarrow (a = steal \vee a = kidnap \vee a = kill \vee a = rape) \wedge \neg q(s) \vee Or(s) \wedge$
$\neg(a = free \vee a = imprison)$

Note that we can deduce $Oq(S_1) \wedge Or(S_1)$, which means that in S_1, it is obligatory that the agent is in prison and that a warning sign is displayed.

In order to represent the CTD obligations, we make some assumptions. For example, the axiom A_3 assumes that p is the only cause that modifies the obligation about q, so the representation not only has an implication but rather an equivalence to satisfy, i.e. the constraint C_3'. $\forall s\ (\neg p(s) \leftrightarrow Oq(s))$ must be considered. In particular $\neg p(do(a,s)) \leftrightarrow Oq(do(a,s))$ must be satisfied for all a and s. Substituting $p(do(a,s))$ for the right hand side of its corresponding successor state axiom, we have $\neg(\Upsilon_p^+(a,s) \vee (p(s) \wedge \neg \Upsilon_p^-(a,s))) \leftrightarrow Oq(do(a,s))$. However, $\neg(\Upsilon_p^+(a,s) \vee (p(s) \wedge \neg \Upsilon_p^-(a,s))) \leftrightarrow \Upsilon_p^-(a,s) \vee (\neg p(s) \wedge \neg \Upsilon_p^+(a,s))$. Thus we have $(\Upsilon_p^-(a,s) \vee (\neg p(s) \wedge \neg \Upsilon_p^+(a,s))) \leftrightarrow Oq(do(a,s))$. Finally, replacing $\neg p(s)$ by its equivalent formula $Oq(s)$, we obtain the axiom A_3. An analogous method can be used to find the representation of the evolution of Fq.

When the conditions that modify the obligation depend not only on a fluent, as in C_5, the constraint representing the CTD obligation is also considered as an equivalence. Implicitly we make the casual completeness assumption [5]. So we consider the case that p and q are all of the causes that can modify Or, i.e. the constraint C_5'. $\forall s(\neg p(s) \wedge \neg q(s) \leftrightarrow Or(s))$ must be satisfied. This assumption seems too strong, however its intuitive interpretation corresponds with desired facts. For example, the warning sign "delinquent on the loose" must exist if and only if there is a delinquent and she is not in prison. Concerning Or, in particular we have $\neg p(do(a,s)) \wedge \neg q(do(a,s)) \leftrightarrow Or(do(a,s))$ for all a and s. Substituting $p(do(a,s))$ and $q(do(a,s))$ for the right hand side of their corresponding successor state axioms, we have $\neg(\Upsilon_p^+(a,s) \vee (p(s) \wedge \neg \Upsilon_p^-(a,s))) \wedge \neg(\Upsilon_q^+(a,s) \vee (q(s) \wedge \neg \Upsilon_q^-(a,s))) \leftrightarrow Or(do(a,s))$ which can be reduced to A_5.

Intuitively the CTD obligations take effect when a primary obligation is violated. Thus Oq comes into force when Op is violated: $Op \wedge \neg p(S_1)$. Also Or comes into force when Oq is violated: $Oq(S_1) \wedge \neg q(S_1)$, recall that $Oq(s) \leftrightarrow \neg p(s)$. In general, the first violation must be done on an ideal obligation. So when the agent abandons the ideal world she is obliged to "pay" the consequences of her behaviour, the "price" (sanction) is allocated by a situation dependent obligation, if she does not pay a second situation dependent obligation can increase the "debt", and so on.

6   Conclusion

We have proposed a representation of the Chisholm set, in the framework of the situation calculus, that avoids the paradox and other intrinsic problems such as pragmatic oddity. In order to close the gap between the theoretical and realistic implementation of rational agent design, we have avoided the use of modal logic for formalising deontic notions and have explored this alternative.

An important advantage of this proposal is that the regression mechanism that deals with fluents [5] can be extended in order to obtain a tractable automated deontic reasoning implementation.

A disadvantage, which accrues from the representations used in Prakken and Sergot's approach [8], is the context-dependence of logical form. It is unclear how multiple levels of CTD can be handled by the approach. Unlike Prakken and Sergot's approach the proposal supplies a uniform representation of deontic conditionals.

We suppose that the conditions changing the truth value of p, $\Upsilon_p^+(a, s)$ and $\Upsilon_p^-(a, s)$ do not depend (directly or indirectly) on the deontic fluent Oq. In general, we suppose that the fluents are not affected by the deontic fluents. In other words, the real world is not affected by the ideals defined by the law. However, it is clear that mental states are influenced by ideals. Thus, one possible extension is the inclusion of obligations in a cognitive model based on the situation calculus such as in [3]. This may assist in the determination of an agent's behaviour, in particular, in the determination of her intentions or in the adoption of goals. Also, an analysis of the philosophical issues will be carried out in our future investigations.

References

1. Chisholm, R.: Contrary-to-duty imperatives and deontic logic. Analysis **24** (1963) 33–36
2. Reiter, R.: The frame problem in the situation calculus: a simple solution (sometimes) and a completeness result for goal regression. In Lifschitz, V., ed.: Artificial Intelligence and Mathematical Theory of Computation: Papers in Honor of John McCarthy, Academic Press (1991) 359–380
3. Pozos Parra, P., Nayak, A., Demolombe, R.: Theories of Intentions in the framework of Situation Calculus. In: Proc. of the Workshop on Declarative Agent Languages and Technologies at AAMAS, New York, USA (2004)
4. Demolombe, R., Herzig, A.: Obligation change in dependence logic and situation calculus. In: Workshop on Deontic Logic and Computer Science. (2004)
5. Reiter, R.: Knowledge in Action: Logical Foundations for Specifying and Implementing Dynamical Systems. The MIT Press (2001)
6. Carmo, J., Jones, A.: Deontic logic and different levels of ideality. RRDMIST **1/95** (1995)
7. Carmo, J., Jones, A.: Deontic logic and contrary-to-duties. In: Handbook of Philosophical Logic. Volume 8., Kluwer (2001)
8. Prakken, H., Sergot, M.: Contrary-to-duty obligations. Studia Logica **57** (1996) 91–115

A Logic Approach for LTL System Modification

Yulin Ding and Yan Zhang

School of Computing & Information Technology,
University of Western Sydney,
Kingswood, N.S.W. 1797, Australia
{yding, yan}@cit.uws.edu.au

Abstract. Model checking has been successfully applied to system verification. However, there are no standard and universal tools to date being applied for system modification. This paper introduces a formal approach called the Linear Temporal Logic (LTL) model update for system modification. In contrast to previous error repairing methods, which were usually simple program debugging and specialized technical methods, our LTL model update modifies the existing LTL model of an abstracted system to correct automatically the errors occurring within this model. We introduce three single operations to represent, update, and simplify the updating problem. The minimal change rules are then defined based on such update operations. We show how our approach can eventually be applied in system modifications by illustrating an example of program corrections and characterizing some frequently used properties in the LTL Kripke model.

Keywords: Logic for Artificial Intelligence, belief revision and update, temporal reasoning, model update, model checking.

1 Introduction

Model checking is rather mature in both theoretical and practical research. Currently, model checkers with SMV or Promela [7] series as their specification languages are widely available for research, experiment, and partial industry purposes. Nowadays SMV [3], NuSMV, Cadence SMV [9] and SPIN [7] have been well accepted as the state of the art model checkers. In most model checkers, counterexamples are the major mechanisms to report errors. However, in Cadence SMV, the counterexample-free concept is introduced [9].

Model checking is a tool to report errors of a designed system. The next step is to repair the errors. In 1998, Stumptner and Wotawa presented an overview of Artificial Intelligence approaches to the development of intelligent debugging systems in [10]. However, most of the previous methods concerning system repair were localized or detailed methods oriented. Recently, error diagnosis and repair are starting to employ a formal methods approach. Buccafurri et. al. [2] applied Artificial Intelligence techniques to model checking and error repairing. They used abductive model revision techniques, repairing errors in concurrent programs. It is a new approach towards automated diagnosis and integrated repair

M.-S. Hacid et al. (Eds.): ISMIS 2005, LNAI 3488, pp. 435–444, 2005.
© Springer-Verlag Berlin Heidelberg 2005

on model checking. It aims at using techniques and concepts from model checking by combining them with AI principles. Harris and Ryan [5] recently proposed another attempt of system modification, which designed update operations to tackle feature integration performing theory change and belief revision.

The update of the knowledge base has been extensively researched. Winslett [12] was a pioneer of the update of the knowledge base and used series update and minimal change methods for databases. Hezig and Rifi [6] conducted extensive surveys about updates of the knowledge base and their development before 1999. They listed ten update operations, based on propositional logic and further characteristics. Recently, the update of the knowledge base is enhanced by the modality update by Baral and Zhang [1]. They discussed knowledge update and its minimal change, based on modal logic $S5$. Both the update of the knowledge base and the knowledge update are at the stage of theoretical research.

We intend to apply knowledge update to practice and develop a universal method to repair errors automatically as the main contribution of our research. In particular, we propose a general method of the Linear Temporal Logic (LTL) model update, by integrating the ideas of knowledge update and model checking in this paper.

This paper is organized as follows: Section 2 reviews LTL syntax and semantics, with the state of the art LTL model checking. Section 3 introduces two major definitions for model update. Section 4 introduces the minimal change principles of model update. Section 5 characterizes two important properties in the LTL model for its update. Finally, the paper concludes with Section 6.

2   LTL Kripke Model Checking

2.1   Knowledge About LTL

Definition 1. *[3] Let AP be a set of atomic propositions. A Kripke model M over AP is a four tuple $M = (S, S_0, R, L)$ where*

1. *S is a finite set of states.*
2. *$S_0 \subseteq S$ is the set of initial states.*
3. *$R \subseteq S \times S$ is a transition relation.*
4. *$L : S \rightarrow 2^{AP}$ is a function that assigns each state with a set of atomic propositions.*

Definition 2. *[8] Linear-time temporal logic (LTL) has the following syntax given in Backus naur form:*

$$\phi ::= p|(\neg\phi)|(\phi \wedge \phi)|(\phi \cup \phi)|(G\phi)|(F\phi)|(X\phi)$$

where p is any propositional atom.

An LTL formula is evaluated on a path, a sequence of states, or a set of paths. Consider the path $\pi \overset{def}{=} [s_0, s_1, s_2, \cdots]$; we write π^i for the suffix starting at s_i, i.e. π^i is $[s_i, s_{i+1}, \cdots]$, and $\pi^{[i]}$ for the prefix ending at s_i, i.e. $\pi^{[i]} = [s_0, \cdots, s_{i-1}, s_i]$. We write $(s_i, s_{i+1}) \subseteq \pi$ and $s_i \in \pi$, if $\pi = [s_0, \cdots, s_i, s_{i+1}, \cdots]$.

Definition 3. *[8] Let $M = (S, S_0, R, L)$ be a Kripke model. Then a path of M is $\pi = [s_0, s_1, s_2, \cdots]$, where for all $i = 0, 1, \cdots$, we have $s_0 \in S_0$, and $(s_i, s_{i+1}) \in R$. We define when π satisfies an LTL formula via the satisfaction relation $\models$ for LTL formulas as follows:*

1. *$\pi \models \top$.*
2. *$\pi \models p$ iff $p \in L(s_0)$.*
3. *$\pi \models \neg\phi$ iff $\pi \not\models \phi$.*
4. *$\pi \models \phi_1 \wedge \phi_2$ iff $\pi \models \phi_1$ and $\pi \models \phi_2$.*
5. *$\pi \models X\phi$ iff $\pi^1 \models \phi$.*
6. *$\pi \models G\phi$ holds iff, for all $i \geq 0$, $\pi^i \models \phi$.*
7. *$\pi \models F\phi$ holds iff, for some $i \geq 0$, $\pi^i \models \phi$.*
8. *$\pi \models \phi \cup \psi$ holds iff there is some $i \geq 0$ such that $\pi^i \models \psi$ and for all $j = 1, ..., i - 1$ we have $\pi^j \models \phi$.*

We say M satisfies ϕ, denoted as $M \models \phi$, if for each path π of M, starting from an initial state, $\pi \models \phi$.

Although the syntax of LTL is thought of as only one path at a time, the semantic viewpoint of LTL is that all paths are considered [8]. In this paper, all the update operations are executed one path at a time, from the syntax viewpoint of LTL. The update and the minimal change methods only apply to finite paths. The LTL representations of software systems in examples within this paper are done by identical methods as the first software system represented in CTL in [11]. That is, one state represents one changed value of the variable in the running process of a software system.

2.2 LTL Model Checking: An Overview

In the context of model checking, a designed system is represented by the CTL or LTL Kripke structure M. Then M should satisfy a certain property ϕ. The function of a model checker is to check whether M really satisfies ϕ. If it does not, the counterexamples [3] report the errors. The describing languages to perform the model checking are, for example, SMV for LTL and CTL, and Promela for LTL.

Parallel to CTL model checking, LTL model checking is extensively studied. One of the main streams is to perform LTL model checking through SMV. In the early stages, Clarke et al. in [3] translated LTL to CTL model checking with fairness constraints, adding a translator into SMV. In recent years, new model checkers such as NuSMV, Cadence SMV and MCK [4] use similar functions of Clarke's LTL-to-CTL translation. Another main stream for LTL model checking is to translate LTL into automata, such as the current popular LTL model checker SPIN. For SPIN, Promela is its specification language in contrast to SMV. SPIN supports the design and verification of asynchronous process software systems. It performs on-the-fly model checking. We have investigated that LTL model checking is well developed for research purposes and perceived as a potential industrial technique. However, model update based on LTL systems has not been explored by researchers yet. We address in the following sections detailed ideas and methods for LTL model updating.

3   The LTL Kripke Model Update: Formal Definitions

Model update is a new concept for system verification and modification. If a designed system M does not satisfy a property ϕ after model checking(See Fig. 1.), the model updater automatically corrects errors in M, updating M to the new model M'. Thus, $M' \models \phi$. Model update is implemented by the model updater. Now we define three update operations for LTL model update on the basis of state of an LTL Kripke model, which is a Kripke model with syntax in Defintion 2 and semantics in Definition 3.

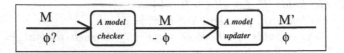

Fig. 1. The relationship of a model checker and a model updater

Definition 4. (Simple Modification). *Given an LTL Kripke structure, $M = (S, S_0, R, L)$ over AP, where $S_0 \subseteq S$. A simple modification on M is defined as one of the following three single operations:* [1]

-**State Addition:** $add(M, s_{new}, s_k, s_{k+1}) = M' = (S', S_0', R', L')$ *over AP, where*

$S' = S \cup \{s_{new}\};$

$S'_0 = \begin{cases} S_0 \cup \{s_{new}\} - \{s_{k+1}\}, & \text{if } s_{k+1} \in S_0 \text{ and } s_{new} \in S_0'; \\ S_0, & \text{otherwise}; \end{cases}$

$R' = \begin{cases} R \cup \{(s_{new}, s_{k+1})\}, & \text{if } s_{k+1} \in S_0; \\ R \cup \{(s_k, s_{new})\}, & \text{if } (s_k, s_{k+1}) \notin R; \\ R \cup \{(s_k, s_{new}), (s_{new}, s_{k+1})\} - \{(s_k, s_{k+1})\}, & \text{otherwise}; \end{cases}$

$L' : S' \to 2^{AP}$, *where $\forall s \in S'$, if $s \in S$, then $L'(s) = L(s)$, else $L'(s_{new}) = \tau(s_{new})$, where τ is the truth assignment related to s_{new}.*

-**State Deletion:** $delete(M, s_k) = M' = (S', S_0', R', L')$ *over AP, where*

$S' = S - \{s_k\};$

$S'_0 = \begin{cases} S_0 - \{s_k\}, & \text{if } s_k \in S_0; \\ S_0, & \text{otherwise}; \end{cases}$

$R' = \begin{cases} R - \{(s_k, s_{k+1})\}, & \text{if } s_k \in S_0 \text{ and } (s_k, s_{k+1}) \in R; \\ R - \{(s_{k-1}, s_k)\}, & \text{if } (s_k, s_{k+1}) \notin R \text{ and } (s_{k-1}, s_k) \in R; \\ (R - \{(s_{k-1}, s_k), (s_k, s_{k+1})\}) \cup \{(s_{k-1}, s_{k+1})\}, & \text{otherwise}; \end{cases}$

---

[1] In the following statement, s_{k-1}, s_k and s_{k+1} are refered to the $k-1$-th, k-th and $k+1$-th states of a path in M. If s_k is the first state of a path, S_{k-1} is assumed not to exist on this path. If s_k is the last state of a path, s_{k+1} is assumed not to exist on this path.

$L' : S' \rightarrow 2^{AP}$, where $\forall s \in S'$, if $s \in S$, then $L'(s) = L(s)$, else
$L'(s_{new}) = \tau(s_{new})$, where τ is the truth assignment related to s_{new}.

-State Substitution: $sub(M, s_{new}, s_k) = M' = (S', S'_0, R', L')$ over AP, where

$$S' = (S - \{s_k\}) \cup \{s_{new}\};$$

$$S'_0 = \begin{cases} (S_0 - \{s_k\}) \cup s_{new}, & \text{if } s_k \in S_0; \\ S_0, & \text{otherwise;} \end{cases}$$

$$R' = \begin{cases} (R - \{(s_k, s_{k+1})\}) \cup \{(s_{new}, s_{k+1})\}, & \text{if } s_k \in S_0 \text{ and } (s_k, s_{k+1}) \in R; \\ (R - [(o_{k-1}, s_k)]) \cup \{(s_{k-1}, s_{new})\}, & \text{if } (s_k, s_{k+1}) \notin R \text{ and } (s_{k-1}, s_k) \in R; \\ R - \{(s_{k-1}, s_k), (s_k, s_{k+1})\} \cup \{(s_{k-1}, s_{new}), (s_{new}, s_{k+1})\}, & \text{otherwise;} \end{cases}$$

$L' : S' \rightarrow 2^{AP}$, where $\forall s \in S'$, if $s \in S$, then $L'(s) = L(s)$, else
$L'(s_{new}) = \tau(s_{new})$, where τ is the truth assignment related to s_{new}.

A simple modification δ denotes one of the above three single operations. $\delta(M)$ denotes the resulting LTL Kripke model after the simple modification δ is applied on M. For Definition 4, we illustrate "State addition" and "State deletion" operations in detail. "State substitution" is actually the combination of the former two operations and for brevity its illustration is omitted.

In Fig. 2, the original LTL model is $M = (S, S_0, R, L)$, where $S = \{s_0, s_1, s_2, s_3\}$, $S_0 = \{s_0\}$, $R = \{(s_0, s_1), (s_1, s_2), (s_2, s_3)\}$ and L assigns all states s_0, s_1, s_2 and s_3 in M with $\{a\}$, $\{b\}$, $\{c\}$, and $\{d\}$ respectively. We suppose that there are three different simple modifications under the addition operation $add(M, s_{new}, s_k, s_{k+1})$ as (A),(B) and (C) in this figure.

In (A), $s_k = s_1$ and $s_{k+1} = s_2$; the modified LTL model is $M' = (S', S'_0, R', S')$, where $S' = \{s_0, s_1, s_2, s_3, s_{new}\}$, $S'_0 = \{s_0\}$, $R' = \{(s_0, s_1), (s_1, s_{new}), (s_{new}, s_2), (s_2, s_3)\}$ and L' assigns all states s_0, s_1, s_2, s_3 and s_{new} in M' with $\{a\}$, $\{b\}$, $\{c\}$, $\{d\}$ and $\{new\}$ respectively.

In (B), $s_k = \emptyset$ and $s_{k+1} = s_0$; the modified LTL model is $M' = (S', S'_0, R', S')$, where $S' = \{s_0, s_1, s_2, s_3, s_{new}\}$, $S'_0 = \{s_{new}\}$, $R' = \{(s_{new}, s_0), (s_0, s_1), (s_1, s_2), (s_2, s_3)\}$ and L' assigns all states s_0, s_1, s_2, s_3 and s_{new} in M' with $\{a\}$, $\{b\}$, $\{c\}$, $\{d\}$ and $\{new\}$ respectively.

In (C), $s_k = s_3$ and $s_{k+1} = \emptyset$; the modified LTL model is $M' = (S', S'_0, R', S')$, where $S' = \{s_0, s_1, s_2, s_3, s_{new}\}$, $S'_0 = \{s_0\}$, $R' = \{(s_0, s_1), (s_1, s_2), (s_2, s_3), (s_3, s_{new})\}$ and L' assigns all states s_0, s_1, s_2, s_3 and s_{new} in M' with $\{a\}$, $\{b\}$, $\{c\}$, $\{d\}$ and $\{new\}$ respectively.

In Fig. 3, the deletion operation $delete(M, s_k)$ works on the same LTL model as above. (A), (B) and (C) in this figure are three different simple modifications from the deletion operation with $s_k = s_2$, $s_k = s_0$, and $s_k = s_3$ respectively.

The modified LTL model in (A) is $M' = (S', S'_0, R', S')$, where $S' = \{s_0, s_1, s_3\}$, $S'_0 = \{s_0\}$, $R' = \{(s_0, s_1), (s_1, s_3)\}$ and L' assigns all states s_0, s_1, s_3 of M' with $\{a\}$, $\{b\}$ and $\{d\}$ respectively.

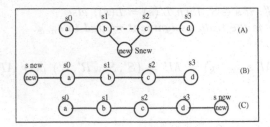

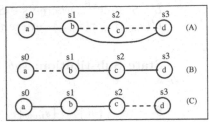

Fig. 2. The illustration of the addition operation

Fig. 3. The illustration of the deletion operation

The modified LTL model in (B) is $M' = (S', S'_0, R', S')$, where $S' = \{s_1, s_2, s_3\}$, $S'_0 = \{s_1\}$, $R' = \{(s_1, s_2), (s_2, s_3)\}$ and L' assigns all states s_1, s_2, and s_3 of M' with $\{b\}$, $\{c\}$, $\{d\}$ respectively.

The modified LTL model in (C) is $M' = (S', S'_0, R', S')$, where $S' = \{s_0, s_1, s_2\}$, $S'_0 = \{s_0\}$, $R' = \{(s_0, s_1), (s_1, s_2)\}$ and L' assigns all states s_0, s_1 and s_2 of M' with $\{a\}, \{b\}$, and $\{c\}$ respectively.

Definition 5. *(Update) Given an LTL Kripke model M and an LTL formula ϕ. An update of M with ϕ, denoted as $Update(M, \phi)$, is a new LTL Kripke model M', such that*

1. there exists a sequence of simple modifications $(\delta_0, \delta_1, \delta_2, \cdots, \delta_n)$ for $(M_0, M_1, M_2, \cdots, M_{n-1}, M_n)$ respectively, where $M_0 = M$. The simple modifications are $\delta_0(M_0) = M_1$, $\delta_1(M_1) = M_2$, $\cdots$, $\delta_i(M_i) = M_{i+1}, \cdots$, and $\delta_n(M_n) = M'$ respectively, where $0 \le i \le n$. M' is the result of the $(n+1)^{th}$ simple modification;

2. $M' \models \phi$.

In Definition 5, the update $Update(M, \phi)$ will result in a new LTL model M', which satisfies ϕ. The method of update is to apply any one of the three single operations in Definition 4 $n+1$ times, until $M' \models \phi$. The process is viewed as the sequence: $M_0 \xrightarrow{\delta_0} M_1 \xrightarrow{\delta_1} M_2, \cdots, M_n \xrightarrow{\delta_n} M_{n+1}$, where we suppose the first simple modification δ_0 by using a single operation, the second one δ_1, and so on, the last one δ_n. Consequently, the first simple modification works on M, denoted as $\delta_0(M) = M_1$; the second one δ_1 works on M_1, denoted as $\delta_1(M_1) = M_2$ and so on; the last one δ_n works on M_n, denoted as $\delta_n(M_n) = M'$, which satisfies ϕ. In other words, $Update(M, \phi)$ consists of the sequence of simple modifications $\delta_0, \delta_1, \cdots, \delta_n$, and gives a final result M'.

4   The Principles of Minimal Change

In order to eliminate possible undesirable update results from the modifications in the previous section, we need to provide justified semantic criterion on LTL model updating. Basically, we prefer to select only those new models that have the least change compared with the original models. In belief revision and update research, various minimal change principles have been developed based on classical propositional logic such as described in [12]. It has been observed that these principles are usually not directly applicable for updating on modal logic based systems such as those described in [1], which works on the $S5$ modal logic Kripke model. In this section, we propose a new minimal change definition for the LTL Kripke model update, based on both logic structure comparison and state differences of LTL Kripke models.

Given a set X, $|X|$ denotes the cardinality of X. Given an integer, N, which could be either positive or negative. $||N||$ denotes its absolute value. e.g., $||-3|| = ||3|| = 3$. Given any two sets X and Y, the *symmetric difference* between X and Y is denoted as $Diff(X,Y) = (X - Y) \cup (Y - X)$.

Definition 6. *(Ordering on Relations)*
Given three LTL models $M = (S, S_0, R, L)$, $M_1 = (S_1, S_{1_0}, R_1, L_1)$ and $M_2 = (S_2, S_{2_0}, R_2, L_2)$, we say relation R_1 in M_1 is as close to relation R in M as relation R_2 in M_2, denoted as $R_1 \leq_R R_2$, if

1. $\forall (s_i, s_{i+1}) \in (R - R_1)$, $(s_i, s_{i+1}) \in (R - R_2)$, and
2. $||(|R| - |R_1|)|| \leq ||(|R| - |R_2|)||$.

Furthermore, $R_1 =_R R_2$ iff $R_1 \leq_R R_2$ and $R_2 \leq_R R_1$; $R_1 <_R R_2$ if $R_1 \leq_R R_2$ and $R_1 \neq_R R_2$.

In Definition 6, condition 1 means that any element of R that is not retained in R_1 is also not retained in R_2; condition 2 indicates that the different number of elements between R and R_1 is less than or at most the same as those between R and R_2.

To illustrate how this definition works, let us consider Figure 4. It is easy to see that $R - R_1 = \{(s_2, s_3), (s_3, s_4)\}$ and $R - R_2 = \{(S_1, S_2)), (S_2, S_3), (S_3, S_4)\}$. Thus $R - R_1 \subset R - R_2$, and condition 1 in Definition 6 is satisfied. Also we have $||(|R| - |R_1|)|| = ||4 - 3|| = 1$, and $||(|R| - |R_2|)|| = ||4 - 2|| = 2$. That is $||(|R| - |R_1|)|| < ||(|R| - |R_2|)||$, so condition 2 is also satisfied. Therefore, we have $R_1 \leq_R R_2$. In other words, in terms of relations, model M_1 is closer to M than model M_2.

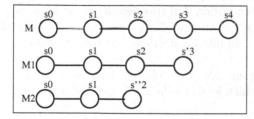

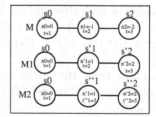

Fig. 4. The illustration of Definition 6

Fig. 5. Illustrate minimal changed update for example 1 and Definition 7

Definition 7. *(Ordering on Models)* *Giving M, M_1, and M_2, we say M_1 is as close to M as M_2, which is denoted as $M_1 \leq_M M_2$, if the following conditions hold:*

Boolean *positive*;
int $t = 1$, $n = 0$;
for(;n! = -2, t! = 3;n - -,t + +)
{if($n \geq 0$) *positive* := 1;
else *positive* := 0;}

Boolean *positive*;
int $t = 1$, $n = 0$;
for(;n! = 2, t! = 3;n + +,t + +)
{if($n \geq 0$) *positive* := 1;
else *positive* := 0;}

Fig. 6. The original code for example 1   **Fig. 7.** The updated code for example 1

1. $R_1 <_R R_2$, or
2. if $R_1 =_R R_2$, then, for $\forall (s_i, s_{i+1}) \in R$, $\exists (s'_i, s'_{i+1}) \in R_1$, such that, $\forall (s''_i, s''_{i+1}) \in R_2$, $Diff(s_i, s'_i) \subseteq Diff(s_i, s''_i)$ implies $Diff(s_{i+1}, s'_{i+1}) \subseteq Diff(s_i, s''_{i+1})$.

We denote $M_1 <_M M_2$ iff $M_1 \leq_M M_2$ and $M_2 \not\leq_M M_1$.

Definition 8. (**Admissible Update**) *Given an LTL Kripke model M and an LTL formula ϕ, an update of M with ϕ, denoted as $Update(M, \phi)$, is called admissible, if any resulting model M', obtained from $Update(M, \phi)$, has the following properties:*

1. $M' \models \phi$;
2. *There does not exist a resulting model M'' from other update of M with ϕ, such that $M'' \models \phi$ and $M'' <_M M'$.*

Example 1. Consider the software code illustrated in Figure 6. We need the software system M to satisfy the property: $M \models G(positive)$, which means "$positive = True$" when all states of path π in M contain "n=positive number". We denote $\phi = G(positive)$.

Now, we have model $M = (S, S_0, R, L)$ in Figure 5 to represent the code in Figure 6, and $M \not\models \phi$. We give up most other obvious none minimal changed updated models and pick up two updated models $M_1 \models \phi$ and $M_2 \models \phi$ in the figure for comparison. To result in both new models, the operation $sub(M, S_{new}, s_k)$,i.e., the simple modification should be applied twice in each. Now we shall pick out a minimal changed model between M_1 and M_2.

Under Definition 6, we have $R_1 =_R R_2$. We need to apply Definition 7 to decide the desirable update. Under condition 2 of this definition, $Diff(s_1, s'_1) = \{n_1 = -1, n'_1 = 1,\}$ and $Diff(s_1, s''_1) = (n_1 = -1, n'_1 = 1, t = 2, t = 3)$ resulting in $Diff(s_1, s'_1) \subset Diff(s_1, s''_1)$. Similarly, it is easy to see $Diff(s_2, s'_2) \subset Diff(s_2, s''_2)$.

Thus, from the above comparison, $M_1 <_M M_2$, we have final admissible minimal changed model $M_1 \models \phi$, which leads to the final updated software code in Fig. 7.

5   Characterization

In this section, we will characterize the update of the LTL Kripke model with $F\phi$ and $\phi \cup \psi$, which are two of the most common and frequently used path formulae in LTL model checking. For simplicity, we consider those LTL Kripke models that only contain a single initial state. However, our results can easily be extended to the general case. The characterizations significantly simplify the underlying update process for these specific formulas.

Theorem 1. *Given* $M = (S, \{s_0, \}, R, L)$ *with a path* $\pi = [s_0, \cdots, s_{k-1}, s_k, s_{k+1}, \cdots]$, *where* s_{k+1} *is not the final state, and* $M \not\models F\phi$. *Update*$(M, F\phi) = M'$, *where* $M' \models F\phi$ *and* $M' = (S', \{s_0\}, R', L')$, *is admissible if the update generates one of the following resulting models by applying the simple modifications:*

1. *Addition operation* $add(M, s_{new}, s_k, s_{k+1})$. *The updated model* M' *has a path* $\pi' = [s_0, \cdots, s_k, s_{new}, s_{k+1}, \cdots]$, *such that,*
   - $S' = S \cup \{s_{new}\}$, $R' = R - \{(s_k, s_{k+1})\} \cup \{(s_k, s_{new}), (s_{new}, s_{k+1})\}$, *and* $L' : S' \to 2^{AP}$, *where* $\forall s \in S'$, *if* $s \in S$, *then* $L'(s) = L(s)$;
   - $Diff(S_{k+1}, s_{new})$ *is minimal and* $s_{new} \models \phi$.
2. *Substitution operation* $sub(M, s_{new}, s_k)$. *The updated model* M' *has a path* $\pi' = [s_0, \cdots, s_{k-1}, s_{new}, s_{k+1}, \cdots]$, *such that,*
   - $S' = S - \{s_k\} \cup \{s_{new}\}$,
     $R' = R - \{(s_{k-1}, s_k), (s_k, s_{k+1})\} \cup \{(s_{k-1}, s_{new}), (s_{new}, s_{k+1})\}$, *and* $L': S' \to 2^{AP}$, *where* $\forall s \in S'$, *if* $s \in S$, *then* $L'(s) = L(s)$;
   - $Diff(S_k, s_{new})$ *is minimal and* $s_{new} \models \phi$.

Theorem 2. *Given* $M = (S, \{s_0, \}, R, L)$ *with a path* $\pi = [s_0, \cdots, s_k, \cdots, s_j, \cdots]$, *where* $M \not\models \phi \cup \psi$. *An update* $Update(M, \phi \cup \psi) = M'$, *where* $M' \models \phi \cup \psi$, *is admissible by applying the simple modification: substitution* $sub(M, s'_k, s_k)$ *to any state* s_k *before* s_j *in* M, *where* $s_k \not\models \phi$, s_j *is the first state with* $s_j \models \psi$ *in* π, *and* $Diff(s_k, s'_k)$ *is minimal. The resulting model* $M' = (S', \{s'_0\}, R', L')$ *with* $\pi' = [s'_0, \cdots, s'_k, \cdots, s_j, \cdots]$ *such that,*

- $S' = S - \{s_k | k < j, s_k \not\models \phi\} \cup \{s'_k | k < j, s'_k \models \phi\}$,
- $s'_0 = s_0$ *if* $s_0 \models \phi$, *otherwise,* $s'_0 \models \phi$ *and* $Diff(s'_0, s_0)$ *is minimal,*
- $R' = R - \{(s_k, s_{k+1}) | k \leq (j-1), s_k \not\models \phi$ *or* $s_{k+1} \not\models \phi\} \cup \{(s'_k, s'_{k+1}) | k \leq (j-1), and(s'_k, s'_{k+1}) \subseteq \pi'\}$, *and*
- $L': S' \to 2^{AP}$, *where* $\forall s \in S'$, *if* $s \in S$, *then* $L'(s) = L(s)$.

6   Conclusions, Related Work and Further Research

In this paper, we have described a new approach of system modification for LTL representation. The LTL model updater achieves its modification task by three single operations. A principle of minimal change is also presented for our LTL model update approach. We further demonstrate examples and characterize two important properties of the LTL model to illustrate the update and minimal change criterion.

Our work presented in this paper can be viewed as a further development of enhanced model checking for system repair by AI techniques, as shown in [2], which introduced the concept of a system repair problem. The authors in that paper integrated the techniques from model checking and abductive AI principles to tackle automated diagnosis. However, as declared by the authors themselves, their approach may not be general enough for other system modification problems. The other related work is due to Harris and Ryan's work [5]. In that paper, model checking is formalized as belief updating operator ◇ to satisfy classical proposition knowledge update KM postulates $U1$-$U8$. However, it is not clear how their model update operator can be implemented for practical system modification.

In order to further develop our research, we will aim to perform an extensive case study of the LTL model update to provide strong supportive evidence for the general principles proposed in this paper. We will apply the LTL model update method to more complex software systems such as concurrent systems [2]. We will also consider alternative methods to formalize the minimal change criterion to enlarge the LTL model update application domain. After this stage of research, we will extend our current approach to the research of CTL model update, which will be more of a challenge and the main focus of our research.

References

1. Baral, C. and Zhang, Y. (2005). Knowledge updates: Semantics and complexity issues. To appear Artificial Intelligence (AIJ), 2005.
2. Buccafurri, F. et al. (1999). Enhancing model checking in verification by AI techniques. Artificial Intelligence 112(1999) 57-104.
3. Clarke, E. Jr., Grumberg, O. and Peled, D. (1999). Model Checking. The MIT Press, Cambridge, Massachusetts London, England.
4. Gammie, P. and van der Meyden, R.(2004). MCK-Model checking the logic of knowledge. In proceeding of 16th International conference on Computer Aided Verification.
5. Harris,H. and Ryan,M.(2003). Theoretical foundations of updating systems. In the prodeeding of the 18th IEEE International Conference on Automated Software Engineering.
6. Herzig, A. and Rifi, O. (1999). Propositional belief base update and minimal change. Artificial Intelligence 115(1999)107-138. Elsevier Science.
7. Holzmann, G. (2003). The SPIN Model Checker: Primer and Reference Manual. Addison-Wesley Professional.
8. Huth, M. and Ryan, M. (2000). Logic in Computer Science: Modelling and Reasoning about Systems. University Press, Canbridge.
9. McMillan,K. and Amla,N.(2002). Automatic abstraction without counterexamples. Cadence Berkeley Labs, Cadence Design Systems.
10. Stumptner,M. and Wotawa,F.(1998). A survey of intelligent debugging. AI Communications, 11(1),1998.
11. Vaziri-Farahani, M. (1995). Using symbolic model checking to verify cache coherence in a distributed file system. Tech. Rep. CMU-CS-95-156, Carnegie Mellon Computer Science Department. Bachelor's Thesis.
12. Winslett, M. (1990). Updating logical databases. Cambridge University Press.

Anticipatory Agents
Based on Anticipatory Reasoning

Feng Shang and Jingde Cheng

Department of Information and Computer Sciences, Saitama University,
Saitama, 338-8570, Japan
{frank, cheng}@aise.ics.saitama-u.ac.jp

Abstract. Anticipatory agents are agents, which are capable of some-how make predictions in advance based on their own knowledge at present and use the predictions about future to guide their current actions. To construct such an agent, we propose an approach based on temporal relevant logic. We analyze the requirements for logic systems to under-lie anticipatory reasoning at first. Secondly, we present a logic family, named "temporal relevant logic," which can satisfy these requirements. And then we propose a conceptual architecture based on anticipatory reasoning in the framework of temporal relevant logic. At last, we present solutions to some issues about automation of anticipatory reasoning.

1 Introduction

Anticipatory Agent[8, 9, 12, 13] is a hybrid concept of *Agent* and *Anticipatory System* which is a system whose current state is determined by not only past/present states but also predicted future states[19].

According to different applications, it might be not necessary for agents to be anticipatory, but in multi-agent systems running in a protean environment, anticipation is certainly a desirable feature. Thus, an agent must face other agents, among which some are cooperating with it, some are competing with it, and some do not have concerns about it at all; also an agent must face various states of the environment, among which some are favorable, and some are not. If it could somehow "know" what the situation is going to be, such as what others are going to do, what the environment is going to be, an agent would make better decisions to cooperate with other agents or take advantage of competing agents or favorable states of environment; on the other hands, devise better counter-measures beforehand to compete with other agents or overcome the obstacles, even threats brought by unfavorable states of environment. By anticipation, it could pursue interests of itself or a group of agents in a more economic way, or just increase the income, or mitigate loss caused by competing agents or unfavorable environments.

Sinceanticipatory agent is a favorable type of agents, we need some methods to implement it. There are some formal logics proposed for *agents*[14, 23], but these formal logics are not sufficient or totally impossible to be used by anticipatory agents based on temporal reasoning. These are also some direct approaches

M.-S. Hacid et al. (Eds.): ISMIS 2005, LNAI 3488, pp. 445–455, 2005.
© Springer-Verlag Berlin Heidelberg 2005

to anticipatory agent, such as linearly anticipatory autonomous agents[9] which is rule based and requires a complete and consistent set of rules about the world — generally the agents could not have one. So from the formal logic perspective, we here present an approach to anticipatory agents based on anticipatory reasoning on *temporal relevant logic*, which can work with incomplete and/or inconsistent information about world.

We analyze the requirements for the logic system to to provide agents with a criterion of logical validity as well as a representation and specification language in anticipatory reasoning, and present a logic family, named "temporal relevant logic," which can satisfy these requirements in section 2. We also apply the formal logic systems in a conceptual architecture based on anticipatory reasoning in section 3. At last, we discuss some implementation issues in section 4.

2   The Logical Basis for Anticipatory Reasoning

Reasoning is the *process* of drawing *new conclusions* from given premises, which are already known facts or previously assumed hypotheses to provide some *evidence* for the conclusions. *Anticipatory reasoning* is the *reasoning*[1] to draw new, previous unknown and/or unrecognized conclusions about some future event or events whose occurrence and truth are uncertain at the point when the reasoning is being performed. The logic system to underlying anticipatory reasoning must satisfy the following four essential requirements.:

1. As a general logical criterion for the validity of reasoning as well as proving, the logic must be able to underlie relevant reasoning as well as truth-preserving reasoning in the sense of conditional.
2. The logic must be able to underlie ampliative reasoning, but not circular and/or tautological reasoning in the sense that the truth of conclusion of the reasoning should be recognized after the completion of the reasoning process but not be invoked in deciding the truth of premises of the reasoning.
3. The logic must be able to underlie paracomplete reasoning and paraconsistent reasoning. In particular, the so-called principle of *Explosion* that everything follows from a contradiction cannot be accepted by the logic as a valid principle. This is because that, in general, our knowledge about a domain as well as a scientific discipline may be incomplete and/or inconsistent in many ways. An anticipatory agent inevitably suffers the same problem.
4. Straightforwardly, the logic must be able to underlie temporal reasoning.

Classical mathematical logic (**CML**) was established based on the classical account of validity — *truth-preservation*. Since the relevance between the premises and conclusion of an argument is not accounted for, a reasoning based on **CML** is not necessarily relevant. In **CML**, the notion of conditional, which

---

[1] There are other notions, such as *proving, argument, conditional, entailment*, etc., refer to [7] for the definitions.

is intrinsically intensional but not truth-functional, is represented by the notion of material implication, which is intrinsically an extensional truth-function. This leads to the problem of "implicational paradoxes" [1, 2, 10, 16, 17].

CML cannot satisfy any of the above four essential requirements because of:

1. A reasoning based on **CML** is not necessarily relevant;
2. The classical truth-preserving property of a reasoning based on **CML** is meaningless in the sense of conditional; a reasoning based on **CML** must be circular and/or tautological but not ampliative;
3. Reasoning under inconsistency is impossible within the framework of **CML**[5, 6, 7].

These facts are also true to those classical conservative extensions or non-classical alternatives of **CML** where the classical account of validity is adopted and the notion of conditional is virtually represented by the material implication, such as some temporal (classical) logics[3, 21, 22] and some other modal and/or epistemic logic systems [14, 23].

Traditional relevant (or relevance) logics (**RLs**)[1, 2, 10, 16, 17] have a primitive intensional connective to represent the notion of (relevant) conditional (entailment). A reasoning based on **RLs** is ampliative but not circular and/or tautological. Also they satisfy *relevance principle*, thus to exclude those implicational paradoxes from logical axioms or theorems of **RLs**. Moreover, because **RLs** reject the principle of *Explosion*, they can certainly underlie paraconsistent reasoning.

Some strong relevant (or relevance) logics (**SRLs**), named **Rc**, **Ec**, and **Tc** are proposed as a modification of **RLs** [5, 6, 7]. **SRLs** are based on *strong relevance principle* which require the antecedent part and consequent part share all propositional variables. They reject all conjunction-implicational and disjunction-implicational paradoxes in **RLs**. In **SRLs**, if a reasoning is valid, then both the relevance between its premises and its conclusion and the validity of its conclusion in the sense of conditional can be guaranteed in a certain sense of strong relevance. Although **SRLs** can satisfy the first three of the essential requirements, they cannot satisfy the fourth.

From the discussions above, we can see that what we need is a suitable combination of strong relevant logics and temporal logics such that it can satisfy the all four requirements for the fundamental logic system.

Cheng proposed a new family of relevant logic systems, named *temporal relevant logic* (TRL), which can satisfy the all four essential requirements[7]. Based on this family of logic systems, we substitute temporal operators (**F**, **P**, **G**, **H**) with *since* (**S**) and *Until* (**U**) [15] as primitive temporal operators and corresponding axiom schemata, and further constraint the axiom schemata to be valid only on linear discrete time flow.

The logical connectives, temporal operators, axiom schemata, and inference rules are as follows:

Primitive logical connectives: entailment ($\Rightarrow$), negation ($\neg$), extensional conjunction($\wedge$)

Defined logical connectives: intensional conjunction($\otimes$), intensional disjunction($\oplus$), intensional equivalence($\Leftrightarrow$), extensional disjunction($\vee$), material implication($\rightarrow$), extensional equivalence($\leftrightarrow$)

Primitive temporal operators: until operator(U), since operator(S)

Defined temporal operators: future-tense sometime operator(F), past-tense sometime operator(P), future-tense always operator(G), past-tense always operator(H), tomorrow operator(T), yesterday operator(Y)

Axiom schemata: The axiom schemata from **SRLs** (**RcQ**, **EcQ**, and **TcQ**)[2], and followings:

T1	$G(A \Rightarrow B) \Rightarrow (U(A,C) \Rightarrow U(B,C))$
T2	$H(A \Rightarrow B) \Rightarrow (S(A,C) \Rightarrow S(B,C))$
T3	$G(A \Rightarrow B) \Rightarrow (U(C,A) \Rightarrow U(C,B))$
T4	$H(A \Rightarrow B) \Rightarrow (S(C,A) \Rightarrow S(C,B))$
T5	$(A \wedge U(B,C)) \Rightarrow U(B \wedge S(A,C),C)$
T6	$(A \wedge S(B,C)) \Rightarrow S(B \wedge U(A,C),C)$
T7	$(FA \wedge FB) \Rightarrow F(A \wedge FB) \vee F(A \wedge B) \vee F(FA \wedge B)$
T8	$(PA \wedge PB) \Rightarrow P(A \wedge PB) \vee P(A \wedge B) \vee P(PA \wedge B)$
T9	$GA \Rightarrow G(GA)$
T10	$HA \Rightarrow H(HA)$
T11	$(A \wedge HA) \Leftrightarrow T(HA)$
T12	$(A \wedge GA) \Leftrightarrow Y(GA)$
T13	$GA \Rightarrow TA$
T14	$HA \Rightarrow YA$
T15	$TA \Rightarrow FA$
T16	$YA \Rightarrow PA$
T17	$A \Leftrightarrow Y(TA)$
T18	$A \Leftrightarrow T(YA)$
TQ1	$\forall x GA \Rightarrow G\forall x A$
TQ2	$\forall x HA \Rightarrow H\forall x A$

Inference rules: include inference rules from **RcQ**, **EcQ**, and **TcQ**, and followings:

TG: "from A to infer GA and HA" (Temporal Generalization)

IRR: "from $\neg q \wedge Hq \Rightarrow A$ to infer A", where atom q not in A (Irreflexivity)

The minimal or weakest propositional (first column) and predicate (second column) TRLs can be obtained by following combinations:

$T_0Tc = Tc + \{T1{\sim}T6\} + TG$ $T_0TcQ = TcQ + \{T1{\sim}T6, TQ1, TQ2\} + TG$

$T_0Ec = Ec + \{T1{\sim}T6\} + TG$ $T_0EcQ = EcQ + \{T1{\sim}T6, TQ1, TQ2\} + TG$

$T_0Rc = Rc + \{T1{\sim}T6\} + TG$ $T_0RcQ = RcQ + \{T1{\sim}T6, TQ1, TQ2\} + TG$

---

[2] For the full list of axiom schemata and inference rules, please refer to [4, 6, 7].

Note that the minimal or weakest temporal classical logic $\mathbf{S,U/K_0}$[15] = all axiom schemata for $\mathbf{CML} + \Rightarrow\mathbf{E} + $ T1$\sim$T6 + TG.

$\mathbf{T_0TcQ}$, $\mathbf{T_0EcQ}$ and $\mathbf{T_0RcQ}$ are valid on all classes of time flows. By adding extra characteristic axiom schemata, we can get following propositional (first column) and predicate (second column) TRLs which are only valid on integer time flows:

$$T_iTc = T_0Tc + \{T7\sim T18\} + IRR \qquad T_iTcQ = T_0TcQ + \{T7\sim T18\} + IRR$$
$$T_iEc = T_0Ec + \{T7\sim T18\} + IRR \qquad T_iEcQ = T_0EcQ + \{T7\sim T18\} + IRR$$
$$T_iRc = T_0Rc + \{T7\sim T18\} + IRR \qquad T_iRcQ = T_0RcQ + \{T7\sim T18\} + IRR$$

The TRLs ($\mathbf{T_iTcQ}$, $\mathbf{T_iEcQ}$ and $\mathbf{T_iRcQ}$) above keep the essential characteristics of $\mathbf{T_0TcQ}$, $\mathbf{T_0EcQ}$ and $\mathbf{T_0RcQ}$[7]: as conservative extensions of strong relevant logics satisfying the strong relevance principle, the logics underlie relevant reasoning as well as truth-preserving reasoning in the sense of conditional, ampliative reasoning, paracomplete reasoning, and paraconsistent reasoning about temporal objects. The use of primitive temporal operators ($\mathbf{S}$, $\mathbf{U}$) enhance expressive power; and the resulted logic systems with extra temporal axioms for integer time flows are more convenient to specify, verify and reason about objects in the agent world.

3   A Conceptual Architecture of Anticipatory Agent

To construct anticipatory agents, we here propose a conceptual architecture which is developed from the basic idea which takes anticipatory reasoning on TRLs to make predictions.

The architecture (shown in Fig. 1) is basically constructed under consideration of component/function, and coupled two-layered structure is adopted: lower part — a traditional reactive subsystem and upper part — a anticipatory reasoning subsystem.

The reactive subsystem can consist of four components:

- **Sensor/measurers** perceive the states of environment and itself.
- **Communicator** encodes received raw data from sensor/measurers, and eliminates the "noise" and pick up the useful and important data for further processing; also, it is in charge of exchanging data with other agents, and the received data help the agent get a more comprehensive and accurate grasp of the world.
- **Enactor** match the received situations to the situation-action rules to select appropriate actions to take.
- **Actuactors** are a set of components which can finish certain kinds of task respectively. They realize actions specified in instructions from the enactor.

The components mentioned above are physical units with certain functions; and on the other hand, there are indispensable data — the abstract rules and theories, more generally "knowledge," just like encoding/filtering rules and situation-action rules. The lower part is closely dependent on application domains, it can

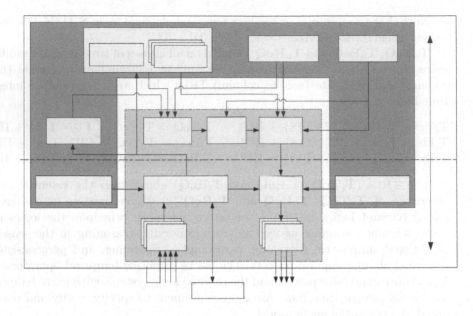

Fig. 1. A Conceptual Architecture of Anticipatory Agent

be implemented by the expert in those domains, so the implementation of its internal components is out of our major concern, all what we need are the *sensory data interface* and *instruction interface*.

The anticipatory reasoning subsystem is where the TRLs is applied, and is our major concern. It can consist of following components[3]:

- **Anticipatory Reasoning Engine** (ARE) gets large quantity of conclusions from history data, world model and general theories through anticipatory reasoning based on TRLs.
- **Formula Identifier** (FI) takes conclusions (formulas) from ARE, and identify some conclusions as predictions, according to the agent's interests.
- **Decision-maker** takes world model, predictions, general theories, system economic model and system goal/interests into account, select appropriate actions, and send instructions to guide enactor.

There also are indispensable data used by components in the anticipatory reasoning subsystem.

- **History data** contains the events/situation agent encountered, actions agent took, and the situation after the actions. It is actually a set of atomic formulas.

---

[3] Here we will use the notions of *formula(s)* and *theorem(s)*, and they are all well-formed formulas represented in the language of TRLs with some extra application-dependent symbols, such as propositions or predicates.

- **World models** contain the frameworks of the world, including models of the agent itself and other agents. The framework is a collection of world change patterns and agents' behavior patterns. It is a set of relevant empirical theorems.
- **General theories** are those of universal truth. It is a set of logical theorems acquired by applying inference rules on axioms of TRLs.
- **Goal/Interest & Economic model** include the purposes/interests of the agent, the actions that system is capable to take, and the efficiency and effectivity of the actions, and some action strategies under certain situations. Some contents of this data can also be formularised as a set of relevant empirical theorems, whereas some cannot.

Summarily, from the constructive aspect, especially using today's computer science, we can constitute an anticipatory agent with:

- **A repository** contains formulas and information of other forms (in the dark gray frame in Fig. 1).
- **A set of physical components (processes)** is capable to use the contents in the repository to finish certain task (in the light gray frame in Fig. 1).

This architecture shows that an anticipatory agent is actually acquired by simply coupling an anticipatory reasoning subsystem on a reactive subsystem. With this architecture, the high-efficiency and high-effectivity of normal routine reactions are guaranteed in reactive subsystem; also, the anticipatory feature of overall system is manifested under the guidance of the anticipatory reasoning. Therefore the anticipatory reasoning subsystem is intrinsically the more important part what we are focusing on, because just this part take anticipations by anticipatory reasoning, and make a reactive agent anticipatory.

Being a part of a multi-agent system, an anticipatory agent can perceive the world by data directly from its sensors and data shared by other agents; with the data, the anticipatory agent gets "interesting" predication about what the environment is going to be and what other agents are going to do by its ARE and FI; the predictions influence the choice of course of actions of the anticipatory agent: to cooperate, to compete, to do something irrelevant, or to do nothing at all; the actions can be observed by other agents or explicitly notified to other agents by the anticipatory agents, and are taken into account in choosing of course of actions by other agents. For the whole multi-agent system, this pattern will loop again and again.

In next section, we discuss some issues of implementation in detail.

4   Some Implementation Issues

Here we focus on the upper part of the architecture in last section. We have mentioned different categories of data used in the upper part, and among them: World Model and Goal/Interests&Ecnomic could be manually prepared as empirical theorems by experts in application domains; General Theories could be generated by ARE.

4.1   Anticipatory Reasoning Engine

ARE takes some logical theorems of TRL and empirical theorems as primises, deduces on TRL, and finally get the logical theorems and empirical theorems.

In general, both the logical theorems of a logic system and empirical theorems deduced based on the logic from some premises are infinite sets of formulas, even though the premises are finite. In order to develop a computational tool for reasoning about logical and empirical entailments, Cheng constraints the conclusions to a set of formulas with low *(entailment) degree*[5]. This strategy can be applied to computational tools that reason about SRLs, so ARE can also adopt this strategy.

Because ARE carries out reasoning on TRLs, we can further constraint the conclusions to a set of formulas with low *temporal degree*. Literally, *temporal degree* of a formula is the nesting depth of temporal operators in that formula. *temporal degree*(D_t) of a formula can be formally defined as:

- $D_t(A)=0$ if and only if there is no temporal operator in A;
- If A has the form of $\Psi(B, C)$, where Ψ is one of binary temporal operator, then $D_t(A)=max(D_t(B), D_t(C)) + 1$;
- If A has the form of ΦB, where Φ is one of unary temporal operator, then $D_t(A)=D_t(B) + 1$;
- If A has the form of ϕB, where ϕ is one of unary logical connectives, then $D_t(A)=D_t(B)$
- If A has the form of $B\psi C$, where ψ is one of binary logical connectives, then $D_t(A)=max(D_t(B), D_t(C))$
- If A has the form of $\sigma x B$, where σ is one of quantifiers, then $D_t(A)=D_t(B)$

If $D_t(A) = i$ where i is a natural number, A is called a ith *temporal degree formula*.

Let $(F(L), \vdash_L, Th(L))$ be one of TRLs, and k be a natural number. The kth *temporal degree fragment* of L, denoted by $Th^{,k}(L)$, is a set of logical theorems of L which is inductively defined as follows (in the terms of Hilbert style formal system):

1. if A is an axiom of L, then $A \in Th^{,k}(L)$
2. if A is a $j^{th}(j < k)$ degree formula which is the result of applying an inference rule of L to some members of $Th^{,k}(L)$, then $A \in Th^{,k}(L)$
3. Nothing else are members of $Th^{,k}(L)$.

Obviously, the definition of the kth *temporal degree fragment* of logic L is constructive.

Let $(F(L), \vdash_L, Th(L))$ be one of TRLs, premise $P \subset F(L)$, and k and j be two natural numbers. A formula A is said to be j^{th}-*temporal-degree-deducible* from P based on $Th^{,k}(L)$ if and only if there is an finite sequence of formulas $f_1, ..., f_n$ such that $f_n = A$ and for all $i(i < n)$ 1)$f_i \in Th^{,k}(L)$, or 2)$f_i \in P$ or 3)f_i whose temporal degree is not higher than j is the result of applying an inference rule to some members $f_{j1}, ..., f_{jm}(ji, ..., jm < i)$ of the sequence.

If $P \neq \phi$, then the set of all formulas which are j^{th}-temporal-degree-deducible from P based on $Th^{,k}(L)$ is called the jth temporal degree fragment with premises P based on $Th^{,k}(L)$, denoted by $T^j_{Th^{,k}(L)}(P)$.

To carry out anticipatory reasoning in ARE, we can combine this strategy based on *temporal degree* with the strategy based on (entailment) *degree* in order to further narrow down the searching space of possible candidates for predictions.

ARE here actually has two roles: when given only logical theorems, it can be an independent tool to prepare General Theories; when given both logical and empirical theorems, it acts as an active component of anticipatory agents. We have developed an automated forward deduction system for general-purpose entailment calculus, name "EnCal"[5], which can reason out the logical and empirical theorem based on SRLs, and it is being expanding to reason on TRLs, so it has the potential to act as an ARE.

4.2   Formula Identifier

We have devised strategies to narrow down the searching space of possible candidates for predictions, where the possible candidates are actually formulas deduced after the reasoning process. However, the quantity of these formulas may still be vary large, and some of them may have no influence on decision-making of the agent. It is the FI which picks up interesting formulas out of numerous candidates. So we devise a strategy to discriminate these formulas.

Before introducing the strategy, we need the notions of *Antecedent Part*(AP) and *Consequent Part*(CP) of a formula[1]. Here we extend its definition:

1. if $\Psi(B, C)$ is a $CP(AP)$ of A, where Ψ is one of binary temporal operator, then B and C are $CP(AP)$ of A;
2. if ΦB is a $CP(AP)$ of A, where Φ is one of unary temporal operator , then B is a $CP(AP)$ of A.

Also there is a property of S and U over integer time flow. If there is not $\Rightarrow$, $\otimes$, $\oplus$ and $\Leftrightarrow$ appearing in the scope of temporal operators in a formula A, then A can be rewritten in an equivalent way as a boolean combination of *pure formulas*, each of which depends only on a single time region[15]. In our case, these formulas are *pure (past|present|future) formulas*.

Now we describe our strategy. Fundamental assumption of this strategy is that an agent is interested in some certain affairs, which can be formalized as propositions, predicates or predicates of some certain instances of variables, called *interesting terms*. And all the affairs interested the agent is the formulas with interesting terms appearing in pure present or pure future formulas in their consequent parts, can be called *interesting formulas*, so FI just takes them as predictions. An *interesting formula* A(IF) to agent's interests can be defined as follows:

- interesting terms (atomic formulas) are IFs;
- If one if the consequent parts of A is an IF, then A is an IF;
- If A are an IF, then ϕA is an IF, where ϕ is a unary logic connective, i.e., $\{\neg\}$;

- If A or B is IFs, then $U(A, B)$ is an IF;
- If A is an IF, then $\forall x A$ and $\exists x A$ is IFs.
- If A is an IF, then ΦA is an IF, where Φ is one of $\{G, F, T\}$.

Given interesting terms by users, the formula identifier is able to choose predictions among deduced formulas by the anticipatory reasoning engine.

5   Concluding Remarks

In this paper, we have proposed an approach to construct anticipatory agents based on anticipatory reasoning on temporal relevant logics, and discuss some implementation issues under the frame of the approach.

Anticipatory agents can be applied in many fields, one of them could be a proactive security guard in computer networks. Actually, this is our preliminary attempt on this subject, There are many challenging theoretical and technical problems that have to be solved, such as we left out issues about decision-maker, since TRLs and anticipatory reason on TRLs are not enough to support decision making.

References

1. Anderson, A.R., Belnap Jr., N.D.: Entailment: The Logic of Relevance and Necessity, Vol. I. Princeton University Press, Princeton (1975)
2. Anderson, A.R., Belnap Jr., N.D., Dunn, J. M.: Entailment: The Logic of Relevance and Necessity, Vol. II. Princeton University Press, Princeton (1992)
3. Burgess, J. P.: Basic Tense Logic. In: Gabbay, D., Guenthner F. (eds.): Handbook of Philosophical Logic, 2nd edition, Vol. 7. Kluwer Academic, Dordrecht (2002) 1-42
4. Cheng, J.: The Fundamental Role of Entailment in Knowledge Representation and Reasoning. Journal of Computing and Information, Vol. 2, No. 1, Special Issue: Proc. of the 8th International Conference of Computing and Information. Waterloo (1996) 853-873
5. Cheng, J.: EnCal: An Automated Forward Deduction System for General-Purpose Entailment Calculus. In: Terashima, N., Altman, E. (eds.): Advanced IT Tools, Proc. IFIP World Conference on IT Tools, IFIP 96 14th World Computer Congress. Chapman & Hall, (1996) 507-514
6. Cheng, J.: A Strong Relevant Logic Model of Epistemic Processes in Scientific Discovery. In: Kawaguchi, E., Kangassalo, H., Jaakkola, H., Hamid, I.A. (eds.): Information Modelling and Knowledge Bases XI. (2000) 136-159
7. Cheng, J.: Temporal Relevant Logic as the Logical Basis of Anticipatory Reasoning-Reacting Systems. In: Daniel M. Dubois (ed.): COMPUTING ANTICIPATORY SYSTEMS: CASYS 2003 - Sixth International Conference. AIP Conference Proceedings, Vol. 718, American Institute of Physics, Melville (2004) 362-375
8. Davidsson, P., Astor, E., Ekdahl, B.: A Framework for Autonomous Agents Based On the Concept of Anticipatory Systems, (ed.)R. Trappl, Cybernetics and Systems '94, pages 1427-1434, World Scientific, (1994)

9. Davidsson, P.: Linearly Anticipatory Autonomous Agents, In: Dubios, D.(ed.) Proc. of 1st International Conference on Computing Anticipatory Systems, CASYS'97, pp. 490-491, NY: American Institute of Physics, (1997)

10. Dunn, J.M., Restall, G.: Relevance Logic. In: Gabbay, D., Guenthner, F. (eds.): Handbook of Philosophical Logic, 2nd Edition, Vol. 6. Kluwer Academic, (2002) 1-128

11. Egenhoger, M.J., Golledge, R.G. (eds.): Spatial and Temporal Reasoning in Geographic Information Systems. Oxford University Press, (1998)

12. Ekdahl, B., Astor, E., Davidsson, P.: Towards Anticipatory Agents, In: Wooldridge, W., Jennings, N.R.(eds.): INtellegentc Agents- Thoeries, Architechtures, and Languages (LNAI890), pp. 191-202, Springer-Verlag: Heidelberg, Germany, 1995

13. Ekdahl, B.: Agent as Anticipatory Systems, 4th World Multiconference on Systemic, Cybernetics and Informatics(SCI2000) and 6th International Conference on Information Systems Analyis and Synthesis(ISAS2000), July 23-26,2000, Orlando, Florida, USA

14. Fagin, R., Halpern, J.Y., Moses, Y., Vardi, M.Y.: Reasoning About Knowledge. The MIT Press, Cambridge (1999)

15. Gabbary, D.M., Hodkinson, I., Reynolds, M.: Temporal logic: Mathematical Foundations and Computational Aspects, Vol. 1, Oxford Science Publications (1994)

16. Mares, E.D., Meyer, R.K.: Relevant Logics. In: Goble, L. (ed.): The Blackwell Guide to Philosophical Logic. Blackwell, Oxford (2001) 280-308

17. Read, S.: Relevant Logic: A Philosophical Examination of Inference. Basil Blackwell, Oxford (1988)

18. Riegler, A.: The Role of Anticipation in Cognition, Proc. of 4th International Conference on Computing Anticipatory Systems, CASYS'00, (ed.) D. M. Dubois, pp. 534-541, NY:the American Institute of Physics (2000)

19. Rosen, R.: Anticipatory Systems, Pergamon Press, (1985)

20. Stock, O. (ed.): Spatial and Temporal Reasoning. Kluwer Academic, (1997)

21. van Benthem, J.: Temporal Logic. In: Gabbay, D.M., Hogger, C.J., Robinson, J.A. (eds.): Handbook of Logic in Artificial Intelligence and Logic Programming, Vol. 4. Oxford University Press, Oxford (1995) 241-350

22. Venema, Y.: Temporal Logic. In: Goble, L. (ed.): The Blackwell Guide to Philosophical Logic, Blackwell, Oxford (2001) 203-223

23. Wooldridge, M.: Reasoning about Rational Agents. The MIT Press, Cambridge (2000)

Extracting Emotions from Music Data

Alicja Wieczorkowska[1], Piotr Synak[1], Rory Lewis[2], and Zbigniew W. Raś[2,1]

[1] Polish-Japanese Institute of Information Technology, Koszykowa 86,
02-008 Warsaw, Poland
{alicja, synak}@pjwstk.edu.pl
[2] University of North Carolina, Charlotte, Computer Science Dept., 9201 University,
City Blvd., Charlotte, NC 28223, USA
{rorlewis, ras}@uncc.edu

Abstract. Music is not only a set of sounds, it evokes emotions, subjectively perceived by listeners. The growing amount of audio data available on CDs and in the Internet wakes up a need for content-based searching through these files. The user may be interested in finding pieces in a specific mood. The goal of this paper is to elaborate tools for such a search. A method for the appropriate objective description (parameterization) of audio files is proposed, and experiments on a set of music pieces are described. The results are summarized in concluding chapter.

1 Introduction

Extracting information on emotions from music is difficult for many reasons. First of all, music itself is a subjective quality, related to culture. Music can be defined in various ways, for instance, as an artistic form of auditory communication incorporating instrumental or vocal tones in a structured and continuous manner [31], or as the art of combining sounds of voices or instruments to achieve beauty of form and expression of emotion [6]. Therefore, music is inseparably related to emotions. Musical structures itself communicate emotions, and also synthesized music aims at expressive performance [13], [19].

The experience of music listening can be considered within three levels of human emotion [12]:

- autonomic level,
- denotative (connotative) level, and
- interpretive (critical) level.

According to [17], music is heard:

- as sound. The constant monitoring of auditory stimuli does not switch off when people listen to music; like any other stimulus in the auditory environment, music is monitored and analyzed.
- as human utterance. Humans have an ability to communicate and detect emotion in the contours and timbres of vocal utterances; a musical listening experience does not annihilate this ability.

M.-S. Hacid et al. (Eds.): ISMIS 2005, LNAI 3488, pp. 456–465, 2005.
© Springer-Verlag Berlin Heidelberg 2005

- in context. Music is always heard within the context of knowledge and environment, which can contribute to an emotional experience.
- as narrative. Listening to music involves the integration of sounds, utterances and context into dynamic, coherent experience. Such integration is underpinned by generic narrative processes (not specific to music listening).

Although music is such a delicate subject of scientific experiments, research has been already performed on automatic composition in given style [23], discovering principles of expressive music performance from real recordings [29], and labeling music files with metadata [24]. Also, research on recognizing emotions in audio files has been performed on speech data [7], [20], [27]. Emotions communicated in speech are quite clear. However, in experiments described by Dellaert et al. in [7] human listeners performed recognition of emotions in speech with about 80% correctness, in experiments with over a 1000 utterances from different speakers, classified into 4 categories: happy, sad, anger, and fear. The results obtained in machine classification were very similar, also reaching 80% correctness. Tato et al. [27] also obtained recognition rate approaching 80%, for 3 classes regarding levels of activation: high (angry, happy), medium (neutral), and low (sad, bored). The database of about 2800 utterances was used in these experiments.

Research on discovering emotions from music audio data have also been recently performed [18]. Li and Ogihara reported in [18] on detecting emotions in music, using 499 sound files representing 13 classes, labeled by a single subject. The accuracy ranged for particular classes from about 50% to 80%. Since emotions in music are more difficult to discover than in speech, and even the listener labeling the data reported difficulties with performing the classification task, the obtained results are very good.

2   Audio Data Parameterization

Parameterization of audio data for classification purposes can be based on various descriptors. For instance, Tato et al. in [27] applied speech-specific prosodic features, derived from pitch, loudness, and duration, which they associated with the activation or arousal dimension, and quality features, i.e. phonation type, articulation manner, voice timbre, which they associated with the evaluation and pleasure dimension. They achieved most important results for the speaker-independent recognition and three classes, with a accuracy about 80%.

In case of music audio data, other descriptors are used, see for instance [25], [28], [30]. These features include structure of the spectrum, time domain features, and also time-frequency description. Since the research on automatic detection of emotions in music is very recent, there is no significant comparison of descriptor sets and their performance for this purpose. Li and Ogihara applied parameters provided in [28], describing timbral texture features, rhythmic content features, and pitch content features. The dimension of the final feature vector was 30.

In our research, we based on assumption that emotions depend on chords and timbre, using Western music as audio samples. Long analyzing frame (32768 samples taken from the left channel of stereo recording, for 44100 Hz sampling frequency and 16-bit resolution), in order obtain more precise spectral bins, and to describe longer time fragment. Hanning window was applied to the analyzed frame. Spectral components up to 12 kHz were taken into account.

The following set of descriptors was calculated [30]:

- *Frequency*: dominating fundamental frequency of the sound
- *Level*: maximal level of sound in the analyzed frame
- *Tristimulus*1, 2, 3: Tristimulus parameters calculated for *Frequency*, given by [26]:

$$Tristimulus1 = \frac{A_1^2}{\sum_{n=1}^{N} A_n^2} \tag{1}$$

$$Tristimulus2 = \frac{\sum_{n=2,3,4} A_n^2}{\sum_{n=1}^{N} A_n^2} \tag{2}$$

$$Tristimulus3 = \frac{\sum_{n=5}^{N} A_n^2}{\sum_{n=1}^{N} A_n^2} \tag{3}$$

where A_n denotes the amplitude of the nth harmonic, N is the number of harmonics available in spectrum, $M = \lfloor N/2 \rfloor$ and $L = \lfloor N/2 + 1 \rfloor$

- *EvenHarm* and *OddHarm*: Contents of even and odd harmonics in the spectrum, defined as

$$EvenHarm = \frac{\sqrt{\sum_{k=1}^{M} A_{2k}^2}}{\sqrt{\sum_{n=1}^{N} A_n^2}} \tag{4}$$

$$OddHarm = \frac{\sqrt{\sum_{k=2}^{L} A_{2k-1}^2}}{\sqrt{\sum_{n=1}^{N} A_n^2}} \tag{5}$$

- *Brightness*: brightness of sound - gravity center of the spectrum, defined as

$$Brightness = \frac{\sum_{n=1}^{N} n A_n}{\sum_{n=1}^{N} A_n} \tag{6}$$

- *Irregularity*: irregularity of spectrum, defined as [9], [16]

$$Irregularity = \log \left(20 \sum_{k=2}^{N-1} \left| \log \frac{A_k}{\sqrt[3]{A_{k-1} A_k A_{k+1}}} \right| \right) \tag{7}$$

- *Frequency*1, *Ratio*1, ..., 9: for these parameters, 10 most prominent peaks in the spectrum are found. The lowest frequency within this set is chosen as *Frequency*1, and proportions of other frequencies to the lowest one are denoted as *Ratio*1, ..., 9

– *Amplitude*1, *Ratio*1, ..., 9: the amplitude of *Frequency*1 in decibel scale, and differences in decibels between peaks corresponding to *Ratio*1, ..., 9 and *Amplitude*1. These parameters describe relative strength of the notes in the music chord.

Since the emotions in music also depend on the evolution of sound, it is recommended to observe changes of descriptor values in time, especially with respect to music chords, roughly represented by parameters *Frequency*1, *Ratio*1, ..., 9; we plan such extension of our feature set in further experiments.

3   Data Labeling

One of difficulties in experiments on recognition of emotions in music is labeling of the data. The emotions can be described in various ways. One of the possibilities is presented in Figure 1, proposed by Hevner [11]. This labeling consists of 8 classes, although not all adjectives in a single group are synonyms, see for instance pathetic and dark in class 2.

Other labeling is also used. For instance, Li and Ogihara in [18] use 13 classes, each labeled by one, two, or three adjectives. These groups are based on redefined

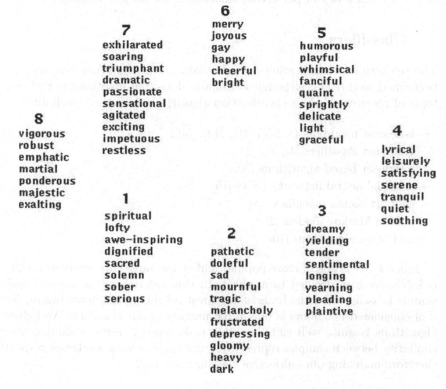

Fig. 1. Adjective Circle according to K. Hevner [11]

(by Farnsworth) Hevner adjectives, supplemented with 3 additional classes. Altogether, the following adjectives were used in this research: cheerful, gay, happy, fanciful, light, delicate, graceful, dreamy, leisurely, longing, pathetic, dark, depressing, sacred, spiritual, dramatic, emphatic, agitated, exciting, frustrated, mysterious, spooky, passionate, and bluesy [18].

Emotions can be also represented in 2 or 3 dimensional space, thus allowing labeling along the chosen axes. For instance, Tato et al. [27] performed research on detecting emotions in speech along activation dimension, using the following adjectives: angry, happy, neutral, sad, bored.

Apart from problem with choosing the appropriate representation, another issue to deal with is labeling the data by subjects, i.e. human listeners. Since emotions may vary from subject to subject, various listeners may provide different labeling. Labeling with emotions is inevitably subjective, and it is very difficult to compare objectively the classification results [5]. Also, even a single subject may have difficulties with choosing the most appropriate label, so multiple labels are usually needed for the same sample of the data. In our research, we decided to use single labeling of classes by a single subject. Such a setup allows checking exactly the quality of parameterization chosen as a tool for finding dependencies between subjective and objective audio description. When this is done, multiple labeling and multi-subject assessment can be performed, in order to check consistency of perceiving emotions from subject to subject.

4   Classifiers

The research on classification of audio data of various types has already been performed worldwide, although automatic detecting emotions is rather recent topic of research. Various classification algorithms were used, including:

- k-nearest neighbors (k-NN) [10], [14], [30],
- Gaussian classifiers [4], [8], [21],
- rough-set based algorithms [30],
- artificial neural networks (NN) [15],
- support vector machines [18],
- hidden Markov models [2],
- and other algorithms [10].

Since k-NN is one of more popular and at the same time successful algorithm is k-NN, we also decided to apply it. In this algorithm, the class of unknown sample is assigned on the basis of k nearest neighbors of known origin. Number k of considered neighbors is one of parameters of our classifier. We believe this algorithms is quite well suited to this task, since it reflects similarity or dissimilarity between samples representing the same or various classes respectively, therefore matching our subjective classification task.

5   Experiments and Results

The research described in this paper was performed using specially collected data. The audio files were gathered from personal collection and labeled by a single male subject, one of the authors (R. Lewis), a practicing musician. We decided to follow labeling used by Li and Ogihara in [18], since the class names they used cover a big set of possible emotions in music, yet represented by reasonable number of classes. Therefore, the experiments we performed were based on the classifying audio data into the following 13 classes:

- cheerful, gay, happy,
- fanciful, light,
- delicate, graceful,
- dreamy, leisurely,
- longing, pathetic,
- dark, depressing,
- sacred, spiritual,
- dramatic, emphatic,
- agitated, exciting,
- frustrated,
- mysterious, spooky,
- passionate,
- bluesy.

The collections consists of 303 music pieces. Each class is represented by 6 (dark and spooky) - 86 (dramatic) pieces, from CDs or bought iTunes [1]. Number of pieces for each class is shown in Figure 2.

Since some of the classes are underrepresented in comparison with the others, we decided to join the data into 6 superclasses as follows (see [18]):

1. happy and fanciful,
2. graceful and dreamy,
3. pathetic and passionate,
4. dramatic, agitated, and frustrated,

Class	No. of objects	Class	No. of objects
Agitated	16	Graceful	14
Bluesy	18	Happy	24
Dark	6	Passionate	18
Dramatic	88	Pathetic	32
Dreamy	20	Sacred	17
Fanciful	34	Spooky	7
Frustrated	17		

Fig. 2. Representation of classes in the collection of musical recordings for the research on automatic classifying emotions

Class	No. of objects	k-NN	Correctness
1. happy, fanciful	57	k=11	81.33%
2. graceful, dreamy	34	k=5	88.67%
3. pathetic, passionate	49	k=9	83.67%
4. dramatic, agitated, frustrated	117	k=7	62.67%
5. sacred, spooky	23	k=7	92.33%
6. dark, bluesy,	23	k=5	92.33%

Fig. 3. Results of automatic classification of emotions for the investigated database

5. sacred and spooky,
6. dark and bluesy.

The pieces were ripped into MP3 format using iTunes and Windows Media Player [22]. Before parameterization, they were converted to au/snd format. As we mentioned in Section 2, sampling frequency 44100 Hz was chosen and 32768 samples (2^{15}) frame length for analysis was selected. Parameterization was performed at the signal frame taken 30 seconds after the beginning of the piece; since Li and Ogihara in [18] also parameterized the same fragment, thus allows more reliable comparison of results.

Twenty-nine parameters were extracted for such a frame, according to description given in Section 2. The spectrum was limited to 11025 Hz (half of available spectrum) and to no more than 100 harmonics, since higher harmonics did not contribute significantly to the spectrum.

The obtained data set was next used in experiments with classification, using k-NN algorithm with k varying within range 1..20. The best k in each experiment was chosen. Standard CV-5 cross-validation was applied to test the classifier, i.e. 20% of data was removed from the set to train the classifier and then used for the tests; such procedure was repeated 5 times and the result was averaged. Since Li and Ogihara always divided data into 2 classes (the tested one against the rest of the data), we also followed the same technique, so these experiments and results can be quite easily compared. Such binary technique is a good basis for further classification, i.e. for construction of a general classifier, based on a set of binary classfiers [3]. The results of our experiments are presented in Figure 3.

To compare with, Li and Ogihara obtained accuracy ranging from 51% to 80% (for various classes), with use of 50% of data for training and the remaining 50% of data for testing of 599 sound files, with labeling into 13 classes, and then into 6 the same classes, also assigned by a single subject (39 year old male, i.e. comparable with our subject) and 30-element feature vector [18]. Our general accuracy in test with 6 classes tested in parallel (i.e. classic k-NN test) yielded 37% correctness. These result suggest necessity of further work. Especially, more balanced representation of all classes should be gathered, and evolution of sound features in time should be observed, in order to improve the quality of audio description.

We also performed similar experiments on the audio data obtained from M. Ogihara. These data (872 audio files) are presented in Figure 4. The best results

Class	No. of objects	Class	No. of objects
Agitated	74	Graceful	45
Bluesy	66	Happy	36
Dark	31	Passionate	40
Dramatic	101	Pathetic	155
Dreamy	46	Sacred	11
Fanciful	38	Spooky	77
Frustrated	152		

Fig. 4. Representation of classes in Ogihara's database

Class	No. of objects	Correctness
1. happy, fanciful	74	95.97%
2. graceful, dreamy	91	89.77%
3. pathetic, passionate	195	71.72%
4. dramatic, agitated, frustrated	327	64.02%
5. sacred, spooky	88	89.88%
6. dark, bluesy,	97	88.80%

Fig. 5. Results of automatic classification of emotions for the Ogihara's database

of binary classification for these data, grouped into 6 classes as previously, were obtained in k-NN experiments for $k = 13$. The results are presented in Figure 5. As we can see, the results are comparable or even better than for our database, albeit the size of the data was increased. These results convince us that our parameterization and classification perform quite well, although the final accuracy still is not satisfying, so our methods should be improved in further research.

6   Summary and Conclusions

Discovering emotions in music is a difficult issue for many reasons. First of all, emotions perceived with music are subjective and depend on numerous factors. Additionally, the same piece may evoke various emotions not only for various human listeners, but even the same person may feel various emotions when listening to this same piece of music. Therefore, our experiments may be extended if we ask other subjects to label the same data, here labeled by a single subject.

The purpose of our research was to perform parameterization of audio data for the purpose of automatic recognition of emotions in music, and the special collection of music pieces was gathered and turned into a data set. In order to check quality of parameterization, single labeling by a single subject was performed. As a classification algorithm k-NN was chosen, since this algorithm performed well in other experiments regarding classification of music, and since it also allows easy extension in case of increasing the size of the data set, which is our plan for the nearest future.

We are going to continue our investigations with use of other classifiers. Since support vector machines gain increasing popularity in audio classification research, we would also like to apply this method to our data. Also, neural networks could be applied in this research, since neural classifiers may perform well in such tasks, and decision trees. Additionally, we can analyze sequences of short audio samples, in order to follow changes of emotions in a music piece. Since we would like to obtain more universal classification, we also plan further listening experiments and labeling of the same data by other subjects. Although multi-label classification is more challenging in the training phase, the results should be more useful, i.e. better suited to emotions that various user may feel while listening to the same music.

Acknowledgements

This research was partially supported by the National Science Foundation under grant IIS-0414815, and by the Research Center at the Polish-Japanese Institute of Information Technology, Warsaw, Poland.

The authors express thanks to Professor Mitsunori Ogihara from the University of Rochester for supplying them with his valuable audio database.

References

1. Apple: iTunes (2004). http://www.apple.com/itunes/
2. Batlle, E. and Cano, P.: Automatic Segmentation for Music Classification using Competitive Hidden Markov Models. Proceedings of International Symposium on Music Information Retrieval, Plymouth, MA (2000). Available at http://www.iua.upf.es/mtg/publications/ismir2000-eloi.pdf
3. Berger, A.: Error-correcting output coding for text classification. IJCAI'99: Workshop on machine learning for information filtering. Stockholm, Sweden (1999). Available at http://www-2.cs.cmu.edu/ aberger/pdf/ecoc.pdf
4. Brown, J. C.: Computer identification of musical instruments using pattern recognition with cepstral coefficients as features. J. Acoust. Soc. of America 105 (1999), 1933–1941
5. Carletta, J.: Assessing agreement on classification tasks: the kappa statistic. Computational Linguistics 22 (2) (1996), 249–254. Available at http://homepages.inf.ed.ac.uk/jeanc/squib.pdf
6. Cross, I.: Music, cognition, culture and evolution. Annals of the New York Academy of Sciences, 930 (2001), 28–42. Available at http://www-ext.mus.cam.ac.uk/ ic108/PDF/IRMCNYAS.pdf
7. Dellaert, F., Polzin, T., Waibel, A.: Recognizing Emotion in Speech. Proc. ICSLP 96 3 (1996), 1970–1973.
8. Eronen, A. and Klapuri, A.: Musical Instrument Recognition Using Cepstral Coefficients and Temporal Features. Proc. IEEE International Conference on Acoustics, Speech and Signal Processing ICASSP 2000, Plymouth, MA (2000). 753–756
9. Fujinaga, I., McMillan, K.: Realtime recognition of orchestral instruments. Proceedings of the International Computer Music Conference (2000) 141–143

10. Herrera, P., Amatriain, X., Batlle, E., and Serra X.: Towards instrument segmentation for music content description: a critical review of instrument classification techniques. In Proc. of International Symposium on Music Information Retrieval ISMIR 2000, Plymouth, MA (2000)

11. Hevner, K.: Experimental studies of the elements of expression in music. American Journal of Psychology **48** (1936) 246–268

12. Huron, D.: Sound, music and emotion: An introduction to the experimental research. Seminar presentation, Society for Music Perception and Cognition Conference. Massachusetts Institute of Technology, Cambridge, MA (1997).

13. Juslin, P., Sloboda, J. (eds.): Music and Emotion: Theory and Research. Series in Affective Science. Oxford University Press (2001)

14. Kaminskyj, I.: Multi-feature Musical Instrument Classifier. MikroPolyphonie **6** (2000).)nline journal at http://www.mikropol.net/

15. Kostek, B. and Czyzewski, A.: Representing Musical Instrument Sounds for Their Automatic Classification. J. Audio Eng. Soc. **49(9)** (2001). 768–785

16. Kostek, B, Wieczorkowska, A.: Parametric Representation Of Musical Sounds. Archives of Acoustics **22, 1** (1997) 3–26

17. Lavy, M. M.: Emotion and the Experience of Listening to Music. A Framework for Empirical Research. PhD. dissertation, Jesus College, Cambridge (2001).

18. Li, T., Ogihara, M.: Detecting emotion in music. 4th International Conference on Music Information Retrieval ISMIR, Washington, D.C., and Baltimore, MD (2003).

19. Mantaras, R. L. de, Arcos, J. L.: AI and Music. From Composition to Expressive Performance. AI Magazine, Fall 2002 (2002) 43–58

20. Marasek, K.: private communication (2004).

21. Martin, K. D., Kim, Y. E.: Musical instrument identification: A pattern-recognition approach. 136 meeting of the Acoustical Soc. of America, Norfolk, VA (1998)

22. Microsoft Corp.: Windows Media Player (2004). http://www.microsoft.com/

23. Pachet, F.: Beyond the Cybernetic Jam Fantasy: The Continuator. IEEE Computers Graphics and Applications, Jan./Feb. 2004, spec. issue on Emerging Technologies.

24. Pachet, F.: Knowledge Management and Musical Metadata. In: Schwartz, D. (Ed.), Encyclopedia of Knowledge Management. Idea Group (2005).

25. Peeters, G. Rodet, X.: Automatically selecting signal descriptors for Sound Classification. ICMC 2002 Goteborg, Sweden (2002)

26. Pollard, H. F., Jansson, E. V.: A Tristimulus Method for the Specification of Musical Timbre. Acustica **51** (1982) 162–171

27. Tato, R., Santos, R., Kompe, R., Pardo, J. M.: Emotional Space Improves Emotion Recognition. 7th International Conference on Spoken Language Processing ICSLP 2002, Denver, Colorado (2002).

28. Tzanetakis, G., Cook, P.: Marsyas: A framework for audio analysis. Organized Sound **4(3)** (2000) 169-175.

29. Widmer, G.: Discovering Simple Rules in Complex Data: A Meta-learning Algorithm and Some Surprising Musical Discoveries. Artificial Intelligence **146(2)** (2003)

30. Wieczorkowska, A., Wroblewski, J., Slezak, D., Synak, P.: Application of temporal descriptors to musical instrument sound recognition. Journal of Intelligent Information Systems **21(1)**, Kluwer (2003), 71–93

31. WordIQ Dictionary (2004). The Internet http://www.wordiq.com/dictionary/

An Intelligent System for Assisting Elderly People

Alberto Tablado, Arantza Illarramendi, Miren I. Bagüés*,
Jesús Bermúdez, and Alfredo Goñi**

University of the Basque Country, Donostia, Spain

Abstract. In this paper we present the main features of AINGERU, a
system that we have developed and that provides a new kind of tele-
assistance service to elderly people. AINGERU, apart from the functionalities offered by the current tele-assistance services, also provides a high
quality, anywhere and at any time assistance. We rate the assistance as
high quality because AINGERU allows the monitoring of vital signs and
a local detection of anomalous situations by the device that the person carries in real time. Therefore, it sends alarms autonomously when
necessary.

Through this paper we explain the three main functionalities offered
by AINGERU: universal assistance anywhere and at any time, monitoring
of vital signs irrespective of location or time and remote monitoring by
allowing authorized external persons to consult data about monitored
persons using the Internet. Moreover we show how those functionalities
are achieved by making use of PDAs (Personal Digital Assistant), wireless communication, Semantic Web, Web services and agent technologies.

1 Introduction

The social, demographic and technological changes that are taking place promote
innovative developments in different areas such as financial, sanitary, etc. More
specifically in the sanitary area, new methods for diagnosis, new ways to assist
patients (tele-medicine, tele-assistance) and so forth, are generating a revolution
in the way the sanitary aspects are considered. In this paper we concentrate
on the tele-assistance services for elderly people and we present a system called
AINGERU[1] which, while taking advantages of new advances in mobile computing,
Semantic Web and agent technologies, gives a step forward in the tele-assistance
services.

---

* This work is supported by a grant of the Basque Government.
** All authors are members of the Interoperable DataBases Group, online at
http://siul02.si.ehu.es. This work is also supported by the University of the Basque
Country, Diputación Foral de Gipuzkoa (cosupported by the European Social Fund)
and the Spanish Ministry of Education and Science TIN 2004-0799-C02-01.
[1] AINGERU is the word in the Basque language for expressing the notion of guardian
angel.

M.-S. Hacid et al. (Eds.): ISMIS 2005, LNAI 3488, pp. 466–474, 2005.
© Springer-Verlag Berlin Heidelberg 2005

It is widely confirmed that the industrialized countries are aging (e.g. percentage of people older than 60: Sweden 22,9 %, France 20,5 % [1]), a circumstance that is forcing the different governments first, to be worried about this situation and then, to take the adequate measures. One of such measures is to favor that elderly people can live alone in their own houses, leading a normal life, while, they feel taken care of at the same time. With that purpose tele-assistance services supported by private or public organizations are becoming quite popular (for example Assistel [2] in Spain, Locapharm [3] in France).

Most of the existing tele-assistance services are based on the use, on the one hand, of a device which is set up at the user's home and connected to the wired public phone network (an example of this kind of device appears in http://www.intervox.fr/eng/home.php) ; and, on the other hand, of a center of tele-assistance, where an operator attends to the user's requirements. Although, those kind of tele-assistance services accomplish an interesting and necessary function, they present the following main shortcomings: they are *passive*, i.e. they mainly react when the user demands it; their *coverage is limited*, normally constrained to the person's home; and they *do not monitor vital signs*. Due to this, they do not fulfill the aim of a *high-quality*, *anywhere* and at *any time* assistance.

AINGERU, our proposal for a new type of tele-assistance service, arises in this scenario. Apart from supporting the functionalities provided by current tele-assistance services, the AINGERU system also offers an *active assistance* by using stationary agents that behave in the face of anomalous situations without a direct intervention of the user; an *anywhere* and at *any time* assistance by using wireless communications and PDAs; and the *monitoring of vital signs* by using sensors that capture the values of those signs and feed a decision support system in the PDA that analyzes them and generates an alarm when necessary.

Concerning related works we want to mention the following ones: TeleCare [4] that tries to offer an active assistance by developing a configurable framework for virtual communities focused on supporting assistance to elderly people; Sensatex [5] and SILC [6] that promote an anywhere and at any time assistance using different devices (Sensatex uses a SmartShirt and SILC a wrist-worn device); doc@HOME [7] and TeleMediCare [8] that also promote an anywhere and at any time assistance, but in this case making use of PDAs (Personal Digital Assistants); MobilHealth project [9] that has developed a vital signs monitoring system based on a Body Area Network (BAN) and a mobile-health service platform. However, as far as we know, none of them, considers the whole set of the functionalities provided by AINGERU.

In the rest of this paper we present first how the traditional tele-assistance services functionality is supported by AINGERU and how it is improved by incorporating the *anywhere* and at *any time* features. Then, we show the main characteristics of the monitoring of vital signs and how this is accomplished. Next, we present the opportunities that AINGERU offers to authorized external people to consult data about the assisted persons using the Internet. Finally, we sum up our conclusions.

2   Current Tele-assistance Services

In this section we explain how the functionality offered by current tele-assistance services is supported by AINGERU and the way in which AINGERU improves it.

2.1   Provided Functionality

As we mentioned in the introduction, current tele-assistance services install a device that is plugged to the public telephone network at the user's home. They also offer to the users a kind of *panic* button, that can be embedded into a wrist strap or a necklace, which the user presses when he feels sick or wants to contact with the Control Center (that button uses a radio frequency to establish contact with the device which generates a call to the Control Center using the telephone network).

AINGERU offers a PDA which presents an interface with a button (see Fig. 1 a) that can be pressed when the user wants to contact with the Control Center[2], on the touchscreen. It is a friendly interface designed taken into account experts opinion. The only necessary interaction of the user with the PDA is that interface so, technical details of PDAs can be transparent for the users. From the system implementation point of view, there is a *MajordomoAgent*, running at the PDA, which generates a message and sends it to the Control Center (see Fig. 1 b) when detects that the user has pressed the button. This message can be sent in different ways: for example, a WiFi connection can be used inside hospitals or buildings that have this kind of networks. Moreover, the PDA can use cellular communications (like GSM or GPRS) when the user is outdoors.

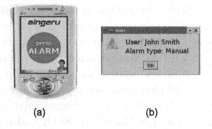

(a)   (b)

Fig. 1. (a) Interface at the user's PDA. (b) Interface at the Control Center

2.2   A Step Forward

Taking into account that the provided device is a PDA, the user can carry it wherever he goes. Therefore the user is assisted not only at his home (as it happens nowadays) but anywhere. We have verified that this feature is actually appreciated by elderly people who so feel more secure anywhere[3] One constraint

---

[2] Although buttons of the existing tele-assistance services are not incorporated in the current prototype, there are no technological obstacles to incorporate them.

[3] We have realized real tests with persons that are attended by an organization specialized in elderly people care (http://www.matiaf.net/).

of nowadays PDAs is the battery life. In the experiments that we have performed we have observed that in average the autonomy of a PDA is about seven hours when it is in complete operating mode. In our modest opinion this period of time comes up to the elderly people's expectations when they are outdoors. Also, if some battery saving measures are taken, operating time is increased to more than 24 hours.

3   Monitoring of Vital Signs

A remarkable functionality of the AINGERU system is the monitoring of the user vital signs performed locally at the PDA using state-of-the-art technologies. We want to remark that the local monitoring is not supported by the other works (eg. [7] and [8]) that also promote the use of PDAs. Bio-sensors are used for measuring vital signs and connection technologies such as Bluetooth, or Wi-Fi are considered for transmitting data. The monitoring process implies the collaboration of different agents, which, in the case of the AINGERU system, communicate using a FIPA-compliant agent communication language, explained in [10]. More details about agents cooperating in AINGERU can be found in [11], here we only introduce a sketchy presentation of some of them in order to focus on the core functionality of the system.

Connection with sensors is wrapped up with a *SensorCommunicationAgent* for each kind of connecting technology. *SensorAgents* deal with raw data captured by sensors and transmitted by the *SensorCommunicationAgents*. *SensorAgents* transform data into a manageable format before they send them to other agents. The main customer of a *SensorAgent* is the *ConditionCheckerAgent*. However, the *ConditionCheckerAgent* can also serve data to non-AINGERU agents that request its services. Let us explain the steps followed when a *SensorAgent* informs to the *ConditionCheckerAgent* which is the user's pulse.

Upon reception of new data about the state of the user, the *ConditionCheckerAgent* may ask for the most recently data to all *SensorAgent* and asserts the received knowledge into the knowledge base (ontology description) and a reasoning process starts in order to determine whether an alarm state is recognized

Currently, we are dealing with a "toy" ontology, called MedOnt (created by experts), that includes descriptions of states of illnesses that elderly people usually suffer from as well as descriptions of states considered thresholds for caution. If the ontology is well designed false alarms cannot be generated. The MedOnt ontology is specified in OWL [12] to take advantage of the Semantic Web technology and its richer primitives for class and property descriptions. We decided to use Semantic Web techniques because they are well suited for conceptual design and furthermore they favor the interoperability of our system with other systems at two levels: domain knowledge and communication. Moreover, the MedOnt ontology can be customized for each person.

For the reasoning process we have selected the RACER [13] system, which covers every OWL constructor we need. Moreover, it deals with reasoning about individuals of classes, which is crucial in our framework[4]. The interaction with the RACER system is done through the Java library JRACER [14].

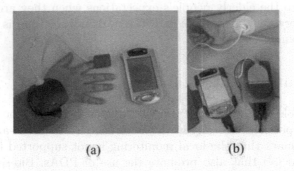

(a)   (b)

Fig. 2. (a) Pulse Oximeter sensor. (b) Monitoring ECG signals

The current prototype can deal with data sent by different kind of sensors (see Fig. 4a in the case of a pulse sensor). Data sent by ECG sensors (see Fig. 4b) require an elaborated treatment. In [15] we explain in detail a real-time classification of ECGs on a PDA.

Using a pulse sensor we have performed real tests with 20 persons and we have verified that once the data are captured and sent by the sensor to the PDA the reasoning process in the PDA is correct in all the cases. Moreover, we show in figure 3 the time that takes the reasoning process in the PDA. Notice that usually is under 1 second so in case of alarms we can say that they are detected as soon as they are generated.

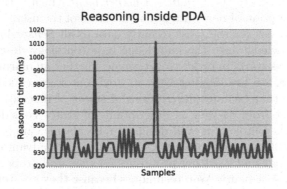

Fig. 3. Time used to analyze vital signs data

---

[4] We have accomplished the goal of running RACER in a PDA. We thank Volker Haarslev and Ralf Möller for their help.

4   Remote Data Access

It is widely accepted that monitoring systems should offer some facilities so that authorized users could access data, retrieved or calculated by the monitoring system, without having to be physically close to the monitored user, that is, in a remote way. In a tele-assistance system like AINGERU, where some vital signs are continuously monitored, a remote data access provided is of great interest because it allows the following possibilities:

1. physicians and social workers can know more about the current values of vital signs after the users had pressed the *panic* button, and therefore they have more information to cope with manually generated alarms;
2. relatives can know more about the current state of the user if they are worried about him/her: if it is late and the user is not at home yet, if the user does not answer the phone, etc:
3. care givers can know the current position of the user when an ambulance must be sent;
4. care givers and relatives can know if users have taken their medicines;
5. care givers can access to historical data about the user before taking any decision;
6. or more generally, care givers can retrieve statistical information about patients in order to make epidemiological studies.

In AINGERU remote data access is provided through Web Services.

Fig. 4. Interface of the Medicines Web Service

4.1   Web Services

In order to provide physicians, care givers and relatives with functionalities mentioned above, a set of web services have been developed. Fig. 4 shows one screen, obtained with a browser in which information about taken medicines is displayed.

Notice that the results provided by the web services correspond to data obtained by the user's PDA (which reads the vital signs values sent by the sensors

and it also stores the answers provided by the user, for example, when he is re-
minded of taking the medicines). Moreover, that data access is remote because
those results are visualized in any of authorized user browsers connected to the
Internet.

4.2 Architecture and Implementation of the Web Services Using Agents

In Fig. 5 part of the system architecture related to the web services is shown.
The browser must be installed in a client node where the physicians or rela-
tives execute the desired functionality. In fact, they load a Java Server Page
(JSP) that offers that functionality. Each JSP is stored in a web server that
is able to work with JSP pages and that is located in the Technical Center of
AINGERU. Although our web services could execute the operations needed to get
the required data, we have decided to make use of agents to retrieve those data.
In order to facilitate the integration of web services and agents, we have used
WSAI [16],which is a project that offers some tools that permit the publication
of agents as web services.

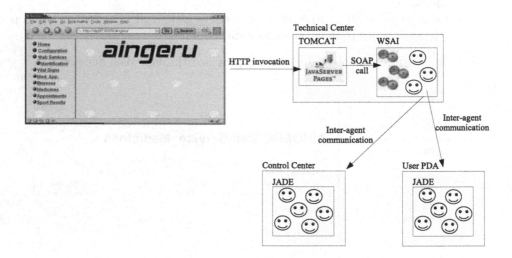

Fig. 5. Architecture of AINGERU Web Services

Why are we using agents in the implementation of the web services? The
answer to this question is related to the fact that PDAs can be disconnected
at a given time. Most of the previous web services require to access data that
reside in the PDA: vital signs, location, etc. However, at a particular moment,
the user's PDA that is connected via a wireless link could be in fact in a disconnected state, due to a coverage problem. An incorrect implementation could
generate a blocking situation if the web service were waiting for the PDA to be
connected. Agents help in the implementation of different interesting alternatives

like accessing to the last known data (stored at the Control Center) instead of the last data known at the PDA. Notice that this requires an intelligent and efficient refreshment of values whenever there is coverage. This task can be properly performed by agents.

4.3 Security Issues

It is commonly accepted that medical data are very sensitive. AINGERU system has been designed with that principle in mind. All communications are performed by using secured data links. Although Internet is used, Virtual Private Networks are established and the information is encrypted end-to-end. All center nodes in which AINGERU takes part implement the necessary measures in order to assure confidentiality, like user authentication, etc.

Moreover, PDAs are small devices that may be lost or stolen and that can contain confidential medical information about the user. However, that would not generate a confidentiality loss problem in AINGERU because the agents do not store sensitive information into a non-volatile memory in the PDA that could be inspected by a non-authorized person. Agents maintain those sensitive data with them into the volatile memory and they do not reveal them to not authorized users.

5   Conclusions

Taking advantage of new advances in the fields of mobile computing, networking and artificial intelligence (Semantic Web and agent technologies) we believe that a new generation of intelligent systems can be developed. In this sense, we have built AINGERU, a system that actually helps elderly people to improve their quality of life by providing them a kind of security when they are alone, at home or outdoors, and even more freedom to carry on with their own normal life when they need some of their vital signs to be monitored.

From the technical point of view, within the AINGERU system, we have made new proposals in the Semantic Web area that favor the interoperability among heterogeneous agent based systems.

References

[1] *The world health report 2003 - shaping the future*, World Health Organization Std., 2004. [Online]. Available: http://www.who.int/whr/2003/en/index.html
[2] (2004) Assistel, teleasistencia domiciliaria. [Online]. Available: http://www.asisttel.com/asisttel3.html
[3] (2004) Locapharm, la référence prestataire auprés des patients et des acteurs de santé. [Online]. Available: http://www.locapharm.fr/site_grand_public/prestations/sommaires.asp
[4] (2004, Feb.) Telecare, a multi-agent tele-supervision system for elderly care. [Online]. Available: http://www.uninova.pt/~telecare
[5] (2004, Feb.) Sensatex. [Online]. Available: http://www.sensatex.com

[6] (2004, Feb.) Supporting Independently Living Citizens. [Online]. Available: http://www.fortec.tuwien.ac.at/silcweb/SILC.htm

[7] (2004, Feb.) doc@HOME. [Online]. Available: http://www.docobo.com

[8] (2004, Feb.) TelemediCare. [Online]. Available: http://www.telemedicare.net

[9] A. van Halteren, R. Bults, K. Wac, et al., "Mobile patient monitoring: The mobihealth system," in *The Journal of Information Technology in Helath Care 2004*, 2004, paper 2(5), pp. 365–373.

[10] M. I. Bagüés, J. Bermúdez, A. Tablado, A. Illarramendi, and A. Goñi, "A new mechanism for the interoperability of data systems," in *1st International Conference on Semantics of a Networked World, Semantics for Grid Databases*, V. K. Mokrane Bouzeghoug, Carole Goble and S. Spaccapietra, Eds., June 2004, pp. 229–247.

[11] A. Tablado, A. Illarramendi, M. I. Bagüés, J. Bermúdez, and A. Goñi, "Agents in a system for monitoring elderly people," in *ECAI 2004 16th European conference on Artificial Intelligence. Workshop 7: Agents Applied in Health Care*, J. Nealon, A. Moreno, J. Fox, and U. Cortés, Eds., August 2004, pp. 47–53.

[12] *Web Ontology Language (OWL) Guide Version 1.0*, World Wide Web Consortium Std., 2004, http://www.w3.org/2001/sw/WebOnt/guide-src/Guide.html.

[13] R. Möller and V. Haarslev. (2004, Feb.) RACER: Renamed ABox and Concept Expression Reasoner. [Online]. Available: http://www.fh-wedel.de/~mo/racer/

[14] J. Alvarez. (2004, Feb.) JRacer library. [Online]. Available: http://www.fh-wedel.de/~mo/racer/jracer-1-7.zip

[15] J. Rodríguez, A. Goñi, and A. Illarramendi, "Real-time classification of ECGs on a PDA," *IEEE Transactions on Information Technology in Biomedicine*, 2004, to appear on March 2005.

[16] (2004) Web services agent integration project. [Online]. Available: http://wsai.sourceforge.net/

Multi-strategy Instance Selection
in Mining Chronic Hepatitis Data

Masatoshi Jumi[1], Einoshin Suzuki[1], Muneaki Ohshima[2], Ning Zhong[2],
Hideto Yokoi[3], and Katsuhiko Takabayashi[4]

[1] Electrical and Computer Engineering, Yokohama National University, Japan
jumi@slab.dnj.ynu.ac.jp, suzuki@ynu.ac.jp
[2] Faculty of Engineering, Maebashi Institute of Technology, Japan
ohshima@wi-lab.com, zhong@maebashi-it.ac.jp
[3] Department of Medical Informatics, Kagawa University Hospital, Japan
yokoi@med.kagawa-u.ac.jp
[4] Division of Medical Informatics, Chiba University Hospital, Japan
takaba@ho.chiba-u.ac.jp

Abstract. In this paper, we propose a method which splits examples
into typical and exceptional by mainly assuming that an example represents a case. The split is based on our previously developed data mining
methods and a novel likelihood-based criterion. Such a split represents
a highly intellectual activity thus the method is assumed to support the
users, who are typically medical experts. Experiments with the chronic
hepatitis data showed that our proposed method is effective and promising from various viewpoints.

1 Introduction

It is a consensus among data miners that data preprocessing requires most of
the labors in a KDD process. This subprocess involves several tasks including
deletion of inappropriate data and addition of required data. For instance, in
mining medical test data, the former corresponds to removing cases or medical
tests which are irrelevant to the objective of the mining task and the latter corresponds to adding relevant cases or medical tests. While data selection specifies
relatively rough conditions such as periods of medical tests or ages of cases, data
preprocessing requires specification of detailed data by considering the mining
objectives. This is considered to be one of the main reasons that the latter is
laborious.

In the example, the cases who are irrelevant to the objectives of data mining can be classified into those with symptoms mainly from other diseases and
those with symptoms dissimilar to typical cases. Detection of both types of patients should be based on overall judgment of various factors thus intervention
of medical experts in the process is considered to be mandatory. Especially the
latter represents a highly intellectual activity in which both modeling of typical
patients and determination of degrees of anomalies for removing cases are done

M.-S. Hacid et al. (Eds.): ISMIS 2005, LNAI 3488, pp. 475–484, 2005.
© Springer-Verlag Berlin Heidelberg 2005

simultaneously. Typical target data for medical data mining are, however, relatively "dirty" since they are obtained from daily diagnosis and huge enough to refuse detailed analysis by medical experts. In order to circumvent these problems, this paper proposes an instance selection method based on a multistrategy approach by mainly assuming the detection problem of cases who are irrelevant to the objectives of data mining.

2   Chronic Hepatitis Data and Liver Cirrhosis Prediction

2.1   Chronic Hepatitis Data

Chronic hepatitis represents a disease in which liver cells become inflamed and harmed by virus infection. In case the inflammation lasts a long period, the disease comes to an end which is called a liver cirrhosis (LC). During the process to an LC, the degree of fibrosis, which consists of five stages ranging from F0 (no fibrosis) to F4 (LC), represents an index of the progress. The degree of fibrosis can be inspected by biopsy which picks liver tissue by inserting an instrument directly into liver. A biopsy, however, cannot be frequently performed since it requires a short-term admission to a hospital and involves danger such as hemorrhage. Therefore, if we can predict the degree of fibrosis with a conventional medical test such as a blood test, it would be highly beneficial in medicine.

A time sequence A represents a list of values $\alpha_1, \alpha_2, \cdots, \alpha_I$ sorted in chronological order. A data set D consists of n examples $e_1, e_2, \cdots, e_n$, and each example e_i is described by m attributes $a_1, a_2, \cdots, a_m$ and a class attribute c. We assume that an attribute a_j originally represents a time-series attribute which takes a time sequence as its value. The class attribute c represents a nominal attribute and its value is called a class. We show an example of a data set which consists of time-series attributes in Figure 1. The data set consists of examples 84, 85, 930, each of which represents a case and is described with time-series attributes GPT, ALB, PLT, and a class.

In classification, the objective represents induction of a classifier, which predicts the class of an example e, given a training data set D. In this paper, we assume liver cirrhosis (LC) and non-liver cirrhosis (non-LC) as classes. Based on the discussions in the previous section, the objective of our classification is to induce a classifier which predicts the class from blood test data.

2.2   Instance Selection in Liver Cirrhosis Prediction

The definition of the problem in the previous section corresponds to learning from example and can be considered as belonging to traditional machine learning instead of data mining. It should be noted that, in medical treatment, it is generally agreed that pathological diagnosis such as a biopsy cannot be totally replaced by blood tests since the latter have too many confounding factors. Alternatively stated, it is interesting to investigate its possibility by removing cases with confounding factors and knowledge obtained in the process can be precious. We, therefore, believe that our problem represents one of the important tasks in data mining.

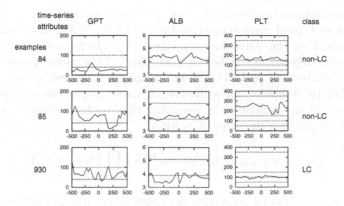

Fig. 1. Data set which consists of time-series attributes

In medical treatment, a case is subject to multiple diseases and anomalies. For instance, in the chronic hepatitis data [3], several cases exhibit symptoms of acute hepatitis or nefroze and they correspond to the cases with symptoms mainly from other diseases in section 1. In diagnosis, a physician understands the status of a case by inferring and verifying various assumptions. On the other hand, in data mining, we try to obtain hypothesis on the definition of the disease by removing inappropriate cases. Such a definition is useful in diagnosis, treatment, and medicine.

Special attention is required for removing cases with symptoms dissimilar to typical cases in section 1. Each physician has his/her own image of a disease and removing atypical cases corresponds to confirming the image. The obtained definition thus cannot deal with the cases outside the image. Selection of typical cases represents a highly intellectual activity in which these factors should be considered. As far as we know, deletion of such cases is left to the experts under the name of data preprocessing. Few attempts try to systematically support such activities and fewer reports are found in the literature.

3   Proposed Method

3.1   Overall Architecture

In order to circumvent the problem in the previous section, we propose a method based on a multistrategy approach. Our use of a multistrategy approach can be justified since exceptional cases have various reasons and considered to exhibit various exceptionalities. Such methods that we employ in this paper are a peculiarity-oriented mining method [14], a time-series decision tree induction method [13], and a PrototypeLines visualization method [12]. These mainly consider peculiar data, time-series form, and related blood tests respectively and expected to contribute to detection of exceptional cases from different perspectives.

Our method classifies input cases into typical cases and exceptional cases[1]. The set of typical cases is employed in definition of LC in the chronic hepatitis data based on the naive Bayes method [5], which shows high accuracy even for a relatively small number of examples[2]. This choice is justified since two of us, Takabayashi and Yokoi, who are physicians, feel natural to use such a probabilistic definition for a disease. A naive Bayes classifier predicts a class $\hat{c}_{NBayes,i}$ of an example e_i by assuming that each attribute a_j is independent. Here v_{ij} represents the value of e_i for a_j.

$$\hat{c}_{NBayes,i} = \operatorname{argmax}_c \Pr(c) \prod_{j=1}^{m} \Pr(a_j = v_{ij} | c) \qquad (1)$$

Another reason for employing the naive Bayes method is that it enables us to use an estimated conditional probability $\hat{\Pr}(c|p)$ of a class c given a case p. By comparing $\hat{\Pr}(c|p)$ with his/her actual class c_p, we can detect candidates of cases with symptoms dissimilar to typical cases. Since this estimation is related with the result of the naive Bayes method, we repeat it iteratively until convergence. Selecting exceptional cases from candidates of them should be left to medical experts since it requires consideration of various factors.

From above, the overall process is determined as follows. First, we apply, to the input set of cases, the peculiarity-oriented mining method, the time-series decision tree induction method, and the PrototypeLines visualization method in order to detect candidates of exceptional cases. These candidates are shown to the medical experts, who select exceptional cases among them. We apply the naive Bayes method to the remaining cases and detect candidates of exceptional cases based on a criterion defined in section 3.2, and again medical experts select exceptional cases among them. The last process is iterated until the result of the naive Bayes method converges.

3.2   Detection Criteria of Exceptional Cases

In a classification problem in general, an example can be intuitively regarded as "typical" or "atypical". The typicalness $\Phi(p)$, which is based on the right-hand side of Eq. (1), of a case p represents a degree to which p belongs to its class c_p compared with the other class $\overline{c_p}$.

$$\Phi(p) = \frac{\Pr(c_p) \prod_{j=1}^{m} \Pr(a_j = v_{ij} \mid c_p)}{\Pr(\overline{c_p}) \prod_{j=1}^{m} \Pr(a_j = v_{ij} \mid \overline{c_p})} \qquad (2)$$

The larger $\Phi(p)$ is, the more certain that p belongs to its class c_p.

If a naive Bayes classifier is relatively accurate for the class c_p, the typicalness $\Phi(p)$ tends to be large and vice versa. Thus the typicalness $\Phi(p)$ is relative since it depends on the preciseness of a naive Bayes classifier in terms of the class

---

[1] Candidates of typical cases are detected with a method presented in section 3.2.

[2] The chronic hepatitis data is huge for this sort of medical data but its number of examples is small for a problem in data mining.

c_p. The degree how a naive Bayes classifier is precise for c can be measured by the degree of correct classification and the degree of incorrect classification. For c and $\bar{c}$, we represent the number of correctly-predicted examples by the naive Bayes method $\mu_{\hat{c}}$ and $\mu_{\hat{\bar{c}}}$ respectively. Likewise, for c and $\bar{c}$, we represent the number of incorrectly-predicted examples by the naive Bayes method $\nu_{\hat{c}}$ and $\nu_{\hat{\bar{c}}}$ respectively. The preciseness $\Psi(\hat{c})$ of a naive Bayes classifier of the estimated class $\hat{c}$ represents the ratio of the precision for c and the precision for $\bar{c}$, where use used Laplace correction in order to cope with the 0-occurrence problem [5].

$$\Psi(\hat{c}) = \frac{(\mu_{\hat{c}} + 1)(\mu_{\hat{\bar{c}}} + \nu_{\hat{\bar{c}}} + 2)}{(\mu_{\hat{c}} + \nu_{\hat{c}} + 2)(\nu_{\hat{\bar{c}}} + 1)} \tag{3}$$

For our LC prediction problem, we define a degree of exception $E(p, \hat{c}_p)$ for a case p and his/her estimated class $\hat{c}_p$ as follows in order to discriminate exceptional cases from typical cases. In the definition, $\lceil x \rceil$ represents the smallest integer that is equal to or greater than x.

$$E(p, \hat{c}_p) = \lceil -\log_{\Psi(\hat{c}_p)} \Phi(p) \rceil \tag{4}$$

Intuitively, $E(p, \hat{c}_p)$ represents an evaluation index which is equal to the number of upvaluated digits below the decimal point when we measure the typicalness $\Phi(p)$ of a case p in terms of the preciseness $\Psi(\hat{c}_p)$ of a naive Bayes classifier of the estimated class $\hat{c}_p$. When prediction of the naive Bayes method is accurate, $\Psi(\hat{c}_p)$ tends to be large, and the absolute value of $E(p, \hat{c}_p)$ is relatively small even if the absolute value of $\Phi(p)$ is large. This fits our intuition that certain information rarely leads to an extreme degree of exception[3].

In each application of the naive Bayes method, cases whose degrees of exception are no less than a user-specified threshold are detected as exceptional. The loop continues until there are no exceptional cases among the detected examples. As the result, we obtain a list of typical cases, conditional probabilities for typical cases, and a list of exceptional cases.

4   Experimental Evaluation

4.1   Data Preparation and Initial Experiments

In the experiments, we followed advice of medical experts and used data from 180 days before the first biopsy to the day of the first biopsy. The numbers of LC and non-LC cases who have at least a value in this period and whose degrees of fibrosis are known are 159 and 112 respectively. In our experiment, we used 46 LC cases and 54 non-LC cases each of whom has test values for all of 14 blood tests in Table 1.

For the classifier, we followed advice of medical experts and first averaged each time sequence then discretized each value. We use for each attribute value

---

[3] We admit that we need further (experimental) research so that our evaluation index becomes fully justified.

U: extremely high, V: very high, H: high, N: normal, L: low, v: very low, and u: extremely low. Each conditional probability is estimated by using Laplace correction. A missing value is ignored both in estimating probabilities and in classifying an example.

We initially performed experiments by employing Yokoi as the medical expert and obtained preliminary results [8]. This time, another expert Takabayashi joined Yokoi in the experiments.

4.2   Application of the Preprocess Methods

First, we applied the peculiarity-oriented mining method in section 3.1 to the data, and showed 13 cases to the medical experts. In the previous experiment, Yokoi had removed four cases as exceptional cases mainly due to their blood test results on ALB, CHE, TP, T-CHO, WBC, and PLT. In the judgment, a bicytopenia, a case who shows low values for at least two of ALB, CHE, TP, T-CHO and a case with blood mass index decrease in terms of WBC and PLT had been considered as a typical LC case. This time, Takabayashi agreed with Yokoi after discussions.

Second, the medical expert investigated display result of PrototypeLines from 500 days before the first biopsy to 500 days after the first biopsy. In the previous experiment, Yokoi had recognized five cases as candidates of exceptional cases. This time, they removed three cases and classified the reasons to the judgment, fatty liver, and an acute aggravation or an uninterpretable disease.

Third, we applied our peculiarity-oriented mining method to non-LC cases in order to detect peculiar cases in this class. In the previous experiment, Yokoi had postponed the decision and judged exceptional cases by using other results. This time, the experts concluded that five cases are exceptional mainly with the judgment method, which became sophisticated in the analysis.

Fourth, the medical experts inspected misclassified cases from the time-series decision tree. As the result, two cases were removed as exceptions. It should be noted that other two cases, who were detected with other methods, were again detected with this method.

Fifth, the medical experts investigated six cases detected by our peculiarity-oriented mining method which was applied to LC cases. Two cases were removed mainly with the judgment method, and one of them was suspected to have hemorrhage stool.

At this moment, the experts revised their criteria and concluded that if at least two of ALB, CHE, PLT are low, they tend to judge a case as LC. An additional judgment is based on values for T-CHO and WBC. They consider that TP is relatively inadequate for the judgment.

4.3   Iterative Application of the Naive Bayes Method

The naive Bayes learner was iteratively applied to the remaining data, and the detection criterion in section 3.2 was employed in order to detect candidates of exceptional cases, in which we used 3 as the value of the threshold.

In the first application, 7 cases showed degrees of exception no less than 3. The experts evaluated the cases individually, and they judged to remove all cases except one. Though they first disagreed on the last case, they agreed to keep him/her as a border limit of an LC case. In the second application, one case was detected with the same procedure and they agreed to remove this case. Since no case was detected in the third application, the procedure terminated at this point.

We show the final conditional probabilities of the naive Bayes classifier in Table 1. In the Table, for each blood test a and a category v, "$\hat{Pr}(a=v|\text{non-LC})$ $(n(a=v|\text{non-LC}))$ | $\hat{Pr}(a=v|\text{LC})$ $(n(a=v|\text{LC}))$" are shown, where $n(\cdot)$ represents the corresponding number of examples in the data set. For instance, there are 6 non-LC cases and 2 LC cases for ZTT=N. The probabilities are obtained by using Laplace correction since there are 48 non-LC cases and 33 LC cases in the data set which corresponds to the Table. Each blood test is assumed to represent an ordinal scale. In the Table, we emphasize categories each of which shows more than 3 times of difference and no smaller than 10 % with boldface and with underline for non-LC predominant and LC predominant respectively. Since each blood test is assumed to represent an ordinal scale, we marked higher/lower categories of the categories appropriately.

Table 1. Conditional probabilities (%) and numbers of examples for typical cases, where each category shows "$\hat{Pr}(a=v|\text{non-LC})$ $(n(a=v|\text{non-LC}))$ | $\hat{Pr}(a=v|\text{LC})$ $(n(a=v|\text{LC}))$"

GOT	N: **34.6(17)** 2.7(0)	H: 40.4(20) 37.8(13)	V: 21.2(10) 54.1(19)	U: 3.8(1) 5.4(1)
GPT	N: 15.4(7) 5.4(1)	H: 50.0(25) 21.6(7)	V: 23.1(11) 62.2(22)	U: 11.5(5) 10.8(3)
TTT	N: 40.4(20) 24.3(8)	H: 28.8(14) 45.9(16)	V: 26.9(13) 10.8(3)	U: 3.8(1) 18.9(6)
ZTT	N: 13.5(6) 8.1(2)	H: 69.2(35) 70.3(25)	V: 13.5(6) 18.9(6)	U: 3.8(1) 2.7(0)
D-BIL	N: **88.5(45)** 40.5(14)	H: 7.7(3) 43.2(15)	V: 1.9(0) 10.8(3)	U: 1.9(0) 5.4(1)
I-BIL	N: 96.1(48) 75.0(26)	H: 2.0(0) 19.4(6)	V: 2.0(0) 5.6(1)	
T-BIL	N: 96.1(48) 69.4(24)	H: 2.0(0) 25.0(8)	V: 2.0(0) 5.6(1)	
ALB	L: 14.0(6) 54.3(18)	N: 86.0(42) 45.7(15)		
CHE	v: 1.9(0) 8.1(2)	L: 3.8(1) 45.9(16)	N: 90.4(46) 43.2(15)	H: 3.8(1) 2.7(0)
TP	L: 3.9(1) 2.8(0)	N: 92.2(46) 83.3(29)	H: 3.9(1) 13.9(4)	
T-CHO	L: 3.8(1) 13.5(4)	N: 86.5(44) 81.1(29)	H: 5.8(2) 2.7(0)	V: 3.8(1) 2.7(0)
WBC	u: 1.9(0) 5.3(1)	v: 1.9(0) 5.3(1)	L: 9.4(4) 13.2 (4)	N: 83.0(43) 71.1(26) / H: 3.8(1) 5.3(1)
PLT	u: 1.9(0) 8.1(2)	v: 5.8(2) 45.9(16)	L: 28.8(14) 35.1(12)	N: **63.5(32)** 10.8(3)
HGB	L: 4.0(1) 17.1(5)	N: 96.0(47) 82.9(28)		

4.4 Analysis of Experimental Results

The apparent merit of the proposed method is to output the disease definition and a list of exceptional cases. The former can be used to understand the disease and the latter can be used for further investigation.

In data mining, discovered knowledge is typically more important than high accuracy. Previous experiments have revealed that detection of exceptional cases could be done by searching for asynchronism in blood tests ALB, CHE, T-CHO, WBC, PLT; and HGB might be ignored. This piece of knowledge was elaborated in the experiments and the experts first check whether at least two of CHE, ALB,

PLT are low then ascertain their decisions with results on T-CHO and WBC. According to them, PLT is the most important blood test and the value 150 K is important as a threshold value. They consider that ALB is also important and T-CHO is relatively unreliable since it tends to be influenced by meals. From these facts, they realized that traditional rules of thumb are highly valuable.

They felt as if they were educated by the cases shown by our data mining method and even called the process "expert learning/training" instead of machine learning. The process gave them novel hypotheses on the LC prediction problem, but evaluating validness of the hypotheses requires systematic experiments followed by a traditional statistical approach. Anyway they were pleased to sharpen their capability for this problem and have the new hypotheses.

After the experiments, the medical experts inspected the obtained set of typical cases and found six cases who were recognized as exceptional cases. Five of them are due to relatively unimportant blood tests, similar stage (i.e. F3) to LC, and inadequate thresholds for ALB and T-CHO. The last case shows limitation of using average values: s/he had known a period with high PLT thus was recognized as non-LC. We believe that these mistakes are due to data handling, which is not directly related with our proposed method. Anyway, seeing the number of exceptional cases that our method detected, these results are considered to confirm effectiveness of our approach.

The separation into typical and exceptional cases can be also validated by measuring predictive accuracy with cross validation. For the prediction problem, we have considered a two-step process, which we call a separate prediction model [8]. Given a novel case, the process judges him/her as an exception if a similar case exists by using a 1-nearest neighbor (1-NN) method for time-series classification [13]. Otherwise, the naive Bayes method is applied to predict his/her class.

For the experimental results in the previous section, the accuracy of the separate prediction model is 72.4 %. More precisely, the accuracies for exceptional cases and typical cases were 40.2 % and 79.0 % respectively. The overall accuracy is similar to that of a conventional naive Bayes classifier, but it should be noted that the predictive accuracy for LC cases is higher than the predictive accuracy obtained by a conventional naive Bayes classifier. The accuracies for LC and non-LC cases were 77.8 % and 67.9 % respectively mostly because the correctly predicted cases with the 1-NN method were all LC. Our separate prediction model, which first applies the 1-NN method for predicting the class of exceptional cases, regards LC cases important since it is adequate in predicting exceptional LC cases due to the nature of its dissimilarity measure[4]. This fits the nature of the LC prediction problem in which overlooking of LC cases costs more than misprediction of non-LC cases.

Although it is impossible to detect an exceptional LC case who shows good results for all blood tests, our 1-NN method could detect exceptional LC cases relatively accurately. A partial LC case who shows partial aggravation of blood

---

[4] Exceptional LC cases are relatively stable in their time sequences and are more easily predicted with the 1-NN method.

tests was known among medical experts only empirically, but we have succeeded in detecting several of them. Such cases might suffer from genetic problems, and detailed inspection can be expected to reveal their true causes.

5   Related Work

Liu and Motoda classified instance selection mainly into sampling, methods associated with classification, methods associated with clustering, and instance labeling [9]. Our criterion-based method in section 3.2 belongs to the second approach. The removal of irrelevant data in classification is mainly pursued in nearest-neighbor methods and instance-based learners [1, 4, 10]. However, our objective is separation of irrelevant examples in classification instead of reduction of data and we assume that the users are involved in our data mining process.

Various methods for density estimation are based on likelihood, e.g. [6]. While these methods assume that examples are identically distributed, we assume that our examples follow either of two distributions. Moreover, instead of assuming density of the example space, we consider to which distribution an example belongs in the context of medical data mining.

Several supports for instance selection in a KDD process are considered and presented in [11] in a general manner. We mainly assume medical data mining and obtained promising results in a specific problem related with the chronic hepatitis data.

Outlier detection has a long history in statistics [2, 7]. Our approach differs from them in that we use KDD methods and domain experts under the framework of a KDD process.

6   Conclusions

In this paper, we have described our endeavor for instance selection in mining chronic hepatitis data. The motivation is based on our previous endeavor, from which we had come to believe that exceptional cases exist for physicians. However, our work for this article has deepened our idea on exceptional cases in medical data mining. Currently, we consider that typical cases are useful in defining a target disease while each exceptional case requires individual investigation but might lead to interesting discoveries.

Among conventional prediction methods for LC cases, ALB such as Child Pugh classification is the most frequently used[5] and PLT is also known a good indicator. Blood chemistry and complete blood count tests such as CHE, T-CHO, WBC were known to decrease as liver cirrhosis progresses, but various factors have prohibited their quantitative evaluation. We believe that our endeavor is expected to contribute to such analysis and actually contributed to

---

[5] It should be noted that the Child Pugh classification is useful in detecting typical LC cases but is not so effective in detecting LC cases in their early stages. The chronic hepatitis data mainly contain the latter sort of cases.

creation of new hypotheses. It should be also noted that rules obtained in our endeavor should be regarded as different from those obtained from conventional rule discovery methods. Our rules are result of careful inspection of individual cases in which our instance selection played a crucial role.

Acknowledgments

This work was partially supported by the grant-in-aid for scientific research on priority area "Active Mining" from the Japanese Ministry of Education, Culture, Sports, Science and Technology.

References

1. D. W. Aha, D. Kibler, and M. K. Albert, "Instance-Based Learning Algorithms", *Machine Learning*, Vol. 6, No. 1, pp. 37-66, 1991.
2. V. Barnett and T. Lewis: *Outliers in Statistical Data*, John Wiley and Sons (1994).
3. P. Berka: ECML/PKDD 2003 Discovery Challenge, Download Data about Hepatitis, *http://lisp.vse.cz/challenge/ecmlpkdd2003/* (current April 26th, 2003)
4. H. Brighton and C. Mellish: "Advances in Instance Selection for Instance-Based Learning Algorithms", *Data Mining and Knowledge Discovery*, Vol. 6, No. 2, pp. 131–152, 2002.
5. P. Domingos and M. Pazzani: On the Optimality of the Simple Bayesian Classifier under Zero-One Loss, *Machine Learning*, Vol. 29, No. 2/3, pp. 103–130 (1997).
6. D. Fragoudis, D. Meretakis, and S. Kokothanassis: "Integrating Feature and Instance Selection for Text Classification", *Proc. Eighth ACM SIGKDD Int'l Conf. Knowledge Discovery and Data Mining (KDD)*, pp. 501–506, 2002.
7. D. Hawkins: *Identification of Outliers*, Chapman and Hall, London (1980).
8. M. Jumi, E. Suzuki, M. Ohshima, N. Zhong, H. Yokoi, and K. Takabayashi: "Spiral Discovery of a Separate Prediction Model from Chronic Hepatitis Data", *Proc. Third International Workshop on Active Mining (AM)*, pp. 1–10, 2004.
9. H. Liu and H. Motoda: "On Issues of Instance Selection", *Data Mining and Knowledge Discovery*, Vol. 6, No. 2, pp. 115–130, 2002.
10. D. Madigan et al.: "Likelihood-Based Data Squashing: A Modeling Approach to Instance Construction", *Data Mining and Knowledge Discovery*, Vol. 6, No. 2, pp. 173–190, 2002.
11. T. Reinartz: "A Unifying View on Instance Selection", *Data Mining and Knowledge Discovery*, Vol. 6, No. 2, pp. 191–210, 2002.
12. E. Suzuki, T. Watanabe, H. Yokoi, and K. Takabayashi: Detecting Interesting Exceptions from Medical Test Data with Visual Summarization, *Proc. Third IEEE International Conference on Data Mining (ICDM)*, pp. 315-322 (2003).
13. Y. Yamada, E. Suzuki, H. Yokoi, and K. Takabayashi: Decision-tree Induction from Time-series Data Based on a Standard-example Split Test, *Proc. Twentieth International Conference on Machine Learning (ICML)*, pp. 840-847 (erratum http://www.slab.dnj.ynu.ac.jp/erratumicml2003.pdf) (2003).
14. N. Zhong, Y. Y. Yao, and M. Ohshima: Peculiarity Oriented Multi-Database Mining, *IEEE Transaction on Knowledge and Data Engineering*, Vol. 15, No. 4, pp. 952-960 (2003).

A Probabilistic Approach to Finding Geometric Objects in Spatial Datasets of the Milky Way

Jon Purnell, Malik Magdon-Ismail, and Heidi Jo Newberg

Rensselaer Polytechnic Institute

Abstract. Data from the Sloan Digital Sky Survey has given evidence of structures within the Milky Way halo from other nearby galaxies. Both the halo and these structures are approximated by densities based on geometric objects. A model of the data is formed by a mixture of geometric densities. By using an EM-style algorithm, we optimize the parameters of our model in order to separate out these structures from the data and thus obtain an accurate dataset of the Milky Way.

1 Introduction

Recent surveys of the Milky Way halo have given astronomers a better idea of the distribution of stars in the galaxy and the location of structures that come from other nearby galaxies. In Newberg & Yanny [1, 2], the data from the Sloan Digital Sky Survey (SDSS) has a distribution inconsistent with the power-law distribution that is commonly used and also indicates the presence of a tidal stream from the Sagittarius galaxy.

A great deal of effort is spent fitting various models to this large dataset. The need arises for a tool that can automatically extract the background distribution of the galaxy stars as well as find certain structures of astronomical importance. Also, such a tool can also yield more insight to how well a given distribution fits the Milky Way halo.

We formulate the problem of simultaneously identifying the galaxy stellar distribution and finding structures of astronomical interest as a *mixture density estimation* problem. The observed stellar density (from which the stars are "sampled") is a mixture of the parameterized densities representing the geometric objects and the background stars. We assume that the observed stellar distribution forms an *i.i.d* random sample from the mixture, and the task is to extract each of the mixture components.

Our Contributions. In this paper we focus on a single structure (a tidal stream) in a background, i.e. a mixture of two densities. We use an EM-style algorithm to optimize for the model parameters to determine the position, orientation and size (number of stars) of the stream, in addition to the parameters describing the distribution of the background stars. In the past, in order to obtain the background distribution, one had to be careful to "look" in a direction that would avoid the stream. By *simultaneously* obtaining both distributions,

M.-S. Hacid et al. (Eds.): ISMIS 2005, LNAI 3488, pp. 485–493, 2005.
© Springer-Verlag Berlin Heidelberg 2005

we avoid this complication, and can use all the data. As a result, our estimates should be more accurate.

We give experimental results on synthetic as well as real data, which indicate that this approach performs well at automatically and simultaneously extracting both the background and structure.

2   Mixture Model for the Galaxy

The first step is to define the probability distributions of stars in the galaxy and in the tidal stream (the geometric object of intent). The following distributions are chosen both for their close approximation to the true distribution of stars as well as for their analytic simplicity (integrability and invertibility).

2.1   Galaxy (Background) Stellar Density

The formula for the galactic, or background, distribution, P_b, is a generalized version of the Hernquist equation:

$$P_b(x, y, z) = \frac{1}{r^\alpha (r + r_o)^{3-\alpha+\delta}} \tag{1}$$

where $r = \sqrt{x^2 + y^2 + (z/q)^2}$

When $\alpha = 1$ and $\delta = 1$, our formula becomes the standard Hernquist equation. q controls the scaling of the galaxy model along the z-axis and r_o controls the density of stars near the origin.

2.2   Tidal Stream Density

To represent the stars in the tidal stream, we use a longitudinal elliptical density with a two-dimensional Gaussian cross-sectional density. This has the effect of "smearing" the stars along the ellipse. The ellipse is defined by three vectors that represent its displacement and two axes. Let $\mathbf{x}$ be a generic point on the ellipse. The parametric equation for the ellipse is then

$$\mathbf{x} = \mathbf{c} + \mathbf{a}\cos t + \mathbf{b}\sin t \quad t \in [0, 2\pi] \tag{2}$$

In order to describe the probability density for the stream, consider $P_s(\mathbf{z})$, for a generic point $\mathbf{z}$. Let $\mathbf{x}^*$ be the closest point on the stream to $\mathbf{z}$, and suppose that $\mathbf{x}^* = \mathbf{c} + \mathbf{a}\cos t^* + \mathbf{b}\sin t^*$. We define a cross sectional basis $\{\mathbf{E}_1, \mathbf{E}_2\}$ for the stream at the point $\mathbf{x}^*$ by the two unit vectors

$$\mathbf{E}_1 = \frac{\mathbf{a} \times \mathbf{b}}{\| \mathbf{a} \times \mathbf{b} \|} \quad \mathbf{E}_2 = \frac{\mathbf{E}_1 \times \dot{\mathbf{x}}^*}{\| \mathbf{E}_1 \times \dot{\mathbf{x}}^* \|} = \frac{\mathbf{E}_1 \times (-\mathbf{a}\sin t^* + \mathbf{b}\cos t^*)}{\| \mathbf{E}_1 \times (-\mathbf{a}\sin t^* + \mathbf{b}\cos t^*) \|} \tag{3}$$

where $-\mathbf{a}\sin\alpha + \mathbf{b}\cos\alpha$ is the tangent vector at $\mathbf{x}^*$. We can then write

$$\mathbf{z} = \mathbf{c} + \mathbf{a}\cos t^* + \mathbf{b}\sin t^* + x\mathbf{E}_1 + y\mathbf{E}_2, \tag{4}$$

where

$$x = (\mathbf{z} - \mathbf{c} - \mathbf{a}\cos t^* - \mathbf{b}\sin t^*) \cdot \mathbf{E_1} \tag{5}$$
$$y = (\mathbf{z} - \mathbf{c} - \mathbf{a}\cos t^* - \mathbf{b}\sin t^*) \cdot \mathbf{E_2} \tag{6}$$

We then have

$$P_s(\mathbf{z}) = \frac{1}{2\pi} \cdot \frac{1}{2\pi\sqrt{\det \Sigma}} e^{-\frac{1}{2}\mathbf{y}^T \Sigma^{-1}\mathbf{y}},$$

where $\mathbf{y} = \begin{bmatrix} x \\ y \end{bmatrix}$. This density corresponds to choosing t uniformly in $[0, 2\pi]$ along the ellipse, and then adding Gaussian cross-sectional noise with variance covariance matrix Σ. We will simplify this general model to assume that the cross-section is spherically symmetric, in which case we get the simpler density

$$P_s(\mathbf{z}) = \frac{1}{2\pi} \cdot \frac{1}{2\pi\sigma^2} e^{-\frac{1}{2\sigma^2}(x^2+y^2)}.$$

σ corresponds to the "thickness" of the tidal stream.

2.3   Mixture Model Density

The mixture density is obtained by combining the galaxy and tidal stream densities. To combine the distributions, they must be both normalized within the region of interest and weighted by a mixing parameter ϵ. Normalization is achieved by dividing the distributions by their integral over the region of interest. These integrals can be calculated analytical for simple densities and by numerical integration for more complex densities. The final mixture density is given by:

$$P_m(\mathbf{x}) = \epsilon \frac{P'_b(\mathbf{x})}{\int P'_b} + (1 - \epsilon)\frac{P'_s(\mathbf{x})}{\int P'_s} \tag{7}$$

where $P'_b(\mathbf{x}) = \rho(\mathbf{x})P_b(\mathbf{x})$ and $P'_s(\mathbf{x}) = \rho(\mathbf{x})P_s(\mathbf{x})$. $\rho(\mathbf{x})$ is an efficiency which corresponds to the probability that a star is detected given that it is at position $\mathbf{x}$. Thus the presence of stars at large distances in our dataset indicates that the density there must be higher because fewer of these stars are detected.

2.4   Normalization

In normalizing our probabilities, we calculate the integral of each distribution over the area of our dataset. In our physical application, the dataset is in a wedge shape that pivots at our Sun given by:

$$307 \leq \theta < 436 \quad -1.25 \leq \phi < 1.25 \quad 1.4 \leq r < 57.5 \tag{8}$$

The analytical solution to the normalization integrals is not easy. Also, if we were to change the distributions, we would have to re-calculate the solution. For these reasons, we choose a numerical integration approach.

The integrals are obtained by dividing the wedge into several smaller volume elements and computing the Rieman sum approximation to the integrals. The small volume elements we used are defined by:

$$\Delta\theta = \frac{436 - 307}{490} \approx 0.26 \tag{9}$$

$$\Delta\phi = \frac{1.25 + 1.25}{10} = 0.25 \tag{10}$$

$$\Delta r = \frac{57.5 - 1.4}{180} \approx 0.31 \tag{11}$$

Let A represent a generic small volume element, V_A its volume and $\mathbf{O}_A$ its center. Then the Rieman approximation to the integral is given by:

$$\int P'_b = \sum_A P'_b(\mathbf{O}_A)V_A \qquad \int P'_s = \sum_A P'_s(\mathbf{O}_A)V_A \tag{12}$$

2.5   Data Efficiency

The ratio of the number of stars in our dataset to the number of actual stars in the galaxy is called the efficiency of our dataset and is a function of distance from the sun, r_S, which is measured in parsecs. By comparing overlapping runs, and the number of matched stars, we can estimate the efficiency function. Figure 1 shows a plot of the efficiency versus g^* where:

$$g^* = 5\log_{10}(r_S/10) + 4.2 \tag{13}$$

The solid line in Figure 1 is the result of fitting a function to these data points. This derived efficiency formula is given by:

$$\rho(g^*) = \frac{0.9402}{e^{1.6171(g^* - 23.5877)} + 1} \tag{14}$$

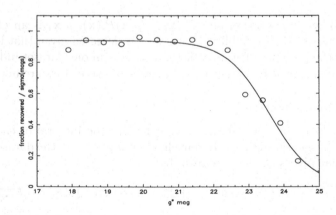

Fig. 1. Completeness of the dataset where the color is in the range of (0.1,0.3). The circles indicate the completeness estimated by comparing two overlapping runs. The solid line is the function fitted to these estimates

3   Maximum Likelihood Estimation

We use maximum likelihood density estimation to estimate the parameters in our model. The dataset is composed of the stars $\{\mathbf{x}_i\}_{i=1}^{N}$. The likelihood is given by $P[\{\mathbf{x}_i\}_{i=1}^{N} \mid Parameters] = \prod_i P_m(\mathbf{x}_i)$. Taking the logarithm and dividing by N, we then maximize $\mathcal{E}(Parameters) = \frac{1}{N} \sum_{i=1}^{N} \log P_m(\mathbf{x}_i)$.

4   Parameter Optimization

To maximize $\mathcal{E}$, we use a standard conjugate gradient optimization algorithm together with the line search algorithm [3] described in [4].

Each step taken in the conjugate gradient algorithm involves calculating a direction vector based on the gradient at the current parameter set, finding the maximum probability that can be obtained along this direction and then testing whether the stopping conditions have been met. We use a simple finite difference scheme to obtain the gradient.

$$\left(\frac{\partial \mathcal{E}}{\partial \mathbf{p}_i}\right)_{\pm} = \pm \left(\frac{\mathcal{E}(\mathbf{p} \pm h_i \mathbf{e}_i) - \mathcal{E}(\mathbf{p})}{h_i}\right) \tag{15}$$

where $\mathbf{e}_i$ is the standard unit vector.

Since $\mathcal{E}$ has varying sensitivities to the different parameters there is no single value for h that we can use. In fact, due to the normalization constants in our probability distributions, we may find ourselves near a non-differentiable cusp on the error surface. To get around this, we start with a sufficiently large value for h, for each parameter $\mathbf{p}_i$. We find $\mathcal{E}$ with that parameter at its current value, $\mathbf{p}_i$, and at the values of $\mathbf{p}_i \pm h$. If the signs of $\left(\frac{\partial \mathcal{E}}{\partial \mathbf{p}_i}\right)_{+}$ and $\left(\frac{\partial \mathcal{E}}{\partial \mathbf{p}_i}\right)_{-}$ are different, we know that we are near a local minimum or maximum and that our value for h is too large. In this case we decrease h by half and check the signs of the gradients again. This process continues until either the signs of the gradients agrees or until the value of h falls below a precision tolerance. If the signs agree, we use either gradient as shown in Equation (15). If h falls below the precision tolerances, we must be sufficiently close to a maximum or minimum and so we consider the gradient to be 0 with respect to $\mathbf{p}_i$.

4.1   Parameter Representation

There are two aspects of our parameters that can help us increase the efficiency of our algorithm. First is that some parameters are redundant and can be eliminated. The second aspect is that some parameters can only take on a particular range of values. Converting these parameters into variables without constrained ranges allows us to use more efficient unconstrained optimization techniques.

Reducing the Number of Parameters. Our first reduction takes advantage of the orthogonality condition between $\mathbf{a}$ and $\mathbf{b}$. Since $\mathbf{a} \cdot \mathbf{b} = 0$ we can define $\mathbf{b}$

with a magnitude d_b and an angle θ_b and remove one parameter. The second reduction is from the assumption that the cross-section of the stream is circular. So, we reduce both width values to just one parameter, σ.

Removing Parameter Constraints. Since the constraints on our parameters are relatively simple bound constraints, we can optimize with respect to unconstrained parameters by explicitly incorporating the constraints in the objective function as follows. Suppose α is a parameter in $\mathcal{E}$, i.e. $\mathcal{E} = \mathcal{E}(\alpha)$ (we only show the α dependence). Suppose that α has a bound constraint $\alpha \in [A, B]$. We can write $\mathcal{E}(\alpha)$ in terms of an unconstrained parameter β by $\mathcal{E}(\alpha) \rightarrow \mathcal{E}(\alpha(\beta))$ where $\alpha(\beta) = A + (B - A)e^{-\beta^2}$. β now becomes an unconstrained parameter in the optimization and α can easily be obtained from β. Such bound constraints apply to $\epsilon \in [0, 1]$ and $q \in [0, 1]$. An unbound constraint of the form $\alpha \in [A, \infty)$ can also be incorporated using the mapping $\alpha(\beta) = A + \beta^2$. Such an unbound constraint applies to $\delta \in [0, \infty)$.

5   Results

We applied our algorithm to two datasets, one synthesized and one from a 2.5 degree thick wedge along the Celestial equator of the SDSS dataset. For each dataset we initialized the algorithm with a parameter set that was close to the optimal value but randomized. The algorithm then ran until the maximum component of the gradient was less that 0.002.

5.1   Synthetic Data

The synthetic data was generated using the exact model mixture density for a particular setting of the parameters. For each star generated, a random number determined whether it was to be a stream star or a background star. If the star is a stream star, three random numbers are generated to determine α, x, and y in (4). If the star is a background star, three random numbers are generated to determine the coordinates of the star, the z-axis component being multiplied by q to take squashness into account.

The synthetic data was generated with the following parameters:

$$\mathbf{c} = (6.9, 10.23, 0.166) \quad \mathbf{a} = (19.4, 9.8, 35.5) \quad \mathbf{b} = (18.5, -2.45, -9.43)$$

$$\sigma = 5.0 \quad q = 0.65 \quad r_o = 13.5 \quad \epsilon = -2.197$$

The algorithm ran for 19 iterations and ended with the following parameters and probability:

$$\mathbf{c} = (7.32, 6.43, -4.72) \quad \mathbf{a} = (22.26, 9.99, 33.08) \quad \mathbf{b} = (15.40, -9.64, -7.45)$$

$$\sigma = 3.32 \quad q = 0.78 \quad r_o = 13.65 \quad \epsilon = -2.78 \quad \mathcal{E} = -3.38358$$

Figure 2 shows the generated synthetic data. Figure 3 shows the separation.

All wedge 82 stars in xy−plane

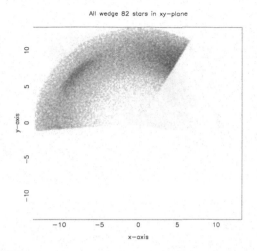

Fig. 2. Density plot of synthetic data in log space

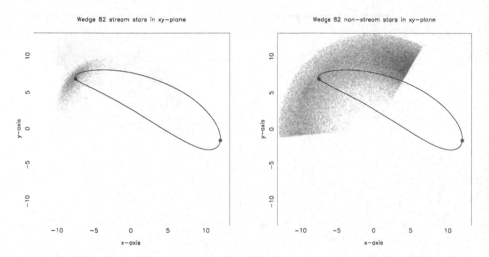

Fig. 3. Separation plot of the synthetic data. The left plot shows the stars labeled as stream stars and the right plot shows the stars labeled as background, or galactic, stars. The line indicates the ellipse of the stream and the circles indicate the point where the stream intersects the plane of the data

5.2   Real Data

With the real data, the algorithm ran for 10 iterations and ended with the following parameters and probability:

$$\mathbf{c} = (6.06, 12.85, -0.039) \quad \mathbf{a} = (19.49, 13.34, 35.70) \quad \mathbf{b} = (19.76, -4.26, -9.20)$$
$$\sigma = 6.21 \quad q = 0.71 \quad r_o = 14.43 \quad \epsilon = -2.38 \quad \mathcal{E} = -3.39434$$

Figure 4 shows a plot of the real data. Figure 5 shows the separation.

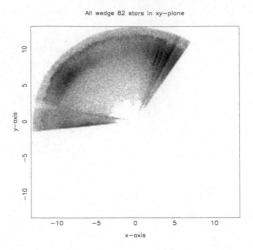

Fig. 4. Density plot of real data from SDSS

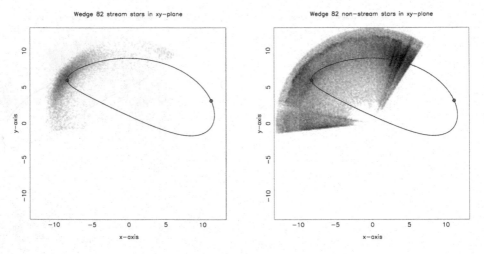

Fig. 5. Separation plot of real data. The left plot shows the stars labeled as stream stars and the right plot shows the stars labeled as background, or galactic, stars. The line indicates the ellipse of the stream and the circles indicate the point where the stream intersects the plane of the real data

6   Conclusion

We have presented a probabilistic approach to finding geometric objects in spatial databases. From these results we can get a clear idea of the direction and size of the tidal stream as well as the distribution of stars in the halo of the Milky Way. Future plans for this work are to increase the number and types of structures that are included in the mixture model, and to scale it up to handle millions of stars. A further direction is to investigate non-parametric estimates of the background densities and resulting geometric structures.

With this approach, astronomers, for the first time, have a tool for extracting the stream from the entire collection of stars, and hence the ability to study separately the stream structure (without being obscured by galaxy structure.

7 Related Works

Previous research has used mixture models and EM algorithms for clustering in large databases [5, 6]. Our techniques similarly uses mixture models but instead use conjugate gradients to solve the maximum likelihood problem. Additionally, our task is not to cluster the data, but to find the parameter set that best fits our model to the data.

Acknowledgement

Initial work on this topic was done in May 2003 by Fred Liu. Also, various parts of the mathematics behind the algorithm were implemented by undergraduates at Rensselaer Polytechnic Institute. We would like to acknowledge them here: Adam Gennett, Warren Hayashi, Jim Wisniewski. Final results were obtained with the help of Nate Cole.

References

1. Brian Yanny Heidi Jo Newberg. The ghost of sagittarius and lumps in the halo of the milky way. *The Astrophysical Journal*, 2002.
2. Brian Yanny Heidi Jo Newberg. Sagittarius tidal debris 90 kiloparsecs from the galactic center. *The Astrophysical Journal*, 2003.
3. Christopher M. Bishop. *Neural Networks for Pattern Recognition*. Oxford University Press, 1995.
4. R.P. Brent. *Algorithms for Minimization without Derivatives*. Prentice-Hall, 1973.
5. M. Jorgensen L. Hunt. Mixture model clustering for mixed data with missing information. *Computational Statistics and Data Analysis*, 2003.
6. C. Reina P. Bradley, U. Fayyad. Clustering very large databases using em mixture models. *Proc. 15th International Conference on Pattern Recognition*, 2000.

Towards Ad-Hoc Rule Semantics for
Gene Expression Data

Marie Agier[1,2], Jean-Marc Petit[2], and Einoshin Suzuki[3]

[1] DIAGNOGENE, 15000 Aurillac, France
[2] LIMOS, UMR 6158 CNRS, Univ. Clermont-Ferrand II, 63177 Aubière, France
[3] Electrical And Computer Engineering, Yokohama National University
79-5 Tokiwadai, Hodogaya, Yokohama 240-8501, Japan

Abstract. The notion of rules is very popular and appears in different flavors, for example as association rules in data mining or as functional (or multivalued) dependencies in databases. Their syntax is the same but their semantics widely differs. In this article, we focus on semantics for which Armstrong's axioms are sound and complete. In this setting, we propose a unifying framework in which any "well-formed" semantics for rules may be integrated. We do not focus on the underlying data mining problems posed by the discovery of rules, rather we prefer to emphasize the expressiveness of our contribution in a particular domain of application: the understanding of gene regulatory networks from gene expression data. The key idea is that biologists have the opportunity to choose - among some predefined semantics - or to define the meaning of their rules which best fits into their requirements. Our proposition has been implemented and integrated into an existing open-source system named MeV of the TIGR environment devoted to microarray data interpretation.

1   Introduction

Microarray technology provides biologists with the ability to measure the expression levels of thousands of genes in a single experience. It is believed that genes of similar function yield similar expression patterns in microarray experiences [1]. As data from such experiences accumulates, it is essential to have accurate means for assigning functions to genes. Also, the interpretation of large-scale gene expression data provides opportunities for developing novel mining methods for selecting for example good drug candidates (all genes are potentially drug targets) from among tens of thousands of expression patterns [2, 3].

However, one real challenge lies in inferring important functional relationships from these data. Beyond the cluster analysis [4], a more ambitious purpose of genetic inference is to find out the underlying regulatory interactions from the expression data, using efficient inference procedures.

Rules between genes are a promising knowledge to reveal regulatory interactions from gene expression data. The conjecture that association rules could be a model for the discovery of gene regulatory networks has been partially validated in [5, 6, 7, 8, 9, 10, 11]. Nevertheless, we believe that many different kinds of rules could be useful to cope with

M.-S. Hacid et al. (Eds.): ISMIS 2005, LNAI 3488, pp. 494–503, 2005.
© Springer-Verlag Berlin Heidelberg 2005

different biological objectives and the restricted setting of association rules could not be enough.

Clearly, the notion of *rules* is very popular and appears in different flavors, the two more famous examples being association rules in data mining and functional dependencies in databases. A simple remark can be done on these rules: their syntax is the same but their semantics i.e. their meaning widely differs.

In this paper, we propose a unifying framework in which any "well-formed" semantics for rules may be integrated. The key features of our approach are the following:

1. Given a dataset, defining a semantics in collaboration with domain experts (e.g. biologists and physicians).
2. Verifying if the semantics fits into our framework, i.e. if Armstrong's axiom system is sound and complete for this semantics [12].
3. Discovering the rules from the dataset, more precisely a cover for exact rules [13, 14] and a cover for approximate rules [15, 16].
4. Computing in a post-processing step, several quality measures for the obtained rules.

Note that we do not focus on the underlying data mining problems posed by the discovery of rules, rather we prefer to emphasize the expressiveness of our contribution in a particular application domain: the understanding of gene regulatory networks from *gene expression data.*

Due to space limitation, we introduce only one semantics based on a pairwise comparison of experiences to analyze *variations* of gene expression levels [5]. This semantics is close to the semantics of functional dependencies extended to deal with gene expression data. For others semantics, the reader is referred to [10, 17].

Our proposition has been implemented in a friendly graphical user interface to make it useful by biologists. We chose to integrate it as a module into a microarray data analysis open-source software: MeV. This tool is a part of an application suite, called TM4, developed by The Institute for Genomic Research (TIGR) [18].

Paper Organization. In Section 2, the framework of our approach is given. In Section 3, one semantics for rules is detailed and its compliance with the framework is shown in Section 4. Implementation details are given in Section 5 and we conclude in Section 6.

2   Framework of Our Approach

Our approach is based on the notion of *rule*, also called *implication*. A *rule* is an expression of the shape $X \rightarrow Y$ i.e. "X implies Y" and the *semantics* of the rule is the signification one wants to give to this implication. For example, association rules in data mining or functional dependencies in databases are two types of semantics.

In this paper, we focus on special kinds of rules, which exhibit nice properties, i.e. Armstrong's axiom system is sound and complete for the considered semantics. Such a semantics for rules is called "well-formed" in the sequel. We have chosen to focus on Armstrong's axioms since they apply obviously for functional dependencies but also for *implications* defined on a closure system [19] and thus turn out to have many practical applications (see examples given in [19]).

Practical interests of a well-formed semantics are twofold:

- Firstly, we can perform some kind of *reasoning* on rules from the Armstrong's axioms: From a set of rules F, it is possible to know if a rule is *implied* by this set of rules [20]. This problem is known as the implication problem and a linear time algorithm does exist for this problem. Thus, if there is a relation r which satisfies F then we know that all the rules that can be deduced from F thanks to the Armstrong's axioms will be satisfied in this relation.
- We can also work on "small" *covers* of rules [21, 22] and propose a discovery process specific to the considered cover, but applicable to *all* well-formed semantics. It is also possible to propose covers for non-satisfied rules [23].

The theoretical framework that we propose to use for the generation of rules defined with well-formed semantics, comes from the inference of functional dependencies [24, 14]. Basically, since by definition the Armstrong's axioms apply for any well-formed semantics, the augmentation axiom implies a *monotone property*: given an attribute A, $X \rightarrow A \Rightarrow \forall Y \supset X, Y \rightarrow A$.

That is to say that the predicate "X implies A" is monotone with respect to set inclusion, thus the predicate "X does not imply A" is anti-monotone. So well known characterization may be used to produce the rules [25].

In other words, the largest left-hand sides not implying A constitute the *positive border* of the predicate "X does not imply A" and the smallest left-hand sides implying A constitute its *negative border*. Consequently, this negative border gives a subset of the canonical cover (i.e. rules with minimal left-hand sides and A as right-hand side) while the positive border gives a subset of the Gottlob and Libkin cover [23] (i.e. rules with maximal left-hand sides and A as right-hand side).

Details on the generation of rules are out of the scope of this paper, interested readers are referred to [13, 14, 25].

Moreover, an important key point of our approach is to take into account characteristics of gene expression data. Indeed, from the microarray analysis domain, two underlying "constraints" have to be understood: firstly, the number of experiences is small (a few hundreds at most) whereas the number of genes is large (several thousands). Such a constraint differs widely from those usually held in databases or data mining where the number of tuples can be huge whereas the number of attributes (i.e. genes in the context of this paper) remains rather small. That is why for example our approach does not take into account a minimum support threshold as usual for association rules. Statistical measures are computed *a posteriori* on the discovered rules.

Secondly, data pre-processing steps on gene expression data are not fully understood yet and therefore, we have to take into account noisy data. Thus microarray technology delivers numerical values with a relatively small confidence on these values, biologists have to interpret the data, for example as levels of expression, which implies a discretization step. In this setting, we propose to deal with noise in data not as an explicit pre-treatment step but implicitly within the semantics of the rules.

3   Example of Semantics for Rules

Our approach consists to interact with biologists in order to establish a semantics for the rules which fits into their objectives and requirements.

In the sequel, we restrict ourselves to one semantics studying similar variations of gene expression levels. In [17], we propose two others semantics for rules specially defined for gene expression data.

In many cases, it does make sense to compare experiences in a pairwise fashion to find some regularities between experiences. Such kind of reasoning is well known in the database community through the notion of *functional dependencies*. However, in our context, the FD satisfaction - its meaning - has to be relaxed to take into account noise in gene expression data. Since a crisp FD $X \rightarrow Y$ can be rephrased as "equal X-values correspond to equal Y-values", we would like to obtain something like "close X-values correspond to close Y-values". Thus, instead of requiring strong equality between attribute values, we admit an error less or equal to the absolute value of the difference (obviously, other norms should have been taken). This leads to the following definition.

Definition 1. *(pairwise comparison semantics) Let $X, Y \subseteq \mathbb{G}$, be two sets of genes and r a relation over $\mathbb{G}$. A rule $X \rightarrow Y$ is satisfied in r with the semantics pc defined with two thresholds ϵ_1 and ϵ_2, denoted by $r \models_{pc} X \rightarrow Y$, if and only if $\forall t_1, t_2 \in r$, if $\forall g \in X, \epsilon_1 \leq |t_1[g] - t_2[g]| \leq \epsilon_2$ then $\forall g \in Y, \epsilon_1 \leq |t_1[g] - t_2[g]| \leq \epsilon_2$.*

Classical satisfaction of functional dependencies is achieved when $\epsilon_1 = \epsilon_2 = 0$.

Thus, $X \rightarrow Y$ can be interpreted in our context as follows: for each gene g of X, each time g has a similar expression level in two experiences of r, then for each gene g of Y, g has also a similar expression level in those experiences.

Example 1. Let us consider a running example made of a set of 6 experiences (t_1, t_2, t_3, t_4, t_5 and t_6) over a set of 8 genes ($g_1, g_2, g_3, g_4, g_5, g_6, g_7$ and g_8) as depicted in Table 1.

Table 1. A running example

r	g_1	g_2	g_3	g_4	g_5	g_6	g_7	g_8
t_1	1.9	0.4	1.4	-1.5	0.3	1.8	0.8	-1.4
t_2	1.7	1.5	1.2	-0.3	1.4	1.6	0.7	0.0
t_3	1.8	-0.7	1.3	0.8	-0.1	1.7	0.9	0.6
t_4	-1.8	0.4	1.7	1.8	0.6	-0.4	1.0	1.5
t_5	-1.7	-1.4	0.9	0.5	-1.8	-0.2	1.2	0.2
t_6	0.0	1.9	-1.9	1.7	1.6	-0.5	1.1	1.3

Let us suppose that the biologists are interested in low variations of expression levels between experiences. Thresholds should be defined as follows: $\epsilon_1 = 0.0$ and $\epsilon_2 = 0.2$. The hypothesis is that a gene does not vary for two experiences if the difference of the expression levels is between 0.0 and 0.2.

The expression levels of the genes g_6 and g_7 are plotted in Figure 1. In that case, the rule $g_6 \rightarrow g_7$ is satisfied in the relation r (on the other hand the rule $g_7 \rightarrow g_6$ is not satisfied because of the variation between the experiences e_3 and e_4).

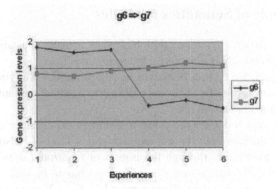

Fig. 1. Expression levels of the genes g_6 and g_7

The rule $g_6 \to g_7$ is interpreted in the following way: for some two experiences, if the expression level of the gene g_6 does not vary then the expression level of the gene g_7 does not vary neither.

4   Well-Formed Semantics

The second step of the process is to verify the well-formedness of the semantics defined by domain experts, i.e. verify that this semantics can be used within our framework.

This step is very important since many semantics could be defined, some of them verifying these requirements, others not (cf Theorem 2).

Definition 2. *A semantics s is* well-formed *if Armstrong's axiom system is sound and complete for s.*

Let us recall the Armstrong's axiom system for a set of rules F defined over a set of attributes (i.e. genes in our context) $\mathbb{G}$:

1. (reflexivity) if $X \subseteq Y \subseteq \mathbb{G}$ then $F \vdash Y \to X$
2. (augmentation) if $F \vdash X \to Y$ and $W \subseteq \mathbb{G}$, then $F \vdash XW \to YW$
3. (transitivity) if $F \vdash X \to Y$ and $F \vdash Y \to Z$ then $F \vdash X \to Z$

The notation $F \vdash X \to Y$ means that a proof of $X \to Y$ can be obtained using Armstrong's axiom system from F. Moreover, given a semantics s, the notation $F \models_s X \to Y$ means that for all relations r over $\mathbb{G}$, if $r \models_s F$ then $r \models_s X \to Y$.

As expected, the semantics previously introduced verify these requirements.

Theorem 1. *The semantics pc is* well-formed.

We need to show that Armstrong's axiom system is sound and complete for pc.

Lemma 1. *Armstrong's axiom system is sound for pc.*

Proof. Let F be a set of rules. We need to show that if $F \vdash X \to Y$ then $F \models_{pc} X \to Y$.

Let r be a relation over a set of genes $\mathbb{G}$.

1. (reflexivity) evident.
2. (augmentation) Let $t_1, t_2 \in r$ such that $\forall g \in X \cup W, \epsilon_1 \leq |t_1[g] - t_2[g]| \leq \epsilon_2$. We need to show that $\forall g \in Y \cup W, \epsilon_1 \leq |t_1[g] - t_2[g]| \leq \epsilon_2$, which implies that $r \models_{pc} XW \to YW$. By assumption $F \vdash X \to Y$, then we have $\forall g \in Y, \epsilon_1 \leq |t_1[g] - t_2[g]| \leq \epsilon_2$. The result follows.
3. (transitivity) Let $t_1, t_2 \in r$ such that $\forall g \in X, \epsilon_1 \leq |t_1[g] - t_2[g]| \leq \epsilon_2$. We need to show that $\forall g \in Z, \epsilon_1 \leq |t_1[g] - t_2[g]| \leq \epsilon_2$, which implies that $r \models_{pc} X \to Z$. By assumption, $F \vdash X \to Y$ and $F \vdash Y \to Z$, then $\forall g \in Y, \epsilon_1 \leq |t_1[g] - t_2[g]| \leq \epsilon_2$ and $\forall g \in Z, \epsilon_1 \leq |t_1[g] - t_2[g]| \leq \epsilon_2$ respectively. The result follows.

Lemma 2. *Armstrong's axiom system is complete for pc.*

Proof. We need to show that if $F \models_{pc} X \to Y$ then $F \vdash X \to Y$ or equivalently, if $F \not\vdash X \to Y$ then $F \not\models_{pc} X \to Y$. As a consequence, assuming that $F \not\vdash X \to Y$, it is enough to give a counter-example relation r such that $r \models_{pc} F$ but $r \not\models_{pc} X \to Y$.

Let r over $\mathbb{G}$ be the relation shown in Table 2, with $\epsilon_1 = 0.0$ and $\epsilon_2 = 0.2$.

Table 2. Counter-example

X^+		$U - X^+$	
0.1	... 0.1	0.1	... 0.1
0.2	... 0.2	1.2	... 1.2

Firstly, we have to show that $r \models_{pc} F$. We suppose the contrary that $r \not\models_{pc} F$ and thus, $\exists V \to W \in F$ such that $r \not\models_{pc} V \to W$. It follows by the construction of r that $V \subseteq X^+$ and $\exists A \in W$ such that $A \in U - X^+$. Since $V \in X^+$, we have $F \vdash X \to V$ and since $F \vdash V \to W$, we have $F \vdash V \to A$. Thus, by the transitivity rule, $F \vdash X \to A$ and thus $A \in X^+$. This leads to a contradiction since $A \in W$, and thus $r \models_{pc} F$.

Secondly, we have to show that $r \not\models_{pc} X \to Y$. We suppose the contrary that $r \models_{pc} X \to Y$. It follows by the construction of r that $Y \subseteq X^+$ and thus $F \vdash X \to Y$. It leads to a contradiction since $F \not\vdash X \to Y$ was assumed, and thus $r \not\models_{pc} X \to Y$.

As an example of semantics which does not fit into our framework, let us consider the following semantics, noted pc', which extends the semantics pc with an additional constraint:

Definition 3. *(pc') Let $X, Y \subseteq \mathbb{G}$, be two sets of genes and r a relation over $\mathbb{G}$. A rule $X \to Y$ is satisfied in r with the semantics pc' defined with two thresholds ϵ_1 and ϵ_2, denoted by $r \models_{pc'} X \to Y$, if and only if $\forall t_1, t_2 \in r$, if $\forall g \in X, \epsilon_1 \leq |t_1[g] - t_2[g]| \leq \epsilon_2$ then $\forall g \in Y, \epsilon_1 \leq |t_1[g] - t_2[g]| \leq \epsilon_2$ AND $\exists t_1, t_2 \in r$ such that $\forall g \in X, \epsilon_1 \leq |t_1[g] - t_2[g]| \leq \epsilon_2$.*

We have the following result:

Theorem 2. *The semantics pc' is not* well-formed.

Proof. Let F be a set of rules and $X \subseteq \mathbb{G}$, we have $F \vdash X \rightarrow X$ by the reflexivity axiom. Nevertheless, $F \not\models_{pc'} X \rightarrow X$. Let us consider the following counter-example made of 4 experiences (t_1, t_2, t_3 and t_4) over a set of 2 genes (g_1 and g_2) as depicted in Table 3.

Table 3. Counter-example for pc'

r	g_1	g_2
t_1	-1.8	1.8
t_2	-1.7	0.2
t_3	0.2	-1.4
t_4	0.3	-1.8

Let us consider the thresholds $\epsilon_1 = 0.0$ and $\epsilon_2 = 0.2$. We can see that $r \not\models_{pc'} g_2 \rightarrow g_2$ because $\nexists\ t_1, t_2 \in r$ such that $0.0 \leq |t_1[g_2] - t_2[g_2]| \leq 0.2$. By the way, the result is proved since the reflexivity axiom is not sound.

5   Implementation

We have implemented the generation of rules as a C++/STL modules integrated into an open-source freeware devoted to microarray data analysis: MeV (MultiExperimentViewer) [18]. This tool is a part of an application suite, called TM4, developed by The Institute for Genomic Research (TIGR). These tools devoted to microarray data propose various functions such as storing the data, image analysis, normalization, interpretation of the results.

MeV is the application devoted to the analysis of gene expression data. Furthermore, MeV takes in input several file formats resulting from various image analysis software, has an important number of functionalities already integrated and is based on a GUI easy to use for biologists.

For the interface, we chose to limit as much as possible the options proposed to the users to make it easier. An example of the graphical user interface developed on top of MeV is presented in Figure 2.

The software was tested on several datasets and we were naturally interested in the post-treatment of rules. Without being exhaustive, four quality measures (support, confidence, dependence and lift) are computed to be able to sort the rules following these criterion. We plan to integrate some other quality measures of rules [26]. The user looks at only the rules he considers interesting according to these various indications.

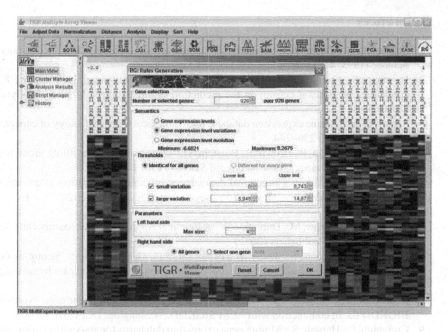

Fig. 2. Graphical user interface of the software

An application has been performed on expression profiles of a sub-sample of genes from breast cancer tumors. The results are presented in [17].

6   Conclusion

In order to attempt a reverse engineering of gene regulatory networks from gene expression data, we have proposed an on-going work aiming at defining different semantics of rules between genes, fitting in the same theoretical framework. Such rules form a complementary and hopefully new knowledge with respect to classical unsupervised techniques used so far [4].

The framework proposed in this paper, based on Armstrong's axiom system, is able to deal with different kinds of semantics in a unified manner. The semantics proposed for gene expression data were implemented as an extension of a free software dedicated to the analysis of microarray data (MeV of TIGR Institute).

For the time being, soundness and completeness of the Armstrong's axiom system have to be proved for every new semantics. We are currently working on a generic definition of a semantics which ensures that a semantics is well-formed if and only if it complies with this definition.

Moreover we are working on a more interactive process of discovery of rules, which would consist in requiring to the biologists some "templates" for the rules they are interested in, and then determining the semantics for which these rules are satisfied.

References

1. Shena, M., al.: Quantitative monitoring of gene expression patterns with a cdna microarray. Science (1995) 467–470
2. Fuhrman, S., Cunningham, M., Wen, X., Zweiger, G., Seilhamer, J., Somogyi, R.: The application of shannon entropy in the prediction of putative drug targets. BioSystems 55 (2000) 5–14
3. Scherf, U., al.: A gene expression database for the molecular pharmacology of cancer. Nature Genetics 24 (2000) 236–244
4. Eisen, M., Spellman, P., Brown, P., Botstein, D.: Gene expression profiling predicts clinical outcome of breast cancer. Proc Natl Acad Sci 95 (1998) 14863–14868
5. Aussem, A., Petit, J.M.: ε-functional dependency inference: application to dna microarray expression data. In Pucheral, P., ed.: Bases de données avancées (BDA'02), Evry, France (2002)
6. Berrar, D.P., Granzow, M., Dubitzky, W.: A Practical Approach to Microarray Data Analysis. Kluwer Academic Publishers (2002)
7. Becquet, C., Blachon, S., Jeudy, B., Boulicaut, J.F., Gandrillon, O.: Strong-association-rule mining for large-scale gene-expression data analysis: a case study on human sage data. Genome Biology 3 (2002)
8. Icev, A., Ruiz, C., Ryder, E.F.: Distance-enhanced association rules for gene expression. In: BIOKDD'03, in conjunction with ACM SIGKDD, Washington, DC, USA. (2003)
9. Creighton, C., Hanash, S.: Mining gene expression databases for association rules. Bioinformatics 19 (2003) 79–86
10. Agier, M., Chabaud, V., Petit, J.M., Sylvain, V., D'Incan, C., Vidal, V., Bignon, Y.J.: Towards meaningful rules between genes from gene expression data. In: poster, MGED'03, Aix en Provence. (2003)
11. Cong, G., Xu, X., Pan, F., A.K.H.Tung, Yang, J.: Farmer: Finding interesting rule groups in microarray datasets. In: SIGMOD. (2004)
12. Armstrong, W.W.: Dependency structures of data base relationships. In: Proc. of the IFIP Congress 1974. (1974) 580–583
13. Mannila, H., Räihä, K.J.: Algorithms for Inferring Functional Dependencies from Relations. DKE 12 (1994) 83–99
14. Demetrovics, J., Thi, V.: Some remarks on generating Armstrong and inferring functional dependencies relation. Acta Cybernetica 12 (1995) 167–180
15. Eiter, T., Gottlob, G.: Identifying the minimal transversals of a hypergraph and related problems. SIAM Journal on Computing 24 (1995) 1278–1304
16. Lopes, S., Petit, J.M., Lakhal, L.: Functional and approximate dependencies mining: Databases and FCA point of view. JETAI 14 (2002) 93–114
17. Agier, M., Petit, J.M., Chabaud, V., Pradeyrol, C., Bignon, Y.J., Vidal, V.: Vers différents types de règles pour les données d'expression de gènes-Application à des données de tumeurs mammaires. In: Actes du Congrès INFORSID'04, Biarritz. (2004)
18. Saeed, A., Sharov, V., White, J., Li, J., Liang, W., Bhagabati, N., Braisted, J., Klapa, M., Currier, T., Thiagarajan, M., Sturn, A., Snuffin, M., Rezantsev, A., Popov, D., Ryltsov, A., Kostukovich, E., Borisovsky, I., Liu, Z., Vinsavich, A., Trush, V., Quackenbush, J.: TM4: a free, open-source system for microarray data management and analysis. Biotechniques 34 (2003) 374–78
19. Ganter, B., Wille, R.: Formal Concept Analysis. Springer-Verlag (1999)
20. Beeri, C., Berstein, P.: Computational problems related to the design of normal form relation schemes. ACM TODS 4 (1979) 30–59
21. Maier, D.: Minimum covers in the relational database model. JACM 27 (1980) 664–674

22. Guigues, J.L., Duquenne, V.: Familles minimales d'implications informatives résultant d'un tableau de données binaires. Math. Sci. Humaines **24** (1986) 5–18
23. Gottlob, G., Libkin, L.: Investigations on Armstrong relations, dependency inference, and excluded functional dependencies. Acta Cybernetica **9** (1990) 385–402
24. Mannila, H., Räihä, K.J.: Algorithms for inferring functional dependencies from relations. DKE **12** (1994) 83–99
25. Mannila, H., Toivonen, H.: Levelwise search and borders of theories in knowledge discovery. DMKD **1** (1997) 241–258
26. Tan, P.N., Kumar, V., Srivastava, J.: Selecting the right objective measure for association analysis. Information Systems **29** (2004) 293–313

Flexible Pattern Discovery with (Extended) Disjunctive Logic Programming

Luigi Palopoli[1], Simona Rombo[2], and Giorgio Terracina[3]

[1] DEIS - Università della Calabria, Via Pietro Bucci, 87036 Rende (CS), Italy
[2] DIMET, Università "Mediterranea" di Reggio Calabria, Via Graziella, Località Feo di Vito, 89060 Reggio Calabria, Italy
[3] Dipartimento di Matematica, Università della Calabria, Via Pietro Bucci, 87036 Rende (CS), Italy
palopoli@deis.unical.it, rombo@ing.unirc.it, terracina@mat.unical.it

Abstract. The post-genomic era showed up a wide range of new challenging issues for the areas of knowledge discovery and intelligent information management. Among them, the discovery of complex pattern repetitions in string databases plays an important role, specifically in those contexts where even what are to be considered the interesting pattern classes is unknown. This paper provides a contribution in this precise setting, proposing a novel approach, based on disjunctive logic programming extended with several advanced features, for discovering interesting pattern classes from a given data set.

1 Introduction

In the last few years, a particular class of raw data stored in string databases, namely *genomic data*, is assuming a prominent role. The completion of the human genome sequencing showed up a wide range of new challenging issues involving sequence analysis. Genome databases mainly consist of sets of strings representing DNA or protein sequences (biosequences) and most of these strings still require to be "interpreted".

In this context, discovering common patterns in sets of biologically related sequences (i.e., motifs) is important because the presence of conserved regions provides insights into the biological function played by the corresponding macromolecules, e.g., for identifying gene regulatory processes [1, 5, 15].

Recently, a particular class of motifs, called structured motifs [16, 15], received much attention since it has been observed [7] that the relative positions of motif regions (we call these regions *boxes* in the following) are characterized when they participate in biological processes. For instance, the most frequently observed prokaryotic promoter regions are in general composed by two boxes positioned approximately 10 and 35 bases upstream from the transcription start. Moreover, since mutations are quite common and, often, important for the evolution, it is mandatory to allow mismatches among boxes in the analysis of their similarity. Clearly, as the complexity of the considered organisms increases, also

M.-S. Hacid et al. (Eds.): ISMIS 2005, LNAI 3488, pp. 504–513, 2005.
© Springer-Verlag Berlin Heidelberg 2005

the complexity of potentially interesting motifs increases [1] e.g., it is interesting to consider motifs with variable length boxes, or with unconstrained distances between boxes and so on.

In the literature, several algorithms for pattern discovery and several classes of patterns have been considered. As an example, [2, 4, 9, 10, 12] deal with simple (i.e., unstructured) motifs; other approaches consider structured motifs [8, 11, 17] but do not allow mismatches; others identify structured motifs allowing also mismatches [6, 15, 18][1].

All those approaches are tailored on specific classes of patterns and, as with most algorithms, even slight changes in the pattern class to be dealt with may cause significant problems in their effectiveness. Generally speaking, algorithms are available that are very efficient and effective when the class of patterns of interest is quite well defined (e.g., for prokaryotic promoter regions), but when the class of interest is unknown (e.g., in eukaryotes) the problem shifts away from motif extraction to the selection of the right approach to apply.

This paper is concerned with the definition and the implementation of a framework allowing for defining and resolving under-specified motif extraction problems where, for instance, the number and the length of boxes can be variable. Our framework *(i)* is general in that it covers a wide range of pattern classes; *(ii)* the computed results can be exploited to guide the selection of specific, efficient, algorithms tailored on the resulting pattern classes; *(iii)* it can be exploited as a "fast prototyping" approach to quickly verify the relevance of new pattern classes in specific biological domains. Notice that, given the complexity of the problem at hand, it is not expected that our approach will be particularly *efficient in solving* the motif discovery problem. Rather, it is mainly oriented to *verify the existence* of some kinds of interesting motif classes in available data.

Our framework is based on automatically generating logic programs starting from user-defined under-specified extraction problems for locating various kinds of motifs in a set of sequences. In this setting, we exploit disjunctive logic programming extended with a variety of features to obtain a sufficiently high language expressiveness allowing for dealing with a large variety of pattern classes. To the best of our knowledge, this is the first attempt in this direction.

We have developed a prototype implementing the proposed approach; in particular we exploited DLV [13] as the core inference engine and Java to equip the system with an easy, user-friendly interface.

2   Problem Statement and Supported Pattern Classes

In this section we illustrate the pattern classes currently supported in our framework. As pointed out in the Introduction, the main purpose of our approach is the identification of significant patterns frequently occurring in a set of input sequences; generally speaking, we look for *portions* of the input sufficiently similar to a number of other *portions* under some user-defined specifications. It

---

[1] A classification of the approaches for motif discovery is presented in [3].

Fig. 1. Example of structured patterns

is possible to identify two main categories of specifications, namely, structural specifications and affinity specifications.

Structural specifications refer to the structure the patterns must have in order to be considered interesting. In its simplest form, a pattern is composed by l contiguous symbols which are all interesting and must be taken into account in pattern repetitions. However, such kind of patterns is practically of low relevance. Indeed, it has been observed that often biologically relevant patterns are constituted by two or more relevant regions (we call these regions *boxes* in the rest of the paper) separated by a number of irrelevant symbols. Figure 1 graphically shows this concept. It indicates that the pattern constituted by the box 'AAA' followed by a number of irrelevant symbols, followed by the box 'TATT' is repeated in two of the three input sequences. In this setting, the following structural specifications can be defined:

Box number, denoting the number of distinct relevant regions the pattern must have in order to be considered interesting.

Box length, indicating the number of symbols in each box; in particular, different boxes may have different lengths and each box length may vary within a given interval.

Distance between boxes, indicating the number of irrelevant symbols separating two consecutive boxes; the framework allows both different distances for different box pairs and intervals of variations for each distance.

In several application contexts, it is useful to fix the content of some boxes to denote "anchors" in the pattern discovery process; as a consequence, the framework allows for the definition of the following specification:

Anchor box, which imposes that a pattern must contain precisely a certain, given content at a certain given position in order to be considered interesting.

In the following, for the sake of clarity, we shall use the notation $b_{l_1} X(d_1) b_{l_2} X(d_2)...X(d_{r-1}) b_{l_r}$ for representing pattern structure specifications; here, each b_{l_i} indicates a box of length l_i, each $X(d_j)$ indicates the sequence of d_j irrelevant symbols separating b_{l_j} from $b_{l_{j+1}}$, and r is the number of boxes. Both l_i, d_j and r can be intervals. We say that the box b_{l_i} is at position i within the pattern specification.

If structural specifications determine the characteristics of each pattern, *affinity specifications* fix the relationships that must hold between two patterns (or portions thereof) in order for them to be considered similar. We distinguish between two kinds of affinities: *(i)* single box affinity and *(ii)* whole pattern affinity.

Single box affinity tells when two boxes of two patterns can be considered similar. So, let s_1 and s_2 be two strings. The *Hamming Distance* $\mathcal{H}$ between

Skips Changing Box Order Inverse Box

Fig. 2. Examples of whole pattern affinity specifications

them is the minimum number of symbol substitutions to be applied on s_1 to obtain s_2, whereas the *Levenshtein Distance* $\mathcal{L}$ between them is the minimum number of *edit operations* (i.e. symbol substitutions, insertions and deletions) to be applied on s_1 to obtain s_2. As an example, '*AAGT*' and '*ACGA*' are at Hamming distance $\mathcal{H} = 2$, whereas the Levenshtein distance between '*misspell*' and '*mistell*' is $\mathcal{L} = 2$.

Single box affinities we consider are the following:

Exact match, that implies that two boxes must be exactly equal in order to be considered similar.

Hamming distance, for which two boxes are considered similar if their Hamming distance is less than a given threshold.

Levenshtein distance, for which two boxes are considered similar if their 14Levenshtein distance is less than a given threshold.

As far as *whole pattern affinity* is concerned, if no specifications are provided, it is assumed that two patterns p_1 and p_2 are similar if each pair of boxes b'_{l_i} of p_1 and b''_{l_i} of p_2 (i.e., boxes in the same positions within their patterns) are similar. In this case, we say that a basic similarity holds between p_1 and p_2.

Otherwise, the following whole pattern affinity specifications can be defined:

Allow Skips: two patterns p_1 and p_2 are considered similar even if a certain number of boxes of p_1 are not similar to the corresponding ones of p_2; the user can specify the maximum allowed number of skips.

Allow Changing Box Order: two patterns p_1 and p_2 are considered similar even if a certain number of changing box order occur; a changing box order occurs if the relative positions of two consecutive boxes in p_1 must be exchanged in order to obtain a basic similarity between p_1 and p_2.

Allow Inverse Box: two patterns p_1 and p_2 are considered similar even if the content of some (or all) boxes of p_1 must be inverted to obtain a basic similarity between p_1 and p_2.

Figure 2 graphically shows the above presented concepts. We are now ready to state the problem addressed in this paper.

Problem Statement. Given a collection of input sequences SC, a set of specifications and an integer Q, find all motifs in SC, that is all patterns satisfying the structural specifications and similar (w.r.t., the provided box affinity and whole pattern affinity specifications) to at least other Q patterns, each of which

obtained from a distinct sequence of *SC*. Q is called *quorum* and indicates the
minimum support a pattern must have within *SC*.   □

It is worth pointing out that most of the existing pattern discovery approaches
do not consider at all neither the Levenshtein distance for box affinity, nor whole
pattern affinity specifications introduced in this section.

Finally, note that since allowed affinity specifications are such that pattern
similarity is not transitive, it may happen that two patterns are similar but only
one of them is also a motif.

3   Automatic Generation of Logic Programs

3.1   Preliminaries

As pointed out in the Introduction, we exploit the DLV system [13] as the core
inference engine to implement our pattern discovery system, as it provides several
advanced features such as, *(i)* disjunctive rules, *(ii)* constraints, *(iii)* arithmetic
predicates, *(iv)* aggregate predicates and *(v)* external functions.

We assume the reader is familiar with (disjunctive) logic programming (see
[14] for a good source of background material). Some basic issues of the DLV
language are recalled next [13]. In DLV, a disjunctive rule a ∨ b :- c indicates
that if c is true, then either a or b must be true. Constraints of the form :- r
tell that condition r must be false in all models. Arithmetic predicates #int,
#succ, +, * allow to perform operations on integer valued variables. Aggregate
predicates can be computed over sets of elements. They can occur in the bodies
of rules and constraints, possibly negated by negation-as-failure. As an example,
the rule q(X) :- a(X), #count{Z : b(X,Z,k)} < 3 tells that q(X) is true
for each X such that a(X) is true and the number of times that b(X,Z,k) is
true is less than 3. Finally, external functions are linked dynamically to the logic
programs and are executed as standard imperative programs. We have tried
to obtain a good trade-off between declarativeness and efficiency limiting the
exploitation of external functions.

3.2   Program Generation

A first, important, issue to consider is how to represent the patterns satisfying
structural specifications that can be derived from the input sequences. Indeed,
the formalization of the whole approach depends on this representation.

We assume a pattern is represented as a list of ordered boxes; each box is
identified by the predicate box(B,IDS,Pos,Idx,L), where B represents the box
content, IDS is the identifier of the sequence B has been obtained from, Pos is the
starting position of B within IDS, whereas Idx specifies the position (index) of B
within the pattern; finally, L is the number of symbols in B. This last information is maintained only for efficiency matters, since it might be anyway derived
from B.

Before describing how the set of boxes is obtained by the program, it is necessary to introduce the set of facts automatically generated from the user inputs, that are:

(1) `string(IDS,''sequence'')`

(2) `boxNumber(R)`

(3) `quorum(Q)`

(4) `boxLength(Idx,Lmin,Lmax)`

(5) `boxDistance(Idx1,Idx2,Dmin,Dmax)`

(6) `error(Idx,Emax)`

(7) `skipNumber(Nskips)`

(8) `minStartPosition(Idx,PosMin,IDS)`

(9) `maxStartPosition(Idx,PosMax,IDS)`

There is a fact of type (1) for each input sequence; each *sequence* is associated with an identifier IDS. Facts (2) and (3) tell the number of boxes allowed for each pattern and the quorum, respectively. Facts of type (4) indicate the minimum and the maximum length each box might have; here, `Idx` indicates the position of the box within the pattern and varies between 1 and R. Analogously, facts of type (5) specify the allowed number of irrelevant symbols separating consecutive boxes. Facts of type (6) tell, for each box, the maximum allowed Hamming or Levenshtein distance for box affinity (it is set to 0 if selected box affinity is *exact match*) whereas, fact (7) encodes the maximum number of skips allowed in whole pattern affinity specification. Finally, facts of type (8) (resp., (9)) are obtained from both the structural specifications and the input sequences and state, for each box, its minimum (resp., maximum) allowed starting position within the input sequence IDS; this allows to reduce the search space. As an example for patterns of the form $b_3X(5)b_4$ the minimum starting position for a second box in a sequence is 9.

It is now possible to describe how boxes are represented:

```
(10) box(B,IDS,Pos,Idx,L) :- string(IDS,Str), #int(L), Lmin<=L, L<=Lmax,
     boxLength(Idx,Lmin,Lmax), minStartPosition(Idx,PosMin,IDS),
     maxStartPosition(Idx,PosMax,IDS), #int(Pos), Pos>=PosMin,
     Pos<=PosMax, #substring(Str,Pos,L,B)
```

Here, `#substring` is an external function used to store in B the substring of Str of length L starting from position Pos. At the basis of our pattern discovery approach there is a guess and check strategy. In particular, we guess a combination of Q+1 good patterns (where Q is the required quorum) such that one of them (the candidate pattern) is similar to the others Q (repetition patterns); moreover, each pattern must be taken from a distinct sequence. Now, since a pattern is represented as an ordered list of R boxes, the approach must guess (Q+1)× R boxes.

More precisely, the following rules are automatically generated:

```
(11) in(B,IDS,Pos,Idx,L) ∨ out(B,IDS,Pos,Idx,L) :- box(B,IDS,Pos,Idx,L)
(12) candidate(IDS) ∨ notCandidate(IDS) :- string(IDS,_)
(13) :- not #count{IDS: candidate(IDS)}=1
(14) :- inPredicates(N), not #count{B,Pos: in(B,IDS,Pos,Idx,L)}=N
(15) inPredicates(N) :- quorum(Q), boxNumber(R), #succ(Q,Q1),*(Q1,R,N)
(16) :- in(_,IDS,_,_,_), index(I), not #count{B,Pos: in(B,IDS,Pos,I,L)}=1
(17) index(I) :- boxLength(I,_,_)
```

where the in (resp., out) predicate represents selected (resp., discarded) boxes, whereas candidate specifies which is the pattern (taken from the sequence IDS) to be considered as a candidate motif[2]. Constraint (13) guarantees that only one candidate is selected. Rules (14) and (15) are used to assure that the number of in predicates evaluated *true* is exactly N=(Q+1)× R, whereas rules (16) and (17) guarantee that exactly one pattern is selected from each of the considered sequences.

Now, in order to complete the verification of structural specifications, only the following constraint is needed, dealing with the position of consecutive boxes in a pattern; indeed, the other structural specifications, namely *box length* and *box number*, are implicitly verified in rules (10) and (14-17).

```
(18) :- in(B1,IDS,Pos1,Idx1,L), in(B2,IDS,Pos2,Idx2,_), #succ(Idx1,Idx2),
        EndB1=Pos1+L,boxDistance(Idx1,Idx2,Dmin,Dmax),
        MinAllowedPosB2=EndB1+Dmin,MaxAllowedPosB2=EndB1+Dmax,
        outOfRange(MinAllowedPosB2,MaxAllowedPosB2,Pos2)
```

Here, outOfRange evaluates *true* if, given the position Pos1 of the first box B1, its length L and the allowed distances Dmin and Dmax between B1 and B2, the position Pos2 within IDS of the second box B2 is out of the allowed range.

If the user specifies an anchor box, a constraint stating that a model is valid only if that anchor is found in the pattern must be added in the program. As an example, if the user wants for the second box to be equal to 'TATA', the following constraint must be added:

```
(19) :- candidate(IDS), in(B,IDS,_,2,_), B!='TATA'
```

All the rules mentioned above are common to every combination of structural specifications defined by the user and constitute the *core program*. In order to handle affinity specifications, suitable rules are added depending on the kinds of options selected by the user. As far as single box affinity is concerned, the following rules are exploited:

```
(20) repetition(IDS) :- in(_,IDS,_,_,_), notCandidate(IDS)
(21) matchPair(IDS2,Idx) :- candidate(IDS1), repetition(IDS2),
        in(B1,IDS1,_,Idx,_), in(B2,IDS2,_,Idx,_), error(Idx,E),
        #distanceFunction(B1,B2,E)
```

Here, rule (20) singles out the Q sequences where repetitions of the candidate pattern are searched for (that there are exactly Q selected sequences derives from rules (14-17) above), whereas rule (21) defines when two boxes B1 and B2 belonging, respectively, to the candidate pattern and to a repetition pattern, are to be considered similar. B1 and B2 must satisfy the following conditions: *(i)* they must have the same position (Idx) within the pattern, *(ii)* the computed distance between B1 and B2 must be less than or equal to E. In particular, if the

---

[2] Note that, since we guess exactly one pattern from a sequence, there is a one-to-one correspondence between IDS and the corresponding pattern.

user specifies the *Hamming* (resp., *Levenshtein*) distance, `#distanceFunction` denotes the call to the external function `#Hamming` (resp., `#Levenshtein`) which computes the Hamming (resp., the Levenshtein) distance D between B1 and B2 and evaluates *true* if `D<=E` and *false* otherwise. On the contrary, if the user specifies as box affinity the *exact match*, `#distanceFunction` reduces to the expression `B1==B2`.

Finally, in order to handle whole pattern affinity specifications, the following rules are generated. If no specific option is selected, i.e. only basic similarity is required, only the following constraint is necessary:

(22) `:- boxNumber(R), repetition(IDS),`
     `not #count{Idx: matchPair(IDS,Idx)}=R`

It imposes that for each repetition string `IDS`, `matchPair` evaluates *true* for every box. This means that each box of a repetition pattern, matches (w.r.t. the selected box affinity) the corresponding box of the candidate pattern.

If the user wants to allow some skips to occur in repetitions, constraint (22) is substituted by the following:

(23) `:- boxNumber(R), repetition(IDS), skipNumber(Nskips),`
     `not #count{Idx: matchPair(IDS,Idx)}>=R-NSkips`

In order to handle changing box order, the following rules must be exploited:

(24) `matchPair(IDS2,I)  :- changeOrder(IDS2,I)`
(25) `matchPair(IDS2,J)  :- index(J), #succ(I,J), changeOrder(IDS2,I)`
(26) `changeOrder(IDS2,I)  :- candidate(IDS1), repetition(IDS2),`
     `in(B11,IDS1,_,I,_), in(B12,IDS1,_,J,_)`
     `in(B21,IDS2,_,I,_), in(B22,IDS2,_,J,_),`
     `#succ(I,J), error(I,E1), error(J,E2),`
     `#distanceFunction(B11,B22,E1),#distanceFunction(B12,B21,E2)`

Here, `#distanceFunction` must be substituted by the proper function for verifying box affinity, as shown for rule (21). Note that rule (26) compares pairs of boxes having crossing indexes; if a change of order occurs, *one* `matchPair` evaluates *true* for *each* of the two involved indexes I and J (remember that J=I+1). Finally, in order to handle inverse boxes, the following rule must be added:

(27) `matchPair(IDS2,Idx)  :- candidate(IDS1), repetition(IDS2),`
     `in(B1,IDS1,_,Idx,_), in(B2,IDS2,_,Idx,_), error(Idx,E),`
     `#inverse(B1,B1I), #distanceFunction(B1I,B2,E)`

where the external function `#inverse` evaluates always *true* and stores in `B1I` the inverse string of B1 and `#distanceFunction` must be substituted by the proper function for verifying box affinity, as described above.

It is worth pointing out that the system generates a valid model for each guess satisfying all the introduced constraints. As a consequence, the set of all valid models generated by the system, corresponds to the set of motifs occurring in the input sequences satisfying user specifications.

4   Conclusions

In this paper we have shown a novel approach based on (extended) disjunctive logic programming for discovering interesting pattern classes from a given data set. The approach is flexible in that a wide range of pattern classes are supported. A specialized GUI makes using the system particularly user-friendly and the logic program generation task is completely transparent to the user.

Currently the system is exploited at the *Cellular Biology Department* of Università della Calabria in advanced biological research issues, such as the thermodynamic stability of Human Genome macromolecules. In the future we plan to further extend the supported pattern classes and to provide the system with refined post-elaboration features to support an in-depth analysis of the obtained results.

Acknowledgments. This work was partially funded by the Italian Ministry of Education, University and Research under the COFIN'03 project "Tecniche di induzione di regole, metaquerying ed estrazione di pattern strutturati su database biologici". The Authors gratefully thank Adele Losso for providing the Human Genome sequences and Nicola Leone and Pasquale Grimaldi for their precious help and comments in the development of this work.

References

1. M.I. Arnone and E.H. Davidson. The hardwiring of development: organization and function of genomic regulatory systems. *Development*, 124:1851–1864, 1997.
2. T.L. Bailey and C. Elkan. Unsupervised learning of multiple motifs in biopolymers using expectation maximization. *Machine Learning*, 21(1-2):51–80, 1995.
3. A. Brazma, I. Jonassen, I. Eidhammer, and D. Gilbert. Approaches to the automatic discovery of patterns in biosequences. *Journal of Computational Biology*, 5(2):277–304, 1998.
4. J. Buhler and M. Tompa. Finding motifs using random projections. In *Proceedings of Fifth Annual International Conference on Computational Molecular Biology (RECOMB01)*, pages 69–76, 2001.
5. I. Erill, M. Escribano, S. Campoy, and J. Barb. In silico analysis reveals substantial variability in the gene contents of the gamma proteobacteria lexa-regulon. *Bioinformatics*, 19(17):2225–2236, 2003.
6. E. Eskin and P.A. Pevzner. Finding composite regulatory patterns in DNA sequences. In *Proceedings of the Tenth International Conference on Intelligent Systems for Molecular Biology (ISMB-2002)*, pages 354–363, 2002.
7. C.A. Gross, M. Lonetto, and R. Losick. Bacterial sigma factors. *Transcriptional Regulation*, 1:129–176, 1992.
8. J. van Helden, A.F. Rios, and J. Collado-Vides. Discovering regulatory elements in non-coding sequences by analysis of spaced dyads. *Nucleic Acids Research*, 28(8):1808–1818, 2000.
9. G. Hertz, G. Stormo. Identifying DNA and protein patterns with statistically significant alignments of multiple sequences. *Bioinformatics*, 15(7-8):563–577, 1999.

10. J. Hughes, P. Estep, S. Tavazoie, and G. Church. Computational identification of cis-regulatory elements associated with groups of functionally related genes in saccharomyces cerevisiae. *Journal of Computational Biology*, 10:1205–1214, 2000.

11. I. Jonassen, J.F. Collins, and D.G. Higgins. Finding flexible patterns in unaligned protein sequences. *Protein Science*, 4:1587–1595, 1995.

12. U. Keich and P.A. Pevzner. Finding motifs in the twilight zone. In *Proceedings of the Sixth Annual International Conference on Computational Biology (RECOMB02)*, pages 195–204, 2002.

13. N. Leone, G. Pfeifer, W. Faber, T. Eiter, G. Gottlob, S. Perri, and F. Scarcello. The DLV System for Knowledge Representation and Reasoning. *ACM Transactions on Computational Logic*, 2004. To appear. Available via http://www.arxiv.org/ps/cs.AI/0211004.

14. Vladimir Lifschitz. Foundations of Logic Programming. In G. Brewka, editor, *Principles of Knowledge Representation*, pages 69–127. CSLI Publications, Stanford, 1996.

15. L. Marsan and M.F. Sagot. Algorithms for extracting structured motifs using a suffix tree with application to promoter and regulatory site consensus identification. *Journal of Computational Biology*, 7:345–360, 2000.

16. S. Robin, J.J. Daudin, H. Richard, M.F. Sagot, and S. Schbath. Occurrence probability of structured motifs in random sequences. *Journal of Computational Biology*, 9:761–773, 2003.

17. H.O. Smith, T.M. Annau, and S. Chandrasegaran. Finding sequence motifs in groups of functionally related proteins. In *Proc. of National Academy of Science*, pages 826–830, U.S.A., 1990.

18. G. Terracina. A fast technique for deriving frequent structured patterns from biological data sets. *Information Sciences*, Forthcoming.

Interactive SOM-Based Gene Grouping:
An Approach to Gene Expression Data Analysis

Alicja Gruździ, Aleksandra Ihnatowicz, and Dominik Ślęzak

Department of Computer Science, University of Regina,
Regina, SK, S4S 0A2 Canada,
Polish-Japanese Institute of Information Technology,
Koszykowa 86, 02-008, Warsaw, Poland

Abstract. We propose an approach to clustering and visualization of the DNA microarray-based gene expression data. We implement the self-organizing map (SOM) handling similarities between genes in terms of their expression characteristics. The resulting algorithmic toolkit is enriched with graphical interface enabling the user to interactively support the entire learning process. Preliminary calculations and consultations with biomedical experts positively verify applicability of our method.

Keywords: Self-Organizing Maps, Gene Expression Data, Interactive Visualization of Dependencies, Mutual Information Entropy Measures.

1 Introduction

The DNA microarray technology provides enormous quantities of biological information about genetically conditioned susceptibility to diseases [2]. The data sets acquired from microarrays refer to genes via their expression levels. Comparison of expressions of different genes in various conditions and for various organisms can be very helpful while formulating biomedical hypotheses.

Analysis of the DNA microarrays is difficult because of extremely large number of genes. A typical gene expression data set has a small number of experiments, while the number of attributes is counted in thousands. Another challenge is in defining functional similarities between genes, which is complex from the genetic point of view, with no commonly approved methodology existing.

The appropriate choice of a gene expression similarity function is important, in particular, in case of the unsupervised grouping algorithms, such as hierarchical clustering [22], Bayesian clustering [12], or, e.g., self-organizing maps (SOM) [24]. Clustering techniques are applied in the gene expression data analysis to group the experiments (cf. [3]) or genes (cf. [23]), depending on application.

Genes with similar functions are expected to be grouped together. For instance, for data about tumors, we would like to obtain the groups of *oncogenes* and *suppressors*, hypothetically considered as tumor indicators [4, 6]. A perfect situation is when every single indicator discriminates experiments related to diseased and healthy cases. However, the gene expressions do not provide such

M.-S. Hacid et al. (Eds.): ISMIS 2005, LNAI 3488, pp. 514–523, 2005.
© Springer-Verlag Berlin Heidelberg 2005

information. Also, genes seem to be able to exchange their functions in patho-logical cases [20]. This is why the analysis of groups of genes may help.

While grouping genes it is important to provide visualization enabling the bio-medical experts to interact with the algorithmic framework. A number of learning methods providing graphical models can be applied with that respect [7, 25]. We focus on the above-mentioned SOM method, as it directly expresses similarities graphically [3, 11]. It simplifies visualization and interpretation by producing a non-linear mapping of the data to a (usually) two-dimensional grid, well usable for generating hypotheses on the gene relationships.

We develop the *Gene-Organizing Map* system (*GenOM*) for mapping rela-tionships between genes derived from DNA microarrays. The SOM architecture is adapted to model the expression characteristics within the grid locations. The similarity functions to be mapped in the grid are calculated as various attribute relationships, beginning from the Euclidean-style comparison, through statistical correlations [8], up to the information theoretic measures [10]. We also implement GUI enabling the expert to work interactively with the SOM learning process.

Calculations performed for the data set related to a selected type of soft tissue tumor [1, 17][1], further referred to as to the *Synovial Sarcoma* data, illustrate the proposed approach. The results do not have a confirmed biomedical value yet, for knowledge about the gene expression relationships is still limited. The only possibility of a future full verification is to cooperate further with the domain experts. On the other hand, even the presented initial illustrative calculations show GenOM's advantages with regards to development of such cooperation.

The article is organized as follows: In Section 2 we present the basics of the DNA microarrays. In Section 3 we consider various distance/correlation func-tions for measuring the gene similarities. In Section 4 we introduce our interac-tive SOM-based framework for the gene similarities. In Section 5 we discuss the results and in Section 6 we summarize the main features of our approach.

2   Basics of DNA Microarrays

The DNA microarray technology [2, 19] enables simultaneous analysis of charac-teristics of thousands of genes in the biological samples of interest. It is au-tomated, quicker, and less complicated than the previous methods of mole-cular biology, allowing scientists to study no more than a few genes at a time.

Microarrays have different formats, but all of them rely on DNA sequences fabricated on glass slides, silicon chips or nylon membranes [19]. Each slide (DNA chip) contains samples of many genes at fixed locations. Each spot on the slide corresponds to a single gene. It may represent cDNA (the most popular, used also in our calculations), DNA or oligonucleotide (a short fragment of a single-stranded DNA that is typically 5 to 50 nucleotides long).

---

[1] Downloaded from http://genome-www.stanford.edu/sarcoma/. We would like to thank the data suppliers for opportunity to run calculations using this data set.

The microarray production starts with preparing two samples of mRNA. The actual sample of interest is paired with a healthy control sample. The fluorescent labels are applied to both the control (green) and the actual (red) samples. The procedure of mixing two labeled samples is repeated for each of thousands of genes on the slide. Then the slide is washed and the color intensities of every gene-spot are scanned. Fluorescence of red and green colors indicates to what extent particular genes are expressed. Fig. 1 roughly illustrates this process.

We obtain the gene expression data system $\mathbb{A} = (U, A)$, where U is the set of experiments and A – the set of genes. Every gene $a \in A$ corresponds to the function $a : U \to \mathbb{R}$ labeling experiments with their expression levels. The data can be represented in various ways (here we use the notation proposed in [14] for information systems), often in a transposed form. Then, as displayed in Fig. 1, genes correspond to the rows and experiments – to the data table's columns.

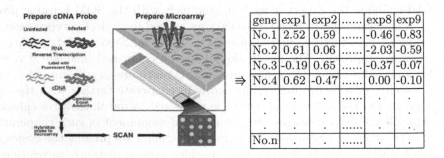

gene	exp1	exp2	......	exp8	exp9
No.1	2.52	0.59	......	-0.46	-0.83
No.2	0.61	0.06	......	-2.03	-0.59
No.3	-0.19	0.65	......	-0.37	-0.07
No.4	0.62	-0.47	......	0.00	-0.10
.	.	.	......	.	.
.	.	.	......	.	.
.	.	.	......	.	.
No.n	.	.	......	.	.

Fig. 1. Microarrays provide the gene expression data. A sample of 9 experiments from the *Synovial Sarcoma* data is illustrated. We have $n = 5520$ genes in this data set

The analysis of such prepared data can lead to discoveries of important dependencies in gene sequences, structures, and expressions. For instance, the cDNA microarray data sets are often analyzed to track down the changes of the gene activations for different types of tumors. This information could be then applied to identifying tumor-specific and tumor-associated genes [20].

3   Gene Expression Similarities

The process of retrieving meaningful cluster-based information demands the appropriate distance metrics. This non-trivial problem becomes even more complicated in the case of a model so unexplored and complex as genes. Defining biologically natural and understandable similarities is very challenging, mostly from the fact that we still know little about genes' functions.

At the current level of genetic knowledge we can just compare the analytical results with the experts' directions and commonly known medical facts. Let us select three genes regarded as relevant to the soft tissue tumor studies [1, 17]:

1. 113533 SRCL scavenger receptor with C-type lectin Hs.29423
2. 109299 SRCL scavenger receptor with C-type lectin Hs.29423
3. 111192 TP53 tumor protein p53 (Li-Fraumeni syndrome) Hs.1846

Fig. 2 illustrates relationships between expressions of these gene examples. As a reference, a gene totally unrelated to the *Synovial Sarcoma* tumor is added.

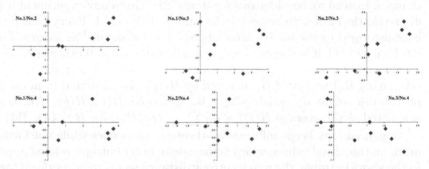

Fig. 2. The higher three plots visualize the sampled expression data distributions for pairs of the above-mentioned three genes known from the *Synovial Sarcoma* tumor studies. The lower plots put them against a tumor irrelevant gene 103806 ESTs Hs.47047

We test how available mathematical functions reflect similarities between genes. We consider the Euclidean distance, as well as the Pearson and Spearman (rank order) correlations [8]. The results are provided in Fig. 3, where we order the gene pairs beginning with most similar (closest or most correlated) ones.

Similarity based on	most similar pairs $\longrightarrow$ least similar pairs
Euclidean distance	(2,3) (1,4) (3,4) (1,2) (1,3) (2,4)
Pearson correlation	(2,3) (3,4) (1,2) (1,3) (2,4) (1,4)
Spearman correlation	(2,3) (1,2) (3,4) (1,3) (2,4) (1,4)
Rough entropy distance	(2,3) (1,2) (1,3) (1,4) (3,4) (2,4)

Fig. 3. Similarities between the gene expression patterns obtained using four measures. Numbers 1,2,3 in the second column correspond to the above-mentioned three *Synovial Sarcoma*-related genes. Number 4 denotes the tumor-irrelevant gene added in Fig. 2

The above example confirms intuition that we should focus on catching the global gene transcription profile changes rather than local differences in expressions. Local differences are reflected by the Euclidean-like distances. Global changes can be captured by statistical correlations, although they may be inaccurate because of imprecise measurements and diversified data origin [1, 17].

The fourth method in Fig. 3, *rough entropy distance*, refers to the well known information-theoretic measures [10]. In its simplest form it is defined

518   A. Gruźdź, A. Ihnatowicz, and D. Ślęzak

as $\varrho_U(a,b) = H(a|b) + H(b|a) = 2H(a,b) - H(a) - H(b)$, where $H(a)$, $H(b)$ are entropies of genes $a, b \in A$, and $H(a,b)$ is the entropy of the product variable (a,b). Using the classical entropy formula for qualitative data, we obtain that $\varrho_U(a,b) \geq 0$, where equality holds if and only if a and b determine each other.

Normally, such entropy-based $\varrho_U(a,b)$ would require *discretization* of quantitative expression data or proceeding with parameterized probabilistic density estimates. Both approaches, however, seem to be too sensitive to the parameter changes. Instead we consider *rough entropy* [21]. Given any experiment $u \in U$, we discretize the data with respect to its values $a(u)$, $a \in A$. Every gene $a : U \to \mathbb{R}$ is transformed to the binary attribute $a_u : U \to \mathbb{R}$ defined as follows: For every $e \in U$, $a_u(e) = 1$ if and only if $a(e) \geq a(u)$, and $a_u(e) = 0$ otherwise.

Given $B \subseteq A$ and $u \in U$, we denote by B_u the set of u-discretized genes taken from B. Entropy of B_u, denoted by $H(B_u)$, is calculated from the product probabilities of binary variables $a_u \in B_u$. Entropies $H(a)$, $H(b)$, $H(a,b)$ are then calculated as the average $H(B) = \frac{1}{|U|} \sum_{u \in U} H_U(B_u)$, for $B = \{a\}$, $\{b\}$, $\{a,b\}$.

Rough entropy keeps information-theoretic properties while not focusing too much on the actual values, which is the case of other entropy-related approaches. In the above example, the rough entropy distance seems to outperform the Spearman correlation. However, obviously, more calculations are needed to decide which method is most suitable to model the gene dependencies.

4   SOM-Based Gene Grouping

Given functions studied in previous section with regards to capturing the gene similarities, we develop the self-organizing map (SOM) [3, 11] framework for calculating and visualizing the gene expression clusters. Every SOM forms a nonlinear mapping of a high dimensional data manifold into a regular, low-dimensional (usually 2D) grid. Both researchers and practitioners find that kind of display as useful for understanding the compound dependencies in data.

Let us consider a gene expression data system $\mathbb{A} = (U, A)$. For any function $\varrho_U : A \times A \to [0, +\infty)$ measuring the gene distances, we consider the following optimization problem: For every $g \in A$, find the 2D-grid coordinates (x_g, y_g) such that the grid distances $\varrho_{2D}(a,b) = \sqrt{(x_a - x_b)^2 + (y_a - y_b)^2}$ reflect *optimally* the actual distances $\varrho_U(a,b)$, for all possible pairs of genes $a, b \in A$.

To optimize the gene grid locations, a standard learning procedure proposed by Kohonen [11] can be applied. Every grid position (i,j) is first initiated with randomly generated artificial gene expressions $a_{ij} : U \to \mathbb{R}$, $i, j = 1, \ldots, N$, where N reflects the grid size. Then the following heuristic steps are repeated:

- For a randomly chosen $a \in A$, find (using possibly a randomized method) the ϱ_U-closest artificial gene a_{ij}, where $\varrho_U(a, a_{ij})$ is calculated as if $a_{ij} \in A$. Remember the obtained (i,j) as the current a's grid location.
- Change a_{ij} to a'_{ij} in such a way that $\varrho_U(a, a'_{ij}) \leq \varrho_U(a, a_{ij})$. Do the same with the neighboring grid locations (k,l). The decrease of $\varrho_U(a, a'_{kl})$ with respect to $\varrho_U(a, a_{kl})$ should be opposite to the distance $\sqrt{(i-k)^2 + (j-l)^2}$.

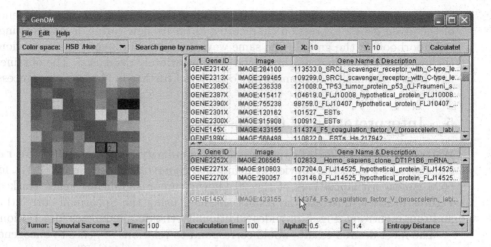

Fig. 4. Graphical GenOM interface. The left part provides the grid of clusters grouping together the most similar genes. Currently highlighted clusters are displayed in detail in the right part. There, the user can drag&drop genes between clusters. Quick recalculation of the map settings after such an operation is automatically supported

The procedure results in the set of the gene grid locations obtained after appropriately many above-described steps. Obviously, a lot of technical issues must be decided while handling the grid neighborhoods and, most of all, while modifying the expression characteristics to control appropriately the values of ϱ_U. We implement and adjust all those parameters within our algorithmic framework called the *Gene-Organizing Map* system, abbreviated as *GenOM*.

To summarize, at GenOM learning level, optimization of the genes' locations within the grid is standard, except operations measuring the distances and updating the grid position characteristics. At GenOM display level, relationships between the groups of similar genes are presented on a scalable 2D image, illustrated by Fig. 4. While selecting the cluster(s), the Gene Cards database [18] is automatically queried to provide information about its (their) elements.

GenOM is regarded as intuitive by the experts. Drag&drop function enables them to interact with the system and easily express assumptions about the gene dependencies. In this way, the following problems are solved, at least partially:

- The space of possible solutions – the grid locations of genes – is enormous. There is no guarantee that the heuristic procedure described in the previous section leads to optimum. A kind of correcting guidance would be helpful.
- Microarrays do not provide complete information about genes. They refer to genes indirectly, via their expressions. Moreover, those expressions can be imprecise depending on the applied microarray technology. An additional tool for interactive involvement of the expert knowledge seems to be required.

An important GenOM's computational feature is that drag&drop leads to the fast grid recalculation with compliance of the manually introduced changes.

The program modifies the grid settings by increasing the mathematical influence
of the given gene's expression characteristics on its new (after drag&dropping)
neighborhood in the grid. In the same way, the gene's influence on its previous
(before drag&dropping) neighborhood is appropriately decreased. The obtained
new map's settings are automatically considered further in the learning process.

5   Interpretation of the Results

We tested our system by applying various similarity representations. We ran
calculations against the previously mentioned *Synovial Sarcoma* data [1, 17], for
5520 genes, with positions of the 20 known tumor significant genes tracked.
Figures 6 and 5 illustrate the results obtained using the Spearman correlation
and rough entropy. Fig. 5 provides additionally the detailed genes' description.

The most desired results would correspond to relations of genes to oncogenes
and suppressors. However, only a few of them are known [4, 6]. The objective for
now is rather to get clusters of genes with similar functionality, possibly coding
the same proteins. In Fig. 5, the interesting sets of genes are well recognizable by
their group names (like e.g. FLT1 for microarray locations 280413 and 67221),

IMAGE	Gene Description	Entr.	Spea.
280413	115575 FLT1 fms-related tyrosine kinase 1	0 x 4	0 x 0
154472	101364 FGFR1 fibroblast growth factor receptor 1	9 x 3	6 x 6
711857	119431 FGFR1 fibroblast growth factor receptor 1	9 x 6	7 x 3
196282	102991 CSF1R colony stimulating factor 1 receptor	4 x 2	7 x 3
713974	101986 CSF1R colony stimulating factor 1 receptor	9 x 0	0 x 4
1637226	99123 FLT3LG fms-related tyrosine kinase 3 ligand	0 x 4	4 x 2
67221	107367 FLT1 fms-related tyrosine kinase 1	0 x 4	0 x 0
358531	111813 JUN v-jun avian sarcoma virus 17 oncogene homolog	9 x 4	1 x 8
122428	100044 JUNB jun B proto-oncogene	1 x 0	6 x 9
309864	115464 JUNB jun B proto-oncogene	4 x 2	6 x 9
265060	99028 KIT v-kit feline sarcoma viral 4 oncogene homolog	7 x 9	1 x 1
147075	100337 MDM2, human homolog of p53-binding protein	9 x 8	4 x 9
40303	119774 SHC1 SHC transforming protein 1	3 x 0	1 x 1
77133	111828 SHC1 SHC transforming protein 1	4 x 1	2 x 5
770794	116399 SHB SHB adaptor protein	6 x 6	3 x 0
236338	121008 TP53 tumor protein p53 (Li-Fraumeni syndrome)	9 x 3	1 x 9
24415	111192 TP53 tumor protein p53 (Li-Fraumeni syndrome)	9 x 3	0 x 8
284100	113533 SRCL scavenger receptor with C-type lectin	9 x 4	8 x 9
299465	109299 SRCL scavenger receptor with C-type lectin	0 x 1	0 x 6
193913	118000 LYN v-yes Yamaguchi sarcoma viral 1 oncogene homol.	1 x 0	9 x 9

Fig. 5. Twenty out of the known tumor significant genes. Column *IMAGE* uniquely
identifies genes by their microarray locations. Images 284100, 299465, 24415 correspond
to genes No.1,2,3 discussed in Section 3. Columns *Entr.* and *Spea.* provide the genes'
coordinates within the entropy and Spearman correlation-based maps from Fig. 6

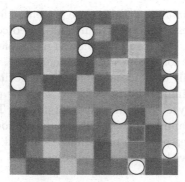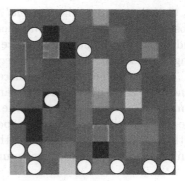

Fig. 6. GenOM maps for 5520-gene *Synovial Sarcoma* data obtained using the rough entropy distance (left) and the Spearman correlation (right) over the 10x10 grid. The clusters where the tumor significant genes belong to are marked by white circles. Black areas correspond to the map coordinates where there are no genes located

as well as additional functional descriptions (like e.g. a relation to the *tyrosine kinase* protein in case of 280413 and 67221, but also 1637226). Comparison of the grid coordinates of such genes seems to be a good verification criterion.

Both the rough entropy and Spearman-related methods provide promising results, although some obvious errors occur (like in case of genes 196282 and 713974, or 284100 and 193913 – those mistakes might have the origin in the quality of data). In other cases, the two considered measures seem to be complementary, as reflecting different aspects of similarity (two genes belonging to the JUNB group are clustered together by the Spearman correlation, but in case of, e.g., the SHC1 group the rough entropy distance is better).

Once we obtain the genes clustered together by both the rough entropy and Spearman correlation (like in case of groups FLT1 + FLT3LG, although 1637226 is not so close to the others when that latter measure is applied), we may formulate a hypothesis about a functional relationship. Obviously, such hypotheses are most valuable when involving genes with yet unrecognized functions, especially in case they occur together with some already documented indicators.

6   Conclusions

We developed a new framework for visualization of the gene expression data obtained from the DNA microarrays. We implemented the Gene-Organizing Map (GenOM) system, which maps compound gene expression similarities onto the two-dimensional grid by using a modified SOM-based technique. We designed the interface enabling the experts to interactively tune up the GenOM data analysis process by drag&dropping the genes between clusters. A novel computational method for combining such graphically expressed experts' suggestions with the standard self-organizing map learning algorithms was proposed.

Calculations over the *Synovial Sarcoma* data [1, 17] were presented for the two most promising (dis)similarity measures – the Spearman rank-based correlation and a new rough entropy distance [21]. The results, although incomplete at this stage of research, show some directions for future improvements.

The obtained errors do not necessarily depend on the applied algorithms. The gene expression characteristics can be influenced in different ways by particular tumors or even by locations of the analyzed cells in a given organism. Therefore, the actual verification of the proposed approach is possible only via cooperation with the domain experts. From this perspective, both analytical and graphical components of GenOM seem to meet with practical requirements.

Acknowledgements. Supported by the research grant from Natural Sciences and Engineering Research Council of Canada awarded to the third author, and by the Research Centre of Polish-Japanese Institute of Information Technology. Special thanks to the geneticists and oncologists we consulted with.

References

1. Alizadeh, A.A., et al : Distinct types of diffuse large B-cell lymphoma identified by gene expression profiling. Nature 403 (2000) pp. 503–511.
2. Baldi, P., Hatfield, W.G.: DNA Microarrays and Gene Expression: From Experiments to Data Analysis and Modeling. Cambridge University Press (2002).
3. Burger, M., Graepel, T., Obermayer, K.: Self-organizing maps: Generalizations and new optimization techniques. Neurocomputing 20 (1998) pp. 173–190.
4. Cooper, G.M.: Oncogenes. Jones & Bartlett Publishers (1995).
5. Draghici, S.: Data Analysis Tools for DNA Microarray. Chapman & Hall (2003).
6. El-Deiry, W.S.: Tumor Suppresor Genes: Regulation, Function and Medical Applications. Humana Press (2003).
7. Eriksen, K.A., Hornquist, M., Sneppen, K.: Visualization of large-scale correlations in gene expressions. Funct Integr Genomics 4/4 (2004) pp. 241–245.
8. Friedman, J.H., Hastie, T., Tibshirani, R.: The Elements of Statistical Learning: Data Mining, Inference, and Prediction. Springer Verlag (2001).
9. Friedman, N., Linial, M., Nachman, I., Pe'er, D.: Using Bayesian networks to analyze expression data. Journal of Computational Biology 7 (2000) pp. 601–620.
10. Kapur, J.N., Kesavan, H.K.: Entropy Optimization Principles with Applications. Academic Press (1992).
11. Kohonen, T.: Self-organized formation of topologically correct feature maps. Biological Cybernetics 43 (1982) pp. 59–69.
12. Liu, J.S., Zhang, J.L., Palumbo, M.J., Lawrence, C.E.: Bayesian Clustering with Variable and Transformation Selections. In: Bayesian Statistics 7. Oxford University Press (2003) pp. 249–275.
13. Oja, E., Kaski, S.: Kohonen Maps. Elsevier Science (1999).
14. Pawlak, Z.: Rough sets – Theoretical aspects of reasoning about data. Kluwer Academic Publishers (1991).
15. Rampal, J.B.: DNA Arrays: Methods and Protocols (Methods in Molecular Biology). Humana Press (2001).
16. Rebhan, M., Chalifa-Caspi, V., Prilusky, J., Lancet, D.: GeneCards: encyclopedia for genes, proteins and diseases. Weizmann Institute of Science, Bioinformatiecs Unit and Genome Center (1997).

17. Ross, D.T., et al : Systematic variation in gene expression patterns in human cancer cell lines. Nature Genetics 24 (2000) pp. 227–235.
18. Safran, M., et al : Human Gene-Centric Databases at the Weizmann Institute of Science: GeneCards, UDB, CroW 21 and HORDE. Nucleic Acids Res. 31/1 (2003) pp. 142–146.
19. Schena, M.: Microarray Biochip Technology. Eaton Publishing Company / Biotechniques Books (2000).
20. Senn, H.J., Morant, R.: Tumor Prevention and Genetics (Recent Results in Cancer Research). Springer-Verlag (2003).
21. Ślęzak, D.: Rough entropy – non-parametric approach to measuring dependencies in quantitative data. In preparation.
22. Spellman, P.T., et al : Comprehensive identification of cell cycle-regulated genes of the yeast Saccharomyces cerevisiae by microarray hybridization. Mol Biol Cell, Dec 9 (1998) pp. 3273–3297.
23. Spellman, P.T., et al : Functional clustering of genes using microarray gene expression data. Nature Genetics 23/75 (1999) Poster Abstracts.
24. Tamayo, P., et al : Interpreting patterns of gene expression with self-organizing maps: methods and application to hematopoietic differentiation. In: Proc Natl Acad Sci USA, 96/6 (1999) pp. 2907–2912.
25. Zimmer, D.P., Paliy, O., Thomas, B., Gyaneshwar, P., Kustu, S.: Genome image programs: visualization and interpretation of Escherichia coli microarray experiments. Genetics 167/4 (2004) pp. 2111–2119.

Some Theoretical Properties of Mutual Information for Student Assessments in Intelligent Tutoring Systems

Chao-Lin Liu

Dept. of Computer Science, Nat'l Chengchi Univ., Taipei 11605, Taiwan
chaolin@nccu.edu.tw

Abstract. This paper presents recently discovered properties of mutual information between concepts and dichotomous test items. The properties generalize some common intuitions for comparing test items, and provide principled foundations for designing item-selection heuristics for student assessments in computer-assisted educational systems. We compare performance profiles achieved by systems that adopt mutual information and the Mahalanobis distance in the assessment task. Experimental results reveal that, all else being equal, the mutual information based methods offer better performance profiles. In addition, experimental results suggest that, when computing mutual information online is considered computationally costly, heuristics that are designed based on our theoretical findings serve as a good delegate for exact mutual information.

1 Introduction

When we have a test-item database available for assessing students' competence of a set of concepts, we face the problem of selecting the best subset of the items in the database so that we can effectively assess the subject student. Possible applications of the assessment include, but not limited to, assigning scores to students and diagnosing students' incompetence of some concepts [1]. In this paper we concern ourselves with the latter application. Assuming that there is a limited number of types of students and that members belonging to each type share competence patterns, we propose methods for identifying types of students based on their item-response patterns in an interactive environment. This is a *latent class analysis* problem, and the literature has seen ample research work in this regard, e.g., [2]. As a result, we are in no position to do a broad review on this research field, but choose to turn attention to our target problem.

Test items are designed to probe students' competence of some target concepts, and test administrators rely on students' responses to test items to assess the students. In the ideal case, students always respond correctly to the items for the concepts that the students already understand and can apply, and always respond incorrectly to items for concepts that they do not understand or cannot apply. In such an ideal world, there will be few difficulty, if any, in diagnosing students' deficiency by their item-response patterns. A rule-based system will suffice. In the real world, students' item-response patterns are "fuzzy" [3] because students may *slip* (responding incorrectly to items that they are supposed to respond correctly) and *guess* (responding correctly to items that the students do not have necessary knowledge). Hence, reasoning about students' knowledge levels with such fuzzy item-response patterns can be challenging.

M.-S. Hacid et al. (Eds.): ISMIS 2005, LNAI 3488, pp. 524–534, 2005.
© Springer-Verlag Berlin Heidelberg 2005

Researchers have proposed probability-based approaches to confront this uncertainty problem, e.g., [1, 4]. In previous work, using Bayesian networks, we adaptively select test items that are more likely to reveal students' mastery of concepts and students' types in a simulated environment [5]. Guiding the item selection process with a mutual information-based measure, our system was able to classify students into their unobservable types with less number of administrated items than another system that was guided by a Euclidean distance-based measure. A main concern for the previous work is that computing mutual information can be time consuming and may become impractical in an interactive environment when the Bayesian networks become sufficiently complex. Computing exact and approximate probability values in general Bayesian networks are NP-hard [6]. Even when the deployed Bayesian network is simple enough, we will have to compute the mutual information between the variable of interest and each test item in a real test-item database, thereby making the computation task potentially costly in real-world applications.

In this paper, we extend theoretical properties of mutual information. These properties shed light on the nature of item comparison. In addition, experimental results show that the mutual information-based heuristics, that are designed based on the theoretical properties, provide better performance when we compare them with some Mahalanobis distance-based heuristics.

Section 2 defines our target application and its formulation with Bayesian networks. Section 3 discusses mutual information-based item selection methods, and investigates theoretical properties of mutual information. In Section 4, we present item-selection heuristics designed based on the theoretical analysis, and, in Section 5, we discuss experimental results of evaluating the heuristics.

2   Modelling with Bayesian Networks

2.1   Problem Definition

We consider a set of concepts $\mathfrak{C} = \{C_1, C_2, \cdots, C_n\}$ and a test-item database $\mathfrak{I}$ that contains a set of test items for $\mathfrak{C}$. We call some of the concepts in $\mathfrak{C}$ **basic** concepts, and others **composite**. The composite concepts require students to integrate some basic concepts. For instance, in Table 1, we have seven different concepts—Three basic ones (cA, cB, and cC) and four composite ones (dAB, dBC, dAC, and $dABC$). A composite concept $dABC$ is the result of integrating knowledge about cA, cB, and cC. For each concept C_j, we have a subset $\mathfrak{I}_j = \{I_{j,1}, I_{j,2}, \cdots, I_{j,m_j}\}$ of $\mathfrak{I}$ for testing students' competence of C_j. For easier reference, we call C_j the **parent concept** of items in $\mathfrak{I}_j$ and of C_j's composite concepts. We assume that students demonstrate special patterns in their competence of concepts in $\mathfrak{C}$, and those who share the same competence patterns form a **subgroup**. We adopt the convention of Q-matrix [1], that originally was proposed for representing the relationships between concepts and items, for encoding subgroup's competence of basic concepts and integrating basic concepts into composite ones. We assume that students form a limited number of subgroups, although there could be 2^n subgroups in principle. Let $group$ be the variable whose value comes from the set of possible student subgroups in the problem. Our target problem is to identify the true value of $group$, that is unobservable by the test administrators, by observing students' fuzzy item-response patterns. Moreover, we are interested in achieving high classification accuracy while administrating the minimal possible number of test items.

Table 1. An example of competence patterns for student subgroups

Subgroup ID	Competence of (integrating) concepts						
	cA	cB	cC	dAB	dBC	dAC	dABC
1	1	1	1	1	1	1	1
2	1	1	1	1	1	0	0
3	1	1	1	0	0	1	1
4	1	1	0	1	0	0	0
5	0	1	1	0	1	0	0
6	1	0	1	0	0	1	0
7	1	1	1	0	0	0	0

2.2   Formulation with Bayesian Networks

Let C be the random variable that encodes the degree of the mastery of a concept, and X the random variable representing the outcomes of using an item for testing the mastery of C. In this paper, we assume that variables for both concepts and items are dichotomous. A variable for a concept takes the value of either **good** or **bad**, and a variable for the response to an item takes the value of either **correct** or **incorrect**. For simplicity of notation, we use a small letter of the variable to denote the "positive" value of a random variable, and a small letter with a bar to denote the "negative" value of the variable. For instance, $\Pr(x|c)$ denotes $\Pr(X{=}correct|C{=}good)$, and $\Pr(\overline{x}|\overline{c})$ $\Pr(X{=}incorrect|C{=}bad)$. We use a bold symbol **Pr** and capital names of random variables to denote the probability values of all possible combinations of the values of the involved random variables, e.g., $\mathbf{Pr}(X|C)$ denotes $\{\Pr(x|c), \Pr(x|\overline{c}), \Pr(\overline{x}|c), \Pr(\overline{x}|\overline{c})\}$. Similarly, we use simplified notation for the conditional probability of a composite concept, whose state depends on its parent concepts. For instance, we use $\Pr(dab|\overline{ca})$ for $\Pr(dAB{=}correct|cA{=}incorrect)$.

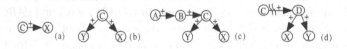

Fig. 1. Examples of Bayesian networks marked with qualitative signs

We use the very simple Bayesian network shown in Figure 1(a) to represent that C is the parent concept of a test item X. In practice, we have no reason to assume that the probability of answering X correctly would decrease when a particular student gets a hand on C. Therefore, in Figure 1(a), we also have $\Pr(x|c) \geq \Pr(x|\overline{c})$, and we show this *positive influence* of C on X by marking the link between them with the "+" symbol, following the tradition of Qualitative Probabilistic Networks (QPNs) [7]. We can use the network shown in Figure 1(b) when we have two items available for testing the competence of C. Notice that, when we accept Figure 1(b), we assume that the student's responses to X and Y become independent given the information about the student's mastery of C, and this is a common practice for systems that adopt the item-response theory (IRT) [8]. When we believe that mastering a parent concept, e.g., B in Figure 1(c), helps the mastery of C, we can add a node for B and draw a link with a plus sign from B to C as well. According to the inference rules for QPNs, we can infer that mastering concept A in Figure 1(c) indirectly improves the mastery of C, and increases the chances of responding to X correctly. In written form, we use $S^+(A, X)$ and $S^+(C, X)$ to denote the positive influences of A and C on X, respectively. We will not discuss Figure 1(d) until Section 3.2.

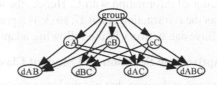

Fig. 2. Concept levels of a Bayesian network for the example in Table 1

The Bayesian network shown in Figure 2 can encode the competence patterns listed in Table 1. In this network, *group* represents students' groups. Nodes cX represents the mastery of basic concept X, and nodes dY the mastery of composite concepts in Y. For clarity, Figure 2 does not include the nodes for the test items that are designed for assessing mastery of the concepts. The network would have 21 more nodes if each concept has three test items. Note that, by such a formulation, the responses to test items are *not* independent given the student's group identity, as many systems that rely on the IRT [8] may have assumed, although the responses to items of a particular concept is still independent given the mastery of that concept. Hence, Bayesian networks provide a more general formulation of the assessment task than the IRT [9].

The links in the network reflect the direct dependence relationship among the nodes. Since different subgroups of students demonstrate different competence patterns, the value of *group* influences whether the values for cX nodes will be *good* or *bad*. For composite concepts, the mastery of the basic concepts will influence the mastery of the composite concepts. In addition, *group* influences the values of nodes for composite concepts because some subgroups may lack the knowledge of integrating the basic concepts. We could have put a "+" mark on the links from basic to composite concepts, as increasing the mastery of basic concepts increases the chance of mastering the composite concepts. Figure 2 does not include these marks for readability of the figure.

We still need to provide a conditional probability table (CPT) for each node in the network. We can use statistical methods to estimate these parameters, e.g., [10]. Once the numerical information becomes available, the network is ready to serve our applications.

3   Mutual Information-Based Item Selection

3.1   Adaptive Item Selection

For the extremely simple case shown in Figure 1(b), it would be helpful if we have a principled way for determining whether we should administrate X or Y for assessing the subject student's competence of C. We can use the mutual information $\mathbb{I}(X;C)$ [11] between C and X for item comparison with a Bayesian network.

$$\mathbb{I}(X;C) = \sum_{c \in C} \sum_{x \in X} \Pr(c,x) \log \frac{\Pr(c,x)}{\Pr(c)\Pr(x)}$$

Since $H(C|X) = H(C) - \mathbb{I}(X;C)$ [11], where $H(C)$ denotes the entropy of a random variable C, we reduce more uncertainty about C if we obtain information about the test item that has larger mutual information with C. Hence, the information about X allows less entropy of C than the information about Y, so X is a preferred. We compute mutual information with a Bayesian network in the following adaptive procedure [5].

Procedure for Adaptive Item Selection and Student Classification

1. Ask simulees to answer the item that has the largest mutual information with *group*
2. Select the most probable subgroup in *group* as the student's subgroup, based on the posterior probability distribution over *group*, updated for the simulees' responses to the selected items
3. Stop the classification task, if every item has been used
4. Compute the mutual information between each untested item and *group*, given the simulees' responses to all previously tested items
5. Ask simulees to answer the item that has the next largest condition mutual information with *group*, and return to step 2

Although we achieved high accuracy of classification in [5], the computational costs of step 4 remain a concern. The computation of a particular mutual information between a pair of random variables may need just one propagation in the Bayesian network , but this "one propagation" can be quite costly as computing either exact or approximate probabilities in Bayesian networks is NP-hard [6]. The problem will be exacerbated when we need to compute the mutual information between each test item and the random variable of interest. In Figure 2, we have to compute the mutual information between each untested item with *group*, and there may be hundreds or thousands of test items available in a realistic test-item database. We investigate theoretical properties of mutual information that shed light on the nature of item comparison and help us to design heuristics for item selection next.

3.2   Useful Properties of Mutual Information

We assume that all variables are dichotomous in this section. Our theorem and corollaries originate from the following theorem and lemma.

Theorem 1 ([11]). *Let* $\Pr(c,x) = \Pr(c)\Pr(x|c)$ *be the joint distribution of* C *and* X. *The mutual information* $\mathbb{I}(X;C)$ *is a concave function of* $\mathbf{Pr}(C)$ *for fixed* $\mathbf{Pr}(X|C)$ *and a convex function of* $\mathbf{Pr}(X|C)$ *for fixed* $\mathbf{Pr}(C)$.

Lemma 1. $\Pr(x|c) = \Pr(x|\bar{c}) \Rightarrow \mathbb{I}(X; C) = 0$. ($\because$ *independence between C and X).*

Theorem 2. *For a fixed $\Pr(c)$, when $\Pr(x|c) \geq \Pr(x|\bar{c})$, $\mathbb{I}(X; C)$ is a monotonically increasing function of $\Pr(x|c)$ for a fixed $\Pr(x|\bar{c})$, and a monotonically decreasing function of $\Pr(x|\bar{c})$ for a fixed $\Pr(x|c)$.*

Proof. *Consider the space of $\Pr(x|c)$ and $\Pr(x|\bar{c})$ shown in Figure 3. Each point in the space represents a pair of $\Pr(x|c)$ and $\Pr(x|\bar{c})$ for a particular distribution $\mathbf{Pr}(X|C)$. The square contains all possible combinations of $\Pr(x|c)$ and $\Pr(x|\bar{c})$, and the diagonal line segment represents the situation when $\Pr(x|c) = \Pr(x|\bar{c})$.*

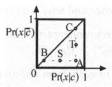

Fig. 3. The space for $\mathbf{Pr}(X|C)$ represented by $(\Pr(x|c), \Pr(x|\bar{c}))$

Let $\mathbf{Pr}_a(X|C), \mathbf{Pr}_b(X|C), \mathbf{Pr}_c(X|C), \mathbf{Pr}_s(X|C)$, and $\mathbf{Pr}_t(X|C)$, respectively, denote the probability distributions represented by A, B, C, S, and T in Figure 3. Assume that B, S, and A are on a horizontal line segment, and that C, T, and A are on a vertical line segment. The coordinates of S must be a linear combination of coordinates of the terminals of the line segment where S resides, and this geometric fact applies to T analogously. As a result, we can express $\mathbf{Pr}_a(X|C), \mathbf{Pr}_b(X|C), \mathbf{Pr}_c(X|C), \mathbf{Pr}_s(X|C)$, and $\mathbf{Pr}_t(X|C)$ in the following manner, where $n \leq m$ and $0 \leq \gamma, \delta \leq 1$.

$$\mathbf{Pr}_a(X|C) = (m, n); \qquad \mathbf{Pr}_b(X|C) = (n, n); \qquad \mathbf{Pr}_c(X|C) = (m, m)$$

$$\mathbf{Pr}_s(X|C) = \gamma \mathbf{Pr}_a(X|C) + (1 - \gamma)\mathbf{Pr}_b(X|C) \tag{1}$$

$$\mathbf{Pr}_t(X|C) = \delta \mathbf{Pr}_a(X|C) + (1 - \delta)\mathbf{Pr}_c(X|C) \tag{2}$$

Let $\mathbb{I}_a(X; C), \mathbb{I}_b(X; C), \mathbb{I}_c(X; C), \mathbb{I}_s(X; C)$, and $\mathbb{I}_t(X; C)$, be the mutual information $\mathbb{I}(X; C)$ when $\mathbf{Pr}(X|C)$ takes on the distribution represented by A, B, C, S, and T, respectively. Applying Lemma 1, $\mathbb{I}_b(X; C)$ and $I_c(X; C)$ must be zero. Because $\mathbf{Pr}_s(X|C)$ is a linear combination of $\mathbf{Pr}_a(X|C)$ and $\mathbf{Pr}_b(X|C)$ in (1), the following inequality must hold according to Theorem 1.

$$\mathbb{I}_s(X; C) \leq \gamma \mathbb{I}_a(X; C) + (1 - \gamma)\mathbb{I}_b(X; C) \Rightarrow \mathbb{I}_s(X; C) \leq \gamma \mathbb{I}_a(X; C) \because \mathbb{I}_b(X; C) = 0$$

$$\Rightarrow \mathbb{I}_a(X; C) \geq \mathbb{I}_s(X; C) \because 0 \leq \gamma \leq 1$$

In Figure 3, the only difference between A and S is that the $\Pr(x|c)$ of A is larger than that of S. Hence we have shown that, when $\Pr(x|c) \geq \Pr(x|\bar{c})$, $\mathbb{I}(X; C)$ is a monotonically increasing function of $\Pr(x|c)$ for fixed $\Pr(c)$ and $\Pr(x|\bar{c})$.

Analogously, the following inequality must hold according to Theorem 1 because $\mathbf{Pr}_t(X|C)$ *is a linear combination of* $\mathbf{Pr}_a(X|C)$ *and* $\mathbf{Pr}_c(X|C)$ *in (2).*

$$\mathbb{I}_t(X;C) \leq \delta\,\mathbb{I}_a(X;C) + (1-\delta)\mathbb{I}_c(X;C) \Rightarrow \mathbb{I}_t(X;C) \leq \delta\,\mathbb{I}_a(X;C) \because \mathbb{I}_c(X;C)=0$$
$$\Rightarrow \mathbb{I}_a(X;C) \geq \mathbb{I}_t(X;C) \because 0 \leq \delta \leq 1$$

In Figure 3, the only difference between A and T is that the $\Pr(x|\bar{c})$ *of A is smaller than that of T. Hence we have shown that, when* $\Pr(x|c) \geq \Pr(x|\bar{c})$, $\mathbb{I}(X;C)$ *is a monotonically decreasing function of* $\Pr(x|\bar{c})$ *for fixed* $\Pr(c)$ *and* $\Pr(x|c)$. ∎

Theorem 2 provides a basis for preferring one test item over others without having to compute the mutual information. The following corollary of the theorem allows us to compare two items by examining their associated CPTs in Bayesian networks, and is applicable for determining when and why we should prefer X to Y in Figure 1(b).

Corollary 1. *Let C be the parent concept of items X and Y. We have* $\mathbb{I}(X;C) \geq \mathbb{I}(Y;C)$ *if* $\Pr(x|c) \geq \Pr(y|c) \geq \Pr(y|\bar{c}) \geq \Pr(x|\bar{c})$.

Proof. *This corollary results directly from Theorem 2.* ∎

As an extreme case, when $\Pr(x|c) = 1$ and $\Pr(x|\bar{c}) = 0$, the item X will have the highest mutual information with C. On the other hand, when $\Pr(x|c) = \Pr(x|\bar{c})$, no item offers less amount of information with C, so X is the worst item to administrate. Hence, Corollary 1 generalizes intuitions for item comparison. Nevertheless Corollary 1 does not allow us to obtain a total ordering of the mutual information between the test items and the given concept. The distribution $\mathbf{Pr}_a(X|C)$, represented by A in Figure 3, offers the largest $\mathbb{I}(X;C)$ among all points within the $\triangle ABC$ area, according to the theorem. Our experiments show that the mutual information offered by other points outside of the triangle can have any possible relationship with that offered by A, depending on the numerical peculiarities.

Figure 1(d) shows an additional scenario when Theorem 2 applies. The tilted short curves means that C and D do not have to have a direct relationship. In this figure, D is the parent concept of two dichotomous items, X and Y, and there is a concept C that positively influences D. The following corollary shows when an item is better than the other for assessing the mastery of a related concept. Corollary 2 holds as long as C positively influences D, as is defined in QPNs.

Corollary 2. *We have* $\mathbb{I}(X;C) \geq \mathbb{I}(Y;C)$ *if* $\Pr(x|d) \geq \Pr(y|d) \geq \Pr(y|\bar{d}) \geq \Pr(x|\bar{d})$ *and* $\Pr(d|c) \geq \tau \geq \Pr(d|\bar{c})$, *where*

$$\tau = \frac{\Pr(y|\bar{d}) - \Pr(x|\bar{d})}{(\Pr(x|d) - \Pr(y|d)) + (\Pr(y|\bar{d}) - \Pr(x|\bar{d}))}.$$

Proof. *This corollary extends Corollary 1. The proof involves algebraic manipulations, but is not provided due to page limits.* ∎

Corollary 2 dictates that even if X is more related to D than Y is *does not* imply that X is more related to C than Y is. This is against what one might have intuitively thought. In realistic assessment, test administrators need to watch whether $\Pr(d|c) \geq \tau \geq \Pr(d|\bar{c})$ really holds in the tests to make sound inference about students' competence based on their item responses.

4   Other Heuristics for Item Selection and Student Classification

Given two items, X and Y, and their parent concept C, a slightly incorrect interpretation of Corollary 1 suggests that X has more mutual information with C than Y does, if $\Pr(x|c) - \Pr(x|\bar{c}) \geq \Pr(y|c) - \Pr(y|\bar{c})$. Corollary 2 further suggests that items that have larger mutual information with their parent concepts may have larger mutual information with a concept that is related to their parent concepts, when $\Pr(d|c) \geq \tau \geq \Pr(d|\bar{c})$ holds. Putting these together, an item X with larger $\Pr(x|c) - \Pr(x|\bar{c})$ may have larger mutual information with a concept that is remotely related with C, under ideal circumstances. The heuristic score of an item X, with C as its parent concept, is thus defined as follows.

$$s(X) = \Pr(x|c) - \Pr(x|\bar{c}) \tag{3}$$

When the ideal conditions do not hold, we may select a non-optimal item. The heuristic is also a static measure that does not change with the students' item responses on the fly as the procedure presented in Section 3.1 would.

The previous heuristic helps us to pick the best item designed for a particular concept, but does not provide clues for selecting items of which concept that we should examine. At present, we rely on the "distance among concepts" to select the concept, and define a distance measure based on the information contained in the Q-matrix. Let $Q_{j,k}$ denote the cell at j^{th} row and the kth column in the Q-matrix. Assuming that there are γ subgroups of students, the inner summation in (4) computes the distance between concepts C_m and C_t, and the whole formula in (4) computes the distance between concept C_m to a subset $\mathfrak{C}' \subset \mathfrak{C}$. If $C_m \in \mathfrak{C}'$, $d_2(C_m, \mathfrak{C}') = 0$.

$$d_2(C_m, \mathfrak{C}') = \sum_{C_t \in \mathfrak{C}'} [\sum_{s=1}^{\gamma} (Q_{s,m} - Q_{s,t})^2]^{1/2}, \quad \text{when } C_m \notin \mathfrak{C}' \tag{4}$$

Assume that $\mathfrak{C}' \subset \mathfrak{C}$ is the set of parent concepts of the administrated items. The item that is designed for a concept $C \notin \mathfrak{C}'$ helps us to gather more unknown information than a $C' \in \mathfrak{C}'$. Moreover, among all items for such untested concepts, we prefer the concept that has the largest $d_2(C, \mathfrak{C}')$ because such a C appears to be most dissimilar to concepts in $\mathfrak{C}'$. Since there are more items than concepts, we reset $\mathfrak{C}'$ to an empty set every time one item of each concept has been administrated, whenever necessary.

For comparison purposes, we evaluate the possibility of classifying students without relying on inferencing with Bayesian networks. We use a Mahalanobis distance-based measure for student classification. Given a student's item-response pattern, we create a *competence pattern* $R = (rC_1, rC_2, \cdots, rC_n)$, where rC_j is the proportion of the student's correct responses to items for C_j. In the extreme cases, rC_j will be, respectively, 1 and 0, if the student responds to all administrated items for C_j correctly and incorrectly. rC_j will be 0.5, if either no item for C_j is administrated yet or the student responds correctly to half of the items for C_j. Given a vector R, we compute the distance between the competence patterns of the student and each subgroup g_k of *group* with the Mahalanobis distance [12].

$$d_4(R, g_k) = [(R - \mu_k)\Sigma_k^{-1}(R - \mu_k)^T]^{1/2} \tag{5}$$

In (5), μ_k and Σ_k are, respectively, the mean and the variance-covariance matrix of the competence patterns of students in subgroup g_k, and $(R - \mu_k)^T$ is the transpose of the row vector $(R - \mu_k)$. Recall that $\{C_1, C_2, \cdots, C_n\}$ is the set of concepts of interest in Section 2.1, so μ_k and Σ_k are, respectively, an $n \times 1$ row vector and an $n \times n$ matrix. The advantages of the Mahalanobis distance come at some extra costs, and our system has to learn these statistics from students' test records with standard statistical methods.

5   Simulation-Based Evaluation

Similar to some previous work, e.g., [13], we used simulated students in the experiments. We adopt the term *simulee* coined by VanLehn in places of simulated students. Due to page limits, we can only claim that we appropriately generate the simulees with the help of a random number generator and take into account the Bayesian network similar to that shown in 2. Details of the simulator is provided in [9]. We will provide more details, including more simulated results, during the conference presentation.

The charts in Figure 4 show the experimental results of using data in Table 1 and the network in Figure 2. The charts depict typical performance profiles achieved by our heuristics in many experiments that we have tried. For both (a) and (b), *groupGuess* and *groupSlip* were 0.1 , and *slip* and *guess* were 0.2 [14] in (a) and 0.1 in (b). For both (a) and (b), we used a total of 10000 simulees in ten experiments, and the charts show profiles of averaged classification accuracy.

The names of the curves contain two parts. The first part denotes the way we classified students, and the second the heuristics for item selection. In the first part, **Bn** means that we used the Bayesian network to compute the probability distribution over *group* to select the most probable subgroup, and **MD** that we relied on the distance-based measure in (5) to guess the simulee's subgroup. In the second part, **Mi** means that we computed the conditional mutual information, **HMi** that we used both the distance-based measure in (4) for selecting concepts and the heuristic mutual information in (3) for selecting items, and **Rand** that items were randomly selected for randomly chosen concepts. The curve **BnMi** was achieved by the procedure presented in Section 3.1.

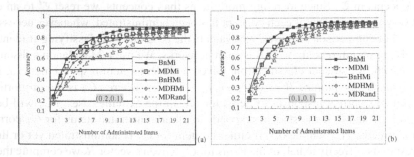

Fig. 4. Evaluation of heuristics for student classification

Due to the randomness in generating the simulees, about 10% of simulees in (a) (and 5% in (b)) showed typical behavior of other subgroups in the current setup, and were impossible for correct classification. Hence, all methods actually performed as well as possible when all 21 items were used up. Since there were seven student subgroups, a blind guess should hit the correct answer about 14.3% of the time. All of the studied methods did better than this baseline.

Chart (a) indicates that **Bn** provides better or comparable performance than **MD** for student classification, and that **HMi** provides pretty good performance for adaptive item selection when computing exact mutual information online is considered computationally costly. Chart (b) exhibits similar trends but the differences between different strategies are relatively squeezed in a narrower range. The differences between **BnMi** and **MDMi** and between **BnHMi** and **MDHMi** show the payoff for using the Bayesian network for inferring students' subgroups. The differences between **MDMi**, **MDHMi**, and **MDRand** illustrates the effectiveness of different strategies for item selection.

We must admit that the aforementioned comparisons were based solely on a few experimental results. Nevertheless, we have conducted experiments using other network structures and parameter settings, and, based on results of these extra experiments, we are convinced the applicability of the reported results. The realistic values of such parameters as *guess* and *slip* depend on many real-world factors, including the pedagogical goals, the student population, etc., so effectiveness of our proposed methods awaits field tests for the final proof of their viability.

6   Conclusion

The main contribution of this paper is the theoretical foundation for comparing the effectiveness of test items based on mutual information. Theorem 2 turns out to be a good vehicle for explaining some intuitions for item comparison, and provides a basis for adaptive student assessments. In addition, the theorem and its corollaries allow us to design heuristics when computing exact values of mutual information online is considered too costly. Although simulated experiments cannot establish decisive conclusions for viability of mutual information-based heuristics for item selection, the current results are definitely encouraging.

There is room for future work. For instance, including mutual information in a decision theory-based system is clearly an option, e.g., [15]. What structure of the Bayesian network should be used to realize the competence patterns in Table 1 deserves a lengthy discussion, and we have begun our investigation in this regard, but we cannot provide details due to page limits. Also due the page limits, we cannot provide details about how we learned the Bayesian networks from data [16].

Acknowledgements

This research was supported in part by Grants NSC-92-2213-E-004-004 and NSC-93-2213-E-004-004 from the National Science Council of Taiwan. We are grateful for the reviewers' comments, but we cannot add all requested material due to page limits.

References

1. Yan, D., Almond, R.G., Mislevy, R.J.: Empirical comparisons of cognitive diagnostic models. unpublished draft of Educational Testing Service (2003) http://www.ets.org/research/dload/aera03-yan.pdf.
2. Rost, J., Langeheine, R., eds.: Applications of Latent Trait and Latent Class Models in the Social Sciences. Waxmann (1997)
3. Birenbaum, M., Kelly, A.E., Tatsuoka, K.K., Gutvirtz, Y.: Attribute-mastery patterns from rule space as the basis for student models in algebra. Int'l J. of Human-Computer Studies **40** (1994) 497–508
4. VanLehn, K., Martin, J.: Evaluation of an assessment system based on Bayesian student modeling. IJAIED **8** (1997) 179–221
5. Liu, C.L.: Using mutual information for adaptive student assessments. Proc. of the 4th IEEE Int'l Conf. on Advanced Learning Technologies (2004) 585–589
6. Jensen, F.V.: Bayesian Networks and Decision Graphs. Springer-Verlag (2001)
7. Wellman, M.P.: Fundamental concepts of qualitative probabilistic networks. Artificial Intelligence **44** (1990) 257–303
8. Hambleton, R.K., Swaminathan, H., Rogers, H.J.: Fundamentals of Item Response Theory. SAGE Publications (1991)
9. Liu, C.L., Wang, Y.T., Liu, Y.C.: A Bayesian network-based simulation environment for investigating assessment issues in intelligent tutoring systems. Proc. of the Int'l Computer Symposium (2004) 234–239
10. Mislevy, R.J., Almond, R.G., Yan, D., Steinberg, L.S.: Bayes nets in educational assessment: Where do the numbers come from? Proc. of the 15th Conf. on Uncertainty in Artificial Intelligence (1999) 437–446
11. Cover, T.M., Thomas, J.A.: Elements of Information Theory. John Wiley & Sons (1991)
12. Duda, R.O., Hart, P.E., Stork, D.G.: Pattern Classification. Wiley (2001)
13. VanLehn, K., Ohlsson, S., Nason, R.: Applications of simulated students: An exploration. IJAIED **5** (1994) 135–175
14. Collins, J.A., Greer, J.E., Huang, S.X.: Adaptive assessment using granularity hierarchies and Bayesian nets. Proc. of the 3rd Int'l Conf. on ITS (1996) 569–577
15. Mayo, M., Mitrovic, A.: Optimising ITS behaviour with Bayesian networks and decision theory. IJAIED **12** (2001) 124–153
16. Lauritzen, S.L.: The EM algorithm for graphical association models with missing data. Computational Statistics & Data Analysis **19** (1995) 191–201

IJAIED: Int'l J. of Artificial Intelligence in Education; ITS: Intelligent Tutoring Systems.

Cooperative Query Answering for RDF

Adrian Tanasescu

LIRIS - Université Claude Bernard Lyon 1, 43 Bld. du 11 Novembre 1918
69422 VILLEURBANNE Cedex – FRANCE
Adrian.Tanasescu@liris.cnrs.fr

Abstract. The interest of representing data for the Semantic Web has
generated standards for expressing knowledge on the Web. RDF, as one
of those standards, has become a recommendation of the W3C. Even
if it was designed to be human and machine readable (XML encoding,
triples, labeled graphs), RDF was not provided with querying and reasoning services. Most work on querying RDF has concentrated on the
use of logic programming evaluation techniques and SQL extensions.
We take a new look at the problem of querying and reasoning on RDF
statements and find that order-sorted feature (OSF) terms apply to this
problem because OSF have been tailored for efficiency and their semantics is compatible with the isomorphic representation (triples) of RDF
statements. This transformation allows to compute an ordering on resources and thus provide better answering mechanisms when querying
RDF.

Keywords: RDF, order-sorted features, ψ-terms, interrogation, cooperative answers.

1 Introduction

RDF provides a basic way to represent data for the semantic Web. When we
talk about the semantic Web today, then we mainly refer to an effort of bringing
back structure to the information that is available on the World Wide Web. This
time, structures do not come in the shape of well-defined database schemas but
in terms of semantic annotations that conform to a specific, often loosely defined
schema or even to an explicit specification of the intended meaning of a piece
of information. The first real results of semantic Web research are languages for
encoding such annotations.

However, a knowledge representation format alone is not enough to enable a
large community of potential users to process RDF effectively. Query languages
and reasoning support are needed to enable the creation of RDF-aware applications. It is possible to identify two main approaches: (1) in the SQL/XQL-like
approach, RDF data are viewed as a relational (or XML) database, and (2) in the
logic-based approach, RDF data can be thought of as the equivalent of ground
facts in a logic-based language. The mapping into predicate calculus consists of
a simple rule for translating RDF statements into first-order relational sentences

M.-S. Hacid et al. (Eds.): ISMIS 2005, LNAI 3488, pp. 535–543, 2005.
© Springer-Verlag Berlin Heidelberg 2005

and a set of first-order axioms that restrict the allowable interpretations of the
non-logical symbols.

In this paper, we take a new look at the problem of querying and reasoning
on RDF statements and find that order-sorted feature (OSF) terms apply to
this problem because OSF have been tailored for efficiency and their semantics
is compatible with the isomorphic representation (triples) of RDF statements.
The ability to express RDF statements using order-sorted feature terms provides
a mechanism to compute an ordering on resources and thus the possibility to
handle approximations when querying RDF.

Furthermore, queries formulated on RDF documents may not provide satisfying answers. Nevertheless, very often, several RDF documents can contribute
together to deliver an exact or approximate answer. Let us consider the following
example. We assume that our database is composed of the two RDF documents
represented as labeled graphs in figure 1. We also consider the following formulated query written as a ψ-term [1].

```
Q : ISMIS05 (type -> X;
             editor -> Y (affiliation -> Z))
```

A classical query answering mechanism would search for an homomorphism
in each of the two RDF documents. As we can see, none of the two documents
can provide a complete answer to the query. Nevertheless, the combination of
parts of the two documents (highlighted by dotted lines in figure 1) will provide
an answer to the query.

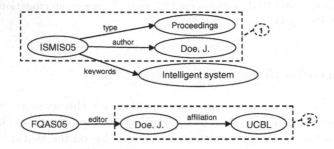

Fig. 1. Sample RDF documents

We propose in this paper a framework that provide such cooperative answers
when querying RDF documents. All documents are translated into ψ-terms that
can be seen as conjunctions of constraints. Then, we propose an algorithm, based
on constraint propagation, to evaluate queries formulated on RDF documents.
This algorithm allows assembling fragments of answers from several RDF documents in order to provide a complete answer to the query.

The rest of the paper is organized as follows. Section 2 shortly discusses the
related work. Section 3 gives some relevant preliminaries to our approach. In Section 4 we present, through some examples, how RDF statements can be rewritten into order-sorted features (ψ-terms). Section 5 develops constraint propagation based mechanisms for query answers over RDF statements. We conclude in
Section 6.

2   Related Work

Our work relates to querying and reasoning on RDF statements. We shortly discuss some of the proposed approaches to tackle these problems. This section is intended to be illustrative. We apologize if we left out other relevant proposals.

The use of Frame-logic [2] as a logic language for expressing RDF data was proposed in [3]. RDF data is translated into F-logic terms, and queries can be issued against these terms. Some limitations of this approach were investigated in a second proposal by Yang and Kifer [4]. This proposal considers an extension of F-logic that supports anonymous resources and reification. The language has a simple and natural paradox-free semantics and a proof theory.

In [5] TRIPLE is presented as an RDF query, inference, and transformation language created as a syntactical extension of Horn logic, similar to F-Logic. Its main purpose is to query web resources in a declarative way. By translating RDF statements into logical rules, TRIPLE enables querying RDF data. Furthermore, TRIPLE rules can be represented in RDF allowing rules to be (re)distributed on the Web.

Karvounarakis et al. [6] proposed an RDF query language called RQL. It is a typed functional language (à la OQL) and relies on a formal model for directed labeled graphs allowing the interpretation of superimposed resource descriptions by means of one or more RDF schemas. RQL adapts the functionality of semistructured/XML query languages to the peculiarities of RDF but, foremost, it enables to uniformly query both resource descriptions and schemas.

Broekstra et al. [7] developed an architecture for storing and querying of RDF and RDFS information called SESAME. It allows persistent storage of RDF data and schema information, and provides access methods to that information through export and querying modules. Support for concurrency control is also offered.

Our work complements those approaches in the sense that it is the first effort towards providing cooperative query answering for RDF.

3   Preliminaries

3.1   RDF Data Model

RDF [8] is an assertional language intended to be used to express propositions using precise formal vocabularies, particularly using RDFS (RDF Schema), for access and use over the World Wide Web, and is intended to provide a basic foundation for more advanced assertional languages with a similar purpose.

RDF data model can be represented as triples, as a graph, or in XML [8]. These representations have equivalent meaning. An RDF document is a finite set of statements of the form {predicate, subject, object}, where predicate is a property, subject is a resource, and object is a resource or a literal.

A way to specify a semantics is to give a translation from RDF into a formal logic with a model theory already attached, as it were. This "axiomatic semantics" approach has been suggested and used previously with various alternative versions of the target logical language [9, 10]. The axiomatic semantics style has some advantages for machine processing and may be more readable, but in the event that any axiomatic semantics fails to conform to the model-theoretic semantics, the model theory should be taken as normative.

3.2   Order-Sorted Features

In [11], ψ-terms were proposed as flexible record structures for logic programming. However, ψ-terms are of wider use (see [1, 12, 13, 14]). The easiest way to describe a ψ-term is with an example. Here is a ψ-term that may be used to describe a generic person object:

P:person(name⇒id(first⇒string,

$$\text{last} \Rightarrow \text{S:string}),$$

age⇒30,

spouse⇒person(name⇒id(last⇒S),

spouse⇒P)).

In words: a 30 year-old person who has a name in which the first and last parts are strings, and whose spouse is a person sharing his or her last name, the latter person's spouse being the first person in question.

This expression looks like a record structure. Like a typical record, it has field names; i.e., the symbols on the left of ⇒. We call these feature symbols. In contrast with conventional records, however, ψ-terms can carry more information. Namely, the fields are attached to sort symbols (e.g., person, id, string, 30, etc.). These sorts may indifferently denote individual values (e.g., 30) or sets of values (e.g., person, string). Sorts are partially ordered so as to reflect set inclusion; e.g., employee < person means that all employees are persons. Finally, sharing of structure can be expressed with variables (e.g., P and S). This sharing may be circular (e.g., P).

ψ-terms represent the basis of a logic of record structures called OSF logic. The latter is, in fact, the most primitive form of the constraint language called LIFE (Logic, Inheritance, Functions and Equations). The fundamental idea behind OSF logic is that it allows establishing a subsumption relation between OSF terms, which turns out to be relevant, in our approach, to reason about RDF statements.

ψ-terms can also be seen as conjunctions of constraints. The sample ψ-term presented above could be directly written as the following set of constraints :

```
{(P, Id1):name; (Id1, string):first; (Id1, S):last; (P, 30):age;
(P, P2):spouse; (P2, Id2):name; (Id2, S):last; (P2, P):spouse }
```
with P < person, S < string, Id1<id, Id2<id.

The possibility of translation from ψ-terms to constraints allows us to build an algorithm that is able to provide cooperative answers for RDF queries (see section 5).

4   Translation of RDF-Statements into ψ-Terms

In this section, we show, through simple examples, how RDF statements can be rewritten into ψ-terms. Furthermore, we show how RDF statements that use anonymous resources or special constructors as Bag, Alt, Seq and List can be translated into ψ-terms. We will consider translating examples presented in [8].

4.1   RDF Sentences with Named or Anonymous Resources

The following statement :

Ora Lassila is the creator of the resource http://www.w3c.org/Lassila/

can be translated into the ψ-term :

```
'http://www.w3c.org/Home/Lassila/'(creator =>'Ora Lassila').
```

In RDF statements, anonymous resources are considered as unique. This means that two such resources finding themselves in different ψ-terms can never be considered as the same resource. Nevertheless, the possibility of representing an anonymous resource more than once in the same ψ-term is needed.

When translating RDF documents into ψ-terms, we note an anonymous resource by #_. To distinguish among several anonymous resources in the same ψ-term we use digits after the symbol #_ (i.e. #_1, #_2, etc). Here is an example:

The individual whose name is Ora Lassila, email lassila@w3c.org is the creator of http://.../Lassila/ is translated into the ψ-term

```
'http://.../Lassila/'(creator => #_ (name =>'Ora Lassila';
                                     email =>'lassila@w3c.org').
```

4.2   Containers and Collections in RDF Statements

Containers and collections are used in RDF to describe groups of things. Thus, containers represent open groups (of resources or literals), while collections represent closed groups, that are described in RDF statements. RDF defines three types of containers: (1) Bag - a group of resources or literals where there is no significance in the order of the members; (2) Seq - a group of resources or literals where the order of the members is significant; (3) Alt - a group of resources or literals that are alternatives. RDF provides the types and properties that can be used to construct the RDF graphs to describe each type of container. RDF has no more built-in understanding of what a resource of type Bag (Alt or Seq) is.

We introduce an extension in the OSF logic for representing these containers and we show how these new extensions will be able to follow subsumption rules that govern OSF terms. For the four constructors we create global types (**Bag, Alt, Seq** and **List**) allowing to define containers and collections in ψ-terms as their subtypes. These terms become reserved and can no longer be used in the definition of types when building ψ-terms.

Expressing Containers and Collections as Types

```
X : Book ( title => 'Modern Information Retrieval' ;
            Authors=> Bag1;
            editor =>'ACM Press')
   Bag1 := {'R. Baeza-Yates'; 'B. Ribeiro-Neto'}
   Bag1 < Bag
```

In this example, the group of authors of a book is defined in the container Bag1. We clearly state that this container is a subset of the global type Bag.

The translation of the three other RDF types is syntactically similar. The semantic interpretation corresponding to each type is made by the application that computes the ψ-terms. Therefore we provide subsumption rules that apply to each of the four types.

Subsumption Between Containers or Collections

1. Subsumption between Bag containers
   Let Bag1 < Bag and Bag2 < Bag.
   Bag1 < Bag2 iff : $\forall t_1 \in$ Bag1, $\exists t_2 \in$ Bag2 $\mid t_1 \leq t_2$
   Ex: {Mary, John} < {Mary, John, Tom}

As collections are also unordered sets of resources, the same rule applies for the subsumption between List collections.

2. Subsumption between Alt containers
   Let Alt1 < Alt and Alt2 < Alt.
   Alt1 $\leq$ Alt2 iff : $\exists t_1 \in$ Alt1, $\exists t_2 \in$ Alt2 $\mid t_1 \leq t_2$
   Ex: {Mary, John} $\leq$ {John, Tom}

3. Subsumption between Seq containers
   Let Seq1 < Seq and Seq2 < Seq.
   Seq1 < Seq2 iff :
   $\quad \forall t_i \in$ Seq1, $\exists t'_j \in$ Seq2$\mid (t_i \leq t'_j)$
   $\quad$ and (if ($\exists t_k \in Seq1$, $\exists t'_m \in Seq2$, $k <^n i$, $t_k \leq t'_m$) then $m <^n j$)
   Ex: {Mary, Fred, Tom} < {Mary, John, Fred, Tom}
   $\quad\quad$ {Mary, Tom, Fred} $\not<$ {Mary, John, Fred, Tom}
   We use < to denote subsumption order and $<^n$ to denote numbers order.

5   RDF Queries and Cooperative Answers

RDF was designed to be (amongst many other things) an appropriate data representation formalism for logic/inference applications on the Web. A number of papers and tools already exist that explore the relationship between the W3C's RDF and the worlds of knowledge representation and logic programming (see, among others, [15, 16, 9]). Our aim here is to continue this effort by investigating additional reasoning services that can be performed over RDF statements. As already stated, RDF statements can be represented as ψ-terms.

We develop a mechanism that is able to provide cooperative answers for RDF queries. Classical query mechanisms consider RDF documents individually and search for an homomorphism of the query in each document. Our approach consists in decomposing RDF documents into individual sentences and thus may provide exact answers by combining RDF sentences from different documents.

5.1 Query Answering Algorithm

We consider that all RDF documents, already translated into ψ-terms, are rewritten as constraints. The answering mechanism consists in two phases: (1) the propagation phase in which we search for constraints that satisfy those of the formulated query, and (2) the validation phase that verifies that the returned answers really exist in the RDF documents.

Let F be the set of facts (resulting from the rewriting of all ψ-terms as constraints) in the form $(s_i, s_j) : label_n$.

Let G be the set of constraints of the query expressed in the form : $(s_i, X) : label_n$, $(X, s_j) : label_n$ or $(X, Y) : label_n$, where X, Y are variables of the constraints. The following set of rules allows to compute values for variables in constraints.

1. Propagation phase

R1 (direct match):
$$\left. \begin{array}{l} if\ (s_i, X) : label_n \in G \\ and\ \exists\ (s_i, s_j) : label_n \in F \end{array} \right\} \Rightarrow G = G \mid X = s_j\ (X\ is\ replaced\ with\ s_j\ in\ G)$$

R2 (approximation on types):
$$\left. \begin{array}{l} if\ (s_i, X) : label_n \in G \\ and\ \exists\ (s_k, s_j) : label_n \in F \\ and\ LUB(s_k, s_i) = s_i \end{array} \right\} \Rightarrow G = G \mid X = s_j$$

R3 (approximation on features):
$$\left. \begin{array}{l} if\ (s_i, X) : label_n \in G \\ and\ \exists\ (s_i, s_j) : label_m \in F \\ and\ LUB(label_m, label_n) = label_n \end{array} \right\} \Rightarrow G = G \mid X = s_j$$

Constraints with one variable are considered first. The rules are triggered according to the order specified here. If a rule satisfies a constraint, the following rules are skipped and a new query constraint is treated. Rules R2 and R3 use a predefined order on the types and features in order to provide approximate query answers.

2. Validation phase

$$\left. \begin{array}{l} if\ (s_i, s_j) : label_n \in G \\ and\ (s_k, s_l) : label_m \in F \\ with\ s_k \leq s_i,\ s_l \leq s_j,\ label_m \leq label_n \end{array} \right\} \Rightarrow G = G \setminus \{(s_i, s_j) : label_n\}$$

If at the end of the validation phase $G = \emptyset$, we have a complete answer. Otherwise, the answer is partial and the set G contains the parts of the query with no answer in the RDF documents.

5.2   Example

We consider the following ψ-terms base obtained from the translation of RDF documents:

```
ψ₁ : ISMIS (type -> proceedings;
              author -> John;
              keywords -> 'Intelligent systems')
ψ₂ : FQAS (editor -> John (affiliation -> UCBL))
```

All ψ-terms are translated into a set of constraints (facts) named F. We formulate the following query :

```
Q : ISMTS (type -> X;
            editor -> Y (affiliation -> Z))
```

that is translated into the following set of constraints (goals) named G:

```
G = {(ISMIS, X) : type, (ISMIS, Y) : editor, (Y, Z) : affiliation}
```

We also have a predefined order on features : `author < editor`.
In the following we simulate the execution of the algorithm. We begin with the propagation phase.

- 1st query constraint : `(ISMIS, X) : type`
  $\rightarrow$ R1 finds an answer : `(ISMIS,proceedings):type` $\Rightarrow X = proceedings$
  $\Rightarrow G = \{$ *(ISMIS, proceedings) : type, (ISMIS, Y) : editor, (Y, Z) : affiliation}*
- 2nd query constraint : `(ISMIS, Y) : editor`
  $\rightarrow$ R3 finds an answer : `(ISMIS,John T.):author` $\Rightarrow Y = John$
  $\Rightarrow G = \{$ *(ISMIS, proceedings) : type, (ISMIS, John) : editor,*
             (John, Z) : affiliation}
- 3rd query constraint : `(John, Z) : affiliation`
  $\rightarrow$ R1 finds an answer : `(John, UCBL) : affiliation` $\Rightarrow Z = UCBL$
  $\Rightarrow G = \{$ *(ISMIS, proceedings) : type, (ISMIS, John) : editor,*
             (John, UCBL) : affiliation}

In our example the validation phase finds all constraints of G in the documents base. This means that we found a complete answer to the query. This answer is built in the validation phase by considering constraints removed from G.

6   Conclusion

In this paper we have addressed issues concerning RDF querying and inferencing that are not investigated in previous approaches. We have demonstrated that order-sorted features (i.e., ψ-terms) provide a nice basis to express approximate descriptions and reason about them. We have developed an approach to provide cooperative answers when querying RDF documents. Therefore we have translated these documents into ψ-terms in order to allow approximation of query answers. We have presented an algorithm for constraints solving that enables better answering to queries formulated on RDF documents. The approach presented in this paper is part of our current research that aims to provide a complete semantics to RDF by using OSF terms. This would allow semantic querying of different kinds of complex data that can be expressed using RDF.

There are at least to issues to pursue. (1) The properties of the proposed algorithm will be investigated together with optimization strategies. That is, an efficient way for selecting constraints during the propagation phase. (2) We will devise a compact database representation for RDF statements. Then, we will provide retrieval algorithms based on abstract interpretation of the ψ-terms unification process.

References

1. H. Ait-Kaci and A. Podelski. Towards the meaning of LIFE. In J. Maluszynski and M. Wirsing, editors, *Proceedings on 3rd International Symposium on Programming Language Implementation and Logic Programming, Berlin*, pages 255–274, 1991.
2. M. Kifer, G. Lausen, and J. Wu. Logical foundations of object-oriented and frame-based languages. *Journal of the ACM*, 42(4):741–843, july 1995.
3. S. Decker, D. Brickley, J. Saarela, and J. Angele. A query and inference service for RDF. In *QL'98 - The Query Languages Workshop*, December 1998.
4. G. Yang and M. Kifer. Reasoning about anonymous resources and meta statements on the semantic web. In *Journal of Data Semantics*, 2003.
5. M. Sintek and S. Decker. TRIPLE - An RDF Query, Inference, and Transformation Language. In *Deductive Databases and Knowledge Management (DDLP'2001)*, October 2001.
6. G. Karvounarakis, A. Magkanaraki, S. Alexaki, V. Christophides, D. Plexousakis, M. Scholl, and K. Tolle. Querying the Semantic Web with RQL. *Computer Networks and ISDN Systems Journal*, 42(5):617–640, 2003.
7. J. Broekstra, A. Kampman, and F. van Harmelen. Sesame: An Architecture for Storing and Querying RDF and RDF Schema. In *Proceedings of the First International Semantic Web Conference (ISWC 2002), Sardinia, Italy*, pages 54–68, June 9-12 2002.
8. O. Lassila and R. Swick. RDF Model and Syntax Specification. http://www.w3.org/TR/1999/REC-rdf-syntax-19990222/, 1999.
9. M. Marchiori and J. Saarela. Query + metadata + logic = metalog. QL'98 : The Query Language Workshop, http://www.w3.org/TandS/QL/QL98/pp/metalog.html, 1998.
10. D. L. McGuinness, R. Fikes, J. Hendler, and L. A. Stein. DAML+OIL:An Ontology Language for the Semantic Web. *IEEE Intelligent Systems*, 17(5), 2002.
11. H. Ait-Kaci and R. Nasr. LOGIN: A logic programming language with built-in inheritance. *The Journal of Logic Programming*, 3(3):185–215, 1986.
12. H. Ait-Kaci and Y. Sasaki. An Axiomatic Approach to Feature Term Generalization. In *Proceedings of the 12th European Conference on Machine Learning, Freiburg, Germany*, pages 1–12, September 5-7 2001.
13. M. Holsheimer, Rolf A. de By, and H. Ait-Kaci. A Database Interface for Complex Objects. In *Proceedings of the Eleventh International Conference on Logic Programming, Santa Margherita Ligure, Italy*, pages 437–455, June 13-18 1994.
14. H. Ait-Kaci and A. Podelski. Logic Programming with Functions over Order-Sorted Feature Terms. In *Proceedings of the Third Workshop on Extensions of Logic Programming, ELP'92, Bologna, Italy*, pages 100–119, February 26-28 1992.
15. J. Peer. *Knowledge Transformation for the Semantic Web*, volume 95 of *Frontiers in Artificial Intelligence and Applications*. IOS Press, 2003.
16. R. Fikes and D. L. McGuinness. An Axiomatic Semantics for RDF, RDF Schema, and DAML+OIL. KSL Technical REport KSL-01-01, 2001.

Intelligent Information Retrieval
for Web-Based Design Data Repository[1]

Huijae Lee and Sang Bong Yoo

School of Computer Science, Inha University, Incheon, Korea
fax: 82-32-874-1435
cyberelf@islabs.inha.ac.kr, syoo@inha.ac.kr

Abstract. As the networks (i.e., Internet and Intranet) proliferate all over the world, it is inevitable to move some (or all) enterprise activities into the virtual spaces. Although the core in this new enterprise environment is at ready and effective exchange of information, it is not an easy task due to the heterogeneity of information resources. In this paper, a Web-based design data repository is presented for facilitating seamless sharing of product data among application systems in virtual enterprises. Two types of knowledge, that is, metadata and ontology, and applications of these to intelligent information retrieval of design data are explained. That knowledge provides users with a dynamically reconfigurable map of design data that helps them to locate proper information and enables a content-based search that can improve search effectiveness throughout the product life cycle.

1 Introduction

As the networks (i.e., Internet and Intranet) proliferate all over the world, it is inevitable to move some (or all) enterprise activities into the virtual spaces. One issue in realizing this is how to support the exchange of product information among application systems or personnel involved in the virtual activities. This is important to obtain the agility for improving the competitiveness of firms. There are two types of data that the enterprises need to properly manage, i.e., business data (e.g., accounting and personnel data) and product data (e.g., CAD and CAM data). Many modern enterprises have enough experience in dealing with business data, but it is not the case for product data, in particular when the product data need to be exchanged throughout the whole product life cycle with systems dealing with the business data. Product data used to be managed only by the design and production activities. However, for the virtual enterprises the product data need to be used in later stages of product life cycle (e.g., Web catalog and service manual).

Differently from business data, product data have complex semantics and thus are not properly exchanged by different application programs. Even though some neutral formats of product data have been developed by standard organizations, translating them among various application programs still needs the comprehensive

---

[1] This work was supported (in part) by the Ministry of Information & Communications, Korea, under the Information Technology Research Center (ITRC) Support Program.

M.-S. Hacid et al. (Eds.): ISMIS 2005, LNAI 3488, pp. 544–552, 2005.
© Springer-Verlag Berlin Heidelberg 2005

understanding of the complex semantics. Recently, it is widely recognized that capturing more knowledge is the next step to overcome the current difficulties on sharing product data. In this paper, we present Web-based knowledge management that facilitates seamless sharing of product data among various application programs including business-oriented and engineering-oriented systems in virtual enterprises.

The knowledge we consider is different from that used by most conventional knowledge-based systems that operate based on if-then rules and inference engines. As the Web enables users or application programs to access the enormous amount of heterogeneous information on global networks, it becomes essential to have proper knowledge to handle that information. This significant change of computing environment has brought active researches on various new types of knowledge representation, some of which includes ontology, metadata, and agents. We have investigated how these approaches can be applied to improve sharing product data among various application systems.

This paper presents extracting, storing, and applying the metadata and ontology of product data. The design and tooling information included in STEP-NC files is focused as an example. By analyzing the relationship among the product data, the RDF Schema [16] is designed first. Based on the schema, metadata is extracted and stored in XML files. As the applications of the stored ontology and metadata, we provides the users content search tools and reconfigure the sitemaps of product data repositories. As well as the users perform content searches; they can select the view that they are interested in (e.g., the views from products, tools, persons, or a current location). With such various views of a product data repository, the users can access the specific data more effectively.

2 Related Work

In conventional knowledge-based systems, knowledge is represented in the form of if-then rules, which are reasoned by inference engines and applied to problem solving. Most of such knowledge-based systems (e.g., expert systems) suffer from several problems such as insufficient understanding of the structure of knowledge-based systems, expensive knowledge acquisition, and focus on complete (but narrow) solutions [12]. However, as the Internet connects the worldwide computing resources each other, the needs to capture various knowledge are increased rapidly. It brings about recent active researches and applications of new encoding methods for the knowledge in various application areas.

Various metadata standards have been developed in order to describe the data resources in application domains. Some examples are GILS (Government Information Locator Service), FGDC (Federal Data Geographic Committee), MARC (Machine Readable Card), DC (Doublin Core), and CIMI (Consortium for the Interchange of Museum Information). These standards have different semantics and syntaxes, and could not interoperate each other. RDF (Resource Description Framework) [15] is the emerging standard from W3C, which defines a general mechanism to represent the metadata of various application areas [9]. Using the syntax of XML, RDF can represent the various metadata on the Web.

The base element of the RDF model is the triple: a resource (the subject) is linked to another resource (the object) through an arc labeled with a third resource (the predicate). RDF triples are designed to easily represent the relationship among objects. Current research and developments of RDF can be considered in two groups. The first group focuses on the development of various applications such as library catalogs, worldwide directories, and syndication and aggregation of news, software, or personal collections [6]. In order to build applications, projects like Doublin Core[5] defines the terminology and hierarchy of metadata. Software tools such as a RDF parser and a browser are also actively developed.

The second group works on enhancing RDF by adding some knowledge processing features such as ontology or logic [7, 10, 17]. Ontology mainly consists of a vocabulary of basic terms and a precise specification of what those terms mean. OWL is an example of Web ontology language, which defines a set of ontology in order to facilitate the exchange of knowledge that is defined with different terminology [14]. In order to utilize the power of declarativeness and inference, logical rules have been extensively studied for artificial intelligence, expert systems and deductive databases [4]. Even though many practical applications have been implemented, the need of high computing power and expensive knowledge acquisition prevent the rule-based systems from becoming general-purpose problem solving tools. Number of proposals have been made to incorporate the general logic into the Semantic Web [1, 3]. However the notorious computational complexity of general-purpose inference is also well acknowledged. A practical compromise would be to apply the logical rules only to the applications where we can control the computational complexity.

There are several researches for agent-based knowledge sharing focusing on enabling collaboration among software agents. Usually a predefined language such as ACL (Agent Communication Language) is used for communication and collaboration among agents. In the SHARE projects, KQML (Knowledge Query Manipulation Language) was used to support design teams to share the understanding of design process [13]. VWL (Virtual Workspace Language) was used for communication and collaboration among designers [2].

The above list is not the exhaustive one of knowledge representation. For example, model-based knowledge acquisition and libraries of problem solving methods are not included. Among the various forms of knowledge, in this paper we focus on the use of metadata and ontology for sharing product data. The other main feature of this paper is that all the interfaces are designed for the Web. User interfaces and other modules are built as applets that can be downloaded from Web pages. Employing these new W3C standards will enable the proposed approaches to be applied for many related applications in the future.

3   Knowledge for Sharing Product Data

In information technology, ontology is the working model of entities and interactions in some particular domain of knowledge or practices. In a broader sense, the metadata presented in the previous subsection can be included in ontology. We use ontology as the meaning and relationship of vocabulary to improve the search capability in product databases. Because products are designed by designers with various backgrounds, different terminologies can be used for the same concept or same terminology can be used for different concepts. For example, 'resource' represents slightly different concept in workflow systems and process planning systems [11]. In some workflow systems, a resource means the information that is used to make necessary decisions. In process planning systems, a resource means a person or machine that will perform a given task. In order to understand the vocabulary used in product data precisely, we should consider the context in which it is used.

Other than the keywords defined in standardized product models, engineers can select one of several synonyms to represent the same meaning. For example, [car, auto, automobile, motorcar] is an example of the synonym list. Usually product designs have short descriptions about the product, which in general include the name, usage, specification, and special features of the product. Because the description is written in natural language, any word in a synonym list can be used. In content (or associative) search, we can significantly improve the results by using the synonym list.

The other common relationship among vocabulary is the *part-of* relationship. When an entity *A* is included in another entity *B*, entities *A* and *B* have the *part-of* relationship. Figure 1 shows an example of this relationship. An automobile consists of chassis and body. The chassis consists of engine, transmission, and wheel, and the body consists of hood, door, and window. Such *part-of* relationships can also be used to improve the search results. For example, when a user request product data of transmissions, the search engine can return the product data for chassis and automobile as well.

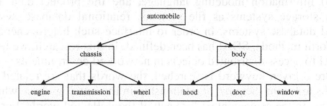

Fig. 1. An example of *part-of* relationship

Still another application of ontology is searching product data created even in different languages. Engineers from different countries use different languages. For example, the country "Korea" is written as "한국" in Korean and "韓國" in Chinese and Japanese. Because proper nouns such as personal or geographical names are often written in native languages, the translation relationship could help for engineers from different country to search or understand the product data from foreign countries. Recent information systems such as Windows NT and STEP employ the Unicode to encode the multi-byte character codes (e.g., Korean and Chinese).

4   Web-Based Knowledge Interface

As an application of metadata and ontology, we present reconfigurable sitemaps in this section. Different views of sitemaps and reconfiguring algorithm are discussed first. A prototype of a reconfigurable sitemaps is also presented.

4.1 Content Search with Ontology Expansion

Product data can be stored in either the standard neutral formats (e.g., STEP and IGES) or proprietary data formats. The standard neutral formats have been developed by standard organizations such as ISO and ANSI. The proprietary file formats, used in commercial systems (e.g. ACIS or AutoCAD™), are not suitable for data exchange among different systems because their structures are not open. Utilizing the open architecture and data models of STEP, we can implement the content search system. With the functionality of content search, users can search the product data with the characteristics (such as name, material, and functions) of the products.

However, as pointed out in the previous section, words can be used with different concepts in different application domains. This might cause that traditional query does not perform satisfactory search or that wrong products are selected for given queries. In order to improve the accuracy of the search we need to consider the context of given keywords. We can also leverage the content search by incorporating product structures. The contexts and product structures are defined in the ontology discussed in Section 3.2. By considering the ontology of given keywords, we can promote the utilization of existing design knowledge stored in the design database.

In STEP, all the product models are defined by EXPRESS [8] which is an object-oriented information modeling language, and the product data are stored in such various storage systems as file systems, relational database systems, and object-oriented database systems. In order to interface such heterogeneous storage systems by uniform methods, SDAI has been defined. In this research, we use the IDL binding of SDAI to access distributed objects in networked environments.

Before a given keyword is searched, the words that are related with the keyword are collected from the *part_of* relationship in the ontology base while considering the synonyms in the same context for each of the collected words. For example, suppose that a keyword and context pair is given as (chassis, AP214), where AP214 is the name of STEP application protocol for automotive mechanical design processes. Assuming that we have the *part_of* relationship and such synonym lists as [car, auto, automobile, motorcar] and [chassis, frame], the given keyword can be expanded into a list [(chassis, AP214), (frame, AP214), (automobile, AP214), (car, AP214), (auto, AP214), (motorcar, AP214)]. This expanded list is sent to the search engine and content search for each word and context pair is performed in turn. Figure 2 shows a user interface for content search.

Fig. 2. An RDF instance represented by a directed labeled graph

4.2 Reconfiguring Sitemaps

Sitemaps usually have hierarchical structures. However, the structure of the schema for product data is a general graph that includes cycles. For drawing this graph as a sitemap, we have several choices to select a node to be the root node. According to the selection of the root node, different hierarchical structures result as in Figure 3. There are 3 different structures in Figure 3; each of them starts from nodes Model, Tool, and Person, respectively. Because different users may have different views of interests, it would be very useful to enable the users to select a particular node as the root in a sitemap.

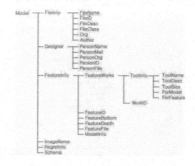

(a) Structure from node Model

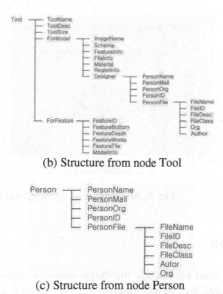

(b) Structure from node Tool

(c) Structure from node Person

Fig. 3. Different structures of RDF model from various nodes

Figure 4 depicts a screen capture of the prototype. After the user logged in, he or she can select the type of sitemaps (e.g., model view, tool view, and person view).

The screen captured in Figure 4 is an example of model view. When the user clicks the ImageName (i.e., 20021313oh.jpg in Figure 4), the image file is on the browser as in Figure 5. In Figure 5, we can see a link named "From Here". When this link is clicked, the sitemap from the current location is displayed as in Figure 5. This is an example of dynamic sitemap that draws a hierarchical structure of data from the current location. For dynamic sitemap the same algorithm can be applied as for reconfigurable sitemaps.

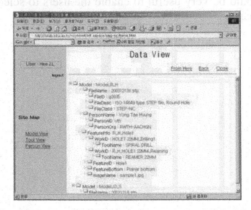

Fig. 4. An example of sitemap from the node Model

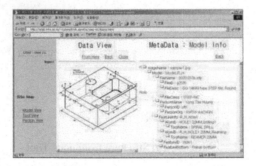

Fig. 5. An example of dynamic sitemap

5   Conclusion

We have investigated knowledge that helps users or application systems share product data in a distributed and virtual enterprise environment, and developed a prototype of intelligent information retrieval for Web-based design data repository. The knowledge we have considered is metadata and ontology. The metadata provides a map of product data space that can facilitate navigation of the product data. The concept of ontology is adopted to supplement the representation of product data. We have defined context, synonym, part-of, and translation relationships, which can significantly improve search capability by extending traditional keyword-based query into content- or product structure-based search of product databases. While implementing our system that can manage the three types of knowledge, we take advantage of the STEP standard. Some knowledge is automatically extracted from STEP data, and users may manually register others. Once the knowledge is set up, users or application programs can get assistance from the system.

As an application of metadata and ontology represented in RDF and RDFS, respectively, content search and dynamically reconfigurable sitemaps are presented in this paper. In virtual enterprise environments, there are mainly two types of data, i.e., business data and engineering data. As for the business data we have enough experience to organize and handle them effectively. However, because the structures of engineering data are usually general graphs including cycles, representing their structure hierarchically is not trivial. According to the interests of the users different views of sitemaps are more helpful. The contribution of this paper can be summarized as follows.

- Models the metadata and ontology in RDF and RDFS, respectively, for data repositories.
- Designs and implements a content search method for product data.
- Presents a prototype of data repositories that support the reconfigurable and dynamic sitemaps.

Prospected application areas of the proposed system are almost all data repositories with complicated structures and relationship among stored data. Most engineering data repositories (e.g., CAD, CAM, e-manufacturing systems, GIS, LBS, real-time systems, monitoring systems, and tracking systems) have these characteristics. In order to be more powerful, it needs to be extended with various development tools. Novice users may have difficulties to model the metadata and ontology in RDF and RDFS, respectively. Some user-friendly designed GUI tools could make the system more effective.

References

1. Boley, S. Tabet, and G. Wagner, "Design Rationale for RuleML: A Markup Language for Semantic Web Rules," Proc. of Semantic Web Symposium, Stanford University, July 2001.
2. Case and S. Lu, "The discourse model for collaborative engineering design," Computer-Aided Design 28(5), 333 – 345, 1996.
3. S. Cohen, J. Mamou, Y. Kanza and Y. Sagiv, "XSEarch: A Semantic Search Engine for XML," Proceedings of 29th International conference on Very Large Data Bases, pp. 45-56, September 2003.
4. A. Datta and S.H. Son, "A study of concurrency control in real-time, active database systems," IEEE Trans. on Knowledge and Data Engineering, Vol. 14, Issue 3, May/Jun 2002, pp. 465-484.
5. Doublin Core Metadata Initiative website http://dublincore.org/
6. Andreas Eberhart, Survey of RDF data on the Web, Dec 2001, available at http://www.i-u.de/schools/eberhart/rdf/
7. R. Fikes and D. McGuinness, An Axiomatic Semantics for RDF, RDF Schema, and DAML+OIL, Technical Report KSL-01-01, Knowledge Systems Laboratory, Stanford University, 2001.

8. ISO, 1994, Industrial automation systems and integration product data representation and exchange part 11: Description methods: The EXPRESS language reference manual (ISO, Geneva).

9. Lassila, O. and Swick, R., 1999, Resource description framework (RDF) model and syntax specification (W3C Recommendation), Available in http://www.w3.org/TR/REC-rdf-syntax/.

10. Drew McDemott and Dejing Dou, Embedding Logic in DAML/RDF, Nov. 2001, available at ftp://ftp.cs.yale.edu/pub/mcdermott/papers/wwwconf.pdf

11. Schlenoff, C., Ivester, R., and Knutilla, A., 1998, A robust process ontology for manufacturing systems integration, in *Proceedings of 2nd International Conference on Engineering Design and Automation*, Maui, Hawaii.

12. Swartout, B., 1996, Future directions in knowledge-based systems, ACM Computing Surveys 28(4es).

13. G. Toye, M. Cutkosky, L.J. Leifer, J. Tenenbaum and J. Glicksman, "SHARE: A methodology and environment for collaborative product development," International Journal of Intelligent & Cooperative Information Systems 3(2), 129-53, 1993.

14. World Wide Web Consortium, OWL Web Ontology Language Reference, W3C Recommendation, February 2004, available at http://www.w3.org/TR/2004/REC-owl-ref-20040210/.

15. World Wide Web Consortium, RDF/XML Syntax Specification, W3C Recommendation, February 2004, available at http://www.w3.org/TR/2004/REC-rdf-syntax-grammar-20040210/.

16. World Wide Web Consortium, RDF Vocabulary Description Language 1.0: RDF Schema, W3C Recommendation, February 2004, available at http://www.w3.org/TR/2004/REC-rdf-schema-20040210/.

17. Sang Bong Yoo, In Han Kim, "Application of Active Real-Time Objects and Rules in Semantic Web," Lecture Notes in Computer Science, Vol. 2822, September 2003.

Incremental Collaborative Filtering for Highly-Scalable Recommendation Algorithms

Manos Papagelis[1, 2], Ioannis Rousidis[2], Dimitris Plexousakis[1, 2], and Elias Theoharopoulos[3,*]

[1] Institute of Computer Science, Forth, Heraklion, Greece
{papaggel, dp}@ics.forth.gr
[2] Computer Science Department, University of Crete, Heraklion, Greece
rousidis@csd.uoc.gr
[3] School of Informatics, University of Edinburgh, Edinburgh, Scotland
e.theoharopoulos@sms.ed.ac.uk

Abstract. Most recommendation systems employ variations of Collaborative Filtering (CF) for formulating suggestions of items relevant to users' interests. However, CF requires expensive computations that grow polynomially with the number of users and items in the database. Methods proposed for handling this scalability problem and speeding up recommendation formulation are based on approximation mechanisms and, even when performance improves, they most of the time result in accuracy degradation. We propose a method for addressing the scalability problem based on incremental updates of user-to-user similarities. Our Incremental Collaborative Filtering (ICF) algorithm (i) is not based on any approximation method and gives the potential for high-quality recommendation formulation (ii) provides recommendations orders of magnitude faster than classic CF and thus, is suitable for online application.

1 Introduction

Recommendation algorithms are extensively adopted by both research and e-commerce applications, in order to provide an intelligent mechanism to filter out the excess of information available in a domain [1]. Collaborative filtering (CF) [3], almost certainly, is the key method to effortlessly find out items that users will probably like according to their logged history of prior transactions.

However, CF requires computations that are very expensive and grow polynomially with the number of users and items in a system. Therefore, in order to bring recommendation algorithms effectively on the web, and succeed in providing recommendations with high accuracy and acceptable performance, sophisticated data structures and advanced, scalable architectures are required [7]. To address this scalability problem, we present an incremental CF method, based on incremental updates of user-to-user similarities which is also able to recommend items orders of magnitude faster than classic CF, while maintaining the recommendation quality.

---

* Work conducted while at ICS-FORTH.

M.-S. Hacid et al. (Eds.): ISMIS 2005, LNAI 3488, pp. 553–561, 2005.
© Springer-Verlag Berlin Heidelberg 2005

The remainder of the paper is organized as follows: Section 2 elaborates on the scalability challenge and explains the weaknesses of already proposed methods. Section 3 presents our Incremental CF method. Section 4 argues about complexity issues of the algorithms, while Section 5 presents our experimental evaluation. Section 6 concludes our work and discusses further research directions.

2   The Scalability Challenge for Collaborative Filtering

Classic CF algorithm generates recommendations based on a subset of users that are most similar to the active user. The formulation of a single recommendation is a two-step computation. First, the algorithm needs to compute the similarity between the active user and all other users, based on their co-rated items, so as to pick the ones with similar behavior. Subsequently, the algorithm recommends to the active user items that are highly rated by his or her most similar users. In order to compute the similarities between users, a variety of similarity measures have been proposed, such as Pearson correlation, cosine vector similarity, Spearman correlation, entropy-based uncertainty measure and mean-square difference. However, Breese et al. [4] and Herlocker et Al. [5] suggest that Pearson correlation performs better than all the rest.

If we define the user-item matrix as the matrix having as elements the ratings of users to items, then a user's model is represented in this matrix as an n-dimensional vector, where n is the number of items in the database. This vector is extremely sparse for most users, since, even ones that are very active result in rating just a few of the total number of items available in a database. If we define the subset of items that users u_x and u_y have co-rated as $I'=\{i_x: x=1, 2, ..., n' \text{ and } n' \leq n\}$, where n is the total number of items in the database, r_{u_x,i_h} as the rating of user u_x to item i_h and $\overline{r_{u_x}}$, $\overline{r_{u_y}}$ as the average ratings of users u_x and u_y respectively, then the similarity between two users is defined as the Pearson correlation of their associated rows in the user-item matrix and is given by equation 1 [14].

	i_1	...	i_x	...	i_y	...	i_n
...							
u_x	$r_{x,1}$		$r_{x,x}$		$r_{x,y}$		$r_{x,n}$
...							
u_y	$r_{y,1}$		$r_{y,x}$		$r_{y,y}$		-
...							

$$sim(u_x,u_y) = \frac{\sum_{h=1}^{n'} (r_{u_x,i_h} - \overline{r_{u_x}})(r_{u_y,i_h} - \overline{r_{u_y}})}{\sqrt{\sum_{h=1}^{n'} (r_{u_x,i_h} - \overline{r_{u_x}})^2} \sqrt{\sum_{h=1}^{n'} (r_{u_y,i_h} - \overline{r_{u_y}})^2}} \quad (1)$$

Classic CF fails to scale up its computation with the growth of both the number of users and items in the database. To deal with the scalability problem Breese et al [4] and Ungar et al [8] utilize Bayesian network and clustering approaches, while Sarwar et al [6, 11] apply folding in Singular Value Decomposition (SVD) to reduce the dimensionality of the user-item matrix. It is also possible to address these scaling issues by data reduction or data focusing techniques. Yu et al [12] and Zeng et al [9] adopt instance selection for removing the irrelevant and redundant instances. Moreover, content-boosted CF approaches reduce the number of items examined, by partitioning the item space according to item category or subject classification. Finally, more greedy approaches concentrate on randomly sampling users, discarding users with few ratings or discarding very popular or unpopular items.

Unfortunately, even when these methods achieve improved performance, they also reduce recommendation quality in several ways. Bayesian networks may prove practical for environments in which user preferences change slowly with respect to the time needed to build the model, but are not suitable for environments in which user preference models must be updated frequently. Clustering-based methods suffer from poor accuracy. It is possible to improve their quality by using numerous fine-grained segments [13], but then online user segment classification becomes almost as expensive as finding similar users using the classic CF. SVD-based work focuses mainly on accuracy rather than efficiency. Data focusing and reduction approaches, such as instance selection or item-space partitioning, experience reduced accuracy due to loss of information. If an algorithm discards the most popular or unpopular items, there may be items that will never be recommended to some users. Obviously, to gain in computation one needs to lose in recommendation quality and vice versa. Appropriate trade-offs must be considered.

3   Incremental Collaborative Filtering

In this section, we present a method to deal with the scalability challenge of Classic CF without compromising its recommendation quality. We refer to this method as Incremental Collaborative Filtering (ICF), because it is based on incremental updates of the user-to-user similarities. ICF can be employed to effectively bring highly scalable and accurate recommendation algorithms on the Web.

Whenever a user u_x submits a new rating or updates the value of an already submitted rating, his or her similarity value with the rest of the users may need to be re-computed. Our objective is to express the new similarity value between two users in relation to their old similarity value. This describes an incremental update of their associated similarity. To smoothen the progress of this task we adopt the following notation for the Pearson Correlation similarity measure of equation 1:

$$A = \frac{B}{\sqrt{C}\sqrt{D}} \Rightarrow A = sim(u_x, u_y), \quad B = \sum_{k=1}^{n'} (r_{u_x, i_k} - \overline{r_{u_x}})(r_{u_y, i_k} - \overline{r_{u_y}}), \quad C = \sum_{i=1}^{n'} (r_{u_x, i_h} - \overline{r_{u_x}})^2, \quad D = \sum_{i=1}^{n'} (r_{u_y, i_h} - \overline{r_{u_y}})^2$$

Actually, we split the similarity measure into three factors B, C, D, independently calculate the new values of each factor B', C', D' and then combine these values so as to obtain the value of the new similarity A' as shown below:

$$A' = \frac{B'}{\sqrt{C'}\sqrt{D'}} \Rightarrow A' = \frac{B+e}{\sqrt{C+f}\sqrt{D+g}}, \quad B' = B+e, \quad C' = C+f, \quad D' = D+g$$

where e, f, g are *increments* that need to be computed after either the submission of a new or the update of an existing rating. Next, we split our study, so as to consider the different computations needed for the two special cases. Table 1 shows the increments to be computed and the Appendix provides proof of equations 2-13.

Submission of a new rating: To calculate the similarity of u_a and u_y, when the active user u_a submits a *new rating* for the active item i_a, we distinguish between two cases:

i. u_y had rated i_a: B, C, D are updated due to the new average of u_a, the new rating of u_a to i_a and the new number of co-rated items

ii. u_y had not rated i_a: B, C are updated due to the new average of u_a.

Table 1. Summary of the increments that need to be calculated

		Submission of a new rating		Update of an existing rating	
u_y had rated i_a	e	$e = (r_{u_a,i_a} - \overline{r_{u_a}}')(r_{u_y,i_a} - \overline{r_{u_y}})$ $-\sum_{h=1}^{n'} d\overline{r_{u_a}}(r_{u_y,i_h} - \overline{r_{u_y}})$	(2)	$e = dr_{u_a,i_a}(r_{u_y,i_a} - \overline{r_{u_y}})$ $-\sum_{h=1}^{n'} d\overline{r_{u_a}}(r_{u_y,i_h} - \overline{r_{u_y}})$	(8)
	f	$f = (r_{u_a,i_a} - \overline{r_{u_a}}')^2 + \sum_{h=1}^{n'} d\overline{r_{u_a}}^2$ $-2\sum_{h=1}^{n'} d\overline{r_{u_a}}(r_{u_a,i_h} - \overline{r_{u_a}})$	(3)	$f = dr_{u_a,i_a}^2 + 2dr_{u_a,i_a}(r_{u_a,i_a} - \overline{r_{u_a}}')$ $+\sum_{h=1}^{n'} d\overline{r_{u_a}}^2 - 2\sum_{h=1}^{n'} d\overline{r_{u_a}}'(r_{u_a,i_h} - \overline{r_{u_a}})$	(9)
	g	$g = (r_{u_y,i_a} - \overline{r_{u_y}})^2$	(4)	$g = 0$	(10)
u_y had not rated i_a	e	$e = -\sum_{h=1}^{n'} d\overline{r_{u_a}}(r_{u_y,i_h} - \overline{r_{u_y}})$	(5)	$e = -\sum_{h=1}^{n'} d\overline{r_{u_a}}(r_{u_y,i_h} - \overline{r_{u_y}})$	(11)
	f	$f = \sum_{h=1}^{n'} d\overline{r_{u_a}}^2 - 2\sum_{h=1}^{n'} d\overline{r_{u_a}}(r_{u_a,i_h} - \overline{r_{u_a}})$	(6)	$f = \sum_{h=1}^{n'} d\overline{r_{u_a}}^2 - 2\sum_{h=1}^{n'} d\overline{r_{u_a}}'(r_{u_a,i_h} - \overline{r_{u_a}})$	(12)
	g	$g = 0$	(7)	$g = 0$	(13)

Table 2. Computation of factors that appear in increments e, f and g

Factors	Calculation
B, C, D	Cached Information (For all pairs of users)
q	Cached Information (The number of the items that a user has rated)
$\overline{r_{u_a}}, \overline{r_{u_y}}$	Cached information (Average ratings of all users in database)
$\sum_{h=1}^{n'} r_{u_y,i_h}, \sum_{h=1}^{n'} r_{u_a,i_h}$	Cached Information (For each pair of users, the sum of their ratings to co-rated items is cached)
$\overline{r_{u_a}}'$	New average rating of active user: • Submission of a new rating: $\overline{r_{u_a}}' = \dfrac{r_{u_a,i_a}}{q+1} + \dfrac{q}{q+1}\overline{r_{u_a}}$ • Update of existing rating: $\overline{r_{u_a}}' = \dfrac{dr_{u_a,i_h}}{q} + \overline{r_{u_a}}$
r_{u_a,i_a}	Interface (Actual rating of the active user u_a to the active item i_a)
$d\overline{r_{u_a}}$	$d\overline{r_{u_a}} = \overline{r_{u_a}}' - \overline{r_{u_a}} \Leftrightarrow \overline{r_{u_a}}' = \overline{r_{u_a}} + d\overline{r_{u_a}}$ (The difference of user's previous and current average rating)
r_{u_y,i_a}	Database query. (The rating of the user u_y to the item i_a)

Update of an existing rating: To calculate the similarity of u_a and u_y, when the active user u_a updates a rating for the active item i_a, we distinguish between two cases:

  i. u_y had rated i_a: B, C are updated due to the new average of u_a and the new rating of u_a to i_a

  ii. u_y had not rated i_a: B, C are updated due to the new average of u_a

We expressed B', C' and D' using the former values of B, C and D and the respective increments e, f, g. However, to enable the incremental computation of the new similarities with trivial operations we need to employ an appropriate data structure. We define a caching scheme, in terms of tables in a database, which permits to store the values of B, C and D for all pairs of users. Furthermore, we cache the average rating and the number of items that each user has rated. Cached information needs to be updated after the submission of a new or the update of an existing rating. Table 2 explains how each factor of e, f, g increments is computed.

4 Complexity Issues

In this section, we discuss the computational complexity of the classic CF and ICF algorithms. We initially present worst cases and then try to give approximations of the algorithms under real conditions. For each case our study spans in two directions: the one refers to the complexity of maintaining the user similarities matrix and the other refers to the complexity of formulating one recommendation to an active user.

In case of Classic CF, if m is the number of users and n the number of items in the database, then the computation complexity of maintaining the user similarities matrix is $O(m^2n)$, since we need to compute the similarity between each pair of users according to the subset of their co-rated items. In order to deal with this task, major e-commerce systems prefer to carry out expensive computations offline and feed the database with updated information periodically [2]. In this way, they succeed in providing quick recommendations to users, based on pre-computed similarities. These recommendations however, are not of the highest accuracy as ratings submitted between two offline computations are not considered. Thus, the offline computation method may be detrimental to new or obscure users and items due to their almost undeveloped profile. Alternatively, if user similarities are not pre-computed offline, they may be computed at the time a recommendation is requested. In this case, instead of computing the whole user similarities matrix, we need to only compute the similarities between the active user and all the rest or a set of training users. The cost of this computation is $O(mn)$. The cost of generating a recommendation using the Classic CF is the cost of finding the most similar users to the active user and scanning their rated items to find the ones that are highly rated. This computation costs $O(n)$ when similarities are pre-computed offline and $O(mn)$ otherwise.

In the case of the ICF algorithm, user-to-user similarities are computed incrementally at the time of rating activity and not at the time that a recommendation is requested. The complexity of this operation is $O(mn)$, as at most $m-1$ similarities need to be updated and at most n items need to be examined for each user. Since user similarities are considered pre-computed, the cost of generating a recommendation using ICF is $O(n)$, as n items need to be examined in the worst case.

Due to the high sparsity levels in recommendation systems, it is essential to also consider approximations of the complexities under real conditions. Thus, we define: m', with $m'<<m$, the number of users with whom the active user has at least one co-rated item; n', with $n'<<n$, the number of items that have not been rated by the active user and have been rated by at least one of its similar users; n'', with $n''<<n$, the number of co-rated items of the active user and another user.

According to these definitions, we can set up the approximations of the complexities following the discussion of the previous paragraph. Worst case and approximation complexities of Classic CF and ICF are summarized in Table 3.

Table 3. Worst case and approximation complexities of Classic CF and ICF

	Classic CF		Incremental CF	
	Worst	Approximation	Worst	Approximation
Complexity for maintaining the Similarity Matrix	$O(m^2n)$	$O(mm'n'')$	$O(mn)$	$O(m'n')$
Complexity for providing a recommendation to active user	$O(mn)$	$O(m'n'')+O(n')$	$O(n)$	$O(n')$
	Pre-computed Offline			
	$O(n)$	$O(n')$		

5 Experimental Evaluation

As complexity computation fails to give real-time performance and behavior of the algorithms described, we set up an experimental scenario for evaluating the performance of our ICF algorithm as opposed to the Classic CF. The evaluation is carried out according to *response time* and *accuracy* metrics as defined below:

Response time: The time required by the algorithm to formulate a recommendation.

Accuracy: The percentage of items an algorithm recommends from the set of items that are recommended by the Classic CF that considers the whole dataset available.

The assumption made here is that recommendations based on the whole dataset are of the highest quality, which is not necessarily true. Indeed, we define this to demonstrate the potential that ICF gives for formulating recommendations based on the complete information in a database and not only a part of it.

The experimental scenario is set up so as to depict the level of scalability that both algorithms demonstrate when the active user requests a single recommendation. We employ sparsity level of 92% and consider a user to be similar to the active user if their associated Pearson correlation coefficient is greater than 0.65 (in a range of -1 to 1). The values selected represent typical values for recommendation systems and do not influence the results of the experiments. Table 4 presents the results of our experiments for user-item matrix of size 100x100 and 1000x1000 respectively. Experiments have been carried out on a 2.80 Mhz, 1G RAM PC.

Table 4. Response time and accuracy performance of Classic CF and ICF

User-item matrix size	Classic CF (Based on sampling)			Incremental CF	
	Samples (#users)	Time (sec)	Accuracy	Time (sec)	Accuracy
100 users x 100 items	10	0.17	22%	0.045	100%
	30	0.55	49.5%		
	50	0.765	67.5%		
	99	1.38	100%		
1000 users x 1000 items	100	6.81	26,7%	0.46	100%
	300	20	53,8%		
	500	33	66.8%		
	999	66	100%		

The following remarks can be drawn from Table 4 about the performance of CF and ICF:

Remark 1: The trade-off between performance and accuracy in case of Classic CF is confirmed. Indeed, Classic CF is very sensitive to the size of samples used. As the sample size increases, accuracy is improved, but the response time also increases and vice versa. Large sample sizes are impractical for online applications due to the slow response time, while small sample sizes are impractical due to accuracy degradation. On the other side, the accuracy of ICF remains as high as 100%, since it is applied to the whole information available.

Remark 2: ICF proves to be highly scalable, as its response time remains acceptable even for a very large data set. For instance, it provides a recommendation in 0.46 seconds for a matrix size of 1000x1000. Classic CF requires extremely disproportional time to reach a satisfactory accuracy level for large matrix sizes. For instance, when an accuracy level of 66.8% is intended, using a sample of 500 users, in a 1000x1000 matrix Classic CF performs 71 times slower than ICF.

Remark 3: The performance of ICF grows linearly with the number of items, thus in case of a *very* large matrix an approximation method may need to be employed.

6 Conclusions and Future Work

High dimensionality seems to be the "Achilles' heel" for most of the CF-based recommendation systems. For dealing with this scalability problem, we proposed an incremental method that replaces expensive vector operations with a scalar operation, able to speed-up computations of high dimensional user-item matrices. We named this method Incremental Collaborative Filtering (ICF). ICF is not based on any approximation method and thus, provides the potential of formulating high-quality recommendations. Moreover, pre-computed user-to-user similarities allow recommendations to be delivered orders of times faster than with classic CF. ICF appears to be suitable for online applications, while the methodology described is general and may be easily adopted to scale the application of CF in other areas. As future directions of our research we consider the development of a method for alleviating the *sparsity* problem of CF. The main idea of the method is to infer trust between users through profile similarities for constructing a denser user-item matrix.

References

1. Sarwar, B., Karypis, G., Konstan, J., Riedl J.: Analysis of recommendation algorithms for e-commerce. Proc. of ACM Electronic Commerce (2000)
2. Linden, G., Smith, B., York, J.: Amazon.com Recommendations: Item-to-Item Collaborative Filtering. IEEE Internet Computing, January 2003
3. Herlocker, J. L., Konstan, J. A., Riedl, J.: Explaining Collaborative Filtering Recommendations. Proc. of the ACM Conf.on CSCW (2000)
4. Breese, J. S., Heckerman, D., Kadie, C.: Empirical analysis of predictive algorithms for collaborative filtering. Proc. of the UAI (1998)
5. Herlocker, J. L., Konstan, J. A., Borchers, A., Riedl, J.: An Algorithmic Framework for Performing Collaborative Filtering. Proc. of ACM SIGIR (1999)
6. Sarwar, B. M., Karypis, G., Konstan, J. A., Riedl, J. T.: Application of Dimensionality Reduction in Recommender System: A Case Study. Proc. of ACM SIGKDD (2000)
7. Papagelis M, Plexousakis D.: Qualitative Analysis of User-based and Item-based Prediction Algorithms for Recommendation Agents. Proc. of CIA (2004)
8. Ungar, L., Foster, D.: Clustering Methods for Collaborative Filtering. Proc. of Workshop on Recommendation Systems, AAAI Press (1998)
9. Zeng, C., Xing, C., Zhou, L.: Similarity Measure and Instance Selection for Collaborative Filtering. Proc. of WWW (2003)
10. Sarwar, B.M., Karypis, G., Konstan, J., Riedl, J.: Incremental SVD-Based Algorithms for Highly Scaleable Recommender Systems. Proc.of ICCIT (2002).
11. Deerwester, S., Dumais, S. T., Furnas, G. W., Landauer, T. K., Harshman, R.: Indexing by Latent Semantic Analysis. JASIS 41(6) (1990)
12. Yu, K., Xu, X., Tao, J., Ester, M., Kriegel H.: Instance Selection Techniques for Memory-Based Collaborative Filtering. Proc. of SDM (2002).
13. Jung, S. Y., Kim, T.: An Incremental Similarity Computation Method in Agglomerative Hierarchical Clustering. Proc. of ISAIS (2001)
14. Pearson K.: Mathematical contribution to the theory of evolution: VII, on the correlation of characters not quantitatively measurable. Phil. Tr. R. Soc. Lond. A, 195, 1-47, 1900

Appendix: Proof of Equations 2-13

Proof of Equation 2

$$B' = \sum_{h=1}^{n'} (r_{u_a,i_h} - \overline{r_{u_a}}')(r_{u_y,i_h} - \overline{r_{u_y}}) \Leftrightarrow B' = (r_{u_a,i_a} - \overline{r_{u_a}}')(r_{u_y,i_a} - \overline{r_{u_y}}) + \sum_{h=1}^{n'} (r_{u_a,i_h} - \overline{r_{u_a}}')(r_{u_y,i_h} - \overline{r_{u_y}}) \Leftrightarrow$$

$$B' = (r_{u_a,i_a} - \overline{r_{u_a}}')(r_{u_y,i_a} - \overline{r_{u_y}}) + B - \sum_{h=1}^{n'} d\overline{r_{u_a}}(r_{u_y,i_h} - \overline{r_{u_y}}) \Rightarrow e = (r_{u_a,i_a} - \overline{r_{u_a}}')(r_{u_y,i_a} - \overline{r_{u_y}}) - \sum_{h=1}^{n'} d\overline{r_{u_a}}(r_{u_y,i_h} - \overline{r_{u_y}})$$

Proof of Equation 3

$$C' = \sum_{h=1}^{n'} (r_{u_a,i_h} - \overline{r_{u_a}}')^2 \Leftrightarrow C' = (r_{u_a,i_a} - \overline{r_{u_a}}')^2 + \sum_{h=1}^{n'} (r_{u_a,i_h} - \overline{r_{u_a}}')^2 \Leftrightarrow$$

$$C' = (r_{u_a,i_a} - \overline{r_{u_a}}')^2 + C + \sum_{h=1}^{n'} d\overline{r_{u_a}}^2 - 2\sum_{h=1}^{n'} d\overline{r_{u_a}}(r_{u_a,i_h} - \overline{r_{u_a}}) \Rightarrow f = (r_{u_a,i_a} - \overline{r_{u_a}}')^2 + \sum_{h=1}^{n'} d\overline{r_{u_a}}^2 - 2\sum_{h=1}^{n'} d\overline{r_{u_a}}(r_{u_a,i_h} - \overline{r_{u_a}})$$

Proof of Equation 4

$$D' = \sum_{h=1}^{n'} (r_{u_y,i_h} - \overline{r_{u_y}})^2 \Leftrightarrow D' = (r_{u_y,i_a} - \overline{r_{u_y}})^2 + \sum_{h=1}^{n'} (r_{u_y,i_h} - \overline{r_{u_y}})^2 \Leftrightarrow D' = (r_{u_y,i_a} - \overline{r_{u_y}})^2 + D \Rightarrow g = (r_{u_y,i_a} - \overline{r_{u_y}})^2$$

Proof of Equation 5, 6, 7

In the case that user u_y has not rated the item i_a, the values of B, C and D are proved in way similar to equations 2, 3 and 4 respectively. In this case the increments e, f and g equal to:

$$e = -\sum_{h=1}^{n'} d\overline{r_{u_a}}(r_{u_y,i_h} - \overline{r_{u_y}}), \quad f = \sum_{h=1}^{n'} d\overline{r_{u_a}}^2 - 2\sum_{h=1}^{n'} d\overline{r_{u_a}}(r_{u_a,i_h} - \overline{r_{u_a}}), \quad g = 0$$

Proof of Equation 8

$$B' = \sum_{h=1}^{n'} (r_{u_a,i_h} - \overline{r_{u_a}}')(r_{u_y,i_h} - \overline{r_{u_y}}) \Leftrightarrow B' = (r_{u_a,i_a}' - \overline{r_{u_a}}')(r_{u_y,i_a} - \overline{r_{u_y}}) + \sum_{h=1}^{n'-1} (r_{u_a,i_h} - \overline{r_{u_a}}')(r_{u_y,i_h} - \overline{r_{u_y}})$$

$$B' = dr_{u_a,i_a}(r_{u_y,i_a} - \overline{r_{u_y}}) + (r_{u_a,i_a} - \overline{r_{u_a}}')(r_{u_y,i_a} - \overline{r_{u_y}}) + \sum_{h=1}^{n'-1} (r_{u_a,i_h} - \overline{r_{u_a}}')(r_{u_y,i_h} - \overline{r_{u_y}}) \Leftrightarrow$$

$$B' = dr_{u_a,i_a}(r_{u_y,i_a} - \overline{r_{u_y}}) + \sum_{h=1}^{n'} (r_{u_a,i_h} - \overline{r_{u_a}}')(r_{u_y,i_h} - \overline{r_{u_y}}) \Leftrightarrow B' = dr_{u_a,i_a}(r_{u_y,i_a} - \overline{r_{u_y}}) + B - \sum_{h=1}^{n'} d\overline{r_{u_a}}(r_{u_y,i_h} - \overline{r_{u_y}})$$

$$\Rightarrow e = dr_{u_a,i_a}(r_{u_y,i_a} - \overline{r_{u_y}}) - \sum_{h=1}^{n'} d\overline{r_{u_a}}(r_{u_y,i_h} - \overline{r_{u_y}})$$

Proof of Equation 9

$$C' = \sum_{h=1}^{n'} (r_{u_a,i_h} - \overline{r_{u_a}}')^2 \Leftrightarrow C' = (r_{u_a,i_a}' - \overline{r_{u_a}}')^2 + \sum_{h=1}^{n'-1} (r_{u_a,i_h} - \overline{r_{u_a}}')^2 \Leftrightarrow C' = dr_{u_a,i_a}^2 + 2dr_{u_a,i_a}(r_{u_a,i_a} - \overline{r_{u_a}}') + (r_{u_a,i_a} - \overline{r_{u_a}}')^2 + \sum_{h=1}^{n'-1} (r_{u_a,i_h} - \overline{r_{u_a}}')^2 \Leftrightarrow$$

$$C' = dr_{u_a,i_a}^2 + 2dr_{u_a,i_a}(r_{u_a,i_a} - \overline{r_{u_a}}') + \sum_{h=1}^{n'} (r_{u_a,i_h} - \overline{r_{u_a}}')^2 \Leftrightarrow C' = dr_{u_a,i_a}^2 + 2dr_{u_a,i_a}(r_{u_a,i_a} - \overline{r_{u_a}}') + C + \sum_{h=1}^{n'} d\overline{r_{u_a}}^2 - 2\sum_{h=1}^{n'} d\overline{r_{u_a}}(r_{u_a,i_h} - \overline{r_{u_a}}) \Leftrightarrow$$

$$\Rightarrow f = dr_{u_a,i_a}^2 + 2dr_{u_a,i_a}(r_{u_a,i_a} - \overline{r_{u_a}}') + \sum_{h=1}^{n'} d\overline{r_{u_a}}^2 - 2\sum_{h=1}^{n'} d\overline{r_{u_a}}(r_{u_a,i_h} - \overline{r_{u_a}})$$

Proof of Equation 10

$$D' = \sum_{h=1}^{n'} (r_{u_y,i_h} - \overline{r_{u_y}})^2 \Leftrightarrow D' = D \Rightarrow g = 0$$

Proof of Equation 11, 12, 13

In the case that user u_y has not rated the item i_a, the values of B, C and D are proved in way similar to equations 8, 9 and 10 respectively. In this case the increments e, f and g equal to:

$$e = -\sum_{h=1}^{n'} d\overline{r_{u_a}}(r_{u_y,i_h} - \overline{r_{u_y}}), \quad f = \sum_{h=1}^{n'} d\overline{r_{u_a}}^2 - 2\sum_{h=1}^{n'} d\overline{r_{u_a}}'(r_{u_a,i_h} - \overline{r_{u_a}}), \quad g = 0$$

A Distance-Based Algorithm for Clustering Database User Sessions

Qingsong Yao, Aijun An, and Xiangji Huang*

Department of Computer Science, York University, Toronto, M3J 1P3, Canada
{qingsong, aan}@cs.yorku.ca, jhuang@yorku.ca

Abstract. In this paper, we present a distance-based clustering algorithm for grouping database user sessions. The algorithm considers both local and global similarities between sessions and incorporates three distance metrics in the computation of the distance between two sessions. We describe the three metrics and discuss the rational for combining them. The algorithm is evaluated on two datasets. One is a clinic OLTP workload file and the other is the TPC-W benchmark. The evaluation results are reported.

1 Introduction

Analysis of database workloads provides insight into how database systems are used. The results of the analysis can be used to improve the performance of database systems. A *database user session* is a sequence of queries issued by a user (or an application) to achieve a certain task. It consists of one or more database transactions, which are in turn a sequence of operations performed as a logical unit of work. Analysis of sessions allows us to discover high-level patterns that stem from the structure of the task the user is solving. In this paper, we assume that a set of database user sessions are already obtained from database workloads. We propose a distance-based session clustering algorithm to group sessions into different classes. The distance between two sessions is measured according to three similarity metrics/scores: *the coefficient score, the alignment score* and *the neighborhood score*. This approach considers not only the local similarity between sessions (the coefficient score and the alignment score), but also the global similarity (the neighborhood score). The rest of the paper is organized as follows. Related work is discussed in Sect. 2. In Sect. 3, a distance-based session clustering algorithm is proposed, and three similarity scores are discussed. We analyze our clustering algorithm and give experimental results in Sect. 4. We conclude the paper in Sect. 5.

2 Related Work

The work presented in this paper is part of a research project that investigates how data mining techniques can be used to improve database system performance. We particularly

---

* This work is supported by Communications and Information Technology Ontario (CITO) and the Natural Sciences and Engineering Research Council of Canada (NSERC).

M.-S. Hacid et al. (Eds.): ISMIS 2005, LNAI 3488, pp. 562–572, 2005.
© Springer-Verlag Berlin Heidelberg 2005

focus on finding user access patterns from database workloads and using them to improve system performance. Sessions can be identified from database workload. Clustering database sessions is an important step in this process. After session groups are generated, we build a model for each class. The discovered models can be used to predict incoming user queries [6, 12, 15] and to redesign and rewrite queries to achieve better performance [16].

Clustering is a subject of active research in several fields such as statistics and data mining. A review of clustering techniques is given in [9]. A survey on data clustering algorithms can be found in [3]. The session clustering algorithm presented in the paper is based on the idea of *Jaccard Coefficient* measurement [8], sequence alignment [10], and common neighbors between sessions [7]. Guha et al. [7] present a clustering algorithm, *ROCK* (Robust Clustering using linKs), that deals with categorical data in which each data point is a set of items. The algorithm is based on *links* between data points instead of distance-based metrics or the Jaccard coefficient. Wang and ZaAne [14] and Birgit and Vanhoof [5] use the sequence alignment technique to cluster web user sessions. However, their similarity scores are different from the one in our approach.

Clustering is one of the common techniques used in characterizing the workload in DBMS environments. Transactions can be grouped according to their consumption of system resources [17], or according to their resource reference patterns [18]. Artis [1] characterizes the workload of an IBM MVS system with the aim of determining its capacity and developing cluster descriptions of the transaction workload. Nikolaou et al. [11] propose several clustering algorithms that can classify OLTP transactions according to their database reference patterns. However, these works focus on grouping transactions according to consumed resources instead of clustering user sessions according to the high-level requests (i.e. SQL queries).

3   Distance-Based Session Clustering

A database user session usually performs certain task and is controlled by certain business logic. Table 1 shows a user session that retrieves and displays a user's treatment schedule. We observe that the queries within a session have certain order, and the query parameters have certain relationships (e.g. *customer id '1074' is shared by all queries*). Thus, it is necessary to group them into different session classes and to use a model to represent the query orders and their relationships. Given an SQL query, we can transform it into two parts: a *query template* and a set of *parameters*. For example, the template of the first query is *("select authority from* employee *where employee_id =%",x)*, and the value of parameter x is *'1025'*. Thus, we can ignore the data value in a user session by treating each request as a query template represented by a template label. For example, the session instance shown in Table 1 corresponds to a template sequence: *30-09-10-20-47-49*. Our objective in this paper is to group user sessions so that each group contains similar sequences of query templates and these sequences are dissimilar to the ones in other clusters.

Table 1. An instance of schedule display session procedure

Label	Statement
30	select authority from *employee* where employee_id ='**1025**'
09	select count(*) as num from *customer* where cust_num = '**1074**'
10	select card_name from *customer* t1, *member_card* t2 where t1.cust_num = '**1074**' and t1.card_id = t2.card_id
20	select contact_last, contact_first from *customer* where cust_num = '**1074**'
47	select t1.branch ,t2.* from *record* t1, *treatment* t2 where t1.contract_no = t2.contract_no and t1.cust_id ='**1074**' and check_in_date = '**2003/03/04**' and t1.branch ='**scar**'
49	select top **10** contract_no from *treatment_schedule* where cust_id = '**1074**'

3.1   Session Similarity

We first consider each session as a session class, and calculate the distance between them. Then, the session groups are merged according to their intra-group distances, and the intra-group distances are updated correspondingly. The clustering procedure stops when all intra-group distances become more than a pre-defined distance threshold (β_1). The distance between two sessions, s_i and s_j, is defined as:

$$1.0 - \alpha_1 \times csim(s_i, s_j) - \alpha_2 \times asim(s_i, s_j) - \alpha_3 \times nsim(s_i, s_j),$$

where *csim, asim, nsim* are *the coefficient score*, *the alignment score*, and *the neighborhood score*, respectively, and α_1, α_2, and α_3 are the similarity parameters, the sum of which is 1.0. The coefficient score is based on the *Jaccard Coefficient* method. *Jaccard Coefficient* [8] can be used to measure the similarity between sets, in which the similarity between two sets A and B is defined as the fraction of the common items between them, i.e., $\frac{|A \cap B|}{|A \cup B|}$. We treat each session as an un-order request set, then the coefficient score, $csim(s_i, s_j)$, is defined as $\frac{|s_i \cap s_j|}{|s_i \cup s_j|}$. The objective of coefficient score is based on the assumption that sessions belonging to the same session class usually have a large amount of common requests.

We observe that if two sessions belong to the same group, they are very likely to have similar request sequence. But the coefficient score does not reflect the request order. Therefore, we propose another scoring scheme based on the idea of sequence alignment, referred to as *the alignment score*. Sequence alignment is a crucial operation in bioinformatics. In sequence alignment, two or more strings are aligned together in order to get the highest similarity score. Gaps may be inserted into a string in order to shift the remaining characters into better matches. For example, given two sequences X=*"ABCDD"* and Y=*"ABED"*, the aligned sequences can be: $\frac{ABCDD}{ABED-}$. In this paper, we use the *Needleman-Wunsch* algorithm [10], a well-known sequence alignment algorithm, to align two sessions. Once the optimal alignment is obtained, we calculate the alignment score based on aligned session sequences as follows. We believe that the session sequences are controlled by certain logic/programming code. The code may contain branches (such as *if-else* and *switch-case* statements) or cycles (such as *for-loop* and *do-while* statements) that may cause the requests to be executed repeatedly. The branches and cycles can be observed from the aligned sessions. For example, from alignment sequences $\frac{ABCDD}{ABED-}$, we can see two matches (A and B), one branch (C/E) and one cycle (DD/D). We assign each match with a score of 2, each branch with a score of 1, and each cycle with a score of 1. To normalize the score, we divide the assigned value with the length of the aligned sessions. The length is defined as *2 × (num. of matches + num. of branches + num. of cycles)*. Then, the final alignment score is *6/8 = 0.75* in our example. The hidden logic/code in the real application is more complex than the above example, but the principle is still applicable.

The neighborhood score used in our distance metric is defined to take global similarity into consideration. We call two sessions s_i and s_j "neighbors" if the *local distance* between them is within a pre-defined threshold β_2. The local distance can be estimated by using the combination of the coefficient score and the alignment score. Thus, each session has a set of neighbors. Each session pair, $< s_i, s_j >$, has a neighborhood score, $nsim(s_i, s_j)$, which is the faction of common neighbors between them.

3.2   Group Representation and Similarity

The step of session distance computing has a high space and time complexity. For example, given a data set that contains k sessions, k^2 scores need to be calculated. To align two sequences with length m and n, the *Needleman-Wunsch* algorithm requires $O((m + 1) \times (n + 1))$ space to store a matrix, and $O(m \times n)$ time to compute the matrix and then $O(m + n)$ time to find an optimal path. Thus, data sampling is used to reduce computing complexity and space requirement. Furthermore, we observe that there are repeated sessions in the data set (i.e., their request sequences are the same). These sessions are in the same session class. Thus, we can represent repeated sessions by using a single session s_i associated with the occurrence frequency, $freq(s_i)$.

With regard to session class representation, it is implausible to use all sessions of a session class to represent it. Thus, we use two sets, the request set rset(g_j) and the session set sset(g_j), to represent a session class g_i. rset(g_j) contains all distinct requests in g_j, and sset(g_j) contains a set of representative sessions. We observe that if session groups g_i and g_j are likely to be merged, they should have a large part of common requests. Thus, we do not consider merging two groups (g_i and g_j) if $\frac{|rset(g_i) \cap rset(g_j)|}{|rset(g_i) \cup rset(g_j)|}$ is less than a pre-defined threshold (β_3). sset(g_j) contains frequent sessions, i.e., the sessions with high frequency value, and is used to compute the distance between session groups. The distance between two session groups is then defined as:

$$distance(g_i, g_j) = \frac{\sum_{s_m \in sset(g_i)} \sum_{s_n \in sset(g_j)} distance(s_m, s_n) \times freq(s_m) \times freq(s_n)}{\sum_{s_m \in sset(g_i)} \sum_{s_n \in sset(g_j)} freq(s_m) \times freq(s_n)}$$

When two session groups are merged, the *sset* and *rest* are updated correspondingly.

3.3   Session Clustering Algorithm

The distance-based session clustering algorithm contains three steps. In the first step, a set of N sessions are randomly chosen from the data set. Then, repeated sessions are merged, session frequencies are updated, and a set of sessions S:($s_1, s_2, ..., s_M$), is obtained. We calculate three similarity scores and distances for each pair of sessions, and an $M \times M$ similarity matrix is obtained. We treat each session as a session group and calculate the distance between the groups. Then, we agglomerate the session groups until the distance threshold β_1 is reached. During this step, a hash table is constructed. The entry of the table has a format of $<seq, grp>$, where seq is a session sequence, grp is the group id. The hash table will be used in the next step to assign the sessions on the disk. When there is no space in the hash table, infrequent items, i.e., sessions with low frequency, are replaced. This step is illustrated in Algorithm 1.

Algorithm 1 clustering_step1(data,N,β_1,β_2,β_3,α_1,α_2,α_3)

Input: session *data*, sampling rate N, similarity parameters and distance thresholds
Output: a set of session groups $G : (g_1, g_2, ..., g_m)$ and a hash table $H : \{< seq, grp >\}$
 1: $G = \{\}, H = \{\}$
 2: random sample N session, generate a set of distinct session instances $S : (s_1, s_2, ..., s_M)$
 3: **for all** $(s_i, s_j), s_i, s_j \in S$ **do**
 4:    calculate $csim(s_i, s_j)$ and $asim(s_i, s_j)$
 5:    $distance(s_i, s_j) = 1 - \alpha_1 * csim(s_i, s_j) + \alpha_2 * asim(s_i, s_j)$
 6:    **if** $distance(s_i, s_j) < \beta_2$ **then**
 7:       mark s_i and s_j as neighbor
 8:    **end if**
 9: **end for**
10: **for all** $(s_i, s_j), s_i, s_j \in S$ **do**
11:    calculate $nsim(s_i, s_j)$
12:    $distance(s_i, s_j) = distance(s_i, s_j) - \alpha_3 * nsim(s_i, s_j)$
13: **end for**
14: **for all** $s_k \in S$ **do**
15:    $G = G + \{s_k\}$;
16:    $H = H+ < s_k, \{s_k\} >$
17: **end for**
18: find groups g_m, and g_n that have the minimal intra-group distance.
19: **while** $distance(g_m, g_n) < \beta_1$ **do**
20:    $g_a = g_m \cup g_n$
21:    $G = G + \{g_a\} - \{g_m\} - \{g_n\}$
22:    update $H, rset(g_a), sset(g_a)$, and group distances related to g_a
23:    find groups g_m, and g_n that have the minimal intra-group distance
24: **end while**

In the second step, we assign the sessions residing on the disk to identified session groups. If a given session is contained in the hash table, we will find the target group directly. Otherwise, we will find a set of candidate groups. Then, the distance between a candidate group and session is estimated, and a group with minimal distance is selected. If the minimal distance is larger than the distance threshold β_1, we create a new session group for the session. In this step, the neighborhood score can not be used as part of the distance since it is implausible to calculate them. This step is illustrated in Algorithm 2.

We observe that some sessions are very short. These sessions are either noise data, or belonging to certain session classes. Thus, we ignore short sessions in step 1 and step 2, and processes them in the final step. The sessions are either discarded, merged into a session class, or constructed as a new session class. In addition, session classes with

Algorithm 2 clustering_step2(data,G,H,β_1,β_2,β_3,α_1,α_2,α_3)

Input: session *data*, similarity parameters ,distance thresholds, session classes G, hash table H
Output: clustering sessions in *data* into different session classes
```
 1: for all s_i ∈ data do
 2:    if ∃ < s_i, g >⊂ H then
 3:       put s_i in g, and update g
 4:    else
 5:       candidates ={ }; g_i = {s_i}
 6:       for all g_j ∈ G do
 7:          if |rset(g_i)∩rset(g_j)| / |rset(g_i)∪rset(g_j)| > β_3 then
 8:             candidates = candidates + { g_j }
 9.          end if
10:       end for
11:       for all g_j ∈ candidates do
12:          estimate distance(g_i, g_j)
13:       end for
14:       find g that have minimal with g_i
15:       if distance(g, g_i) > β_1 then
16:          G = G + g_i
17:       else
18:          put s_i in g, update g
19:       end if
20:    end if
21: end for
```

small number of sessions (the number is smaller than a predefined threshold), are treated as noise data, and are removed.

4   Algorithm Analysis and Experimental Results

The performance of our algorithm depends on the size of input data, the sampling size (N), the number of unique sessions (M) in the sampled data, the average session length (L), where L is usually less than M. The choice of sampling size may affect the performance of our algorithm. If the size is too small, many session clusters will not be identified, which can cause low clustering accuracy. However, if the size is too large, the time and space complexity will increase. Alignment score calculating takes most of the time, the space requirement of clustering step 1 is $O(M^2)$, and the time complexity is $O(M^2 * L^2)$. The time and space requirement of clustering step 2 vary with the given sessions. In the worst case, we have to calculate the distance with each identified session group. However, such a case will seldom occurs.

The performance of our algorithm depends on the selection of three distance threshold values and session similarity parameters. Among the three distance thresholds, the value of β_1 is the most important one since the other two values are related to β_1, and can be derived from it. If distance thresholds are too low, many session classes are generated. If they are too high, many sessions that belong to different classes may be merged into a single session group. The selection of threshold values depends on the specific application. Small threshold values can be used for application in which the difference between session classes is significant, i.e., the distance between them is "far", otherwise, large threshold values are used since it can discriminate the trivial difference between session classes. The distance threshold also depends on the values of parameters which are an important factor in our algorithm. The parameters can be viewed as the weights of the three similarity scores. Different applications may have different parameter values, and the adjustment of these parameters accordingly is necessary.

Another clustering validation and evaluation approach is actually an assessment of the data domain. For this approach, we can build user access graph, a weighted directed graph, to represent each session class. In this sense, we can evaluate user access graphs instead of session classes based on the *prediction of next request*. The evaluation methods are described as follows. Given a request sequence $r :< r_1, ..., r_n >$, that is part of a given session s in the test data, we can estimate the possibility of r belonging to a session class g_i, and the possibility of the next request is r_m from the corresponding models (user access graphs). The next request r_{n+1} can be obtained from the test data. We say it is a "hit", if r_m and r_{n+1} are the same. In some cases, we will not predict the next request because of the limited request history or too many random requests in the history. The performance measurement is referred to as *F-measure*, which is defined as

$$F\text{-}Measure = \frac{2 * precision * recall}{precision + recall},$$

where *precision* is defined as the ratio of the number of correctly predicted requests to the total predicted requests, and the *recall* is the hit-rate, that is the ratio of the number of correctly predicted requests to the total number of requests to be predicted. A higher F-measure value means a better overall performance. This approach can be viewed as statistics based cluster interpretation technique.

4.1   Results for an OLTP Application

To test our ideas in the project, we have uesd a clinic OLTP application as a test bed. We obtain a OLTP database trace log (400M bytes) that contains *81,417* events belonging to 9

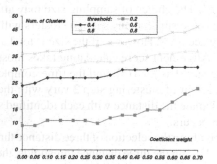

Fig. 1. Number of clusters v.s various similarity parameter values

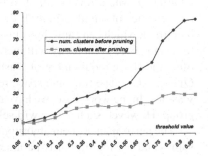

Fig. 2. Number of clusters v.s various threshold values (pruning threshold =10)

different applications, such as front-end sales, daily report, monthly report, data backup, and system administration. The target application of the paper is the front-end sales application. After preprocessing the trace log, we obtain 7,244 SQL queries, 18 database connection instances of the front-end sales application. The queries are classified into 190 query templates, and 18 request sequences are obtained (one sequence per connection). 1510 sessions are obtained from the 18 request sequences. In the experiments, we choose 721 sessions that belong to 4 request sequences as the input of the clustering algorithm, and the other 789 sessions as the test data of the algorithm.

We first test the number of clusters generated with different similarity parameters in the sampling step. We set the neighborhood similarity parameter as 0.3, and the coefficient parameter is dynamically changed from 0.0 to 0.7, and the alignment parameter is changed correspondingly. The result is shown in Fig. 1. The figure shows that more clusters are generated when the coefficient parameter is large, and fewer clusters are generated when the alignment parameter is large. In the next step, we use $0.4,0.3,0.3$ as similarity parameters in clustering step 1, and use $0.5,0.5, 0.0$ in clustering step 2. Finally, we remove any clusters with less than 10 sessions. We use different threshold values (β_1) to cluster sessions. The result is shown in Fig. 2. From the figure, we observe that the number of clusters increases when the threshold value increases. However, the increasing rate after pruning is less than that before pruning.

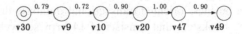

Fig. 3. An Example of User Access Graph

Table 2. Performance comparison of different similarity parameters

Case	Methods	Similarity Parameters	Best Threshold	Best F-measure	Average F-measure
1	Proposed	0.4/0.3/0.3	0.45	0.73	0.70
2	Coefficient	1.0/0.0/0.0	0.5	0.67	0.63
3	Alignment	0.0/1.0/0.0	0.3	0.65	0.61
4	Coefficient+ Alignment	0.5/0.5/0.0	0.4	0.70	0.65
5	Neighborhood	0.01/0.01/0.98	0.6	0.68	0.45

After grouping sessions, we build a user access graph for each session class. Figure 3 shows an example of user access graphs obtained from our test data. Each node in the graph is a query template, and an edge is associated with a confidence value $\sigma_{v_i \to v_j}$ which is the probability of v_j following v_i. Then, we use the other 789 sessions as the test data to test the proposed algorithm. We evaluate the performance based on request prediction performance of the corresponding user access graphs. We test the performance of our algorithm with following methods: 1) using all scores together, 2) using only coefficient score, 3) using only alignment score, 4) using coefficient score + alignment score, 5) mainly using neighborhood score[1]. The experimental result is shown in Table 2, which gives the best and average F-measures for each method and the threshold (β_1) value corresponding to the best performance. The result shows that using coefficient score and alignment score together is better than using one score, and our proposed clustering method achieves the best among these measurement scores. The best performance of neighborhood is comparable to the other methods, but the average performance is the worst.

We analyze the result as follows. The coefficient score treats session {a - b -c} and session {c - b -a} as the same although they have different orders. Also it is likely to treat session {a - b -c - d} and session {a - b -e -f} as the different session type although the sessions may belong to the same cluster which contains a conditional branch. But for the alignment score, it may treat two sessions {a -.... - d} and {a -.... - d} as the same although the two sessions only have two common requests a and d. Thus, the combination of the two scores obtain a better performance. Meanwhile, the introduction of neighborhood makes the similarity scores more accurate, and thus gain the best performance. However, simply using neighborhood score will not get better performance since it treats the local similarity between two sessions as 0 or 1, thus loses useful information.

4.2   Results for TPC-W Benchmark

TPC Benchmark^{TW} (TPC-W) [13] is a transactional web benchmark that simulates the activities of a business oriented transactional database-driven web server. TPC-W models an on-line bookstore that consists of 14 browser/web server interactions, and each interaction consists of a sequence of SQL queries. Among these web-interactions, *Home* web interaction does not contains SQL queries, where *Product Detail* and Admin Request interaction both have the same kind of requests/queries. Thus, there are *12* kinds of sessions in the workload. TPC-W simulates three different profiles/users by varying the ratio of browse to buy: primarily shopping (WIPS), browsing (WIPSb) and web-based ordering (WIPSo). In [4], a TPC-W Java implementation is proposed. The remote browser emulation (RBE) and web merchant application logic are implemented completely in Java language. We adopt the implementation to *Tomcat* application server, and *Microsoft SQL Server 2000* database. In the original implementation, the queries in a web interaction do not share common connections. We modify the implementation to make all queries in a web interaction share the same connection which enables us to find sessions efficiently. We collect two different TPC-W database workloads which contain the mix of 15 concurrent RBEs, over 2 hour's observation time. One is for shopping and the other for ordering.

We test the number of clusters generated with different similarity parameters and distance thresholds. We set the neighborhood similarity parameter as 0.3, and the coefficient parameter is dynamically changed from 0.0 to 0.7, and the alignment parameter is changed correspondingly. The result is shown in Fig. 4 and 5. From the figure, we observe that in order to achieve better performance, the coefficient score and alignment score are both important. Also, different workload have different best parameters.

---

[1] The sampling rate becomes 100% which means that every session is loaded in order to get neighborhood scores.

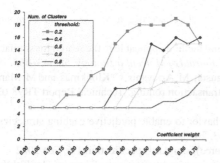

Fig. 4. Number of clusters v.s various similarity parameter values in Shopping Workload

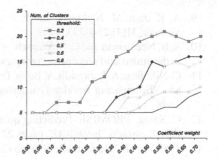

Fig. 5. Number of clusters v.s various similarity parameter values in Ordering Workload

5   Conclusion

In this paper, we discuss our approach to clustering database user sessions. The algorithm is a bottom-up agglomerative hierarchical algorithm. Session similarity is based on the three kinds of similarity scores. This approach considers not only the local similarity between sessions (the coefficient score and the alignment score) but also the global similarity (the neighborhood score) between them. Each session class is represented by a request set and a representative session set. This approach can reduce computation complexity. The idea presented in the paper can be used in any database-based application, such as the *ERP* or *CRM* applications that may contain hundreds or even thousands different types of sessions. It can also be used on Web user session analysis and DNA sequence analysis.

References

1. H. P. Artis. Capacity planning for MVS computer systems. In L. S. Wright and J. P. Buzen, editors, *Int. CMG Conference*, pages 209–226. Computer Measurement Group, 1978.
2. A. Behm, S. Rielau, and R. Swagerman. Returning modified rows - SELECT statements with side effects. In *VLDB 2004, Toronto, Canada*, 2004.
3. P. Berkhin. Survey of clustering data mining techniques. Technical report, Accrue Software, San Jose, CA, 2002.
4. T. Bezenek, H. Cain, R. Dickson, T. Heil, M. Martin, C. McCurdy, R. Rajwar, E. Weglarz, C. Zilles, and M. Lipasti. Characterizing a Java implementation of TPC-W. In *Third CAECW Workshop*, 2000.
5. G. W. Birgit Hay and K. Vanhoof. Clustering navigation patterns on a website using a sequence alignment method. In *IJCAI Workshop on Intelligent Techniques for Web Personalization*, 2001.
6. I. T. Bowman and K. Salem. Optimization of query streams using semantic prefetching. In *Proceedings of the 2004 ACM SIGMOD conference*, pages 179–190. ACM Press, 2004.
7. S. Guha, R. Rastogi, and K. Shim. ROCK: A robust clustering algorithm for categorical attributes. *Information Systems*, 25(5):345–366, 2000.
8. P. Jaccard. The distribution of the flora in the alpine zone. *New Phytologist*, 11:37–50, 1912.

9. A. K. Jain, M. N. Murty, and P. J. Flynn. Data clustering: a review. *ACM Computing Surveys*, 31(3):264–323, 1999.

10. S. B. Needleman and C. D. Wunsch. A general method applicable to the search for similarities in the amino acid sequence of two proteins. *Journal of Molecular Biology*, 58:443–453, 1970.

11. C. Nikolaou, A. Labrinidis, V. Bohn, D. Ferguson, M. Artavanis, C. Kloukinas, and M. Marazakis. The impact of workload clustering on transaction routing. Technical Report TR98-0238, 1998.

12. C. Sapia. PROMISE: Predicting query behavior to enable predictive caching strategies for OLAP systems. In *DAWAK*, pages 224–233, 2000.

13. TPC-W. TPC Benchmark W (Web Commerce), standard specification 1.6, Feb 2002.

14. W. Wang and O. R. ZaAne. Clustering web sessions by sequence alignment. In *13th International Workshop on Database and Expert Systems Applications (DEXA'02)*, 2002.

15. Q. Yao and A. An. Using user access patterns for semantic query caching. In *Database and Expert Systems Applications (DEXA)*, 2003.

16. Q. Yao and A. An. Characterizing database user's access patterns, accepted for database and expert systems applications, 2004.

17. P. S. Yu and A. Dan. Impact of workload partitionability on the performance of coupling architectures for transaction processing. In *Proc. of the Fourth IEEE SPDP Conference*, pages 40–49, 1992.

18. P. S. Yu and A. Dan. Performance analysis of affinity clustering on transaction processing coupling architecture. *IEEE TKDE*, 6(5):764–786, 1994.

User-Interest-Based Document Filtering via Semi-supervised Clustering

Na Tang and V. Rao Vemuri

Computer Science Dept.,
University of California, Davis,
Davis, CA 95616, USA
{natang, rvemuri}@ucdavis.edu

Abstract. This paper studies the task of user-interest-based document filtering, where users target to find some documents of a specific topic among a large document collection. This is usually done by a text categorization process, which divides all the documents into two categorizes: one containing all the desired documents (called positive documents) and the other containing all the other documents (called negative documents). However, in many cases, some documents among the negative documents are close enough to the positive documents, prompting a re-consideration (called *deviating negative* documents). Simply treating them as negative documents would deteriorate the categorization accuracy. We modify and extend a semi-supervised clustering method to conduct the categorization. Compared to the original method, our approach incorporates more informative initialization and constraints and in a result leads to better clustering results. The experiments show that our approach retrieves better (sometimes significantly improved) categorization accuracy than the original method in the presence of the *deviating negative* documents.

1   Introduction

A document filtering process is required in many information systems and applications (e.g. [11, 8, 2]), where users target to find some documents of a specific topic that they are interested in from a large document collection. This task of user-interest-based document filtering usually divides the document collection into two categories: positive documents and negative documents, where the former are those that users are interested in and the latter are those that users are not interested in. With increasingly maturing information retrieval and text mining techniques, this task of document categorization can be automated to a certain degree. The task can be done by representing the document collection in a vector space and then applying some learning algorithm to the vector space. The learning algorithms used for document categorization are usually divided into supervised learning, unsupervised learning and semi-supervised learning. Document categorization based on supervised learning is usually called document

M.-S. Hacid et al. (Eds.): ISMIS 2005, LNAI 3488, pp. 573–582, 2005.
© Springer-Verlag Berlin Heidelberg 2005

classification, in which case the model constructed from a set of labeled documents categorizes new unlabeled documents. Document categorization based on unsupervised learning is usually called document clustering, in which case no labeled documents are available and the model categorizes all the unlabeled documents based on some clustering technique. Usually document clustering does not give as good categorization accuracy as document classification but it saves the effort of manual labeling. Semi-supervised document categorization, a case in which only limited labeled documents are available, provides a compromised solution; it requires some small effort in labeling, but still obtains good categorization results.

In realistic situations, quite often people show medium interest in some documents. These documents are hard to be categorized as positive or negative. Strictly speaking, they belong to the negative documents because they are not exactly what users look for. But they stand closer to the positive documents than to the other negative documents. For example, if users are looking for some documents talking about how to play tennis, then the documents that are not related to tennis definitely belong to negative documents. We call this kind of documents *pure negative* documents. During the searching process they might also get the documents that explain the history of tennis. These documents are also negative documents but they are biased toward the positive documents in some degree. We call this kind of documents *deviating negative* documents. It would deteriorate the categorization accuracy if they are simply considered as negative documents. In this paper, we propose a semi-supervised document clustering method to deal with this issue of borderline documents, namely *deviating negative* documents. Our approach performs a user-interest-based document retrieval task in the presence of *deviating negative* documents by modifying the semi-supervised clustering approach in [3].

The semi-supervised method in [3] made improvements to the standard K-means clustering by incorporating user supervision to the initialization process and the distance measure based on a probabilistic framework. Like [3], the proposed approach is also based on a probabilistic framework while taking advantage of more informative labeled data. Basically the documents are still divided into two classes, positive and negative, but in this paper we recognize the *deviating negative* documents among the negative documents while labeling documents. The initial cluster centroids are estimated from the labeled data. The cluster centroid of the negative documents is estimated from both the pure negative documents and *deviating negative* documents with a bias toward the pure negative documents. While assigning the instances to the clusters at each iteration, it is sensitive to the constraints provided by the more informative labeled data. In addition, it applies adaptive distance learning to be aware of the constraints and at the same time incorporate data variance. The experiments show that our approach is able to deal with the case when *deviating negative* documents are present. Compared to the semi-supervised clustering which does not recognize *deviating negative* documents, the proposed approach increases the categorization accuracy.

The rest of the paper is organized as follows: Section 2 describes the semi-supervised algorithm for the user-interest-based document filtering task. The experimental results are shown at section 3. The related work is described section 4 and we conclude and discuss the future work at section 5.

2   Algorithm/Framework

This section explains how the standard K-means algorithm partitions documents into two clusters: the one containing positive documents and the one containing negative documents. And it then introduces how we incorporate a limited amount of labeled data into the clustering procedure while being aware of the *deviating negative* documents.

2.1   Standard K-Means for Document Partition

K-means clustering can best be described as a partitioning method, which partitions N data points into K mutually exclusive clusters that minimize the total distance between the data points and their cluster centroids. For the user-interest-based document filtering task, each document is treated as a data point; only two clusters are expected to be generated among the documents: C_1 (the cluster with positive documents) and C_{-1} (the cluster with negative documents). These 2-class clustering procedure via K-means can be described as: *1)* Randomly partition the documents into two clusters C_1 and C_{-1}; Estimate the centroids. *2)* For each document xi, calculate the distance (named D_{ij}) from x_i to each cluster centroid of C_j. If the x_i is closest to its own cluster, do nothing; otherwise, move it into the closest cluster. *3)* Re-estimate both the cluster centroids. *4)* Repeat *2)* and *3)* until no documents move from one cluster to another.

2.2   Semi-supervised Clustering with *Deviating Negative* Documents

The proposed approach incorporates labeled data into the K-means clustering framework to improve the clustering results. In this paper, the labeled data consists of the positive documents and the negative documents, where the latter includes the pure negative documents as well as the *deviating negative* documents. Based on these labeled documents, the clustering process is improved through three aspects: 1) initialization; 2) constraint-sensitive distance measure and 3) adaptive distance learning. These three improvements are explained in the following subsections. In the rest of the paper, the following notations are used: documents $\{x_i\}_{i \in P}$ are the labeled positive documents, documents $\{x_i\}_{i \in DN}$ are the *deviating negative* documents, documents $\{x_i\}_{i \in PN}$ are the pure negative documents and documents $\{x_i\}_{i \in U}$ are unlabeled documents. Here P, DN, PN, U are four disjoint subsets of $\{1, ..., N\}$ and $P + DN + PN + U = \{1, ..., N\}$. The function $l(x_i)$ stands for the label of document x_i, where

$$l(x_i) = \begin{cases} 1, & i \in P \\ 0, & i \in DN \\ -1, & i \in PN \\ unknown, & i \in U \end{cases}$$

Initialization. The existence of the labeled data can provide prior information about the cluster distribution at the initial time and often results in good clustering. Therefore, instead of randomly initializing cluster centroids (section 2.1 step 1), the proposed approach estimates the cluster centroids from the limited labeled data. The cluster centroid of the positive documents is initialized with the mean of $\{x_i\}_{i \in P}$: $\frac{1}{|P|} \sum_{i \in P} x_i$. Because the topic of the *deviating negative* documents is close to that of the positive documents to some extent, if the cluster centroid is set to be the mean of all the negative documents, then the cluster centroid would be dragged toward that of the positive documents. Therefore, the proposed method initializes the cluster centroid of the negative documents with a weighted mean of the pure negative documents and the *deviating negative* documents: $\frac{1}{w_1 \cdot |DN| + w_2 \cdot |PN|} (w_1 \sum_{i \in DN} x_i + w_2 \sum_{i \in PN} x_i)$ where $w_1 < w_2$, which makes the cluster centroid of the negative documents biased toward the pure negative documents.

Constraint-sensitive Distance Measure. The proposed approach enforces constraints that are induced by the labeled documents into the clustering procedure. As it is explained in section 2.1, the K-means algorithm for our document partition task aims to find the document clusters that minimize the overall distance of the documents from the cluster centroids. It modifies the distance measure so that the incorrect assignment of any labeled document x_i to cluster C_j ($j = \pm 1$) results in a certain degree of penalty, i.e., some increase in the distance of x_i from the centroid of C_j. By considering the similarity between the *deviating negative* documents and the positive documents, the proposed method weights the constraints so that the incorrect assignment of the *deviating negative* documents (i.e. assigning the *deviating negative* documents to the cluster of the positive documents) result in lighter penalty than the incorrect assignment of the pure negative documents. As it is mentioned in the original K-means algorithm, D_{ij} is the distance of a document x_i from the cluster centroid of C_j. The K-means assigns document x_i to cluster C_j with the minimum D_{ij} for any C_j. In the proposed method, instead of the pure distance D_{ij}, each document x_i is assigned to C_j to minimize the distortion NEW_D_{ij}, which is defined as:

$$NEW\_D_{ij} = D_{ij} + D_{ij} \cdot penalty(x_i, C_j),$$

where the penalty function is:

$$penalty(x_i, C_j) = \begin{cases} 0, & \text{if } l(x_i) = unknown \parallel \text{if } j = l(x_i) \parallel (j = -1 \text{ \&\& } l(x_i) = 0) \\ p_1, & \text{if } j = 1 \text{ \&\& } l(x_i) = 0 \\ p_2, & otherwise \end{cases}$$

Here the constants satisfy the condition $p_1 < p_2$. The iterated conditional modes (ICM), applied in [3] to find the optimal assignment based on the distance measure, is not used in this paper because the exact label of the documents under supervision are known while only pairwise constraints (must-link and cannot-link) are provided in [3]. Because of the same reason, the constraints are enforced in the clustering procedure in a simpler way than [3, 12]. Furthermore, the weight function is sensitive to the distance of the point from the cluster centroid and it also provides lighter penalty (p_1) for the incorrect assignment of the *deviating negative* documents, in which case $j = 1$ and $l(x_i) = 0$.

In general, the constraint-sensitive distance measure discourages constraint violations while being aware of the real distance between points. In addition, the penalty of violations by *deviating negative* documents is differentiated from the penalty of violations by pure negative documents by taking into account the topic closeness between *deviating negative* documents and positive documents.

Adaptive Distance Learning. The pure distance D_{ij} from document x_i to cluster C_j can be estimated from any distance measure such as Euclidean distance, Cosine distance, I-divergence and so on. However, instead of using the static distance, which may fails to capture the real notion of distance in a clustering procedure, parameterized distance measures are used to incorporate the user-specified constraints and data variance.

One of the commonly used distance measure - Euclidean distance - is parameterized in this paper. Suppose the centroid of cluster C_j is c_j, the pure Euclidean distance is defined as:

$$D_{ij} = \sqrt{(x_i - c_j)^T (x_i - c_j)}$$

Then the parameterized Euclidean distance is defined as follows:

$$D_{ij}^A = \sqrt{(x_i - c_j)^T \cdot A \cdot (x_i - c_j)},$$

where A is a positive diagonal matrix. Therefore, the final distortion NEW_D_{ij}, which the clustering process tries to minimize for each document x_i, is parameterized as:

$$\text{NEW\_}D_{ij}^A = \sqrt{(x_i - c_j)^T \cdot A \cdot (x_i - c_j)},$$

The parameter matrix A is first initialized with an identity matrix and then updated at each iteration after the cluster centroids are re-estimated. The updating rule is:

$$a_k = a_k + \frac{\partial New\_D}{\partial a_k}$$
$$= a_k + (\sum_{i=1}^{N} \frac{\partial D_{i,assigned\_l(x_i)}}{\partial a_k} + penalty(x_i, assigned\_l(x_i)) \cdot \sum_{i=1}^{N} \frac{\partial D_{i,assigned\_l(x_i)}}{\partial a_k}),$$

where $assigned\_l(x_i)$ stands for the assigned label for document x_i at the current iteration and

$$\frac{\partial D_{i,assigned\_l(x_i)}}{\partial a_k} = \frac{x_{ik} c_{assigned\_l(x_i),k}}{2\sqrt{(x_i - c_j)^T \cdot A \cdot (x_i - c_j)}}.$$

In essence, the adaptive distance learning brings similar documents closer and pushes dissimilar documents further apart. In this way more cohesive clusters are generated, which facilitate the partitioning process.

As a whole, combined with these three improvements, the proposed algorithm is summarized in the following chart:

Semi-supervised Clustering with Deviating Negative Documents

Input: Set of documents $\{x_i\}_{i=1}^N$, index of labeled positive
documents, deviating negative documents and pure
negative documents respectively: P, DN, PN

Output: Disjoint 2-partitioning of $\{x_i\}_{i=1}^N$

1. Initialize centroids of clusters C_1 and C_{-1} with $\dfrac{1}{|P|}\sum_{i\in P}x_i$ and

$$\dfrac{1}{w_1\cdot|DN|+w_2\cdot|PN|}(w_1\sum_{i\in DN}x_i+w_2\sum_{i\in PN}x_i)\text{ respectively.}$$

2. For each $i\in\{1,...N\}$, calculate the parameterized distance from
document i to cluster C_j, i.e., $New\_D_{ij}^A$. If document i is closest
to its own cluster, do nothing; otherwise, move it into the closest
cluster.

3. Re-estimate the cluster centroids with $c_j=\dfrac{1}{|C_j|}\sum_{x_i\in C_j}x_i$;

Update parameter matrix A.

4. Repeat 2 & 3 until no documents moving from one cluster to
another.

---

3   Experiments

Experiments are conducted on the Syskill and Webert Web Page Ratings (SW) [9], the 20 Newsgroup data set (20NG) [1] and the heart-disease webpage set (HD) from [11]. SW contains four data sets of HTML pages relating to four different topics. A user rated each page in a 3-point scale (hot, median and cold) which indicates his interest in that page. We select 3 sets from SW (*bands, biomedical, goats*) and treat the "hot" documents as positive documents, "median" documents as *deviating negative* documents, "cold" documents as pure negative documents. The 20NG data set contains about 20,000 documents on different subjects from 20 UseNet discussion groups. We select 2 subsets from 20NG: *ibm_gra_mac* and *ibm_x_mac*. The subset *ibm_gra_mac* contains 600 documents, 200 randomly selected from the group *comp.sys.ibm.hardware* as positive documents, 200 randomly selected from the group *comp.sys.mac.hardware* as *deviating negative* documents and 200 randomly selected from the group *comp.graphics* as pure negative documents. The subset *ibm_x_mac* also contains 600 documents. The 200 positive and 200 *deviating negative* documents are randomly selected from the same groups as *ibm_gra_mac* while the 200 pure negative documents are randomly selected from the group *comp.windows.x*. HD contains 288 HTML pages that are divided into positive documents, *deviating negative* documents and *pure negative* documents based on a user's interest. For each data set, 10% of documents are chosen as the labeled data, and the remaining as the unlabeled data.

The preprocessing includes document representation and feature selection. We represent each document as a vector via a TF-IDF model (Term Frequency - Inverse Document Frequency). With the TF-IDF vector representation, each *j*th item of the vector *i* (representing document *i*) is determined by the number of times that it appears in document *i* (TF) as well as the number of documents that this word appears (IDF). The dimension of the vectors is decided by the vocabulary size, which tends to be large even with a small set of documents. Instead of using all the words, a smaller number of best words can be selected for further clustering. This can lead to significant savings of computer resources and processing time. It is called feature selection because each word is considered as a feature for clustering. In the proposed method, the following equation (see [7]) is used for feature selection. It evaluates the quality of a word *w*:

$$q(w) = \sum_{i=1}^{N} f_i^2 - \frac{1}{N} \left[\sum_{i=1}^{N} f_i \right]^2.$$

Here f_i is the frequency of word w in document d_i and N is the total number of documents. In our experiments, the dimension of the vectors is set to be 128.

The pair of weights for initialization (w_1, w_2) prevents the centroid of negative documents from biased toward positive documents, while the pair of penalties for constraint-sensitive distance (p_1, p_2) provides more sensitive constraints with the presence of *deviating negative* documents. The selection of the initialization parameters, namely the weights and penalties, is a problem that is yet to be addressed. Like the learning parameter in many machine learning methods, these values are likely to be problem dependent. Some local search is probably involved. For expediency, both (w_1, w_2) and (p_1, p_2) are set at $(0.5, 1)$ in this study, which satisfies $w_1 < w_2$ and $p_1 < p_2$.

The categorization accuracies with different document sets and different methods are shown at Table 1. The method "K-means_3C" is the standard K-means algorithm by treating *deviating negative* documents as a separated class (totally 3 classes) while the method "K-means_2C" is the standard K-means algorithm with only 2 classes: the positive class and the negative class. Similarly, the method "semi_K-means_3C" and "semi_K-means_2C" is the semi-supervised K-means approach presented in [3] with 3 classes and 2 classes respectively. The method "semi_K-means_DND" is the proposed approach, i.e., the semi-supervised K-means by assuming 2 classes while considering *deviating negative* documents (DND) during clustering procedure.

Table 1. A Comparison of categorization accuracies with different methods and document set

	bands	biomedical	goats	ibm_gra_mac	ibm_x_mac	HD
K-means_3C	0.557	0.588	0.500	0.453	0.521	0.535
semi_K-means_3C	0.574	0.611	0.557	0.588	0.640	0.552
K-means_2C	0.656	0.595	0.500	0.652	0.548	0.563
semi_K-means_2C	0.672	0.687	0.529	0.731	0.598	0.689
semi_K-means_DND	**0.754**	**0.702**	**0.571**	**0.740**	**0.688**	**0.693**

The experimental results show that both "K-means" and "semi_K-means" with 2 classes offer better performance than those with 3 classes (by treating *deviating negative* documents as a separated class). The reason is that the topic of *deviating negative* documents are not totally separated from either *pure negative* documents or *positive* documents, which confuses the 3-class clustering. The results also show that, among all the approaches with 2 classes, our approach retrieves the best categorization accuracies over all the document sets. It indicates that the 2-class clustering and the additional semi-supervision on the *deviating negative* documents, which are the documents similar to positive documents but not exactly what users want, is able to give more informative constraints and in a result lead to better clustering accuracy for filtering purpose.

4   Related Work

Some other semi-supervised clustering algorithms [3, 4, 6, 12] and semi-supervised classification algorithms [8, 10, 5] are available and can be applied to the user-interest-based document filtering task. Basically semi-supervised clustering incorporate limited labeled data to guide the clustering process while semi-supervised classification uses unlabeled data to improve classification. However, none of them consider the issue of *deviating negative* documents. Ignorance of this kind of documents may deteriorate the categorization results. This paper deals with this issue under a limited amount of user supervision.

5   Conclusion and Discussion

This paper presented a semi-supervised clustering approach to user-interest-based document filtering. It modifies a semi-supervised clustering algorithm in [3] in order to be sensitive to user interest especially to the presence of the *deviating negative* documents. This approach was empirically tested with the Syskill and Webert Web Page Ratings, the 20 Newsgroup data set and a webpage set from [11]. The experiments show that our approach retrieves better categorization accuracy than the method in [3] with the presence of the *deviating negative* documents.

A number of interesting problems are left for future research:

1. Labeling data selection: Selecting appropriate documents for labeling would have an influence in the clustering results. We propose to incorporate an active learning algorithm to actively select samples for labeling in the future.
2. Feature selection: The labeled data may have a good insight about the feature selection. By combining the method used in this paper and the information gain technique, which is usually used for classification when adequate labeled data is available, we may get words of better quality for categorization.
3. Incremental documents clustering: The information environments tend to be dynamic and it is desirable to have an adaptive clustering method to deal with continuously growing document set.
4. Other applications: Besides document categorization and document filtering, some other applications involving 2-class classification may also take advantage of the proposed method to deal with the issue of *deviating negative* instances, which are the instances belonging to the negative class but close to the positive instances.

References

1. 20 newsgroup data set. http://people.csail.mit.edu/ jrennie/20Newsgroups, last visited Jan. 19th, 2005.
2. Baldi, P., Frasconi, P. and Smyth, P.: Modeling the Internet and theWeb: Probabilistic Methods and Algorithms. Chapter 4: Text Analysis. Wiley, (2003).
3. Basu, S., Bilenko, M. and Mooney, R.J.: A probabilistic framework for semi-supervised clustering. In Proceedings of the Tenth ACM SIGKDD International Conference on Knowledge Discovery and Data Mining (KDD-2004). Seattle, WA, (2004).
4. Basu, S., Banerjee, A. and Mooney, R.J.: Semi-supervised Clustering by Seeding. In Proceedings of the 19th International Conference on Machine Learning (ICML-2002). Sydney, Australia, (2002).
5. Blum, A. and Mitchell, T.: Combining labeled and unlabeled data with co-training. In Proceedings of the 11th Annual Conference on Computational Learning Theory. (1998).
6. Cohn, D., Caruana, R. and McCallum, A.: Semi-supervised clustering with user feedback. Technical Report TR2003-1892, Cornell University, (2003).
7. Dhillon, I., Kogan, J. and Nicholas, C.: Feature Selection and Document Clustering, in Survey of Text Mining. Springer-Verlag, New York. (2004) Chapter 4.
8. Liu, B., Dai, Y., Li, X., Lee, W. S. and Yu, P. S.: Building Text Classifiers Using Positive and Unlabeled Examples. In Proceedings of the Third IEEE International Conference on Data Mining. Melbourne, Florida, (2003).
9. Pazzani, M.: Syskill and Webert Web Page Ratings.http://ncdm171.lac.uic.edu: 16080/kdd/databases/SyskillWebert/SyskillWebert.task.html, last visited Jan. 19th, 2005.
10. Nigam, K., McCallum, A. K., Thrun, S. and Mitchell, T.: Text Classification from Labeled and Unlabeled Documents using EM. Machine Learning. Vol. 39. (2000).

11. Tang, N. and Vemuri, V. R.: Web-based Knowledge Acqusition to Impute Missing Values for Classification. In Proceedings of the 2004 IEEE/WIC/ACM International Joint Conference on Web Intelligence and Intelligent Agent Technology (WI/IAT-2004). Beijing, China, (2004).
12. Wagstaff, K., Cardie, C., Rogers, S. and Schroedl, S.: Constrained K-Means Clustering with Background Knowledge. In Proceedings of 18th International Conference on Machine Learning (ICML-2001), (2001).

A Filter Feature Selection Method for Clustering

Pierre-Emmanuel Jouve and Nicolas Nicoloyannis

LABORATOIRE ERIC, Université Lumière - Lyon2,
Bâtiment L, 5 avenue Pierre Mendès-France, 69 676 BRON cedex France
pierre.jouve@eric.univ-lyon2.fr, nicoloyannis@univ-lyon2.fr
http://eric.univ-lyon2.fr

Abstract. High dimensional data is a challenge for the KDD community. Feature Selection (FS) is an efficient preprocessing step for dimensionality reduction thanks to the removal of redundant and/or noisy features. Few and mostly recent FS methods have been proposed for clustering. Furthermore, most of them are "wrapper" methods that require the use of clustering algorithms for evaluating the selected features subsets. Due to this reliance on clustering algorithms that often require parameters settings (such as number of clusters), and due to the lack of a consensual suitable criterion to evaluate clustering quality in different subspaces, the wrapper approach cannot be considered as a universal way to perform FS within the clustering framework. Thus, we propose and evaluate in this paper a "filter" FS method. This approach is consequently completely independent of any clustering algorithm. It is based upon the use of two specific indices that allow to assess the adequacy between two sets of features. As these indices exhibit very specific and interesting properties as far as their computational cost is concerned (they just require one dataset scan), the proposed method can be considered as an effective method not only from the point of view of the results quality but also from the execution time point of view.

1 Introduction

High dimensional data is a common problem for data miners. Feature Selection (FS) enables to choose the relevant original features and is an effective dimensionality reduction technique. A relevant feature for a learning task can be defined as one whose removal degrades the learning accuracy. By removing the non relevant features, data sizes reduce, while learning accuracy and comprehensibility may improve or, at least, remain the same. Learning can occur within two contexts : supervised or unsupervised (clustering). While there are several methods for FS in supervised context [1], there are only very few, mostly recent, FS methods for the unsupervised context. This may be explained by the fact that it is easier to select features for supervised learning than for clustering: in supervised context, you know a priori what has to be learned whereas it is not the case for clustering and thus it might be hard to determine which features are relevant to the learning task. FS for clustering may then be described as the task of selecting relevant features for the underlying clusters [3].

M.-S. Hacid et al. (Eds.): ISMIS 2005, LNAI 3488, pp. 583–593, 2005.
© Springer-Verlag Berlin Heidelberg 2005

Among the proposed FS methods [2][4][9][5][11][3] most of them are "wrapper" methods. These methods evaluate the candidate feature subsets by the learning algorithm itself which later uses the selected features for efficient learning. In clustering, a wrapper method evaluates the candidate feature subsets by a clustering algorithm (For example, Kmeans are used in [2][9], EM algorithm in [5]). Although wrapper methods for supervised learning have several disadvantages: computational cost, lack of robustness across different learning algorithms, they are still interesting in applications where accuracy is important. But, unlike supervised learning which owns a consensual way for evaluating accuracy, there is no unanimous criterion to estimate the accuracy of clustering. Furthermore, this criterion would have to perform well in different subspaces. These limitations make wrapper methods for clustering very disadvantageous. In this paper we propose and evaluate a 'filter' method for FS. A filter method, by definition, is independent of clustering algorithms, and thus completely avoids the issue about lack of unanimity in the choice of clustering criterion. The proposed method is based on two indices for assessing the adequacy between two sets of attributes (i.e. to determine if two sets of features include the same information). Moreover the proposed method just needs one data set scan which confers it a great advantages over other method as far as the execution time is concerned.

2   Introductory Concepts and Formalisms

This section is essential for the presentation of our FS method, it consists in the presentation of two indices for evaluating to which extent two sets of attributes include the same information. In the rest of this paper, this evaluation is named adequacy assessment between two sets of attributes. Through the rest of the paper we consider a clustering problem involving a dataset DS composed by a set (O) of n objects described by a set (SA) of l attributes.

Notation 1. $O = \{o_i, i = 1..n\}$ *a set of* n *objects (of a given dataset)*
$SA = \{A_1, .., A_l\}$ *the set of* l *attributes (features) describing the objects of* O.
$o_i = [o_{i_1}, .., o_{i_l}]$ *an object of* O, o_{i_j} *corresponds to the value of* o_i *for attribute (feature)* A_j, *this value may be numerical or categorical.*

2.1   Notion of Link

In categorical data framework, the notion of similarity between objects of a dataset is used; in this paper, we substitute for it an extension of this notion that may be applied to any type of data (categorical or quantitative). It is named link according to an attribute and defined as follows :

Definition 1 *Link between 2 objects: We associate to each attribute* A_i *a function noted* $link_i$ *which defines a link (a kind of similarity) or a non-link (a kind of dissimilarity) according to the attribute* A_i *between two objects of* O:

$$link_i(o_{a_i}, o_{b_i}) = \begin{cases} 1 \text{ if a particular condition which determines a link} \\ \quad \text{(according to } A_i) \text{ between objects } o_a \text{ and } o_b \text{ is verified} \\ 0 \text{ otherwise (non-link)} \end{cases} \quad (1)$$

EXAMPLES :

- For a categorical attribute A_i, we can naturally define $link_i$ as follows :
$$link_i(o_{a_i}, o_{b_i}) = \begin{cases} 1 \text{ if } o_{a_i} = o_{b_i} \\ 0 \text{ otherwise} \end{cases}$$
- For a quantitative attribute A_i, we can for instance define $link_i$ as follows :
$$link_i(o_{a_i}, o_{b_i}) = \begin{cases} 1 \text{ if } |o_{a_i} - o_{b_i}| \leq \delta, \text{ with } \delta \text{ a threshold fixed by the user} \\ 0 \text{ otherwise} \end{cases}$$
- For a quantitative attribute A_i, we can also think about discretizing it and subsequently use the definition of $link_i$ proposed for categorical attributes.

2.2 Assessment of the Adequacy Between a Set of Attributes SA and a Subset SA⋆ of SA (SA⋆ ⊆ SA)

To assess the adequacy between $SA = \{A_1, .., A_l\}$ (the whole set of attributes describing the objects of the dataset DS) and $SA_\star = \{A_{\star_1}, .., A_{\star_m}\}$ a subset of SA ($SA_\star \subseteq SA$) we use four indices defined in [7]. Thus, these indices allow to assess in which extent those two sets of attributes contain the same information concerning the objects of the dataset. They are first presented in a relatively intuitive way and their mathematical formulation is given afterwards.

Let's consider couples $((o_a, o_b), (A_{\star_j}, A_i))$ composed by : (1) a couple of objects (o_a, o_b) such that $a < b$; (2) a couple of attributes $(A_{\star_j}, A_i)$ constituted by an attribute $A_{\star_j} \in SA_\star$ and an attribute $A_i \in SA$ such that $A_{\star_j} \neq A_i$. The indices are then "intuitively" defined as follows:

- **LL(SA⋆, SA)** counts the number of couples $((o_a, o_b), (A_{\star_j}, A_i))$ such that :
  1. there is a **link** according to $A_{\star_j}$ between o_a and o_b : $link_{\star_j}(o_{a_{\star_j}}, o_{b_{\star_j}}) = 1$,
  2. there is a **link** according to A_i between o_a and o_b : $link_i(o_{a_i}, o_{b_i}) = 1$.
- **L̄L̄(SA⋆, SA)** counts the number of couples $((o_a, o_b), (A_{\star_j}, A_i))$ such that:
  1. there is a **non-link** according to $A_{\star_j}$ between o_a and o_b: $link_{\star_j}(o_{a_{\star_j}}, o_{b_{\star_j}}) = 0$,
  2. there is a **non-link** according to A_i between o_a and o_b : $link_i(o_{a_i}, o_{b_i}) = 0$.
- **LL̄(SA⋆, SA)** counts the number of couples $((o_a, o_b), (A_{\star_j}, A_i))$ such that :
  1. there is a **link** according to $A_{\star_j}$ between o_a and o_b : $link_{\star_j}(o_{a_{\star_j}}, o_{b_{\star_j}}) = 1$,
  2. there is a **non-link** according to A_i between o_a and o_b : $link_i(o_{a_i}, o_{b_i}) = 0$.
- **L̄L(SA⋆, SA)** counts the number of couples $((o_a, o_b), (A_{\star_j}, A_i))$ such that :
  1. there is a **non-link** according to $A_{\star_j}$ between o_a and o_b: $link_{\star_j}(o_{a_{\star_j}}, o_{b_{\star_j}}) = 0$,
  2. there is a **link** according to A_i between o_a and o_b : $link_i(o_{a_i}, o_{b_i}) = 1$.

More Formally, indices are defined as follows :

$$LL(SA_\star, SA) = \sum_{a=1..n} \sum_{b=a+1..n} \sum_{i=1..l} \sum_{\substack{j=1..m \\ j \text{ such that } A_{\star_j} \neq A_i}} link_i(o_{a_i}, o_{b_i}) \times link_j(o_{a_{\star_j}}, o_{b_{\star_j}})$$

$$(2)$$

$$\overline{LL}(SA_\star, SA) = \sum_{a=1..n} \sum_{b=a+1..n} \sum_{i=1..l} \sum_{\substack{j=1..m \\ j \text{ such that } A_{\star_j} \neq A_i}} (1 - link_i(o_{a_i}, o_{b_i})) \times (1 - link_j(o_{a_{\star_j}}, o_{b_{\star_j}}))$$

$$(3)$$

$$L\overline{L}(SA_\star, SA) = \sum_{a=1..n} \sum_{b=a+1..n} \sum_{i=1..l} \sum_{\substack{j=1..m \\ j \text{ such that } A_{\star j} \neq A_i}} link_i(o_{a_i}, o_{b_i}) \times (1 - link_j(o_{a_j}, o_{b_j}))$$

$$(4)$$

$$\overline{L}L(SA_\star, SA) = \sum_{a=1..n} \sum_{b=a+1..n} \sum_{i=1..l} \sum_{\substack{j=1..m \\ j \text{ such that } A_{\star j} \neq A_i}} (1 - link_i(o_{a_i}, o_{b_i})) \times link_j(o_{a_{\star j}}, o_{b_{\star j}})$$

$$(5)$$

It is shown in [7] that the level of adequacy between $SA_\star$ and SA can be characterized by the previous indices (LL, $\overline{L}L$, $L\overline{L}$, $\overline{LL}$) and that a strong adequacy between SA and $SA_\star$ is associated with high values for LL and $\overline{LL}$. However, the meaning of high values is not completely intuitive, so we have also determined in [7] the statistical laws (two different binomial laws) followed by indices LL and $\overline{LL}$ under the assumption of non-adequacy. This has then allowed us to derive (thanks to a normal approximation and a standardisation) two indices $Aq_1(SA_\star, SA)$ and $Aq_2(SA_\star, SA)$ which respectively characterize how significantly high are LL and $\overline{LL}$. Under the non-adequacy assumption, both these indices follow a standardized normal law ($N(0,1)$). They are defined as follows:

$$Aq_1(SA_\star, SA) = \frac{LL - \frac{(LL + L\overline{L})(LL + \overline{L}L)}{LL + \overline{L}L + L\overline{L} + \overline{LL}}}{\sqrt{\frac{(LL + \overline{L}L)(LL + L\overline{L})}{LL + \overline{L}L + L\overline{L} + \overline{LL}} \times \left(1 - \frac{LL + L\overline{L}}{LL + \overline{L}L + L\overline{L} + \overline{LL}}\right)}}, Aq_1(SA_\star, SA) \hookrightarrow N(0,1)$$

$$Aq_2(SA_\star, SA) = \frac{\overline{LL} - \frac{(\overline{L}L + \overline{LL})(L\overline{L} + \overline{LL})}{LL + \overline{L}L + L\overline{L} + \overline{LL}}}{\sqrt{\frac{(\overline{L}L + \overline{LL})(L\overline{L} + \overline{LL})}{LL + \overline{L}L + L\overline{L} + \overline{LL}} \times \left(1 - \frac{L\overline{L} + \overline{LL}}{LL + \overline{L}L + L\overline{L} + \overline{LL}}\right)}}, Aq_2(SA_\star, SA) \hookrightarrow N(0,1)$$

Consequently, we can say that the adequacy between $SA_\star$ and SA is strong if both values $Aq_1(SA_\star, SA)$ and $Aq_2(SA_\star, SA)$ are simultaneously significantly high. To simplify, the more $Aq_1(SA_\star, SA)$ and $Aq_2(SA_\star, SA)$ values are simultaneously high the more the adequacy between $SA_\star$ and SA is high.

IMPORTANT REMARK:
We have shown in [7] that $Aq_1(SA_\star, SA)$ and $Aq_2(SA_\star, SA)$ indices exhibit a very interesting and specific property concerning their computation:

IF [$\frac{l(l-1)}{2}$ specific contingency tables crossing each attributes of SA are built] (this only requires one dataset scan, and $O(\frac{l(l-1)}{2}n)$ (resp. $O(\frac{l(l-1)}{2}n^2)$) comparisons if all attributes of SA are categorical (resp. if some attributes of SA are numerical and not-discretized))

THEN : it is possible to compute $Aq_1(SA_\star, SA)$ and $Aq_2(SA_\star, SA)$ for any subset of SA without accessing the original dataset. This may be done with a complexity in $o(\frac{l(l-1)}{2})$ just by accessing the $\frac{l(l-1)}{2}$ specific contingency tables.

3   The New Filter Feature Selection Method for Clustering

The method we propose is based upon $Aq_1(SA_\star, SA)$ and $Aq_2(SA_\star, SA)$ indices. The basic idea is to discover the subset of SA which is the most adequate with SA (that is to say the subset which seems to best carry the information of SA). To do so, we use indices $Aq_1(SA_\star, SA)$ and $Aq_2(SA_\star, SA)$ to derive a unique new measure which reflects the adequacy between SA and $SA_\star$ ($SA_\star \subseteq SA$). Then the aim is to discover the subset of SA which optimizes this new measure.

The New Adequacy Measure, named $fit(SA, SA_\star)$ is based upon the fact that a great adequacy between $SA_\star$ and SA is characterized by simultaneously very high values for $Aq_1(SA_\star, SA)$ and $Aq_2(SA_\star, SA)$. It is defined as follows :

$$fit(SA, SA_\star) = \begin{cases} \sqrt{(a\tilde{q}_1 - Aq_1(SA_\star, SA))^2 + (a\tilde{q}_2 - Aq_2(SA_\star, SA))^2}, \\ \text{if } Aq_1(SA_\star, SA) > 0 \text{ and } Aq_2(SA_\star, SA) > 0 \\ +\infty \text{ otherwise} \end{cases}$$

We can see that, in a certain way, this function corresponds to a "distance" between two subsets of attributes from the adequacy with SA point of view. More precisely, this measure may be seen as the "distance" from the adequacy with SA point of view between : a virtual subset of attributes whose values for Aq_1 and Aq_2 would be respectively $a\tilde{q}_1$ and $a\tilde{q}_2$ and the set of attributes $SA_\star$.

Indeed, we set $a\tilde{q}_1 = a\tilde{q}_2 = high\ values$ in order to confer to the particular virtual set of attributes the aspect of a kind of ideal set of attributes from the point of view of the adequacy with SA. Consequently, the weaker is the value for this measure (i.e. the weaker is the "distance"), the more the adequacy between SA and $SA_\star$ can be considered to be high.

The Filter Method for Feature Selection for Clustering that we propose is based upon the use of this measure : it consists in looking for the subset of SA which minimizes $fit(SA, SA_\star)$ function.

This search might be exhaustive but it would imply a far too high computational cost. To reduce it we decided to use a genetic algorithm (GA) in order to perform only a partial exploration of the space composed by subsets of SA [1].

The GA used is defined as follows:

(1) a chromosome codes (corresponds to) a subset of SA;
(2) each gene of the chromosome codes an attribute of SA (so, there are l genes);
(3) each gene of a chromosome has a binary value: the gene value is 1 (resp. 0) if its associated attribute is present (resp. absent) in the subset of SA coded by the chromosome.

---

[1] Note that we could have used any other optimization method and that we made a debatable arbitrary choice. Using other greedy approaches would allow one to limit the computational cost in a greater extent. However, this choice is not the point here.

The FS method algorithm is given next page. We should note that:

(1) it only requires one scan of the dataset (due to properties of Aq_1 and Aq_2);
(2) it needs to store some contingency tables (due to $Aq_1 \& Aq_2$) but that corresponds to a small memory amount (it typically fits into computer main memory);
(3) its complexity is small due to properties of Aq_1 and Aq_2 (it is quadratic according to the number of attributes of the dataset and completely independent from the number of objects once the needed contingency tables have been built);
(4) it can deal with either numerical, categorical or mixed categorical and numerical data. However, we should note that the computational cost associated to the creation of the needed contingency tables may appear excessive in case of quantitative attributes since the complexity is quadratic with the number of objects; and that it is more interesting to treat categorical data or discretized numerical data since the complexity of contingency tables creation is thereafter linear with the number of objects.

Algorithm : *Filter Feature Selection for Clustering*

(1) In only one scan of the dataset derive the $\frac{l(l-1)}{2}$ contingency tables necessary for computing the previously presented adequacy indices.
(2) Run the Genetic Algorithm using the fitness function $fit(SA, SA_\star)$.
(3) Select the best subspace found by the Genetic Algorithm

4   Experimental Evaluations

We experimented our method both on synthetic datasets and on UCI[10] datasets.

4.1   Experiment #1: Experimental Evaluation on Synthetic Datasets

Description: The objective was to test whether or not our method is able to detect the relevant attributes. So, we built synthetic datasets including 1000 objects characterized by 9 relevant attributes (A_1, A_2, A_3, A_4, A_5, A_6, A_7, A_8, A_9) and by a set of $(l - 9)$ noisy attributes. More precisely : objects o_1 to o_{250} (resp. o_{251} to o_{500}) (resp. o_{501} to o_{750}) (resp. o_{751} to o_{1000}) all have the same value D for attributes A_1, A_2, A_3 (resp. A_3, A_4, A_5) (resp. A_5, A_6, A_7) (resp. A_7, A_8, A_9); as for the remaining attributes, a value among A, B and C is randomly assigned to the objects (the probability of assignment of each value is 1/3). We illustrate in figure 1, the composition of the datasets. We can thus see that only the first 9 attributes are relevant, and, the four clusters datasets' structures.

The experiments were the following : we ran several FS processes for 6 datasets made up of the 1000 objects characterized by attributes A_1, A_2, A_3, A_4, A_5, A_6, A_7, A_8, A_9 and respectively by 9, 18, 27, 36, 81 and 171 noisy attributes. Consequently, the datasets were respectively composed by 18 attributes (50%

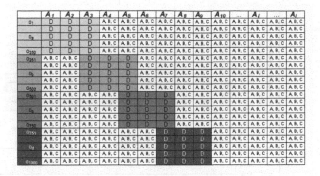

Fig. 1. Synthetic Datasets

of them are relevant), 27 attributes ($\frac{1}{3}$ of them are relevant), 36 attributes (25% of them are relevant), 45 attributes (20% of them are relevant), 90 attributes (10% of them are relevant), 180 attributes (5% of them are relevant). For each of the 6 datasets, we then ran 5 series of 5 FS processes, each series being characterized by the number of generations for the GA used. Thus, for the first series, the number of generations for the GA was 50; this number was set to 100, 500, 1000 and 2500 for the second, third, fourth and fifth series. The other parameters of the GA were : *number of chromosomes per generation = 30; cross-over rate = 0.98; mutation rate = 0,4; elitism = yes.*

Analysis of the Results:

Results are presented in figure 2. Let us note first that each of the $(6 \times 5 \times 5 = 150)$ FS processes led to a subset of attributes including the 9 relevant attributes $(A_1,...,A_9)$.

Thus, the various curves of figure 2. describe how many noisy attributes were simultaneously selected with the 9 relevant attributes for each series of 5 FS processes. They detail for each series: **(1)** the average percentage of noisy attributes selected by the 5 FS processes of the series; **(2)** the smallest percentage of selected noisy attributes (percentage of noisy attributes selected by the "best" FS process of the series); **(3)** the greatest percentage of selected noisy attributes (percentage of noisy attributes selected by the "worst" FS process of the series).

The first interesting point is the ability of the method not to omit relevant attributes in its selection, even when there are very few relevant attributes (5%) and when simultaneously the number of generations of the GA is very small (50) (for so low numbers of generations one can really consider that the optimization process of the GA did not reach its end).

As for the percentage of selected non relevant (noisy) attributes, we see that:

  – it is null (resp. nearly null) for datasets including at least 25% (resp. 20%) of relevant attributes (even for very small numbers of generations (50);

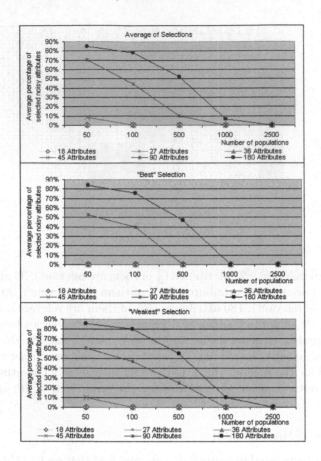

Fig. 2. Experiments on Synthetic Datasets

- concerning datasets including 10% or less than 10% of relevant attributes, the selection of the optimal subset of attributes ($SA_\star = \{A_1, A_2, A_3, A_4, A_5, A_6, A_7, A_8, A_9\}$) is obtained for numbers of generations greater or equal to 1000.

Thus, on these (relatively naive) synthetic examples the method which we propose seems very efficient, because, the indices as well as the used fitness function really give an account of what is a good subset of attributes, and, the used optimization process allows the discovery of the optimal subset while not implying a disproportionate computing time.

Finally, note that using clustering algorithms on the "reduced" dataset would lead to the "good" clustering in 4 clusters and that the associated computing time would be reduced by a factor from 2 to 20 (resp. 4 to 400) in case of algorithms having a linear complexity (resp. quadratic) in the number of attributes.

4.2   Experiment #2: Experimental Evaluation on UCI Datasets

Description: The objective of these experiments was to determine if clusterings obtained by considering a subset of the whole set of attributes (a subset of SA) selected thanks to our FS methods exhibit an equivalent or better level of quality than clusterings obtained by considering the whole set of attributes (SA).

For this, we used two famous datasets of the UCI Repository [10]: Mushrooms dataset and Small Soybean Diseases dataset. More precisely, we used our FS method in order to select a subset of the attributes of these datasets:

- For Small Soybean Diseases, 9 attributes (plantstand, precip., temp, area-damaged, stem-cankers, canker-lesion, int-discolor, sclerotia, fruit-pods) have been selected among the 35 initial attributes
- For Mushrooms, 15 attributes (bruises, odor, gill-color, stalk-shape, stalk-root, stalk-surface-above-boxing ring, stalk-surfacebelow-boxing ring, stalk-color-above-boxing ring, stalk-color-below-boxing ring, veil-type, sporeprint-color, population, habitat) have been selected among the 22 initial attributes.

Then, we clustered objects of the Small Soybean Diseases (resp. Mushrooms) dataset by considering either the whole set of 35 (resp. 22) attributes or by considering the 9 (resp. 15) attributes selected by our FS method. We used K-Modes [6] categorical data clustering method. Different parameters (different numbers of clusters) were used so as to generate clusterings having different numbers of clusters [2]. To sum up, for Mushrooms (resp. Small Soybean Diseases) dataset, we performed clusterings (using K-Modes method) into 2, 3, 4, ..., 24, 25 (resp. 2, 3, ..., 9, 10) clusters either by considering the whole set of attributes or by considering the selected subset.

To assess the quality of these clusterings we used an internal validity measure: the QKM criterion [3]. Obviously, we computed the value for this criterion by taking into account the whole set of attributes of the considered dataset even if the clustering was obtained by considering only the selected subset.

Analysis of the Results:

Mushrooms Dataset:
We see (Fig.3) that the quality of clusterings (according to QKM criterion) obtained either by performing clustering on the whole set of attributes or on the selected subset is quite similar. This shows the efficiency of our method since clusterings obtained with the FS pre-processing step are as good as those obtained without this step.

Small Soybean Diseases Dataset:
Results (Fig. 4) are similar to those obtained with Mushrooms dataset, it gives another piece of evidence about the quality of the selected subset and of our

---

[2] For each parameter setting (number of clusters), we carried out 10 different experiments and kept the clustering corresponding to the best value for criterion QKM (see note 3.).This was done to minimize the initialization effect on the K-Modes.

[3] QKM is the criterion to be optimized (minimized) by the K-Modes method.

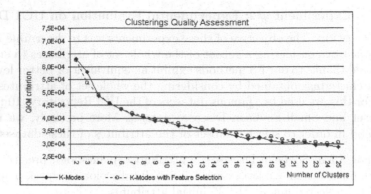

Fig. 3. Experiments on Mushrooms Dataset

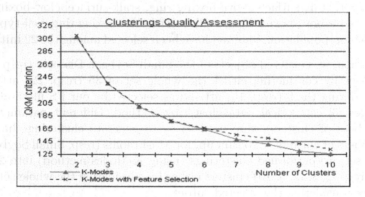

Fig. 4. Experiments on S. S. Diseases Dataset

method. Note also that the number of selected attributes is quite low (about 25% of the initial attributes).

REMARK: More extensive experiments involving different criterions and methodologies for quality checking (such as external validity measures) and also involving different clustering methods such as Kerouac method [8]) are presented in [7]. These experiments also confirm the efficiency of our FS method. Further experiments, concerning the composition in term of objects of each cluster of the obtained clusterings, show that, for a given number of clusters, clustering obtained by treating the whole set of attributes and those obtained by treating the selected subset do have a very similar composition.

5   Further Discussion and Conclusion

In short, we propose a new filter FS method for clustering which, in addition to classical filter methods advantages, exhibits several other interesting points: **(1)** it only requires one scan of the dataset contrary to almost all other filter approaches; **(2)** it has a small memory cost; **(3)** its algorithmic complexity is rather low and completely independent from the number of objects once some needed contingency tables have been built; **(4)** it can deal with either numerical, categorical or mixed categorical and numerical data contrary to other filter FS methods such as [3]; **(5)** similarly to [3] this method allows one to select attributes of the initial set of attributes and not a selection of new virtual attributes like approaches based on factorial analysis or multi-dimensional scaling. This is particularly interesting if one wants to build an easily interpretable model.

Experiments have shown the efficiency of our approach concerning clusterings quality, dimensionality reduction, noisy data handling, and computing time. We do think that the power of this method essentially lies in the efficiency of Aq_1 and Aq_2 indices. Therefore many potential improvements may be investigated such as substituting a greedy optimization method to the GA, modifying the structure of the GA in order not to seek the "optimal" subset of attributes but the best subset of attributes such that it includes a fixed number of attributes.

References

1. M. Dash and H. Liu : Feature selection for classification. Int. Journal of Intelligent Data Analysis, 1(3), (1997)
2. M. Dash and H. Liu : Feature selection for clustering. In Proc. of Fourth PacificAsia Conference on Knowledge Discovery and Data Mining, (PAKDD) (2000)
3. M. Dash, K. Choi, P. Scheuermann and H. Liu : Feature Selection for Clustering-A Filter Solution. Proc. of Int. Conference on Data Mining (ICDM02), (2002), 115–122
4. M. Devaney and A. Ram : Efficient feature selection in conceptual clustering. In Proc. of the International Conference on Machine Learning (ICML), (1997) 92–97
5. J. G. Dy and C. E. Brodley :Visualization and interactive feature selection for unsupervised data. In Proc. of the International Conference on Knowledge Discovery and Data Mining (KDD), (2000) 360–364
6. Z. Huang : A Fast Clustering Algorithm to Cluster VeryLarge Categorical Data Sets in Data Mining. Research Issues on Data Mining and Knowledge Discovery, (1997)
7. P. E. Jouve: Clustering and Knowledge Discovery in Databases. PhD thesis, Lab. ERIC, University Lyon II, France, (2003)
8. P.E. Jouve and N. Nicoloyannis : KEROUAC, an Algorithm for Clustering Categorical Data Sets with Practical Advantages. In. Proc. of International Workshop on Data Mining for Actionable Knowledge (PAKDD03), (2003)
9. Y. S. Kim, W. N. Street, and F. Menczer : Feature selection in unsupervised learning via evolutionary search. In Proc. of ACM SIGKDD International Conference on Knowledge and Discovery, (2000) 365–369
10. Merz, C., Murphy, P.: UCI repository of machine learning databases. http://www.ics.uci.edu/#mlearn/mlrepository.html. (1996)
11. L. Talavera: Feature selection and incremental learning of probabilistic concept hierarchies. In Proc. of International Conference on Machine Learning (ICML), (2000)

Automatic Determination of the Number of Fuzzy Clusters Using Simulated Annealing with Variable Representation

Sanghamitra Bandyopadhyay

Machine Intelligence Unit, Indian Statistical,
Institute, Kolkata 700 108, India
sanghami@isical.ac.in

Abstract. In this article a simulated annealing based approach for automatically clustering a data set into a number of fuzzy partitions is proposed. This is in contrast to the widely used fuzzy clustering scheme, the fuzzy C-Means (FCM) algorithm, which requires the a priori knowledge of the number of clusters. The said approach uses a real-coded variable representation of the cluster centers encoded as a state of the simulated annealing, while optimizing the Xie-Beni cluster validity index. In order to automatically determine the number of clusters, the perturbation operator is defined appropriately so that it can alter the cluster centers, and increase as well as decrease the encoded number of cluster centers. The operators are designed using some domain specific information. The effectiveness of the proposed technique in determining the appropriate number of clusters is demonstrated for both artificial and real-life data sets.

Keywords: Pattern recognition, fuzzy clustering, cluster validity index, variable number of clusters, simulated annealing.

1 Introduction

Clustering [1], also known as unsupervised learning, is a process of assigning labels to a set of n patterns in $X = \{x_1, x_2, \ldots, x_n\} \subset I\!\!R^N$, such that patterns that are similar are assigned the same label, while those that are dissimilar get different labels. A c-partition of X can be conveniently represented by a $c \times n$ matrix called the partition matrix $U = [u_{ik}]$. In fuzzy partitioning, the following condition must hold:

$$0 \leq u_{ik} \leq 1 \;\; \forall i,k, \;\; \text{and} \;\; \sum_{i=1}^{c} u_{ik} = 1 \;\; \forall k. \tag{1}$$

Here, u_{ik} is the fuzzy membership of the kth point in the ith cluster, which represents the probability $p(i|x_k)$ that, given x_k, it came from class i.

Fuzzy C-means (FCM) [2] is a widely used fuzzy clustering technique. However, it suffers from two major limitations. First of all, FCM requires the a

M.-S. Hacid et al. (Eds.): ISMIS 2005, LNAI 3488, pp. 594–602, 2005.
© Springer-Verlag Berlin Heidelberg 2005

priori specification of the number of clusters. Secondly, it often gets stuck at sub-optimal solutions. Here, we aim to develop an algorithm that will automatically find the fuzzy partitions, and will be able to come out of local optima. It may be noted that in many real life situations, the number of clusters is unknown. As a consequence, development of a technique that can automatically determine this number (as proposed in this article) is extremely important. Since, the number of clusters is variable, the optimizing criterion of the FCM algorithm cannot be used in this scenario. Therefore, we propose to utilize a fuzzy cluster validity index as the optimizing criterion. Some validity measures in the context of fuzzy clustering are the *partition coefficient, partition entropy, uniform data function, Fukuyama-Sugeno index, partition index, Xie-Beni index* [3, 4, 5, 6, 7, 8, 9, 10]. In this article, we use the Xie-Beni (XB) cluster validity index as the underlying optimizing criterion since it was found to be better able to indicate the correct number of clusters. The searching capability of simulated annealing (SA) is used for determining an appropriate set of cluster centers, such that the XB index associated with the corresponding fuzzy partition is minimized.

Simulated Annealing (SA) [11, 12] belongs to a class of local search algorithm. It utilizes the principles of statistical mechanics, regarding the behaviour of a large number of atoms at low temperature, for finding minimal cost solutions to large optimization problems by minimizing the associated energy. Let $E(q, T)$ be the energy at temperature T when the system is in the state q. Let a new state s be generated. Then state s is accepted in favour of state q with a probability $p_{qs} = \frac{1}{1+e^{\frac{-(E(q,T)-E(s,T))}{T}}}$. Application of simulated annealing or deterministic annealing for clustering has also been tackled by researchers [13, 14, 15, 16]. However, previous attempts, in general, restrict attention to partitioning the data into crisp and/or fixed number of clusters. In contrast, here we propose a real-coded SA based clustering technique, SACLUS, where a configuration or state encodes the centers of a variable number of fuzzy clusters, and the XB-index of the corresponding partition is used to measure its energy value. The perturbation operator is redefined appropriately in order to be able to both increase and decrease the number of clusters. Experimental results are demonstrated for several artificial and real-life data sets with number of dimensions ranging from two to nine and number of clusters ranging from two to ten.

2   Fuzzy Clustering Model

In most of the real life cases cluster boundaries are not well defined, and unambiguous assignment of patterns to clusters is difficult. In such situations the principles of fuzzy set theory, which permits an object to belong to a cluster with a grade of membership, are applied to provide fuzzy clustering algorithms [2]. One such widely used algorithm, the fuzzy C-Means (FCM), is first described in this section. Thereafter, some cluster validity indices are explained.

FCM Algorithm

The minimizing criterion used to define good clusters for fuzzy c-means partitions is the FCM function, defined as

$$J_m(U, V) = \sum_{i=1}^{c}\sum_{k=1}^{n}(u_{ik})^m D_{ik}^2(v_i, x_k). \tag{2}$$

Here $U \in M_{fcn}$ is a fuzzy partition matrix; $m \in [1, \infty]$ is the weighting exponent on each fuzzy membership; $V = [v_1, \ldots, v_c]$ represents c cluster centers; $v_i \in I\!\!R^N$; and $D_{ik}(v_i, x_k)$ is the distance from x_k to the ith cluster center. The Fuzzy c-Means theorem [2] states that if $D_{ik} > 0$, for all i and k, then (U, V) may minimize J_m, only if when $m > 1$

$$u_{ik} = \frac{1}{\sum_{j=1}^{c}(\frac{D_{ik}(v_i, x_k)}{D_{jk}(v_j, x_k)})^{\frac{2}{m-1}}}, \quad \text{for } 1 \le i \le c;\ 1 \le k \le n, \tag{3}$$

and

$$v_i = \frac{\sum_{k=1}^{n}(u_{ik})^m x_k}{\sum_{k=1}^{n}(u_{ik})^m}, \quad i \le i \le c. \tag{4}$$

A common strategy for generating the approximate solutions of the minimization problem in Eqn. 2 is by iterating through Eqns. 3 and 4 (also known as Picard iteration technique). A detailed description of the FCM algorithm may be found in [2].

Fuzzy Cluster Validity Index

Cluster validity index is often used to indicate the goodness of a partitioning of a data set as obtained by a clustering algorithm. Xie and Beni [10] proposed one such validity measure which is defined as the ratio of the total variation σ to the minimum separation sep of the clusters, where σ and sep can be written as

$$\sigma(U, V; X) = \sum_{i=1}^{c}\sum_{k=1}^{n}u_{ik}^2\|x_k - v_i\|^2, \quad \text{and} \quad sep(V) = \min_{i \ne j}\{\|v_i - v_j\|^2\}. \tag{5}$$

The XB index is then written as

$$XB(U, V; X) = \frac{\sigma(U, V; X)}{n\ sep(V)} = \frac{\sum_{i=1}^{c}\sum_{k=1}^{n}u_{ik}^2\|x_k - v_i\|^2}{n(min_{i \ne j}\{\|v_i - v_j\|^2\})}. \tag{6}$$

When the partitioning is compact and good, value of σ should be low while sep should be high resulting in low values of the Xie-Beni (XB) index.

3   SACLUS: Simulated Annealing for Automatic Clustering

The basic steps of simulated annealing are shown in Fig. 1. Here T_{max} and T_{min} are the initial and final temperatures respectively, k is the number of iterations

```
Begin
      generate the initial configuration randomly = q
      Let T = Tmax and E(q,T) the energy of q
      while (T ≥ Tmin)
            for i = 1 to k
                  Perturb the configuration q to yield s with energy E(s,T)
                  Set q ← s with probability  1/(1+e^{-(E(q,T)-E(s,T))/T})
            end for
            T = rT
      end while
      Decode the configuration q to provide the solution of the problem.
End
```

Fig. 1. Steps of Simulated Annealing

carried out at each temperature, and the temperature is decreased using the cooling schedule $T = rT$, where $0 < r < 1$.

For the purpose of clustering, the cluster centers, whose number can vary, constitute a configuration (state) in SA. In order to generate the initial state of the SACLUS, a random integer, c, is selected from the range $[c_{min}, c_{max}]$ and c randomly selected points from the data constitute the initial cluster centers. For determining the energy, the centers encoded in a string are first extracted and the corresponding membership values are computed using Eqn. 3. The energy is then computed using the Xie-Beni (XB) index as defined in Eqn. 6. Thereafter, the new cluster centers are computed using Eqn. 4, which are used to replace the original cluster centers encoded in the SA state.

In order to generate a new state from the current one, a perturbation function is applied. This is defined in such a way that it has the capability of perturbing a cluster center (*PerturbCenter*), reducing the number of clusters by deleting a cluster (*DeleteCenter*) as well as splitting an existing cluster (*SplitCenter*) with equal probability. These three operations are described below.

PerturbCenter: Here, a cluster center is picked at random from the string, and its value on every feature, v, is allowed to change by atmost f percent.

DeleteCenter: For this purpose, the smallest cluster is chosen, and it is deleted from the string. The size of a cluster C_i is defined as the sum of the membership values of all the points assigned to C_i, or equivalently its fuzzy cardinality. That is $|C_i| = \sum_{k=1}^{n} u_{ik}$.

SplitCenter: In this function, the largest cluster, i, computed using the above equation, is selected, and the corresponding center, say v_i, is replaced by two centers, v_{i1} and v_{i2}, as follows. A point, say x_k, whose membership to cluster i is smaller than but closest to 0.5 is found. Note that all points closer to v_i than this point have membership values greater than 0.5. The extent of the cluster along all the dimensions is computed as $extent[j] = |(x_k[j] - v_i[j])|$, $j = 0, 1, \ldots, N-1$, where N is the number of dimensions. The two new cluster centers resulting from the splitting of cluster i are computed as $v_i \pm extent$.

After the new state is generated, its energy (or, the XB index value for the corresponding fuzzy partitioning of the data) is computed. In case, the energy of the new state is lower than that of the previous state, then the new state is accepted. In case the energy of the new state is greater than or equal to that of the previous state, the new state is accepted with the probability defined earlier.

4   Experimental Results

The effectiveness of the proposed algorithm in automatically clustering a data set is demonstrated for two artificial and two real-life data sets. The data sets, along with the implementation parameters, are first described in this section. Subsequently, the partitionings provided by the proposed technique, and its comparison with FCM is provided.

4.1   Data Sets and Implementation Parameters

The two artificial data sets that have been used in this article are *AD_10_2* and *AD_9_2* and the two real-life data sets are *Cancer* and *Kalaazar*. Note that results on several other data sets are also available, but could not be included in order to restrict the size of the article. *AD_10_2* is a two dimensional overlapping data set with 10 clusters and 500 points. Fig. 2 shows the data set. *AD_9_2* is a two-dimensional, nine class data with triangular distribution of data points. All the classes are assumed to have equal *a priori* probabilities ($= 1/9$). The $X - Y$ ranges for classes 1-9 are [-3.3, -0.7] × [0.7, 3.3], [-1.3, 1.3] × [0.7, 3.3], [0.7, 3.3] × [0.7, 3.3], [-3.3, -0.7] × [-1.3, 1.3], [-1.3, 1.3] × [-1.3, 1.3], [0.7, 3.3] × [-1.3, 1.3], [-3.3, -0.7] × [-3.3, -0.7], [-1.3, 1.3] × [-3.3, -0.7], and [0.7, 3.3] × [-3.3, -0.7] respectively. The data set is shown in Fig. 3. We have chosen the classes in such a way that each class has some overlap with everyone of its adjacent classes. In any direction the non-overlapping portion is 1.4 units and the overlapping portion is 1.2 units.

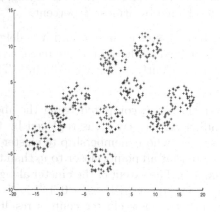

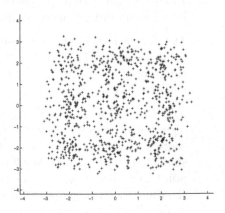

Fig. 2. *AD_10_2*   **Fig. 3.** *AD_9_2*

The *Cancer* data has 683 pattern in nine features (*clump thickness, cell size uniformity, cell shape uniformity, marginal adhesion, single epithelial cell size, bare nuclei, bland chromatin, normal nucleoli* and *mitoses*), and two classes malignant and benign. The two classes are known to be linearly inseparable. The data set is available in [http://www.ics.uci.edu/~mlearn/MLRepository.html]. The *Kalaazar* data [17] consists of 68 patterns in four dimensions with two classes: diseased and normal/cured. The four features are the measurements of blood urea (mg%), serum creatinine (mg%), urinary creatinine (mg%) and creatinine clearance (ml/min).

The parameters of the SACLUS algorithm are as follows: $T_{max} = 100$, $T_{min} = 0.0001$, $\alpha = 0.7$, and #iterations at each temperature $= 30$. The number of clusters, c, is varied from 2 to $\sqrt{n}$ (since c is usually assumed to be less than or equal to $\sqrt{n}$), where n is the size of the data set.

4.2   Comparative Results with FCM

Tables 1(a) - 2(b) provide the comparative results of SACLUS and FCM for *AD_10_2*, *AD_9_2*, *Cancer* and *Kalaazar* respectively. Table 3 summarizes the number of clusters provided by the two techniques when the minimum value of XB-index is achieved, and the corresponding value of m for the five data sets. As can be seen from Tables 1(a) - 2(b), the SACLUS technique generally provides

Table 1. Comparative Values of Number of Clusters and XB-index for

(a) *AD_10_2*

m	FCM		SACLUS	
	# clusters	XB	# clusters	XB
1.6	9	0.0998	9	0.0968
1.8	9	0.0857	10	0.0835
2.0	9	0.0828	10	0.0758
2.2	9	0.0903	10	0.0785
2.4	8	0.1056	10	0.0880

(b) *AD_9_2*

m	FCM		SACLUS	
	# clusters	XB	# clusters	XB
1.6	9	0.0892	9	0.0885
1.8	9	0.0788	9	0.0787
2.0	9	0.0765	9	0.0739
2.2	9	0.0817	9	0.0793
2.4	9	0.0921	9	0.0954

Table 2. Comparative Values of Number of Clusters and XB-index for

(a) *Cancer*

m	FCM		SACLUS	
	# clusters	XB	# clusters	XB
1.6	2	0.1167	2	0.1125
1.8	2	0.1116	2	0.1093
2.0	2	0.1103	2	0.1059
2.2	2	0.1117	2	0.1073
2.4	2	0.1150	2	0.1101

(b) *Kalaazar*

m	FCM		SACLUS	
	# clusters	XB	# clusters	XB
1.6	5	0.2034	2	0.1570
1.8	5	0.2067	2	0.1448
2.0	5	0.2192	2	0.1333
2.2	5	0.2353	2	0.1379
2.4	5	0.3033	2	0.1440

600   S. Bandyopadhyay

Table 3. Number of Clusters, m and Value of XB-index Obtained by SACLUS and FCM

Data Set	SACLUS			FCM		
	# clusters	m	XB	# clusters	m	XB
AD_10_2	10	2.0	0.0758	9	2.0	0.0828
AD_9_2	9	2.0	0.0739	9	2.0	0.0765
Cancer	2	2.0	0.1059	2	2.0	0.1103
Kalaazar	2	2.0	0.1333	5	1.6	0.2034

lower values of the XB-index for all values of m for all the data sets, except for except for AD_9_2 when $m = 2.4$. Moreover, as can be seen from Table 3, the SA based method provides the correct number of clusters for all the data sets. In contrast, FCM fails to provide this for AD_10_2 and $Kalaazar$, where it yields 9 and 5 clusters respectively. Note that the number of clusters provided by FCM for a particular value of m was obtained by varying c, the number of clusters, from $\max[2, c^* - 2]$ to $c^* + 2$, where c^* is equal to the actual number of clusters present in the data. The value of c for which the minimum value of the XB-index was obtained was considered to be the number of clusters provided by FCM. For the purpose of illustration, Figures 4 (a) and (b) demonstrate the variation of the value of the XB-index with the number of clusters for different values of m for AD_10_2 and $Cancer$ respectively when FCM is used for clustering. The values of the number of clusters for FCM, as provided in Tables 1(a) and 2 (and similarly for the other data sets), are obtained from the above figures.

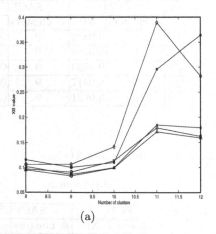
(a)

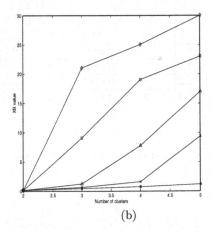
(b)

Fig. 4. Variation of XB-index with Number of Clusters for Different Values of m ('*' - $m = 1.6$, 'x' - $m = 1.8$, '$\triangle$' - $m = 2.0$, '$\square$' - $m = 2.2$, '$\lozenge$' - $m = 2.4$) for (a) AD_10_2 (b) $Cancer$

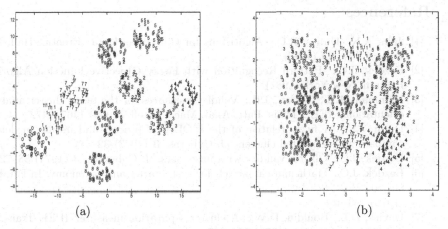

(a)   (b)

Fig. 5. Clustered Data Using SACLUS with the XB Index (a) AD_10_2 When 10 Clusters Were Obtained Labeled 0-9, (b) AD_9_2 When 9 Clusters Were Obtained Labeled 1-9

It may be noted from Table 3 that, in general, the lowest value of the XB-index corresponds to $m = 2.0$. The only exception is for the Kalaazar data set, where this is obtained for $m = 1.6$ when FCM is used. Figures 5 (a) and (b) demonstrate the clustered AD_10_2 and AD_9_2 for the purpose of illustration.

5   Discussion and Conclusions

In this article, an unsupervised fuzzy classification algorithm has been proposed for automatic determination of the number of clusters as well as the proper partitioning of the data. Simulated annealing has been used as the underlying search strategy as it has the capability of coming out of local optima. Since the number of clusters is not known *a priori*, it is kept variable in the representation. Therefore, in order to perturb the current state, several perturbation operators, namely, *PerturbCenter, DeleteCenter* and *SplitCenter* are proposed. Xie-Beni index has been used as the minimizing criterion, since it has been previously shown to be better able to indicate the correct number of clusters. Experimental results demonstrating the effectiveness of the proposed technique along with a comparison with the FCM algorithm, that requires the *a priori* knowledge of the number of clusters, has been provided for several artificial and real-life data sets.

As a scope of further research, a detailed comparative analysis needs to be carried out with other ways computing the validity indices as well as other similar search techniques in order to justify the use of a particular index and an underlying search tool for a given problem. Application of the proposed technique in different domains, e.g., for image segmentation, may be studied in future.

References

[1] Jain, A.K., Dubes, R.C.: Algorithms for Clustering Data. Prentice-Hall, Englewood Cliffs, NJ (1988)

[2] Bezdek, J.C.: Pattern Recognition with Fuzzy Objective Function Algorithms. Plenum, New York (1981)

[3] Hammah, R.E., Curran, J.H.: Validity measures for the fuzzy cluster analysis of orientations. IEEE Trans. Patt. Anal. Mach. Intell. (2000) 1467–1472

[4] Dunn, J.C.: A fuzzy relative of the ISODATA process and its use in detecting compact well-separated clusters. J. Cyberns. **3** (1973) 32–57

[5] Bezdek, J.C.: Cluster validity with fuzzy sets. J. Cybernet. **3** (1974) 58–72

[6] Bezdek, J.C.: Mathematical models for systematics and taxonomy. In Estabrook, G., ed.: Proc. 8th Intl. Conf. Numerical Taxonomy. Freeman, San Francisco, CA (1975) 143–166

[7] Davies, D.L., Bouldin, D.W.: A cluster separation measure. IEEE Trans. Patt. Anal. Mach. Intell. **1** (1979) 224–227

[8] Windham, M.P.: Cluster validity for the fuzzy c-means clustering algorithm. IEEE Trans. Patt. Anal. Mach. Intell. **4** (1982) 357–363

[9] Bensaid, A.M., Hall, L.O., Bezdek, J.C., Clarke, L.P., Silbiger, M.L., Arrington, J.A., Murtagh, R.F.: Validity-guided (re)clustering with applications to image segmentation. IEEE Trans. Fuzzy Systs. **4** (1996) 112–123

[10] Xie, X.L., Beni, G.: A validity measure for fuzzy clustering. IEEE Trans. Patt. Anal. Mach. Intell. **13** (1991) 841–847

[11] Kirkpatrik, S., Gelatt, C., Vecchi, M.: Optimization by simulated annealing. Science **220** (1983) 671–680

[12] van Laarhoven, P.J.M., Aarts, E.H.L.: Simulated Annealing: Theory and Applications. Kluwer Academic Publisher (1987)

[13] Bakker, B., Heskes, T.: Model clustering by deterministic annealing. In: European Symposium on Artificial Neural Networks, Bruges, Belgium (1999) 87–92

[14] Lukashin, A.V., Fuchs, R.: Analysis of temporal gene expression profiles: clustering by simulated annealing and determining the optimal number of clusters. Bioinformatics **17** (2001) 405–419

[15] Bandyopadhyay, S., Maulik, U., Pakhira, M.K.: Clustering using simulated annealing with probabilistic redistribution. International Journal of Pattern Recognition and Artificial Intelligence **15** (2001) 269–285

[16] Hermes, L., Buhmann, J.M.: Semi-supervised image segmentation by parametric distributional clustering. In: Energy Minimization Methods in Computer Vision and Pattern Recognition. Volume LNCS 2683. Springer (2003) 229–245

[17] Mitra, S., Pal, S.K.: Fuzzy multi-layer perceptron, inferencing and rule generation. IEEE Trans. Neural Networks **6** (1995) 51–63

Experimental Analysis of the Q-Matrix Method in Knowledge Discovery

Tiffany Barnes[1], Donald Bitzer[2], and Mladen Vouk[2,*]

[1] Computer Science Dept., University of North Carolina at Charlotte,
Charlotte, NC, 28223, USA
tbarnes2@uncc.edu
[2] Computer Science Dept., North Carolina State University, Raleigh, NC 27695, USA

Abstract. The q-matrix method, a new method for data mining and knowledge discovery, is compared with factor analysis and cluster analysis in analyzing fourteen experimental data sets. This method creates a matrix-based model that extracts latent relationships among observed binary variables. Results show that the q-matrix method offers several advantages over factor analysis and cluster analysis for knowledge discovery. The q-matrix method can perform fully unsupervised clustering, where the number of clusters is not known in advance. It also yields better error rates than factor analysis, and is comparable in error to cluster analysis. The q-matrix method also allows for automatic interpretation of the data sets. These results suggest that the q-matrix method can be an important tool in automated knowledge discovery.

1 Introduction

Knowledge discovery and data mining are increasingly important tools [4,5]. We present the q-matrix method, a tool used in the automatic analysis of educational data, and analyze this method in several experiments to explore its use as a knowledge discovery tool.

The q-matrix method is a clustering method used in fault-tolerant teaching systems for the adaptation of online tutorials to student knowledge [1]. It was originally developed through research in student modeling and knowledge remediation [1,2,3,6,11] and is related to theories of knowledge representation as in [12]. The advantage of this method over other intelligent tutoring systems is its generality: The q-matrix method can be applied to any tutorial independent of topic. The method can also be set to remain static or to modify itself as new data are collected. In addition to its use in computer-based educational applications, q-matrices can also be used to understand data in other settings. This research presents the first interpretation of the q-matrix method as a knowledge discovery and data mining tool, and compares it with two other analysis techniques.

---

* This work was partially supported by NSF grants #9813902 and #0204222.

M.-S. Hacid et al. (Eds.): ISMIS 2005, LNAI 3488, pp. 603–611, 2005.
© Springer-Verlag Berlin Heidelberg 2005

In our previous research, we explored the literature related to the q-matrix method and presented our results for testing its validity for use in directing student progress in computer-based tutorials [1]. In this research, the first to consider the method as a clustering method, we compare the q-matrix method with factor analysis and k-means cluster analysis for fitting and understanding data in fourteen experiments. Using this comparison, we verify the validity of the relationships found by the q-matrix method, and determine the factors that affect its performance. These experiments use data collected from online tutorials, where the goal is to automatically assess student knowledge and determine the next step in student learning. Throughout this work we will refer to the utility of the q-matrix method in this application. However, we believe this application is not unique to the education domain. In other words, the automatic extraction of latent relationships in the data set, and the concept model created, could be used in automatic data processing in many applications.

2 Data Collection

Data were collected from several computer-based tutorials on the NovaNET [9] educational network, which are required for the authors' Discrete Mathematics course in Fall 2002. One tutorial in binary relations contains three sections: binq1, binq2, and binq3. The second tutorial, count, is one on basic combinations and permutations. In these four experiments, data are student answer vectors, where a 1 corresponds to a correct answer and a 0 corresponds to an incorrect answer for a particular question. A sample answer vector in binq1 of 11010 corresponds to a student answering questions 1,2, and 4 correctly and 3 and 5 incorrectly.

The third tutorial is a formal logic proof checker. Solutions to its ten proof problems are lists of successive rule applications, with references to the rules and lines used in each step. For one proof, a solution is translated into an "answer vector" by listing the rules that were used in a proof, and then placing a 1 in a student's answer vector if they used that rule and a 0 otherwise. This resulted in 10 separate experiments, pf1-pf10.

In each experiment, approximately 100 student answer vectors were analyzed using three methods: the q-matrix method, factor analysis, and cluster analysis.

3 Q-Matrix Method

Static q-matrix models created by content experts were originally developed to explain relationships between the concepts students learn in arithmetic to questions they solve on tests [2], and they are now used in intelligent tutoring systems to relate underlying concepts to problems [12]. Q-matrices were originally binary matrices but were adapted and interpreted as probabilities by Brewer in his experiment on simulated students [3] and by Sellers in its first application with a small set of real students [11].

A q-matrix is a matrix that represents relationships between a set of observed variables (e.g. questions), and latent variables that relate these observations. We call

Table 1. Example q-matrix

	q1	q2	q3	q4	q5	q6	q7
c1	1	0	0	0	0	1	1
c2	1	1	0	1	0	0	1
c3	1	1	1	0	0	0	0

these latent variables "concepts." An example q-matrix is given in Table 1 below. In this q-matrix, the observed variables are 7 questions q1-q7, and the concepts are c1-c3. For simplicity, this example is given with binary values.

For a given q-matrix Q, the value of Q(Con,Ques) represents the conditional probability that Ques will be TRUE given that the underlying concept Con is not present. In the context of our educational experiment, this is the probability that a student will miss the question Ques given that they do not understand concept Con. In Table 1, this means that question q1 will not be answered correctly unless a student understands all three concepts c1-c3. Question q2 will not be answered correctly unless a student understands concepts c2 and c3, even if the student does not understand concept c1. In contrast, question q5 can be answered correctly without understanding any of the concepts c1-c3. This indicates that prerequisite knowledge not represented in the q-matrix affects the answer to q5. In a more general setting, "concepts" can be thought of similarly to the components extracted in PCA (principal components analysis), since they represent abstract data vectors that can be used to understand a larger set. These concepts can also be used to describe different clusters of observed data.

Each cluster in the q-matrix method is represented by its concept state, a vector of bits where the kth bit is 0 if the students do not understand concept k, and a 1 if they do. Each concept state also has associated with it an ideal response vector (IDR), or representative vector, that is determined using the concept state and the q-matrix. For each question q in the q-matrix we examine the concepts needed to answer that question. If the concept state contains all those needed for q, we set bit q in the IDR to 1, and otherwise to 0. There are 2^{NumCon} concept states for a q-matrix with NumCon concepts. A concept state's ideal response vector (IDR) is the answer we predict a student in that state would give under ideal conditions (e.g. he does not make any slips or guesses).

Mathematically, given a q-matrix Q with NumCon concepts, and a concept state Con, where Con(k) denotes whether concept k is understood or not, we calculate the ideal response (IDR) for each question Ques as:

$$\text{IDR(Ques)} = \prod_{k=1}^{NumCon} \begin{cases} 1 & Con(k)=1 \\ 1-Q(k,Ques) & Con(k)=0 \end{cases}. \tag{1}$$

Table 2 lists the IDRs for all the possible concept states for the q-matrix given in Table 1. The all-zero concept state 000 describes the "default" knowledge not accounted for in the model, while the all-one concept state 111 describes full understanding of all concepts. Concept state 011's IDR corresponds to a binary OR

Table 2. Ideal Response Vectors for each Concept State

Concept State	IDR	Concept State	IDR
000	0000100	100	0000110
001	0010100	101	0010110
010	0001100	110	0001111
011	0111100	111	1111111

of the IDRs for concept states 001 and 010, plus the addition of a 1 for q2, which requires both concepts c2 and c3 for a correct outcome.

3.2 Q-Matrix Model Evaluation

To evaluate the fit of a given q-matrix to a data set, we compute its concept states and IDRs as in Table 2 and determine each data point's nearest neighbor from the set of IDRs. The data point is then assigned to the corresponding concept state, with an associated error, which is the L_1 distance between the IDR and the data point. In other words, the distance d(p,IDR) between data point p and its IDR is:

$$d(p,IDR) = \sum_q |p(q) - IDR(q)| \tag{2}$$

For example, for a data vector 0111110 and the q-matrix given in Table 1, the nearest IDR would be 0111100 in concept state 011, and the error associated with this assignment is 1, since there is only one difference between the data point and its nearest IDR. The total error for a q-matrix on a given data set is the sum of the errors over all data points.

3.3 Q-Matrix Model Extraction

The q-matrix method of model extraction is a heuristic hill-climbing method that varies q-matrix values to minimize the error in student answer predictions, as first suggested in [2]. The method described in this research is that used in [11], but modified to ignore data with all-zero or all-ones responses. These data are not important in fitting the data, since their assigned concept states will be either concept state 0 (in the all-zero case), or the highest-numbered concept state (in the all-ones case).

To find an optimal q-matrix, we iterate the algorithm given in Table 3 for a set number of concepts, NumCon, until we meet a pre-set stopping criterion. Here, the average error per student should be less than 1. The parameter NumStarts allows enough random starts to avoid local minima. In the interior loop of the algorithm, single values in the q-matrix are optimized (by Delta at a time) while the rest of the q-matrix is held constant. Therefore, several (NumIter) passes through the entire q-matrix are made. In these experiments, NumStarts was set to 50, Delta was set to 0.1, and NumIter was set to 5.

Table 3. Q-matrix method pseudo-code for fixed NumCon

```
Set MinError = LargeNumber;
For Starts= 1 to NumStarts
    Randomly initialize Q[NumCon][NumQues];
    Set Q* = Q; Set CurrError = Error(Q) ;
    For Iter = 1 to NumIter;
        For c= 1 to NumCon
            For q= 1 to NumQues
                Q*[c][q] = Q[c][q] + Delta;
                If (Error(Q*) < CurrError)
                Do
                    Set Q=Q*; Set CurrError = Error(Q*);
                    Q*[c][q] = Q[c][q] + Delta;
                    While (Error(Q*) < CurrError);
                Else
                    Q*[c][q] = Q[c][q] - Delta;
                    While (Error(Q*) < CurrError)
                        Set Q=Q*; Set CurrError = Error(Q*);
                        Q*[c][q] = Q[c][q] - Delta;
    If (CurrError < MinError)
        Set BestQ = Q; Set MinError = CurrError;
```

These parameters usually yielded consistent outcomes for the final q-matrix when run several times on the same data. In other experiments, these parameters will have to be adjusted according to the size of the data set and the number of questions.

The efficiency of the algorithm is roughly quadratic in the size of the input data (number of student responses * number of questions). The number of concept states is usually close to the number of questions, so therefore the number of concepts extracted will be approximately the logarithm of the number of questions. A more detailed analysis of the running time of this algorithm is left for future work.

4 Comparison with Factor Analysis

Factor analysis is a statistical process, often used in the social sciences, that attempts to extract latent (i.e. unknown and unobservable) variables from observed data [8]. The final results of a factor analysis include a factor matrix and factor loadings, respectively, the eigenvectors and eigenvalues of the correlation matrix of the observed data. The factor matrix is typically interpreted to demonstrate which observed variables correspond to the latent, or underlying, factors that caused the observations. If the magnitude of a factor matrix score is 0.3 or more, then the corresponding variable is related to the factor, and otherwise it is not. Before interpretation, the factor matrix has been "rotated" to yield distinct factors that account for most of the observed variance [8].

SAS was used to perform a factor analysis on student answers for fourteen online tutorials [10]. The SAS "proc factor" was used with "PRIORS=max" and the percent of variance stopping criterion. (Note: with PRIORS set to 1, factor analysis is equivalent to PCA, principle components analysis). Most of the experiments yielded four factors.

For a fair comparison of the methods, each q-matrix analysis was performed with the number of concepts equal to the number of extracted factors. Then, the factor and q-matrix results were converted to binary by rounding scores less than 0.3 to 0, and those higher to 1. We note that the q-matrix scores were already near 0 and 1 values.

The error for both the q-matrix and factor analysis methods, calculated as described above for a q-matrix, is shown in Fig. 1. The errors per student for the q-matrix method are all less than 1.25, while the errors for factor analysis range up to almost 3 errors per student. With less than 10 questions in each experiment, an error rate of 2 per student is more than 20% error in answer prediction. Our goal is less than 1 error per student, or in other words, less than 1 error per data point on average in each experiment. This is much more consistently attained using the q-matrix method.

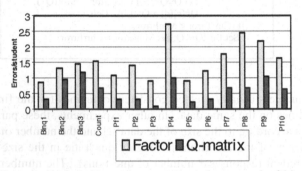

Fig. 1. Factor analysis and q-matrix errors per student on each of 14 experiments

Fig. 2 shows that the difference in performance between the factor analysis and q-matrix methods can be primarily understood by examining the relative number of distinct observations made in each experiment. For each experiment, the first column plotted, "# diff ans/max," is the actual number of distinct observations, scaled by the maximum number of distinct observations made. The second column represents a ratio of the q-matrix error over the factor analysis error. The lower the number of distinct observations, the better the q-matrix method performed relative to factor analysis.

In 1996, Brewer compared factor analysis with the q-matrix method on simulated student data and found that factor analysis requires 10 to 100 times more data than the q-matrix method does to achieve an equivalent fit [3]. Our work confirms and expands this finding on real student data, and shows that the q-matrix method nalso outperforms factor analysis when fewer distinct observations exist in the data set. This difference in performance can be explained simply through an examination of the two methods of model extraction. In factor analysis we pre-process the data to create a correlation matrix. This prevents the model from explaining the differences in individual responses as the q-matrix can, since the q-matrix method builds its model by minimizing the sum of all individual errors.

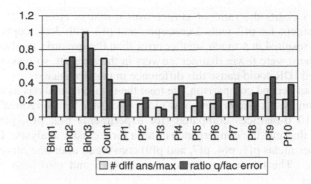

Fig. 2. Ratio of q-matrix to factor error and relative # of distinct observations

5   Comparison with Cluster Analysis

Cluster analysis is a common data mining technique to group data based on a distance criterion, providing a way to classify data without a priori knowledge of the classification types. Although k-means cluster analysis is not the best technique for clustering binary data [7], we were interested in whether the q-matrix method error statistics would be comparable to those found in a typical cluster analysis.

For each experiment, we ran a cluster analysis using the SAS procedure fastclus, with parameters least = 1 and maxclusters is set to the number of clusters found in the q-matrix analysis for a fair comparison. The "least = 1" parameter corresponds to the L_1 distance metric, where the distance is the number of differing bits between two vectors.

The proc fastclus algorithm is an iterative algorithm. First, a random seed is chosen from the data set for each cluster. Then, each observation is assigned to the cluster whose seed is nearest. At the end of an iteration, each seed is reset to be the cluster median. The observation clusters are recalculated, and cluster seeds reset, iteratively, until the maximum relative change in the cluster seeds is less than 0.0001 [10].

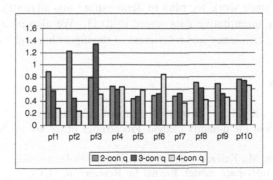

Fig. 3. Ratio of cluster over q-matrix error for 2, 3, & 4 concepts

Fig. 3 charts the ratio of cluster over q-matrix error for 10 experiments. In all cases, except for pf2 with 2 concepts, and pf3 with 3 concepts, the cluster analysis method resulted in a much smaller error than the q-matrix method. In the exceptional cases, there were fewer distinct answers in the data set, so a skew towards a q-matrix predicted IDR could cause this difference in performance.

For our second comparison, we treat the q-matrix analysis as one step in a k-means cluster analysis to determine how close to cluster "convergence" we might be. Four of the 10 q-matrices compared (for experiments pf2, pf3, pf8, and pf10) formed clusters that met the convergence criteria for a cluster analysis. Four more q-matrices (for experiments pf1, pf4, pf7, and pf9) converged after one more iteration of a cluster analysis. The two remaining q-matrices (pf5 and pf6) converged after two more iterations.

These convergence results indicate that the clusters formed by a q-matrix analysis are similar to those formed by a cluster analysis. Not all of the cluster formations created by the q-matrix analysis meet the convergence criterion since there are relationships imposed on the clusters. Using these relationships, the q-matrix model can explain the clusters using approximately the log of the number of clusters for its number of concepts. This advantage outweighs the difference in error for the two models. In addition, since the q-matrix method may generate more clusters than are actually used, this method may be more flexible when applied to new data.

6 Final Remarks

Our results suggest that the q-matrix method has several advantages over factor analysis and cluster analysis for knowledge discovery in the selected experiments. The q-matrix method builds an interpretable model for data, without a priori knowledge of concepts or clusters needed, in a fully automated process. It requires less data than factor analysis (which is important in educational applications), and may be less sensitive to over-fitting than cluster analysis. Like these other methods, the q-matrix method forms reasonable clusters of data, but imposes a structure to these clusters that has been used in adaptive systems [1]. We believe that this structure can offer a great advantage over cluster analysis in the knowledge discovery process. In future work we plan to demonstrate this advantage on a variety of data sets, including quantitative data scaled to [0,1]. We also plan to perform a detailed analysis of the efficiency and robustness of the algorithm and its convergence criteria.

References

1. Barnes, T. & Bitzer, D. (2003). Fault tolerant teaching and knowledge assessment: Evaluation of the q-matrix method. Proceedings of the 40th ACMSE, Raleigh, NC, April 2003.
2. Birenbaum, M., Kelly, A., & Tatsuoka, K. (1993). Diagnosing knowledge state in algebra using the rule-space model. Journal for Research in Mathematics Education, 24(5), 442-459.
3. Brewer, P. (1996). Methods for concept mapping in computer based education. Computer Science Masters Thesis, North Carolina State University.

4. Elder, J.F., & Abbott, D.W. (1998). A comparison of leading data mining tools. Proc. 4th Intl. Conf. on Knowledge Discovery and Data Mining.
5. Erlich, Z., Gelbard, R. & Spiegler, I. (2002). Data Mining by Means of Binary Representation: A Model for Similarity and Clustering. Information Systems Frontiers, 4(2): 187-197, July 2002.
6. Jones, S. (1996). Computer assisted learning of mathematical recursion. Computer Science Masters Thesis, North Carolina State University.
7. Kauffman, L. & P.J. Rousseeuw. (1990). Finding groups in data. Wiley, New York.
8. Kline, P. (1994). An easy guide to factor analysis. Rutledge, London.
9. NovaNET educational network. Online. [http://www.pearsondigital.com/novanet/]
10. Statistical Analysis Software (SAS) and Help System. Online. [http://www.sas.com]
11. Sellers, J. (1998). An empirical evaluation of a fault-tolerant approach to computer-assisted teaching of binary relations. Computer Science Masters Thesis, North Carolina State University.
12. VanLehn, K., Niu, Z., Siler, S., & Gertner, A. (1998). Student modeling from conventional test data: A Bayesian approach without priors. Intelligent Tutoring Systems, p. 434-443.

Clustering Time-Series Medical Databases Based on the Improved Multiscale Matching

Shoji Hirano and Shusaku Tsumoto

Department of Medical Informatics, Shimane University, School of Medicine,
89-1 Enya-cho, Izumo, Shimane 693-8501, Japan
hirano@ieee.org, tsumoto@computer.org

Abstract. This paper presents a novel method called modified multiscale matching, that enable us to multiscale structural comparison of irregularly-sampled, different-length time series like medical data. We revised the conventional multiscale matching algorithm so that it produces sequence dissimilarity that can be further used for clustering. The main improvements are: (1) introduction of a new segment representation that elude the problem of shrinkage at high scales, (2) introduction of a new dissimilarity measure that directly reflects the dissimilarity of sequence values. We examined the usefulness of the method on the cylinder-bell-funnel dataset and chronic hepatitis dataset. The results demonstrated that the dissimilarity matrix produced by the proposed method, combined with conventional clustering techniques, lead to the successful clustering for both synthetic and real-world data.

1 Introduction

Temporal data mining [1] has been receiving much attention in medical domain since it provides a new, data-oriented way of discovering interesting knowledge useful for diagnosis; for example relationships between the temporal course of examination results and onset time of diseases. Especially, data mining concerning chronic diseases such as viral hepatitis B and C attracts much interest of physicians since it enables us the large-scale comparison of chronic temporal courses over patients. However, despite its significance, the cross-patient comparison of the time-series examination results of chronic disease patients has rarely been performed due to the following difficulties. (1) Temporal irregularity of the data: Intervals of laboratory examinations can vary depending on the patient's condition over long time. Therefore, the sampling interval of a time-series is in nature irregular, and, the length of the sequences is also different. This prevents the use of conventional point-to-point comparison based methods. (2) Coexistence of short-term and long-term events. For example in chronic viral hepatitis, short-term changes induced by interferon treatment can be observed during several months, while long-term changes by virus can be observed for several years. Comparison should be performed by taking the correspondence between events into account. Namely, in order to compare such inhomogeneous

M.-S. Hacid et al. (Eds.): ISMIS 2005, LNAI 3488, pp. 612–621, 2005.
© Springer-Verlag Berlin Heidelberg 2005

time-series medical data, we have to partly change our observation scales according to the granularity of data and the possible size of events.

Dynamic Time Warping (DTW) [3, 2] is a well-known method that compares irregular-length sequences without any discretization. It makes pairs of the nearest points, one from each sequence, allowing one-to-many matching. However, the comparison scheme of DTW is basically local dissimilarity and thus it does not perform structural comparison of the time series. Another well-known approach is subsequence clustering [4], that compares subsequences of the original sequences generated using a sliding window of the fixed width. However, it is pointed out that the representatives of clusters obtained using this approach do not correctly reflect the common features of sequences [5]. Frequency-domain based approaches [6, 7] can also be applied to time series analysis. However, in general they do not recognize the structural features of a sequence, for example, the place of inflection points. Therefore, it is difficult to represent and visualize the correspondence between partial sequences used for comparison.

This paper presents the modified multiscale matching, a pattern recognition-based comparison method that solves the above problems.

2 Modified Multiscale Matching

Multiscale matching is a method for observing and comparing two curves at various scales, from detail to gross. There are various methods for multiscale representation including the frequency-based methods. Among them, a method based on scale-space filtering [8, 12] is widely used, because (1) it employs curvature, which is a fundamental feature of planar curves [10], and (2) it preserves monotonicity of the structural changes induced by scale increase [11]. Later, Ueda et al. [13] enabled the use of discrete scales and comparison of largely distorted curves by introducing a segment-based matching, where a segment corresponds to a subsequence between two adjacent inflection points.

In this section, we present a method called modified multiscale matching, which enables us the multiscale comparison of time series. The main improvements are: (1) introduction of a new segment representation that elude the problem of shrinkage [14] at high scales, (2) introduction of a new dissimilarity measure that directly reflects the dissimilarity of sequence values.

2.1 Multiscale Description Using the Modified Bessel Function

Let t denote a time parameter and $x(t)$ denote a time series of examination results. Let σ denote an observation scale and $g(t, \sigma)$ be a Gaussian with variance σ^2. Then the time series at scale σ, $X(t, \sigma)$, is obtained by convoluting $x(t)$ with $g(t, \sigma)$ as follows.

$$X(t, \sigma) = x(t) \otimes g(t, \sigma) = \int_{-\infty}^{+\infty} x(u) \frac{1}{\sigma\sqrt{2\pi}} e^{-(t-u)^2/2\sigma^2} du \qquad (1)$$

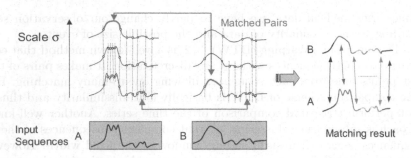

Fig. 1. Illustrative example of multiscale matching.

Figure 1 shows an example of multiscale description. Increase of scale corresponds to the increase of deviance in Gaussian function. Therefore, it induces the decrease of weights for neighbors, and smoothing over wide area. Consequently, simplified time series with less inflection points are obtained. Curvature of the time series at time point t is defined by

$$K(t,\sigma) = \frac{X''}{(1 + X'^2)^{3/2}} \tag{2}$$

where X' and X'' denotes the first- and second-order derivatives of $X(t,\sigma)$. The m-th order derivative of $X(t,\sigma)$, $X^{(m)}(t,\sigma)$, is defined by

$$X^{(m)}(t,\sigma) = \frac{\partial^m X(t,\sigma)}{\partial t^m} = x(t) \otimes g^{(m)}(t,\sigma) \tag{3}$$

It should be noted that many of the real-world time-series data, including medical data, can be discrete in time domain. Thus, a sampled Gaussian kernel is generally used for calculation of 1, changing an integral to summation. However, Lindeberg [9] pointed out that, a sampled Gaussian may lose some of the properties that a continuous Gaussian has, for example, non-creation of local extrema with the increase of scale. Additionally, in a sampled Gaussian kernel, the center value can be relatively large and imbalanced when the scale is very small. Ref. [9] suggests the use of kernel based on the modified Bessel function, as it is derived by incorporating the discrete property. Since this it influence the description ability of detailed structure of time series, we employed the Lindeberg's kernel and derive $X(t,\sigma)$ as follows.

$$X(t,\sigma) = \sum_{n=-\infty}^{\infty} e^{-\sigma} I_n(\sigma) x(t-n) \tag{4}$$

where $I_n(\sigma)$ denote the modified Bessel function of order n. The first- and second-order derivatives of $X(t,\sigma)$ are obtained as follows.

$$X'(t, \sigma) = \sum_{n=-\infty}^{\infty} -\frac{n}{\sigma} e^{-\sigma} I_n(\sigma) x(t - n) \tag{5}$$

$$X''(t, \sigma) = \sum_{n=-\infty}^{\infty} \frac{1}{\sigma} (\frac{n^2}{\sigma} - 1) e^{-\sigma} I_n(\sigma) x(t - n) \tag{6}$$

2.2   Trace of Segment Hierarchy and Matching

For each time series represented by multiscale description, we obtain the places of inflection points according to the sign of curvature. Then we divide each time series into a set of convex/concave segments, where both ends of a segment correspond to adjacent inflection points. Let A be a sequence at $\sigma^{(k)}$ composed of N segments. Then A is represented by $\mathbf{A}^{(k)} = \{a_i^{(k)} \mid i = 1, 2, \cdots, N^{(k)}\}$, where $a_i^{(k)}$ denotes i-th segment at scale $\sigma^{(k)}$. Similarly, Another sequence B at scale $\sigma^{(h)}$ is represented by $\mathbf{B}^{(h)} = \{b_j^{(h)} \mid j = 1, 2, \cdots, M^{(h)}\}$.

Next, we chase the cross-scale correspondence of inflection points from top scales to bottom scale. It defines the hierarchy of segments and enables us to guarantees connectivity of segments obtained from different scales. For details of algorithms for checking segment hierarchy, see ref. [13]. In order to apply the algorithm for closed curve to 1D time series, we allow replacement of odd number of segments at sequence ends, since cyclic property of a set of inflection points can be lost.

The main procedure of multiscale matching is to search the best set of segment pairs that satisfies both of the following conditions:

1. Complete Match: By concatenating all segments, original sequence should be completely formed without any gaps or overlaps.
2. Minimal Difference: The sum of segment dissimilarities over all segment pairs should be minimized.

The search is performed throughout all scales. For example, in 1, five contiguous segments at the lowest scale of Sequence A are integrated into one segment at the highest scale, and the integrated segments well match to one segment in Sequence B at the lowest scale. Thus the set of the five segments in Sequence A and the one segment in Sequence B will be considered as a candidate for corresponding subsequences. While, another pair of segments will be matched at the lowest scale. In this way, if segment pairs present short-term similarity, they are matched at a lower scale, and if they present long-term similarity, they are matched at a higher scale.

2.3   A New Segment Representation for Time Series and New Segment Difference

As described previously, the primary factor for selecting the best segment pairs is minimization of the accumulated dissimilarities. Therefore, the definition of segment dissimilarity is critical. Generally, the dissimilarity is derived by parameterizing the features of spaces, for example, curvature, length etc., and calculating the difference of two segments w.r.t. these parameters. It means that shape parameters of a segment are derived using the shape of smoothed curve at each scale. This approach includes the following problems when applied to time series.

- Shrinkage: If scale becomes higher, the shape of a time series will shrink toward a line or point, due to excessive smoothing with neighbors [14]. Sequence at a high scale contains almost flat segments, for which shape parameters becomes very small. Consequently, high-scale match will be too much facilitated. A cost can be added for suppressing excessive mergence of segments [13], however, it would make the dissimilarity measure be cost-sensitive.
- Mixture of multiple attributes in the resultant dissimilarity:
  In order to evaluate the structural dissimilarity of segments, different types of geometric features should be parameterized and included in the dissimilarity measure. However, this allows the presence of different attributes in the accumulated (total) dissimilarity, making it difficult to reversely interpret the contribution of each factors from the clustering results.

In order to solve these problems, we have developed a new segment representation and a new dissimilarity measure for time-series.

Shape Parameters Using Base Segments. According to the segment hierarchy, each segment can be exactly associated with one or more segments at the lowest scale, which we call base segments. Focusing on this feature, we derive shape parameters of each segment using those of the base segments. The main difference compared to the previous approach is that the smoothed curves are used only for determining places of inflection points and for tracing segment hierarchy, and never used for deriving segment shape parameters. By this we exclude the corruption of shapes induced by shrinkage at high scales.

The new shape parameters consist of the following four components.

- **Amplitude(amp)**: Vertical amplitude from the peak point to baseline.
- **Width (width)**: Width between both ends.
- **Vertical shift (height)**: Vertical shift between both ends.
- **Phase (phase)**: Phase at the left end.

Figure 2 left illustrates the shape parameters for a single base segment $a_i^{(0)}$. For simplicity, we omit the scale notation ($^{(0)}$) for base segments and represent $a_i^{(0)}$ as a_i. Amplitude of a base segment a_i, $amp(a_i)$, is measured from the peak point $pk[a_i]$ to the base line connecting both ends $left[a_i]$ and $right[a_i]$. The shape parameters of base segments will be inherited toward segments at a higher scale, until the base segments will be merged and replaced into another segment by smoothing. Thus the parameters will be preserved for scale changes that do not induce replacement of segments.

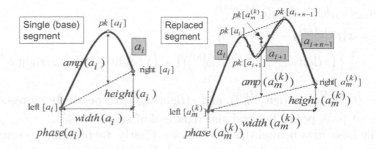

Fig. 2. Segment parameters: left: single (base) segment, right: replaced segments

Figure 2 right illustrates the shape parameters for a segment $a_m^{(k)}$ at scale k, that replaces n contiguous base segments $\{a_i, a_{i+1}, \ldots, a_{i+n-1}\}$. The peak point $pk[a_m^{(k)}]$ of the merged segment $a_m^{(k)}$ is assigned to the centroid of the peak points of the base segments $pk[a_i]$, $pk[a_{i+1}]$, $\ldots$, $pk[a_{i+n-1}]$. Segment $a_m^{(k)}$ inherits both ends left$[a_m^{(k)}]$ and right$[a_m^{(k)}]$ form the set of base segments. According to these three feature points, we obtain parameters $amp(a_m^{(k)})$, $phase(a_m^{(k)})$, $width(a_m^{(k)})$, and $height(a_m^{(k)})$.

$$d(a_m^{(k)}, b_l^{(h)}) = \max(d_{amp}, d_{width}, d_{height}, d_{phase}) + \gamma(\text{cost}(a_m^{(k)}) + \text{cost}(b_l^{(h)})) \quad (7)$$

where d_{amp} represents the difference of amplitude $d_{amp} = \left| amp(a_m^{(k)}) - amp(b_l^{(h)}) \right|$. Similarly, d_{width}, d_{height}, and d_{phase} represent the differences on width, vertical shift and phase respectively. The term $\text{cost}(a_m^{(k)})$ is a replacement cost added to the dissimilarity for suppressing excessive mergence of segments. We define it by the kurtosis of end points of all base segments and ratio of amplitude before/after replacement.

$$\text{cost}(a_m^{(k)}) = \text{kurt}(\mathbf{x_p}) + n \frac{\sum_{s=i}^{i+n-1} |amp(a_s)|}{\left| amp(a_m^{(k)}) \right|} \quad (8)$$

where $\mathbf{x_p}$ denotes a set of data values at all ends of base segments. $\{a_i, a_{i+1}, \ldots, a_{i+n-1}\}$. By this cost we facilitate replacement that increases amplitude, while suppressing mergence of vertically lined segments like sine curves.

Separation of Matching Parameters from Total Dissimilarity of Sequences. After obtaining the best set of segment pairs, we calculate the value-based total dissimilarity of the two time series, $D_{val}(A, B)$, defined by

$$D_{val}(A, B) = \frac{1}{Np} \sum_{i=1}^{Np} d_{val}(a_p, b_p). \quad (9)$$

where N_p denotes the number of matched segment pairs, $d_{val}(a_p, b_p)$ denotes the value-based difference for p-th segment pair. $d_{val}(a_p, b_p)$ is defined by

$$d_{val}(a_p, b_p) = d_{val}(a_m^{(k)}, b_l^{(h)})$$

$$= x(pk[a_m^{(k)}]) - x(pk[b_l^{(h)}])$$

$$+ \frac{1}{2}\left\{\left(x(\text{left}[a_m^{(k)}]) - x(\text{left}[b_l^{(h)}])\right) + \left(x(\text{right}[a_m^{(k)}]) - x(\text{right}[b_l^{(h)}])\right)\right\} \quad (10)$$

where $x(pk[a_m^{(k)}])$, $x(\text{left}[a_m^{(k)}])$, and $x(\text{right}[a_m^{(k)}])$ respectively represent the data values at peak point, left end and right end of segment $a_m^{(k)}$.

The basic idea behind this is as follows. Firstly, we obtain the correspondence of segments according to the structural dissimilarity represented by the four shape parameters. After that, we obtain the differences of data values for each of the segment pairs, and use their mean value as the value-based total dissimilarity of the two time series.

3   Experimental Results

We examined the usefulness of the proposed method on two types of data sets. The first data set was cylinder-bell-funnel data set [16] [17]; a simple synthetic data set which is well-known and frequently used in the temporal data mining community. The another data set is chronic hepatitis data set, a real-world medical data set that includes time-series laboratory examination results of the patients of chronic viral hepatitis B and C.

3.1   CBF Dataset

Experiments were performed as follows. (1) Generate a data set containing a total of 384 sequences; 128 sequences for each of the three classes, cylinder, bell, and funnel. (2) Compute the dissimilarities for all pairs of sequences in the data sets using the proposed method. This produced a 384×384 symmetric dissimilarity matrix. (3) Remove one sequence, and predict its class according to the class label of the nearest sequence. The nearest sequence is selected according to the dissimilarity matrix. (4) Repeat step (3) for each of the 384 sequences, and evaluate the prediction error rate. Namely, we performed the leave-one-out validation with 1-Nearest Neighbor classification algorithm, using the dissimilarity matrix obtained by the proposed method as in [18].

Before applying MSM, all of the input sequences were normalized in both horizontal and vertical directions by dividing by their standard deviation (because the length of sequences in cylinder-bell-funnel dataset were all the same, we simply normalized them in horizontal direction by dividing their length). The parameters in MSM were set as follows: starting scale = 0.1, scale interval = 0.5, number of scales = 100, cost weight $\gamma = 0.15$.

The error rate was 0.054, which is quite better compared to the results summarized in [18] (2nd best below the Euclidean distance, whose error rate = 0.003; we also reproduced the same result).

Next, we evaluated whether the dissimilarity matrix can be used to form meaningful clusters. We modified parts (3)-(4) of the above experimental procedures as follows. (3) remove one sequence, and using the 383×383 matrix, perform conventional average-linkage agglomerative clustering [19] specifying the number of clusters to 3. (4) assign class label to each of the three clusters by the voting. (5) Perform 1-Nearest Neighbor classification for the removed sequence, and evaluate the classification accuracy. (6) remove another sequence and perform the same procedure. This is applied to all the 384 sequences.

The error rate was 0.042, similar to the previous experiment. We also performed the same experiments using the Euclidean distance, and its error rate was 0.216. This relatively high error rate of Euclidean distance implied that the dissimilarity matrix failed to form the clusters representing correct class distributions.

3.2   Chronic Hepatitis Dataset

We applied the proposed method to the chronic hepatitis dataset [15], which was used as a common dataset at ECML/PKDD Discovery Challenge 2002-2004. Due to space limitation, we just present a piece of the results. Figure 3 shows examples of the clustered Platelet (PLT) sequences, obtained using modified MSM as a comparison method and average-linkage AHC as a grouping method.

Figure 3 left shows cluster 4, that contains three F1 (fibrosis stage 1; larger number means severer stage) cases and one F1 cases. Common decreasing trend was clearly observed. The middle of Figure 3 is cluster 6, that contains one F1, one F3 and one F4 cases. Similarity to cluster 4, clear decreasing trend was observed; however, the method captured differences on their mean levels, and could differentiate from cluster 4. It also demonstrates that the method correctly captures common features among sequences of different length. The right of the figure shows cluster 10, that contains increasing cases. For details, see ref. [20].

Fig. 3. Examples of the clustered sequences. Left: cluster 4 (4 cases), middle: 6 (3 cases), right: 10 (5 cases).

4   Conclusions

In this paper, we have presented a new analysis method of long time-series medical databases based on the improved multiscale matching. The method enabled us to compare sequences by partly changing observation scales. We have introduced a new representation of segment parameters directly induced from the base segments, in order to elude the problem of shrinkage occurs at high scales. Experiments on the chronic hepatitis data showed the usefulness of this method. The future work include validation of the method using other datasets and detailed analysis of the computational complexity.

Acknowledgments

This work was supported in part by the Grant-in-Aid for Scientific Research on Priority Area (B)(13131208)" Development of the Active Mining System in Medicine Based on Rough Sets" by the Ministry of Education, Culture, Science and Technology of Japan.

References

1. E. Keogh (2001): Mining and Indexing Time Series Data. Tutorial at the 2001 IEEE International Conference on Data Mining.
2. S. Chu and E. J. Keogh and D. Hart and M. J. Pazzani (2002): Iterative Deepening Dynamic Time Warping for Time Series. In Proc. the Second SIAM Int'l Conf. Data Mining, 148–156.
3. D. Sankoff and J. Kruskal (1999): Time Warps, String Edits, and Macromolecules. CLSI Publications.
4. G. Das and K. Lin and H. Mannila and G. Renganathan and P. Smyth (1998): Rule Discovery from Time Series. Knowledge Discovery and Data Mining, 16–22.
5. E. Keogh and J. Lin and W. Truppel (2003): Clustering of Time Series Subsequences is Meaningless: Implications for Previous and Future Research. Proc. the IEEE ICDM 2003, 115–122.
6. K. P. Chan and A. W. Fu (2003): Efficient Time Series Matching by Wavelets. Proc the IEEE ICDM 1999, 126–133.
7. K. Kawagoe and T. Ueda (2002): A Similarity Search Method of Time Series Data with Combination of Fourier and Wavelet Transforms. Proc. the IEEE TIME-2002, 86–92.
8. A. P. Witkin (1983): Scale-space filtering. Proc. the Eighth IJCAI, 1019–1022.
9. T. Lindeberg (1990): Scale-Space for Discrete Signals. IEEE Trans. PAMI, 12(3):234–254.
10. G. Dudek and J. K. Tostsos (1997) Shape Representation and Recognition from Multiscale Curvature. Comp. Vis. Img Understanding, 68(2):170–189.
11. J. Babaud and A. P. Witkin and M. Baudin and O. Duda (1986): Uniqueness of the Gaussian kernel for scale-space filtering. IEEE Trans. PAMI, 8(1):26–33.
12. F. Mokhtarian and A. K. Mackworth (1986): Scale-based Description and Recognition of planar Curves and Two Dimensional Shapes. IEEE Transactions on Pattern Analysis and Machine Intelligence, PAMI-8(1): 24-43.
13. N. Ueda and S. Suzuki (1990):http://lisp.vse.cz/challenge/ecmlpkdd2002/
A Matching Algorithm of Deformed Planar Curves Using Multiscale Convex/Concave Structures. IEICE Transactions on Information and Systems, J73-D-II(7): 992–1000.
14. Lowe, D.G (1980): Organization of Smooth Image Curves at Multiple Scales. International Journal of Computer Vision, 3:119–130.
15. URL: http://lisp.vse.cz/challenge/
16. N. Saito (1994): Local Feature Extraction and Its Application using a Library of Bases. Ph.D. Thesis, Yale University.
17. P. Geurts (2001): Pattern Extraction for Time-Series Classification. Proceedings of PAKDD-01 115-127.

18. E. Keogh and S. Kasetty (2003): On the Need for Time Series Data Mining Benchmarks: A Survey and Empirical Demonstration. Data Mining And Knowledge Discovery 7:349-371.
19. B. S. Everitt, S. Landau, and M. Leese (2001): Cluster Analysis Fourth Edition. Arnold Publishers.
20. S. Tsumoto, S. Hirano, and K. Takabayashi (2005): Development of the Active Mining System in Medicine Based on Rough Sets. Journal of Japan Society of Artificial Intelligence (in press).

Efficient Causal Interaction Learning with Applications in Microarray

Yong Ye and Xintao Wu*

UNC Charlotte
{yye, xwu}@uncc.edu

Abstract. The prediction and identification of physical and genetic interactions from gene expression data is one of the most challenging tasks of modern functional genomics. Although various interaction analysis methods have been well studied in data mining and statistics fields, we face new challenges in applying these methods to the analysis of microarray data. In this paper, we investigate an enhanced constraint based approach for causal structure learning. We integrate with graphical gaussian modeling and use its independence graph as input of next phase's causal analysis. We also present graphical decomposition techniques to further improve the performance. The experimental results show that our enhanced method makes it feasible to explore causal interactions interactively for applications with a large number of variables (e.g., microarray data analysis).

1 Introduction

The prediction and identification of physical and genetic interactions from gene expression data is one of the most challenging tasks of modern functional genomics. Although various interaction analysis methods (e.g., Causal Probabilistic Networks [11, 6], Graphical Gaussian Modeling [9], Loglinear Modeling [12], Association Rule [1] etc.) have been well studied in data mining and statistics fields, we face new challenges in applying these methods to the analysis of microarray data. First, genes in rows of gene expression matrices are of very high dimensionality (e.g., 10^3 - 10^4 genes) while samples in columns are of relatively low dimensionality (e.g., 10^1 - 10^2 samples). Second, the microarray data are usually corrupted with a substantial amount of measurement noise. Third, although most of the genes with significant differential expression were included, these only cover about 3 % of the whole genome - still there are also other potentially relevant hidden factors. Therefore, there is a great need for new tools to explore and analyze complex gene interactions in a highly interactive environment, which requires the computational aspects of modeling both efficient and effective.

As causal network learned can present the knowledge embedded in the microarray data in a manner that is intuitive and familiar to biologists (e.g., edges between any two variables in the graph denote direct causal relationships between the two variables.),

---

* This research was supported, in part, by funds provided by the University of North Carolina at Charlotte.

M.-S. Hacid et al. (Eds.): ISMIS 2005, LNAI 3488, pp. 622–630, 2005.
© Springer-Verlag Berlin Heidelberg 2005

many causal network construction algorithms have been investigated and applied in genetic regulatory network analysis. Generally, these algorithms come into two flavors: Bayesian (search and score) approaches [6], and constraint-based conditional independence approaches [11].

Bayesian approaches use heuristic searching methods to construct a model and then evaluate it using different scoring criteria (e.g., bayesian scoring, entropy, and minimum description length etc.). While bayesian model averaging over the space of structures (or even just variable orders) is computationally intractable, constraint-based conditional independence test approaches, which do not search the space of models, seem an appealing alternative. Generally, they start from the complete undirected graph, then thin that graph by removing edges conditional independence relations in various orders. The advantage is that they are able to produce a single representation of the knowledge inferable from the microarray data. However, these approaches need to take a long time to finish when a large amount of variables are present, which makes interactive exploration of microarray data impossible.

In this paper, we propose an enhanced constraint based approach to learn causal interactions from microarray. As constraint based causal learning approaches are with high computational cost, we use the undirected independence graph which is the output of graphical gaussian modeling, rather than the complete graph. To further improve performance and support better interactive exploration, we apply graph decomposition techniques to decompose large independence graph into subgraphs and apply causal modeling method on each component to derive causal interactions respectively.

2   Constraint-Based Causal Modeling Revisited

Let $S = \{s_1, s_2, \cdots, s_m\}$ be a set of samples or conditions and $G = \{g_1, g_2, \cdots, g_n\}$ be a set of genes. The microarray data can be represented as $X = \{x_{ij} \| i = 1, \cdots, n, j = 1, \cdots, m\}(n \gg m)$, where x_{ij} corresponds to the expression value of gene g_i in sample s_j. In this section, we revisit constraint based causal modeling which will be used in our paper.

The constraint-based approaches use data to make categorical decisions about whether particular conditional-independence constraints hold and then pieces these decisions together by looking for those sets of causal structures that are consistent with the constraints. In [11] Spirtes et al. proposed a PC constraint based method which starts from the complete undirected graph, then thins that graph by removing edges with zero order conditional independence relations, thins again with first order conditional independence relations, and so on. The set of variables conditioned on need only to be a subset of the set of variables adjacent to one or the other of the variables conditioned. Figure 1 shows the algorithm (The correctness of the procedure is given by Theorem 3.4 on page 47 of [11]).

The complexity of the PC constraint-based causal modeling method is bounded by the largest degree in the undirected graph. In the worst case, the number of conditional independence tests required by the algorithm is bounded by $\frac{n^2(n-1)^{k-1}}{(k-1)!}$ where k be the maximal degree of any vertex and n be the number of vertices [11].

PC
BEGIN
1   Form the complete undirected graph G
2   For each edge $e = (X, Y)$
3   If variables X and Y are independent
4   remove e from G
5       $G_1 = G$
6       $i = 1$
7   While(no more edges can be removed)
8   For each remaining edge $e = (X, Y)$
9   If variables X and Y are independent conditional on
                one subset s ($| s | = i$) of their adjacent neighbor
10   remove e from G_i
11          $G_{i+1} = G_i$
12   i = i+ 1
13   For each triple X, Y, Z such that $X - Y - Z$ is in graph but $X - Z$ is not
14   If Y is not in the d-separated subset(X, Z)
15   orient $X - Y - Z$ as $X \rightarrow Y \leftarrow Z$
16   While (no more edges can be oriented)
17   If $A \rightarrow B, B - C, A$ and C are not adjacent, and there is no arrowhead at B
18   orient $B - C$ as $B \rightarrow C$
19   If there is directed path from A to B, and an edge between A and B
20   orient $A - B$ as $A \rightarrow B$
END

Fig. 1. PC constraint-based causal modeling algorithm revisited

3   Our Enhanced *GGM+PC* Method

3.1   Outline of *GGM+PC*

Our approach is outlined as follows.

1. Preprocessing: we subject the input data $\mathcal{X}$ to clustering or association rule mining, prior to analyzing gene interactions.
2. GGM: For each cluster
   - Compute the variance matrix $\mathcal{V}$ where v_{ij}, $i, j = 1, \cdots, n$, corresponds to covariance between gene g_i and g_j.
   - Compute its inverse $\mathcal{S} = \mathcal{V}^{-1}$.
   - Scale $\mathcal{S}$ to have a unit diagonal and compute partial correlations $pr_{x_i x_j \cdot g}$.
   - Draw the independence graph according to the rule that no edge is included in the graph if the absolute value of partial correlation coefficient is less than some threshold s.

3. Decomposition: For those graphs with large number of vertices, decompose those independence graphs into components.
4. Causal Modeling: For each component, apply *PC* (line 7-20 of Figure 1) with its independence graph as input.

We have two major enhancements. First, we use the undirected independence graph which is the output of graphical gaussian modeling, rather than the complete graph suggested in *PC* algorithm, as input. The advantage of graphical gaussian modeling is that it can generate an undirected independence graph for a relatively large set of genes very quickly. The independence graph is much simpler than the complete graph, which can significantly decrease searching complexity. Second, the independence graph can even further be decomposed into components and the causal analysis is done over each small component. We leave the discussion of this part in Section 3.3. The motivation here is that though many biological pathways and processes are known to involve interactions among a relatively large number of genes the genetic network topology is dominated by a few highly connected nodes which link the rest of the less connected nodes.

One potential problem here is that it becomes infeasible to use graphical gaussian modeling when the size of genes exceeds that of samples. This is because the correlation matrix is generally degenerate as the matrix rank is bounded by the sample size. In our system, we apply various existing clustering methods and frequent item set mining to get gene clusters priori applying graphical gaussian modeling. Though this preprocessing step is not our focus in this paper, we would emphasize this step is very important. The number of genes contained in the resulting clusters or frequent itemsets is expected to be less than the size of samples, thus avoiding the matrix rank problem.

3.2   Graphical Gaussian Modeling

Graphical gaussian model [9], also known as covariance selection model, assumes multivariate normal distribution for underlying data and satisfies the pairwise conditional independence restrictions which are shown in the independence graph of a jointly normal set of random variables. The independence graph is defined by a set of pairwise conditional independence relationships that determine the edge set of the graph. A crucial concept of applying graphical gaussian model is *partial correlation*, which measures the correlation between two variables after the common effects of all other variables in the genome are removed.

$$pr_{xy.z} = \frac{r_{xy} - r_{xz}r_{yz}}{\sqrt{(1 - r_{xz}^2)(1 - r_{yz}^2)}} \tag{1}$$

Equation 1 shows the form for partial correlation of two genes, g_x and g_y, while controlling for a third gene variable g_z, where r_{xy} denotes Pearson's correlation coefficient. The partial correlation, $pr_{xy.z}$ of genes g_x and g_y with respect to gene g_z may be considered to be the correlation r_{xy} of g_x and g_y, after the effect of g_z is removed. Partial correlations that remain significantly different from zero may be taken as indicators of a possible causal link.

When a set of genes g are present, the partial correlation can be computed by $pr_{xy.g} = -\frac{s_{xy}}{\sqrt{s_{xx}s_{yy}}}$, where s_{xy} is the xy-th element of the inverse of variance matrix ($\mathcal{S} = \mathcal{V}^{-1}$). It is known that conditional independence constraints are equivalent to specifying zeros in the inverse variance. Under the assumption of multivariate normality, tests for vanishing partial correlation are equivalent as tests for conditional independence, i.e., $pr_{xy \cdot g} = 0 \iff x \perp y \mid g$. The independence graph is then determined according to the rule that no edge is included in the graph if Fisher's z test is less than the specified threshold. It is important to note that partial correlation is different from standard correlation, indicates better evidence for genetic regulatory links than standard correlation, as shown from our previous results [13], and is in agreement with biological interpretation.

3.3   Graphical Decomposition

It has become increasingly clear that signaling pathways interact with one another and the final biological response is shaped by interaction between pathways. It is expected that the relatively large independence graph generated from graphical gaussian modeling may show the interactions among different pathways and the inter-pathway interactions is not as strong as gene interactions within each pathway. This suggests we may decompose the independence graph into basic, irreducible components and each component may respond to a single pathway.

Graph-theoretical results show that if a graph corresponding to a graphical model is decomposable into subgraphs by a clique separator [1], the maximum likelihood estimates for the parameters of the model can easily be derived by combining the estimates of the models on the simpler subgraphs. Hence, applying a divide-and-conquer approach based on the decompositions will make the procedure applicable to much larger subsets of genes.

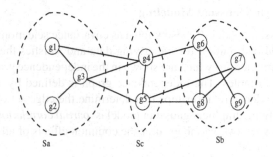

Fig. 2. Graphical decomposition

The theory may be interpreted in the following way as shown in Figure 2: if two disjoint subsets of vertices S_a and S_b are separated by a subset S_c in the sense that all paths from S_a to S_b go through S_c, then the variables in S_a are conditionally independent of those in S_b given the variables in S_c. The subgraphs may be further decomposed into subgraphs $S_a \cup S_c$ and $S_b \cup S_c$. The requirement that the subgraph on S_c is complete

---

[1] A clique is a subset of vertices which induce a complete subgraph for which the addition of any further vertex renders the induced subgraph incomplete. A graph is complete if all vertices are joined with undirected edges. In other words, the clique is maximally complete.

implies that there is no further independence constraints on the elements of S_c, so that this factorization contains all the information about the joint distribution.

4   Experimental Results

The experiments were conducted in a DELL Precision 340 Workstation (Redhat Linux 9.0 operating system), with one 2.4G processor, and 1G bytes of RAM. We used Yeast data set which contains expression profiles for 6316 transcripts corresponding to 300 diverse mutations and chemical treatments in yeast [7].

4.1   Performance Analysis

Figure 3 shows the execution time of our enhanced method of *GGM+PC* with gene clusters with different sizes. We randomly chose ten clusters with size varying from 10 to 150 respectively. Please note the maximum of genes contained in one single cluster is 300 as we only have 300 samples in this Yeast data set. For each cluster, we varied threshold s used for vanishing partial correlation in independence graph and reported their execution times respectively. We also included the execution time of original *PC* method. As the original *PC* method uses complete graph as input and does not use graphical decomposition, its effect is equivalent to our *GGM+PC* with threshold s = 0. Figure 3 shows for all Yeast clusters with size exceeding 50, our enhanced method *GGM+PC* is significantly better than that of original *PC* while there is no much difference when cluster size is less than 50. For example, our *GGM+PC* needs few seconds to process cluster with 150 genes while the original *PC* needs 228 seconds. This significant improvement of performance makes interactive exploration feasible. For cluster with 260 genes, the original *PC* needs more than 5 hours while our enhanced method needs only about 1 minute.

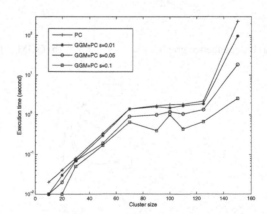

Fig. 3. Execution time vs. varying cluster size for original *PC* and $GGM + PC$ with different thresholds s

4.2   Causal Interaction Analysis

The performance of our method was further evaluated by how well our predictions agree with the currently available protein interaction databases. As an example, we chose the cluster that shows potential interactions between SNO and SNZ family proteins. Figure 4(a) shows independence graph generated from graphical gaussian modeling for one selected gene group with 12 genes . Note we used dashed lines to indicate a negative partial correlation and solid line to indicate a positive partial correlation. The negative correlation (e.g., between YMR095C and YBR250C) in Figure 4(a) indicates that the functions of each pair of genes may counteract with each other (activators and repressors) of the biosynthesis/metabolism pathways or their expression is negatively regulated by the other gene in each pair.

Many causal interactions in our graphs receive some solid biological explanations. Furthermore, our results of causal interactions have revealed some previously unknown gene interactions that have solid biological explanations. Figure 4(b) and 4(c) show causal networks learned from *GGM+PC* and original *PC* respectively. We can see both causal graphs agree on most causal interactions among genes. The only difference is that YMR095C and YJR025C are among causes of YIL116W which is a cause of YKL218C

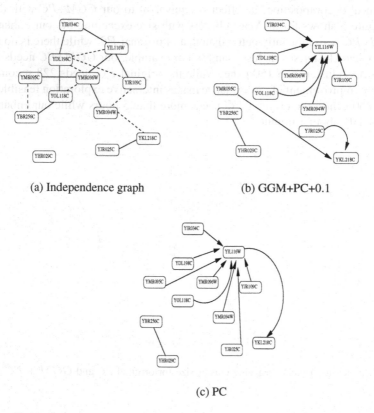

(a) Independence graph   (b) GGM+PC+0.1

(c) PC

Fig. 4. Comparison of causal structures learned from *GGM+PC* and *PC*

in Figure 4(c) while YMR095C and YJR025C are two causes of YKL218C and there is no causal relationship between YIL116W and YKL218C in Figure 4(b). Since the biological function of YKL218C is unknown, we speculate that YKL218C might be involved in NAD biosynthesis pathway since its expression correlates with that of YJR025C.

5   Related Work

Gene clusters from various clustering methods can be interpreted as a network of co-regulated genes, which may encode interacting proteins that are involved in the same biological processes. However, clustering methods cannot address gene interactions as they cannot give the information on how one gene influences other genes in the same cluster. In [4], association rules [1] are applied to investigate how the expression of one gene may be associated with the expression of a set of genes. Recently, loglinear modeling has been investigated to overcome the limitations of support-based association algorithms [12] and was applied in micorarray data analysis [13]. This method can be used to reveal all significant high order non-linear combinatorial interactions (e.g., a gene is over expressed only if several genes are jointly over expressed, but not if at least one of them is not over expressed). However, both association rule and loglinear modeling require a discretization of the data, which may cause some information loss during discretization. Furthermore, interactions learned are undirected instead of directed causal interactions investigated in this paper.

Bayesian network has recently been investigated for gene regulatory networks [5]. Basically, the techniques rely on a matching score to evaluate the networks with respect to the data and search for the network with the optimal score. The difficulty with this technique is that learning the bayesian network structure is an NP-hard problem, as the number of DAGs is superexponential in the number of genes, and exhaustive search is intractable. Currently causal learning techniques only scale up to a few hundred variables in the best case. For example, the public available versions of the PC [11] and the TPDA [3] algorithms accept datasets with only 100 and 255 variables respectively. In [10], the authors investigate the problem of determining causal relationships, instead of mere associations, when mining market basket data. However, it focuses more on inferring the lack of causality than inferring causality. Other methods such as Boolean Networks, differential equations, stochastic master equations, and rule based formalisms are discussed in [8].

6   Conclusions and Future Work

In this paper we presented an enhanced causal structure learning approach, which allows users to analyze complex gene interactions in a highly interactive environment, permitting exploration. Experiments demonstrated that our method is both efficient and effective. There are some aspects of this work that merit further research. Among them, we will compare our constraint based approach with bayesian based approach in detail for microarray data where gene expressions usually are noisy and stochastic. We have run our constraint based approach and bayesian based appproach respectively using ALARM data, a bayesian network used in medical diagnosis decision support system

[2] and found causal structures learned are very similar. However, we got very different causal networks on yeast data using constraint based and bayesian based approaches. Another problem is the dimensionality problem. We are trying to relieve this problem by incorporating apriori knowledge during the modeling process. From the existing protein-protein interaction databases, users may already know some causal interaction relationships. Those apriori known relationships will be incorporated as the input, which can make the method more effective and efficient.

References

1. R. Agrawal, T. Imilienski, and A. Swami. Mining association rules between sets of items in large databases. In *Proceedings of the ACM SIGMOD International Conference on Management of Database*, pages 207–216, 1993.
2. I. Beinlich, H. Suermondt, and et al. The alarm monitoring system: A case study with two probabilistic inference techniques for belief netowrks. In *Proceedings of the Second European Conference ub Artificial Intelligence in Medicine*, 1989.
3. J. Cheng, R. Greiner, J. Kelly, D. Bell, and W. Liu. Learning bayesian networks from data: An information theory based approach. *Artificial Intelligence*, 137:43–90, 2002.
4. C. Creighton and S. Hanash. Mining gene expression databases for association rules. *Bioinformatics*, 19-1:79–86, 2003.
5. N. Friedman, M. Linial, I. Nachman, and D. Peer. Using bayesian networks to analyze expression data. In *Proceedings of the fourth Annual International Conference on Computational Molecular Biology*, 2000.
6. D. Heckerman. Bayesian networks for data mining. *Data Mining and Knowledge Discovery*, 1:79–119, 1997.
7. T. Hughes, M. Marton, A. R. Jones, C. Roberts, R. Stoughton, C. Armour, H. Bennett, E. Coffey, H. Dai, Y. He, M. J. Kidd, and A. M. King. Functional discovery via a compendium of expression profiles. *Cell*, 102:109–126, 2000.
8. H. D. Jong. Modeling and simulation of genetic regulatory systems: a literature review. *Journal of Computational Biology*, 9(1):67–103, 2002.
9. S. Lauritzen. *Graphical Models*. Oxford University Press, 1996.
10. C. Silverstein, S. Brin, R. Motwani, and J. Ullman. Scalable techniques for mining causal structures. In *Proceedings of the International Conference on Very Large Data Bases*, pages 594–605, 1998.
11. P. Spirtes, C. Glymour, and R. Scheines. *Causation, Prediction, and Search*. The MIT Press, 2000.
12. X. Wu, D. Barbará, and Y. Ye. Screening and interpreting multi-item associations based on log-linear modeling. In *Proceedings of the ACM SIGKDD International Conference on Knowledge Discovery and Data Mining*, pages 276–285. Washington, DC, August 2003.
13. X. Wu, Y. Ye, and L. Zhang. Graphical modeling based gene interaction analysis for microarray data. *KDD Explorations*, 5(2):91–100, 2003.

A Dynamic Adaptive Sampling Algorithm (DASA) for Real World Applications: Finger Print Recognition and Face Recognition

Ashwin Satyanarayana and Ian Davidson

State University of New York, Albany,
Department of Computer Science , LI-67A,
1400 Washington Ave, Albany, NY-12222
{ashwin, davidson}@cs.albany.edu

Abstract. In many real world problems, data mining algorithms have access to massive amounts of data (defense and security). Mining all the available data is prohibitive due to computational (time and memory) constraints. Thus, the smallest sufficient training set size that obtains the same accuracy as the entire available dataset remains an important research question. Progressive sampling randomly selects an initial small sample and increases the sample size using either geometric or arithmetic series until the error converges, with the sampling schedule determined apriori. In this paper, we explore sampling schedules that are adaptive to the dataset under consideration. We develop a general approach to determine how many instances are required at each iteration for convergence using Chernoff Inequality. We try our approach on two real world problems where data is abundant: face recognition and finger print recognition using neural networks. Our empirical results show that our dynamic approach is faster and uses much fewer examples than other existing methods. However, the use of Chernoff bound requires the samples at each iteration to be independent of each other. Future work will look at removing this limitation which should further improve performance.

1 Introduction

Many mining algorithms have the property that as the training set size increase, the accuracy increases until at some point there is no benefit to training set size increase. This plot of the number of training set instances as a function of predictive accuracy is commonly referred to as a learning curve.

Given a dataset, a sampling procedure, and an induction algorithm, we define n_{min} to be the size of the smallest sufficient training set such that:

(1) models built with smaller training sets have lower accuracy than the model built with training set of size n_{min} and

(2) models built with larger training sets have no significant higher accuracy than the model built with training set of size n_{min} (see **Fig. 1**).

M.-S. Hacid et al. (Eds.): ISMIS 2005, LNAI 3488, pp. 631–640, 2005.
© Springer-Verlag Berlin Heidelberg 2005

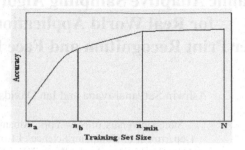

Fig. 1. A hypothetical plot of predictive accuracy versus training set size

Determining this smallest sufficient training sample size remains an important open question. A too small training set will result in sub-optimal generalization performance. A too large training set will be time consuming to learn from. The typical solution that is employed is to start with a small random sample of data and to add new instances until a test of convergence is passed. This approach is referred to as *Progressive sampling* [4]. The two fundamental parts to learning curve convergence are testing whether the error has stabilized and if not, determining how many more instances to add. Previous work added data points in a geometric [4] or arithmetic series [2] with convergence simply defined as no significant increase in training accuracy [2][3]. In all these schemes the sampling schedule is fixed apriori and does not change adaptively, based on the dataset under consideration. In this paper, we will be focusing more on the second part, which deals with how to adaptively create the sampling schedule dependent on the dataset.

Our contributions in this paper include a principled dynamic adaptive sampling approach that estimates the number of instances required for learning curve convergence at each iteration. We then implement our and other approaches for training Neural Networks (for face recognition and finger print recognition).

The format of the paper is as follows. We begin by surveying previous work on the learning curve phenomenon. In section 2, we present background information for confidence bounds and Chernoff inequality. We then provide our motivation and methodology in section 3. In section 4, we derive our adaptive schedule, the stopping criteria and show our algorithm. We discuss Neural Networks for recognizing patterns in section 5. We then perform experiments on real datasets in the next section. We finally summarize our results and conclude.

1.1 Prior Learning Curve Literature

Empirical work by John and Langley [2] compare *Arithmetic sampling* with *Static sampling*. *Static sampling* computes n_{min} without progressive sampling, based on a sample's statistical similarity to the entire dataset. *Arithmetic sampling* uses a schedule $S_a = \{|D_1|, |D_1|+\beta, |D_1|+2\beta \dots |D_1|+k.\beta\}$, where $|D_1|$ is the starting sample size, and β is the fixed difference between successive terms. They show that arithmetic sampling produces more accurate models than static sampling. However, as argued by Provost et al [4] the main drawback of arithmetic sampling is that if n_{min} is a large multiple of $|D_1|$ then the approach will require many runs of the underlying induction algorithm. Provost, Jensen & Oates [4] consider incrementally adding a geometrically increasing number of cases. *Geometric sampling* uses the schedule $S_g = a^k.|D_1| = \{|D_1|,a.|D_1|,a^2.|D_1|,a^3.|D_1|....a^k.|D_1|\}$, where 'a' is the common ratio. More recently, the work of Meek, Theisson & Heckerman [3] discusses their 'learning curve sampling method' in which they: 1) Monitor the increasing costs and performance as larger and larger amounts of data are used for training, and 2) Terminate learning when future costs outweigh future benefits. In their work they still use geometric sampling but with an enhanced convergence test that depends on the problem.

The computational learning theory community [1], is largely interested in determining apriori the total number of training examples required by the learner. That is, no progressive sampling occurs. The results of their work are primarily limited to PAC learners.

Though the above research has provided many key insights into the learning curve phenomenon it does not generally address a dynamic, adaptive (that varies with the problem) approach to determine the number of instances required at each iteration. We answer this question with our work and define an associated convergence test.

2 Background: Confidence Bounds and Chernoff Inequality

In this section we introduce the utility confidence bound and the Chernoff Inequality and show how we can relate these two concepts.

Definition 1: (*utility confidence interval* [6]) *Let* u *be the utility function. Let* u(D) *denote the true quality when using all of the data, and let* û(D_i) *denote its estimated quality based on a sample* $D_i \subseteq D$ *of size m. Then* θ *is a utility confidence bound for* u *iff for any* δ, *0< δ ≤ 1,*

$$\Pr[\,|u(D) - û(D_i)| \geq \theta\,] \leq \delta \tag{1}$$

Equation (1) says that θ provides a two-sided confidence interval on û(D_i) with confidence δ. In other words, the probability of drawing a sample D_i (when drawing instances independently and identically distributed from D), such that the difference between true and estimated utility of any hypothesis disagree by θ or more (in either direction) lies below δ.

In this paper, the utility function we consider is the average over all instances, of some instance function $f(x_i)$, where $x_i \in D$. The utility is then defined as

$$u(D) = \frac{1}{|D|}\sum_{i=1}^{|D|} f(x_i) \text{ (the average over the entire dataset), and} \tag{2}$$

$$û(D_i) = \frac{1}{|D_i|}\sum_{i=1}^{|D_i|} f(x_i) \text{ (the average over the sample } D_i).$$

The instance function $f(x_i)$ used in this paper is the *classification accuracy* (where $f(x_i)$ is 0 or 1).

Definition 2: (*Chernoff Inequality* [7]) *Consider the independent Bernoulli trials* $X_1,X_2,....,X_m$ *with* $\Pr[X_i=1] = p$ *(probability of success) and* $\Pr[X_i=0] = 1-p$

(probability of failure).Let X *be the sum of the outcomes of these 'm' trials:* $X = X_1+X_2+....+X_m$. *If we denote* p' *as X/m, then the general form of Chernoff Bounds (where the expected value of* X, E[X]= mp) *is:*

$$\Pr[|\,p - p'| \geq \varepsilon] \leq e^{-mp\varepsilon^2/2} \tag{3}$$

Chernoff inequality is used to bound the chance that an arbitrary random variable X takes a value that is far away from its expected value E[X]. We now, combine the two concepts, namely, confidence bounds and the Chernoff inequality as:

(a) We are using a 0-1 loss function as the classification accuracy for each example,
(b) The utility function is the average over all the instances of the 0-1 loss function.

Combining Equation (1) and Equation (3) we get:

$$\Pr[|\,u(D) - \hat{u}(D_i)\,| \geq \varepsilon] \leq e^{-mp\varepsilon^2/2} \leq \delta \tag{4}$$

Bounds such as Chernoff , Hoeffding, Rademacher and Chebycheff bounds have been used in other areas such as error bound calculation [1], finding interesting patterns in a database [6], determining the number of models in an ensemble [8], learning from infinite data in finite time [10] and Rademacher sampling [5].

3 Motivation and Methodology

There are three fundamental goals that we would like to achieve:

(a) An adaptive sampling schedule, that *hill-climbs* along the learning curve, towards the optimum $n_{min.}$ in as *few steps as possible.*
(b) An adaptive *stopping criterion* to determine when the learning curve has reached optimum point in the learning curve (the plateau region).
(c) Geometric or arithmetic sampling approach runs the risk of overshooting n_{min}. Therefore, we would like to minimize the amount of overshooting over n_{min}.

The two key questions that we have to address here are: (a) When do we *stop* adding more instances? (b) How do we determine *how many* instances are required convergence? To address these questions, our work describes a general sampling algorithm, DASA, that hill climbs to $n_{min,.}$ Given the approximation and confidence parameters, ε and $\delta > 0$, DASA efficiently determines a sampling schedule adaptively, adding instances at each iteration. We describe our methodology in this section.

From an initial sample, D_1 whose size is $1/10^{th}$ the size of the entire dataset (determining the starting sample size is an open problem), we apply some learning algorithm (e.g. back propagation for neural networks) to it, gather utility measures— classification accuracy — of that initial sample and then determine whether to add in more number of instances. When to stop this process is a sequential decision problem, either stop learning or add more points.

Let D_{opt} be the oracle-optimal sample whose size is n_{min} the smallest sufficient sample size (i.e. $|D_{opt}| = n_{min}$). Ideally we would stop when $|u(D_{opt}) - \hat{u}(D_i)| < \varepsilon$, (for some sample D_i), that is, when we are within ε distance from the optimal utility measure

$u(D_{opt})$ (in either direction). Since we do not know $u(D_{opt})$, we use the "myopic" strategy (look one step at a time) where we assume that the current utility measure is the optimal one. Consider the current stage i, previous stage $i-1$ and their corresponding utility measures $\hat{u}(D_i)$ and $\hat{u}(D_{i-1})$ obtained from the samples D_i and D_{i-1} respectively. If $|\hat{u}(D_i) - \hat{u}(D_{i-1})| < \varepsilon$, then according to our assumption we have reached convergence as the utility has stabilized. If $|\hat{u}(D_i) - \hat{u}(D_{i-1})| \geq \varepsilon$ then more instances are needed. How many instances to add can be derived from Chernoff Inequality (Equation (3)):

$$\Pr\left[|\hat{u}(D_i) - \hat{u}(D_{i-1})| \geq \varepsilon\right] \leq e^{-mp\varepsilon^2/2}$$

The Chernoff inequality gives us an estimate for total number of instances (m) to ensure that the difference will be within distance ε of the optimum utility. We can upper bound the above equation by δ which is the chance of failure and solve for m. We then **create a new sample** (drawn randomly) for our incremental algorithm, apply our learner and calculate the utility $\hat{u}(D_{i+1})$. If $|\hat{u}(D_{i+1}) - \hat{u}(D_i)| < \varepsilon$ then the learner's utility has stabilized and we need not add any more instances. If this is not the case, the process repeats until the utility has stabilized. It is important to note that to use the Chernoff inequality, the samples D_i and D_{i-1} must be independent hence our creation of a new sample at each iteration of the algorithm. Future work will explore using an appropriate bound so that D_i is a superset of D_{i-1}.

4 Derivation of the DASA Algorithm

(a) Adaptive Sampling Schedule

In this section we determine how to adaptively come up with the sampling schedule. As was motivated in section 3, we determine how many instances to add at each iteration. We use the terminology $\hat{u}(D_i)$ to represent the utility at stage i and $\hat{u}(D_{i-1})$ the utility at stage $i-1$ to reflect our approach The probability of failure that the distance between these utilities differ greater by *distance* ε is:

$$\Pr[\hat{u}(D_i) - \hat{u}(D_{i-1}) \geq \varepsilon] \tag{5}$$

Using Chernoff Inequality (Definition 2), we set $p = \hat{u}(D_i)$ and $p' = \hat{u}(D_{i-1})$:

$$\Pr[\,|p - p'| \geq \varepsilon] \leq e^{-mp\varepsilon^2/2}$$

We can upper bound this expression by δ, the chance of failure (from section 2):

$$e^{-mp\varepsilon^2/2} \leq \delta$$

Rearranging terms and solving for m we get:

$$m \geq \frac{2}{p}\left[\frac{1}{\varepsilon^2}\log\frac{1}{\delta}\right]$$

We replace p with $\hat{u}(D_i)$ to get:

$$m \geq \frac{2}{\hat{u}(D_i)} \left[\frac{1}{\varepsilon^2} \log \frac{1}{\delta} \right] \qquad (6)$$

Recall that the utility function $\hat{u}(D_i)$ is the average over all instances in the sample D_i, of the instance function $f(x_i)$, where $x_i \in D$. The instance function used here is the classification accuracy (i.e. $f(x_i)$ is 0 -1 loss function).

(b) Stopping Criteria

An important ingredient for sampling algorithms is how to determine when to stop at a particular sample size. As was motivated in section 3, we use the "myopic" (look only one step ahead at each iteration) strategy for determining when to stop. According to the myopic strategy, if the expected utility in moving from stage i to i+1 is less than a small number, we stop. That is, we would stop when:

$$\mid \hat{u}(D_{i+1}) - \hat{u}(D_i) \mid \leq \varepsilon$$

Using the definition of utility from Equation (2), and setting $f(x_i) = acc(x_i)$, the classification accuracy (a 0-1 loss function), we obtain: We refer to ε as the stopping threshold and Equation (7) as the stopping criterion.

$$\left| \frac{1}{\mid D_{i+1} \mid} \sum_{i=1}^{|D_{i+1}|} acc(x_i) - \frac{1}{\mid D_i \mid} \sum_{i=1}^{|D_i|} acc(x_i) \right| \leq \varepsilon \qquad (7)$$

(c) DASA Algorithm

Algorithm DASA(D, ε, δ)
Input: Training dataset D, ε and δ
Output: Total number of instances and mean computation time (for convergence)
Step 0: $\hat{u}(D_0) \leftarrow 0$
Step 1: Randomly select $(1/10)*|D|$ instances $(=|D_1|)$. Apply the learner (Neural network), determine $\hat{u}(D_1)$ (using Equation (2))
Step 2: For each iteration i (≥ 1) do:
    (a) Check for convergence using the criteria:

$$\left| \frac{1}{\mid D_i \mid} \sum_{i=1}^{|D_i|} acc(x_i) - \frac{1}{\mid D_{i-1} \mid} \sum_{i=1}^{|D_{i-1}|} acc(x_i) \right| < \varepsilon$$

    IF   the above test succeeds then we have reached convergence (return the mean computation time and the number of instances and EXIT)
    ELSE
        (We have to add more instances)
        Compute m using Equation (6).
    (b) Randomly draw $m+|D_i|$ instances to form the new sample D_{i+1}. (Note: that D_i and D_{i+1} are independent of one another.)
    (c) Apply learner and determine $\hat{u}(D_{i+1})$.

5   Neural Networks for Recognizing Patterns

(a) Motivation

Neural networks [9][11] are highly desirable as they are capable of modelling extremely complex functions. Algorithms such as *Back-propagation* [11] use gradient descent to tune network parameters to best fit a training set of input-output pairs. A properly trained neural network is able to compare fingerprints and faces successfully even if the pixels are slightly offset of one another, as the network will look for the pattern of pixels rather than their exact position.

(b) Drawbacks

The two major drawbacks of training Neural Networks are:
(a)   Longer Training times [9][11]: Training times depends on factors such as the number of weights in the network, the number of instances considered and the settings of the various learning parameters. Hence they are infeasible for training massive amount of data. (b) Memory constraint [9][11]: Reading *all the patterns* into memory before the training is started and keeping them there all the time uses up valuable memory.

(c) Our Work

In this paper, we address both the drawbacks of neural networks and show that given a neural network (e.g. Multilayer perceptron [9]), we obtain results with the same predictive accuracy with much fewer training examples, and lesser computational time as compared to using the entire training dataset.

6   Empirical Results Using Neural Networks

We now try our experiments on neural networks (for finger print recognition and face recognition). We compare our convergence method with other methods, which are as follows:

(Full): $S_N = \{N\}$, a single sample with all the instances. This is the most commonly used method. This method suffers from both speed and memory drawbacks.

(Arith): Arithmetic Sampling [2], $S_a = \{|D_1|, |D_1|+\beta, |D_1|+2\beta, \ldots\ldots |D_1|+k.\beta\}$ where β is the fixed number of instances to add until we reach convergence. In our experiments, we use $|D_1| = \beta = 100$, as was used by John and Langley in their experiments.

(Geo): Geometric Sampling [3][4], in which the training set size is increased *geometrically*, $Sg = \{|D_1|, a.|D_1|, a^2.|D_1|, a^3.|D_1|\ldots.a^k.|D_1|\}$ until convergence is reached. In our experiments, we use $|D_1|=100$, and a=2 as per the Provost et' al study.

(DASA): Our adaptive sampling approach using Chernoff Bounds. We use $\varepsilon = 0.001$ and $\delta = 0.05$ (95% probability) in all our experiments.

(Oracle): $S_o = \{n_{min}\}$, the optimal schedule determined by an omniscient oracle; we determined n_{min} empirically by analyzing the full learning curve beforehand. We use these results to empirically compare the optimum performance with other methods.

We compare these methods using the following two performance criteria:

(a) The *mean computation time*[1]: Averaged over 20 runs for each dataset.
(b) The *total number of instances needed to converge*: If the sampling schedule, is as follows: $S=\{|D_1|,|D_2|,|D_3|....|D_k|\}$, then the total number of instances would be $|D_1|+|D_2|+|D_3|....+|D_k|$.

6.1 Fingerprint Recognition

We consider datasets from two different sources. The first source is from an international competition on fingerprint verification - FVC2004 (http://bias.csr.unibo.it/fvc2004). And the other source is the Fingerprint Samples for NIST Special Database 4 (http://www.nist.gov/srd/nistsd4.htm) and Special Database 9 (http://www.nist.gov/srd/nistsd9.htm). **Table 1** shows running times in seconds (averaged over 20 runs) to obtain the *same accuracy* using the different sampling methods. **Table 2** shows the total number of instances (averaged over 20 runs) used by each sampling method for convergence. Before each run the order of the instances were randomized.

Table 1. Comparison of the mean computation time required for the different methods to obtain the same accuracy (averaged over 20 runs of the experiment)

Mean Computation Time	Full: $S_N=\{N\}$	Arith: $S_a=|D_1|+k.\beta$	Geo $S_g=a^k.|D_1|$	DASA	Oracle $S_O=\{n_{min}\}$
FVC2004 DB3	1821.3	956.7	870.2	353.4	312.1
FVC2004 DB4	1188.7	854.3	765.2	336.5	265.6
NIST Special DB 4	3580.4	4730.7	2082.3	991.5	887.6
NIST Special DB 9	2591.6	1753.9	1387.9	616.9	564.2

Table 2. Comparison of the total number of instances required for the different methods to reach convergence

Avg. No. of instances	Full: $S_N=\{N\}$	Arith: $S_a=|D_1|+k.\beta$	Geo $S_g=a^k.|D_1|$	DASA	Oracle $S_O=\{n_{min}\}$
FVC2004 DB3	880	312	297	136	116
FVC2004 DB4	880	614	582	269	233
NIST Special DB 4	2000	3609	1497	686	585
NIST Special DB 9	1500	1083	717	316	232

---

[1] As measured the by the user component of the LINUX time command.

6.2 Face Recognition

The first dataset is from the Mitchell FACES database. Images of 20 different people were collected, including 32 images per person. The data for these experiments were obtained from http://www-2.cs.cmu.edu/afs/cs.cmu.edu/user/ mitchell. For the second dataset we use is the ORL database (http://www.uk.research.att.com/facedatabase. html). The results are as shown in **Table 3** and **Table 4** below:

Table 3. Comparison of the mean computation time required for the different methods to obtain the same accuracy over 20 runs of the experiment

Mean Computation Time	Full: $S_N=\{N\}$	Arith: $S_a=|D_1|+k.\beta$	Geo $S_g=a^k.|D_1|$	DASA	Oracle $S_O=\{n_{min}\}$
MITCHELL DB	362.1	229.5	127.2	63.2	58.2
ORL DB	176.5	148.8	95.8	38.6	29.5

Table 4. Comparison of the total number of instances required for the different methods used

Avg. No. of instances	Full: $S_N=\{N\}$	Arith: $S_a=|D_1|+k.\beta$	Geo $S_g=a^k.|D_1|$	DASA	Oracle $S_O=\{n_{min}\}$
MITCHELL DB	640	600	640	381	210
ORL DB	400	316	300	146	124

7 Discussion

1) *Geometric Sampling:* Geometric sampling is between one and two times faster in terms of the computation time than learning with all of the data *(Full)*. It also is usually between one and three times faster than arithmetic sampling *(Arith)*.
2) (a) *DASA v/s Full:* The adaptive scheduling approach is between three and six times faster than learning with all of the data to obtain the same accuracy.
   (b) *DASA v/s Arith*: We find that DASA is between two and five times faster than Arithmetic Sampling.
   (c) *DASA v/s Geo:* We find that DASA is between two and three times faster than Geometric Sampling.
   (d) In all datasets, DASA is only between one and two times slower than the optimum performance as given by S_O.

8 Conclusion

Computing the smallest sufficient training set size is a fundamental question to answer in data mining. The prior learning literature allows for a fixed apriori specification of the number of instances for the sampling schedule. Our contributions in this paper include a principled dynamic adaptive sampling approach, that addresses two key questions: 1) Has convergence occurred and 2) If not, how many more are required. In this paper we address these two questions together using Chernoff bounds. We showed that for finger print recognition and face recognition (using neural networks), this approach outperforms other approaches with respect to number of instances required and computation time. In this paper we have used the approach of drawing the samples of different size **independently** from one another. This is required as we are using the Chernoff inequality and reasonable since neural networks are typically non-incremental learners. Future work will look at extending the work so that a new sample is a superset of the previous sample which may require the use of other bounds. In particular we intend to explore the application of dynamic adaptive sampling to semi-supervised learning.

References

1. Haussler,D., Kearns,M., Seung,H.S., Tishby,N.: *Rigorous Learning Curve Bounds from Statistical Mechanics*. In Proc. 7th ACM Workshop on Comp. Learning Theory (1994)
2. John,G., Langley,P.: *Static versus dynamic sampling for data mining*. In Proc. of the 2nd International Conference on Knowledge Discovery and Data Mining, pp 367–370. (1996)
3. Meek,C., Theisson,B., Heckerman,D.: *The learning-curve sampling method applied to model- based clustering,* The Journal of Machine Learning Research (2002)
4. Provost,F., Jensen,D., Oates,T.: *Efficient progressive sampling*. In Proceedings of the Fifth International Conference on Knowledge Discovery and Data Mining, pp 23–32 (1999)
5. Elomaa,T., Kaariainen,M.: *Progressive rademacher sampling*. In Proc. 18th national conference on Artificial intelligence, Edmonton, Alberta, Canada. pp: 140 – 145 (2002)
6. Scheffer,T., Wrobel,S.: *Finding the Most Interesting Patterns in a Database Quickly by Using Sequential Sampling*. Journal of Machine Learning Research 3, pp 833-862 (2002)
7. Chernoff,H.: *A measure of asymptotic efficiency for tests of a hypothesis based on the sums of observations*. Annals of Mathematical Statistics, 23:493-507 (1952)
8. Davidson,I.: *An Ensemble Approach for Stable Learners*, The National Conference on A.I. (AAAI), San Jose, (2004)
9. Tarassenko,L.: *A guide to Neural Computing Applications*. (1998)
10. Hulten,G., Domingos,P.: *Learning from infinite data in finite time*. In Advances in Neural Information Processing Systems 14, pages 673--680, Cambridge, MA (2002)
11. Mitchell,T.: *Machine Learning*, The McGraw Hill Companies, Inc. (1997)

Catching the Picospams*

Matthew Chang and Chung Keung Poon

Dept. of Computer Science, City U. of Hong Kong, China
{kcmchang, ckpoon}@cs.cityu.edu.hk

Abstract. In this paper, we study the problem of filtering unsolicited
bulk emails, also known as spam emails. We apply a k-NN algorithm with
a similarity measure called *resemblance* and compare it with the naive
Bayes and the k-NN algorithm with TF-IDF weighting. Experimental
evaluation shows that our method produces the lowest cost results under
different cost models of classification. Compared with TF-IDF weighting, our method is more practical in a dynamic environment. Also, our
method successfully catches a notorious class of spams called *picospams*.
We believe that it will be a useful member in a hybrid classifier.

1 Introduction

The proliferation of unsolicited bulk emails, also known as spams, has become
an irritating problem in recent years. Various studies (e.g. [1]) indicate that the
problem is getting worse quickly. By far, the most popular technical anti-spam
solution is spam filtering based on the message content. This will be the focus
of this paper.

1.1 Previous Work

Early anti-spam filters rely on hand-crafted rules to detect patterns that often
appear in spam messages. Since constructing the rules manually is cognitively demanding and periodic updating of the rules is necessary to cope with the changing characteristics of the spam messages, various machine learning techniques
for text categorization have been applied to learn the patterns automatically.

Drucker et al. [7] and Hidalgo [9] have experimentally found that support
vector machines (SVM's) are more accurate than many other classification algorithms, including Ripper, Rocchio and boosting C4.5 trees. Unfortunately,
SVM's are impractical for a dynamic data set: feature reduction is often needed
to reduce the processing time of a SVM but the subset of the most relevant
features is dynamic. See [5] for discussion.

In contrast, the naive Bayes classifier summarizes each class by a probability
distribution which can be updated incrementally as new samples arrive. Studies by Sahami et al. [13], Androutsopoulos et al. [2, 3] and Pantel and Lin [10]

---

* This research was fully supported by a grant from the Research Grants Council of
the Hong Kong SAR, China [CityU 1198/03E].

M.-S. Hacid et al. (Eds.): ISMIS 2005, LNAI 3488, pp. 641–649, 2005.
© Springer-Verlag Berlin Heidelberg 2005

showed that the naive Bayes classifier is rather efficient and accurate. Androutsopoulos et al. also proposed the *cost-sensitive* performance measure to capture the asymmetric penalty between misclassifying a legitimate email as spam and misclassifying a spam as legitimate. Usually, the former cost is much higher than the latter.

Androutsopoulos et al. [3] and Sakkis et al. [15] argued that a folder of spam messages is often heterogeneous and as such, memory-based algorithms should be at least as effective as naive Bayes classifier that attempts to learn unifying characteristics of the spam messages. However, a memory-based algorithm requires much computational overhead (both processing time and storage) due to its "lazy" processing style. Thus feature reduction is needed and consequently, it suffers from the same non-adaptive problem as SVM's.

1.2   Our Contributions

Resemblance: In this paper, we follow the memory-based approach but with *resemblance* as the similarity measure between emails. Previously, the same approach has been used for the more general problem of email classification ([11]). Here we investigate the applicability of this approach for the special case of spam filtering and compare it with two other popular methods, namely, the *k*-NN with TF-IDF weighting and the naive Bayes. One advantage of our method over TF-IDF weighting is that feature reduction is achieved by a careful random sampling process in which each email is reduced to a *sketch* based on its local information only. Thus we avoid the need to examine the whole email corpus as needed in traditional feature selection methods such as *information gain*. Nor do we need to maintain the TF-IDF's of each vector as the corpus evolves. The random sampling needs to be coordinated among emails but the coordination is easily achieved by agreeing on a common random hash function beforehand (i.e., before seeing the emails).

Picospams: In our experiments, we choose a publicly available dataset called Ling-Spam[1], a privately collected email corpus and two randomly generated sets of *picospams* (to be explained in Section 2) accompanied by legitimate emails from the Ling-Spam corpus. These last two sets of data are motivated by the observation in [8] that half of the spams that sneaked through their variant of naive Bayes classifier in 2003 are the so-called *picospams*. Effective countermeasures are needed to stop such spams. Experimental results show that our classifier is more accurate in filtering the picospams than the other two classifiers.

The rest of the paper is organized as follows. Section 2 describes the test collections, including the picospams. Section 3 describes the preprocessing of emails, the TF-IDF weighting and resemblance measure. Section 4 describes the naive Bayes and *k*-NN classifier. Section 5 explains our experimental set up and presents our results. Section 6 is conclusion.

---

[1]   Ling-Spam corpus is available at http://www.aueb.gr/users/ion/data

2   Test Collections

The Ling-Spam is a publicly available corpus containing 2893 messages, of which 481 are spam and 2412 are legitimate. The messages are collected from the Linguist list, a mailing list about the science and profession of linguistics. The topics of messages includes job postings, software availability announcements, and even flame-like responses.

The Private corpus is our collection, which includes 2903 messages with 1307 legitimate messages related to teaching and 1596 spam messages of advertisements, on-line newsletters and conference announcements. This collection instantiates the situation in which the number of spam messages we received is larger than that of the legitimate ones.

The last two data sets both consist of 2893 messages and include the 2412 legitimate messages of Ling-Spam. The 481 spam messages of both sets are randomly generated picospams, each of which generated by embedding an advertising link (of 5 to 7 components) in a text of 200 random words. One set of the random words is from a dictionary with 45425 words; and the other set is from a stopword list with 319 words.

3   Message Preprocessing and Representation

In our experiments, we only consider the message body and ignore any header information. For the message body, we remove any formatting information such as HTML or XML tags and then extract words by treating blanks, punctuation marks and special characters as word separators. After this, an email becomes a sequence of words separated by blanks. For simplicity, lemmatization is not done. We will remove stop-shingles (defined as a shingle containing only stopwords) before mapping the emails into vectors. Next, we will describe the TF-IDF weighting with cosine measure and the shingling representation with resemblance measure.

3.1   TF-IDF Weighting and Cosine Measure

In this representation, we map each email to a vector of term weightings for terms present in the email corpus. Attribute weight of the ith term in the jth document is defined as: $w_{ij} = t_{ij} \times \log_2 (N/d_i)$ where N is the total number of documents in the email corpus, t_{ij} (the *term frequency*) is the frequency of the ith term in the jth document, and d_i (the *document frequency*) is the number of documents containing the ith term. Thus, the jth document is represented by the vector $(w_{1j}, w_{2j}, \ldots)$. Having mapped the emails into vectors, the distance between two emails can be measured by the cosine similarity measure (i.e., the dot product of the two vectors normalized by the product of their lengths).

3.2   Shingling and Resemblance

The resemblance measure was originally introduced by Broder [4] to detect duplicated web sites. Instead of considering individual keywords, this measure considers w-shingles (or w-grams). A w-shingle of a document is a contiguous sequence of w words in the document. The w-shingling of a document A, denoted $S_w(A)$, is defined as the multi-set of all w-shingles in A. Alternatively, we can view $S_w(A)$ as a vector of w-shingle weights in which the weighting function is the frequency of occurrences in the document. Given two documents A and B with w-shingling $S_w(A)$ and $S_w(B)$ respectively, their w-*resemblance* (or simply *resemblance* if w is understood) is defined as $r_w(A, B) = |S_w(A) \cap S_w(B)| / |S_w(A) \cup S_w(B)|$. Thus, the resemblance is a value between 0 (the least similar) and 1 (the most similar). In general, the larger value of w, the more stringent requirement we impose on A and B in order to classify them as similar. In the original application in duplication detection, a larger value of w is chosen so that the definition is more sensitive to permutation changes. In our application here, we concentrate on $w = 2$ and 3.

For a document A with n words, the size of $S_w(A)$ is $n - w + 1$. Storing $S_w(A)$ requires storing $w(n - w + 1)$ (English) words, which is larger than the original document by a factor of w. Alternatively, one may use a vector representation in which each distinct w-shingle in the email corpus corresponds to a component in the vector. A huge vector is needed.

To reduce the storage cost and computation time, we use a sampling and fingerprinting techniques described in [4]. More precisely, for each email, we apply Rabin's fingerprinting technqiue [12] to hash each shingle of the w-shingling of the email into an l-bit integer (the fingerprint). Then we take a sample of a fixed number, s, of fingerprints. Moreover, the samplings are coordinated among different emails so that the resemblance between any pair of emails can be estimated from their samples. This is achieved by applying the same random hash function to each shingle when forming the fingerprints, followed by taking the smallest s fingerprints from each shingling. Let $f(S)$ denote the set of fingerprint samples for a set S of shingles. Then the resemblance, $r_w(A, B)$, of two documents A and B is approximately $|f(S_w(A)) \cap f(S_w(B))| / |f(S_w(A)) \cup f(S_w(B))|$. In total, each email requires only $s \cdot l$ bits of storage. The hash function (which is simply an irreducible polynomial) is chosen randomly before seeing the emails. Storing the hash function requires only l bits. From our previous experience, choosing $l = 64$ and taking a sample of $s = 200$ shingles suffice to give a satisfactory result. For more detail explanation of the mathematical foundation, see [4].

4   Classification Methods

Naive Bayes: Each class of emails is represented as a probability distribution of words in which the probability of a word is proportional to its frequency in the class. Let S and L denote the spam and legitimate class respectively. Then given an email $A = (w_1, w_2, \ldots, w_n)$, the probability that A belongs to S is $Pr(S|A) = Pr(A|S)Pr(S)/Pr(A)$. Assuming each word of A is drawn from S independently, $Pr(A|S)$ can be estimated as $\prod_i Pr(w_i|S)$. Thus, to determine which class the email A should belong, we compare $Pr(S) \prod_i Pr(w_i|S)$ and

$Pr(L) \prod_i Pr(w_i|L)$ and choose the larger one. If A contains a word w_i not present in a class C_k, we apply Laplace smoothing: $Pr(w_i|C_k) = 1/(n_k + s_i)$, where n_k is the number of words in C_k, and s_i is the number of distinct words in the corpus.

Memory-Based: A number of classified instances called *examplars* are stored in the memory. To classify a new email, we compare it with the exemplar emails in the system and take the majority vote among the k nearest ones. The variant that weighs the vote by the similarity measure is usually more noise-tolerant than the one with pure binary vote. The algorithm is suitable for folders with multi-topics such as a spam folder because the distance of a new email with a folder is determined not by the average distance over all members but by the nearest members in it.

5   Experimental Evaluation

We tested the classifiers in an incremental supervised-learning environment: new emails are given one at a time for classification and the user's feedback is given immediately before taking the next email. We believe that this model better reflects the real scenario in which the classifier is deployed for a period of time during which the user will feedback to the classifier. Human feedback is necessary because it is likely that users will examine the classification themselves so as to avoid missing an important legitimate email as spam and to weed out the spams that get through the filter. For each classification, the incoming email is classified as spam, legitimate, or unknown; where unknown class collects emails having no similarity with any existing email or probability with any class.

For k-NN classifiers, we implement the algorithm with $k = 1$ and 10. For TF-IDF weighting, we perform feature reduction by selecting the top 700 terms based on TF-IDF weightings and mapping all emails into the 700-attribute vector space model. This feature selection method is similar to that used in [15] except that their feature scoring function is information gain. For resemblance measure, we take the best result among $w = 2$ and 3. For naive Bayes, no parameter setting is needed.

5.1   Performance Criteria

Following Sakkis's [15] framework, we denote by $N_{L \to S}$ the number of legitimate emails classified as spam and by $N_{S \to L}$ the number of spams classified as legitimate. Furthermore, we define $c(L \to S)$ and $c(S \to L)$ as the cost of an $L \to S$ error and $S \to L$ error respectively. The *weighted cost* for the classification of a corpus is then defined as: $cost = c(L \to S) \cdot N_{L \to S} + c(S \to L) \cdot N_{S \to L}$. Usually $c(L \to S) \gg c(S \to L)$. Although we expect the user to examine the spam emails, the collection of spam emails is huge and people tend to skim through them quickly and delete them. Thus it is possible that misclassified legitimate emails are deleted. Even if not, it may take a long time to recover a misclassified legitimate email from a huge list of spams. Therefore, we set the $c(S \to L) : c(L \to S)$ as $1 : 1$, $1 : 10$ and $1 : 100$ in our experiments.

To deal with this cost-sensitive classification problem, we introduce a parameter $\lambda \geq 1$ in the classification algorithms. For the k-NN approach, the resemblance or the cosine similarity of an incoming email with a legitimate message is multiplied by λ (while that with a spam message is not adjusted). Similarly, for naive Bayes, the probability of the incoming email being in the class of legitimate emails is multiplied by λ before comparing with that of spam. We tested different values of λ from 1.0 to 9999.9 and take the smallest value that minimizes the weighted cost.

5.2   Efficiency

Our first experiment compares the efficiency of the memory-based algorithms. Since we do not concentrate on the classification accuracy, we only perform our tests on one set of data, namely the Ling-Spam corpus. The results are shown in Table 1.

Table 1. Average Processing Time (in milli-seconds) of Ling-Spam email

	$tf \cdot idf$ local=200	Resemblance local=200	$tf \cdot idf$ global=700
k-NN	681.1376	242.8925	236.8521
Nearest Neighbour	680.6402	242.0415	236.6792

To compare the efficiency of the TF-IDF weighting and resemblance measure in a dynamic setting, we modify the feature selection method of TF-IDF weighting so that each email locally selects 200 attributes. The number of features is chosen to match the number of fingerprints sampled in the resemblance measure. During the testing, the TF's and DF's of all the terms are maintained and when computing the cosine measure of two emails, we take the current TF's and DF's value of their common terms. The processing times are shown in the leftmost column. The rightmost column shows the processing time for the TF-IDF measure when 700 features are selected globally. Comparing the leftmost two columns, the resemblance measure seems to be faster due to its simplicity. Without feature selection, the TF-IDF measure would even be slower. Comparing the rightmost two columns, the resemblance measure is roughly as efficient as the TF-IDF weighting. Comparing the two rows of the table, we found that k-NN with $k = 1$ and $k = 10$ are essentially the same in efficiency.

5.3   Accuracy

Tables 2 shows the recall and precision for the spam class as well as the weighted cost for each classifier. Note that, the result of cost ratio 1:10 and 1:100 is not shown individually because the results are similar to that of cost ratio 1:1 except the total cost. The classifier "NN+resemblance" represents the k-NN classifier with $k = 1$.

First, we observe that our algorithm performs the best in all four data sets. The k-NN with resemblance successfully filters all the picospams from the legitimate messages at the cost ratio 1:1, 1:10, and 1:100. It achieves 100% precision and about 99% recall for both sets of picospams, while its costs are zeroes with only a few of the messages classified as unknown. For the naive Bayes classifier, it performs very well for the picospam corpora at the cost ratio 1:1 and 1:10 but less well for higher cost ratio 1:100. In particular, the rightmost column of Table 2 shows that it is unable to prevent misclassifying legitimate emails without letting through a lot of picospams. Furthermore, it misclassifies a lot of legitimates as spam in Ling-Spam corpus for all cost models. It attains only 78.07% spam precision for the corpus. For k-NN with TF-IDF weighting, its cost is similar to that of k-NN with resemblance for small cost ratio in Private and Ling-Spam corpora but somewhat inferior for cost ratio 1:100. This is again due to the fact that it cannot prevent misclassifying a legitimate email without letting a lot of spams to pass through.

Table 2. Results with cost measure $c(S \rightarrow L) : c(L \rightarrow S) = 1 : 1, 1 : 10$, and $1 : 100$

Corpus	Spam Classifier	w	λ	Spam Recall	Spam Precision	Cost 1:1	Cost 1:10	Cost 1:100
Private	NN + Resemblance	2	1.0	0.9969	0.9969	9	54	504
	k-NN + Resemblance	2	1.0	0.9975	0.9956	10	73	703
	NN + TF-IDF	-	1.0	0.9950	0.9857	31	238	2308
	k-NN + TF-IDF	-	1.0	0.9969	0.9791	39	345	3405
	naive Bayes	-	1.0	0.9261	0.9919	130	238	1318
Ling-Spam	NN + Resemblance	2	1.0	0.8836	0.9279	89	386	3356
	k-NN + Resemblance	2	1.0	0.8711	0.9744	73	162	972
	NN + TF-IDF	-	1.0	0.8981	0.9076	93	489	4449
	k-NN + TF-IDF	-	1.0	0.9189	0.9485	63	279	2439
	naive Bayes	-	99999.9	0.9771	0.7807	143	1331	13211
PicoSpam (Dictionary)	NN + Resemblance	3	1.0	0.9938	1.0	0	0	0
	k-NN + Resemblance	3	1.0	0.9938	1.0	0	0	0
	NN + TF-IDF	-	1.0	0.8108	0.7831	199	1171	10891
	k-NN + TF-IDF	-	1.0	0.8565	0.9763	79	169	1069
	naive Bayes	-	1.0	0.9979	0.9917	5	41	401
PicoSpam (Stopword)	NN + Resemblance	3	1.0	0.9938	1.0	0	0	0
	k-NN + Resemblance	3	1.0	0.9938	1.0	0	0	0
	NN + TF-IDF	-	1.0	0.9917	1.0	4	4	4
	k-NN + TF-IDF	-	1.0	0.9917	1.0	4	4	4
	naive Bayes	-	9999.9	0.9979	0.9959	3	21	201

We also observe that the resemblance measure is very sensitive to sequences of words. On careful examination of our experimental data, we found that a picospam typically matches five to seven 3-shingles (mostly due to the advertising link) with the nearest previously classified picospam but matches none of the 3-shingles with any legitimate email. Therefore, most of the picospams are caught and none of the legitimate emails are misclassified. The TF-IDF classifier also performs well at the picospam generated by stopword but it performs the worst among all classifiers at the picospam generated by dictionary. It shows that a lot of the random stopwords are removed and the words in the spam link are retained during the initial (global) feature selection. However, if we are testing the picospam generated by dictionary, the initial feature selection is unable to locate and retain the important features, namely, the spam link terms.

6   Conclusions

In this paper, we investigated the applicability of k-NN with resemblance in spam filtering and found it to be competitive with two other common text classifiers, namely, naive Bayes and k-NN with TF-IDF weighting. Our method is more practical than k-NN with TF-IDF weighting for a dynamic data set. The excellent performance of our approach in catching picospams has some ramifications. Recently, researchers are considering the combination of more than one classifier to achieve better accuracy. For example, [14] considered a set of classifiers whose individual decisions are combined in some way to classify new emails. If the classifiers err on different types of emails, their combination may give rise to a better overall classifier. Thus, it is conceivable that a k-NN classifier with resemblance can be a member for catching the picospams.

References

1. Spam war. *Technology Review*, July/August 2003.
2. I. Androutsopoulos, J. Koutsias, K. Chandrinos, and C. Spyropoulos. An experimental comparison of naive bayesian and keywordbased anti-spam filtering with personal email messages. In *SIGIR'00*, pp 160–167, 2000.
3. I. Androutsopoulos, G. Paliouras, V. Karkaletsis, G. Sakkis, C. Spyropoulos, and P. Stamatopoulos. Learning to filter spam e-mail: A comparison of a naive bayesian and a memory-based approach. In *Proc. of the Workshop on Machine Learning and Textual Information Access PKDD-2000*, 2000.
4. A.Z. Broder. On the resemblance and containment of documents. In *SEQUENCES'97*, pp 21–29. IEEE Computer Society, 1997.
5. C. Brutlag and J. Meek. Challenges of the email domain for text classification. In *17th ICMP*, pp 103–110, July 2000.
6. L.F. Cranor and B.A. LaMacchia. Spam! *Communications of the ACM*, 41(8):103–110, August 1998.
7. H. Drucker, D. Wu, and V.N. Vapnik. Support vector machines for spam categorization. *IEEE Trans. on Neural Networks*, 10(5):1048–1054, September 1999.
8. J. Graham-Cumming. How to beat an adaptive spam filter. In *MIT Spam Conference*, January 2004.
9. J. Maria Gomez Hidalgo. Evaluating cost-sensitive unsolicited bulk email categorization. In *Proc. of ACM Symp. on Applied computing*, pp 615–620, 2002.
10. P. Pantel and D. Lin. A spam classification and organization program. In *Proc. of AAAI-98 Workshop on Learning for Text Categorization*, pp 95–98, 1998.

11. C. K. Poon and M. Chang. An email classifier based on resemblance. In *Proc. of 14th ISMIS*, pp 334–338, 2003.
12. M.O. Rabin. Fingerprint by random polynomials. Technical Report TR-15-81, Center for Research in Computing Technology, Harvard University, 1981.
13. M. Sahami, S. Dumais, D. Heckerman, and E. Horvitz. A bayesian approach to filtering junk e-mail. In *Proc. of AAAI-98 Workshop on Learning for Text Categorization*, 1998.
14. G. Sakkis, I. Androutsopoulos, G. Paliouras, V. Karkaletsis, C. D. Spyropoulos, and P. Stamatopoulos. Stacking classifiers for anti-spam filtering of e-mail. In *6th Conf. on EMNLP*, pp 44–50, Carnegie Mellon U., Pittsburgh, USA, 2001.
15. G. Sakkis, I. Androutsopoulos, G. Paliouras, V. Karkaletsis, C. D. Spyropoulos, and P. Stamatopoulos. A memory-based approach to anti-spam filtering for mailing lists. *Information Retrieval*, pp 49–73, 2003.

Personalized Peer Filtering for a Dynamic Information Push

Melanie Gnasa, Sascha Alda, Nadir Gül, and Armin B. Cremers

Institute of Computer Science III,
University of Bonn, Römerstrasse 164,
53117 Bonn, Germany
{gnasa, alda, guel, abc}@cs.uni-bonn.de

Abstract. Due to the anonymity of the user during Web searching, no support for long-term information needs exists. First attempts for personalized Web retrieval are made, however these approaches are limited to static objects and no individual recommendations from a dynamic data set can be determined. Peer-to-peer architectures build a promising platform for a personalized information filtering system, where all steps during information exchange are transparent to the user. Our approach assists active requests in the form of an information pull as well as a system initiated information push. In a cooperative manner all peers have the function of information providers and consumers. The ranking of recommendations is established by a community-based filtering approach.

1 Motivation

The prognosis that peer-to-peer (P2P) networks are the next stage of the evolution in the development of the Internet, is attributed to the term frequently discussed in the recent history of information technology. Peer-to-peer networks form the infrastructure for virtual communities in a collaborative working environment, in which resources are divided and information is exchanged. The success of such virtual communities depends considerably on the efficiency of the integrated procedures for accessing information. In this regard, the function of an integrated procedure is the acquisition of accurate descriptions of information needs. According to Belkin and Croft [Belkin and Croft, 1992] information needs can be distinguished between one-time or long-time-goals. On one side, information retrieval processes are typically concerned with dynamic information needs requesting stable information sources [Oard, 1997]. On the other, information filtering assists stable information needs, which are continuously used to detect relevant documents in dynamic information sources. Today, no major Web search engine addresses both information detection processes. Regarding a traditional Web search, a user formulates his information need with a query and as result he gets a list of documents, which every user gets for the same query at the moment. At the same time, other users with comparable information needs pass through the same search steps. From the users' point-of-view,

M.-S. Hacid et al. (Eds.): ISMIS 2005, LNAI 3488, pp. 650–659, 2005.
© Springer-Verlag Berlin Heidelberg 2005

no awareness features are integrated to detect other users and changes of the information sources. In this paper, we present a strategy to model dynamic information sources, which assists dynamic and stable information needs of a group of users. Each index of a Web search engine is continuously updated, and each user gets a subset of relevant documents at the moment of request. For a user with stable information needs, only the document offset since his last request would be of special interest. This offset should be provided each user in a personalized manner. Common client-server architectures of Web search engines do not offer such time-constraints regarding the indexing time of documents. Furthermore, it would be desirable to excuse the user from a pull of information by a conscious initiation. In contrast to this attempt, the usage of an information push [Cheverst and Smith, 2001] assumes the passive attitude of a user, where any information flow occurs unexpectodly by the user. The push technology has first been proposed by H. P. Luhn [Luhn, 1958] as "selective dissemination of information" (SDI) in 1961. According to Bates [Bates, 2002], hundreds of millions of dollars have been invested during the Internet boom, but the push technology has largely failed. Many of these services failed because of information flooding for the user. Additionally, users received an information push only for predefined topics like news, sports etc. Hence, for the implementation of a push service, which is dynamically adapted to the users' individual information needs, peer-to-peer architectures are a promising platform.

Our approach introduces a hybrid peer-to-peer network with on the one side, a highly-available search service and an index of several billion Web sites (in our case, Google) and on the other, peers describing a dynamic data set based on a local peer profile (cf. Section 2). In Section 3 this paper emphasizes the dynamic information push strategy to determine relevant results for a passive user and implemented with the prototype called "MyPush" (cf. Section 4). Finally, we deal with related work in Section 5, and we conclude future plans in Section 6.

2   Topology of a Hybrid Peer-to-Peer Network

For the assistance of both information detection processes, we want to improve existing Web search facilities in order to model dynamic information sources. All common Web search engines have a client-server architecture, where no interaction among users is feasible. This scenario is depicted with the 'User Layer' and a 'Web Layer' in Figure 1. A user selects one or more search servers, and all retrieved documents provide an access point for a navigation through the World Wide Web. On this account, the user performs a conscious selection of an information source, which has a stable collection of documents at the moment of request. The interaction among users is limited to an information pull. For the assistance of pull und push services, we propose a hybrid peer-to-peer network. The main advantages of this network is the support of interaction among users. It is a hybrid network, because existing Web search engines are integrated for an efficient information pull. The effectiveness can be enriched by the interaction of users and their exchange of relevant documents in a 'Virtual P2P Network'

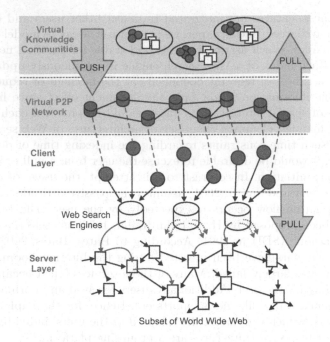

Fig. 1. Topology of a Hybrid Peer-to-Peer Network

(cf. Figure 1). For a tracking of new information sources, an additional layer of 'Virtual Knowledge Communities' is proposed, in order to restrict the push to selected users, which are organized in a community as depicted in Figure 1.

2.1   Modelling User Interaction

Modelling user interaction is a first step towards a dynamic information push beyond Web search engines. The main shortcoming of existing client-server architectures, which assist no user interaction during search, is a missing local personalization strategy. An essential task of the information retrieval process is the display of useful information sources to the user. We enhance this task, in order to collect explicit relevance feedback. In a local database, the Peer Search Memory [Gnasa et al., 2004b], stores all queries and their relevant documents of a user. This leads to a transaction matrix with validated results of a user. Recently, a Web search server can log all requests and viewed documents of their users, although these assessments are based on implicit feedback [Oard and Kim, 1998]. If a user requests different Web servers, only with a local personalization strategy the overall usage information can be stored. In general, user interaction should be independent of a special server, which assists such an interaction among its users, and should not be limited to special topics. In our hybrid peer-to-peer network, each user can use his favorite Web search engine, and there is no restriction to special search topics. In addition to the 'User Layer' in Figure 1, all Peer

Search Memories are organized in a virtual network. We assume that each peer represents only one user. Hence, this network provides an exchange platform of document assessments and their context is independent of the requested search servers. Each query is interpreted as context information [Lawrence, 2000], and it can be used to group users with similar interests. With these local feedback information, dynamic information sources exists on each peer. The query, which results from a dynamic information need, can be performed in our network by a traditional Web search engine. Furthermore, Virtual Knowledge Communities [Gnasa et al., 2003] transfer all dynamic information on all peers into a consistent state. Each community brings together users and their relevant documents for a special context. These grouping will only be proposed to the users, if a set of documents have a high degree of commitment by a representative number of users. Both, communities as well as Web search engines are requested, if an information pull is initiated by the user. As a result, we present a summary of all server selected documents with additional user assessments from our network, if they are available, and all documents of a community, which matche the information need. In difference to the single server results, a hit of a Virtual Knowledge Community leads only to a small set of validated documents. Thus, an interaction beyond server boundaries is feasible with our approach.

2.2   Towards a Hyper Peer Graph

Beyond the support of user interaction, the hybrid peer-to-peer network encourages the grouping of users and validated results into communities. Web communities can be detected by spectral or non-spectral metrics [Flake et al., 2003], which are widely used. In our system, such techniques can be enhanced by additional nodes that represent users, all query contexts and their evaluated results. On the Web layer in Figure 1, information is provided by users on Web pages. The linkage structure can be used to compute subsets of the Web graph, which represent special topics based on their Peer Search Memory. This information can also be regarded for the computation of subsets of the Web graph. In Figure 2, we depicted a meta-graph of such an usage graph as well as an example instance. This instantiated example graph shows the usage information of a Web log that collects all queries of users and their viewed documents. The most frequently retrieved Web site in this collection was a German-English dictionary. In total, 64 users selected in 136 query sessions the URL http://dict.leo.org. The result was retrieved by 45 distinct queries. Figure 2 presents four of the most frequently requested queries. Traditional Web community algorithms only analyze the linkage structure between Web sites. If all usage information is integrated, additional incoming links can be detected and weighted. The enhancement of the Web graph with usage information leads to a *Hyper Peer Graph* with additional vertices and edges.

Common Web community algorithms consider no content-based analysis of Web pages. With our topology, the decentralization of all usage information assists the distributed computation of weights between different kinds of vertices. In the Hyper Peer Graph, we distinguish between *page*, *user*, and *context*

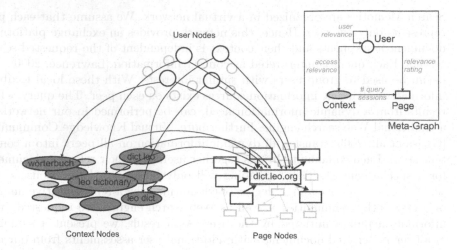

Fig. 2. Meta-graph of the Hyper Peer Graph and an example instance

vertices. Between these nodes, three directed edges are annotated. First, a directed edge between a context and a page is weighted with the *number of query sessions*, in which the selected page was relevant. Second, an *access relevance* [Gnasa et al., 2004b] is used to determine personalized issues like last access time and frequency of usage of a relevant document. Third, all peers compute implicit feedback information for each local document association, in order to assign a *relevance rating* [Gnasa et al., 2004b]. All three edge annotations are based on collected information of the Peer Search Memory. During the recommendation process, the interaction between users leads to additional information about the usability of recommended results. This means, if a user gets a list of recommended documents, and if one of these documents is stored in his Peer Search Memory, the *user relevance* (UserRel) [Gnasa et al., 2004b] of the recommending peer is increased. This user relevance defines the degree of relationships between two users, and this leads to a linkage network between users.

Summarizing, the Hyper Peer Graph unifies content providers and consumers. Our future work leads to the integration of new algorithms to compute subsets of this graph. Each subset will represent a common topic of interest for a user group and relevant documents, which have a commitment in this group. A first community algorithms is already implemented and discussed in [Gnasa et al., 2003]. Independently of the process to detect communities, our dynamic information push strategy assumes groups of users, in order to decrease the number of potential information sources and the information flooding through a dynamic adaption of the algorithm.

3   Dynamic Information Push

Unlike traditional collaborative filtering approaches, our system is based on a hybrid peer-to-peer architecture. If a user wants an automatic detection of relevant information, all peers are involved in a collaborative manner. The cooperation between all peers requires the definition of two essential roles. On this account, a scheduler differentiates on each peer between active and passive tasks. An information pull is interpreted as active mode of a peer. Likewise, an information push for other peers is the passive part. To serve many peers at the same time several passive instances at each peer exists, whereas a peer can only be in one active mode. In contrast to central systems, efficient techniques for parallelization enable the simultaneous processing of active and passive tasks. According to the definition of an information push [Cheverst and Smith, 2001] the user has a passive attitude during the peer filtering, and the role of a peer can not be assigned to a user. In terms of a cooperative pull-push cycle [Gnasa et al., 2004a], an active peer initiates a recommendation request to all peers with a membership to the same group as the active peer. For this task, we assume the Virtual Knowledge Communities (VKC), detected in the Hyper Peer Graph, for a context-driven global prefiltering of peers. This preselection of peers mainly decreases the network load by considering affiliated peers on a semantic layer. All preselected and accessible peers interpret a request of an active peer and fade to the passive mode. At the same time these peers can request other peers of the group in their active mode. The number of recommended documents mainly depends on the number of peers in a community. If a community has many members, the recommendation process can be adapted by a threshold, which depends on the actual number of members and influences the maximal number of recommended documents.

Due to the requesting of peers of the same Virtual Knowledge Community, the network load is minimized and a context-specific selection of requested peers is the goal. Hence, an information flooding can be avoided, and a dynamic set of data is mapped to a static snapshot of fundamental associations for a set of peers. This static set is used as a basis for an enhanced collaborative filtering approach, where all explicit and implicit ratings, as well as all peer relevances are considered. The peer recommendation task proceeds in the active mode of a peer, and starts after the receiving of suggested results of all passive peers which are online. To overcome existing shortcomings of content-based and collaborative filtering approaches, we use a *community-based filtering* approach, in order to utilize the similarity between members of the same community in respect to their documents ratings as well as their content, which are relevant for the community. For a user $u \in U$ with memberships to the groups $C_i \subset VKC$, a prediction for a recommended document d is computed over all peers c of the group C_i

$$cof_{u,d} = \overline{r_u} + \frac{\sum_{c \in C_i} (sim(u,c) + UserRel_{u,c})(r_{c,d} - \overline{r_c})}{\sum_{c \in C_i} (sim(u,c) + UserRel_{u,c})}$$

The prediction weight *cof* is used for a ranking of all recommendations. In this regard, a high value represents a high relevance of a document d. The similarity of two peers can be computed with standard similarity measures [Rijsberg, 1979].

Finally, after weighting all suggested results of a peer group, an information push is initiated by the system.

4   MyPush - Prototype

A first Java-based prototype of our proposed system has been implemented and evaluated, which incorporates the JXTA framework[1] by Sun as the fundamental architecture. The JXTA framework proposes basic protocols and common standards for the development of peer-to-peer architectures. For the implementation of our prototype, mainly two protocols have been utilized: the pipe protocol and the peergroup protocol.

The pipe protocol is used for establishing a channel-based communication among peers. These channels, so-called *pipes* are used for pushing information about documents (recommendations) pertaining to virtual communities to all subscribed users (see Figure 3). In fact, our push algorithm is based on a conventional periodic pull protocol. Within the MyPush environment, a component called Information Gatherer is responsible to address all virtual communities, which the corresponding user has subscribed and, eventually, to request all new recommendations. These results are preprocessed and displayed to the user in a graphical user interface component. So, from the user's perspective, the arrival of new recommendations appears as a true push service, which can be compared to a conventional email client.

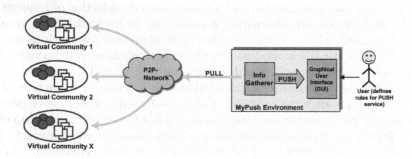

Fig. 3. The push service in the MyPush prototype

Virtual communities are represented by so-called peergroups. Peergroups are made of a set of peers, which have agreed on common topics or interests. In our system, member peers share all relevant parts of their locally stored associations with other members of that group. JXTA integrates protocols for discovering, joining, and creating new peergroups. This way, new groups can be discovered throughout an entire (given) P2P-network.

---

[1] http://www.jxta.org

5   Related Work

The system Outride [Pitkow et al., 2002] pursues a widespread personalization strategy characterized with "You know what I know, show me what I do not know". However, the sharing of previously-visited URL's is not assisted in a collaborative manner. Beyond these actual approaches, other systems concentrate either on one-time or long-time information needs. For one-time goals, Chakrabarti et al. [Chakrabarti et al., 2000] provide a Web browsing assistant for individual users and groups with focused information needs. It is based on a client-server architecture, and no information about topics that has not already been requested by other users, can be provided. On this account, no collaborative support exists. The goal of the system WebView [Cockburn et al., 1999] is the assistance of the user for revisiting relevant Web sites. A mapping of relevant Web sites to individual information needs is not available. Bawa et al. [Bawa et al., 2003] propose a peer-to-peer approach for collaborative retrieval. It supports the aggregation of peers into overlapping (user defined) groups, and the search through specific groups. This restriction is not desirable in order to achieve a flexible clustering of topics. For the support of long-time goals, traditional information filtering systems can be found in the context of push services, recommender systems, and awareness. GroupLens [Resnick et al., 1994] filters NetNews articles by the personal interest of a user. Collaborative filtering [Goldberg et al., 1992] is used to generate recommendations, but no content of the messages is analyzed in this central system. Although the need of personalization and collaboration is taken up by several systems, there are no aspects for a transparent information exchange and user interaction as conceived in this work.

6   Future Work

With this paper we presented an approach for dynamic information push. Based on explicit result rankings, a hybrid peer-to-peer network ensures a transparent filtering on each peer. Future work on the prototype will lead in three directions. First, we will investigate the impact of a global peer relevance. Actually, a peer gets no feedback about the usefulness of recommended documents for other peers. This information will lead to an intra-clustering of users to detect experts. For the implementation of an answer the MyPush protocol can be extended so that the satisfaction of an active peer is sent as a reply to the passive peers. Furthermore, we plan the integration of a *collaborative peer relevance* in order to assist a global perception of all users of a peer group. Second, in addition to the basic implicit weighting of associations, a combination between explicit and implicit weighting of associations and peer relevances is conceivable. On this account, the explicit influence of a user can be enhanced whereby the profile of the user comes to the forefront. Additionally, all results explicitly flagged as not relevant should be considered. Third, the actuality of long-time goals needs further investigation. A possible strategy would be the classification of local associations monitoring user behavior.

References

[Bates, 2002] Bates, M. (2002). After the dot-bomb: Getting web information retrieval right this time. *First Monday*, 7(7).

[Bawa et al., 2003] Bawa, M., Bayardo, Jr., R. J., Rajagopalan, S., and Shekita, E. J. (2003). Make it fresh, make it quick: searching a network of personal webservers. In *Proceedings of the twelfth international conference on World Wide Web*, pages 577–586. ACM Press.

[Belkin and Croft, 1992] Belkin, N. J. and Croft, W. B. (1992). Information filtering and information retrieval: two sides of the same coin? *CACM*, 35(12):29–38.

[Chakrabarti et al., 2000] Chakrabarti, S., Srivastava, S., Subramanyam, M., and Tiwari, M. (2000). Memex: A browsing assistant for collaborative archiving and mining of surf trails. In *VLDB 2000, Proceedings of the 26th International Conference on Very Large Data Bases*, pages 603–606, Cairo, Egypt.

[Cheverst and Smith, 2001] Cheverst, K. and Smith, G. (2001). Exploring the notion of information push and pull with respect to the user intention and disruption. In *International workshop on Distributed and Disappearing User Interfaces in Ubiquitous Computing*, pages 67–72.

[Cockburn et al., 1999] Cockburn, A., Greenberg, S., McKenzie, B., Smith, M., and Kaasten, S. (1999). Webview: A graphical aid for revisiting web pages. In *Proceedings of the OZCHI'99 Australian Conference on Human Computer Interaction*, Wagga Wagga (Australia).

[Flake et al., 2003] Flake, G. W., Tsioutsioulilis, K., and Zhukov, L. (2003). Methods for miming web communities: Bibliometric, spectral, and flow. In Levene, M. and Poulovassilis, A., editors, *Web Dynamics*, pages 45–68. Springer-Verlag.

[Gnasa et al., 2003] Gnasa, M., Alda, S., Grigull, J., and Cremers, A. B. (2003). Towards virtual knowledge communities in peer-to-peer networks. In *SIGIR 2003 Workshop on Distributed Information Retrieval*, Toronto, Canada. Springer-Verlag. LNCS.

[Gnasa et al., 2004a] Gnasa, M., Gül, N., Grigull, J., Alda, S., and Cremers, A. B. (2004a). Cooperative pull-push cycle for searching a hybrid p2p network. In *Proceedings of the 4th IEEE International Conference on Peer-to-Peer Computing*.

[Gnasa et al., 2004b] Gnasa, M., Won, M., and Cremers, A. B. (2004b). Three pillars for congenial web searching - continuous evaluation for enhancing web search effectiveness. *Journal of Web Engineering*, 3(3&4):252–280.

[Goldberg et al., 1992] Goldberg, D., Nichols, D., Oki, B. M., and Terry, D. (1992). Using collaborative filtering to weave an information tapestry. *CACM*, 35(12):61–70.

[Lawrence, 2000] Lawrence, S. (2000). Context in web search. *IEEE Data Engineering Bulletin*, 23(3):25–32.

[Luhn, 1958] Luhn, H. (1958). A business intelligent system. *IBM Journal of Research and Development*, 2(4):314–319.

[Oard, 1997]   Oard, D. W. (1997). The state of the art in text filtering. *User Modeling and User-Adapted Interaction*, 7(3):141–178.

[Oard and Kim, 1998]   Oard, D. W. and Kim, J. (1998). Implicit feedback for recommender systems. In *Proceedings of the AAAI Workshop on Recommender Systems*.

[Pitkow et al., 2002] Pitkow, J., Schütze, H., Cass, T., Cooley, R., Turnbull, D., Edmonds, A., Adar, E., and Breuel, T. (2002). Personalized search. *CACM*, 45(9):50–55.

[Resnick et al., 1994] Resnick, P., Iacovou, N., Suchak, M., Bergstorm, P., and Riedl, J. (1994). GroupLens: An Open Architecture for Collaborative Filtering of Netnews. In *Proceedings of ACM 1994 Conference on Computer Supported Cooperative Work*, pages 175–186, Chapel Hill, North Carolina. ACM.

[Rijsberg, 1979]   Rijsberg, C. J. V. (1979). *Information Retrieval*. Butterworths.

Getting Computers to See Information Graphics So Users Do Not Have to

Daniel Chester[1] and Stephanie Elzer[2]

[1] University of Delaware, Newark DE 19716, USA
chester@cis.udel.edu
http://cis.udel.edu/~chester
[2] Dept. of Computer Science, Millersville University, Millersville PA 17551, USA
elzer@cs.millersville.edu

Abstract. Information graphics such as bar, line and pie charts appear frequently in electronic media and often contain information that is not found elsewhere in documents. Unfortunately, sight-impaired users have difficulty accessing and assimilating information graphics. Our goal is an interactive natural language system that provides effective access to information graphics for sight-impaired individuals. This paper describes how image processing has been applied to transform an information graphic into an XML representation that captures all aspects of the graphic that might be relevant to extracting knowledge from it. It discusses the problems that were encountered in analyzing and categorizing components of the graphic, and the algorithms and heuristics that were successfully applied. The resulting XML representation serves as input to an evidential reasoning component that hypothesizes the message that the graphic was intended to convey.

1 Introduction

Information graphics (line charts, bar charts, etc.) frequently occur in popular media such as newspapers, magazines, and newsletters. Moreover, they generally contain information that is not part of any accompanying text. Although most people easily acquire knowledge from information graphics, this is not the case for individuals with sight impairments. Several research projects have investigated devices for conveying graphics in an alternative medium, such as tactile images or soundscapes[1, 2], but these approaches have serious limitations. For example, generation of a tactile image requires specialized equipment that is expensive. Soundscapes are ineffective at conveying intersection points of multiple lines. In order to avoid disenfranchising a segment of our population, methods must be developed that enable sight-impaired users to effectively access and assimilate information graphics.

The primary goal of our project is a methodology that enables sight-impaired individuals to assimilate the content of an information graphic with relative ease. While previous research has concentrated on rendering graphical elements in an

M.-S. Hacid et al. (Eds.): ISMIS 2005, LNAI 3488, pp. 660–668, 2005.
© Springer-Verlag Berlin Heidelberg 2005

alternative medium, our goal is to provide the user with the knowledge that one would gain from actually viewing the graphic rather than enabling the user to access what the graphic "looks like." Thus we are developing an interactive system that hypothesizes the intended message of the information graphic, uses spoken language to convey this message along with other related significant features of the graphic, and responds to follow-up questions about more detailed aspects of the graphic.

Section 2 discusses related work and describes potential applications of our system. Section 3 presents the overall architecture of our system. Section 4 focuses on the initial processing of the graphical image to construct an XML representation of the components of the graphic and their relation to one another. It discusses the goals of the image processing component, the problems that were encountered in analyzing and categorizing components of the graphic, and the algorithms and heuristics that were successfully applied. Section 5 describes the current status of our implementation and discusses future work that will extend the kind of graphics that the system can handle.

2   Overview

Limited attention has been given to summarizing information graphics. Reiter[3] used pattern recognition techniques to summarize interesting features of automatically generated graphs of time-series data from a gas turbine engine; however, Reiter started with the underlying data, not the graphical image. St. Amant[4] developed a system, VisMap, for manipulating a visual display that allowed interaction through a graphical user interface. VisMap could take pixel-level input from a screen display and recognize the interface objects displayed on the screen, such as menus and buttons. Futrelle [5, 6, 7, 8] developed a constraint grammar to define components of diagrams and parse the diagram. However, Futrelle was interested in a sophisticated mechanism for parsing complex vector diagrams (including finite state automata and gene diagrams); our work is limited to information graphics such as bar and line charts, and thus we can focus on simpler mechanisms that will have high success and be efficient on our real-world problem.

There are several useful applications for a system that can summarize information graphics at different levels of granularity. First, as the primary motivation for our work, it will facilitate an interactive natural language system that can provide the user with the primary content of the graphic (its intended message along with significant related features) and then respond to follow-up questions that address more detailed aspects of the graphic. For digital libraries, the initial summary of the graphic will be used in conjunction with summaries of the document text to provide a more complete representation of the content of the document for searching and indexing. In the case of environments with low-bandwidth transmission and miniature viewing facilities, such as cellular telephones for accessing the web, the initial summary and follow-up capability will provide an alternative modality for access to the document.

3   Architecture

Our current work is concerned with simple bar, line and pie charts, although eventually we will handle other kinds of graphics. The visual extraction module (VEM) analyzes the graphic and provides an XML representation of the graphic to the intention recognition module (IRM). The IRM is responsible for recognizing the intended message of the information graphic and sending it to the content planning module (CPM), which will augment the intended message of the graphic with related interesting features. The message organization module (MOM) then organizes the most salient propositions into a coherent summary, which will be rendered in natural language and conveyed to the user via speech synthesis. The follow-up question module (FQM) will provide the user with the opportunity to interactively seek additional information about the graphic. Details and status of the overall system may be found elsewhere [9, 10, 11, 12].

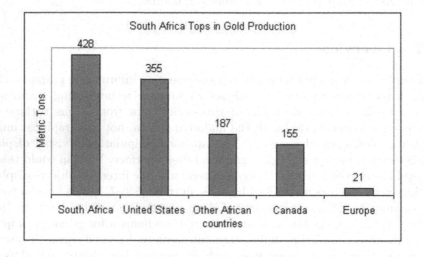

Fig. 1. A sample information graphic image (from USA Today)

The focus of this paper is on the processing done by the visual extraction module, which converts a graphic from its image format to a text format more suitable for the other modules to process. First the raw drawing components that are extracted from the image are described. Next, how the components are simplified and grouped to obtain the graphic components, and how these are used to identify the information graphic as a bar, line or pie chart is explained. Then the construction of an XML representation of the information content implicit in the graphic components is discussed. Finally several unresolved issues are addressed.

The information graphics that VEM handles are bar, line and pie charts that have been created by spreadsheet or drawing software. The graphics have been saved in an uncompressed image format and converted to pgm format, making them easy to read into internal arrays of pixels. The images are presently assumed to be one of the three chart types, with no textured regions, i.e., all areas are uniformly filled with one gray level. They are also free of noise and are not blurry, and components do not overlap. A typical example of such an input is the image shown in Fig. 1. One should note that although the graphic in this figure contains a useful caption, our analysis of a corpus of information graphics confirms research by Corio[13] that showed captions to be often nonexistent or unhelpful. Thus the graphic itself must be analyzed to convey its intent to the user.

4   Visual Extraction

When an information graphic is designed, it is built from abstract components like axes, bars, labels, titles, data points connected by lines, and wedges, depending on the graphic type. An image, however, is, at its simplest, just an array of gray level values. The task of the VEM is to extract the graphic components from the pixel array and present them in a textual form. The abstract components of an information graphic are themselves composed of entities, however, consisting of text, line segments, arcs, curves and filled regions in combination. For example, a bar in a bar chart typically has a filled rectangular region, a border of a different color, and labels that identify the attribute-value pair that the bar represents. The strategy of the VEM is to find these raw components and then to combine them into the graphic components at the level of abstraction that the designer was working with. Once these graphic components, together with their relationships to each other, have been found, it is a simple matter to describe them in a textual format.

4.1   Raw Component Extraction

As Fig. 1 shows, the images typically produced by spreadsheets have a small number of distinct gray level values, and they are usually well-spaced in the range of possible values. This makes it easy to separate an image into connected regions where each region has a uniform gray level. The first step in processing an image is identifying these connected uniform regions which we call *plateaus*. Examination of a histogram of the gray levels in the image with special attention to pixels near the edges identifies the background color, which is white in this example. In addition, the border of each plateau is computed by finding all the points in the plateau that are not completely surrounded by pixels with the same gray level.

Once the plateaus have been extracted, they have to be classified as text, or as chart elements that have to be broken down further into their drawing primitives. The text in a graphic consists of isolated plateaus, each of which is a character (or sometimes two characters run together). To identify these plateaus, we apply the heuristic that textual elements typically occupy small bounding boxes and take up a small percentage of space in those boxes or are short, thin horizontal or vertical line segments, which could be characters "I", "l" or the main part of "i", depending on the font. We identify these textual elements with a rather simple optical character recognition algorithm; much work has been done on the OCR problem, so we anticipate that one of the commercial OCR programs can be adapted to our needs in a future version of our software, but we have put that effort off because identifying the characters in an information graphic is only a small part of what has to be done. Instead, we use a simple template matching algorithm so that we can concentrate on sketching out the other steps needed for identifying the components of an information graphic image.

The smallest meaningful textual elements, however, are words, so we must group the text plateaus into word groups. We tried the irregular pyramid approach of Tan and Loo[14] to address this problem, but it was slow and ineffective. We devised a heuristic approach based on an analysis of information graphics in popular media. We create a new image in which the bounding boxes surrounding the text plateaus are filled rectangles, all having the same gray level. These rectangular plateaus are then dilated, which merges those that are close together. The modified plateaus are extracted from this modified image and the characters that fit inside of each modified plateau are grouped together as a word.

The highest level of meaningful text in an information graphic is the phrase level, where the phrase serves as a title or label of some nontextual element such as a bar or pie wedge. We extract titles with a simple heuristic: The words that are topmost with a horizontal orientation are sorted from left to right to form the title of the graphic and words that are leftmost with a vertical orientation are sorted from bottom to top to form the title for the Y-axis of the graphic. To facilitate extraction of visual components of a graphic, we make a new copy of the plateau list with all the text plateaus removed.

While the text plateaus can be treated as the textual primitives, the chart element plateaus in a graphic are actually compound entities. Since the shape information of a chart element plateau is entirely in its border, chart element plateaus that are not already lines are replaced by their borders for the rest of the extraction process. The graphic can now be thought of as a line drawing with an overlay of texts. But the chart element plateaus, which are now lines of various sorts, are still compound entities; they have to be broken down into simple drawing primitives like straight line segments and arcs before we can recognize what the plateaus are. In Fig. 1, for example, the X and Y axes are composed of two long lines and many smaller lines which serve as tick marks. We need to break these plateaus into straight line segments before we can recognize what parts of the X axis plateau are the tick marks and what part is the X axis itself. One way to break a compound line into straight line segments is to vectorize it, but the vectorizing programs available on the World Wide Web were not satisfactory to our purpose, so we devised our own way of decomposing the chart element plateaus. Each chart element plateau is traced in a clockwise direction and is broken into chains of pixels that are straight line segments or curves. They terminate when certain changes in the trend of the line is observed and when a junction is encountered. This breaks up most borders into small pieces. In Fig. 1, the borders that include the X and Y axes are broken up into the Y axis, the tick marks, and the segments of the X axis that lie between the tick marks. Straight lines are fitted to all chains using least squares. Connected sequences of short straight lines that slowly change orientation from one line to the next are recognized as curves. The end result is a representation of the line drawing part of the graphic as a set of straight line segments and simple arcs, which when drawn would reproduce the graphic minus the texts and without closed regions being filled in with gray levels other than the background color. Now that the graphic is decomposed into texts and line primitives that accurately capture all the information in a graphic (because they reproduce the graphic when drawn), the graphic is ready for the recognition phase of the visual extraction.

4.2   Component Regrouping

The line primitives have to be regrouped into recognizable components of bar, line and pie charts. Both bar charts and line charts are expected to have an X axis and a Y axis. Bar charts are expected to have bars that are laid out either vertically or horizontally. Line graphs are expected to have irregular sequences of straight line segments connecting the data points. Pie charts are expected to have wedge-shaped regions that belong to a circular region. There may be other graphical elements present also. For example, grid lines are often present to help the viewer read data off the graphic. Our task is to look for these components of information graphics and see how they are compositions of the line primitives that have been found.

The most perspicuous features of bar and line charts, apart from the bars and data lines, are the X and Y axes. We expect these to be a long horizontal and a long vertical line, respectively. To find these features, we start at the lower left corner of the graphic and look for the nearest vertical and horizontal line segments. These line segments are extended when possible with other line segments that are parallel to and in line with them. Extension is necessary because axes with tick marks get segmented as explained above. If the line segments grow into a line that is long enough, say, about four tenths of the width or height of the graphic, they are grouped together as one line and labeled the X axis or Y axis, depending on their orientation. Small line segments that are next to but perpendicular to one of these lines are grouped with that line as its tick marks. Finding the axes is helpful because they generally mark two sides of the rectangular region where the graphic's data is displayed. In a similar manner, other horizontal and vertical lines that are the same length as the axes are found and classified as grid lines. It is important to get rid of these lines so that the data region is left uncluttered, containing only informative graphic components.

The other graphic elements we look for are bars, data lines, wedges and legends. Small horizontal and vertical line segments have to be grouped when possible into rectangles. Sometimes several line segments have to be grouped together to make one side of a rectangle because there are junction points on the side when other rectangles are adjacent. Furthermore, some line segments may be part of more than one rectangle, again when rectangles are adjacent, such as when bars are drawn touching each other. If a rectangle is found that contains other rectangles with text near them, that cluster of objects is made into a single component and classified as a legend. The remaining rectangles are expected to be bars in a bar graph.

To recognize the wedges in a pie chart, we look for one straight line segment that has a curve connecting its two ends (a wedge that is half a pie) or two straight line segments that touch at one end and are connected to each other at the other end by a curve.

The data lines in line charts are the least structured of all the graphic components we look for, since they are just a sequence of connected line segments that can wander in any direction across the graphic. We recognize them by looking for connected line segments among the line segments that have not already been found to be parts of an axis, tick marks, parts of rectangles, or parts of wedges.

Finally, after axes, tick marks, rectangles, legends, wedges and data lines have been found, we are able to categorize an information graphic as to type; if there are rectangles that are not legends, the graphic is a bar chart; if it contains one or more data lines, it is a line chart; if it contains one or more wedges, it is a pie chart.

4.3   XML Formatted Output

With the information graphic dissected into its meaningful visual and textual components, we finally have to generate an XML representation of the graphic. Once we know what type of chart we are dealing with, it is straightforward to describe the chart. There are just a few additional pieces of information that have to be extracted from the relative locations of the visual and textual components.

In the case of bar charts, each bar has to be described in terms of its essential properties. These are the color (gray level) of the bar, its length (if horizontal) or height (if vertical) in centimeters, the text near its axis end, and any annotation text at its other end. If the bar has no annotation text, the value represented by its height must be computed. The ticks associated with the measurement axis are scanned for nearby text that are recognizable as numbers. The value of the bar is then computed by interpolating the projected length or height of the bar between the ticks. Figure 2 shows the XML representation of the middle bar in Fig. 1.

In the case of a line chart, each data line is represented by a sequence of points (expressed as the pixel location coordinates in the original image). The X coordinate of each point is projected down to the X axis and the text near that location is paired with the value obtained by projecting the Y coordinate onto the Y axis and estimating the value from the numerical texts and tick marks found there. These pairs are the data that are conveyed by the data line.

```
<Bar>
        <Label>
                <Content>Other African countries</Content>
                <Color>0</Color>
                <Bold>false</Bold>
        </Label>
        <Color>128</Color>
        <Height>2.72</Height>
        <AxisDistance>7.69</AxisDistance>
        <SightLine>false</SightLine>
        <Annotation>
                <Content>187</Content>
                <Color>0</Color>
                <Bold>false</Bold>
        </Annotation>
</Bar>
```

Fig. 2. XML representation of a bar in bar chart

5   Current Status

The present visual extraction system can handle simple black and white bar charts and line charts that have been produced by spreadsheet or drawing software and saved into an uncompressed image file. While pie charts are recognized, their transcription into XML output is not complete. Also, legends, although they are identified, produce no output.

In the future we intend to handle color images and make character recognition more robust. Allowing for regions to be filled in with textured color instead of only solid color is a more distant goal. A more immediate goal, however, is to make the system more robust in the presence of noise in the graphic image. Computer generated images can be noise-free and they can be transmitted over the Internet without becoming contaminated with noise, but most images on the Internet are stored in a lossy compressed format such as JPEG. The lossy compression process introduces artifacts when the image is decompressed that are an unusual kind of structured noise, which is different from the kinds that are commonly addressed in image processing. Most notably, the artifacts create barely noticeable dots around the characters in the image and faint ghost lines next to long lines. These ghost lines are not noticeable to the human eye, but they are glaring to the computer eye. Filtering out this special kind of noise will be the focus of our future work.

6   Summary

In this paper we have outlined the visual extraction module of an interactive dialog system for making information graphics accessible to sight-impaired users. Numerous heuristics are used to break down easily extracted regions (regions that are connected and have uniform gray level) into characters and line segments which serve as primitive elements from which the graphic elements, such as axes, bars, data lines and pie wedges are composed. We have shown that fairly simple techniques can be used to identify the components of an information graphic and produce an XML representation of its visual content. Much work remains, however, to extend the module to be more robust, particularly to be able to ignore the artifacts that are created by lossy compressed image formats and to deal with the artistic license of graphics designers, who often don't follow rules of good design.

References

1. Meijer, P.: An Experimental System for Auditory Image Representations. IEEE Transactions on Biomedical Engineering **39** (1992) 291–300
2. Kennel, A.: Audiograf: A diagram-reader for the blind. Proc. of the International Conference on Intelligent User Interfaces (1996) 51–56
3. Yu, J., Hunter, J., Reiter, E., Sripada, S.: Recognising Visual Patterns to Communicate Gas Turbine Time-Series Data. ES2002 (2002) 105–118
4. St. Amant, R., Riedl, M.: A Perception/Action Substrate for Cognitive Modeling in HCI. International Journal of Human-Computer Studies **55** (2000) 15–39
5. Futrelle, R., Kakadiaris, I., Alexander, J., Futrelle, J., Carriero, C., Nikolakis, N.: Understanding Diagrams in Technical Documents. IEEE Computer **25** (1992) 75–78
6. Futrelle, R., Nikolakis, N.: Diagram Analysis using Context-Based Constraint Grammars. Technical Report NC-CCS-96-01, College of Computer Science, Northeastern University (1996)
7. Futrelle, R.: Ambiguity in Visual Language Theory and its Role in Diagram Parsing. A Proceedings of the IEEE Symposium on Visual Languages (1999) 172–175
8. Futrelle, R.: Summarization of Diagrams in Documents. Advances in Automated Text Summarization, Mani, I., Maybury, M., eds., MIT Press (1999) 403–421
9. Carberry, S., Elzer, S., Green, N., McCoy K., Chester, D.: Understanding information graphics: a discourse-level problem. Proceedings of the Fourth SIGDial Workshop on Discourse and Dialogue (2003) 1–12
10. Elzer, S., Green, N., Carberry, S., McCoy, K.: Extending plan inference techniques to recognize intentions in information graphics. Proceedings of the Nineth International Conference on user Modeling (2003) 122–132
11. Carberry, S., Elzer, S., Green, N., McCoy K., Chester, D.: Extending document summarization to information graphics. Proceedings of the ACL Workshop on Text Summarization (2004)
12. Elzer, S., Green, N., Carberry, S., Hoffman, J.: Incorporating perceptual task effort into the recognition of intention in information graphics. Diagrammatic Representation and Inference: Third International Conference on the Theory and Application of Diagrams (LNAI 2980) (2004) 255–270
13. Corio, M., Lapalme, G.: Generation of texts for information graphics. Proceedings of the 7th European Workshop on Natural Language Generation (EWNLG'99) (1999) 49–58
14. Tan, C., Loo, P.: Word Extraction Using Irregular Pyramid. Proceedings of SPIE–Volume 4307 Document Recognition and Retrieval VIII, Kantora, P., Lopresti, D., Zhou, J., eds. (2000) 363–371

A Data Model Based on Paraconsistent Intuitionistic Fuzzy Relations

Haibin Wang and Rajshekhar Sunderraman

Department of Computer Science,
Georgia State University,
Atlanta, GA 30302, USA
hwang17@student.gsu.edu, raj@cs.gsu.edu

Abstract. Paraconsistent intuitionistic fuzzy set is an extension of intuitionistic fuzzy set or interval-valued fuzzy set. It relaxes the require ment that $t + f \leq 1$, where t is grade of truth-membership and f is grade of false-membership. In paraconsistent intuitionistic fuzzy set, $t, f \in [0, 1], 0 \leq t + f \leq 2$. In this paper, we present a generalization of the relational model of data based on paraconsistent intuitionistic fuzzy set. Our data model is capable of manipulating incomplete as well as inconsistent information. Associated with each relation there are two membership functions which keep track of the extent to which we believe the tuple is in the relation and the extent to which we believe that it is not in the relation. In order to handle inconsistent situations, we propose an operator, called "split", to transform inconsistent paraconsistent intuitionistic fuzzy relations into pseudo-consistent paraconsistent intuitionistic fuzzy relations. We may then manipulate these pseudo-consistent paraconsistent intuitionistic fuzzy relations by performing set-theoretic and relation-theoretic operations on them. Finally, we can use another operator, called "combine", to transform the results back to paraconsistent intuitionistic fuzzy relations. For this model, we define algebraic operators that are generalization of the usual operators such as union, selection, join on fuzzy relations. Our data model can underlie any database management system that deals with incomplete or inconsistent information.

1   Introduction

The relational model was proposed by Ted Codd's in his pioneering paper [1]. This data model usually takes care of only well-defined and unambiguous data. However, imperfect information is prevalent in many situations and approaches to deal with such imperfect data need to be devised.

In order to represent and manipulate various forms of incomplete information in relational databases, several extensions of the classical relational model have been proposed [2, 3, 4]. In some of these extensions, a variety of "null values" have been introduced to model unknown or not-applicable data values. Attempts have also been made to generalize operators of relational algebra to manipulate such extended data models [3, 5]. Fuzzy set theory and fuzzy logic proposed by Zadeh

M.-S. Hacid et al. (Eds.): ISMIS 2005, LNAI 3488, pp. 669–677, 2005.
© Springer-Verlag Berlin Heidelberg 2005

[6] provides a requisite mathematical framework for dealing with incomplete and imprecise information. Later on, the concept of interval-valued fuzzy sets was proposed to capture the fuzziness of grade of membership itself [7]. In 1986, Atanassov introduced the intuitionistic fuzzy set [8] which is a generalization of fuzzy set and provably equivalent to interval-valued fuzzy set. The intuitionistic fuzzy set considers both truth-membership t and false-membership f with $t, f \in [0,1]$ and $t + f \leq 1$. Because of this restirction, fuzzy sets, interval-valued fuzzy sets and intuitionistic fuzzy sets cannot handle inconsistent information. Some authors [9, 10, 11, 12, 13, 14] have studied relational databases in the light of fuzzy set theory with an objective to accommodate a wider range of real-world requirements and to provide closer man-machine interactions.

However, unlike incomplete, imprecise, and uncertain information, inconsistent information has not enjoyed enough research attention. In fact, inconsistent information exists in a lot of applications. For example, in data warehousing application, inconsistency will appear when trying to integrate data from many different sources. Another example is that of expert systems, where the knowledge base itself may contain facts which are inconsistent with each other. Generally, two basic approaches have been followed in solving the inconsistency problem in knowledge bases: belief revision and paraconsistent logics. The goal of the first approach is to make an inconsistent theory consistent, either by revising it or by representing it by a consistent semantics. On the other hand, the paraconsistent approach allows reasoning in the presence of inconsistency and contradictory information can be derived or introduced without trivialization [15]. Bagai and Sunderraman [16] proposed a paraconsistent relational data model to deal with incomplete and inconsistent information. This data model is based on paraconsistent logics.

In this paper, we present a new relational data model - paraconsistent intuitionistic fuzzy relational data model (PIFRDM). Our model is based on the intuitionistic fuzzy set theory [8] and is capable of manipulating incomplete as well as inconsistent information. Let X be the universe of discourse. We use both grade of truth membership α and grade of false membership β to denote the status of a tuple of a certain relation with $\alpha(x), \beta(x) \in [0,1]$ and $\alpha(x) + \beta(x) \leq 2$ for all $x \in X$. PIFRDM is the generalization of fuzzy relational data model (FRDM). That is, when $\alpha(x) + \beta(x) = 1$ for all $x \in X$, paraconsistent intuitionistic fuzzy relation is the ordinary fuzzy relation. This generalization is distinct from paraconsistent relational data model (PRDM), in fact it can be easily shown that PRDM is a special case of PIFRDM. That is, when $\alpha(x), \beta(x) = 0$ or 1 for all $x \in X$, paraconsistent intuitionistic fuzzy relation is just paraconsistent relation.

We introduce paraconsistent intuitionistic fuzzy relations, which are the fundamental mathematical structures underlying our model. These structures are strictly more general than classical fuzzy relations, in that for any fuzzy relation there is a paraconsistent intuitionistic fuzzy relation with the same information content, but not *vice versa*. The claim is also true for the relationship between paraconsistent intuitionistic fuzzy relations and paraconsistent relations. We define algebraic operators over paraconsistent intuitionistic fuzzy relations that extend the standard operators, such as selection, join, union, over fuzzy relations.

2   Paraconsistent Intuitionistic Fuzzy Relations

In this section, we generalize fuzzy relations and paraconsistent relations in such a manner that we are now able to assign a measure of belief and a measure of doubt to each tuple. We shall refer to these generalized relations as *paraconsistent intuitionistic fuzzy relations*. So, a tuple in a paraconsistent intuitionistic fuzzy relation is assigned a measure $\langle \alpha, \beta \rangle$, $0 \leq \alpha, \beta \leq 1$. α will be referred to as the *belief* factor and β will be referred to as the *doubt* factor. The interpretation of this measure is that we believe with confidence α and doubt with confidence β that the tuple is in the relation. The belief and doubt confidence factors for a tuple need not add to exactly 1. This allows for incompleteness and inconsistencies to be represented. If the belief and doubt factors add up to less than 1, we have incomplete information regarding the tuple's status in the relation and if the belief and doubt factors add up to more than 1, we have inconsistent information regarding the tuple's status in the relation.

We now formalize the notion of a paraconsistent intuitionistic fuzzy relation.

Let a *relation scheme* (or just *scheme*) Σ be a finite set of *attribute names*, where for any attribute $A \in \Sigma$, $dom(A)$ is a non-empty *domain* of values for A. A *tuple* on Σ is any map $t : \Sigma \to \cup_{A \in \Sigma} dom(A)$, such that $t(A) \in dom(A)$, for each $A \in \Sigma$. Let $\tau(\Sigma)$ denote the set of all tuples on Σ.

Definition 1. *A **paraconsistent intuitionistic fuzzy relation** R on scheme Σ is any subset of $\tau(\Sigma) \times [0,1] \times [0,1]$. For any $t \in \tau(\Sigma)$, we shall denote an element of R as $\langle t, R(t)^+, R(t)^- \rangle$, where $R(t)^+$ is the belief factor assigned to t by R and $R(t)^-$ is the doubt factor assigned to t by R. Let $\mathcal{V}(\Sigma)$ be the set of all paraconsistent intuitionistic fuzzy relations on Σ.*

Definition 2. *A paraconsistent intuitionistic fuzzy relation R on scheme Σ is **consistent** if $R(t)^+ + R(t)^- \leq 1$, for all $t \in \tau(\Sigma)$. Let $\mathcal{C}(\Sigma)$ be the set of all consistent paraconsistent intuitionistic fuzzy relations on Σ. R is said to be **complete** if $R(t)^+ + R(t)^- \geq 1$, for all $t \in \tau(\Sigma)$. If R is both consistent and complete, i.e. $R(t)^+ + R(t)^- = 1$, for all $t \in \tau(\Sigma)$, then it is a **total** paraconsistent intuitionistic fuzzy relation, and let $\mathcal{T}(\Sigma)$ be the set of all total paraconsistent intuitionistic fuzzy relations on Σ.*

Definition 3. *R is said to be **pseudo-consistent** if*
$\max\{b_i | (\exists t \in \tau(\Sigma))(\exists d_i)(\langle t, b_i, d_i \rangle \in R)\} + \max\{d_i | (\exists t \in \tau(\Sigma))(\exists b_i)(\langle t, b_i, d_i \rangle \in R)\} > 1$, *where for these $\langle t, b_i, d_i \rangle$, $b_i + d_i = 1$. Let $\mathcal{P}(\Sigma)$ be the set of all pseudo-consistent paraconsistent intuitionistic fuzzy relations on Σ.*

It should be observed that total paraconsistent intuitionistic fuzzy relations are essentially fuzzy relations where the uncertainty in the grade of membership is eliminated. Let $\mathcal{F}(\Sigma)$ be the set of all fuzzy relations over scheme Σ. We make this relationship explicit by defining an one-one correspondence $\lambda_\Sigma : \mathcal{T}(\Sigma) \to \mathcal{F}(\Sigma)$, given by $\lambda_\Sigma(R)(t) = R(t)^+$, for all $t \in \tau(\Sigma)$. This correspondence is used frequently in the following discussion.

Operator Generalisations

It is easily seen that paraconsistent intuitionistic fuzzy relations are a generalisation of fuzzy relations, in that for each fuzzy relation there is a paraconsistent intuitionistic fuzzy relation with the same information content, but not *vice versa*. It is thus natural to think of generalising the operations on fuzzy relations, such as union, join, projection etc., to paraconsistent intuitionistic fuzzy relations. However, any such generalisation should be intuitive with respect to the belief system model of paraconsistent intuitionistic fuzzy relations. We now construct a framework for operators on both kinds of relations and introduce two different notions of the generalisation relationship among their operators.

An n-ary *operator on fuzzy relations with signature* $\langle \Sigma_1, \ldots, \Sigma_{n+1} \rangle$ is a function $\Theta : \mathcal{F}(\Sigma_1) \times \cdots \times \mathcal{F}(\Sigma_n) \to \mathcal{F}(\Sigma_{n+1})$, where $\Sigma_1, \ldots, \Sigma_{n+1}$ are any schemes. Similarly, an n-ary *operator on paraconsistent intuitionistic fuzzy relations with signature* $\langle \Sigma_1, \ldots, \Sigma_{n+1} \rangle$ is a function $\Psi : \mathcal{V}(\Sigma_1) \times \cdots \times \mathcal{V}(\Sigma_n) \to \mathcal{V}(\Sigma_{n+1})$.

Definition 4. *An operator Ψ on paraconsistent intuitionistic fuzzy relations with signature $\langle \Sigma_1, \ldots, \Sigma_{n+1} \rangle$ is* **totality preserving** *if for any total paraconsistent intuitionistic fuzzy relations $R_1, \ldots, R_n$ on schemes $\Sigma_1, \ldots, \Sigma_n$, respectively, $\Psi(R_1, \ldots, R_n)$ is also total.*

Definition 5. *A totality preserving operator Ψ on paraconsistent intuitionistic fuzzy relations with signature $\langle \Sigma_1, \ldots, \Sigma_{n+1} \rangle$ is a* **weak generalisation** *of an operator Θ on fuzzy relations with the same signature, if for any total paraconsistent intuitionistic fuzzy relations $R_1, \ldots, R_n$ on schemes $\Sigma_1, \ldots, \Sigma_n$, respectively, we have*

$$\lambda_{\Sigma_{n+1}}(\Psi(R_1, \ldots, R_n)) = \Theta(\lambda_{\Sigma_1}(R_1), \ldots, \lambda_{\Sigma_n}(R_n)).$$

The above definition essentially requires Ψ to coincide with Θ on total paraconsistent intuitionistic fuzzy relations (which are in one-one correspondence with the fuzzy relations). In general, there may be many operators on paraconsistent intuitionistic fuzzy relations that are weak generalisations of a given operator Θ on fuzzy relations. The behavior of the weak generalisations of Θ on even just the consistent paraconsistent intuitionistic fuzzy relations may in general vary. We require a stronger notion of operator generalisation under which, when restricted to consistent paraconsistent intuitionistic fuzzy relations, the behavior of all the generalised operators is the same. Before we can develop such a notion, we need that of 'representations' of a paraconsistent intuitionistic fuzzy relation.

We associate with a consistent paraconsistent intuitionistic fuzzy relation R the set of all (fuzzy relations corresponding to) total paraconsistent intuitionistic fuzzy relations obtainable from R by filling in the gaps between the belief and doubt factors for each tuple. Let the map $\mathbf{reps}_\Sigma : \mathcal{C}(\Sigma) \to 2^{\mathcal{F}(\Sigma)}$ be given by

$$\mathbf{reps}_\Sigma(R) = \{ Q \in \mathcal{F}(\Sigma) \mid \bigwedge_{t_i \in \tau(\Sigma)} (R(t_i)^+ \le Q(t_i) \le 1 - R(t_i)^-) \}.$$

The set $\mathbf{reps}_\Sigma(R)$ contains all fuzzy relations that are 'completions' of the consistent or pseudo-consistent paraconsistent intuitionistic fuzzy relation R. Observe that $\mathbf{reps}_\Sigma$ is defined only for consistent paraconsistent intuitionistic fuzzy relations and produces sets of fuzzy relations. Then we have following observation.

Proposition 1. *For any consistent paraconsistent intuitionistic fuzzy relation R on scheme Σ, $\mathbf{reps}_\Sigma(R)$ is the singleton $\{\lambda_\Sigma(R)\}$ iff R is total.*

We now need to extend operators on fuzzy relations to sets of fuzzy relations. For any operator $\Theta : \mathcal{F}(\Sigma_1) \times \cdots \times \mathcal{F}(\Sigma_n) \to \mathcal{F}(\Sigma_{n+1})$ on fuzzy relations, we let $\mathcal{S}(\Theta) : 2^{\mathcal{F}(\Sigma_1)} \times \cdots \times 2^{\mathcal{F}(\Sigma_n)} \to 2^{\mathcal{F}(\Sigma_{n+1})}$ be a map on sets of fuzzy relations defined as follows. For any sets $M_1, \ldots, M_n$ of fuzzy relations on schemes $\Sigma_1, \ldots, \Sigma_n$, respectively,

$$\mathcal{S}(\Theta)(M_1, \ldots, M_n) = \{\Theta(R_1, \ldots, R_n) \mid R_i \in M_i, \text{ for all } i, 1 \le i \le n\}.$$

In other words, $\mathcal{S}(\Theta)(M_1, \ldots, M_n)$ is the set of Θ-images of all tuples in the cartesian product $M_1 \times \cdots \times M_n$. We are now ready to lead up to a stronger notion of operator generalisation.

Definition 6. *An operator Ψ on paraconsistent intuitionistic fuzzy relations with signature $\langle \Sigma_1, \ldots, \Sigma_{n+1} \rangle$ is* **consistency preserving** *if for any consistent or pseudo-consistent paraconsistent intuitionistic fuzzy relations $R_1, \ldots, R_n$ on schemes $\Sigma_1, \ldots, \Sigma_n$, respectively, $\Psi(R_1, \ldots, R_n)$ is also consistent or pseudo-consistent.*

Definition 7. *A consistency preserving operator Ψ on paraconsistent intuitionistic fuzzy relations with signature $\langle \Sigma_1, \ldots, \Sigma_{n+1} \rangle$ is a* **strong generalisation** *of an operator Θ on fuzzy relations with the same signature, if for any consistent or pseudo-consistent paraconsistent intuitionistic fuzzy relations $R_1, \ldots, R_n$ on schemes $\Sigma_1, \ldots, \Sigma_n$, respectively, we have*

$$\mathbf{reps}_{\Sigma_{n+1}}(\Psi(R_1, \ldots, R_n)) = \mathcal{S}(\Theta)(\mathbf{reps}_{\Sigma_1}(R_1), \ldots, \mathbf{reps}_{\Sigma_n}(R_n)).$$

Given an operator Θ on fuzzy relations, the behavior of a weak generalisation of Θ is 'controlled' only over the total paraconsistent intuitionistic fuzzy relations. On the other hand, the behavior of a strong generalisation is 'controlled' over all consistent or pseudo-consistent paraconsistent intuitionistic fuzzy relations. This itself suggests that strong generalisation is a stronger notion than weak generalisation. The following proposition makes this precise.

Proposition 2. *If Ψ is a strong generalisation of Θ, then Ψ is also a weak generalisation of Θ.*

Proof. Let $\langle \Sigma_1, \ldots, \Sigma_{n+1} \rangle$ be the signature of Ψ and Θ, and let $R_1, \ldots, R_n$ be any total paraconsistent intuitionistic fuzzy relations on schemes $\Sigma_1, \ldots, \Sigma_n$, respectively. Since all total relations are consistent, and Ψ is a strong generalisation of Θ, we have that

$$\mathbf{reps}_{\Sigma_{n+1}}(\Psi(R_1, \ldots, R_n)) = \mathcal{S}(\Theta)(\mathbf{reps}_{\Sigma_1}(R_1), \ldots, \mathbf{reps}_{\Sigma_n}(R_n)),$$

Proposition 1 gives us that for each i, $1 \leq i \leq n$, $\mathbf{reps}_{\Sigma_i}(R_i)$ is the singleton set $\{\lambda_{\Sigma_i}(R_i)\}$. Therefore, $\mathcal{S}(\Theta)(\mathbf{reps}_{\Sigma_1}(R_i), \ldots, \mathbf{reps}_{\Sigma_n}(R_n))$ is just the singleton set: $\{\Theta(\lambda_{\Sigma_1}(R_1), \ldots, \lambda_{\Sigma_n}(R_n))\}$. Here, $\Psi(R_1, \ldots, R_n)$ is total, and $\lambda_{\Sigma_{n+1}}(\Psi(R_1, \ldots, R_n)) = \Theta(\lambda_{\Sigma_1}(R_1), \ldots, \lambda_{\Sigma_n}(R_n))$, i.e. Ψ is a weak generalisation of Θ.   □

Though there may be many strong generalisations of an operator on fuzzy relations, they all behave the same when restricted to consistent or pseudo-consistent paraconsistent intuitionistic fuzzy relations. In the next section, we propose strong generalisations for the usual operators on fuzzy relations. The proposed generalised operators on paraconsistent intuitionistic fuzzy relations correspond to the belief system intuition behind paraconsistent intuitionistic fuzzy relations.

First we will introduce two special operators on paraconsistent intuitionistic fuzzy relations called "split" and "combine" to transform inconsistent paraconsistent intuitionistic fuzzy relations into pseudo-consistent paraconsistent intuitionistic fuzzy relations and transform pseudo-consistent paraconsistent intuitionistic fuzzy relations into inconsistent paraconsistent intuitionistic fuzzy relations, respectively.

Definition 8 (Split). *Let R be a paraconsistent intuitionistic fuzzy relation on scheme Σ. Then,*
$\triangle(R) = \{\langle t, b, d \rangle | \langle t, b, d \rangle \in R \text{ and } b + d \leq 1\} \cup \{\langle t, b', d' \rangle | (\exists b)(\exists d)(\langle t, b, d \rangle \in R \text{ and } b + d > 1 \text{ and } b' = b \text{ and } d' = 1 - b)\} \cup \{\langle t, b', d' \rangle | (\exists b)(\exists d)(\langle t, b, d \rangle \in R \text{ and } b + d > 1 \text{ and } b' = 1 - d \text{ and } d' = d)\}.$

Definition 9 (Combine). *Let R be a paraconsistent intuitionistic fuzzy relation on scheme Σ. Then,*
$\nabla(R) = \{\langle t, b, d \rangle | (\exists b')(\exists d')(((\langle t, b', d \rangle \in R \text{ and } (\forall b_i)(\forall d_i)(\langle t, b_i, d_i \rangle \in R \to d \geq d_i)) \text{ and } (\langle t, b, d' \rangle \in R \text{ and } (\forall b_i)(\forall d_i)(\langle t, b_i, d_i \rangle \in R \to b \geq b_i)))\}.$

Note that strong generalization defined above only holds for consistent or pseudo-consistent paraconsistent intuitionistic fuzzy relations. For any paraconsisent intuitionistic fuzzy relations, we should first use split operation to transform them into consistent or pseudo-consistent paraconsistent intuitionistic fuzzy relations and apply the set-theoretic and relation-theoretic operations on them and finally use combine operation to transform the result into paraconsistent intuitionistic fuzzy relation. For the simplification of notation, the following generalized algebra is defined under such assumption.

3   Generalized Algebra on Paraconsistent Intuitionistic Fuzzy Relations

In this section, we present one strong generalisation each for the fuzzy relation operators such as union, join, projection. To reflect generalisation, a hat is placed over a fuzzy relation operator to obtain the corresponding paraconsistent intuitionistic fuzzy relation operator. For example, ⋈ denotes the natural join among fuzzy relations, and $\widehat{\bowtie}$ denotes natural join on paraconsistent intuitionistic fuzzy relations. These generalized operators maintain the belief system intuition behind paraconsistent intuitionistic fuzzy relations.

Set-Theoretic Operators

We first generalize the two fundamental set-theoretic operators, union and complement.

Definition 10. *Let R and S be paraconsistent intuitionistic fuzzy relations on scheme Σ. Then,*

(a) *the* **union** *of R and S, denoted $R \,\widehat{\cup}\, S$, is a paraconsistent intuitionistic fuzzy relation on scheme Σ, given by*

$$(R \,\widehat{\cup}\, S)(t) = \langle \max\{R(t)^+, S(t)^+\}, \min\{R(t)^-, S(t)^-\}\rangle, \text{ for any } t \in \tau(\Sigma);$$

(b) *the* **complement** *of R, denoted $\widehat{-}\, R$, is a paraconsistent intuitionistic fuzzy relation on scheme Σ, given by*

$$(\widehat{-}\, R)(t) = \langle R(t)^-, R(t)^+\rangle, \text{ for any } t \in \tau(\Sigma).$$

Proposition 3. *The operators $\widehat{\cup}$ and unary $\widehat{-}$ on paraconsistent intuitionistic fuzzy relations are strong generalisations of the operators $\cup$ and unary $-$ on fuzzy relations.*

Definition 11. *Let R and S be paraconsistent intuitionistic fuzzy relations on scheme Σ. Then,*

(a) *the* **intersection** *of R and S, denoted $R \,\widehat{\cap}\, S$, is a paraconsistent intuitionistic fuzzy relation on scheme Σ, given by*

$$(R \,\widehat{\cap}\, S)(t) = \langle \min\{R(t)^+, S(t)^+\}, \max\{R(t)^-, S(t)^-\}\rangle, \text{ for any } t \in \tau(\Sigma);$$

(b) *the* **difference** *of R and S, denoted $R \,\widehat{-}\, S$, is a paraconsistent intuitionistic fuzzy relation on scheme Σ, given by*

$$(R \,\widehat{-}\, S)(t) = \langle \min\{R(t)^+, S(t)^-\}, \max\{R(t)^-, S(t)^+\}\rangle, \text{ for any } t \in \tau(\Sigma);$$

Relation-Theoretic Operators

We now define some relation-theoretic algebraic operators on paraconsistent intuitionistic fuzzy relations.

Definition 12. *Let R and S be paraconsistent intuitionistic fuzzy relations on schemes Σ and Δ, respectively. Then, the* **natural join** *(further for short called join) of R and S, denoted $R \,\widehat{\bowtie}\, S$, is a paraconsistent intuitionistic fuzzy relation on scheme $\Sigma \cup \Delta$, given by*

$$(R \bowtie S)(t) = \langle \min\{R(\pi_\Sigma(t))^+, S(\pi_\Delta(t))^+\}, \max\{R(\pi_\Sigma(t))^-, S(\pi_\Delta(t))^-\}\rangle,$$

where π is the usual projection of a tuple.

It is instructive to observe that, similar to the intersection operator, the minimum of the belief factors and the maximum of the doubt factors are used in the definition of the join operation.

Proposition 4. $\bowtie$ *is a strong generalisation of* $\bowtie$.

Definition 13. *Let R be a paraconsistent intuitionistic fuzzy relation on scheme Σ, and $\Delta \subseteq \Sigma$. Then, the* **projection** *of R onto Δ, denoted $\widehat{\pi}_\Delta(R)$, is a paraconsistent intuitionistic fuzzy relation on scheme Δ, given by*

$$(\widehat{\pi}_\Delta(R))(t) = \langle \max\{R(u)^+ | u \in t^\Sigma\}, \min\{R(u)^- | u \in t^\Sigma\}\rangle.$$

The belief factor of a tuple in the projection is the maximum of the belief factors of all of the tuple's extensions onto the scheme of the input paraconsistent intuitionistic fuzzy relation. Moreover, the doubt factor of a tuple in the projection is the minimum of the doubt factors of all of the tuple's extensions onto the scheme of the input paraconsistent intuitionistic fuzzy relation.

Definition 14. *Let R be a paraconsistent intuitionistic fuzzy relation on scheme Σ, and let F be any logic formula involving attribute names in Σ, constant symbols (denoting values in the attribute domains), equality symbol $=$, negation symbol $\neg$, and connectives $\vee$ and $\wedge$. Then, the* **selection** *of R by F, denoted $\widehat{\sigma}_F(R)$, is a paraconsistent intuitionistic fuzzy relation on scheme Σ, given by*

$$(\widehat{\sigma}_F(R))(t) = \langle \alpha, \beta \rangle, \text{ where}$$

$$\alpha = \begin{cases} R(t)^+ & \text{if } t \in \sigma_F(\tau(\Sigma)) \\ 0 & \text{otherwise} \end{cases} \quad \text{and} \quad \beta = \begin{cases} R(t)^- & \text{if } t \in \sigma_F(\tau(\Sigma)) \\ 1 & \text{otherwise} \end{cases}$$

where σ_F is the usual selection of tuples satisfying F from ordinary relations.

If a tuple satisfies the selection criterion, its belief and doubt factors are the same in the selection as in the input paraconsistent intuitionistic fuzzy relation. In the case where the tuple does not satisfy the selection criterion, its belief factor is set to 0 and the doubt factor is set to 1 in the selection.

Proposition 5. *The operators $\widehat{\pi}$ and $\widehat{\sigma}$ are strong generalisations of π and σ, respectively.*

4   Conclusions

We have presented a generalization of fuzzy relations and paraconsistent relations, called paraconsistent intuitionistic fuzzy relations, in which we allow the representation of confidence (belief and doubt) factors with each tuple. The algebra on fuzzy relations is appropriately generalized to manipulate paraconsistent intuitionistic fuzzy relations.

Our data model can be used to represent relational information that may be incomplete or inconsistent. As usual, the algebraic operators can be used to construct queries to any database systems for retrieving imprecise information.

References

1. Codd, E.: A relational model for large shared data banks. Communications of the ACM **13** (1970) 377–387
2. Brodie, M.L., Mylopoulous, J., Schmidt, J.W.: On the development of data models. On Conceptual Modelling (1984) 19–47
3. Biskup, J.: A foundation of codds relational maybe–operations. ACM Trans. Database Syst. 8 **4** (1983) 608–636
4. Imieliński, T., Lipski, W.: Incomplete information in relational databases. Journal of the ACM **31** (1984) 761–791
5. Codd, E.: Extending the database relational model to capture more meaning. ACM Transactions of Database Systems 4 (1979) 397–434
6. Zadeh, L.A.: Fuzzy sets. Inf. Control 8 (1965) 338–353
7. Turksen, I.: Interval valued fuzzy sets based on normal forms. Fuzzy Sets and Systems **20** (1986) 191–210
8. Atanassov, K.: Intuitionistic fuzzy sets. Fuzzy Sets and Systems **20** (1986) 87–96
9. Bosc, P., Prade, H.: An introduction to fuzzy set and possibility theory-based approaches to treatment of uncertainty and imprecision in database management systems. In: Proc. Workshop Uncertainty Management in Information Systems. (1993)
10. Bosc, P., Pivert, O.: Sqlf: A relational database language for fuzzy querying. IEEE Transactions on Fuzzy Systems **3** (1995)
11. Kacprzyk, J., Ziolkowski, A.: Database queries with fuzzy linguistic quantifiers. IEEE Trans. Syst. Man Cybern. SMC-16 **3** (1986) 474–479
12. Prade, H., Testemale, C.: Representation of soft constraints and fuzzy attribute values by means of possibility distributions in databases. Analysis of Fuzzy Information, Volume II, Artificial Intelligence and Decision Systems (1987) 213–229
13. Raju, K.V.S.V.N., Majumdar, A.K.: Fuzzy functional dependencies and lossless join decomposition of fuzzy relational database systems. ACM Trans. on Database Syst. 13 **2** (1988) 129–166
14. Vila, M., Cubero, J., Medina, J., Pons, O.: Logic and fuzzy relational databases: a new language and a new definition. In Bosc, P., Kacprzyk, J., eds.: Fuzziness in Database Management Systems. (Physica-Verlag)
15. de Amo, S., Carnielli, W., Marcos, J.: A logical framework for integrating inconsistent information in multiple databasses. In: Proc. PoIKS'02, LNCS 2284. (2002) 67–84
16. Bagai, R., Sunderraman, R.: A paraconsistent relational data model. International Journal of Computer Mathematics **55** (1995)

Logical Data Independence Reconsidered
(Extended Abstract)

James J. Lu

Emory University, Atlanta, GA 30332
jlu@mathcs.emory.edu

Abstract. Logical data independence is central to a number of database research problems including data integration and keyword search. In this paper, a data model that unifies several of the most widely adopted data models is studied. The key is to disassociate metadata from particular roles. A high-level, context-based (or semantically-based) query language is introduced, and applications to the aforementioned areas of research are demonstrated briefly.

Keywords: data model, context-based query language, universal relation, data integration, keyword searches, information retrieval.

1 Introduction

A basic tenet of data management systems is that data exist in contexts and in relationships to one another. For example, in relational databases, contexts are given through relation and attribute names, and relationships by grouping data into tuples and linked via foreign keys. In XML, contexts are given through element and attribute names, and relationships by organizing data into trees and subtrees.

Contexts provide the means through which information can be queried, but traditional data management systems associate, in addition, specific roles to contexts. In relational databases, the roles of attributes and relations are reflected in the standard SQL query explicitly:

```
select <attributes> from <relations> where ...
```

One must know which contexts have been assigned the role of attribute, and which the role of relation in order to write a correct query. A relation name in the `select` clause, for instance, is not allowed. Similarly, in XPath queries, notions of root, ancestor, descendent, and other axes reflect the roles that are, either absolutely or relatively, associated with elements and attributes.

Practically, role assignments impose unnecessary restrictions and have hindered the development of query languages that are transparent to the logical structures of the data. To motivate, we observe that the following two English queries are equivalent.

1. Find all first and last names (of authors) in the Atlanta area.
2. Find all authors (first and last names) in the Atlanta area.

M.-S. Hacid et al. (Eds.): ISMIS 2005, LNAI 3488, pp. 678–687, 2005.
© Springer-Verlag Berlin Heidelberg 2005

In the first query, the word "authors" qualifies the names that are being searched, and in the second query, the phrase "first and last names" specifies that part of the author information of interest. In both cases, parenthesized texts provide context to the attributes desired, but switching the roles of attributes and their contexts do not, in fact, change the meaning of the query. However, to represent the above data in, say, relational databases requires either we associate the role of relation to author and attribute to first and last names, or unconventionally as the two relations constrained by a foreign key between the two id attributes: $\begin{array}{|c|c|}\hline \textbf{firstname} \\ \hline \text{author} & \text{id} \\ \hline \end{array} \leftarrow \begin{array}{|c|c|}\hline \textbf{lastname} \\ \hline \text{id} & \text{author} \\ \hline \end{array}$. Firstname and lastname are now relations linked via an attribute id, and author is an attribute in each relation.

Under certain assumptions about database designs, relationless query languages have been investigated since the early 80's within the relational data model in a series of foundational papers (e.g., [8, 6, 9]). Yet the basic question of how to achieve logical data independence has remained at the core of numerous data and information management research issues, including modern problems such as heterogeneous data integration and keyword based querying. In this paper, we revisit the idea of "structureless" databases based on the observation that many of the popular logical data models (e.g., relational, ERD, XML) can be unified into a single conceptual model by simply removing role assignments to contexts. Our primary objective is to *provide an abstraction that facilitates structure-independent querying without imposing assumptions on data designs*. The practical benefits of the accompanying query language include (1) the blurring of structured (in a sense similar to SQL and XPath) and unstructured (in the sense of keyword searches) queries, and (2) providing a single, logically transparent interface to accessing heterogeneous data sources.

In Section 2, we develop the basic model of our database. A query language and its algebraic foundation for the data model is introduced in Section 3. Sections 4 and 5 illustrate applications in simple data integration and keyword searching scenarios.

2   Basics

We assume disjoint sets V and S called *values* and *context identifiers* respectively. Intuitively, values are the data in the database including strings, integers, booleans, etc., and sets of context identifiers make up a context for a value. We assume that V contains the distinguished element $\perp$ (the null value).

Definition 1. A *context* is a subset of S.[1] Each context c has an associated subset, $\text{Dom}(c)$, of V, called the *domain* of c. The null value is assumed to be in the domain of every context.

Definition 2. A unit is a function u that maps a finite number of contexts to non-null values while satisfying the condition $u(c) \in \text{Dom}(c)$, for every context c. If $u(c) \neq \perp$, we say that c is a *well-defined context* for u, denoted by $u(c) \downarrow$. A unit u is well-defined if $u(c) \downarrow$ for some context c.[2]

---

[1] Singleton contexts are sometimes written without braces.

[2] A topic of ongoing study is to generalize the definition to map contexts to subsets of V.

We define a partial ordering $\preceq$ on a set of units $\mathcal{U}$:

Definition 3. Unit u_1 is a *subunit* of unit u_2 iff for each context c such that $u_1(c) \downarrow$, there is a context $c' \supseteq c$ that satisfiy $u_2(c') = u_1(c)$. We denote the subunit relation with the symbol $\preceq$.

We adopt a generalization of the notational convention used in relational databases for representing units: Let $c_1, ..., c_m$ be all the well-defined contexts for u. Then, u can be written $< c_1 : v_1, ..., c_m : v_m >$ where $u(c_i) = v_i$, for $1 \leq i \leq m$.

Definition 4. A *universal database* (UDB) is a quadruple $(\mathcal{V}, \mathcal{S}, \text{Dom}, \mathbf{U})$ where $\mathbf{U}$ is a finite collection of units.

Example 1 (Modeling RDB). Consider the relational database, DB_1, that contains the following two relations. We assume **Contract**.Author is a foreign key to **Writer**.SSN.

<table>
<tr><th colspan="2">Writer</th><th colspan="3">Contract</th></tr>
<tr><td>Name</td><td>SSN</td><td>Publisher</td><td>Book</td><td>Author</td></tr>
<tr><td>Diana</td><td>1234</td><td>Prentice</td><td>Diana</td><td>1111</td></tr>
<tr><td>Mary</td><td>1111</td><td>Addison</td><td>XML</td><td>1111</td></tr>
</table>

We can model DB_1 as the UDB $(\mathcal{V}, \mathcal{S}, \text{Dom}, \mathbf{U})$ where

1. $\mathcal{V}$ is the set of all data that can appear in the two relations (e.g., Diana, 1234, Prentice, XML, etc.);
2. $\mathcal{S} = \{$Writer, Contract, Name, SSN, Publisher, Book, Author$\}$;
3. Dom maps contexts to non-empty sets of values. For example, Dom($\{$Writer,Name$\}$) includes $\{$Diana, Mary$\}$.
4. The well-defined units of the UDB are as follows.
   $<\{$Writer,Name$\}$:Diana,$\{$Writer,SSN$\}$:1234$>$
   $<\{$Contract,Author$\}$:1111,$\{$Contract,Publisher$\}$:Prentice,$\{$Contract,Book$\}$:Diana$>$
   $<\{$Writer,Name$\}$:Mary,$\{$Writer,SSN$\}$:1111$>$
   $<\{$Contract,Author$\}$:1111,$\{$Contract,Publisher$\}$:Addison,$\{$Contract,Book$\}$:XML$>$

The mapping to UDB from any relational database is now straightforward.

Definition 5. Given a relational database R, we construct a UDB as follows.

1. Define $\mathcal{V}$ to be the union of the domains that appear in R.
2. Define $\mathcal{S}$ to be the set of all relation and attribute names.
3. For each context $\{r, a\}$ where r is the name of a relation in R and a an attribute of r, define Dom($\{r, a\}$) to be the same as the domain of $r.a$ (but include $\bot$).
4. If t is a tuple of a relation over the schema $r(a_1, ..., a_m)$ in R, then put the unit u_t in the UDB where $u_t =< \{r, a_1\} : t(a_1), ..., \{r, a_m\} : t(a_m) >$.

A particularly simple UDB model $(\mathcal{V}, \mathcal{S}, \text{Dom}, \mathbf{U})$ for XML documents is to create one unit for each document. First, given an XML tree $T =< V, E >$ (corresponding to some document) and a vertex $v \in V$, let $path(v)$ denote the set of vertices along the path from the root of T to v. The label of v (i.e., element or attribute names if v is an internal node, or data value otherwise) is denoted $lab(v)$, and the *context associated with* v, $con(v)$, is the set $\{lab(v') \mid v' \in path(v) - v\}$.

Definition 6. Given an XML tree T, define $\mathcal{V}$ to be the set of labels associated with the leaves of T, and $\mathcal{S}$ the set of labels associated with non-leaf nodes of T. Then, the only well-defined unit maps, for each leaf node l, $con(l)$ to $lab(l)$.[3]

Example 2 (Modeling XML). Suppose $\mathcal{V}$ includes, among other values, "Election", "Fiction", "Tom", "Perrota", and "1997", and suppose $\mathcal{S}$ is the set $\{b,a,f,l,t,p,@g,@f\}$ that represent elements book, author, firstname, lastname, title, published, and attributes @genre, @format, respectively. The unit

$$< \{b,@g\}\text{:Fiction, } \{b,a,f\}\text{:Tom, } \{b,a,l\}\text{:Perrota, } \{b,t\}\text{:Election, } \{b,p\}\text{:1997} >$$

models the document:

```
<book genre="Fiction">
  <author>
    <firstname> Tom </firstname>
    <lastname> Perrota </lastname>
  </author>
  <title> Election </title>
  <published> 1997 </published>
</book>
```

As we will see, the context-based query language introduced next will enable subunits to be extracted as well as larger units to be created from existing ones.

3   A Context-Based Query Language (CBQL) for UDB

We take as our starting point the basic syntax of the query language proposed for the Universal Relation [8]: retrieve <attributes> where <condition>, and extend it to allow for context specifications. Moreover, each query is written with respect to a set of units, e.g., the entire database. Thus, we allow for the optional in clause, as the following example shows.[4]

```
retrieve (firstname, lastname) {author}
with title {book} = "Election"
in UDB
```

Each of the two attributes firstname and lastname is a context, and is further qualified by the context author. The context title is qualified by book. The in clause specifies that the query ranges over all units. This clause may be omitted if

---

[3] To accomodate paths with duplicate labels, more sophisticated definitions of context may be appropriate [10].

[4] As we will see, the keyword with is adopted in place of where because it reads more naturally in some queries.

By convention, non-terminals with names of the form `<X list>` consist of any number of comma-separated X's.

```
<query> → <retrieve> <with> [<in>] | <query> <set op> <query>
          "(" <query> ")" [<modifer> <context>]
<set op> → union | intersect | minus
<modifier> → @ | . | !
<retrieve> → retrieve (<attribute list> | *)
<attribute> → (ID | "("<ID list>")") ["{"<ID list>"}"]
<with> → with <boolean>
<boolean> → <condition> | not <boolean>
          | <boolean> (and|or) <boolean>
<condition> → <expr> (-|<|>|<=|>=|!=) <expr> | <or context>
<expr> → literal | <context>
<or context> → <context> | "["<context list>"]"
<context> → ID ["{"<ID list>"}"] | "{"<ID list>"}"
<in> → in <units list>
<units> → (ID | * | "(" <query> ")") [<modifier> <context>]
```

Fig. 1. BNF for CBQL

the range of units are understood. The result of the query with respect to the UDB in Example 2 is the unit: $< \{b,a,f\}:\text{Tom}, \{b,a,l\}:\text{Perrota} >$.

Note that contexts appearing in qualifications can be switched with those that appear outside without changing the meaning of the query. This flexibility is similar to those found in natural languages (as discussed earlier), and is afforded to our query language by the absence of role assignments to contexts.

The BNF for the core query language is given in Figure 1. In the remainder of this section, we summarize the algebraic foundation of the language. The operations in the language generalize familiar operations in the relational algebra. At the core of these operations is the manipulation of units.

Selection: The operation λ selects units based on conditions over context identifiers and values. First, we extend the syntax of ordinary boolean expressions. A *term* is either a context or a value.

Definition 7. A *boolean expression* is formed recursively:

1. A context is a boolean expression.
2. If $\bullet \in \{=, <, >, \leq, \geq, \neq\}$ and b_1 and b_2 are terms, then $b_1 \bullet b_2$ is a boolean expression.
3. If b_1 and b_2 are boolean expressions, then so are $b_1 \wedge b_2$, $b_1 \vee b_2$, $\neg b_1$.

Definition 8. A unit u satisfies the boolean expression b, written $u \models b$, if the following conditions hold.

1. If b is a context, then there exists a superset c of b such that $u(c) \downarrow$.
2. If b has the form $b_1 \bullet b_2$, then
   - if b_1, b_2 are contexts, then $u(c_1) \bullet u(c_2)$ for some $c_1 \supseteq b_1$ and $c_2 \supseteq b_2$;
   - if b_1 is a value and b_2 is a context, then $b_1 \bullet u(c_2)$ for some $c_2 \supseteq b_2$;
   - if b_1 is a context and b_2 is a value, then $u(c_1) \bullet b_2$ for some $c_1 \supseteq b_1$;
   - if b_1, b_2 are values, then $b_1 \bullet b_2$.
3. If b has the form $b_1 \wedge b_2$, then u satisfies both b_1 and b_2.
4. If b has the form $b_1 \vee b_2$, then u satisfies either b_1 or b_2.
5. If b has the form $\neg b_1$, then u does not satisfy b_1.

Proposition 1. *Suppose $u \models b$ and $u \preceq u'$. Then $u' \models b$.*

Definition 9. Suppose b is a boolean expression and $\mathcal{U}$ is a set of units. The query $\lambda_b \mathcal{U}$ is defined to be the set: $\{u \in \mathcal{U} \mid u \models b\}$.

Example 3. Consider Example 1. The query $\lambda_{\{Name,Writer\}} = 'Diana' \text{UDB}$ finds information about writers named Diana. Observe that the only unit returned from the query is $<\{Writer,Name\}:Diana,\{Writer,SSN\}:1234>$.

As a special case of λ, if c is a context, we write $\mathcal{U}@c$ to denote $\lambda_c \mathcal{U}$. For the above example, an equivalent query is $\lambda_{Name} = 'Diana' \text{UDB} @ Writer$.

Suppose $\text{ans}(Q)$ is the sets of units computed from a query Q. The following is an immediate consequence of Proposition 1.

Corollary 1. *Suppose $u, u' \in \mathcal{U}$ and $u \preceq u'$. If $u \in \text{ans}(\lambda_b \mathcal{U})$, then $u' \in \text{ans}(\lambda_b \mathcal{U})$.*

Projection: Given a unit u and a set of contexts $\mathcal{C}$, we denote by $(u|\mathcal{C})$ the unit that satisfies the following.

1. If $c \supseteq c'$ for some $c' \in \mathcal{C}$, then $(u|\mathcal{C})(c) = u(c)$.
2. $(u|\mathcal{C})(c'') = \perp$ for all other contexts c''.

Definition 10. Suppose $\mathcal{C}$ is a set of contexts and $\mathcal{U}$ is a set of units. The query $\mu_c \mathcal{U}$ consists of the set $\{u' \mid u \in \mathcal{U} \text{ and } u' = (u|\mathcal{C})\}$.

Example 4. To find all SSNs of writers in Example 1: $\mu_{SSN} \text{UDB} @ Writer$. The resulting set is $\{<\{Writer,SSN\}:1234>, <\{Writer,SSN\}:1111>\}$.

If $\mathcal{C}$ is a singleton $\{c\}$, we abbreviate $\mu_c \mathcal{U}$ by $\mathcal{U}.c$. As a variation, we write $\mathcal{U}!c$ to denote the set of units $\mathcal{U}'$ obtained from $\mathcal{U}.c$ as follows: If $u \in \mathcal{U}.c$, then the unit u' such that $u'(c' - c) = u(c')$ for every context c' is in $\mathcal{U}'$. The intuition of this last operation is, since c is a subcontext of every well-defined context in u, it may be unncessary to "display" c. Consider Example 3 again, the query $\lambda_{Name} = 'Diana' \text{UDB}!Writer$ computes $<\{Name\}:Diana,\{SSN\}:1234>$.

Join and Set Operations: Join and set theoretic operators can be similarly defined for sets of units. The latter operators involve no special notation: Given unit sets $\mathcal{U}_1, \mathcal{U}_2$, the expressions $\mathcal{U}_1 \cup \mathcal{U}_2$, $\mathcal{U}_1 \cap \mathcal{U}_2$, and $\mathcal{U}_1 - \mathcal{U}_2$ are all well-defined.[5]

We say two units u_1 and u_2 are *consistent* if whenever $u_1(c) \downarrow$ and $u_2(c) \downarrow$ for some context c, then $u_1(c) = u_2(c)$. Given a unit u, define $graph(u) = \{(c, u(c)) \mid u(c) \downarrow\}$. The join of $\mathcal{U}_1$ and $\mathcal{U}_2$, denoted $\mathcal{U}_1 \diamond \mathcal{U}_2$, is the set of all units u such that there exist $u_1 \in \mathcal{U}_1, u_2 \in \mathcal{U}_2$ where u_1 and u_2 are consistent and $graph(u) = graph(u_1) \cup graph(u_2)$.

Example 5. To find books and their authors in Example 1, we first join the units that have the contexts Contract and Writer before selecting units that have matching SSN and Author: $\lambda_{\text{SSN} = \text{Author}}(\text{UDB.Contract} \diamond \text{UDB.Writer})$.

Connections to the Context-Based Query Language: Properties of the algebra, including its connections to the relational algebra and XPath, will be detailed in the full paper. Many of the rewriting properties of the relational algebra also carry over to the current language. Here, we return to the relationship between the CB-query language shown in Figure 1 and the algebra. In general, CBQL contains a number of syntactic shorthands for writing multiple contexts and boolean expressions, but the basic CBQL statement:

```
retrieve <contexts> with <conditions> in <u1>, <u2>
```

computes the query $\mu_{\text{<contexts>}}(\lambda_{\text{<conditions>}}(\text{<u1>} \diamond \text{<u2>}))$.

Example 6. The query in Example 5 can be written:

```
retrieve * with Author = SSN
in *.Writer, *.Contract                    (QJ)
```

Note that nested queries are allowed, as shown in the next example:

```
retrieve * with Author = SSN
in *.Writer, (retrieve * with Contract)
```

4 Structured vs Search Queries

So far, the examples have only illustrated the flexibilities of CBQL in terms of formatting queries. But more powerfully, we may use CBQL to express inexact queries – queries that may retrieve incorrect answers. In the extreme case, we may write CB queries to perform keyword based searches. This is an area of growing interest. Examples of systems that perform keyword based searches over relational databases include those described in [3], [1], and [2]. We borrow some basic concepts from information retrieval.

Definition 11. Suppose Q_1 and Q_2 and are queries.

1. The *precision* of Q_1 with respect to Q_2 is that portion of the units computed by Q_1 that is in the units computed by Q_2: $|\text{ans}(Q_1) \cap \text{ans}(Q_2)| / |\text{ans}(Q_1)|$.

---

[5] More general versions may be desirable in some situations. We do not go into details here due to space constraints.

2. The *recall* of Q_1 with respect to Q_2 is that portion of all units computed by Q_2 included in the units computed from Q_1: $|\text{ans}(Q_1) \cap \text{ans}(Q_2)|/|\text{ans}(Q_2)|$.

Intuitively, precision and recall give us a way to measure the accuracy of a query with respect to a (not necessarily known) set of desired units. In the definition, Q_2 is intended to denote a query that computes this set exactly. Of course, to write such a query requires, in general, complete knowledge about all well-defined contexts (and presumably their intended meanings) for each unit. A query that achieves total recall with respect to any query that retrieves only the explicitly defined units can be formulated easily: `retrieve * with {}`. A slight variation is a query to perform a keyword search based on a data value v: `retrieve * with {} = v`.

More interestingly, the series of queries in Figure 2 illustrate a range of precisions for finding all books and their authors in Example 1 based on different amounts of knowledge that the query designer has (described to the right of each query).

Query	Assumed Knowledge

(1) `retrieve *`
`with SSN = Contract`
`in *.Writer, *`
	Units are grouped into Contract and Writer, and SSN is a valid context in Writer.

(2) `retrieve *`
`with Writer = Contract`
`in *, *`
	Units are grouped into Contract and Writer, but no further context information is known within these groups.

(3) `retrieve *`
`with Book and Name`
`in *, *`
	Units are grouped into two groups (with names unknown), and there is no information other than that Book and Name are valid contexts in the result.

Fig. 2. Precise and Imprecise Query Examples

Not surprisingly, the more contexts are provided, the better the precision. If the de facto query for the information desired is (QJ) in Example 6, then the precision for each of the three queries are 1, 2/3, and 1/2, respectively, with respect to (QJ). Note that for query (2), the following unit will be returned due to the inadvertent match between the contexts {Writer,Name} and {Contract,Book}.

< {Writer,Name}:Diana,{Writer,SSN}:1234,{Contract,Author}:1111,
   {Contract,Publisher}:Prentice,{Contract,Book}:Diana   >

Compared to the Universal Relation data model, a disadvantage of our model is that the system does not pre-determine connections among contexts (i.e., the Relationship Uniqueness Assumption of Maier *et. al.* [9]), and hence explicit calculation of connections among units may be necessary. On the other hand, we gain in flexibility since we may choose the connection desired. In addition, as the examples illustrate, our query language uniformly provides structured as well as unstructured (i.e., information retrieval) forms of querying.

5   Data Integration

Data integration remains one of the most studied yet challenging research topic in databases (see [4, 11, 12, 7] for surveys of this broad area of research). In the simplest case, an integration of two UDBs is just the union of the units in the two databases. Even without semantic reconciliation [11], this naive approach in combination with search-based querying will allow reasonable queries to be written under limited knowledge about the data sources.

For example, consider the union of the two UDBs in Examples 1 and 2. We assume the latter UDB contains a number of additional units with the same structure as the one shown in Example 2. To find the names of all writers that have authored a book under the (rather extreme) assumption that the only information the query designer has are the following.

- One of the databases separates book information from writer information, and
- author and name are relevant contexts for the requested information, but which context belongs to which data source is unknown.

The query retrieve * with [author,name] in *,* will return all units derived from the UDB of Example 2, and eight units from the relational source (of which two are relevant).

6   Conclusion

We have presented a universal data model that unifies several of the most popular data models, and have introduced a versatile query language that can form the basis for addressing some important database research problems. Ongoing and future work include the design and implementation of a prototype based on the model [5], and to explore ways of ranking the results of queries.

Acknowledgement

Many thanks to the reviewers' helpful comments and suggestions.

References

1. B. Aditya, Gaurav Bhalotia, Soumen Chakrabarti, Arvind Hulgeri, Charuta Nakhe, and S. Sudarshan Parag. Banks: Browsing and keyword searching in relational databases. In *Proceedings of VLDB*, pages 1083–1086, 2002.
2. V. Hristidis, Luis Gravano, and Y. Papakonstantinou. Efficient ir-style keyword search over relational databases. In *Proceedings of VLDB*, pages 850–861, 2003.

3. V. Hristidis and Y. Papakonstantinou. Discover: Keyword search in relational databases. In *Proceedings of VLDB*, pages 670–681, 2002.
4. Richard Hull. Managing semantic heterogeneity in databases: a theoretical prospective. In *Proceedings of PODS*, pages 51–61, 1997.
5. Charles Travers Franckle Jr. A data management system for data without structures, May 2005. Emory University Master Thesis.
6. Henry F. Korth, Gabriel M. Kuper, Joan Feigenbaum, Allen Van Gelder, and Jeffrey D. Ullman. System/u: A database system based on the universal relation assumption. *ACM Trans. Database Syst.*, 9(3):331–347, 1984.
7. Maurizio Lenzerini. Data integration: A theoretical perspective. In *PODS*, pages 233–246, 2002.
8. David Maier, David Rozenshtein, Sharon C. Salveter, Jacob Stein, and David Scott Warren. Toward logical data independence: A relational query language without relations. In Mario Schkolnick, editor, *Proceedings of the 1982 ACM SIGMOD International Conference on Management of Data, Orlando, Florida, June 2-4, 1982*, pages 51–60. ACM Press, 1982.
9. David Maier, Jeffrey D. Ullman, and Moshe Y. Vardi. On the foundations of the universal relation model. *ACM Trans. Database Syst.*, 9(2):283–308, 1984.
10. John McCarthy and Sasa Buvac. Formalizing context (expanded notes). Technical report, 1994.
11. M. Tamer Özsu and Patrick Valduriez. *Principles of Distributed Database Systems*. Prentice Hall, second edition, 1999.
12. Sriram Raghavan and Hector Garcia-Molina. Integrating diverse information management systems: A brief survey. *IEEE Data Engineering Bulletin*, 24(4):44–52, 2001.

Estimation of the Density of Datasets
with Decision Diagrams

Ansaf Salleb[1] and Christel Vrain[2]

[1] IRISA-INRIA Campus Universitaire de Beaulieu 35042 Rennes Cedex - France
Ansaf.Salleb@irisa.fr[**]
[2] LIFO, Université d'Orléans, B.P. 6759, 45067 Orléans Cedex 2 - France
Christel.Vrain@lifo.univ-orleans.fr

We dedicate this paper to our colleague Zahir Maazouzi
who participated to that work.

Abstract. We address the problem of loading transactional datasets into main memory and estimating the density of such datasets. We propose BoolLoader, an algorithm dedicated to these tasks; it relies on a compressed representation of all the transactions of the dataset. For sake of efficiency, we have chosen Decision Diagrams as the main data structure to the representation of datasets into memory. We give an experimental evaluation of our algorithm on both dense and sparse datasets. Experiments have shown that BoolLoader is efficient for loading some dense datasets and gives a partial answer about the nature of the dataset before time-consuming patterns extraction tasks.

Keywords: Transactional dataset, boolean function, decision diagram, density

1 Introduction

Many works have addressed the problem of efficiently mining frequent itemsets and frequent association rules in transactional databases (for instance [1, 3, 8, 16, 21]). One of the key problems is to find an appropriate data structure for loading the transactional database into main memory, and the efficiency depends on the nature of the database, e.g., density / sparseness. Indeed, choosing the right algorithm is difficult without *a priori* information on the database.

In this paper, we develop two points. First, we study the interest of *Binary Decision Diagrams (BDDs)* as a data structure for representing and loading transactional datasets. Then we introduce a coefficient, called the *sparseness coefficient* and we experimentally show that it could be an interesting measure for evaluating the density of a database. In our framework, a dataset is viewed as a vectorial function, thus allowing, when possible, to load only this vectorial function in memory by means of a BDD. Such a structure has already been successfully used for representing boolean functions in various applications of Computer Science such as very large scale integration systems. As far as we know, it

---

[**] This work was done while the first author was a PhD student at LIFO, University of Orléans.

M.-S. Hacid et al. (Eds.): ISMIS 2005, LNAI 3488, pp. 688–697, 2005.
© Springer-Verlag Berlin Heidelberg 2005

has not yet been studied in the field of mining transactional databases. For the time being, four tendencies for representing and handling transactional datasets can be distinguished:

- **Horizontal format:** Used in the *Apriori* algorithm [1], this format is considered as the classical representation. The dataset is seen as a succession of transactions, each one identified by an identifier *tid*. This format is also used for mining maximal frequent itemsets in algorithms such as *MaxMiner* [3].
- **Vertical format:** It is used by *Eclat* [21] and *Partition* [16]. It consists in representing the dataset vertically by giving to each item its *tidset*, *i.e.* the set of transactions containing this item. Another recent vertical format named *Diffset* has been proposed in [20]. It consists in keeping only track of differences between tidsets.
- **Bitvectors:** Bitvectors are used in the algorithm *Mafia* [5] and *Viper* [17]. This format consists in representing data as bitvectors compressed using a strategy called *Run Length Encoding*.
- **Fp-tree:** This data structure is an extended prefix-tree structure for storing compressed and crucial information about frequent patterns. This data structure has been used in the *Fp-growth* [8] algorithm for mining frequent patterns.

In this paper, we are interested in developing a new representation and we propose an algorithm, called BoolLoader, to load transactional datasets. We also give an experimental evaluation on both sparse and dense datasets. It shows that BoolLoader is particularly efficient for loading dense datasets which are considered as challenging datasets in mining frequent itemsets. Moreover, comparing the size of the BDD and the initial size of the database gives an interesting measure for evaluating its density, and can be very important information on the nature of the dataset before working on it.

The remainder of this paper is organized as follows: In § 2 we give some basic definitions concerning itemsets and transactional datasets. We then show in § 3 how to represent a dataset by a vectorial function. § 4 is devoted to the BDD data structure. In § 5, we propose an algorithm for moving from a given dataset to a BDD. Details on implementation and experimental tests are given in § 6. We finally conclude in § 7.

2   Transactional Datasets and Frequent Itemsets

This section recall some definitions concerning the frequent itemset mining task. An *item* is an element of a finite set $\mathcal{I} = \{x_1, ..., x_n\}$. A subset of $\mathcal{I}$ is called an *itemset*. The set of all possible itemsets ordered by set inclusion forms a lattice $(\mathcal{P}(\mathcal{I}), \subseteq)$. A *transaction* is a subset of $\mathcal{I}$, identified by a unique transaction identifier *tid*. $\mathcal{T}$ denotes the set of all transaction identifiers. A transactional database is a finite set of pairs (y, X_y) where y is a transaction identifier and X_y is an itemset; in the following, it is denoted by *BDT*. The *frequency* of an itemset X in a BDT $\mathcal{D}$ is the number of transactions in $\mathcal{D}$ containing X. An itemset X is said to be frequent in $\mathcal{D}$ when its frequency is greater than a given threshold.

Table 1. A transactional dataset and its corresponding truth table

Item	Movie	Producer
x_1	Harry Potter	C. Columbus
x_2	Star Wars II	G. Lucas
x_3	Catch me if you can	S. Spielberg
x_4	A Beautiful Mind	R. Howard

$\mathcal{D}$

Tid	Transaction
1	x_1, x_2
2	x_1, x_2, x_4
3	x_1, x_2
4	x_3, x_4
5	x_1, x_2
6	x_3, x_4
7	x_1, x_3, x_4
8	x_1, x_2, x_3
9	x_1, x_2
10	x_1, x_3, x_4
11	x_1, x_2
12	x_1, x_2, x_3
13	x_1, x_2
14	x_1, x_3, x_4
15	x_3, x_4

$\wp \longrightarrow$

e_1	e_2	e_3	e_4	f
0	0	0	0	0
0	0	0	1	0
0	0	1	0	0
0	0	1	1	3
0	1	0	0	0
0	1	0	1	0
0	1	1	0	0
0	1	1	1	0
1	0	0	0	0
1	0	0	1	0
1	0	1	0	0
1	0	1	1	3
1	1	0	0	6
1	1	0	1	1
1	1	1	0	2
1	1	1	1	0

Example 1. Let us consider the BDT given in Table 1 and let us suppose that it stores movies recently seen by 15 spectators. The dataset $\mathcal{D}$ is defined on the set of items (movies) $\mathcal{I} = \{x_1, x_2, x_3, x_4\}$. The set of tids is given by $\mathcal{T} = \{1, 2, \cdots, 15\}$. Each line in $\mathcal{D}$ associates a set of movies to the spectator identified by the corresponding tid. For instance, the spectator 1 has recently seen *Harry Potter* and *Star Wars II*. The itemset $\{x_1, x_2\}$, written $x_1 x_2$ for sake of simplicity, is frequent relatively to the threshold 2 since it appears 9 times in $\mathcal{D}$.

3   From Transactional Datasets to Vectorial Functions

Our framework relies on the Stone's representation theorem for Boolean algebras [18]:

Theorem 1. Lattice isomorphism *The lattice* $(\mathcal{P}(\mathcal{I}), \subseteq)$ *where* $\mathcal{I}$ *is a set of n items is isomorphic to the lattice* $(\mathbb{B}^n, \leq)$ *where* $\mathbb{B} = \{0, 1\}$ *and* $(b_1, \ldots, b_n) \leq (b'_1, \ldots, b'_n)$ *when for all* i, $b_i \leq b'_i$.

The bijective function $\wp$ is defined by $\wp(X) = (b_1, b_2, \cdots, b_n)$ where $b_i = 1$ if $x_i \in X$, 0 *otherwise*. Thus, each bit expresses whether the corresponding item x_i is included in that combination or not. Let us consider a truth table $\mathbb{T}^n = [e_1, \ldots, e_n]$, where for each index j, $1 \leq j \leq n$, e_j is a 2^n-bits vector representing the jth vector of $\mathbb{T}^n$. In $\mathbb{T}^n$ each line corresponds to a possible combination of $b_1, \ldots, b_n$, thus to an itemset. We can associate to this truth table a vectorial function f, which gives for each line of the truth table (a combination of items), the number of times the transaction corresponding to that itemset appears in $\mathcal{D}$. Since the structure of the truth table is fixed when n is fixed and when the variables are ordered, the function f is then sufficient to express the entire set of transactions of $\mathcal{D}$.

Example 2. The BDT $\mathcal{D}$ of table 1 is represented by $\mathbb{T}^4 = [e_1, \ldots, e_4]$ where:

$$e_1 = 0000\ 0000\ 1111\ 1111 \quad e_2 = 0000\ 1111\ 0000\ 1111$$
$$e_3 = 0011\ 0011\ 0011\ 0011 \quad e_4 = 0101\ 0101\ 0101\ 0101$$

with the output function $f = 0003\ 0000\ 0003\ 6120$.

For instance, the transaction $\{x_1, x_2, x_3\}$ exists twice in $\mathcal{D}$, it is then represented by the 15th line (1110) in the truth table and the value of f is equal to 2. In the same way, the transaction $\{x_1, x_2, x_3, x_4\}$ does not exist in $\mathcal{D}$, it will be represented by the last line (1111) in the truth table with 0 as output function.

The vector f represents a new form of the dataset. It is then interesting to study whether it is possible to load it into memory instead of loading the dataset itself. This seems very difficult since the size of f may be very large. For instance, for a dataset defined on 100 items, the size of the corresponding vectorial function is equal to 2^{100}, so greater than 10^{30} unsigned integers. But, a compact representation, called BDD, has been introduced by Lee [9] and Akers [2]. Moreover, we show in Section 5 that it is possible to build the BDD directly from the dataset without computing f.

4   Binary and Algebraic Decision Diagrams

A Binary Decision Diagram (BDD) is a graph-based representation of boolean functions. It is a directed acyclic graph with 2 terminal nodes 1 and 0. Each non-terminal node has an index to identify a variable of the boolean function, and has two outgoing edges; the dashed one means that the variable is fixed to 0 whereas the other one means that the variable is fixed to 1. A BDD represents a disjunctive normal form of a boolean function: each path from the root of a BDD till a leaf indexed by number 1 gives a conjunction of literals (where a literal is either a variable or the negation of a variable) that is true for that boolean function. Given a boolean function, it is possible to represent it by a canonical graph, using the following rules [11] (Figure 1):

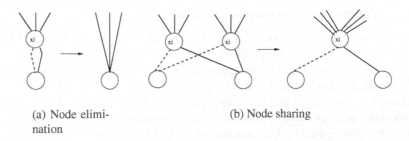

(a) Node elimi-
nation

(b) Node sharing

Fig. 1. Reduction rules

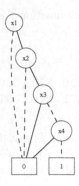

Fig. 2. BDD of $x_1 \wedge x_2 \wedge \neg x_3 \wedge \neg x_4$

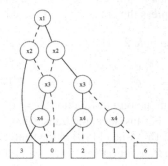

Fig. 3. BDD corresponding to the vector f

1. Choose an order on variables: $x_1 \prec x_2 \prec \ldots \prec x_n$; variables appear in this order in all the paths of the graph and no variable appears more than once in a path.
2. Eliminate all the redundant nodes whose two edges point to the same node.
3. Share all equivalent subgraphs.

Operations (AND ($\wedge$), OR ($\vee$), etc.) on BDDs have been defined in [4]. For example, the BDD of the expression $x_1 \wedge x_2 \wedge \neg x_3 \wedge \neg x_4$ given in Figure 2 is obtained by first generating the trivial BDDs of x_1, x_2, $\neg x_3$ and $\neg x_4$, and then by computing the AND operation between these basic BDDs. In our case, we have to handle vectorial functions from $\mathbb{B}^n$ to $\mathbb{N}$. We use an extension of BDD, called Algebraic Decision Diagrams (ADD) [6, 13] that handles such functions: in ADDs, leaves are indexed by integers. In the following, we still use the term BDD instead of ADD, since it is more commonly used.

Example 3. Figure 3 gives the BDD of the function f of Table 1. For instance, the rightmost path expresses that there are 6 spectators who have seen *Harry Potter* (x_1) and *Stars Wars* (x_2) but who have not seen the other movies (x_3, x_4). The leftmost path expresses that no spectator has seen *Stars Wars* without having seen *Harry Potter*.

5   From Datasets to Decision Diagrams

5.1   Building a Binary Decision Diagram

The construction of a BDD representing a dataset is done by scanning only once the dataset. For each transaction, a BDD is constructed and added to the final BDD using the operation $\vee$ between BDDs. Although not shown in the algorithm, reduction rules (eliminating redundant nodes and sharing equivalent subgraphs) (Figure 1) are used during the construction process in order to get a compact BDD. Let us notice that **the function f is never computed**; in fact, we transform directly a transactional dataset into its corresponding BDD. The construction of a BDD associated to a BDT is given by the algorithm *BDT2BDD*.

```
    Algorithm BDT2BDD
Input :  a dataset D
Output : a decision diagram BDD_D

1.  BDD_D=NULL
2.  For each transaction t ∈ D do
3.       BDD_t=NULL
4.       For i=1 to n do
5.            If x_i ∈ t then BDD_t=BDD_t ∧ BDD_{x_i}
6.            else BDD_t=BDD_t∧ BDD_{¬x_i}
7.       BDD_D=BDD_D ∨ BDD_t
```

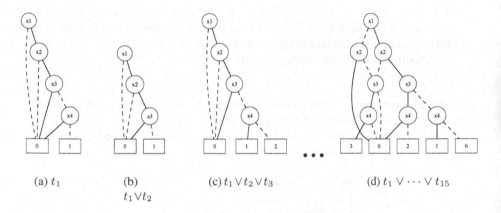

(a) t_1 (b)   (c) $t_1 \vee t_2 \vee t_3$ (d) $t_1 \vee \cdots \vee t_{15}$
            $t_1 \vee t_2$

Fig. 4. Example of construction of a reduced BDD of D

Example 4. Figure 4 represents the construction steps of the BDD of Table 1, considering the transactions one by one. Figure 4(a) represents the BDD of transaction 1, (b) shows the BDD of the two first transactions, (c) the three first transactions and so on. Finally, the BDD in (d) represents all the transactions of the database. For more details about the operations between BDDs representing transactions see [15].

5.2   A Measure of Sparseness

We introduce a measure, called the Sparseness coefficient, defined as follows:

$$\text{Sparseness coefficient} = \frac{\#\text{nodes in BDD}}{\#\text{transactions} \times \#\text{items}}\%$$

It compares the size of the BDD with the size of the database, expressed by the two dimensions that are: the number of items and the number of transactions. It gives an evaluation of the sparseness of the database; a low coefficient would be an indication of a dense database.

6   Implementation and Experimental Results

We developed a prototype, called BoolLoader to load transactional datasets. It has been developed in C and it uses ADDs as the main data structure for representing datasets and shared BDDs [10] to optimize memory. Our implementation relies on the CUDD[1] library. This free library can manage BDDs with a number of nodes up to 2^{28}, *i.e.*, more than 250 million nodes! The nodes have a size of 16 bytes, one of the smallest sizes of the existing libraries. The maximal number of variables managed by CUDD is equal to 2^{16}, i.e., 65 536 variables. The aim of the experiments is twofold: first, to test whether that data structure is suitable for loading transactional datasets, second, to study the sparseness coefficient introduced in Section 5 as an estimation of the density of the database. Experiments have been performed on a PC Pentium 4, 2.66 GHz processor with 512 Mb of main memory, running under Linux Mandrake 9.2. We have tested BoolLoader on real and artificial datasets (Table 2). Artificial datasets have been generated using the *IBM generator*[2]. Concerning real dense datasets, we have experimented BoolLoader on some known benchmarks [12]: *Mushroom, Chess, Connect, Pumsb*. With our current implementation, we can handle databases of about $D \times N = 10^7$ where D is the number of transactions and N the number of items.

Table 2. Experimental results on real and artificial datasets. For artificial ones, T denotes the average items per transaction, I the average length of maximal patterns and D the number of transactions. When I is close to T, *i.e.* when the dataset is dense, BoolLoader is more efficient than when I is smaller than T. All the given times include both system and user time

Database	#items	T	#transactions	#nodes	Time(s)	Spars. Coef.(%)
Mushroom	120	23	8 124	3225	1.47	0.334
Connect	130	43	67 557	171 662	26.39	1.970
Chess	76	37	3 196	18 553	0.54	7.741
T10I4D10K	50	10	9 823	102 110	1.56	20.79
	100	10	9 824	316 511	2.94	32.21
	500	10	9 853	2 557 122	25.83	51.90
	1000	10	9 820	5 480 596	59.57	58.81
T10I4D100K	50	10	98 273	479 382	2.32	9.75
	100	10	98 394	1 985 437	55.41	20.17
	150	10	98 387	4 131 643	93.04	28.18
T10I8D100K	50	10	84 824	442 671	17.15	10.43
	100	10	84 823	1 694 029	41.84	19.97
	150	10	85 027	3 228 899	68.77	25.48
T20I6D100K	50	20	99 913	916 315	27.84	18.34
	100	20	99 919	4 198 947	62.52	42.02
	150	20	99 924	7 479 490	stopped at 95 000 trans.	52.84
T20I18D100K	50	20	81 428	632 518	19.99	15.53
	100	20	81 472	2 485 199	46.10	30.50
	150	20	81 639	4 330 529	72.02	35.60
T40I10D100K	50	40	100 000	617 024	27.85	12.34
	100	40	100 000	5 561 767	72.28	55.61
	150	40	100 000	9 070 580	stopped at 90 000 trans.	67.64
T40I35D100K	50	40	85 445	470 245	20.75	11.00
	100	40	85 410	3 175 313	50.72	37.17
	150	40	85 646	5 574 661	88.04	43.68

[1] http://www.bdd-portal.org/cud.html
[2] http://www.almaden.ibm.com/cs/quest/syndata.html

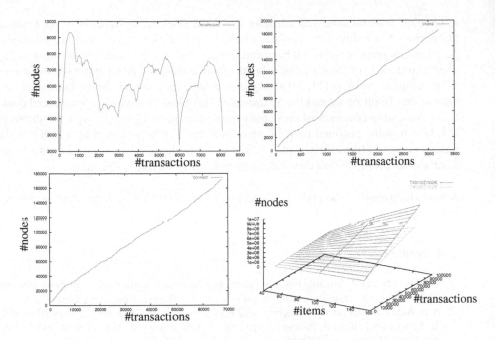

Fig. 5. Evolution of the number of nodes according to the number of transactions in the datasets: mushroom, connect, chess, T40I10D100K and T40I35D100K

Some datasets, such as Pumsb, seem to be intractable by BoolLoader. We have studied the evolution of the number of nodes according to the number of already processed transactions (Figure 5) and we have noticed a quite linear relationship between these two dimensions, except for mushroom. Concerning mushroom, we observe in Figure 5 that this dataset shows a particular evolution during the loading process. In fact, in mushroom, maximal itemsets are long (about 22 items [7]) which is quite the average length of a transaction. This means that in the corresponding BDD, many paths are shared and this explains the few number of nodes and the very low value of the sparseness coefficient of that dataset.

On the other hand, mushroom, connect and chess are known to be dense (with long maximal itemsets) and their spareseness coefficient is less than 10% whereas sparse synthetic datasets, such as T10I4D10KN1000, have high coefficient. In order to study the link between sparseness and our coefficient, we have generated several artificial datasets. Our study (Figure 5) shows that artificial databases do not behave as real databases (they are too smooth); this point has already been pointed out in [22].

7   Conclusion and Future Works

In this paper we present BoolLoader, a tool for representing a transactional database by a BDD. Our aim when designing that tool was to investigate the use of such a data structure for data mining. For the time being, we have studied the feasability of that representation: it seems to be well suited for some databases but we have also given limits of that approach in terms of the number of items and the number of transactions. In our experiments no preprocessing has been done on the datasets. It could be interesting to find a "good ordering" of the variables to build a more condensed BDD, but it is known to be a NP-complete problem [11, 19] and heuristics have to be found. Beyond this study, we believe that BoolLoader and the Sparseness Coefficient that we have introduced could be an interesting estimator of the density of the database. Moreover, we have shown in [14] how to mine maximal frequent itemsets in datasets represented by a BDD. In the future, we would like to study other strategies for building a BDD from a transactional database but also to design clever algorithms to mine such data structure.

Acknowledgments. The authors would like to thank the referees for their comments and suggestions.

References

1. R. Agrawal and R. Srikant. Fast algorithms for mining association rules. In *Proc. 20th Int. Conf. Very Large Data Bases, VLDB*, pages 487–499. Morgan Kaufmann, 1994.
2. S.B. Akers. Binary decision diagrams. *IEEE Transactions on Computers*, 27:509–516, 1978.
3. R. J. Bayardo. Efficiently mining long patterns from databases. In *Proc. 1998 ACM-SIGMOD Int. Conf. Management of Data*, pages 85–93, Seattle, Washington, June 1998.
4. R.E. Bryant. Graph-based algorithms for boolean functions manipulation. *IEEE Trans. on Computers*, C-35(8):677–691, August 1986.
5. D. Burdick, M. Calimlim, and J. Gehrke. Mafia: A maximal frequent itemset algorithm for transactional databases. In *Proceedings of the 17th International Conference on Data Engineering*, pages 443–452, Heidelberg, Germany, April 2001.
6. E. Clarke, M. Fujita, P. McGeer, K. McMillan, J. Yang, and X. Zhao. Multi terminal binary decision diagrams: An efficient data structure for matrix representation. In *Int. Workshop on Logic Synth.*, pages P6a:1–15, 1993.
7. K. Gouda and M. J. Zaki. Efficiently mining maximal frequent itemsets. In *Proceedings of 1st IEEE International Conference on Data Mining*, San Jose, November 2001.
8. J. Han, J. Pei, and Y. Yin. Mining frequent patterns without candidate generation. *Proc. of Int. Conf. on Management of Data*, pages 1–12, May 2000.
9. C.Y. Lee. Representation of Switching Circuits by Binary-Decision Programs. *Bell Systems Technical Journal*, 38:985–999, July 1959.
10. S. Minato. Shared binary decision diagram with attributed edges for efficient boolean function manipulation. In *Proc. 27th Design Automation Conference*, pages 52–57, June 1990.
11. S. Minato. *Binary Decision Diagrams and Applications for VLSI CAD*. Kluwer Academic Publishers, 1996.
12. P. M. Murphy and D. W. Aha. *UCI Repository of Machine Learning Databases*. Machine-readable collection, Dept of Information and Computer Science, University of California, Irvine, 1995. [Available by anonymous ftp from ics.uci.edu in directory pub/machine-learning-databases].
13. R.I. Bahar, E.A. Frohm, C.M. Gaona, G.D. Hachtel, E. Macii, A. Pardo, and F. Somenzi. Algebraic decision diagrams and their applications. In *IEEE/ACM International Conference on CAD*, pages 188–191, Santa Clara, California, 1993. IEEE Computer Society Press.
14. A. Salleb, Z. Maazouzi, and C. Vrain. Mining maximal frequent itemsets by a boolean approach. In *Proceedings of the 15th European Conference on Artificial Intelligence ECAI*, pages 385–389, Lyon, France, 2002.

15. A. Salleb and C. Vrain. Can We Load Efficiently Dense Datasets ? Technical Report RR-2004-02, LIFO, Université d'Orléans, 2004.
16. A. Savasere, E. Omiecinsky, and S. Navathe. An efficient algorithm for mining association rules in large databases. *In 21st Int'l Conf. on Very Large Databases (VLDB)*, 1995.
17. P. Shenoy, J. Haritsa, S. Sudarshan, G. Bhalotia, M. Bawa, , and D. Shah. Turbo-charging vertical mining of large databases. In *Proc. of Int.. Conf. on Management of Data*, 2000.
18. M. H. Stone. Boolean algebras and their relation to topology. *Proceedings of National Academy of Sciences*, 20:37–111, 1934.
19. S. Tani, K. Hamaguchi, and S. Yajima. The complexity of the optimal variable ordering problems of shared binary decision diagrams. In *ISAAC: 4th International Symposium on Algorithms and Computation Algorithms)*, 1993.
20. M. J. Zaki and K. Gouda. Fast vertical mining using diffsets. In *9th International Conference on Knowledge Discovery and Data Mining*, Washington, DC, August 2003.
21. M. J. Zaki, S. Parthasarathy, M. Ogihara, and W. Li. New algorithms for fast discovery of association rules. In *3rd Intl. Conf. on Knowledge Discovery and Data Mining*, pages 283–296. AAAI Press, 1997.
22. Z. Zheng, R. Kohavi, and L. Mason. Real world performance of association rule algorithms. In *Proceedings of the Seventh ACM SIGKDD International Conference on Knowledge Discovery and Data Mining*, pages 401–406, 2001.

Author Index

Agier, Marie   494
Alda, Sascha   650
An, Aijun   562
Andreasen, Troels   74
Angelis, Lefteris   219
Appice, Annalisa   342

Bagüés, Miren I.   466
Bandyopadhyay, Sanghamitra   594
Barnes, Tiffany   603
Basile, T.M.A.   373
Bentayeb, Fadila   65
Berardi, Margherita   342
Bermúdez, Jesús   466
Biermann, Alan W.   1
Bitzer, Donald   603
Bonnaire, Xavier   83
Bosc, Patrick   314
Botta, Maco   47
Braynova, Elena   364
Bright, Damien   170
Bui, Linh H.   14
Bulskov, Henrik   74

Carbonell, Jaime G.   29, 142
Caruso, Costantina   131
Ceci, Michelangelo   342
Chang, Matthew   641
Chen, Jianhua   323
Chen, Peter   323
Chen, Qijun   391
Chen, Yaohua   210
Cheng, Betty Yee Man   29
Cheng, Jingde   445
Chester, Daniel   660
Cho, Sung-Bae   92
Cozzolongo, G.   404
Cremers, Armin B.   650

Dardzińska, Agnieszka   152
Davidson, Ian   631
Debnath, Sandip   285
De Carolis, B.   404
Demolombe, Robert   425
Deogun, Jitender S.   121, 332

de Souza, Jano Moreira   294
Di Mauro, N.   373
Ding, Guoli   323
Ding, Yulin   435

Eick, Christoph F.   248
Elomaa, Tapio   228
Elzer, Stephanie   660
Erik Rosenthal, Erik   304
Esposito, Floriana   102, 373

Favie, Cécile   65
Ferilli, S.   373
Ferster, Ryan   14

Galassi, Ugo   47
Giles, C. Lee   285
Giordana, Attilio   47
Gnasa, Melanie   650
Goh, Chong   112
Goñi, Alfredo   466
Greco, S.   413
Gruźdź, Alicja   514
Gul, Nadir   650

Hähnle, Reiner   304
Hayes, Phil   142
Hershkop, Shlomo   14
Hirano, Shoji   38, 612
Hooijmaijers, Dennis   170
Huang, Xiangji   562

Ihnatowicz, Aleksandra   514
Illarramendi, Arantza   466
Inouye, R. Bryce   1

Jiang, Liying   121
Jin, Chun   142
Jouve, Pierre-Emmanuel   583
Jumi, Masatoshi   475

Kacprzyk, Janusz   200
Kim, Kyung-Joong   92
Klein-Seetharaman, Judith   29
Knappe, Rasmus   74
Koivistoinen, Heidi   228

Lalmas, Mounia   257
Lax, Robert   323
Lee, Huijae   544
Lee, Wol Young   266
Lewis, Rory   456
Li, Dan   332
Lisi, Francesca A.   102
Liu, Chao-Lin   524
Lu, James J.   678
Luo, Xiao   161

Magdon-Ismail, Malik   485
Malerba, Donato   131, 342
McKenzie, Ashley   1
Mitra, Prasenjit   285
Mitschang, Bernhard   294
Monteiro, Rodrigo Salvador   294
Murray, Neil V.   182, 304

Newberg, Heidi Jo   485
Nicoloyannis, Nicolas   583

Ohshima, Muneaki   475
Orihara, Ryohei   112

Pallis, George   219
Palopoli, Luigi   504
Papagelis, Manos   553
Papagni, Davide   131
Park, Sanghyun   237
Pozos-Parra, Pilar   425
Pendharkar, Hemant   364
Petit, Jean-Marc   494
Pivert, Olivier   314
Pizzutilo, S.   404
Plantamura, V.L.   404
Plexousakis, Dimitris   553
Poon, Chung Keung   641
Purnell, Jon   485

Raś, Zbigniew W.   152, 456
Riff, María-Cristina   83
Rocacher, Daniel   314
Rombo, Simona   504
Rosenthal, Erik   182, 304
Rousidis, Ioannis   553
Ruan, Chun   191

Saitta, Lorenza   47
Sakurai, Shigeaki   112
Salleb, Ansaf   688
Satyanarayana, Ashwin   631

Schwarz, Holger   294
Seo, Minkoo   237
Shang, Feng   445
Ślęzak, Dominik   354, 514
Spyns, Peter   276
Stolfo, Salvatore J.   14
Sunderraman, Rajshekhar   669
Suzuki, Einoshin   475, 494
Synak, Piotr   456
Szkatula, Grażyna   200

Tablado, Alberto   466
Takabayashi, Katsuhiko   475
Tanasescu, Adrian   535
Tang, Na   573
Terracina, Giorgio   504
Theoharopoulos, Elias   553
Trubitsyna, I.   413
Tsikrika, Theodora   257
Tsumoto, Shusaku   38, 56, 612

Vakali, Athena   219
Varadharajan, Vijay   191
Vemuri, V. Rao   573
Vouk, Mladen   603
Vrain, Christel   688

Wang, Haibin   669
Wang, Ke   14
Wang, Yongge   382
Wieczorkowska, Alicja   456
Won, Jung-Im   237
Wu, Xindong   391
Wu, Xintao   382, 622

Yao, Qingsong   562
Yao, Yiyu   210
Ye, Yong   622
Yokoi, Hideto   475
Yong, Hwan Seung   266
Yoo, Ji-Oh   92
Yoo, Sang Bong   544

Zeidat, Nidal   248
Zhang, Yan   435
Zheng, Yuliang   382
Zhong, Ning   475
Zhu, Xingquan   391
Zimbrão, Geraldo   294
Zincir-Heywood, A. Nur   161
Zumpano, E.   413

Lecture Notes in Artificial Intelligence (LNAI)

Vol. 3501: B. Kégl, G. Lapalme (Eds.), Advances in Artificial Intelligence. XV, 458 pages. 2005.

Vol. 3492: P. Blache, E. Stabler, J. Busquets, R. Moot (Eds.), Logical Aspects of Computational Linguistics. X, 363 pages. 2005.

Vol. 3488: M.-S. Hacid, N.V. Murray, Z.W. Raś, S. Tsumoto (Eds.), Foundations of Intelligent Systems. XIII, 700 pages. 2005.

Vol. 3452: F. Baader, A. Voronkov (Eds.), Logic for Programming, Artificial Intelligence, and Reasoning. XI, 562 pages. 2005.

Vol. 3419: B. Faltings, A. Petcu, F. Fages, F. Rossi (Eds.), Constraint Satisfaction and Constraint Logic Programming. X, 217 pages. 2005.

Vol. 3416: M. Böhlen, J. Gamper, W. Polasek, M.A. Wimmer (Eds.), E-Government: Towards Electronic Democracy. XIII, 311 pages. 2005.

Vol. 3415: P. Davidsson, B. Logan, K. Takadama (Eds.), Multi-Agent and Multi-Agent-Based Simulation. X, 265 pages. 2005.

Vol. 3403: B. Ganter, R. Godin (Eds.), Formal Concept Analysis. XI, 419 pages. 2005.

Vol. 3398: D.-K. Baik (Ed.), Systems Modeling and Simulation: Theory and Applications. XIV, 733 pages. 2005.

Vol. 3397: T.G. Kim (Ed.), Artificial Intelligence and Simulation. XV, 711 pages. 2005.

Vol. 3396: R.M. van Eijk, M.-P. Huget, F. Dignum (Eds.), Agent Communication. X, 261 pages. 2005.

Vol. 3394: D. Kudenko, D. Kazakov, E. Alonso (Eds.), Adaptive Agents and Multi-Agent Systems II. VIII, 313 pages. 2005.

Vol. 3392: D. Seipel, M. Hanus, U. Geske, O. Bartenstein (Eds.), Applications of Declarative Programming and Knowledge Management. X, 309 pages. 2005.

Vol. 3374: D. Weyns, H.V.D. Parunak, F. Michel (Eds.), Environments for Multi-Agent Systems. X, 279 pages. 2005.

Vol. 3371: M.W. Barley, N. Kasabov (Eds.), Intelligent Agents and Multi-Agent Systems. X, 329 pages. 2005.

Vol. 3369: V.R. Benjamins, P. Casanovas, J. Breuker, A. Gangemi (Eds.), Law and the Semantic Web. XII, 249 pages. 2005.

Vol. 3366: I. Rahwan, P. Moraitis, C. Reed (Eds.), Argumentation in Multi-Agent Systems. XII, 263 pages. 2005.

Vol. 3359: G. Grieser, Y. Tanaka (Eds.), Intuitive Human Interfaces for Organizing and Accessing Intellectual Assets. XIV, 257 pages. 2005.

Vol. 3346: R.H. Bordini, M. Dastani, J. Dix, A.E.F. Seghrouchni (Eds.), Programming Multi-Agent Systems. XIV, 249 pages. 2005.

Vol. 3345: Y. Cai (Ed.), Ambient Intelligence for Scientific Discovery. XII, 311 pages. 2005.

Vol. 3343: C. Freksa, M. Knauff, B. Krieg-Brückner, B. Nebel, T. Barkowsky (Eds.), Spatial Cognition IV. XIII, 519 pages. 2005.

Vol. 3339: G.I. Webb, X. Yu (Eds.), AI 2004: Advances in Artificial Intelligence. XXII, 1272 pages. 2004.

Vol. 3336: D. Karagiannis, U. Reimer (Eds.), Practical Aspects of Knowledge Management. X, 523 pages. 2004.

Vol. 3327: Y. Shi, W. Xu, Z. Chen (Eds.), Data Mining and Knowledge Management. XIII, 263 pages. 2005.

Vol. 3315: C. Lemaître, C.A. Reyes, J.A. González (Eds.), Advances in Artificial Intelligence – IBERAMIA 2004. XX, 987 pages. 2004.

Vol. 3303: J.A. López, E. Benfenati, W. Dubitzky (Eds.), Knowledge Exploration in Life Science Informatics. X, 249 pages. 2004.

Vol. 3276: D. Nardi, M. Riedmiller, C. Sammut, J. Santos-Victor (Eds.), RoboCup 2004: Robot Soccer World Cup VIII. XVIII, 678 pages. 2005.

Vol. 3275: P. Perner (Ed.), Advances in Data Mining. VIII, 173 pages. 2004.

Vol. 3265: R.E. Frederking, K.B. Taylor (Eds.), Machine Translation: From Real Users to Research. XI, 392 pages. 2004.

Vol. 3264: G. Paliouras, Y. Sakakibara (Eds.), Grammatical Inference: Algorithms and Applications. XI, 291 pages. 2004.

Vol. 3259: J. Dix, J. Leite (Eds.), Computational Logic in Multi-Agent Systems. XII, 251 pages. 2004.

Vol. 3257: E. Motta, N.R. Shadbolt, A. Stutt, N. Gibbins (Eds.), Engineering Knowledge in the Age of the Semantic Web. XVII, 517 pages. 2004.

Vol. 3249: B. Buchberger, J.A. Campbell (Eds.), Artificial Intelligence and Symbolic Computation. X, 285 pages. 2004.

Vol. 3248: K.-Y. Su, J. Tsujii, J.-H. Lee, O.Y. Kwong (Eds.), Natural Language Processing – IJCNLP 2004. XVIII, 817 pages. 2005.

Vol. 3245: E. Suzuki, S. Arikawa (Eds.), Discovery Science. XIV, 430 pages. 2004.

Vol. 3244: S. Ben-David, J. Case, A. Maruoka (Eds.), Algorithmic Learning Theory. XIV, 505 pages. 2004.

Vol. 3238: S. Biundo, T. Frühwirth, G. Palm (Eds.), KI 2004: Advances in Artificial Intelligence. XI, 467 pages. 2004.

Vol. 3230: J.L. Vicedo, P. Martínez-Barco, R. Muñoz, M. Saiz Noeda (Eds.), Advances in Natural Language Processing. XII, 488 pages. 2004.

Vol. 3229: J.J. Alferes, J. Leite (Eds.), Logics in Artificial Intelligence. XIV, 744 pages. 2004.

Vol. 3228: M.G. Hinchey, J.L. Rash, W.F. Truszkowski, C.A. Rouff (Eds.), Formal Approaches to Agent-Based Systems. VIII, 290 pages. 2004.

Vol. 3215: M.G.. Negoita, R.J. Howlett, L.C. Jain (Eds.), Knowledge-Based Intelligent Information and Engineering Systems, Part III. LVII, 906 pages. 2004.

Vol. 3214: M.G.. Negoita, R.J. Howlett, L.C. Jain (Eds.), Knowledge-Based Intelligent Information and Engineering Systems, Part II. LVIII, 1302 pages. 2004.

Vol. 3213: M.G.. Negoita, R.J. Howlett, L.C. Jain (Eds.), Knowledge-Based Intelligent Information and Engineering Systems, Part I. LVIII, 1280 pages. 2004.

Vol. 3209: B. Berendt, A. Hotho, D. Mladenic, M. van Someren, M. Spiliopoulou, G. Stumme (Eds.), Web Mining: From Web to Semantic Web. IX, 201 pages. 2004.

Vol. 3206: P. Sojka, I. Kopecek, K. Pala (Eds.), Text, Speech and Dialogue. XIII, 667 pages. 2004.

Vol. 3202: J.-F. Boulicaut, F. Esposito, F. Giannotti, D. Pedreschi (Eds.), Knowledge Discovery in Databases: PKDD 2004. XIX, 560 pages. 2004.

Vol. 3201: J.-F. Boulicaut, F. Esposito, F. Giannotti, D. Pedreschi (Eds.), Machine Learning: ECML 2004. XVIII, 580 pages. 2004.

Vol. 3194: R. Camacho, R. King, A. Srinivasan (Eds.), Inductive Logic Programming. XI, 361 pages. 2004.

Vol. 3192: C. Bussler, D. Fensel (Eds.), Artificial Intelligence: Methodology, Systems, and Applications. XIII, 522 pages. 2004.

Vol. 3191: M. Klusch, S. Ossowski, V. Kashyap, R. Unland (Eds.), Cooperative Information Agents VIII. XI, 303 pages. 2004.

Vol. 3187: G. Lindemann, J. Denzinger, I.J. Timm, R. Unland (Eds.), Multiagent System Technologies. XIII, 341 pages. 2004.

Vol. 3176: O. Bousquet, U. von Luxburg, G. Rätsch (Eds.), Advanced Lectures on Machine Learning. IX, 241 pages. 2004.

Vol. 3171: A.L.C. Bazzan, S. Labidi (Eds.), Advances in Artificial Intelligence – SBIA 2004. XVII, 548 pages. 2004.

Vol. 3159: U. Visser, Intelligent Information Integration for the Semantic Web. XIV, 150 pages. 2004.

Vol. 3157: C. Zhang, H. W. Guesgen, W.K. Yeap (Eds.), PRICAI 2004: Trends in Artificial Intelligence. XX, 1023 pages. 2004.

Vol. 3155: P. Funk, P.A. González Calero (Eds.), Advances in Case-Based Reasoning. XIII, 822 pages. 2004.

Vol. 3139: F. Iida, R. Pfeifer, L. Steels, Y. Kuniyoshi (Eds.), Embodied Artificial Intelligence. IX, 331 pages. 2004.

Vol. 3131: V. Torra, Y. Narukawa (Eds.), Modeling Decisions for Artificial Intelligence. XI, 327 pages. 2004.

Vol. 3127: K.E. Wolff, H.D. Pfeiffer, H.S. Delugach (Eds.), Conceptual Structures at Work. XI, 403 pages. 2004.

Vol. 3123: A. Belz, R. Evans, P. Piwek (Eds.), Natural Language Generation. X, 219 pages. 2004.

Vol. 3120: J. Shawe-Taylor, Y. Singer (Eds.), Learning Theory. X, 648 pages. 2004.

Vol. 3097: D. Basin, M. Rusinowitch (Eds.), Automated Reasoning. XII, 493 pages. 2004.

Vol. 3071: A. Omicini, P. Petta, J. Pitt (Eds.), Engineering Societies in the Agents World. XIII, 409 pages. 2004.

Vol. 3070: L. Rutkowski, J. Siekmann, R. Tadeusiewicz, L.A. Zadeh (Eds.), Artificial Intelligence and Soft Computing - ICAISC 2004. XXV, 1208 pages. 2004.

Vol. 3068: E. André, L. Dybkjær, W. Minker, P. Heisterkamp (Eds.), Affective Dialogue Systems. XII, 324 pages. 2004.

Vol. 3067: M. Dastani, J. Dix, A. El Fallah-Seghrouchni (Eds.), Programming Multi-Agent Systems. X, 221 pages. 2004.

Vol. 3066: S. Tsumoto, R. Słowiński, J. Komorowski, J.W. Grzymała-Busse (Eds.), Rough Sets and Current Trends in Computing. XX, 853 pages. 2004.

Vol. 3065: A. Lomuscio, D. Nute (Eds.), Deontic Logic in Computer Science. X, 275 pages. 2004.

Vol. 3060: A.Y. Tawfik, S.D. Goodwin (Eds.), Advances in Artificial Intelligence. XIII, 582 pages. 2004.

Vol. 3056: H. Dai, R. Srikant, C. Zhang (Eds.), Advances in Knowledge Discovery and Data Mining. XIX, 713 pages. 2004.

Vol. 3055: H. Christiansen, M.-S. Hacid, T. Andreasen, H.L. Larsen (Eds.), Flexible Query Answering Systems. X, 500 pages. 2004.

Vol. 3048: P. Faratin, D.C. Parkes, J.A. Rodríguez-Aguilar, W.E. Walsh (Eds.), Agent-Mediated Electronic Commerce V. XI, 155 pages. 2004.

Vol. 3040: R. Conejo, M. Urretavizcaya, J.-L. Pérez-de-la-Cruz (Eds.), Current Topics in Artificial Intelligence. XIV, 689 pages. 2004.

Vol. 3035: M.A. Wimmer (Ed.), Knowledge Management in Electronic Government. XII, 326 pages. 2004.

Vol. 3034: J. Favela, E. Menasalvas, E. Chávez (Eds.), Advances in Web Intelligence. XIII, 227 pages. 2004.

Vol. 3030: P. Giorgini, B. Henderson-Sellers, M. Winikoff (Eds.), Agent-Oriented Information Systems. XIV, 207 pages. 2004.

Vol. 3029: B. Orchard, C. Yang, M. Ali (Eds.), Innovations in Applied Artificial Intelligence. XXI, 1272 pages. 2004.

Vol. 3025: G.A. Vouros, T. Panayiotopoulos (Eds.), Methods and Applications of Artificial Intelligence. XV, 546 pages. 2004.

Vol. 3020: D. Polani, B. Browning, A. Bonarini, K. Yoshida (Eds.), RoboCup 2003: Robot Soccer World Cup VII. XVI, 767 pages. 2004.

Vol. 3012: K. Kurumatani, S.-H. Chen, A. Ohuchi (Eds.), Multi-Agents for Mass User Support. X, 217 pages. 2004.

Vol. 3010: K.R. Apt, F. Fages, F. Rossi, P. Szeredi, J. Váncza (Eds.), Recent Advances in Constraints. VIII, 285 pages. 2004.

Vol. 2990: J. Leite, A. Omicini, L. Sterling, P. Torroni (Eds.), Declarative Agent Languages and Technologies. XII, 281 pages. 2004.

Vol. 2980: A. Blackwell, K. Marriott, A. Shimojima (Eds.), Diagrammatic Representation and Inference. XV, 448 pages. 2004.